Lecture Notes in Computer Science 12110

More information about this series at http://www.springer.com/series/7410

Aggelos Kiayias · Markulf Kohlweiss ·
Petros Wallden · Vassilis Zikas (Eds.)

Public-Key Cryptography – PKC 2020

23rd IACR International Conference
on Practice and Theory of Public-Key Cryptography
Edinburgh, UK, May 4–7, 2020
Proceedings, Part I

Springer

Editors
Aggelos Kiayias
University of Edinburgh
Edinburgh, UK

Markulf Kohlweiss
University of Edinburgh
Edinburgh, UK

Petros Wallden
University of Edinburgh
Edinburgh, UK

Vassilis Zikas
University of Edinburgh
Edinburgh, UK

ISSN 0302-9743 ISSN 1611-3349 (electronic)
Lecture Notes in Computer Science
ISBN 978-3-030-45373-2 ISBN 978-3-030-45374-9 (eBook)
https://doi.org/10.1007/978-3-030-45374-9

LNCS Sublibrary: SL4 – Security and Cryptology

This Springer imprint is published by the registered company Springer Nature Switzerland AG
The registered company address is: Gewerbestrasse 11, 6330 Cham, Switzerland

Preface

The 23rd IACR International Conference on Practice and Theory of Public-Key Cryptography (PKC 2020) was held during May 4–7, 2020, in Edinburgh, Scotland, UK. This conference series is organized annually by the International Association of Cryptologic Research (IACR). It is the main annual conference with an explicit focus on public-key cryptography sponsored by IACR. The proceedings are comprised of two volumes and include the 44 papers that were selected by the Program Committee.

A total of 180 submissions were received for consideration for this year's program. Three submissions were table rejected due to significant deviations from the instructions of the call for papers. Submissions were assigned to at least three reviewers, while submissions by Program Committee members received at least four reviews.

The review period was divided in three stages, the first one reserved for individual reviewing that lasted five weeks. It was followed by the second stage, where the authors were given the opportunity to respond to the reviews. Finally in the third stage, which lasted about 5 weeks, the Program Committee members engaged in discussion taking into account the rebuttal comments submitted by the authors. In addition to the rebuttal, in a number of occasions, the authors of the papers were engaged with additional questions and clarifications. Seven of the papers were conditionally accepted and received a final additional round of reviewing. The reviewing and paper selection process was a difficult task and I am deeply grateful to the members of the Program Committee for their hard and thorough work. Additionally, my deep gratitude is extended to the 252 external reviewers who assisted the Program Committee. The submissions included two papers with which the program chair had a soft conflict of interest (they included in their author list researchers based at the University of Edinburgh). For these two papers, the chair abstained from the management of the discussion and delegated this task to a Program Committee member. I am grateful to Helger Lipmaa for his help in managing these two papers. I would like to also thank Shai Halevi for his web submission and review software which we used for managing the whole process very successfully.

The invited talk at PKC 2020, entitled "How low can we go?" was delivered by Yuval Ishai. I would like to thank Yuval for accepting the invitation and contributing to the program this year as well as all the authors who submitted their work. I would like to also thank my good colleagues and co-editors of these two volumes, Markulf Kohlweiss, Petros Wallden, and Vassilis Zikas who served as general co-chairs this year. A special thanks is also due to Dimitris Karakostas who helped with the website of the conference, Gareth Beedham who assisted in various administrative tasks, and all

---

This proceedings volume was prepared before the conference took place and it reflects its original planning, irrespective of the disruption caused by the COVID-19 pandemic.

PhD students at the School of Informatics who helped with the conference organization. Finally, I am deeply grateful to our industry sponsors, listed in the conference's website, who provided generous financial support.

May 2020 Aggelos Kiayias

Organization

The 23rd IACR International Conference on Practice and Theory in Public-Key Cryptography (PKC 2020) was organized by the International Association for Cryptologic Research and sponsored by the Scottish Informatics and Computer Science Alliance.

General Chairs

Markulf Kohlweiss	University of Edinburgh, UK
Petros Wallden	University of Edinburgh, UK
Vassilis Zikas	University of Edinburgh, UK

Program Chair

Aggelos Kiayias	University of Edinburgh, UK

Program Committee

Gorjan Alagic	UMD, USA
Gilad Asharov	Bar-Ilan University, Israel
Nuttapong Attrapadung	AIST, Japan
Joppe Bos	NXP, Germany
Chris Bruszka	TU Hamburg, Germany
Liqun Chen	University of Surrey, UK
Kai-Min Chung	Academia Sinica, Taiwan
Dana Dachman-Soled	UMD, USA
Sebastian Faust	TU Darmstadt, Germany
Dario Fiore	IMDEA Software Institute, Spain
Marc Fischlin	TU Darmstadt, Germany
Georg Fuchsbauer	ENS Paris, France
Steven Galbraith	Auckland University, New Zealand
Junqing Gong	CNRS and ENS, France
Kyoohyung Han	Coinplug, South Korea
Aggelos Kiayias	University of Edinburgh, UK
Stephan Krenn	AIT, Austria
Benoît Libert	CNRS and ENS de Lyon, France
Helger Lipmaa	Simula UiB, Norway
Ryo Nishimaki	NTT Secure Platform Lab, Japan
Miyako Okhubo	NICT, Japan
Emmanuela Orsini	KUL, Belgium
Omkant Pandey	Stonybrook University, USA

Charalampos Papamanthou	UMD, USA
Christophe Petit	University of Birmingham, UK
Thomas Prest	PQ Shield Ltd., USA
Carla Ràfols	University of Bristol, UK
Arnab Roy	Universitat Pompeu Fabra, Spain
Simona Samardjiska	Radboud University, The Netherlands
Yongsoo Song	Microsoft Research, USA
Rainer Steinwandt	Florida Atlantic University, USA
Berk Sunar	Worcester Polytechnic Institute, USA
Atsushi Takayasu	University of Tokyo, Japan
Serge Vaudenay	EPFL, Switzerland
Daniele Venturi	Sapienza Università di Roma, Italy
Frederik Vercauteren	KUL, Belgium
Chaoping Xing	Nanyang Technological University, Singapore
Thomas Zacharias	University of Edinburgh, UK
Hong Sheng Zhou	VCU, USA

External Reviewers

Aydin Abadi
Behzad Abdolmaleki
Masayuki Abe
Kamalesh Acharya
Shashank Agrawal
Younes Talibi Alaoui
Erdem Alkim
Miguel Ambrona
Myrto Arapinis
Thomas Attema
Shi Bai
Foteini Baldimtsi
Fatih Balli
Subhadeep Banik
Khashayar Barooti
Andrea Basso
Balthazar Bauer
Carsten Baum
Ward Beullens
Rishiraj Bhattacharyya
Nina Bindel
Olivier Blazy
Carl Bootland
Colin Boyd
Andrea Caforio
Sergiu Carpov
Ignacio Cascudo
Wouter Castryck
Andrea Cerulli
Rohit Chatterjee
Hao Chen
Long Chen
Rongmao Chen
Jung Hee Cheon
Ilaria Chillotti
Gwangbae Choi
Heewon Chung
Michele Ciampi
Aloni Cohen
Ran Cohen
Alexandru Cojocaru
Simone Colombo
Anamaria Costache
Craig Costello
Wei Dai
Dipayan Das
Poulami Das
Thomas Debris-Alazard
Thomas Decru
Ioannis Demertzis
Amit Deo
Yarkin Doroz

Yfke Dulek
F. Betül Durak
Stefan Dziembowski
Fabian Eidens
Thomas Eisenbarth
Naomi Ephraim
Andreas Erwig
Leo Fan
Xiong Fan
Antonio Faonio
Pooya Farshim
Prastudy Fauzi
Tamara Finogina
Danilo Francati
Cody Freitag
Eiichiro Fujisaki
Jun Furukawa
Ameet Gadekar
Chaya Ganesh
Wei Gao
Pierrick Gaudry
Romain Gay
Huijing Gong
Alonso Gonzalez
Alonso González
Cyprien de Saint Guilhem
Mohammad Hajiabadi
Shuai Han
Abida Haque
Patrick Harasser
Carmit Hazay
Javier Herranz
Kristina Hostakova
Dongping Hu
Loïs Huguenin-Dumittan
Shih-Han Hung
Ilia Iliashenko
Mitsugu Iwamoto
Kiera Jade
Aayush Jain
Christian Janson
David Jao
Jinhyuck Jeong
Dingding Jia
Yanxue Jia
Charanjit Jutla
Dimitris Karakostas
Nada El Kassem
Shuichi Katsumata
Marcel Keller
Thomas Kerber
Nguyen Ta Toan Khoa
Ryo Kikuchi
Allen Kim
Dongwoo Kim
Duhyeong Kim
Jiseung Kim
Miran Kim
Taechan Kim
Mehmet Kiraz
Elena Kirshanova
Fuyuki Kitagawa
Susumu Kiyoshima
Karen Klein
Dimitris Kolonelos
Ilan Komargodski
Venkata Koppula
Toomas Krips
Mukul Kulkarni
Péter Kutas
Norman Lahr
Nikolaos Lamprou
Fei Li
Jiangtao Li
Zengpeng Li
Zhe Li
Xiao Liang
Wei-Kai Lin
Yeo Sze Ling
Orfeas Thyfronitis Litos
Julian Loss
Zhenliang Lu
Vadim Lyubashevsky
Fermi Ma
Yi-Hsin Ma
Bernardo Magri
Christian Majenz
Nathan Manohar
William J. Martin
Chloe Martindale
Ramiro Martínez
Daniel Masny

Simon Masson
Takahiro Matsuda
Sogol Mazaheri
Simon-Philipp Merz
Peihan Miao
Takaaki Mizuki
Fabrice Mouhartem
Yi Mu
Pratyay Mukherjee
Koksal Mus
Michael Naehrig
Khoa Nguyen
Ariel Nof
Luca Notarnicola
Adam O'Neill
Erdinc Ozturk
Tapas Pal
Alain Passelègue
Alice Pellet–Mary
Ray Perlner
Thomas Peters
Zaira Pindado
Rafael del Pino
Federico Pintore
Antoine Plouviez
Yuriy Polyakov
Chen Qian
Luowen Qian
Yuan Quan
Sebastian Ramacher
Joost Renes
Thomas Ricosset
Felix Rohrbach
Mélissa Rossi
Dragos Rotaru
Sujoy Sinha Roy
Cyprien Delpech de Saint-Guilhem
Yusuke Sakai
Katerina Samari
Kai Samelin
Olivier Sanders
Benjamin Schlosser
Jacob Schuldt
Peter Schwabe
Jae Hong Seo
Ido Shahaf
Yu-Ching Shen
Kazumasa Shinagawa
Janno Siim
Javier Silva
Luisa Siniscalchi
Daniel Slamanig
Azam Soleimanian
Yongha Son
Claudio Soriente
Pierre-Jean Spaenlehauer
Florian Speelman
Akshayaram Srinivasan
Shravan Srinivasan
Martijn Stam
Igors Stephanovs
Noah Stephens-Davidowitz
Christoph Striecks
Shifeng Sun
Koutarou Suzuki
Alan Szepieniec
Katsuyuki Takashima
Rajdeep Talapatra
Qiang Tang
Titouan Tanguy
Phuc Thai
Radu Titiu
Junichi Tomida
Nikos Triandopoulos
Yiannis Tselekounis
Jorge L. Villar
Christine van Vredendaal
Sameer Wagh
Michael Walter
Yuntao Wang
Yuyu Wang
Yohei Watanabe
Gaven Watson
Florian Weber
Charlotte Weitkämper
Weiqiang Wen
Benjamin Wesolowski
Jeroen van Wier
Jan Winkelmann
Fredrik Winzer
Keita Xagawa
Chaoping Xing

Shota Yamada
Takashi Yamakawa
Avishay Yanai
Rupeng Yang
Eylon Yogev
Kazuki Yoneyama
Chen Yuan
Alexandros Zacharakis
Michal Zajac
Bingsheng Zhang
Yupeng Zhang
Zhenfei Zhang
Yi Zhao
Haibin Zheng
Arne Tobias Ødegaard
Morten Øygarden

This proceedings volume was prepared before the conference took place and it reflects its original planning, irrespective of the disruption caused by the COVID-19 pandemic.

How Low Can We Go? (Invited Talk)

Yuval Ishai

Computer Science Department, Technion
yuvali@cs.technion.il

Abstract. Given a cryptographic task, such as encrypting a message or securely computing a given function, a natural question is to find the "minimal cost" of carrying out this task. The question can take a variety of forms, depending on the cost measure. For instance, one can try to minimize computation, communication, rounds, or randomness. In the case of computational cost, one can consider different computation models, such as circuits or branching programs, and different cost metrics, such as size or depth. The answer to the question may further depend on the type of computational assumptions one is willing to make.

The study of this question, for different cryptographic tasks and clean asymptotic cost measures, has led to a rich body of work with useful and often unexpected results. The talk will survey some of this work, highlighting connections between different research areas in cryptography and relevance beyond cryptography.

In addition to the direct interest in minimizing well-motivated complexity measures, there are cases in which "high-end" cryptographic tasks, such as secure multiparty computation or program obfuscation, call for minimizing different cost measures of lower-end primitives that would otherwise seem poorly motivated. I will give some examples of this kind.

Finally, I will make the case that despite the progress already made, there is much more to be explored. Research in this area can greatly benefit from more cooperation between theoretical and applied cryptographers, as well as between cryptographers and researchers from other fields, including computational complexity, algorithms, computational learning theory, coding and information theory.

Supported by ERC Project NTSC (742754), NSF-BSF grant 2015782, BSF grant 2018393, and a grant from the Ministry of Science and Technology, Israel and Department of Science and Technology, Government of India.

Contents – Part I

Functional Encryption

Fast, Compact, and Expressive Attribute-Based Encryption 3
Junichi Tomida, Yuto Kawahara, and Ryo Nishimaki

Adaptive Simulation Security for Inner Product Functional Encryption 34
Shweta Agrawal, Benoît Libert, Monosij Maitra, and Radu Titiu

Verifiable Inner Product Encryption Scheme. 65
Najmeh Soroush, Vincenzo Iovino, Alfredo Rial, Peter B. Roenne, and Peter Y. A. Ryan

A New Paradigm for Public-Key Functional Encryption for Degree-2 Polynomials. 95
Romain Gay

Identity-Based Encryption

Master-Key KDM-Secure IBE from Pairings 123
Sanjam Garg, Romain Gay, and Mohammad Hajiabadi

Hierarchical Identity-Based Encryption with Tight Multi-challenge Security 153
Roman Langrehr and Jiaxin Pan

Obfuscation and Applications

The Usefulness of Sparsifiable Inputs: How to Avoid Subexponential iO 187
Thomas Agrikola, Geoffroy Couteau, and Dennis Hofheinz

Witness Maps and Applications 220
Suvradip Chakraborty, Manoj Prabhakaran, and Daniel Wichs

Encryption Schemes

Memory-Tight Reductions for Practical Key Encapsulation Mechanisms 249
Rishiraj Bhattacharyya

Toward RSA-OAEP Without Random Oracles 279
Nairen Cao, Adam O'Neill, and Mohammad Zaheri

Public-Key Puncturable Encryption: Modular and Compact Constructions . . . 309
Shi-Feng Sun, Amin Sakzad, Ron Steinfeld, Joseph K. Liu, and Dawu Gu

Secure Channels

Flexible Authenticated and Confidential Channel Establishment (fACCE): Analyzing the Noise Protocol Framework . . . 341
Benjamin Dowling, Paul Rösler, and Jörg Schwenk

Limits on the Efficiency of (Ring) LWE Based Non-interactive Key Exchange . . . 374
Siyao Guo, Pritish Kamath, Alon Rosen, and Katerina Sotiraki

PAKEs: New Framework, New Techniques and More Efficient Lattice-Based Constructions in the Standard Model . . . 396
Shaoquan Jiang, Guang Gong, Jingnan He, Khoa Nguyen, and Huaxiong Wang

Basic Primitives with Special Properties

Constraining and Watermarking PRFs from Milder Assumptions. . . . 431
Chris Peikert and Sina Shiehian

Bringing Order to Chaos: The Case of Collision-Resistant Chameleon-Hashes . . . 462
David Derler, Kai Samelin, and Daniel Slamanig

Proofs and Arguments I

Concretely-Efficient Zero-Knowledge Arguments for Arithmetic Circuits and Their Application to Lattice-Based Cryptography . . . 495
Carsten Baum and Ariel Nof

Updateable Inner Product Argument with Logarithmic Verifier and Applications . . . 527
Vanesa Daza, Carla Ràfols, and Alexandros Zacharakis

On Black-Box Extensions of Non-interactive Zero-Knowledge Arguments, and Signatures Directly from Simulation Soundness . . . 558
Masayuki Abe, Miguel Ambrona, and Miyako Ohkubo

On QA-NIZK in the BPK Model . . . 590
Behzad Abdolmaleki, Helger Lipmaa, Janno Siim, and Michał Zając

Lattice-Based Cryptography

Improved Discrete Gaussian and Subgaussian Analysis for Lattice Cryptography 623
Nicholas Genise, Daniele Micciancio, Chris Peikert, and Michael Walter

Almost Tight Security in Lattices with Polynomial Moduli – PRF, IBE, All-but-many LTF, and More 652
Qiqi Lai, Feng-Hao Liu, and Zhedong Wang

Author Index 683

Contents – Part II

Lattice-Based Cryptography

The Randomized Slicer for CVPP: Sharper, Faster, Smaller, Batchier 3
Léo Ducas, Thijs Laarhoven, and Wessel P. J. van Woerden

Tweaking the Asymmetry of Asymmetric-Key Cryptography on Lattices: KEMs and Signatures of Smaller Sizes 37
Jiang Zhang, Yu Yu, Shuqin Fan, Zhenfeng Zhang, and Kang Yang

MPSign: A Signature from Small-Secret Middle-Product Learning with Errors 66
Shi Bai, Dipayan Das, Ryo Hiromasa, Miruna Rosca, Amin Sakzad, Damien Stehlé, Ron Steinfeld, and Zhenfei Zhang

Proofs and Arguments II

Witness Indistinguishability for Any Single-Round Argument with Applications to Access Control 97
Zvika Brakerski and Yael Kalai

Boosting Verifiable Computation on Encrypted Data 124
Dario Fiore, Anca Nitulescu, and David Pointcheval

Isogeny-Based Cryptography

Lossy CSI-FiSh: Efficient Signature Scheme with Tight Reduction to Decisional CSIDH-512 157
Ali El Kaafarani, Shuichi Katsumata, and Federico Pintore

Threshold Schemes from Isogeny Assumptions 187
Luca De Feo and Michael Meyer

Multiparty Protocols

Topology-Hiding Computation for Networks with Unknown Delays 215
Rio LaVigne, Chen-Da Liu-Zhang, Ueli Maurer, Tal Moran, Marta Mularczyk, and Daniel Tschudi

Sublinear-Round Byzantine Agreement Under Corrupt Majority 246
T.-H. Hubert Chan, Rafael Pass, and Elaine Shi

Bandwidth-Efficient Threshold EC-DSA 266
Guilhem Castagnos, Dario Catalano, Fabien Laguillaumie, Federico Savasta, and Ida Tucker

Secure Computation and Related Primitives

Blazing Fast OT for Three-Round UC OT Extension. 299
Ran Canetti, Pratik Sarkar, and Xiao Wang

Going Beyond Dual Execution: MPC for Functions with Efficient Verification 328
Carmit Hazay, Abhi Shelat, and Muthuramakrishnan Venkitasubramaniam

Mon$\mathbb{Z}_{2^k}$a: Fast Maliciously Secure Two Party Computation on $\mathbb{Z}_{2^k}$ 357
Dario Catalano, Mario Di Raimondo, Dario Fiore, and Irene Giacomelli

Post-Quantum Primitives

Generic Authenticated Key Exchange in the Quantum Random Oracle Model 389
Kathrin Hövelmanns, Eike Kiltz, Sven Schäge, and Dominique Unruh

Threshold Ring Signatures: New Definitions and Post-quantum Security 423
Abida Haque and Alessandra Scafuro

Tight and Optimal Reductions for Signatures Based on Average Trapdoor Preimage Sampleable Functions and Applications to Code-Based Signatures. 453
André Chailloux and Thomas Debris-Alazard

Cryptanalysis and Concrete Security

Faster Cofactorization with ECM Using Mixed Representations 483
Cyril Bouvier and Laurent Imbert

Improved Classical Cryptanalysis of SIKE in Practice 505
Craig Costello, Patrick Longa, Michael Naehrig, Joost Renes, and Fernando Virdia

A Short-List of Pairing-Friendly Curves Resistant to Special TNFS at the 128-Bit Security Level 535
Aurore Guillevic

Privacy-Preserving Schemes

Privacy-Preserving Authenticated Key Exchange and the Case of IKEv2 567
Sven Schäge, Jörg Schwenk, and Sebastian Lauer

Linearly-Homomorphic Signatures and Scalable Mix-Nets 597
Chloé Hébant, Duong Hieu Phan, and David Pointcheval

Efficient Redactable Signature and Application to Anonymous Credentials. . . 628
Olivier Sanders

Author Index 657

Functional Encryption

Fast, Compact, and Expressive Attribute-Based Encryption

Junichi Tomida(✉), Yuto Kawahara, and Ryo Nishimaki

NTT Secure Platform Laboratories, Tokyo, Japan
{junichi.tomida.vw,yuto.kawahara.yk,ryo.nishimaki.zk}@hco.ntt.co.jp

Abstract. Attribute-based encryption (ABE) is an advanced cryptographic tool and useful to build various types of access control systems. Toward the goal of making ABE more practical, we propose key-policy (KP) and ciphertext-policy (CP) ABE schemes, which first support unbounded sizes of attribute sets and policies with negation and multi-use of attributes, allow fast decryption, and are adaptively secure under a standard assumption, simultaneously. Our schemes are more expressive than previous schemes and efficient enough. To achieve the adaptive security along with the other properties, we refine the technique introduced by Kowalczyk and Wee (Eurocrypt'19) so that we can apply the technique more expressive ABE schemes. Furthermore, we also present a new proof technique that allows us to remove redundant elements used in their ABE schemes. We implement our schemes in 128-bit security level and present their benchmarks for an ordinary personal computer and smartphones. They show that all algorithms run in one second with the personal computer when they handle any policy or attribute set with one hundred attributes.

Keywords: Attribute-based encryption · Standard assumption · Non-monotone · Unbounded · Multi-use · Random oracle model

1 Introduction

Attribute-based encryption (ABE) [17] is an advanced form of public key encryption (PKE), which yields fine-grained access control over encrypted data. More concretely, ABE allows us to embed an attribute x into a ciphertext when we encrypt a message. An authority that has a master secret key can issue a secret key that is associated with a predicate y. The ciphertext can be decrypted with the secret key only if x and y satisfy some relation R.

Previously, ABE schemes have been proposed for various relations, such as equality [9], threshold [29], orthogonality of vectors [19], and so on. One of the most notable relations among them is that expressed by an access structure [7,17]. In a key-policy ABE (KP-ABE) scheme, for instance, one can embed an access structure in a secret key such as (YEAR:1991–2000 AND CATEGORY:jazz). The secret key can decrypt ciphertexts that have attributes YEAR:1991–2000 and

A. Kiayias et al. (Eds.): PKC 2020, LNCS 12110, pp. 3–33, 2020.
https://doi.org/10.1007/978-3-030-45374-9_1

CATEGORY:jazz but cannot ones that only have at most one of them. Ciphertext-policy ABE (CP-ABE) is a dual of KP-ABE and allows us to embed an access structure into ciphertexts.

Recently, Agrawal and Chase proposed practical KP-ABE and CP-ABE schemes named FAME [1], which are the first schemes that simultaneously:

1. have no restriction on sizes of policies and attribute sets (unboundedness);
2. allow an arbitrary string as an attribute (large universe);
3. are based on the fast Type-III pairings;
4. need a small number of pairings for decryption;
5. satisfy the adaptive security under standard assumptions.

All these properties are arguably important in practice. We briefly explain the reasons. The first two properties say about scalability. It is not uncommon that we extend a system to add new attributes to a database in operation. In such cases, scalability is essential property because if the scheme does not have the scalability, we need a redeployment of the scheme. The second two properties say about efficiency. The efficiency of building blocks directly affects that of the entire system. Thus, efficient cryptographic schemes are desirable. The final property says about security. In contrast to the selective security, the adaptive security considers a model that captures a natural attack of an adversary against a scheme. Additionally, standard assumptions are based on well-studied hard problems and thus reliable. Hence, the adaptive security under standard assumptions guarantees that schemes are secure enough.

1.1 Our Contribution

Toward the goal to make ABE schemes more usable and realistic, we propose more expressive schemes. More precisely, we propose KP-ABE and CP-ABE schemes that satisfy all the above properties and additionally allow us to use

6. negation *in a natural form* (non-monotonicity);
7. the same attribute more than once (multi-use of attributes or compactness);

in a policy. These properties allow us to use more fine-grained policies that are commonly used in practice. Negation is essential for access control by blacklisting. Multi-use of attributes in policies is indispensable to express certain types of policies such as (A AND B) OR (A AND C) OR (B AND D), where A, B, C, D are Boolean variables.

Thanks to great works on ABE [3,21,27], we have several ABE schemes that can handle unbounded sizes of attribute sets and policies in prime-order groups. To our knowledge, however, there are no schemes that achieve all the properties listed above simultaneously. We summarize previous schemes and ours in Table 1.

One note is that our schemes require the random oracle model for security analysis as well as FAME. Whereas a random oracle cannot be replaced with any implemented hash function in some particular cases [11], it is still a widely accepted and standard methodology to analyze the security of cryptographic

Table 1. Comparison of unbounded KP and CP-ABE schemes based on prime-order groups.

Scheme	Unbounded-ness	Large universe	Type-III	Fast Dec	Standard assump.	Non monotonicity	Multi-use	w/o RO
OT12 [27]	✓	✓	✓	×	✓	✓	×	✓
AC17 [1]	✓	✓	✓	✓	✓	×	×	×
CGKW18 [13]	✓	✓	✓	×	✓	×	×	✓
KW19 [21]	✓	✓	✓	×	✓	×	✓	✓
Att19 [3]	✓	✓	✓	×	×	×[a]	✓	✓
Ours	✓	✓	✓	✓[b]	✓	✓	✓	×

[a]The scheme that is explicitly described by Attrapadung [3] can handle negation, but it is not the natural form that we consider.

[b]The number of pairings in decryption of our schemes does not depend on the size of policies or the number of attributes but only depends on the number of multi-use of labels in a policy. Thus, as long as considering the same setting as FAME, which imposes one-use restriction on policies, the decryption requires only a constant number of pairings.

schemes. Actually, many practical schemes that are used in the real world require the random oracle model for their security analysis [5,6,15].

In the following, we elaborate on the last two properties.

Non-monotonicity. Previously, there are several works that consider access structures including negation (non-monotone access structures) in ABE [3,4, 24,26–28,32]. Among them, only the negation form defined by Okamoto and Takashima (OT negation) [26,27] is different from that by the others (non-OT negation). Considering an example is the best way to describe the difference. Let attributes consist of a pair of a label and value, e.g., YEAR:1991–2000, where YEAR is a label and 1991–2000 is a value. Suppose there are two labels YEAR and CATEGORY in an access control system supported by KP-ABE. Then, non-OT negation is like (NOT YEAR:1991–2000) whereas OT negation is like (YEAR:NOT 1991–2000). Semantically, the former implies that the secret key can decrypt a ciphertext if it does not have attribute YEAR:1991–2000. On the other hand, the latter implies that a ciphertext is decryptable if it has an attribute on label YEAR and its attribute is not 1991–2000.

When we consider large universe ABE, which is exactly the desirable case in practice, the natural negation form is arguably OT negation. In large universe ABE, it is unreasonable to fix all attributes used in a system at the setup phase because the most significant advantage of large universe ABE is that we can utilize an exponentially large number of attributes. Associating strings with attributes that the ABE scheme handles in an ad-hoc way by a hash function would be a better solution. However, if we use non-OT negation in the system, we have to fix all attributes that the system supports at the setup phase. This is because a secret key whose policy is negation of an attribute that the system has not supported before can decrypt all ciphertexts generated so far. More concretely, in the above example, we consider the case where we add a new label ARTIST in the system. Then, if an authority issues a key whose policy is (NOT ARTIST:The Beatles), all previous ciphertexts are decrypted by the key even if the underlying content is by The Beatles because they do not have an attribute on label Artist. On the other hand, OT negation does not cause this inconvenience because a key whose policy is (Artist:NOT The Beatles) is useless to decrypt ciphertexts without an attribute on label Artist. Thus, we refer to OT negation as a natural form.

Note that we can use monotone ABE as non-monotone ABE by preparing attributes for both positive and negative if they are small-universe constructions, in which the number of attributes are polynomially bounded. That is, non-possession of attributes can be expressed by possession of negative attributes. However, this is not the case in large-universe constructions because we cannot attach an exponentially large number of negative attributes to a ciphertext or secret key. Hence, monotone ABE and non-monotone ABE are completely different things in the context of large-universe constructions.

Multi-use of Attributes (Compactness). Many ABE schemes whose security relies on the dual system methodology [30] have a one-use restriction on access structures [12,13,23,26,27]. In an ABE scheme with the one-use restriction, one can use only policies in which all attributes appear once. That is, one cannot embed a policy into a ciphertext or secret key such as ((Year:1991–2000 AND Category:jazz) OR (Year:2001–2010 AND Category:jazz) OR (Year:2001–2010 AND Artist:The Beatles)) because attributes Category:jazz and Year:2001–2010 appear twice in the policy.

One way to circumvent this restriction is to prepare multiple nominal attributes for each single attribute in advance like Category:jazz-1, ..., Category:jazz-d for Category:jazz. However, this solution has two problems. The first is that the maximum number d of multi-use is fixed at the setup phase. Thus, the access structures that the scheme supports are still limited. The second is that, in KP-ABE, for instance, the solution increases the sizes of ciphertexts proportionally to the maximum number of multi-use, and it leads to efficiency loss. This prevents the solution to set a sufficiently large number for the limit.

On the other hand, in an ABE scheme that supports multi-use of attributes, we have no restrictions on policies and can combine any attributes in an arbitrary way to generate a policy. In KP-ABE, for instance, the sizes of ciphertexts are independent of policies and thus satisfies "compactness" [21].

1.2 Design of Our ABE Schemes

In the following, we focus on the design our KP-ABE scheme, and the CP-ABE scheme is similarly constructed. The relation R of our ABE is close to that by Okamoto and Takashima in [27]. As we mentioned, an attribute consists of a label and value. A predicate is an arbitrary Boolean formula that is a combination of variables by operations AND, OR, and NOT such as ((Year:1991–2000 AND Category:jazz) OR (Year:1991–2000 AND Artist:NOT The Beatles)). A formal definition of R is described in Definition 2.5.

Our scheme is based on the dual system encryption, which we can instantiate from either composite-order or prime-order bilinear groups [12,25,30,31]. Our actual scheme is based on prime-order bilinear groups following the framework by Chen et al. [12] to utilize the dual system methodology in prime-order groups and the technique by Agrawal and Chase [1] to utilize a random oracle in asymmetric prime-order bilinear groups. For ease of exposition, we describe the composite-order variant of our scheme here. Let $N = p_1 p_2$ for primes p_1 and p_2, and (G, H, G_T) be bilinear groups of order N. Let g and h be generators of G and H, and g_i and h_i be generators of subgroups G_i and H_i of order p_i for $i = \{1, 2\}$, respectively. Let $R : \{0,1\}^* \to G_1 \times G_1$ be a hash function modeled as a random oracle, and its input is a label. We denote the output of $R(i)$ by $(g_1^{u_i}, g_1^{h_i})$. Then, our scheme can be written as

$$\mathsf{pk} = (g_1, h_1, e(g_1, h_1)^{\alpha})$$

$$\mathsf{ct} = (h_1^s, \underbrace{\{g_1^{s(x_i u_i + h_i)}}_{\text{ct of IBE}}\}_{i \in S}, e(g_1, h_1)^{s\alpha} M)$$

$$\mathsf{sk} = \left(\{h_1^{r_i}\}_{i \in [n]}, \left\{ \underbrace{g^{\alpha_i} \cdot g_1^{r_i(y_i u_{\psi(i)} + h_{\psi(i)})}}_{\mathsf{sk}\text{ of IBE}} \text{ or } \underbrace{\begin{matrix} g^{-\alpha_i} \cdot g_1^{r_i u_{\psi(i)}}, \\ g^{y_i \alpha_i} \cdot g_1^{r_i h_{\psi(i)}} \end{matrix}}_{\mathsf{sk}\text{ of NIBE}} \right\}_{i \in [n]} \right),$$

where S is the set of labels, n is the number of variables in the formula, $\psi : [n] \to \{0,1\}^*$ is a function that specifies the label of each variable, α_i is a share of the secret α, and x_i and y_i are the values for label i. Note that the reason ct and sk contain both elements in G and H is to utilize a hash function in asymmetric groups as FAME [1].

The high-level idea of the construction is a combination of secret sharing (SS) and two-mode identity-based encryption (TIBE) [32]. TIBE is obtained by just combining identity-based encryption (IBE) and negation of IBE (NIBE). Our scheme can instantiate an arbitrary number of TIBE on the fly by leveraging hash function R, and each instance corresponds to each label. A secret key of our scheme consists of secret keys of IBE and NIBE, and each secret key hides a share α_i of a master secret α generated by SS according to the formula. A ciphertext of ABE consists of ciphertexts of IBE, which have the same form as those in Boneh-Boyen IBE [8]. Note that ciphertexts of IBE and NIBE are identical, and thus we do not need to include both ciphertexts of IBE and NIBE in a ciphertext of our scheme. In decryption, one computes $\{e(g_1, h_1)^{s\alpha_i}\}_i$ for labels in which the relation of (in)equality between the ciphertext and secret keys is satisfied. Note that one cannot compute $e(g_1, h_1)^{s\alpha_i}$ if the relation of (in)equality does not hold in label i, thanks to the security of underlying TIBE. If $e(g_1, h_1)^{s\alpha}$ is recovered via reconstruction of SS, which means that the policy in the secret key is satisfied by the attribute in the ciphertext, one can decrypt the ciphertext of ABE. By the construction, $e(g_1, h_1)^{s\alpha_i}$ cannot be computed if a ciphertext of ABE does not contain a ciphertext of TIBE for label i, and this property yields OT negation.

1.3 Our Main Technique

We can easily prove the adaptive security of our scheme from a standard assumption by the dual system methodology and the predicate encoding framework as in [31] if ψ is injective, or the scheme has the one-use restriction of labels in policies. However, if it is not the case, to prove the adaptive security of the scheme from standard assumptions becomes quite difficult and had been a long-standing open problem. Very recently, Kowalczyk and Wee brought a breakthrough for this problem (KW19) [21]. More precisely, they proposed a methodology to prove the adaptive security of the most simple ABE scheme, which supports monotone NC_1 circuits (or equivalently Boolean formulae) for a small attribute universe. The scheme can be written in composite-order groups as

$$\begin{aligned}\mathsf{pk} &= (g_1, h_1, g_1^{w_1}, \ldots, g_1^{w_\ell}, e(g_1, h_1)^{\alpha})\\ \mathsf{ct} &= (g_1^s, \{g_1^{sw_i}\}_{i \in S}, e(g_1, h_1)^{s\alpha} M)\\ \mathsf{sk} &= (\{h_1^{r_i}\}_{i \in [n]}, \{h^{\alpha_i} \cdot h_1^{r_i w_{\psi(i)}}\}_{i \in [n]}).\end{aligned}$$

Roughly speaking, this scheme can be seen as KP-ABE whose ingredients are ElGamal-like encryption whereas the counterpart of our scheme corresponds to TIBE.

We briefly recall the framework by KW19. Their framework follows the dual system methodology, which is the standard technique to achieve the adaptive security. In the methodology, we change the challenge ciphertext and secret keys into the semi-functional form. Roughly speaking, semi-functional ciphertexts and secret keys have an additional structure in G_2 and H_2 as follows:

$$\begin{aligned}\mathsf{ct} &= (g^s, \{g^{sw_i}\}_{i \in S}, e(g, h)^{s\alpha} M)\\ \mathsf{sk} &= (\{h_1^{r_i}\}_{i \in [n]}, \{h^{\alpha_i} \cdot h_1^{r_i w_{\psi(i)}} \cdot h_2^{\gamma_i}\}_{i \in [n]}),\end{aligned}$$

where γ_i is a share of a random secret γ.

In the dual system methodology, we consider a series of hybrids where we first change the challenge ciphertext into the semi-functional form and then the secret keys into the semi-functional form one by one. In the latter part, the methodology allows us to focus on only one secret key by leveraging components in G_2 and H_2. Therefore, to show the following indistinguishability for the adaptive choice of ct and the one key sk is sufficient to change the target secret key into a semi-functional form:

$$\left\{\begin{array}{l}\mathsf{ct} : (g_2^s, \{g_2^{sw_i}\}_{i \in S}),\\ \mathsf{sk} : (\{h_2^{r_i}\}_{i \in [n]}, \{h_2^{r_i w_{\psi(i)} + \boxed{\gamma_{0,i}}}\}_{i \in [n]})\end{array}\right\} \approx_c \left\{\begin{array}{l}(g_2^s, \{g_2^{sw_i}\}_{i \in S}),\\ (\{h_2^{r_i}\}_{i \in [n]}, \{h_2^{r_i w_{\psi(i)} + \boxed{\gamma_{1,i}}}\}_{i \in [n]})\end{array}\right\}$$

where $\gamma_{0,i}$ is a share of secret 0 and $\gamma_{1,i}$ is a share of secret γ. This core component is called core 1-ABE.

The difficulty of showing the indistinguishability of core 1-ABE from a standard assumption arises from the fact that we need to embed a computational problem into sk depending on ct. That is, if an adversary first asks for sk, a simulator has no idea on how to embed the computational problem into sk. Their framework tells us how to construct a series of hybrids to show the above indistinguishability. In each transition of hybrids, the simulator guesses a part of the adversary's output that has sufficient information to embed the problem into sk. Simultaneously, the part must be so small that the simulator can guess it with non-negligible probability. In our case, the part tells the correct element in sk where the simulator embeds the problem. Observe that each γ_i is masked by ElGamal-like encryption in H_2. Thus, we can embed the DDH problem based on the guess and gradually change shares $\{\gamma_i\}_{i\in[n]}$.

At a glance, their framework seems applicable to our scheme directly, but actually, it does not work. The main problem is the fact that whereas their framework tells us the location and its label where we should embed the problem in sk, it does not tell us the value of the label in ct. In other words, the difficulty of directly applying their framework to our scheme seems essentially the same as that of proving the adaptive security of Boneh-Boyen IBE, which was proven secure only in the selective setting. This problem does not occur in the scheme by KW19 because the corresponding part is just the ElGamal-like encryption, that is, public-key encryption.

To overcome the problem, we introduce new usage of KW19 framework that allows us to utilize the dual system methodology more beneficially. As we mentioned previously, a secret key of our scheme contains many secret keys of TIBE based on the dual system encryption. Furthermore, the framework tells us which secret key should be changed in each hybrid in the core 1-ABE. Thus, we can gradually randomize the component in H_2 of each element in sk by the dual system methodology instead of the DDH problem in H_2.

For simplicity, we show the case where we apply our new technique to the scheme by KW19. In our technique, we consider the following indistinguishability of core 1-ABE:

$$\left\{\begin{array}{l}(g^s, \{g^{sw_i}\}_{i\in S}),\\ (\{h_1^{r_i}\}_{i\in[n]}, \{h_1^{r_i w_{\psi(i)}} \cdot h_2^{\boxed{\gamma_{0,i}}}\}_{i\in[n]})\end{array}\right\} \approx_c \left\{\begin{array}{l}(g^s, \{g^{sw_i}\}_{i\in S}),\\ (\{h_1^{r_i}\}_{i\in[n]}, \{h_1^{r_i w_{\psi(i)}} \cdot h_2^{\boxed{\gamma_{1,i}}}\}_{i\in[n]})\end{array}\right\}.$$

The difference from the original core 1-ABE is that our core 1-ABE considers both normal space (G_1 and H_1) and semi-functional space (G_2 and H_2), whereas the original one considers only semi-functional space. We use the dual system methodology to randomize the component in H_2. Let i^* be the location where γ_{i^*} is supposed to be changed in some two hybrids, which means that $i^* \notin S$. Then, from the subgroup assumption, the dual system methodology argue that $(h_1^{r_{i^*}}, h_1^{r_{i^*} w_{\psi(i^*)}} \cdot h_2^{\gamma_{i^*}}) \approx_c (h^{r_{i^*}}, h^{r_{i^*} w_{\psi(i^*)}} \cdot h_2^{\gamma_{i^*}})$. Then, we can observe that $w_{\psi(i^*)}$ mod p_2 in sk is randomly distributed in $\mathbb{Z}_{p_2}$ from the Chinese remainder theorem and the fact $i^* \notin S$. Thus, term γ_i is completely hidden by term $r_{i^*} w_{\psi(i^*)}$. Unlike the framework by KW19, we can apply this technique to our scheme similarly.

1.4 Other Techniques

Furthermore, we give the following technical contributions:

- reducing the number of pairings in decryption;
- reducing the number of shares of secret sharing;
- making the proof simpler;
- presenting our CP-ABE scheme.

Number of Pairings. Our scheme described in Sect. 1.2 requires $O(n)$ pairings in decryption. To reduce the number, we employ the construction by Agrawal and Chase in [2]. That is, we use an exponent $r_{\pi(i)}$ instead of r_i, where $\pi(i) = |\{j \mid \psi(j) = \psi(i), j \leq i\}|$. In this construction, we need $O(d)$ pairings in decryption where $d = \max \pi(i)$ is the maximum number of multi-use of labels in the policy. Because our scheme in prime-order groups follows the construction, it allows fast decryption for secret keys with a small number of multi-use of labels. We show that we can prove the security of our schemes under standard assumptions even if we use this construction. Note that the construction by Agrawal and Chase relies on a q-type assumption.

Number of Shares. In the scheme by KW19, they use a secret sharing scheme where the number of shares corresponds to the summation of the numbers of gates and input wires when we capture a Boolean formula as a circuit. On the other hand, our schemes employ a secret sharing scheme where the number of shares corresponds to only the number of input wires. Their framework derives from the technique to prove the adaptive security of secret sharing for monotone circuits by Jafargholi et al. [18], which requires the same number of shares as in KW19. We guess that this is why their construction employs such a secret sharing scheme. However, we show that we do not need shares for the gates in secret sharing schemes for Boolean formulae to utilize the framework.

Simpler Proof. Our scheme follows the technique of FAME to make our scheme unbounded by a hash function [1]. We show that we can utilize a pseudorandom function (PRF) to significantly ease the security proof. Concretely, we can skip the part that corresponds to Hyb_0 to $\mathsf{Hyb}_{2,3,q}$ in their security proof [1, Appendix C]. Note that the additional computational cost by the modification is quite small compared with the whole procedure of the key generation because it requires only small numbers of PRF evaluations and multiplications in $\mathbb{Z}_p$ for each element in a secret key.

CP-ABE Scheme. We present our CP-ABE scheme and its security proof (described in the full version). Note that the security proof of our CP-ABE scheme is more complicated than that of our KP-ABE scheme, because we need two hidden spaces as in [13,16] due to a technical reason.

1.5 Implementation and Evaluation

We implement our KP and CP-ABE schemes in 128-bit security level and measure benchmarks for an ordinary personal computer and two smartphones: iPhone XR and Pixel 3. In our schemes, a running time of each algorithm is affected by the numbers of negation and multi-use of labels in a policy as well as the number of attributes. To show the effects of these factors, we present benchmarks for four types of policies that differ in the existence of negation and multi-use.

We roughly describe the running times of our schemes when we handle a policy or attribute set with 100 attributes on a personal computer. In all cases, our KP-ABE (resp. CP-ABE) scheme takes about 0.4 to 0.7 s (resp. 0.4 to 0.9 s) for encryption and key generation. Decryption is heavily affected by a type of policy, and our schemes take only about 0.02 s (KP & CP) in the fastest case and 0.5 (KP) or 0.7 s (CP) even in the slowest case. Thus, we can conclude that our schemes take less than 1 s in any process and any cases with 100 attributes.

We also implement KP and CP-ABE schemes by Okamoto and Takashima (OT12), which are the only known ABE schemes that support OT negation and the unboundedness [27]. There are no known schemes that are as expressive as ours (see Table 1), and OT12 seems to have a closet functionality. This is why we choose OT12 to compare. The comparison between our schemes and OT12 shows that our schemes achieve significant speedups for each algorithm.

2 Preliminaries

2.1 Notation

For a natural number $n \in \mathbb{N}$, $[n]$ denotes a set $\{1, \dots, n\}$. For a set S, $s \leftarrow S$ denotes that s is uniformly chosen from S. For matrices with the same number of rows $\mathbf{A}_1$ and $\mathbf{A}_2$, $(\mathbf{A}_1||\mathbf{A}_2)$ denotes the matrix generated by their concatenation. We denote the whole space spanned by all columns of matrix $\mathbf{A}$ by $\mathsf{span}(\mathbf{A})$. For a matrix $\mathbf{A} := (a_{j,\ell})_{j,\ell}$ over $\mathbb{Z}_p$, $[\mathbf{A}]_i$ $(i \in \{1, 2, T\})$ denotes a matrix over G_i whose (j, ℓ) entry is $g_i^{a_{j,\ell}}$, and we apply the similar notation to vectors and scalars. We denote $([\mathbf{A}]_1, [\mathbf{A}]_2)$ by $[\mathbf{A}]_{1,2}$. For matrices $\mathbf{A}$ and $\mathbf{B}$ where $\mathbf{A}^\top\mathbf{B}$ is defined, we abuse the pairing notation in the following way: $e([\mathbf{A}]_1, [\mathbf{B}]_2) = [\mathbf{A}^\top\mathbf{B}]_T$. A function $f : \mathbb{N} \to \mathbb{R}$ is called negligible if $f(\lambda) = \lambda^{-\omega(1)}$ and denotes $f(\lambda) \leq \mathsf{negl}(\lambda)$. For families of distributions $X := \{X_\lambda\}_{\lambda\in\mathbb{N}}$ and $Y := \{Y_\lambda\}_{\lambda\in\mathbb{N}}$, $X \approx_c Y$ means that they are computationally indistinguishable.

2.2 Basic Tools

Boolean Formula and NC^1. A monotone Boolean formula can be represented by a Boolean circuit whose all gates have fan-in 2 and fan-out 1. We can specify a monotone Boolean formula $f : \{0,1\}^n \to \{0,1\}$ as $f = (n, w, v, G)$, where $n, m, v \in \mathbb{N}$ and $G : [v] \to \{\text{AND, OR}\} \times [w]^3$. This means the Boolean formula f has n input wires, w wires including the input wires, and v gates. We number the wires $1, \dots, w$ and the gates $1, \dots, v$. The function G specifies a type, incoming wires, and an outgoing wire of each gate. That is, for $G(i) = (T, a, b, c)$ such that $a < b < c$, T specifies a type of gate i, a and b specify the incoming wires, and c specifies the outgoing wire. A non-monotone Boolean formula additionally contains NOT gates, which have fan-in 1 and fan-out 1. It is well-known that we can express all non-monotone Boolean formulae by one in which all NOT gates are put on the input wires, and we only consider such formulae in this paper. Thus, we can specify a non-monotone Boolean formula $f' : \{0,1\}^n \rightarrow \{0,1\}$ as $f' = (f, t)$, where $f = (n, w, v, G)$ is a monotone Boolean formula and $t : [n] \rightarrow \{0,1\}$ specifies input gates that connect to a NOT gate. That is, input wire i connects to a NOT gate if $t(i) = 0$ and does not if $t(i) = 1$.

Standard complexity theory tells us that circuit complexity class NC^1 and Boolean formulae are equivalent. It is known also that NC^1 is equivalent to the class captured by log-depth Boolean formulae (see e.g., [21]). Thus, the circuit complexity class captured by Boolean formulae is equivalent to the class captured by log-depth Boolean formulae.

Definition 2.1 (Pseudorandom Functions). *A pseudorandom function (PRF) family $\mathcal{F} := \{F_K\}_{K \in \mathcal{K}_\lambda}$ with a key space $\mathcal{K}_\lambda$, a domain $\mathcal{X}_\lambda$, and a range $\mathcal{Y}_\lambda$ is a function family that consists of functions $F_K : \mathcal{X}_\lambda \rightarrow \mathcal{Y}_\lambda$. Let $\mathcal{R}_\lambda$ be a set of functions consisting of all functions whose domain and range are $\mathcal{X}_\lambda$ and $\mathcal{Y}_\lambda$ respectively. For any PPT adversary $\mathcal{A}$, the following condition holds,*

$$\mathsf{Adv}_{\mathcal{A}}^{\mathsf{PRF}}(\lambda) := |\Pr[1 \leftarrow \mathcal{A}^{F_K(\cdot)}] - \Pr[1 \leftarrow \mathcal{A}^{R(\cdot)}]| \leq \mathsf{negl}(\lambda),$$

where $K \leftarrow \mathcal{K}_\lambda$ and $R \leftarrow \mathcal{R}_\lambda$.

Definition 2.2 (Bilinear Groups). *A description of bilinear groups $\mathbb{G}:=(p, G_1, G_2, G_T, g_1, g_2, e)$ consist of a prime p, cyclic groups G_1, G_2, G_T of order p, generators g_1 and g_2 of G_1 and G_2 respectively, and a bilinear map $e : G_1 \times G_2 \rightarrow G_T$, which has two properties.*

- *(Bilinearity): $\forall h_1 \in G_1, h_2 \in G_2, a, b \in \mathbb{Z}_p, e(h_1^a, h_2^b) = e(h_1, h_2)^{ab}$.*
- *(Non-degeneracy): For g_1 and g_2, $g_T := e(g_1, g_2)$ is a generator of G_T.*

A bilinear group generator $\mathcal{G}_{\mathsf{BG}}(1^\lambda)$ takes a security parameter 1^λ and outputs a description of bilinear groups $\mathbb{G}$ with $\Omega(\lambda)$ bit prime. In this paper, we refer to Type-I groups, where efficient isomorphisms exist in both way between G_1 and G_2, as symmetric bilinear groups, and Type-III groups, where no efficient isomorphisms exist between them, as asymmetric bilinear groups.

For the proofs of our schemes, we utilize the $\mathcal{D}_k$-MDDH assumption [14], which is generalization of the DDH assumption. There are mainly two types of $\mathcal{D}_k$-MDDH assumption families for asymmetric bilinear groups. In the first one, an instance contains unilateral group elements such as the SXDH assumption. The other one consists of assumptions that are involved with bilateral group elements such as the DLIN assumption used in [1], which is sometimes called the XDLIN assumption. In our paper, we utilize the latter type.

Definition 2.3 ($\mathcal{D}_{j,k}$-MDDH Assumption). *For $j > k$, let $\mathcal{D}_{j,k}$ be a matrix distribution over $\mathbb{Z}_p^{j\times k}$ that outputs full rank matrix with overwhelming probability. We can assume that, wlog, the first k rows of a matrix $\mathbf{A}$ chosen from $\mathcal{D}_{j,k}$ form an invertible matrix. We consider the following distribution:*

$$\mathbb{G} \leftarrow \mathcal{G}_{\mathsf{BG}}(1^\lambda),\ \ \mathbf{A} \leftarrow \mathcal{D}_k,\ \ \mathbf{v} \leftarrow \mathbb{Z}_p^k,\ \ \mathbf{t}_0 := \mathbf{A}\mathbf{v},\ \ \mathbf{t}_1 \leftarrow \mathbb{Z}_p^j,$$
$$P_\beta := (\mathbb{G}, [\mathbf{A}]_{1,2}, [\mathbf{t}_\beta]_{1,2}).$$

We say that the bilateral $\mathcal{D}_{j,k}$-MDDH assumption holds with respect to $\mathcal{G}_{\mathsf{BG}}$ if, for any PPT adversary $\mathcal{A}$,

$$\mathsf{Adv}_{\mathcal{A},\mathsf{bi}}^{\mathcal{D}_{j,k}\text{-}\mathsf{MDDH}}(\lambda) := |\Pr[1 \leftarrow \mathcal{A}(P_0)] - \Pr[1 \leftarrow \mathcal{A}(P_1)]| \le \mathsf{negl}(\lambda).$$

We denote $\mathcal{D}_{k+1,k}$ by $\mathcal{D}_k$. Let $\mathcal{U}_{j,k}$ be a uniform distribution over full rank matrices in $\mathbb{Z}_p^{j\times k}$. Then, the following relations hold with tight reductions; $\mathcal{D}_k$-MDDH $\Rightarrow \mathcal{U}_k$-MDDH $\Rightarrow \mathcal{U}_{j,k}$-MDDH.

For an appropriate distribution $\mathcal{D}_k$, the $\mathcal{D}_k$-MDDH assumption generically holds in k-linear groups [14]. Thus, in asymmetric bilinear groups, we can utilize the bilateral $\mathcal{D}_k$-MDDH assumption for $k \ge 2$.

Matrix Notation. For a matrix $\mathbf{A} \in \mathcal{D}_k$, we define a matrix $\mathbf{A}^*$ and vectors $\mathbf{a}_1$ and $\mathbf{a}_1^*$ as follows. Vector $\mathbf{a}_1$ is a $k+1$ dimensional vector whose last entry is 1 and the others are 0. Then, it is not hard to see that $\overline{\mathbf{A}} := (\mathbf{A}||\mathbf{a}_1)$ forms a basis of $\mathbb{Z}_p^{k+1}$ because the first k rows of a matrix $\mathbf{A}$ chosen from $\mathcal{D}_k$ form an invertible matrix. $\mathbf{A}^*$ and $\mathbf{a}_1^*$ are the matrix that consists of the left k columns of $(\overline{\mathbf{A}}^\top)^{-1}$ and the vector that consists of right one column of $(\overline{\mathbf{A}}^\top)^{-1}$, respectively. Note that we have $\mathbf{A}^\top\mathbf{A}^* = \mathbf{I}_k$, $\mathbf{A}^\top\mathbf{a}_1^* = \mathbf{0}$, and $\mathbf{A}^*\mathbf{A}^\top + \mathbf{a}_1^*\mathbf{a}_1^\top = \mathbf{I}_{k+1}$. We use a similar notation for a matrix $\overline{\mathbf{B}} \in \mathsf{GL}_{k+\eta}(\mathbb{Z}_p)$ where $\eta \in \mathbb{N}$. $\mathbf{B}$ and $\mathbf{b}_i$ denote a matrix consists of the first k columns of $\overline{\mathbf{B}}$ and a vector consists of the $k+i$-th column of $\overline{\mathbf{B}}$, respectively. Similarly, $\mathbf{B}^*$, $\mathbf{b}_i^*$ denote a matrix consists of the first k columns of $(\overline{\mathbf{B}}^\top)^{-1}$ and a vector consists of the $k+i$-th column of $(\overline{\mathbf{B}}^\top)^{-1}$, respectively. For the convenience, we denote $(\mathbf{b}_1||\mathbf{b}_2)$ by $\mathbf{B}_{12}$, and this notation is applied to other cases similarly.

2.3 Attribute-Based Encryption

Definition 2.4 (Attribute-Based Encryption). *An attribute-based encryption (ABE) scheme for relation $R : \mathcal{X} \times \mathcal{Y} \to \{0, 1\}$ consists of four algorithms, where $\mathcal{X}$ and $\mathcal{Y}$ are an attribute universe and predicate universe, respectively.*

$\mathsf{Setup}(1^\lambda)$: *It takes a security parameter 1^λ and outputs a public key pk and a master secret key msk. pk specifies a message space $\mathcal{M}$.*

$\mathsf{Enc}(\mathsf{pk}, x, m)$: *It takes pk, an attribute $x \in \mathcal{X}$ and a message $m \in \mathcal{M}$ and outputs a ciphertext ct_x.*

$\mathsf{KeyGen}(\mathsf{pk}, \mathsf{msk}, y)$: *It takes $\mathsf{pk}, \mathsf{msk}$, and a predicate $y \in \mathcal{Y}$ and outputs a secret key sk_y.*

$\mathsf{Dec}(\mathsf{pk}, \mathsf{ct}_x, \mathsf{sk}_y)$: *It takes $\mathsf{pk}, \mathsf{ct}_x$ and sk_y and outputs a message m' or $\perp$.*

Correctness. *An ABE scheme is correct if it satisfies the following condition. For all* $\lambda \in \mathbb{N}$, $x \in \mathcal{X}$, $y \in \mathcal{Y}$ *such that* $R(x, y) = 1$, *and* $m \in \mathcal{M}$, *we have*

$$\Pr\left[m = m' \,\middle|\, \begin{array}{l} (\mathsf{pk}, \mathsf{msk}) \leftarrow \mathsf{Setup}(1^\lambda) \\ \mathsf{ct}_x \leftarrow \mathsf{Enc}(\mathsf{pk}, x, m) \\ \mathsf{sk}_y \leftarrow \mathsf{KeyGen}(\mathsf{pk}, \mathsf{msk}, y) \\ m' := \mathsf{Dec}(\mathsf{pk}, \mathsf{ct}_x, \mathsf{sk}_y) \end{array} \right] = 1.$$

Security. *An ABE scheme is adaptively secure if it satisfies the following condition. That is, the advantage of* $\mathcal{A}$ *defined as follows is negligible in* λ *for all stateful PPT adversary* $\mathcal{A}$:

$$\mathsf{Adv}_{\mathcal{A}}^{\mathsf{ABE}}(\lambda) := \left| \Pr\left[\beta = \beta' \,\middle|\, \begin{array}{l} \beta \leftarrow \{0,1\} \\ (\mathsf{pk}, \mathsf{msk}) \leftarrow \mathsf{Setup}(1^\lambda) \\ (x^*, m_0, m_1) \leftarrow \mathcal{A}^{\mathsf{KeyGen}(\mathsf{pk}, \mathsf{msk}, \cdot)}(\mathsf{pk}) \\ \mathsf{ct}_{x^*} \leftarrow \mathsf{Enc}(\mathsf{pk}, x^*, m_\beta) \\ \beta' \leftarrow \mathcal{A}^{\mathsf{KeyGen}(\mathsf{pk}, \mathsf{msk}, \cdot)}(\mathsf{ct}_{x^*}) \end{array} \right] - \frac{1}{2} \right|,$$

where $\{y_i\}_{i \in [q_{\mathsf{sk}}]}$ *on which* $\mathcal{A}$ *queries* KeyGen *must satisfy* $R(x^*, y_i) = 0$.

A relation for ABE that we consider in our paper is expressed by a non-monotone Boolean formula over the equivalence relation in $\mathbb{Z}_p$. More specifically, each input of the Boolean formula is decided by whether certain components in an attribute and predicate are equal. Then, the relation is decided by the output of the formula. Our relation is very close to that formulated by Okamoto and Takashima in [27], though their scheme has one-use restriction on labels in policies. One caveat is that we can use only a non-monotone Boolean formula for a predicate in our scheme, whereas the relation by Okamoto and Takashima allows us to use a more powerful non-monotone span program for a predicate. In the following, we consider only non-monotone Boolean formulae where NOT gates exist only on input wires.

Definition 2.5 (Relation R). *Relations* R_{KP} *and* R_{CP} *for our KP and CP-ABE schemes, respectively, are defined as follows. Let* $R : \mathcal{X} \times \mathcal{Y} \to \{0,1\}$ *be a relation defined as follows:*

- $\mathcal{X} = \bigcup_{i \in \mathbb{N}} \mathbb{Z}_p^i \times \Phi_i$, *where* Φ_i *consists of all injective functions such that* $\phi : [i] \to \{0,1\}^*$.
- $\mathcal{Y} = \bigcup_{i \in \mathbb{N}} \mathbb{Z}_p^i \times \mathcal{F}_i \times \Psi_i \times \mathcal{T}_i$, *where* $\mathcal{F}_i$ *consists of all monotone Boolean formulae whose input lengths are* i, *and* Ψ_i *and* $\mathcal{T}_i$ *consist of all functions such that* $\psi : [i] \to \{0,1\}^*$ *and* $t : [i] \to \{0,1\}$, *respectively.*
- *For* $x = (\mathbf{x} \in \mathbb{Z}_p^m, \phi)$ *and* $y = (\mathbf{y} \in \mathbb{Z}_p^n, f, \psi, t)$, *we define* $b = (b_1, \ldots, b_n) \in \{0,1\}^n$ *as* $b_i := \begin{cases} t(i) \odot \mathrm{true}(x_{\phi^{-1}(\psi(i))} = y_i) & \psi(i) \subseteq \mathrm{Im}(\phi) \\ 0 & \psi(i) \not\subseteq \mathrm{Im}(\phi) \end{cases}$, *where* $\odot$ *denotes xnor. Then,* $R(x, y) = 1 \Leftrightarrow f(b) = 1$.

Then, $R_{\mathsf{KP}} : \mathcal{X}_{\mathsf{KP}} \times \mathcal{Y}_{\mathsf{KP}} \to \{0,1\}$ *is defined as* $\mathcal{X}_{\mathsf{KP}} := \mathcal{X}$*,* $\mathcal{Y}_{\mathsf{KP}} := \mathcal{Y}$*, and* $R_{\mathsf{KP}}(x,y) = R(x,y)$*, whereas* $R_{\mathsf{CP}} : \mathcal{X}_{\mathsf{CP}} \times \mathcal{Y}_{\mathsf{CP}} \to \{0,1\}$ *is defined as* $\mathcal{X}_{\mathsf{CP}} := \mathcal{Y}$*,* $\mathcal{Y}_{\mathsf{CP}} := \mathcal{X}$*, and* $R_{\mathsf{CP}}(x,y) = R(y,x)$*.*

For $\mathcal{X}$, each element of $\mathbf{x} \in \mathbb{Z}_p^m$ corresponds to a value for some label, and ϕ specifies which label each element of $\mathbf{x}$ is associated with. For instance, when we consider an attribute (AGE:22, HOBBY:tennis), $x = (\mathbf{x}, \phi)$ can be set as $\mathbf{x} := (22, H_1(\text{tennis}))$, $\phi(1) :=$ AGE, and $\phi(2) :=$ HOBBY where $H_1 : \{0,1\}^* \to \mathbb{Z}_p$ is a collision resistant hash function.

For $\mathcal{Y}$, each element of $\mathbf{y} \in \mathbb{Z}_p^n$ corresponds to the value for each input wire of f, and ψ specifies which label each input wire of f is associated with. Additionally, t specifies whether each input wire connects to a NOT gate. For instance, let us consider a predicate (AGE:25 AND HOBBY:NOT baseball). Then, $y = (\mathbf{y}, f, \psi, t)$ can be set as $\mathbf{y} := (25, H_1(\text{baseball}))$, f is a formula with a single AND gate, $\psi(1) :=$ AGE and $\psi(2) :=$ HOBBY, and $t(1) = 1$ and $t(2) = 0$.

Definition 2.6 (Linear Secret Sharing Scheme). *A linear secret sharing scheme (LSSS) for a function class* $\mathcal{F}$ *consists of two algorithms* Share *and* Rec*.*

Share$(f, \mathbf{k})$**:** *It takes a function* $f \in \mathcal{F}$ *where* $f : \{0,1\}^n \to \{0,1\}$ *and a vector* $\mathbf{k} \in \mathbb{Z}_p^\ell$*. Then, outputs shares* $\mathbf{k}_1, \ldots, \mathbf{k}_n \in \mathbb{Z}_p^\ell$*.*

Rec$(f, x, \{\mathbf{k}_i\}_{x_i=1})$**:** *It takes* $f : \{0,1\}^n \to \{0,1\}$*, a bit string* $x := (x_1, \ldots, x_n) \in \{0,1\}^n$ *and shares* $\{\mathbf{k}_i\}_{x_i=1}$*. Then, outputs a vector* $\mathbf{k}'$ *or* $\perp$*.*

In particular, Rec *computes a linear function on shares to reconstruct a secret;* $\mathbf{k} = \sum_{x_i=1} a_i \mathbf{k}_i$ *where each* a_i *is determined by* f*. A LSSS has two properties.*

Correctness: *For any* $f \in F$*,* $x \in \{0,1\}^n$ *such that* $f(x) = 1$*,*

$$\Pr[\mathsf{Rec}(f, x, \{\mathbf{k}_i\}_{x_i=1}) = \mathbf{k} \mid \mathbf{k}_1, \ldots, \mathbf{k}_n \leftarrow \mathsf{Share}(f, \mathbf{k})] = 1.$$

Security: *For any* $f \in F$*,* $x \in \{0,1\}^n$ *such that* $f(x) = 0$*, and* $\mathbf{k}_1, \ldots, \mathbf{k}_n \leftarrow$ Share$(f, \mathbf{k})$*, shares* $\{\mathbf{k}_i\}_{x_i=1}$ *have no information about* $\mathbf{k}$*.*

2.4 Piecewise Guessing Framework

Here, we briefly recall the piecewise guessing framework by Kowalczyk and Wee [21], which is based on the framework by Jafargholi et al. [18]. The framework helps us to prove adaptive security of cryptographic schemes that are selectively secure.

Definition 2.7 (Interactive Game). *An interactive game* G *is a game between an adversary* $\mathcal{A}$ *and a challenger* $\mathcal{C}$*. In the game,* $\mathcal{A}$ *and* $\mathcal{C}$ *send messages interactively, and the messages sent by* $\mathcal{C}$ *depend on the game* G*. After the interaction,* $\mathcal{A}$ *outputs* $\beta \in \{0,1\}$*. We denotes the output of* $\mathcal{A}$ *in* G *by* $\langle \mathcal{A}, \mathsf{G} \rangle$*. Let* $z \in \{0,1\}^R$ *be a part of messages supposed to be sent by* $\mathcal{A}$ *in the game. In the adaptive game* G*,* $\mathcal{A}$ *can send* z *at arbitrary points as long as it follows a rule of the game. We define the selective variant of* G*, denoted by* $\widehat{\mathsf{G}}$*, to be the same as* G *except that* $\mathcal{A}$ *has to declare* z *that will be sent in the game, at the beginning of the interaction.*

Suppose we want to show that adaptive games G_0 and G_1 are computationally indistinguishable, i.e.,

$$|\Pr[\langle \mathcal{A}, \mathsf{G}_0 \rangle = 1] - \Pr[\langle \mathcal{A}, \mathsf{G}_1 \rangle = 1]| \leq \mathsf{negl}(\lambda).$$

Then, we consider a series of selective hybrids $\widehat{\mathsf{H}}^{h_0}, \ldots, \widehat{\mathsf{H}}^{h_L}$ such that

$$\widehat{\mathsf{G}}_0 = \widehat{\mathsf{H}}^{h_0} \approx_c \widehat{\mathsf{H}}^{h_1} \approx_c, \ldots, \approx_c \widehat{\mathsf{H}}^{h_L} = \widehat{\mathsf{G}}_1,$$

where $h_0, \ldots, h_L : \{0,1\}^R \to \{0,1\}^{R'}$ for some $R' \ll R$, and $\widehat{\mathsf{H}}^{h_\iota}$ is an interactive game in which $\mathcal{C}$'s messages depend on $u := h_\iota(z)$. Additionally, h_0 and h_L need to be constant functions. Note that $\mathcal{C}$ can generate messages depending on u because z is declared at the beginning of the interaction. Next, we define variants of $\widehat{\mathsf{H}}^{h_\iota}$, namely, $\widehat{\mathsf{H}}_0^{h_\iota}$ and $\widehat{\mathsf{H}}_1^{h_\iota}$ as follows. In $\widehat{\mathsf{H}}_\beta^{h_\iota}$ for $\beta \in \{0,1\}$, $\mathcal{A}$ has to declare $h_{\iota-1+\beta}(z)$ and $h_{\iota+\beta}(z)$ instead of z at the beginning of the game. Then, $\mathcal{C}$ interacts with $\mathcal{A}$ setting $u := h_\iota(z)$ in both $\widehat{\mathsf{H}}_0^{h_\iota}$ and $\widehat{\mathsf{H}}_1^{h_\iota}$. In other words, $\widehat{\mathsf{H}}_\beta^{h_\iota}$ is the same as $\widehat{\mathsf{H}}^{h_\iota}$ except that only partial information of z is declared by $\mathcal{A}$. Now we are ready to state the adaptive security lemma.

Lemma 2.1 (Adaptive Security Lemma [21]). *Let G_0 and G_1 be adaptive interactive games and $\{\widehat{\mathsf{H}}^{h_i}\}_{0 \leq i \leq L}$ be selective hybrids defined above. Suppose they satisfy the two properties:*

- *$\mathsf{G}_0 = \mathsf{H}^{h_0}$ and $\mathsf{G}_1 = \mathsf{H}^{h_L}$, where H^{h_0} and H^{h_L} are the same as $\widehat{\mathsf{H}}^{h_0}$ and $\widehat{\mathsf{H}}^{h_L}$, respectively, except that $\mathcal{A}$ does not declare z at the beginning. Note that $\mathcal{C}$'s messages can be correctly defined because h_0 and h_L are constant functions.*
- *For all PPT adversary $\mathcal{A}$ and all $\iota \in L$, we have*

$$|\Pr[\langle \mathcal{A}, \widehat{\mathsf{H}}_1^{h_{\iota-1}} \rangle = 1] - \Pr[\langle \mathcal{A}, \widehat{\mathsf{H}}_0^{h_\iota} \rangle = 1]| \leq \epsilon.$$

Then, we have

$$|\Pr[\langle \mathcal{A}, \mathsf{G}_0 \rangle = 1] - \Pr[\langle \mathcal{A}, \mathsf{G}_1 \rangle = 1]| \leq 2^{2R'} L\epsilon.$$

2.5 Pebbling Strategy for Boolean Formula

A pebbling strategy is used for a guide of how to construct a series of hybrids in the piecewise guessing framework.

Definition 2.8 (Pebbling Game). *A player of the pebbling game is given a monotone Boolean formula $f : \{0,1\}^n \to \{0,1\}$ and input $b = (b_1, \ldots, b_n) \in \{0,1\}^n$ such that $f(b) = 0$. The goal of the game is to reach the state where a pebble is placed on only the output gate (the gate with the output wire), starting from the state with no pebbles on the Boolean formula f, following a pebbling rule. The rule is defined as follows.*

1. *We can place or remove a pebble on input wire i whose input corresponds to 0, i.e., $b_i = 0$.*

2. *We can place or remove a pebble on an AND gate if at least one of its incoming wires comes from a gate or input wire with a pebble on it.*
3. *We can place or remove a pebble on an OR gate if both of its incoming wires come from a gate or input wire with a pebble on it, respectively.*
4. *We can pass the turn, which allows us to increase the total number of steps in the game without changing the pebbling strategy.*

Definition 2.9 (Pebbling Record). *A pebbling record $\mathcal{R} := (r_0, \ldots, r_L) \in (\{0,1\}^{R'})^L$ is a list of all pebbling configuration that a player took from the start to the goal in the pebbling game. R'-bit string r_ι specifies the configuration at the ι-th step in the play. Thus, r_0 specifies the state with no pebbles and r_L specifies the state with one pebble on the output gate. It also means that the player takes L steps to reach the goal, and all pebbling configurations that the player took can be specified by an R'-bit string.*

The following lemma says that, for any monotone Boolean formula and input, there exists a pebbling strategy where all pebbling configurations can be specified with a "short" bit string.

Lemma 2.2 (Pebbling Lemma [21]). *Let $f : \{0,1\}^n \to \{0,1\}$ be any monotone Boolean formula with a depth $d \leq B$, and $b \in \{0,1\}^n$ be any bit string such that $f(b) = 0$. Then, there exists a deterministic algorithm $\mathsf{PebRec}(f, b)$ that takes f and b and outputs a record $\mathcal{R}$ consisting of 8^B strings whose lengths are $3B$ bits.*

3 Our KP-ABE Scheme

First, we describe a linear secret sharing scheme that we use in our schemes as a building block.

3.1 Linear Secret Sharing for Boolean Formulae

Our secret sharing scheme for monotone Boolean formulae is described in Fig. 1, which is essentially the same as the scheme in [22, Appendix G]. Note that it works similarly if all vectors in Fig. 1 are group elements. Let f be a formula and $b = (b_1, \ldots, b_n)$ be a bit string such that $f(b) = 1$. Then, for reconstruction, it is not difficult to see that there exists a set $S \subseteq \{i \mid b_i = 1\}$ such that $\sum_{i \in S} \boldsymbol{\sigma}_i = \mathbf{k}$.

Clearly, the number of shares for formula f corresponds to the number of its input wires. The secret sharing scheme employed by Kowalczyk and Wee is different from ours [20], where the number of shares corresponds to the summation of the numbers of input wires and gates in f. We show that we can utilize their framework even if we replace the secret sharing scheme to ours.

We use the following lemma on the secret sharing scheme in the security proof of our scheme.

$\mathsf{Share}(f, \mathbf{k})$
Input: A monotone Boolean formula $f = (n, w, v, G)$ and a secret $\mathbf{k} \in \mathbb{Z}_p^{\ell}$.
1. Set a vector $\boldsymbol{\sigma}_{\mathsf{out}} := \mathbf{k}$ on the output wire.
2. For each AND gate g with incoming wires a, b and an outgoing wire c where a vector $\boldsymbol{\sigma}_c$ is set on c, choose $\mathbf{u}_g \leftarrow \mathbb{Z}_p^{\ell}$ and set $\boldsymbol{\sigma}_a := \boldsymbol{\sigma}_c - \mathbf{u}_g$ and $\boldsymbol{\sigma}_b := \mathbf{u}_g$ on a and b, respectively.
3. For each OR gate g with incoming wires a, b and an outgoing wire c where a vector $\boldsymbol{\sigma}_c$ is set on c, set $\boldsymbol{\sigma}_a := \boldsymbol{\sigma}_c$ and $\boldsymbol{\sigma}_b := \boldsymbol{\sigma}_c$ on a and b, respectively.
4. Output shares $\boldsymbol{\sigma}_1, \ldots, \boldsymbol{\sigma}_n$, which are set on the input wires $1, \ldots, n$.

Fig. 1. Our linear secret sharing scheme for Boolean formulae.

Lemma 3.1. *Let* Share *be the algorithm defined in Fig. 1. For all* $\ell, n \in \mathbb{N}$, *monotone Boolean formulae* $f = (n, w, v, G)$, $\mathbf{k}, \mathbf{a} \in \mathbb{Z}_p^{\ell}$, *and* $\mu \in \mathbb{Z}_p$, *we define the following distribution.*

$$\mathbf{k}_1, \ldots, \mathbf{k}_n \leftarrow \mathsf{Share}(f, \mathbf{k} + \mu\mathbf{a}), \quad \mathbf{k}'_1, \ldots, \mathbf{k}'_n \leftarrow \mathsf{Share}(f, \mathbf{k}),$$
$$\sigma_1, \ldots, \sigma_n \leftarrow \mathsf{Share}(f, \mu).$$

Then, the two distributions are identical:

$$\{\mathbf{k}_1, \ldots, \mathbf{k}_n\} \text{ and } \{\mathbf{k}'_1 + \sigma_1\mathbf{a}, \ldots, \mathbf{k}'_n + \sigma_n\mathbf{a}\}.$$

The proof of Lemma 3.1 is presented in the full version.

3.2 Construction

For generality, we describe our scheme using a matrix distribution $\mathcal{D}_k$. When we instantiate our scheme from asymmetric pairings, we typically choose the k-Lin family $\mathcal{L}_k$ with $k = 2$. In this case, we can set matrices as

$$\mathbf{A} = \begin{pmatrix} a_1 & 0 \\ 0 & a_2 \\ 1 & 1 \end{pmatrix}, \quad \mathbf{A}^* = \begin{pmatrix} \frac{1}{a_1} & 0 \\ 0 & \frac{1}{a_2} \\ 0 & 0 \end{pmatrix}, \quad \mathbf{a}_1^* = \begin{pmatrix} -\frac{1}{a_1} \\ -\frac{1}{a_2} \\ 1 \end{pmatrix},$$

where $a_1, a_2 \leftarrow \mathbb{Z}_p$. Let $H : \{0,1\}^* \rightarrow G_1^{(k+1)\times k} \times G_1^{(k+1)\times k}$ be a hash function modeled as a random oracle. Let $F_K : \{0,1\}^* \rightarrow \mathbb{Z}_p^{k+1} \times \mathbb{Z}_p^{k+1}$ be a PRF with a secret key K. Let $\mathcal{K}_\lambda$ be a key space of the PRF. Let Share be the LSSS described in Fig. 1. Note that we can instantiate H from a hash function $H' : \{0,1\}^* \rightarrow G_1$ by generating each output group element of H with H'. More precisely, each output group element of $H(i)$ is defined by $H'(i||\$||j)$, where $\$$ is a special symbol and $j \in [2k(k+1)]$ specifies the location of the matrices. The symbol $\$$ can be expressed by encoding, e.g., $0 \rightarrow 00$, $1 \rightarrow 11$, and $\$ \rightarrow 01$. Our scheme for R_{KP} is described as follows.

$\mathsf{Setup}(1^\lambda)$: It takes a security parameter 1^λ and outputs pk and msk as follows.

$$\mathbb{G} \leftarrow \mathcal{G}_{\mathsf{BG}}(1^\lambda),\;\; \mathbf{A} \leftarrow \mathcal{D}_k,\;\; \mathbf{B} \leftarrow \mathbb{Z}_p^{(k+1)\times k},\;\; \mathbf{k} \leftarrow \mathbb{Z}_p^{k+1},\;\; K \leftarrow \mathcal{K}_\lambda,$$
$$\mathsf{pk} := (\mathbb{G}, [\mathbf{A}]_2, [\mathbf{A}^\top \mathbf{k}]_T),\;\; \mathsf{msk} := (\mathbf{A}^*, \mathbf{a}_1^*, \mathbf{B}, \mathbf{k}, K).$$

$\mathsf{Enc}(\mathsf{pk}, x, M)$: It takes pk, an attribute $x = (\mathbf{x} \in \mathbb{Z}_p^m, \phi)$, and a message $M \in G_T$ and outputs ct_x as follows.

$$\mathbf{s} \leftarrow \mathbb{Z}_p^k,\;\; ([\mathbf{U}_{\phi(i),0}]_1, [\mathbf{U}_{\phi(i),1}]_1) := H(\phi(i)),$$
$$c_1 := [\mathbf{A}\mathbf{s}]_2,\;\; c_{2,i} := [(x_i \mathbf{U}_{\phi(i),0} + \mathbf{U}_{\phi(i),1})\mathbf{s}]_1,\;\; c_3 := [\mathbf{s}^\top \mathbf{A}^\top \mathbf{k}]_T M,$$
$$\mathsf{ct}_x := (x, c_1, \{c_{2,i}\}_{i\in[m]}, c_3).$$

$\mathsf{KeyGen}(\mathsf{pk}, \mathsf{msk}, y)$: It takes pk, msk, and a predicate $y = (\mathbf{y} \in \mathbb{Z}_p^n, f, \psi, t)$ and outputs sk_y as follows. Let $\pi : [n] \to \mathbb{N}$ be a function such that $\pi(i) := |\{j \mid \psi(j) = \psi(i), j \le i\}|$. Let d be the maximum number of multi-use of labels in f, i.e., $d := \max_{i\in[n]} \pi(i)$.

$$\mathbf{r}_1, \ldots, \mathbf{r}_d \leftarrow \mathbb{Z}_p^k,\;\; k_{1,j} := [\mathbf{B}\mathbf{r}_j]_2,\;\; \mathbf{k}_1, \ldots, \mathbf{k}_n \leftarrow \mathsf{Share}(f, \mathbf{k}) \in \mathbb{Z}_p^{k+1},$$
$$([\mathbf{U}_{\psi(i),0}]_1, [\mathbf{U}_{\psi(i),1}]_1) := H(\psi(i)),\;\; (\mathbf{u}_{\psi(i),0}, \mathbf{u}_{\psi(i),1}) := F_K(\psi(i)),$$
If $t(i) = 1$:
$$k_{2,i} := [\mathbf{k}_i + \mathbf{A}^*(y_i \mathbf{U}_{\psi(i),0}^\top + \mathbf{U}_{\psi(i),1}^\top)\mathbf{B}\mathbf{r}_{\pi(i)} + \mathbf{a}_1^*(y_i \mathbf{u}_{\psi(i),0}^\top + \mathbf{u}_{\psi(i),1}^\top)\mathbf{B}\mathbf{r}_{\pi(i)}]_1,$$
If $t(i) = 0$:
$$k_{2,i} := (k_{2,i,1}, k_{2,i,2}) := \begin{pmatrix} [-\mathbf{k}_i + \mathbf{A}^*\mathbf{U}_{\psi(i),0}^\top \mathbf{B}\mathbf{r}_{\pi(i)} + \mathbf{a}_1^* \mathbf{u}_{\psi(i),0}^\top \mathbf{B}\mathbf{r}_{\pi(i)}]_1, \\ [y_i \mathbf{k}_i + \mathbf{A}^*\mathbf{U}_{\psi(i),1}^\top \mathbf{B}\mathbf{r}_{\pi(i)} + \mathbf{a}_1^* \mathbf{u}_{\psi(i),1}^\top \mathbf{B}\mathbf{r}_{\pi(i)}]_1 \end{pmatrix}$$
$$\mathsf{sk}_y := (y, \{k_{1,j}\}_{j\in[d]}, \{k_{2,i}\}_{i\in[n]}).$$

$\mathsf{Dec}(\mathsf{pk}, \mathsf{ct}_x, \mathsf{sk}_y)$: It takes pk, ct_x, and sk_y. It computes $b \in \{0,1\}^n$ from x and y as in Definition 2.5. If $f(b) = 0$, it outputs $\perp$. Otherwise, computes a set $S \subseteq \{i \mid b_i = 1\}$ such that $\mathbf{k} = \sum_{i\in S} \mathbf{k}_i$. Let $S_1 := S \cap \{i \mid t(i) = 1\}$ and $S_0 := S \cap \{i \mid t(i) = 0\}$. Then outputs M' as follows.

$$D_{1,j} := e\left(\sum_{\substack{\pi(i)=j \\ i\in S_1}} k_{2,i} + \sum_{\substack{\pi(i)=j \\ i\in S_0}} \frac{1}{y_i - x_{\phi^{-1}(\psi(i))}} (x_{\phi^{-1}(\psi(i))} k_{2,i,1} + k_{2,i,2}), c_1 \right)^\top$$

$$D_{2,j} := e\left(\sum_{\substack{\pi(i)=j \\ i\in S_1}} c_{2,\phi^{-1}(\psi(i))} + \sum_{\substack{\pi(i)=j \\ i\in S_0}} \frac{1}{y_i - x_{\phi^{-1}(\psi(i))}} c_{2,\phi^{-1}(\psi(i))}, k_{1,j} \right)$$

$$M' := c_3 / \prod_{j\in[d]} (D_{1,j}/D_{2,j}).$$

Correctness: For honestly generated ct_x and sk_y such that $R(x, y) = 1$,

$$D_{1,j} = \left[\begin{array}{l} \sum_{\substack{\pi(i)=j \\ i \in S_1}} \left(\mathbf{s}^\top \mathbf{A}^\top \mathbf{k}_i + \mathbf{s}^\top (y_i \mathbf{U}^\top_{\psi(i),0} + \mathbf{U}^\top_{\psi(i),1}) \mathbf{B} \mathbf{r}_j \right) \\ + \sum_{\substack{\pi(i)=j \\ i \in S_0}} \left(\mathbf{s}^\top \mathbf{A}^\top \mathbf{k}_i + \frac{1}{y_i - x_{\phi^{-1}(\psi(i))}} \mathbf{s}^\top (x_{\phi^{-1}(\psi(i))} \mathbf{U}^\top_{\psi(i),0} + \mathbf{U}^\top_{\psi(i),1}) \mathbf{B} \mathbf{r}_j \right) \end{array} \right]_T$$

$$D_{2,j} = \left[\begin{array}{l} \sum_{\substack{\pi(i)=j \\ i \in S_1}} \left(\mathbf{s}^\top (x_{\phi^{-1}(\psi(i))} \mathbf{U}^\top_{\psi(i),0} + \mathbf{U}^\top_{\psi(i),1}) \mathbf{B} \mathbf{r}_j \right) \\ + \sum_{\substack{\pi(i)=j \\ i \in S_0}} \left(\frac{1}{y_i - x_{\phi^{-1}(\psi(i))}} \mathbf{s}^\top (x_{\phi^{-1}(\psi(i))} \mathbf{U}^\top_{\psi(i),0} + \mathbf{U}^\top_{\psi(i),1}) \mathbf{B} \mathbf{r}_j \right) \end{array} \right]_T.$$

In the above, we use the relations $\mathbf{A}^\top \mathbf{A}^* = \mathbf{I}_k$ and $\mathbf{A}^\top \mathbf{a}_1^* = \mathbf{0}$. Because $x_{\phi^{-1}(\psi(i))} = y_i$ for $i \in S_1$, we have $\prod_{j \in [d]} (D_{1,j}/D_{2,j}) = [\mathbf{s}^\top \mathbf{A}^\top \sum_{j \in [d]} \sum_{\substack{i \in S \\ \pi(i)=j}} \mathbf{k}_i]_T = [\mathbf{s}^\top \mathbf{A}^\top \mathbf{k}]_T$. Thus, $M' = M$.

3.3 Security

Theorem 3.1. *Let B be the maximum depth of formulae on which $\mathcal{A}$ queries* KeyGen. *Let q_{sk} be the maximum number of $\mathcal{A}$'s queries to* KeyGen. *Then, our scheme is adaptively secure as long as $B = O(\log \lambda)$. More precisely, for any PPT adversary $\mathcal{A}$, there exist PPT algorithms $\mathcal{B}_1$ and $\mathcal{B}_2$ such that*

$$\mathsf{Adv}^{\mathsf{ABE}}_{\mathcal{A}}(\lambda) \leq \mathsf{Adv}^{\mathsf{PRF}}_{\mathcal{B}_1}(\lambda) + (2^{9B+2} q_{\mathsf{sk}} + 1)(\mathsf{Adv}^{\mathcal{D}_k\text{-}\mathsf{MDDH}}_{\mathcal{B}_2,\mathsf{bi}}(\lambda) + 2^{-\Omega(\lambda)}).$$

Proof Overview. We prove Theorem 3.1 following the standard dual system methodology. To do so, we first replace the PRF with a random function. Then, our scheme basically follows the construction on the dual system group from prime-order groups in [12]. Concretely, we can rewrite $c_{2,i}$ and $k_{2,i}$ in the challenge ciphertext and secret keys as

$$c_{2,i} = [(x_i \mathbf{W}^\top_{\phi(i),0} + \mathbf{W}^\top_{\phi(i),1}) \mathbf{A} \mathbf{s}]_1,$$
$$k_{2,i} := [\mathbf{k}_i + (y_i \mathbf{W}_{\psi(i),0} + \mathbf{W}_{\psi(i),1}) \mathbf{B} \mathbf{r}_{\pi(i)}]_1 \ \text{ if } t(i) = 1,$$
$$k_{2,i} := \begin{pmatrix} [-\mathbf{k}_i + \mathbf{W}_{\psi(i),0} \mathbf{B} \mathbf{r}_{\pi(i)}]_1, \\ [y_i \mathbf{k}_i + \mathbf{W}_{\psi(i),1} \mathbf{B} \mathbf{r}_{\pi(i)}]_1 \end{pmatrix} \ \text{ if } t(i) = 0,$$

where $\mathbf{W}_{i,b} \in \mathbb{Z}_p^{(k+1)\times(k+1)}$. Next, we change the challenge ciphertext into a semi-functional form, where $\mathbf{A}\mathbf{s}$ is replaced with a vector $\mathbf{c} \leftarrow \mathbb{Z}_p^{k+1}$. That is, the elements in a ciphertext are

$$c_1 = [\mathbf{c}]_2,\ c_{2,i} = [(x_i \mathbf{W}^\top_{\phi(i),0} + \mathbf{W}^\top_{\phi(i),1}) \mathbf{c}]_1,\ c_3 = [\mathbf{c}^\top \mathbf{k}]_T M.$$

The indistinguishability directly follows from the $\mathcal{D}_k$-MDDH assumption. After that, we gradually change the secret keys into a semi-functional form, where $\mathbf{k}_i$ is a share of secret $\mathbf{k}+\mu\mathbf{a}_1^*$ instead of $\mathbf{k}$ for $\mu \leftarrow \mathbb{Z}_p$. To prove each indistinguishability, we utilize the KW technique [21]. In the final hybrid, we can argue that $\mathbf{c}^\top\mathbf{k}$ in the challenge ciphertext is statistically close to a uniform randomness.

Proof. We consider a series of hybrids H_0, H_1, H_2, and $\mathsf{H}_{3,\iota}$ for $i \in \{0, \ldots, q_{\mathsf{sk}}\}$, where H_0 is the real game and $\mathsf{H}_{3,q_{\mathsf{sk}}}$ is the final game. In the following, we denote the event $\beta = \beta'$ in hybrid H by $\langle \mathcal{A}, \mathsf{H}\rangle_{\mathsf{win}}$, where β is a random bit chosen by the challenger, and β' is the output of $\mathcal{A}$. Note that we have

$$|\Pr[\langle \mathcal{A}, \mathsf{H}_0\rangle_{\mathsf{win}}] - 1/2| = \mathsf{Adv}_{\mathcal{A}}^{\mathsf{ABE}}(\lambda). \tag{1}$$

$\underline{\mathsf{H}_1}$. We define H_1 as the same as H_0 except replacing PRF F_K in KeyGen with a random function $R : \{0,1\}^* \to \mathbb{Z}_p^{k+1} \times \mathbb{Z}_p^{k+1}$. From the definition of PRFs, we have

$$|\Pr[\langle \mathcal{A}, \mathsf{H}_0\rangle_{\mathsf{win}}] - \Pr[\langle \mathcal{A}, \mathsf{H}_1\rangle_{\mathsf{win}}]| \leq \mathsf{Adv}_{\mathcal{B}}^{\mathsf{PRF}}(\lambda). \tag{2}$$

$\underline{\mathsf{H}_2}$. Next, we define H_2. We change the behavior of random oracle H and random function R. Consider another random oracle $H' : \{0,1\}^* \to \mathbb{Z}_p^{(k+1)\times(k+1)} \times \mathbb{Z}_p^{(k+1)\times(k+1)}$ that only the challenger can access. We denote the first and second elements of $H'(i)$ by $\mathbf{W}_{i,0}$ and $\mathbf{W}_{i,1}$, respectively. In H_2, $H(i)$ outputs $([\mathbf{W}_{i,0}^\top\mathbf{A}]_1, [\mathbf{W}_{i,1}^\top\mathbf{A}]_1)$, and $R(i)$ outputs $(\mathbf{W}_{i,0}^\top\mathbf{a}_1, \mathbf{W}_{i,1}^\top\mathbf{a}_1)$. Then, we have

$$\Pr[\langle \mathcal{A}, \mathsf{H}_1\rangle_{\mathsf{win}}] = \Pr[\langle \mathcal{A}, \mathsf{H}_2\rangle_{\mathsf{win}}]. \tag{3}$$

It is not difficult to confirm that the above equality holds because $\overline{\mathbf{A}} = (\mathbf{A}||\mathbf{a}_1)$ is a regular matrix, and thus $\mathbf{W}_{i,b}^\top\overline{\mathbf{A}}$ is randomly distributed in $\mathbb{Z}_p^{(k+1)\times(k+1)}$ for $\mathcal{A}$. By this conceptual change, we can rewrite $c_{2,i}$ and $k_{2,i}$ in the challenge ciphertext and secret keys as follows:

$$\begin{aligned}
c_{2,i} &= [(x_i\mathbf{W}_{\phi(i),0}^\top + \mathbf{W}_{\phi(i),1}^\top)\mathbf{A}\mathbf{s}]_1,\\
k_{2,i} &:= [\mathbf{k}_i + (y_i\mathbf{W}_{\psi(i),0} + \mathbf{W}_{\psi(i),1})\mathbf{B}\mathbf{r}_{\pi(i)}]_1 \ \text{ if } t(i) = 1,\\
k_{2,i} &:= \begin{pmatrix} [-\mathbf{k}_i + \mathbf{W}_{\psi(i),0}\mathbf{B}\mathbf{r}_{\pi(i)}]_1,\\ [y_i\mathbf{k}_i + \mathbf{W}_{\psi(i),1}\mathbf{B}\mathbf{r}_{\pi(i)}]_1 \end{pmatrix} \ \text{ if } t(i) = 0
\end{aligned}$$

In the above, we use the relations $\mathbf{A}^*\mathbf{A}^\top + \mathbf{a}_1^*\mathbf{a}_1^\top = \mathbf{I}_{k+1}$.

$\underline{\mathsf{H}_{3,\iota}}$. To describe $\mathsf{H}_{3,\iota}$, we define some distributions on ciphertexts and secret keys as follows. Concretely, we define two types of ciphertexts and secret keys, namely, normal and semi-functional. A normal ciphertext is one generated as in H_2. That is,

$$c_1 = [\mathbf{A}\mathbf{s}]_2,\ c_{2,i} = [(x_i\mathbf{W}_{\phi(i),0}^\top + \mathbf{W}_{\phi(i),1}^\top)\mathbf{A}\mathbf{s}]_1,\ c_3 = [\mathbf{s}^\top\mathbf{A}^\top\mathbf{k}]_T M.$$

A semi-functional ciphertext is the same as the normal one except that $\mathbf{As}$ is replaced with $\mathbf{c} \leftarrow \mathbb{Z}_p^{k+1}$. That is,

$$c_1 = [\mathbf{c}]_2,\ c_{2,i} = [(x_i \mathbf{W}_{\phi(i),0}^\top + \mathbf{W}_{\phi(i),1}^\top)\mathbf{c}]_1,\ c_3 = [\mathbf{c}^\top \mathbf{k}]_T M.$$

Similarly, a normal secret key is one generated as in H_2. That is,

$$\begin{aligned} k_{1,j} &= [\mathbf{B}\mathbf{r}_j]_2, \\ k_{2,i} &:= [\mathbf{k}_i + (y_i \mathbf{W}_{\psi(i),0} + \mathbf{W}_{\psi(i),1})\mathbf{B}\mathbf{r}_{\pi(i)}]_1 \ \text{ if } t(i) = 1, \\ k_{2,i} &:= \begin{pmatrix} [-\mathbf{k}_i + \mathbf{W}_{\psi(i),0}\mathbf{B}\mathbf{r}_{\pi(i)}]_1, \\ [y_i \mathbf{k}_i + \mathbf{W}_{\psi(i),1}\mathbf{B}\mathbf{r}_{\pi(i)}]_1 \end{pmatrix} \ \text{ if } t(i) = 0 \end{aligned} \tag{4}$$

Especially, $\mathbf{k}_1, \ldots, \mathbf{k}_n$ in $k_{2,i}$ is outputs of $\mathsf{Share}(f, \mathbf{k})$. On the other hand, in a semi-functional secret key, $\mathbf{k}_1, \ldots, \mathbf{k}_n$ in $k_{2,i}$ is outputs of $\mathsf{Share}(f, \mathbf{k} + \mu \mathbf{a}_1^*)$ where $\mu \leftarrow \mathbb{Z}_p$. Then, $\mathsf{H}_{3,\iota}$ is the same as H_2 except that the challenge ciphertext and the first ι keys that $\mathcal{A}$ is given are semi-functional.

Lemma 3.2

$$|\Pr[\langle \mathcal{A}, \mathsf{H}_2 \rangle_{\mathsf{win}}] - \Pr[\langle \mathcal{A}, \mathsf{H}_{3,0} \rangle_{\mathsf{win}}]| \leq \mathsf{Adv}_{\mathcal{B},\mathsf{bi}}^{\mathcal{D}_k\text{-}\mathsf{MDDH}}(\lambda). \tag{5}$$

Proof. To show this, we describe $\mathcal{B}$, which is given an instance of the $\mathcal{D}_k$-MDDH problem $(\mathbb{G}, [\mathbf{A}]_{1,2}, [\mathbf{t}_\beta]_{1,2})$. Let $H' : \{0,1\}^* \rightarrow \mathbb{Z}_p^{(k+1)\times(k+1)} \times \mathbb{Z}_p^{(k+1)\times(k+1)}$ be a random oracle simulated by $\mathcal{B}$ that $\mathcal{A}$ cannot access.

1. $\mathcal{B}$ generates $\mathbf{B}$ and $\mathbf{k}$ by itself.
2. $\mathcal{B}$ computes $\mathsf{pk} = (\mathbb{G}, [\mathbf{A}]_2, e([\mathbf{A}]_1, [\mathbf{k}]_2))$ and gives it to $\mathcal{A}$.
3. For query $H(i)$, $\mathcal{B}$ answers with $([\mathbf{W}_{i,0}^\top \mathbf{A}]_1, [\mathbf{W}_{i,1}^\top \mathbf{A}]_1)$, where $(\mathbf{W}_{i,0}, \mathbf{W}_{i,1})$ is an output of $H'(i)$.
4. For query $\mathsf{KeyGen}(\mathsf{pk}, \mathsf{msk}, y)$, $\mathcal{B}$ computes sk_y as in Eq. (4). Note that $\mathcal{B}$ can generate sk without the random function R because it does not contain terms related to $\mathbf{A}$ any more.
5. For the challenge query with the attribute $x^* = (\mathbf{x}, \phi)$, $\mathcal{B}$ flip the coin $\delta \leftarrow \{0,1\}$ and generates ct_{x^*} as

$$c_1 = [\mathbf{t}_\beta]_2,\ c_{2,i} = [(x_i \mathbf{W}_{\phi(i),0}^\top + \mathbf{W}_{\phi(i),1}^\top)\mathbf{t}_\beta]_1,\ \ c_3 = e([\mathbf{t}_\beta]_1, [\mathbf{k}]_2) M_\delta.$$

6. $\mathcal{B}$ outputs true$(\delta = \delta')$, where δ' is an output of $\mathcal{A}$.

The case $\beta = 0$ corresponds to H_2 and the case $\beta = 1$ corresponds to $\mathsf{H}_{3,0}$. □

In the next lemma, we prove the indistinguishability between $\mathsf{H}_{3,\iota-1}$ and $\mathsf{H}_{3,\iota}$. That is, all PPT adversaries cannot distinguish whether the ι-th secret key is normal or semi-functional. To prove this one-secret-key indistinguishability, we introduce core 1-ABE game $\mathsf{G}_\beta^{\text{1-ABE}}$ where $\beta \in \{0,1\}$ such that $\mathsf{G}_0^{\text{1-ABE}}$ and $\mathsf{G}_1^{\text{1-ABE}}$ are computationally indistinguishable. Roughly speaking, the core 1-ABE game is designed so that we can construct a distinguisher between $\mathsf{G}_0^{\text{1-ABE}}$ and $\mathsf{G}_1^{\text{1-ABE}}$ if there exists an adversary that can distinguish $\mathsf{H}_{3,\iota-1}$ and $\mathsf{H}_{3,\iota}$.

It is convenient for us to parametrize the core 1-ABE game by $\eta \in \{1,2\}$ because we also use it in the security proof of our CP-ABE scheme. We use the game with $\eta = 1$ in the security proof of our KP-ABE scheme, and that with $\eta = 2$ in the security proof of our CP-ABE scheme.

Definition 3.1 (Core 1-ABE). *For $\eta \in \{1,2\}$ and $\beta \in \{0,1\}$, we define $\mathsf{G}^{1\text{-}ABE}_{\eta,\beta}$ as Fig. 2. In $\mathsf{G}^{1\text{-}ABE}_{\eta,\beta}$, $\mathcal{A}$ can query $\mathcal{O}_X$ and $\mathcal{O}_F$ only once whereas $\mathcal{A}$ can query $\mathcal{O}_R$ polynomially many times. All queries can be done adaptively. Furthermore, $x \in \mathcal{X}$ and $y \in \mathcal{Y}$ on which $\mathcal{A}$ queries $\mathcal{O}_X$ and $\mathcal{O}_F$ must satisfy $R(x,y) = 0$. $\mathcal{X}$ and $\mathcal{Y}$ are defined in Definition 2.5. Note that the difference between $\mathsf{G}^{1\text{-}ABE}_{\eta,0}$ and $\mathsf{G}^{1\text{-}ABE}_{\eta,1}$ lies in the input of* Share *in $\mathcal{O}_F$. We define the advantage of $\mathcal{A}$ against $\mathsf{G}^{1\text{-}ABE}_{\eta,\beta}$ as follows:*

$$\mathsf{Adv}^{\mathsf{1\text{-}ABE}}_{\mathcal{A},\eta}(\lambda) := |\Pr[\langle \mathcal{A}, \mathsf{G}^{1\text{-}ABE}_{\eta,0}\rangle = 1] - \Pr[\langle \mathcal{A}, \mathsf{G}^{1\text{-}ABE}_{\eta,1}\rangle = 1]|.$$

We defer the proof of the indistinguishability between the two games to Sect. 4.

Lemma 3.3. *For $\iota \in [q_{\mathsf{sk}}]$, we have*

$$|\Pr[\langle \mathcal{A}, \mathsf{H}_{3,\iota-1}\rangle_{\mathsf{win}}] - \Pr[\langle \mathcal{A}, \mathsf{H}_{3,\iota}\rangle_{\mathsf{win}}]| \le \mathsf{Adv}^{\mathsf{1\text{-}ABE}}_{\mathcal{B},1}(\lambda). \tag{6}$$

Proof. We consider an adversary $\mathcal{B}$ against $\mathsf{G}^{1\text{-}ABE}_{1,\beta}$ where $\eta = 1$. We describe $\mathcal{B}$'s behavior.

1. $\mathcal{B}$ is given $(\mathbb{G}, \mathbf{A}, [\mathbf{B}]_{1,2}, \mathsf{d}, \mathbf{W})$ from the 1-ABE game.
2. $\mathcal{B}$ sets $\mathsf{k} := \mathbf{W}\mathsf{d}$ and gives $\mathsf{pk} = (\mathbb{G}, [\mathbf{A}]_2, [\mathbf{A}^\top \mathbf{k}]_T)$ to $\mathcal{A}$.
3. For query $H(i)$, $\mathcal{B}$ makes a query $\mathcal{O}_R(i)$ and answers with $([\mathbf{W}_{i,0}^\top \mathbf{A}]_1, [\mathbf{W}_{i,1}^\top \mathbf{A}]_1)$.
4. For the challenge query with an attribute x^*, $\mathcal{B}$ flips the coin $\delta \leftarrow \{0,1\}$. Then, $\mathcal{B}$ obtains $(A_0, \{A_i\}_{i\in[m]})$ as the reply of $\mathcal{O}_X(x^*)$. $\mathcal{B}$ returns ct_{x^*} as
$$\mathsf{ct}_{x^*} := \left([A_0]_2, \{[A_i]_1\}_{i\in[m]}, [A_0^\top \mathbf{k}]_T M_\delta\right).$$
5. For the ℓ-th query $\mathsf{KeyGen}(\mathsf{pk}, \mathsf{msk}, y)$, where $\ell < \iota$ and $y = (\mathbf{y}, f, \psi, t)$, $\mathcal{B}$ computes sk_y as in Eq. (4) by setting $\mathbf{k}_1, \ldots, \mathbf{k}_n \leftarrow \mathsf{Share}(f, \mathbf{k} + \mu \mathbf{a}_1^*)$ with a fresh randomness $\mu \leftarrow \mathbb{Z}_p$.
6. For the ℓ-th query $\mathsf{KeyGen}(\mathsf{pk}, \mathsf{msk}, y)$, where $\ell = \iota$ and $y = (\mathbf{y}, f, \psi, t)$, $\mathcal{B}$ obtains $(P_0, \{P_i\}_{i\in[n]})$ as the reply of $\mathcal{O}_F(y)$. Then, $\mathcal{B}$ returns sk_y as
$$\mathsf{sk}_y := (P_0, \{P_i\}_{i\in[n]}).$$
7. For the ℓ-th query $\mathsf{KeyGen}(\mathsf{pk}, \mathsf{msk}, y)$, where $\ell > \iota$ and $y = (\mathbf{y}, f, \psi, t)$, $\mathcal{B}$ computes sk_y as in Eq. (4) by setting $\mathbf{k}_1, \ldots, \mathbf{k}_n \leftarrow \mathsf{Share}(f, \mathbf{k})$.
8. $\mathcal{B}$ outputs $\mathrm{true}(\delta = \delta')$, where δ' is an output of $\mathcal{A}$.

$\underline{\mathsf{G}^{\text{1-ABE}}_{\eta,\beta}}$

$\mathbb{G} \leftarrow \mathcal{G}_{\mathsf{BG}}(1^\lambda),\ \mu' \leftarrow \mathbb{Z}_p,\ \mathbf{A} \leftarrow \mathcal{D}_k,\ \overline{\mathbf{B}} \leftarrow \mathbb{Z}_p^{(k+\eta)\times(k+\eta)}$

$\mathbf{d} \leftarrow \mathbb{Z}_p^{k+\eta},\ \mathbf{W} \leftarrow \mathbb{Z}_p^{(k+1)\times(k+\eta)},\ L := \emptyset$

$$\mathsf{param} := \begin{cases} (\mathbb{G}, \mathbf{A}, [\mathbf{B}]_{1,2}, \mathbf{d}, \mathbf{W}) & \eta = 1 \\ (\mathbb{G}, \mathbf{A}, [\mathbf{B}]_{1,2}, \mathbf{d}, \mathbf{W}, \mathbf{b}_2^*) & \eta = 2 \end{cases}$$

$\beta' \leftarrow \mathcal{A}^{\mathcal{O}_X(\cdot),\mathcal{O}_F(\cdot),\mathcal{O}_R(\cdot)}(\mathsf{param})$

$\underline{\mathcal{O}_X(\cdot)}$

Input: $x = (\mathbf{x} \in \mathbb{Z}_p^m, \phi) \in \mathcal{X}$

$A_0 := \mathbf{c} \leftarrow \mathbb{Z}_p^{k+1}$

For $i \in [m]$:

If $(\phi(i), *, *) \notin L$:

$\mathbf{W}_{\phi(i),0}, \mathbf{W}_{\phi(i),1} \leftarrow \mathbb{Z}_p^{(k+1)\times(k+\eta)}$

$L := L \cup (\phi(i), \mathbf{W}_{\phi(i),0}, \mathbf{W}_{\phi(i),1})$

$A_i := (x_i \mathbf{W}_{\phi(i),0}^\top + \mathbf{W}_{\phi(i),1}^\top)\mathbf{c}$

Output $(A_0, \{A_i\}_{i\in[m]})$

$\underline{\mathcal{O}_F(\cdot)}$

Input: $y = (\mathbf{y} \in \mathbb{Z}_p^n, f, \psi, t) \in \mathcal{Y}$

$\mathbf{k}_1, \ldots, \mathbf{k}_n \leftarrow \mathsf{Share}(f, \mathbf{W}\mathbf{d}),\ \sigma_1, \ldots, \sigma_n \leftarrow \boxed{\mathsf{Share}(f, \beta\mu')}$

$\pi(i) := |\{j \mid \psi(j) = \psi(i), j \leq i\}|$

$d := \max_{i\in[n]} \pi(i)$

$\mathbf{r}_1, \ldots, \mathbf{r}_d \leftarrow \mathbb{Z}_p^k$

$\mathbf{v}_i := \mathbf{B}\mathbf{r}_i$

$P_0 := ([\mathbf{v}_1]_2, \ldots, [\mathbf{v}_d]_2)$

For $i \in [n]$:

If $(\psi(i), *, *) \notin L$:

$\mathbf{W}_{\psi(i),0}, \mathbf{W}_{\psi(i),1} \leftarrow \mathbb{Z}_p^{(k+1)\times(k+\eta)}$

$L := L \cup (\psi(i), \mathbf{W}_{\psi(i),0}, \mathbf{W}_{\psi(i),1})$

If $t(i) = 1$:

$P_i := [\mathbf{k}_i + \sigma_i \mathbf{a}_1^* + (y_i \mathbf{W}_{\psi(i),0} + \mathbf{W}_{\psi(i),1})\mathbf{B}\mathbf{r}_{\pi(i)}]_1$

If $t(i) = 0$:

$P_i := \big([-(\mathbf{k}_i + \sigma_i \mathbf{a}_1^*) + \mathbf{W}_{\psi(i),0}\mathbf{B}\mathbf{r}_{\pi(i)}]_1,\ [y_i(\mathbf{k}_i + \sigma_i \mathbf{a}_1^*) + \mathbf{W}_{\psi(i),1}\mathbf{B}\mathbf{r}_{\pi(i)}]_1\big)$

Output $(P_0, \{P_i\}_{i\in[n]})$

$\underline{\mathcal{O}_R(\cdot)}$

Input: $i \in \{0,1\}^*$

If $(i, *, *) \notin L$:

$\mathbf{W}_{i,0}, \mathbf{W}_{i,1} \leftarrow \mathbb{Z}_p^{(k+1)\times(k+\eta)},\ L := L \cup (i, \mathbf{W}_{i,0}, \mathbf{W}_{i,1})$

Output $([\mathbf{W}_{i,0}^\top \mathbf{A}]_1, [\mathbf{W}_{i,1}^\top \mathbf{A}]_1, [\mathbf{W}_{i,0}\mathbf{B}]_1, [\mathbf{W}_{i,1}\mathbf{B}]_1)$

Fig. 2. Core 1-ABE game.

From Lemma 3.1, the term $\mathbf{k}_i + \sigma_i \mathbf{a}_1^*$ in the reply of $\mathcal{O}_F$ is identically distributed with the i-th output of $\mathsf{Share}(\mathbf{k} + \beta\mu\mathbf{a}_1^*)$. Thus, if the oracles are those in $\mathsf{G}^{\text{1-ABE}}_{1,0}$, $\mathcal{A}$'s view corresponds to $\mathsf{H}_{3,\iota-1}$, and otherwise, it corresponds to $\mathsf{H}_{3,\iota}$. □

Lemma 3.4

$$|\Pr[\langle \mathcal{A}, \mathsf{H}_{3,q_{\mathsf{sk}}}\rangle_{\mathsf{win}}] - 1/2| \leq 2^{-\Omega(\lambda)}. \tag{7}$$

Proof. Because $(\mathbf{A}^*||\mathbf{a}_1^*)$ forms a basis, redefining $\mathbf{k}$ as $\mathbf{k} := \mathbf{A}^*\mathbf{z} + z\mathbf{a}_1^*$ where $\mathbf{z} \leftarrow \mathbb{Z}_p^k$ and $z \leftarrow \mathbb{Z}_p$ does not change its distribution. Recall that the information on $\mathbf{k}$ that $\mathcal{A}$ obtains throughout the game is $\mathbf{A}^\top\mathbf{k}$ in pk, $\mathsf{Share}(f, \mathbf{k}+\mu\mathbf{a}_1^*)$ in sk_y, and $\mathbf{c}^\top\mathbf{k}$ in ct_{x^*}. However, $\mathbf{A}^\top\mathbf{k}$ does not contain the information on z because $\mathbf{A}^\top\mathbf{a}_1^* = \mathbf{0}$. Similarly, each $\mathbf{k} + \mu\mathbf{a}_1^*$ also does not contain the information on z because it is masked by fresh randomness μ. Thus, $z\mathbf{c}^\top\mathbf{a}_1^*$ is randomly distributed in $\mathbb{Z}_p$ for $\mathcal{A}$, and so is $\mathbf{c}^\top\mathbf{k}$, unless $\mathbf{c}^\top\mathbf{a}_1^* = 0$. Since $\mathbf{c}$ is randomly chosen from $\mathbb{Z}_p^{k+1}$, $\mathbf{c}^\top\mathbf{a}_1^* = 0$ with a probability $2^{-\Omega(\lambda)}$. If it is not the case, ct_{x^*} does not have information on β, and the lemma holds. □

Thanks to Eqs. (1) to (3) and (5) to (7) and Lemma 4.1, Theorem 3.1 holds. □

4 Adaptive Security for Core Component

In this section, we prove the indistinguishability between $\mathsf{G}_{\eta,0}^{\text{1-ABE}}$ and $\mathsf{G}_{\eta,1}^{\text{1-ABE}}$ defined in Definition 3.1. This is formally stated in the following lemma.

Lemma 4.1 (Core 1-ABE Security). *Let B be the maximum depth of formula f for all choice of f by $\mathcal{A}$. For any PPT adversary $\mathcal{A}$ and $\eta \in \{1,2\}$, there exists a PPT algorithm $\mathcal{B}$ such that*

$$\mathsf{Adv}_{\mathcal{A},\eta}^{\text{1-ABE}}(\lambda) \leq 2^{9B+2}(\mathsf{Adv}_{\mathcal{B},\mathsf{bi}}^{\mathcal{D}_k\text{-MDDH}}(\lambda) + 2^{-\Omega(\lambda)}).$$

Proof. We prove Lemma 4.1 by extending the KW technique [21]. We omit the variable η from the notation of hybrid games for conciseness, but all hybrids are parametrized by η. Following the piecewise guessing framework, we define a series of selective hybrids $\widehat{\mathsf{H}}^{h_0}$ to $\widehat{\mathsf{H}}^{h_L}$, where $L = 8^B$, and two intermediate games $\mathsf{G}_{\mathsf{M0}}^{\text{1-ABE}}$ and $\mathsf{G}_{\mathsf{M1}}^{\text{1-ABE}}$, which satisfy

- $\widehat{\mathsf{G}}_0^{\text{1-ABE}} = \widehat{\mathsf{H}}^{h_0} \approx_c, \ldots, \approx_c \widehat{\mathsf{H}}^{h_L} = \widehat{\mathsf{G}}_{\mathsf{M0}}^{\text{1-ABE}}$
- $\mathsf{G}_{\mathsf{M0}}^{\text{1-ABE}} = \mathsf{G}_{\mathsf{M1}}^{\text{1-ABE}}$.

Let $z := (x, y) \in \{0,1\}^R$ on which $\mathcal{A}$ queries $\mathcal{O}_X$ and $\mathcal{O}_F$, respectively. Let $b \in \{0,1\}^n$ be a string computed from z following Definition 2.5. Note that $f(b) = 0$ because the game imposes the condition $R(x,y) = 0$ on $\mathcal{A}$. Let $\mathcal{R}$ be the pebbling record generated as $\mathcal{R} = (r_1, \ldots, r_L) = \mathsf{PebRec}(f, b)$ as defined in Lemma 2.2. Then, we define $h_\iota : \{0,1\}^R \to \{0,1\}^{3B}$ as $h_\iota(z) := r_\iota$. Note that h_0 and h_L are constant functions because they specify the pebbling configurations where no pebbles on it and a pebble is placed on only the output gate, respectively.

The hybrids and intermediate games only differ in the Share algorithm in $\mathcal{O}_F$ as follows. That is, $\widehat{\mathsf{H}}^{h_\iota}$ is the same as $\widehat{\mathsf{G}}_0^{\text{1-ABE}}$ except that $\mathsf{Share}(f, 0)$ is replaced with $\widetilde{\mathsf{Share}}(f, 0, h_\iota(z))$, which is described in Fig. 3. $\mathsf{G}_{\mathsf{M0}}^{\text{1-ABE}}$ is the same as H^{h_L}, and $\mathsf{G}_{\mathsf{M1}}^{\text{1-ABE}}$ is the same as $\mathsf{G}_{\mathsf{M0}}^{\text{1-ABE}}$ except that $\widetilde{\mathsf{Share}}(f, 0, h_L(z))$ is replaced with $\widetilde{\mathsf{Share}}(f, \mu, h_L(z))$.

We prove that

- $\mathsf{G}_0^{\text{1-ABE}} \approx_c \mathsf{G}_{\mathsf{M0}}^{\text{1-ABE}}$,
- $\mathsf{G}_{\mathsf{M0}}^{\text{1-ABE}} = \mathsf{G}_{\mathsf{M1}}^{\text{1-ABE}}$,
- $\mathsf{G}_{\mathsf{M1}}^{\text{1-ABE}} \approx_c \mathsf{G}_1^{\text{1-ABE}}$.

First, we prove item 2, then prove item 1. We omit the proof of item 3 because it is almost the same as that of item 1. Then, we are done.

$\widetilde{\mathsf{Share}}(f, \mathbf{k}, u)$
Input: $f = (n, w, v, G)$ with a depth B, $\mathbf{k} \in \mathbb{Z}_p^\ell$, and $u \in \{0,1\}^{3B}$

1. Set a vector $\boldsymbol{\sigma}_{\mathsf{out}} := \mathbf{k}$ on the output wire.
2. Interpret u as a pebbling configuration on f.
3. For each gate g with a pebble that has incoming wires a, b and an outgoing wire c where a vector $\boldsymbol{\sigma}_c$ is set on c, choose $\mathbf{u}_{g,1}, \mathbf{u}_{g,2} \leftarrow \mathbb{Z}_p^\ell$ and set $\boldsymbol{\sigma}_a := \mathbf{u}_{g,1}$ and $\boldsymbol{\sigma}_b := \mathbf{u}_{g,2}$ on a and b, respectively.
4. For each AND gate g with no pebble that has incoming wires a, b and an outgoing wire c where a vector $\boldsymbol{\sigma}_c$ is set on c, choose $\mathbf{u}_g \leftarrow \mathbb{Z}_p^\ell$ and set $\boldsymbol{\sigma}_a := \boldsymbol{\sigma}_c - \mathbf{u}_g$ and $\boldsymbol{\sigma}_b := \mathbf{u}_g$ on a and b, respectively.
5. For each OR gate g with no pebble that has incoming wires a, b and an outgoing wire c where a vector $\boldsymbol{\sigma}_c$ is set on c, set $\boldsymbol{\sigma}_a := \boldsymbol{\sigma}_c$ and $\boldsymbol{\sigma}_b := \boldsymbol{\sigma}_c$ on a and b, respectively.
6. For each input wire i with a pebble, replace $\boldsymbol{\sigma}_i$ with a random vector $\mathbf{u}_i \leftarrow \mathbb{Z}_p^k$.
7. Output shares $\boldsymbol{\sigma}_1, \ldots, \boldsymbol{\sigma}_n$, which are set on the input wires $1, \ldots, n$.

Fig. 3. Description of $\widetilde{\mathsf{Share}}$.

$\underline{\mathsf{G}_{\mathsf{M0}}^{\text{1-ABE}} = \mathsf{G}_{\mathsf{M1}}^{\text{1-ABE}}}$**.** Recall that the difference between the two games lies in the input of $\widetilde{\mathsf{Share}}$, namely, $(f, 0, h_L(z))$ or $(f, \mu, h_L(z))$. First, we note that $u = h_L(z)$ is a constant that specifies the pebbling configuration on f where a pebble is placed on only the output gate. In this case, it is not difficult to see that the output of $\widetilde{\mathsf{Share}}$ is independent of the second argument of the input. This is because the values set on the two incoming wires of the output gate are chosen independently of σ_{out} when a pebble is placed on the output gate (see item 3 in Fig. 3). Then, the values to be set on the rest of wires are computed based on these values set on the incoming wires of the output gate. Thus, the output of $\widetilde{\mathsf{Share}}$ is identically distributed in both games, and the claim holds.

$\underline{\mathsf{G}_0^{\text{1-ABE}} \approx_c \mathsf{G}_{\mathsf{M0}}^{\text{1-ABE}}}$**.** Following Lemma 2.1, we prove the two properties:

1. $\mathsf{G}_0^{\text{1-ABE}} = \mathsf{H}^{h_0}$ and $\mathsf{H}^{h_L} = \mathsf{G}_{\mathsf{M0}}^{\text{1-ABE}}$,
2. $\widehat{\mathsf{H}}_1^{h_{\iota-1}} \approx_c \widehat{\mathsf{H}}_0^{h_\iota}$ for $\iota \in [L]$.

where $\widehat{\mathsf{H}}_\beta^{h_i}$ for $\beta \in \{0,1\}$ is defined in Sect. 2.4. For item 1, the latter holds because we defined $\mathsf{G}_{\mathsf{M0}}^{\text{1-ABE}}$ in such a way. To show the former, we need to confirm that the output of $\mathsf{Share}(f, 0)$ and $\widetilde{\mathsf{Share}}(f, 0, h_0(z))$ is identically distributed. Recall that h_0 is a constant function that specifies the pebbling configuration where no pebbles on it. In this case, no gates correspond to item 3 or 6 in Fig. 3, and the remaining procedures are exactly the same as $\mathsf{Share}(f, 0)$. Thus, the former also holds.

The remaining thing is to prove $\widehat{\mathsf{H}}_1^{h_{\iota-1}} \approx_c \widehat{\mathsf{H}}_0^{h_\iota}$. Formally, we show that, for any PPT adversary $\mathcal{A}$, there exists a PPT adversary $\mathcal{B}$ such that

$$|\Pr[\langle \mathcal{A}, \widehat{\mathsf{H}}_1^{h_{\iota-1}} \rangle = 1] - \Pr[\langle \mathcal{A}, \widehat{\mathsf{H}}_0^{h_\iota} \rangle = 1]| \leq 2\mathsf{Adv}_{\mathcal{B},\mathsf{bi}}^{\mathcal{D}_k\text{-MDDH}}(\lambda) + 2^{-\Omega(\lambda)}.$$

To show this, we additionally consider three intermediate selective hybrids $\widehat{\mathsf{H}}_{1,1}^{h_\iota-1}$ to $\widehat{\mathsf{H}}_{1,3}^{h_\iota-1}$.

In the following, we denote the pebbling configuration on f that is specified by a bit string u by $C(f,u)$. Let u_0 and u_1 be the committed values by $\mathcal{A}$, which correspond to $h_{\iota-1}(z)$ and $h_\iota(z)$ for z chosen by $\mathcal{A}$. Then, $C(f,u_0)$ and $C(f,u_1)$ are adjacent pebbling configurations for some input $b \in \{0,1\}^n$ for f. In other words, there exists b such that u_0 and u_1 correspond to $r_{\iota-1}$ and r_ι where $(r_0,\ldots,r_L) = \mathsf{PebRec}(f,b)$. Thus, $C(f,u_0)$ can be changed to $C(f,u_1)$ in one step following the rule defined in Definition 2.8. Recall that the difference between $\widehat{\mathsf{H}}_1^{h_\iota-1}$ and $\widehat{\mathsf{H}}_0^{h_\iota}$ is the input of $\widetilde{\mathsf{Share}}$. That is, the input is $(f,0,u_0)$ in $\widehat{\mathsf{H}}_1^{h_\iota-1}$ and $(f,0,u_1)$ in $\widehat{\mathsf{H}}_0^{h_\iota}$. Thus, in case of $u_0 = u_1$, $\widehat{\mathsf{H}}_1^{h_\iota-1}$ and $\widehat{\mathsf{H}}_0^{h_\iota}$ are clearly identical. In the following, we consider the case of $u_0 \neq u_1$.

Let an object O be either a gate g or an input wire i^*, in which the difference between $C(f,u_0)$ and $C(f,u_1)$ lies. We consider only the case where a pebble is placed on g or i^*, since the case where a pebble is removed is just the reverse of the former case. Intermediate hybrids $\widehat{\mathsf{H}}_{1,1}^{h_\iota-1}$ to $\widehat{\mathsf{H}}_{1,3}^{h_\iota-1}$ are different from $\widehat{\mathsf{H}}_1^{h_\iota-1}$ only in $\mathcal{O}_F$ as shown in Fig. 4. That is, when O is a gate, $\widehat{\mathsf{H}}_{1,1}^{h_\iota-1}$ to $\widehat{\mathsf{H}}_{1,3}^{h_\iota-1}$ are the same as $\widehat{\mathsf{H}}_1^{h_\iota-1}$. When O is an input wire, these hybrids are defined as follows:

- $\widehat{\mathsf{H}}_{1,1}^{h_\iota-1}$ is the same as $\widehat{\mathsf{H}}_1^{h_\iota-1}$ except that $\mathbf{v}_{\pi(i^*)} \leftarrow \mathsf{span}(\mathsf{B},\mathsf{b}_1)$,
- $\widehat{\mathsf{H}}_{1,2}^{h_\iota-1}$ is the same as $\widehat{\mathsf{H}}_{1,1}^{h_\iota-1}$ except that random value u is added to σ_{i^*},
- $\widehat{\mathsf{H}}_{1,3}^{h_\iota-1}$ is the same as $\widehat{\mathsf{H}}_{1,2}^{h_\iota-1}$ except that $\mathbf{v}_{\pi(i^*)} := \mathbf{B}\mathbf{r}_{\pi(i^*)}$ for $\mathbf{r}_{\pi(i^*)} \leftarrow \mathbb{Z}_p^k$.

Thanks to Lemmas 4.2 to 4.5 and observations so far, Lemma 4.1 holds. □

Lemma 4.2. $|\Pr[\langle\mathcal{A},\widehat{\mathsf{H}}_1^{h_\iota-1}\rangle = 1] - \Pr[\langle\mathcal{A},\widehat{\mathsf{H}}_{1,1}^{h_\iota-1}\rangle = 1]| \leq \mathsf{Adv}_{\mathcal{B},\mathsf{bi}}^{\mathcal{D}_k\text{-}\mathsf{MDDH}}(\lambda)$.

Lemma 4.3. $|\Pr[\langle\mathcal{A},\widehat{\mathsf{H}}_{1,1}^{h_\iota-1}\rangle = 1] - \Pr[\langle\mathcal{A},\widehat{\mathsf{H}}_{1,2}^{h_\iota-1}\rangle = 1] \leq 2^{-\Omega(\lambda)}$.

Lemma 4.4. $|\Pr[\langle\mathcal{A},\widehat{\mathsf{H}}_{1,2}^{h_\iota-1}\rangle = 1] - \Pr[\langle\mathcal{A},\widehat{\mathsf{H}}_{1,3}^{h_\iota-1}\rangle = 1]| \leq \mathsf{Adv}_{\mathcal{B},\mathsf{bi}}^{\mathcal{D}_k\text{-}\mathsf{MDDH}}(\lambda)$.

Lemma 4.5. $\Pr[\langle\mathcal{A},\widehat{\mathsf{H}}_{1,3}^{h_\iota-1}\rangle = 1] = \Pr[\langle\mathcal{A},\widehat{\mathsf{H}}_0^{h_\iota}\rangle = 1]$.

We present the proof of Lemmas 4.2, 4.3 and 4.5 in the full version. We omit the proof of Lemma 4.4 because the proof of this lemma is almost the same as that of Lemma 4.2.

5 Implementation and Evaluation

We implement our KP-ABE and CP-ABE schemes and measure the benchmarks of our schemes on an ordinary personal computer (PC) and two smartphones, Apple iPhone XR and Google Pixel 3. The details of our implementation are described in the full version.

$\widehat{\mathsf{H}}_1^{h_\iota-1}$, $\boxed{\widehat{\mathsf{H}}_{1,1}^{h_\iota-1}}$, $\widehat{\mathsf{H}}_{1,2}^{h_\iota-1}$, $\widehat{\mathsf{H}}_{1,3}^{h_\iota-1}$

$\underline{\mathcal{O}_F(\cdot)}$

Input: $y = (\mathbf{y} \in \mathbb{Z}_p^n, f, \psi, t) \in \mathcal{Y}$

$\mathbf{k}_1, \ldots, \mathbf{k}_n \leftarrow \mathsf{Share}(f, \mathbf{Wd})$, $\sigma_1, \ldots, \sigma_n \leftarrow \widetilde{\mathsf{Share}}(f, 0, u_0)$

$\pi(i) := |\{j \mid \psi(j) = \psi(i), j \leq i\}|$

$d := \max_{i\in[n]} \pi(i)$

$\mathbf{r}_1, \ldots, \mathbf{r}_d \leftarrow \mathbb{Z}_p^k$

$\mathbf{v}_i := \mathbf{Br}_i$ for $i \in [d]$

$\boxed{\mathbf{v}_i := \mathbf{Br}_i \text{ for } i \in [d]\backslash\pi(i^*), \quad \mathbf{v}_{\pi(i^*)} \leftarrow \mathsf{span}(\mathbf{B}, \mathbf{b}_1)}$

$P_0 := ([\mathbf{v}_1]_2, \ldots, [\mathbf{v}_d]_2)$

For $i \in [n]$:

  If $(\psi(i), *, *) \notin L$:

    $\mathbf{W}_{\psi(i),0}, \mathbf{W}_{\psi(i),1} \leftarrow \mathbb{Z}_p^{(k+1)\times(k+\eta)}$

    $L := L \cup (\psi(i), \mathbf{W}_{\psi(i),0}, \mathbf{W}_{\psi(i),1})$

  If $i = i^*$

    $\boxed{u \leftarrow \mathbb{Z}_p, \quad \sigma_i := \sigma_i + u}$

  If $t(i) = 1$:

    $P_i := [\mathbf{k}_i + \sigma_i \mathbf{a}_1^* + (y_i \mathbf{W}_{\psi(i),0} + \mathbf{W}_{\psi(i),1})\mathbf{v}_{\pi(i)}]_1$

  If $t(i) = 0$:

    $P_i := \big([-(\mathbf{k}_i + \sigma_i \mathbf{a}_1^*) + \mathbf{W}_{\psi(i),0}\mathbf{v}_{\pi(i)}]_1, \ [y_i(\mathbf{k}_i + \sigma_i \mathbf{a}_1^*) + \mathbf{W}_{\psi(i),1}\mathbf{v}_{\pi(i)}]_1\big)$

Output $(P_0, \{P_i\}_{i\in[n]})$

Fig. 4. Description of O_F in hybrids.

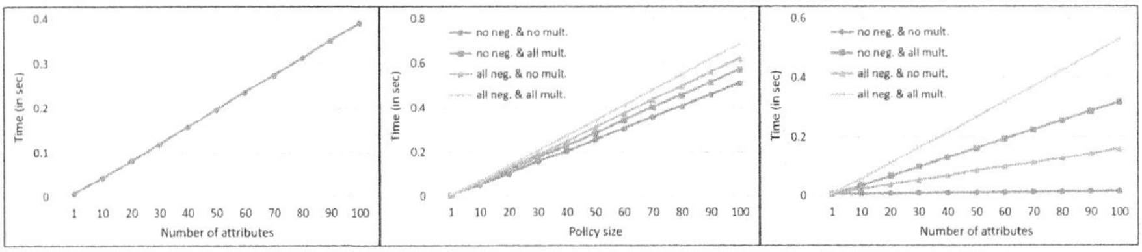

(a) Enc (b) KeyGen (c) Dec

Fig. 5. Benchmarks of our KP-ABE on PC.

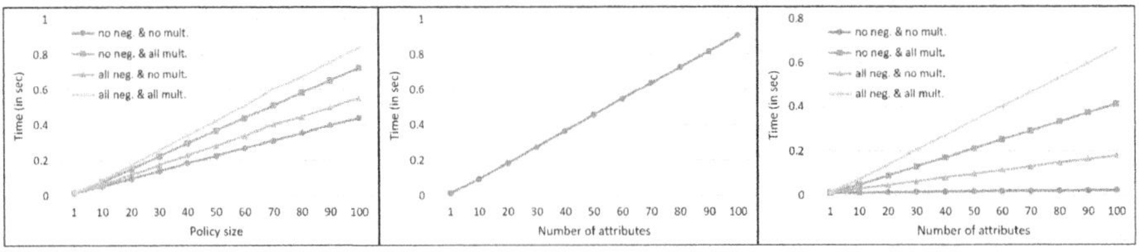

(a) Enc (b) KeyGen (c) Dec

Fig. 6. Benchmarks of our CP-ABE on PC.

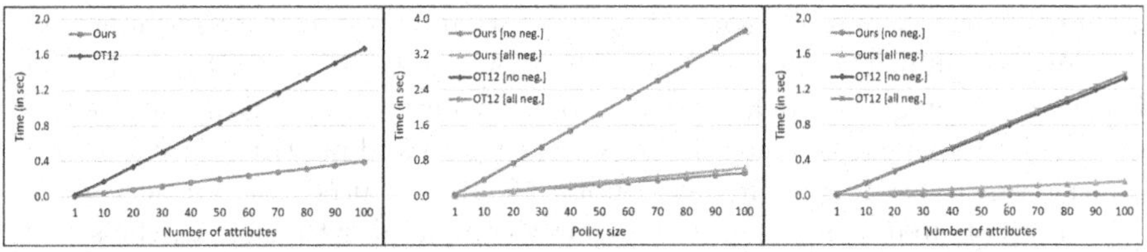

(a) Enc (b) KeyGen (c) Dec

Fig. 7. Comparison of KP-ABE between ours and OT12 on PC.

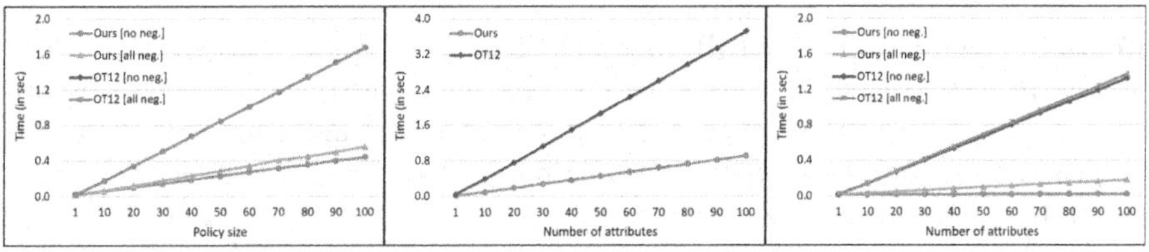

(a) Enc (b) KeyGen (c) Dec

Fig. 8. Comparison of CP-ABE between ours and OT12 on PC.

The efficiency of KeyGen and Dec in KP-ABE (resp. Enc and Dec in CP-ABE) is affected by formula f used in a secret key (resp. a ciphertext). More concretely, in KeyGen of our KP-ABE and Enc of our CP-ABE, the numbers of exponentiation in G_1 and G_2 increase proportionally to those of negation and multi-use, respectively. On the other hand, the number of hashing decreases proportionally to that of multi-use. In Dec, the numbers of exponentiation and pairings increase proportionally to the numbers of negation and multi-use, respectively.

To clarify the effects of these factors, we consider the four types of formulae.

1. no negations and multi-uses (no neg. & no mult.):
   i.e., (LABEL-1:v_1 AND LABEL-2:v_2 AND ...),
2. all negations and no multi-uses (all neg. & no mult.):
   i.e., (LABEL-1:NOT v_1 AND LABEL-2:NOT v_2 AND ...),
3. no negations and all multi-uses (no neg. & all mult.):
   i.e., (LABEL-1:v_1 AND LABEL-1:v_1 AND ...),
4. all negations and multi-uses (all neg. & all mult.):
   i.e., (LABEL-1:NOT v_1 AND LABEL-1:NOT v_2 AND ...).

We present the benchmarks on the PC in Figs. 5 and 6 and smartphones in the full version. The figures show the benchmarks with respect to a formula or attribute set with $1, 10, 20, \ldots, 100$ attributes for each case listed above. Enc in KP-ABE and KeyGen in CP-ABE are not affected by the types of formula, and we measure the benchmark for encryption/key generation with attributes LABEL-1:$v_1, \ldots,$ LABEL-n:v_n.

In all cases, our KP-ABE (resp. CP-ABE) scheme takes about 0.4 to 0.7s (resp. 0.4 to 0.9s) for encryption and key generation on the PC to handle 100 attributes. Our schemes allow very fast decryption for a monotone formula without multi-use (item 1), and they take only about 0.02s (KP & CP) for a formula with 100 attributes. We can assume that our schemes allow similarly fast decryption also for a formula in which the ratio of negation and multi-use is small. Even in the slowest case (item 4), it takes about 0.5 (KP) or 0.7s (CP) for decryption.

Because of small computational resource compared with the PC, the smartphones take more time for each algorithm. The benchmarks show that running times on iPhone XR are relatively close to those on the PC, and they are approximately 1.5 times slower. Google Pixel 3 takes further more time and its running times are 3 to 3.5 times as slow as those on the PC.

Effects of Negation and Multi-use. The benchmarks for KeyGen in KP-ABE and Enc in CP-ABE show that both negation and multi-use slow the running time down. It is reasonable that negation slows the running time down because it increases the number of exponentiation in G_1. In contrast, multi-use decreases the number of hashing to G_1 whereas it increases that of exponentiation in G_2. The benchmarks show that the former effect is smaller than the latter in our implementation. However, multi-use can shorten the running time in a platform where exponentiation in G_2 is more efficient or hashing to G_1 is less efficient.

In Dec, both negation and multi-use extend the running time, and the effect of multi-use is larger. This is since the number of negation affects that of exponentiation in G_1 while the number of multi-use affects that of heavier pairings.

Comparison with OT12. We also implement KP and CP schemes by Okamoto and Takashima in [27] (OT12), which are the only schemes that support OT negation and unboundedness, and thus whose functionalities are the closest to our schemes among known ABE schemes. The comparison between our schemes and OT12 on PC is presented in Figs. 7 and 8, which shows that our schemes achieve significant speedups in every algorithm. We compare them in the one-use restriction of labels (no multi-use), which corresponds to item 1 and item 2 in the four cases, since OT12 does not support multi-use of labels. Hence, the blue and gray lines in Fig. 5 are the same as those in Fig. 7 up to scale (similarly in Figs. 6 and 8). In contrast to our schemes, negation hardly affects the efficiency in OT12. Note that although we can utilize a bounded number of multi-use of labels by preparing multiple nominal labels for each single label in OT12, this significantly affects the efficiency. For example, when we set the bound as 10, this slows down Enc in KP-ABE or KeyGen in CP-ABE by 10 times.

CCA Security. In practice, the chosen ciphertext attack (CCA) security is a de facto standard and desirable security requirement. The Fujisaki-Okamoto conversion [15] is not suitable for our case because it requires the decryption algorithm to run the encryption algorithm, which causes a significant efficiency loss. However, our schemes can be efficiently converted to CCA secure ones via Boneh-Katz conversion [10] in a similar manner to [26].

References

1. Agrawal, S., Chase, M.: FAME: fast attribute-based message encryption. In: Thuraisingham, B.M., Evans, D., Malkin, T., Xu, D. (eds.) ACM CCS 2017, pp. 665–682. ACM Press, October/November 2017
2. Agrawal, S., Chase, M.: Simplifying design and analysis of complex predicate encryption schemes. In: Coron, J.-S., Nielsen, J.B. (eds.) EUROCRYPT 2017, Part I. LNCS, vol. 10210, pp. 627–656. Springer, Cham (2017). https://doi.org/10.1007/978-3-319-56620-7_22
3. Attrapadung, N.: Unbounded dynamic predicate compositions in attribute-based encryption. In: Ishai, Y., Rijmen, V. (eds.) EUROCRYPT 2019, Part I. LNCS, vol. 11476, pp. 34–67. Springer, Cham (2019). https://doi.org/10.1007/978-3-030-17653-2_2
4. Attrapadung, N., Libert, B., de Panafieu, E.: Expressive key-policy attribute-based encryption with constant-size ciphertexts. In: Catalano, D., Fazio, N., Gennaro, R., Nicolosi, A. (eds.) PKC 2011. LNCS, vol. 6571, pp. 90–108. Springer, Heidelberg (2011). https://doi.org/10.1007/978-3-642-19379-8_6
5. Bellare, M., Rogaway, P.: Optimal asymmetric encryption. In: De Santis, A. (ed.) EUROCRYPT 1994. LNCS, vol. 950, pp. 92–111. Springer, Heidelberg (1995). https://doi.org/10.1007/BFb0053428
6. Bellare, M., Rogaway, P.: The exact security of digital signatures: how to sign with RSA and Rabin. In: Maurer, U.M. (ed.) EUROCRYPT 1996. LNCS, vol. 1070, pp. 399–416. Springer, Heidelberg (1996). https://doi.org/10.1007/3-540-68339-9_34
7. Bethencourt, J., Sahai, A., Waters, B.: Ciphertext-policy attribute-based encryption. In: 2007 IEEE Symposium on Security and Privacy, pp. 321–334. IEEE Computer Society Press, May 2007
8. Boneh, D., Boyen, X.: Secure identity based encryption without random oracles. In: Franklin, M. (ed.) CRYPTO 2004. LNCS, vol. 3152, pp. 443–459. Springer, Heidelberg (2004). https://doi.org/10.1007/978-3-540-28628-8_27
9. Boneh, D., Franklin, M.K.: Identity-based encryption from the Weil pairing. SIAM J. Comput. **32**(3), 586–615 (2003)
10. Boneh, D., Katz, J.: Improved efficiency for CCA-secure cryptosystems built using identity-based encryption. In: Menezes, A. (ed.) CT-RSA 2005. LNCS, vol. 3376, pp. 87–103. Springer, Heidelberg (2005). https://doi.org/10.1007/978-3-540-30574-3_8
11. Canetti, R., Goldreich, O., Halevi, S.: The random oracle methodology, revisited. J. ACM **51**(4), 557–594 (2004)
12. Chen, J., Gay, R., Wee, H.: Improved dual system ABE in prime-order groups via predicate encodings. In: Oswald, E., Fischlin, M. (eds.) EUROCRYPT 2015, Part II. LNCS, vol. 9057, pp. 595–624. Springer, Heidelberg (2015). https://doi.org/10.1007/978-3-662-46803-6_20
13. Chen, J., Gong, J., Kowalczyk, L., Wee, H.: Unbounded ABE via bilinear entropy expansion, revisited. In: Nielsen, J.B., Rijmen, V. (eds.) EUROCRYPT 2018, Part I. LNCS, vol. 10820, pp. 503–534. Springer, Cham (2018). https://doi.org/10.1007/978-3-319-78381-9_19
14. Escala, A., Herold, G., Kiltz, E., Ràfols, C., Villar, J.L.: An algebraic framework for Diffie-Hellman assumptions. J. Cryptol. **30**(1), 242–288 (2017). https://doi.org/10.1007/s00145-015-9220-6
15. Fujisaki, E., Okamoto, T.: Secure integration of asymmetric and symmetric encryption schemes. J. Cryptol. **26**(1), 80–101 (2013). https://doi.org/10.1007/s00145-011-9114-1

16. Gong, J., Dong, X., Chen, J., Cao, Z.: Efficient IBE with tight reduction to standard assumption in the multi-challenge setting. In: Cheon, J.H., Takagi, T. (eds.) ASIACRYPT 2016, Part II. LNCS, vol. 10032, pp. 624–654. Springer, Heidelberg (2016). https://doi.org/10.1007/978-3-662-53890-6_21
17. Goyal, V., Pandey, O., Sahai, A., Waters, B.: Attribute-based encryption for fine-grained access control of encrypted data. In: Juels, A., Wright, R.N., De Capitani di Vimercati, S. (eds.) ACM CCS 2006, pp. 89–98. ACM Press, October/November 2006. Available as Cryptology ePrint Archive Report 2006/309
18. Jafargholi, Z., Kamath, C., Klein, K., Komargodski, I., Pietrzak, K., Wichs, D.: Be adaptive, avoid overcommitting. In: Katz, J., Shacham, H. (eds.) CRYPTO 2017, Part I. LNCS, vol. 10401, pp. 133–163. Springer, Cham (2017). https://doi.org/10.1007/978-3-319-63688-7_5
19. Katz, J., Sahai, A., Waters, B.: Predicate encryption supporting disjunctions, polynomial equations, and inner products. J. Cryptol. **26**(2), 191–224 (2013). https://doi.org/10.1007/s00145-012-9119-4
20. Kim, T., Barbulescu, R.: Extended tower number field sieve: a new complexity for the medium prime case. In: Robshaw, M., Katz, J. (eds.) CRYPTO 2016, Part I. LNCS, vol. 9814, pp. 543–571. Springer, Heidelberg (2016). https://doi.org/10.1007/978-3-662-53018-4_20
21. Kowalczyk, L., Wee, H.: Compact adaptively secure ABE for NC^1 from k-lin. In: Ishai, Y., Rijmen, V. (eds.) EUROCRYPT 2019, Part I. LNCS, vol. 11476, pp. 3–33. Springer, Heidelberg (2019). https://doi.org/10.1007/978-3-030-17653-2_1
22. Lewko, A., Waters, B.: Decentralizing attribute-based encryption. Cryptology ePrint Archive, Report 2010/351 (2010). http://eprint.iacr.org/2010/351
23. Lewko, A.B., Okamoto, T., Sahai, A., Takashima, K., Waters, B.: Fully secure functional encryption: attribute-based encryption and (hierarchical) inner product encryption. In: Gilbert, H. (ed.) EUROCRYPT 2010. LNCS, vol. 6110, pp. 62–91. Springer, Heidelberg (2010). https://doi.org/10.1007/978-3-642-13190-5_4
24. Lewko, A.B., Sahai, A., Waters, B.: Revocation systems with very small private keys. In: 2010 IEEE Symposium on Security and Privacy, pp. 273–285. IEEE Computer Society Press, May 2010
25. Lewko, A.B., Waters, B.: New techniques for dual system encryption and fully secure HIBE with short ciphertexts. In: Micciancio, D. (ed.) TCC 2010. LNCS, vol. 5978, pp. 455–479. Springer, Heidelberg (2010). https://doi.org/10.1007/978-3-642-11799-2_27
26. Okamoto, T., Takashima, K.: Fully secure functional encryption with general relations from the decisional linear assumption. In: Rabin, T. (ed.) CRYPTO 2010. LNCS, vol. 6223, pp. 191–208. Springer, Heidelberg (2010). https://doi.org/10.1007/978-3-642-14623-7_11
27. Okamoto, T., Takashima, K.: Fully secure unbounded inner-product and attribute-based encryption. In: Wang, X., Sako, K. (eds.) ASIACRYPT 2012. LNCS, vol. 7658, pp. 349–366. Springer, Heidelberg (2012). https://doi.org/10.1007/978-3-642-34961-4_22
28. Ostrovsky, R., Sahai, A., Waters, B.: Attribute-based encryption with non-monotonic access structures. In: Ning, P., De Capitani di Vimercati, S., Syverson, P.F. (eds.) ACM CCS 2007, pp. 195–203. ACM Press, October 2007
29. Sahai, A., Waters, B.R.: Fuzzy identity-based encryption. In: Cramer, R. (ed.) EUROCRYPT 2005. LNCS, vol. 3494, pp. 457–473. Springer, Heidelberg (2005). https://doi.org/10.1007/11426639_27

30. Waters, B.: Dual system encryption: realizing fully secure IBE and HIBE under simple assumptions. In: Halevi, S. (ed.) CRYPTO 2009. LNCS, vol. 5677, pp. 619–636. Springer, Heidelberg (2009). https://doi.org/10.1007/978-3-642-03356-8_36
31. Wee, H.: Dual system encryption via predicate encodings. In: Lindell, Y. (ed.) TCC 2014. LNCS, vol. 8349, pp. 616–637. Springer, Heidelberg (2014). https://doi.org/10.1007/978-3-642-54242-8_26
32. Yamada, S., Attrapadung, N., Hanaoka, G., Kunihiro, N.: A framework and compact constructions for non-monotonic attribute-based encryption. In: Krawczyk, H. (ed.) PKC 2014. LNCS, vol. 8383, pp. 275–292. Springer, Heidelberg (2014). https://doi.org/10.1007/978-3-642-54631-0_16

Adaptive Simulation Security for Inner Product Functional Encryption

Shweta Agrawal[1], Benoît Libert[2,3(✉)], Monosij Maitra[1], and Radu Titiu[3,4]

[1] IIT Madras, Chennai, India
[2] CNRS, Laboratoire LIP, Lyon, France
[3] ENS de Lyon, Laboratoire LIP (U. Lyon, CNRS, ENSL, Inria, UCBL), Lyon, France
benoit.libert@ens-lyon.fr
[4] Bitdefender, Bucharest, Romania

Abstract. Inner product functional encryption (IPFE) [1] is a popular primitive which enables inner product computations on encrypted data. In IPFE, the ciphertext is associated with a vector $\boldsymbol{x}$, the secret key is associated with a vector $\boldsymbol{y}$ and decryption reveals the inner product $\langle \boldsymbol{x}, \boldsymbol{y} \rangle$. Previously, it was known how to achieve adaptive *indistinguishability* (IND) based security for IPFE from the DDH, DCR and LWE assumptions [8]. However, in the stronger simulation (SIM) based security game, it was only known how to support a restricted adversary that makes all its key requests either before or after seeing the challenge ciphertext, but not both. In more detail, Wee [46] showed that the DDH-based scheme of Agrawal *et al.* (Crypto 2016) achieves *semi-adaptive* simulation-based security, where the adversary must make all its key requests *after* seeing the challenge ciphertext. On the other hand, O'Neill showed that all IND-secure IPFE schemes (which may be based on DDH, DCR and LWE) satisfy SIM based security in the restricted model where the adversary makes all its key requests *before* seeing the challenge ciphertext.

In this work, we resolve the question of SIM-based security for IPFE by showing that variants of the IPFE constructions by Agrawal *et al.*, based on DDH, Paillier and LWE, satisfy the strongest possible *adaptive* SIM-based security where the adversary can make an unbounded number of key requests both before and after seeing the (single) challenge ciphertext. This establishes optimal security of the IPFE schemes, under all hardness assumptions on which it can (presently) be based.

Keywords: Functional encryption · Inner-products · Simulation-based security · Standard assumptions

1 Introduction

Functional Encryption (FE) [15,37] is a modern cryptographic paradigm that allows fine-grained access to encrypted data, unlike traditional public-key encryption, where decryption offers all-or-nothing access to data. In FE, a secret key

A. Kiayias et al. (Eds.): PKC 2020, LNCS 12110, pp. 34–64, 2020.
https://doi.org/10.1007/978-3-030-45374-9_2

sk_f corresponds to function f, and ciphertext $\mathsf{ct}(\boldsymbol{x})$ corresponds to some input $\boldsymbol{x}$ from the domain of f. Given a function key sk_f and a ciphertext $\mathsf{ct}(\boldsymbol{x})$, a user can run the decryption algorithm to learn $f(\boldsymbol{x})$. Security of FE guarantees that beyond $f(\boldsymbol{x})$, nothing about $\boldsymbol{x}$ is revealed.

Functional encryption has been studied extensively, yielding a plethora of constructions that achieve various tradeoffs between generality, security and hardness assumptions. Assuming the existence of the powerful multilinear maps [22] or indistinguishability obfuscation [23], FE can be constructed for all polynomial sized circuits achieving the strongest possible definition of security [23,24]. However, from standard assumptions, which is the focus of this work, constructions are only known for restricted classes of functionalities or achieving restricted notions of security. We discuss each of these aspects next.

On the Definition of Security. In the papers that introduced functional encryption [15,37], the authors discussed the subtleties involved in formulating the *right* definition of security for FE. Traditionally, an "indistinguishability" (IND) style definition had been used for constructing various special cases of functional encryption, which roughly requires that no efficient adversary that has oracle access to the key generation algorithm should be able to distinguish between encryptions of two messages $\boldsymbol{x}_0$ and $\boldsymbol{x}_1$. However, [15] showed that this notion was too weak for functional encryption in some cases. Specifically, they gave an FE construction that could be proved secure with respect to the IND security requirement, but was intuitively insecure.

[15,37] proposed the study of *simulation-based* (SIM) security which asks that the view of the adversary be simulated by a simulator that is given access to pairs $(f_i, f_i(\boldsymbol{x}^\star))$ where f_i are the functions for which the adversary requests keys, and $\boldsymbol{x}^\star$ is the challenge message. SIM security captured the intuition that nothing about $\boldsymbol{x}^\star$ be revealed except for the function output value, and ruled out the insecure scheme that IND security could not. However, it was soon shown that for general functionalities, SIM-based security is impossible to achieve [7,15].

Additionally, other restricted notions of security have also been studied, that limit either (i) the number of key requests – *bounded collusion* FE [26], (ii) the "type" of key requests – *one sided FE or "predicate encryption"* where the adversary may only request keys for functions f such that $f(\boldsymbol{x}^\star) = 0$ [10,28], or (iii) that allow for part of the input vector to be public – *public index or "attribute-based encryption"* [6,14,28,29,31]. While these restricted notions are meaningful for different applications, it remains desirable to obtain security in an unrestricted security game, if only for specialized functionalities.

Restricting the Functionality. Aside from different security notions, constructions of FE also vary in the functionality they support. Many special cases of FE have been studied before and since its formalization as an abstract primitive [15,37] – identity-based encryption (IBE) [13,42] fuzzy identity-based encryption [5,41] attribute-based encryption (ABE) [27,29,31] predicate encryption (PE) [28,30,31], bounded-key functional encryption [25,26]. However, excepting [30], the security of all these schemes was restricted in one of the three ways discussed above.

Abdalla, Bourse, De Caro and Pointcheval [1] introduced the primitive of inner product functional encryption (IPFE). In IPFE the ciphertext is associated with a vector $\boldsymbol{x}$, the secret key is associated with a vector $\boldsymbol{y}$ and decryption reveals $\langle \boldsymbol{x}, \boldsymbol{y} \rangle$. Since its introduction, IPFE has been studied extensively [1,8,11, 12,17,19,43,44] due to its feasibility under well-established assumptions [1,8], its natural applications [1] and extensions [2,3,18,21], its use as a building block for more advanced functionalities [3,4,9,32,33], and the fact that it admits an unrestricted security definition (more on this below).

Security of IPFE. Abdalla et al. [1] constructed practical schemes for IPFE under well studied hardness assumptions like the Decisional Diffie-Hellman (DDH) and Learning With Errors (LWE). Their constructions achieved security in a game which did not place any restriction on the number or type of key requests, nor necessitated making any part of the input public. Given the paucity of schemes that achieve these features, this was good news.

However, despite its positive features, the security game considered by [1] had shortcomings – their constructions were only proven to be *selectively secure* in the IND model, which means that the adversary has to announce the challenge messages before it even sees the public key of the scheme. This result was improved by Agrawal, Libert and Stehlé [8] who constructed adaptive AD-IND functional encryption for the same inner product functionality, under DDH, LWE and also from Paillier's Decision Composite Residuosity (DCR). Thus, the result of [8] established optimal security of IPFE in the IND-based game, from all hardness assumptions on which it can (presently) be based.

In the domain of SIM-based security for IPFE, much less is known. On one hand, O'Neill [37] showed that for IPFE,[1] IND security implies SIM security in a model where the adversary is restricted to making all its key queries *before* it sees the challenge ciphertext. On the other hand, Wee [46] recently proved that the DDH-based FE scheme from [8] achieves simulation-based security in a model where the adversary is restricted to making all its key queries *after* it sees the challenge ciphertext, in the so-called *semi-adaptive* game. Datta *et al.* [20] subsequently extended Wee's ideas so as to prove simulation-security against adaptive adversaries in predicate encryption schemes [30] based on bilinear maps [34–36]. In the IPFE setting, known proofs of SIM security break down in the natural *adaptive* model where the adversary is allowed to make key queries adaptively, both before and after seeing the challenge ciphertext. Moreover, Wee's result is not generic and only applies to the DDH-based construction of [8] as well as in specific pairing-based constructions of predicate encryption.

For a functionality as basic as IPFE, this state of affairs is quite dissatisfying. Specifically, the following fundamental question remains to be answered:

Is it possible to achieve the strongest notion of security, namely AD-SIM *security for* IPFE, *which permits the adversary an unbounded number of key requests before and after seeing the (single) challenge ciphertext? Moreover, can*

[1] Or, more generally, the class of *preimage sampleable functinalities* of which inner product is a special case.

we achieve AD-SIM *security from all the assumptions on which* IPFE *can be based, namely* DDH *(in groups without a bilinear map),* DCR *and* LWE*?*

In the present work, we resolve this question in the affirmative.

Our Results. In this work, we prove adaptive simulation-security (AD-SIM) for an unbounded number of key queries and a single challenge ciphertext, for IPFE schemes, based on the DDH, DCR and LWE assumptions. We place no restrictions on when the adversary may query for keys with respect to the challenge ciphertext. Thus, our security game achieves the "best of" both security games considered by Wee [46] and O'Neill [37], where the former permits post-challenge key requests but not pre, and the latter permits pre-challenge key requests but not post. By providing constructions under all assumptions on which IPFE schemes may presently be based, we improve a result by Wee [46], which achieved semi-adaptive SIM based security for DDH-based IPFE.

In more detail, we prove that the DDH based scheme of Agrawal et al. [8] (unmodified) achieves AD-SIM rather than just AD-IND security. Next, we show how to modify the DCR based scheme of [8] so that it satisfies AD-SIM security. Finally, we construct a new scheme for IPFE mod p based on LWE which leverages the LWE scheme of [8] (almost) generically to achieve AD-SIM security. Note that the impossibility from [15] rules out AD-SIM for many challenge messages, but our proofs work for a single challenge message (as does [46]). Moreover, [7] shows that AD-SIM security for one challenge message is impossible for *all* circuits, but this does not contradict our results since our proofs apply for a restricted class of functionality. Since our schemes achieve the strongest possible SIM security notion for IPFE under all assumptions on which it can currently be based, we finally settle the question of optimal security for IPFE.

Technical Overview. Next, we provide a technical overview of our constructions in turn.

DDH-Based IPFE: The DDH-based IPFE scheme of Agrawal *et al.* [8] was shown to provide indistinguishability-based security against adaptive adversaries (or AD-IND security for short). Later on, Abdalla *et al.* [3] proved it simulation-secure against selective adversaries. Wee [46] subsequently gave a proof of semi-adaptive simulation-based security for the same construction. Here, we show that the scheme can actually be proved simulation-secure against adaptive adversaries without any modification.

In Wee's proof [46], the simulator can create a dummy challenge ciphertext as an encryption of the all-zeroes vector. In the semi-adaptive setting, the simulated challenge ciphertext does not have to be consistent with pre-challenge queries because functional key queries are only allowed *after* the challenge phase. For a post-challenge key query $\boldsymbol{y} \in \mathbb{Z}_q^\ell$, the simulator has to respond with a key that decrypts the dummy ciphertext to the value $z_{\boldsymbol{y}} = f_{\boldsymbol{y}}(\boldsymbol{x}^\star) = \langle \boldsymbol{y}, \boldsymbol{x}^\star \rangle$ supplied by the oracle. To do this, it can embed the value $z_{\boldsymbol{y}} = \langle \boldsymbol{x}^\star, \boldsymbol{y} \rangle$ in the modified secret key which is obtained as an appropriate shift of the actual secret key. Namely, if the master public key is $g^{\boldsymbol{s}} \cdot h^{\boldsymbol{t}} \in \mathbb{G}^\ell$ and the master secret key consists of

$(\boldsymbol{s}, \boldsymbol{t}) \in_R \mathbb{Z}_q^\ell \times \mathbb{Z}_q^\ell$, the real functional secret key for $\boldsymbol{y} \in \mathbb{Z}_q^\ell$ is comprised of $(s_{\boldsymbol{y}}, t_{\boldsymbol{y}}) = (\langle \boldsymbol{s}, \boldsymbol{y} \rangle, \langle \boldsymbol{t}, \boldsymbol{y} \rangle)$. In order to "program" $z_{\boldsymbol{y}} = \langle \boldsymbol{x}^\star, \boldsymbol{y} \rangle$ in the simulated post-challenge keys, the simulator can define

$$s'_{\boldsymbol{y}} := \langle \boldsymbol{s}, \boldsymbol{y} \rangle + \alpha \cdot z_{\boldsymbol{y}} \bmod q \qquad t'_{\boldsymbol{y}} := \langle \boldsymbol{t}, \boldsymbol{y} \rangle + \beta \cdot z_{\boldsymbol{y}} \bmod q,$$

for carefully chosen coefficients $\alpha, \beta \in \mathbb{Z}_q$. From the adversary's view, this is equivalent to changing the master secret key into $\boldsymbol{s}' = \boldsymbol{s} + \alpha \cdot \boldsymbol{x}^\star \bmod q$ and $\boldsymbol{t}' = \boldsymbol{t} + \beta \cdot \boldsymbol{x}^\star \bmod q$, which is consistent with the master public key and responses to key queries for all vectors $\boldsymbol{y}$. Using a careful analysis, it was shown [46] that, under the DDH assumption, the simulation is indistinguishable from the real experiment, even if the message $\boldsymbol{x}^\star$ is adaptively chosen after seeing the public parameters, but before making any key query.

In order to prove simulation-based security for adaptive adversaries, we use the same approach as [46], but we modify the generation of the simulated ciphertext. Now, the dummy ciphertext should not only decrypt to the values dictated by the oracle under post-challenge keys, but it also needs to be consistent with responses to pre-challenge queries. To achieve this, our simulator answers pre-challenge key queries by running the real functional key generation algorithm. For each key query $\boldsymbol{y} \in \mathbb{Z}_q^\ell$, it replies with $(s_{\boldsymbol{y}}, t_{\boldsymbol{y}}) = (\langle \boldsymbol{s}, \boldsymbol{y} \rangle, \langle \boldsymbol{t}, \boldsymbol{y} \rangle)$. In the challenge phase, the simulator has to create a ciphertext that is compatible with all the pre-challenge queries without having access to the challenge message $\boldsymbol{x}^\star \in \mathbb{Z}_q^\ell$. For this purpose, it encrypts an arbitrary dummy message $\bar{\boldsymbol{x}}$ that satisfies the relations $\langle \bar{\boldsymbol{x}}, \boldsymbol{y} \rangle = \langle \boldsymbol{x}^\star, \boldsymbol{y} \rangle \bmod q$, for any pre-challenge query $\boldsymbol{y} \in \mathbb{Z}_q^\ell$. Our observation is that, although the DDH-based scheme of [8] encrypts vectors $\boldsymbol{x} \in \mathbb{Z}^\ell$ with small entries (because functional secret keys only make it possible to recover the inner product $\langle \boldsymbol{x}, \boldsymbol{y} \rangle$ when it lives in a polynomial-size interval), the dummy message does not have to be small. This implies that, given the function evaluation $\{z_{\boldsymbol{y}} = f_{\boldsymbol{y}}(\boldsymbol{x}^\star) = \langle \boldsymbol{x}^\star, \boldsymbol{y} \rangle\}_{\boldsymbol{y}}$ corresponding to all pre-challenge queries $\boldsymbol{y}$, the simulator can easily compute a compatible dummy message using linear algebra over $\mathbb{Z}_q$. Once the simulator is committed to the challenge ciphertext, it has to "program" the post-challenge functional keys in such a way that they decrypt the dummy ciphertext to the real function evaluations $z_{\boldsymbol{y}} = f_{\boldsymbol{y}}(\boldsymbol{x}^\star) = \langle \boldsymbol{x}^\star, \boldsymbol{y} \rangle$. Given a post-challenge query $\boldsymbol{y} \in \mathbb{Z}_q^\ell$ and the corresponding function evaluation $z_{\boldsymbol{y}} = \langle \boldsymbol{x}^\star, \boldsymbol{y} \rangle$, the value $z_{\boldsymbol{y}}$ is embedded in the simulated functional key in such a way that the difference $z_{\boldsymbol{y}} - \langle \bar{\boldsymbol{x}}, \boldsymbol{y} \rangle$ between $z_{\boldsymbol{y}}$ and the function evaluation $f_{\boldsymbol{y}}(\bar{\boldsymbol{x}})$ serves as a shift of the real actual key: namely, the simulator returns $\mathsf{sk}_{\boldsymbol{y}} = (s'_{\boldsymbol{y}}, t'_{\boldsymbol{y}})$, where

$$\begin{aligned} \boldsymbol{s}'_{\boldsymbol{y}} &:= \langle \boldsymbol{s}, \boldsymbol{y} \rangle + \alpha \cdot (z_{\boldsymbol{y}} - \langle \bar{\boldsymbol{x}}, \boldsymbol{y} \rangle) \bmod q \\ \boldsymbol{t}'_{\boldsymbol{y}} &:= \langle \boldsymbol{t}, \boldsymbol{y} \rangle + \beta \cdot (z_{\boldsymbol{y}} - \langle \bar{\boldsymbol{x}}, \boldsymbol{y} \rangle) \bmod q. \end{aligned} \tag{1.1}$$

By exploiting the linearity properties of the scheme, the shift terms $\alpha \cdot (z_{\boldsymbol{y}} - \langle \bar{\boldsymbol{x}}, \boldsymbol{y} \rangle)$ and $\beta \cdot (z_{\boldsymbol{y}} - \langle \bar{\boldsymbol{x}}, \boldsymbol{y} \rangle)$ ensure that $\mathsf{sk}_{\boldsymbol{y}} = (s'_{\boldsymbol{y}}, t'_{\boldsymbol{y}})$ will decrypt the dummy ciphertext to the oracle-supplied $z_{\boldsymbol{y}}$. As in [46], we can prove that this shift of post-challenge keys is equivalent to a shift of the master secret key from the adversary's view:

namely, $\mathsf{msk} = (\boldsymbol{s}, \boldsymbol{t})$ is traded for $\mathsf{msk}' = (\boldsymbol{s}', \boldsymbol{t}')$, where $\boldsymbol{s}' = \boldsymbol{s} + \alpha \cdot (\boldsymbol{x}^\star - \bar{\boldsymbol{x}})$ and $\boldsymbol{t}' = \boldsymbol{t} + \beta \cdot (\boldsymbol{x}^\star - \bar{\boldsymbol{x}})$. By applying complexity leveraging argument in a statistical setting (as previously done in, e.g., [11,45,46]), we can prove that the two master secret keys of $(\boldsymbol{s}', \boldsymbol{t}')$ and $(\boldsymbol{s}, \boldsymbol{t})$ are identically distributed in the adversary's view, even if the adversary chooses $\boldsymbol{x}^\star$ adaptively, after having seen the public parameters and responses to pre-challenge queries.

DCR-Based IPFE: The above ideas can be adapted to the Composite Residuosity assumption (DCR) [38] so as to prove simulation-based security in (a variant of) the Paillier-based construction of Agrawal *et al.* [8]. One difficulty is that functional secret keys $s_{\boldsymbol{y}} = \langle \boldsymbol{s}, \boldsymbol{y} \rangle$ have to be computed over the integers since the group order is hidden. When we want to prove that the simulation is indistinguishable from the real experiment, this makes it harder to create simulated functional secret keys $s'_{\boldsymbol{y}} := \langle \boldsymbol{s}, \boldsymbol{y} \rangle + \alpha \cdot (z_{\boldsymbol{y}} - \langle \bar{\boldsymbol{x}}, \boldsymbol{y} \rangle)$ that are statistically indistinguishable from the real keys $s_{\boldsymbol{y}} := \langle \boldsymbol{s}, \boldsymbol{y} \rangle$. In particular, since the functional secret keys are computed over $\mathbb{Z}$, the simulator cannot easily compute a small-norm dummy message $\bar{\boldsymbol{x}}$ which is consistent with responses to pre-challenge queries (indeed, it does not have a short basis for the lattice induced by these queries). However, the simulator can still use the pre-challenge queries to compute a dummy message $\bar{\boldsymbol{x}} \in \mathbb{Z}^\ell$ with large entries. Although $\bar{\boldsymbol{x}} \in \mathbb{Z}^\ell$ does not fit in $\mathbb{Z}_N^\ell$, we can still encrypt $\bar{\boldsymbol{x}} \bmod N$ and obtain a simulated ciphertext which is compatible with responses to pre-challenge queries. When it comes to simulating post-challenge keys, we can have the simulator compute $s'_{\boldsymbol{y}} := \langle \boldsymbol{s}, \boldsymbol{y} \rangle + \alpha \cdot (z_{\boldsymbol{y}} - \langle \bar{\boldsymbol{x}}, \boldsymbol{y} \rangle)$ and argue that, from the adversary's view, this is equivalent to trading the master secret key $\boldsymbol{s} \in \mathbb{Z}^\ell$ for $\boldsymbol{s}' := \boldsymbol{s} + \alpha \cdot (\boldsymbol{x}^\star - \bar{\boldsymbol{x}})$. By computing an upper bound for $\|\boldsymbol{x}^\star - \bar{\boldsymbol{x}}\|_\infty$, we can increase the magnitude of the master secret key $\boldsymbol{s} \in \mathbb{Z}^\ell$ so as to make sure that the statistical distance between $\boldsymbol{s} \in \mathbb{Z}^\ell$ and $\boldsymbol{s}' \in \mathbb{Z}^\ell$ negligible. This is actually possible by sampling the entries of the master secret key $\boldsymbol{s} \in \mathbb{Z}^\ell$ from a large interval, so that its bitlength becomes $O(\ell^3 \cdot \lambda^3/\text{polylog}(\lambda))$ if ℓ is the dimension of encrypted vectors.

LWE-Based IPFE mod p: We now outline our adaptation of the LWE-based construction for IPFE [8] to achieve adaptive SIM-based security. We focus on the construction of IPFE modulo a prime p, [8, Sec 4.2], where the ciphertext contains a vector $\boldsymbol{x} \in \mathbb{Z}_p^\ell$, the key contains a vector $\boldsymbol{y} \in \mathbb{Z}_p^\ell$ and decryption reveals $\langle \boldsymbol{x}, \boldsymbol{y} \rangle \bmod p$. Our construction is generic except that it requires the underlying scheme IPFE to satisfy the property that functional keys for vectors that are linearly dependent on previously queried vectors may be computed as the linear combination of previously returned keys. In more detail, say that the adversary queries vectors $\boldsymbol{y}_1, \ldots, \boldsymbol{y}_k \in \mathbb{Z}_p^\ell$ and then submits a query $\boldsymbol{y}$ such that $\boldsymbol{y} = \sum_{j \in [k]} k_j \cdot \boldsymbol{y}_j \pmod p$, for some $k_j \in \mathbb{Z}_p$. Then, the secret key $\mathsf{sk}_{\boldsymbol{y}} \in \mathbb{Z}^m$ can be computed as $\mathsf{sk}_{\boldsymbol{y}} = \sum_{j \in [k]} k_j \cdot \mathsf{sk}_{\boldsymbol{y}_j} \in \mathbb{Z}^m$. This property is satisfied by the LWE-based construction that evaluates inner products over $\mathbb{Z}_p$ in [8, Sec 4.2].

Since secret keys of linearly dependent vectors are computed as linear combinations of previously returned keys[2], it suffices to consider an adversary that

[2] As in [8], this results in a stateful key generator.

only requests for $\ell - 1$ linearly independent keys. Let us refer to the key requests made in the pre-challenge phase as $\boldsymbol{y}^{\mathsf{pre}}$ and those in the post-challenge phase as $\boldsymbol{y}^{\mathsf{post}}$.

To begin, we set $L = 2\ell$ and instantiate the adaptive IND secure IPFE of [8, Sec 4.2] with message length L. Given a message vector $\boldsymbol{x} \in \mathbb{Z}_p^\ell$, we extend it to $\widehat{\boldsymbol{x}} \in \mathbb{Z}_p^L$ to make one slot corresponding to each independent key queried up to $\ell - 1$ keys. The simulated challenge ciphertext $\mathbf{c}^*$ encrypts the extended vector $\widehat{\bar{\boldsymbol{x}}} = (\bar{\boldsymbol{x}}, -r_1, \ldots, -r_{\ell-1}, 1)$ for a dummy message $\bar{\boldsymbol{x}}$, where $\{r_i \leftarrow \mathbb{Z}_p\}_{i \in [\ell-1]}$ are chosen uniformly at random, while simulating the setup phase of the real protocol.

Pre-challenge keys for vectors $\boldsymbol{y}^{\mathsf{pre}} \in \mathbb{Z}_p^\ell$ are handled as in the real scheme. In more detail, for the ith independent pre-challenge key $\boldsymbol{y}_i^{\mathsf{pre}}$ the underlying IPFE scheme is used to compute keys for the vector $(\boldsymbol{y}_i^{\mathsf{pre}}, \mathbf{e}_i, r_i)$, where $\mathbf{e}_i \in \mathbb{Z}_p^{\ell-1}$ is the i-th canonical vector and $\{r_i \leftarrow \mathbb{Z}_p\}_{i \in [\ell-1]}$ are as above. The challenge ciphertext is handled by computing a message $\bar{\boldsymbol{x}}$ that is consistent with only the keys associated with the pre-challenge vectors $\boldsymbol{y}^{\mathsf{pre}}$. For handling post-challenge queries, let $\Delta_i = \langle \boldsymbol{x}^\star - \bar{\boldsymbol{x}}, \boldsymbol{y}_i^{\mathsf{post}} \rangle$ be the difference in decryption using the i-th post-challenge key corresponding to a linearly independent vector $\boldsymbol{y}_i^{\mathsf{post}}$. To compensate this difference, we extend the vector $\boldsymbol{y}_i^{\mathsf{post}}$ to $(\boldsymbol{y}_i^{\mathsf{post}}, \mathbf{e}_i, \Delta_i + r_i)$. Note that the randomizer r_i in the i-th slot of the extended message vector hides Δ_i in the i-th post-challenge key.

For post challenge keys, the decryption outputs

$$\langle \bar{\boldsymbol{x}}, \boldsymbol{y}_i^{\mathsf{post}} \rangle + \langle -r_i, 1 \rangle + \langle 1, \Delta_i + r_i \rangle = \langle \bar{\boldsymbol{x}}, \boldsymbol{y}_i^{\mathsf{post}} \rangle + \Delta_i = \langle \boldsymbol{x}^\star, \boldsymbol{y}_i^{\mathsf{post}} \rangle$$

as desired. It is easy to verify that this also works if a post-challenge vector $\boldsymbol{y}^{\mathsf{post}}$ is a linear combination of possibly any arbitrary subset of pre-challenge and post-challenge keys queried so far. As for pre-challenge queries, the simulated keys properly decrypt the simulated ciphertext since the r_i simply get cancelled (i.e., $\Delta_i = 0$). Also, note that the simulated keys work for any honestly generated ciphertext since this contains $\mathbf{0}$ in the extended slots and do not "activate" the extended slots in the keys. For the detailed proof, please see Sect. 5.

DCR-Based IPFE mod N: In the description of our construction from LWE, we assumed that the modulus p is prime. However, the same technique can also be applied to the Paillier-based construction of [8, Section 5.2], which evaluates inner products over $\mathbb{Z}_N$. As a result, it provides a simulation-secure IPFE with stateful key generation for inner products over $\mathbb{Z}_N$, whereas our scheme in Sect. 4 is stateless but computes inner products over $\mathbb{Z}$. When we switch to composite moduli $N = pq$, we need to take into account that $\mathbb{Z}_N$ is not a field when the simulator has to solve a linear system over $\mathbb{Z}_N$ in order to compute a dummy message. Fortunately, inversion over $\mathbb{Z}_N$ is always possible with overwhelming probability when factoring N is hard.

2 Preliminaries

In this section we define the preliminaries that we require in this work.

Notation. We begin by defining the notation that we will use throughout the paper. We use bold letters to denote vectors and the notation $[1, n]$ or $[n]$ or $\{1, \ldots, n\}$ interchangeably to denote the set of first n positive integers. We denote by $U([n])$ the uniform distribution over the set $[n]$ and $u \hookleftarrow \mathcal{D}$ or $u \leftarrow \mathcal{D}$ interchageably to sample an element u from distribution $\mathcal{D}$. Concatenation is denoted by the symbol $\|$ or $|$ interchangeably. We say a function $f(n)$ is *negligible*, denoted by $\text{negl}(n)$, if it is $O(n^{-c})$ for all $c > 0$. We say an event occurs with *overwhelming probability* if its probability is $1 - \text{negl}(n)$.

2.1 Useful Lemmas

We will rely on a few simple but useful lemmas, which are stated hereunder.

Lemma 1. *Let M, m be positive integers, $M = m \cdot q + r$ with $0 \le r < m$. The statistical distance between the distributions $(U(\mathbb{Z}_M) \bmod m)$ and $U(\mathbb{Z}_m)$ is bounded by $\Delta(U(\mathbb{Z}_M) \bmod m, U(\mathbb{Z}_m)) \le \frac{r}{M}$.*

Proof. Let $M = mq + r$, with $0 \le r < m$. Observe that for $i \in \mathbb{Z}_m$ we can compute the number of integers of the form $i + jm$, smaller than $M - 1$, by $\lfloor \frac{M-1-i}{m} \rfloor + 1$ which is also equal to $\lfloor q + \frac{r-1-i}{m} \rfloor + 1$. So the probability of getting $i \in \mathbb{Z}_m$ by sampling from $U(\mathbb{Z}_M) \bmod m$ is equal to $\frac{q+1}{M}$ if $i < r$ or equal to $\frac{q}{M}$ if $i \ge r$. So the statistical distance that we want to evaluate is equal to:

$$\Delta = \frac{1}{2}\left(\sum_{i<r}\left|\frac{q+1}{M} - \frac{1}{m}\right| + \sum_{i \ge r}\left|\frac{q}{M} - \frac{1}{m}\right|\right) = \frac{r(m-r)}{Mm} \le \frac{r}{M}.$$

□

Lemma 2. *Let $a, b, c \in \mathbb{Z}$ such that $b > a$. We have $\Delta\left(U_{[a,b]}, U_{c+[a,b]}\right) \le \frac{|c|}{b-a}$, where $U_{[\alpha,\beta]}$ is the uniform distribution on $[\alpha, \beta] \cap \mathbb{Z}$.*

Lemma 3. *For any $\mathbf{A} \in \mathbb{R}^{m \times n}$, let $\alpha := \max_{i,j} |a_{i,j}|$. Then, we have the inequality $\det(\mathbf{A}\mathbf{A}^\top) \le (n \cdot \alpha^2)^m$.*

Proof. Since $\mathbf{A}\mathbf{A}^\top \in \mathbb{R}^{m \times m}$ is positive definite, we know that it has positive eigenvalues $\lambda_1, \lambda_2, \ldots, \lambda_m \ge 0$. By the mean inequality, we have $\sqrt[m]{\lambda_1 \lambda_2 \cdots \lambda_m} \le \frac{\lambda_1 + \cdots + \lambda_m}{m}$. This can be interpreted as $\det(\mathbf{A}\mathbf{A}^\top) \le \left(\frac{\text{Tr}\mathbf{A}\mathbf{A}^\top}{m}\right)^m$ and the right hand side term can be bounded by $(n\alpha^2)^m$. □

Lemma 4. *Let $\mathbf{Y} \in \mathbb{Z}^{k \times \ell}$ be a full rank matrix such that $\max_{i,j} |y_{ij}| \le Y$. There exists an efficient algorithm that finds a basis $\{\mathbf{x}_1, \mathbf{x}_2, \ldots, \mathbf{x}_{\ell-k}\} \subset \mathbb{Z}^\ell$ of the lattice $\mathbf{Y}^\perp := \{\mathbf{x} \in \mathbb{Z}^\ell : \mathbf{Y} \cdot \mathbf{x} = \mathbf{0}\}$ such that*

$$\|\mathbf{x}_j\|_\infty \le (\sqrt{k}Y)^k \ , \ j \in \{1, \ldots, \ell - k\}.$$

Proof. We assume w.l.o.g. that $\mathbf{Y} = [\mathbf{A}|\mathbf{B}]$, for a full rank matrix $\mathbf{A} \in \mathbb{Z}^{k\times k}$ and for some $\mathbf{B} \in \mathbb{Z}^{k\times(\ell-k)}$ such that $\max_{i,j}|a_{i,j}| \leq Y$ and $\max_{i,j}|b_{i,j}| \leq Y$. If $\mathbf{x} = (z_1,\ldots,z_k,\lambda_1,\ldots,\lambda_{\ell-k})^\top$ satisfies $\mathbf{Y}\cdot\mathbf{x} = \mathbf{0}$, Cramer's rule implies

$$z_i = \frac{-1}{\det \mathbf{A}} \sum_{j=1}^{\ell-k} \lambda_j \cdot \det \mathbf{A}_{ij},$$

where the matrix $\mathbf{A}_{ij} \in \mathbb{Z}^{k\times k}$ is obtained by replacing the i-th column of $\mathbf{A}$ by the j-th column of $\mathbf{B}$. By choosing $(\lambda_1,\lambda_2,\ldots,\lambda_{\ell-k}) \in \mathbb{Z}^{\ell-k}$ from the set

$$\{\det \mathbf{A}\cdot(1,0,\ldots,0), \det \mathbf{A}\cdot(0,1,\ldots,0),\ldots,\det \mathbf{A}\cdot(0,0,\ldots,1)\},$$

we obtain the desired basis. Concretely, for every $j \in \{1,2,\ldots,\ell-k\}$, we define

$$\mathbf{x}_j = (-\det \mathbf{A}_{1j}, -\det \mathbf{A}_{2j},\ldots,-\det \mathbf{A}_{kj},\ \mathbf{e}_j\cdot\det \mathbf{A}) \in \mathbb{Z}^\ell.$$

By using Lemma 3 we get the bounds on the size of each basis vector $\mathbf{x}_j$. □

Corollary 1. *Let a full rank* $\mathbf{Y} \in \mathbb{Z}^{k\times\ell}$ *such that* $|y_{ij}| \leq Y$ *and* $\mathbf{z} \in \mathbb{Z}^k$. *If there exists a solution* $\mathbf{x}_0 \in \mathbb{Z}^\ell$ *to the system* $\mathbf{Y}\cdot\mathbf{x}_0 = \mathbf{z}$, *then there exists an efficient algorithm that computes a solution* $\mathbf{x} \in \mathbb{Z}^\ell$ *such that* $\|\mathbf{x}\|_\infty \leq (\ell-k)\cdot(\sqrt{k}Y)^k$.

Proof. By Lemma 4, we can efficiently find a basis $\{\mathbf{x}_1,\ldots,\mathbf{x}_{\ell-k}\}$ of the lattice $\mathbf{Y}^\perp$ such that $\|\mathbf{x}_j\|_\infty \leq (\sqrt{k}Y)^k$. Reducing the solution $\mathbf{x}_0$ modulo this basis, we obtain $\mathbf{x} := \mathbf{x}_0 \bmod \mathbf{Y}^\perp$ such that $\|\mathbf{x}\|_\infty \leq \sum_{k=1}^{\ell-k}\|\mathbf{x}_j\|_\infty \leq (\ell-k)\cdot(\sqrt{k}Y)^k$. □

2.2 Functional Encryption

Definition 1. *A Functional Encryption (FE) scheme over a class of functions* $\mathcal{F} = \{f : \mathcal{X} \to \mathcal{Z}\}$ *consists of the* PPT *algorithms* (Setup, KeyGen, Encrypt, Decrypt)*:*

Setup$(1^\lambda, \mathcal{F})$: *Outputs a public key* mpk *and a master secret key* msk.

Keygen(msk, f) : *Given the master secret key and a functionality* $f \in \mathcal{F}$, *the algorithm outputs a secret key* sk_f.

Encrypt(mpk, $\boldsymbol{x}$) : *On input the public key and a message* $\boldsymbol{x} \in \mathcal{X}$ *from the message space, the algorithm outputs a ciphertext* $\boldsymbol{c}$.

Decrypt(mpk, sk_f, $\boldsymbol{c}$) : *Given a ciphertext and a secret key corresponding to some functionality* $f \in \mathcal{F}$, *the algorithm outputs* $\boldsymbol{z} \in \mathcal{Z}$.

Correctness: We require that for $(\mathsf{mpk},\mathsf{msk}) \leftarrow \mathsf{Setup}(1^\lambda,\mathcal{F})$, for all $\boldsymbol{x} \in \mathcal{X}$, all $f \in \mathcal{F}$, $\boldsymbol{c} \leftarrow \mathsf{Encrypt}(\mathsf{mpk},\boldsymbol{x})$ and $\mathsf{sk}_f \leftarrow \mathsf{Keygen}(\mathsf{msk},f)$, with overwhelming probability, we have $\mathsf{Decrypt}(\mathsf{mpk},\mathsf{sk}_f,\boldsymbol{c}) = f(\boldsymbol{x})$.

In some cases, we will also give a state st as input to algorithm Keygen, so that a stateful authority may reply to key queries in a way that depends on the queries that have been made so far. In that situation, algorithm Keygen may additionally update state st.

2.3 Security

Next, we define security of functional encryption. Security comes in two flavours – indistinguishability-based and simulation-based – we define each in turn.

INDISTINGUISHABILITY-BASED SECURITY. We first define the weaker notion of indistinguishability-based security [15]. In this notion, one asks that no efficient adversary be able to differentiate encryptions of $\boldsymbol{x}_0$ and $\boldsymbol{x}_1$ without obtaining secret keys sk_f such that $f(\boldsymbol{x}_0) \neq f(\boldsymbol{x}_1)$.

Definition 2 (Indistinguishability-based security). *A functional encryption scheme* $\mathcal{FE} = (\mathsf{Setup}, \mathsf{Keygen}, \mathsf{Encrypt}, \mathsf{Decrypt})$ *provides semantic security under chosen-plaintext attacks (or IND-CPA security) if no* PPT *adversary has non-negligible advantage in the following game, where* $q_1 \leq q \in \mathsf{poly}(\lambda)$*:*

1. *The challenger runs* $(\mathsf{mpk}, \mathsf{msk}) \leftarrow \mathsf{Setup}(1^\lambda)$ *and the master public key* mpk *is given to the adversary* $\mathcal{A}$.
2. *The adversary adaptively makes secret key queries to the challenger. At each query, adversary* $\mathcal{A}$ *chooses a function* $f \in \mathcal{F}$ *and obtains* $\mathsf{sk}_f \leftarrow \mathsf{Keygen}(\mathsf{msk}, f)$.
3. *Adversary* $\mathcal{A}$ *chooses distinct messages* $\boldsymbol{x}_0, \boldsymbol{x}_1$ *subject to the restriction that, if* $\{f_i\}_{i=1}^{q_1}$ *denotes the set of secret key queries made by* $\mathcal{A}$ *at Stage 2, it holds that* $f_i(\boldsymbol{x}_0) = f_i(\boldsymbol{x}_1)$ *for each* $i \in \{1, \ldots, q_1\}$*. Then, the challenger flips a fair coin* $\beta \hookleftarrow \{0,1\}$ *and computes* $\mathbf{c}^\star \leftarrow \mathsf{Encrypt}(\mathsf{mpk}, \boldsymbol{x}_\beta)$ *which is sent as a challenge to* $\mathcal{A}$.
4. *Adversary* $\mathcal{A}$ *makes further secret key queries for arbitrary functions* $f \in \mathcal{F}$*. However, it is required that* $f(\boldsymbol{x}_0) = f(\boldsymbol{x}_1)$ *at each query* $f \in \{f_{q_1+1}, \ldots, f_q\}$.
5. *Adversary* $\mathcal{A}$ *eventually outputs a bit* $\beta' \hookleftarrow \{0,1\}$ *and wins if* $\beta' = \beta$.

The adversary's advantage is defined to be $\mathbf{Adv}_{\mathcal{A}}(\lambda) := |\Pr[\beta' = \beta] - 1/2|$*, where the probability is taken over all coin tosses.*

Definition 2 captures *adaptive* security in that the adversary is allowed to choose the messages $\boldsymbol{x}_0, \boldsymbol{x}_1$ at Stage 3.

As pointed out in [15], indistinguishability-based security is not fully satisfactory in general as it may fail to rule out constructions that are intuitively insecure. They argue that, whenever it is possible at all, one should prefer a stronger notion of simulation-based security. We recall this notion hereunder.

SIMULATION-BASED SECURITY: For a FE scheme defined as above, a PPT adversary $\mathcal{A} = (A_1, A_2)$ and a PPT simulator $\mathsf{Sim} = (\mathsf{Setup}^\star, \mathsf{KeyGen}_0^\star, \mathsf{Encrypt}^\star, \mathsf{KeyGen}_1^\star)$, consider the following experiments:

$\mathsf{Exp}^{\mathsf{Real}}_{\mathsf{FE},\mathcal{A}}(1^\lambda)$	$\mathsf{Exp}^{\mathsf{Ideal}}_{\mathsf{FE},\mathcal{A}}(1^\lambda)$
1. $(\mathsf{mpk}, \mathsf{msk}) \leftarrow \mathsf{Setup}(1^\lambda, \mathcal{F})$	1. $(\mathsf{mpk}^\star, \mathsf{msk}^\star) \leftarrow \mathsf{Setup}^\star(1^\lambda, \mathcal{F})$
2. $(\boldsymbol{x}^\star, \mathsf{st}) \leftarrow A_1^{\mathsf{Keygen}(\mathsf{msk},\cdot)}(\mathsf{mpk})$	2. $(\boldsymbol{x}^\star, \mathsf{st}) \leftarrow A_1^{\mathsf{Keygen}_0^\star(\mathsf{msk}^\star,\cdot)}(\mathsf{mpk}^\star)$ Let $\mathcal{V} = \{(f_i, f_i(\boldsymbol{x}^\star), \mathsf{sk}_{f_i})\}_{i=1}^k$
3. $\boldsymbol{c} \leftarrow \mathsf{Encrypt}(\mathsf{mpk}, \boldsymbol{x}^\star)$	3. $(\boldsymbol{c}^\star, \mathsf{st}') \leftarrow \mathsf{Encrypt}^\star(\mathsf{mpk}^\star, \mathsf{msk}^\star, \mathcal{V}, 1^{\lvert \boldsymbol{x}^\star \rvert})$
4. $\alpha \leftarrow A_2^{\mathsf{KeyGen}(\mathsf{msk},\cdot)}(\mathsf{mpk}, \boldsymbol{c}, \mathsf{st})$	4. $\alpha \leftarrow A_2^{\mathsf{KeyGen}_1^\star(\mathsf{msk}^\star,\mathsf{st}',\cdot)}(\mathsf{mpk}^\star, \boldsymbol{c}^\star, \mathsf{st})$

In the Ideal experiment above, the $\{f_i \in \mathcal{F}\}_{i=1}^k$ are the functionalities for which the adversary requests their corresponding keys, $\{\mathsf{sk}_{f_i}\}_{i=1}^k$. An FE scheme achieves **adaptive simulation-based** (AD-SIM) security if there exists a PPT simulator Sim such that, for any PPT adversary $\mathcal{A}$, the Real and the Ideal experiments are computationally indistinguishable.

We stress that we consider simulators that run in polynomial time. For the knowledgeable reader, it was shown by Boneh, Sahai and Waters [15] that AD-SIM-security is impossible to achieve for many challenge messages. While [15] provided the lower bound for the IBE functionality, the same argument easily extends to IPFE. Thus, as in [46], our security game must also be restricted to a single challenge ciphertext. Note that AD-SIM for a single ciphertext implies AD-IND for a single ciphertext, which in turn implies AD-IND for many ciphertexts [26]. Hence, AD-SIM for a single ciphertext is still the strongest definition of security for IPFE.

2.4 Hardness Assumptions

Our first scheme relies on the standard Decision Diffie-Hellman DDH assumption in ordinary (i.e., non-pairing-friendly) cyclic groups.

Definition 3. *In a cyclic group* $\mathbb{G}$ *of prime order* p*, the* **Decision Diffie-Hellman Problem** *(DDH) in* $\mathbb{G}$*, is to distinguish the distributions* (g, g^a, g^b, g^{ab}) *and* (g, g^a, g^b, g^c)*, with* $a, b, c \hookleftarrow \mathbb{Z}_p$*. The* **Decision Diffie-Hellman** *assumption is the intractability of DDH for any* PPT *algorithm* $\mathcal{D}$*.*

Our second scheme relies on Paillier's composite residuosity assumption.

Definition 4 ([38]). *Let* p, q *be prime numbers and* $N = pq$*. The* **Decision Composite Residuosity** (DCR) *assumption states that the following two distributions are computationally indistinguishable:*

$$\{t_0^N \bmod N^2 \mid t_0 \leftarrow U(\mathbb{Z}_N^\star)\} \overset{c}{\approx} \{t \mid t \leftarrow U(\mathbb{Z}_{N^2}^\star)\}$$

Our third construction builds on the Learning-With-Errors (LWE) problem, which is known to be at least as hard as certain standard lattice problems in the worst case [16,40].

Definition 5. *Let q, α, m be functions of a parameter n. For a secret $\mathbf{s} \in \mathbb{Z}_q^n$, the distribution $A_{q,\alpha,\mathbf{s}}$ over $\mathbb{Z}_q^n \times \mathbb{Z}_q$ is obtained by sampling $\mathbf{a} \hookleftarrow \mathbb{Z}_q^n$ and an $e \hookleftarrow D_{\mathbb{Z},\alpha q}$, and returning $(\mathbf{a}, \langle \mathbf{a}, \mathbf{s}\rangle + e) \in \mathbb{Z}_q^{n+1}$. The* **Learning With Errors** *(LWE) problem $\mathsf{LWE}_{q,\alpha,m}$ is as follows: For $\mathbf{s} \hookleftarrow \mathbb{Z}_q^n$, the goal is to distinguish between the distributions:*

$$D_0(\mathbf{s}) := U(\mathbb{Z}_q^{m\times(n+1)}) \quad and \quad D_1(\mathbf{s}) := (A_{q,\alpha,\mathbf{s}})^m.$$

We say that a PPT algorithm $\mathcal{A}$ solves $\mathsf{LWE}_{q,\alpha}$ if it distinguishes $D_0(\mathbf{s})$ and $D_1(\mathbf{s})$ with non-negligible advantage (over the random coins of $\mathcal{A}$ and the randomness of the samples), with non-negligible probability over the randomness of $\mathbf{s}$.

3 Adaptive Simulation-Based Security from DDH

In this section, we first recall the IPFE scheme of [8]. Abdalla *et al.* [3] previously showed that this construction provides simulation-based security for selective adversaries. In [46], Wee gave a proof of simulation-based security for semi-adaptive adversaries. We provide a proof that handles adaptive adversaries without any modification in the original scheme.

Setup$(1^\lambda, 1^\ell)$**:** Choose a cyclic group $\mathbb{G}$ of prime order $q > 2^\lambda$ with generators $g, h \hookleftarrow U(\mathbb{G})$. Then, for each $i \in \{1, \ldots, \ell\}$, sample $s_i, t_i \hookleftarrow U(\mathbb{Z}_q)$ and compute $h_i = g^{s_i} \cdot h^{t_i}$. Define $\mathsf{msk} := \{s_i, t_i\}_{i=1}^{\ell}$ and

$$\mathsf{mpk} := \Big(\mathbb{G}, g, h, \{h_i\}_{i=1}^{\ell}\Big).$$

Keygen$(\mathsf{msk}, \boldsymbol{y})$**:** To generate a key for the vector $\boldsymbol{y} = (y_1, \ldots, y_\ell) \in \mathbb{Z}_q^\ell$, compute $\mathsf{sk}_{\boldsymbol{y}} = (s_{\boldsymbol{y}}, t_{\boldsymbol{y}}) = (\sum_{i=1}^{\ell} s_i \cdot y_i, \sum_{i=1}^{\ell} t_i \cdot y_i) = (\langle \boldsymbol{s}, \boldsymbol{y}\rangle, \langle \boldsymbol{t}, \boldsymbol{y}\rangle)$.

Encrypt$(\mathsf{mpk}, \boldsymbol{x})$**:** To encrypt a vector $\boldsymbol{x} = (x_1, \ldots, x_\ell) \in \mathbb{Z}_q^\ell$, sample $r \hookleftarrow \mathbb{Z}_q$ and compute

$$C = g^r, \qquad D = h^r, \qquad \{E_i = g^{x_i} \cdot h_i^r\}_{i=1}^{\ell}.$$

Return $C_{\boldsymbol{x}} = (C, D, E_1, \ldots, E_\ell)$.

Decrypt$(\mathsf{mpk}, \mathsf{sk}_{\boldsymbol{y}}, C_{\boldsymbol{x}})$**:** Given $\mathsf{sk}_{\boldsymbol{y}} = (s_{\boldsymbol{y}}, t_{\boldsymbol{y}})$, compute

$$E_{\boldsymbol{y}} = (\prod_{i=1}^{\ell} E_i^{y_i})/(C^{s_{\boldsymbol{y}}} \cdot D^{t_{\boldsymbol{y}}}).$$

Then, compute and output $\log_g(E_{\boldsymbol{y}})$.

Correctness. Note that $\prod_{i=1}^{\ell} E_i^{y_i} = g^{\langle \boldsymbol{x}, \boldsymbol{y}\rangle} \cdot g^{r\langle \boldsymbol{s}, \boldsymbol{y}\rangle} \cdot h^{r\langle \boldsymbol{t}, \boldsymbol{y}\rangle} = g^{\langle \boldsymbol{x}, \boldsymbol{y}\rangle} \cdot C^{s_{\boldsymbol{y}}} \cdot D^{t_{\boldsymbol{y}}}$, which implies $E_{\boldsymbol{y}} = g^{\langle \boldsymbol{x}, \boldsymbol{y}\rangle}$. The decryption algorithm can thus recover $\langle \boldsymbol{x}, \boldsymbol{y}\rangle \bmod q$ by solving a discrete logarithm instance in a small interval, by restricting messages and keys so as to have $|\langle \boldsymbol{x}, \boldsymbol{y}\rangle| \leq L$, for some polynomially bounded $L = \mathsf{poly}(\lambda)$. In this case, the inner product $\langle \boldsymbol{x}, \boldsymbol{y}\rangle$ can be recovered in $\tilde{O}(L^{1/2})$ time using [39].

Theorem 1. *The scheme provides simulation-based security against adaptive adversaries under the* DDH *assumption.*

Proof. To prove the result, we first describe a PPT simulator before showing that, under the DDH assumption, the adversary cannot distinguish the ideal experiment from the real experiment.

In both experiments, we know that the adversary $\mathcal{A}$ can obtain private keys for up to $\ell - 1$ linearly independent vectors. We assume w.l.o.g. that $\mathcal{A}$ makes private keys queries for exactly $\ell - 1 = \ell_0 + \ell_1$ independent vectors, which we denote by $\boldsymbol{y}_1, \ldots, \boldsymbol{y}_{\ell-1} \in \mathbb{Z}_q^\ell$. Among these vectors, we denote by $\boldsymbol{y}_1, \ldots, \boldsymbol{y}_{\ell_0}$ the vectors queried by $\mathcal{A}$ *before* the challenge phase while $\boldsymbol{y}_{\ell_0+1}, \ldots, \boldsymbol{y}_{\ell_0+\ell_1}$ stand for the post-challenge private key queries. In the challenge phase, we denote by $\boldsymbol{x}^\star = (x_1^\star, \ldots, x_\ell^\star) \in \mathbb{Z}_q^\ell$ the message chosen by $\mathcal{A}$. The simulator $(\mathsf{Setup}^\star, \mathsf{Keygen}_0^\star, \mathsf{Encrypt}^\star, \mathsf{Keygen}_1^\star)$ proceeds in the following way.

$\mathsf{Setup}^\star(1^\lambda, 1^\ell)$: This algorithm is identical to Setup except that $\omega = \log_g(h)$ is included in the master secret key. It outputs

$$\mathsf{mpk}^\star := \Big(\mathbb{G}, g, h, \{h_i\}_{i=1}^{\ell}\Big).$$

and $\mathsf{msk}^\star = (\omega, \boldsymbol{s}, \boldsymbol{t})$.

$\mathsf{Keygen}_0^\star(\mathsf{msk}^\star, \boldsymbol{y})$: This algorithm is used to answer private key queries before the challenge phase and proceeds exactly like Keygen in the real scheme.

$\mathsf{Encrypt}^\star(\mathsf{mpk}^\star, \mathsf{msk}^\star, \mathcal{V}, \{1^{|x_i^\star|}\}_{i=1}^{\ell})$: This algorithm takes as input $\mathsf{mpk}^\star, \mathsf{msk}^\star$, the lengths $\{1^{|x_i^\star|}\}_{i=1}^{\ell}$ of all coordinates of $\boldsymbol{x}^\star$ and a set

$$\mathcal{V} = \Big\{\{\boldsymbol{y}_j, z_j = \langle \boldsymbol{x}^\star, \boldsymbol{y}_j\rangle, \mathsf{sk}_{\boldsymbol{y}_j}\}_{j=1}^{\ell_0}\Big\}$$

containing all pre-challenge independent queries $\{\boldsymbol{y}_j\}_{j=1}^{\ell_0}$, the returned keys and the corresponding linear function evaluations $\{z_j = \langle \boldsymbol{x}^\star, \boldsymbol{y}_j\rangle\}_{j=1}^{\ell_0}$ for the challenge message $\boldsymbol{x}^\star$. The challenge ciphertext $(C^\star, D^\star, E_1^\star, \ldots, E_\ell^\star)$ is simulated as follows.

1. Letting $\boldsymbol{z}_{\mathsf{pre}} = (z_1, \ldots, z_{\ell_0})^\top \in \mathbb{Z}_q^{\ell_0}$, compute an arbitrary $\bar{\boldsymbol{x}} \in \mathbb{Z}_q^\ell$ such that $\mathbf{Y}_{\mathsf{pre}} \cdot \bar{\boldsymbol{x}} = \boldsymbol{z}_{\mathsf{pre}} \bmod q$, where

$$\mathbf{Y}_{\mathsf{pre}} = \begin{bmatrix} \boldsymbol{y}_1^\top \\ \vdots \\ \boldsymbol{y}_{\ell_0}^\top \end{bmatrix} \in \mathbb{Z}_q^{\ell_0 \times \ell}.$$

   Note that $\bar{\boldsymbol{x}} = (\bar{x}_1, \ldots, \bar{x}_\ell)^\top$ does not have to be small and can be obtained via Gaussian elimination.
2. Compute the ciphertext by sampling $r, r' \hookleftarrow U(\mathbb{Z}_q)$ uniformly and computing $(C^\star, D^\star) = (g^r, h^{r'})$ as well as

$$E_i^\star = g^{\bar{x}_i} \cdot C^{\star s_i} \cdot D^{\star t_i} \qquad \forall i \in [\ell].$$

Output the simulated ciphertext $(C^\star, D^\star, E_1^\star, \ldots, E_\ell^\star)$ together with the state information $\mathsf{st}' = (\bar{\boldsymbol{x}}, r, r')$.

$\mathsf{Keygen}_1^\star(\mathsf{msk}^\star, \boldsymbol{y}, z = \langle \boldsymbol{x}^\star, \boldsymbol{y}\rangle, \mathsf{st}')$: On input of $\mathsf{msk}^\star = (\omega, \boldsymbol{s}, \boldsymbol{t})$, a post-challenge query $\boldsymbol{y} \in \mathbb{Z}_q^\ell$, the evaluation $z = \langle \boldsymbol{x}^\star, \boldsymbol{y}\rangle$ of the linear function $f_{\boldsymbol{y}}(\boldsymbol{x}^\star)$ on the message $\boldsymbol{x}^\star$ and the state information $\mathsf{st}' = (\bar{\boldsymbol{x}}, r, r') \in \mathbb{Z}_q^\ell \times \mathbb{Z}_q^2$, this algorithm computes

$$t'_{\boldsymbol{y}} = \langle \boldsymbol{t}, \boldsymbol{y}\rangle + \frac{1}{\omega \cdot (r' - r)} \cdot (\langle \bar{\boldsymbol{x}}, \boldsymbol{y}\rangle - z) \mod q. \tag{3.1}$$

$$s'_{\boldsymbol{y}} = \langle \boldsymbol{s}, \boldsymbol{y}\rangle - \frac{1}{(r' - r)} \cdot (\langle \bar{\boldsymbol{x}}, \boldsymbol{y}\rangle - z) \mod q.$$

and returns $\mathsf{sk}_{\boldsymbol{y}} = (s'_{\boldsymbol{y}}, t'_{\boldsymbol{y}})$.

Observe that the ciphertext $(C^\star, D^\star, E_1^\star, \ldots, E_\ell^\star)$ produced by $\mathsf{Encrypt}^\star$ is distributed in such a way that $(C^\star, D^\star) = (g^r, g^{\omega\cdot(r+(r'-r))})$ and

$$(E_1^\star, \ldots, E_\ell^\star) = g^{\bar{\boldsymbol{x}} + \omega\cdot(r'-r)\cdot \boldsymbol{t}} \cdot (h_1, \ldots, h_\ell)^r,$$

so that, for any $\boldsymbol{y} = (y_1, \ldots, y_\ell)^\top \in \mathbb{Z}_q^\ell$, we have

$$\prod_{i=1}^{\ell} E_i^{\star y_i} = g^{\langle \bar{\boldsymbol{x}}, \boldsymbol{y}\rangle + \omega\cdot(r'-r)\cdot\langle \boldsymbol{t}, \boldsymbol{y}\rangle} \cdot (g^{\langle \boldsymbol{s}, \boldsymbol{y}\rangle} \cdot h^{\langle \boldsymbol{t}, \boldsymbol{y}\rangle})^r,$$

which implies

$$\prod_{i=1}^{\ell} E_i^{\star y_i} / (C^{\star s'_{\boldsymbol{y}}} \cdot D^{\star t'_{\boldsymbol{y}}}) = g^z.$$

This shows that decrypting the simulated ciphertext $(C^\star, D^\star, E_1^\star, \ldots, E_\ell^\star)$ using the simulated key $\mathsf{sk}_{\boldsymbol{y}} = (s'_{\boldsymbol{y}}, t'_{\boldsymbol{y}})$ yields $z = \langle \boldsymbol{x}^\star, \boldsymbol{y}\rangle$, as required.

We now proceed to show that the simulation is computationally indistinguishable from the real experiment under the DDH assumption.

The proof uses a sequence of games that begins with a game in which the challenger interacts with the adversary as in real experiment and ends with a game where the challenger interacts with the adversary as in the ideal experiment. For Game_i and Game_j we denote by $\mathsf{Adv}_{ij}(\mathcal{A})$ the advantage of a PPT algorithm $\mathcal{A}$ in distinguishing between Game_i and Game_j. Formally the challenger $\mathcal{C}$ flips a coin $b \hookleftarrow \{0, 1\}$. If $b = 0$ it interacts with the adversary as in Game_i, else it interacts as in Game_j. At the end of the interaction $\mathcal{A}$ will have to make its guess $b' \in \{0, 1\}$. We define $\mathsf{Adv}_{ij}(\mathcal{A}) := \left|\Pr[b' = b] - \frac{1}{2}\right|$.

Game_0: In this game the challenger interacts with the adversary as in the real experiment.

Game_1: We modify the generation of the ciphertext $C_{\boldsymbol{x}}^\star = (C^\star, D^\star, E_1^\star, \ldots, E_\ell^\star)$. Namely, the experiment $\mathcal{B}$ first computes

$$C^\star = g^r \text{ and } D^\star = h^r, \tag{3.2}$$

for a randomly sampled $r \hookleftarrow \mathbb{Z}_q$. Then, it uses $\mathsf{msk} := \{s_i, t_i\}_{i=1}^{\ell}$ to compute

$$E_i^\star = g^{x_i^\star} \cdot C^{\star s_i} \cdot D^{\star t_i}. \tag{3.3}$$

It can be observed that $C_{\boldsymbol{x}}^\star = (C^\star, D^\star, E_1^\star, \ldots, E_\ell^\star)$ has the same distribution as in Game 0. We hence have $\mathsf{Adv}_{01}(\mathcal{A}) = 0$.

Game$_2$: We modify again the generation of $C_{\boldsymbol{x}}^\star = (C^\star, D^\star, E_1^\star, \ldots, E_\ell^\star)$. Namely, instead of computing the pair $(C^\star, D^\star)$ as in (3.2), the experiment samples $r, r' \hookleftarrow U(\mathbb{Z}_q)$ and sets

$$C^\star = g^r \quad \text{and} \quad D^\star = h^{r'}.$$

The ciphertext components $(E_1^\star, \ldots, E_\ell^\star)$ are still computed as per (3.3). Under the DDH assumption, this modification should not significantly affect $\mathcal{A}$'s view and we have $\mathsf{Adv}_{12}(\mathcal{A}) \leq \mathsf{Adv}_{\mathcal{B}}^{\mathsf{DDH}}(1^\lambda)$.

Game$_3$: In this game, the challenger runs exactly the ideal experiment with the adversary. Lemma 5 shows that $\mathsf{Adv}_{23}(\mathcal{A}) = 0$.

Combining the above, we find

$$|\Pr[1 \leftarrow \mathbf{Exp}_{\mathcal{A}}^{\mathsf{Real}}(1^\lambda)] - \Pr[1 \leftarrow \mathbf{Exp}_{\mathcal{A}}^{\mathsf{Ideal}}(1^\lambda)]| \leq \mathbf{Adv}_{\mathcal{B}}^{\mathsf{DDH}}(1^\lambda),$$

as claimed. □

Lemma 5. *The advantage of an adversary $\mathcal{A}$ in distinguishing between* Game$_2$ *and* Game$_3$ *is* 0.

Proof. To prove the result, we define the following two variants of these games.

Game$_2'$: This game is identical to Game$_2$ except that, at the outset of the game, the challenger chooses a random vector $\boldsymbol{\Delta x} \hookleftarrow U(\mathbb{Z}_q^\ell)$. It interacts with $\mathcal{A}$ as in Game$_2$ until the challenge phase, at which point it samples an arbitrary vector $\bar{\boldsymbol{x}} \in \mathbb{Z}_q^\ell$ satisfying $\mathbf{Y}_{\mathsf{pre}} \cdot \bar{\boldsymbol{x}} = \mathbf{Y}_{\mathsf{pre}} \cdot \boldsymbol{x}^\star \bmod q$, where $\mathbf{Y}_{\mathsf{pre}} \in \mathbb{Z}_q^{\ell_0 \times \ell}$ is the matrix whose rows are the first ℓ_0 independent key queries. At this point, the challenger checks whether $\boldsymbol{\Delta x} = \bar{\boldsymbol{x}} - \boldsymbol{x}^\star \bmod q$ (we call Guess this event). If not, it aborts the interaction with $\mathcal{A}$ and replaces $\mathcal{A}$'s output with 0. Otherwise, it proceeds like Game$_2$ and outputs whatever $\mathcal{A}$ outputs. Since $\boldsymbol{\Delta x}$ is drawn uniformly and independently of $\mathcal{A}$'s view, we have $\Pr[\mathsf{Guess}] = 1/q^\ell$.

Game$_3'$: This game is like Game$_3$, except that, at the very beginning of the game, the challenger chooses a random $\boldsymbol{\Delta x} \hookleftarrow U(\mathbb{Z}_q^\ell)$. It proceeds like Game$_3$ until the challenge phase, at which point it samples an arbitrary $\bar{\boldsymbol{x}} \in \mathbb{Z}_q^\ell$ satifying $\mathbf{Y}_{\mathsf{pre}} \cdot \bar{\boldsymbol{x}} = \boldsymbol{z}_{\mathsf{pre}} \bmod q$. Then, it checks whether $\boldsymbol{\Delta x} = \bar{\boldsymbol{x}} - \boldsymbol{x}^\star \bmod q$ (we call Guess this event). If not, it aborts and replaces $\mathcal{A}$'s output with 0. Otherwise, it proceeds identically to Game$_3$ and outputs the same result as $\mathcal{A}$.

Now, we claim that Game$_2'$ and Game$_3'$ are identical. To see this, we first note that, conditionally on $\neg$Guess, both games output 0. If Guess occurs, we observe that Game_3' is identical to Game_2' when the master secret key is replaced by $(\boldsymbol{s}', \boldsymbol{t}') \in \mathbb{Z}_q^\ell \times \mathbb{Z}_q^\ell$, where

$$\begin{aligned} t_i' &= t_i + \frac{1}{\omega \cdot (r' - r)} \cdot \boldsymbol{\Delta x} \\ &= t_i + \frac{1}{\omega \cdot (r' - r)} \cdot (\bar{x}_i - x_i^\star) \mod q \qquad\qquad \forall i \in [\ell] \\ s_i' &= s_i - \frac{1}{r' - r} \cdot \boldsymbol{\Delta x} \\ &= s_i - \frac{1}{r' - r} \cdot (\bar{x}_i - x_i^\star) \mod q. \end{aligned}$$

Indeed, $(\boldsymbol{s}', \boldsymbol{t}')$ has the same distribution as $(\boldsymbol{s}, \boldsymbol{t})$ conditionally on mpk. By construction, we also have $\langle \boldsymbol{s}', \boldsymbol{y} \rangle = \langle \boldsymbol{s}, \boldsymbol{y} \rangle$ and $\langle \boldsymbol{t}', \boldsymbol{y} \rangle = \langle \boldsymbol{t}, \boldsymbol{y} \rangle$ in all pre-challenge queries $\boldsymbol{y} \in \mathbb{Z}_q^\ell$. Moreover, we have

$$g^{\bar{\boldsymbol{x}} + \omega \cdot (r' - r) \cdot \boldsymbol{t}} \cdot (h_1, \ldots, h_\ell)^r = g^{\boldsymbol{x}^\star + \omega \cdot (r' - r) \cdot \boldsymbol{t}'} \cdot (h_1, \ldots, h_\ell)^r.$$

Finally, answering post-challenge queries $\boldsymbol{y} \in \mathbb{Z}_q^\ell$ using $(\boldsymbol{s}', \boldsymbol{t}')$ gives exactly the distribution (3.1). This implies that the games are indeed identical, therefore $\mathsf{Adv}_{23}' = 0$.

To conclude, notice that any adversary $\mathcal{A}$ that can distinguish between Game_2 and Game_3 can be used to distinguish between Game_2' and Game_3', with a loss factor of q^ℓ in the advantage:

$$\mathsf{Adv}_{23}' = \frac{1}{q^\ell} \cdot \mathsf{Adv}_{23}(\mathcal{A})$$

This holds since the probability that $\mathcal{A}$ outputs the correct bit b' when distinguishing between Game_2' and Game_3' is equal to:

$$\Pr[b' = b] = \Pr[b' = b | \mathsf{Guess}] \cdot \Pr[\mathsf{Guess}] + \Pr[b' = b | \overline{\mathsf{Guess}}] \cdot \Pr[\overline{\mathsf{Guess}}]$$

which is equivalent to:

$$\Pr[b' = b] - \frac{1}{2} = \left(\Pr[b' = b | \mathsf{Guess}] - \frac{1}{2} \right) \cdot \Pr[\mathsf{Guess}]$$

By considering the equality in absolute value, we get the desired relation between the advantages. □

While efficient and based on a standard assumption, the scheme of [8] is restricted to the evaluation of inner products confined in a small interval. In the next section, we show that our proof can be adapted to the Paillier-based constructions of [8,11], which make it possible to evaluate inner products over exponentially large intervals.

4 Adaptive Simulation-Based Security for Inner Products over $\mathbb{Z}$ from DCR

This section shows that a variant of the Paillier-based IPFE scheme of Agrawal *et al.* [8] can also be proved simulation-secure for adaptive adversaries. Like the first DCR-based construction of [8], it evaluates inner products over the integers. Our variant differs from [8] in that master secret keys are no longer sampled from a Gaussian distribution but are rather sampled uniformly in a large interval.

In [11], Benhamouda *et al.* also considered secret keys sampled from a uniform distribution over an interval. Their motivation was to obtain indistinguishability-based security under chosen-ciphertext attacks for adaptive adversaries. Our goal differs from theirs in that we do not consider chosen-ciphertext attacks but rather focus on achieving simulation-based security. To this end, we have to sample master secret keys from a significantly larger interval.

The reason why we need larger master secret keys is that, in the challenge phase, our simulator has to sample a dummy message $\bar{\boldsymbol{x}} \in \mathbb{Z}^\ell$ that should satisfy an equation of the form $\mathbf{Y}_{\mathsf{pre}} \cdot \bar{\boldsymbol{x}} = \boldsymbol{z}_{\mathsf{pre}} \in \mathbb{Z}^k$, for some given $\mathbf{Y}_{\mathsf{pre}} \in \mathbb{Z}^{k \times \ell}$ and $\boldsymbol{z}_{\mathsf{pre}} \in \mathbb{Z}^k$, in order to be consistent with responses $\boldsymbol{z}_{\mathsf{pre}} = (z_1, \ldots, z_k)$ to all pre-challenge queries. For lack of a short basis for the lattice $\mathbf{Y}_{\mathsf{pre}}^\perp := \{\boldsymbol{x} \in \mathbb{Z}^\ell : \mathbf{Y}_{\mathsf{pre}} \cdot \boldsymbol{x} = \mathbf{0}\}$, our simulator can only sample a dummy message $\bar{\boldsymbol{x}} \in \mathbb{Z}^\ell$ with large entries. At each post-challenge query $\boldsymbol{y} \in \mathbb{Z}^\ell$, the simulator has to "program" the returned functional secret key in such a way that it decrypts the simulated ciphertext to the value $z = \langle \boldsymbol{x}^\star, \boldsymbol{y} \rangle$ dictated by the oracle. For this purpose, the "programmed" key $\mathsf{sk}'_{\boldsymbol{y}}$ must consist of the sum (over $\mathbb{Z}$) of the real key $\mathsf{sk}_{\boldsymbol{y}} = \langle \boldsymbol{s}, \boldsymbol{y} \rangle$ and a multiple of the difference $z - \langle \bar{\boldsymbol{x}}, \boldsymbol{y} \rangle$ between the function evaluation $f_{\boldsymbol{y}}(\bar{\boldsymbol{x}}) = \langle \bar{\boldsymbol{x}}, \boldsymbol{y} \rangle$ and the oracle value $z = \langle \boldsymbol{x}^\star, \boldsymbol{y} \rangle$. Since $z - \langle \bar{\boldsymbol{x}}, \boldsymbol{y} \rangle$ may be large over $\mathbb{Z}$, we need to sample the entries of $\boldsymbol{s} \in \mathbb{Z}^\ell$ from a sufficiently wide interval so as to "drown" the statistical discrepancy between the distributions of the master secret $\boldsymbol{s} \in \mathbb{Z}^\ell$ and its shifted variant $\boldsymbol{s}' = \boldsymbol{s} + \gamma \cdot (\boldsymbol{x}^\star - \bar{\boldsymbol{x}}) \in \mathbb{Z}^\ell$ for which $\mathsf{sk}'_{\boldsymbol{y}} = \langle \boldsymbol{s}', \boldsymbol{y} \rangle$. Since RSA moduli should asymptotically contain $\lambda^3/\mathrm{polylog}(\lambda)$ bits to resist factorization attacks, we need to sample each entry of $\boldsymbol{s} \in \mathbb{Z}^\ell$ from an interval of cardinality $O(2^{\ell^2 \cdot \lambda^3/\mathrm{polylog}(\lambda)})$. Despite somewhat large secret keys, the scheme remains computationally efficient as only one exponentiation with a large exponent $\mathsf{sk}_{\boldsymbol{y}}$ suffices to decrypt. We see it as an interesting open problem to obtain shorter keys while retaining simulation-based security.

Setup$(1^\lambda, 1^\ell, X, Y)$**:** Choose safe primes $p = 2p' + 1$ and $q = 2q' + 1$ with p', q' also primes, such that $\ell XY < N/2$, where $N = pq$. Sample $g' \leftarrow U(\mathbb{Z}_{N^2}^*)$ and set $g := g'^{2N} \bmod N^2$. Next for each $i \in [\ell]$ sample $s_i \leftarrow U([-S, S] \cap \mathbb{Z})$, where $S = 2^{\lambda + \ell - 1} \cdot \bar{X}^{\ell - 1} \cdot \ell N^2$ and $\bar{X} := X + \ell \cdot (\sqrt{\ell} Y)^\ell$ and then compute $h_i = g^{s_i} \bmod N^2$. Define $\mathsf{msk} := \boldsymbol{s} = (s_1, \ldots, s_\ell)^\top \in \mathbb{Z}^\ell$ and $\mathsf{mpk} := (N, g, \{h_i\}_{i=1}^\ell, X, Y)$.

Keygen$(\mathsf{msk}, \boldsymbol{y})$**:** To generate a secret key from the vector $\boldsymbol{y} \in [-Y, Y]^\ell$ using $\mathsf{msk} = \boldsymbol{s} = (s_1, \ldots, s_\ell)^\top$, compute $\mathsf{sk}_{\boldsymbol{y}} := \langle \boldsymbol{s}, \boldsymbol{y} \rangle = \sum_{i=1}^\ell s_i \cdot y_i \in \mathbb{Z}$.

Encrypt(mpk, $\boldsymbol{x}$)**:** Given the public key mpk, to encrypt a message $\boldsymbol{x} \in [-X, X]^\ell$, sample $r \leftarrow U(\{0, 1, \ldots, N/4\})$ and compute

$$c_0 = g^r \bmod N^2, \qquad c_i = (1 + x_i N) \cdot h_i^r \bmod N^2 \qquad \forall i \in [\ell]$$

and output $\mathbf{c} = (c_0, \{c_i\}_{i=1}^{\ell}) \in \left(\mathbb{Z}_{N^2}^*\right)^{\ell+1}$.

Decrypt(mpk, $\mathsf{sk}_{\boldsymbol{y}}$, $\mathbf{c}$)**:** On input of a functional decryption key $\mathsf{sk}_{\boldsymbol{y}}$ and a ciphertext $\mathbf{c} = (c_0, c_1, \ldots, c_\ell)$, compute

$$\mathbf{c}_{\boldsymbol{y}} = c_0^{-\mathsf{sk}_{\boldsymbol{y}}} \cdot \prod_{i=1}^{\ell} c_i^{y_i} \bmod N^2$$

Then output $\log_{1+N}(\mathbf{c}_{\boldsymbol{y}}) = \frac{\mathbf{c}_{\boldsymbol{y}} - 1 \mod N^2}{N}$.

Correctness: Suppose that we want to decrypt $\boldsymbol{c} = \{c_i\}_{i=0}^{\ell}$ using $\mathsf{sk}_{\boldsymbol{y}} = \langle \boldsymbol{s}, \boldsymbol{y} \rangle$. Observe that we have the following equalities modulo N^2:

$$\prod_{i=1}^{\ell} c_i^{y_i} = \prod_{i=1}^{\ell} (1 + x_i N)^{y_i} \cdot g^{r \cdot s_i y_i} = (1 + N)^{\langle \boldsymbol{x}, \boldsymbol{y} \rangle} \cdot g^{r \cdot \langle \boldsymbol{s}, \boldsymbol{y} \rangle} = (1 + N)^{\langle \boldsymbol{x}, \boldsymbol{y} \rangle} \cdot c_0^{\langle \boldsymbol{s}, \boldsymbol{y} \rangle},$$

so that $\boldsymbol{c}_{\boldsymbol{y}} = (1 + N)^{\langle \boldsymbol{x}, \boldsymbol{y} \rangle} \bmod N^2$. Recall that $(1 + N)^{\langle \boldsymbol{x}, \boldsymbol{y} \rangle} = 1 + \langle \boldsymbol{x}, \boldsymbol{y} \rangle \cdot N \bmod N^2$, so that computing discrete logarithms in the subgroup generated by $1 + N$ is easy. This enables the computation of $\langle \boldsymbol{x}, \boldsymbol{y} \rangle \bmod N$. By the choice of parameters we have $|\langle \boldsymbol{x}, \boldsymbol{y} \rangle| \leq \ell \cdot \|\boldsymbol{x}\|_\infty \|\boldsymbol{y}\|_\infty \leq \ell \cdot X \cdot Y < N/2$, so we actually recover $\langle \boldsymbol{x}, \boldsymbol{y} \rangle$ computed over $\mathbb{Z}$.

Theorem 2. *Under the* DCR *assumption, the above construction achieves adaptive simulation-based security.*

Proof. To prove the theorem we first describe the PPT simulator and show that under the DCR assumption the real experiment is indistinguishable from the ideal experiment. The simulator proceeds as follows.

Setup$^\star(1^\lambda, 1^\ell, X, Y)$**:** This algorithm chooses safe primes $p = 2p' + 1$ and $q = 2q' + 1$ such that $\ell XY < N/2$, and sets $N = pq$. It samples $g' \leftarrow U(\mathbb{Z}_{N^2}^*)$ and sets $g := g'^{2N} \bmod N^2$. Next, for each $i \in [\ell]$, it samples $s_i \leftarrow U([-S, S] \cap \mathbb{Z})$, where $S = 2^{\lambda+\ell-1} \cdot \bar{X}^{\ell-1} \cdot \ell N^2$ and $\bar{X} := X + \ell \cdot (\sqrt{\ell} Y)^\ell$, and computes $h_i = g^{s_i} \bmod N^2$. It defines the master secret key $\mathsf{msk}^\star = (\boldsymbol{s}, p, q)$, where $\boldsymbol{s} = (s_1, \ldots, s_\ell)^\top$, and the master public key $\mathsf{mpk}^\star = \big(N, g, \{h_i\}_{i=1}^{\ell}, X, Y\big)$.

Keygen$_0^\star(\mathsf{msk}^\star, \boldsymbol{y})$**:** This algorithm is used to generate all the pre-challenge functional decryption queries. To generate a secret key for $\boldsymbol{y} \in [-Y, Y]^\ell$, it computes and outputs $\mathsf{sk}_{\boldsymbol{y}} := \langle \boldsymbol{s}, \boldsymbol{y} \rangle = \sum_{i=1}^{\ell} s_i \cdot y_i \in \mathbb{Z}$.

Encrypt$^\star(\mathsf{mpk}^\star, \mathsf{msk}^\star, \{(\boldsymbol{y}_1, z_1), (\boldsymbol{y}_2, z_2), \ldots, (\boldsymbol{y}_k, z_k)\})$**:** Given $\mathsf{mpk}^\star$, $\mathsf{msk}^\star$ and all the pre-challenge pairs $(\boldsymbol{y}_j, z_j) \in [-Y, Y]^\ell \times \mathbb{Z}$, where $z_j = \langle \boldsymbol{x}^\star, \boldsymbol{y}_j \rangle \in \mathbb{Z}$ and $\boldsymbol{x}^\star$ is the challenge message, it first computes a dummy message $\bar{\boldsymbol{x}} \in \mathbb{Z}^\ell$ such that $\langle \bar{\boldsymbol{x}}, \boldsymbol{y}_j \rangle = z_j$ for all $j \in [k]$ by applying Corollary 1. Note that

$\|\bar{\boldsymbol{x}}\|_\infty \leq (\ell - k) \cdot (\sqrt{k}Y)^k \leq \ell \cdot (\sqrt{\ell}Y)^\ell$. Next, it samples $a \leftarrow U(\mathbb{Z}_N^*)$ and $b \leftarrow U(\mathbb{Z}_{N'})$, where $N' = p'q'$, and computes

$$c_0^\star = (1 + aN) \cdot g^b \bmod N^2, \qquad c_i^\star = (1 + \bar{x}_i N) \cdot (c_0^\star)^{s_i} \bmod N^2 \qquad \forall i \in [\ell].$$

It outputs the simulated ciphertext $\mathbf{c}^\star = \left(c_0^\star, \{c_i^\star\}_{i=1}^\ell\right) \in \left(\mathbb{Z}_{N^2}^*\right)^{\ell+1}$ together with the state information $\mathsf{st} := (\bar{\boldsymbol{x}}, a, N')$.

$\mathsf{Keygen}_1^\star(\mathsf{msk}^\star, (\boldsymbol{y}, z = \langle \boldsymbol{y}, \boldsymbol{x}^\star \rangle), \mathsf{st})$: This algorithm handles post-challenge key queries as follows. Upon receiving a pair $(\boldsymbol{y}, z = \langle \boldsymbol{x}^\star, \boldsymbol{y} \rangle)$, it first computes $u, v \in \mathbb{Z}$ such that $uN + vN' = 1$ and $\gamma := (a^{-1} \bmod N) \cdot vN' \bmod NN'$ then computes and outputs

$$\mathsf{sk}_{\boldsymbol{y}}' := \langle \boldsymbol{s}, \boldsymbol{y} \rangle - \gamma \cdot (z - \langle \bar{\boldsymbol{x}}, \boldsymbol{y} \rangle) \in \mathbb{Z}.$$

In order to prove that the real experiment is computationally indistinguishable from the ideal experiment, we use a sequence of games. We denote by $\mathsf{Adv}_{ij}(\mathcal{A})$ the advantage of an adversary $\mathcal{A}$ in distinguishing between Game_i and Game_j. More precisely, a challenger $\mathcal{C}$ flips a coin $b \leftarrow \{0,1\}$. If $b = 0$ the challenger interacts with the adversary $\mathcal{A}$ as in Game_i while, if $b = 1$, it interacts as in Game_j. At the end of the interaction, $\mathcal{A}$ outputs $b' \in \{0,1\}$. The advantage is defined as $\mathsf{Adv}_{ij}(\mathcal{A}) := \left|\Pr[b' = b] - \frac{1}{2}\right|$.

Game_0: This is the real game in which the challenger generates the parameters and interacts with the adversary as in the real experiment.

Game_1: This game is exactly as the previous one except that the challenge ciphertext is computed as follows: $r \leftarrow U(\{0, 1, \ldots, N/4\})$ is sampled and

$$c_0^\star = g^r \bmod N^2, \qquad c_i^\star = (1 + x_i^\star N) \cdot (c_0^\star)^{s_i} \bmod N^2, \text{ for } i \in [\ell]$$

This is possible since the challenger knows the secret key $\mathsf{msk} = \left(\{s_i\}_{i=1}^\ell\right)$. Notice that Game_0 is identical to Game_1. So, $\mathsf{Adv}_{01}(\mathcal{A}) = 0$.

Game_2: In this game, we modify the computation of $c_0^\star$. In the challenge phase, the challenger samples $r \leftarrow U(\mathbb{Z}_{N'})$, where $N' = p'q'$, and computes $c_0^\star := g^r \bmod N^2$. By Lemma 1, the statistical distance between $U(\{0,1,2,\ldots,N/4\}) \bmod N'$ and $U(\mathbb{Z}_{N'})$ is $< \frac{1}{p} + \frac{1}{q}$, which is negligible. Hence, Game_1 and Game_2 are statistically indistinguishable. More precisely, we have $\mathsf{Adv}_{12}(\mathcal{A}) < 1/p + 1/q$.

Game_3: The game is like Game_2, except that $c_0^\star$ is generated by sampling $t \hookleftarrow U(\mathbb{Z}_{N^2}^*)$ and computing $c_0^\star := t^2 \bmod N^2$. Under the DCR assumption, Game_2 and Game_3 are computationally indistinguishable. Indeed, in Game_2, as long as g has order N', the distribution $\{g^r \mid r \hookleftarrow U(\mathbb{Z}_{N'})\}$ is the uniform distribution in the subgroup of $2N$-th residues. The DCR assumption implies that the latter distribution computationally indistinguishable from the distribution $\{t^2 \bmod N^2 \mid t \hookleftarrow U(\mathbb{Z}_{N^2}^*)\}$. Since a random $2N$-th residue g generates the entire subgroup of $2N$-th residues with probability $\frac{\varphi(N')}{N'} = 1 - \frac{1}{p'} - \frac{1}{q'} + \frac{1}{N'}$, we obtain

$$\left(1 - \frac{1}{p'} - \frac{1}{q'} + \frac{1}{N'}\right) \cdot \mathsf{Adv}_{23}(\mathcal{A}) \leq \mathsf{Adv}^{\mathsf{DCR}}(\mathcal{B}).$$

Game_4: In this game, we sample $a \leftarrow U(\mathbb{Z}_N^*)$ and $b \leftarrow U(\mathbb{Z}_{N'})$ and compute $c_0^\star := (1 + aN) \cdot g^b \bmod N^2$. Observe that $\{t^2 \bmod N^2 \mid t \hookleftarrow U(\mathbb{Z}_{N^2}^*)\}$ is the same as the distribution $\{(1+\alpha N) \cdot g^\beta \bmod N^2 \mid \alpha \hookleftarrow U(\mathbb{Z}_N),\ \beta \hookleftarrow U(\mathbb{Z}_{N'})\}$. Therefore the statistical distance between the view of the adversary in Game_3 and Game_4 is bounded by $\Delta(a, \alpha) < \frac{1}{p} + \frac{1}{q}$. So, these games are statistically indistinguishable and $\mathsf{Adv}_{34}(\mathcal{A}) < 1/p + 1/q$.

Game_5: This is the ideal experiment where the adversary interacts with the simulator. Lemma 6 shows that Game_5 and Game_4 are statistically indistinguishable, which yields the stated result.

Putting the above altogether, we obtain that a PPT adversary $\mathcal{A}$ that can distinguish between the real and the ideal experiment implies an efficient DCR distinguisher $\mathcal{B}$ such that

$$\begin{aligned}\mathsf{Adv}^{\mathsf{Real\text{-}Ideal}}(\mathcal{A}) &= |\Pr[1 \leftarrow \mathbf{Exp}_{\mathcal{A}}^{\mathsf{Real}}(1^\lambda)] - \Pr[1 \leftarrow \mathbf{Exp}_{\mathcal{A}}^{\mathsf{Ideal}}(1^\lambda)]| \\ &\leq \frac{N'}{\varphi(N')} \cdot \mathsf{Adv}_{\mathcal{B}}^{\mathsf{DCR}}(1^\lambda) + \frac{2}{p} + \frac{2}{q} + 2^{-\lambda}.\end{aligned}$$

□

Lemma 6. *The advantage of any distinguisher between* Game_4 *and* Game_5 *is statistically negligible and* $\mathsf{Adv}_{45}(\mathcal{A}) \leq 2^{-\lambda}$.

Proof. In order to prove the claim, we simultaneously define Game_4' and Game_5' as follows. For each $k \in \{4, 5\}$, define Game_k' identically to Game_k except that, at the outset of the game, the challenger samples $\Delta\boldsymbol{x} \hookleftarrow U([-\bar{X}, \bar{X}]^\ell)$, where $\bar{X} = X + \ell \cdot (\sqrt{\ell}Y)^\ell$. Before generating the challenge ciphertext, the challenger uses Corollary 1 to compute $\bar{\boldsymbol{x}} \in \mathbb{Z}^\ell$ such that $\mathbf{Y}_{\mathsf{pre}} \cdot \bar{\boldsymbol{x}} = \mathbf{Y}_{\mathsf{pre}} \cdot \boldsymbol{x}^\star$, where $\mathbf{Y}_{pre}$ is the matrix obtained by stacking up the (linearly independent) transposed vectors $\boldsymbol{y}^\top$ occurring in pre-challenge queries. If $\Delta\boldsymbol{x} = \boldsymbol{x}^\star - \bar{\boldsymbol{x}}$ (we call this event Guess), the challenger proceeds as in Game_k. Otherwise, the challenger aborts the game and replaces $\mathcal{A}$'s output b' by a random bit. We claim that any adversary $\mathcal{A}$ that can distinguish between Game_4 and Game_5 with advantage $\mathsf{Adv}_{45}(\mathcal{A})$ can be used to distinguish between Game_4' and Game_5' with advantage

$$\mathsf{Adv}_{45}'(\mathcal{A}) = \frac{1}{(2\bar{X})^\ell} \cdot \mathsf{Adv}_{45}(\mathcal{A}). \tag{4.1}$$

Indeed, the probability that $\mathcal{A}$ outputs the correct bit b' when distinguishing between Game_4' and Game_5' is equal to

$$\Pr[b' = b] = \Pr[b' = b|\mathsf{Guess}] \cdot \Pr[\mathsf{Guess}] + \Pr[b' = b|\overline{\mathsf{Guess}}] \cdot \Pr[\overline{\mathsf{Guess}}]$$

which is equivalent to

$$\Pr[b' = b] - \frac{1}{2} = \left(\Pr[b' = b|\mathsf{Guess}] - \frac{1}{2}\right) \cdot \Pr[\mathsf{Guess}]$$

By considering the equality in absolute value, we obtain (4.1).

Next, we claim that $\mathsf{Adv}'_{45}(\mathcal{A}) \le (2\bar{X})^{-\ell} \cdot 2^{-\lambda}$, which implies that Game_4 and Game_5 are indistinguishable. To see this, observe that, when Guess occurs, Game'_5 is identical to a modification of Game'_4 where the master secret key has been replaced by

$$s'_i = s_i - \gamma \cdot \Delta \boldsymbol{x}_i \in \mathbb{Z}, \qquad \forall i \in [\ell]$$

where $\gamma = (a^{-1} \bmod N) \cdot vN' \bmod NN'$ is determined by the Bézout coefficient v for which $uN + vN' = 1$ (and thus $vN' = 1 \bmod N$) and the element $a \in \mathbb{Z}_N^*$ which used to compute $c_0^\star = (1 + aN) \cdot g^b \bmod N^2$ in the challenge ciphertext. (Note that a and v can be chosen by the challenger at the beginning of the game, so that we can define a game where the challenger uses $\{s'_i\}_i$ instead of $\{s_i\}_i$). With this new master secret key $\boldsymbol{s}' = (s'_1, \ldots, s'_\ell)$, we have $g^{s_i} = g^{s'_i} \bmod N^2$ for all $i \in [\ell]$ and $\langle \boldsymbol{s}, \boldsymbol{y} \rangle = \langle \boldsymbol{s}', \boldsymbol{y} \rangle$ for all pre-challenge queries $\boldsymbol{y} \in \mathbb{Z}^\ell$. We thus obtain

$$\mathsf{Adv}'_{45}(\mathcal{A}) \le \Delta(\boldsymbol{s}', \boldsymbol{s}) \le (2\bar{X})^{-\ell} \cdot 2^{-\lambda},$$

where the last inequality follows from the fact that

$$\Delta(\boldsymbol{s}', \boldsymbol{s}) \le \sum_{i=1}^{\ell} \Delta(s'_i, s_i) \overset{\text{Lemma 2}}{\le} \ell \cdot \frac{\|\gamma \cdot \Delta \boldsymbol{x}\|_\infty}{2S} \le \frac{NN' \cdot \bar{X}}{2^{\lambda+\ell} \cdot \bar{X}^{\ell-1} \cdot N^2} \le (2\bar{X})^{-\ell} \cdot 2^{-\lambda}.$$

□

The above DCR-based construction is stateless and evaluates inner products over $\mathbb{Z}$. In Sect. 5, we describe a generic construction of simulation-secure IPFE with stateful key generation, which allows evaluating inner products modulo a prime or a composite. This generic construction can be instantiated under the DCR and LWE assumptions.

5 Adaptive Simulation-Based Security for Inner Products Mod P from LWE

In this section we construct an adaptively simulation secure FE scheme ($\mathsf{AdSimIPFE}$) for inner products modulo some prime p. In more detail, the messages and keys are chosen from $\mathbb{Z}_p^\ell$ and the inner product is computed over $\mathbb{Z}_p$.

We denote our scheme by $\mathsf{AdSimIPFE} = (\mathsf{Setup}, \mathsf{Keygen}, \mathsf{Encrypt}, \mathsf{Decrypt})$. Our construction is based on the scheme of Agrawal *et al.* [8] for inner products modulo a prime p satisfying adaptive indistinguishability from LWE. We denote this scheme by $\mathsf{IPFE} = (\mathsf{IPFE.Setup}, \mathsf{IPFE.Keygen}, \mathsf{IPFE.Encrypt}, \mathsf{IPFE.Decrypt})$, and require it to support messages and keys of length $L = 2\ell$.

Our construction is generic except that it requires the underlying scheme IPFE to satisfy the property that functional keys for vectors that are linearly dependent on previously queried vectors may be computed as the linear combination of previously returned keys. In more detail, say that $\mathsf{sk}_{\boldsymbol{y}} \in \mathbb{Z}^m$.[3]

[3] The precise ring in which $\mathsf{sk}_{\boldsymbol{y}}$ lives is not important. We choose this to be $\mathbb{Z}$ for concreteness and compatibility with [8].

Say that the adversary queries vectors $\boldsymbol{y}_1, \ldots, \boldsymbol{y}_k \in \mathbb{Z}_p^\ell$ and then submits a query $\boldsymbol{y}$ such that $\boldsymbol{y} = \sum_{j\in[k]} k_j \cdot \boldsymbol{y}_j \pmod p, \forall k_j \in \mathbb{Z}_p$. Then, the secret key $\mathsf{sk}_{\boldsymbol{y}}$ is computed as $\mathsf{sk}_{\boldsymbol{y}} = \sum_{j\in[k]} k_j \cdot \mathsf{sk}_{\boldsymbol{y}_j} \in \mathbb{Z}^m$. This property is satisfied by the LWE-based construction that evaluates inner products over $\mathbb{Z}_p$ in [8, Sec 4.2].

In the description hereunder, we assume that the modulus p is prime. However, the construction can also be applied to the Paillier-based construction of [8, Section 5.2], which evaluates inner products over $\mathbb{Z}_N$. As a result, it provides a simulation-secure IPFE with stateful key generation for inner products over $\mathbb{Z}_N$, whereas our scheme in Sect. 4 is stateless but computes inner products over $\mathbb{Z}$. When we switch to composite moduli $N = pq$, we need to take into account that $\mathbb{Z}_N$ is not a field when the simulator has to solve a linear system over $\mathbb{Z}_N$ in order to compute a dummy message. Fortunately, inversion over $\mathbb{Z}_N$ is always possible with overwhelming probability when factoring N is hard.

5.1 Construction

Below, we provide our construction of AdSimIPFE.

Setup$(1^\lambda, 1^\ell, p)$**:** Given the security parameter λ, the supported message and key lengths ℓ and a prime integer p, do the following:
1. Set $L = 2\ell$ and obtain $(\mathsf{IPFE.mpk}, \mathsf{IPFE.msk}) \leftarrow \mathsf{IPFE.Setup}(1^\lambda, 1^L, p)$.
2. Output $(\mathsf{mpk}, \mathsf{msk}) := (\mathsf{IPFE.mpk}, \mathsf{IPFE.msk})$.

Keygen$(\mathsf{msk}, \boldsymbol{y}, \mathsf{st})$**:** Given the msk, a vector $\boldsymbol{y} = (y_1, \ldots, y_\ell)^\top \in \mathbb{Z}_p^\ell$ to obtain a key and an internal state st, do the following:
1. Parse the master secret key as $\mathsf{msk} = \mathsf{IPFE.msk}$.
2. The internal state st contains tuples $\left(\widehat{\boldsymbol{y}}_j, \boldsymbol{y}_j, \mathsf{sk}_{\boldsymbol{y}_j}, r_j\right)$ for some $j \in [\ell-1]$ corresponding to (a subset of the) key queries made so far. If no queries have been made before $\boldsymbol{y}$, st is empty.
3. If $|\mathsf{st}| = i-1$ for $i \in [\ell-1]$ and $\boldsymbol{y} = \sum_{j=1}^{i-1} k_j \cdot \boldsymbol{y}_j \pmod p$ for some $k_j \in \mathbb{Z}_p$, $j \in [i-1]$, set $\widehat{\boldsymbol{y}} = \sum_{j=1}^{i-1} k_j \cdot \widehat{\boldsymbol{y}}_j \pmod p$ and compute the secret key as $\mathsf{IPFE.sk}_{\widehat{\boldsymbol{y}}} \leftarrow \mathsf{IPFE.Keygen}(\mathsf{IPFE.msk}, \widehat{\boldsymbol{y}})$. Set $\mathsf{sk}_{\boldsymbol{y}} := \mathsf{IPFE.sk}_{\widehat{\boldsymbol{y}}}$.
4. Else, if $|\mathsf{st}| = i-1$ for some $i \in [\ell-1]$, set $\boldsymbol{y}_i = \boldsymbol{y}$. Then, construct the extended vector $\widehat{\boldsymbol{y}}_i = (\boldsymbol{y}_i, \mathbf{e}_i, r_i) \in \mathbb{Z}_p^L$, where $\mathbf{e}_i \in \mathbb{Z}_p^{\ell-1}$ is the i-th canonical vector and $r_i \leftarrow \mathbb{Z}_p$ is chosen uniformly at random. Next, compute a secret key $\mathsf{IPFE.sk}_{\widehat{\boldsymbol{y}}_i} \leftarrow \mathsf{IPFE.Keygen}(\mathsf{IPFE.msk}, \widehat{\boldsymbol{y}}_i)$ and set $\mathsf{sk}_{\boldsymbol{y}} := \mathsf{IPFE.sk}_{\widehat{\boldsymbol{y}}_i}$. Update the internal state as $\mathsf{st} \leftarrow \mathsf{st} \cup \{(\widehat{\boldsymbol{y}}_i, \boldsymbol{y}_i, \mathsf{sk}_{\boldsymbol{y}_i}, r_i)\}$.
5. Output the secret key $\mathsf{sk}_{\boldsymbol{y}}$.

Encrypt$(\mathsf{mpk}, \boldsymbol{x})$**:** Given the mpk and a message $\boldsymbol{x} = (x_1, \ldots, x_\ell) \in \mathbb{Z}_p^\ell$ to encrypt, do the following:
1. Parse the master public key as $\mathsf{mpk} = \mathsf{IPFE.mpk}$.
2. Construct the extended vector $\widehat{\boldsymbol{x}} = (\boldsymbol{x}, \mathbf{0}, 0) \in \mathbb{Z}_p^L$, where $\mathbf{0} \in \mathbb{Z}_p^{\ell-1}$ is the all-zeroes vector.
3. Compute a ciphertext $\mathsf{IPFE.ct} \leftarrow \mathsf{IPFE.Encrypt}(\mathsf{IPFE.mpk}, \widehat{\boldsymbol{x}})$.
4. Output the ciphertext $\boldsymbol{c} := \mathsf{IPFE.ct}$.

Decrypt(mpk, $\mathsf{sk}_{\boldsymbol{y}}, \boldsymbol{c}$)**:** Given mpk, a secret key $\mathsf{sk}_{\boldsymbol{y}}$ and a ciphertext $\boldsymbol{c}$, do the following:

1. Parse the secret key as $\mathsf{sk}_{\boldsymbol{y}} = \mathsf{IPFE.sk}_{\widehat{\boldsymbol{y}}}$ and the ciphertext as $\boldsymbol{c} = \mathsf{IPFE.ct}$.
2. Compute and output $z = \mathsf{IPFE.Decrypt}(\mathsf{IPFE.sk}_{\widehat{\boldsymbol{y}}}, \mathsf{IPFE.ct})$.

Correctness. The correctness of AdSimIPFE is implied by the correctness of the underlying IPFE scheme as follows. For a message vector $\boldsymbol{x}$ and the i-th linearly independent vector $\boldsymbol{y} \in \mathbb{Z}_p^\ell$, let $\widehat{\boldsymbol{x}} = (\boldsymbol{x}, \mathbf{0}, 0), \widehat{\boldsymbol{y}} = (\boldsymbol{y}, \mathbf{e}_i, r_i) \in \mathbb{Z}_p^L$. When $\boldsymbol{y} \in \mathbb{Z}_p^\ell$ is linearly dependent on the previously queried vectors $\{\boldsymbol{y}_j \in \mathbb{Z}_p^\ell\}_{j \in [i-1]}$ for some $i \in [\ell - 1]$, we have $\widehat{\boldsymbol{y}} = \sum_{j=1}^{i-1} k_j \cdot \widehat{\boldsymbol{y}}_j \pmod p = \sum_{j=1}^{i-1} k_j \cdot (\boldsymbol{y}_j, \mathbf{e}_j, r_j) \pmod p$.

The Decrypt algorithm takes mpk, $\mathsf{sk}_{\boldsymbol{y}} = \mathsf{IPFE.sk}_{\widehat{\boldsymbol{y}}}$ and $\boldsymbol{c} = \mathsf{IPFE.ct}$ as input, where we have the following.

$$\mathsf{IPFE.sk}_{\widehat{\boldsymbol{y}}} \leftarrow \mathsf{IPFE.Keygen}(\mathsf{IPFE.msk}, \widehat{\boldsymbol{y}})$$
$$\mathsf{IPFE.ct} \leftarrow \mathsf{IPFE.Encrypt}(\mathsf{IPFE.mpk}, \widehat{\boldsymbol{x}})$$

Hence, the correctness of IPFE decryption algorithm forces the output to be $\mathsf{IPFE.Decrypt}(\mathsf{IPFE.sk}_{\widehat{\boldsymbol{y}}}, \mathsf{IPFE.ct}) = \langle \widehat{\boldsymbol{x}}, \widehat{\boldsymbol{y}} \rangle = \langle (\boldsymbol{x}, \mathbf{0}, 0), (\boldsymbol{y}, \mathbf{e}_i, r_i) \rangle = \langle \boldsymbol{x}, \boldsymbol{y} \rangle \in \mathbb{Z}_p$ as desired.

Efficiency. The efficiency of AdSimIPFE is inherited from the efficiency of the underlying IPFE scheme. The ciphertext and secret key sizes grow proportionally to $L = 2\ell = O(\ell)$.

5.2 Proof of Security for AdSimIPFE

Theorem 3. *The* AdSimIPFE *scheme achieves adaptive simulation based security, as long as the underlying* IPFE *scheme satisfies full adaptive indistinguishability based security.*

Proof. We assume w.l.o.g. that $\mathcal{A}$ makes secret key queries for linearly independent vectors only. In particular, we assume that $\mathcal{A}$ issues secret key queries for Q_{pre} independent vectors in the *pre-challenge* phase, which we denote by $\boldsymbol{y}_1^{\mathsf{pre}}, \ldots, \boldsymbol{y}_{Q_{\mathsf{pre}}}^{\mathsf{pre}} \in \mathbb{Z}_p^\ell$ while the i-th vector for the *post-challenge* independent secret key query is denoted as $\boldsymbol{y}_i^{\mathsf{post}} \in \mathbb{Z}_p^\ell$ such that $i \in [\ell - 1] \setminus [Q_{\mathsf{pre}}]$. Note that this simplification implies that there are no repetition in the key queries. We denote by $\boldsymbol{x}^\star = (x_1^\star, \ldots, x_\ell^\star) \in \mathbb{Z}_p^\ell$ the message chosen by $\mathcal{A}$ in the challenge phase.

The Simulator: To simulate the real world scheme, the simulator uses the following tuple of PPT algorithms: $(\mathsf{Setup}^\star, \mathsf{Keygen}_0^\star, \mathsf{Encrypt}^\star, \mathsf{Keygen}_1^\star)$. Note that $\mathsf{Keygen}_0^\star$ and $\mathsf{Keygen}_1^\star$ denote the simulated key generation algorithms to answer secret key queries in the pre-challenge and post-challenge phases respectively. The simulator then proceeds as follows.

Setup$^\star(1^\lambda, 1^\ell, p)$: This algorithm is identical to **Setup** except that the simulator also samples $r_i \leftarrow \mathbb{Z}_p$ for all $i \in [\ell-1]$ and maintains the internal state as the set of tuples $\mathsf{st}^\star = \{(\cdot,\cdot,\cdot,r_i)\}_{i\in[\ell-1]}$. In particular, it outputs the key pair as $(\mathsf{mpk}^\star, \mathsf{msk}^\star) := (\mathsf{IPFE.mpk}, \mathsf{IPFE.msk})$ while keeping $\mathsf{st}^\star$ to itself.

Keygen$_0^\star(\mathsf{msk}^\star, \boldsymbol{y}^{\mathsf{pre}}, \mathsf{st}^\star)$: This algorithm runs almost identical to **Keygen**. In particular, on input a pre-challenge vector $\boldsymbol{y}^{\mathsf{pre}}$, it does the following:

1. The internal state $\mathsf{st}^\star$ contains tuples $\left(\widehat{\boldsymbol{y}}_j^{\mathsf{pre}}, \boldsymbol{y}_j^{\mathsf{pre}}, \mathsf{sk}_{\boldsymbol{y}_j^{\mathsf{pre}}}, r_j\right)$ for some $j \in [\ell-1]$ corresponding to (a subset of the) key queries made so far. If no query has been made before $\boldsymbol{y}^{\mathsf{pre}}$, $\mathsf{st}^\star$ is empty.
2. If $|\mathsf{st}| = i-1$ for some $i \in [\ell-1]$, set $\boldsymbol{y}_i^{\mathsf{pre}} = \boldsymbol{y}^{\mathsf{pre}}$. Then, construct the extended vector $\widehat{\boldsymbol{y}}_i^{\mathsf{pre}} = (\boldsymbol{y}_i^{\mathsf{pre}}, \mathbf{e}_i, r_i) \in \mathbb{Z}_p^L$. Next, compute a secret key $\mathsf{IPFE.sk}_{\widehat{\boldsymbol{y}}_i^{\mathsf{pre}}} \leftarrow \mathsf{IPFE.Keygen}(\mathsf{IPFE.msk}, \widehat{\boldsymbol{y}}_i^{\mathsf{pre}})$ and set $\mathsf{sk}_{\boldsymbol{y}_i^{\mathsf{pre}}} := \mathsf{IPFE.sk}_{\widehat{\boldsymbol{y}}_i^{\mathsf{pre}}}$. Update the internal state as $\mathsf{st}^\star \leftarrow \left(\mathsf{st}^\star \cup \{(\widehat{\boldsymbol{y}}_i^{\mathsf{pre}}, \boldsymbol{y}_i^{\mathsf{pre}}, \mathsf{sk}_{\boldsymbol{y}_i^{\mathsf{pre}}}, r_i)\}\right) \setminus \{(\cdot,\cdot,\cdot,r_i)\}$.
3. Output the simulated secret key as $\mathsf{sk}_{\boldsymbol{y}_i^{\mathsf{pre}}}$.

Encrypt$^\star(\mathsf{mpk}^\star, \mathsf{msk}^\star, \mathcal{V}, \{1^{|x_i^\star|}\}_{i=1}^{\ell}, \mathsf{st}^\star)$: This algorithm takes $\mathsf{mpk}^\star = \mathsf{IPFE.mpk}$, $\mathsf{msk}^\star$, the lengths $\{1^{|x_i^\star|}\}_{i\in[\ell]}$ of all coordinates of the challenge message $\boldsymbol{x}^\star$ as input, the internal state $\mathsf{st}^\star$ and a set

$$\mathcal{V} = \left\{ \left(\boldsymbol{y}_j^{\mathsf{pre}}, z_j^{\mathsf{pre}} = \langle \boldsymbol{x}^\star, \boldsymbol{y}_j^{\mathsf{pre}} \rangle, \mathsf{sk}_{\boldsymbol{y}_j^{\mathsf{pre}}} \right)_{j\in[Q_{\mathsf{pre}}]} \right\}$$

containing all pre-challenge independent queries $\{\boldsymbol{y}_j^{\mathsf{pre}}\}_{j\in[Q_{\mathsf{pre}}]}$, the returned keys and the corresponding linear function evaluations $\{z_j^{\mathsf{pre}} = \langle \boldsymbol{x}^\star, \boldsymbol{y}_j^{\mathsf{pre}}\rangle\}_{j\in[Q_{\mathsf{pre}}]}$ for the challenge message $\boldsymbol{x}^\star$. The challenge ciphertext $\boldsymbol{c}^\star$ is simulated as follows.

1. Letting $\boldsymbol{z}_{\mathsf{pre}} = (z_1^{\mathsf{pre}}, \ldots, z_{Q_{\mathsf{pre}}}^{\mathsf{pre}})^\top \in \mathbb{Z}_p^{Q_{\mathsf{pre}}}$, it computes an arbitrary solution $\bar{\boldsymbol{x}} = (\bar{x}_1, \ldots, \bar{x}_\ell)^\top \in \mathbb{Z}_p^\ell$ of the system $\mathbf{Y}_{\mathsf{pre}} \cdot \bar{\boldsymbol{x}} = \boldsymbol{z}_{\mathsf{pre}} \pmod p$, where
$$\mathbf{Y}_{\mathsf{pre}} = \left[\boldsymbol{y}_1^{\mathsf{pre}} || \cdots || \boldsymbol{y}_{Q_{\mathsf{pre}}}^{\mathsf{pre}}\right]^\top \in \mathbb{Z}_p^{Q_{\mathsf{pre}} \times \ell}.$$
Note that $\bar{\boldsymbol{x}}$ can be obtained via Gaussian elimination over $\mathbb{Z}_p$.
2. Construct the extended message vector $\widehat{\bar{\boldsymbol{x}}} = (\bar{\boldsymbol{x}}, -\mathbf{r}, 1) \in \mathbb{Z}_p^L$, where $\mathbf{r} = (r_1, \ldots, r_{\ell-1}) \in \mathbb{Z}_p^{\ell-1}$.[4]
3. Compute a ciphertext $\mathsf{IPFE.ct} \leftarrow \mathsf{IPFE.Encrypt}(\mathsf{IPFE.mpk}, \widehat{\bar{\boldsymbol{x}}})$.
4. Output the simulated ciphertext $\boldsymbol{c}^* := \mathsf{IPFE.ct}$.

Keygen$_1^\star(\mathsf{msk}^\star, \boldsymbol{y}_i^{\mathsf{post}}, z_i^{\mathsf{post}}, \mathsf{st}^\star)$: On input a post-challenge vector $\boldsymbol{y}_i^{\mathsf{post}} \in \mathbb{Z}_p^\ell$, where $i \in \{Q_{\mathsf{pre}}+1, \ldots, \ell-1\}$, the linear function evaluation $z_i^{\mathsf{post}} = \langle \boldsymbol{x}^\star, \boldsymbol{y}_i^{\mathsf{post}}\rangle$ for the challenge message $\boldsymbol{x}^\star \in \mathbb{Z}_p^\ell$ and internal state $\mathsf{st}^\star$, it does the following:

1. The internal state $\mathsf{st}^\star$ now contains Q_{pre} tuples of the form $\left(\widehat{\boldsymbol{y}}_j^{\mathsf{pre}}, \boldsymbol{y}_j^{\mathsf{pre}}, \mathsf{sk}_{\boldsymbol{y}_j^{\mathsf{pre}}}, r_j\right)$ and tuples of the form $\left(\widehat{\boldsymbol{y}}_k^{\mathsf{post}}, \boldsymbol{y}_k^{\mathsf{post}}, \mathsf{sk}_{\boldsymbol{y}_k^{\mathsf{post}}}, r_k\right)$ for

[4] For readability, we denote $-\mathbf{r} = (-r_1, \ldots, -r_{\ell-1}) = \mathbf{r}' \in \mathbb{Z}_p^{\ell-1}$ such that $\mathbf{r} + \mathbf{r}' = \mathbf{0} \bmod p$.

some $k \in [\ell-1] \setminus [Q_{\mathsf{pre}}]$ corresponding to (a subset of the) post-challenge key queries made so far. If $i = Q_{\mathsf{pre}} + 1$, then $\mathsf{st}^\star = \left\{ \left(\widehat{\boldsymbol{y}}_j^{\mathsf{pre}}, \boldsymbol{y}_j^{\mathsf{pre}}, \mathsf{sk}_{\boldsymbol{y}_j^{\mathsf{pre}}}, r_j \right)_{j \in [Q_{\mathsf{pre}}]}, (\cdot,\cdot,\cdot,r_k)_{k \in [\ell-1] \setminus [Q_{\mathsf{pre}}]} \right\}$.

2. Construct the extended vector $\widehat{\boldsymbol{y}}_i^{\mathsf{post}} = (\boldsymbol{y}_i^{\mathsf{post}}, \mathbf{e}_i, \Delta_i + r_i)$, where $\mathbf{e}_i \in \mathbb{Z}_p^{\ell-1}$ is the i-th canonical vector, and $\Delta_i = z_i^{\mathsf{post}} - \langle \bar{\boldsymbol{x}}, \boldsymbol{y}_i^{\mathsf{post}} \rangle$. Next, compute a secret key $\mathsf{IPFE.sk}_{\widehat{\boldsymbol{y}}_i^{\mathsf{post}}} \leftarrow \mathsf{IPFE.Keygen}(\mathsf{IPFE.msk}, \widehat{\boldsymbol{y}}_i^{\mathsf{post}})$ and set $\mathsf{sk}_{\boldsymbol{y}_i^{\mathsf{post}}} := \mathsf{IPFE.sk}_{\widehat{\boldsymbol{y}}_i^{\mathsf{post}}}$. Update the internal state as $\mathsf{st}^\star \leftarrow \left(\mathsf{st}^\star \cup \left\{ \left(\widehat{\boldsymbol{y}}_i^{\mathsf{post}}, \boldsymbol{y}_i^{\mathsf{post}}, \mathsf{sk}_{\boldsymbol{y}_i^{\mathsf{post}}}, r_i \right) \right\} \right) \setminus \{(\cdot,\cdot,\cdot,r_i)\}$.
3. Output the simulated secret key as $\mathsf{sk}_{\boldsymbol{y}_i^{\mathsf{post}}}$.

The Hybrids. We now prove that the simulation is computationally indistinguishable from the real experiment assuming full indistinguishability of IPFE. The proof proceeds via a sequence of games ($\mathbf{Game}_0, \mathbf{Game}_1, \mathbf{Game}_2, \mathbf{Game}_3$). $\mathbf{Game}_0$ describes the interaction between the challenger and the adversary as in real experiment $\mathbf{Exp}^{\mathsf{Real}}_{\mathsf{AdSimIPFE},\mathcal{A}}(1^\lambda)$ while $\mathbf{Game}_3$ describes the same as in the ideal experiment $\mathbf{Exp}^{\mathsf{Ideal}}_{\mathsf{AdSimIPFE},\mathcal{A}}(1^\lambda)$.

In the following, let E_i denote the event that $\mathcal{A}$ wins in $\mathbf{Game}_i$. To prove the result, we will show that $\Pr[\mathsf{E}_0] = \Pr[\mathsf{E}_1] = \Pr[\mathsf{E}_2]$ and $|\Pr[\mathsf{E}_2] - \Pr[\mathsf{E}_3]| \leq \text{negl}(\lambda)$, which implies $|\Pr[\mathsf{E}_0] - \Pr[\mathsf{E}_3]| \leq \text{negl}(\lambda)$.

$\mathbf{Game}_0$: In this game the challenger interacts with the adversary as in the real experiment.

$\mathbf{Game}_1$: In this game the setup phase is modified as follows. Beside computing $(\mathsf{mpk}, \mathsf{msk})$ as in the real experiment, the challenger now also precomputes $r_i \leftarrow \mathbb{Z}_p, \forall i \in [\ell-1]$ for answering at most $\ell-1$ linearly independent key queries as well as the challenge ciphertext query. It maintains an internal state $\mathsf{st}^\star = \{(\cdot,\cdot,\cdot,r_i)\}_{i \in [\ell-1]}$.

$\mathbf{Game}_2$: In this game the challenger changes the way the post-challenge keys are generated. It generates the pre-challenge keys as in $\mathbf{Game}_1$ with the precomputed randomness in $\mathsf{st}^\star$. It also generates the challenge ciphertext as before. As for post-challenge queries, they are answered as follows.

1. The challenger first computes $\bar{\boldsymbol{x}} \in \mathbb{Z}_p^\ell$ that is consistent with the Q_{pre} key vectors it encountered in the pre-challenge phase. In particular, letting $\boldsymbol{z}_{\mathsf{pre}} = (z_1^{\mathsf{pre}}, \ldots, z_{Q_{\mathsf{pre}}}^{\mathsf{pre}})^\top \in \mathbb{Z}_p^{Q_{\mathsf{pre}}}$ corresponding to the function evaluations $\{z_j^{\mathsf{pre}}\}_{j \in [Q_{\mathsf{pre}}]}$ on pre-challenge keys, it computes $\bar{\boldsymbol{x}} \in \mathbb{Z}_p^\ell$ such that

$$\mathbf{Y}_{\mathsf{pre}} \cdot \bar{\boldsymbol{x}} = \boldsymbol{z}_{\mathsf{pre}} (\text{mod } p), \text{ where } \mathbf{Y}_{\mathsf{pre}} = \left[\boldsymbol{y}_1^{\mathsf{pre}} || \cdots || \boldsymbol{y}_{Q_{\mathsf{pre}}}^{\mathsf{pre}} \right]^\top \in \mathbb{Z}_p^{Q_{\mathsf{pre}} \times \ell}.$$

2. For all $i \in [\ell-1] \setminus [Q_{\mathsf{pre}}]$, the i-th post-challenge vector $\boldsymbol{y}_i^{\mathsf{post}}$ is now extended as $\widehat{\boldsymbol{y}}_i^{\mathsf{post}} = (\boldsymbol{y}_i^{\mathsf{post}}, \mathbf{e}_i, \Delta_i + r_i)$, where $\Delta_i = z_i^{\mathsf{post}} - \langle \bar{\boldsymbol{x}}, \boldsymbol{y}_i^{\mathsf{post}} \rangle$.
3. The secret key is computed as $\mathsf{IPFE.sk}_{\widehat{\boldsymbol{y}}_i^{\mathsf{post}}} \leftarrow \mathsf{IPFE.Keygen}(\mathsf{IPFE.msk}, \widehat{\boldsymbol{y}}_i^{\mathsf{post}})$.

4. The internal state is updated as

$$\mathsf{st}^\star \leftarrow \left(\mathsf{st}^\star \cup \left\{ \left(\widehat{\boldsymbol{y}}_i^{\mathsf{post}}, \boldsymbol{y}_i^{\mathsf{post}}, \mathsf{sk}_{\boldsymbol{y}_i^{\mathsf{post}}}, r_i\right) \right\}\right) \setminus \{(\cdot,\cdot,\cdot,r_i)\}.$$

Game$_3$: In this game the challenger computes everything as before in **Game**$_2$ except that the challenge ciphertext is modified as follows. Instead of encrypting the extended message $\widehat{\boldsymbol{x}}^\star = (\boldsymbol{x}^\star, \mathbf{0}, 0)$, the challenger now encrypts $\widehat{\bar{\boldsymbol{x}}} = (\bar{\boldsymbol{x}}, -\mathbf{r}, 1)$ to compute $\boldsymbol{c}^\star := \mathsf{IPFE.ct} \leftarrow \mathsf{IPFE.Encrypt}(\mathsf{IPFE.mpk}, \widehat{\bar{\boldsymbol{x}}})$.

We now prove the following lemmas in order to complete the proof.

Lemma 7. *We have* $\Pr[\mathsf{E}_0] = \Pr[\mathsf{E}_1]$.

Proof. The change introduced here is only conceptual, where for all $i \in [\ell-1]$, the randomness $r_i \in \mathbb{Z}_p$ are precomputed in the setup phase. Thus, the lemma follows trivially. □

Lemma 8. *We have* $\Pr[\mathsf{E}_1] = \Pr[\mathsf{E}_2]$.

Proof. We note that **Game**$_2$ only differs from **Game**$_1$ in the treatment of post-challenge queries. Specifically, the simulator $\mathcal{B}$ simulates $\mathcal{A}$'s view in the two games as follows.

1. On input $(1^\lambda, 1^\ell, p)$ from $\mathcal{A}$, $\mathcal{B}$ sets $L = 2\ell$ and computes $\mathsf{IPFE.Setup}(1^\lambda, 1^L, p)$ to obtain $(\mathsf{IPFE.mpk}, \mathsf{IPFE.msk})$. It sets $(\mathsf{mpk}, \mathsf{msk}) = (\mathsf{IPFE.mpk}, \mathsf{IPFE.msk})$, computes $r_i \leftarrow \mathbb{Z}_p$, for all $i \in [\ell-1]$ to maintain its internal state as $\mathsf{st}^\star = \{(\cdot,\cdot,\cdot,r_i)\}_{i\in[\ell-1]}$. Finally, it sends mpk to $\mathcal{A}$.
2. When $\mathcal{A}$ requests a pre-challenge key for $\boldsymbol{y}_i^{\mathsf{pre}}$, $\mathcal{B}$ first computes the extended vector $\widehat{\boldsymbol{y}}_i^{\mathsf{pre}} = (\boldsymbol{y}_i^{\mathsf{pre}}, \mathbf{e}_i, r_i) \in \mathbb{Z}_p^L$, where $\mathbf{e}_i \in \mathbb{Z}_p^{\ell-1}$ is the i-th canonical vector. Using $\mathsf{msk} = \mathsf{IPFE.msk}$, it then obtains a secret key for $\widehat{\boldsymbol{y}}_i^{\mathsf{pre}}$ as $\mathsf{IPFE.sk}_{\widehat{\boldsymbol{y}}_i^{\mathsf{pre}}} \leftarrow \mathsf{IPFE.Keygen}(\mathsf{IPFE.msk}, \widehat{\boldsymbol{y}}_i^{\mathsf{pre}})$. $\mathcal{B}$ then updates $\mathsf{st}^\star \leftarrow \left(\mathsf{st}^\star \cup \left\{(\widehat{\boldsymbol{y}}_i^{\mathsf{pre}}, \boldsymbol{y}_i^{\mathsf{pre}}, \mathsf{sk}_{\boldsymbol{y}_i^{\mathsf{pre}}}, r_i)\right\}\right) \setminus \left\{(\cdot,\cdot,\cdot,r_i)\right\}$, sets $\mathsf{sk}_{\boldsymbol{y}_i^{\mathsf{pre}}} = \mathsf{IPFE.sk}_{\widehat{\boldsymbol{y}}_i^{\mathsf{pre}}}$ and sends $\mathsf{sk}_{\boldsymbol{y}_i^{\mathsf{pre}}}$ to $\mathcal{A}$.
3. When $\mathcal{A}$ requests a challenge ciphertext for a message $\boldsymbol{x}^\star \in \mathbb{Z}_p^\ell$, $\mathcal{B}$ first computes an extended message $\widehat{\boldsymbol{x}}^\star = (\boldsymbol{x}^\star, \mathbf{0}, 0) \in \mathbb{Z}_p^L$, where $\mathbf{0} \in \mathbb{Z}_p^{\ell-1}$ is the all-zero vector. Using $\mathsf{mpk} = \mathsf{IPFE.mpk}$, it then obtains a ciphertext as $\mathsf{IPFE.ct} \leftarrow \mathsf{IPFE.Encrypt}(\mathsf{IPFE.mpk}, \widehat{\boldsymbol{x}}^\star)$, sets $\boldsymbol{c}^\star = \mathsf{IPFE.ct}$ and sends $\boldsymbol{c}^\star$ to $\mathcal{A}$.
4. In the post-challenge phase, when $\mathcal{A}$ queries a key for a vector $\boldsymbol{y}_i^{\mathsf{post}} \in \mathbb{Z}_p^\ell$, with $i \in [\ell-1] \setminus [Q_{\mathsf{pre}}]$, for which the corresponding function evaluation is $z_i^{\mathsf{post}} = \langle \boldsymbol{x}^\star, \boldsymbol{y}_i^{\mathsf{post}} \rangle$, the challenger $\mathcal{B}$ responds as follows:
   - To simulate $\mathcal{A}$'s view in **Game**$_1$, $\mathcal{B}$ computes the extended vector $\widehat{\boldsymbol{y}}_i^{\mathsf{post}} = (\boldsymbol{y}_i^{\mathsf{post}}, \mathbf{e}_i, r_i)$.
   - To simulate $\mathcal{A}$'s view in **Game**$_2$, $\mathcal{B}$ first computes $\bar{\boldsymbol{x}} \in \mathbb{Z}_p^\ell$ as described in **Game**$_2$ such that $\bar{\boldsymbol{x}}$ is consistent the Q_{pre} pre-challenge key vectors. It then extends the vector $\boldsymbol{y}_i^{\mathsf{post}}$ as $\widehat{\boldsymbol{y}}_i^{\mathsf{post}} = (\boldsymbol{y}_i^{\mathsf{post}}, \mathbf{e}_i, \Delta_i + r_i)$, where $\Delta_i = \langle \boldsymbol{x}^\star - \bar{\boldsymbol{x}}, \boldsymbol{y}_i^{\mathsf{post}} \rangle$.

Using $\mathsf{msk} = \mathsf{IPFE.msk}$, $\mathcal{B}$ obtains a secret key for $\widehat{\boldsymbol{y}}_i^{\mathsf{post}}$ as $\mathsf{IPFE.sk}_{\widehat{\boldsymbol{y}}_i^{\mathsf{post}}} \leftarrow \mathsf{IPFE.Keygen}(\mathsf{IPFE.msk}, \widehat{\boldsymbol{y}}_i^{\mathsf{post}})$ and sets $\mathsf{sk}_{\boldsymbol{y}_i^{\mathsf{post}}} = \mathsf{IPFE.sk}_{\widehat{\boldsymbol{y}}_i^{\mathsf{post}}}$. It then updates its internal state as $\mathsf{st}^\star \leftarrow \left(\mathsf{st}^\star \cup \left\{(\widehat{\boldsymbol{y}}_i^{\mathsf{post}}, \boldsymbol{y}_i^{\mathsf{post}}, \mathsf{sk}_{\boldsymbol{y}_i^{\mathsf{post}}}, r_i)\right\}\right) \setminus \left\{(\cdot,\cdot,\cdot,r_i)\right\}$ and sends $\mathsf{sk}_{\boldsymbol{y}_i^{\mathsf{post}}}$ to $\mathcal{A}$.

Recall that the only change between the two games is the way post-challenge keys are generated. In particular, the last co-ordinate of the i-th post-challenge key vector is set to r_i in $\mathbf{Game}_1$ while it is set to $(r_i + \Delta_i)$ in $\mathbf{Game}_2$. Note that each r_i is chosen uniformly in $\mathbb{Z}_p$ in the setup phase and is unique for each post challenge key query $i \in [\ell - 1] \setminus [Q_{\mathsf{pre}}]$. Hence, the computation $r_i + \Delta_i$ being done modulo p, it follows that the two distributions $\{r_i \mid r_i \leftarrow \mathbb{Z}_p\}_{i \in [\ell-1]\setminus[Q_{\mathsf{pre}}]}$ and $\{r_i + \Delta_i \mid r_i \leftarrow \mathbb{Z}_p, \Delta_i \in \mathbb{Z}_p\}_{i \in [\ell-1]\setminus[Q_{\mathsf{pre}}]}$ are perfectly indistinguishable.

Further, any post-challenge key $\mathsf{sk}_{\boldsymbol{y}^{\mathsf{post}}}$ in $\mathbf{Game}_2$ always correctly decrypts any honestly generated ciphertext because such a ciphertext contains $\mathbf{0} \in \mathbb{Z}_p^\ell$ in its extended slots, which nullifies the extended slots of the keys. The two games are thus perfectly indistinguishable, which implies $\Pr[\mathsf{E}_1] = \Pr[\mathsf{E}_2]$. □

Lemma 9. *We have* $|\Pr[\mathsf{E}_2] - \Pr[\mathsf{E}_3]| \leq \mathrm{negl}(\lambda)$.

Proof. Let us assume that $|\Pr[\mathsf{E}_2] - \Pr[\mathsf{E}_3]|$ is non-negligible. We then construct an adversary $\mathcal{B}$ that breaks the indistinguishability-based security of the underlying IPFE scheme as follows:

1. On input $(1^\lambda, 1^\ell, p)$ from $\mathcal{A}$, $\mathcal{B}$ sets $L = 2\ell$ and relays $(1^\lambda, 1^L, p)$ to the IPFE challenger. Upon receiving $\mathsf{IPFE.mpk}$, it sets $\mathsf{mpk}^\star = \mathsf{IPFE.mpk}$ and randomly chooses $r_i \leftarrow \mathbb{Z}_p$ for all $i \in [\ell - 1]$ to maintain the internal state as $\mathsf{st}^\star = \{(\cdot,\cdot,\cdot,r_i)\}_{i\in[\ell-1]}$. It sends $\mathsf{mpk}^\star$ to $\mathcal{A}$.
2. When $\mathcal{A}$ requests a pre-challenge key for $\boldsymbol{y}_i^{\mathsf{pre}}$, $\mathcal{B}$ computes the extended vector $\widehat{\boldsymbol{y}}_i^{\mathsf{pre}} = (\boldsymbol{y}_i^{\mathsf{pre}}, \mathbf{e}_i, r_i) \in \mathbb{Z}_p^L$, where $\mathbf{e}_i \in \mathbb{Z}_p^{\ell-1}$ is the i-th canonical vector. It then queries the IPFE challenger with $\widehat{\boldsymbol{y}}_i^{\mathsf{pre}}$ for a secret key and receives $\mathsf{IPFE.sk}_{\widehat{\boldsymbol{y}}_i^{\mathsf{pre}}}$. Then, $\mathcal{B}$ updates $\mathsf{st}^\star \leftarrow \left(\mathsf{st}^\star \cup \left\{(\widehat{\boldsymbol{y}}_i^{\mathsf{pre}}, \boldsymbol{y}_i^{\mathsf{pre}}, \mathsf{sk}_{\boldsymbol{y}_i^{\mathsf{pre}}}, r_i)\right\}\right) \setminus \left\{(\cdot,\cdot,\cdot,r_i)\right\}$, sets $\mathsf{sk}_{\boldsymbol{y}_i^{\mathsf{pre}}} = \mathsf{IPFE.sk}_{\widehat{\boldsymbol{y}}_i^{\mathsf{pre}}}$ and sends $\mathsf{sk}_{\boldsymbol{y}_i^{\mathsf{pre}}}$ to $\mathcal{A}$.
3. When $\mathcal{A}$ requests a challenge ciphertext, $\mathcal{B}$ sets $\boldsymbol{z}_{\mathsf{pre}} = (z_1^{\mathsf{pre}}, \ldots, z_{Q_{\mathsf{pre}}}^{\mathsf{pre}})^\top \in \mathbb{Z}_p^{Q_{\mathsf{pre}}}$ and then computes an arbitrary solution $\bar{\boldsymbol{x}} = (\bar{x}_1, \ldots, \bar{x}_\ell)^\top \in \mathbb{Z}_p^\ell$ of the linear system $\mathbf{Y}_{\mathsf{pre}} \cdot \bar{\boldsymbol{x}} = \boldsymbol{z}_{\mathsf{pre}} (\bmod\ p)$, where
$$\mathbf{Y}_{\mathsf{pre}} = \left[\boldsymbol{y}_1^{\mathsf{pre}} || \cdots || \boldsymbol{y}_{Q_{\mathsf{pre}}}^{\mathsf{pre}}\right]^\top \in \mathbb{Z}_p^{Q_{\mathsf{pre}} \times \ell}.$$
Next, it constructs the extended message vector $\widehat{\bar{\boldsymbol{x}}} = (\bar{\boldsymbol{x}}, -\mathbf{r}, 1) \in \mathbb{Z}_p^L$, where $\mathbf{r} = (r_1, \ldots, r_{\ell-1}) \in \mathbb{Z}_p^{\ell-1}$ to output $\boldsymbol{x}_0 = (\boldsymbol{x}^\star, \mathbf{0}, 0) \in \mathbb{Z}_p^L$ and $\boldsymbol{x}_1 = \widehat{\bar{\boldsymbol{x}}}$ as the pair of challenge messages to the IPFE challenger. The latter returns a challenge ciphertext $\mathsf{IPFE.ct}$ and $\mathcal{B}$ sets $\boldsymbol{c}^\star = \mathsf{IPFE.ct}$, which is returned to $\mathcal{A}$.
4. When $\mathcal{A}$ requests for a post-challenge key for $\boldsymbol{y}_i^{\mathsf{post}} \in \mathbb{Z}_p^\ell, i \in [\ell - 1] \setminus [Q_{\mathsf{pre}}]$ with its corresponding function evaluation z_i^{post}, $\mathcal{B}$ computes $\Delta_i = z_i^{\mathsf{post}} - \langle \bar{\boldsymbol{x}}, \boldsymbol{y}_i^{\mathsf{post}} \rangle$ and the extended vector $\widehat{\boldsymbol{y}}_i^{\mathsf{post}} = (\boldsymbol{y}_i^{\mathsf{post}}, \mathbf{e}_i, \Delta_i + r_i)$. It then queries

the IPFE challenger with $\widehat{\boldsymbol{y}}_i^{\mathsf{post}}$ for a secret key and receives $\mathsf{IPFE.sk}_{\widehat{\boldsymbol{y}}_i^{\mathsf{post}}}$. Then, $\mathcal{B}$ updates

$$\mathsf{st}^\star \leftarrow \left(\mathsf{st}^\star \cup \left\{ \left(\widehat{\boldsymbol{y}}_i^{\mathsf{post}}, \boldsymbol{y}_i^{\mathsf{post}}, \mathsf{sk}_{\boldsymbol{y}_i^{\mathsf{post}}}, r_i\right) \right\}\right) \setminus \{(\cdot,\cdot,\cdot,r_i)\},$$

sets $\mathsf{sk}_{\boldsymbol{y}_i^{\mathsf{post}}} = \mathsf{IPFE.sk}_{\widehat{\boldsymbol{y}}_i^{\mathsf{post}}}$ and sends $\mathsf{sk}_{\boldsymbol{y}_i^{\mathsf{post}}}$ to $\mathcal{A}$.
5. $\mathcal{B}$ outputs the same bit as $\mathcal{A}$.

Note that the ciphertext $\boldsymbol{c}^\star$ encodes the message $\boldsymbol{x}_0 = (\boldsymbol{x}^\star, \mathbf{0}, 0) \in \mathbb{Z}_p^L$ in $\mathbf{Game}_2$ and $\boldsymbol{x}_1 = \widehat{\bar{\boldsymbol{x}}} = (\bar{\boldsymbol{x}}, -\mathbf{r}, 1) \in \mathbb{Z}_p^L$ in $\mathbf{Game}_3$. The message $\bar{\boldsymbol{x}}$ in both games is computed maintaining the consistency with all the pre-challenge keys $\{\mathsf{sk}_{\boldsymbol{y}_i^{\mathsf{pre}}}\}_{i\in[Q_{\mathsf{pre}}]}$. Thus, upon decryption of $\boldsymbol{c}^\star$, it yields $\langle \boldsymbol{x}_0, \widehat{\boldsymbol{y}}_i^{\mathsf{pre}}\rangle = \langle \boldsymbol{x}^\star, \boldsymbol{y}_i^{\mathsf{pre}}\rangle = z^{\mathsf{pre}} \pmod p$ in $\mathbf{Game}_2$ as well as $\langle \boldsymbol{x}_1, \widehat{\boldsymbol{y}}_i^{\mathsf{pre}}\rangle = \langle \bar{\boldsymbol{x}}, \boldsymbol{y}_i^{\mathsf{pre}}\rangle + \langle -\mathbf{r}, \mathbf{e}_i\rangle + r_i = z^{\mathsf{pre}} \pmod p$ in $\mathbf{Game}_3$ as required. Further, note that in both games, for each $i \in [\ell-1] \setminus [Q_{\mathsf{pre}}]$, the i-th post-challenge key $\mathsf{sk}_{\boldsymbol{y}_i^{\mathsf{post}}}$ is a secret key for the vector $\widehat{\boldsymbol{y}}_i^{\mathsf{post}} = (\boldsymbol{y}_i^{\mathsf{post}}, \mathbf{e}_i, \Delta_i + r_i)$, where

$$\Delta_i = z_i^{\mathsf{post}} - \langle \bar{\boldsymbol{x}}, \boldsymbol{y}_i^{\mathsf{post}}\rangle,$$

which implies $\Delta_i + \langle \bar{\boldsymbol{x}}, \boldsymbol{y}_i^{\mathsf{post}}\rangle = z_i^{\mathsf{post}}$. Hence, upon decrypting $\boldsymbol{c}^\star$, we have

$$\langle \boldsymbol{x}_0, \widehat{\boldsymbol{y}}_i^{\mathsf{post}}\rangle = \langle \boldsymbol{x}^\star, \boldsymbol{y}_i^{\mathsf{post}}\rangle + \langle \mathbf{0}, \mathbf{e}_i\rangle + 0 \cdot (\Delta_i + r_i) = z_i^{\mathsf{post}} (\mathrm{mod}\ p),$$

in $\mathbf{Game}_2$, and

$$\langle \boldsymbol{x}_1, \widehat{\boldsymbol{y}}_i^{\mathsf{post}}\rangle = \langle \bar{\boldsymbol{x}}, \boldsymbol{y}_i^{\mathsf{post}}\rangle + \langle -\mathbf{r}, \mathbf{e}_i\rangle + 1 \cdot (\Delta_i + r_i) = z_i^{\mathsf{post}} (\mathrm{mod}\ p)$$

in $\mathbf{Game}_3$, as required. This proves that $\mathcal{B}$ is an admissible IPFE adversary in the indistinguishability-based security game. If the IPFE challenger returned a challenge ciphertext for the vector $\boldsymbol{x}_0$, $\mathcal{A}$'s view is as in $\mathbf{Game}_2$. Otherwise, $\mathcal{A}$'s view is the same as in $\mathbf{Game}_3$. Consequently, $\mathcal{B}$ breaks the adaptive indistinguishability-based security of the scheme if $\mathcal{A}$ can distinguish between the two games with noticeable advantage. □

Acknowledgements. Part of this work was funded by the French ANR ALAMBIC project (ANR-16-CE39-0006) and by BPI-France in the context of the national project RISQ (P141580). This work was also supported by the European Union PROMETHEUS project (Horizon 2020 Research and Innovation Program, grant 780701).

References

1. Abdalla, M., Bourse, F., De Caro, A., Pointcheval, D.: Simple functional encryption schemes for inner products. In: Katz, J. (ed.) PKC 2015. LNCS, vol. 9020, pp. 733–751. Springer, Heidelberg (2015). https://doi.org/10.1007/978-3-662-46447-2_33
2. Abdalla, M., Catalano, D., Fiore, D., Gay, R., Ursu, B.: Multi-input functional encryption for inner products: function-hiding realizations and constructions without pairings. In: Shacham, H., Boldyreva, A. (eds.) CRYPTO 2018. LNCS, vol. 10991, pp. 597–627. Springer, Cham (2018). https://doi.org/10.1007/978-3-319-96884-1_20

3. Abdalla, M., Gay, R., Raykova, M., Wee, H.: Multi-input inner-product functional encryption from pairings. In: Coron, J.-S., Nielsen, J.B. (eds.) EUROCRYPT 2017. LNCS, vol. 10210, pp. 601–626. Springer, Cham (2017). https://doi.org/10.1007/978-3-319-56620-7_21
4. Agrawal, S., Bhattacherjee, S., Phan, D.-H., Stehlé, D., Yamada, S.: Efficient public trace and revoke from standard assumptions. In: ACM-CCS (2017)
5. Agrawal, S., Boyen, X., Vaikuntanathan, V., Voulgaris, P., Wee, H.: Functional encryption for threshold functions (or fuzzy IBE) from lattices. In: Fischlin, M., Buchmann, J., Manulis, M. (eds.) PKC 2012. LNCS, vol. 7293, pp. 280–297. Springer, Heidelberg (2012). https://doi.org/10.1007/978-3-642-30057-8_17
6. Agrawal, S., Freeman, D.M., Vaikuntanathan, V.: Functional encryption for inner product predicates from learning with errors. In: Lee, D.H., Wang, X. (eds.) ASIACRYPT 2011. LNCS, vol. 7073, pp. 21–40. Springer, Heidelberg (2011). https://doi.org/10.1007/978-3-642-25385-0_2
7. Agrawal, S., Gorbunov, S., Vaikuntanathan, V., Wee, H.: Functional encryption: new perspectives and lower bounds. In: Canetti, R., Garay, J.A. (eds.) CRYPTO 2013. LNCS, vol. 8043, pp. 500–518. Springer, Heidelberg (2013). https://doi.org/10.1007/978-3-642-40084-1_28
8. Agrawal, S., Libert, B., Stehlé, D.: Fully secure functional encryption for inner products, from standard assumptions. In: Robshaw, M., Katz, J. (eds.) CRYPTO 2016. LNCS, vol. 9816, pp. 333–362. Springer, Heidelberg (2016). https://doi.org/10.1007/978-3-662-53015-3_12
9. Agrawal, S., Rosen, A.: Functional encryption for bounded collusions, revisited. In: Kalai, Y., Reyzin, L. (eds.) TCC 2017. LNCS, vol. 10677, pp. 173–205. Springer, Cham (2017). https://doi.org/10.1007/978-3-319-70500-2_7. http://eprint.iacr.org/
10. Agrawal, S.: Stronger security for reusable garbled circuits, general definitions and attacks. In: Katz, J., Shacham, H. (eds.) CRYPTO 2017. LNCS, vol. 10401, pp. 3–35. Springer, Cham (2017). https://doi.org/10.1007/978-3-319-63688-7_1
11. Benhamouda, F., Bourse, F., Lipmaa, H.: CCA-secure inner-product functional encryption from projective hash functions. In: Fehr, S. (ed.) PKC 2017. LNCS, vol. 10175, pp. 36–66. Springer, Heidelberg (2017). https://doi.org/10.1007/978-3-662-54388-7_2
12. Bishop, A., Jain, A., Kowalczyk, L.: Function-hiding inner product encryption. In: Iwata, T., Cheon, J.H. (eds.) ASIACRYPT 2015. LNCS, vol. 9452, pp. 470–491. Springer, Heidelberg (2015). https://doi.org/10.1007/978-3-662-48797-6_20
13. Boneh, D., Franklin, M.: Identity-based encryption from the Weil pairing. SIAM J. Comput. **32**(3), 586–615 (2003)
14. Boneh, D., et al.: Fully key-homomorphic encryption, arithmetic circuit ABE and compact garbled circuits. In: Nguyen, P.Q., Oswald, E. (eds.) EUROCRYPT 2014. LNCS, vol. 8441, pp. 533–556. Springer, Heidelberg (2014). https://doi.org/10.1007/978-3-642-55220-5_30
15. Boneh, D., Sahai, A., Waters, B.: Functional encryption: definitions and challenges. In: Ishai, Y. (ed.) TCC 2011. LNCS, vol. 6597, pp. 253–273. Springer, Heidelberg (2011). https://doi.org/10.1007/978-3-642-19571-6_16
16. Brakerski, Z., Langlois, A., Peikert, C., Regev. O., Stehlé, D.: On the classical hardness of learning with errors. In: STOC (2013)
17. Castagnos, G., Laguillaumie, F., Tucker, I.: Practical fully secure unrestricted inner product functional encryption modulo p. In: Peyrin, T., Galbraith, S. (eds.) ASIACRYPT 2018. LNCS, vol. 11273, pp. 733–764. Springer, Cham (2018). https://doi.org/10.1007/978-3-030-03329-3_25

18. Chotard, J., Dufour Sans, E., Gay, R., Phan, D.H., Pointcheval, D.: Decentralized multi-client functional encryption for inner product. In: Peyrin, T., Galbraith, S. (eds.) ASIACRYPT 2018. LNCS, vol. 11273, pp. 703–732. Springer, Cham (2018). https://doi.org/10.1007/978-3-030-03329-3_24
19. Datta, P., Dutta, R., Mukhopadhyay, S.: Functional encryption for inner product with full function privacy. In: Cheng, C.-M., Chung, K.-M., Persiano, G., Yang, B.-Y. (eds.) PKC 2016. LNCS, vol. 9614, pp. 164–195. Springer, Heidelberg (2016). https://doi.org/10.1007/978-3-662-49384-7_7
20. Datta, P., Okamoto, T., Takashima, K.: Adaptively simulation-secure attribute-hiding predicate encryption. In: Peyrin, T., Galbraith, S. (eds.) ASIACRYPT 2018. LNCS, vol. 11273, pp. 640–672. Springer, Cham (2018). https://doi.org/10.1007/978-3-030-03329-3_22
21. Datta, P., Okamoto, T., Tomida, J.: Full-hiding (unbounded) multi-input inner product functional encryption from the k-linear assumption. In: Abdalla, M., Dahab, R. (eds.) PKC 2018. LNCS, vol. 10770, pp. 245–277. Springer, Cham (2018). https://doi.org/10.1007/978-3-319-76581-5_9
22. Garg, S., Gentry, C., Halevi, S.: Candidate multilinear maps from ideal lattices. In: Johansson, T., Nguyen, P.Q. (eds.) EUROCRYPT 2013. LNCS, vol. 7881, pp. 1–17. Springer, Heidelberg (2013). https://doi.org/10.1007/978-3-642-38348-9_1
23. Garg, S., Gentry, C., Halevi, S., Raykova, M., Sahai, A., Waters, B.: Candidate indistinguishability obfuscation and functional encryption for all circuits. In: FOCS (2013)
24. Garg, S., Gentry, C., Halevi, S., Zhandry, M.: Functional encryption without obfuscation. In: Kushilevitz, E., Malkin, T. (eds.) TCC 2016. LNCS, vol. 9563, pp. 480–511. Springer, Heidelberg (2016). https://doi.org/10.1007/978-3-662-49099-0_18
25. Goldwasser, S., Kalai, Y.T., Popa, R.A., Vaikuntanathan, V., Zeldovich, N.: Reusable garbled circuits and succinct functional encryption. In: STOC, pp. 555–564 (2013)
26. Gorbunov, S., Vaikuntanathan, V., Wee, H.: Functional encryption with bounded collusions via multi-party computation. In: Safavi-Naini, R., Canetti, R. (eds.) CRYPTO 2012. LNCS, vol. 7417, pp. 162–179. Springer, Heidelberg (2012). https://doi.org/10.1007/978-3-642-32009-5_11
27. Gorbunov, S., Vaikuntanathan, V., Wee, H.: Attribute-based encryption for circuits. In: STOC (2013)
28. Gorbunov, S., Vaikuntanathan, V., Wee, H.: Predicate encryption for circuits from LWE. In: Gennaro, R., Robshaw, M. (eds.) CRYPTO 2015. LNCS, vol. 9216, pp. 503–523. Springer, Heidelberg (2015). https://doi.org/10.1007/978-3-662-48000-7_25
29. Goyal, V., Pandey, O., Sahai, A., Waters, B.: Attribute-based encryption for fine-grained access control of encrypted data. In: ACM-CCS (2006)
30. Katz, J., Sahai, A., Waters, B.: Predicate encryption supporting disjunctions, polynomial equations, and inner products. In: Smart, N. (ed.) EUROCRYPT 2008. LNCS, vol. 4965, pp. 146–162. Springer, Heidelberg (2008). https://doi.org/10.1007/978-3-540-78967-3_9
31. Lewko, A., Okamoto, T., Sahai, A., Takashima, K., Waters, B.: Fully secure functional encryption: attribute-based encryption and (hierarchical) inner product encryption. In: Gilbert, H. (ed.) EUROCRYPT 2010. LNCS, vol. 6110, pp. 62–91. Springer, Heidelberg (2010). https://doi.org/10.1007/978-3-642-13190-5_4
32. Lin, H.: Indistinguishability obfuscation from SXDH on 5-linear maps and locality-5 PRGs. In: Katz, J., Shacham, H. (eds.) CRYPTO 2017. LNCS, vol. 10401, pp. 599–629. Springer, Cham (2017). https://doi.org/10.1007/978-3-319-63688-7_20

33. Lin, H., Vaikuntanathan, V.: Indistinguishability obfuscation from DDH-like assumptions on constant-degree graded encodings. In: FOCS (2016)
34. Okamoto, T., Takashima, K.: Hierarchical predicate encryption for inner-products. In: Matsui, M. (ed.) ASIACRYPT 2009. LNCS, vol. 5912, pp. 214–231. Springer, Heidelberg (2009). https://doi.org/10.1007/978-3-642-10366-7_13
35. Okamoto, T., Takashima, K.: Fully secure functional encryption with general relations from the decisional linear assumption. In: Rabin, T. (ed.) CRYPTO 2010. LNCS, vol. 6223, pp. 191–208. Springer, Heidelberg (2010). https://doi.org/10.1007/978-3-642-14623-7_11
36. Okamoto, T., Takashima, K.: Adaptively attribute-hiding (hierarchical) inner product encryption. In: Pointcheval, D., Johansson, T. (eds.) EUROCRYPT 2012. LNCS, vol. 7237, pp. 591–608. Springer, Heidelberg (2012). https://doi.org/10.1007/978-3-642-29011-4_35
37. O'Neill, A.: Definitional issues in functional encryption. Cryptology ePrint Archive, Report 2010/556 (2010). http://eprint.iacr.org/
38. Paillier, P.: Public-key cryptosystems based on composite degree residuosity classes. In: Stern, J. (ed.) EUROCRYPT 1999. LNCS, vol. 1592, pp. 223–238. Springer, Heidelberg (1999). https://doi.org/10.1007/3-540-48910-X_16
39. Pollard, J.: Kangaroos, monopoly and discrete logarithms. J. Cryptol. **13**, 433–447 (2000). https://doi.org/10.1007/s001450010010
40. Regev, O.: On lattices, learning with errors, random linear codes, and cryptography. J. ACM **56**(6), 1–40 (2009)
41. Sahai, A., Waters, B.: Fuzzy identity-based encryption. In: Cramer, R. (ed.) EUROCRYPT 2005. LNCS, vol. 3494, pp. 457–473. Springer, Heidelberg (2005). https://doi.org/10.1007/11426639_27
42. Shamir, A.: Identity-based cryptosystems and signature schemes. In: Blakley, G.R., Chaum, D. (eds.) CRYPTO 1984. LNCS, vol. 196, pp. 47–53. Springer, Heidelberg (1985). https://doi.org/10.1007/3-540-39568-7_5
43. Tomida, J., Abe, M., Okamoto, T.: Efficient functional encryption for inner-product values with full-hiding security. In: Bishop, M., Nascimento, A.C.A. (eds.) ISC 2016. LNCS, vol. 9866, pp. 408–425. Springer, Cham (2016). https://doi.org/10.1007/978-3-319-45871-7_24
44. Tomida, J., Takashima, K.: Unbounded inner product functional encryption from bilinear maps. In: Peyrin, T., Galbraith, S. (eds.) ASIACRYPT 2018. LNCS, vol. 11273, pp. 609–639. Springer, Cham (2018). https://doi.org/10.1007/978-3-030-03329-3_21
45. Wee, H.: Dual system encryption via predicate encodings. In: Lindell, Y. (ed.) TCC 2014. LNCS, vol. 8349, pp. 616–637. Springer, Heidelberg (2014). https://doi.org/10.1007/978-3-642-54242-8_26
46. Wee, H.: Attribute-hiding predicate encryption in bilinear groups, revisited. In: Kalai, Y., Reyzin, L. (eds.) TCC 2017. LNCS, vol. 10677, pp. 206–233. Springer, Cham (2017). https://doi.org/10.1007/978-3-319-70500-2_8

Verifiable Inner Product Encryption Scheme

Najmeh Soroush[1(✉)], Vincenzo Iovino[1,2], Alfredo Rial[1], Peter B. Roenne[1], and Peter Y. A. Ryan[1]

[1] SnT, University of Luxembourg, Luxembourg City, Luxembourg
{najmeh.soroush,alfredo.rial,peter.roenne,peter.ryan}@uni.lu
[2] University of Salerno, Salerno, Italy
vinciovino@gmail.com

Abstract. In the standard setting of functional encryption (FE), we assume both the Central Authority (CA) and the encryptors to run their respective algorithms faithfully. Badrinarayanan *et al.* [ASIACRYPT 2016] proposed the concept of verifiable FE, which essentially guarantees that dishonest encryptors and authorities, even when colluding together, are not able to generate ciphertexts and tokens that give "inconsistent" results. They also provide a compiler turning any perfectly correct FE into a verifiable FE, but do not give efficient constructions.

In this paper we improve on this situation by considering Inner-Product Encryption (IPE), which is a special case of functional encryption and a primitive that has attracted wide interest from both practitioners and researchers in the last decade. Specifically, we construct the first *efficient* verifiable IPE (VIPE) scheme according to the inner-product functionality of Katz, Sahai and Waters [EUROCRYPT 2008]. To instantiate the general construction of Badrinarayanan *et al.* we need to solve several additional challenges. In particular, we construct the first efficient *perfectly correct* IPE scheme. Our VIPE satisfies *unconditional* verifiability, whereas its privacy relies on the DLin assumption.

Keywords: Inner-product encryption · Verifiability · Functional commitments

1 Introduction

Functional encryption (FE) is a new encryption paradigm that was first proposed by Sahai and Waters [23] and formalized by Boneh, Sahai and Waters [7]. Informally, in an FE system, a decryption key allows a user to learn a *function* of the original message. More specifically, in a FE scheme for functionality $F : K \times \mathcal{M} \rightarrow \mathcal{CT}$, defined over *key space* $\mathcal{K}$, *message space* $\mathcal{M}$ and *output space* $\mathcal{CT}$, for every *key* $k \in K$, the owner of the master secret key MSK associated with master public key MPK can generate a token $\mathtt{Tok}_k$ that allows the computation of $F(k, m)$ from a ciphertext of x computed under the master public key MPK.

This research were supported by the Luxembourg National Research Fund (FNR).

A. Kiayias et al. (Eds.): PKC 2020, LNCS 12110, pp. 65–94, 2020.
https://doi.org/10.1007/978-3-030-45374-9_3

A notable special case of FE is that of *inner product encryption* (IPE). In IPE [8,18,19,21,22] the message is a pair $(m, \boldsymbol{x})$, with $m \in \mathcal{M}$, the *payload message* and $\boldsymbol{x}$ is an attribute vector in the set Σ and the token is associated with a vector $\boldsymbol{v} \in \Sigma$. The functionality is $F(\boldsymbol{v}, (m, \boldsymbol{x})) = f_{\boldsymbol{v}}(\boldsymbol{x}, m)$ which returns m if $\langle \boldsymbol{x}, \boldsymbol{v} \rangle = 0$ (i.e,. the two vectors are orthogonal) or $\perp$ otherwise. IPE is a generalization of Identity-Based Encryption [6,9,24] and Anonymous Identity-Based Encryption [1,5], and has been the subject of extensive studies in the last decade.

In FE and IPE, the encryptors and the Central Authority (CA) that generate the tokens are assumed to be honest. Indeed, as noticed by Badrinarayanan *et al.* in presence of any dishonest party (that is, either the party that generates the token or the party who encrypts the message), the decryption outputs may be inconsistent and this raises serious issues in practical applications (e.g., auditing). For instance, a dishonest authority might be able to generate a faulty token $\mathsf{Tok}_{\boldsymbol{v}}$ for a vector $\boldsymbol{v}$ such that $\mathsf{Tok}_{\boldsymbol{v}}$ enables the owner to decrypt a ciphertext for a vector $\boldsymbol{x}$ that is not orthogonal to $\boldsymbol{v}$. Or a dishonest encryptor might generate a faulty ciphertext that decrypts to an incorrect result with an honestly computed token. These issues are particularly severe in the applications to functional commitments that we will see later.

Verifiable Inner Product Encryption (VIPE) overcomes those limitations by adding strong verifiability guarantees to IPE. VIPE is a special case of Verifiable Functional Encryption (VFE), firstly proposed by Badrinarayanan *et al.* [2] for general functionalities. Informally speaking, in VIPE there are public verification algorithms to verify that the output of the setup, encryption and token generation algorithms are computed honestly. Intuitively, if the master public key MPK and a ciphertext CT pass a public verification test, it means there exists some message m and a unique vector $\boldsymbol{x}$ – up to parallelism – such that for all vectors $\boldsymbol{v}$, if a token $\mathsf{Tok}_{\boldsymbol{v}}$ for $\boldsymbol{v}$ is accepted by the verification algorithm then the following holds:

$$\forall \boldsymbol{v} : \mathsf{Dec}(\mathsf{Tok}_{\boldsymbol{v}}, \mathsf{CT}) = f_{\boldsymbol{v}}(\boldsymbol{x}, m)$$

The main component we employ for constructing a VIPE scheme is an IPE scheme. However, it is worth mentioning that most IPE schemes cannot be made verifiable following the general compiler of Badrinarayanan *et al.* because this compiler requires the IPE scheme to have perfect correctness. We will later discuss in depth why this property is crucial in constructing VIPE.

1.1 Our Results and Applications

Our Contribution. In this paper we construct an efficient VIPE scheme from bilinear maps. Towards this goal, we build a perfectly correct IPE scheme that may be of independent interest. To our knowledge, all IPE schemes known in literature do *not* satisfy perfect correctness. Our perfectly correct IPE scheme is based on standard assumptions over bilinear groups.

We assume the reader to be familiar with the construction of Badrinarayanan *et al.* [2] that transforms a generic perfectly correct FE scheme to a VFE scheme for the same functionality. They employ four duplicates of the underlying FE scheme adding NIWI proofs for verifiabilty with trapdoor statements to ensure privacy. We will use this transform explicitly in Sect. 4. This transform, for the case of the inner-product functionality of [18], requires a perfectly correct IPE scheme and non-interactive witness-indistinguishable (NIWI) proofs for the relations we will define in Sect. 5. Therefore, constructing an efficient VIPE scheme boils down to building an efficient perfectly correct IPE scheme and efficient NIWI proofs for specific relations. The rest of the paper is devoted to achieving these goals.

Motivating Applications. IPE has numerous applications, including Anonymous Identity-Based Encryption [5], Hidden-Vector Encryption [8], and predicate encryption schemes supporting polynomial evaluation [18]. As shown by Badrinarayanan *et al.* [2], making FE schemes verifiable enables more powerful applications. As an example, in this section we show that VIPE can be used to construct what we call *polynomial commitment scheme* which corresponds to a functional commitment of Badrinarayanan *et al.* for the polynomial evaluation *predicate*. The same construction can easily be adapted to construct functional commitments for the inner-product predicate.

Perfectly Binding Polynomial Commitments. Using a polynomial commitment scheme (see also [17]), Alice may publish a commitment to a polynomial $\mathsf{poly}(x)$ with coefficients in $\mathbb{Z}_p$. If later Bob wants to know $\mathsf{poly}(m)$ for some value m, that is the evaluation of the polynomial at some point, he sends m to Alice who replies with the claimed evaluation y and a proof that $y = \mathsf{poly}(m)$. The proof guarantees that the claimed evaluation is consistent with the committed polynomial. We require the scheme to be *perfectly binding.*

We construct a polynomial commitment scheme for polynomials of degree at most d from a VIPE scheme for vectors of dimension $d+2$ in the following way. Let $\mathsf{VIP} = \langle \mathsf{VIP.SetUp}, \mathsf{VIP.TokGen}, \mathsf{VIP.Enc}, \mathsf{VIP.Dec} \rangle$ be a VIPE scheme. We define the following algorithms:

- Commitment Phase: To commit to a polynomial $\mathsf{poly}(x) = a_d x^d + a_{d-1} x^{d-1} + \ldots + a_1 x + a_0 \in \mathbb{Z}_p[X]$, run $\mathsf{VIP.SetUp}(1^\lambda, d+2)$ to generate $(\mathsf{MPK}, \mathsf{MSK})$, compute the attribute $\boldsymbol{x} := (a_d, a_{d-1}, \ldots, a_1, a_0, 1) \in \mathbb{Z}_p^{d+2}$ and ciphertext $\mathsf{CT} \rightarrow \mathsf{VIP.Enc}(\mathsf{MPK}, \boldsymbol{x})$, and output the commitment $:= (\mathsf{MPK}, \mathsf{CT})$.
- Opening phase: In this phase, a party requests a query (m, y) to check if the commitment corresponds to a polynomial poly such that $\mathsf{poly}(m) = y$. The Committer runs the token-generator algorithm of VIP for vector $\boldsymbol{v} := (m^d, m^{d-1}, \ldots, m, 1, -y)$ and sends $\mathsf{Tok}_{\boldsymbol{v}}$ as the opening. Note that $\langle \boldsymbol{x}, \boldsymbol{v} \rangle = a_d m^d + a_{d-1} m^{d-1} + \ldots + a_1 m + a_0 - y = \mathsf{poly}(m) - y$, therefore $\mathsf{VIP.Dec}(\mathsf{CT}, \mathsf{Tok}_{\boldsymbol{v}}) = 0$ iff $\mathsf{poly}(m) = y$.

It is straightforward to see that the above algorithms form a functional commitment (in the sense of [2]) for the polynomial evaluation predicate. We refer the reader to [2] for more details on functional commitments.

1.2 Technical Overview

To instantiate the transform of Badrinarayanan *et al.* we need to build an IPE scheme with perfect correctness. Our starting point to construct a perfectly correct IPE scheme is the IPE scheme of Park [22] which only enjoys statistical correctness. The reason for choosing this IPE is that it is conceptually simple and its security is based on standard assumptions over bilinear groups. However, to make the Park's scheme compatible with the Badrinarayanan *et al.*'s transform we need to solve several technical challenges, in particular:

i. The master public key needs to be verifiable.
ii. The scheme has to satisfy perfect correctness.

This requires substantial modification of all main algorithms: setup, token generation, encryption and decryption.

Verification of Algorithm Outputs. A VIPE scheme requires public verification algorithms that can verify the outputs of the setup, encryption and token generation algorithms, in particular check whether these algorithms were run honestly. In more detail, if any string (master public key, ciphertext or token) passes the corresponding verification algorithm, it means it was a proper output of the corresponding algorithm (setup, encryption or token generation). Each party who runs the setup, encryption or token generation algorithm needs to provide a proof that it executed the algorithm honestly without revealing harmful information about the secret parameters or the randomness used in the algorithm.

Usually non-interactive Zero-Knowledge (NIZK) proofs are used in this context. Unfortunately, NIZK proofs cannot used for verifiable FE as they rely on a trusted CRS (Common Reference String) or random oracles and we aim at *perfect verifiability* which has to hold despite any collusion and computing power. The transform of Badrinarayanan *et al.* solves the issue by employing NIWI-proofs in a clever way.

Following the transform of [2], our VIPE consists of four instances of an IPE scheme. In the VIPE's encryption algorithm we first run the IPE's encryption algorithm four times to generate four ciphertexts and then we prove that all these four ciphertexts are the encryption of the same message or that some other trapdoor predicate is satisfied (the latter is needed for message indistinguishability and will be detailed later).

For the sake of argument, let us assume the VIPE scheme consists only of two (instead of four) parallel perfectly correct IPE scheme instantiations IP and $\hat{\mathsf{IP}}$. The master public key of the Park's scheme [22] contains a component $\Lambda = e(g, g')$ in which g is public but g' needs to be kept secret. An honestly computed ciphertext CT in IP includes $\mathsf{ct}_1 = g^{-s}$ and $\mathsf{ct}_7 = \Lambda^{-s} \cdot m$ among its components (we here ignore the other components). We first provide proof that CT (resp. $\hat{\mathsf{CT}}$ in $\hat{\mathsf{IP}}$) is well-formed. Then we need to prove that the two ciphertexts are both encryptions of the same message M (i.e., $m = \hat{m} = M$). We reduce the problem to proving that the following property holds:

$$\frac{\mathsf{ct}_7}{\hat{\mathsf{ct}}_7} = \frac{e(g, g')^{-s} \cdot m}{e(\hat{g}, \hat{g}')^{-\hat{s}} \cdot \hat{m}} = \frac{e(\hat{\mathsf{ct}}_1, \hat{g}')}{e(\mathsf{ct}_1, g')} = \frac{e(\hat{g}^{\hat{s}}, \hat{g}')}{e(g^s, g')}$$

However, since g' and $\hat{g}'$ are not public, the party who runs the encryption algorithm would be unable to prove this property. We solve this issue in the following way: We add to the master public key of IP two elements g_1, g_2 (and $\hat{g}_1, \hat{g}_2$ for $\hat{\mathsf{IP}}$) satisfying $\Lambda = e(g, g') = e(g_1, g_2), \hat{\Lambda} = e(\hat{g}, \hat{g}') = e(\hat{g}_1, \hat{g}_2)$. Then, we add the following equations for the new secret variables $\mathcal{X}_3 = g_1^s, \hat{\mathcal{X}}_3 = \hat{g}_1^{\hat{s}}$:

$$\mathsf{ct}_7^{-1} \cdot \hat{\mathsf{ct}}_7 = e(\mathcal{X}_3, g_2) \cdot e(\hat{\mathcal{X}}_3, \hat{g}_2)^{-1}, e(g, \mathcal{X}_3) = e(\mathsf{ct}_1, g_1), e(\hat{g}, \hat{\mathcal{X}}_3) = e(\hat{\mathsf{ct}}_1, \hat{g}_1)$$

It is easy to see that these equations are satisfied iff $m = \hat{m}$, and now they can be proven by the encryptor. Having modified Park's scheme, we thus have to prove that the modified scheme is $\mathsf{IND\text{-}secure}$. This is done in Sect. 3.1 in which we reduce the IND-Security of the scheme to the Decision Linear assumption.

Achieving Perfect Correctness. For the Badrinarayanan *et al.*'s transform to work, it is crucial that the underlying IPE scheme have perfect correctness. If the IPE scheme had a negligible probability of decryption error rather than perfect correctness, then dishonest parties might collude with each other so that invalid results would be accepted by the verification algorithms. Contrast this with the aforementioned functional commitments. In the latter primitive, the committer is the same party who generates the ciphertext (the commitment) and the token (the decommitment) and thus might profit from a negligible space of decryption error to prove false assertions on its committed value. To our knowledge, all IPE schemes[1] known in the literature have a negligible probability of error which makes cheating possible and so not directly usable to construct verifiable functional encryption and functional commitments for the IPE functionality.

In more detail, in most pairing-based IPE schemes the encryption and decryption algorithms work as follows:

$$\mathsf{Enc}(\mathsf{MPK}, \boldsymbol{x}, \mathbf{m}) \rightarrow \mathsf{CT}, \quad \mathsf{Dec}(\mathsf{Tok}_{\boldsymbol{v}}, \mathsf{CT}) \rightarrow m^* = m \cdot (\mathbf{r})^{\langle \boldsymbol{x}, \boldsymbol{v} \rangle},$$

in which $\mathbf{r}$ is some random value that depends on the randomness used by the token generator and encryption algorithms. Thus, even in case of honest parties, there is a negligible probability that $\mathbf{r} = 1$ and so, even if $\langle \boldsymbol{x}, \boldsymbol{v} \rangle \neq 0$, the decryption algorithm may output a valid message $\mathbf{m}$ instead of $\perp$.

In case of dishonest parties, it may happen that two parties (the encryptor and the token generator) collude with each other to create randomness such that $\mathbf{r}$ equals 1. In this case, the parties would be able to provide valid proofs of the fact that they followed the protocol correctly and invalid results would pass the verification algorithms. A similar problem also appears in the context of MPC in the head [16], where the soundness of the ZK protocol built from MPC strongly relies on the perfect correctness of the underlying MPC. To cope with statistical correctness in MPC in the head, a coin tossing protocol can be employed, while in a completely non-interactive scenario like ours this is more challenging. Hence, to obtain a VIPE scheme it is crucial to construct an IPE scheme satisfying perfect correctness.

Recall that the decryption algorithm in the IPE scheme of Park [22] works as follows:

$$\mathsf{Dec}(\mathsf{Tok}_{\boldsymbol{v}}, \mathsf{CT} = \mathsf{Enc}(\boldsymbol{x}, m)) \longrightarrow m^* = m \cdot \mathbf{e}(g, h)^{(\lambda_1 s_3 + \lambda_2 s_4)\langle \boldsymbol{x}, \boldsymbol{v} \rangle}$$

[1] Recall that we refer to the IPE functionality of Katz, Sahai and Waters [18].

in which λ_1, λ_2 are random values used in the token generation algorithm and s_3, s_4 are random values used in the encryption algorithm. To decide whether to accept the output of the decryption or not, the first attempt would be the following. Generate two ciphertexts $\mathsf{ct}, \mathsf{ct}'$ with two independent random values $\{s_i\}, \{s_i'\}$, decrypt both ct and ct' to get M and M' and if $M = M'$ accept the result, or output $\perp$ otherwise. In more detail:

$$M = m \cdot e(h,g)^{(\lambda_1 s_3 + s_4 \lambda_2)\langle \boldsymbol{x}, \boldsymbol{v} \rangle}, M' = m \cdot e(h,g)^{(\lambda_1 s_3' + s_4' \lambda_2)\langle \boldsymbol{x}, \boldsymbol{v} \rangle}$$

However, in case $\langle \boldsymbol{x}, \boldsymbol{v} \rangle \neq 0$ there is non-zero probability for which:

$$\lambda_1 s_3 + s_4 \lambda_2 = \lambda_1 s_3' + \lambda_2 s_4' \neq 0 \Rightarrow M = M' \neq m$$

To avoid this issue, we choose the random values in such a way that the above equality can never occur. To do so, in the encryption algorithm we choose non-zero random values $s_1, \ldots, s_4$ and $s_1', \ldots, s_4'$ such that $s_3 \neq s_3'$, and $s_4 = s_4'$. In this case, we have:

$$\lambda_1 s_3 + s_4 \lambda_2 = \lambda_1 s_3' + \lambda_2 s_4 \Rightarrow \lambda_1 (s_3 - s_3') = 0 \Rightarrow (\lambda_1 = 0) \vee (s_3 = s_3')$$

Based on the way λ_1, s_3, s_3' have been chosen, neither $(\lambda_1 = 0)$ nor $(s_3 = s_3')$ may happen, hence the decryption algorithm outputs m if and only if $\langle \boldsymbol{x}, \boldsymbol{v} \rangle = 0$. The resulting IPE scheme satisfies perfect correctness as wished and we prove that it is still selectively indistinguishability-secure under the DLin Assumption. When constructing a VIPE scheme from such IPE scheme, these additional constraints in the encryption and token generation procedures will correspond to more constraints in the proofs of correct encryption and token generation.

Furthermore, an additional challenge we will have to address is that some of the proofs in the Badrinarayanan *et al.* transform are for relations that consist of a generalized form of disjunction and thus standard techniques to implement disjunctions for GS proofs cannot be directly applied, see Sect. 5.1.

1.3 Related Work and Comparison

Verifiable functional encryption has been introduced by Badrinarayanan *et al.* [2], who provide a construction for general functionalities.

Recently, [3] introduced a new FE scheme that supports an extension of the inner-product functionality. The scheme is perfectly correct assuming the message space to be short. However, notice that when employing the scheme in order to construct an IPE scheme (according to the functionality of Katz, Sahai and Waters [18]) the perfect correctness is *lost*. In essence, the IPE constructed from the scheme in [3] would encrypt some additional random value r so that the decryption would return the value $m + r \cdot \langle \boldsymbol{x}, \boldsymbol{v} \rangle$. In this way, if the vectors $\boldsymbol{x}$ and $\boldsymbol{v}$ are orthogonal then the payload message m is obtained, otherwise a random value is returned.

As corollary of our VIPE, we obtain functional commitments (in the sense of [2]) for the polynomial evaluation and inner-product *predicate*. A similar form of commitments has been proposed by Libert *et al.* [20] but differs from ours in different aspects. In the Libert *et al.*'s scheme, the decommitter reveals the evaluations of the inner-product of the committed vector with any vector of its choice, whereas in ours just the binary value of the inner-product predicate (i.e whether the two vectors are orthogonal or not) is leaked. Our functional commitments are perfectly binding rather than computational binding as in Libert *et al.* Moreover, ours are not based on any trust assumption, whereas in [20] the generator of the public-key can completely break the binding property.

Tang and Ji [26] constructed an Attribute-based Encryption scheme that enjoys a weaker form of verifiability limited to the secret keys.

Roadmap. In Sect. 2 we provide the building blocks and the basic terminology used in this paper. In Sect. 3 we construct our perfectly correct IPE scheme and prove its security based on the Decisional Bilinear Diffie-Hellman and DLin assumptions. In Sect. 4 we define VIPE and present one candidate construction built on perfectly correct IPE and the NIWI proofs of Sect. 5.

2 Preliminaries

Notation. Throughout the paper, we use $\lambda \in \mathbb{N}$ as a security parameter. For any integer $n > 0$, we denote by $[n]$ the set $\{1, \ldots, n\}$. PPT stands for probabilistic polynomial time algorithm and $\mathsf{negl}(\lambda)$ denotes a negligible function in λ.

2.1 Building Blocks

Definition 1 (Bilinear group [6]). A bilinear group consists of a pair of groups $\mathbb{G}$ and $\mathbb{G}_T$ of prime order p with a map $\mathbf{e} : \mathbb{G} \times \mathbb{G} \rightarrow \mathbb{G}_T$ satisfying:

1. Bilinearity: for all $a, b \in \mathbf{Z}$, $e(g^a, g^b) = e(g, g)^{ab}$ for any $g \in \mathbb{G}$.
2. Non-degeneracy: $e(g, g) \neq 1_{\mathbb{G}_T}$ for any $g \in \mathbb{G}$.
3. Efficiency: there exists an efficient algorithm to compute the map.

Definition 2 (NIWI). *A non-interactive witness indistinguishable proof system (NIWI) is a pair of PPT algorithms $\langle \mathcal{P}, \mathcal{V} \rangle$ for a NP-relation R_L satisfying the following properties:*

1. *Completeness: for all $(x, w) \in R_L$, $\Pr[\, \mathcal{V}(x, \pi) = 1 \mid \pi \longleftarrow \mathcal{P}(x, w)\,] = 1$.*
2. *Perfect soundness: for every $x \notin L$ and $\pi \in \{0,1\}^*$, $\Pr[\, \mathcal{V}(x, \pi) = 1\,] = 0$.*
3. *Witness indistinguishability: for any sequence $\{(x_n, w_{1,n}, w_{2,n})\}_{n \in \mathbb{N}}$, which $x_n \in \{0,1\}^n, w_{1,n}, w_{2,n} \in R_L(x_n)$, the following holds:* $n \in \mathbb{N} : \{\pi_{1,n} |\ \pi_{1,n} \leftarrow \mathcal{P}(x_n, w_{1,n})\}_n \approx_c \{\pi_{2,n} |\ \pi_{2,n} \leftarrow \mathcal{P}(x_n, w_{2,n})\}_n$.

*Groth and Sahai (GS) [14] provide NIWI systems for the satisfiability of what they call "**Pairing Products Equations**" that can be used to instantiate the relations needed in our VIPE construction (cf. Construction 7). Using the techniques of [13], such proofs may be made perfectly sound.*

IPE Scheme: For any $n > 0$, let Σ_n be a set of vectors of length n defined over some field and let $\mathcal{M}$ be a message space. For any vector $\boldsymbol{v} \in \Sigma_n$, the function $f_{\boldsymbol{v}} : \Sigma_n \times \mathcal{M} \rightarrow \mathcal{M} \cup \{\perp\}$ is

$$f_{\boldsymbol{v}}(\boldsymbol{x}, m) = \begin{cases} m \text{ If } \langle \boldsymbol{x}, \boldsymbol{v} \rangle = 0 \\ \perp \text{ If } \langle \boldsymbol{x}, \boldsymbol{v} \rangle \neq 0 \end{cases} .$$

Both $\mathcal{M}$, n and the field size can depend on the security parameter λ but for simplicity hereafter we will skip this detail. IPE can be seen as a FE scheme for the previous functionality. More concretely, an IPE scheme is defined as follows.

Definition 3 (IPE Scheme). *An IPE scheme* IP *for a message space* $\mathcal{M}$ *and for a family of sets* $\Sigma = \{\Sigma_n\}_{n>0}$ *consisting of sets of vectors of length* n *over some field is a tuple of four PPT algorithms* $\mathsf{IP} = \{\mathsf{IP.SetUp}, \mathsf{IP.TokGen}, \mathsf{IP.Enc}, \mathsf{IP.Dec}\}$ *with the following syntax and satisfying the correctness property below.*

- $\mathsf{IP.SetUp}(1^\lambda, n) \longrightarrow (\mathsf{MPK}, \mathsf{MSK})$*: the setup algorithm, on input the security parameter* λ *and the vector length* n*, generates master public key* MPK *and master secret key* MSK *for that parameter.*
- $\mathsf{IP.TokGen}(\mathsf{MPK}, \mathsf{MSK}, \boldsymbol{v}) \longrightarrow \mathsf{Tok}_{\boldsymbol{v}}$*: on input master keys and vector* $\boldsymbol{v} \in \Sigma_n$*, the token generation algorithm generates the token* $\mathsf{Tok}_{\boldsymbol{v}}$*.*
- $\mathsf{IP.Enc}(\mathsf{MPK}, \overrightarrow{x}, m) \longrightarrow \mathsf{CT}$*: the encryption algorithm encrypts message* $m \in \mathcal{M}$ *and vector* $\boldsymbol{x} \in \Sigma_n$ *under the master public key.*
- $\mathsf{IP.Dec}(\mathsf{MPK}, \mathsf{Tok}_{\boldsymbol{v}}, \mathsf{CT}) \longrightarrow m' \in \mathcal{M} \cup \{\perp\}$.
- Perfect correctness: IP *is perfectly correct if for all* $\lambda, n > 0, \boldsymbol{x}, \boldsymbol{v} \in \Sigma_n$ *and all* $m \in \mathcal{M}$ *the following holds:*

$$\Pr\left[\begin{array}{l} \mathsf{IP.Dec}(\mathsf{MPK}, \mathsf{Tok}_{\boldsymbol{v}}, \mathsf{CT}) \\ = f_{\boldsymbol{v}}(\boldsymbol{x}, m) \end{array} \middle| \begin{array}{l} (\mathsf{MPK}, \mathsf{MSK}) \longleftarrow \mathsf{IP.SetUp}(1^\lambda, n), \\ \mathsf{Tok}_{\boldsymbol{v}} \longleftarrow \mathsf{IP.TokGen}(\mathsf{MPK}, \mathsf{MSK}, \boldsymbol{v}), \\ \mathsf{CT} \longleftarrow \mathsf{IP.Enc}(\mathsf{MPK}, \boldsymbol{x}, m) \end{array}\right] = 1$$

Security. To model security we adopt the indistinguishability-based (IND) notion of security [8], in particular selective security [4]. Boneh, Sahai, and Waters [7] showed deficiencies of this notion *in general* and impossibility results for the more general notion of simulation-based security; see also [7,10,11,15] for general techniques to overcome the known impossibility results in different settings. Nonetheless, to our knowledge no practical attacks are known for natural schemes. Selective security is sufficient for CCA-security [4] and for our application of verifiable polynomial commitments of Sect. 1.1.

The selectively indistinguishability-based notion of security for an IPE scheme over the vector space Σ and message space $\mathcal{M}$ is formalized by means of the game $\mathsf{IND}^{\mathcal{A},\mathcal{C},\lambda,n}$ in Fig. 1, between an adversary $\mathcal{A}$ and a challenger $\mathcal{C}$ (defined in the game) parameterized by security parameter λ and dimension n. The advantage of $\mathcal{A}$ in this game is $\mathsf{Adv}_{\mathsf{IP},\lambda,n}(\mathcal{A}) = \left|\Pr\left[\mathsf{IND}^{\mathcal{A},\mathsf{IP},\lambda,n} = 1\right] - \frac{1}{2}\right|$.

Definition 4. *An IPE scheme* IP *is selectively-indistinguishable secure (*IND*-Secure) if for all* $n > 0$ *and all PPT adversaries* $\mathcal{A}$*,* $\mathsf{Adv}_{\mathsf{IP},\lambda,n}(\mathcal{A})$ *is a negligible function of* λ*.*

- **Selective Challenge Phase.** $\mathcal{A}(1^\lambda, n) \longrightarrow \boldsymbol{x}_0, \boldsymbol{x}_1 \in \Sigma_n$. Then $\mathcal{A}$ sends these two vectors to the challenger.
- **Setup Phase.** The challenger $\mathcal{C}$ generates the pair $(\mathsf{MSK}, \mathsf{MPK})$ by invoking the setup algorithm on input $(1^\lambda, n)$. Then $\mathcal{C}$ sends MPK to $\mathcal{A}$.
- **Query Phase 1.** $\mathcal{A}$ asks for the token for a vector $\boldsymbol{v_i} \in \Sigma_n$.
- **Challenge Phase.** $\mathcal{A}$ sends to the challenger two messages $m_0, m_1 \in \mathcal{M}$ of the same length.
- $\mathcal{C}$ flips a coin to generate random bit b and send $\mathsf{CT} = \mathsf{Enc}(\mathsf{MPK}, \boldsymbol{x}_b, m_b)$.
- **Query Phase 2.** Query Phase 2: same as Query Phase 1.
- **Output Phase.** $\mathcal{A}$ outputs a bit b'.
- **Winning Condition.** $\mathcal{A}$ wins the game if $b' = b$ and the following condition is met. It is required that if $m_0 \neq m_1$, $\langle \boldsymbol{x}_0, \boldsymbol{v}_i \rangle, \langle \boldsymbol{x}_1, \boldsymbol{v}_i \rangle \neq 0$ for all the vectors $\boldsymbol{v}_i$ queried in both query phase 1 and 2, or $\langle \boldsymbol{v}_i, \boldsymbol{x}_0 \rangle = 0$ iff $\langle \boldsymbol{v}_i, \boldsymbol{x}_1 \rangle = 0$ otherwise. If the winning condition is satisfied the output of the game is 1 or 0 otherwise.

Fig. 1. Security Game $\mathsf{IND}^{\mathcal{A},\mathsf{IP},\lambda,n}$

2.2 Hardness Assumptions

We conjecture that the following problems hold relative to some bilinear group generator $\mathsf{GroupGen}(1^\lambda) \rightarrow (p, \mathbb{G}, \mathbb{G}_T, e)$ that takes security parameter λ as input and outputs λ-bit prime p, the descriptions of two groups $\mathbb{G}$ and $\mathbb{G}_T$ of order p and a bilinear map $e : \mathbb{G} \times \mathbb{G} \rightarrow \mathbb{G}_T$.

Assumption 1. *The Decisional Bilinear Diffie-Hellman assumption (DBDH) in bilinear groups $(p, \mathbb{G}, \mathbb{G}_T, e)$ states the hardness for PPT adversaries of solving the following problem. On input $(g, g^\alpha, g^\beta, g^\gamma, Z) \in \mathbb{G}^4 \times \mathbb{G}_T$, decide whether $Z = e(g, g^{\alpha\beta\gamma})$ or Z is a random element in $\mathbb{G}_T$.*

Assumption 2. *The Decisional Linear assumption (DLin) in a bilinear group $(p, \mathbb{G}, \mathbb{G}_T, e)$ states the hardness for PPT adversaries of solving the following problem. On input $(g, g^\alpha, g^\beta, g^{\alpha\tau}, g^{\beta\eta}, Z) \in \mathbb{G}^6$, decide whether $Z = g^{\eta+\tau}$ or a random element in $\mathbb{G}$.*

In this paper we use the following equivalent formulation of DLin given in [22]: on input $(g, g^\alpha, g^\beta, g^\tau, g^{\alpha\eta}, Z) \in \mathbb{G}^6$ decide whether $Z = g^{\beta(\eta+\tau)}$ or a random element.

Note that DLin is stronger than DBDH. In the rest of this paper we assume the existence of a bilinear group generator $\mathsf{GroupGen}$ such that DLin (and thus DBDH) holds relative to it.

3 Our Perfectly Correct Inner-Product Encryption

In this section we construct our perfectly correct IPE, the key ingredient for building verifiable inner-product encryption (see Sect. 4).

Let $\mathsf{GroupGen}(1^\lambda) \longrightarrow (p, \mathbb{G}, \mathbb{G}_T, e)$ be a bilinear group generator, and $n \in \mathbb{N}$ be the vector length. We construct a perfectly correct IPE scheme $\mathsf{IP} = \langle \mathsf{IP.SetUp}, \mathsf{IP.Enc}, \mathsf{IP.TokGen}, \mathsf{IP.Dec} \rangle$ for the set $\mathbb{Z}_p^n$ of vectors of length n over $\mathbb{Z}_p$ and for message space $\mathcal{M} = \mathbb{G}_T$.

Construction 1 [Our perfectly correct IPE scheme IP]

- $\mathsf{IP.SetUp}(1^\lambda, n) \longrightarrow (\mathsf{MSK}, \mathsf{MPK})$:
  For security parameter λ, $i \in [n]$ and $b \in [2]$, compute what follows:
  1. Run $\mathsf{GroupGen}(1^\lambda)$ (cf. Sect. 2.2) to generate a tuple $\langle p, \mathbb{G}, \mathbb{G}_T, e \rangle$.
  2. Pick $g, g' \leftarrow \mathbb{G}$ and $\delta_1, \theta_1, \delta_2, \theta_2, w_{1,i}, t_{1,i}, f_{b,i}, h_{b,i}, k \leftarrow \mathbb{Z}_p^*$.
  3. Pick $\Omega \leftarrow \mathbb{Z}_p$ and compute $\{w_{2,i}, t_{2,i}\}_{i \in [n]}$ such that:
  $$\Omega = \delta_1 w_{2,i} - \delta_2 w_{1,i} = \theta_1 t_{2,i} - \theta_2 t_{1,i}.$$
  4. For $i \in [n], b[2]$ set:
  $$W_{b,i} = g^{w_{b,i}}, \quad F_{b,i} = g^{f_{b,i}}, \quad K_1 = g^k, \quad U_b = g^{\delta_b}, \quad h = g^{\Omega},$$
  $$T_{b,i} = g^{t_{b,i}}, \quad H_{b,i} = g^{h_{b,i}}, \quad K_2 = g'^{\frac{1}{k}}, \quad V_b = g^{\theta_b}, \quad \Lambda = \mathbf{e}(g, g').$$
  5. Set:
  $$\begin{aligned} \mathsf{MPK} =& [(p, \mathbb{G}, \mathbb{G}_t, e), (g, h, \{W_{b,i}, F_{b,i}, T_{b,i}, H_{b,i}, U_b, V_b\}_{b \in [2], i \in [n]}, \\ & K_1, K_2, \Lambda) \in \mathbb{G}^{8n+8} \times \mathbb{G}_T], \\ \mathsf{MSK} =& (\{w_{b,i}, f_{b,i}, t_{b,i}, h_{b,i}, \delta_b, \theta_b\}_{b \in [2], i \in [n]}, g') \in \mathbb{Z}_p^{8n+4} \times \mathbb{G}. \end{aligned}$$
  6. Return $(\mathsf{MPK}, \mathsf{MSK})$.
- $\mathsf{IP.Enc}(\mathsf{MPK}, \boldsymbol{x}, m) \longrightarrow \mathsf{CT}$:
  1. For $\boldsymbol{x} = (x_1, \ldots, x_n) \in \mathbb{Z}_p^n$ and a message $m \in \mathbb{G}_T$, pick random elements $s_1, \ldots s_4, s'_1, \ldots, s'_3 \leftarrow \mathbb{Z}_p^*$ such that $s_3 \neq s'_3$ and compute what follows:
  $$\begin{aligned} & \mathsf{ct}_1 = g^{s_2}, \ \mathsf{ct}_2 = h^{s_1}, \\ & \left\{ \begin{matrix} \mathsf{ct}_{3,i} = W_{1,i}^{s_1} \cdot F_{1,i}^{s_2} \cdot U_1^{x_i s_3}, & \mathsf{ct}_{4,i} = W_{2,i}^{s_1} \cdot F_{2,i}^{s_2} \cdot U_2^{x_i s_3} \\ \mathsf{ct}_{5,i} = T_{1,i}^{s_1} \cdot H_{1,i}^{s_2} \cdot V_1^{x_i s_4}, & \mathsf{ct}_{6,i} = T_{2,i}^{s_1} \cdot H_{2,i}^{s_2} \cdot V_2^{x_i s_4} \end{matrix} \right\}_{i \in [n]}, \\ & \mathsf{ct}_7 = \mathbf{e}(g^{s_3}, g^{s_4}), \ \mathsf{ct}_8 = \Lambda^{-s_2} \cdot m. \\ & \mathsf{ct}'_1 = g^{s'_2}, \ \mathsf{ct}'_2 = h^{s'_1}, \\ & \left\{ \begin{matrix} \mathsf{ct}'_{3,i} = W_{1,i}^{s'_1} \cdot F_{1,i}^{s'_2} \cdot U_1^{x_i s'_3}, & \mathsf{ct}'_{4,i} = W_{2,i}^{s'_1} \cdot F_{2,i}^{s'_2} \cdot U_2^{x_i s'_3} \\ \mathsf{ct}'_{5,i} = T_{1,i}^{s'_1} \cdot H_{1,i}^{s'_2} \cdot V_1^{x_i s_4}, & \mathsf{ct}'_{6,i} = T_{2,i}^{s'_1} \cdot H_{2,i}^{s'_2} \cdot V_2^{x_i s_4} \end{matrix} \right\}_{i \in [n]}, \\ & \mathsf{ct}'_7 = \mathbf{e}(g^{s'_3}, g^{s_4}), \ \mathsf{ct}'_8 = \Lambda^{-s'_2} \cdot m. \end{aligned}$$
  2. Set:
  $$\mathsf{ct} = \left(\mathsf{ct}_1, \mathsf{ct}_2, \left\{ \begin{matrix} \mathsf{ct}_{3,i}, \mathsf{ct}_{4,i} \\ \mathsf{ct}_{5,i}, \mathsf{ct}_{6,i} \end{matrix} \right\}, \mathsf{ct}_7, \mathsf{ct}_8\right),$$
  $$\mathsf{ct}' = \left(\mathsf{ct}'_1, \mathsf{ct}'_2, \left\{ \begin{matrix} \mathsf{ct}'_{3,i}, \mathsf{ct}'_{4,i} \\ \mathsf{ct}'_{5,i}, \mathsf{ct}'_{6,i} \end{matrix} \right\}, \mathsf{ct}'_7, \mathsf{ct}'_8\right).$$

3. Output $\mathsf{CT} = (\mathsf{ct}, \mathsf{ct}')$.

- $\mathsf{IP.TokGen}(\mathsf{MSK}, \boldsymbol{v}) \longrightarrow \mathsf{Tok}_{\boldsymbol{v}}$:
  1. Pick $\lambda_1, \lambda_2 \leftarrow \mathbb{Z}_p^*$ and for any $i \in [n]$ pick $\{r_i\}$, $\{\Phi_i\} \leftarrow \mathbb{Z}_p^*$.
  2. Set $\mathsf{Tok}_{\boldsymbol{v}} = (K_A, K_B, \left\{\begin{matrix} K_{3,i}\ ,\ K_{4,i} \\ K_{5,i}\ ,\ K_{6,i} \end{matrix}\right\}_{i\in[n]})$ as follows and return $\mathsf{Tok}_{\boldsymbol{v}}$.

$$K_A = g' \cdot \prod_{i=1}^{n} K_{3,i}^{-f_{1,i}} \cdot K_{4,i}^{-f_{2,i}} \cdot K_{5,i}^{-h_{1,i}} \cdot K_{6,i}^{-h_{2,i}}, \qquad K_B = \prod_{i=1}^{n} g^{-(r_i+\Phi_i)}.$$
$$K_{3,i} = g^{-\delta_2 r_i} \cdot g^{\lambda_1 v_i w_{2,i}}, \qquad K_{4,i} = g^{\delta_1 r_i} \cdot g^{-\lambda_1 v_i w_{1,i}}.$$
$$K_{5,i} = g^{-\theta_2 \Phi_i} \cdot g^{\lambda_2 v_i t_{2,i}}, \qquad K_{6,i} = g^{\theta 1 \Phi_i} \cdot g^{-\lambda_2 v_i t_{1,i}}.$$

- $\mathsf{IP.Dec}(\mathsf{CT}, \mathsf{Tok}_{\boldsymbol{v}})$:
  Let $\mathsf{CT} = (\mathsf{ct}, \mathsf{ct}')$, such that $\mathsf{ct} = (\mathsf{ct}_1, \mathsf{ct}_2, \{\mathsf{ct}_{3,i}, \mathsf{ct}_{4,i}, \mathsf{ct}_{5,i}, \mathsf{ct}_{6,i}\}, \mathsf{ct}_7, \mathsf{ct}_8)$, $\mathsf{ct}' = (\mathsf{ct}'_1, \mathsf{ct}'_2, \{\mathsf{ct}'_{3,i}, \mathsf{ct}'_{4,i}, \mathsf{ct}'_{5,i}, \mathsf{ct}'_{6,i}\}, \mathsf{ct}_7, \mathsf{ct}_8)$
  1. If $\mathsf{ct}_7 = \mathsf{ct}'_7$ output $\perp$ and stop, otherwise go to the next step.
  2. Compute:

$$\begin{aligned} \Upsilon =& \mathsf{ct}_8 \cdot \mathbf{e}(\mathsf{ct}_1, K_A) \cdot \mathbf{e}(\mathsf{ct}_2, K_B) \cdot \\ & \prod_{i=1}^{n} \mathbf{e}(\mathsf{ct}_{3,i}, K_{3,i}) \cdot \mathbf{e}(\mathsf{ct}_{4,i}, K_{4,i}) \cdot \mathbf{e}(\mathsf{ct}_{5,i}, K_{5,i}) \cdot \mathbf{e}(\mathsf{ct}_{6,i}, K_{6,i}). \\ \Upsilon' =& \mathsf{ct}'_8 \cdot \mathbf{e}(\mathsf{ct}'_1, K_A) \cdot \mathbf{e}(\mathsf{ct}'_2, K_B) \cdot \\ & \prod_{i=1}^{n} \mathbf{e}(\mathsf{ct}'_{3,i}, K_{3,i}) \cdot \mathbf{e}(\mathsf{ct}'_{4,i}, K_{4,i}) \cdot \mathbf{e}(\mathsf{ct}'_{5,i}, K_{5,i}) \cdot \mathbf{e}(\mathsf{ct}'_{6,i}, K_{6,i}). \end{aligned}$$

  3. If $\Upsilon = \Upsilon'$ output Υ otherwise output $\perp$.

Perfect Correctness: We now show that an honestly generated ciphertext decrypts correctly with probability 1. Since $F_{1,i}^{-s_2} \cdot \mathsf{ct}_{3,i} = W_{1,i}^{s_1} \cdot U_1^{s_3 x_i}$, we get

$$\mathbf{e}(F_{1,i}^{-s_2} \cdot \mathsf{ct}_{3,i}, K_{3,i}) = \mathbf{e}(g,g)^{s_1\lambda_1 v_i w_{1,i} w_{2,i} - s_3 x_i \delta_1 \delta_2} \cdot \mathbf{e}(g,g)^{-s_1 r_i \delta_2 w_{1,i} + s_3 \lambda_1 v_i \delta_1 w_{2,i}}$$

$$\mathbf{e}(F_{2,i}^{-s_2} \cdot \mathsf{ct}_{4,i}, K_{4,i}) = \mathbf{e}(g,g)^{-s_1\lambda_1 v_i w_{1,i} w_{2,i} + s_3 x_i \delta_1 \delta_2} \cdot \mathbf{e}(g,g)^{s_1 r_i \delta_1 w_{2,i} - s_3 \lambda_1 v_i \delta_2 w_{1,i}}$$

We then get

$$\begin{aligned} &\mathbf{e}(F_{1,i}^{-s_2} \cdot \mathsf{ct}_{3,i}, K_{3,i}) \cdot \mathbf{e}(F_{2,i}^{-s_2} \cdot \mathsf{ct}_{4,i}, K_{4,i}) = \\ &\qquad \Big(\mathbf{e}(g^{s_1}, g^{r_i}) \cdot \mathbf{e}(g^{x_i s_3}, g^{\lambda_1 v_i})\Big)^{\delta_1 w_{2,i} - \delta_2 w_{1,i}} = \\ &\qquad \mathbf{e}(h^{s_1}, g^{r_i}) \cdot \mathbf{e}(h^{s_3 \lambda_1}, g^{x_i v_i}) = \mathbf{e}(\mathsf{ct}_2, g^{r_i}) \cdot \mathbf{e}(h^{\lambda_1 s_3}, g^{x_i v_i}) \end{aligned}$$

The same computation gives us

$$\mathbf{e}(H_{1,i}^{-s_2} \cdot \mathsf{ct}_{5,i}, K_{5,i}) \cdot \mathbf{e}(H_{2,i}^{-s_2} \cdot \mathsf{ct}_{6,i}, K_{6,i}) = \mathbf{e}(\mathsf{ct}_2, g^{\Phi_i}) \cdot \mathbf{e}(h^{\lambda_2 s_4}, g^{x_i v_i})$$

As a conclusion we have the following:

$$\mathbf{e}(\mathsf{ct}_1, K_A) \cdot \prod_{i=1}^{n} \mathbf{e}(\mathsf{ct}_{3,i}, K_{3,i}) \cdot \mathbf{e}(\mathsf{ct}_{4,i}, K_{4,i}) \cdot \mathbf{e}(\mathsf{ct}_{5,i}, K_{5,i}) \cdot \mathbf{e}(\mathsf{ct}_{6,i}, K_{6,i}) =$$
$$= \Lambda^{s_2} \prod_{i=1}^{n} \mathbf{e}(F_{1,i}^{-s_2}, K_{3,i})\mathbf{e}(F_{1,i}^{-s_2}, K_{4,i}) \cdot \mathbf{e}(H_{1,i}^{-s_2}, K_{5,i}) \cdot \mathbf{e}(H_{1,i}^{-s_2}, K_{6,i}) =$$
$$= \Lambda^{s_2} \cdot \mathbf{e}(\mathsf{ct}_2, K_B^{-1}) \cdot \mathbf{e}(h,g)^{(\lambda_1 s_3 + \lambda_2 s_4)\langle \boldsymbol{x}, \boldsymbol{v} \rangle}$$

Plugging this into the decryption algorithm we get

$$\Upsilon = m \cdot \mathbf{e}(h,g)^{(\lambda_1 s_3 + \lambda_2 s_4)\langle \boldsymbol{x}, \boldsymbol{v} \rangle}, \; \Upsilon' = m \cdot \mathbf{e}(h,g)^{(\lambda_1 s_3' + s_4 \lambda_2)\langle \boldsymbol{x}, \boldsymbol{v} \rangle}$$

First note that it cannot happen that $\mathsf{ct}_7 \neq \mathsf{ct}_7'$ for honestly generated ciphertexts. Clearly, $\langle \boldsymbol{x}, \boldsymbol{v} \rangle = 0 \Rightarrow (\Upsilon = \Upsilon' = m)$. All we need to check is thus that if $\langle \boldsymbol{x}, \boldsymbol{v} \rangle \neq 0$, we get output $\perp$. We could only get a wrong output if it happens that $\Upsilon = \Upsilon'$, but this is impossible since it implies (using $\lambda_1 \neq 0, s_3 \neq s_3'$)

$$\mathbf{e}(h,g)^{(\lambda_1 s_3 - \lambda_1 s_3')\langle \boldsymbol{x}, \boldsymbol{v} \rangle} = 1_{\mathbb{G}_T} \Rightarrow \lambda_1(s_3 - s_3')\langle \boldsymbol{x}, \boldsymbol{v} \rangle \equiv_p 0 \;\Rightarrow \langle \boldsymbol{x}, \boldsymbol{v} \rangle \equiv_p 0.$$

3.1 Security Reduction to DLin and DBDH

In this section we prove our IPE scheme is IND-Secure under the standard computational assumptions.

Theorem 1. *The IPE scheme* IP *of Construction 1 is* IND*-Secure if the DBDH and DLin assumptions hold relative to* GroupGen.

To prove the theorem we define a series of hybrid experiments $\mathsf{H}_0, \ldots, \mathsf{H}_{12}$ in which H_0 corresponds to the real experiment with challenge bit $b = 0$ and H_{12} corresponds to the real experiment with challenge bit $b = 1$, and we show that they are computationally indistinguishable. We provide the full proof of Theorem 1 in the full version of this paper [25].

- **Hybrid** H_0: this hybrid is identical to the real game with challenge bit $b = 0$. Precisely, the ciphertext is computed for message m_0 and vector $\boldsymbol{x}$ as follows:

$$\mathsf{ct} = (g^{s_2}, h^{s_1}, \{W_{b,i}^{s_1} \cdot F_{b,i}^{s_2} \cdot U_b^{x_i s_3}, T_{b,i}^{s_1} \cdot H_{b,i}^{s_2} \cdot V_b^{x_i s_4}\}_{b \in [2], i \in [n]}, \mathbf{e}(g^{s_3}, g^{s_4}), \Lambda^{-s_2} \cdot m_0)$$
$$\mathsf{ct}' = (g^{s_2'}, h^{s_1'}, \{W_{b,i}^{s_1'} \cdot F_{b,i}^{s_2'} \cdot U_b^{x_i s_3'}, T_{b,i}^{s_1'} \cdot H_{b,i}^{s_2'} \cdot V_b^{x_i s_4}\}_{b \in [2], i \in [n]}, \mathbf{e}(g^{s_3'}, g^{s_4}), \Lambda^{-s_2'} \cdot m_0)$$

- **Hybrid** H_1: this hybrid is identical to the previous hybrid except that instead of $\mathbf{e}(g,g)^{s_3 s_4}, \mathbf{e}(g,g)^{s'_3 s_4}$, the ciphertext contains two random elements $R_1, R'_1 \leftarrow \mathbb{G}_T$. Precisely, the ciphertext is computed as follows:

$$\begin{aligned}\mathsf{ct} =& (g^{s_2}, h^{s_1}\{W_{b,i}^{s_1} \cdot F_{b,i}^{s_2} \cdot U_b^{x_i s_3}, T_{b,i}^{s_1} \cdot H_{b,i}^{s_2} \cdot V_b^{x_i s_4}\}_{b\in[2],i\in[n]}, \boxed{R_1}, \\ & \Lambda^{-s_2} \cdot m_0) \\ \mathsf{ct}' =& (g^{s'_2}, h^{s'_1}, \{W_{b,i}^{s'_1} \cdot F_{b,i}^{s'_2} \cdot U_b^{x_i s'_3}, T_{b,i}^{s'_1} \cdot H_{b,i}^{s'_2} \cdot V_b^{x_i s_4}\}_{b\in[2],i\in[n]}, \boxed{R'_1}, \\ & \Lambda^{-s'_2} \cdot m_0)\end{aligned}$$

- **Hybrid** H_2: this hybrid is identical to the previous hybrid except that instead of $\Lambda^{-s_2} \cdot m_0, \Lambda^{-s'_2} \cdot m_0$, the ciphertext contains two random elements $R, R' \leftarrow \mathbb{G}_T$. Precisely, the ciphertext is computed as follows:

$$\mathsf{ct} = (g^{s_2}, h^{s_1}, \{W_{b,i}^{s_1} \cdot F_{b,i}^{s_2} \cdot U_b^{x_i s_3}, T_{b,i}^{s_1} \cdot H_{b,i}^{s_2} \cdot V_b^{x_i s_4}\}_{b\in[2],i\in[n]}, R_1, \boxed{R})$$
$$\mathsf{ct}' = (g^{s'_2}, h^{s'_1}, \{W_{b,i}^{s'_1} \cdot F_{b,i}^{s'_2} \cdot U_b^{x_i s'_3}, T_{b,i}^{s'_1} \cdot H_{b,i}^{s'_2} \cdot V_b^{x_i s_4}\}_{b\in[2],i\in[n]}, R'_1, \boxed{R'})$$

- **Hybrid** H_3: this hybrid is identical to the previous hybrid except that instead of $T_{b,i}^{s_1} \cdot H_{b,i}^{s_2} \cdot V_b^{x_i s_4}, T_{b,i}^{s'_1} \cdot H_{b,i}^{s'_2} \cdot V_b^{x_i s_4}$, the ciphertext contains $T_{b,i}^{s_1} \cdot H_{b,i}^{s_2}, T_{b,i}^{s'_1} \cdot H_{b,i}^{s'_2}$. Precisely, the ciphertext is computed as follows:

$$\mathsf{ct} = (g^{s_2}, h^{s_1}, \{W_{b,i}^{s_1} \cdot F_{b,i}^{s_2} \cdot U_b^{x_i s_3}, \boxed{T_{b,i}^{s_1} \cdot H_{b,i}^{s_2}}\}_{b\in[2],i\in[n]}, R_1, R)$$
$$\mathsf{ct}' = (g^{s'_2}, h^{s'_1}, \{W_{b,i}^{s'_1} \cdot F_{b,i}^{s'_2} \cdot U_b^{x_i s'_3}, \boxed{T_{b,i}^{s'_1} \cdot H_{b,i}^{s'_2}}\}_{b\in[2],i\in[n]}, R'_1, R')$$

- **Hybrid** H_4: this hybrid is identical to the previous hybrid except that instead of $T_{b,i}^{s_1} \cdot H_{b,i}^{s_2}, T_{b,i}^{s'_1} \cdot H_{b,i}^{s'_2}$, the ciphertext contains $T_{b,i}^{s_1} \cdot H_{b,i}^{s_2} \cdot V_b^{y_i s_4}, T_{b,i}^{s'_1} \cdot H_{b,i}^{s'_2} \cdot V_b^{y_i s_4}$. Precisely, the ciphertext is computed as follows:

$$\mathsf{ct} = (g^{s_2}, h^{s_1}, \{W_{b,i}^{s_1} \cdot F_{b,i}^{s_2} \cdot U_b^{x_i s_3}, \boxed{T_{b,i}^{s_1} \cdot H_{b,i}^{s_2} \cdot V_b^{y_i s_4}}\}_{b\in[2],i\in[n]}, R_1, R)$$
$$\mathsf{ct}' = (g^{s'_2}, h^{s'_1}, \{W_{b,i}^{s'_1} \cdot F_{b,i}^{s'_2} \cdot U_b^{x_i s'_3}, \boxed{T_{b,i}^{s'_1} \cdot H_{b,i}^{s'_2} \cdot V_b^{y_i s_4}}\}_{b\in[2],i\in[n]}, R'_1, R')$$

- **Hybrid** H_5: $\mathsf{CT}_6 = (\mathsf{ct}, \mathsf{ct}')$, This hybrid is identical to the previous hybrid except that the power of V_b in ct is s_4 and its power in ct' is s'_4. Precisely, the ciphertext is computed as follows:

$$\mathsf{ct} = (g^{s_2}, h^{s_1}, \{W_{b,i}^{s_1} \cdot F_{b,i}^{s_2} \cdot U_b^{x_i s_3}, T_{b,i}^{s_1} \cdot H_{b,i}^{s_2} \cdot V_b^{y_i s_4}\}_{b\in[2],i\in[n]}, R_1, R)$$
$$\mathsf{ct}' = (g^{s'_2}, h^{s'_1}, \{W_{b,i}^{s'_1} \cdot F_{b,i}^{s'_2} \cdot U_b^{x_i s'_3}, \boxed{T_{b,i}^{s'_1} \cdot H_{b,i}^{s'_2} \cdot V_b^{y_i s'_4}}\}_{b\in[2],i\in[n]}, R'_1, R')$$

- **Hybrid** H_6: this hybrid is identical to the previous hybrid except that $s_3 = s'_3$. Precisely:

$$\mathsf{ct} = (g^{s_2}, h^{s_1}, \{W_{b,i}^{s_1} \cdot F_{b,i}^{s_2} \cdot U_b^{x_i s_3}, T_{b,i}^{s_1} \cdot H_{b,i}^{s_2} \cdot V_b^{y_i s_4}\}_{b\in[2],i\in[n]}, R_1, R)$$
$$\mathsf{ct}' = (g^{s'_2}, h^{s'_1}, \{\boxed{W_{b,i}^{s'_1} \cdot F_{b,i}^{s'_2} \cdot U_b^{x_i s_3}}, T_{b,i}^{s'_1} \cdot H_{b,i}^{s'_2} \cdot V_b^{y_i s'_4}\}_{b\in[2],i\in[n]}, R'_1, R')$$

- **Hybrid** H_7: This hybrid is identical to the previous hybrid except we replace s_3 with 0.

$$\mathsf{ct} = (g^{s_2}, h^{s_1}, \{ W_{b,i}^{s_1} \cdot F_{b,i}^{s_2}, T_{b,i}^{s_1} \cdot H_{b,i}^{s_2} \cdot V_b^{y_i s_4} \}_{b\in[2], i\in[n]}, R_1, R)$$

$$\mathsf{ct}' = (g^{s_2'}, h^{s_1'}, \{ W_{b,i}^{s_1'} \cdot F_{b,i}^{s_2'}, T_{b,i}^{s_1'} \cdot H_{b,i}^{s_2'} \cdot V_b^{y_i s_4'} \}_{b\in[2], i\in[n]}, R_1', R')$$

- **Hybrid** H_8: This hybrid is identical to the previous hybrid except that instead of $W_{b,i}^{s_1} \cdot F_{b,i}^{s_2}, W_{b,i}^{s_1'} \cdot F_{b,i}^{s_2'}$, we set $W_{b,i}^{s_1} \cdot F_{b,i}^{s_2} \cdot U_b^{y_i s_3}, W_{b,i}^{s_1'} \cdot F_{b,i}^{s_2'} \cdot U_b^{y_i s_3}$. Precisely:

$$\mathsf{ct} = (g^{s_2}, h^{s_1}, \{ W_{b,i}^{s_1} \cdot F_{b,i}^{s_2} \cdot U_b^{y_i s_3}, T_{b,i}^{s_1} \cdot H_{b,i}^{s_2} \cdot V_b^{y_i s_4} \}_{b\in[2], i\in[n]}, R_1, R)$$

$$\mathsf{ct}' = (g^{s_2'}, h^{s_1'}, \{ W_{b,i}^{s_1'} \cdot F_{b,i}^{s_2'} \cdot U_b^{y_i s_3}, T_{b,i}^{s_1'} \cdot H_{b,i}^{s_2'} \cdot V_b^{y_i s_4'} \}_{b\in[2], i\in[n]}, R_1', R')$$

- **Hybrid** H_9: this hybrid is identical to the previous hybrid except that instead of $W_{b,i}^{s_1} \cdot F_{b,i}^{s_2}, W_{b,i}^{s_1'} \cdot F_{b,i}^{s_2'}$, we set $W_{b,i}^{s_1} \cdot F_{b,i}^{s_2} \cdot U_b^{y_i s_3}, W_{b,i}^{s_1'} \cdot F_{b,i}^{s_2'} \cdot U_b^{y_i s_3'}$. Precisely:

$$\mathsf{ct} = (g^{s_2}, h^{s_1}, \{W_{b,i}^{s_1} \cdot F_{b,i}^{s_2} \cdot U_b^{y_i s_3}, T_{b,i}^{s_1} \cdot H_{b,i}^{s_2} \cdot V_b^{y_i s_4} \}_{b\in[2], i\in[n]}, R_1, R)$$

$$\mathsf{ct}' = (g^{s_2'}, h^{s_1'}, \{ W_{b,i}^{s_1'} \cdot F_{b,i}^{s_2'} \cdot U_b^{y_i s_3'}, T_{b,i}^{s_1'} \cdot H_{b,i}^{s_2'} \cdot V_b^{y_i s_4'} \}_{b\in[2], i\in[n]}, R_1', R')$$

- **Hybrid** H_{10}: this hybrid is identical to the previous hybrid except that instead of $W_{b,i}^{s_1} \cdot F_{b,i}^{s_2}, W_{b,i}^{s_1'} \cdot F_{b,i}^{s_2'}$, we set $W_{b,i}^{s_1} \cdot F_{b,i}^{s_2} \cdot U_b^{y_i s_3}, W_{b,i}^{s_1'} \cdot F_{b,i}^{s_2'} \cdot U_b^{y_i s_3'}$. Precisely:

$$\mathsf{ct} = (g^{s_2}, h^{s_1}, \{W_{b,i}^{s_1} \cdot F_{b,i}^{s_2} \cdot U_b^{y_i s_3}, T_{b,i}^{s_1} \cdot H_{b,i}^{s_2} \cdot V_b^{y_i s_4} \}_{b\in[2], i\in[n]}, R_1, R)$$

$$\mathsf{ct}' = (g^{s_2'}, h^{s_1'}, \{W_{b,i}^{s_1'} \cdot F_{b,i}^{s_2'} \cdot U_b^{y_i s_3'}, T_{b,i}^{s_1'} \cdot H_{b,i}^{s_2'} \cdot V_b^{y_i s_4} \}_{b\in[2], i\in[n]}, R_1', R')$$

- **Hybrid** H_{11}: this hybrid is identical to the previous hybrid except that instead of choosing $R, R' \leftarrow \mathbb{G}_T$, we set $R = \Lambda^{-s_2} \cdot m_1, R' = \Lambda^{-s_2'} \cdot m_1$. Precisely, the ciphertext is computed as follows:

$$\mathsf{ct} = (g^{s_2}, h^{s_1}, \{W_{b,i}^{s_1} \cdot F_{b,i}^{s_2} \cdot U_b^{y_i s_3}, T_{b,i}^{s_1} \cdot H_{b,i}^{s_2} \cdot V_b^{y_i s_4} \}_{b\in[2], i\in[n]}, R_1, \Lambda^{-s_2} \cdot m_1)$$

$$\mathsf{ct}' = (g^{s_2'}, h^{s_1'}, \{W_{b,i}^{s_1'} \cdot F_{b,i}^{s_2'} \cdot U_b^{y_i s_3'}, T_{b,i}^{s_1'} \cdot H_{b,i}^{s_2'} \cdot V_b^{y_i s_4} \}_{b\in[2], i\in[n]}, R_1', \Lambda^{-s_2'} \cdot m_1)$$

- **Hybrid** H_{12}: this hybrid is identical to the previous hybrid except that instead of R_1, R_1', we set $\mathbf{e}(g^{s_3}, g^{s_4}), \mathbf{e}(g^{s_3'}, g^{s_4})$, which is identical to the real game with challenge bit $b = 1$, in particular for message m_1 and vector $\boldsymbol{y}$. Precisely, the ciphertext is computed as follows:

$$\mathsf{ct} = (g^{s_2}, h^{s_1}, \{W_{b,i}^{s_1} \cdot F_{b,i}^{s_2} \cdot U_b^{y_i s_3}, T_{b,i}^{s_1} \cdot H_{b,i}^{s_2} \cdot V_b^{y_i s_4} \}_{b\in[2], i\in[n]}, \mathbf{e}(g^{s_3}, g^{s_4}), \Lambda^{-s_2} \cdot m_1)$$

$$\mathsf{ct}' = (g^{s_2'}, h^{s_1'}, \{W_{b,i}^{s_1'} \cdot F_{b,i}^{s_2'} \cdot U_b^{y_i s_3'}, T_{b,i}^{s_1'} \cdot H_{b,i}^{s_2'} \cdot V_b^{y_i s_4} \}_{b\in[2], i\in[n]}, \mathbf{e}(g^{s_3'}, g^{s_4}), \Lambda^{-s_2'} \cdot m_1)$$

Proposition 2. *If the DLin assumption holds relative to* GroupGen, *then* H_0 *is computationally indistinguishable from* H_1.

Proof. Let us assume there exists a PPT adversary $\mathcal{A}$ which distinguishes between H_0 and H_1 with non-negligible advantage. We describe a simulator $\mathcal{B}$ which uses $\mathcal{A}$, on input $(g, A = g^{\alpha}, B = g^{\beta}, C = g^{\tau}, D = g^{\alpha\eta}, Z) \in \mathbb{G}^6$, output 1 if $Z = g^{\beta(\eta+\tau)}$ and 0 if Z is a random element in $\mathbb{G}$. $\mathcal{B}$ interacts with $\mathcal{A}$ as follows:

SetUp Phase. The adversary $\mathcal{A}$ sends to the simulator, $\mathcal{B}$, two vectors $\boldsymbol{x}, \boldsymbol{y} \in \mathbb{Z}_p^n$. The simulator picks $g' \leftarrow \mathbb{G}$ and $\tilde{\Omega}, k, \tilde{\delta}_b, \theta_b, \{w_{1,i}, \tilde{t}_{1,i}, f_{b,i}, h_{b,i}\}_{i\in[n],b\in[2]} \leftarrow \mathbb{Z}_p$, compute $\{w_{2,i}, \tilde{t}_{2,i}\}_{i\in[n]}$ such that for each i, $\tilde{\Omega} = \tilde{\delta}_1 w_{2,i} - \tilde{\delta}_2 w_{1,i} = \theta_1 \tilde{t}_{2,i} - \theta_2 \tilde{t}_{1,i}$. Compute the master public key components as follows and returns it:

$$\{W_{b,i} = g^{w_{b,i}}, F_{b,i} = g^{f_{b,i}}\}_{b\in[2],i\in[n]}, \{U_b = A^{\tilde{\delta}_b}\}_{b\in[2]}, h = A^{\tilde{\Omega}}, \Lambda = \mathbf{e}(g, g').$$
$$\{T_{b,i} = A^{\tilde{t}_{b,i}}, H_{b,i} = g^{h_{b,i}}\}_{b\in[2],i\in[n]}, \{V_b = g^{\theta_b}\}_{b\in[2]}, K_1 = g^k,\ K_2 = g'^{\frac{1}{k}}.$$

By doing so, $\mathcal{B}$ implicitly sets $\delta_b = \alpha\tilde{\delta}_b, t_{b,i} = \alpha\tilde{t}_{b,i}$ for $b \in [2], i \in [n]$ and $\Omega = \alpha\tilde{\Omega}$, which shows that each element of the master public key is independently and uniformly distributed in $\mathbb{Z}_p$. Also notice that for each $i \in [n]$, we have: $\delta_1 w_{2,i} - \delta_2 w_{1,i} = \alpha\tilde{\delta}_1 w_{2,i} - \alpha\tilde{\delta}_2 w_{1,i} = \theta_1\alpha\tilde{t}_{2,i} - \theta_2\alpha\tilde{t}_{1,i} = \theta_1 t_{2,i} - \theta_2 t_{1,i} = \alpha\tilde{\Omega} = \Omega$. hence the output has the same structure as the output of the real setup algorithm.

Token Query Phase. All the secret parameters except $\{\delta_b, t_{b,i}\}_{b\in[2],i\in[n]}, \Omega$ are known by $\mathcal{B}$. When $\mathcal{A}$ asks for a query for a vector $\boldsymbol{v}$, $\mathcal{B}$ picks $\lambda_1, \tilde{\lambda}_2, \{\tilde{r}_i, \Phi_i\}_{i\in[n]} \leftarrow \mathbb{Z}_p^\star$. In generating $\mathsf{Tok}_{\boldsymbol{v}}$, the simulator implicitly sets $\lambda_2 = \alpha\tilde{\lambda}_2, r_i = \alpha\tilde{r}_i$ which are independently and uniformly distributed in $\mathbb{Z}_p^\star$. Token elements are set as follows:

$$K_{3,i} = A^{-\tilde{\delta}_2 r_i} \cdot g^{\lambda_1 v_i w_{2,i} x_i} = \text{(by the above settings)} = g^{-\delta_2 r_i} \cdot g^{v_i w_{2,i}\lambda_1}.$$
$$K_{5,i} = g^{-\theta_2\phi_i} \cdot A^{\lambda_2 v_i \tilde{t}_{2,i} x_i} = \text{(by the above settings)} = g^{-\theta_2\phi_i} \cdot g^{\lambda_2 v_i t_{2,i} x_i}.$$
$$\text{Similarly, } K_{4,i} = A^{\tilde{\delta}_1 r_i} \cdot g^{-\lambda_1 v_i w_{1,i} x_i}, K_{6,i} = g^{\theta_1 r_i} \cdot A^{-\lambda_2 v_i \tilde{t}_{1,i} x_i}.$$
$$K_B = \prod_{i=1}^{n} A^{-r_i} g^{-\Phi_i} = \prod_{i=1}^{n} g^{-(\alpha\tilde{r}_i + \Phi_i)} = \prod_{i=1}^{n} g^{-(r_i+\Phi_i)}.$$

$\mathcal{B}$ knows $\{f_{b,i}, h_{b,i}\}_{b\in[2],i\in[n]}$, hence it can compute K_A.

Generating the Challenge Ciphertext. $\mathcal{A}$ sends message m_0 to $\mathcal{B}$. To generate a challenge ciphertext, $\mathcal{B}$ picks $s_1, s_2, s_1', s_2', \tilde{s}_3, \tilde{s}_4, \tilde{s}_{3'} \leftarrow \mathbb{Z}_p^\star$ such that $\tilde{s}_3 \neq \tilde{s}_3'$. $\mathcal{B}$ implicitly sets $s_3 = \eta\tilde{s}_3, s_4 = \beta\tilde{s}_4$ and computes the ciphertext as follows:

$$\begin{array}{ll}
\mathsf{ct}_1 = g^{s_2}, \mathsf{ct}'_1 = g^{s'_2} & , \mathsf{ct}_2 = h^{s_1}, \mathsf{ct}'_2 = h^{s'_1}. \\
\mathsf{ct}_{3,i} = W_{1,i}^{s_1} \cdot F_{1,i}^{s_2} \cdot D^{\tilde{\delta}_1 \tilde{s}_3 x_i} & , \mathsf{ct}'_{3,i} = W_{1,i}^{s'_1} \cdot F_{1,i}^{s'_2} \cdot D^{\tilde{\delta}_1 x_i \tilde{s}'_3}. \\
\mathsf{ct}_{4,i} = W_{2,i}^{s_1} \cdot F_{2,i}^{s_2} \cdot D^{\tilde{\delta}_2 \tilde{s}_3 x_i} & , \mathsf{ct}'_{4,i} = W_{2,i}^{s'_1} \cdot F_{2,i}^{s'_2} \cdot D^{\tilde{\delta}_2 x_i \tilde{s}'_3}. \\
\mathsf{ct}_{5,i} = T_{1,i}^{s_1} \cdot H_{1,i}^{s_2} \cdot B^{\theta_1 \tilde{s}_4 x_i} & , \mathsf{ct}'_{5,i} = T_{1,i}^{s'_1} \cdot H_{1,i}^{s'_2} \cdot B^{\theta_1 \tilde{s}_4 x_i}. \\
\mathsf{ct}_{6,i} = T_{2,i}^{s_1} \cdot H_{2,i}^{s_2} \cdot B^{\theta_2 \tilde{s}_4 x_i} & , \mathsf{ct}'_{6,i} = T_{2,i}^{s'_1} \cdot H_{2,i}^{s'_2} \cdot B^{\theta_2 \tilde{s}_4 x_i}. \\
\mathsf{ct}_7 = (\frac{\mathsf{e}(Z,g)}{\mathsf{e}(B,C)})^{\tilde{s}_3 \tilde{s}_4}, & , \mathsf{ct}'_7 = (\frac{\mathsf{e}(Z,g)}{\mathsf{e}(B,C)})^{\tilde{s}_{3'} \tilde{s}_4}, \\
\mathsf{ct}_8 = \mathsf{e}(g, g')^{-s_2} \cdot m_0 & , \mathsf{ct}'_8 = \mathsf{e}(g, g')^{-s'_2} \cdot m_0
\end{array}$$

Since $D^{\tilde{\delta}_b x_i \tilde{s}_3} = g^{\alpha \tilde{\delta}_b \eta \tilde{s}_3 x_i} = U_b^{x_i s_3}, B^{\theta_b \tilde{s}_4 x_i} = V_1^{\beta \tilde{s}_4 x_i} = V_b^{s_4 x_i}$, for each $i \in [n]$ the values $\mathsf{ct}_{3,i}, \mathsf{ct}'_{3,i}, \ldots, \mathsf{ct}_{6,i}, \mathsf{ct}'_{6,i}$ are computed properly.

Analysing the Game: Let us analyze the two events, $Z = g^{\beta(\tau+\eta)}$ or $Z \leftarrow \mathbb{G}$:

- $Z = g^{\beta(\tau+\eta)} \Rightarrow \dfrac{\mathsf{e}(Z,g)}{\mathsf{e}(B,C)} = \dfrac{\mathsf{e}(g^{\beta(\tau+\eta)}, g)}{\mathsf{e}(g^\beta, g^\tau)} = \dfrac{\mathsf{e}(g^\beta, g^\tau) \cdot \mathsf{e}(g^\beta, g^\eta)}{\mathsf{e}(g^\beta, g^\tau)} = \mathsf{e}(g^\eta, g^\beta)$
  $\Rightarrow \mathsf{ct}_7 = (\dfrac{\mathsf{e}(Z,g)}{\mathsf{e}(B,C)})^{\tilde{s}_3 \tilde{s}_4} = \mathsf{e}(g^{\eta \tilde{s}_3}, g^{\beta \tilde{s}_4}) = \mathsf{e}(g^{s_3}, g^{s_4}), \mathsf{ct}'_7 = \mathsf{e}(g^{s'_3}, g^{s_4})$
  $\Rightarrow \mathcal{A}$ interacting with H_0.
- $Z \leftarrow \mathbb{G} \Rightarrow \mathsf{ct}_7, \mathsf{ct}'_7$ random elements in $\mathbb{G}_T \Rightarrow \mathcal{A}$ interacting with H_1. □

Proposition 3. *If the DBDH assumption holds relative to* GroupGen, *then* H_1 *is computationally indistinguishable from* H_2.

Proposition 4. *If the DLin assumption holds relative to* GroupGen, *then* H_2 *is computationally indistinguishable from* H_3.

Proposition 5. *If the DLin assumption holds relative to* GroupGen, *then* H_3 *is computationally indistinguishable from* H_4.

The Propositions 3, 4, 5 are proved in the full version [25].

Proposition 6. *If the DLin assumption holds relative to* GroupGen, *then* H_4 *is computationally indistinguishable from* H_5.

Proof. The simulator takes as input $(g, A = g^\alpha, B = g^\beta, C = g^\tau, D = g^{\alpha\eta}, Z \stackrel{?}{=} g^{\beta(\eta+\tau)})$ and by interacting with the adversary $\mathcal{A}$, distinguish between the two cases $Z = g^{\beta(\eta+\tau)}$ and $Z \stackrel{\$}{\leftarrow} \mathbb{G}$, a random element of the group.

SetUp and Token Query Phase. $\mathcal{B}$ runs as in the SetUp phase and token query phase in Proposition 5.

Generating the Challenge Ciphertext. $\mathcal{B}$ chooses random elements $\tilde{s}_1, \tilde{s}_2, \tilde{s}_3, \tilde{s}_4, \tilde{s}'_1, \tilde{s}'_2, \tilde{s}'_3, k \leftarrow \mathbb{Z}_p^\star$ and computes the challenge ciphertext as follows:

- $\mathsf{ct}_1 = C \cdot g^{\tilde{s}_2} = g^{\tau+\tilde{s}_2} \Rightarrow s_2 = \tau + \tilde{s}_2$, • $\mathsf{ct}'_1 = C^k \cdot g^{\tilde{s}_{2'}} = g^{k\tau+\tilde{s}'_2} \Rightarrow s'_2 = k\tau + \tilde{s}_2$
- $\mathsf{ct}_2 = D^{\tilde{\Omega}} \cdot A^{\tilde{\Omega}\tilde{s}_1} = (g^{\alpha\tilde{\Omega}})^{(\eta+\tilde{s}_1)} = h^{\eta+\tilde{s}_1} \Rightarrow s_1 = \eta + \tilde{s}_1$
- $\mathsf{ct}'_2 = D^{k\tilde{\Omega}} \cdot A^{\tilde{\Omega}\tilde{s}'_1} = (g^{\alpha\tilde{\Omega}})^{(k\eta+\tilde{s}'_1)} = h^{k\eta+\tilde{s}'_1} \Rightarrow s'_1 = k\eta + \tilde{s}'_1$
- $\mathsf{ct}_{3,i} = W_{1,i}^{\tilde{s}_1} \cdot F_{1,i}^{\tilde{s}_2} \cdot U_1^{\tilde{s}_3 x_i} \cdot D^{\tilde{w}_{1,i}} \cdot C^{f_{1,i}} = W_{1,i}^{\tilde{s}_1} \cdot F_{1,i}^{\tilde{s}_2+\tau} \cdot U_1^{\tilde{s}_3 x_i} \cdot g^{\eta\alpha\tilde{w}_{1,i}} \cdot F_{1,i}^{\tau} =$
$= W_{1,i}^{\tilde{s}_1} \cdot F_{1,i}^{\tilde{s}_2+\tau} \cdot U_1^{\tilde{s}_3 x_i} \cdot g^{\eta(w_{1,i}-\beta\delta_1 x_i)} = W_{1,i}^{\tilde{s}_1+\eta} \cdot F_{1,i}^{\tilde{s}_2+\tau} \cdot U_1^{(\tilde{s}_3-\eta\beta)x_i}$
$\Rightarrow s_3 = -\eta\beta + \tilde{s}_3$
- $\mathsf{ct}_{4,i} = W_{2,i}^{\tilde{s}_1} \cdot F_{2,i}^{\tilde{s}_2} \cdot U_2^{\tilde{s}_3 x_i} \cdot D^{\tilde{w}_{2,i}} \cdot C^{f_{2,i}}$, (similar computation as $\mathsf{ct}_{3,i}$)
- $\mathsf{ct}'_{3,i} = W_{1,i}^{\tilde{s}'_1} \cdot F_{1,i}^{\tilde{s}'_2} \cdot U_1^{\tilde{s}'_3 x_i} \cdot D^{k\tilde{w}_{1,i}} \cdot C^{kf_{1,i}} = W_{1,i}^{\tilde{s}'_1} \cdot F_{1,i}^{\tilde{s}'_2} \cdot U_1^{\tilde{s}'_3 x_i} \cdot g^{k\eta\alpha\tilde{w}_{1,i}} \cdot F_{1,i}^{k\tau}$
$= W_{1,i}^{\tilde{s}'_1} \cdot F_{1,i}^{\tilde{s}'_2+k\tau} \cdot U_1^{\tilde{s}'_3 x_i} \cdot g^{k\eta(w_{1,i}-\beta\delta_1 x_i)} = W_{1,i}^{\tilde{s}'_1+k\eta} \cdot F_{1,i}^{\tilde{s}'_2+k\tau} \cdot U_1^{(\tilde{s}'_3-k\eta\beta)x_i}$
$\Rightarrow s'_3 = -k\eta\beta + \tilde{s}'_3$
- $\mathsf{ct}'_{4,i} = W_{2,i}^{\tilde{s}'_1} \cdot F_{2,i}^{\tilde{s}'_2} \cdot U_2^{\tilde{s}'_3 x_i} \cdot D^{k\tilde{w}_{2,i}} \cdot C^{kf_{2,i}}$, (similar computation as $\mathsf{ct}'_{3,i}$)
- $\mathsf{ct}_{5,i} = T_{1,i}^{\tilde{s}_1} \cdot D^{\tilde{t}_{1,i}} \cdot H_{1,i}^{\tilde{s}_2} \cdot C^{\tilde{h}_{1,i}} \cdot Z^{\theta_1 y_i} \cdot g^{\tilde{s}_4\theta_1 y_i}$
- $\mathsf{ct}'_{5,i} = T_{1,i}^{\tilde{s}'_1} \cdot D^{k\tilde{t}_{1,i}} \cdot H_{1,i}^{\tilde{s}'_2} \cdot C^{k\tilde{h}_{1,i}} \cdot Z^{k\theta_1 y_i} \cdot g^{\tilde{s}_4\theta_1 y_i}$
- $\mathsf{ct}_{6,i} = T_{2,i}^{\tilde{s}_1} \cdot D^{\tilde{t}_{2,i}} \cdot H_{2,i}^{\tilde{s}_2} \cdot C^{\tilde{h}_{2,i}} \cdot Z^{\theta_2 y_i} \cdot g^{\tilde{s}_4\theta_2 y_i}$
- $\mathsf{ct}'_{6,i} = T_{2,i}^{\tilde{s}'_1} \cdot D^{k\tilde{t}_{2,i}} \cdot H_{2,i}^{\tilde{s}'_2} \cdot C^{k\tilde{h}_{2,i}} \cdot Z^{k\theta_2 y_i} \cdot g^{\tilde{s}_4\theta_2 y_i}$

Analysis of the Game: First, notice that:

$$D^{\tilde{t}_{1,i}} = g^{\eta\alpha\tilde{t}_{1,i}} = g^{\eta(t_{1,i}-\beta\theta_1 y_i)} = T_{1,i}^{\eta} \cdot g^{-\beta\eta\theta_1 y_i}, D^{k\tilde{t}_{1,i}} = T_{1,i}^{k\eta} \cdot g^{-k\beta\eta\theta_1 y_i}$$

$$C^{\tilde{h}_{1,i}} = g^{\tau(h_{1,i}-\beta\theta_1 y_i)} = H_{1,i}^{\tau} \cdot g^{-\beta\tau\theta_1 y_i}, C^{k\tilde{h}_{1,i}} = H_{1,i}^{k\tau} \cdot g^{-k\beta\tau\theta_1 y_i} \Rightarrow$$

$$\begin{aligned} \mathsf{ct}_{5,i} &= T_{1,i}^{\tilde{s}_1} \cdot D^{\tilde{t}_{1,i}} \cdot H_{1,i}^{\tilde{s}_2} \cdot C^{\tilde{h}_{1,i}} \cdot (Z \cdot g^{\tilde{s}_4})^{\theta_1 y_i} \\ &= T_{1,i}^{\eta+\tilde{s}_1} \cdot H_{1,i}^{\tau+\tilde{s}_2} \cdot (g^{-\beta(\tau+\eta)} \cdot Z \cdot g^{\tilde{s}_4})^{\theta_1 y_i} \\ &= T_{1,i}^{s_1} \cdot H_{1,i}^{s_2} \cdot (g^{(-\beta(\tau+\eta))} \cdot Z \cdot g^{\tilde{s}_4})^{\theta_1 y_i} \\ \mathsf{ct}'_{5,i} &= T_{1,i}^{s'_1} \cdot H_{1,i}^{s'_2} \cdot (g^{(-k\beta(\tau+\eta))} \cdot Z^k \cdot g^{\tilde{s}_4})^{\theta_1 y_i} \end{aligned}$$

$$\text{If } Z = g^{\beta(\eta+\tau)} \quad \Rightarrow \begin{cases} g^{-\beta(\tau+\eta)} \cdot Z \cdot g^{\tilde{s}_4} = g^{\tilde{s}_4} \Rightarrow \mathsf{ct}_{5,i} = T_{1,i}^{s_1} \cdot H_{1,i}^{s_2} \cdot U_1^{s_4 y_i} \\ g^{(-k\beta(\tau+\eta))} \cdot Z^k \cdot g^{\tilde{s}_4} = g^{\tilde{s}_4} \Rightarrow \mathsf{ct}_{5,i} = T_{1,i}^{s'_1} \cdot H_{1,i}^{s'_2} \cdot U_1^{s_4 y_i} \end{cases}$$

$\Rightarrow$ The adversary interacts with hybrid H_4

$$\text{If } Z = g^r \quad \Rightarrow \begin{cases} g^{-\beta(\tau+\eta)} \cdot Z \cdot g^{\tilde{s}_4} = g^{r+\tilde{s}_4} \Rightarrow \mathsf{ct}_{5,i} = T_{1,i}^{s_1} \cdot H_{1,i}^{s_2} \cdot U_1^{s_4 y_i} \\ g^{(-k\beta(\tau+\eta))} \cdot Z^k \cdot g^{\tilde{s}_4} = g^{kr+\tilde{s}_4} \Rightarrow \mathsf{ct}_{5,i} = T_{1,i}^{s'_1} \cdot H_{1,i}^{s'_2} \cdot U_1^{s'_4 y_i} \end{cases}$$

$\Rightarrow$ The adversary interacts with hybrid H_5. □

4 Verifiable Inner-Product Encryption

Firstly, we present a formal definition of a VIPE scheme. Essentially, VIPE is similar to IPE except that it is endowed with extra verification algorithms $\mathsf{VrfyCT}, \mathsf{VrfyTok}$ and $\mathsf{VrfyMPK}$.

Definition 5. *A verifiable inner product encryption scheme for a message space $\mathcal{M}$ and for a family $\Sigma = \{\Sigma_n\}_{n>0}$ of vectors over some field is a tuple of PPT algorithms (here called* VIP*)* $\mathsf{VIP} = \{\mathsf{VIP.SetUp}, \mathsf{VIP.TokGen}, \mathsf{VIP.Enc}, \mathsf{VIP.Dec}, \mathsf{VIP.VrfyMPK}, \mathsf{VIP.VrfyCT}, \mathsf{VIP.VrfyTok}\}$ *with the syntax and properties below:*

- $\mathsf{VIP.SetUp}(1^\lambda, n) \rightarrow (\mathsf{MPK}, \mathsf{MSK})$*: as for IPE.*
- $\mathsf{VIP.TokGen}(\mathsf{MPK}, \mathsf{MSK}, \boldsymbol{v}) \longrightarrow \mathsf{Tok}_{\boldsymbol{v}}$*: as for IPE.*
- $\mathsf{VIP.Enc}(\mathsf{MPK}, \overrightarrow{x}, m) \rightarrow \mathsf{CT}$*: as for IPE.*
- $\mathsf{VIP.Dec}(\mathsf{MPK}, \mathsf{Tok}_{\boldsymbol{v}}, \mathsf{CT}) \rightarrow m \in \mathcal{M} \cup \{\perp\}$*: as for IPE.*
- $\mathsf{VIP.VrfyMPK}(\mathsf{MPK}) \rightarrow \{0, 1\}$*: this is a deterministic algorithm that outputs* 1 *if* MPK *was correctly generated, or outputs* 0 *otherwise.*
- $\mathsf{VIP.VrfyCT}(\mathsf{MPK}, \mathsf{CT}) \rightarrow \{0, 1\}$*: this is a deterministic algorithm that outputs* 1 *if* CT *was correctly generated using the master public key on input some m in the message space $\mathcal{M}$ and a vector $\boldsymbol{x}$, or outputs* 0 *otherwise.*
- $\mathsf{VIP.VrfyTok}(\mathsf{MPK}, \boldsymbol{v}, \mathsf{Tok}_{\boldsymbol{v}}) \longrightarrow \{0, 1\}$*: this is a deterministic algorithm that outputs* 1 *if* $\mathsf{Tok}_{\boldsymbol{v}}$ *was correctly generated using the master secret key on input vector $\boldsymbol{v}$, or outputs* 0 *otherwise.*
- Perfect correctness: *as for IPE.*
- Verifiability: VIP *is verifiable if for all* $\mathsf{MPK} \in \{0, 1\}^*$*, all* $\mathsf{CT} \in \{0, 1\}^*$*, there exists $n > 0, (\boldsymbol{x}, m) \in \Sigma_n \times \mathcal{M}$ such that for all $\boldsymbol{v} \in \Sigma_n$ and* $\mathsf{Tok}_{\boldsymbol{v}} \in \{0, 1\}^*$*, the following holds:*

$$\begin{pmatrix} \mathsf{VIP.VrfyMPK}(\mathsf{MPK}) = 1 \wedge \\ \mathsf{VIP.VrfyCT}(\mathsf{MPK}, \mathsf{CT}) = 1 \wedge \\ \mathsf{VIP.VrfyTok}(\mathsf{MPK}, \boldsymbol{v}, \mathsf{Tok}_{\boldsymbol{v}}) = 1 \end{pmatrix} \Rightarrow \Pr\begin{bmatrix} \mathsf{VIP.Dec}(\mathsf{MPK}, \mathsf{Tok}_{\boldsymbol{v}}, \mathsf{CT}) \\ = f_{\boldsymbol{v}}(\boldsymbol{x}, m) \end{bmatrix} = 1$$

Intuitively verifiability states that each ciphertext (possibly with a maliciously generated public key) should be associated with a unique message $(\boldsymbol{x}, m)$ and decryption for a function $f_{\boldsymbol{v}}$ using any possibly maliciously generated token $\mathsf{Tok}_{\boldsymbol{v}}$ should result in $f_{\boldsymbol{v}}(\boldsymbol{x}, m)$ for the unique message associated with the ciphertext [2].

4.1 Our Construction

Our VIPE is based on a perfectly correct IPE (cf. our IPE scheme of Construction 1), a perfectly binding commitment scheme such as the commitment scheme proposed in [13] and NIWI proofs for some specific relations that will be detailed below.

Let $n \in \mathbb{N}$ be the vector length and λ the security parameter. Let IP be a perfectly correct IPE scheme, Com be a perfectly binding commitment scheme and $\mathsf{NIWI}^{\mathsf{mpk}} = \langle \mathcal{P}^{\mathsf{mpk}}, \mathcal{V}^{\mathsf{mpk}} \rangle$, $\mathsf{NIWI}^{\mathsf{enc}} = \langle \mathcal{P}^{\mathsf{enc}}, \mathcal{V}^{\mathsf{enc}} \rangle$ and $\mathsf{NIWI}^{\mathsf{tok}} = \langle \mathcal{P}^{\mathsf{tok}}, \mathcal{V}^{\mathsf{tok}} \rangle$ be NIWI proofs systems for, resp., the relations $\mathcal{R}^{\mathsf{mpk}}$, $\mathcal{R}^{\mathsf{enc}}$ and $\mathcal{R}^{\mathsf{tok}}$, that are essentially instantiations of analogous relations in [2]. The construction of these NIWI systems is provided in Sect. 5.

- $\mathrm{R}^{\mathsf{mpk}}_{\mathsf{IP}}(\overbrace{\mathsf{mpk}}^{x}, \overbrace{(\mathsf{msk}, \mathsf{r}^{\mathsf{mpk}})}^{w}) = \mathsf{TRUE} \iff (\mathsf{mpk}, \mathsf{msk}) = \mathsf{IP.SetUp}(1^\lambda, n; \mathsf{r}^{\mathsf{mpk}})$
- $\mathrm{R}^{\mathsf{tok}}_{\mathsf{IP}}\Big(\overbrace{(\mathsf{mpk}, t, \boldsymbol{v})}^{x}, \overbrace{(\mathsf{msk}, \mathsf{r}^{\mathsf{mpk}}, \mathsf{r}^{\mathsf{token}})}^{w}\Big) = \mathsf{TRUE}$
$\iff \begin{pmatrix} (\mathsf{mpk}, (\mathsf{msk}, \mathsf{r}^{\mathsf{mpk}})) \in \mathrm{R}^{\mathsf{mpk}}_{\mathsf{IP}} \wedge \\ t = \mathsf{IP.TokGen}(\mathsf{MSK}, \boldsymbol{v}; \mathsf{r}^{\mathsf{tok}}) \end{pmatrix}$
- $\mathrm{R}^{k,\mathsf{ct}}_{\mathsf{IP}}\Big(\overbrace{((\mathsf{ct}_1, \mathsf{mpk}_1), \ldots, (\mathsf{ct}_k, \mathsf{mpk}_k))}^{x}, \overbrace{(\boldsymbol{x}, m, \mathsf{r}^{\mathsf{enc}}_1, \ldots, \mathsf{r}^{\mathsf{enc}}_k)}^{w}\Big) = \mathsf{TRUE}, k \in [4]$
$\iff \forall i \in [k]\ \mathsf{ct}_i = \mathsf{IP.Enc}(\mathsf{mpk}_i, \boldsymbol{x}, m; \mathsf{r}^{\mathsf{enc}}_i)$
- $\mathrm{R}^{\mathsf{enc}}(x, w) = \mathsf{TRUE} \iff \mathsf{P}^{\mathsf{enc}}_1(x, w) \vee \mathsf{P}^{\mathsf{enc}}_2(x, w)$, with
$\mathsf{P}^{\mathsf{enc}}_1\Big((\{c_i\}_{i\in[4]}, \{a_i\}_{i\in[4]}, z_0, z_1), (m, \boldsymbol{x}, \{\mathsf{r}^{\mathsf{enc}}_i\}_{i\in[4]}, i_1, i_2, \mathsf{r}^{\mathsf{com}}_0, \mathsf{r}^{\mathsf{com}}_1)\Big) = \mathsf{TRUE}$
$\iff \Big(((c_1, a_1), \ldots, (c_4, a_4)), (\boldsymbol{x}, m, \{\mathsf{r}^{\mathsf{enc}}_i\}_{i\in[4]})\Big) \in \mathrm{R}^{4,\mathsf{ct}}_{\mathsf{IP}}$
$\mathsf{P}^{\mathsf{enc}}_2\Big((\{c_i\}_{i\in[4]}, \{a_i\}_{i\in[4]}, z_0, z_1), (m, \boldsymbol{x}, \{\mathsf{r}^{\mathsf{enc}}_i\}_{i\in[4]}, i_1, i_2, \mathsf{r}^{\mathsf{com}}_0, \mathsf{r}^{\mathsf{com}}_1)\Big) = \mathsf{TRUE}$
$\iff \begin{pmatrix} i_1, i_2 \in [4] \wedge (i_1 \neq i_2) \wedge \Big(\left((c_{i_1}, a_{i_1}), (c_{i_2}, a_{i_2})\right), (\boldsymbol{x}, m, \mathsf{r}^{\mathsf{enc}}_i)\Big) \in \mathrm{R}^{2,\mathsf{ct}}_{\mathsf{IP}} \\ \wedge\ z_0 = \mathsf{Com}(\{c_i\}_{i\in[4]}; \mathsf{r}^{\mathsf{com}}_0) \wedge z_1 = \mathsf{Com}(0; \mathsf{r}^{\mathsf{com}}_1) \end{pmatrix}$
- $\mathrm{R}^{\mathsf{tok}}(x, w) = \mathsf{TRUE} \iff \mathsf{P}^{\mathsf{tok}}_1(x, w) \vee \mathsf{P}^{\mathsf{tok}}_2(x, w)$, with, where

$$\mathsf{P}^{\mathsf{tok}}_1\Big((\boldsymbol{v}, \{t_i\}_{i\in[4]}, \{a_i\}_{i\in[4]}, z_0, z_1),$$
$$(\{b_i\}_{i\in[4]}, \{\mathsf{r}^{\mathsf{mpk}}_i\}_{i\in[4]}, \{\mathsf{r}^{\mathsf{tok}}_i\}_{i\in[4]}, i_1, i_2, i_3, \mathsf{r}^{\mathsf{com}}_0, \mathsf{r}^{\mathsf{com}}_1)\Big) = \mathsf{TRUE}$$
$$\iff \begin{pmatrix} \forall i \in [4] : \big((a_i, (b_i, \mathsf{r}^{\mathsf{mpk}}_i)\big) \in \mathrm{R}^{\mathsf{mpk}} \wedge \\ ((a_i, t_i, \boldsymbol{v}_i), (b_i, \mathsf{r}^{\mathsf{mpk}}_i, \mathsf{r}^{\mathsf{tok}}_i))) \in \mathrm{R}^{\mathsf{tok}}_{\mathsf{IP}} \\ \wedge\ z_1 = \mathsf{Com}(1; \mathsf{r}^{\mathsf{com}}_1) \end{pmatrix}, \text{ and}$$
$$\mathsf{P}^{\mathsf{tok}}_2((\boldsymbol{v}, \{t_i\}_{i\in[4]}, \{a_i\}_{i\in[4]}, z_0, z_1),$$
$$\Big(\{b_i\}_{i\in[4]}, \{\mathsf{r}^{\mathsf{mpk}}_i\}_{i\in[4]}, \{\mathsf{r}^{\mathsf{tok}}_i\}_{i\in[4]}, i_1, i_2, i_3, \mathsf{r}^{\mathsf{com}}_0, \mathsf{r}^{\mathsf{com}}_1\Big)) = \mathsf{TRUE}$$
$$\iff \begin{pmatrix} i_1, i_2, i_3 \in [4] \wedge\ (i_1 \neq i_2) \wedge (i_1 \neq i_3) \wedge (i_2 \neq i_3) \\ \forall j \in [3] : \big(a_{i_j}, (b_{i_j}, \mathsf{r}^{\mathsf{mpk}}_{i_j})\big) \in \mathrm{R}^{\mathsf{mpk}} \wedge \\ \Big(\left(a_{i_j}, t_{i_j}, \boldsymbol{v}_{i_j}\right), \left(b_{i_j}, \mathsf{r}^{\mathsf{mpk}}_{i_j}, \mathsf{r}^{\mathsf{tok}}_{i_j}\right)\Big) \in \mathrm{R}^{\mathsf{tok}}_{\mathsf{IP}} \\ \wedge\ z_0 = \mathsf{Com}(\{c_i\}_{i\in[4]}; \mathsf{r}^{\mathsf{com}}_1) \wedge \\ \exists m \in \mathcal{M}\ \forall i \in [4]\ \mathsf{IP.Dec}(c_i, t_i) = f_{\boldsymbol{v}}(m) \end{pmatrix}$$

Construction 7 [Our VIPE VIP]

- $\mathsf{VIP.SetUp}(1^\lambda, n) \to (\mathsf{MPK}, \mathsf{MSK})$:
  1. For $i \in [4]$, run $\mathsf{IP.SetUp}(1^\lambda, n)$ to generate $(\mathsf{MPK}_i, \mathsf{MSK}_i)$.
  2. Run the commitment algorithm to generate $\mathsf{Z}_0 = \mathsf{Com}(0; \mathsf{r}^{\mathsf{com}}_0)$ and $\mathsf{Z}_1 = \mathsf{Com}(1; \mathsf{r}^{\mathsf{com}}_1)$.

3. Output $\mathsf{VIP.MPK} = (\{\mathsf{MPK}_i\}_{i\in[4]}, \mathsf{Z}_0, \mathsf{Z}_1), \mathsf{VIP.MSK} = (\{\mathsf{MSK}_i\}_{i\in[4]}, \mathsf{r}_0^{\mathsf{com}}, \mathsf{r}_1^{\mathsf{com}})$.

- $\mathsf{VIP.Enc}(\mathsf{MPK}, m, \boldsymbol{x}) \to \mathsf{CT}$:
  1. For $i \in [4]$, run the encryption algorithm to compute $\mathsf{CT}_i = \mathsf{IP.Enc}(\mathsf{MPK}, m, \boldsymbol{x}; \mathsf{r}_i^{\mathsf{enc}})$.
  2. Set $x = (\{\mathsf{CT}_i\}_{i\in[4]}, \{\mathsf{MPK}_i\}_{i\in[4]}, \mathsf{Z}_0, \mathsf{Z}_1), w = (m, \boldsymbol{x}, \{\mathsf{r}_i^{\mathsf{enc}}\}_{i\in[4]}, 0, 0, 0^{|u_0|}, 0^{|u_1|})$, and run $\mathcal{P}^{\mathsf{enc}}(x, w)$ to generate π_{ct} for relation $\mathcal{R}^{\mathsf{enc}}(x, w)$. Note that $\mathsf{P}_1^{\mathsf{enc}}(x, w) = \mathsf{TRUE}$.
  3. Output ciphertext $\mathsf{CT} = (\{\mathsf{CT}_i\}_{i\in[4]}, \pi_{\mathsf{ct}})$.
- $\mathsf{VIP.TokGen}(\mathsf{MPK}, \mathsf{MSK}, f_v)$:
  1. For $i \in [4]$, run $\mathsf{IP.TokGen}(\mathsf{MSK}, \boldsymbol{v}; \mathsf{r}_i^{\mathsf{tok}})$ to generate Tok_v^i.
  2. $x = (\boldsymbol{v}, \{\mathsf{Tok}_v^i\}_{i\in[4]}, \{\mathsf{MPK}_i\}_{i\in[4]}, \mathsf{Z}_0, \mathsf{Z}_1), w = (\{\mathsf{MSK}_i\}_{i\in[4]}, \{\mathsf{r}_i^{\mathsf{tok}}\}_{i\in[4]}, 0, 0, 0, 0^{|\mathsf{r}_0^{\mathsf{com}}|}, |\mathsf{r}_1^{\mathsf{com}}|)$ run $\mathcal{P}^{\mathsf{tok}}$ to generate π_{tok} to prove $\mathcal{R}^{\mathsf{tok}}(x, w) = \mathsf{TRUE}$. Note that $\mathsf{P}_1^{\mathsf{tok}}(x, w) = \mathsf{TRUE}$
  3. Output token $\mathsf{Tok}_v = (\{\mathsf{Tok}_v^i\}_{i\in[4]}, \pi_{\mathsf{tok}})$.
- $\mathsf{VIP.Dec}(\mathsf{MPK}, f_v, \mathsf{Tok}_v, \mathsf{CT})$:
  1. Run the verification algorithms $\mathcal{V}^{\mathsf{mpk}}, \mathcal{V}^{\mathsf{enc}}, \mathcal{V}^{\mathsf{tok}}$ on input the corresponding pairs of statement and proof (the proof for the verification of the master public key is set to the empty string). If some verification algorithms fails, then stop and output $\perp$ or go to the next step otherwise.
  2. For all $i \in [4]$, compute $m^{(i)} = \mathsf{IP.Dec}(\mathsf{Tok}_v^{(i)}, \mathsf{CT}_i)$ and output the following:
     $$\begin{cases} \texttt{If } \exists i_1, i_2, i_3 \in [4] \;\; s.t. \;\; m = m^{(i_1)} = m^{(i_2)} = m^{(i_3)} \Rightarrow \texttt{Output } m. \\ \texttt{If } \nexists i_1, i_2, i_3 \in [4] \;\; s.t. \;\; m^{(i_1)} = m^{(i_2)} = m^{(i_3)} \Rightarrow \texttt{Output } \perp. \end{cases}$$
- $\mathsf{VIP.VrfyMPK}(\mathsf{MPK})$: run $\mathcal{V}^{\mathsf{mpk}}(\mathsf{MPK}, \epsilon)$ and output its result.
- $\mathsf{VIP.VrfyCT}\big((\{\mathsf{CT}_i\}_{i\in[4]}, \{\mathsf{MPK}_i\}_{i\in[4]}, \mathsf{Z}_0, \mathsf{Z}_1), \pi_{\mathsf{ct}})\big)$:
  run $\mathcal{V}^{\mathsf{enc}}\big((\{\mathsf{CT}_i\}_{i\in[4]}, \{\mathsf{MPK}_i\}_{i\in[4]}, \mathsf{Z}_0, \mathsf{Z}_1), \pi_{\mathsf{ct}}\big)$ and output its result.
- $\mathsf{VIP.VrfyTok}\big((\boldsymbol{v}, \{\mathsf{Tok}_v^i\}_{i\in[4]}, \{\mathsf{MPK}_i\}_{i\in[4]}, \mathsf{Z}_0, \mathsf{Z}_1), \pi_{\mathsf{tok}}\big)$:
  run $\mathcal{V}^{\mathsf{tok}}\big((\boldsymbol{v}, \{\mathsf{Tok}_v^i\}_{i\in[4]}, \{\mathsf{MPK}_i\}_{i\in[4]}, \mathsf{Z}_0, \mathsf{Z}_1), \pi_{\mathsf{tok}}\big)$ and output its result.

Correctness of VIP follows from perfect correctness of IP. IND-Security and Verifiability of VIP follows as corollary (following Theorem 2) from the verifiability and IND-Security of the construction of [2] for general functions.

Theorem 2. *If* IP *is a perfectly correct* IND*-Secure IP scheme for message space* $\mathcal{M}$ *and for the set* $\mathbb{Z}_p^n$ *of vectors of length* n *over* $\mathbb{Z}_p$*, and* $\mathsf{NIWI}^{\mathsf{mpk}}, \mathsf{NIWI}^{\mathsf{ct}}, \mathsf{NIWI}^{\mathsf{tok}}$ *are NIWI systems resp. for the relations* $\mathcal{R}^{\mathsf{mpk}}, \mathcal{R}^{\mathsf{enc}}, \mathcal{R}^{\mathsf{tok}}$ *and* Com *is a non-interactive perfectly binding and computationally hiding commitment scheme, then* VIP *is an* IND*-Secure VIPE scheme for the class of inner product functionality over* $\mathcal{M}$ *and* $\mathbb{Z}_p^n$.

5 NIWI Proofs and Verification Algorithms

In this section we present the proof systems that we used in our VIP scheme, to prove membership of relations $\mathcal{R}^{\mathsf{mpk}}$, $\mathcal{R}^{\mathsf{tok}}$ and $\mathcal{R}^{\mathsf{enc}}$. For each of our relations[2], we need to define a system of equations such that satisfiability of that system and the membership in the relation are equivalent. Then, the GS generic prover and verifier algorithms, $\mathsf{NIWI}_{\mathsf{GS}} = \langle \mathcal{P}_{\mathsf{GS}}, \mathcal{V}_{\mathsf{GS}} \rangle$, can be used for such equations. In this section, for each of our relations of Sect. 4, we will either define a corresponding system of equations or we will show how to implement directly (without using GS proofs).

Definition 6 (Pairing Product System of Equations). *Consider a bilinear map* $\mathbf{e} : \mathbb{G} \times \mathbb{G} \to \mathbb{G}_T$. *The following system of equation with* k *equations over* m *variables* $\mathcal{X}_i \in \mathbb{G}, i \in [m]$ *and constants* $B_i^{(t)} \in \mathbb{G}, \tau^{(t)} \in \mathbb{G}_T$ *and* $\gamma_{ij}^{(t)} \in \mathbb{Z}_p$ *for* $i \in [m], t \in [k]$ *is called a* pairing product system of equations *over* $(\mathbb{G}, \mathbb{G}_T, e)$*:*

$$\mathsf{E} : \begin{cases} \prod_{i=1}^{m} \mathbf{e}(\mathcal{X}_i, B_i^{(1)}) \cdot \prod_{i=1}^{m} \prod_{j=1}^{m} \mathbf{e}(\mathcal{X}_i, \mathcal{X}_j)^{\gamma_{ij}^{(1)}} = \tau^{(1)} \\ \dots \\ \prod_{i=1}^{m} \mathbf{e}(\mathcal{X}_i, B_i^{(k)}) \cdot \prod_{i=1}^{m} \prod_{j=1}^{m} \mathbf{e}(\mathcal{X}_i, \mathcal{X}_j)^{\gamma_{ij}^{(k)}} = \tau^{(k)} \end{cases} \tag{1}$$

$(g_1, g_2, \dots, g_m) \in \mathbb{G}^m$ *is a solution for the equation* E *iff*

$$\Big(\mathsf{E}[(g_1, \dots, g_m)] = \mathsf{TRUE}\Big) = \begin{cases} \prod_{i=1}^{m} \mathbf{e}(g_i, B_i^{(1)}) \cdot \prod_{i=1}^{m} \prod_{j=1}^{m} \mathbf{e}(g_i, g_j)^{\gamma_{ij}^{(1)}} = \tau^{(1)} \\ \dots \\ \prod_{i=1}^{m} \mathbf{e}(g_i, B_i^{(k)}) \cdot \prod_{i=1}^{m} \prod_{j=1}^{m} \mathbf{e}(g_i, g_j)^{\gamma_{ij}^{(k)}} = \tau^{(k)} \end{cases}$$

We define the following relation for pairing product system of equations:

$$\mathcal{R}_{\mathsf{E}} = \{(x, w) |\ x = \mathsf{E}, w = (g_1, \dots, g_m) : \mathsf{E}[(g_1, \dots, g_m)] = \mathsf{TRUE}\}$$

Throughout the paper, we denote by $\mathsf{NIWI}_{\mathsf{GS}} = \langle \mathcal{P}_{\mathsf{GS}}, \mathcal{V}_{\mathsf{GS}} \rangle$ a Groth-Sahai [14] NIWI-proof system. Precisely:

- $\mathcal{P}_{\mathsf{GS}}(x = \mathsf{E}, w = (g_1, \dots, g_m)) \to \pi_{\mathsf{E}}$
- $\mathcal{V}_{\mathsf{GS}}(x, \pi_{\mathsf{E}}) \to \begin{cases} 1 : & \texttt{If } (x, w) \in \mathcal{R}_{\mathsf{E}} \\ 0 : & \texttt{Otherwise} \end{cases}$

5.1 How to Handle Generalized or Statements

Some of our relations of Sect. 4 consist of a generalized form of disjunction (OR) of two predicates, let us say P_1 and P_2. Suppose that we have equivalent systems

[2] Actually, we will implement some or part of them not directly using GS proofs.

of equations for each of the two predicate, that is a system of equations E_1 (resp. E_2) representing predicate P_1 (resp. P_2). Consider the following relation:

$$\begin{aligned}\mathcal{R}_{\mathsf{OR}} =&\{(x,w)|\ x=(\mathsf{E}_1,\mathsf{E}_2), w=(\mathsf{idx},w_1,w_2) : \mathsf{idx}\in\{1,2\}\ \wedge \\ &(\mathsf{E}_{\mathsf{idx}}, w_{\mathsf{idx}})\in \mathcal{R}_{\mathsf{E}}\ \wedge\ w_{\bar{\mathsf{idx}}}\in\mathbb{G}^3\},\end{aligned}$$

where $\bar{\mathsf{idx}}$ means $\{1,2\}/\{\mathsf{idx}\}$.

Notice that the relation is not exactly a disjunction of pairing product equations because we need to make sure that the statement that holds is the one selected by the index in the witness, so we cannot use the technique of Groth [12] and we will follow a different approach.

By hypothesis $\mathcal{P}_{\mathsf{GS}}$ takes as input a system of equations E as statement and a solution $(g_1,\ldots,g_m)$ as witness and provides a NIWI-proof of membership of $(\mathsf{E},w)\in\mathcal{R}_{\mathsf{E}}$. Therefore, to use $\mathsf{NIWI}_{\mathsf{GS}}$ to generate a NIWI-proof for relation $\mathcal{R}_{\mathsf{OR}}$, we need to define a third system of equation E_{OR} with the following properties:

1. $\mathsf{E}_{\mathsf{OR}}\approx\mathcal{R}_{\mathsf{OR}}$. With this notation, we mean that there exist two efficiently computable functions f and g such that:

$$\exists w=(\mathsf{idx},w_1,w_2)\ \big(x=(\mathsf{E}_1,\mathsf{E}_2),w\big)\in\mathcal{R}_{\mathsf{OR}}\Leftrightarrow\exists\tilde{w}\ \big(\mathsf{E}_{\mathsf{OR}}=f(x),\tilde{w}\big)\in\mathcal{R}_{\mathsf{E}}.$$

$$\big(x,w\big)\in\mathcal{R}_{\mathsf{OR}}\Rightarrow\big(f(x),g(x,w)\big)\in\mathcal{R}_{\mathsf{OR}}.$$

The latter properties guarantee that a proof for relation $\mathcal{R}_{\mathsf{OR}}$ computed using $\mathsf{NIWI}_{\mathsf{GS}}$ satisfies completeness and soundness. For WI to hold, we need the following property.

2. The function f is efficiently invertible.

Now we show how to construct the system of equations E_{OR} with the aforementioned properties. Consider two systems of pairing product equations E_1 and E_2 - same structure as in 1. For simplicity, we assume the equations are over two variables (the general case is straightforward).

$$\mathsf{E}_1:\mathbf{e}(\mathcal{X}_1,a_1)\cdot\mathbf{e}(\mathcal{X}_2,a_2)=\tau_1\ ,\mathsf{E}_2:\mathbf{e}(\mathcal{Y}_1,b_1)\cdot\mathbf{e}(\mathcal{Y}_2,b_2)=\tau_2$$

We define the new system of equations E_{OR} with 4 new variables $\mathcal{Z}_{11},\mathcal{Z}_{12}$, $\mathcal{Z}_{21},\mathcal{Z}_{22}$ as follows:

$$\mathsf{E}_{\mathsf{OR}}:\begin{cases}\mathbf{e}(\mathcal{X}_1,a_1)\cdot\mathbf{e}(\mathcal{X}_2,a_2)\cdot\mathbf{e}(\mathcal{Z}_{11},\mathcal{Z}_{12})=\tau_1\\ \mathbf{e}(\mathcal{Y}_1,b_1)\cdot\mathbf{e}(\mathcal{Y}_2,b_2)\cdot\mathbf{e}(\mathcal{Z}_{21},\mathcal{Z}_{22})=\tau_2\\ \mathbf{e}(\mathcal{Z}_{11},\mathcal{Z}_{22})=1\\ \mathbf{e}(\mathcal{Z}_{11},g)\cdot\mathbf{e}(\mathcal{Z}_{\mathsf{idx}},g)=\mathbf{e}(g,g)\\ \mathbf{e}(\mathcal{Z}_{22},g)\cdot\mathbf{e}(\mathcal{Z}_{\mathsf{idx}},g)=\mathbf{e}(g^2,g)\end{cases}$$

Analysis of the Equations: Consider $(\mathcal{Z}_{\mathsf{idx}}\hookleftarrow g_{\mathsf{idx}},\mathcal{X}_1\hookleftarrow g_1,\mathcal{X}_2\hookleftarrow g_2,\mathcal{Y}_1\hookleftarrow g_3,\mathcal{Y}_2\hookleftarrow g_4,\mathcal{Z}_{11}\hookleftarrow g_{11},\ldots,\mathcal{Z}_{22}\hookleftarrow g_{22})$ as a solution for E_{OR}. So, there exist values $\mathsf{idx}, z_{11}, z_{22} \in \mathbb{Z}_p$ such that $g_{\mathsf{idx}} = g^{\mathsf{idx}}, g_{11} = g^{z_{11}}, g_{22} = g^{z_{22}}$ and for $t \in [k]$ there exist values α_t such that $\tau_t = \mathbf{e}(g, \alpha_t)$.

- $\mathbf{e}(\mathcal{Z}_{11}, g) \cdot \mathbf{e}(\mathcal{Z}_{\mathsf{idx}}, g) = \mathbf{e}(g, g) \Rightarrow \mathbf{e}(g^{z_{11}+\mathsf{idx}-1}, g) = 1$
  $\Rightarrow z_{11} = 1 - \mathsf{idx}$ and similarly $z_{22} = 2 - \mathsf{idx}$.
- $\mathbf{e}(\mathcal{Z}_{11}, \mathcal{Z}_{22}) = 1 \Rightarrow (z_{11} = 0 \;\vee\; z_{22} = 0)$
- $z_{11} = 0 \;\wedge\; z_{11} = 1 - \mathsf{idx} \Rightarrow \mathbf{e}(\mathcal{X}_1 \hookleftarrow g_1, a_1) \cdot \mathbf{e}(\mathcal{X}_2 \hookleftarrow g_2, a_2) = \tau_1$
  $\Rightarrow (\mathsf{E}_1[g_1, g_2] = \mathsf{TRUE} \;\wedge\; \mathsf{idx} = 1)$
- Similarly, $z_{22} = 0 \;\wedge z_{22} = 2 - \mathsf{idx}$
  $\Rightarrow \mathbf{e}(\mathcal{Z}_{21}, \mathcal{Z}_{22}) = 1 \Rightarrow (\mathsf{E}_2[g_3, g_4] = \mathsf{TRUE} \;\wedge\; \mathsf{idx} = 2)$

The above facts imply that:

$$\mathsf{E}_{\mathsf{OR}}[(g_{\mathsf{idx}}, g_1, \ldots, g_4, g_{11}, \ldots, g_{22})] = \mathsf{TRUE} \Rightarrow$$
$$\Big(\big(\mathsf{E}_1[g_1, g_2, \alpha_1] = \mathsf{TRUE} \;\wedge\; \mathsf{idx} = 1\big) \vee \big(\mathsf{E}_2[g_3, g_4, \alpha_2] = \mathsf{TRUE} \;\wedge\; \mathsf{idx} = 2\big)\Big),$$

as it was to show. It is also easy to see that the previous transformation is efficiently invertible.

For the other direction, suppose w.l.o.g that $w_1 = (g_1, g_2, \alpha_1)$ is a solution to $x = \mathsf{E}_1$ (the other case is symmetrical and we omit it), namely $(x, w_1) \in \mathcal{R}'$. Suppose also that $w_2 = (g_3, g_4, \alpha_2) \in \mathbb{G}^3$ is an arbitrary triple of elements of $\mathbb{G}$. Therefore $(1, w_1, w_2)$ is a witness to $(\mathsf{E}_1, \mathsf{E}_2)$ with respect to relation $\mathcal{R}_{\mathsf{OR}}$. Then, setting $(\mathcal{Z}_{\mathsf{idx}} \hookleftarrow g^1, \mathcal{X}_1 \hookleftarrow g_1, \mathcal{X}_2 \hookleftarrow g_2, \mathcal{Y}_1 \hookleftarrow g^0, \mathcal{Y}_2 \hookleftarrow g^0, \mathcal{Z}_{11} \hookleftarrow g^0, \mathcal{Z}_{12} \hookleftarrow g^1, \mathcal{Z}_{21} \hookleftarrow \alpha_2, \mathcal{Z}_{22} \hookleftarrow g^1)$, we have that:

$$\mathsf{E}_{\mathsf{OR}}[(g_{\mathsf{idx}}, g_1, \ldots, g_4, g_{11}, \ldots, g_{22})] = \mathsf{TRUE}.$$

(Notice that we implicitly defined a transformation g as needed.)

5.2 OR Proof in the General Case

If the number of pairing products (m) in each of the two equations is greater than 1, such as:

$$\mathsf{E}_1 : \begin{cases} \mathbf{e}(\mathcal{X}_1, a_1) \cdot \mathbf{e}(\mathcal{X}_2, a_2) = \tau_1 \\ \mathbf{e}(\mathcal{X}_1, a'_1) \cdot \mathbf{e}(\mathcal{X}_2, a'_2) = \tau'_1 \end{cases}, \quad \mathsf{E}_2 : \begin{cases} \mathbf{e}(\mathcal{Y}_1, b_1) \cdot \mathbf{e}(\mathcal{Y}_2, b_2) = \tau_2 \\ \mathbf{e}(\mathcal{Y}_1, b'_1) \cdot \mathbf{e}(\mathcal{Y}_2, a'_2) = \tau'_2 \end{cases}$$

then E_{OR} can be defined as:

$$\mathsf{E}_{\mathsf{OR}} : \begin{cases} \mathbf{e}(\mathcal{X}_1, a_1) \cdot \mathbf{e}(\mathcal{X}_1, a_2) \cdot \mathbf{e}(\mathcal{Z}_{11}, \mathcal{Z}_{12}) = \tau_1 \\ \mathbf{e}(\mathcal{X}_1, a'_1) \cdot \mathbf{e}(\mathcal{X}_2, a'_2) \cdot \mathbf{e}(\mathcal{Z}_{11}, \mathcal{Z}_{13}) = \tau'_1 \\ \mathbf{e}(\mathcal{Y}_1, b_1) \cdot \mathbf{e}(\mathcal{Y}_2, b_2) \cdot \mathbf{e}(\mathcal{Z}_{21}, \mathcal{Z}_{22}) = \tau_2 \\ \mathbf{e}(\mathcal{Y}_1, b'_1) \cdot \mathbf{e}(\mathcal{Y}_2, b'_2) \cdot \mathbf{e}(\mathcal{Z}_{23}, \mathcal{Z}_{22}) = \tau'_2 \\ \mathbf{e}(\mathcal{Z}_{11}, \mathcal{Z}_{22}) = 1 \\ \mathbf{e}(\mathcal{Z}_{11}, g) \cdot \mathbf{e}(\mathcal{Z}_{\mathsf{idx}}, g) = \mathbf{e}(g, g) \\ \mathbf{e}(\mathcal{Z}_{22}, g) \cdot \mathbf{e}(\mathcal{Z}_{\mathsf{idx}}, g) = \mathbf{e}(g^2, g) \end{cases}$$

We omit further details.

Notations: For the rest of this section, let us fix $n \in \mathbb{N}$ as dimension of the vector space and let $i \in [n], b \in [2]$. Note we can efficiently check whether a string is a valid group element. We recall what follows.

$$\begin{aligned}
&\mathsf{mpk} = (g, h, \{W_{b,i}, F_{b,i}, T_{b,i}, H_{b,i}, U_b, V_b\}, K_1, K_2, \Lambda) \in \mathbb{G}^{4n+8} \times \mathbb{G}_T \\
&\mathsf{msk} = (\{w_{b,i}, f_{b,i}, t_{b,i}, h_{b,i}, \delta_b, \theta_b\}, \Omega, k) \in \mathbb{Z}_p^{4n+6} \\
&\mathsf{tok} = (K_A, K_B, \{K_{3,i}, K_{4,i}, K_{5,i}, K_{6,i}\}_i) \in \mathbb{G}^{4n+2} \\
&\mathsf{ct} = \Big((\mathsf{ct}_1, \mathsf{ct}_2, \begin{Bmatrix} \mathsf{ct}_{3,i} , \mathsf{ct}_{4,i} \\ \mathsf{ct}_{5,i} , \mathsf{ct}_{6,i} \end{Bmatrix}, \mathsf{ct}_7, \mathsf{ct}_8), \\
&\qquad (\mathsf{ct}'_1, \mathsf{ct}'_2, \begin{Bmatrix} \mathsf{ct}'_{3,i} , \mathsf{ct}'_{4,i} \\ \mathsf{ct}'_{5,i} , \mathsf{ct}'_{6,i} \end{Bmatrix}, \mathsf{ct}'_7, \mathsf{ct}'_8)\Big) \in \mathbb{G}^{8n+6} \times \mathbb{G}_T^2
\end{aligned}$$

5.3 Master Public Key Verification

Let $x = \mathsf{mpk}$. Since g and $\mathbf{e}(g,g)$ are generators for the groups $\mathbb{G}$ and $\mathbb{G}_T$ of prime order p, we can represent all components of x as a power of either g or $\mathbf{e}(g,g)$. That is, there exist $\Omega, k', \{w_{b,i}, f_{b,i}, t_{b,i}, h_{b,i}\}, \{\delta_b, \theta_b, k_b\}$ for $i \in [n]$ and $b \in [2]$, in $\mathbb{Z}_p$ such that: $h = g^{\Omega}, \Lambda = \mathbf{e}(g,g)^{k'}, W_{b,i} = g^{w_{b,i}}, F_{b,i} = g^{f_{b,i}}, T_{b,i} = g^{t_{b,i}}, H_{b,i} = g^{h_{b,i}}, U_b = g^{\delta_b}, V_b = g^{\theta_b}, K_b = g^{k_b}$. The following holds:

$$\begin{aligned}
&\mathbf{e}(g,h) = \mathbf{e}(U_1, W_{2,i}) \cdot \mathbf{e}(U_2, W_{1,i})^{-1} = \mathbf{e}(V_1, T_{2,i}) \cdot \mathbf{e}(V_2, T_{1,i})^{-1} \Rightarrow \\
&\mathbf{e}(g, g^{\Omega}) = \mathbf{e}(g^{\delta_1}, g^{w_{2,i}}) \cdot \mathbf{e}(g^{\delta_2}, g^{-w_{1,i}}) = \mathbf{e}(g^{\theta_1}, g^{t_{2,i}}) \cdot \mathbf{e}(g^{\theta_2}, g^{-t_{1,i}}) \\
&\Rightarrow \Omega = \delta_1 w_{2,i} - \delta_2 w_{1,i} = \theta_1 t_{2,i} - \theta_2 t_{1,i}. \\
&\mathbf{e}(K_1, K_2) = \mathbf{e}(g^{k_1}, g^{k_2}) = \Lambda = \mathbf{e}(g, g^{k'}) \Rightarrow k' = k_1 k_2 \\
&\text{By defining } g' = g^{k'}, K_1 = g^{k_1}, K_2 = g^{k_2}, \text{it follows that:} \\
&\Lambda = e(K_1, K_2), K_1 = g^k, K_2 = g'^{\frac{1}{k}}
\end{aligned}$$

Hence, we have the verification algorithm in Fig. 2 for master public key.

Input: mpk, **Output:** 1 if mpk is a well-generated master public key for IP scheme and 0 otherwise

(1) If $\Lambda \neq \mathbf{e}(K_1, K_2)$. output 0 otherwise go to the next step

(2) For $i = 1$ to n do :

  ($i.a$) If $\mathbf{e}(U_1, W_{2,i}) \cdot \mathbf{e}(U_2, W_{1,i})^{-1} \neq \mathbf{e}(h, g)$ output 0 else go to the next step

  ($i.b$) If $\mathbf{e}(V_1, T_{2,i}) \cdot \mathbf{e}(V_2, T_{1,i})^{-1} \neq \mathbf{e}(h, g)$ output 0 else go to the next step

(3) Output 1.

Fig. 2. Master public key verification algorithm. (membership in relation $\mathrm{R}_{\mathsf{IP}}^{\mathsf{mpk}}$)

5.4 Token Verification Algorithms

As it was defined in Sect. 4, there are two relations for tokens, $\mathsf{R}_{\mathsf{IP}}^{\mathsf{tok}}$ and $\mathsf{R}^{\mathsf{tok}}$. The algorithm in Fig. 3 verifies membership in relation $\mathsf{R}_{\mathsf{IP}}^{\mathsf{tok}}$.

Input: $\mathsf{MPK}, \boldsymbol{v} = (v_1, \dots, v_n) \neq \mathbf{0}, \mathsf{tok}$
Output: 1 if tok is a well-generated token for IP scheme and 0 otherwise

1. If $\boldsymbol{v} = \mathbf{0}$ output 0 else let i^* be an index such that $v_{i^*} \neq 0$
2. Compute $\Lambda_1^* = \mathbf{e}(K_{3,i}, U_1) \cdot \mathbf{e}(K_{4,i}, U_2)$ and $\Lambda_2^* = \mathbf{e}(K_{5,i}, V_1) \cdot \mathbf{e}(K_{6,i}, V_2)$
3. If $\Lambda_1^* = 1_{\mathbb{G}_T}$ OR $\Lambda_2^* = 1_{\mathbb{G}_T}$ output $\perp$
4. For $i = 1$ to n do:
   (a) If $\Big(\mathbf{e}(K_{3,i}, U_1) \cdot \mathbf{e}(K_{4,i}, U_2)\Big)^{v_{i^*}} \neq (\Lambda_1^*)^{v_i}$ output 0
   (b) If $\Big(\mathbf{e}(K_{5,i}, V_1) \cdot \mathbf{e}(K_{6,i}, V_2)\Big)^{v_{i^*}} \neq (\Lambda_2^*)^{v_i}$ output 0
5. If $\Lambda \prod_{i=1}^{n} \mathbf{e}(K_{3,i}, F_{1,i})^{-1} \cdot \mathbf{e}(K_{4,i}, F_{2,i})^{-1} \cdot \mathbf{e}(K_{5,i}, H_{1,i})^{-1} \mathbf{e}(K_{6,i}, H_{2,i})^{-1} \neq \mathbf{e}(K_A, g)$ output 0.
6. If $\prod_{i=1}^{n} \mathbf{e}(K_{3,i}, W_{1,i}) \cdot \mathbf{e}(K_{4,i}, W_{2,i}) \cdot \mathbf{e}(K_{5,i}, T_{1,i}) \cdot \mathbf{e}(K_{6,i}, T_{2,i}) \neq \mathbf{e}(h, K_B)^{-1}$ output 0.
7. Output 1.

Fig. 3. First token verification algorithm. (membership in relation $\mathsf{R}_{\mathsf{IP}}^{\mathsf{tok}}$)

Correctness of the algorithm: For simplicity let's assume $v_1 \neq 0$ and $i^* = 1$.

- $\Lambda_1^*, \Lambda_2^* \in \mathbb{G}_T \Rightarrow \exists \lambda_1, \lambda_2 \in \mathbb{Z}_p$ *s.t.* $\Lambda_1^* = e(g,h)^{\lambda_1 v_1}, \Lambda_2^* = e(g,h)^{\lambda_2 v_1}$
- $\forall i \in [n]\ \exists r_i, r_i' \in \mathbb{Z}_p$ *s.t.* $K_{3,i} = g^{-\delta_2 r_i} \cdot g^{\lambda_1 v_i w_{2,i}}, K_{4,i} = g^{\delta_1 r_i'} \cdot g^{-\lambda_1 v_i w_{1,i}}$

$$\Rightarrow \mathbf{e}(K_{3,i}, U_1) \cdot \mathbf{e}(K_{4,i}, U_2) = \mathbf{e}(g^{-\delta_2 r_i} \cdot g^{\lambda_1 v_i w_{2,i}}, g^{\delta_1}) \cdot \mathbf{e}(g^{\delta_1 r_i'} \cdot g^{-\lambda_1 v_i w_{1,i}}, g^{\delta_2}) = \mathbf{e}(g,g)^{\delta_1\delta_2(r_i'-r_i)} \cdot \mathbf{e}(g,h)^{\lambda_1 v_i} =$$

$$\Rightarrow \Big(\mathbf{e}(K_{3,i}, U_1) \cdot \mathbf{e}(K_{4,i}, U_2)\Big)^{v_1} = \mathbf{e}(g,g)^{v_1\delta_1\delta_2(r_i'-r_i)} \cdot \mathbf{e}(g,h)^{\lambda_1 v_1 v_i}$$

- **Step 3:** $\Lambda_1^* \neq 1_{\mathbb{G}_T}, \Lambda_2^* \neq 1_{\mathbb{G}_T} \Rightarrow \lambda_1 \neq 0, \lambda_2 \neq 0$
- **Step 4.a:** If $\Big(\mathbf{e}(K_{3,i}, U_1) \cdot \mathbf{e}(K_{4,i}, U_2)\Big)^{v_1} = (\Lambda_1^*)^{v_i} \Rightarrow \mathbf{e}(g,g)^{v_1\delta_1\delta_2(r_i'-r_i)} \cdot \mathbf{e}(h,g)^{\lambda_1 v_1 v_i} = \mathbf{e}(g,h)^{\lambda_1 v_1 v_i} \Rightarrow \mathbf{e}(g,g)^{v_1\delta_1\delta_2(r_i'-r_i)} = 1_{\mathbb{G}_T} \Rightarrow \forall i \in [n] : r_i = r_i' \Rightarrow K_{3,i} = g^{-\delta_2 r_i} \cdot g^{\lambda_1 v_i w_{2,i}}, K_{4,i} = g^{\delta_1 r_i} \cdot g^{-\lambda_1 v_i w_{1,i}}$ And similar computations show that the equality in step (4.b) holds for all $i \in [n]$. Then we conclude that there exists $\phi_i \in \mathbb{Z}_p$ such that: $K_{5,i} = g^{-\theta_2\phi_i} \cdot g^{\lambda_2 v_i t_{2,i}}, K_{6,i} = g^{\theta_1\phi_i} \cdot g^{-\lambda_2 v_i t_{1,i}}$.

- **Step 5**

$$K_A = g' \prod_{i=1}^{n} K_{3,i}^{-f_{1,i}} K_{4,i}^{-f_{2,i}} K_{5,i}^{-h_{1,i}} K_{6,i}^{-h_{2,i}}$$
$$\Longleftrightarrow \mathbf{e}(K_A, g) = \mathbf{e}(g' \prod_{i=1}^{n} K_{3,i}^{-f_{1,i}} K_{4,i}^{-f_{2,i}} K_{5,i}^{-h_{1,i}} K_{6,i}^{-h_{2,i}}, g)$$
$$\Longleftrightarrow \mathbf{e}(K_A, g) = \Lambda \cdot \prod_{i=1}^{n} \mathbf{e}(K_{3,i}, F_{1,i})^{-1}.\mathbf{e}(K_{4,i}, F_{2,i})^{-1}.\mathbf{e}(K_{5,i}, H_{1,i})^{-1}$$
$$\mathbf{e}(K_{6,i}, H_{2,i})^{-1}.$$

- **Step 6**

$$\prod_{i=1}^{n} \mathbf{e}(K_{3,i}, W_{1,i}) \cdot \mathbf{e}(K_{4,i}, W_{2,i}) \cdot \mathbf{e}(K_{5,i}, T_{1,i}) \cdot \mathbf{e}(K_{6,i}, T_{2,i}) = \mathbf{e}(h, K_B)^{-1}$$
$$= \prod_{i=1}^{n} \mathbf{e}(g^{r_i(\delta_1 w_{2,i} - \delta_2 w_{1,i})}, g) \cdot \mathbf{e}(g^{\phi_i(\theta_1 t_{2,i} - \theta_2 t_{1,i})}, g) = \mathbf{e}(h, K_B)^{-1}$$
$$= \prod_{i=1}^{n} \mathbf{e}(g, h)^{r_i + \phi_i} = \mathbf{e}(h, K_B)^{-1} \Rightarrow K_B = \prod_{i=1}^{n} g^{-(r_i + \phi_i)}$$

The second relation is a disjunction of two predicates, $\mathfrak{R}^{\mathsf{tok}}(x, w) = P_1^{\mathsf{tok}} \vee P_2^{\mathsf{tok}}$. The proof of membership for this relation can be implemented using the equations for the token verification algorithm for relation $\mathfrak{R}_{\mathsf{IP}}^{\mathsf{tok}}$ Fig. 3 and assuming to have pairing product equations corresponding to the commitments in the two aforementioned predicates. We skip further details.

5.5 $\mathsf{NIWI}^{\mathsf{enc}} = \langle \mathcal{P}^{\mathsf{enc}}, \mathcal{V}^{\mathsf{enc}} \rangle$: NIWI-Proof for Encryption Algorithm

For the relation $\mathfrak{R}_{\mathsf{IP}}^{\mathsf{ct}}$, we first provide a proof of satisfiability for a system of equations related to a single ciphertext, that is $k = 1$, and we will later extend it to the case of two ciphertexts, that is $k = 2$. For $k > 2$, the algorithm is similar to the case $k = 2$.

Let $x = (\mathsf{mpk}, \mathsf{ct})$. We define the following variables for $i \in [n]$:

$$\mathcal{S}_1 = g^{s_1}, \mathcal{S}_3 = g^{s_3}, \mathcal{S}_4 = g^{s_4}, \mathcal{X}_i = g^{x_i}, \mathcal{S}_1' = g^{s_1'}, \mathcal{S}_3' = g^{s_3'}, \mathcal{U}_1 = U_1^{s_3},$$
$$\mathcal{U}_2 = U_2^{s_3}, \mathcal{V}_1 = V_1^{s_4}, \mathcal{V}_2 = V_2^{s_4}, \mathcal{U}_1' = U_1^{s_3'}, \mathcal{U}_2' = U_2^{s_3'}, \mathcal{K}_1 = K_1^{s_2}, \mathcal{K}_1' = K_1^{s_2'}$$

We have the following Equations related to component $\mathsf{ct}_2 (\mathsf{ct}_2')$:

$$\mathbf{e}(\mathsf{ct}_2, g) = \mathbf{e}(h^{s_1}, g) = \mathbf{e}(h, g^{s_1}) = \mathbf{e}(h, \mathcal{S}_1), \left(\mathbf{e}(\mathsf{ct}_2', g) = \mathbf{e}(h, \mathcal{S}_1')\right)$$

and related equation to $\mathsf{ct}_{3,i}$ for $i \in [n]$: (Same computation results the same equations for $\mathsf{ct}_{j,i}, \mathsf{ct}'_{j,i}$ for $j = 3, 4, 5, 6$)

$$\begin{aligned}\mathsf{e}(\mathsf{ct}_{3,i}, g) &= \mathsf{e}(W_{1,i}^{s_1}, g) \cdot \mathsf{e}(F_{1,i}^{s_2}, g) \cdot \mathsf{e}(U_1^{s_3 x_i}, g) \\ &= \mathsf{e}(W_{1,i}, g^{s_1}) \cdot \mathsf{e}(F_{1,i}, g^{s_2}) \cdot \mathsf{e}(U_1^{s_3}, g^{x_i}) \\ &= \mathsf{e}(W_{1,i}, \mathcal{S}_1) \cdot \mathsf{e}(F_{1,i}, \mathsf{ct}_1) \cdot \mathsf{e}(\mathcal{U}_1, \mathcal{X}_i) \\ \Rightarrow &\mathsf{e}(\mathsf{ct}_{3,i}, g) \cdot \mathsf{e}(F_{1,i}, \mathsf{ct}_1)^{-1} = \mathsf{e}(W_{1,i}, \mathcal{S}_1) \cdot \mathsf{e}(\mathcal{U}_1, \mathcal{X}_i)\end{aligned}$$

The equations show that the exponent of $U_b^{s_3}$ and $V_b^{s_4}$ in $\mathsf{ct}_{3,i}, \mathsf{ct}_{4,i}, \mathsf{ct}_{5,i}, \mathsf{ct}_{6,i}$ are x_i. So we have the following equation:

$$\mathsf{e}(\mathcal{U}_1, U_2) \cdot \mathsf{e}(U_1^{-1}, \mathcal{U}_2) = \mathsf{e}(U^{s_3}, U_2) \cdot \mathsf{e}(U_1^{-1}, U_2^{s_3}) = \mathsf{e}(U_1, U_2)^{s_3 - s_3} = 1_{\mathbb{G}_T}$$
$$\mathsf{e}(\mathcal{V}_1, V_2) \cdot \mathsf{e}(V_1^{-1}, \mathcal{V}_2) = \mathsf{e}(V^{s_4}, V_2) \cdot \mathsf{e}(V_1^{-1}, V_2^{s_4}) = \mathsf{e}(V_1, V_2)^{s_4 - s_4} = 1_{\mathbb{G}_T}$$

The equation related to $\mathsf{ct}_7 = \mathsf{e}(g^{s_3}, g^{s_4})$ is the following:

$$\mathsf{ct}_7 = \mathsf{e}(g^{s_3}, g^{s_4}) = \mathsf{e}(\mathcal{S}_3, \mathcal{S}_4), \mathsf{ct}'_7 = \mathsf{e}(g^{s'_3}, g^{s_4}) = \mathsf{e}(\mathcal{S}'_3, \mathcal{S}_4)$$

To prove $s_3 \neq s'_3$, we just need to check whether $\mathsf{ct}_7 \neq \mathsf{ct}'_7$ or not.

$$\mathsf{ct}_7 \neq \mathsf{ct}'_7 \Rightarrow \mathsf{e}(g^{s_3}, g^{s_4}) \neq \mathsf{e}(g^{s'_3}, g^{s_4}) \Rightarrow s_3 \neq s'_3.$$

The equation related to $\mathsf{ct}_8, \mathsf{ct}'_8$ is the following:

$$\mathsf{ct}_8 = \Lambda^{-s_2} \cdot m, \mathsf{ct}'_8 = \Lambda^{-s'_2} \cdot m \Rightarrow \mathsf{ct}_8^{-1} \cdot \mathsf{ct}'_8 = \Lambda^{s_2} \cdot m^{-1} \Lambda^{-s'_2} \cdot m = \Lambda^{s_2 - s'_2}$$
$$\Rightarrow \mathsf{ct}_8^{-1} \cdot \mathsf{ct}'_8 = \mathsf{e}(K_1, K_2)^{s_2 - s'_2} = \mathsf{e}(K_1, K_2^{s_2}) \cdot \mathsf{e}(K_1^{-1}, K_2^{s'_2}) = \mathsf{e}(K_1, \mathcal{K}_2) \cdot \mathsf{e}(K_1^{-1}, \mathcal{K}'_1)$$

And to prove that $\mathsf{ct}_1 = g^{s_2}$ and $\mathsf{ct}_8 = \lambda^{-s_2} \cdot m$, we add the following equation:

$$\mathsf{e}(\mathsf{ct}_1, K_1) = \mathsf{e}(g, \mathcal{K}_1), \mathsf{e}(\mathsf{ct}'_1, K_1) = \mathsf{e}(g, \mathcal{K}'_1)$$

So we have the following system of equations for one single ciphertext.

$$\mathsf{E}_{\mathsf{ct}}: \begin{cases} \mathsf{e}(\mathsf{ct}_2, g) = \mathsf{e}(h, \mathcal{S}_1), \mathsf{e}(\mathsf{ct}'_2, g) = \mathsf{e}(h, \mathcal{S}'_1) \\ \mathsf{e}(\hat{\mathsf{ct}}_2, \hat{g}) = \mathsf{e}(\hat{h}, \hat{\mathcal{S}}_1), \mathsf{e}(\hat{\mathsf{ct}}'_2, \hat{g}) = \mathsf{e}(\hat{h}, \hat{\mathcal{S}}'_1) \\ \mathsf{e}(\mathsf{ct}_{3,i}, g) \cdot \mathsf{e}(F_{1,i}, \mathsf{ct}_1)^{-1} = \mathsf{e}(W_{1,i}, \mathcal{S}_1) \cdot \mathsf{e}(\mathcal{U}_1, \mathcal{X}_i) \\ \mathsf{e}(\mathsf{ct}'_{3,i}, g) \cdot \mathsf{e}(F_{1,i}, \mathsf{ct}'_1)^{-1} = \mathsf{e}(W_{1,i}, \mathcal{S}'_1) \cdot \mathsf{e}(\mathcal{U}'_1, \mathcal{X}_i) \\ \mathsf{e}(\mathsf{ct}_{4,i}, g) \cdot \mathsf{e}(F_{2,i}, \mathsf{ct}_1)^{-1} = \mathsf{e}(W_{2,i}, \mathcal{S}_1) \cdot \mathsf{e}(\mathcal{U}_2, \mathcal{X}_i) \\ \mathsf{e}(\mathsf{ct}'_{4,i}, g) \cdot \mathsf{e}(F_{2,i}, \mathsf{ct}'_1)^{-1} = \mathsf{e}(W_{2,i}, \mathcal{S}'_1) \cdot \mathsf{e}(\mathcal{U}'_2, \mathcal{X}_i) \\ \mathsf{e}(\mathsf{ct}_{5,i}, g) \cdot \mathsf{e}(H_{1,i}, \mathsf{ct}_2)^{-1} = \mathsf{e}(T_{1,i}, \mathcal{S}_1) \cdot \mathsf{e}(\mathcal{V}_1, \mathcal{X}_i) \\ \mathsf{e}(\mathsf{ct}'_{5,i}, g) \cdot \mathsf{e}(H_{1,i}, \mathsf{ct}'_2)^{-1} = \mathsf{e}(T_{1,i}, \mathcal{S}'_1) \cdot \mathsf{e}(\mathcal{V}_1, \mathcal{X}_i) \\ \mathsf{e}(\mathsf{ct}_{6,i}, g) \cdot \mathsf{e}(H_{2,i}, \mathsf{ct}_2)^{-1} = \mathsf{e}(T_{2,i}, \mathcal{S}_1) \cdot \mathsf{e}(\mathcal{V}_2, \mathcal{X}_i) \\ \mathsf{e}(\mathsf{ct}'_{6,i}, g) \cdot \mathsf{e}(H_{2,i}, \mathsf{ct}'_2)^{-1} = \mathsf{e}(T_{2,i}, \mathcal{S}'_1) \cdot \mathsf{e}(\mathcal{V}_2, \mathcal{X}_i) \\ \mathsf{ct}_7 = \mathsf{e}(\mathcal{S}_3, \mathcal{S}_4), \mathsf{ct}'_7 = \mathsf{e}(\mathcal{S}'_3, \mathcal{S}_4), \hat{\mathsf{ct}}_7 = \mathsf{e}(\hat{\mathcal{S}}_3, \hat{\mathcal{S}}_4), \hat{\mathsf{ct}}'_7 = \mathsf{e}(\hat{\mathcal{S}}'_3, \hat{\mathcal{S}}_4) \\ \mathsf{ct}_8^{-1} \cdot \mathsf{ct}'_8 = \mathsf{e}(K_1, \mathcal{K}_2) \cdot \mathsf{e}(K_1^{-1}, \mathcal{K}'_1), \hat{\mathsf{ct}}_8^{-1} \cdot \hat{\mathsf{ct}}'_8 = \mathsf{e}(\hat{K}_1, \hat{\mathcal{K}}_2) \cdot \mathsf{e}(\hat{K}_1^{-1}, \hat{\mathcal{K}}'_1) \\ \mathsf{e}(\mathsf{ct}_1, K_1) = \mathsf{e}(g, \mathcal{K}_1), \mathsf{e}(\mathsf{ct}'_1, K_1) = \mathsf{e}(g, \mathcal{K}'_1) \end{cases}$$

Now we need to provide a proof that two ciphertexts $\mathsf{ct}, \hat{\mathsf{ct}}$ are the encryption of a single message m and a single attribute $\boldsymbol{x}$:

$$\mathcal{X}_i = g^{x_i}, \hat{\mathcal{X}}_i = \hat{g}^{x_i} \Rightarrow \mathbf{e}(\mathcal{X}_i, \hat{g}) = \mathbf{e}(g, \hat{\mathcal{X}}_i) \Rightarrow \mathbf{e}(\mathcal{X}_i, \hat{g}) \cdot \mathbf{e}(g, \hat{\mathcal{X}}_i)^{-1} = 1_{\mathbb{G}_T}$$

Notice that $\mathsf{ct}_8, \mathsf{ct}'_8$ are the only components of the ciphertext which are related to the message, m, so we have:

$$\left(\mathsf{ct}_8 = \Lambda^{-s_2}\mathbf{m}, \hat{\mathsf{ct}}_8 = \hat{\Lambda}^{-\hat{s}_2}\mathbf{m}\right) \Rightarrow \mathsf{ct}_8\hat{\mathsf{ct}}_8^{-1} = \Lambda^{-s_2} \cdot \hat{\Lambda}^{\hat{s}_2} =$$
$$\mathbf{e}(K_1^{s_2}, K_2^{-1}) \cdot \mathbf{e}(\hat{K}_1^{\hat{s}_2}, \hat{K}_2) == \mathbf{e}(\mathcal{K}_1, K_2^{-1}) \cdot \mathbf{e}(\hat{\mathcal{K}}_1, \hat{K}_2) = \mathbf{e}(K_1^{-1}, \mathcal{K}_2) \cdot \mathbf{e}(\hat{K}_1, \hat{\mathcal{K}}_2)$$

So the prover has to provide a proof for the following system of equations:

$$\mathsf{E}_{\mathsf{ct}-\hat{\mathsf{ct}}}: \begin{cases} \mathsf{ct}_8\hat{\mathsf{ct}}_8^{-1} = \mathbf{e}(\mathcal{K}_1, K_2^{-1},) \cdot \mathbf{e}(\hat{\mathcal{K}}_1, \hat{K}_2) \\ \mathsf{ct}_8\hat{\mathsf{ct}}_8^{-1} = \mathbf{e}(K_1^{-1}, \mathcal{K}_2) \cdot \mathbf{e}(\hat{K}_1, \hat{\mathcal{K}}_2) \\ \mathbf{e}(g, \mathcal{K}_1) = \mathbf{e}(\mathsf{ct}_1, K_1)\ , \mathbf{e}(\hat{g}, \hat{\mathcal{K}}_1) = \mathbf{e}(\hat{\mathsf{ct}}_1, \hat{K}_1) \\ \mathbf{e}(\mathcal{X}_i, \hat{g}) \cdot \mathbf{e}(g, \hat{\mathcal{X}}_i)^{-1} = 1_{\mathbb{G}_T} \end{cases}$$

Summing up, to provide the NIWI-proof system for encryption algorithm the prover uses Groth-Sahai proof-system for the system of equations, $\mathsf{E}_{\mathsf{CT}} = \mathsf{Ect} \wedge \mathsf{E}_{\mathsf{ct}-\hat{\mathsf{ct}}}$.

6 Conclusion

Our main contribution is the first *efficient* verifiable (attribute-hiding) IPE scheme from bilinear groups. The privacy of our scheme is based on the standard DLIN assumption whereas its verifiability is unconditional. Towards this goal, we also constructed the first perfectly correct inner product encryption scheme for plaintexts of arbitrary length. Our VIPE scheme is selectively secure only; we leave as an interesting open problem the construction of a fully secure one.

Acknowledgments. We would like to thank the Luxembourg National Research Fund (FNR) for funding this reserach. In particular N. Soroush and V. Iovino were supported by the FNR CORE project FESS (no. C16/IS/11299247). A. Rial was supported by the FNR CORE project SZK (no. C17/11650748) and P. Roenne was supported by the INTER-SURCVS project.

References

1. Abdalla, M., et al.: Searchable encryption revisited: consistency properties, relation to anonymous IBE, and extensions. In: Shoup, V. (ed.) CRYPTO 2005. LNCS, vol. 3621, pp. 205–222. Springer, Heidelberg (2005). https://doi.org/10.1007/11535218_13
2. Badrinarayanan, S., Goyal, V., Jain, A., Sahai, A.: Verifiable functional encryption. In: Cheon, J.H., Takagi, T. (eds.) ASIACRYPT 2016, Part II. LNCS, vol. 10032, pp. 557–587. Springer, Heidelberg (2016). https://doi.org/10.1007/978-3-662-53890-6_19

3. Baltico, C.E.Z., Catalano, D., Fiore, D., Gay, R.: Practical functional encryption for quadratic functions with applications to predicate encryption. In: Katz, J., Shacham, H. (eds.) CRYPTO 2017, Part I. LNCS, vol. 10401, pp. 67–98. Springer, Cham (2017). https://doi.org/10.1007/978-3-319-63688-7_3
4. Boneh, D., Canetti, R., Halevi, S., Katz, J.: Chosen-ciphertext security from identity-based encryption. SIAM J. Comput. **36**(5), 1301–1328 (2007)
5. Boneh, D., Di Crescenzo, G., Ostrovsky, R., Persiano, G.: Public key encryption with keyword search. In: Cachin, C., Camenisch, J.L. (eds.) EUROCRYPT 2004. LNCS, vol. 3027, pp. 506–522. Springer, Heidelberg (2004). https://doi.org/10.1007/978-3-540-24676-3_30
6. Boneh, D., Franklin, M.K.: Identity-based encryption from the Weil pairing. In: Kilian, J. (ed.) CRYPTO 2001. LNCS, vol. 2139, pp. 213–229. Springer, Heidelberg (2001). https://doi.org/10.1007/3-540-44647-8_13
7. Boneh, D., Sahai, A., Waters, B.: Functional encryption: definitions and challenges. In: Ishai, Y. (ed.) TCC 2011. LNCS, vol. 6597, pp. 253–273. Springer, Heidelberg (2011). https://doi.org/10.1007/978-3-642-19571-6_16
8. Boneh, D., Waters, B.: Conjunctive, subset, and range queries on encrypted data. In: Vadhan, S.P. (ed.) TCC 2007. LNCS, vol. 4392, pp. 535–554. Springer, Heidelberg (2007). https://doi.org/10.1007/978-3-540-70936-7_29
9. Cocks, C.: An identity based encryption scheme based on quadratic residues. In: Honary, B. (ed.) Cryptography and Coding 2001. LNCS, vol. 2260, pp. 360–363. Springer, Heidelberg (2001). https://doi.org/10.1007/3-540-45325-3_32
10. De Caro, A., Iovino, V.: On the power of rewinding simulators in functional encryption. Des. Codes Cryptogr. **84**(3), 373–399 (2016). https://doi.org/10.1007/s10623-016-0272-x
11. De Caro, A., Iovino, V., Jain, A., O'Neill, A., Paneth, O., Persiano, G.: On the achievability of simulation-based security for functional encryption. In: Canetti, R., Garay, J.A. (eds.) CRYPTO 2013, Part II. LNCS, vol. 8043, pp. 519–535. Springer, Heidelberg (2013). https://doi.org/10.1007/978-3-642-40084-1_29
12. Groth, J.: Simulation-sound NIZK proofs for a practical language and constant size group signatures. In: Lai, X., Chen, K. (eds.) ASIACRYPT 2006. LNCS, vol. 4284, pp. 444–459. Springer, Heidelberg (2006). https://doi.org/10.1007/11935230_29
13. Groth, J., Ostrovsky, R., Sahai, A.: Non-interactive zaps and new techniques for NIZK. In: Dwork, C. (ed.) CRYPTO 2006. LNCS, vol. 4117, pp. 97–111. Springer, Heidelberg (2006). https://doi.org/10.1007/11818175_6
14. Groth, J., Sahai, A.: Efficient non-interactive proof systems for bilinear groups. In: Smart, N. (ed.) EUROCRYPT 2008. LNCS, vol. 4965, pp. 415–432. Springer, Heidelberg (2008). https://doi.org/10.1007/978-3-540-78967-3_24
15. Iovino, V., Żebroski, K.: Simulation-based secure functional encryption in the random oracle model. In: Lauter, K., Rodríguez-Henríquez, F. (eds.) LATINCRYPT 2015. LNCS, vol. 9230, pp. 21–39. Springer, Cham (2015). https://doi.org/10.1007/978-3-319-22174-8_2
16. Ishai, Y., Kushilevitz, E., Ostrovsky, R., Sahai, A.: Zero-knowledge from secure multiparty computation. In: Proceedings of the 39th Annual ACM Symposium on Theory of Computing, San Diego, California, USA, 11–13 June 2007, pp. 21–30 (2007)
17. Kate, A., Zaverucha, G.M., Goldberg, I.: Constant-size commitments to polynomials and their applications. In: Abe, M. (ed.) ASIACRYPT 2010. LNCS, vol. 6477, pp. 177–194. Springer, Heidelberg (2010). https://doi.org/10.1007/978-3-642-17373-8_11

18. Katz, J., Sahai, A., Waters, B.: Predicate encryption supporting disjunctions, polynomial equations, and inner products. In: Smart, N. (ed.) EUROCRYPT 2008. LNCS, vol. 4965, pp. 146–162. Springer, Heidelberg (2008). https://doi.org/10.1007/978-3-540-78967-3_9
19. Lewko, A.B., Okamoto, T., Sahai, A., Takashima, K., Waters, B.: Fully secure functional encryption: attribute-based encryption and (hierarchical) inner product encryption. In: Gilbert, H. (ed.) EUROCRYPT 2010. LNCS, vol. 6110, pp. 62–91. Springer, Heidelberg (2010). https://doi.org/10.1007/978-3-642-13190-5_4
20. Libert, B., Ramanna, S.C., Yung, M.: Functional commitment schemes: from polynomial commitments to pairing-based accumulators from simple assumptions. In: 43rd International Colloquium on Automata, Languages, and Programming, ICALP 2016, 11–15 July 2016, Rome, Italy, pp. 30:1–30:14 (2016)
21. Okamoto, T., Takashima, K.: Adaptively attribute-hiding (hierarchical) inner product encryption. In: Pointcheval, D., Johansson, T. (eds.) EUROCRYPT 2012. LNCS, vol. 7237, pp. 591–608. Springer, Heidelberg (2012). https://doi.org/10.1007/978-3-642-29011-4_35
22. Park, J.H.: Inner-product encryption under standard assumptions. Des. Codes Cryptogr. **58**(3), 235–257 (2011). https://doi.org/10.1007/s10623-010-9405-9
23. Sahai, A., Waters, B.: Fuzzy identity-based encryption. In: Cramer, R. (ed.) EUROCRYPT 2005. LNCS, vol. 3494, pp. 457–473. Springer, Heidelberg (2005). https://doi.org/10.1007/11426639_27
24. Shamir, A.: Identity-based cryptosystems and signature schemes. In: Blakley, G.R., Chaum, D. (eds.) CRYPTO 1984. LNCS, vol. 196, pp. 47–53. Springer, Heidelberg (1985). https://doi.org/10.1007/3-540-39568-7_5
25. Soroush, N., Iovino, V., Rial, A., Roenne, P.B., Ryan, P.Y.A.: Verifiable inner product encryption scheme. Cryptology ePrint Archive, Report 2020/122 (2020). https://eprint.iacr.org/2020/122
26. Tang, Q., Ji, D.: Verifiable attribute-based encryption. IJ Netw. Secur. **10**(2), 114–120 (2010)

A New Paradigm for Public-Key Functional Encryption for Degree-2 Polynomials

Romain Gay(✉)

Cornell Tech, New York, NY, USA
romain.gay@cornell.edu

Abstract. We give the first public-key functional encryption that supports the generation of functional decryption keys for degree-2 polynomials, with succinct ciphertexts, whose semi-adaptive simulation-based security is proven under standard assumptions. At the heart of our new paradigm lies a so-called partially function-hiding functional encryption scheme for inner products, which admits public-key instances, and that is sufficient to build functional encryption for degree-2 polynomials. Doing so, we improve upon prior works, such as the constructions from Lin (CRYPTO 17) or Ananth Sahai (EUROCRYPT 17), both of which rely on function-hiding inner product FE, that can only exist in the private-key setting. The simplicity of our construction yields the most efficient FE for quadratic functions from standard assumptions (even those satisfying a weaker security notion). The interest of our methodology is that the FE for quadratic functions that builds upon any partially function-hiding FE for inner products inherits the security properties of the latter. In particular, we build a partially function-hiding FE for inner products that enjoys simulation security, in the semi-adaptive setting, where the challenge sent from the adversary can be chosen adaptively after seeing the public key (but before corrupting functional decryption keys). This is in contrast from prior public-key FE for quadratic functions from Baltico et al. (CRYPTO 17), which only achieved an indistinguishability-based, selective security. As a bonus, we show that we can obtain security against Chosen-Ciphertext Attacks straightforwardly. Even though this is the de facto security notion for encryption, this was not achieved by prior functional encryption schemes for quadratic functions, where the generic Fujisaki Okamoto transformation (CRYPTO 99) does not apply.

R. Gay—Supported in part by NSF Award SATC-1704788 and in part by the Office of the Director of National Intelligence (ODNI), Intelligence Advanced Research Projects Activity (IARPA), via 2019-19-020700006. The views and conclusions contained herein are those of the authors and should not be interpreted as necessarily representing the official policies, either expressed or implied, of ODNI, IARPA, or the U.S. Government. The U.S. Government is authorized to reproduce and distribute reprints for governmental purposes notwithstanding any copyright annotation therein.

A. Kiayias et al. (Eds.): PKC 2020, LNCS 12110, pp. 95–120, 2020.
https://doi.org/10.1007/978-3-030-45374-9_4

1 Introduction

Functional Encryption [O'N10, BSW11](in short: FE) is a general paradigm where restricted decryption keys are generated, that let users learn specific functions of the encrypted data. Namely, each decryption key sk_f is associated with a function f, and the decryption of an encrypted message x with sk_f recovers $f(x)$, and nothing else. The scheme must be resistant to any collusion of decryption keys sk_f for different functions f: such group of keys should not learn anything more than the information leaked by each key sk_f, individually. This security property makes FE schemes both hard to build and extremely useful, provided the class of function they handle is large. In fact, it has been shown [BV15, AJ15] that general purpose functional encryption gives a construction of Indinstiguishability Obfuscation [BGI+01, GGG+14] (in short: iO) for all circuits, a powerful object that has been remarkably successful at providing an all-purpose tool for solving cryptographic problems [SW14]. Surprisingly, even FE for smaller classes of functions are powerful. Recently, [LT17] has shown that succinct FE supporting degree-3 functions is sufficient to build iO, together with additional assumptions on the existence of special kind of pseudo-random generators[1]. However, there is no construction of such FE schemes from standard, well understood assumptions. All known constructions rely on either multilinear maps, or iO itself. Can we build FE for rich classes of functions from standard assumptions?

Beyond the case of predicate encryption [BW07, KSW08, GVW15], little is known about standard-based FE constructions. [ABDP15] gave the first construction of FE for inner products, where the encryption of a vector $\mathbf{x} \in \mathbb{Z}^n$, together with a decryption key associated with vector $\mathbf{y} \in \mathbb{Z}^n$, yields the inner product of $\mathbf{x}$ and $\mathbf{y}$. That is, their scheme can generate decryption keys that compute a weighted sum on encrypted data. They prove selective security, a useful but artificial security notion where the adversary has to commit to its challenge ciphertext beforehand. Later, [ALS16] gave constructions with full security (aka adaptive security, where the adversary can request decryption keys and the challenge ciphertext adaptively). Both constructions use standard assumptions (DDH, LWE, DCR). Note that inner products already capture constant depth circuits, by simply expressing circuits as polynomials, and encrypting all the monomials (of constant degree). However, for most applications, and in particular to obtain iO, one needs to recursively apply the FE scheme to itself. This bootstrapping requires the ciphertexts to be succinct, that is, their size should only depend on the underlying message, and not on the function to be evaluated. Following this quest for succinct FE for richer classes of functions, [BCFG17] (concurrently [AS17, Lin17] in the private-key setting), gave the first construction of succinct FE that supports the evaluation of quadratic functions on ciphertexts. All of these constructions are proven secure under an indistinguishability-based security definition, which is cumbersome to use, and is too weak to meaningful security for some functionality. Moreover, all these schemes either achieve only selective security, or assume the generic group model.

[1] Namely, the existence of pseudo-random generators of block-wise locality 3.

Our Contributions. We build the first simulation-secure FE in the semi-adaptive setting, whose security relies on a standard assumption, that supports a functionality beyond inner products, or predicate encryption. In our scheme, ciphertexts are associated with two vectors $\mathbf{x} \in \mathbb{Z}^n$ and $\mathbf{y} \in \mathbb{Z}^m$, and decryption keys are associated with a matrix $\mathbf{F} \in \mathbb{Z}^{n \times m}$. The decryption of a ciphertext $\mathsf{ct}_{\mathbf{x},\mathbf{y}}$ with a decryption key $\mathsf{sk}_{\mathbf{F}}$ recovers $\mathbf{x}^\top \mathbf{F} \mathbf{y} \in \mathbb{Z}$. The ciphertext size is $O(n+m)$ group elements, and security relies on pairings (DLIN) (Fig. 1).

Scheme:	public-key	security	assumption
[AS17]	✗	SEL-IND	GGM
[Lin17]	✗	SEL-IND	SXDH
[BCFG17]	✓	SEL-IND	SXDH & 3-PDDH
[BCFG17,DGP18]	✓	AD-IND	GGM
ours	✓	SAD-SIM	DLIN

Fig. 1. Quadratic FE. Here, {AD, SAD, SEL}-{IND, SIM} stands for {adaptive, semi-adaptive, selective}-{indistinguishability, simulation} security. GGM stands for Generic Group Model .

To build our quadratic FE, we deploy a new paradigm that uses at its core a so-called partially function-hiding inner-product FE, where decryption keys partially hide their underlying function (in the case of inner product, their underlying vector). This approach allows us to obtain public-key FE, as opposed to prior work [AS17,Lin17] relying on full-fledged function-hiding inner-product FE, which is inherently private-key.

We then build a partially function-hiding inner-product FE with simulation security. This security notion implies its indistinguishability-based counterpart, and drastically simplifies the proof compared to previous works relying on indistinguishability-secure inner-product FE (for instance [Lin17]). This simplicity is illustrated by short ciphertexts and keys (see Fig. 2). We obtain simulation security in the semi-adaptive setting, where an adversary is restricted to choose its challenge before querying any secret keys. This is the best we can hope for: a simple extension of [BSW11,AGVW13] shows that adaptively simulation secure partially function-hiding inner-product FE are impossible to achieve from standard assumptions (note this impossibility result doesn't apply to schemes proved in the generic group model, such as the inner-product FE from [KLM+18]). As shown in [BSW11], indistiguishability-based security is inadequate for some functionality. For instance, if a ciphertext encrypts the seed of a PRG, and each functional decryption key is associated with one position of the output of the PRG, simulation-based security ensure that only the output of the PRG is revealed, whereas indistinguishability-based security is essentially useless, since it only proves that an encryption of a seed is computationally indistinguishable from an encryption of seed' if PRG(seed) = PRG(seed'). This example is relevant in the context of quadratic FE, since our construction is expressive enough to evaluate the output of a PRG (see Remark 1). This indicates that simulation security is qualitatively stronger than its indistinguisahbility-based counterpart.

Scheme:	$\|ct\|$	$\|sk\|$	sec., assump.
[BCFG17]	$2n\|\mathbb{G}_1\| + (2m+2)\|\mathbb{G}_2\|$	$2\|\mathbb{G}_1\| + \|\mathbb{G}_2\|$	AD-IND, GGM
[BCFG17]	$(6n+1)\|\mathbb{G}_1\| + (6m+1)\|\mathbb{G}_2\|$	$\|\mathbb{G}_1\| + [\mathbb{G}_2\|$	SEL-IND, SDXH & 3-PDDH
[DGP18]	$(2n+1)\|\mathbb{G}_1\| + 2m\|\mathbb{G}_2\|$	$\mathbb{G}_2$	AD-IND, GGM
ours	$(4n+2m+2)\|\mathbb{G}_1\| + m\|\mathbb{G}_2\|$	$(3n+2m+2)\|\mathbb{G}_2\|$	SAD-SIM, DLIN

Fig. 2. Efficiency comparison between public-key quadratic FE, where ciphertext encrypt $(\mathbf{x}, \mathbf{y}) \in \mathbb{Z}^n \times \mathbb{Z}^m$ and decryption keys are associated with $\mathbf{F} \in \mathbb{Z}^{n \times m}$. {AD, SAD, SEL}-{IND, SIM} stands for {adaptive, semi-adaptive, selective}-{indistinguishability, simulation} security. GGM stands for Generic Group Model. SXDH stands for Symmetric eXternal Diffie Hellman, 3-PDDH stands for 3-Party Decisional Diffie Hellman, DLIN stands for Decisional LINear, both of which are standards assumptions in pairing groups.

Another benefit of our new approach is that many properties of the underlying partially function-hiding inner-product FE can be lifted to the overall quadratic FE. This is case of the semi-adaptive simulation-based security, but we also show that if the partially function-hiding inner-product FE is secure against Chosen-Ciphertext Attacks (CCA-security), then so is the resulting quadratic FE. CCA-security is the de facto security notion for encryption, as it captures active or man-in-the-middle attacks, as opposed to CPA security. However, previous quadratic FE only prove CPA security. Note that generic transformation, such as Fujisaki Okamoto transform [FO99], cannot be applied here, since it relies on hybrid encryption, which is incompatible with functional encryption, which permits selective computation on encrypted data, as opposed to the all-or-nothing access provided by typical encryption. The CHK transform [CHK04] has been extended in [GPSW06] to obtain CCA-security for Attribute-Based Encryption (ABE) with some delegatability property. This property has been relaxed in [YAHK11]. However, these techniques only apply to ABE, where a decryption secret key recovers the encrypted plaintext entirely, or not at all, which is different in nature from the Functional Encryption we are studying here, where only partial information about the plaintext is recovered. The only generic transformation that seems to apply in our case is the dual encryption methodology from [NY90], which has the disadvantage of doubling the size of ciphertexts, and relying on (simulation-sound) non-interactive zero knowledge proofs. [BBL17] avoids using the Naor Yung paradigm, and builds the first CCA-secure FE (beyond the case of ABE), which handles inner product, and is based on efficient hash-proof systems. Their security proof crucially relies on structural (linearly homomorphic) properties of hash proofs system, which is tailored to FE for inner products. Indeed, none of these techniques seem to be applicable to existing quadratic FE, such as [BCFG17]. Our construction strikes by its simplicity: it suffices to build a CCA-secure partially function-hiding inner-product FE, which can be simply obtained by adding an Quasi-Adaptive Non-Interactive Zero Knowledge argument for the simple language of DDH tuples, without doubling the size of the ciphertext as required by Naor Yung dual encryption methodology. Instantiating these with arguments from [KW15] only adds 2 group elements in the ciphertexts, and requires no extra assumption. Surely, this is made easy by the use of pairings, which are not used by [BBL17]. In fact, we do not consider CCA-security to be the main technical contribution of this paper, but rather an illustration of the interest of building quadratic FE from inner-product FE, as is done in our new paradigm.

Technical Overview

Quadratic FE. Our quadratic FE uses a pairing group $\mathbb{G}_1 \times \mathbb{G}_2 \rightarrow \mathbb{G}_T$, where the encryption of $\mathbf{x}, \mathbf{y}$ contains an encryption $\mathsf{Enc}_1(\mathbf{x}; r)$ of $\mathbf{x}$ under randomness r, that consists of elements in $\mathbb{G}_1$, and an encryption $\mathsf{Enc}_2(\mathbf{y}; s)$ of $\mathbf{y}$ under randomness s, which consists of elements in $\mathbb{G}_2$. Thanks to the pairing $e : \mathbb{G}_1 \times \mathbb{G}_2 \rightarrow \mathbb{G}_T$, we can compute the product of $\mathsf{Enc}_1(\mathbf{x}, r)$ and $\mathsf{Enc}_2(\mathbf{y}, s)$ to obtain the output $\mathbf{x}^\top \mathbf{F} \mathbf{y}$ in the group $\mathbb{G}_T$, masked by some extra terms, that can be expressed as the inner product of a vector that only depends on the input $\mathbf{x}, \mathbf{y}$, and the randomness r, s used by the encryption, together with another vector which only depends on the secret key of these encryptions, and the matrix $\mathbf{F}$. Both vectors have a dimension that is *linear* in the dimension of the vectors $\mathbf{x}$ and $\mathbf{y}$. Thus, as in [AS17,Lin17], we can use an inner-product FE to compute the masking term. Such inner-product FE needs to be function-hiding, since revealing the secret key would compromise the security of the encryptions Enc_1 and Enc_2. However, function-hiding FE is an inherently private-key primitive, since a public encryption would allow to recover the function underlying each decryption key, simply by encrypting well-chosen vectors and decrypting them using the decryption key. To obtain a public key quadratic FE, we make the crucial observation that the underlying function-hiding FE for inner products is only used for vectors that lie in some specific subspace. Thus, we create, and make public, a restricted encryption key that can only generate ciphertexts for these vectors, while still providing some meaningful function-hiding. In particular, we obtain a public-key inner-product FE where decryption keys *partially* hide their underlying vector, which turns out to be sufficient for the security proof of the quadratic FE. Roughly speaking, the security of the inner-product FE proves that only the masking terms are revealed, along with some partial information on the secret keys that do not compromise security of the encryptions Enc_1, Enc_2. Thus, we obtain security of the quadratic FE using the security of the latter encryptions.

Partially Function-Hiding Inner-Product FE. We now highlight the construction of our new public-key, partially function-hiding inner-product FE. Our starting point is the FE for inner products from [ALS16], where decrypting an encryption $\mathsf{Enc}(\mathbf{x})$ of a vector $\mathbf{x}$ with a decryption key $\mathsf{KeyGen}(\mathbf{y})$ associated with vector $\mathbf{y}$ yields the inner product $\mathbf{x}^\top \mathbf{y}$. Their scheme is not function-hiding since $\mathbf{y}$ is part of the decryption key generated by $\mathsf{KeyGen}(\mathbf{y})$. As in [Lin17, Section 6.3], we use the fact that the decryption computes the inner product of $\mathsf{Enc}(\mathbf{x})$ and $\mathsf{KeyGen}(\mathbf{y})$

to obtain $\mathbf{x}^\top \mathbf{y}$. Namely, we replace the vector $\mathbf{y}$ in each decryption key by an ALS encryption of $\mathbf{y}$, and $\mathbf{x}$ in each ciphertext is replaced by an ALS decryption key for $\mathbf{x}$ (see Fig. 3). Function-Hiding (hiding $\mathbf{y}$) follows from the security of the inner ALS FE, whereas security (hiding $\mathbf{x}$) follows from the security of the outter ALS FE. [Lin17] uses a similar approach, where the entire decryption key is encrypted using an outter inner-product FE (see Fig. 3), and the underlying inner-product FE [ABDP15] are only selective indistinguishability secure.

ours	[Lin17]
$\mathsf{ct}_{\mathbf{x}} = \mathsf{Enc}^{\mathsf{out}}\Big(\mathsf{KeyGen}^{\mathsf{in}}(\mathbf{x})\Big)$	$\mathsf{ct}_{\mathbf{x}} = \mathsf{KeyGen}^{\mathsf{out}}\Big(\mathsf{Enc}^{\mathsf{in}}(\mathbf{x})\Big)$
$\mathsf{sk}_{\mathbf{y}} = \mathsf{KeyGen}^{\mathsf{out}}\Big(\mathsf{Enc}^{\mathsf{in}}(\mathbf{y})\Big)$	$\mathsf{sk}_{\mathbf{y}} = \mathsf{Enc}^{\mathsf{out}}\Big(\mathsf{KeyGen}^{\mathsf{in}}(\mathbf{y})\Big)$

Fig. 3. Function-Hiding FE for inner products. In the leftmost column (resp. rightmost column) $(\mathsf{Enc}^{\mathsf{out}}, \mathsf{KeyGen}^{\mathsf{out}})$ and $(\mathsf{Enc}^{\mathsf{in}}, \mathsf{KeyGen}^{\mathsf{in}})$ are two independent instances of [ALS16] (resp. [ABDP15]) FE for inner products.

To make our scheme public-key, we publish a restricted secret key for the inner layer FE that lets $\mathsf{KeyGen}^{\mathsf{in}}(\mathbf{x})$ run on vectors $\mathbf{x}$ that lie in some subspace. To be of use in our quadratic FE scheme, our function-hiding FE needs to be simulation secure (this is stronger than the classical indistinguishability based security for FE). We prove simulation security using the simulation security of [ALS16], which was proved in [AGRW17, Wee17] in the selective setting.

CCA-Security. As a bonus, we show that we can easily obtain CCA-security for our partially function-hiding inner-product FE, and that security property is transferred to the overall quadratic FE. We use Quasi-Adaptive Non-Interactive arguments for the simple language of DDH tuples, which must fulfill one-time simulation-soundness, in order to boost the security of our partially function-hiding FE for inner products to handle Chosen Ciphertext Attacks. This QANIZK argument can be instantiated with [KW15, Section 3.3], which only adds two group elements in the ciphertexts (this is the case $k = 1$ in their paper) and rely on the Kernel assumption, implied by SXDH (this is competitive with Fiat Shamir NIZKs, and does not rely on the random oracle model). Recall that prior constructions fail to obtain CCA-security even in the random oracle model, since the Fujisaki Okamoto transform, which relies on hybrid encryption (that is incompatible with functional encryption, where only a partial information on the plaintext is recovered during decryption), is of no help here.

Conclusion, and Perspective. Summarizing, we exhibit a new paradigm to build quadratic FE from partially function-hiding FE for inner products, a newly introduced primitive that bypasses impossibility results of public-key function-hiding FE. This gives stronger, desirable security guarantees that were previously not achieved. Moreover, its simplicity is appealing, not only because it gives constructions that outperform previous standard-based schemes in terms of ciphertext size, but also because it transfers properties from inner-product FE to quadratic FE. An important exception is adaptive security. Even though there are adaptively-secure inner-product FE (in fact we claim, without proof, that our semi-adaptive partially function-hiding FE for inner products can be extended to the adaptive, indistinguishability-based setting, up to doubling the size of the ciphertexts, as done in [LV16]), our quadratic FE fails at achieving adaptive security. Despite this shortcomings, we are optimistic this new approach will shed light on the largely unexplored domain of building functional encryption for richer functionalities from standard assumptions.

Road-Map. The rest of this paper is organized as follows. After giving some relevant technical preliminaries in Sect. 2, we define partially function-hiding public-key FE for inner products, and generically use it to build a quadratic FE, in Sect. 3. Then, in Sect. 4, we give concrete instances of such partially function-hiding FE for inner products, using standard assumptions on pairing groups.

2 Preliminaries

2.1 Notations

For any set S, we denote by $a \leftarrow_{\mathrm{R}} S$ a uniformly random element a in S. PPT stands for Probabilistic Polynomial Time. For any PPT algorithm $\mathcal{A}$, we denote by $x \leftarrow \mathcal{A}$ a random output from $\mathcal{A}$. We use $\approx_c$ to denote computational indistinguishability, and $\equiv$ to denote equality between distributions.

2.2 Pairing Groups

Let PGGen be a PPT algorithm that on input the security parameter 1^λ, returns a description $\mathcal{PG} = (\mathbb{G}_1, \mathbb{G}_2, \mathbb{G}_T, p, P_1, P_2, e)$ where for all $s \in \{1, 2, T\}$, $\mathbb{G}_s$ is an additive cyclic group of order p for a 2λ-bit prime p. $\mathbb{G}_1$ and $\mathbb{G}_2$ are generated by P_1 and P_2 respectively, and $e : \mathbb{G}_1 \times \mathbb{G}_2 \to \mathbb{G}_T$ is an efficiently computable (non-degenerate) bilinear map. Define $P_T := e(P_1, P_2)$, which is a generator of $\mathbb{G}_T$, of order p. We use implicit representation of group elements. For $s \in \{1, 2, T\}$ and $a \in \mathbb{Z}_p$, define $[a]_s = a \cdot P_s \in \mathbb{G}_s$ as the implicit representation of a in G_s. More generally, for a matrix $\mathbf{A} = (a_{ij}) \in \mathbb{Z}_p^{n \times m}$ we define $[\mathbf{A}]_s$ as the implicit representation of $\mathbf{A}$ in $\mathbb{G}_s$:

$$[\mathbf{A}]_s := \begin{pmatrix} a_{11} \cdot P_s \ldots a_{1m} \cdot P_s \\ \\ a_{n1} \cdot P_s \ldots a_{nm} \cdot P_s \end{pmatrix} \in \mathbb{G}_s^{n \times m}.$$

Given $[a]_1$ and $[b]_2$, one can efficiently compute $[a \cdot b]_T$ using the pairing e. For matrices $\mathbf{A}$ and $\mathbf{B}$ of matching dimensions, define $e([\mathbf{A}]_1, [\mathbf{B}]_2) := [\mathbf{AB}]_T$. For any matrix $\mathbf{A}, \mathbf{B} \in \mathbb{Z}_p^{n \times m}$, any group $s \in \{1, 2, T\}$, we denote by $[\mathbf{A}]_s + [\mathbf{B}]_s = [\mathbf{A} + \mathbf{B}]_s$.

For any prime p, we define the following distributions. The DDH distribution over $\mathbb{Z}_p^2$: $a \leftarrow_{\mathrm{R}} \mathbb{Z}_p$, outputs $\mathbf{a} := \binom{1}{a}$. The DLIN distribution over $\mathbb{Z}_p^{3\times 2}$: $a, b \leftarrow_{\mathrm{R}} \mathbb{Z}_p$, outputs $\mathbf{A} := \begin{pmatrix} a & 0 \\ 0 & b \\ 1 & 1 \end{pmatrix}$.

Definition 1 (DDH assumption). *For any adversary $\mathcal{A}$, any group $s \in \{1, 2, T\}$ and any security parameter λ, let*

$$\mathrm{Adv}^{\mathsf{DDH}}_{\mathbb{G}_s,\mathcal{A}}(\lambda) := |\Pr[1 \leftarrow \mathcal{A}(\mathcal{PG}, [\mathbf{a}]_s, [\mathbf{a}r]_s)] - \Pr[1 \leftarrow \mathcal{A}(\mathcal{PG}, [\mathbf{a}]_s, [\mathbf{u}]_s)]|,$$

where the probabilities are taken over $\mathcal{PG} \leftarrow_R \mathsf{GGen}(1^\lambda, d)$, $\mathbf{a} \leftarrow_R \mathsf{DDH}$, $r \leftarrow_R \mathbb{Z}_p$, $\mathbf{u} \leftarrow_R \mathbb{Z}_p^2$, and the random coins of $\mathcal{A}$. We say DDH holds in $\mathbb{G}_s$ if for all PPT adversaries $\mathcal{A}$, $\mathrm{Adv}^{\mathsf{DDH}}_{\mathbb{G}_s,\mathcal{A}}(\lambda)$ is a negligible function of λ.

Definition 2 (SXDH assumption). *For any security parameter λ and any pairing group $\mathcal{PG} = (\mathbb{G}_1, \mathbb{G}_2, \mathbb{G}_T, p, P_1, P_2, e) \leftarrow_R \mathsf{PGGen}(1^\lambda)$, we say SXDH holds in $\mathcal{PG}$ if DDH holds in $\mathbb{G}_1$ and $\mathbb{G}_2$.*

Definition 3 (bilateral DLIN). *For any adversary $\mathcal{A}$, any security parameter λ, let*

$$\mathrm{Adv}^{\mathsf{DLIN}}_{\mathcal{A}}(\lambda) := |\Pr[1 \leftarrow \mathcal{A}\left(\mathcal{PG}, \{[\mathbf{A}]_s, [\mathbf{Ar}]_s, \}_{s\in\{1,2\}}\right) \\ - \Pr[1 \leftarrow \mathcal{A}\left(\mathcal{PG}, \{[\mathbf{A}]_s, [\mathbf{u}]_s\}_{s\in\{1,2\}}\right)]|,$$

with where the probabilities are taken over $\mathcal{PG} \leftarrow_R \mathsf{GGen}(1^\lambda, d)$, $\mathbf{A} \leftarrow_R \mathsf{DLIN}$, $\mathbf{r} \leftarrow_R \mathbb{Z}_p^2$, $\mathbf{u} \leftarrow_R \mathbb{Z}_p^3$, and the random coins of $\mathcal{A}$. We say bilateral DLIN holds relative to $\mathcal{PG}$ if for all PPT adversaries $\mathcal{A}$, $\mathrm{Adv}^{\mathsf{DLIN}}_{\mathcal{A}}(\lambda)$ is a negligible function of λ.

2.3 Functional Encryption

A functional encryption scheme for a functionality $\mathcal{F} : \mathcal{X} \to \mathcal{Z}$ is a tuple of PPT algorithms:

- $\mathsf{Setup}(1^\lambda, \mathcal{F})$: on input the security paramter λ, the functionality $\mathcal{F}$, returns a public key pk (which is implicitly an input of all other algorithms), and a master secret key msk.
- $\mathsf{Enc}(x \in \mathcal{X})$: returns ct_x, an encryption of x.
- $\mathsf{KeyGen}(\mathsf{msk}, f \in \mathcal{F})$: returns sk_f, a decryption key for f.
- $\mathsf{Dec}(\mathsf{ct}_x, \mathsf{sk}_f)$: deterministic algorithm that returns a value in $\mathcal{Z}$, or $\perp$ if it fails.

An FE scheme is said to be private-key if Enc requires msk as additional input, otherwise, it is public-key.

Correctness. For any security paramter λ, any functionality $\mathcal{F} : \mathcal{X} \to \mathcal{Z}$, any $x \in \mathcal{X}$, and $f \in \mathcal{F}$, $\Pr[\mathsf{Dec}(\mathsf{ct}_x, \mathsf{sk}_f) = f(x)] = 1$, where the probability is taken over $(\mathsf{pk}, \mathsf{msk}) \leftarrow \mathsf{Setup}(1^\lambda, \mathcal{F})$, $\mathsf{ct}_x \leftarrow \mathsf{Enc}(x)$, $\mathsf{sk}_f \leftarrow \mathsf{KeyGen}(\mathsf{msk}, f)$.

Security. We recall the notion of simulation security, which implies its indistinguishability counterpart. Both notions were originally introduced in [BSW11, O'N10]. We work in the semi-adaptive setting, where the adversary sends its challenge x before querying any secret keys, but after receiving the public key. Semi-adaptive security has been introduced in [CW14] in the context of Attribute-Based Encryption, and subsequently studied in [GKW16]. It implies traditional selective security (where the adversary sends x before seeing the public key and querying secret keys), and is implied by the full-fledged adaptive security (where the adversary can query secret keys before sending its challenge x). We give both Chosen-Plaintext Attack (CPA) and Chosen-Ciphertext Attack variants of simulation security.

Definition 4 (Simulation CPA security). *For any FE scheme* FE *for functionality $\mathcal{F}$, any security parameter λ, any PPT simulator $\mathcal{S} := (\widetilde{\mathsf{Setup}}, \widetilde{\mathsf{Enc}}, \widetilde{\mathsf{KeyGen}})$, and any PPT stateful adversary $\mathcal{A}$, we define the following two experiments.*

$\mathsf{Real}^{\mathsf{CPA\text{-}FE}}_{\mathcal{A}}(1^\lambda)$:	$\mathsf{Ideal}^{\mathsf{CPA\text{-}FE}}_{\mathcal{A},\mathcal{S}}(1^\lambda)$:
$(\mathsf{pk}, \mathsf{msk}) \leftarrow \mathsf{Setup}(1^\lambda, \mathcal{F})$	$(\widetilde{\mathsf{pk}}, \widetilde{\mathsf{msk}}) \leftarrow \widetilde{\mathsf{Setup}}(1^\lambda, \mathcal{F})$
$x^\star \leftarrow \mathcal{A}(1^\lambda, \mathsf{pk})$	$x^\star \leftarrow \mathcal{A}(1^\lambda, \widetilde{\mathsf{pk}})$
$\mathsf{ct}^\star \leftarrow \mathsf{Enc}(x^\star)$	$\mathsf{ct}^\star \leftarrow \widetilde{\mathsf{Enc}}(\widetilde{\mathsf{msk}})$
$\alpha \leftarrow \mathcal{A}^{\mathcal{O}_{\mathsf{KeyGen}}(\cdot)}(\mathsf{ct}^\star)$	$\alpha \leftarrow \mathcal{A}^{\mathcal{O}_{\mathsf{KeyGen}}(\cdot)}(\mathsf{ct}^\star)$

In the real experiment, the key generation oracle $\mathcal{O}_{\mathsf{KeyGen}}$, when given as input $f \in \mathcal{F}$, returns $\mathsf{KeyGen}(\mathsf{msk}, f)$. In the ideal experiment, the key generation oracle $\mathcal{O}_{\mathsf{KeyGen}}$, when given as input $f \in \mathcal{F}$, computes $f(x^\star)$, and returns $\widetilde{\mathsf{KeyGen}}(\widetilde{\mathsf{msk}}, f, f(x^\star))$.

We say an FE scheme is CPA-SIM secure if there exists a PPT simulator $\mathcal{S} := (\widetilde{\mathsf{Setup}}, \widetilde{\mathsf{Enc}}, \widetilde{\mathsf{KeyGen}})$ such that for all PPT adversaries $\mathcal{A}$, we have:

$$\mathrm{Adv}^{\mathsf{CPA\text{-}SIM}}_{\mathsf{FE},\mathcal{A}}(\lambda) := |\Pr[1 \leftarrow \mathsf{Real}^{\mathsf{CPA\text{-}FE}}_{\mathcal{A}}(1^\lambda)] - \Pr[1 \leftarrow \mathsf{Ideal}^{\mathsf{CPA\text{-}FE}}_{\mathcal{A},\mathcal{S}}(1^\lambda)]| = \mathsf{negl}(\lambda).$$

Definition 5 (Simulation CCA security). *For any FE scheme* FE *for functionality $\mathcal{F}$, any security parameter λ, any PPT simulator $\mathcal{S} := (\widetilde{\mathsf{Setup}}, \widetilde{\mathsf{Enc}}, \widetilde{\mathsf{KeyGen}}, \widetilde{\mathsf{Dec}})$, and any PPT stateful adversary $\mathcal{A}$, we define the following two experiments.*

$\mathsf{Real}^{\mathsf{CCA\text{-}FE}}_{\mathcal{A}}(1^\lambda)$:	$\mathsf{Ideal}^{\mathsf{CCA\text{-}FE}}_{\mathcal{A},\mathcal{S}}(1^\lambda)$:
$(\mathsf{pk}, \mathsf{msk}) \leftarrow \mathsf{Setup}(1^\lambda, \mathcal{F})$	$(\widetilde{\mathsf{pk}}, \widetilde{\mathsf{msk}}) \leftarrow \widetilde{\mathsf{Setup}}(1^\lambda, \mathcal{F})$
$x^\star \leftarrow \mathcal{A}(1^\lambda, \mathsf{pk})$	$x^\star \leftarrow \mathcal{A}(1^\lambda, \widetilde{\mathsf{pk}})$
$\mathsf{ct}^\star \leftarrow \mathsf{Enc}(x)$	$\mathsf{ct}^\star \leftarrow \widetilde{\mathsf{Enc}}(\widetilde{\mathsf{msk}})$
$\alpha \leftarrow \mathcal{A}^{\mathcal{O}_{\mathsf{KeyGen}}(\cdot), \mathcal{O}_{\mathsf{Dec}}(\cdot,\cdot)}(\mathsf{ct}^\star)$	$\alpha \leftarrow \mathcal{A}^{\mathcal{O}_{\mathsf{KeyGen}}(\cdot), \mathcal{O}_{\mathsf{Dec}}(\cdot,\cdot)}(\mathsf{ct}^\star)$

In the real experiment, the oracle $\mathcal{O}_{\mathsf{KeyGen}}$*, when given as input* $f \in \mathcal{F}$*, returns* $\mathsf{KeyGen}(\mathsf{msk}, f)$*; the oracle* $\mathcal{O}_{\mathsf{Dec}}$*, given as input a ciphertext* ct *different from the challenge ciphertext* $\mathsf{ct}^\star$ *and a function* $f \in \mathcal{F}$*, computes* $\mathsf{sk}_f \leftarrow \mathsf{KeyGen}(\mathsf{msk}, f)$*, and returns* $\mathsf{Dec}(\mathsf{ct}, \mathsf{sk}_f)$*. If* $\mathcal{O}_{\mathsf{Dec}}$ *is queried on an input that contains the challenge ciphertext* $\mathsf{ct}^\star$*, it returns* $\perp$*.*

In the ideal experiment, the oracle $\mathcal{O}_{\mathsf{KeyGen}}$*, when given as input* $f \in \mathcal{F}$*, computes* $f(x^\star)$*, and returns* $\widetilde{\mathsf{KeyGen}}(\widetilde{\mathsf{msk}}, f, f(x^\star))$*. The oracle* $\mathcal{O}_{\mathsf{Dec}}$*, when given as input a ciphertext* ct *different from the challenge ciphertext* $\mathsf{ct}^\star$ *and a function* $f \in \mathcal{F}$*, returns* $\widetilde{\mathsf{Dec}}(\widetilde{\mathsf{msk}}, f, \mathsf{ct})$*. If* $\mathcal{O}_{\mathsf{Dec}}$ *is queried on an input that contains the challenge ciphertext* $\mathsf{ct}^\star$*, it returns* $\perp$*.*

We say an FE scheme is CCA-SIM secure if there exists a PPT simulator $\mathcal{S} := (\widetilde{\mathsf{Setup}}, \widetilde{\mathsf{Enc}}, \widetilde{\mathsf{KeyGen}}, \widetilde{\mathsf{Dec}})$ *such that for all PPT adversaries* $\mathcal{A}$*, we have:*

$$\mathrm{Adv}^{\mathsf{CCA\text{-}SIM}}_{\mathsf{FE},\mathcal{A}}(\lambda) := |\Pr[1 \leftarrow \mathsf{Real}^{\mathsf{CCA\text{-}FE}}_{\mathcal{A}}(1^\lambda)] - \Pr[1 \leftarrow \mathsf{Ideal}^{\mathsf{CCA\text{-}FE}}_{\mathcal{A},\mathcal{S}}(1^\lambda)]| = \mathsf{negl}(\lambda).$$

2.4 Quasi-Adaptive Non-Interactive Zero-Knowledge

This part is taken almost verbatim from [KW15]. Quasi-Adaptive NIZK (QA-NIZK) proofs are NIZK proofs where the common reference string (CRS) is allowed to depend on the specific language for which proofs have to be generated [JR13]. The CRS is generated in a specific way and contains a fixed part par, produced by an algorithm $\mathsf{Gen}_{\mathsf{par}}$, and a language-dependent part crs. However, for the zero-knowledge property there should exist a single simulator for the entire class of languages.

For public parameters par produced by $\mathsf{Gen}_{\mathsf{par}}$, let $\mathcal{D}_{\mathsf{par}}$ be a probability distribution over a collection of relations $R = \{R_\rho\}$ parametrized by a string ρ with an associated language $\mathcal{L}_\rho = \{y : \exists x \text{ s.t. } R_\rho(y, x) = 1\}$. We now recall the tag definition of QANIZK for $\mathcal{D}_{\mathsf{par}}$, in its tag-based variant.

Definition 6 (QANIZK Argument). *A* Quasi-adaptive Non-Interactive Zero Knowledge Argument *(QANIZK)* Π *for a language distribution* $\mathcal{D}_{\mathsf{par}}$ *consists of five PPT algorithms* $\Pi = (\mathsf{Gen}_{\mathsf{par}}, \mathsf{Gen}_{\mathsf{crs}}, \mathsf{Prove}, \mathsf{Sim}, \mathsf{Ver})$*:*

- $\mathsf{Gen}_{\mathsf{par}}(1^\lambda)$*: returns the public parameters* par.
- $\mathsf{Gen}_{\mathsf{crs}}(\mathsf{par}, \rho)$*: returns a common reference string* crs*, and a trapdoor* trap*. We assume that* crs *implicitly contains* par *and* ρ*, and that it defines a tag space* $\mathcal{T}$*.*
- $\mathsf{Prove}(\mathsf{crs}, \tau, x, y)$*: on input the* crs*, a tag* $\tau \in \mathcal{T}$*, a witness* x *and a statement* y*, it returns a proof* π*.*
- $\mathsf{Ver}(\mathsf{crs}, \tau, y, \pi)$*: on input* crs*, a tag* $\tau \in \mathcal{T}$*, a statement* y*, and a proof* π*, it returns* 1 *or* 0*, where* 1 *means that* π *is a valid proof of* $y \in \mathcal{L}_\rho$*, with respect to tag* τ*.*
- $\mathsf{Sim}(\mathsf{crs}, \mathsf{trap}, \tau, y)$*: returns a proof* π *for some* $y \in \mathcal{Y}$ *(not necessarily in* $\mathcal{L}_\rho$*).*

We require that the algorithms satisfy the following properties:

Perfect completeness. *For all* λ, *all* par *output by* $\mathsf{Gen}_{\mathsf{par}}(\lambda)$, *all* ρ *output by* $\mathcal{D}_{\mathsf{par}}$, *all* (x, y) *with* $R_\rho(y, x) = 1$, *all* $\tau \in \mathcal{T}$, *we have:*

$$\Pr[\mathsf{Ver}(\mathsf{crs}, \tau, y, \pi) = 1 | (\mathsf{crs}, \mathsf{trap}) \leftarrow_R \mathsf{Gen}_{\mathsf{crs}}(\mathsf{par}, \rho); \pi \leftarrow_R \mathsf{Prove}(\mathsf{crs}, \tau, x, y)] = 1.$$

$$\Pr\left[\mathsf{Ver}(\mathsf{crs}, \tau, y, \pi) = 1 \middle| \begin{array}{l} (\mathsf{crs}, \mathsf{trap}) \leftarrow_R \mathsf{Gen}_{\mathsf{crs}}(\mathsf{par}, \rho) \\ \pi \leftarrow_R \mathsf{Prove}(\mathsf{crs}, \tau, x, y) \end{array}\right] = 1.$$

Perfect zero-knowledge. *For all* λ, *all* par *output by* $\mathsf{Gen}_{\mathsf{par}}(\lambda)$, *all* ρ *output by* $\mathcal{D}_{\mathsf{par}}$, *all* $(\mathsf{crs}, \mathsf{trap})$ *output by* $\mathsf{Gen}_{\mathsf{crs}}(\mathsf{par}, \rho)$, *all* (x, y) *with* $R_\rho(y, x) = 1$, *all tags* $\tau \in \mathcal{T}$, *the distributions*

$$\mathsf{Prove}(\mathsf{crs}, \tau, x, y) \text{ and } \mathsf{Sim}(\mathsf{crs}, \mathsf{trap}, \tau, y)$$

are the same (where the coin tosses are taken over Prove, Sim*).*

Simulation Soundness. *For all PPT adversaries* $\mathcal{A}$ *and any QANIZK argument* Π *the following advantage*

$$\mathrm{Adv}_{\mathcal{A}}^{\Pi}(\lambda) := \Pr\left[\begin{array}{l} \mathsf{Ver}(\mathsf{crs}, \tau^\star, y^\star, \pi^\star) = 1 \\ \wedge y^\star \notin \mathcal{L}_\rho \wedge \tau^\star \notin \mathcal{T}_{\mathsf{sim}} \end{array} \middle| \begin{array}{l} \mathsf{par} \leftarrow_R \mathsf{Gen}_{\mathsf{par}}(\lambda), \rho \leftarrow_R \mathcal{D}_{\mathsf{par}} \\ (\mathsf{crs}, \mathsf{trap}) \leftarrow_R \mathsf{Gen}_{\mathsf{crs}}(\mathsf{par}, \rho) \\ (y^\star, \tau^\star, \pi^\star) \leftarrow \mathcal{A}^{\mathsf{SimO}(\cdot,\cdot)}(\mathsf{crs}) \end{array}\right]$$

is negligible, where $\mathsf{SimO}(\tau, y)$ *returns* $\pi := \mathsf{Sim}(\mathsf{crs}, \mathsf{trap}, \tau, y)$ *and sets* $\mathcal{T}_{\mathsf{sim}} := \mathcal{T}_{\mathsf{sim}} \cup \{\tau\}$, *where* $\mathcal{T}_{\mathsf{sim}}$ *is initially empty.*

One-time Simulation Soundness. For any PPT adversary $\mathcal{A}$ *and QANIZK argument* Π, *we define* $\mathrm{Adv}_{\mathcal{A}}^{\mathsf{OT}\text{-}\Pi}(\lambda)$ *as* $\mathrm{Adv}_{\mathcal{A}}^{\Pi}(\lambda)$, *except the adversary can only make* one query *to the oracle* SimO.

3 Quadratic FE from Inner-Product FE

In this section we build a functional encryption scheme for bounded-norm quadratic functions, namely, for the functionality $\mathcal{F}_{\mathsf{quad},B} : [0, B]^n \times [0, B]^m \to [0, n \cdot m \cdot B^3]$, $\mathcal{X} := [0, B]^n \times [0, B]^m$, $\mathcal{Z} := [0, n \cdot m \cdot B^3]$, such that each $\mathbf{F} \in \mathcal{F}_{\mathsf{quad},B}$ is represented by a matrix in $[0, B]^{n \times m}$, and for all $(\mathbf{x}, \mathbf{y}) \in [0, B]^n \times [0, B]^m$, the output of the function is $\mathbf{x}^\top \mathbf{F} \mathbf{y} \in [0, n \cdot m \cdot B^3]$. We consider B, n, m all polynomials in the security parameter.

Our quadratic FE is built from a so-called partially function-hiding inner product FE. After giving an overview of the quadratic FE, we define partially function-hiding inner-product FE in Sect. 3.1, and we use it build a simulation-secure quadratic FE in Sect. 3.2, based on the DLIN assumption in a type-3 pairing group $e : \mathbb{G}_1 \times \mathbb{G}_2 \to \mathbb{G}_T$.

Overview of the Quadratic FE. To encrypt the pair of vectors $\mathbf{x}$ and $\mathbf{y}$, we provide an encryption of $\mathbf{x}$ which contains group elements from $\mathbb{G}_1$, and an encryption of $\mathbf{y}$, which contains group elements from $\mathbb{G}_2$. Equipped with a pairing $e : \mathbb{G}_1 \times \mathbb{G}_2 \to \mathbb{G}_T$, we multiply these encryptions to obtain the desired value in $\mathbb{G}_T$. A natural starting point is to use the ElGamal encryption [ElG84]. That is, the ciphertext $\mathsf{ct}_{\mathbf{x},\mathbf{y}}$ includes the encryption of $\mathbf{x} \in \mathbb{Z}^n$ in $\mathbb{G}_1$: $\mathsf{ct}_{\mathbf{x}} = (c_1 := [r]_1, c_2 := [\mathbf{x} + \mathbf{a}r]_1)$ with randomness $r \leftarrow_{\mathrm{R}} \mathbb{Z}_p$, public key $[\mathbf{a}]_1 \in \mathbb{G}_1^n$ and secret key $\mathbf{a} \in \mathbb{Z}_p^n$; and an ElGamal encryption of $\mathbf{y} \in \mathbb{Z}^m$ in $\mathbb{G}_2$: $\mathsf{ct}_{\mathbf{y}} = (c_3 := [s]_2, c_4 := [\mathbf{y} + \mathbf{b}s]_2)$, with randomness $s \leftarrow_{\mathrm{R}} \mathbb{Z}_p$, public key $[\mathbf{b}]_2 \in \mathbb{G}_2^m$, and secret key $\mathbf{b} \in \mathbb{Z}_p^m$. Decryption computes the product $c_2^\top \mathbf{F} c_4$, using the pairing, to recover:

$$[\mathbf{x}^\top \mathbf{F}\mathbf{y} + \underbrace{(\mathbf{a}r)^\top \mathbf{F}\mathbf{y} + \mathbf{x}^\top \mathbf{F}\mathbf{b}s + (\mathbf{a}r)^\top \mathbf{F}\mathbf{b}s)}_{\text{extra terms}}]_T,$$

where the output $[\mathbf{x}^\top \mathbf{F}\mathbf{y}]_T$ is masked by extra terms, which can be expressed as the inner product between $\begin{pmatrix} r \cdot \mathbf{y} \\ s \cdot \mathbf{x} \\ r \cdot s \end{pmatrix}$ and $\begin{pmatrix} \mathbf{F}^\top \mathbf{a} \\ \mathbf{F}\mathbf{b} \\ \mathbf{a}^\top \mathbf{F}\mathbf{b} \end{pmatrix}$.

Note that the first vector only contains elements known to the encryptor (the randomness used by the encryption and the input vectors $\mathbf{x}$ and $\mathbf{y}$), while the second vector only contains elements known to the decryption key generator (the master secret key $\mathsf{msk} = (\mathbf{a}, \mathbf{b})$, and the input $\mathbf{F}$ to the key generation algorithm). Besides, the dimension of both vectors are linear in $n + m$. Thus, to compute these extra terms (without compromising succinctness), we use an FE for inner products $\mathsf{IPFE.Enc}, \mathsf{IPFE.KeyGen}$, and we add $\mathsf{IPFE.Enc}\begin{pmatrix} r \cdot \mathbf{y} \\ s \cdot \mathbf{x} \\ r \cdot s \end{pmatrix}$ to the ciphertext $\mathsf{ct}_{\mathbf{x},\mathbf{y}}$, and we define $\mathsf{sk}_{\mathbf{F}} = \mathsf{IPFE.KeyGen}\begin{pmatrix} \mathbf{F}^\top \mathbf{a} \\ \mathbf{F}\mathbf{b} \\ \mathbf{a}^\top \mathbf{F}\mathbf{b} \end{pmatrix}$. This underlying inner-product FE needs to be function-hiding, since revealing the vector input to $\mathsf{IPFE.KeyGen}$, which contains the master secret key $\mathsf{msk} = (\mathbf{a}, \mathbf{b})$, would be fatal for the security of the ElGamal encryptions. However, function-hiding FE is an inherently private-key primitive, since a public encryption would allow to recover $\mathbf{y}$ from the decryption key $\mathsf{sk}_{\mathbf{y}}$, simply by encrypting sufficiently many well-chosen vectors $\mathbf{x}$ and decrypting them using $\mathsf{sk}_{\mathbf{y}}$.

To obtain a public-key quadratic FE, we use an encryption scheme that has more structure than ElGamal, namely, Damgård ElGamal [Dam92]. This gives the possibility to relax the function-hiding property required from the inner-product FE, and bypass the impossibility result for public-key function-hiding FE.

Namely, the ciphertext $\mathsf{ct}_{\mathbf{x},\mathbf{y}}$ contains a Damgård ElGamal encryption in $\mathbb{G}_1$: $\mathsf{ct}_{\mathbf{x}} = (c_1 := [\mathbf{a}r]_1, c_2 := [\mathbf{x} + \mathbf{U}\mathbf{a}r]_1)$ with randomness $r \leftarrow_{\mathrm{R}} \mathbb{Z}_p$, public key $([\mathbf{a}]_1 \in \mathbb{G}_1^2, [\mathbf{U}\mathbf{a}]_1 \in \mathbb{G}_1^n)$, and secret key $\mathbf{U} \in \mathbb{Z}_p^{n \times 2}$; and a Damgård ElGamal encryption of $\mathbf{y} \in \mathbb{Z}^m$ in $\mathbb{G}_2$: $\mathsf{ct}_{\mathbf{y}} = (c_3 := [\mathbf{b}s]_2, c_4 := [\mathbf{y} + \mathbf{V}\mathbf{b}s]_2)$, with randomness $s \leftarrow_R \mathbb{Z}_p$, public key $([\mathbf{b}]_2 \in \mathbb{G}_2, [\mathbf{Vb}]_2 \in \mathbb{G}_2^m)$, and secret key $\mathbf{V} \in \mathbb{Z}_p^{m\times 2}$. Decryption computes the product $c_2^\top \mathbf{F} c_4$, using the pairing, to recover:

$$[\mathbf{x}^\top \mathbf{F}\mathbf{y} + \underbrace{(\mathbf{a}r)^\top(\mathbf{U}^\top\mathbf{F})(\mathbf{y}+\mathbf{Vb}s) + \mathbf{x}^\top(\mathbf{FV})(\mathbf{b}s)}_{\text{extra terms}}]_T,$$

where the output $[\mathbf{x}^\top\mathbf{F}\mathbf{y}]_T$ is masked by extra terms, which can be expressed as the inner product between $\begin{pmatrix}\mathbf{a}r\otimes(\mathbf{y}+\mathbf{Vb}s)\\ \mathbf{x}\otimes\mathbf{b}s\end{pmatrix}$ and $\begin{pmatrix}\mathsf{vect}(\mathbf{U}^\top\mathbf{F})\\ \mathsf{vect}(\mathbf{FV})\end{pmatrix}$, where for any vector $\mathbf{x}\in\mathbb{Z}_p^n$, $\mathbf{y}\in\mathbb{Z}_p^m$, and matrix $\mathbf{M}\in\mathbb{Z}_p^{n\times m}$, we denote by $\mathsf{vect}(\mathbf{M})\in\mathbb{Z}_p^{nm}$ the vector such that the inner product of $\mathbf{x}\otimes\mathbf{y}$ with $\mathsf{vect}(\mathbf{M})$ is $\mathbf{x}^\top\mathbf{My}$.

As before, the first vector only contains elements known to the encryptor (the randomness used by the encryption, the input vectors $\mathbf{x}$ and $\mathbf{y}$, and the public keys), while the second vector only contains elements known to the decryption key generator (the master secret key $\mathsf{msk} = (\mathbf{U},\mathbf{V})$, and the input $\mathbf{F}$ to the key generation algorithm). Besides, the dimension of both vectors are linear in $n+m$.

As before, to compute these extra terms, we use an FE for inner products $\mathsf{IPFE.Enc}$, $\mathsf{IPFE.KeyGen}$, and we add $\mathsf{IPFE.Enc}\begin{pmatrix}\mathbf{a}r\otimes(\mathbf{y}+\mathbf{Vb}s)\\ \mathbf{x}\otimes\mathbf{b}s\end{pmatrix}$ to the ciphertext $\mathsf{ct}_{\mathbf{x},\mathbf{y}}$, and we define $\mathsf{sk}_\mathbf{F} = \mathsf{IPFE.KeyGen}\begin{pmatrix}\mathsf{vect}(\mathbf{U}^\top\mathbf{F})\\ \mathsf{vect}(\mathbf{FV})\end{pmatrix}$.

Now, we make the crucial observation that the underlying function-hiding FE for inner products is only used for vectors that lie in some specific subspace, strictly included in the whole space, namely, vectors (column) spanned by the matrix: $\mathbf{M} := \left(\begin{array}{c|c}\mathbf{a}\otimes(\mathrm{Id}_m|\mathbf{Vb}) & \mathbf{0}\\ \hline \mathbf{0} & \mathrm{Id}_n\otimes\mathbf{b}\end{array}\right)$, where Id_n (resp. Id_m) denotes the identity matrix of dimension n (resp. m). Thus, we create, and make public, a restricted key that can only generate ciphertexts for these vectors, while still providing some meaningful function-hiding. Namely, we prove that only $\mathbf{M}^\top\mathbf{y}$ leaks from a decryption key $\mathsf{sk}_\mathbf{y}$ (in addition to what is supposed to leak by correctness of the scheme), which turns out to be sufficient for the security proof of the overall quadratic FE. [Lin17] also builds quadratic FE from function-hiding FE for inner products, but it uses [ABDP15] encryption of $\mathbf{x}$ and $\mathbf{y}$ in the ciphertext, and it requires a full-fledged function-hiding FE, which can only be private-key.

3.1 Partially Function-Hiding Inner-Product FE

A partially function-hiding functional encryption for inner products is defined with respect to a pairing group $\mathcal{PG} := (\mathbb{G}_1,\mathbb{G}_2,P_1,P_2,e) \leftarrow \mathsf{PGGen}(1^\lambda)$, a full rank matrix $\mathbf{M}\in\mathbb{Z}_p^{n\times m}$, with $n > m$, and such that $\mathbf{M}^\top\mathbf{M}\in\mathbb{Z}_p^{m\times m}$ is invertible; and a tag space $\mathcal{T}$. It consists of the following PPT algorithms:

- $\mathsf{Setup}(1^\lambda, \mathcal{PG}, [\mathbf{M}]_1)$: returns the public key pk (implicitly input of all other algorithms), and the master secret key msk. We assume pk contains a description of $[\mathbf{M}]_1$ and $\mathcal{T}$.

- $\mathsf{Enc}(\mathbf{t} \in \mathbb{Z}_p^m, \tau \in \mathcal{T})$: returns a ciphertext $\mathsf{ct}_{\mathbf{Mt}}$, associated with vector $\mathbf{Mt} \in \mathbb{Z}_p^n$ and tag τ.
- $\mathsf{Enc}'(\mathsf{msk}, [\mathbf{x}]_1 \in \mathbb{G}_1^n, \tau \in \mathcal{T})$: returns a ciphertext $\mathsf{ct}_{\mathbf{x}}$, associated with vector $\mathbf{x} \in \mathbb{Z}_p^n$ and tag τ.
- $\mathsf{KeyGen}(\mathsf{msk}, \mathbf{y} \in \mathbb{Z}_p^n)$: returns a decryption key $\mathsf{sk}_{\mathbf{y}}$.
- $\mathsf{Dec}(\tau, \mathsf{ct}_{\mathbf{x}}, \mathsf{sk}_{\mathbf{y}})$: deterministic algorithm that returns a value in $\mathbb{G}_T$, or $\perp$ if it fails.

Note that Enc is public key, and can only encrypt vectors in the span of $[\mathbf{M}]_1$, while Enc' needs the msk, but can encrypt any vector $[\mathbf{x}]_1 \in \mathbb{G}_1^n$. Another crucial difference is that Enc' works on vector of group elements, while Enc needs to get the exponents as input. We require these two encryption algorithms agree on the their common input space, namely: for all $\mathbf{t} \in \mathbb{Z}_p^m$ and $\tau \in \mathcal{T}$, $\mathsf{Enc}(\mathbf{t}, \tau)$ is identically distributed from $\mathsf{Enc}'(\mathsf{msk}, [\mathbf{Mt}]_1, \tau)$, where $(\mathsf{pk}, \mathsf{msk}) \leftarrow \mathsf{Setup}(1^\lambda, \mathcal{PG}, [\mathbf{M}]_1)$.

To build quadratic FE in Sect. 3, we require a tag-free partially function-hiding inner-product FE (which corresponds to the case $\mathcal{T} := \{\varepsilon\}$). The latter can be obtained generically from any tag-based partially function-hiding inner-product FE, using one-time signature.

Correctness. For all $\mathbf{t} \in \mathbb{Z}_p^m$, $\mathbf{y} \in \mathbb{Z}_p^n$, $\tau \in \mathcal{T}$, $\Pr[\mathsf{Dec}(\tau, \mathsf{ct}_{\mathbf{Mt}}, \mathsf{sk}_{\mathbf{y}}) = [(\mathbf{Mt})^\top \mathbf{y}]_T] = 1$, where the probability is taken over $(\mathsf{pk}, \mathsf{msk}) \leftarrow \mathsf{Setup}(1^\lambda, \mathcal{PG}, [\mathbf{M}]_1)$, $\mathsf{ct}_{\mathbf{Mt}} \leftarrow \mathsf{Enc}(\mathbf{t}, \tau)$, $\mathsf{sk}_{\mathbf{y}} \leftarrow \mathsf{KeyGen}(\mathsf{msk}, \mathbf{y})$.

Security. We define simulation security for partially function-hiding inner-product FE, which captures the fact that the only information that leaks from a ciphertext $\mathsf{ct}_{\mathbf{x}}$ and keys $\mathsf{sk}_{\mathbf{y}}$ is $\mathbf{x}^\top \mathbf{y}$, and some partial information on $\mathbf{y}$, namely, $\mathbf{M}(\mathbf{M}^\top \mathbf{M})^{-1}\mathbf{M}^\top \mathbf{y}$. We give both CPA and CCA variant of security notions.

Definition 7 (partially function-hiding, CPA Simulation security). *For any inner-product FE scheme* FE, *any PPT simulator* $\mathcal{S} := (\widetilde{\mathsf{Setup}}, \widetilde{\mathsf{Enc}}, \widetilde{\mathsf{KeyGen}})$, *and any PPT stateful adversary* $\mathcal{A}$, *we define the following two experiments.*

$\underline{\mathsf{Real}_{\mathcal{A}}^{\mathsf{CPA\text{-}FE}}(1^\lambda)}$:	$\underline{\mathsf{Ideal}_{\mathcal{A},\mathcal{S}}^{\mathsf{CPA\text{-}FE}}(1^\lambda)}$:
$(\mathsf{pk}, \mathsf{msk}) \leftarrow \mathsf{Setup}(1^\lambda, \mathcal{PG}, [\mathbf{M}]_1)$	$(\widetilde{\mathsf{pk}}, \widetilde{\mathsf{msk}}) \leftarrow \widetilde{\mathsf{Setup}}(1^\lambda, \mathcal{PG}, [\mathbf{M}]_1)$
$(\tau^\star, \mathbf{x}) \leftarrow \mathcal{A}(1^\lambda, \mathsf{pk})$	$(\tau^\star, \mathbf{x}) \leftarrow \mathcal{A}(1^\lambda, \widetilde{\mathsf{pk}})$
$\mathsf{ct}^\star \leftarrow \mathsf{Enc}'(\mathsf{msk}, [\mathbf{x}]_1, \tau^\star)$	$\mathsf{ct}^\star \leftarrow \widetilde{\mathsf{Enc}}(\widetilde{\mathsf{msk}}, \tau^\star)$
$\alpha \leftarrow \mathcal{A}^{\mathcal{O}_{\mathsf{KeyGen}}(\cdot)}(\mathsf{ct}^\star)$	$\alpha \leftarrow \mathcal{A}^{\mathcal{O}_{\mathsf{KeyGen}}(\cdot)}(\mathsf{ct}^\star)$

In the real experiment, the key generation oracle $\mathcal{O}_{\mathsf{KeyGen}}$*, when given as input* $\mathbf{y} \in \mathbb{Z}_p^n$*, returns* $\mathsf{KeyGen}(\mathsf{msk}, \mathbf{y})$*. In the ideal experiment, when* $\mathcal{O}_{\mathsf{KeyGen}}$ *is given as input* $\mathbf{y} \in \mathbb{Z}_p^n$*, it computes* $\mathbf{x}^\top \mathbf{y}$*,* $\widetilde{\mathbf{y}} := \mathbf{M}(\mathbf{M}^\top \mathbf{M})^{-1}\mathbf{M}^\top \mathbf{y}$*, and returns* $\widetilde{\mathsf{KeyGen}}(\widetilde{\mathsf{msk}}, \mathbf{x}^\top \mathbf{y}, \widetilde{\mathbf{y}})$.

We say an FE scheme is partially function-hiding simulation-secure if there exists a PPT simulator $\mathcal{S} := (\widetilde{\mathsf{Setup}}, \widetilde{\mathsf{Enc}}, \widetilde{\mathsf{KeyGen}})$ *such that for all PPT adversaries* $\mathcal{A}$, *we have:*

$$\mathrm{Adv}_{\mathsf{FE},\mathcal{A}}^{\mathsf{CPA\text{-}PFH\text{-}SIM}}(\lambda) := |\Pr[1 \leftarrow \mathsf{Real}_{\mathcal{A}}^{\mathsf{CPA\text{-}FE}}(1^\lambda)] - \Pr[1 \leftarrow \mathsf{Ideal}_{\mathcal{A},\mathcal{S}}^{\mathsf{CPA\text{-}FE}}(1^\lambda)]| = \mathsf{negl}(\lambda).$$

Definition 8 (partially function-hiding, CCA Simulation security). *For any inner-product FE scheme* FE, *any PPT simulator* $\mathcal{S} := (\widetilde{\mathsf{Setup}}, \widetilde{\mathsf{Enc}}, \widetilde{\mathsf{KeyGen}}, \widetilde{\mathsf{Dec}})$, *and any PPT stateful adversary* $\mathcal{A}$, *we define the following two experiments.*

$\mathsf{Real}_{\mathcal{A}}^{\mathsf{CCA\text{-}FE}}(1^\lambda)$:	$\mathsf{Ideal}_{\mathcal{A},\mathcal{S}}^{\mathsf{CCA\text{-}FE}}(1^\lambda)$:
$(\mathsf{pk}, \mathsf{msk}) \leftarrow \mathsf{Setup}(1^\lambda, \mathcal{PG}, [\mathbf{M}]_1)$	$(\widetilde{\mathsf{pk}}, \widetilde{\mathsf{msk}}) \leftarrow \widetilde{\mathsf{Setup}}(1^\lambda, \mathcal{PG}, [\mathbf{M}]_1)$
$(\tau^\star, \mathbf{x}) \leftarrow \mathcal{A}(1^\lambda, \mathsf{pk})$	$(\tau^\star, \mathbf{x}) \leftarrow \mathcal{A}(1^\lambda, \widetilde{\mathsf{pk}})$
$\mathsf{ct}^\star \leftarrow \mathsf{Enc}'(\mathsf{msk}, [\mathbf{x}]_1, \tau^\star)$	$\mathsf{ct}^\star \leftarrow \widetilde{\mathsf{Enc}}(\widetilde{\mathsf{msk}}, \tau^\star)$
$\alpha \leftarrow \mathcal{A}^{\mathcal{O}_{\mathsf{KeyGen}}(\cdot), \mathcal{O}_{\mathsf{Dec}}(\cdot,\cdot,\cdot)}(\mathsf{ct}^\star)$	$\alpha \leftarrow \mathcal{A}^{\mathcal{O}_{\mathsf{KeyGen}}(\cdot), \mathcal{O}_{\mathsf{Dec}}(\cdot,\cdot,\cdot)}(\mathsf{ct}^\star)$

In the real experiment, $\mathcal{O}_{\mathsf{KeyGen}}(\mathbf{y} \in \mathbb{Z}_p^n)$ *returns* $\mathsf{KeyGen}(\mathsf{msk}, \mathbf{y})$. *The oracle* $\mathcal{O}_{\mathsf{Dec}}(\tau, \mathsf{ct}, \mathbf{y})$ *returns* $\perp$ *if* $\tau = \tau^\star$; *otherwise, it computes* $\mathsf{sk}_{\mathbf{y}} \leftarrow \mathsf{KeyGen}(\mathsf{msk}, \mathbf{y})$, *and returns* $\mathsf{Dec}(\tau, \mathsf{ct}, \mathsf{sk}_{\mathbf{y}})$.

In the ideal experiment, $\mathcal{O}_{\mathsf{KeyGen}}(\mathbf{y} \in \mathbb{Z}_p^n)$ *computes* $\mathbf{x}^\top\mathbf{y}$, $\widetilde{\mathbf{y}} := \mathbf{M}(\mathbf{M}^\top\mathbf{M})^{-1}\mathbf{M}^\top\mathbf{y}$, *and returns* $\widetilde{\mathsf{KeyGen}}(\widetilde{\mathsf{msk}}, \mathbf{x}^\top\mathbf{y}, \widetilde{\mathbf{y}})$. *The oracle* $\mathcal{O}_{\mathsf{Dec}}(\tau, \mathsf{ct}, \mathbf{y})$ *returns* $\perp$ *if* $\tau \neq \tau^\star$; *otherwise, it computes* $\widetilde{\mathbf{y}} := \mathbf{M}(\mathbf{M}^\top\mathbf{M})^{-1}\mathbf{M}^\top\mathbf{y}$, *and returns* $\widetilde{\mathsf{Dec}}(\tau, \mathsf{ct}, \widetilde{\mathbf{y}})$.

We say an FE scheme is CCA partially function-hiding, simulation secure if there exists a PPT simulator $\mathcal{S} := (\widetilde{\mathsf{Setup}}, \widetilde{\mathsf{Enc}}, \widetilde{\mathsf{KeyGen}}, \widetilde{\mathsf{Dec}})$ *such that for all PPT adversaries* $\mathcal{A}$, *we have:*

$$\mathrm{Adv}_{\mathsf{FE},\mathcal{A}}^{\mathsf{CCA\text{-}PFH\text{-}SIM}}(\lambda) := |\Pr[1 \leftarrow \mathsf{Real}_{\mathcal{A}}^{\mathsf{CCA\text{-}FE}}(1^\lambda)] - \Pr[1 \leftarrow \mathsf{Ideal}_{\mathcal{A},\mathcal{S}}^{\mathsf{CCA\text{-}FE}}(1^\lambda)]| = \mathsf{negl}(\lambda).$$

3.2 Quadratic FE from Partially Function-Hiding Inner-Product FE

We describe our quadratic FE in Fig. 4, for the functionality $\mathcal{F}_{\mathsf{quad},B}$. Its security relies on the security of the underlying partially function-hiding inner-product FE, the bilateral DLIN assumption, and the DDH assumption in $\mathbb{G}_1$.

Correctness. By correctness of the underlying inner-product FE, we have:

$$\begin{aligned} d &= \begin{pmatrix} r \otimes \binom{\mathbf{y}}{\mathbf{s}} \\ \mathbf{x} \otimes \mathbf{s} \end{pmatrix}^\top \mathbf{M}^\top \begin{pmatrix} \mathsf{vect}(\mathbf{U}^\top\mathbf{F}) \\ \mathsf{vect}(\mathbf{F}\mathbf{V}) \end{pmatrix} \\ &= \begin{pmatrix} \mathbf{a}r \otimes \mathsf{ct}_{\mathbf{y}} \\ \mathbf{x} \otimes \mathbf{B}\mathbf{s} \end{pmatrix}^\top \begin{pmatrix} \mathsf{vect}(\mathbf{U}^\top\mathbf{F}) \\ \mathsf{vect}(\mathbf{F}\mathbf{V}) \end{pmatrix} \\ &= (\mathbf{U}\mathbf{a}r)^\top\mathbf{F}\mathsf{ct}_{\mathbf{y}} + \mathbf{x}^\top\mathbf{F}\mathbf{V}\mathbf{B}\mathbf{s}, \end{aligned}$$

$\underline{\mathsf{Setup}(1^\lambda, \mathcal{F}_{\mathsf{quad},B})}$:
$\mathcal{PG} := (\mathbb{G}_1, \mathbb{G}_2, g_1, g_2, p, e) \leftarrow \mathsf{PGGen}(1^\lambda)$, $\mathbf{a} \leftarrow_{\mathrm{R}} \mathsf{DDH}$, $\mathbf{B} \leftarrow_{\mathrm{R}} \mathsf{DLIN}$, $\mathbf{U} \leftarrow_{\mathrm{R}} \mathbb{Z}_p^{n \times 2}$, $\mathbf{V} \leftarrow_{\mathrm{R}} \mathbb{Z}_p^{m \times 3}$
$\mathbf{M} := \begin{pmatrix} \mathbf{a} \otimes (\mathrm{Id}_m | \mathbf{VB}) & \mathbf{0} \\ \mathbf{0} & \mathrm{Id}_n \otimes \mathbf{B} \end{pmatrix}$, $(\mathsf{pk}_{\mathsf{IPFE}}, \mathsf{msk}_{\mathsf{IPFE}}) \leftarrow \mathsf{Setup}_{\mathsf{IPFE}}(1^\lambda, \mathcal{PG}, [\mathbf{M}]_1)$
Return $\mathsf{pk} := ([\mathbf{Ua}]_1, [\mathbf{VB}]_2, \mathsf{pk}_{\mathsf{IPFE}})$, $\mathsf{msk} := (\mathbf{U}, \mathbf{V}, \mathsf{msk}_{\mathsf{IPFE}})$

$\underline{\mathsf{Enc}(\mathbf{x}, \mathbf{y})}$:
$r \leftarrow_{\mathrm{R}} \mathbb{Z}_p$, $\mathsf{ct}_{\mathbf{x}} := \mathbf{x} + \mathbf{U}\mathbf{a}r$, $\mathbf{s} \leftarrow_{\mathrm{R}} \mathbb{Z}_p^2$, $\mathsf{ct}_{\mathbf{y}} := \mathbf{y} + \mathbf{VBs}$,
$\mathsf{ct}_{\mathsf{IPFE}} := \mathsf{Enc}_{\mathsf{IPFE}}\left(\mathsf{pk}_{\mathsf{IPFE}}, \begin{pmatrix} r \otimes \binom{\mathbf{y}}{\mathbf{s}} \\ \mathbf{x} \otimes \mathbf{s} \end{pmatrix}\right)$
Return $\mathsf{ct}_{\mathbf{x},\mathbf{y}} := ([\mathsf{ct}_{\mathbf{x}}]_1, [\mathsf{ct}_{\mathbf{y}}]_2, \mathsf{ct}_{\mathsf{IPFE}})$

$\underline{\mathsf{KeyGen}(\mathsf{msk}, \mathbf{F})}$:
$\mathsf{sk}_{\mathsf{IPFE}} \leftarrow \mathsf{KeyGen}_{\mathsf{IPFE}}\left(\mathsf{msk}_{\mathsf{IPFE}}, \begin{pmatrix} \mathsf{vect}(\mathbf{U}^\top \mathbf{F}) \\ \mathsf{vect}(\mathbf{FV}) \end{pmatrix}\right)$
Return $\mathsf{sk}_{\mathbf{F}} := (\mathbf{F}, \mathsf{sk}_{\mathsf{IPFE}})$

$\underline{\mathsf{Dec}(\mathsf{ct}_{\mathbf{x},\mathbf{y}} := ([\mathsf{ct}_{\mathbf{x}}]_1, [\mathsf{ct}_{\mathbf{y}}]_2, \mathsf{ct}_{\mathsf{IPFE}}), \mathsf{sk}_{\mathbf{F}} := (\mathbf{F}, \mathsf{sk}_{\mathsf{IPFE}}))}$:
$[d]_T \leftarrow \mathsf{Dec}_{\mathsf{IPFE}}(\mathsf{ct}_{\mathsf{IPFE}}, \mathsf{sk}_{\mathsf{IPFE}})$, $[v]_T := e([\mathsf{ct}_{\mathbf{x}}]_1^\top, [\mathbf{F}\mathsf{ct}_{\mathbf{y}}]_2) - [d]_T$
If $v \in [0, n \cdot m \cdot B^3]$, return $\log([v]_T)$. Otherwise, return $\perp$.

Fig. 4. Quadratic FE: Quad. Here, $\mathsf{IPFE} := (\mathsf{Setup}_{\mathsf{IPFE}}, \mathsf{Enc}_{\mathsf{IPFE}}, \mathsf{Enc}'_{\mathsf{IPFE}}, \mathsf{KeyGen}_{\mathsf{IPFE}}, \mathsf{Dec}_{\mathsf{IPFE}})$ is a (tag-free) partially function-hiding inner-product FE, as defined in Sect. 3.1.

which corresponds exactly to the extra terms obtained when computing $\mathsf{ct}_{\mathbf{x}}^\top \mathbf{F} \mathsf{ct}_{\mathbf{y}}$, that is, we have: $\mathsf{ct}_{\mathbf{x}}^\top \mathbf{F} \mathsf{ct}_{\mathbf{y}} = \mathbf{x}^\top \mathbf{F} \mathbf{y} + d$. Finally, Dec computes the discrete log of $[\mathbf{x}^\top \mathbf{F} \mathbf{y}]_T$, which is efficient since the output $\mathbf{x}^\top \mathbf{F} \mathbf{y}$ is bounded by $n \cdot m \cdot B^3$, which is a polynomial in the security parameter.

Theorem 1 (Simulation security of the quadratic FE). *The quadratic FE from Fig. 4 for the functionality is simulation CPA (resp. CCA) secure if the underlying inner-product FE is partially function-hiding CPA (resp. CCA) simulation secure, assuming the bilateral DLIN assumption and the DDH assumption in $\mathbb{G}_1$.*

Namely, for any PPT adversary $\mathcal{A}$, there exist PPT adversaries $\mathcal{B}_1$, $\mathcal{B}_2$, and $\mathcal{B}_3$ such that:

$$\mathrm{Adv}^{\mathsf{CPA\text{-}SIM}}_{\mathsf{Quad},\mathcal{A}} \leq \mathrm{Adv}^{\mathsf{DDH}}_{\mathbb{G}_1,\mathcal{B}_1}(\lambda) + \mathrm{Adv}^{\mathsf{DLIN}}_{\mathcal{PG},\mathcal{B}_2}(\lambda) + \mathrm{Adv}^{\mathsf{CPA\text{-}PFH\text{-}SIM}}_{\mathsf{IPFE},\mathcal{B}_3}(\lambda) + \frac{4}{p}.$$

Besides, for any PPT adversary $\mathcal{A}'$, there exist PPT adversaries $\mathcal{B}'_1$, $\mathcal{B}'_2$, and $\mathcal{B}'_3$ such that:

$$\mathrm{Adv}^{\mathsf{CCA\text{-}SIM}}_{\mathsf{Quad},\mathcal{A}'} \leq \mathrm{Adv}^{\mathsf{DDH}}_{\mathbb{G}_1,\mathcal{B}'_1}(\lambda) + \mathrm{Adv}^{\mathsf{DLIN}}_{\mathcal{PG},\mathcal{B}'_2}(\lambda) + \mathrm{Adv}^{\mathsf{CCA\text{-}PFH\text{-}SIM}}_{\mathsf{IPFE},\mathcal{B}'_3}(\lambda) + \frac{4}{p}.$$

Proof. We prove the second part of the theorem, that is, CCA security. The CPA security proof is a straightforward simplification, hence omitted. Let $\mathcal{A}$ be a PPT adversary against the CCA security of Quad. We use a sequence of hybrid games Game_i for $i \in \{1,2,3,4\}$, defined in Fig. 5, and we denote the advantage $\varepsilon_i := \Pr[1 \leftarrow \mathsf{Game}_i(\mathcal{A}, 1^\lambda)]$. We show that these games are computationally indistinguishable: $\mathsf{Real}_{\mathcal{A}}^{\mathsf{CCA\text{-}Quad}}(1^\lambda) \equiv \mathsf{Game}_1 \approx_c \mathsf{Game}_2 \approx_c \mathsf{Game}_3 \approx_c \mathsf{Game}_4 \approx_s \mathsf{Ideal}_{\mathcal{A},\mathcal{S}}^{\mathsf{CCA\text{-}Quad}}(1^\lambda)$, for the PPT simulator $\mathcal{S} := (\widetilde{\mathsf{Setup}}, \widetilde{\mathsf{Enc}}, \widetilde{\mathsf{KeyGen}}, \widetilde{\mathsf{Dec}})$ defined in Fig. 6.

Game_1*:* is as $\mathsf{Real}_{\mathcal{A}}^{\mathsf{CCA\text{-}Quad}}(1^\lambda)$, except the encryption algorithm Enc' is used instead of Enc. Since these algorithms are identically distributed on input vectors in the span on $[\mathbf{M}]_1$, this does not change the advantage of $\mathcal{A}$:

$$\Pr[1 \leftarrow \mathsf{Real}_{\mathcal{A}}^{\mathsf{CCA\text{-}Quad}}(1^\lambda)] = \varepsilon_1.$$

Game_2*:* we use the DDH assumption in $\mathbb{G}_1$ to switch the distribution of the vector $[\mathbf{a}r]_1$ in the challenge ciphertext to uniformly random over $\mathbb{G}_1^2$. Namely, we build a PPT adversary $\mathcal{B}_1$ against the DDH assumption such that

$$\varepsilon_2 - \varepsilon_1 \leq \mathrm{Adv}_{\mathbb{G}_1,\mathcal{B}_1}^{\mathsf{DDH}}(\lambda).$$

Upon receiving the DDH challenge $(\mathcal{PG}, [\mathbf{a}]_1, [\mathbf{c}]_1)$, $\mathcal{B}_1$ samples $\mathbf{U} \leftarrow_{\mathrm{R}} \mathbb{Z}_p^{n\times 2}$, $\mathbf{V} \leftarrow_{\mathrm{R}} \mathbb{Z}_p^{m\times 3}$, $\mathbf{B} \leftarrow \mathsf{DLIN}$, computes $[\mathbf{M}]_1$ as defined in Fig. 4, and runs $(\mathsf{pk}_{\mathsf{IPFE}}, \mathsf{msk}_{\mathsf{IPFE}}) \leftarrow \mathsf{Setup}_{\mathsf{IPFE}}(1^\lambda, \mathcal{PG}, [\mathbf{M}]_1)$, tanks to which it can simulate the public key pk for $\mathcal{A}$, and answer its queries to $\mathcal{O}_{\mathsf{KeyGen}}$ and $\mathcal{O}_{\mathsf{Dec}}$. When $\mathcal{A}$ submits its challenge $(\mathbf{x}, \mathbf{y})$, $\mathcal{B}_1$ samples $\mathbf{s} \leftarrow_{\mathrm{R}} \mathbb{Z}_p^2$, computes $[\mathsf{ct}_{\mathbf{x}}]_1 := [\mathbf{x} + \mathbf{U}\mathbf{c}]_1$, $[\mathsf{ct}_{\mathbf{y}}]_2 := [\mathbf{y} + \mathbf{V}\mathbf{B}\mathbf{s}]_2$, $[\mathbf{z}]_1 := \begin{bmatrix} \mathbf{c} \otimes \mathsf{ct}_{\mathbf{y}} \\ \mathbf{x} \otimes \mathbf{B}\mathbf{s} \end{bmatrix}_1$ and returns the challenge ciphertext $([\mathsf{ct}_{\mathbf{x}}]_1, [\mathsf{ct}_{\mathbf{y}}]_2, \mathsf{Enc}'_{\mathsf{IPFE}}(\mathsf{msk}_{\mathsf{IPFE}}, [\mathbf{z}]_1))$ to $\mathcal{A}$. When $[\mathbf{c}]_1$ is a real DDH challenge, that is, of the form $[\mathbf{c}]_1 := [\mathbf{a}r]_1$ for some $r \leftarrow_{\mathrm{R}} \mathbb{Z}_p$, $\mathcal{B}_1$ simulates Game_1, whereas it simulates Game_2 when $[\mathbf{c}]_1$ is uniformly random over $\mathbb{G}_1^2$.

Game_3*:* we use the bilateral DLIN assumption to switch the distribution of the vector $[\mathbf{B}\mathbf{s}]_2$ to uniformly random over $\mathbb{G}_2^3$. Namely, we build a PPT adversary $\mathcal{B}_2$ such

$$\varepsilon_3 - \varepsilon_2 \leq \mathrm{Adv}_{\mathcal{PG},\mathcal{B}_2}^{\mathsf{DLIN}}(\lambda).$$

Upon receiving the DLIN challenge $(\mathcal{PG}, \{[\mathbf{B}]_s, [\mathbf{t}]_s\}_{s\in\{1,2\}})$, $\mathcal{B}_2$ samples $\mathbf{U} \leftarrow_{\mathrm{R}} \mathbb{Z}_p^{n\times 2}$, $\mathbf{V} \leftarrow_{\mathrm{R}} \mathbb{Z}_p^{m\times 3}$, $\mathbf{a} \leftarrow_{\mathrm{R}} \mathsf{DDH}$, computes $[\mathbf{M}]_1$ as defined in Fig. 4, and runs $(\mathsf{pk}_{\mathsf{IPFE}}, \mathsf{msk}_{\mathsf{IPFE}}) \leftarrow \mathsf{Setup}_{\mathsf{IPFE}}(1^\lambda, \mathcal{PG}, [\mathbf{M}]_1)$, tanks to which it can simulate the public key pk for $\mathcal{A}$, and answer its queries to $\mathcal{O}_{\mathsf{KeyGen}}$ and $\mathcal{O}_{\mathsf{Dec}}$. When $\mathcal{A}$ submits its challenge $(\mathbf{x}, \mathbf{y})$, $\mathcal{B}$ samples $\mathbf{c} \leftarrow_{\mathrm{R}} \mathbb{Z}_p^2$, computes $[\mathsf{ct}_{\mathbf{x}}]_1 := [\mathbf{x} + \mathbf{U}\mathbf{c}]_1$, $[\mathsf{ct}_{\mathbf{y}}]_2 := [\mathbf{y} + \mathbf{V}\mathbf{t}]_2$, $[\mathbf{z}]_1 := \begin{bmatrix} \mathbf{c} \otimes (\mathbf{y} + \mathbf{V}\mathbf{t}) \\ \mathbf{x} \otimes \mathbf{t} \end{bmatrix}_1$ and returns the challenge ciphertext $([\mathsf{ct}_{\mathbf{x}}]_1, [\mathsf{ct}_{\mathbf{y}}]_2, \mathsf{Enc}'_{\mathsf{IPFE}}(\mathsf{msk}_{\mathsf{IPFE}}, [\mathbf{z}]_1))$ to $\mathcal{A}$. When $\{[\mathbf{t}]_s\}_{s\in\{1,2\}}$ is a real DLIN challenge, that is, of the form $[\mathbf{t}]_s := [\mathbf{B}\mathbf{s}]_s$ for some $\mathbf{s} \leftarrow_{\mathrm{R}} \mathbb{Z}_p^2$, $\mathcal{B}_2$ simulates Game_2, whereas it simulates Game_3 when $[\mathbf{t}]_s$ is uniformly random over $\mathbb{G}_s^2$.

$\boxed{\mathsf{Game}_1, \boxed{\mathsf{Game}_2, \mathsf{Game}_3, \mathsf{Game}_4}}$:

$\mathcal{PG} \leftarrow \mathsf{GGen}(1^\lambda)$, $\mathbf{a} \leftarrow_{\mathrm{R}} \mathsf{DDH}$, $\mathbf{B} \leftarrow_{\mathrm{R}} \mathsf{DLIN}$, $\mathbf{U} \leftarrow_{\mathrm{R}} \mathbb{Z}_p^{n\times 2}$, $\mathbf{V} \leftarrow_{\mathrm{R}} \mathbb{Z}_p^{m\times 3}$

$\mathbf{M} := \begin{pmatrix} \mathbf{a} \otimes (\mathrm{Id}_m | \mathbf{VB}) & \mathbf{0} \\ \mathbf{0} & \mathrm{Id}_n \otimes \mathbf{B} \end{pmatrix}$

$(\mathsf{pk}_{\mathsf{IPFE}}, \mathsf{msk}_{\mathsf{IPFE}}) \leftarrow \mathsf{Setup}_{\mathsf{IPFE}}(1^\lambda, \mathcal{PG}, [\mathbf{M}]_1)$, $\mathsf{pk}' := \mathsf{pk}_{\mathsf{IPFE}}$, $\mathsf{msk}' := \mathsf{msk}_{\mathsf{IPFE}}$

$(\widetilde{\mathsf{pk}}_{\mathsf{IPFE}}, \widetilde{\mathsf{msk}}_{\mathsf{IPFE}}) \leftarrow \widetilde{\mathsf{Setup}}_{\mathsf{IPFE}}(1^\lambda, \mathcal{PG}, [\mathbf{M}]_1)$, $\mathsf{pk}' := \widetilde{\mathsf{pk}}_{\mathsf{IPFE}}$, $\mathsf{msk}' := \widetilde{\mathsf{msk}}_{\mathsf{IPFE}}$

$\mathsf{pk} := ([\mathbf{Ua}]_1, [\mathbf{VB}]_2, \mathsf{pk}')$, $\mathsf{msk} := (\mathbf{U}, \mathbf{V}, \mathsf{msk}')$

$(\mathbf{x}, \mathbf{y}) \leftarrow \mathcal{A}(\mathsf{pk})$

$\mathsf{ct}^\star \leftarrow \mathcal{O}_{\mathsf{Enc}}(\mathbf{x}, \mathbf{y})$

$\alpha \leftarrow \mathcal{A}^{\mathcal{O}_{\mathsf{KeyGen}}(\cdot), \mathcal{O}_{\mathsf{Dec}}(\cdot,\cdot)}(\mathsf{ct}^\star)$

$\underline{\mathcal{O}_{\mathsf{Enc}}(\mathbf{x}, \mathbf{y})}$:

$r \leftarrow_{\mathrm{R}} \mathbb{Z}_p$, $\mathbf{c} := \mathbf{a}r$, $\boxed{\mathbf{c} \leftarrow_{\mathrm{R}} \mathbb{Z}_p^2}$, $\mathsf{ct}_{\mathbf{x}} := \mathbf{x} + \mathbf{Uc}$

$\mathbf{s} \leftarrow_{\mathrm{R}} \mathbb{Z}_p^2$, $\mathbf{t} := \mathbf{Bs}$, $\mathbf{t} \leftarrow_{\mathrm{R}} \mathbb{Z}_p^3$, $\mathsf{ct}_{\mathbf{y}} := \mathbf{y} + \mathbf{Vt}$

$\mathsf{ct}_{\mathsf{IPFE}} := \mathsf{Enc}'_{\mathsf{IPFE}}\left(\mathsf{msk}_{\mathsf{IPFE}}, \begin{bmatrix} \mathbf{c} \otimes \mathsf{ct}_{\mathbf{y}} \\ \mathbf{x} \otimes \mathbf{t} \end{bmatrix}_1\right)$

$\mathsf{ct}_{\mathsf{IPFE}} := \widetilde{\mathsf{Enc}}_{\mathsf{IPFE}}\left(\widetilde{\mathsf{msk}}_{\mathsf{IPFE}}\right)$

Return $([\mathsf{ct}_{\mathbf{x}}]_1, [\mathsf{ct}_{\mathbf{y}}]_2, \mathsf{ct}_{\mathsf{IPFE}})$

$\underline{\mathcal{O}_{\mathsf{KeyGen}}(\mathbf{F})}$:

$\mathsf{sk}_{\mathbf{F}} := \mathsf{KeyGen}(\mathsf{msk}, \mathbf{F})$

$d_{\mathbf{F}} := \mathsf{ct}_{\mathbf{x}}^\top \mathbf{F} \mathsf{ct}_{\mathbf{y}} - \mathbf{x}^\top \mathbf{F} \mathbf{y}$, $\mathbf{v}_{\mathbf{F}} := \mathbf{M}(\mathbf{M}^\top \mathbf{M})^{-1} \mathbf{M}^\top \begin{pmatrix} \mathsf{vect}(\mathbf{U}^\top \mathbf{F}) \\ \mathsf{vect}(\mathbf{FV}) \end{pmatrix}$

$\mathsf{sk}_{\mathbf{F}} := \widetilde{\mathsf{KeyGen}}_{\mathsf{IPFE}}\left(\widetilde{\mathsf{msk}}_{\mathsf{IPFE}}, d_{\mathbf{F}}, \mathbf{v}_{\mathbf{F}}\right)$

Return $\mathsf{sk}_{\mathbf{F}}$

$\underline{\mathcal{O}_{\mathsf{Dec}}(\mathsf{ct} := ([\mathbf{c}_1]_1, [\mathbf{c}_2]_2, \mathsf{ct}_{\mathsf{IPFE}}), \mathbf{F})}$:

$\mathsf{sk}_{\mathbf{F}} := \mathsf{KeyGen}_{\mathsf{IPFE}}\left(\mathsf{msk}_{\mathsf{IPFE}}, \begin{pmatrix} \mathsf{vect}(\mathbf{U}^\top \mathbf{F}) \\ \mathsf{vect}(\mathbf{FV}) \end{pmatrix}\right)$, $[d]_T \leftarrow \mathsf{Dec}_{\mathsf{IPFE}}(\mathsf{ct}_{\mathsf{IPFE}}, \mathsf{sk}_{\mathbf{F}})$

$\mathbf{v}_{\mathbf{F}} := \mathbf{M}(\mathbf{M}^\top \mathbf{M})^{-1} \mathbf{M}^\top \begin{pmatrix} \mathsf{vect}(\mathbf{U}^\top \mathbf{F}) \\ \mathsf{vect}(\mathbf{FV}) \end{pmatrix}$, $[d]_T \leftarrow \widetilde{\mathsf{Dec}}_{\mathsf{IPFE}}(\widetilde{\mathsf{msk}}_{\mathsf{IPFE}}, \mathsf{ct}_{\mathsf{IPFE}}, \mathbf{v}_{\mathbf{F}})$

$[v]_T := [\mathbf{c}_1^\top \mathbf{F} \mathbf{c}_2]_T - [d]_T$

If $v \in [0, n \cdot m \cdot B^3]$, return v; otherwise, return $\perp$.

Fig. 5. Games for the security proof of the quadratic FE from Fig. 4. In each procedure, the components inside a solid (dotted, gray) frame are only present in the games marked by a solid (dotted, gray) frame. $(\widetilde{\mathsf{Setup}}_{\mathsf{IPFE}}, \widetilde{\mathsf{Enc}}_{\mathsf{IPFE}}, \widetilde{\mathsf{KeyGen}}_{\mathsf{IPFE}}, \widetilde{\mathsf{Dec}}_{\mathsf{IPFE}})$ is a PPT simulator for the partially function-hiding SEL-SIM secure inner-product FE: IPFE.

$\underline{\widetilde{\mathsf{Setup}}(1^\lambda, \mathcal{F}_{\mathsf{quad}})}$:
$\mathcal{PG} \leftarrow \mathsf{GGen}(1^\lambda)$, $\mathbf{a} \leftarrow_{\mathrm{R}} \mathsf{DDH}$, $\mathbf{B} \leftarrow_{\mathrm{R}} \mathsf{DLIN}$, $\mathbf{U} \leftarrow_{\mathrm{R}} \mathbb{Z}_p^{n\times 2}$, $\mathbf{V} \leftarrow_{\mathrm{R}} \mathbb{Z}_p^{m\times 3}$
$\mathbf{M} := \left(\begin{array}{c|c} \mathbf{a}\otimes(\mathrm{Id}_m|\mathbf{VB}) & \mathbf{0} \\ \hline \mathbf{0} & \mathrm{Id}_n \otimes \mathbf{B}\end{array}\right)$, $(\widetilde{\mathsf{pk}}_{\mathsf{IPFE}}, \widetilde{\mathsf{msk}}_{\mathsf{IPFE}}) \leftarrow \widetilde{\mathsf{Setup}}_{\mathsf{IPFE}}(1^\lambda, \mathcal{PG}, [\mathbf{M}]_1)$
Return $\widetilde{\mathsf{pk}} := \left([\mathbf{Ua}]_1, [\mathbf{VB}]_2, \widetilde{\mathsf{pk}}_{\mathsf{IPFE}}\right)$, $\widetilde{\mathsf{msk}} := \left(\mathbf{U}, \mathbf{V}, \widetilde{\mathsf{msk}}_{\mathsf{IPFE}}\right)$

$\underline{\widetilde{\mathsf{Enc}}(\widetilde{\mathsf{msk}})}$:
$\mathsf{ct}_{\mathbf{x}} \leftarrow_{\mathrm{R}} \mathbb{Z}_p^n$, $\mathsf{ct}_{\mathbf{y}} \leftarrow_{\mathrm{R}} \mathbb{Z}_p^m$
Return $\mathsf{ct}_{\mathbf{x},\mathbf{y}} := \left([\mathsf{ct}_{\mathbf{x}}]_1, [\mathsf{ct}_{\mathbf{y}}]_2, \widetilde{\mathsf{Enc}}_{\mathsf{IPFE}}\left(\widetilde{\mathsf{msk}}_{\mathsf{IPFE}}\right)\right)$

$\underline{\widetilde{\mathsf{KeyGen}}(\widetilde{\mathsf{msk}}, \mathbf{F}, \mathbf{x}^\top\mathbf{F}\mathbf{y})}$:
$d_{\mathbf{F}} := \mathsf{ct}_{\mathbf{x}}^\top \mathbf{F} \mathsf{ct}_{\mathbf{y}} - \mathbf{x}^\top\mathbf{F}\mathbf{y}$, $\mathbf{v}_{\mathbf{F}} := \mathbf{M}(\mathbf{M}^\top\mathbf{M})^{-1}\mathbf{M}^\top \begin{pmatrix}\mathsf{vect}(\mathbf{U}^\top\mathbf{F}) \\ \mathsf{vect}(\mathbf{FV})\end{pmatrix}$
Return $\widetilde{\mathsf{KeyGen}}_{\mathsf{IPFE}}\left(\widetilde{\mathsf{msk}}_{\mathsf{IPFE}}, d_{\mathbf{F}}, \mathbf{v}_{\mathbf{F}}\right)$

$\underline{\widetilde{\mathsf{Dec}}(\widetilde{\mathsf{msk}}, \mathsf{ct}, \mathbf{F})}$:
$\mathbf{v}_{\mathbf{F}} := \mathbf{M}(\mathbf{M}^\top\mathbf{M})^{-1}\mathbf{M}^\top \begin{pmatrix}\mathsf{vect}(\mathbf{U}^\top\mathbf{F}) \\ \mathsf{vect}(\mathbf{FV})\end{pmatrix}$, $[d]_T \leftarrow \widetilde{\mathsf{Dec}}_{\mathsf{IPFE}}(\widetilde{\mathsf{msk}}_{\mathsf{IPFE}}, \mathsf{ct}, \mathbf{v}_{\mathbf{F}})$,
$[v]_T := [\mathsf{ct}_{\mathbf{x}}^\top \mathbf{F} \mathsf{ct}_{\mathbf{y}}]_T - [d]_T$.
If $v \in [0, n\cdot m\cdot B^3]$, return v; otherwise, return $\perp$.

Fig. 6. PPT simulator for the security proof of the quadratic FE from Fig. 4. Here, $(\widetilde{\mathsf{Setup}}_{\mathsf{IPFE}}, \widetilde{\mathsf{Enc}}_{\mathsf{IPFE}}, \widetilde{\mathsf{KeyGen}}_{\mathsf{IPFE}}, \widetilde{\mathsf{Dec}}_{\mathsf{IPFE}})$ is a PPT simulator for the partially function-hiding, simulation secure inner-product FE, IPFE, used in the quadratic FE.

Game_4*:* we use the simulator $(\widetilde{\mathsf{Setup}}_{\mathsf{IPFE}}, \widetilde{\mathsf{Enc}}_{\mathsf{IPFE}}, \widetilde{\mathsf{KeyGen}}_{\mathsf{IPFE}}, \widetilde{\mathsf{Dec}}_{\mathsf{IPFE}})$ of IPFE, as described in Fig. 5. Namely, there exists a PPT adversary $\mathcal{B}_3$ such that

$$\varepsilon_4 - \varepsilon_3 \leq \mathrm{Adv}_{\mathsf{IPFE},\mathcal{B}_3}^{\mathsf{CCA\text{-}PFH\text{-}SIM}}(\lambda).$$

Adversary $\mathcal{B}_3$ samples $\mathbf{a} \leftarrow_{\mathrm{R}} \mathsf{DDH}$, $\mathbf{B} \leftarrow_{\mathrm{R}} \mathsf{DLIN}$, $\mathbf{U} \leftarrow_{\mathrm{R}} \mathbb{Z}_p^{n\times 2}$, $\mathbf{V} \leftarrow_{\mathrm{R}} \mathbb{Z}_p^{m\times 3}$, and simulates $\mathcal{A}$'s view straightforwardly, using the fact that for all $\mathbf{x} \in \mathbb{Z}_p^n$, $\mathbf{y} \in \mathbb{Z}_p^m$, $\mathbf{F} \in \mathbb{Z}_p^{n\times m}$, $\mathbf{c} \in \mathbb{Z}_p^2$, $\mathbf{t} \in \mathbb{Z}_p^3$, we have:

$$\begin{pmatrix}\mathbf{c}\otimes \mathsf{ct}_{\mathbf{y}} \\ \mathbf{x}\otimes\mathbf{t}\end{pmatrix}^\top \begin{pmatrix}\mathsf{vect}(\mathbf{U}^\top\mathbf{F}) \\ \mathsf{vect}(\mathbf{FV})\end{pmatrix} = \mathsf{ct}_{\mathbf{x}}^\top\mathbf{F}\mathsf{ct}_{\mathbf{y}} - \mathbf{x}^\top\mathbf{F}\mathbf{y},$$

where $\mathsf{ct}_{\mathbf{x}} = \mathbf{x} + \mathbf{Uc}$, and $\mathsf{ct}_{\mathbf{y}} = \mathbf{y} + \mathbf{Vt}$.

$\mathsf{Ideal}_{\mathcal{A},\mathcal{S}}^{\mathsf{CCA\text{-}Quad}}(1^\lambda)$*:* is as Game_4, except that $\mathsf{ct}_{\mathbf{x}}$ and $\mathsf{ct}_{\mathbf{y}}$ in the challenge ciphertext are uniformly distributed. We show that these two games are statistically close. Namely, we show that the vectors $\mathbf{Uc}$ and $\mathbf{Vt}$ are statistically close to uniformly random over $\mathbb{Z}_p^2$ and $\mathbb{Z}_p^3$, respectively.

To prove so, we use the following basis of $\mathbb{Z}_p^2$ and $\mathbb{Z}_p^3$: $(\mathbf{a}|\mathbf{a}^\perp)$ and $(\mathbf{B}|\mathbf{b}^\perp)$ with $\mathbf{a} \leftarrow_{\mathrm{R}} \mathsf{DDH}$, $\mathbf{B} \leftarrow_{\mathrm{R}} \mathsf{DLIN}$, and $\mathbf{a}^\perp \in \mathbb{Z}_p^2$, $\mathbf{b}^\perp \in \mathbb{Z}_p^3$ are such that $\mathbf{a}^\top\mathbf{a}^\perp = 0$

and $\mathbf{B}^\top\mathbf{b}^\perp = \mathbf{0}$. Such basis exist assuming $\mathbf{a}$ and $\mathbf{B}$ are both full rank, which happens with probability at least $1-\frac{2}{p}$ over the choice of $\mathbf{a} \leftarrow_{\mathrm{R}} \mathsf{DDH}$ and $\mathbf{B} \leftarrow_{\mathrm{R}} \mathsf{DLIN}$. We have: $\mathbf{U}^\top := \mathbf{a}\mathbf{u}_0^\top + \mathbf{a}^\perp\mathbf{u}_1^\top$, and $\mathbf{V}^\top := \mathbf{B}\mathbf{V}_0 + \mathbf{b}^\perp\mathbf{v}_1^\top$, with $\mathbf{u}_0, \mathbf{u}_1 \leftarrow_{\mathrm{R}} \mathbb{Z}_p^n$, $\mathbf{V}_0 \leftarrow_{\mathrm{R}} \mathbb{Z}_p^{2\times m}$, and $\mathbf{v}_1 \leftarrow_{\mathrm{R}} \mathbb{Z}_p^m$. We will show that $\mathbf{u}_1$ and $\mathbf{v}_1$ only appear in the adversary view as $(\mathbf{c}^\top\mathbf{a}^\perp)\mathbf{u}_1$ in $\mathsf{ct}_{\mathbf{x}}$, and as $(\mathbf{t}^\top\mathbf{b}^\perp)\mathbf{v}_1$ in $\mathsf{ct}_{\mathbf{y}}$. Since we have $\mathsf{ct}_{\mathbf{x}} = \mathbf{x} + \mathbf{u}_0(\mathbf{c}^\top\mathbf{a}) + \mathbf{u}_1(\mathbf{c}^\top\mathbf{a}^\perp)$ and $\mathsf{ct}_{\mathbf{y}} = \mathbf{y} + \mathbf{V}_0^\top(\mathbf{B}^\top\mathbf{t}) + \mathbf{v}_1(\mathbf{t}^\top\mathbf{b}^\perp)$, when $\mathbf{c}^\top\mathbf{a}^\perp \neq 0$, and $\mathbf{t}^\top\mathbf{b}^\perp \neq 0$, the vectors $\mathsf{ct}_{\mathbf{x}}$ and $\mathsf{ct}_{\mathbf{y}}$ are uniformly random over $\mathbb{Z}_p^2$ and $\mathbb{Z}_p^3$, respectively. With probability $1-\frac{2}{p}$ over the choice of $\mathbf{c} \leftarrow_{\mathrm{R}} \mathbb{Z}_p^2$ and $\mathbf{t} \leftarrow_{\mathrm{R}} \mathbb{Z}_p^3$, we have $\mathbf{c}^\top\mathbf{a}^\perp \neq 0$, and $\mathbf{t}^\top\mathbf{b}^\perp \neq 0$, which proves

$$\varepsilon_4 \leq \Pr\left[1 \leftarrow \mathsf{Ideal}_{\mathcal{A}}^{\mathsf{CCA\text{-}Quad}}(1^\lambda)\right] + \frac{4}{p}.$$

We now show that $\mathbf{u}_1$ and $\mathbf{v}_1$ only appear in $\mathsf{ct}_{\mathbf{x}}$ and $\mathsf{ct}_{\mathbf{y}}$, as indicated above. In the public key, we have $\mathbf{a}^\top\mathbf{U}^\top = \mathbf{a}^\top(\mathbf{a}\mathbf{u}_0^\top + \mathbf{a}^\perp\mathbf{u}_1^\top) = (\mathbf{a}^\top\mathbf{a})\mathbf{u}_0^\top$, and $\mathbf{B}^\top\mathbf{V}^\top = \mathbf{B}^\top(\mathbf{B}\mathbf{V}_0 + \mathbf{b}^\perp\mathbf{v}_1^\top) = (\mathbf{B}^\top\mathbf{B})\mathbf{v}_0^\top$. The information needed to simulate $\mathcal{O}_{\mathsf{KeyGen}}$ and $\mathcal{O}_{\mathsf{Dec}}$ is contained in $\mathbf{F}$, $\mathsf{ct}_{\mathbf{x}}$, $\mathsf{ct}_{\mathbf{y}}$, $\mathbf{x}^\top\mathbf{F}\mathbf{y}$, $\mathbf{M}$, and

$$\mathbf{M}^\top \begin{pmatrix} \mathsf{vect}((\mathbf{a}\mathbf{u}_0^\top + \mathbf{a}^\perp\mathbf{u}_1^\top)\mathbf{F}) \\ \mathsf{vect}(\mathbf{F}(\mathbf{B}\mathbf{V}_0 + \mathbf{b}^\perp\mathbf{v}_1^\top)^\top) \end{pmatrix} = \mathbf{M}^\top \begin{pmatrix} \mathsf{vect}(\mathbf{a}\mathbf{u}_0^\top\mathbf{F}) \\ \mathsf{vect}(\mathbf{F}\mathbf{B}\mathbf{V}_0) \end{pmatrix},$$

where the equality holds by definition of $\mathbf{M}$. That is, the only information about $\mathbf{u}_1$ and $\mathbf{v}_1$ is contained in $\mathsf{ct}_{\mathbf{x}}$, $\mathsf{ct}_{\mathbf{y}}$, which concludes the proof. □

4 Partially-Hiding Inner Product FE

In this section we build a partially-hiding, simulation-secure inner-product FE scheme, as defined in Sect. 3.1, based on the SXDH assumption. Together with the generic construction from Sect. 3, this gives the quadratic FE advertised in Sect. 1, Fig. 2.

Overview of the Partially-Hiding Inner-Product FE. We now highlight the construction of our new partially-hiding public-key FE for inner products. Our starting point is the FE for inner products from [ALS16], described in Fig. 7. It is not function-hiding since $\mathbf{y}$ is part of the decryption keys generated by KeyGen. As in [Lin17, Section 6.3], we use the fact that the decryption computes the inner product of $\mathsf{Enc}(\mathbf{x})$ and $\mathsf{KeyGen}(\mathbf{y})$ to obtain $[\mathbf{x}^\top\mathbf{y}] \in \mathbb{G}$. Namely, we replace the vector $\mathbf{y}$ in each decryption key by an ALS encryption of $\mathbf{y}$, and $\mathbf{x}$ in each ciphertext is replaced by an ALS decryption key for $\mathbf{x}$ (see Fig. 3). Function-Hiding (hiding $\mathbf{y}$) follows from the security of the inner ALS FE, whereas security (hiding $\mathbf{x}$) follows from the security of the outter ALS FE. Note that we use the fact that the KeyGen algorithm from [ALS16] FE can act on vectors in $\mathbb{G}_2$, and the multiplications can be computed using the pairing $e : \mathbb{G}_1 \times \mathbb{G}_2 \rightarrow \mathbb{G}_T$ to recover the inner product of $\mathbf{x}$ and $\mathbf{y}$ in $\mathbb{G}_T$.

$$
\begin{array}{ll}
\mathsf{pk} = [\mathbf{a}], [\mathbf{Ua}] & //[\mathbf{a}] \leftarrow_{\mathrm{R}} \mathbb{G}^2,\ \mathbf{U} \leftarrow_{\mathrm{R}} \mathbb{Z}_p^{d\times 2} \\
\mathsf{Enc}(\mathbf{x} \in \mathbb{Z}^n) = \begin{bmatrix} \mathbf{a}r \\ \mathbf{x} + \mathbf{Ua}r \end{bmatrix} \in \mathbb{G}^{n+2} & //r \leftarrow_{\mathrm{R}} \mathbb{Z}_p \\
\mathsf{KeyGen}(\mathbf{y} \in \mathbb{Z}^n) = \left(\mathbf{y}, \begin{pmatrix} -\mathbf{U}^\top \mathbf{y} \\ \mathbf{y} \end{pmatrix}\right) \in \mathbb{Z}^n \times \mathbb{Z}_p^{n+2} &
\end{array}
$$

Fig. 7. FE for inner products, from [ALS16].

To make our scheme public-key, we need to publish a restricted secret key for the inner layer FE that lets $\mathsf{KeyGen}^{\mathsf{in}}(\mathbf{x})$ run on vectors $\mathbf{x}$ spanned by the matrix $\mathbf{M}$ described in Sect. 3 (recall that $\mathbf{M}$ is a full rank, n times m matrix, with $n > m$). If we denote the master secret key of the inner layer FE by $\mathsf{msk} := \mathbf{U} \in \mathbb{Z}_p^{d\times 2}$, the restricted key would simply be $\mathbf{U}^\top \mathbf{M}$.

We prove simulation security, which is necessary to be of use in our quadratic FE scheme, and which is stronger than the classical indistinguishability based security for FE. To do so, we use the simulation security of [ALS16], which was proven in [AGRW17, Wee17]. We obtain simulation security in the semi-adaptive setting, where the adversary sends its challenge before querying any secret keys, but after receiving the public key. This is the best we can hope for, since a straightforward adaptation of the results from [BSW11, AGVW13] show that simulation security is impossible in the adaptive setting (where the adversary can query secret keys before sending its challenge ciphertext).

[Lin17] also builds function-hiding FE from a two layered FE encryption, but uses [ABDP15] instead of [ALS16], and only obtains indistinguishability security, in the private key setting (see Fig. 3).

Our partially-hiding, simulation-secure inner-product FE is described in Fig. 8.

Correctness. For all $\mathbf{t} \in \mathbb{Z}_p^m$ and $\mathbf{y} \in \mathbb{Z}_p^n$, we have:

$$
\left(\begin{pmatrix} \mathbf{a}r \\ -\mathbf{V}^\top \mathbf{Mt} \\ \mathbf{Mt} \end{pmatrix} + \mathbf{Ua}r\right)^\top \begin{pmatrix} -\mathbf{U}^\top \begin{pmatrix} \mathbf{b}s \\ \mathbf{y} + \mathbf{Vb}s \end{pmatrix} \\ \begin{pmatrix} \mathbf{b}s \\ \mathbf{y} + \mathbf{Vb}s \end{pmatrix} \end{pmatrix} = \begin{pmatrix} -\mathbf{V}^\top \mathbf{Mt} \\ \mathbf{Mt} \end{pmatrix}^\top \begin{pmatrix} \mathbf{b}s \\ \mathbf{y} + \mathbf{Vb}s \end{pmatrix}
$$
$$
= (\mathbf{Mt})^\top \mathbf{y}.
$$

The first equality uses the correctness of the outer ALS encryption, while the second equality uses the correctness of the inner ALS encryption. We conclude using the completeness of the QANIZK argument.

Remark 1 (Large inputs). First, we observe that the encryption algorithm of our partially function-hiding inner product FE can take as input arbitrary vectors $\mathbf{x} \in \mathbb{Z}_p^n$, as opposed to $\mathbf{x} \in [0, B]^n$ for a polynomially bounded B. The decryption

$\underline{\mathsf{Setup}(1^\lambda, \mathcal{PG}, [\mathbf{M}]_1 \in \mathbb{G}_1^{n\times m})}$:

$\mathbf{a}, \mathbf{b} \leftarrow_{\mathrm{R}} \mathsf{DDH}$, $(\mathsf{crs}, \mathsf{trap}) \leftarrow \mathsf{Gen}_{\mathsf{crs}}(\mathsf{par}, [\mathbf{a}]_1)$, $\mathbf{U} \leftarrow_{\mathrm{R}} \mathbb{Z}_p^{(n+2)\times 2}$, $\mathbf{V} \leftarrow_{\mathrm{R}} \mathbb{Z}_p^{n\times 2}$

Return $\mathsf{pk} := ([\mathbf{a}]_1, [\mathbf{Ua}]_1, [\mathbf{V}^\top \mathbf{M}]_1, [\mathbf{M}]_1, \mathsf{crs})$, $\mathsf{msk} := ([\mathbf{b}]_2, \mathbf{V}, \mathbf{U})$

$\underline{\mathsf{Enc}(\mathbf{t} \in \mathbb{Z}^m, \tau)}$:

$r \leftarrow_{\mathrm{R}} \mathbb{Z}_p$, $\mathbf{c} := \mathbf{a}r$, $\pi \leftarrow \mathsf{Prove}(\mathsf{crs}, \tau, [\mathbf{c}]_1, r)$

$$\text{Return } \mathsf{ct} := \left(\begin{bmatrix} \mathbf{c} \\ \begin{pmatrix} -\mathbf{V}^\top \mathbf{M}\mathbf{t} \\ \mathbf{M}\mathbf{t} \end{pmatrix} + \mathbf{Uc} \end{bmatrix}_1, \pi \right)$$

$\underline{\mathsf{Enc}'(\mathsf{msk}, [\mathbf{x}]_1 \in \mathbb{G}_1^n, \tau)}$:

$r \leftarrow_{\mathrm{R}} \mathbb{Z}_p$, $\mathbf{c} := \mathbf{a}r$, $\pi \leftarrow \mathsf{Prove}(\mathsf{crs}, \tau, [\mathbf{c}]_1, r)$

$$\text{Return } \mathsf{ct} := \left(\begin{bmatrix} \mathbf{c} \\ \begin{pmatrix} -\mathbf{V}^\top \mathbf{x} \\ \mathbf{x} \end{pmatrix} + \mathbf{Uc} \end{bmatrix}_1, \pi \right)$$

$\underline{\mathsf{KeyGen}(\mathsf{msk}, \mathbf{y} \in \mathbb{Z}_p^n)}$:

$s \leftarrow_{\mathrm{R}} \mathbb{Z}_p$

$$\text{Return } [\mathsf{sk}_{\mathbf{y}}]_2 := \begin{bmatrix} -\mathbf{U}^\top \begin{pmatrix} \mathbf{b}s \\ \mathbf{y} + \mathbf{Vb}s \end{pmatrix} \\ \begin{pmatrix} \mathbf{b}s \\ \mathbf{y} + \mathbf{Vb}s \end{pmatrix} \end{bmatrix}_2 \in \mathbb{G}_2^{n+4}$$

$\underline{\mathsf{Dec}(\tau, [\mathsf{sk}_{\mathbf{y}}]_2, \mathsf{ct})}$:

Parse $\mathsf{ct} := \left(\begin{bmatrix} \mathbf{c} \\ \mathbf{c}' \end{bmatrix}_1, \pi \right)$, with $[\mathbf{c}]_1 \in \mathbb{G}_1^2$.

If $\mathsf{Ver}(\mathsf{crs}, \tau, \pi, [\mathbf{c}]_1) = 0$, then return $\perp$. Return $e\left(\begin{bmatrix} \mathbf{c} \\ \mathbf{c}' \end{bmatrix}_1^\top, [\mathsf{sk}_{\mathbf{y}}]_2 \right) \in \mathbb{G}_T$.

Fig. 8. Simulation-secure, partially function-hiding inner-product FE. The components highlighted in gray are only present in the CCA secure scheme. Here, we use a QANIZK argument $\Pi := (\mathsf{Gen}_{\mathsf{par}}, \mathsf{Gen}_{\mathsf{crs}}, \mathsf{Prove}, \mathsf{Sim}, \mathsf{Ver})$, where $\mathsf{par} = \mathcal{PG}$, a pairing group $\mathcal{PG} = (\mathbb{G}_1, \mathbb{G}_2, \mathbb{G}_T, p, P_1, P_2, e)$. Given $\rho := [\mathbf{a}]_1$, the language $\mathcal{L}_\rho$ is defined as $\mathcal{L}_\rho = \{[\mathbf{c}]_1 \in \mathbb{G}_1^2 : \exists r \in \mathbb{Z}_p \text{ s.t.} \mathbf{c} = \mathbf{a}r\}$.

is in two step: first $\mathsf{Dec}_{\mathsf{large}}(\mathsf{Enc}(\mathbf{x}), \mathsf{KeyGen}(\mathsf{msk}, \mathbf{y}))$ for arbitrary vectors $\mathbf{x} \in \mathbb{Z}_p^n$ and $\mathbf{y} \in \mathbb{Z}_p^n$, recovers $[\mathbf{x}^\top \mathbf{y}]_T$. The second step solves the discrete logarithm to recover $\mathbf{x}^\top \mathbf{y}$. The second step is only efficient for polynomially bounded output, whereas the first step handles arbitrary large inputs.

The second observation we make is that for all $\mathbf{y} \in \mathbb{Z}_p^n$, $\mathsf{KeyGen}(\mathsf{msk}, \mathbf{y})$ outputs a vector or group elements $[\mathbf{d}]_2 \in \mathbb{G}_2^\ell$, for some dimension ℓ. The algorithm $\widetilde{\mathsf{KeyGen}}$ from the simulator of our scheme described in Fig. 8, when given as input $\widetilde{\mathsf{msk}}$, $\widetilde{\mathbf{y}}$, and $\mathbf{x}^\top \mathbf{y}$, first computes $\mathbf{d} \in \mathbb{Z}_p^\ell$, and then returns $[\mathbf{d}]_2$ as the functional decryption key for $\mathbf{y}$. Moreover, it is a linear function in its input $\widetilde{\mathbf{y}}$ and $\mathbf{x}^\top\mathbf{y}$. Thus, we can run $\widetilde{\mathsf{KeyGen}}(\widetilde{\mathsf{msk}}, [\widetilde{\mathbf{y}}]_2, [\mathbf{x}^\top\mathbf{y}]_2)$ to get the functional decryption key $[\mathbf{d}]_2$. Otherwise stated, we achieved a slightly stronger simulation security than in Definition 7, since the simulator only requires to know the value $[\widetilde{\mathbf{y}}]_2$ and $\mathbf{x}^\top\mathbf{y}]_2$ in $\mathbb{G}_2$, as opposed to the values $\widetilde{\mathbf{y}}$ and $\mathbf{x}^\top\mathbf{y}$ over $\mathbb{Z}_p$.

Consequently, the quadratic FE from Sect. 3 that builds upon our partially function-hiding inner product FE inherits the same properties. Therefore, it can be use to encrypt random vectors $\mathbf{u} \in \mathbb{Z}_p^n$, and $\mathbf{v} \in \mathbb{Z}_p^m$. Each functional decryption key corresponds to a pair of indices $(i, j) \in [n] \times [m]$, and the decryption outputs $[u_i v_j]_T$. Simulation security ensures that the adversary view can be simulated from $[u_i v_j]_2$ only, which are pseudorandom by the DDH assumption in $\mathbb{G}_2$. This allows users to evaluate outputs of a PRG over $\mathbb{G}_T$, which is unachievable with an indistinguishability-based quadratic FE.

Theorem 2 (Security). *The inner-product FE described in Fig. 8 is partially-hiding, CPA simulation-secure, assuming the SXDH assumption. Moreover, if the QANIZK argument Π is one-time simulation sound, then the FE is CCA simulation-secure. Namely, for any PPT adversary $\mathcal{A}$, there exist PPT adversaries $\mathcal{B}_1$ and $\mathcal{B}_2$ such that:*

$$\mathrm{Adv}_{\mathsf{IPFE},\mathcal{A}}^{\mathsf{CPA\text{-}PFH\text{-}SIM}}(\lambda) \leq \mathrm{Adv}_{\mathbb{G}_1,\mathcal{B}_1}^{\mathsf{DDH}}(\lambda) + 2Q_{\mathsf{sk}} \cdot \mathrm{Adv}_{\mathbb{G}_2,\mathcal{B}_2}^{\mathsf{DDH}}(\lambda) + \frac{1+Q_{\mathsf{sk}}}{p},$$

where Q_{sk} denotes the number of queries to $\mathcal{O}_{\mathsf{KeyGen}}$. Moreover, for any PPT adversary $\mathcal{A}'$, there exist PPT adversaries $\mathcal{B}_1'$, $\mathcal{B}_2'$ and $\mathcal{B}_3'$ such that:

$$\begin{aligned}\mathrm{Adv}_{\mathsf{IPFE},\mathcal{A}}^{\mathsf{CCA\text{-}PFH\text{-}SIM}}(\lambda) \leq\ & \mathrm{Adv}_{\mathbb{G}_1,\mathcal{B}_1'}^{\mathsf{DDH}}(\lambda) + 2(Q_{\mathsf{sk}} + Q_{\mathsf{Dec}}) \cdot \mathrm{Adv}_{\mathbb{G}_2,\mathcal{B}_2'}^{\mathsf{DDH}}(\lambda) \\ & + Q_{\mathsf{Dec}} \cdot \mathrm{Adv}_{\mathcal{B}_2'}^{\mathsf{OT}\text{-}\Pi}(\lambda) + \frac{1+Q_{\mathsf{sk}}+Q_{\mathsf{Dec}}}{p},\end{aligned}$$

where Q_{sk} denotes the number of queries to $\mathcal{O}_{\mathsf{KeyGen}}$, and Q_{Dec} denotes the number of queries to $\mathcal{O}_{\mathsf{Dec}}$.

The proof of Theorem 2 is given in the full version of this paper.

References

[ABDP15] Abdalla, M., Bourse, F., De Caro, A., Pointcheval, D.: Simple functional encryption schemes for inner products. In: Katz, J. (ed.) PKC 2015. LNCS, vol. 9020, pp. 733–751. Springer, Heidelberg (2015). https://doi.org/10.1007/978-3-662-46447-2_33

[AGRW17] Abdalla, M., Gay, R., Raykova, M., Wee, H.: Multi-input inner-product functional encryption from pairings. In: Coron, J.-S., Nielsen, J.B. (eds.) EUROCRYPT 2017, Part I. LNCS, vol. 10210, pp. 601–626. Springer, Cham (2017). https://doi.org/10.1007/978-3-319-56620-7_21

[AGVW13] Agrawal, S., Gorbunov, S., Vaikuntanathan, V., Wee, H.: Functional encryption: new perspectives and lower bounds. In: Canetti, R., Garay, J.A. (eds.) CRYPTO 2013, Part II. LNCS, vol. 8043, pp. 500–518. Springer, Heidelberg (2013). https://doi.org/10.1007/978-3-642-40084-1_28

[AJ15] Ananth, P., Jain, A.: Indistinguishability obfuscation from compact functional encryption. In: Gennaro, R., Robshaw, M. (eds.) CRYPTO 2015, Part I. LNCS, vol. 9215, pp. 308–326. Springer, Heidelberg (2015). https://doi.org/10.1007/978-3-662-47989-6_15

[ALS16] Agrawal, S., Libert, B., Stehlé, D.: Fully secure functional encryption for inner products, from standard assumptions. In: Robshaw, M., Katz, J. (eds.) CRYPTO 2016, Part III. LNCS, vol. 9816, pp. 333–362. Springer, Heidelberg (2016). https://doi.org/10.1007/978-3-662-53015-3_12

[AS17] Ananth, P., Sahai, A.: Projective arithmetic functional encryption and indistinguishability obfuscation from degree-5 multilinear maps. In: Coron, J.-S., Nielsen, J.B. (eds.) EUROCRYPT 2017, Part I. LNCS, vol. 10210, pp. 152–181. Springer, Cham (2017). https://doi.org/10.1007/978-3-319-56620-7_6

[BBL17] Benhamouda, F., Bourse, F., Lipmaa, H.: CCA-secure inner-product functional encryption from projective hash functions. In: Fehr, S. (ed.) PKC 2017, Part II. LNCS, vol. 10175, pp. 36–66. Springer, Heidelberg (2017). https://doi.org/10.1007/978-3-662-54388-7_2

[BCFG17] Baltico, C.E.Z., Catalano, D., Fiore, D., Gay, R.: Practical functional encryption for quadratic functions with applications to predicate encryption. In: Katz, J., Shacham, H. (eds.) CRYPTO 2017, Part I. LNCS, vol. 10401, pp. 67–98. Springer, Cham (2017). https://doi.org/10.1007/978-3-319-63688-7_3

[BGI+01] Barak, B., Goldreich, O., Impagliazzo, R., Rudich, S., Sahai, A., Vadhan, S., Yang, K.: On the (Im)possibility of obfuscating programs. In: Kilian, J. (ed.) CRYPTO 2001. LNCS, vol. 2139, pp. 1–18. Springer, Heidelberg (2001). https://doi.org/10.1007/3-540-44647-8_1

[BSW11] Boneh, D., Sahai, A., Waters, B.: Functional encryption: definitions and challenges. In: Ishai, Y. (ed.) TCC 2011. LNCS, vol. 6597, pp. 253–273. Springer, Heidelberg (2011). https://doi.org/10.1007/978-3-642-19571-6_16

[BV15] Bitansky, N., Vaikuntanathan, V.: Indistinguishability obfuscation from functional encryption. In: 56th FOCS, pp. 171–190. IEEE Computer Society Press, October 2015

[BW07] Boneh, D., Waters, B.: Conjunctive, subset, and range queries on encrypted data. In: Vadhan, S.P. (ed.) TCC 2007. LNCS, vol. 4392, pp. 535–554. Springer, Heidelberg (2007). https://doi.org/10.1007/978-3-540-70936-7_29

[CHK04] Canetti, R., Halevi, S., Katz, J.: Chosen-ciphertext security from identity-based encryption. In: Cachin, C., Camenisch, J.L. (eds.) EUROCRYPT 2004. LNCS, vol. 3027, pp. 207–222. Springer, Heidelberg (2004). https://doi.org/10.1007/978-3-540-24676-3_13

[CW14] Chen, J., Wee, H.: Semi-adaptive attribute-based encryption and improved delegation for boolean formula. In: Abdalla, M., De Prisco, R. (eds.) SCN 2014. LNCS, vol. 8642, pp. 277–297. Springer, Cham (2014). https://doi.org/10.1007/978-3-319-10879-7_16

[Dam92] Damgård, I.: Towards practical public key systems secure against chosen ciphertext attacks. In: Feigenbaum, J. (ed.) CRYPTO 1991. LNCS, vol. 576, pp. 445–456. Springer, Heidelberg (1992). https://doi.org/10.1007/3-540-46766-1_36

[DGP18] Dufour Sans, E., Gay, R., Pointcheval, D.: Reading in the dark: classifying encrypted digits with functional encryption. Cryptology ePrint Archive, Report 2018/206 (2018). https://eprint.iacr.org/2018/206

[ElG84] ElGamal, T.: A public key cryptosystem and a signature scheme based on discrete logarithms. In: Blakley, G.R., Chaum, D. (eds.) CRYPTO 1984. LNCS, vol. 196, pp. 10–18. Springer, Heidelberg (1985). https://doi.org/10.1007/3-540-39568-7_2

[FO99] Fujisaki, E., Okamoto, T.: Secure integration of asymmetric and symmetric encryption schemes. In: Wiener, M. (ed.) CRYPTO 1999. LNCS, vol. 1666, pp. 537–554. Springer, Heidelberg (1999). https://doi.org/10.1007/3-540-48405-1_34

[GGG+14] Goldwasser, S., et al.: Multi-input functional encryption. In: Nguyen, P.Q., Oswald, E. (eds.) EUROCRYPT 2014. LNCS, vol. 8441, pp. 578–602. Springer, Heidelberg (2014). https://doi.org/10.1007/978-3-642-55220-5_32

[GKW16] Goyal, R., Koppula, V., Waters, B.: Semi-adaptive security and bundling functionalities made generic and easy. In: Hirt, M., Smith, A. (eds.) TCC 2016, Part II. LNCS, vol. 9986, pp. 361–388. Springer, Heidelberg (2016). https://doi.org/10.1007/978-3-662-53644-5_14

[GPSW06] Goyal, V., Pandey, O., Sahai, A., Waters, B.: Attribute-based encryption for fine-grained access control of encrypted data. In: ACM CCS 2006, pp. 89–98. ACM Press, October/November 2006. Available as Cryptology ePrint Archive Report 2006/309

[GVW15] Gorbunov, S., Vaikuntanathan, V., Wee, H.: Predicate encryption for circuits from LWE. In: Gennaro, R., Robshaw, M. (eds.) CRYPTO 2015, Part II. LNCS, vol. 9216, pp. 503–523. Springer, Heidelberg (2015). https://doi.org/10.1007/978-3-662-48000-7_25

[JR13] Jutla, C.S., Roy, A.: Shorter quasi-adaptive NIZK proofs for linear subspaces. In: Sako, K., Sarkar, P. (eds.) ASIACRYPT 2013, Part I. LNCS, vol. 8269, pp. 1–20. Springer, Heidelberg (2013). https://doi.org/10.1007/978-3-642-42033-7_1

[KLM+18] Kim, S., Lewi, K., Mandal, A., Montgomery, H., Roy, A., Wu, D.J.: Function-hiding inner product encryption is practical. In: Catalano, D., De Prisco, R. (eds.) SCN 2018. LNCS, vol. 11035, pp. 544–562. Springer, Cham (2018). https://doi.org/10.1007/978-3-319-98113-0_29

[KSW08] Katz, J., Sahai, A., Waters, B.: Predicate encryption supporting disjunctions, polynomial equations, and inner products. In: Smart, N. (ed.) EUROCRYPT 2008. LNCS, vol. 4965, pp. 146–162. Springer, Heidelberg (2008). https://doi.org/10.1007/978-3-540-78967-3_9

[KW15] Kiltz, E., Wee, H.: Quasi-adaptive NIZK for linear subspaces revisited. In: Oswald, E., Fischlin, M. (eds.) EUROCRYPT 2015, Part II. LNCS, vol. 9057, pp. 101–128. Springer, Heidelberg (2015). https://doi.org/10.1007/978-3-662-46803-6_4

[Lin17] Lin, H.: Indistinguishability obfuscation from SXDH on 5-linear maps and locality-5 PRGs. In: Katz, J., Shacham, H. (eds.) CRYPTO 2017, Part I. LNCS, vol. 10401, pp. 599–629. Springer, Cham (2017). https://doi.org/10.1007/978-3-319-63688-7_20

[LT17] Lin, H., Tessaro, S.: Indistinguishability obfuscation from trilinear maps and block-wise local PRGs. In: Katz, J., Shacham, H. (eds.) CRYPTO 2017, Part I. LNCS, vol. 10401, pp. 630–660. Springer, Cham (2017). https://doi.org/10.1007/978-3-319-63688-7_21

[LV16] Lin, H., Vaikuntanathan, V.: Indistinguishability obfuscation from DDH-like assumptions on constant-degree graded encodings. In: 57th FOCS, pp. 11–20. IEEE Computer Society Press, October 2016

[NY90] Naor, M., Yung, M.: Public-key cryptosystems provably secure against chosen ciphertext attacks. In: 22nd ACM STOC, pp. 427–437. ACM Press, May 1990

[O'N10] O'Neill, A.: Definitional issues in functional encryption. Cryptology ePrint Archive, Report 2010/556 (2010). http://eprint.iacr.org/2010/556

[SW14] Sahai, A., Waters, B.: How to use indistinguishability obfuscation: deniable encryption, and more. In: 46th ACM STOC, pp. 475–484. ACM Press, May/June 2014

[Wee17] Wee, H.: Attribute-hiding predicate encryption in bilinear groups, revisited. In: Kalai, Y., Reyzin, L. (eds.) TCC 2017, Part I. LNCS, vol. 10677, pp. 206–233. Springer, Cham (2017). https://doi.org/10.1007/978-3-319-70500-2_8

[YAHK11] Yamada, S., Attrapadung, N., Hanaoka, G., Kunihiro, N.: Generic constructions for chosen-ciphertext secure attribute based encryption. In: Catalano, D., Fazio, N., Gennaro, R., Nicolosi, A. (eds.) PKC 2011. LNCS, vol. 6571, pp. 71–89. Springer, Heidelberg (2011). https://doi.org/10.1007/978-3-642-19379-8_5

Identity-Based Encryption

Master-Key KDM-Secure IBE from Pairings

Sanjam Garg[1], Romain Gay[2], and Mohammad Hajiabadi[1](✉)

[1] University of California, Berkeley, USA
mdhajiabadi@berkeley.edu
[2] Cornell Tech, New York, USA

Abstract. Identity-based encryption (IBE) is a generalization of public-key encryption (PKE) by allowing encryptions to be made to user identities. In this work, we seek to obtain IBE schemes that achieve key-dependent-message (KDM) security with respect to messages that depend on the master secret key. Previous KDM-secure schemes only achieved KDM security in simpler settings, in which messages may only depend on user secret keys.

An important motivation behind studying master-KDM security is the application of this notion in obtaining generic constructions of KDM-CCA secure PKE, a primitive notoriously difficult to realize.

We give the first IBE that achieves master-KDM security from standard assumptions in pairing groups. Our construction is modular and combines techniques from KDM-secure PKE based from hash-proof systems, together with IBE that admits a tight security proof in the multi-challenge setting, which happens to be unexpectedly relevant in the context of KDM security. In fact, to the best of our knowledge, this is the first setting where techniques developed in the context of realizing tightly secure cryptosystems have led to a new feasibility result.

As a byproduct, our KDM-secure IBE, and thus the resulting KDM-CCA-secure PKE both enjoy a tight security reduction, independent of the number of challenge ciphertexts, which was not achieved before.

S. Garg—Supported in part from AFOSR Award FA9550-19-1-0200, AFOSR YIP Award, NSF CNS Award 1936826, DARPA and SPAWAR under contract N66001-15-C-4065, a Hellman Award and research grants by the Okawa Foundation, Visa Inc., and Center for Long-Term Cybersecurity (CLTC, UC Berkeley). The views expressed are those of the authors and do not reflect the official policy or position of the funding agencies.

R. Gay—Supported in part by NSF Award SATC-1704788 and in part by the Office of the Director of National Intelligence (ODNI), Intelligence Advanced Research Projects Activity (IARPA), via 2019-19-020700006. The views and conclusions contained herein are those of the authors and should not be interpreted as necessarily representing the official policies, either expressed or implied, of ODNI, IARPA, or the U.S. Government. The U.S. Government is authorized to reproduce and distribute reprints for governmental purposes notwithstanding any copyright annotation therein.

A. Kiayias et al. (Eds.): PKC 2020, LNCS 12110, pp. 123–152, 2020.
https://doi.org/10.1007/978-3-030-45374-9_5

1 Introduction

Key-dependent-message (KDM) security is a strengthening of the classical notion of semantic security, by allowing the adversary to obtain encryptions of messages that depend on the secret key. Originally introduced in [BRS03] in the setting of public/private key encryption, KDM security has since found applications in such contexts as fully-homomorphic encryption [Gen09], function secret sharing [BGI16], and more recently in obtaining CCA-secure PKE and designated-verifier non-interactive zero knowledge (NIZK) [KMT19,LQR+19].

For a function class $\mathcal{F}$, an encryption scheme is $\mathcal{F}$-KDM secure if no adversary can distinguish between encryptions of $f(sk)$, where $f \in \mathcal{F}$ and sk is the secret key, and encryptions of fixed messages. We know how to obtain KDM-secure encryption for arbitrarily-large classes of functions from various specific assumptions. These results are achieved by first realizing KDM security for a 'minimal' class of functions, e.g., affine functions [BHHO08,ACPS09,BG10,BLSV18], and then expanding the function family using KDM-amplification theorems [BHHI10, App11].

KDM Security for Identity-Based Encryption (IBE). Alperin-Sheriff and Peikert [AP12] introduced notions of KDM security in the setting of IBE, under which one may securely encrypt functions of user secret keys (as opposed to the master secret key). In more detail, these notions (that we call *user-KDM security*) extend the semantic-security notion of IBE by allowing the adversary, who has specified a challenge identity id, to ask for encryptions of functions of sk_{id}, the user-specific secret key for id, under id itself. They showed how to build user-KDM secure IBE schemes from the learning with errors (LWE) assumption.

KDM Security for Master Secret Keys. In this work, we seek to realize stronger notions of KDM-security for IBE where the adversary may obtain ciphertexts encrypting functions of the master secret key, as opposed to user secret keys. In more detail, we would like the system to retain security even if the adversary obtains encryptions of functions of the master secret key made with respect to "uncorrupted identities." We call this notion master-KDM security (Definition 3).

Why Should We Care About Master-KDM Secure IBE? Theoretically speaking, we believe that the notion of master-KDM security for IBE is more natural than the user-KDM notion, as it implies KDM-CCA security for public-key encryption, via the transformation of [CHK04]. In other words, just as IBE implies CCA2 security, master-KDM security implies KDM CCA2 security. In contrast, the weaker user-KDM security does not seem to imply KDM-CCA security.

Generically and simultaneously realizing both KDM security and CCA2 security for public-key encryption has been beset with challenges; thus, also pointing to the challenge in realizing master-KDM IBE. One reason that makes this combination challenging is the fact that KDM-secure PKE schemes typically come with *KDM-oblivious* algorithms, which allow one to sample KDM ciphertexts—without knowledge of the secret key—in such a way that such oblivious ciphertexts will even fool a real decryptor who is in possession of the secret key. This obliviousness property is exactly the intuition behind KDM security: that real KDM ciphertexts may be simulated by publicly samplable ciphertexts. On the other hand, this KDM-obliviousness property is exactly what destroys CCA security: an adversary may query the decryption oracle on such oblivious ciphertexts to retrieve the secret key.

Previous works showed how to get around the above obstacle against KDM-CCA2 PKE by using NIZK along with CPA-KDM secure PKE [CCS09], or more directly from pairing-based assumptions [Hof13], or by using the specific properties of hash-proof systems, and hence from DDH, QR and DCR [KT18]. Very recently, the work of [KM19] shows the equivalence of KDM-CPA and KDM-CCA PKE schemes, via non-blackbox constructions that make use of designated-verifier NIZK and garbled circuits. However, it is not yet clear whether the more challenging notion of master-KDM secure IBE is at all realizable in the standard model, and if so from what assumptions. In particular, by trying to build this latter notion from a variety of assumptions, we will have an overarching approach for obtaining KDM-CCA secure PKE.

In summary, in addition to being interesting in its own right, master-KDM secure IBE offers a pathway to realizing new KDM-CCA public-key encryption schemes.

Prior Work on Master-KDM Secure IBE. The observation that master-KDM security for IBE suffices for KDM-CCA secure PKE was first made by [GHV12], who gave constructions of *bounded-master-KDM* secure IBE from pairing assumptions. Their constructions, however, only achieve bounded-KDM in the sense that (a) the number of KDM queries should be bounded beforehand, meaning that the sizes of various IBE parameters do grow with this fixed number; and (b) the set of identities against which KDM encryption are allowed should also be chosen beforehand, and not adaptively.

1.1 Our Contributions and Open Problems

In this work, we show constructions of IBE systems satisfying master-KDM security with respect to affine functions from standard assumptions in bilinear groups. Our construction does not suffer from any of the limitations of [GHV12], which resulted in bounded master-KDM secure IBE. As a special case, our KDM notion allows us to encrypt the bits as well as the negations of the bits of the master secret key. As shown in [BHHI10, App11], KDM security with respect to affine functions is sufficient for obtaining KDM security with respect to any a-priori bounded function family.

At a high level, our construction is obtained via a modular combination of the KDM-secure public-key encryption from [BHHO08] and a tightly-secure IBE inspired by prior works [CW13, HKS15, AHY15, GDCC16]. This connection between tight security and KDM-security is novel to this work and made explicit by abstract definitions that we put forth to capture the modular nature of our construction. Namely, we define a set of properties that our IBE and an abstract underlying public-key encryption must satisfy to obtain KDM security. These properties are naturally fulfilled by prior schemes relying on the standard dual system encryption proof paradigm, introduced by [Wat09] in the context of fully-secure IBE; and by KDM-secure encryption schemes such as [BHHO08,BG10, BGK11] that all rely on hash-proof systems, as unified in [Wee16]. Our IBE is an instance of this new abstract framework with a combination of tightly-secure IBE and the KDM-secure PKE from [BHHO08]. As a byproduct, our IBE also achieves *tight* security. Namely, the security loss is independent of the number of challenge ciphertexts, but is only a small constant times the security parameter. In fact, to the best of our knowledge, this is the first setting where techniques developed in the context of realizing tightly secure cryptosystems have led to new feasibility results.

Moreover, our IBE scheme implies KDM-CCA2 secure public-key encryption scheme. One of the benefits of our approach is that we are able to build on the techniques realized in the context of IBE and leverage them in the context of realizing KDM-CCA2 secure schemes. For example, this gives the first *tightly* secure KDM-CCA2 secure public-key encryption scheme. We give more details on our construction in Sect. 1.2.

Open Problems. The main open problem that arises from our work is to build master-KDM secure IBE from other assumptions such as DDH, or factoring-based assumptions. One possible approach toward this is to investigate what properties will allow us to prove the DDH-based IBE schemes of [DG17b,DG17a,BLSV18] KDM-secure, and whether those properties are realizable under standard assumptions.

1.2 General Overview of Our Construction

Modular Construction of IBE from Public-Key Encryption. We start with the observation that most pairing-based IBE schemes are built upon traditional PKE schemes in the following way. The public key of the IBE is the public key of the underlying PKE, plus some extra components that are generated from the latter and some independently generated parameters params. The master secret key of the IBE is simply the secret key of the underlying PKE. The IBE encryption algorithm outputs a ciphertext ct_0, which is an encryption of the plaintext m under the underlying PKE, and extra components that are generated from ct_0, the identity id, and the parameters params (Fig. 1).

Put simply, it is possible to generate the public key and a ciphertext of the IBE from an existing public key and ciphertext of the underlying public-key encryption, which is not attribute-based, simply by sampling independent parameters params, and running the algorithms $\mathsf{Expand}_{\mathsf{pk}}$ and $\mathsf{Expand}_{\mathsf{ct}}$. The key generation algorithm of the IBE uses as input the master secret key, which is the secret key of the underlying public-key encryption, and the public key of the IBE.

$$(\mathsf{PKE.pk}, \mathsf{PKE.sk}) \leftarrow \mathsf{PKE.Setup}(1^\lambda)$$

$$\mathsf{IBE.msk} := \mathsf{PKE.sk}$$

$$\mathsf{IBE.pk} := (\mathsf{pk}_0, \mathsf{pk}_1)$$
$$\text{with } \mathsf{pk}_0 := \mathsf{PKE.pk}, \mathsf{pk}_1 := \mathsf{Expand}_{\mathsf{pk}}(\mathsf{pk}_0, \mathsf{params})$$

$$\mathsf{IBE.Enc}(m, \mathsf{id}) := (\mathsf{ct}_0, \mathsf{ct}_1)$$
$$\text{with } \mathsf{ct}_0 := \mathsf{PKE.Enc}(\mathsf{PKE.pk}, m), \mathsf{ct}_1 := \mathsf{Expand}_{\mathsf{ct}}(\mathsf{params}, \mathsf{ct}_0, \mathsf{id}).$$

Fig. 1. Modular IBE. Here, $(\mathsf{PKE.Setup}, \mathsf{PKE.Enc}, \mathsf{PKE.Dec})$ is a public-key encryption, and params are parameters that are generated independently.

KDM-Secure IBE. For modular IBE, we can hope to achieve KDM-security by replacing the underlying PKE used in existing schemes with a KDM-secure PKE. This approach actually works for what we call *modular IBE* schemes (Definition 4) whose security proof follows the dual system encryption paradigm, originally put forth in [Wat09], in the simplified security model where the adversary gets to see only *one* challenge ciphertext. Note that in the standard IND-CPA security game, one challenge ciphertext is equivalent to many challenge ciphertexts, using a standard hybrid argument (this is valid for any public-key encryption). However, this argument fails for KDM security, since the plaintexts depend on the secret key. We describe the construction based on the dual system methodology, which is instructive despite the fact that its security only handles one challenge ciphertext. Next, we explain how to modify this first attempt and get KDM security with many challenge ciphertexts.

1.3 First Attempt: Dual System Encryption

Dual System Encryption. For schemes using the dual system encryption paradigm, the security proof makes use of the fact that the master secret key of the IBE consists of two independent components: $\mathsf{IBE.msk} = \mathsf{PKE.sk} := (\mathsf{msk}_\mathsf{N}, \mathsf{msk}_\mathsf{SF})$, typically referred to as normal and semi-functional components, respectively. The corresponding public key $\mathsf{PKE.pk}$ (and thus, honestly generated ciphertexts) only depends on the normal component msk_N. The security proof consists of a sequence of hybrid games, where the first transition switches the distribution of the challenge ciphertext to a semi-functional distribution, where the ciphertext now also depends on the component msk_SF. In the next step of the security proof, the distribution of the functional secret keys is changed so that they do not depend on the semi-functional component msk_SF. This change of distribution should not be noticeable to the adversary, which implies that these semi-functional keys still correctly decrypt honestly generated ciphertext. However, they fail to decrypt the challenge ciphertext, which means the simulator can leverage the adversary's ability to break semantic security on the challenge ciphertext. At this point, the security relies on a statistical argument: the component msk_SF, which only appears in the challenge ciphertext, is used to mask the plaintext (Fig. 2).

Hybrid game:	ct	sk
IND-CPA security game	N	N
game 1	SF	N
game 2	SF	SF

sk \ ct	N	SF
N	✓	-
SF	✓	✗

Fig. 2. The dual system encryption proof paradigm. The leftmost table depicts the sequence of hybrid games used in the security proof, starting with the original IND-CPA security game, and the rightmost table illustrates when decryption succeeds, depending on whether the ciphertexts and keys are normal (N) or semi-functional (SF). We denote by ct here the challenge ciphertext, and by sk the user secret keys generated in the security game.

Making IBE KDM-Secure, for One Challenge Ciphertext. As in prior works [BHHO08, BG10, BGK11], we consider KDM-security for the class of affine functions, where the message space is a group $\mathbb{G}$ of order p, generated by g, and the secret key is of the form $\mathsf{msk} := (g_1, \ldots, g_\ell) \in \mathbb{G}^\ell$, an encoding of an ℓ-bit string. The adversary can choose an affine combination $(w_1, \ldots, w_\ell) \in \mathbb{Z}_p^\ell$ and $M \in \mathbb{G}$, and obtain an encryption of the message $\prod_{i \in [\ell]} g_i^{w_i} \cdot M$. For convenience, we use bracket notations, where for any exponent $a \in \mathbb{Z}_p$, we denote by $[a] := g^a$. With this notation, we can write $\mathsf{msk} := [\mathbf{k}] \in \mathbb{G}^\ell$, and the adversary gets an encryption of $[\mathbf{k}^\top \mathbf{w} + m]$. For simplicity, we focus on the single instance case, where only one public key, secret key pair is generated, and we consider the simplified security model where the adversary gets to see only *one* challenge ciphertext. We will see how to remove that restriction later, thereby allowing the adversary to obtain multiple challenge ciphertexts for many identities and affine combinations of its choice.

We take a modular IBE where the underlying PKE is compatible with the dual system encryption methodology, that is, a PKE whose ciphertext can be turned to a semi-functional distribution, even given the secret key. Thus, the secret key can be used to simulate the user secret keys queried by the adversary during the security proof, as well as the challenge ciphertext, whose underlying plaintext may depend on the secret key. Then, user secret keys of the IBE are turned to semi-functional, following the standard dual system encryption paradigm, except that this must be done with encryption of key-dependent messages. At this point, user secret keys can be generated only knowing the normal component of the secret key msk_N, as opposed to the full master secret key. Finally, we rely on the KDM security of the underlying PKE, which must hold even if the value msk_N is revealed to the adversary. This value permits to simulate semi-functional keys. This is achieved using a statistical argument which only involves msk_SF (and not msk_N). Indeed, since the value msk_SF only shows up in the challenge ciphertext, it can be used to hide the plaintext, and conclude the security proof. As it turns out, most existing KDM-secure encryption, such as [BHHO08, BG10, BGK11] can be shown to satisfy these additional properties (and in fact, as noted in [Wee16], all PKE based on hash-proof systems).

We show a concrete exposition of this technique by combining the modular IBE from [CGW15] and the KDM-secure PKE from [BHHO08], both of which rely on prime-order groups, and thus are compatible. This construction gives some insight and prepares for the IBE satisfying full-fledged KDM security, where the adversary gets to see many challenge ciphertexts, that we present later.

Chen et al. Identity-Based Encryption. We illustrate the dual system encryption methodology with the IBE from [CGW15]. We use a pairing group $e : \mathbb{G}_1 \times \mathbb{G}_2 \to \mathbb{G}_T$, where $\mathbb{G}_1, \mathbb{G}_2, \mathbb{G}_T$ are all cyclic groups of prime order p, generated respectively by g_1, g_2, and $e(g_1, g_2)$, where e is a non-degenerate bilinear map, that is, for all $a, b \in \mathbb{Z}_p$, $e(g_1^a, g_2^b) = e(g_1, g_2)^{ab}$. We use bracket notations, where for all exponents $a \in \mathbb{Z}_p$ and all groups $s \in \{1, 2, T\}$, we denote by $[a]_s$ the group element g_s^a. We generalize this notation for any matrix $\mathbf{A} = \begin{pmatrix} a_{1,1} & \cdots & a_{1,n} \\ & \ddots & \\ a_{m,1} & \cdots & a_{m,n} \end{pmatrix} \in \mathbb{Z}_p^{m \times n}$, that is, we denote by $[\mathbf{A}]_s$ the matrix of group elements $\begin{pmatrix} g_s^{a_{1,1}} & \cdots & g_s^{a_{1,n}} \\ & \ddots & \\ g_s^{a_{m,1}} & \cdots & g_s^{a_{m,n}} \end{pmatrix} \in \mathbb{G}_s^{m \times n}$.

The IBE from [CGW15] is a modular IBE that uses the following underlying public-key encryption, which is essentially Damgård El-Gamal encryption [Dam92], with message space $\mathbb{G}_T$.

- $\mathsf{PKE.Setup}(1^\lambda)$: $\mathbf{a}, \mathbf{k} \leftarrow_{\mathsf{R}} \mathbb{Z}_p^2$, return $\mathsf{pk} := ([\mathbf{a}]_1, [\mathbf{a}^\top \mathbf{k}]_T)$, and $\mathsf{sk} := \mathbf{k}$.
- $\mathsf{PKE.Enc}(\mathsf{pk}, M \in \mathbb{G}_T)$: $r \leftarrow_{\mathsf{R}} \mathbb{Z}_p$, return $([\mathbf{a}r]_1, [\mathbf{a}r^\top \mathbf{k}]_T \cdot M)$.
- $\mathsf{PKE.Dec}(\mathsf{pk}, \mathsf{ct}, \mathbf{k})$: parse $\mathsf{ct} := ([\mathbf{c}]_1 \in \mathbb{G}_1^2, [c']_T \in \mathbb{G}_T)$, and return $[c']_T / e([\mathbf{c}^\top \mathbf{k}]_1, [1]_2)$.

The rest of the IBE parameters are computed as follows. Note that the identity space is $\mathbb{Z}_p$.

- $\mathsf{params} := (\mathbf{W}_0, \mathbf{W}_1)$, where $\mathbf{W}_0, \mathbf{W}_1 \leftarrow_{\mathsf{R}} \mathbb{Z}_p^{2 \times 2}$.
- $\mathsf{Expand}_{\mathsf{pk}}(\mathsf{pk}_0)$: given $\mathsf{pk}_0 := ([\mathbf{a}]_1, [\mathbf{a}^\top \mathbf{k}]_T)$, samples $\mathbf{b} \leftarrow_{\mathsf{R}} \mathbb{Z}_p^2$, and returns $\mathsf{pk}_1 := ([\mathbf{W}_0 \mathbf{a}]_1, [\mathbf{W}_1 \mathbf{a}]_1, [\mathbf{W}_0^\top \mathbf{b}]_2, [\mathbf{W}_1^\top \mathbf{b}]_2)$.
- $\mathsf{Expand}_{\mathsf{ct}}(\mathsf{params}, \mathsf{ct}_0, \mathsf{id} \in \mathbb{Z}_p)$: given $\mathsf{ct}_0 := ([\mathbf{c}]_1, [c']_T)$, returns $\mathsf{ct}_1 := [(\mathbf{W}_0 + \mathsf{id}\mathbf{W}_1)\mathbf{c}]_1$.
- $\mathsf{KeyGen}(\mathsf{msk}, \mathsf{pk}, \mathsf{id} \in \mathbb{Z}_p)$: samples $s \leftarrow_{\mathsf{R}} \mathbb{Z}_p$, and returns $\mathsf{sk}_{\mathsf{id}} := ([\mathbf{b}s]_2, [\mathbf{k} + (\mathbf{W}_0 + \mathsf{id}\mathbf{W}_1)^\top \mathbf{b}s]_2)$.
- $\mathsf{Dec}(\mathsf{mpk}, \mathsf{ct}, \mathsf{sk}_{\mathsf{id}})$: parse $\mathsf{ct} := (\mathsf{ct}_0, \mathsf{ct}_1)$ with $\mathsf{ct}_0 := ([\mathbf{c}]_1, [c']_T)$, $\mathsf{ct}_1 := [\mathbf{c}_1]_1$, $\mathsf{sk}_{\mathsf{id}} := ([\mathbf{d}]_2, [\mathbf{d}']_2)$ and return $[c']_T \cdot e([\mathbf{c}_1]_1^\top, [\mathbf{d}]_2) / e([\mathbf{c}]_1^\top, [\mathbf{d}']_2)$.

We know there is an orthogonal vector $\mathbf{a}^\perp \in \mathbb{Z}_p^2$, such that $\mathbf{a}^\perp \neq \mathbf{0}$, and $\mathbf{a}^\top \mathbf{a}^\perp = 0$. Assuming $\mathbf{a} \leftarrow_{\mathsf{R}} \mathbb{Z}_p^2$ is different from the zero vector $\mathbf{a} \neq \mathbf{0}$, which happens with all but negligible probability over the choice of $\mathbf{a} \leftarrow_{\mathsf{R}} \mathbb{Z}_p^2$, we have that $(\mathbf{a}|\mathbf{a}^\perp)$ is a basis of $\mathbb{Z}_p^2$, and we can write $\mathbf{k} := \mathsf{msk}_{\mathsf{N}} + \mathsf{msk}_{\mathsf{SF}}$, where $\mathsf{msk}_{\mathsf{N}}$, the normal component, is of the form $k_0 \cdot \mathbf{a}$ with $k_0 \leftarrow_{\mathsf{R}} \mathbb{Z}_p$, and $\mathsf{msk}_{\mathsf{SF}}$, the semi-functional component, is of the form $k_1 \cdot \mathbf{a}^\perp$ with $k_1 \leftarrow_{\mathsf{R}} \mathbb{Z}_p$. That is, $\mathsf{msk}_{\mathsf{N}}$ (resp. $\mathsf{msk}_{\mathsf{SF}}$) is the projection of the vector $\mathbf{k}$ onto the vector $\mathbf{a}$ (resp. onto $\mathbf{a}^\perp$). This way, the public key only depends on $\mathsf{msk}_{\mathsf{N}}$, since it only contains $[\mathbf{a}^\top \mathbf{k}]_T$, and $\mathbf{a}^\top \mathbf{a}^\perp = 0$.

The semi-functional distribution of ciphertexts is illustrated in Fig. 3. We can change the distribution of the challenge ciphertext using the DDH assumption in $\mathbb{G}_1$, which says that $([\mathbf{a}]_1, [\mathbf{a}r]_1)$ is computationally indistinguishable from $([\mathbf{a}]_1, [\mathbf{u}]_1)$, where $\mathbf{a}, \mathbf{u} \leftarrow_{\mathsf{R}} \mathbb{Z}_p^2$, and $r \leftarrow \mathbb{Z}_p$. Otherwise stated, DDH is a subgroup membership problem, which states that it is hard to distinguish a vector of group elements that is proportional to $[\mathbf{a}]$, from a uniformly random vector over $\mathbb{G}_1$. The consequence is that the semi-functional ciphertext depends on the component $\mathsf{msk}_{\mathsf{SF}}$, since the vector $[\mathbf{u}]_1$ that is part of the ciphertext (see Fig. 3) is not orthogonal to $\mathbf{a}^\perp$ (with all but negligible probability), unlike $\mathbf{a}$.

Normal:	Semi-functional:
$\mathsf{ct}_0 := ([\mathbf{a}r], [\mathbf{a}r^\top \mathbf{k}]_T \cdot M)$	$\mathsf{ct}_0 := ([\mathbf{u}], [\mathbf{u}^\top \mathbf{k}]_T \cdot M)$

Fig. 3. Normal and semi-functional distributions for the challenge ciphertext. Here, $\mathbf{a}, \mathbf{k}, \mathbf{u} \leftarrow_{\mathsf{R}} \mathbb{Z}_p^2$, and $r \leftarrow_{\mathsf{R}} \mathbb{Z}_p$. The rest of the ciphertext is computed from ct_0 using $\mathsf{Expand}_{\mathsf{ct}}$ and params.

Then, in [CGW15], the distribution of all the user secret keys generated in the security game is changed, so that they depend on $\mathsf{msk}_{\mathsf{N}}$, but are independent of $\mathsf{msk}_{\mathsf{SF}}$. Namely, all the keys are switched from $\mathsf{KeyGen}(\mathbf{k}, \mathsf{pk}, \mathsf{id})$ to $\mathsf{KeyGen}(\mathsf{msk}_{\mathsf{N}}, \mathsf{pk}, \mathsf{id})$. Finally, we can use the component $\mathsf{msk}_{\mathsf{SF}}$ as a one-time pad to mask the plaintext in the challenge ciphertext.

We observe that if we trade the underlying public-key encryption used here, namely Damgård ElGamal [Dam92], for the KDM-secure public-key encryption from [BHHO08], we obtain an overall IBE that enjoys KDM-security. Roughly speaking, the dual system encryption is compatible with the proof techniques used in [BHHO08].

Boneh et al. KDM-Secure Public-Key Encryption. We now recall the public-key encryption from [BHHO08], which is KDM-secure for the class of affine functions. For simplicity, we focus on the single instance case, where only one public key, secret key pair is generated.

It is a modification of the Damgårg ElGamal encryption scheme where the key space is changed to $\mathbb{G}_T^\ell$ instead of $\mathbb{Z}_p^2$, so that affine combinations of the secret key $[\mathbf{k}]_T \in \mathbb{G}_T^\ell$ belong to the message space. To preserve correctness of the encryption scheme, the authors of [BHHO08] choose a secret key $[\mathbf{k}]_T$ where the discrete logarithm $\mathbf{k}$ can be obtained efficiently, and decryption can proceed as for the Damgård ElGamal encryption scheme. Namely, $\mathbf{k} \leftarrow_{\mathsf{R}} \{0,1\}^\ell$. To have enough entropy in the secret key, it is necessary to take a dimension

$\ell = \Theta(\log p)$. The dimension of the vector $[\mathbf{a}]_1$ which is part of the public key is modified accordingly. The security proof follows a similar pattern as outlined previously: the ciphertexts are switched to semi-functional, using a computational assumption that holds even when the secret key is revealed. Then the plaintexts are made independent of the key, using a perfect statistical argument. Finally, $\mathsf{msk}_{\mathsf{SF}}$, the semi-functional component of $\mathbf{k}$, is used to mask the plaintext, using a statistical argument. Namely, we use the Left Over Hash Lemma [ILL89] with entropy source $\mathsf{msk}_{\mathsf{SF}}$. An overview is given Fig. 4.

Hybrid game:	challenge ct:	explanation
KDM security game	$[\mathbf{a}r]_1, [\mathbf{k}^\top \mathbf{a}r]_T \cdot [\mathbf{k}^\top \mathbf{w} + m]_T$	the adversary chooses an affine combination $\mathbf{w} \in \mathbb{Z}_p^\ell$, $[m] \in \mathbb{G}$
Game 1	$[\mathbf{u}]_1, [\mathbf{k}^\top \mathbf{u}]_T \cdot [\mathbf{k}^\top \mathbf{w} + m]_T$	ct is switched to semi-functional using DDH in $\mathbb{G}_1$
Game 2	$[\mathbf{u} - \mathbf{w}]_1, [\mathbf{k}^\top \mathbf{u}]_T \cdot [m]_T$	statistical change, the encrypted plaintext is not key-dependent
Game 3	$[\mathbf{u} - \mathbf{w}]_1, [\mathbf{k}^\top \mathbf{u}]_T$	LOHL, with seed $\mathbf{u} \leftarrow_{\mathsf{R}} \mathbb{Z}_p^\ell$

Fig. 4. KDM security proof of [BHHO08]. Here, $[\mathbf{a}]_1 \leftarrow_{\mathsf{R}} \mathbb{G}_1^\ell$ is part of pk, and the secret key is $[\mathbf{k}]_T$ with $\mathbf{k} \leftarrow_{\mathsf{R}} \{0,1\}^\ell$, $\ell = \Theta(\log p)$, and $\mathbf{w} \in \mathbb{Z}_p^\ell$, $[m] \in \mathbb{G}$ are chosen by the adversary. The randomness $r \leftarrow_{\mathsf{R}} \mathbb{Z}_p$, $\mathbf{u} \leftarrow_{\mathsf{R}} \mathbb{Z}_p^\ell$ is sampled upon creation of the challenge ciphertext. LHOL stands for Left Over Hash Lemma [ILL89].

Combining Boneh et al. PKE with Chen et al. IBE. We change the IBE from [CGW15], which uses as an underlying PKE Damgård ElGamal encryption scheme, to a similar modular IBE which uses the Boneh et al. KDM-secure PKE instead. Namely, we have: $\mathbf{a} \leftarrow_{\mathsf{R}} \mathbb{Z}_p^\ell$, and $\mathbf{k} \leftarrow_{\mathsf{R}} \{0,1\}^\ell$ for $\ell = \Theta(\log p)$, $\mathsf{pk} := ([\mathbf{a}]_1, [\mathbf{k}^\top \mathbf{a}]_T)$, and $\mathsf{sk} := [\mathbf{k}]_T$. The parameters are modified accordingly: $\mathsf{params} := (\mathbf{W}_0, \mathbf{W}_1)$ where $\mathbf{W}_0, \mathbf{W}_1 \leftarrow_{\mathsf{R}} \mathbb{Z}_p^{2\times\ell}$.

This way, we can prove KDM security of the IBE simply by following the first steps of the KDM security proof of [BHHO08]: the challenge ciphertext is switched to semi-functional, then the functional keys are switched to semi-functional; the plaintext is made independent of the master secret key, using a hash proof system style statistical argument; finally we use the Left Over Hash lemma with entropy source $\mathsf{msk}_{\mathsf{SF}}$ to mask the plaintext in the challenge ciphertext. The security proof is illustrated in Fig. 5.

Dual System Encryption, in More Details. The proof of Chen et al. IBE (and more generally, of any scheme using the dual system encryption methodology) crucially relies on the fact that there is only one challenge ciphertext. Recall that this is equivalent to many challenge ciphertexts for IND-CPA public-key IBE, however, this doesn't hold for KDM-secure IBE.

Game:	challenge c_0:	$\mathsf{sk}_{\mathsf{id}}$	explanation
Game 0	$[\mathbf{a}r]_1, [\mathbf{k}^\top \mathbf{a}r]_T \cdot [\mathbf{k}^\top \mathbf{w} + m]_T$	$\mathsf{KeyGen}(\mathsf{mpk}, [\mathbf{k}]_T, \mathsf{id})$	the adversary chooses an affine combination $\mathbf{w} \in \mathbb{Z}_p^\ell$, $[m] \in \mathbb{G}$
Game 1	$[\mathbf{u}]_1, [\mathbf{k}^\top \mathbf{u}]_T \cdot [\mathbf{k}^\top \mathbf{w} + m]_T$	$\mathsf{KeyGen}(\mathsf{mpk}, [\mathbf{k}]_T, \mathsf{id})$	ct is switched to semi-functional using DDH in $\mathbb{G}_1$
Game 2	$[\mathbf{u}]_1, [\mathbf{k}^\top \mathbf{u}]_T \cdot [\mathbf{k}^\top \mathbf{w} + m]_T$	$\mathsf{KeyGen}(\mathsf{mpk}, [\mathsf{msk}_\mathsf{N}]_T, \mathsf{pk}, \mathsf{id})$	$\mathsf{sk}_{\mathsf{id}}$ are switched to semi-functional
Game 3	$[\mathbf{u} - \mathbf{w}]_1, [\mathbf{k}^\top \mathbf{u}]_T \cdot [m]_T$	$\mathsf{KeyGen}(\mathsf{mpk}, [\mathsf{msk}_\mathsf{N}]_T, \mathsf{pk}, \mathsf{id})$	statistical change, the encrypted plaintext is not key-dependent
Game 4	$[\mathbf{u} - \mathbf{w}]_1, [\mathbf{k}^\top \mathbf{u}]_T$	$\mathsf{KeyGen}(\mathsf{mpk}, [\mathsf{msk}_\mathsf{N}]_T, \mathsf{pk}, \mathsf{id})$	LOHL, with seed $\mathbf{u} \leftarrow_{\mathsf{R}} \mathbb{Z}_p^\ell$ and entropy source $\mathsf{msk}_{\mathsf{SF}}$

Fig. 5. KDM security proof of the IBE. Here, $[\mathbf{a}]_1 \leftarrow_{\mathsf{R}} \mathbb{G}_1^\ell$ is part of mpk, and the secret key is $[\mathbf{k}]_T$ with $\mathbf{k} \leftarrow_{\mathsf{R}} \{0,1\}^\ell$, $\ell = \Theta(\log p)$, and $\mathbf{w} \in \mathbb{Z}_p^\ell$, $[m] \in \mathbb{G}$ are chosen by the adversary. The randomness $r \leftarrow_{\mathsf{R}} \mathbb{Z}_p$, $\mathbf{u} \leftarrow_{\mathsf{R}} \mathbb{Z}_p^\ell$ is sampled upon creation of the challenge ciphertext. Recall that $\mathsf{msk} := [\mathbf{k}]_T$, $\mathbf{k} := \mathsf{msk}_\mathsf{N} + \mathsf{msk}_{\mathsf{SF}}$, where msk_N, and $\mathsf{msk}_{\mathsf{SF}}$ are the projections of $\mathbf{k}$ onto $\mathbf{a}$ and $\mathbf{A}^\perp$, respectively.

Indeed, to switch the functional keys to semi-functional, the proof uses an underlying statistical argument that is only valid in the presence of one challenge ciphertext. Namely, the distribution of each functional key is switched to a pseudo distribution, one by one. Doing so releases some entropy from the parameters params in the pseudo functional key, while that entropy remains hidden from all others keys, and from the public key, but not from the challenge ciphertext. At this point, the security relies on the fact the identity of the pseudo key and semi-functional ciphertext don't match, using a statistical *one-time* argument. This argument fails for many semi-functional ciphertexts, the presence of which is unavoidable in the KDM security proof.

More concretely, the pseudo keys in Chen et al. IBE are of the form: $([\mathbf{v}]_2, [\mathbf{k} + (\mathbf{W}_0 + \mathsf{id}\mathbf{W}_1)^\top \mathbf{v}]_2)$, for a uniformly random $[\mathbf{v}]_2 \leftarrow_{\mathsf{R}} \mathbb{G}_2$, instead of $[\mathbf{v}]_2 := [\mathbf{b}s]_2$ with $s \leftarrow_{\mathsf{R}} \mathbb{Z}_p$ in normal keys. This releases entropy from $\mathbf{W}_0, \mathbf{W}_1 \leftarrow_{\mathsf{R}} \mathbb{Z}_p^{\ell \times 2}$ that is not revealed from the public key which only contains $([\mathbf{W}_0\mathbf{a}]_1, [\mathbf{W}_1\mathbf{a}]_1, [\mathbf{W}_0^\top \mathbf{b}]_2, [\mathbf{W}_1^\top \mathbf{b}]_2)$. Namely, the component from these matrices that is orthogonal to $\mathbf{a}$ and $\mathbf{b}$ can be used to perform a statistical one-time argument with the semi-functional challenge ciphertext, which contains: $([\mathbf{u}]_1, [(\mathbf{W}_0 + \mathsf{id}^\star \mathbf{W}_1)\mathbf{u}]_1)$ for $[\mathbf{u}]_1 \leftarrow_{\mathsf{R}} \mathbb{G}_1^\ell$. This essentially uses the fact that the map $\mathsf{id} \to \mathbf{W}_0 + \mathsf{id}\mathbf{W}_1$ is a pairwise independent hash function, aka 2-universal hash function. This argument fails when there are several challenge ciphertexts, each of which associated with a different identity.

1.4 Final Attempt: Handling Many Challenge Ciphertexts

To prove KDM security, we need to consider many challenge ciphertexts simultaneously. Ultimately, in the security proof, we use the entropy from the semi-functional component $\mathsf{msk}_{\mathsf{SF}}$ of the master secret key to hide the plaintexts in all the challenge ciphertexts. Since there number of challenge ciphertexts is unbounded, this will require a computational argument, as opposed to the statistical argument used previously, in the single challenge ciphertext setting. To that end, we first need to make the user secret keys and the plaintexts in the challenge ciphertexts independent from $\mathsf{msk}_{\mathsf{SF}}$. As explained previously, to do so, we make use of the fact that the plaintext in semi-functional challenge ciphertexts can be made independent from the master secret key, statistically (this is the transition from game 2 to game 3 in Fig. 5). Thus, to make the plaintext independent from msk in *all* challenge ciphertexts, we need to switch them to semi-functional distribution *all* at the same time. More details are provided in Sect. 2.1.

Traditional dual system encryption, as explained previously, is incapable of handling many semi-functional challenge ciphertext at once. Instead, we adapt techniques from [HKS15, AHY15, GDCC16] that build IBE where the security proof can handle many challenge ciphertexts at once. These techniques, which builds upon [CW13, BKP14, CGW15], were developed for a whole different purpose than KDM security, namely, they were used to obtain IBE that are secure in the multi-challenge setting, where the security loss is independent of the number of challenge ciphertexts. These tight security reductions yield shorter concrete parameters for a given security level.

2 Preliminaries

2.1 Pairing Groups

Let GGen be a PPT algorithm that on input the security parameter 1^λ, returns a description $\mathcal{PG} = (\mathbb{G}_1, \mathbb{G}_2, \mathbb{G}_T, p, P_1, P_2, e)$ where for all $s \in \{1, 2, T\}$, $\mathbb{G}_s$ is a cyclic group of order p for a 2λ-bit prime p. $\mathbb{G}_1$ and $\mathbb{G}_2$ are generated by P_1 and P_2 respectively, and $e : \mathbb{G}_1 \times \mathbb{G}_2 \rightarrow \mathbb{G}_T$ is an efficiently computable (non-degenerate) bilinear map. Define $P_T := e(P_1, P_2)$, which is a generator of $\mathbb{G}_T$, of order p. We use implicit representation of group elements. For $s \in \{1, 2, T\}$ and $a \in \mathbb{Z}_p$, define $[a]_s = a \cdot P_s \in \mathbb{G}_s$ as the implicit representation of a in G_s. More generally, for a matrix $\mathbf{A} = (a_{ij}) \in \mathbb{Z}_p^{n \times m}$ we define $[\mathbf{A}]_s$ as the implicit representation of $\mathbf{A}$ in $\mathbb{G}_s$:

$$[\mathbf{A}]_s := \begin{pmatrix} a_{11} \cdot P_s \dots a_{1m} \cdot P_s \\ \\ a_{n1} \cdot P_s \dots a_{nm} \cdot P_s \end{pmatrix} \in \mathbb{G}_s^{n \times m}.$$

Given $[a]_1$ and $[b]_2$, one can efficiently compute $[a \cdot b]_T$ using the pairing e. For matrices $\mathbf{A}$ and $\mathbf{B}$ of matching dimensions, define $e([\mathbf{A}]_1, [\mathbf{B}]_2) := [\mathbf{AB}]_T$. For any matrix $\mathbf{A}, \mathbf{B} \in \mathbb{Z}_p^{n \times m}$, any group $s \in \{1, 2, T\}$, we denote by $[\mathbf{A}]_s + [\mathbf{B}]_s = [\mathbf{A} + \mathbf{B}]_s$.

For any prime p, we define the following distributions. The DDH distribution over $\mathbb{Z}_p^2$: $a \leftarrow_{\mathsf{R}} \mathbb{Z}_p$, output $\mathbf{a} := \binom{1}{a}$.

Definition 1 (DDH assumption). *For any adversary $\mathcal{A}$, any group $s \in \{1, 2, T\}$ and any security parameter λ, let*

$$\mathsf{Adv}^{\mathsf{DDH}}_{\mathbb{G}_s,\mathcal{A}}(\lambda) := |\Pr[1 \leftarrow \mathcal{A}(\mathcal{PG}, [\mathbf{a}]_s, [\mathbf{a}r]_s)] - \Pr[1 \leftarrow \mathcal{A}(\mathcal{PG}, [\mathbf{a}]_s, [\mathbf{u}]_s)]|,$$

where the probabilities are taken over $\mathcal{PG} \leftarrow_{\mathsf{R}} \mathsf{GGen}(1^\lambda, d)$, $\boldsymbol{a} \leftarrow_{\mathsf{R}} \mathsf{DDH}$, $r \leftarrow_{\mathsf{R}} \mathbb{Z}_p$, $\mathbf{u} \leftarrow_{\mathsf{R}} \mathbb{Z}_p^2$, and the random coins of $\mathcal{A}$. We say DDH holds in $\mathbb{G}_s$ if for all PPT adversaries $\mathcal{A}$, $\mathsf{Adv}^{\mathsf{DDH}}_{\mathbb{G}_s,\mathcal{A}}(\lambda)$ is a negligible function of λ.

Definition 2 (SXDH assumption). *For a pairing group $\mathcal{PG} = (\mathbb{G}_1, \mathbb{G}_2, \mathbb{G}_T, p, P_1, P_2, e) \leftarrow_{\mathsf{R}} \mathsf{GGen}(1^\lambda)$, we say SXDH holds in $\mathcal{PG}$ if DDH holds in $\mathbb{G}_1$ and $\mathbb{G}_2$.*

We define the (ℓ, Q)-fold DDH assumption below. Note that the DDH assumption corresponds to the $(1, 1)$-fold DDH assumption.

Lemma 1 (Random self reducibility of DDH). *For any $\ell, Q \geq 1$, any PPT adversary $\mathcal{A}$, we define:*

$$\begin{aligned}\mathsf{Adv}^{\ell,Q\text{-}\mathsf{DDH}}_{\mathbb{G}_s,\mathcal{A}}(\lambda) := |&\Pr[1 \leftarrow \mathcal{A}(\mathcal{PG}, [\mathbf{a}]_s, \{[r_i]_s, [\mathbf{a}r_i]_s\}_{i\in[Q]})] \\ &- \Pr[1 \leftarrow \mathcal{A}(\mathcal{PG}, [\mathbf{a}]_s, \{[r_i]_s, [\mathbf{u}_i]_s\}_{i\in[Q]})]|,\end{aligned}$$

where the probabilities are taken over $\mathcal{PG} \leftarrow_{\mathsf{R}} \mathsf{GGen}(1^\lambda, d)$, $\mathbf{a} \leftarrow_{\mathsf{R}} \mathbb{Z}_p^\ell$, $r_i \leftarrow_{\mathsf{R}} \mathbb{Z}_p$, $\mathbf{u}_i \leftarrow_{\mathsf{R}} \mathbb{Z}_p^\ell$ for all $i \in [Q]$, and the random coins of $\mathcal{A}$.

There exists a PPT adversary $\mathcal{B}$ such that

$$\mathsf{Adv}^{\ell,Q\text{-}\mathsf{DDH}}_{\mathbb{G}_s,\mathcal{A}}(\lambda) \leq \mathsf{Adv}^{\mathsf{DDH}}_{\mathbb{G}_s,\mathcal{B}}(\lambda).$$

2.2 Entropy Extraction

We give a particular case of the left over hash lemma, that is tailored to our purpose.

Lemma 2 (Leftover hash lemma [ILL89]). *Let p be a 2λ-bit prime, and $\ell := 4\lceil \log_2(p) \rceil$. The following distribution are within $2^{-\lambda}$ statistical distance:*

$$(\mathbf{a}, \mathbf{b}, \mathbf{u}, \mathbf{k}^\top \mathbf{a}, \mathbf{k}^\top \mathbf{b}, \mathbf{k}^\top \mathbf{u}) \text{ and } (\mathbf{a}, \mathbf{b}, \mathbf{u}, \mathbf{k}^\top \mathbf{a}, \mathbf{k}^\top \mathbf{b}, r),$$

where $\mathbf{a}, \mathbf{b}, \mathbf{u} \leftarrow_{\mathsf{R}} \mathbb{Z}_p^\ell$, $\mathbf{k} \leftarrow_{\mathsf{R}} \{0, 1\}^\ell$, and $r \leftarrow_{\mathsf{R}} \mathbb{Z}_p$.

2.3 Identity Based Encryption

An Identity Based Encryption for identity space $\mathcal{I}$ and message space $\mathcal{M}$ is a tuple of PPT algorithms:

- $\mathsf{Setup}(1^\lambda)$: on input the security parameter λ, returns a master public key mpk which defines an identity space $\mathcal{I}$, and a master secret key msk.
- $\mathsf{Enc}(\mathsf{mpk}, \mathsf{id} \in \mathcal{I}, m \in \mathcal{M})$: returns a ciphertext ct.
- $\mathsf{KeyGen}(\mathsf{mpk}, \mathsf{msk}, \mathsf{id} \in \mathcal{I})$: returns $\mathsf{sk}_{\mathsf{id}}$, a user secret key for identity id.
- $\mathsf{Dec}(\mathsf{mpk}, \mathsf{ct}, \mathsf{sk})$: deterministic algorithm that returns a message, or a special symbol $\perp$ if it fails.

Correctness. For any security parameter λ, any $\mathsf{id} \in \mathcal{I}$, any message m, $\Pr[\mathsf{Dec}(\mathsf{mpk}, \mathsf{ct}, \mathsf{sk}_{\mathsf{id}}) = m] = 1$, where the probability is taken over $(\mathsf{mpk}, \mathsf{msk}) \leftarrow \mathsf{Setup}(1^\lambda)$, $\mathsf{ct} \leftarrow \mathsf{Enc}(\mathsf{mpk}, \mathsf{id}, m)$, $\mathsf{sk}_{\mathsf{id}} \leftarrow \mathsf{KeyGen}(\mathsf{mpk}, \mathsf{msk}, \mathsf{id})$.

Remark 1 (Public-key encryption (PKE)). Note that a public-key encryption is a special case of IBE with identity space $\mathcal{I} := \{\varepsilon\}$. Of course, the interesting case of IBE is when $\mathcal{I}$ is of exponential size in the security parameter.

Definition 3 (Master-KDM security). *An IBE scheme* IBE *for identity space* $\mathcal{I}$ *and message space* $\mathcal{M}$ *is said to be KDM-secure for the class of (efficiently computable) functions* $\mathcal{F}$ *if for all PPT adversaries* $\mathcal{A}$*, the following advantage is a negligible function of the security parameter* λ*:*

$$\mathsf{Adv}^{\mathsf{KDM}}_{\mathsf{IBE},\mathcal{A}}(\lambda) := 2 \cdot \left| 1/2 - \Pr\left[b' = b \;\middle|\; \begin{array}{c} b \leftarrow_{\mathsf{R}} \{0,1\} \\ (\mathsf{mpk}, \mathsf{msk}) \leftarrow \mathsf{Setup}(1^\lambda) \\ b' \leftarrow \mathcal{A}^{\mathsf{O}_{\mathsf{Enc}}(\cdot,\cdot),\mathsf{O}_{\mathsf{KeyGen}}(\cdot)}(\mathsf{mpk}) \end{array} \right] \right|,$$

where the oracle $\mathsf{O}_{\mathsf{Enc}}(\mathsf{id}, f)$*, on input an identity* $\mathsf{id} \in \mathcal{I}$ *and a function* $f \in \mathcal{F}$*, computes* $y := f(\mathsf{msk}) \in \mathcal{M}$*, returns* $\mathsf{Enc}(\mathsf{mpk}, \mathsf{id}, f(\mathsf{msk}))$ *if* $b = 0$*, and computes a uniformly random message* $M \leftarrow_{\mathsf{R}} \mathcal{M}$*, and returns* $\mathsf{Enc}(\mathsf{mpk}, \mathsf{id}, M)$ *if* $b = 1$*; the oracle* $\mathsf{O}_{\mathsf{KeyGen}}(\mathsf{id})$*, on input an identity* $\mathsf{id} \in \mathcal{I}$*, returns* $\mathsf{KeyGen}(\mathsf{mpk}, \mathsf{msk}, \mathsf{id})$*. We require that the identities queried by the adversary to the oracle* $\mathsf{O}_{\mathsf{Enc}}(\cdot, \cdot)$ *are different from the identities queried to* $\mathsf{O}_{\mathsf{KeyGen}}(\cdot)$*. This is in order to avoid trivial attacks, where the adversary can win the game simply using the correctness of the scheme.*

In this paper, as in prior works [BG10, BGK11], we consider the class of affine functions, that is, we consider IBE where the message space is a group $\mathbb{G}$ of order p, and $\mathsf{msk} := [\mathbf{k}] \in \mathbb{G}^\ell$ for some integer ℓ. The adversary is allowed to query encryption of affine functions on msk, that is, encryption of messages of the form $[\mathbf{k}^\top \mathbf{w} + \gamma]$, for $\mathbf{w} \in \mathbb{Z}_p^\ell$, $[\gamma] \in \mathbb{G}$ of its choice. In [App11, BHHI10], the authors showed that this can be boosted to KDM-security with respect to the class of circuits of a-priori bounded size.

The work of Alperin-Sheriff and Peikert [AP12] gives KDM-secure IBE schemes that only support KDM messages that depend on user secret keys.

Also, the work of Galindo et al. [GHV12] only achieved a restricted version of master-KDM security, on in which (a) the number of KDM queries is bounded and (b) the oracle $\mathsf{O}_{\mathsf{KeyGen}}$ may only be called on identities that were fixed at the beginning of the game.

3 KDM-Secure IBE from Pairings

In this section we give our construction of KDM-secure IBE from pairing assumptions. To make our construction modular, we first introduce an intermediate primitive (which we call modular IBE), and show that any modular IBE with some specific properties is already KDM secure. We then show how to realize the notion of modular IBE with those required properties.

3.1 Ingredients of Our Construction

We first start with the definition of modular IBE. Informally, we call an IBE scheme modular if it is built upon a PKE scheme in the sense we define below.

Definition 4 (Modular IBE). *We say an IBE* $(\mathsf{Setup}, \mathsf{Enc}, \mathsf{KeyGen}, \mathsf{Dec})$ *for identity space* $\mathcal{I}$ *is modular if there exists a PKE* $(\mathsf{PKE.Setup}, \mathsf{PKE.Enc}, \mathsf{PKE.Dec})$*, and PPT algorithms* $\mathsf{SampParams}$*,* $\mathsf{Expand}_{\mathsf{pk}}$ *and* $\mathsf{Expand}_{\mathsf{ct}}$ *such that:*

1. $\mathsf{Setup}(1^\lambda)$*:* $(\mathsf{pk}, \mathsf{sk}) \leftarrow \mathsf{PKE.Setup}(1^\lambda)$*,* $\mathsf{params} \leftarrow \mathsf{SampParams}(\mathsf{pk}, \mathcal{I})$*,* $\mathsf{pk}' \leftarrow \mathsf{Expand}_{\mathsf{pk}}(\mathsf{params}, \mathsf{pk})$*,* $\mathsf{mpk} := (\mathsf{pk}, \mathsf{pk}', \mathcal{I})$*,* $\mathsf{msk} := \mathsf{sk}$*, returns* $(\mathsf{mpk}, \mathsf{msk})$*.*
2. *For all identities* $\mathsf{id} \in \mathcal{I}$ *and all messages* m*, the following are identically distributed:*
$$\mathsf{ct} \leftarrow \mathsf{Enc}(\mathsf{mpk}, \mathsf{id}, m),$$
and
$$(\mathsf{ct}_0, \mathsf{ct}_1) \text{ where } \mathsf{ct}_0 \leftarrow \mathsf{PKE.Enc}(\mathsf{pk}, m), \mathsf{ct}_1 \leftarrow \mathsf{Expand}_{\mathsf{ct}}(\mathsf{pk}, \mathsf{params}, \mathsf{ct}_0, \mathsf{id}).$$
In both distributions, we have $(\mathsf{pk}, \mathsf{sk}) \leftarrow \mathsf{PKE.Setup}(1^\lambda)$*,* $\mathsf{params} \leftarrow \mathsf{SampParams}(\mathsf{pk}, \mathcal{I})$*,* $\mathsf{pk}' \leftarrow \mathsf{Expand}_{\mathsf{pk}}(\mathsf{params}, \mathsf{pk})$*, and* $\mathsf{mpk} := (\mathsf{pk}, \mathsf{pk}', \mathcal{I})$*.*

The definition implies that there are two ways to compute the encryption of a message m under identity id: either using Enc on input mpk, id and m; or using the underlying PKE encryption algorithm on input pk and message m, and using the $\mathsf{Expand}_{\mathsf{ct}}$ algorithm that takes as input the PKE ciphertext, pk, and id. These two ways are identically distributed.

We will now define the properties that need to be fulfilled by our IBE and its underlying PKE in order to achieve KDM security. Recall that we denote by $\mathsf{IBE} := (\mathsf{Setup}, \mathsf{Enc}, \mathsf{KeyGen}, \mathsf{Dec})$ the modular IBE, with underlying pke $\mathsf{PKE} := (\mathsf{PKE.Setup}, \mathsf{PKE.Enc}, \mathsf{PKE.Enc})$ whose message space is a group $\mathbb{G}$ of order p, and whose secret key is of the form $\mathsf{sk} := [\mathbf{k}] \in \mathbb{G}^\ell$ for some $\ell \in \mathbb{N}$. We can write $\mathbf{k} := \mathsf{msk}_{\mathsf{N}} + \mathsf{msk}_{\mathsf{SF}} \in \mathbb{Z}_p^\ell$, where $\mathsf{msk}_{\mathsf{N}}$ is the normal component of sk, and $\mathsf{msk}_{\mathsf{SF}}$ is the semi-functional component of sk.

Property 1 (semi-functional encryption). There exists a PPT algorithm $\widetilde{\mathsf{Enc}}$ that takes as input $\mathsf{pk}, \mathsf{sk}, M$ and returns a ciphertext. For all PPT adversaries $\mathcal{A}$, the following advantage is a negligible function of the security parameter λ:

$$\mathsf{Adv}^{\mathsf{SF\text{-}ct}}_{\mathsf{PKE},\mathcal{A}}(\lambda) := 2 \cdot \left| 1/2 - \Pr\left[b' = b \,\middle|\, \begin{array}{c} b \leftarrow_{\mathsf{R}} \{0,1\} \\ (\mathsf{pk}, \mathsf{sk}) \leftarrow \mathsf{PKE.Setup}(1^\lambda) \\ b' \leftarrow \mathcal{A}^{\mathsf{O}_{\mathsf{Enc}}(\cdot)}(\mathsf{pk}, \mathsf{sk}) \end{array} \right] \right|,$$

where the oracle $\mathsf{O}_{\mathsf{Enc}}(M)$, on input a message $M \in \mathbb{G}$, outputs $\mathsf{PKE.Enc}(\mathsf{pk}, M)$ if $b = 0$, or $\widetilde{\mathsf{Enc}}(\mathsf{pk}, \mathsf{sk}, M)$ if $b = 1$. Note that the message M can depend on sk since the latter is given to $\mathcal{A}$.

Property 2 (semi-functional keys). There exists a PPT algorithm $\widetilde{\mathsf{KeyGen}}$ that takes as input $\mathsf{pk}, \mathsf{msk}_{\mathsf{N}}$ where $\mathsf{sk} = [\mathsf{msk}_{\mathsf{N}} + \mathsf{msk}_{\mathsf{SF}}]$ and $(\mathsf{pk}, \mathsf{sk})$ is generated by $\mathsf{Setup}(1^\lambda)$, together with an identity, and outputs a user secret key. We require that for all PPT adversaries $\mathcal{A}$, the following advantage is a negligible function of λ:

$$\mathsf{Adv}^{\mathsf{SF\text{-}sk}}_{\mathsf{IBE},\mathcal{A}}(\lambda) := 2 \cdot \left| 1/2 - \Pr\left[b' = b \,\middle|\, \begin{array}{c} b \leftarrow_{\mathsf{R}} \{0,1\} \\ (\mathsf{pk}, \mathsf{sk}) \leftarrow \mathsf{Setup}(1^\lambda) \\ \mathsf{params} \leftarrow \mathsf{SampParams}(\mathsf{pk}, \mathcal{I}) \\ \mathsf{pk}' \leftarrow \mathsf{Expand}_{\mathsf{pk}}(\mathsf{params}, \mathsf{pk}) \\ \mathsf{mpk} := (\mathsf{pk}, \mathsf{pk}', \mathcal{I}), \mathsf{msk} := \mathsf{sk} \\ b' \leftarrow \mathcal{A}^{\mathsf{O}_{\mathsf{Enc}}(\cdot,\cdot), \mathsf{O}_{\mathsf{KeyGen}}{}^{(b)}(\cdot)}(\mathsf{mpk}) \end{array} \right] \right|,$$

where the oracle $\mathsf{O}_{\mathsf{Enc}}(\mathsf{id}, (\mathbf{w}, [m]))$, on input an identity $\mathsf{id} \in \mathcal{I}$, a vector $\mathbf{w} \in \mathbb{Z}_p^\ell$, and a message $[m] \in \mathbb{G}$, computes $\mathsf{ct}_0 \leftarrow \widetilde{\mathsf{Enc}}(\mathsf{pk}, \mathsf{sk}, [\mathbf{k}^\top \mathbf{w} + m])$, $\mathsf{ct}_1 \leftarrow \mathsf{Expand}_{\mathsf{ct}}(\mathsf{pk}, \mathsf{params}, \mathsf{ct}_0, \mathsf{id})$ an returns $(\mathsf{ct}_0, \mathsf{ct}_1)$. The oracle $\mathsf{O}_{\mathsf{KeyGen}}{}^{(b)}(\mathsf{id})$, on input an identity $\mathsf{id} \in \mathcal{I}$, returns $\mathsf{KeyGen}(\mathsf{mpk}, \mathsf{msk}, \mathsf{id})$ if $b = 0$ or $\widetilde{\mathsf{KeyGen}}(\mathsf{mpk}, [\mathsf{msk}_{\mathsf{N}}], \mathsf{id})$ if $b = 1$. Recall that $\mathsf{msk} := [\mathsf{msk}_{\mathsf{N}} + \mathsf{msk}_{\mathsf{SF}}]$. We require that the identities queried by $\mathcal{A}$ to $\mathsf{O}_{\mathsf{Enc}}$ are distinct to the identities it queries to $\mathsf{O}_{\mathsf{KeyGen}}$.

Property 3 (KDM security). For all PPT adversaries $\mathcal{A}$, the following advantage is a negligible function of the security parameter λ:

$$\mathsf{Adv}^{\mathsf{KDM}}_{\mathsf{PKE},\mathcal{A}}(\lambda) := 2 \cdot \left| 1/2 - \Pr\left[b' = b \,\middle|\, \begin{array}{c} b \leftarrow_{\mathsf{R}} \{0,1\} \\ (\mathsf{pk}, \mathsf{sk}) \leftarrow \mathsf{Setup}(1^\lambda), \\ b' \leftarrow \mathcal{A}^{\mathsf{O}_{\mathsf{Enc}}(\cdot)}(\mathsf{pk}, [\mathsf{msk}_{\mathsf{N}}]_T) \end{array} \right] \right|,$$

where the oracle $\mathsf{O}_{\mathsf{Enc}}(\mathbf{w}, [m])$, on input a vector $\mathbf{w} \in \mathbb{Z}_p^\ell$ and a message $[m] \in \mathbb{G}$, outputs $\widetilde{\mathsf{Enc}}(\mathsf{pk}, \mathsf{sk}, [\mathbf{w}^\top \mathbf{k} + m])$ if $b = 0$, or $\widetilde{\mathsf{Enc}}(\mathsf{pk}, \mathsf{sk}, [r])$ for a fresh random $r \leftarrow_{\mathsf{R}} \mathbb{Z}_p$ if $b = 1$. Recall that $\mathsf{sk} := [\mathbf{k}]$, with $\mathbf{k} := \mathsf{msk}_{\mathsf{N}} + \mathsf{msk}_{\mathsf{SF}}$.

3.2 KDM-Secure IBE Construction

We now give our theorem statement for KDM-secure IBE.

Theorem 1 (KDM-security). *Any modular IBE that satisfies properties 1 to 3 is KDM-secure for the class of affine functions.*

Proof. The proof goes through a hybrid argument, starting with game G_0, which is the KDM security experiment from Definition 3. Let $\mathcal{A}$ be a PPT adversary. For any game G, we denote by $\mathsf{Adv}_{\mathcal{A}}(\mathsf{G})$ the advantage of $\mathcal{A}$ in the game G.

Game G_0**.** This is the KDM security experiment for the class of affine functions. The message space is a group $\mathbb{G}$ of order p, the master secret key is of the form $[\mathbf{k}] \in \mathbb{G}^{\ell}$, and the adversary gets access to encryption of affine combinations of the form $[\mathbf{k}^{\top}\mathbf{w} + m]$, for $\mathbf{w} \in \mathbb{Z}_p^{\ell}$, $[m] \in \mathbb{G}$ of its choice. Namely, the adversary $\mathcal{A}$ first receives mpk. Then it can adaptively query $\mathsf{O}_{\mathsf{Enc}}(\mathsf{id}, (\mathbf{w}, [m]))$, to receive $\mathsf{Enc}(\mathsf{mpk}, \mathsf{id}, [\mathbf{k}^{\top}\mathbf{w} + m])$ if $b = 0$, $\mathsf{Enc}(\mathsf{mpk}, \mathsf{id}, [r])$ for a fresh $[r] \leftarrow_{\mathsf{R}} \mathbb{G}$ if $b = 1$. Upon querying $\mathsf{O}_{\mathsf{KeyGen}}(\mathsf{id})$, $\mathcal{A}$ receives $\mathsf{KeyGen}(\mathsf{mpk}, \mathsf{msk}, \mathsf{id})$.

Game G_1**.** We change the challenge ciphertexts to semi-functional. That is, in game G_0, $\mathsf{O}_{\mathsf{Enc}}(\mathsf{id}, (\mathbf{w}, [m]))$ computes $[m_0] := [\mathbf{k}^{\top}\mathbf{w} + m]$, $[m_1] \leftarrow_{\mathsf{R}} \mathbb{G}$, $\mathsf{ct}_0 := \mathsf{PKE.Enc}(\mathsf{pk}, [m_b])$; whereas $\mathsf{ct}_0 := \widetilde{\mathsf{Enc}}(\mathsf{pk}, \mathsf{sk}, [m_b])$ in game G_1, where $\widetilde{\mathsf{Enc}}$ is the PPT algorithm that generates semi-functional ciphertexts (see Property 1). The rest of the challenge ciphertext is computed as $\mathsf{ct}_1 := \mathsf{Expand}_{\mathsf{ct}}(\mathsf{pk}, \mathsf{params}, \mathsf{ct}_0, \mathsf{id})$ in both games. We show there exists a PPT adversary $\mathcal{B}_0$ such that:

$$|\mathsf{Adv}_{\mathcal{A}}(\mathsf{G}_0) - \mathsf{Adv}_{\mathcal{A}}(\mathsf{G}_1)| \leq \mathsf{Adv}^{\mathsf{SF\text{-}ct}}_{\mathsf{PKE},\mathcal{B}_0}(\lambda),$$

which is negligible by Property 1. The reduction $\mathcal{B}_0$ receives $(\mathsf{pk}, \mathsf{sk} := [\mathbf{k}] \in \mathbb{G}^{\ell})$ from its own experiment, samples $b \leftarrow_{\mathsf{R}} \{0, 1\}$, $\mathsf{params} \leftarrow \mathsf{SampParams}(\mathsf{pk}, \mathcal{I})$, computes $\mathsf{pk}' \leftarrow \mathsf{Expand}_{\mathsf{pk}}(\mathsf{params}, \mathsf{pk})$, and returns $\mathsf{mpk} := (\mathsf{pk}, \mathsf{pk}', \mathcal{I})$ to $\mathcal{A}$. $\mathcal{B}_0$ can simulate the oracle $\mathsf{O}_{\mathsf{KeyGen}}$ straightforwardly using sk and mpk. To simulate $\mathsf{O}_{\mathsf{Enc}}(\mathsf{id}, (\mathbf{w}, [m]))$, it computes $[m_0] := [\mathbf{k}^{\top}\mathbf{w} + m]$, $[m_1] \leftarrow_{\mathsf{R}} \mathbb{G}$, and uses its own encryption oracle on input the message $[m_b]$ to obtain a challenge ciphertext ct_0. Then it computes $\mathsf{ct}_1 \leftarrow \mathsf{Expand}_{\mathsf{ct}}(\mathsf{pk}, \mathsf{params}, \mathsf{ct}_0, \mathsf{id})$, and returns the challenge ciphertext $(\mathsf{ct}_0, \mathsf{ct}_1)$. If $\mathcal{A}$'s guess b' is such that $b' = b$ and identities queried by $\mathcal{A}$ to its encryption oracle are distinct from the identities queried to its key generation oracle, then $\mathcal{B}_0$ returns 1. Otherwise, it returns 0.

Game G_2**.** We change the user secret keys to semi-functional. That is, in game G_1, $\mathsf{O}_{\mathsf{KeyGen}}(\mathsf{id})$ returns $\mathsf{KeyGen}(\mathsf{mpk}, \mathsf{msk}, \mathsf{id})$, whereas it returns $\mathsf{KeyGen}(\mathsf{mpk}, [\mathsf{msk}_{\mathsf{N}}]_T, \mathsf{id})$ in game G_2. Recall that $\mathsf{msk} := [\mathbf{k}]_T$, and $\mathbf{k} := \mathsf{msk}_{\mathsf{N}} + \mathsf{msk}_{\mathsf{SF}}$.

We show there exists a PPT adversary $\mathcal{B}_1$ such that:

$$|\mathsf{Adv}_{\mathcal{A}}(\mathsf{G}_1) - \mathsf{Adv}_{\mathcal{A}}(\mathsf{G}_2)| \leq \mathsf{Adv}^{\mathsf{SF\text{-}sk}}_{\mathsf{IBE},\mathcal{B}_1}(\lambda),$$

which is negligible by Property 2. The reduction $\mathcal{B}_1$ receives mpk from its own experiment, which it forwards to $\mathcal{A}$, and simulates the oracles to $\mathcal{A}$ straightforwardly using its own oracles. Here, we make use of the fact that the the identities queried by $\mathcal{A}$ to its encryption oracle $\mathsf{O}_{\mathsf{Enc}}$ must be distinct to the identities it queries to its key generation oracle $\mathsf{O}_{\mathsf{KeyGen}}$, since this condition must also be fulfilled in the security game from Property 2.

Game G_3**.** We use the KDM security of the underlying PKE to change the challenge ciphertexts to encryptions of random message $[r] \leftarrow_{\mathsf{R}} \mathbb{G}$. That is, $\widetilde{\mathsf{O}_{\mathsf{Enc}}}(\mathsf{id}, (\mathbf{w}, [m]))$ computes $[m_0] := [\mathbf{w}^\top \mathbf{k} + m]$, $[m_1] \leftarrow_{\mathsf{R}} \mathbb{G}$, $\mathsf{ct}_0 := \widetilde{\mathsf{Enc}}(\mathsf{pk}, \mathsf{sk}, [m_b])$ in game G_3, whereas it computes $\widetilde{\mathsf{Enc}}(\mathsf{pk}, \mathsf{sk}, [r])$ for a fresh random $r \leftarrow_{\mathsf{R}} \mathbb{Z}_p$ in game G_3. The rest of the challenge ciphertext is computed as $\mathsf{ct}_1 := \mathsf{Expand}_{\mathsf{ct}}(\mathsf{pk}, \mathsf{params}, \mathsf{ct}_0, \mathsf{id})$ in both games. It is clear that the challenge ciphertexts do not depend on the random bit $b \leftarrow_{\mathsf{R}} \{0,1\}$ chosen by the experiment in game G_3, since the plaintexts are random, regardless of the value of b. Thus, we have:

$$\mathsf{Adv}_{\mathcal{A}}(\mathsf{G}_3) = 0.$$

Now, we show there exists a PPT adversary $\mathcal{B}_3$ such that:

$$|\mathsf{Adv}_{\mathcal{A}}(\mathsf{G}_3) - \mathsf{Adv}_{\mathcal{A}}(\mathsf{G}_3)| \leq \mathsf{Adv}^{\mathsf{KDM}}_{\mathsf{PKE},\mathcal{B}_3}(\lambda),$$

which is negligible by Property 3. The reduction $\mathcal{B}_3$ receives $(\mathsf{pk}, [\mathsf{msk}_{\mathsf{N}}]_T)$ from its own experiment, samples $b \leftarrow_{\mathsf{R}} \{0,1\}$, $\mathsf{params} \leftarrow \mathsf{SampParams}(\mathsf{pk}, \mathcal{I})$, computes $\mathsf{pk}' \leftarrow \mathsf{Expand}_{\mathsf{pk}}(\mathsf{params}, \mathsf{pk})$, and returns $\mathsf{mpk} := (\mathsf{pk}, \mathsf{pk}', \mathcal{I})$ to $\mathcal{A}$. When $\mathcal{A}$ queries $\mathsf{O}_{\mathsf{KeyGen}}(\mathsf{id})$, $\mathcal{B}_3$ returns $\mathsf{KeyGen}(\mathsf{mpk}, [\mathsf{msk}_{\mathsf{N}}]_T, \mathsf{id})$. When $\mathcal{A}$ queries $\mathsf{O}_{\mathsf{Enc}}(\mathsf{id}, (\mathbf{w}, [m]))$, $\mathcal{B}_3$ computes $[m_0] := [m]$, $[m_1] \leftarrow_{\mathsf{R}} \mathbb{G}$, and queries its own encryption oracle on input $(\mathbf{w}, [m_b])$ to obtain a challenge ciphertext ct_0. Then, $\mathcal{B}_3$ computes $\mathsf{ct}_1 \leftarrow \mathsf{Expand}_{\mathsf{ct}}(\mathsf{pk}, \mathsf{params}, \mathsf{ct}_0, \mathsf{id})$ and returns the challenge ciphertext $(\mathsf{ct}_0, \mathsf{ct}_1)$ to $\mathcal{A}$. If $\mathcal{A}$'s guess b' is such that $b' = b$ and identities queried by $\mathcal{A}$ to its encryption oracle are distinct from the identities queried to its key generation oracle, then $\mathcal{B}_0$ returns 1. Otherwise, it returns 0.

Overall, we have:

$$\mathsf{Adv}^{\mathsf{KDM}}_{\mathsf{IBE},\mathcal{A}}(\lambda) \leq \mathsf{Adv}^{\mathsf{SF\text{-}ct}}_{\mathsf{PKE},\mathcal{B}_0}(\lambda) + \mathsf{Adv}^{\mathsf{SF\text{-}sk}}_{\mathsf{IBE},\mathcal{B}_1}(\lambda) + \mathsf{Adv}^{\mathsf{KDM}}_{\mathsf{PKE},\mathcal{B}_3}(\lambda).$$

□

3.3 Concrete Instantiations

We instantiate the framework presented in the previous section with a modular IBE inspired from [CW13], and the KDM-secure PKE from [BHHO08]. Both of them rely on prime-order groups, which make them compatible. In Fig. 6, we give a description of the [BHHO08] when adapted to fit pairing groups, and in Fig. 7, we show how to extent it in a modular way to obtain a KDM-secure IBE. A concrete description of our IBE is given in Fig. 8.

We now proceed to prove the required properties from our concrete instantiation of the modular framework presented in the previous section.

<u>PKE.Setup(1^λ):</u>

$\mathcal{PG} := (\mathbb{G}_1, \mathbb{G}_2, \mathbb{G}_T, p, P_1, P_2, e) \leftarrow \mathsf{GGen}(1^\lambda)$, $\ell := 4\lceil \log_2(p) \rceil$, $\mathbf{a} \leftarrow_{\mathsf{R}} \mathbb{Z}_p^\ell$, $\mathbf{k} \leftarrow_{\mathsf{R}} \{0,1\}^\ell$, return $\mathsf{pk} := (\mathcal{PG}, [\mathbf{a}]_1, [\mathbf{k}^\top \mathbf{a}]_1)$ and $\mathsf{sk} := [\mathbf{k}]_T$.

<u>PKE.Enc(pk, $[m]_T \in \mathbb{G}_T$):</u>

$r \leftarrow_{\mathsf{R}} \mathbb{Z}_p$, return $([\mathbf{a}r]_1, [\mathbf{k}^\top \mathbf{a}r]_T + [m]_T)$

<u>PKE.Dec(pk, sk, ct):</u>

Recover $\mathbf{k} \in \{0,1\}^\ell$ from $\mathsf{sk} := [\mathbf{k}] \in \mathbb{G}_T^\ell$.
Parse $\mathsf{ct} := ([\mathbf{c}_0]_1, [c_1]_T)$, return $[c_1]_T - e([\mathbf{k}^\top \mathbf{c}_0]_1, [1]_2)$.

<u>$\widetilde{\mathsf{Enc}}$(sk, pk, $[m]_T \in \mathbb{G}_T$):</u>

$\mathbf{u} \leftarrow_{\mathsf{R}} \mathbb{Z}_p^\ell$, return $([\mathbf{u}]_1, [\mathbf{k}^\top \mathbf{u}]_T + [m]_T)$

Fig. 6. KDM-secure public-key encryption from [BHHO08].

Property 1 **(semi-functional encryption).** The difference between normal and semi-functional ciphertexts is that the vector $[\mathbf{a}r]_1$, with $r \leftarrow_{\mathsf{R}} \mathbb{Z}_p$ that is part of each challenge ciphertext is switched to a uniformly random vector over $\mathbb{G}_1^\ell$, using the (ℓ, Q)-fold DDH assumption, where Q denotes the number of encryption queries. By Lemma 1, this assumption is implied by the DDH assumption. Upon receiving a (ℓ, Q)-DDH challenge $([\mathbf{a}]_1, \{[\mathbf{z}_i]_1\}_{i \in [Q]})$, where either $[\mathbf{z}_i]_1 = [\mathbf{a}r_i]_1$ for $r_i \leftarrow_{\mathsf{R}} \mathbb{Z}_p$, or $[\mathbf{z}_i]_1 \leftarrow_{\mathsf{R}} \mathbb{G}_1^\ell$, the reduction samples $\mathbf{k} \leftarrow_{\mathsf{R}} \{0,1\}^\ell$, and returns $\mathsf{pk} := ([\mathbf{a}]_1, [\mathbf{k}^\top \mathbf{a}]_T)$ and $\mathsf{sk} := [\mathbf{k}]_T$ to $\mathcal{A}$. On the i'th query $\mathsf{O}_{\mathsf{Enc}}([m]_T \in \mathbb{G}_T)$, the reduction answers with $([\mathbf{z}_i]_1, [\mathbf{k}^\top \mathbf{z}_i]_T + [m]_T)$, for $i \in [Q]$.

Property 2, semi-functional keys. The proof goes through a sequence of hybrid games, defined in Fig. 9. Let $\mathcal{A}$ be a PPT adversary. For each game G, we denote by $\mathsf{Adv}_{\mathcal{A}}(\mathsf{G})$ the advantage of $\mathcal{A}$ if game G. We start with game G_0, which is the security game defined in Property 2.

Game G_1: We change the vector $[\mathbf{u}]_1 \leftarrow_{\mathsf{R}} \mathbb{G}_1^\ell$ used in each challenge ciphertext to $[\mathbf{a}_0 r]$, for $r \leftarrow_{\mathsf{R}} \mathbb{Z}_p$, and $\mathbf{a}_0 \leftarrow_{\mathsf{R}} \mathbb{Z}_p^\ell$, independent of $\mathbf{a}$ used in the public key, using the (ℓ, Q)-fold DDH assumption in $\mathbb{G}_1$, where Q denotes the number of queries to $\mathsf{O}_{\mathsf{Enc}}$. By Lemma 1, this is implied by the DDH assumption. We build a PPT adversary $\mathcal{B}_0$ such that:

$$|\mathsf{Adv}_{\mathcal{A}}(\mathsf{G}_0) - \mathsf{Adv}_{\mathcal{A}}(\mathsf{G}_1)| \leq \mathsf{Adv}_{\mathbb{G}_1, \mathcal{B}_0}^{\ell, Q\text{-}\mathsf{DDH}}(\lambda).$$

Upon receiving a (ℓ, Q)-DDH challenge $([\mathbf{a}_0]_1, \{[\mathbf{z}_i]_1\}_{i \in [Q]}$, $\mathcal{B}_0$ samples $b \leftarrow_{\mathsf{R}} \{0,1\}$, $\mathbf{a} \leftarrow_{\mathsf{R}} \mathbb{Z}_p^\ell$, $\mathbf{k} \leftarrow_{\mathsf{R}} \{0,1\}^\ell$, and for all $i \in [\lambda]$, $b \in \{0,1\}$: $\mathbf{W}_{i,b} \leftarrow_{\mathsf{R}} \mathbb{Z}_p^{2 \times \ell}$, thanks to which it can compute mpk and simulate $\mathsf{O}_{\mathsf{KeyGen}}$ to $\mathcal{A}$ as described in Fig. 9. On the i'th query of $\mathcal{A}$ to $\mathsf{O}_{\mathsf{Enc}}(\mathsf{id}, \mathbf{w}, [m]_T)$, $\mathcal{B}_0$ returns $([\mathbf{z}_i]_1, [\mathbf{W}_{\mathsf{id}} \mathbf{z}_i]_1, [\mathbf{k}^\top \mathbf{z}_i + \mathbf{k}^\top \mathbf{w} + m]_T)$, where $\mathbf{W}_{\mathsf{id}} := \sum_{i \in [\lambda]} \mathbf{W}_{i, \mathsf{id}_i}$.

$\underline{\mathsf{SampParams}(\mathsf{pk}):}$
For all $i \in [\lambda]$, $b \in \{0,1\}$, $\mathbf{W}_{i,b} \leftarrow_{\mathsf{R}} \mathbb{Z}_p^{2\times \ell}$. $\mathbf{b} \leftarrow_{\mathsf{R}}$ DDH. Return $\mathsf{params} := (\mathbf{b}, \{\mathbf{W}_{i,b}\}_{i\in[\lambda],b\in\{0,1\}})$.

$\underline{\mathsf{Expand}_{\mathsf{pk}}(\mathsf{params}, \mathsf{pk}):}$
Parse $\mathsf{pk} := (\mathcal{PG}, [\mathbf{a}]_1, [\mathbf{k}^\top \mathbf{a}]_1)$.
Return $\mathsf{pk}' := ([\mathbf{b}]_2, \{[\mathbf{W}_{i,b}\mathbf{a}]_1, [\mathbf{W}_{i,b}^\top \mathbf{b}]_2\}_{i\in[\lambda],b\in\{0,1\}})$

$\underline{\mathsf{Expand}_{\mathsf{ct}}(\mathsf{pk}, \mathsf{params}, \mathsf{ct}_0, \mathsf{id} \in \{0,1\}^\lambda):}$
Parse $\mathsf{ct}_0 := ([\mathbf{c}]_1, [c']_T)$, return $\mathsf{ct}_1 := \sum_{i\in[\lambda]} [\mathbf{W}_{i,\mathsf{id}_i}\mathbf{c}]_1$.

Fig. 7. KDM-secure modular IBE, for the identity space $\{0,1\}^\lambda$. We denote by id_i the i'th bit of $\mathsf{id} \in \{0,1\}^\ell$. It builds upon the PKE from Fig. 6.

Game G_2: We change the vector $[\mathbf{d}]_2$ in each user secret key from $[\mathbf{b}s]_2$ for $s \leftarrow_{\mathsf{R}} \mathbb{Z}_p$ to uniformly random over $\mathbb{G}_2^2$, using the DDH assumption in $\mathbb{G}_2$. We build a PPT adversary $\mathcal{B}_1$ such that:

$$|\mathsf{Adv}_{\mathcal{A}}(\mathsf{G}_1) - \mathsf{Adv}_{\mathcal{A}}(\mathsf{G}_2)| \leq \mathsf{Adv}_{\mathbb{G}_1,\mathcal{B}_1}^{1,Q_{\mathsf{sk}}\text{-}\mathsf{DDH}}(\lambda),$$

where Q_{sk} denotes the number of queries to $\mathsf{O}_{\mathsf{KeyGen}}$.

Upon receiving a $1, Q_{\mathsf{sk}}$-fold DDH challenge $([\mathbf{b}]_2, \{[\mathbf{z}_i]_2\}_{i\in[Q_{\mathsf{sk}}]})$, $\mathcal{B}_1$ samples $b \leftarrow_{\mathsf{R}} \{0,1\}$, $\mathbf{a}, \mathbf{a}_0 \leftarrow_{\mathsf{R}} \mathbb{Z}_p^\ell$, $\mathbf{k} \leftarrow_{\mathsf{R}} \{0,1\}^\ell$, and for all $i \in [\lambda]$, $b \in \{0,1\}$: $\mathbf{W}_{i,b} \leftarrow_{\mathsf{R}} \mathbb{Z}_p^{2\times\ell}$, thanks to which it can compute mpk and simulate $\mathsf{O}_{\mathsf{Enc}}$ to $\mathcal{A}$ as described in Fig. 9. On the i'th query of $\mathcal{A}$ to $\mathsf{O}_{\mathsf{KeyGen}}(\mathsf{id})$, $\mathcal{B}_0$ returns $([\mathbf{z}_i]_2, [\mathbf{k}_b + \mathbf{W}_{\mathsf{id}}\mathbf{z}_i]_2)$, where $\mathbf{W}_{\mathsf{id}} := \sum_{i\in[\lambda]} \mathbf{W}_{i,\mathsf{id}_i}$, $\mathbf{k}_0 := \mathbf{k}$ and $\mathbf{k}_1 := \frac{\mathbf{k}^\top \mathbf{a}}{\|\mathbf{a}\|_2^2}$.

Game G_3: We change the way $\mathbf{W}_{\mathsf{id}}$ is computed, as described in Fig. 9. In Lemma 3, we show that there exists a PPT adversary $\mathcal{B}_2$ such that:

$$|\mathsf{Adv}_{\mathcal{A}}(\mathsf{G}_2) - \mathsf{Adv}_{\mathcal{A}}(\mathsf{G}_3)| \leq 3\lambda \cdot \mathsf{Adv}_{\mathbb{G}_2,\mathcal{B}_2}^{\mathsf{DDH}}(\lambda) + \frac{2\lambda Q_{\mathsf{sk}}}{p},$$

where Q_{sk} denotes the number of queries to $\mathsf{O}_{\mathsf{KeyGen}}$.

Game G_4: We change the distribution of the user secret keys as described in Fig. 9.

First, we use the fact that the following distributions are statistically $1/p$-close:

$$\mathbf{d} \leftarrow_{\mathsf{R}} \mathbb{Z}_p^2 \text{ and } \gamma \cdot \mathbf{d}, \text{ with } \gamma \leftarrow_{\mathsf{R}} \mathbb{Z}_p, \mathbf{d} \leftarrow_{\mathsf{R}} \mathbb{Z}_p^2.$$

Thus, we can write the output of $\mathsf{O}_{\mathsf{KeyGen}}(\mathsf{id})$ as

$$([\gamma \cdot \mathbf{d}]_2, [\mathbf{k}_b + \sum_{j\in[\lambda]} \mathbf{W}_{j,\mathsf{id}_j}^\top (\gamma \cdot \mathbf{d}) + \mathbf{A}^\perp \gamma \cdot \mathsf{RF}(\mathsf{id}) \cdot (\mathbf{b}^\perp)^\top \mathbf{d}]_2),$$

$\underline{\mathsf{Setup}(1^\lambda)}$:
$\mathcal{PG} := (\mathbb{G}_1, \mathbb{G}_2, \mathbb{G}_T, p, P_1, P_2, e) \leftarrow \mathsf{GGen}(1^\lambda)$, $\ell := 4\lceil \log_2(p) \rceil$, $\mathbf{a} \leftarrow_R \mathbb{Z}_p^\ell$, $\mathbf{b} \leftarrow_R \mathsf{DDH}$, $\mathbf{k} \leftarrow_R \{0,1\}^\ell$. For all $i \in [\lambda]$, $b \in \{0,1\}$, $\mathbf{W}_{i,b} \leftarrow_R \mathbb{Z}_p^{2\times\ell}$.
Return $\mathsf{mpk} := (\mathcal{PG}, [\mathbf{a}]_1, [\mathbf{b}]_2, \{[\mathbf{W}_{i,b}\mathbf{a}]_1, [\mathbf{W}_{i,b}^\top \mathbf{b}]_2\}_{i\in[\lambda], b\in\{0,1\}}, [\mathbf{k}^\top \mathbf{a}]_T)$ and $\mathsf{msk} := [\mathbf{k}]_T$

$\underline{\mathsf{Enc}(\mathsf{mpk}, \mathsf{id} \in \{0,1\}^\lambda, [m]_T \in \mathbb{G}_T)}$:
$r \leftarrow_R \mathbb{Z}_p$, return: $\mathsf{ct} := ([\mathbf{a}r]_1, [\sum_{i\in[\lambda]} \mathbf{W}_{i,\mathsf{id}_i}\mathbf{a}r]_1, [\mathbf{k}^\top \mathbf{a}r]_T + [m]_T)$

$\underline{\mathsf{KeyGen}(\mathsf{msk}, \mathsf{id} \in \{0,1\}^\lambda)}$:
Recover $\mathbf{k}$ from $[\mathbf{k}]_T$, $s \leftarrow_R \mathbb{Z}_p$, return $\mathsf{sk}_{\mathsf{id}} := ([\mathbf{b}s]_2, [\mathbf{k} + \sum_{i\in[\lambda]} \mathbf{W}_{i,\mathsf{id}_i}^\top \mathbf{b}s]_2)$.

$\underline{\mathsf{Dec}(\mathsf{mpk}, \mathsf{ct}, \mathsf{sk}_{\mathsf{id}})}$:
Parse $\mathsf{ct} := ([\mathbf{c}]_1, [\mathbf{c}']_1, [c'']_T) \in \mathbb{G}_1^\ell \times \mathbb{G}_1^2 \times \mathbb{G}_T$ and $\mathsf{sk}_{\mathsf{id}} := ([\mathbf{d}]_2, [\mathbf{d}']_2) \in \mathbb{G}_2^2 \times \mathbb{G}_2^\ell$.
Return $[c'']_T - e([\mathbf{c}]_1^\top, [\mathbf{d}']_2) + e([\mathbf{c}']_1^\top, [\mathbf{d}]_2)$.

Fig. 8. Concrete description of our KDM-secure IBE.

with fresh $\mathbf{d} \leftarrow_R \mathbb{Z}_p^2$ and $\gamma \leftarrow_R \mathbb{Z}_p$. Using the DDH assumption in $\mathbb{G}_2$, for any identity id queried to $\mathsf{O}_{\mathsf{KeyGen}}$ (and therefore, not queried to $\mathsf{O}_{\mathsf{Enc}}$), we can switch $([\gamma]_2, [\mathsf{RF}(\mathsf{id})]_2, [\gamma \cdot \mathsf{RF}(\mathsf{id})]_2)$ to $([\gamma]_2, [\mathsf{RF}(\mathsf{id})]_2, [\mathbf{t}]_2)$, where $\gamma \leftarrow_R \mathbb{Z}_p$ and $\mathbf{t} \leftarrow_R \mathbb{Z}_p^{\ell-1}$. Note that we make crucial use of the fact the value $\mathsf{RF}(\mathsf{id})$ for an identity id queried to $\mathsf{O}_{\mathsf{KeyGen}}$ only appears in the output of $\mathsf{O}_{\mathsf{KeyGen}}(\mathsf{id})$, since this identity must not be queried to $\mathsf{O}_{\mathsf{Enc}}$ by $\mathcal{A}$. This means the output of $\mathsf{O}_{\mathsf{KeyGen}}(\mathsf{id})$ becomes:

$$([\gamma \cdot \mathbf{d}]_2, [\mathbf{k}_b + \sum_{j\in[\lambda]} \mathbf{W}_{j,\mathsf{id}_j}^\top (\gamma \cdot \mathbf{d}) + \mathbf{A}^\perp \mathbf{t} \cdot (\mathbf{b}^\perp)^\top \mathbf{d}]_2),$$

where $\gamma \leftarrow_R \mathbb{Z}_p$, $\mathbf{d} \leftarrow_R \mathbb{Z}_p^2$ and $\mathbf{t} \leftarrow_R \mathbb{Z}_p^{\ell-1}$ are sampled freshly upon generation of each user secret key.

Finally, we switch back $\gamma \cdot \mathbf{d}$ to $\mathbf{d}$, for $\mathbf{d} \leftarrow_R \mathbb{Z}_p^2$, $\gamma \leftarrow_R \mathbb{Z}_p$, which are $1/p$ statistically close, such that $\mathsf{O}_{\mathsf{KeyGen}}(\mathsf{id})$ becomes:

$$([\mathbf{d}]_2, [\mathbf{k}_b + \sum_{j\in[\lambda]} \mathbf{W}_{j,\mathsf{id}_j}^\top \mathbf{d} + \mathbf{A}^\perp \mathbf{t} \cdot (\mathbf{b}^\perp)^\top \mathbf{d}]_2),$$

which exactly as in game G_4. We have successfully transitioned from game G_3 to G_4; overall we have a PPT adversary $\mathcal{B}_4$ such that:

$$|\mathsf{Adv}_{\mathcal{A}}(\mathsf{G}_3) - \mathsf{Adv}_{\mathcal{A}}(\mathsf{G}_4)| \leq \mathsf{Adv}_{\mathbb{G}_2,\mathcal{B}_4}^{\mathsf{DDH}}(\lambda) + \frac{2Q_{\mathsf{sk}}}{p},$$

where Q_{sk} denotes the number of queries to $\mathsf{O}_{\mathsf{KeyGen}}$.

Now, we show that:

$$\mathsf{Adv}_{\mathcal{A}}(\mathsf{G}_4) \leq \frac{Q_{\mathsf{sk}}}{p}.$$

This is due to the fact that in game G_4, the semi-functional component of msk is statistically hidden in the generated user secret keys.

Indeed, $\mathsf{O}_{\mathsf{KeyGen}}(\mathsf{id})$ outputs $([\mathbf{d}]_2, [\mathbf{k}_b + \sum_{j\in[\lambda]} \mathbf{W}_{j,\mathsf{id}_j}^\top \mathbf{d} + \mathbf{A}^\perp \mathbf{t} \cdot (\mathbf{b}^\perp)^\top \mathbf{d}]_2)$, where $\mathbf{d} \leftarrow_{\mathsf{R}} \mathbb{Z}_p^2$, and $\mathbf{t} \leftarrow_{\mathsf{R}} \mathbb{Z}_p^{\ell-1}$ are sampled freshly for each generated user secret key. Using the basis $(\mathbf{a}|\mathbf{A}^\perp)$ of $\mathbb{Z}_p^\ell$, we can write $\mathbf{k} := \mathbf{a} \cdot \mathsf{msk}_{\mathsf{N}} + \mathbf{A}^\perp \cdot \mathsf{msk}_{\mathsf{SF}}$, where $\mathsf{msk}_{\mathsf{N}} \in \mathbb{Z}_p$ and $\mathsf{msk}_{\mathsf{SF}} \in \mathbb{Z}_p^{\ell-1}$ denotes the normal and semi-functional components of $\mathbf{k}$, respectively. The component $\mathsf{msk}_{\mathsf{SF}}$ is completely hidden by the random vector $\mathbf{t} \leftarrow_{\mathsf{R}} \mathbb{Z}_p^{\ell-1}$. Namely, conditioned on the fact that $\mathbf{d}^\top \mathbf{b}^\perp \neq 0$, which holds with probability $1/p$ over the choice of $\mathbf{d} \leftarrow_{\mathsf{R}} \mathbb{Z}_p^2$, the output of $\mathsf{O}_{\mathsf{KeyGen}}(\mathsf{id})$ is identically distributed to:

$$([\mathbf{d}]_2, [\mathbf{a} \cdot \mathsf{msk}_{\mathsf{N}} + \sum_{j\in[\lambda]} \mathbf{W}_{j,\mathsf{id}_j}^\top \mathbf{d} + \mathbf{A}^\perp \mathbf{t} \cdot (\mathbf{b}^\perp)^\top \mathbf{d}]_2),$$

where $\mathsf{msk}_{\mathsf{N}} := \frac{\mathbf{k}^\top \mathbf{a}}{\|\mathbf{a}\|_2^2}$. At this point, the output is independent of the random bit $b \leftarrow_{\mathsf{R}} \{0,1\}$ picked by the experiment. □

Lemma 3 (From game G_2 to game G_3). *There exists a PPT adversary $\mathcal{B}_2$ such that:*

$$|\mathsf{Adv}_{\mathcal{A}}(\mathsf{G}_2) - \mathsf{Adv}_{\mathcal{A}}(\mathsf{G}_3)| \leq 3\lambda \cdot \mathsf{Adv}_{\mathcal{B}_2}^{\mathsf{DDH}}(\lambda) + \frac{2\lambda Q_{\mathsf{sk}}}{p},$$

where Q_{sk} denotes the number of queries to $\mathsf{O}_{\mathsf{KeyGen}}$.

Proof. The proof goes over a series of hybrid games defined in Fig. 10. We progressively increase the entropy in the matrices $\mathbf{W}_{\mathsf{id}}$, originally set as $\mathbf{W}_{\mathsf{id}} := \sum_{j\in[\lambda]} \mathbf{W}_{j,\mathsf{id}_j}$ in game G_2, up to $\mathbf{W}_{\mathsf{id}} := (\sum_{j\in[\lambda]} \mathbf{W}_{j,\mathsf{id}_j}) + (\mathbf{A}^\perp \mathsf{RF}(\mathsf{id}))^\top$ in game G_3, where RF is a random function, computed on the fly by the experiment. Namely, in game $\mathsf{G}_{2.i}$, we have $\mathbf{W}_{\mathsf{id}} := (\sum_{j\in[\lambda]} \mathbf{W}_{j,\mathsf{id}_j}) + (\mathbf{A}^\perp \mathsf{RF}_i(\mathsf{id}))^\top$, where RF_i is a random function that only depends on the first i'th bits on its input. It is clear that $\mathsf{G}_{2.\lambda}$ is the same as G_3. We prove that G_2 is statistically close to $\mathsf{G}_{2.0}$ (note that RF_0 is a constant function, that ignores its input), and we show that for all $i \in [\lambda]$, G_{i-1} is computationally indistinguishable from G_i, in a way that is reminiscent to the security proof from [GHKW16]. One difference here is that the vector $\mathbf{k}$ is not uniformly random over $\mathbb{Z}_p$, which adds technical difficulties.

Game $\mathsf{G}_{2.0}$. This game is as G_1, except the matrix $\mathbf{W}_{\mathsf{id}}$ is switched from $\mathbf{W}_{\mathsf{id}} := \sum_{j\in[\lambda]} \mathbf{W}_{j,\mathsf{id}_j}$ to $\mathbf{W}_{\mathsf{id}} := \sum_{j\in[\lambda]} \mathbf{W}_{j,\mathsf{id}_j} + \mathbf{b}^\perp(\mathbf{A}^\perp \mathsf{RF}_0(\mathsf{id}))^\top$, where $\mathsf{RF}_0(\mathsf{id})$ is a random vector in $\mathbb{Z}_p^{\ell-1}$, independent of id (the extra term is highlighted in gray to better see the difference between G_2 and $\mathsf{G}_{2.0}$). This does change the distribution of the game, since $(\mathbf{W}_{1,0}, \mathbf{W}_{1,1})$ is identically distributed to $(\mathbf{W}_{1,0} + \mathbf{b}^\perp(\mathbf{A}^\perp \mathsf{RF}_0(\mathsf{id}))^\top, \mathbf{W}_{1,1} + \mathbf{b}^\perp(\mathbf{A}^\perp \mathsf{RF}_0(\mathsf{id}))^\top)$. Note that these extra terms don't appear in the public key, since $\mathbf{a}^\top \mathbf{A}^\perp = \mathbf{0}$ and $\mathbf{b}^\top \mathbf{b}^\perp = 0$. Thus, we have:

$$\mathsf{Adv}_{\mathcal{A}}(\mathsf{G}_1) = \mathsf{Adv}_{\mathcal{A}}(\mathsf{G}_{2.0}).$$

Game G_0, $\boxed{\mathsf{G}_1,\ \mathsf{G}_2,\ \mathsf{G}_3, \mathsf{G}_4}$:

$b \leftarrow_R \{0,1\}$, $\mathcal{PG} \leftarrow \mathsf{GGen}(1^\lambda)$, $\ell := 4\lceil \log_2(p) \rceil$, $\mathbf{a} \leftarrow_R \mathbb{Z}_p^\ell$, $\boxed{\mathbf{a}_0 \leftarrow_R \mathbb{Z}_p^\ell}$,
$\mathbf{A}^\perp \leftarrow_R \mathbb{Z}_p^{\ell \times (\ell-1)}$ s.t. $\mathbf{a}^\top \mathbf{A}^\perp = \mathbf{0}$, $\mathbf{b} \leftarrow_R \mathsf{DDH}$, $\mathbf{b}^\perp \leftarrow_R \mathbb{Z}_p^2$ s.t. $\mathbf{b}^\top \mathbf{b}^\perp = \mathbf{0}$,
$\mathbf{k} \leftarrow_R \{0,1\}^\ell$. For all $i \in [\lambda]$, $b \in \{0,1\}$, $\mathbf{W}_{i,b} \leftarrow_R \mathbb{Z}_p^{2 \times \ell}$.
$\mathsf{mpk} := (\mathcal{PG}, [\mathbf{a}]_1, \{[\mathbf{W}_{i,b}\mathbf{a}]_1, [\mathbf{W}_{i,b}^\top \mathbf{b}]_2\}_{i \in [\lambda], b \in \{0,1\}}, [\mathbf{k}^\top \mathbf{a}]_T)$
$b' \leftarrow_R \mathcal{A}^{\mathsf{O}_{\mathsf{Enc}}(\cdot,\cdot), \mathsf{O}_{\mathsf{KeyGen}}{}^{(b)}(\cdot)}(\mathsf{mpk})$
Return 1 if $b' = b$ and identities queried to $\mathsf{O}_{\mathsf{Enc}}$ are distinct from identities queried to $\mathsf{O}_{\mathsf{KeyGen}}$.
Return 0 otherwise.

$\mathsf{O}_{\mathsf{Enc}}(\mathsf{id} \in \{0,1\}^\lambda, \mathbf{w} \in \mathbb{Z}_p^\ell, [m]_T \in \mathbb{G}_T)$: $\quad \mathsf{G}_0$, $\boxed{\mathsf{G}_1,\ \mathsf{G}_2,\ \mathsf{G}_3,\ \mathsf{G}_4}$

$\mathbf{u} \leftarrow_R \mathbb{Z}_p^\ell$, $[\mathbf{c}]_1 := [\mathbf{u}]_1$, $\boxed{r \leftarrow_R \mathbb{Z}_p,\ [\mathbf{c}]_1 := [\mathbf{a}_0 r]_1}$
$\mathbf{W}_{\mathsf{id}} := \sum_{i \in [\lambda]} \mathbf{W}_{i,\mathsf{id}_i} + \mathbf{b}^\perp(\mathbf{A}^\perp \mathsf{RF}(\mathsf{id}))^\top$
$\mathsf{ct} := ([\mathbf{c}]_1, [\mathbf{W}_{\mathsf{id}}\mathbf{c}]_1, [\mathbf{k}^\top \mathbf{c}]_T + [\mathbf{k}^\top \mathbf{w} + m]_T)$

$\mathsf{O}_{\mathsf{KeyGen}}{}^{(b)}(\mathsf{id} \in \{0,1\}^\lambda)$: $\quad \mathsf{G}_0$, G_1, $\boxed{\mathsf{G}_2,\ \mathsf{G}_3,\ \mathsf{G}_4}$

$s \leftarrow_R \mathbb{Z}_p$, $[\mathbf{d}]_2 := [\mathbf{b}s]_2$, $\boxed{[\mathbf{d}]_2 \leftarrow_R \mathbb{G}_2^2}$, $\mathbf{k}_0 := \mathbf{k}$, $\mathbf{k}_1 := \frac{\mathbf{k}^\top \mathbf{a}}{\|\mathbf{a}\|_2^2} \cdot \mathbf{a}$, $\mathbf{t} \leftarrow_R \mathbb{Z}_p^{\ell-1}$
$\mathbf{W}_{\mathsf{id}} := \sum_{i \in [\lambda]} \mathbf{W}_{i,\mathsf{id}_i} + \mathbf{b}^\perp(\mathbf{A}^\perp \mathsf{RF}(\mathsf{id}))^\top + \mathbf{b}^\perp(\mathbf{A}^\perp \mathbf{t})^\top$
Return $\mathsf{sk}_{\mathsf{id}} := ([\mathbf{d}]_2, [\mathbf{k}_b + \mathbf{W}_{\mathsf{id}}^\top \mathbf{d}]_2)$.

Fig. 9. Games for the proof of Property 2. In each procedure, the components inside a solid (dotted, gray) frame are only present in the games marked by a solid (dotted, gray) frame. Here, $\mathsf{RF} : \{0,1\}^\lambda \rightarrow \mathbb{Z}_p^{\ell-1}$ denotes a random function that is computed on the fly.

Games $\mathsf{G}_{2.i-1.1}$, for all $i \in [\lambda+1]$. This game is as $\mathsf{G}_{2.i-1}$, except the vector $[\mathbf{c}]_1$ output $\mathsf{O}_{\mathsf{Enc}}(\mathsf{id}, \mathbf{w}, [m]_T)$ is switched from $[\mathbf{a}_0 r]_1$ to $[\mathbf{a}_{\mathsf{id}_i} r]_1$, with $r \leftarrow_R \mathbb{Z}_p$, where id_i denotes the i'th bit of id, and $\mathbf{a}_0, \mathbf{a}_1 \leftarrow_R \mathbb{Z}_p^\ell$ are two independent random vectors. We use the DDH assumption in $\mathbb{G}_1$, to first switch $[\mathbf{a}_0 r]_1$ to uniformly random over $\mathbb{G}_1^2$ when necessary, that is, when $\mathsf{id}_i = 1$; then we use the DDH assumption again to switch the uniformly random vector to $[\mathbf{a}_1 r]_1$ with $r \leftarrow_R \mathbb{Z}_p$. Overall we have a PPT adversary $\mathcal{B}_i$ such that:

$$|\mathsf{Adv}_{\mathcal{A}}(\mathsf{G}_{2.i-1}) - \mathsf{Adv}_{\mathcal{A}}(\mathsf{G}_{2.i-1.1})| \leq 2 \cdot \mathsf{Adv}_{\mathbb{G}_1, \mathcal{B}_i}^{\mathsf{DDH}}(\lambda).$$

Games $\mathsf{G}_{2.i-1.2}$, for all $i \in [\lambda+1]$. See the description in Fig. 10.

As in the security proof of the CCA-secure pke from [GHKW16], we use a basis $(\mathbf{A}_0^\perp | \mathbf{A}_1^\perp) \in \mathbb{Z}_p^{\ell-1}$ of $\mathbf{A}^\perp$ where $\mathbf{a}_0^\top \mathbf{A}_0^\perp = \mathbf{a}_1^\top \mathbf{A}_1^\perp = \mathbf{0}$, where both $\mathbf{a}_0$ and $\mathbf{a}_1$ are uniformly random vectors from $\mathbb{Z}_p^\ell$, sampled independently.

Namely, we sample $\mathbf{A}_0^\perp \leftarrow_{\mathsf{R}} \mathbb{Z}_p^{\ell\times\ell/2}$ and $\mathbf{A}_1^\perp \leftarrow_{\mathsf{R}} \mathbb{Z}_p^{\ell\times(\ell/2-1)}$ such that $(\mathbf{A}_0^\perp|\mathbf{A}_1^\perp) \in \mathbb{Z}_p^{\ell-1}$ is full rank, and $\mathbf{a}^\top\mathbf{A}_0^\perp = \mathbf{a}_0^\top\mathbf{A}_0^\perp = \mathbf{a}^\top\mathbf{A}_1^\perp = \mathbf{a}_1^\top\mathbf{A}_1^\perp = \mathbf{0}$.

Using this basis, we can decompose $\mathbf{A}^\perp\mathsf{RF}_{i-1}(\mathsf{id}) := \mathbf{A}_0^\perp\mathsf{RF}_{i-1}^{(0)}(\mathsf{id}) + \mathbf{A}_1^\perp\mathsf{RF}_{i-1}^{(1)}(\mathsf{id})$, where $\mathsf{RF}_{i-1}^{(0)} : \{0,1\}^\lambda \rightarrow \mathbb{Z}_p^{\ell/2}$ and $\mathsf{RF}_{i-1}^{(1)} : \{0,1\}^\lambda \rightarrow \mathbb{Z}_p^{\ell/2-1}$ are independent random functions that only read the first $i-1$'th bits of their inputs.

We define

$$\mathsf{RF}_i^{(0)}(\mathsf{id}) := \begin{cases} \mathsf{RF}_{i-1}^{(0)}(\mathsf{id}) + \widetilde{\mathsf{RF}}_{i-1}^{(0)}(\mathsf{id}) & \text{if } \mathsf{id}_i = 0 \\ \mathsf{RF}_{i-1}^{(0)}(\mathsf{id}) & \text{if } \mathsf{id}_i = 1 \end{cases},$$

and

$$\mathsf{RF}_i^{(1)}(\mathsf{id}) := \begin{cases} \mathsf{RF}_{i-1}^{(1)}(\mathsf{id}) & \text{if } \mathsf{id}_i = 0 \\ \mathsf{RF}_{i-1}^{(1)}(\mathsf{id}) + \widetilde{\mathsf{RF}}_{i-1}^{(1)}(\mathsf{id}) & \text{if } \mathsf{id}_i = 1 \end{cases},$$

where $\widetilde{\mathsf{RF}}_{i-1}^{(0)} : \{0,1\}^\lambda \rightarrow \mathbb{Z}_p^{\ell/2}$ and $\widetilde{\mathsf{RF}}_{i-1}^{(1)} : \{0,1\}^\lambda \rightarrow \mathbb{Z}_p^{\ell/2-1}$ are random functions that only read the first $i-1$'th bits of their inputs, that are independent of $\mathsf{RF}_{i-1}^{(0)}$ and $\mathsf{RF}_{i-1}^{(1)}$. Note that the random functions $\mathsf{RF}_i^{(0)}$ and $\mathsf{RF}_i^{(1)}$ now depend on the first i'th bits of their inputs: we added a dependency on the i'th bit. Thus, writing $\mathbf{A}^\perp\mathsf{RF}_i(\mathsf{id}) := \mathbf{A}_0^\perp\mathsf{RF}_i^{(0)}(\mathsf{id}) + \mathbf{A}_1^\perp\mathsf{RF}_i^{(1)}(\mathsf{id})$, we have $\mathbf{A}^\perp\mathsf{RF}_i(\mathsf{id}) = \mathbf{A}^\perp\mathsf{RF}_{i-1}(\mathsf{id}) + \mathbf{A}_{\mathsf{id}_i}^\perp\widetilde{\mathsf{RF}}_{i-1}^{(\mathsf{id}_i)}(\mathsf{id})$. The game $\mathsf{G}_{2.i-1.2}$ is the same as $\mathsf{G}_{2.i-1.1}$, except the latter uses $\mathbf{W}_{\mathsf{id}} := (\sum_{j\in[\lambda]}\mathbf{W}_{j,\mathsf{id}_j}) + \mathbf{b}^\perp(\mathbf{A}^\perp\mathsf{RF}_{i-1}(\mathsf{id}))^\top$, and the former uses $\mathbf{W}_{\mathsf{id}} + \mathbf{A}_{\mathsf{id}_i}^\perp\widetilde{\mathsf{RF}}_{i-1}^{(\mathsf{id}_i)}(\mathsf{id})$.

Note that this change doesn't appear in the challenge ciphertexts, since $\mathsf{O}_{\mathsf{Enc}}(\mathsf{id}, \mathbf{w}, [m]_T)$ outputs:

$$\begin{aligned} \mathsf{ct} : &= ([\mathbf{a}_{\mathsf{id}_i} r]_1, [(\mathbf{W}_{\mathsf{id}} + \mathbf{b}^\perp(\mathbf{A}_{\mathsf{id}_i}^\perp\widetilde{\mathsf{RF}}_{i-1}^{(\mathsf{id}_i)}(\mathsf{id}))^\top\mathbf{a}_{\mathsf{id}_i} r]_1, [\mathbf{k}^\top\mathbf{a}_{\mathsf{id}_i} r + \mathbf{k}^\top\mathbf{w} + m]_T) \\ &= ([\mathbf{a}_{\mathsf{id}_i} r]_1, [(\mathbf{W}_{\mathsf{id}}\mathbf{a}_{\mathsf{id}_i} r]_1, [\mathbf{k}^\top\mathbf{a}_{\mathsf{id}_i} r + \mathbf{k}^\top\mathbf{w} + m]_T), \end{aligned}$$

since $\mathbf{a}_0^\top\mathbf{A}_0^\perp = \mathbf{a}_1^\top\mathbf{A}_1^\perp = \mathbf{0}$. Thus, the output of the oracle $\mathsf{O}_{\mathsf{Enc}}$ is identically distributed in $\mathsf{G}_{2.i-1.1}$ and $\mathsf{G}_{2.i-1.2}$. We now turn our attention to the output of $\mathsf{O}_{\mathsf{KeyGen}}$.

First, we use the fact that the following are identically distributed:

$$\mathbf{d} \leftarrow_{\mathsf{R}} \mathbb{Z}_p^2 \text{ and } \widehat{\mathsf{RF}}_{i-1}(\mathsf{id}) \cdot \mathbf{d}, \text{ with } \mathbf{d} \leftarrow_{\mathsf{R}} \mathbb{Z}_p^2,$$

where $\widehat{\mathsf{RF}}_{i-1} : \{0,1\}^\lambda \rightarrow \mathbb{Z}_p$ is a random function that only reads the first $i-1$'th bits of its input. That is, $\mathsf{O}_{\mathsf{KeyGen}}(\mathsf{id})$ uses a random vector $[\widehat{\mathsf{RF}}_{i-1}(\mathsf{id})\cdot\mathbf{d}]_2$ instead of $[\mathbf{d}]_2 \leftarrow_{\mathsf{R}} \mathbb{G}_2^2$.

Then, we use the fact that following distributions are within statistical distance $1/p$:

$$(\mathbf{W}_{i,0}, \mathbf{W}_{i,1}) \text{ and } (\mathbf{W}_{i,0} + \mathbf{b}^{\perp}(\mathbf{A}_0^{\perp}\mathbf{u}_0)^{\top}, \mathbf{W}_{i,1} + \mathbf{b}^{\perp}(\mathbf{A}_1^{\perp}\mathbf{u}_1)^{\top}),$$

where $\mathbf{W}_{i,0}, \mathbf{W}_{i,1} \leftarrow_{\mathsf{R}} \mathbb{Z}_p^{2\times\ell}$, $\mathbf{u}_0 \leftarrow_{\mathsf{R}} \mathbb{Z}_p^{\ell/2}$, $\mathbf{u}_1 \leftarrow_{\mathsf{R}} \mathbb{Z}_p^{\ell/2-1}$.

Thus, we can re-write the output of $\mathsf{O}_{\mathsf{KeyGen}}(\mathsf{id})$ as:

$$([\mathbf{d} \cdot \widehat{\mathsf{RF}}_{i-1}(\mathsf{id})]_2, [\mathbf{k}_b + \mathbf{W}_{\mathsf{id}}^{\top}\widehat{\mathsf{RF}}_{i-1}(\mathsf{id}) \cdot \mathbf{d} + \mathbf{A}_{\mathsf{id}_i}^{\perp}\mathbf{u}_{\mathsf{id}_i} \cdot \widehat{\mathsf{RF}}_{i-1}(\mathsf{id})(\mathbf{b}^{\perp})^{\top}\mathbf{d}]_2).$$

Note that the vectors $\mathbf{u}_0$ and $\mathbf{u}_1$ do not appear in the public key or the challenge ciphertexts, since $\mathbf{a}_0^{\top}\mathbf{A}_0^{\perp} = \mathbf{a}_1^{\top}\mathbf{A}_1^{\perp} = \mathbf{0}$.

At this point, we use the DDH assumption in $\mathbb{G}_2$ to switch

$$([\widehat{\mathsf{RF}}_{i-1}(\mathsf{id})]_2, [\mathbf{u}_{\mathsf{id}_i} \cdot \widehat{\mathsf{RF}}_{i-1}(\mathsf{id})]_2)$$

to

$$([\widehat{\mathsf{RF}}_{i-1}(\mathsf{id})]_2, [\widetilde{\mathsf{RF}}_{i-1}^{(\mathsf{id}_i)}(\mathsf{id})]_2).$$

The output of $\mathsf{O}_{\mathsf{KeyGen}}(\mathsf{id})$ becomes:

$$([\mathbf{d} \cdot \widehat{\mathsf{RF}}_{i-1}(\mathsf{id})]_2, [\mathbf{k}_b + \mathbf{W}_{\mathsf{id}}^{\top}\widehat{\mathsf{RF}}_{i-1}(\mathsf{id}) \cdot \mathbf{d} + \mathbf{A}_{\mathsf{id}_i}^{\perp}\widetilde{\mathsf{RF}}_{i-1}^{(\mathsf{id}_i)}(\mathsf{id})(\mathbf{b}^{\perp})^{\top}\mathbf{d}]_2).$$

Finally, we reverse the statistical change from $[\widehat{\mathsf{RF}}_{i-1}(\mathsf{id}) \cdot \mathbf{d}]_2$ to $[\mathbf{d}]_2$ in each user secret key, so that the output of $\mathsf{O}_{\mathsf{KeyGen}}(\mathsf{id})$ becomes:

$$\begin{aligned}&([\mathbf{d}]_2, [\mathbf{k}_b + (\sum_{j\in[\lambda]} \mathbf{W}_{j,\mathsf{id}_j})\mathbf{d} + (\mathbf{A}^{\perp}\mathsf{RF}_{i-1}(\mathsf{id}) + \mathbf{A}_{\mathsf{id}_i}^{\perp}\widetilde{\mathsf{RF}}_{i-1}^{(\mathsf{id}_i)}(\mathsf{id}))(\mathbf{b}^{\perp})^{\top}\mathbf{d}]_2) = \\ &([\mathbf{d}]_2, [\mathbf{k}_b + (\sum_{j\in[\lambda]} \mathbf{W}_{j,\mathsf{id}_j})\mathbf{d} + (\mathbf{A}^{\perp}\mathsf{RF}_i(\mathsf{id})(\mathbf{b}^{\perp})^{\top}\mathbf{d}]_2),\end{aligned}$$

exactly as in game $\mathsf{G}_{2.i-1.2}$. Putting everything together, we obtain a PPT adversary $\mathcal{B}_i'$ such that:

$$|\mathsf{Adv}_{\mathcal{A}}(\mathsf{G}_{2.i-1.1}) - \mathsf{Adv}_{\mathcal{A}}(\mathsf{G}_{2.i-1.2})| \leq \mathsf{Adv}_{\mathbb{G}_2,\mathcal{B}_i'}^{\mathsf{DDH}}(\lambda) + \frac{2Q_{\mathsf{sk}}}{p},$$

where Q_{sk} denotes the number of queries to $\mathsf{O}_{\mathsf{KeyGen}}$.

Summing up for all $i \in [\lambda]$, we obtain a PPT adversary $\mathcal{B}_2$ such that:

$$|\mathsf{Adv}_{\mathcal{A}}(\mathsf{G}_2) - \mathsf{Adv}_{\mathcal{A}}(\mathsf{G}_3)| \leq 3\lambda \cdot \mathsf{Adv}_{\mathcal{B}_2}^{\mathsf{DDH}}(\lambda) + \frac{2\lambda Q_{\mathsf{sk}}}{p}.$$

□

Property 3 (KDM security). First, as in the security proof of [BHHO08], we use the fact that the output of $\widetilde{\mathsf{Enc}}(\mathsf{pk}, \mathsf{sk}, [\mathbf{k}^{\top}\mathbf{w}]_T + [m]_T)$, which is of the

Games $\mathsf{G}_{2.i-1}$, $\boxed{\mathsf{G}_{2.i-1.1}}$, $\mathsf{G}_{2.i-1.2}$ (dotted frame) for $i \in [\lambda+1]$:

$b \leftarrow_{\mathsf{R}} \{0,1\}$, $\mathcal{PG} \leftarrow \mathsf{GGen}(1^\lambda)$, $\ell := 4\lceil \log_2(p) \rceil$, $\mathbf{a} \leftarrow_{\mathsf{R}} \mathbb{Z}_p^\ell$, $\mathbf{a}_0 \leftarrow_{\mathsf{R}} \mathbb{Z}_p^\ell$, $\boxed{\mathbf{a}_1 \leftarrow_{\mathsf{R}} \mathbb{Z}_p^\ell}$, $\mathbf{A}^\perp \leftarrow_{\mathsf{R}} \mathbb{Z}_p^{\ell \times (\ell-1)}$ s.t. $\mathbf{a}^\top \mathbf{A}^\perp = \mathbf{0}$, $\mathbf{b} \leftarrow_{\mathsf{R}} \mathsf{DDH}$, $\mathbf{b}^\perp \leftarrow_{\mathsf{R}} \mathbb{Z}_p^2$ s.t. $\mathbf{b}^\top \mathbf{b}^\perp = 0$, $\mathbf{k} \leftarrow_{\mathsf{R}} \{0,1\}^\ell$.

For all $i \in [\lambda]$, $b \in \{0,1\}$, $\mathbf{W}_{i,b} \leftarrow_{\mathsf{R}} \mathbb{Z}_p^{2\times\ell}$. $\mathsf{mpk} := (\mathcal{PG}, [\mathbf{a}]_1, \{[\mathbf{W}_{i,b}\mathbf{a}]_1, [\mathbf{W}_{i,b}^\top \mathbf{b}]_2\}_{i\in[\lambda], b\in\{0,1\}}, [\mathbf{k}^\top \mathbf{a}]_T)$

$b' \leftarrow_{\mathsf{R}} \mathcal{A}^{\mathsf{O}_{\mathsf{Enc}}(\cdot,\cdot), \mathsf{O}_{\mathsf{KeyGen}}(\cdot)}(\mathsf{mpk})$

Return 1 if $b' = b$ and identities queried to $\mathsf{O}_{\mathsf{Enc}}$ are distinct from identities queried to $\mathsf{O}_{\mathsf{KeyGen}}$.

$\mathsf{O}_{\mathsf{Enc}}(\mathsf{id} \in \{0,1\}^\ell, \mathbf{w} \in \mathbb{Z}_p^\ell, [m]_T \in \mathbb{G}_T)$:

$r \leftarrow_{\mathsf{R}} \mathbb{Z}_p$, $[\mathbf{c}]_1 := [\mathbf{a}_0 r]_1$, $\boxed{[\mathbf{c}]_1 := [\mathbf{a}_{\mathsf{id}_i} r]_1}$

$\mathbf{W}_{\mathsf{id}} := (\sum_{j\in[\lambda]} \mathbf{W}_{j,\mathsf{id}_j}) + \mathbf{b}^\perp(\mathbf{A}^\perp \mathsf{RF}_{i-1}(\mathsf{id}))^\top$

$\mathbf{W}_{\mathsf{id}} := (\sum_{j\in[\lambda]} \mathbf{W}_{j,\mathsf{id}_j}) + \mathbf{b}^\perp(\mathbf{A}^\perp \mathsf{RF}_{i}(\mathsf{id}))^\top$ (dotted frame)

$\mathsf{ct} := ([\mathbf{c}]_1, [\mathbf{W}_{\mathsf{id}}\mathbf{c}]_1, [\mathbf{k}^\top \mathbf{c} + \mathbf{k}^\top \mathbf{w} + m]_T)$

$\mathsf{O}_{\mathsf{KeyGen}}(\mathsf{id} \in \{0,1\}^\lambda)$:

$\mathbf{k}_0 := \mathbf{k}$, $\mathbf{k}_1 := \frac{\mathbf{k}^\top \mathbf{a}}{\|\mathbf{a}\|_2^2} \cdot \mathbf{a}$

$\mathbf{W}_{\mathsf{id}} := (\sum_{j\in[\lambda]} \mathbf{W}_{j,\mathsf{id}_j}) + \mathbf{b}^\perp(\mathbf{A}^\perp \mathsf{RF}_{i-1}(\mathsf{id}))^\top$

$\mathbf{W}_{\mathsf{id}} := (\sum_{j\in[\lambda]} \mathbf{W}_{j,\mathsf{id}_j}) + \mathbf{b}^\perp(\mathbf{A}^\perp \mathsf{RF}_{i}(\mathsf{id}))^\top$ (dotted frame)

$\mathbf{d} \leftarrow_{\mathsf{R}} \mathbb{Z}_p^2$, return $\mathsf{sk}_{\mathsf{id}} := ([\mathbf{d}]_2, [\mathbf{k}_b + \mathbf{W}_{\mathsf{id}}^\top \mathbf{d}]_2)$.

Fig. 10. Games for the proof of Lemma 3. In each procedure, the components inside a solid (dotted) frame are only present in the games marked by a solid (dotted) frame. Here, for all $i \in [\lambda]$, $\mathsf{RF}_i : \{0,1\}^\lambda \to \mathbb{Z}_p^{\ell-1}$ denotes a random function that only reads the first i'th bits of its input, and that is computed on the fly.

form $([\mathbf{u}]_1, [\mathbf{k}^\top(\mathbf{u}+\mathbf{w})]_T + [m]_T$ with $[\mathbf{u}]_1 \leftarrow_{\mathsf{R}} \mathbb{G}_1^\ell$, is identically distributed to $([\mathbf{u}-\mathbf{w}]_1, [\mathbf{k}^\top \mathbf{u}]_T + [m]_T)$. That is, we can remove the dependence of the message on the key $\mathbf{k}$ via a statistical argument. At this point, the proof in [BHHO08] relies on the DDH assumption on $[\mathbf{a}]_1$. Namely, the ciphertexts are switched back to normal (as opposed to semi-functional), then a hybrid argument goes over each ciphertext one by one, switching it to semi-functional and using a statistical argument (the Left Over Hash lemma to extract the entropy from $\mathbf{k} \leftarrow_{\mathsf{R}} \{0,1\}^\ell$ and masks the plaintext). However, we cannot use DDH on $[\mathbf{a}]_1$, since the normal component of the master secret key is of the form $\mathsf{msk}_{\mathsf{N}} := \frac{\mathbf{k}^\top \mathbf{a}}{\|\mathbf{a}\|_2^2} \cdot \mathbf{a}$. This value is necessary to generate the user secret keys (see Property 2), and it is not clear how to generate $[\mathsf{msk}_{\mathsf{N}}]_T$ from $[\mathbf{a}]_1$, which prevents to use DDH with respect to $[\mathbf{a}]_1$. Instead, we switch the challenge ciphertexts from $([\mathbf{u}-\mathbf{w}]_1, [\mathbf{k}^\top \mathbf{u}]_T + [m]_T)$ to $([\mathbf{b}s-\mathbf{w}]_1, [\mathbf{k}^\top \mathbf{b}s]_T + [m]_T$, for $s \leftarrow_{\mathsf{R}} \mathbb{Z}_p$, which relies on the DDH assumption with respect to a public vector $[\mathbf{b}]_1 \leftarrow_R \mathbb{G}_1^\ell$ that is independent of $\mathbf{a}$. The rest of the proof is similar to that [BHHO08]. It is given in Lemma 4.

Lemma 4 (Property 3, KDM security). *The PKE from Fig. 6 satisfies Property 3. Namely, for any PPT adversary $\mathcal{A}$, the advantage $\mathsf{Adv}^{\mathsf{KDM}}_{\mathsf{PKE},\mathcal{A}}(\lambda)$ is a negligible function of λ.*

Proof. The proof goes over a series of hybrid games, where for each game G, we denote by $\mathsf{Adv}_{\mathcal{A}}(\mathsf{G})$ the advantage of PPT adversary $\mathcal{A}$ in game G. We start with G_0, which is the security game defined in Property 3. In that game, $\mathcal{A}$ receives $\mathsf{pk} := (\mathcal{PG}, [\mathbf{a}]_1, [\mathbf{k}^\top \mathbf{a}]_T)$ and $[\mathsf{msk}_\mathsf{N}]_T$. Recall that $\mathsf{msk} := [\mathbf{k}]_T$, with $\mathbf{k} := \mathsf{msk}_\mathsf{N} + \mathsf{msk}_\mathsf{SF}$, where msk_N and msk_SF are the projections of $\mathbf{k}$ onto $\mathbf{a}$ and $\mathbf{A}^\perp$, respectively; $\mathbf{a} \leftarrow_R \mathbb{Z}_p^\ell$, and $\mathbf{A}^\perp \leftarrow_R \mathbb{Z}_p^{\ell \times (\ell-1)}$ such that $\mathbf{a}^\top \mathbf{A}^\perp = \mathbf{0}$. For any $\mathbf{w} \in \mathbb{Z}_p^\ell$, $[m]_T \in \mathbb{G}_T$, the oracle $\mathsf{O}_{\mathsf{Enc}}(\mathbf{w}, [m]_T)$ sets $[m_0]_T := [m]_T$, $[m_1]_T \leftarrow_R \mathbb{G}_T$, and returns $\widetilde{\mathsf{Enc}}(\mathsf{sk}, \mathsf{pk}, [\mathbf{k}^\top \mathbf{w}]_T + [m_b]_T)$, where $b \leftarrow_R \{0,1\}$ is chosen by the experiment.

Game G_1. We switch the challenge ciphertexts from $\widetilde{\mathsf{Enc}}(\mathsf{sk}, \mathsf{pk}, [\mathbf{k}^\top \mathbf{w}]_T + [m_b]_T) := ([\mathbf{u}]_1, [\mathbf{k}^\top \mathbf{u}]_T + [\mathbf{k}^\top \mathbf{w} + m_b]_T)$ with $[\mathbf{u}]_1 \leftarrow_R \mathbb{G}_1^\ell$ in game G_0 to $([\mathbf{u} - \mathbf{w}]_1, [\mathbf{k}^\top \mathbf{u}]_T + [m_b]_T)$ in game G_1. Doing so, we remove the dependence of the encrypted messages on $\mathbf{k}$. We show that the two games are identically distributed, so

$$\mathsf{Adv}_{\mathcal{A}}(\mathsf{G}_0) = \mathsf{Adv}_{\mathcal{A}}(\mathsf{G}_1).$$

We use the fact that for any $\mathbf{w} \in \mathbb{Z}_p$, the following distributions are identical:

$$\mathbf{u} \text{ and } \mathbf{u} - \mathbf{w},$$

where $\mathbf{u} \leftarrow_R \mathbb{Z}_p^\ell$. The leftmost distribution corresponds to the game G_0, whereas the rightmost distribution corresponds to the game G_1.

Game G_2. We switch the challenge ciphertexts to $([\mathbf{b}s - \mathbf{w}]_1, [\mathbf{k}^\top \mathbf{b}s]_T + [m_b]_T)$ where $s \leftarrow_R \mathbb{Z}_p$, and $\mathbf{b} \leftarrow_R \mathbb{Z}_p^\ell$, independent of $\mathbf{a}$ used in the public key and in msk_N. Namely, we build a PPT adversary $\mathcal{B}$ such that:

$$|\mathsf{Adv}_{\mathcal{A}}(\mathsf{G}_1) - \mathsf{Adv}_{\mathcal{A}}(\mathsf{G}_2)| \leq \mathsf{Adv}^{\ell, Q\text{-}\mathsf{DDH}}_{\mathbb{G}_1, \mathcal{B}}(\lambda).$$

By Lemma 1, the latter advantage is negligible by the DDH assumption in $\mathbb{G}_1$.

Upon receiving an (ℓ, Q)-fold DDH challenge $([\mathbf{b}]_1, \{[\mathbf{z}_i]_1\}_{i \in [Q]})$, $\mathcal{B}$ samples $b \leftarrow_R \{0,1\}$, $\mathbf{a} \leftarrow_R \mathbb{Z}_p^\ell$, $\mathbf{k} \leftarrow_R \{0,1\}^\ell$, sets $\mathsf{pk} := ([\mathbf{a}]_1, [\mathbf{k}^\top \mathbf{a}]_T)$, $\mathsf{msk}_\mathsf{N} := \frac{\mathbf{k}^\top \mathbf{a}}{\|\mathbf{a}\|_2^2} \cdot \mathbf{a}$, and returns $(\mathsf{pk}, \mathsf{msk}_\mathsf{N})$ to $\mathcal{A}$. On the i'th query $\mathsf{O}_{\mathsf{Enc}}(\mathbf{w}, [m]_T)$, $\mathcal{B}$ computes $[m_0]_T := [m]_T$, $[m_1]_T \leftarrow_R \mathbb{G}_T$, and returns $([\mathbf{z}_i - \mathbf{w}]_1, [\mathbf{k}^\top \mathbf{z}_i + m_b]_T)$ to $\mathcal{A}$.

Game G_3. We switch the challenge ciphertexts to $([\mathbf{b}s - \mathbf{w}]_1, [\gamma s]_T + [m_b]_T)$ where $s \leftarrow_R \mathbb{Z}_p$, and $\mathbf{b} \leftarrow_R \mathbb{Z}_p^\ell$, $\gamma \leftarrow_R \mathbb{Z}_p$ independent of $\mathbf{a}$ used in the public key and in $\mathsf{msk_N}$. We show that the games G_2 and G_3 are statistically close, using the left over hash lemma [ILL89] recalled in Lemma 2, which implies that $(\mathbf{a}, \mathbf{b}, \mathbf{k}^\top\mathbf{a}, \mathbf{k}^\top\mathbf{b})$ is statistically close (within statistical distance $2^{-\lambda}$) from $(\mathbf{a}, \mathbf{b}, \mathbf{k}^\top\mathbf{a}, \gamma)$, where $\gamma \leftarrow_{\mathsf{R}} \mathbb{Z}_p$. The first distribution corresponds to the distribution of the game G_2, whereas the second distribution corresponds to the game G_3. Note that pk and $\mathsf{msk_N}$ can be computed from $(\mathbf{a}, \mathbf{k}^\top\mathbf{a})$. Thus, we have

$$|\mathsf{Adv}_{\mathcal{A}}(\mathsf{G}_2) - \mathsf{Adv}_{\mathcal{A}}(\mathsf{G}_3)| \leq 2^{-\lambda}.$$

Game G_4. We change all the messages in the challenge ciphertexts to uniformly random, regardless of the random bit $b \leftarrow_{\mathsf{R}} \{0,1\}$. Namely, in game G_4, $\mathsf{O}_{\mathsf{Enc}}(\mathbf{w}, [m]_T)$, returns $([\mathbf{b}s]_1, [r]_T)$, where $[r]_T \leftarrow_{\mathsf{R}} \mathbb{G}_T$ and $s \leftarrow_{\mathsf{R}} \mathbb{Z}_p$ are sampled freshly for each query to $\mathsf{O}_{\mathsf{Enc}}$. Clearly:

$$\mathsf{Adv}_{\mathcal{A}}(\mathsf{G}_4) = 0.$$

To prove that game G_4 is computationally indistinguishable from G_3, we use the DDH assumption in $\mathbb{G}_1$ to switch $([s]_1, [\gamma s]_T)$ to $([s]_1, [r]_T)$. Namely, we build a PPT adversary $\mathcal{B}_3$ such that:

$$|\mathsf{Adv}_{\mathcal{A}}(\mathsf{G}_3) - \mathsf{Adv}_{\mathcal{A}}(\mathsf{G}_4)| \leq \mathsf{Adv}_{\mathbb{G}_1,\mathcal{B}_3}^{1,Q_{\mathsf{Enc}}\text{-}\mathsf{DDH}}(\lambda),$$

where Q_{Enc} denotes the number of queries to $\mathsf{O}_{\mathsf{Enc}}$.

Upon receiving a $1, Q_{\mathsf{Enc}}$-fold DDH challenge $\{[s_i]_1, [z_i]_1\}_{i \in [Q_{\mathsf{Enc}}]}$), $\mathcal{B}_3$ samples $b \leftarrow_{\mathsf{R}} \{0,1\}$, $\mathbf{a}, \mathbf{b} \leftarrow_{\mathsf{R}} \mathbb{Z}_p^\ell$, $\mathbf{k} \leftarrow_{\mathsf{R}} \{0,1\}^\ell$, thanks to which it can compute mpk, $\mathsf{msk_N}$, which it forwards to $\mathcal{A}$. On the i'th query of $\mathcal{A}$ to $\mathsf{O}_{\mathsf{Enc}}(\mathsf{id}, \mathbf{w}, [m]_T)$, $\mathcal{B}_3$ sets $[m_0]_T := [m]_T$, $[m_1]_T \leftarrow_{\mathsf{R}} \mathbb{G}_T$, and returns $([\mathbf{b}s_i]_1, [z_i]_T + [m_b]_T)$ to $\mathcal{A}$. When $[z_i]_1$ is of the form $[\gamma s_i]_1$, $\mathcal{B}_3$ simulates the game G_3, whereas it simulates the game G_4 when $[z_i]_1 \leftarrow_{\mathsf{R}} \mathbb{G}_1$. □

References

[ACPS09] Applebaum, B., Cash, D., Peikert, C., Sahai, A.: Fast cryptographic primitives and circular-secure encryption based on hard learning problems. In: Halevi, S. (ed.) CRYPTO 2009. LNCS, vol. 5677, pp. 595–618. Springer, Heidelberg (2009). https://doi.org/10.1007/978-3-642-03356-8_35

[AHY15] Attrapadung, N., Hanaoka, G., Yamada, S.: A framework for identity-based encryption with almost tight security. In: Iwata, T., Cheon, J.H. (eds.) ASIACRYPT 2015, Part I. LNCS, vol. 9452, pp. 521–549. Springer, Heidelberg (2015). https://doi.org/10.1007/978-3-662-48797-6_22

[AP12] Alperin-Sheriff, J., Peikert, C.: Circular and KDM security for identity-based encryption. In: Fischlin, M., Buchmann, J., Manulis, M. (eds.) PKC 2012. LNCS, vol. 7293, pp. 334–352. Springer, Heidelberg (2012). https://doi.org/10.1007/978-3-642-30057-8_20

[App11] Applebaum, B.: Key-dependent message security: generic amplification and completeness. In: Paterson, K.G. (ed.) EUROCRYPT 2011. LNCS, vol. 6632, pp. 527–546. Springer, Heidelberg (2011). https://doi.org/10.1007/978-3-642-20465-4_29

[BG10] Brakerski, Z., Goldwasser, S.: Circular and leakage resilient public-key encryption under subgroup indistinguishability. In: Rabin, T. (ed.) CRYPTO 2010. LNCS, vol. 6223, pp. 1–20. Springer, Heidelberg (2010). https://doi.org/10.1007/978-3-642-14623-7_1

[BGI16] Boyle, E., Gilboa, N., Ishai, Y.: Breaking the circuit size barrier for secure computation under DDH. In: Robshaw, M., Katz, J. (eds.) CRYPTO 2016, Part I. LNCS, vol. 9814, pp. 509–539. Springer, Heidelberg (2016). https://doi.org/10.1007/978-3-662-53018-4_19

[BGK11] Brakerski, Z., Goldwasser, S., Kalai, Y.T.: Black-box circular-secure encryption beyond affine functions. In: Ishai, Y. (ed.) TCC 2011. LNCS, vol. 6597, pp. 201–218. Springer, Heidelberg (2011). https://doi.org/10.1007/978-3-642-19571-6_13

[BHHI10] Barak, B., Haitner, I., Hofheinz, D., Ishai, Y.: Bounded key-dependent message security. In: Gilbert, H. (ed.) EUROCRYPT 2010. LNCS, vol. 6110, pp. 423–444. Springer, Heidelberg (2010). https://doi.org/10.1007/978-3-642-13190-5_22

[BHHO08] Boneh, D., Halevi, S., Hamburg, M., Ostrovsky, R.: Circular-secure encryption from decision Diffie-Hellman. In: Wagner, D. (ed.) CRYPTO 2008. LNCS, vol. 5157, pp. 108–125. Springer, Heidelberg (2008). https://doi.org/10.1007/978-3-540-85174-5_7

[BKP14] Blazy, O., Kiltz, E., Pan, J.: (Hierarchical) identity-based encryption from affine message authentication. In: Garay, J.A., Gennaro, R. (eds.) CRYPTO 2014, Part I. LNCS, vol. 8616, pp. 408–425. Springer, Heidelberg (2014). https://doi.org/10.1007/978-3-662-44371-2_23

[BLSV18] Brakerski, Z., Lombardi, A., Segev, G., Vaikuntanathan, V.: Anonymous IBE, leakage resilience and circular security from new assumptions. In: Nielsen, J.B., Rijmen, V. (eds.) EUROCRYPT 2018, Part I. LNCS, vol. 10820, pp. 535–564. Springer, Cham (2018). https://doi.org/10.1007/978-3-319-78381-9_20

[BRS03] Black, J., Rogaway, P., Shrimpton, T.: Encryption-scheme security in the presence of key-dependent messages. In: Nyberg, K., Heys, H. (eds.) SAC 2002. LNCS, vol. 2595, pp. 62–75. Springer, Heidelberg (2003). https://doi.org/10.1007/3-540-36492-7_6

[CCS09] Camenisch, J., Chandran, N., Shoup, V.: A public key encryption scheme secure against key dependent chosen plaintext and adaptive chosen ciphertext attacks. In: Joux, A. (ed.) EUROCRYPT 2009. LNCS, vol. 5479, pp. 351–368. Springer, Heidelberg (2009). https://doi.org/10.1007/978-3-642-01001-9_20

[CGW15] Chen, J., Gay, R., Wee, H.: Improved dual system ABE in prime-order groups via predicate encodings. In: Oswald, E., Fischlin, M. (eds.) EUROCRYPT 2015, Part II. LNCS, vol. 9057, pp. 595–624. Springer, Heidelberg (2015). https://doi.org/10.1007/978-3-662-46803-6_20

[CHK04] Canetti, R., Halevi, S., Katz, J.: Chosen-ciphertext security from identity-based encryption. In: Cachin, C., Camenisch, J.L. (eds.) EUROCRYPT 2004. LNCS, vol. 3027, pp. 207–222. Springer, Heidelberg (2004). https://doi.org/10.1007/978-3-540-24676-3_13

[CW13] Chen, J., Wee, H.: Fully, (almost) tightly secure IBE and dual system groups. In: Canetti, R., Garay, J.A. (eds.) CRYPTO 2013, Part II. LNCS, vol. 8043, pp. 435–460. Springer, Heidelberg (2013). https://doi.org/10.1007/978-3-642-40084-1_25

[Dam92] Damgård, I.: Towards practical public key systems secure against chosen ciphertext attacks. In: Feigenbaum, J. (ed.) CRYPTO 1991. LNCS, vol. 576, pp. 445–456. Springer, Heidelberg (1992). https://doi.org/10.1007/3-540-46766-1_36

[DG17a] Döttling, N., Garg, S.: From selective ibe to full IBE and selective HIBE. In: Kalai, Y., Reyzin, L. (eds.) TCC 2017, Part I. LNCS, vol. 10677, pp. 372–408. Springer, Cham (2017). https://doi.org/10.1007/978-3-319-70500-2_13

[DG17b] Döttling, N., Garg, S.: Identity-based encryption from the Diffie-Hellman assumption. In: Katz, J., Shacham, H. (eds.) CRYPTO 2017, Part I. LNCS, vol. 10401, pp. 537–569. Springer, Cham (2017). https://doi.org/10.1007/978-3-319-63688-7_18

[GDCC16] Gong, J., Dong, X., Chen, J., Cao, Z.: Efficient IBE with tight reduction to standard assumption in the multi-challenge setting. In: Cheon, J.H., Takagi, T. (eds.) ASIACRYPT 2016, Part II. LNCS, vol. 10032, pp. 624–654. Springer, Heidelberg (2016). https://doi.org/10.1007/978-3-662-53890-6_21

[Gen09] Gentry, C.: Fully homomorphic encryption using ideal lattices. In: 41st ACM STOC, pp. 169–178. ACM Press, May/June (2009)

[GHKW16] Gay, R., Hofheinz, D., Kiltz, E., Wee, H.: Tightly CCA-secure encryption without pairings. In: Fischlin, M., Coron, J.-S. (eds.) EUROCRYPT 2016, Part I. LNCS, vol. 9665, pp. 1–27. Springer, Heidelberg (2016). https://doi.org/10.1007/978-3-662-49890-3_1

[GHV12] Galindo, D., Herranz, J., Villar, J.: Identity-based encryption with master key-dependent message security and leakage-resilience. In: Foresti, S., Yung, M., Martinelli, F. (eds.) ESORICS 2012. LNCS, vol. 7459, pp. 627–642. Springer, Heidelberg (2012). https://doi.org/10.1007/978-3-642-33167-1_36

[HKS15] Hofheinz, D., Koch, J., Striecks, C.: Identity-based encryption with (almost) tight security in the multi-instance, multi-ciphertext setting. In: Katz, J. (ed.) PKC 2015. LNCS, vol. 9020, pp. 799–822. Springer, Heidelberg (2015). https://doi.org/10.1007/978-3-662-46447-2_36

[Hof13] Hofheinz, D.: Circular chosen-ciphertext security with compact ciphertexts. In: Johansson, T., Nguyen, P.Q. (eds.) EUROCRYPT 2013. LNCS, vol. 7881, pp. 520–536. Springer, Heidelberg (2013). https://doi.org/10.1007/978-3-642-38348-9_31

[ILL89] Impagliazzo, R., Levin, L.A., Luby, M.: Pseudo-random generation from one-way functions (extended abstracts). In: 21st ACM STOC, pp. 12–24. ACM Press, May 1989

[KM19] Kitagawa, F., Matsuda, T.: CPA-to-CCA transformation for KDM security. In: Hofheinz, D., Rosen, A. (eds.) TCC 2019, Part II. LNCS, vol. 11892, pp. 118–148. Springer, Cham (2019). https://doi.org/10.1007/978-3-030-36033-7_5

[KMT19] Kitagawa, F., Matsuda, T., Tanaka, K.: CCA security and trapdoor functions via key-dependent-message security. In: Boldyreva, A., Micciancio, D. (eds.) CRYPTO 2019, Part III. LNCS, vol. 11694, pp. 33–64. Springer, Cham (2019). https://doi.org/10.1007/978-3-030-26954-8_2

[KT18] Kitagawa, F., Tanaka, K.: A framework for achieving KDM-CCA secure public-key encryption. In: Peyrin, T., Galbraith, S. (eds.) ASIACRYPT 2018, Part II. LNCS, vol. 11273, pp. 127–157. Springer, Cham (2018). https://doi.org/10.1007/978-3-030-03329-3_5

[LQR+19] Lombardi, A., Quach, W., Rothblum, R.D., Wichs, D., Wu, D.J.: New constructions of reusable designated-verifier NIZKs. In: Boldyreva, A., Micciancio, D. (eds.) CRYPTO 2019, Part III. LNCS, vol. 11694, pp. 670–700. Springer, Cham (2019). https://doi.org/10.1007/978-3-030-26954-8_22

[Wat09] Waters, B.: Dual system encryption: realizing fully secure IBE and HIBE under simple assumptions. In: Halevi, S. (ed.) CRYPTO 2009. LNCS, vol. 5677, pp. 619–636. Springer, Heidelberg (2009). https://doi.org/10.1007/978-3-642-03356-8_36

[Wee16] Wee, H.: KDM-security via homomorphic smooth projective hashing. In: Cheng, C.-M., Chung, K.-M., Persiano, G., Yang, B.-Y. (eds.) PKC 2016, Part II. LNCS, vol. 9615, pp. 159–179. Springer, Heidelberg (2016). https://doi.org/10.1007/978-3-662-49387-8_7

Hierarchical Identity-Based Encryption with Tight Multi-challenge Security

Roman Langrehr[1] and Jiaxin Pan[2(✉)]

[1] ETH Zurich, Zurich, Switzerland
roman.langrehr@inf.ethz.ch
[2] Department of Mathematical Sciences,
NTNU – Norwegian University of Science and Technology, Trondheim, Norway
jiaxin.pan@ntnu.no

Abstract. We construct the *first* hierarchical identity-based encryption (HIBE) scheme with tight adaptive security in the multi-challenge setting, where adversaries are allowed to ask for ciphertexts for multiple adaptively chosen identities. Technically, we develop a novel technique that can tightly introduce randomness into user secret keys for hierarchical identities in the multi-challenge setting, which cannot be easily achieved by the existing techniques for tightly multi-challenge secure IBE.

In contrast to the previous constructions, the security of our scheme is independent of the number of user secret key queries and that of challenge ciphertext queries. We prove the tight security of our scheme based on the Matrix Decisional Diffie-Hellman Assumption, which is an abstraction of standard and simple decisional Diffie-Hellman assumptions, such as the k-Linear and SXDH assumptions.

Finally, we also extend our ideas to achieve tight chosen-ciphertext security and anonymity, respectively. These security notions for HIBE have not been tightly achieved in the multi-challenge setting before.

Keywords: Hierarchical identity-based encryption · Tight security · Multi-challenge security · Chosen-ciphertext security · Anonymity

1 Introduction

Tight Reductions. In public-key cryptography, most of the schemes are constructed with reduction-based security proofs. A security reduction efficiently maps an adversary $\mathcal{A}$ against the security of a scheme with success probability $\varepsilon_{\mathcal{A}}$ to a solver $\mathcal{B}$ that breaks the hardness of a suitable computational problem with success probability $\varepsilon_{\mathcal{B}}$. We call the quotient $\ell := \varepsilon_{\mathcal{A}}/\varepsilon_{\mathcal{B}}$ the security loss of a reduction, which can be viewed as a quantitative measurement of the distance between the security of the scheme and the hardness of the problem. Ideally, we want (1) the underlying problem to be standard and well-established, (2) the security notion to be realistic, and (3) the security of the scheme to be as close to the hardness of the problem as possible, namely, ℓ to be as close to 1 as possible.

R. Langrehr—Parts of the work were done at Karlsruhe Institute of Technology, Karlsruhe, Germany.

A. Kiayias et al. (Eds.): PKC 2020, LNCS 12110, pp. 153–183, 2020.
https://doi.org/10.1007/978-3-030-45374-9_6

We consider a reduction *tight* if ℓ is a small constant and the running time of $\mathcal{B}$ is approximately the same as that of $\mathcal{A}$. Many existing works [8,11–13] consider a notion of tightness called "almost tight security". Different to the (full) tightness, almost tight security allows the security loss ℓ to be a small polynomial, which is usually a linear function of the security parameter, but still independent of the size of $\mathcal{A}$. We do not distinguish these two notions, but we are precise about the security loss in our comparison tables and security proofs.

Tight reductions are not only theoretically interesting but also beneficial in practice. A tight reduction enables us to give universal key-length recommendations that are independent of the size of an application and shorter than the non-tight ones. This is, in particular, useful in the setting where the envisioned size of an application cannot be reasonably bounded a priori. As a result of that, many recent works have been pursuing efficient tightly secure cryptographic schemes, including digital signature [13,21,26], public-key encryption [11,12,20], identity-based encryption [5,8] schemes, and authenticated key exchange protocols [15].

HIBE MEETS TIGHT SECURITY. In this paper, we focus on hierarchical identity-based encryption (HIBE) schemes [14,24]. In an L-level HIBE, an identity is a vector of maximal L identities. It is considered to be more difficult to construct HIBE than IBE and PKE since an HIBE scheme provides more functionalities. For instance, an L-level HIBE scheme allows a user at level $\alpha < L$ to delegate a secret key for its descendants at level $\alpha' > \alpha$.

Constructing tightly secure HIBE appears to be much more challenging. The first tightly secure IBE from standard assumptions was constructed in 2013 [8], while the first tightly secure HIBE was just proposed very recently [28]. We believe that it is not a coincidence. Firstly, Lewko and Waters [32] showed the potential difficulty of constructing tightly secure HIBE. More precisely, they proved that there is a (relatively) large class of HIBE schemes that cannot be tightly proven secure. Secondly, Blazy, Kiltz, and Pan (BKP) [5] made the first attempt to bypass the aforementioned impossibility result. Unfortunately, it has been found that the BKP proof strategy is insufficient for the tight adaptive security of HIBE (cf. [6] and Appendix A of [29]). Adaptive security allows an adversary $\mathcal{A}$ to adaptively choose a challenge identity $\mathsf{id}^\star$ after it sees the master public key and asks for polynomial many user secret keys for identities chosen by $\mathcal{A}$.

Very recently, Langrehr and Pan (LP) proposed the first tightly secure HIBE based on standard assumptions. Their proof strategy improves the one of BKP in the sense that the LP strategy can tightly introduce (suitable) randomness in user secret keys for identities with flexible lengths. Inherently, the LP proof strategy seems to only work tightly in the *single-challenge* setting, where an adversary is restricted to ask for a ciphertext for at most one challenge identity.

FROM SINGLE- TO MULTI-CHALLENGE SECURITY. In the real world, an adversary can learn ciphertexts of multiple challenge identities. This is captured by the more realistic multi-challenge security. We note that single-challenge security implies multi-challenge security via a straightforward, but non-tight reduction. This is mainly the reason why the security of many (H)IBE schemes (e.g. [5,28,30,31,35]) is analyzed in this simple single-challenge setting.

However, this straightforward "single- to multi-challenge" reduction loses a relatively large polynomial factor. Namely, if an adversary makes Q_c many queries for challenge ciphertexts, then the overall security loses a factor of Q_c. This defeats the purpose of establishing tight reductions for the overall scheme in a more realistic setting.

OUR GOAL: HIBE WITH TIGHT MULTI-CHALLENGE SECURITY. We aim at constructing tightly secure HIBE schemes in the more realistic multi-challenge setting. We note that there exist several techniques in constructing tightly multi-challenge secure IBE schemes (for instance [17,18,22,23]) in composite- or prime-order pairing groups. However, as already observed by the LP paper, these techniques cannot be easily used in the HIBE setting. Thus, to achieve our goal, it requires us to develop a new technique for tight multi-challenge security that is useful for HIBE schemes.

1.1 Our Contribution

We construct the *first* tightly chosen-plaintext secure HIBE schemes in the multi-challenge setting. The main novelty of this paper is a new randomization technique that enables us to randomize user secret keys for hierarchical identities in the multi-challenge setting. We highlight that our technique improves the existing techniques [17,18,22,23] for tightly multi-challenge secure IBE schemes in the sense that ours can handle randomization for identities with flexible lengths. We postpone the detailed comparison of these techniques in Sect. 1.3.

Following the "MAC-to-(H)IBE" framework [5,28], we capture our core technique with the notion of affine MACs with levels (which was firstly proposed in [28]) in the multi-challenge setting. By using prime-order pairings and the Matrix Decisional Diffie-Hellman (MDDH) assumption [10], we compile any of these MAC schemes to an HIBE tightly in the multi-challenge setting. We have two main constructions of the affine MACs, MAC_1 and MAC_2, and they give us two HIBE with different advantages and disadvantages, respectively: Considering identity space $\mathcal{ID} := (\{0,1\}^n)^{\leq L}$, our first scheme has constant amount of group elements in the ciphertext, but $\mathbf{O}(nL)$ many elements in the user secret key; and our second scheme has shorter user secret key that contains $\mathbf{O}(L)$ many elements, but its ciphertext contains $\mathbf{O}(L)$ many elements. Both schemes have security loss $\mathbf{O}(n \cdot L^2)$ and independent of the numbers of challenge ciphertext queries and user secret key queries. Table 1 compares our schemes with the existing HIBE schemes in prime-order pairing groups.

We extend our main results in the following directions by using known techniques:

ANONYMITY. Additionally, the first construction of our MACs, MAC_1, has tight anonymity. By using the anonymity-preserving transformation of [5], we construct the *first* tightly secure, anonymous HIBE scheme in the multi-challenge setting. An (H)IBE scheme is anonymous if its challenge ciphertexts hide the corresponding identities. An application of anonymous HIBE is PKE with keyword search [1].

Table 1. Comparison of HIBEs in prime-order pairing groups with adaptive security in the standard model based on static assumptions. The highlighted rows are from this paper. The schemes with $\mathcal{H}$ in the superscript are obtained by hashing the identities as described in the full version of [28].
The hierarchical identity space is $(\{0,1\}^n)^{\leq L}$, and γ is the bit length of the range of a collision-resistant hash function. '$|\mathsf{mpk}|$,' '$|\mathsf{usk}|$,' and '$|\mathsf{C}|$' stand for the size of the master public key, a user secret key and a ciphertext, respectively. We count the number of group elements in $\mathbb{G}_1, \mathbb{G}_2$, and $\mathbb{G}_T$. For a scheme that works in symmetric pairing groups, we write $\mathbb{G}(:= \mathbb{G}_1 = \mathbb{G}_2)$. The schemes that work in asymmetric pairing groups can be instantiated with SXDH = 1-LIN. In the '$|\mathsf{usk}|$' and '$|\mathsf{C}|$' columns p stands for the hierarchy depth of the identity vector. In bounded HIBEs, L denotes the maximum hierarchy depth. In the security loss, Q_{e} denotes the number of user secret key queries by the adversary. The last but one column indicates whether the adversary is allowed to query multiple challenge ciphertexts (✓) or just one (✗). The last column shows the underlying security assumption.

Scheme	$\|\mathsf{mpk}\|$	$\|\mathsf{usk}\|$	$\|\mathsf{C}\|$	Loss	MC	Ass.
Wat05 [35]	$O(nL)\|\mathbb{G}\|$	$O(nL)\|\mathbb{G}\|$	$(1+p)\|\mathbb{G}\|$	$O(nQ_{\mathsf{e}})^L$	✗	DBDH
Wat09 [34]	$O(L)\|\mathbb{G}\|$	$O(p)(\|\mathbb{G}\|+\|\mathbb{Z}_q\|)$	$O(p)(\|\mathbb{G}\|+\|\mathbb{Z}_q\|)$	$O(Q_{\mathsf{e}})$	✗	2-LIN
Lew12 [30]	$60\|\mathbb{G}\|+2\|\mathbb{G}_T\|$	$(60+10p)\|\mathbb{G}\|$	$10p\|\mathbb{G}\|$	$O(Q_{\mathsf{e}}L)$	✗	2-LIN
CW13 [8]	$O(Lk^2)(\|\mathbb{G}_1\|+\|\mathbb{G}_2\|)$	$O(Lk)\|\mathbb{G}_2\|$	$(2k+2)\|\mathbb{G}_1\|$	$O(Q_{\mathsf{e}})$	✗	k-LIN
BKP14 [5]	$O(Lk^2)(\|\mathbb{G}_1\|+\|\mathbb{G}_2\|)$	$O(Lk)\|\mathbb{G}_2\|$	$(2k+2)\|\mathbb{G}_1\|$	$O(Q_{\mathsf{e}})$	✗	k-LIN
GCTC16 [16]	$(6k^2+12k)(\|\mathbb{G}_1\|+\|\mathbb{G}_2\|)$ $+(k+2)\|\mathbb{G}_T\|$	$((6k+12)\lceil p/3\rceil$ $-(k+2)p)\|\mathbb{G}_2\|$	$(3k+6)\lceil p/3\rceil\|\mathbb{G}_1\|$	$O(QL)$	✗	k-LIN
$\mathsf{LP19}_1$ [28]	$O(nL^2k^2)(\|\mathbb{G}_1\|+\|\mathbb{G}_2\|)$	$O(nL^2k)\|\mathbb{G}_2\|$	$(4k+1)\|\mathbb{G}_1\|$	$O(nL^2k)$	✗	k-LIN
$\mathsf{LP19}_1^{\mathcal{H}}$ [28]	$O(\gamma Lk^2)(\|\mathbb{G}_1\|+\|\mathbb{G}_2\|)$	$O(\gamma Lk)\|\mathbb{G}_2\|$	$(4k+1)\|\mathbb{G}_1\|$	$O(\gamma Lk)$	✗	k-LIN
$\mathsf{LP19}_2$ [28]	$O(nL^2k^2)(\|\mathbb{G}_1\|+\|\mathbb{G}_2\|)$	$(3kp+k+1)\|\mathbb{G}_2\|$	$(3kp+k+1)\|\mathbb{G}_1\|$	$O(nLk)$	✗	k-LIN
$\mathsf{LP19}_2^{\mathcal{H}}$ [28]	$O(\gamma Lk^2)(\|\mathbb{G}_1\|+\|\mathbb{G}_2\|)$	$(3kp+k+1)\|\mathbb{G}_2\|$	$(3kp+k+1)\|\mathbb{G}_1\|$	$O(\gamma k)$	✗	k-LIN
HIBKEM_1	$O(nL^2k^2)(\|\mathbb{G}_1\|+\|\mathbb{G}_2\|)$	$O(nL^2k)\|\mathbb{G}_2\|$	$5k\|\mathbb{G}_1\|$	$O(nL^2k)$	✓	k-LIN
$\mathsf{HIBKEM}_1^{\mathcal{H}}$	$O(\gamma Lk^2)(\|\mathbb{G}_1\|+\|\mathbb{G}_2\|)$	$O(\gamma Lk)\|\mathbb{G}_2\|$	$5k\|\mathbb{G}_1\|$	$O(\gamma Lk)$	✓	k-LIN
HIBKEM_2	$O(nL^2k^2)(\|\mathbb{G}_1\|+\|\mathbb{G}_2\|)$	$(3kp+2k)\|\mathbb{G}_2\|$	$(3kp+2k)\|\mathbb{G}_1\|$	$O(nLk)$	✓	k-LIN
$\mathsf{HIBKEM}_2^{\mathcal{H}}$	$O(\gamma Lk^2)(\|\mathbb{G}_1\|+\|\mathbb{G}_2\|)$	$(3kp+2k)\|\mathbb{G}_2\|$	$(3kp+2k)\|\mathbb{G}_1\|$	$O(\gamma k)$	✓	k-LIN

We note that it was unknown how to construct a tightly adaptively secure anonymous HIBE scheme even in the single-challenge setting.

CHOSEN-CIPHERTEXT SECURITY. We note that ciphertexts of our HIBE schemes have compatible structure to use Quasi-Adaptive Non-Interactive Zero-Knowledge (QANIZK) argument for linear subspace systems [2,22,25,27]. Similar to [22], we upgrade our schemes to chosen-ciphertext security by using any tightly unbounded simulation-sound QANIZK scheme. These schemes are the first tightly chosen-ciphertext secure HIBE schemes in the multi-challenge setting. Combining with the technique in the first extension, we also construct a tightly chosen-ciphertext secure and anonymous HIBE.

MORE (MINOR) EXTENSIONS. Additionally, our schemes have tight multi-instance security. In the multi-instance setting, an adversary can get multiple instances of the HIBE scheme. It is trivial that our HIBE schemes are tightly secure in this setting, since, given an instance of our HIBE, it can be easily rerandomized to get multiple instances from it.

In the full version of [28], they use a collision-resistant hash function to further improve the security loss and master public key size of their schemes. Here we can also do the same improvement.

These two extensions are rather minor and we skip the technical details here, but include them in Table 1 for a more complete comparison of different HIBE schemes.

1.2 Technical Details

We give an overview of our main technique in achieving tight adaptive security for HIBE in the multi-challenge setting. Here we restrict ourselves to chosen-plaintext security.

STARTING POINT: THE BKP FRAMEWORK. To set up the stage of our discussion, we recall the BKP framework [5], which transforms an algebraic MAC scheme to an IBE scheme in prime-order pairing groups. The algebraic MAC is called affine MAC, due to its affine structure. Their framework is an abstraction of the Chen-Wee (CW) IBE [8] and can also be viewed as an extension of the "MAC-to-Signature" framework by Bellare and Goldwasser (BG) [4] in the IBE context. In particular, the BKP framework can be viewed as a fine-grained reverse of the Naor transformation [7] on the BG signature scheme.

We give some informal ideas about how an affine MAC can be turned into an IBE. The master public key of an IBE, $\mathsf{pk} := \mathsf{Com}(\mathsf{sk}_{\mathsf{MAC}})$, is a commitment of the MAC secret key, $\mathsf{sk}_{\mathsf{MAC}}$. A user secret key $\mathsf{usk}[\mathsf{id}]$ of an identity id consists of a BG signature, namely, a MAC tag τ_{id} on the message id and a NIZK proof of the validity of τ_{id} w.r.t. the secret key committed in pk. The observation of BKP is that one can implement these commitments and NIZK proofs with the (tuned) Groth-Sahai proof system [19].

Due to the fact that the BKP MAC has affine structures, the NIZK verification involves only linear equations and can be randomized. Indeed, the BKP IBE ciphertext C_{id} can be viewed as a randomized linear combination of pk w.r.t. id. Implicitly, the decryption algorithm is a randomized NIZK verification of the validity of τ_{id} (from $\mathsf{usk}[\mathsf{id}]$): If τ_{id} is valid, then the ciphertext C_{id} can be correctly decrypted.

OBSTACLES IN ACHIEVING OUR GOAL WITH BKP. The BKP framework has a nice property that the security of the IBE scheme can be tightly reduced to the security of the MAC scheme. Thus, we can only focus on constructing tightly secure MAC, which is more fundamental. In particular, the BKP framework has a tightly secure MAC scheme $\mathsf{MAC}_{\mathsf{NR}}$ in the single-challenge setting under a standard assumption. $\mathsf{MAC}_{\mathsf{NR}}$ is implicitly in the CW IBE and borrows some idea from the Naor-Reingold PRF [33]. However, $\mathsf{MAC}_{\mathsf{NR}}$ has limitations that

(a) it can only be used to handle at most one IBE challenge ciphertext, and
(b) it cannot provide tight adaptive security for HIBE.

We recall $\mathsf{MAC_{NR}}$ and give more technical discussion about these two limitations.

Let $\mathbb{G}_2 := \langle P_2 \rangle$ be an additive prime-order group. We use the implicit notation $[x]_2 := xP_2$ as in [10]. $\mathsf{MAC_{NR}}$ chooses $\mathbf{B} \in \mathbb{Z}_q^{(k+1)\times k}$ according to the underlying assumption. $\mathbf{B}$ always has rank k and, for simplicity, we assume that the first k rows of $\mathbf{B}$, denoted by $\overline{\mathbf{B}}$, forms a full-rank square matrix. For message space $\mathcal{M} := \{0,1\}^n$, which is the same as the identity space of the resulting IBE, its secret key is chosen uniformly at random and has the form of

$$\mathsf{sk_{MAC}} := \left((\mathbf{x}_{i,b})_{1\le i\le n, b\in\{0,1\}}, x_0' \right) \in \left(\mathbb{Z}_q^{k\cdot 2}\right)^n \times \mathbb{Z}_q.$$

Its MAC tag $\tau := ([\mathbf{t}]_2, [u]_2)$ contains a random vector $[\mathbf{t}]_2$ and a message-dependent value $[u]_2$ in the form of

$$\begin{aligned} \mathbf{t} &= \overline{\mathbf{B}}\mathbf{s} \in \mathbb{Z}_q^k \qquad \text{for random } \mathbf{s} \in \mathbb{Z}_q^k \\ u &= \sum_i \mathbf{x}_{i,\mathsf{m}_i}^\top \mathbf{t} + x_0' \in \mathbb{Z}_q. \end{aligned} \tag{1}$$

Based on the MDDH assumption, $\mathsf{MAC_{NR}}$ is tightly pseudorandom against chosen-message attacks ($\mathsf{PR\text{-}CMA}$ security), which is a decisional variant of the standard existential unforgeability against chosen-message attacks ($\mathsf{EUF\text{-}CMA}$ security) for MAC schemes [9]. Essentially, the $\mathsf{PR\text{-}CMA}$ security of $\mathsf{MAC_{NR}}$ shows that $[u]_2$ is pseudorandom.

To understand the intuition of the BKP proof strategy, we consider the standard $\mathsf{EUF\text{-}CMA}$ security, where an adversary $\mathcal{A}$ can ask for polynomial many MAC tags $\tau_{\mathsf{m}} := ([\mathbf{t}_{\mathsf{m}}]_2, [u_{\mathsf{m}}]_2)$ on messages m of its adaptive choice and submit a forgery $\tau^\star := ([\mathbf{t}^\star]_2, [u^\star]_2)$ for *one single* verification. The MAC tag query is corresponding to the IBE user secret key query, and the verification query is related to the IBE challenge ciphertext query.

The overall proof strategy of $\mathsf{MAC_{NR}}$ is to gradually randomize all the u values in answering $\mathcal{A}$'s tag queries. During this process, the reduction must be able to compute $u^\star = \sum_i \mathbf{x}_{i,\mathsf{m}_i^\star}^\top \mathbf{t}^\star + x_0'$ for a fresh $\mathsf{m}^\star$, which is the main difficulty in the proof. To solve it, the BKP argument conceptually replace x_0' with a constant random function $\mathsf{RF}_0(\varepsilon)$. Then, by using the MDDH assumption, it develops a random function $\mathsf{RF}_{i+1} : \{0,1\}^{i+1} \to \mathbb{Z}_q$ from another random function $\mathsf{RF}_i : \{0,1\}^i \to \mathbb{Z}_q$ on-the-fly for some integer $0 \le i < n$. After n recursions, a random function $\mathsf{RF} : \{0,1\}^n \to \mathbb{Z}_q$ is developed and thus the security loss of $\mathsf{MAC_{NR}}$ is $\mathbf{O}(n)$. More precisely, in each step, the reduction guesses the $(i+1)$-th bit of $\mathsf{m}^\star$ as $b^\star \in \{0,1\}$ and defines the function RF_{i+1} as:

$$\mathsf{RF}_{i+1}(\mathsf{m}_{|i+1}) := \begin{cases} \mathsf{RF}_i(\mathsf{m}_{|i}) & (\text{if } \mathsf{m}_{i+1} = b^\star) \\ \mathsf{RF}_i(\mathsf{m}_{|i}) + R_{\mathsf{m}_{|i}} & (\text{if } \mathsf{m}_{i+1} = 1 - b^\star) \end{cases}, \tag{2}$$

where $\mathsf{m}_{|i}$ is the first i bits of m and $R_{\mathsf{m}_{|i}}$ is a random value from $\mathbb{Z}_q$ chosen for $\mathsf{m}_{|i}$. Alternatively, the BKP strategy can be viewed as gradually injecting randomness directly into x_0', during developing the random function above.

There are two important observations of this strategy, which lead to Limitations (a) and (b) above. These observations are in the proof step from Hybrid i (using RF_i) to Hybrid $(i+1)$ (using RF_{i+1}):

REASON FOR LIMITATION (a): In this step, the reduction embeds a MDDH problem instance in $[\mathbf{x}_{i+1,1-b^\star}]_2$ and chooses the other $\mathbf{x}_{j,b}$ in $\mathbb{Z}_q$. Thus, $\mathbf{x}_{i+1,1-b^\star}$ in $\mathbb{Z}_q$ is unknown to the reduction during this step, but $\mathbf{x}_{i+1,b^\star}$ is known in $\mathbb{Z}_q$ for verifying the forgery on a single $\mathsf{m}^\star$. However, this strategy cannot work tightly if there is more than one verification queries, which is required in the multi-challenge setting. For instance, after guessing $b^\star$, the reduction fails to answer two verification queries for challenge messages, 0^n and 1^n, respectively.

REASON FOR LIMITATION (b): RF_{i+1} defined via Eq. (2) is a random function for message spaces with fixed length based on the crucial fact that the outputs of RF_{i+1} and RF_i are not revealed at the same time. However, for hierarchical identity spaces, $\mathcal{ID} := (\{0,1\}^n)^{\leq L}$, it is not the case anymore.
As a concrete example, we consider the transition from Hybrids n to $(n+1)$. Via Eq. (2), $\mathsf{RF}_n(\mathsf{m}) = \mathsf{RF}_{n+1}(\mathsf{m}||b^\star)$ and adversaries can learn this by asking MAC tags for m and $\mathsf{m}||b^\star||\mathsf{m}'$ (where $\mathsf{m}' \in \{0,1\}^{n-1}$). Thus, the tags for these two message are not independent and we cannot continue the hybrid argument.

In order to solve our task, we need to develop new techniques to overcome both limitations described above. Our approach essentially has two main steps: In the first step, we target at tight multi-challenge security, and, at the same time, we are looking ahead and making it suitable for handling hierarchical identities; and, in the second step, we upgrade the technique developed in the first step to the HIBE setting.

STEP 1: NEW STRATEGY FOR TIGHT MULTI-CHALLENGE SECURITY. We call this randomization strategy subspace randomization, since it first increases the dimension of $\mathbf{t}$ in the tag so that there exist subspaces, and our crucial randomization happens in some of these subspaces. This subspace randomization is compatible with the independent randomization of Langrehr and Pan [28] and, thus, it gets extended in Step 2 to randomize MAC tags for messages with flexible length, namely, hierarchical identities.

Our starting point of achieving tight multi-challenge security is to design a new randomization strategy that does not depend on any bit of $\mathsf{m}^\star$. To implement this strategy, our first attempt is to choose the random vector $\mathbf{t}$ in the MAC tag from a larger vector space $\mathbb{Z}_q^{2k}$. Accordingly, we choose $\mathbf{x}_{j,b}$ values in $\mathsf{sk}_{\mathsf{MAC}}$ from $\mathbb{Z}_q^{2k}$ and compute $([\mathbf{t}]_2, [u]_2)$ in the MAC tag as

$$\mathbf{t} \xleftarrow{\$} \mathbb{Z}_q^{2k}$$
$$u = \sum_i \mathbf{x}_{i,\mathsf{m}_i}^\top \mathbf{t} + x_0' \in \mathbb{Z}_q. \tag{3}$$

Our proof strategy is rather algebraic and make use of some simple facts about the vector space $\mathbb{Z}_q^{2k}$. We choose two random matrices $\mathbf{B}_0, \mathbf{B}_1 \xleftarrow{\$} \mathbb{Z}_q^{2k \times k}$

and $\mathbf{B}_0^{\perp}, \mathbf{B}_1^{\perp} \in \mathbb{Z}_q^{2k \times k}$ are the corresponding non-zero kernel matrices, respectively. Namely,

$$\mathbf{B}_0^{\top} \cdot \mathbf{B}_0^{\perp} = \mathbf{B}_1^{\top} \mathbf{B}_1^{\perp} = \mathbf{0} \in \mathbb{Z}_q^{k \times k} \tag{4}$$

$(\mathbf{B}_0 \mid \mathbf{B}_1)$ is a basis of $\mathbb{Z}_q^{2k}$. $\mathsf{Span}(\mathbf{B}_0) := \{\mathbf{v} \in \mathbb{Z}_q \mid \exists \mathbf{w} \in \mathbb{Z}_q^k \text{ s.t. } \mathbf{v} = \mathbf{B}_0 \cdot \mathbf{w}\}$ is a linear subspace of $\mathbb{Z}_q^{2k}$ and it is the same for $\mathsf{Span}(\mathbf{B}_1)$.

We note that in the value u the information of the secret $\mathbf{x}_{j,b}$ values is only projected to $\mathbf{t}$. When we answer a tag query on message m, we can switch $\mathbf{t}$ to a suitable subspace (either $\mathsf{Span}(\mathbf{B}_0)$ or $\mathsf{Span}(\mathbf{B}_1)$) by the MDDH assumption. After the switch, some information about $\mathbf{x}_{j,b}$ values is perfectly hidden, and we can use it to gradually randomize the u values. Choosing $\mathbf{t}$ from the suitable subspace depends on the corresponding bit of m, but independent of the guess of $\mathsf{m}^{\star}$.

More precisely, in our Hybrid i, for a tag query on m, our u_{m} has the form

$$u_{\mathsf{m}} := \Big(\sum_j \mathbf{x}_{j,\mathsf{m}_j}^{\top} + \underbrace{\mathsf{OF}_i(\mathsf{m}_{|i})(\mathbf{B}_0^{\perp})^{\top} + \mathsf{ZF}_i(\mathsf{m}_{|i})(\mathbf{B}_1^{\perp})^{\top}}_{=:\mathsf{RF}_i(\mathsf{m}_{|i})} \Big) \mathbf{t}_{\mathsf{m}} + x_0',$$

where $\mathsf{OF}_i, \mathsf{ZF}_i : \{0,1\}^i \to \mathbb{Z}_q^{1 \times k}$ are two independent random functions. Since $(\mathbf{B}_0^{\perp} \mid \mathbf{B}_1^{\perp})^{\top} \in \mathbb{Z}_q^{2k \times 2k}$ is full-rank with overwhelming probability, we can view $\big(\mathsf{OF}_i(\mathsf{m}_{|i}) \mid \mathsf{ZF}_i(\mathsf{m}_{|i})\big)(\mathbf{B}_0^{\perp} \mid \mathbf{B}_1^{\perp})^{\top}$ as a random function $\mathsf{RF}_i : \{0,1\}^i \to \mathbb{Z}_q^{1 \times 2k}$.

In the transition to Hybrid $(i+1)$, we do the following two sub-steps:

- Step 1.1 (using MDDH): If $\mathsf{m}_{i+1} = 0$, then we choose $\mathbf{t}_{\mathsf{m}}$ from $\mathsf{Span}(\mathbf{B}_0)$, otherwise, from $\mathsf{Span}(\mathbf{B}_1)$.
- Step 1.2 (information-theoretic argument): For all tag queries with $\mathsf{m}_{i+1} = 0$, we increase the entropy in OF_i and develop OF_{i+1}. By Eq. (4), this change is perfectly hidden from the adversary $\mathcal{A}$. Similarly, we also develop ZF_{i+1} from ZF_i.

Now we can introduce RF_{i+1} and, after n of these recursions, we can have RF_n to randomize all the tags.

The only thing left is to handle multiple verification queries. To this end, in our scheme, we choose random $\mathbf{X}_{j,b} \in \mathbb{Z}_q^{k \times 2k}$. Compared with $\mathbf{x}_{j,b}^{\top} \in \mathbb{Z}_q^{2k}$, our new $\mathbf{X}_{j,b}$ has more rows such that we can embed the MDDH challenge to randomize multiple verification queries as well. We do not always know all the whole $\mathbf{X}_{j,b}$ values over $\mathbb{Z}_q$. However, different to the BKP or CW strategy, we multiply the unknown part in $\mathbf{X}_{j,b}$ with the suitable kernel matrix, either $\mathbf{B}_0^{\perp}$ or $\mathbf{B}_1^{\perp}$. This is done implicitly. Since, in all the tag queries, $\mathbf{t}_{\mathsf{m}}$ has already been chosen in the correct subspace, the unknown part will not appear, and we can simulate the tag queries. When we answer the verification queries, this unknown part will "react with" these queries and randomize them, which will later be the challenge ciphertext queries of the resulting IBE.

To sum up the discussion above, our strategy increases the dimension of $\mathbf{x}_{j,b}^{\top} \in \mathbb{Z}_q^{1 \times k}$ to $\mathbf{X}_{j,b} \in \mathbb{Z}_q^{k \times 2k}$ in such a way that we have enough entropy from the row vectors to randomize tag queries and, combining it with the entropy from the column vectors, we can handle the verification queries at the same time.

We capture all the above discussion formally by presenting an affine MAC in Sect. 3.1, which can be used to construct a tightly multi-challenge secure IBE. We are not claiming any efficiency improvement with this IBE, but technical achievement, instead, since it has roughly the same efficiency as its counterparts from [17,18,22]. However, our techniques involved in this IBE scheme improves those in [17,18,22] in the sense that ours can be extended to randomize user secret keys for hierarchical identities, while those in [17,18,22] cannot.

STEP 2: UPGRADE TO HIERARCHICAL IDENTITIES. For the random function RF_i developed via the strategy above, an important observation is that its output is only projected in $\mathbf{t}$ during the hybrid argument. This gives us "room" to upgrade the subspace randomization to handle hierarchical identities: By controlling the choice of $\mathbf{t}$, we can make sure that the outputs of RF_i and RF_{i+1} will not appear at the same time via the value u.

The strategy in this step is motivated by the work of Langrehr and Pan [28], where their core technique is to isolate the randomization for messages at different levels (which will be identities at different levels in the HIBE). To implement this, we add a "layer" to $\mathbf{t}$ by choosing $\mathbf{t}$ from $\mathbb{Z}_q^{3k}$. Similar to Step 1, we exploit some properties of the linear space $\mathbb{Z}_q^{3k}$. We choose two random matrices $\mathbf{B}_0, \mathbf{B}_1 \xleftarrow{\$} \mathbb{Z}_q^{3k \times k}$ and decompose $\mathbb{Z}_q^{3k}$ into $\mathsf{Span}(\mathbf{B} \mid \mathbf{B}_0 \mid \mathbf{B}_1)$. The span of $\mathbf{B}^{\perp}$ is decomposed into that of $\mathbf{B}_0^* \in \mathbb{Z}_q^{3k \times k}$ and $\mathbf{B}_1^* \in \mathbb{Z}_q^{3k \times k}$. An overview of the orthogonal relations between all these matrices is given in Fig. 1.

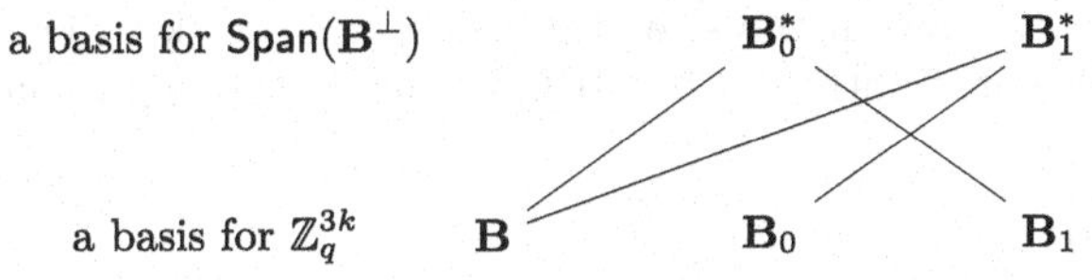

Fig. 1. Solid lines mean orthogonal: $\mathbf{B}^\top \mathbf{B}_0^* = \mathbf{B}_1^\top \mathbf{B}_0^* = \mathbf{0} = \mathbf{B}^\top \mathbf{B}_1^* = \mathbf{B}_0^\top \mathbf{B}_1^* \in \mathbb{Z}_q^{k \times k}$.

The intuition of our technique is that we develop a random function in $\mathsf{Span}(\mathbf{B}^{\perp})$, which is orthogonal to $\mathsf{Span}(\mathbf{B})$. Thus, it is easy to isolate the randomization for messages at level $\alpha(\leq L)$[1] from that at other levels by choosing $\mathbf{t}_{\mathsf{m}}$ from $\mathsf{Span}(\mathbf{B})$ for $\mathsf{m} \in (\{0,1\}^n)^{\alpha'}$ and $\alpha' \neq \alpha$. The randomization with a level α is done similar to Step 1. In particular, $(\mathbf{B}_0, \mathbf{B}_1^*)$ functions similar to $(\mathbf{B}_0, \mathbf{B}_0^{\perp})$ in Step 1, and the same for $(\mathbf{B}_1, \mathbf{B}_0^*)$ vs. $(\mathbf{B}_1, \mathbf{B}_1^{\perp})$.

We only present our intuitions here and refer Sect. 3.2 and the full version for the actual constructions and formal proofs.

1.3 More on Related Works

As we discussed before, there are different techniques [3,17,18,22,23] to achieve tight multi-challenge security for IBE schemes. Schemes in [18,22] are based on

[1] For message space with flexible length $\mathcal{M} := (\{0,1\}^n)^{\leq L}$, a message at level α means $\mathsf{m} \in (\{0,1\}^n)^{\alpha}$.

the BKP framework and close to ours, while the other schemes are either using composite-order pairings [23] or based on stronger, non-standard assumptions [3,17]. We suppose the proof strategy in the work of Hofheinz, Jia, and Pan (HJP) [22] cannot be easily extended to randomize MAC tags for hierarchical identities, since their technique develops the random function RF_i in the full space $\mathbb{Z}_q$ and directly introduce randomness into x_0'. Inherently, in the HIBE setting, this strategy has the same limitation as BKP, namely, the outputs of RF_i and RF_{i+1} are both leaked when identities have different lengths. The work of Gong et al. [18] has the same issue as well. This limitation explains why some proof steps of LP HIBE schemes cannot be done in the multi-challenge setting, even with the HJP technique.

1.4 Open Problems

As mentioned before and observed in Table 1, the tighter security loss of our schemes is $\mathbf{O}(\gamma k)$, but with relatively larger ciphertext. We leave further improving the security loss with compact ciphertext as an open problem.

Another interesting direction is to make our schemes more efficient. A main disadvantage of our schemes is that they require relatively large master public keys. More precisely, ignoring the small constant k, mpk contains either $\mathbf{O}(\alpha L^2)$ or $\mathbf{O}(\gamma L)$ group elements, because of the use of the LP technique [28]. An interesting open problem is to construct a tightly secure HIBE with shorter master public keys, probably first in the single-challenge setting. A similar interesting open problem is to shorten the size of either user secret keys or ciphertexts to have a more efficient, tightly secure HIBE scheme in the multi-challenge setting.

1.5 Roadmap

We recall useful definitions in Sect. 2. Section 3 proposes affine MACs that can be used to construct tightly multi-challenge secure IBE and HIBE, respectively. It presents our core techniques as described above in a detailed and formal manner. Section 4 gives a transformation to HIBE, similar to the BKP framework. Its security proof is in the full version. For completeness of our claims, in the full version, we constructs an anonymous HIBE and a CCA-secure HIBE tightly in the multi-challenge setting. Furthermore, concrete instantiations of our schemes can be found in the full version as well.

2 Preliminaries

NOTATIONS. We use $x \stackrel{\$}{\leftarrow} \mathcal{S}$ to denote the process of sampling an element x from $\mathcal{S}$ uniformly at random if $\mathcal{S}$ is a set and to denote the process of running $\mathcal{S}$ with its internal randomness and assign the output to x if $\mathcal{S}$ is an algorithm. The expression $a \stackrel{?}{=} b$ stands for comparing a and b on equality and returning the result in Boolean value. For positive integers $k, \eta \in \mathbb{N}_+$ and a matrix $\mathbf{A} \in \mathbb{Z}_q^{(k+\eta)\times k}$, we denote the upper square matrix of $\mathbf{A}$ by $\overline{\mathbf{A}} \in \mathbb{Z}_q^{k\times k}$ and the lower

η rows of $\mathbf{A}$ by $\underline{\mathbf{A}} \in \mathbb{Z}_q^{\eta \times k}$. Similarly, for a column vector $\mathbf{v} \in \mathbb{Z}_q^{k+\eta}$, we denote the upper k elements by $\overline{\mathbf{v}} \in \mathbb{Z}_q^k$ and the lower η elements of $\mathbf{v}$ by $\underline{\mathbf{v}} \in \mathbb{Z}_q^{\eta}$. We use $\mathbf{A}^{-\top}$ as shorthand for $(\mathbf{A}^{-1})^\top$. For a matrix $\mathbf{A} \in \mathbb{Z}_q^{n \times m}$, we use $\mathsf{Span}(\mathbf{A}) := \{\mathbf{Av} \mid \mathbf{v} \in \mathbb{Z}_q^m\}$ to denote the linear span of $\mathbf{A}$ and $\mathbf{A}^\perp$ denotes an arbitrary matrix with $\mathsf{Span}(\mathbf{A}^\perp) = \{\mathbf{v} \mid \mathbf{A}^\top \mathbf{v} = \mathbf{0}\}$.

For a set $\mathcal{S}$ and $n \in \mathbb{N}_+$, $\mathcal{S}^n$ denotes the set of all n-tuples with components in $\mathcal{S}$. For a string $\mathsf{m} \in \Sigma^n$, m_i denotes the i-th component of m $(1 \le i \le n)$ and $\mathsf{m}_{|i}$ denotes the prefix of length i of m. Furthermore for a p-tuple of bit strings $\mathsf{m} \in (\{0,1\}^n)^p$, we use $[\![\mathsf{m}]\!]$ to denote the string $\mathsf{m}_1 || \dots || \mathsf{m}_p$. Thus for $1 \le i \le np$, $[\![\mathsf{m}]\!]_i$ denotes the i-th bit of $\mathsf{m}_1 || \dots || \mathsf{m}_p$ and $[\![\mathsf{m}]\!]_{|i}$ denotes the i-bit-long prefix of $\mathsf{m}_1 || \dots || \mathsf{m}_p$.

All algorithms in this paper are probabilistic polynomial-time unless we state otherwise. If $\mathcal{A}$ is an algorithm, then we write $a \stackrel{\$}{\leftarrow} \mathcal{A}(b)$ to denote the random variable outputted by $\mathcal{A}$ on input b.

GAMES. Following [5], we use code-based games to define and prove security. A game G contains procedures INIT and FINALIZE, and some additional procedures $\mathrm{P}_1, \dots, \mathrm{P}_n$, which are defined in pseudo-code. Initially all variables in a game are undefined (denoted by $\perp$), all sets are empty (denote by $\emptyset$), and all partial maps (denoted by $f : A \dashrightarrow B$) are totally undefined. An adversary $\mathcal{A}$ is executed in game G (denote by $\mathsf{G}^{\mathcal{A}}$) if it first calls INIT, obtaining its output. Next, it may make arbitrary queries to P_i (according to their specification), again obtaining their output. Finally, it makes one single call to FINALIZE$(\cdot)$ and stops. We use $\mathsf{G}^{\mathcal{A}} \Rightarrow d$ to denote that G outputs d after interacting with $\mathcal{A}$, and d is the output of FINALIZE.

$T(\mathcal{A})$ denotes the running time of $\mathcal{A}$.

2.1 Pairing Groups and Matrix Diffie-Hellman Assumptions

Let GGen be a probabilistic polynomial-time (PPT) algorithm that on input 1^λ returns a description $\mathcal{G} := (\mathbb{G}_1, \mathbb{G}_2, \mathbb{G}_T, q, P_1, P_2, e)$ of asymmetric pairing groups where $\mathbb{G}_1$, $\mathbb{G}_2$, $\mathbb{G}_T$ are cyclic groups of order q for a λ-bit prime q. The group elements P_1 and P_2 are generators of $\mathbb{G}_1$ and $\mathbb{G}_2$, respectively. The function $e : \mathbb{G}_1 \times \mathbb{G}_2 \to \mathbb{G}_T$ is an efficient computable (non-degenerated) bilinear map. Define $P_T := e(P_1, P_2)$, which is a generator in $\mathbb{G}_T$. In this paper, we only consider Type III pairings, where $\mathbb{G}_1 \neq \mathbb{G}_2$ and there is no efficient homomorphism between them. All constructions in this paper can be easily instantiated with Type I pairings by setting $\mathbb{G}_1 = \mathbb{G}_2$ and defining the dimension k to be greater than 1.

We use the implicit representation of group elements as in [10]. For $s \in \{1, 2, T\}$ and $a \in \mathbb{Z}_q$ define $[a]_s = aP_s \in \mathbb{G}_s$ as the implicit representation of a in $\mathbb{G}_s$. Similarly, for a matrix $\mathbf{A} = (a_{ij}) \in \mathbb{Z}_q^{n \times m}$ we define $[\mathbf{A}]_s$ as the implicit representation of $\mathbf{A}$ in $\mathbb{G}_s$. $\mathsf{Span}(\mathbf{A}) := \{\mathbf{Ar} | \mathbf{r} \in \mathbb{Z}_q^m\} \subset \mathbb{Z}_q^n$ denotes the linear span of $\mathbf{A}$, and similarly $\mathsf{Span}([\mathbf{A}]_s) := \{[\mathbf{Ar}]_s | \mathbf{r} \in \mathbb{Z}_q^m\} \subset \mathbb{G}_s^n$. Note that it is efficient to compute $[\mathbf{AB}]_s$ given $([\mathbf{A}]_s, \mathbf{B})$ or $(\mathbf{A}, [\mathbf{B}]_s)$ with matching dimensions. We define $[\mathbf{A}]_1 \circ [\mathbf{B}]_2 := e([\mathbf{A}]_1, [\mathbf{B}]_2) = [\mathbf{AB}]_T$, which can be efficiently computed given $[\mathbf{A}]_1$ and $[\mathbf{B}]_2$.

Next we recall the definition of the matrix Diffie-Hellman (MDDH) and related assumptions [10].

Definition 1 (Matrix Distribution). *Let $k, \ell \in \mathbb{N}$ with $\ell > k$. We call $\mathcal{D}_{\ell,k}$ a* matrix distribution *if it outputs matrices in $\mathbb{Z}_q^{\ell \times k}$ of full rank k in polynomial time.*

Without loss of generality, we assume the first k rows of $\mathbf{A} \xleftarrow{\$} \mathcal{D}_{\ell,k}$ form an invertible matrix. The $\mathcal{D}_{\ell,k}$-matrix Diffie-Hellman problem is to distinguish the two distributions $([\mathbf{A}], [\mathbf{Aw}])$ and $([\mathbf{A}], [\mathbf{u}])$ where $\mathbf{A} \xleftarrow{\$} \mathcal{D}_{\ell,k}$, $\mathbf{w} \xleftarrow{\$} \mathbb{Z}_q^k$ and $\mathbf{u} \xleftarrow{\$} \mathbb{Z}_q^{\ell}$.

Definition 2 ($\mathcal{D}_{\ell,k}$-matrix Diffie-Hellman Assumption). *Let $\mathcal{D}_{\ell,k}$ be a matrix distribution and $s \in \{1, 2, T\}$. We say that the $\mathcal{D}_{\ell,k}$-*matrix Diffie-Hellman *($\mathcal{D}_{\ell,k}$-*MDDH*)* assumption *holds relative to* PGGen *in group $\mathbb{G}_s$ if for all PPT adversaries $\mathcal{A}$, it holds that*

$$\mathsf{Adv}^{\mathsf{mddh}}_{\mathcal{D}_{\ell,k},\mathsf{PGGen},s}(\mathcal{A}) := |\Pr[\mathcal{A}(\mathcal{PG}, [\mathbf{A}]_s, [\mathbf{Aw}]_s) = 1] - \Pr[\mathcal{A}(\mathcal{PG}, [\mathbf{A}]_s, [\mathbf{u}]_s) = 1]|$$

is negligible where the probability is taken over $\mathcal{PG} \xleftarrow{\$} \mathsf{PGGen}(1^\lambda)$, $\mathbf{A} \xleftarrow{\$} \mathcal{D}_{\ell,k}$, $\mathbf{w} \xleftarrow{\$} \mathbb{Z}_q^k$ and $\mathbf{u} \xleftarrow{\$} \mathbb{Z}_q^{\ell}$.

The uniform distribution is a particular matrix distribution that deserves special attention, as an adversary breaking the $\mathcal{U}_{\ell,k}$ assumption can also distinguish between real MDDH tuples and random tuples for all other possible matrix distributions. For uniform distributions, they stated in [11] that $\mathcal{U}_k$-MDDH and $\mathcal{U}_{\ell,k}$-MDDH assumptions are equivalent.

Definition 3 (Uniform Distribution). *Let $k, \ell \in \mathbb{N}_+$ with $\ell > k$. We call $\mathcal{U}_{\ell,k}$ a* uniform distribution *if it outputs uniformly random matrices in $\mathbb{Z}_q^{\ell \times k}$ of rank k in polynomial time. Let $\mathcal{U}_k := \mathcal{U}_{k+1,k}$.*

Lemma 1 ($\mathcal{U}_{\ell,k}$-MDDH $\Leftrightarrow$ $\mathcal{U}_k$-MDDH [11]). *Let $\ell, k \in \mathbb{N}_+$ with $\ell > k$. An $\mathcal{U}_{\ell,k}$-MDDH instance is as hard as an $\mathcal{U}_k$-MDDH instance. More precisely, for each adversary $\mathcal{A}$ there exists an adversary $\mathcal{B}$ and vice versa with*

$$\mathsf{Adv}^{\mathsf{mddh}}_{\mathcal{U}_{\ell,k},\mathsf{PGGen},s}(\mathcal{A}) = \mathsf{Adv}^{\mathsf{mddh}}_{\mathcal{U}_k,\mathsf{PGGen},s}(\mathcal{B})$$

and $T(\mathcal{A}) \approx T(\mathcal{B})$.

Proof. An $\mathcal{U}_{\ell,k}$-MDDH instance $(\mathcal{PG}, [\mathbf{A}]_s, [\mathbf{v}]_s)$ can be transformed into an $\mathcal{U}_k$-MDDH by picking uniformly random a full-rank matrix $\mathbf{T} \in \mathbb{Z}_q^{(k+1)\times \ell}$ and returning $(\mathcal{PG}, [\mathbf{TA}]_s, [\mathbf{Tv}]_s)$.

For the other direction one picks uniformly random a full-rank matrix $\mathbf{T}' \in \mathbb{Z}_q^{\ell \times (k+1)}$ to turn the $\mathcal{U}_k$-MDDH instance $(\mathcal{PG}, [\mathbf{A}]_s, [\mathbf{v}]_s)$ into an $\mathcal{U}_{\ell,k}$-MDDH instance $(\mathcal{PG}, [\mathbf{T}'\mathbf{A}]_s, [\mathbf{T}'\mathbf{v}]_s)$. □

Lemma 2 **($\mathcal{D}_{\ell,k}$-MDDH $\Rightarrow$ $\mathcal{U}_k$-MDDH [10]).** *Let $\ell, k \in \mathbb{N}_+$ with $\ell > k$ and let $\mathcal{D}_{\ell,k}$ be a matrix distribution. A $\mathcal{U}_k$-MDDH instance is at least as hard as an $\mathcal{D}_{\ell,k}$ instance. More precisely, for each adversary $\mathcal{A}$ there exists an adversary $\mathcal{B}$ with*

$$\mathsf{Adv}^{\mathsf{mddh}}_{\mathcal{U}_k,\mathsf{PGGen},s}(\mathcal{A}) \leq \mathsf{Adv}^{\mathsf{mddh}}_{\mathcal{D}_{\ell,k},\mathsf{PGGen},s}(\mathcal{B})$$

and $T(\mathcal{A}) \approx T(\mathcal{B})$.

For $Q \in \mathbb{N}_+$, $\mathbf{W} \xleftarrow{\$} \mathbb{Z}_q^{k \times Q}, \mathbf{U} \xleftarrow{\$} \mathbb{Z}_q^{\ell \times Q}$, consider the Q-fold $\mathcal{D}_{\ell,k}$-MDDH problem which is distinguishing the distributions $(\mathcal{PG}, [\mathbf{A}], [\mathbf{AW}])$ and $(\mathcal{PG}, [\mathbf{A}], [\mathbf{U}])$. That is, the Q-fold $\mathcal{D}_{\ell,k}$-MDDH problem contains Q independent instances of the $\mathcal{D}_{\ell,k}$-MDDH problem (with the same $\mathbf{A}$ but different $\mathbf{w}_i$). By a hybrid argument, one can show that the two problems are equivalent, where the reduction loses a factor Q. The following lemma gives a tight reduction.

Lemma 3 (Random Self-reducibility [10]). *For $\ell > k$ and any matrix distribution $\mathcal{D}_{\ell,k}$, the $\mathcal{D}_{\ell,k}$-MDDH assumption is random self-reducible. In particular, for any $Q \in \mathbb{N}_+$ and any adversary $\mathcal{A}$ there exists an adversary $\mathcal{B}$ with*

$$\begin{aligned}(\ell - k)\mathsf{Adv}^{\mathsf{mddh}}_{\mathcal{D}_{\ell,k},\mathsf{PGGen},s}(\mathcal{A}) + \frac{1}{q-1} \geq \mathsf{Adv}^{Q\text{-}\mathsf{mddh}}_{\mathcal{D}_{\ell,k},\mathsf{PGGen},s}(\mathcal{B}) :=\\ |\Pr[\mathcal{B}(\mathcal{PG}, [\mathbf{A}], [\mathbf{AW}] \Rightarrow 1)] - \Pr[\mathcal{B}(\mathcal{PG}, [\mathbf{A}], [\mathbf{U}] \Rightarrow 1)]|,\end{aligned}$$

where $\mathcal{PG} \xleftarrow{\$} \mathsf{PGGen}(1^\lambda)$, $\mathbf{A} \xleftarrow{\$} \mathcal{D}_{\ell,k}$, $\mathbf{W} \xleftarrow{\$} \mathbb{Z}_q^{k \times Q}$, $\mathbf{U} \xleftarrow{\$} \mathbb{Z}_q^{(k+1) \times Q}$, and $T(\mathcal{B}) \approx T(\mathcal{A}) + Q \cdot \mathsf{poly}(\lambda)$, where poly is a polynomial independent of $\mathcal{A}$.

To reduce the Q-fold $\mathcal{U}_{\ell,k}$-MDDH assumption to the $\mathcal{U}_k$-MDDH assumption we have to apply Lemma 3 to get from Q-fold $\mathcal{U}_{\ell,k}$-MDDH to standard $\mathcal{U}_{\ell,k}$-MDDH and then Lemma 1 to get from $\mathcal{U}_{\ell,k}$-MDDH to $\mathcal{U}_k$-MDDH. Thus for every adversary $\mathcal{A}$ there exists an adversary $\mathcal{B}$ with

$$\mathsf{Adv}^{Q\text{-}\mathsf{mddh}}_{\mathcal{U}_{\ell,k},\mathsf{PGGen},s}(\mathcal{A}) \leq (\ell - k)\mathsf{Adv}^{\mathsf{mddh}}_{\mathcal{U}_k,\mathsf{PGGen},s}(\mathcal{B}) + \frac{1}{q-1}.$$

The following Lemma is often helpful with the uniform matrix distribution.

Lemma 4.

$$\Pr\left[\mathrm{rank}(\mathbf{A}) = k \mid \mathbf{A} \xleftarrow{\$} \mathbb{Z}_q^{k \times k}\right] \geq 1 - \frac{1}{q-1}$$

A proof can be found in the full version.

2.2 Pseudorandom Functions

For the IBE construction we need pseudorandom functions (PRFs).

Definition 4 (Pseudorandom Function). *A* family of pseudorandom functions *is a tuple $\mathcal{F} := (\mathsf{Gen}_{\mathsf{PRF}}, \mathsf{PRF})$ of polynomial-time algorithms with:*

- $\mathcal{K} \xleftarrow{\$} \mathsf{Gen}_{\mathsf{PRF}}(1^\lambda)$ *is a probabilistic algorithm that gets the security parameter* 1^λ *and returns a (private) key* $\mathcal{K}$.
- PRF *is a deterministic algorithm that gets a key* $\mathcal{K}$ *and an input* $X \in \mathcal{D}$ *and outputs* $\mathsf{PRF}_{\mathcal{K}}(X) \in \mathcal{R}$, *where* $\mathcal{D}$ *is the domain set and* $\mathcal{R}$ *is the finite range set.*

The security notion for pseudorandom functions is pseudorandomness.

Definition 5 (Pseudorandomness). *A family of pseudorandom functions* $\mathcal{F} := (\mathsf{Gen}_{\mathsf{PRF}}, \mathsf{PRF})$ *is* pseudorandom *if for all PPT adversaries* $\mathcal{A}$,

$$\mathsf{Adv}^{\mathsf{pr}}_{\mathcal{F}}(\mathcal{A}) := \left|\Pr\left[\mathcal{A}^{\mathsf{PRF}_{\mathcal{K}}(\cdot)} \Rightarrow 1 \mid \mathcal{K} \xleftarrow{\$} \mathsf{Gen}_{\mathsf{PRF}}(1^\lambda)\right] - \Pr\left[\mathcal{A}^{\mathsf{RF}(\cdot)} \Rightarrow 1\right]\right|$$

is negligible in λ. *The notion* $\mathcal{A}^{f(\cdot)}$ *means* $\mathcal{A}$ *has oracle access to the function* f *and* $\mathsf{RF} : \mathcal{D} \to \mathcal{R}$ *is random function (i.e. a function that maps every input to a uniform random value from* $\mathcal{R}$*).*

2.3 Affine MACs

The HIBEs in this paper are constructed in the BKP framework: The HIBEs are obtained from a Message Authentication Code with suitable algebraic structures (affine MAC with levels). The main work is to achieve tight security in the multi-challenge setting for the MACs.

To achieve this, we need to generalize the structure of the affine MAC with levels slightly and allow that $\mathbf{X}$ can be a matrix (instead of a vector) and $\mathbf{x}'$ can be a vector (instead of only a scalar value). Please note that in the definition in this paper, $\mathbf{X}$ is transposed compared to the original affine MAC with levels definition.

Definition 6 (Affine MAC with Levels). *An* affine MAC with levels MAC *consists of three PPT algorithms* $(\mathsf{Gen}_{\mathsf{MAC}}, \mathsf{Tag}, \mathsf{Ver}_{\mathsf{MAC}})$ *with the following properties:*

- $\mathsf{Gen}_{\mathsf{MAC}}(\mathbb{G}_2, q, P_2)$ *gets a description of a prime-order group* $(\mathbb{G}_2, q, P_2)$ *and returns a secret key* $\mathsf{sk}_{\mathsf{MAC}} := \left(\mathbf{B}, (\mathbf{X}_{l,i,j})_{1\le l\le \ell(p), 1\le i\le L, 1\le j\le \ell'(l,i)}, \mathbf{x}'\right)$ *where* $\mathbf{B} \in \mathbb{Z}_q^{n\times n'}$, $\mathbf{X}_{l,i,j} \in \mathbb{Z}_q^{\eta\times n}$ *for* $l \in \{1,\dots,\ell(L)\}$, $i \in \{1,\dots,L\}$, *and* $j \in \{0,\dots,\ell'(l,i)\}$ *and* $\mathbf{x}' \in \mathbb{Z}_q^{\eta}$.
- $\mathsf{Tag}(\mathsf{sk}_{\mathsf{MAC}}, \mathsf{m} \in \mathcal{S}^{p\le L})$ *returns a tag* $\tau := \left(([\mathbf{t}_l]_2)_{1\le l\le \ell(p)}, [\mathbf{u}]_2\right)$ *where*

$$\mathbf{t}_l := \mathbf{B}\mathbf{s}_l \quad \text{for } \mathbf{s}_l \xleftarrow{\$} \mathbb{Z}_q^{n'} \quad (1 \le l \le \ell(p))$$

$$\mathbf{u} := \sum_{l=1}^{\ell(p)} \left(\sum_{i=1}^{p} \sum_{j=1}^{\ell'(l,i)} f_{l,i,j}(\mathsf{m}_{|i}) \mathbf{X}_{l,i,j} \right) \mathbf{t}_l + \mathbf{x}'. \tag{5}$$

- $\mathsf{Ver}_{\mathsf{MAC}}\left(\mathsf{sk}_{\mathsf{MAC}}, \mathsf{m}, \tau = \left(([\mathbf{t}_l]_2)_{1\le l\le \ell(p)}, [\mathbf{u}]_2\right)\right)$ *checks, whether Eq. (5) holds.*

$\underline{\textsc{Init}_{\mathsf{MAC}}:}$ $\mathcal{PG} \xleftarrow{\$} \mathsf{PGGen}(1^\lambda)$ **parse** $\mathcal{PG} =: (\mathbb{G}_1, \mathbb{G}_2, \mathbb{G}_T, q, P_1, P_2, e)$ $\mathsf{sk}_{\mathsf{MAC}} \xleftarrow{\$} \mathsf{Gen}_{\mathsf{MAC}}(\mathbb{G}_2, q, P_2)$ **parse** $\mathsf{sk}_{\mathsf{MAC}} =: (\mathbf{B}, (\mathbf{X}_j)_{1\le j\le \ell}, \mathbf{x}')$ **return** $\mathcal{PG}$ $\underline{\textsc{Eval}(\mathsf{m} \in \mathcal{S}):}$ $\mathcal{Q}_{\mathcal{M}} := \mathcal{Q}_{\mathcal{M}} \cup \{\mathsf{m}\}$ **return** $\mathsf{Tag}(\mathsf{sk}_{\mathsf{MAC}}, \mathsf{m})$ $\underline{\textsc{Finalize}_{\mathsf{MAC}}(\beta \in \{0,1\}):}$ **return** $(\mathcal{C}_{\mathcal{M}} \cap \mathcal{Q}_{\mathcal{M}} = \emptyset) \wedge \beta$	$\underline{\textsc{Chal}(\mathsf{m}^\star \in \mathcal{S}):}$ $\mathcal{C}_{\mathcal{M}} := \mathcal{C}_{\mathcal{M}} \cup \{\mathsf{m}^\star\}$ $\mathbf{h} \xleftarrow{\$} \mathbb{Z}_q^\eta$ $\mathbf{h}_0 := \left(\sum_{j=1}^{\ell} f_j(\mathsf{m}^\star)\mathbf{X}_j^\top\right)\mathbf{h}$ $\boxed{\mathbf{h}_0 \xleftarrow{\$} \mathbb{Z}_q^n}$ $h_1 = (\mathbf{x}')^\top \mathbf{h} \in \mathbb{Z}_q$ $\boxed{h_1 \xleftarrow{\$} \mathbb{Z}_q}$ **return** $([\mathbf{h}]_1, [\mathbf{h}_0]_1, [h_1]_T)$

Fig. 2. Games $\mathsf{mPR\text{-}CMA}_{\mathsf{real}}$ and $\boxed{\mathsf{mPR\text{-}CMA}_{\mathsf{rand}}}$ for defining mPR-CMA security for affine MACs.

The messages of MAC *have the form* $\mathsf{m} = (\mathsf{m}_1, \ldots, \mathsf{m}_p)$ *where* $p \le L$ *and* $\mathsf{m}_i \in \mathcal{S}$. *After the transformation to an HIBE,* $\mathcal{S}$ *will be the base set of the identity space and* L *will be the maximum number of levels. The functions* $f_{l,i,j} : \mathcal{S}^i \to \mathbb{Z}_q$ *must be public, efficiently computable functions. The parameters* $\ell : \{1, \ldots, p\} \to \mathbb{N}_+$, $n, n', \eta \in \mathbb{N}_+$ *and* $\ell' : \{1, \ldots, p\} \times \{1, \ldots, L\} \to \mathbb{N}_+$ $(1 \le i \le L)$ *are arbitrary, scheme-depending parameters. The function* ℓ *must be monotonous increasing.*

A delegatable affine MAC is an affine MAC with levels with $\ell(p) = 1$ and an affine MAC is a delegatable affine MAC with $L = 1$. We can use affine MACs with levels to build HIBEs, delegatable affine MACs to build anonymous HIBEs and affine MACs to build anonymous IBEs.

Security. To build anonymous IBE, we need an affine MAC that satisfies multi-challenge pseudorandomness against chosen message attacks (mPR-CMA) security. The security notion is defined by the games in Fig. 2.

We require multi-challenge hierarchical pseudorandomness against chosen-message attacks (mHPR-CMA) for affine MACs with levels to obtain mIND-HID-CPA and mIND-HID-CCA secure HIBEs. The security notion is defined by the games in Fig. 3.

Definition 7 (mXPR-CMA **Security**). *An affine MAC (with levels)* MAC *is* mXPR-CMA-secure *for* $X \in \{\varepsilon, \mathsf{H}\}$ *in* $\mathbb{G}_2$ *if for all PPT adversaries* $\mathcal{A}$ *the function*

$$\mathsf{Adv}^{\mathsf{m}x\mathsf{pr\text{-}cma}}_{\mathsf{MAC},\mathbb{G}_2}(\mathcal{A}) := \left|\Pr\left[\mathsf{mXPR\text{-}CMA}^{\mathcal{A}}_{\mathsf{real}} \Rightarrow 1\right] - \Pr\left[\mathsf{mXPR\text{-}CMA}^{\mathcal{A}}_{\mathsf{rand}} \Rightarrow 1\right]\right|$$

is negligible.

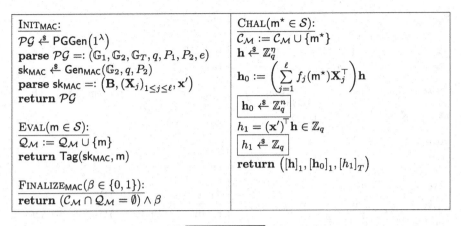

$\underline{\text{INIT}_{\mathsf{MAC}}}$: $\mathcal{PG} \overset{\$}{\leftarrow} \mathsf{PGGen}(1^\lambda)$ **parse** $\mathcal{PG} =: (\mathbb{G}_1, \mathbb{G}_2, \mathbb{G}_T, q, P_1, P_2, e)$ $\mathsf{sk_{MAC}} \overset{\$}{\leftarrow} \mathsf{Gen_{MAC}}(\mathbb{G}_2, q, P_2)$ $\mathsf{sk_{MAC}} =: \left(\mathbf{B}, (\mathbf{X}_{l,i,j})_{1\le l\le \ell(p), 1\le i\le L, 1\le j\le \ell'(l,i)}, \mathbf{x}'\right)$ $\mathsf{dk} := \left([\mathbf{X}_{l,i,j}\mathbf{B}]_2\right)_{1\le l\le \ell(p), 1\le i\le L, 1\le j\le \ell'(l,i)}$ **return** $\left(\mathcal{PG}, [\mathbf{B}]_2, \mathsf{dk}\right)$ $\underline{\text{EVAL}(\mathsf{m} \in \mathcal{S}^p)}$: $\mathcal{Q_M} := \mathcal{Q_M} \cup \{\mathsf{m}\}$ $\left(\left([\mathbf{t}_l]_2\right)_{1\le l\le \ell(p)}, [\mathbf{u}]_2\right) \overset{\$}{\leftarrow} \mathsf{Tag}(\mathsf{sk_{MAC}}, \mathsf{m})$ **for** $l \in \{1, \ldots, \ell(p)\}$, $i \in \{p+1, \ldots, L\}$, $j \in \{1, \ldots, \ell'(l,i)\}$ **do** $\mathbf{d}_{l,i,j} := \mathbf{X}_{l,i,j}\mathbf{t}_l$ $\mathsf{tdk} := \left([\mathbf{d}_{l,i,j}]_2\right)_{1\le l\le \ell(p), p+1\le i\le L, 1\le j\le \ell'(l,i)}$ **return** $\left(\left([\mathbf{t}_l]_2\right)_{1\le l\le \ell(p)}, [\mathbf{u}]_2, \mathsf{tdk}\right)$	$\underline{\text{CHAL}(\mathsf{m}^\star \in \mathcal{S}^p)}$: $\mathcal{C_M} := \mathcal{C_M} \cup \{\mathsf{m}^\star\}$ $\mathbf{h} \overset{\$}{\leftarrow} \mathbb{Z}_q^\eta$ **for** $l \in \{1, \ldots, \ell(p)\}$ **do** $\quad \mathbf{h}_{0,l} := \left(\sum_{i=1}^{L} \sum_{j=1}^{\ell'(l,i)} f_{l,i,j}\left(\mathsf{m}^\star_{\|i}\right)\mathbf{X}_{l,i,j}^\top\right)\mathbf{h}$ $h_1 = (\mathbf{x}')^\top \mathbf{h} \in \mathbb{Z}_q$ $\boxed{h_1 \overset{\$}{\leftarrow} \mathbb{Z}_q}$ **return** $\left([\mathbf{h}]_1, \left([\mathbf{h}_{0,l}]_1\right)_{1\le l\le \ell(p)}, [h_1]_T\right)$ $\underline{\text{FINALIZE}_{\mathsf{MAC}}(\beta \in \{0,1\})}$: **return** $\left(\bigcup_{\mathsf{m}^\star \in \mathcal{C_M}} \mathsf{Prefix}(\mathsf{m}^\star) \cap \mathcal{Q_M} = \emptyset\right) \wedge \beta$

Fig. 3. Games $\mathsf{mHPR\text{-}CMA_{real}}$ and $\boxed{\mathsf{mHPR\text{-}CMA_{rand}}}$ for defining $\mathsf{mHPR\text{-}CMA}$ security for affine MACs with levels.

3 Delegatable Affine MACs with Tight Multi-challenge Security

3.1 Warm-Up: IBE

First, we present the technique to handle multiple challenge queries in the IBE setting ($L = 1$). The MAC is given in Fig. 4. This affine MAC has identity space $\mathcal{S} = \{0,1\}^\alpha$ (for arbitrary $\alpha \in \mathbb{N}_+$) and uses $n = 2k$, $n' = k$, $\eta = k$ and $\ell' = \alpha$. To match the formal definition, $\mathbf{X}_{j,b}$ should be renamed to $\mathbf{X}_{2j-b}$ and $f_{2j-b}(\mathsf{m}) := \left(\mathsf{m}_j \overset{?}{=} b\right)$. The MAC looks very similar to the one in [22] and achieves the same security and very similar efficiency, however the security proof is quite different. A comparison of the resulting IBE with other tightly secure IBEs can be found in Table 2.

As in [22], we need to ensure that the adversary can only query one tag per message. The key generator can ensure this by making the tags deterministic. He can achieve this by storing the generated tags for duplicated queries (stateful scheme) or by generating the randomness with a pseudorandom function. We have done the later in our presentation. The affine MACs with levels we present later solve this by having rerandomizable tags. Of course, they can be used as affine MAC as well by setting $L = 1$, but this comes at the cost of being slightly less efficient.

Table 2. Comparison of IBEs in prime-order pairing groups with tight adaptive IND-ID-CPA-security in the standard model based on static assumptions. The schemes in the last two rows can also be made IND-ID-CCA secure. The second column indicates whether an IBE is anonymous (✓) or not (✗). The identity space is $\{0,1\}^n$. '$|\mathsf{mpk}|$,' '$|\mathsf{usk}|$,' and '$|\mathsf{C}|$' stand for the size of the master public key, the user secret key and a ciphertext, respectively. We count the number of group elements in $\mathbb{G}_1, \mathbb{G}_2$, and $\mathbb{G}_T$. For a scheme that works in symmetric pairing groups, we write $\mathbb{G}(:= \mathbb{G}_1 = \mathbb{G}_2)$. The last but one column indicates whether the adversary is allowed to query multiple challenge ciphertexts (✓) or just one (✗). The last column shows the underlying security assumption.

Scheme	A	$\vert\mathsf{mpk}\vert$	$\vert\mathsf{usk}\vert$	$\vert\mathsf{C}\vert$	Loss	MC	Ass.
CW13 [8]	✗	$2k^2(2n+1)\vert\mathbb{G}_1\vert + k\vert\mathbb{G}_T\vert$	$4k\vert\mathbb{G}_2$	$4k\vert\mathbb{G}_1$	$\mathsf{O}(n)$	✗	k-LIN
BKP14 [5]	✓	$(2nk^2+2k)\mathbb{G}_1\vert$	$(2k+1)\vert\mathbb{G}_2\vert$	$(2k+1)\vert\mathbb{G}_1\vert$	$\mathsf{O}(n)$	✗	k-LIN
AHY15 [3]	✓	$(16n+8)\vert\mathbb{G}_1\vert + 2\vert\mathbb{G}_T\vert$	$8\vert\mathbb{G}_2\vert$	$8\vert\mathbb{G}_1\vert$	$\mathsf{O}(n)$	✓	DLIN
GCD$^+$16$_1$ [17]	✗	$(6nk^2+3k^2))\vert\mathbb{G}_1\vert + k\vert\mathbb{G}_T\vert$	$6k\vert\mathbb{G}_2\vert$	$6k\vert\mathbb{G}_1\vert$	$\mathsf{O}(n)$	✓	k-LIN
GCD$^+$16$_2$ [17]	✗	$(4nk^2+2k^2))\vert\mathbb{G}_1\vert + k\vert\mathbb{G}_T\vert$	$4k\vert\mathbb{G}_2\vert$	$4k\vert\mathbb{G}_1\vert$	$\mathsf{O}(n)$	✓	k-LINAI
GDCC16 [18]	✓	$(2nk^2+3k^2))\vert\mathbb{G}_1\vert + k\vert\mathbb{G}_T\vert$	$4k\vert\mathbb{G}_2\vert$	$4k\vert\mathbb{G}_1\vert$	$\mathsf{O}(n)$	✓	k-LIN
HJP18 [22]	✓	$((3+n)k^2+k)\vert\mathbb{G}_1\vert$	$4k\vert\mathbb{G}_2\vert$	$4k\vert\mathbb{G}_1\vert$	$\mathsf{O}(n)$	✓	k-LIN
Ours	✓	$((2+2n)k^2+k)\vert\mathbb{G}_1\vert$	$4k\vert\mathbb{G}_2\vert$	$4k\vert\mathbb{G}_1\vert$	$\mathsf{O}(n)$	✓	k-LIN

$\underline{\mathsf{Gen}_{\mathsf{MAC}}(\mathbb{G}_2, q, P_2):}$

$\mathcal{K} \xleftarrow{\$} \mathsf{Gen}_{\mathsf{PRF}}(1^\lambda)$

for $j \in \{1, \ldots, \alpha\}$, $b \in \{0,1\}$ **do** $\mathbf{X}_{j,b} \xleftarrow{\$} \mathbb{Z}_q^{k \times 2k}$

$\mathbf{x}' \xleftarrow{\$} \mathbb{Z}_q^k$

return $\mathsf{sk}_{\mathsf{MAC}} := \left(\mathcal{K}, (\mathbf{X}_{j,b})_{1 \le j \le \alpha, b \in \{0,1\}}, \mathbf{x}'\right)$

$\underline{\mathsf{Tag}(\mathsf{sk}_{\mathsf{MAC}}, \mathsf{m} \in \mathcal{S}):}$

parse $\mathsf{sk}_{\mathsf{MAC}} =: \left(\mathcal{K}, (\mathbf{X}_{j,b})_{1 \le j \le \alpha, b \in \{0,1\}}, \mathbf{x}'\right)$

$\mathbf{t} := \mathsf{PRF}_{\mathcal{K}}(\mathsf{m}) \in \mathbb{Z}_q^{2k}$

$\mathbf{u} := \sum_{j=1}^{\alpha} \mathbf{X}_{j,\mathsf{m}_j} \mathbf{t} + \mathbf{x}'$

return $\left([\mathbf{t}]_2, [\mathbf{u}]_2\right)$

$\underline{\mathsf{Ver}_{\mathsf{MAC}}(\mathsf{sk}_{\mathsf{MAC}}, \mathsf{m} \in \mathcal{S}, \tau):}$

parse $\mathsf{sk}_{\mathsf{MAC}} =: \left(\mathcal{K}, (\mathbf{X}_{j,b})_{1 \le j \le \alpha, b \in \{0,1\}}, \mathbf{x}'\right)$

parse $\tau =: \left([\mathbf{t}]_2, [\mathbf{u}]_2\right)$

return $\mathbf{u} \stackrel{?}{=} \sum_{j=1}^{\alpha} \mathbf{X}_{j,\mathsf{m}_j} \mathbf{t} + \mathbf{x}'$

Fig. 4. The new multi-challenge tightly secure affine MAC MAC_{mc}.

Theorem 1 (Security of MAC_{mc}). *MAC_{mc} is tightly $\mathsf{mPR\text{-}CMA}$ secure in $\mathbb{G}_2$ under the $\mathcal{U}_k$-MDDH assumption for $\mathbb{G}_1$, the $\mathcal{U}_k$-MDDH assumption for $\mathbb{G}_2$ and the pseudorandomness of $\mathcal{F} := (\mathsf{Gen}_{\mathsf{PRF}}, \mathsf{PRF})$. More precisely, for all adversaries $\mathcal{A}$ there exists adversaries $\mathcal{B}_1$, $\mathcal{B}_2$ and $\mathcal{B}_3$ with*

$$\mathsf{Adv}^{\mathsf{mpr\text{-}cma}}_{\mathsf{MAC}_{mc}}(\mathcal{A}) \leq 8k\alpha \mathsf{Adv}^{\mathsf{mddh}}_{\mathcal{U}_k,\mathsf{PGGen},2}(\mathcal{B}_1) + (k\alpha + 2k + 1)\mathsf{Adv}^{\mathsf{mddh}}_{\mathcal{U}_k,\mathsf{PGGen},1}(\mathcal{B}_2) + 2\mathsf{Adv}^{\mathsf{pr}}_{\mathcal{F}}(\mathcal{B}_3) + \frac{(Q_c + 10)\alpha + 4}{q-1} + \frac{2Q_e}{q^{2k}}$$

and $T(\mathcal{B}_1) \approx T(\mathcal{B}_2) \approx T(\mathcal{B}_3) \approx T(\mathcal{A}) + (Q_e + Q_c) \cdot \mathsf{poly}(\lambda)$, where Q_e resp. Q_c denotes the number of Eval *resp.* Chal *queries of $\mathcal{A}$ and* poly *is a polynomial independent of $\mathcal{A}$.*

Proof. The proof uses a hybrid argument with the hybrids G_0, G_1, $\mathsf{G}_{2,\hat{\jmath},0}$ for $\hat{\jmath} \in \{0,\dots,\alpha\}$, $\mathsf{G}_{2,\hat{\jmath},1}$–$\mathsf{G}_{2,\hat{\jmath},3}$ for $\hat{\jmath} \in \{0,\dots,\alpha-1\}$ and finally G_3–G_5. They are given in Table 3. They make use of the random functions $\mathsf{RF} : \mathcal{S} \rightarrow \mathbb{Z}_q^{2k}$, $\mathsf{RF}' : \mathcal{S} \rightarrow \mathbb{Z}_q^{k}$, $\mathsf{RF}_{\hat{\jmath}} : \{0,1\}^{\hat{\jmath}} \rightarrow \mathbb{Z}_q^{k\times 2k}$, $\mathsf{ZF}_{\hat{\jmath}} : \{0,1\}^{\hat{\jmath}} \rightarrow \mathbb{Z}_q^{k\times k}$ and $\mathsf{OF}_{\hat{\jmath}} : \{0,1\}^{\hat{\jmath}} \rightarrow \mathbb{Z}_q^{k\times k}$ for $\hat{\jmath} \in \{1,\dots,\alpha\}$ and $\widetilde{\mathsf{RF}} : \mathcal{S} \rightarrow \mathbb{Z}_q^{k}$.

Lemma 5 ($\mathsf{G}_0 \rightsquigarrow \mathsf{G}_1$). *For all adversaries $\mathcal{A}$ there exists an adversary $\mathcal{B}$ with*

$$\left|\Pr\left[\mathsf{G}_0^{\mathcal{A}} \Rightarrow 1\right] = \Pr\left[\mathsf{G}_1^{\mathcal{A}} \Rightarrow 1\right]\right| \leq \mathsf{Adv}^{\mathsf{pr}}_{\mathcal{F}}\mathcal{B}$$

and $T(\mathcal{B}) \approx T(\mathcal{A}) + (Q_e + Q_c) \cdot \mathsf{poly}(\lambda)$.

Proof. The value $\mathbf{t}$ for in the Eval oracle is chosen randomly in game G_1 instead of pseudorandom in game G_0. This leads to a straight forward reduction to the pseudorandomness of $\mathcal{F} := (\mathsf{Gen}_{\mathsf{PRF}}, \mathsf{PRF})$. □

Lemma 6 ($\mathsf{G}_1 \rightsquigarrow \mathsf{G}_{2,0,0}$).

$$\Pr\left[\mathsf{G}_1^{\mathcal{A}} \Rightarrow 1\right] = \Pr\left[\mathsf{G}_{2,0,0}^{\mathcal{A}} \Rightarrow 1\right]$$

Proof. In game G_1 replace $\mathbf{X}_{1,b}$ with $\mathbf{X}_{1,b} + \mathsf{RF}_0(\varepsilon)$ for $b \in \{0,1\}$ to obtain game $\mathsf{G}_{2,0,0}$. □

Lemma 7 ($\mathsf{G}_{2,\hat{\jmath},0} \rightsquigarrow \mathsf{G}_{2,\hat{\jmath},1}$). *For $\hat{\jmath} < \alpha$ and all adversaries $\mathcal{A}$ there exists an adversary $\mathcal{B}$ with*

$$\left|\Pr\left[\mathsf{G}_{2,\hat{\jmath},0}^{\mathcal{A}} \Rightarrow 1\right] - \Pr\left[\mathsf{G}_{2,\hat{\jmath},1}^{\mathcal{A}} \Rightarrow 1\right]\right| \leq 2k\mathsf{Adv}^{\mathsf{mddh}}_{\mathcal{U}_k,\mathsf{PGGen},2}(\mathcal{B}) + \frac{2}{q-1}$$

and $T(\mathcal{B}) \approx T(\mathcal{A}) + (Q_e + Q_c) \cdot \mathsf{poly}(\lambda)$.

A proof can be found in the full version.

Lemma 8 ($\mathsf{G}_{2,\hat{\jmath},1} \rightsquigarrow \mathsf{G}_{2,\hat{\jmath},2}$). *For all adversaries $\mathcal{A}$ there exists an adversary $\mathcal{B}$ with*

$$\left|\Pr\left[\mathsf{G}_{2,\hat{\jmath},1}^{\mathcal{A}} \Rightarrow 1\right] - \Pr\left[\mathsf{G}_{2,\hat{\jmath},2}^{\mathcal{A}} \Rightarrow 1\right]\right| \leq k\mathsf{Adv}^{\mathsf{mddh}}_{\mathcal{U}_k,\mathsf{PGGen},1}(\mathcal{B}) + \frac{Q_c + 2}{q-1}$$

and $T(\mathcal{B}) \approx T(\mathcal{A}) + (Q_e + Q_c) \cdot \mathsf{poly}(\lambda)$.

G_0 | G_1 | $\mathsf{G}_{2,\hat{\jmath},0}$ | $\mathsf{G}_{2,\hat{\jmath},1}$ | $\mathsf{G}_{2,\hat{\jmath},2}$ | $\mathsf{G}_{2,\hat{\jmath},3}$ | G_3 | G_4 | G_5

<u>INIT$_{\mathsf{MAC}}$:</u>
$\mathcal{PG} \xleftarrow{\$} \mathsf{PGGen}(1^\lambda)$
parse $\mathcal{PG} =: (\mathbb{G}_1, \mathbb{G}_2, \mathbb{G}_T, q, P_1, P_2, e)$
$\mathbf{B}_0, \mathbf{B}_1 \xleftarrow{\$} \mathcal{U}_{2k,k}$ such that $\mathbf{B}_0, \mathbf{B}_1$ is a basis of $\mathbb{Z}_q^{2k}$
$\mathcal{K} \xleftarrow{\$} \mathsf{Gen}_{\mathsf{PRF}}(1^\lambda)$
for $j \in \{1, \ldots, \alpha\}$, $b \in \{0,1\}$ **do**
  $\mathbf{X}_{j,b} \xleftarrow{\$} \mathbb{Z}_q^{k \times 2k}$
$\mathbf{x}' \xleftarrow{\$} \mathbb{Z}_q^k$
return $\mathcal{PG}$

<u>CHAL($\mathsf{m}^\star \in \mathcal{S}$):</u>
$\mathcal{C}_\mathcal{M} := \mathcal{C}_\mathcal{M} \cup \{\mathsf{m}^\star\}$
$\mathbf{h} \xleftarrow{\$} \mathbb{Z}_q^k$
$\mathbf{h}_0 := \sum_{j=1}^{\alpha} \mathbf{X}_{j,\mathsf{m}_j^\star}^\top \mathbf{h}$
  $+ \mathsf{RF}_{\hat{\jmath}}(\mathsf{m}^\star_{|\hat{\jmath}})^\top \mathbf{h}$
  $+ \left(\mathbf{B}_1^\perp \mathsf{ZF}_{\hat{\jmath}+1}(\mathsf{m}^\star_{|\hat{\jmath}+1})^\top + \mathbf{B}_0^\perp \mathsf{OF}_{\hat{\jmath}}(\mathsf{m}^\star_{|\hat{\jmath}})^\top\right)\mathbf{h}$
  $+ \left(\mathbf{B}_1^\perp \mathsf{ZF}_{\hat{\jmath}+1}(\mathsf{m}^\star_{|\hat{\jmath}+1})^\top + \mathbf{B}_0^\perp \mathsf{OF}_{\hat{\jmath}+1}(\mathsf{m}^\star_{|\hat{\jmath}+1})^\top\right)\mathbf{h}$
  $+ \mathsf{RF}_\alpha(\mathsf{m}^\star)^\top \mathbf{h}$
$\mathbf{h}_0 \xleftarrow{\$} \mathbb{Z}_q^{2k}$
$h_1 := (\mathbf{x}')^\top \mathbf{h}$
$h_1 \xleftarrow{\$} \mathbb{Z}_q$
return $([\mathbf{h}]_1, [\mathbf{h}_0]_1, [h_1]_T)$

<u>EVAL($\mathsf{m} \in \mathcal{S}$):</u>
$\mathcal{Q}_\mathcal{M} := \mathcal{Q}_\mathcal{M} \cup \{\mathsf{m}\}$
$\mathbf{t} := \mathsf{PRF}_\mathcal{K}(\mathsf{m}) \in \mathbb{Z}_q^{2k}$
$\mathbf{t} := \mathsf{RF}(\mathsf{m}) \in \mathbb{Z}_q^{2k}$
$\mathbf{s} := \mathsf{RF}'(\mathsf{m}) \in \mathbb{Z}_q^k$
if $\mathsf{m}_{\hat{\jmath}+1} = 0$ **then**
  $\mathbf{t} := \mathbf{B}_0 \mathbf{s}$
else
  $\mathbf{t} := \mathbf{B}_1 \mathbf{s}$
$\mathbf{u} := \sum_{j=1}^{\alpha} \mathbf{X}_{j,\mathsf{m}_j} \mathbf{t} + \mathbf{x}'$
  $+ \mathsf{RF}_{\hat{\jmath}}(\mathsf{m}_{|\hat{\jmath}})\mathbf{t}$
  $+ \left(\mathsf{ZF}_{\hat{\jmath}+1}(\mathsf{m}_{|\hat{\jmath}+1})(\mathbf{B}_1^\perp)^\top + \mathsf{OF}_{\hat{\jmath}}(\mathsf{m}_{|\hat{\jmath}})(\mathbf{B}_0^\perp)^\top\right)\mathbf{t}$
  $+ \left(\mathsf{ZF}_{\hat{\jmath}+1}(\mathsf{m}_{|\hat{\jmath}+1})(\mathbf{B}_1^\perp)^\top + \mathsf{OF}_{\hat{\jmath}+1}(\mathsf{m}_{|\hat{\jmath}+1})(\mathbf{B}_0^\perp)^\top\right)\mathbf{t}$
$\mathbf{u} := \widetilde{\mathsf{RF}}(\mathsf{m})$
return $([\mathbf{t}]_2, [\mathbf{u}]_2)$

<u>FINALIZE$_{\mathsf{MAC}}$($\beta \in \{0,1\}$):</u>
return $(\mathcal{C}_\mathcal{M} \cap \mathcal{Q}_\mathcal{M} = \emptyset) \wedge \beta$

Fig. 5. Hybrids for the security proof of MAC_{mc}.

Proof. First of all, we replace the term $\mathsf{RF}_{\hat{\jmath}}(\mathsf{m}_{|\hat{\jmath}})$ in $\mathsf{G}_{2,\hat{\jmath},1}$ with $\mathsf{ZF}_{\hat{\jmath}}(\mathsf{m}_{|\hat{\jmath}})(\mathbf{B}_1^\perp)^\top + \mathsf{OF}_{\hat{\jmath}}(\mathsf{m}_{|\hat{\jmath}})(\mathbf{B}_0^\perp)^\top$. This does not change the distribution, since $\mathbf{B}_1^\perp, \mathbf{B}_0^\perp$ is a basis of $\mathbb{Z}_q^{2k}$. To show this, we assume $(\mathbf{B}_1^\perp | \mathbf{B}_0^\perp)$ does not have full rank. Since both

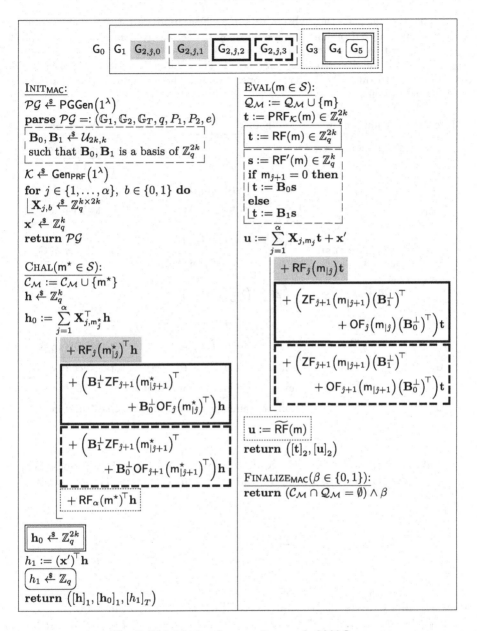

Table 3. Summary of the hybrids of Fig. 5. Non-duplicated EVAL queries draw (pseudo-)randomly $\mathbf{t}$ from the set described by the second column and add the randomness $r_{\mathbf{u}}(\mathsf{m})\mathbf{t}$ to $\mathbf{u}$ or choose $\mathbf{u}$ uniform random. The CHAL queries add the term $r_{\mathbf{h}_0}(\mathsf{m}^\star)^\top\mathbf{h}$ to $\mathbf{h}_0$ or choose $\mathbf{h}_0$ uniform random. The column "Transition" displays how we can switch to this hybrid from the previous one. The background color indicates repeated transitions.

Hybrid	$\mathbf{t}$ uniform in	$r_{\mathbf{u}}(\mathsf{m})$	$r_{\mathbf{h}_0}(\mathsf{m})$	Transition
G_0	$\mathbb{Z}_q^{2k}$ (pseudorandom)	0		Original game
G_1	$\mathbb{Z}_q^{2k}$	0		PRF
$\mathsf{G}_{2,\hat{\jmath},0}$	$\mathbb{Z}_q^{2k}$	$\mathsf{RF}_{\hat{\jmath}}(\mathsf{m}_{\mid\hat{\jmath}})$		Identical
$\mathsf{G}_{2,\hat{\jmath},1}$	**if** $\mathsf{m}_{\hat{\jmath}+1}=0$ **then** $\mathsf{Span}(\mathbf{B}_0)$ **else** $\mathsf{Span}(\mathbf{B}_1)$	$\mathsf{RF}_{\hat{\jmath}}(\mathsf{m}_{\mid\hat{\jmath}})$		$\mathcal{U}_k$-MDDH in $\mathbb{G}_2$
$\mathsf{G}_{2,\hat{\jmath},2}$		$\left(\mathsf{ZF}_{\hat{\jmath}+1}(\mathsf{m}_{\mid\hat{\jmath}+1})(\mathbf{B}_1^\perp)^\top + \mathsf{OF}_{\hat{\jmath}}(\mathsf{m}_{\mid\hat{\jmath}})(\mathbf{B}_0^\perp)^\top\right)$		$\mathcal{U}_k$-MDDH in $\mathbb{G}_1$
$\mathsf{G}_{2,\hat{\jmath},3}$		$\left(\mathsf{ZF}_{\hat{\jmath}+1}(\mathsf{m}_{\mid\hat{\jmath}+1})(\mathbf{B}_1^\perp)^\top + \mathsf{OF}_{\hat{\jmath}+1}(\mathsf{m}_{\mid\hat{\jmath}+1})(\mathbf{B}_0^\perp)^\top\right)$		$\mathcal{U}_k$-MDDH in $\mathbb{G}_1$
$\mathsf{G}_{2,\hat{\jmath}+1,0}$	$\mathbb{Z}_q^{2k}$	$\mathsf{RF}_{\hat{\jmath}+1}(\mathsf{m}_{\mid\hat{\jmath}+1})$		$\mathcal{U}_k$-MDDH in $\mathbb{G}_2$
G_3	$\mathbb{Z}_q^{2k}$	uniform random	$\mathsf{RF}_\alpha(\mathsf{m})$	Statistically close
G_4	$\mathbb{Z}_q^{2k}$	uniform random	uniform random	$\mathcal{U}_k$-MDDH in $\mathbb{G}_1$
G_5	$\mathbb{Z}_q^{2k}$	uniform random	uniform random	$\mathcal{U}_k$-MDDH in $\mathbb{G}_1$

$\mathbf{B}_1^\perp$ and $\mathbf{B}_0^\perp$ have rank k, there is a non-zero vector $\mathbf{v} \in \mathsf{Span}(\mathbf{B}_1^\perp) \cap \mathsf{Span}(\mathbf{B}_0^\perp)$ such that $(\mathbf{B}_0|\mathbf{B}_1)\mathbf{v} = 0$, which contradicts the fact that $\mathbf{B}_0, \mathbf{B}_1$ is a basis of $\mathbb{Z}_q^{2k}$.

Define

$$\mathsf{ZF}_{\hat{\jmath}+1}(\mathsf{m}_{\mid\hat{\jmath}+1}) := \begin{cases} \mathsf{ZF}_{\hat{\jmath}}(\mathsf{m}_{\mid\hat{\jmath}}) & \text{if } \mathsf{m}_{\hat{\jmath}+1} = 0 \\ \mathsf{ZF}_{\hat{\jmath}}(\mathsf{m}_{\mid\hat{\jmath}}) + \mathsf{ZF}'_{\hat{\jmath}}(\mathsf{m}_{\mid\hat{\jmath}}) & \text{if } \mathsf{m}_{\hat{\jmath}+1} = 1 \end{cases},$$

where $\mathsf{ZF}'_{\hat{\jmath}} : \{0,1\}^{\hat{\jmath}} \to \mathbb{Z}_q^{1\times k}$ is another independent random function. Since $\mathsf{ZF}_{\hat{\jmath}}$ does not appear in game $\mathsf{G}_{2,\hat{\jmath},2}$ anymore, $\mathsf{ZF}_{\hat{\jmath}+1}$ is a random function.

Let $([\mathbf{D}]_1, [\mathbf{f}_1]_1, \ldots, [\mathbf{f}_{kQ_c}]_1)$ be a (kQ_c)-fold $\mathcal{U}_{2k,k}$-MDDH challenge and define $\mathbf{F}_c := (\mathbf{f}_{(c-1)k+1}|\ldots|\mathbf{f}_{ck})$ to get Q_c $2k \times k$ matrices, whose column vectors are uniformly random chosen from either $\mathsf{Span}(\mathbf{D})$ or $\mathbb{Z}_q^{2k}$. Then the reduction in Fig. 6 can be used to bound the difference between $\mathsf{G}_{2,\hat{\jmath},1}$ and $\mathsf{G}_{2,\hat{\jmath},2}$.

EVAL queries are distributed identically in game $\mathsf{G}_{2,\hat{\jmath},1}$ and $\mathsf{G}_{2,\hat{\jmath},2}$: If $\mathsf{m}_{\hat{\jmath}+1} = 0$, they are the same by the definition of $\mathsf{ZF}_{\hat{\jmath}+1}$. If $\mathsf{m}_{\hat{\jmath}+1} = 1$, $\mathbf{t} \in \mathsf{Span}(\mathbf{B}_0)$ and thus the term $\mathsf{ZF}_{\hat{\jmath}}(\mathsf{m}_{\mid\hat{\jmath}})(\mathbf{B}_1^\perp)^\top$ resp. $\mathsf{ZF}_{\hat{\jmath}+1}(\mathsf{m}_{\mid\hat{\jmath}+1})(\mathbf{B}_1^\perp)^\top$ cancels out in this query. Note that $\mathsf{ZF}'_{\hat{\jmath}}$ is not evaluated in EVAL queries.

$\underline{\text{INIT}_{\text{MAC}}:}$
parse $\mathcal{PG} =: (\mathbb{G}_1, \mathbb{G}_2, \mathbb{G}_T, q, P_1, P_2, e)$
$\mathbf{B}_0, \mathbf{B}_1 \xleftarrow{\$} \mathcal{U}_{2k,k}$
such that $\mathbf{B}_0, \mathbf{B}_1$ is a basis of $\mathbb{Z}_q^{2k}$
for $j \in \{1, \ldots, \alpha\}$, $b \in \{0,1\}$ **do**
$\quad \mathbf{J}_{j,b} \xleftarrow{\$} \mathbb{Z}_q^{k \times 2k}$
$\quad$**if** $(j,b) \neq (\hat{\jmath}+1, 1)$ **then** $\mathbf{X}_{j,b} := \mathbf{J}_{j,b}$
// Implicit: $\mathbf{X}_{\hat{\jmath}+1,1} := \mathbf{J}_{\hat{\jmath}+1,1} + \left(\mathbf{B}_1^{\perp}\underline{\mathbf{D}}\overline{\mathbf{D}}^{-1}\right)^{\top}$
$\mathbf{x}' \xleftarrow{\$} \mathbb{Z}_q^k$
return $\mathcal{PG}$
 	
$\underline{\text{EVAL}(\mathsf{m} \in \mathcal{S}):}$
$\mathcal{Q}_{\mathcal{M}} := \mathcal{Q}_{\mathcal{M}} \cup \{\mathsf{m}\}$
$\mathbf{s} := \mathsf{RF}'(\mathsf{m}) \in \mathbb{Z}_q^k$
if $\mathsf{m}_{\hat{\jmath}+1} = 0$ **then**
$\quad \mathbf{t} := \mathbf{B}_0\mathbf{s}$
else
$\quad \mathbf{t} := \mathbf{B}_1\mathbf{s}$
$\mathbf{u} := \left(\sum_{j=1}^{\alpha} \mathbf{J}_{j,\mathsf{m}_j} + \mathsf{ZF}_{\hat{\jmath}}(\mathsf{m}_{\lvert\hat{\jmath}})(\mathbf{B}_1^{\perp})^{\top} + \mathsf{OF}_{\hat{\jmath}}(\mathsf{m}_{\lvert\hat{\jmath}})(\mathbf{B}_0^{\perp})^{\top}\right)\mathbf{t} + \mathbf{x}'$
return $([\mathbf{t}]_2, [\mathbf{u}]_2)$
	$\underline{\text{CHAL}(\mathsf{m}^\star \in \mathcal{S}):}$
	$\mathcal{C}_{\mathcal{M}} := \mathcal{C}_{\mathcal{M}} \cup \{\mathsf{m}^\star\}$
	Let c be the index of the first CHAL query on a message with prefix $\mathsf{m}^\star_{\lvert\hat{\jmath}}$.
	$\mathbf{h}' \xleftarrow{\$} \mathbb{Z}_q^k$
	$\mathbf{h} := \overline{\mathbf{F}_c}\mathbf{h}'$
	$\mathbf{h}_0 := \left(\sum_{j=1}^{\alpha} \mathbf{J}_{j,\mathsf{m}^\star_j}^{\top} + \mathbf{B}_1^{\perp}\mathsf{ZF}_{\hat{\jmath}}(\mathsf{m}^\star_{\lvert\hat{\jmath}})^{\top} + \mathbf{B}_0^{\perp}\mathsf{OF}_{\hat{\jmath}}(\mathsf{m}^\star_{\lvert\hat{\jmath}})^{\top}\right)\mathbf{h}$
	if $\mathsf{m}^\star_{\hat{\jmath}+1} = 1$ **then** $\mathbf{h}_0 := \mathbf{h}_0 + \mathbf{B}_1^{\perp}\underline{\mathbf{F}_c}\mathbf{h}'$
	$h_1 := (\mathbf{x}')^{\top}\mathbf{h}$
	return $([\mathbf{h}]_1, [\mathbf{h}_0]_1, [h_1]_T)$
	
	$\underline{\text{FINALIZE}_{\text{MAC}}(\beta \in \{0,1\}):}$
	return $(\mathcal{C}_{\mathcal{M}} \cap \mathcal{Q}_{\mathcal{M}} = \emptyset) \wedge \beta$

Fig. 6. Reduction for the transition from $\mathsf{G}_{2,\hat{\jmath},1}$ to $\mathsf{G}_{2,\hat{\jmath},2}$ to the kQ_c-fold $\mathcal{U}_{2k,k}$MDDH challenge $([\mathbf{D}]_1, [\mathbf{F}_1]_1, \ldots, [\mathbf{F}_{Q_c}]_1)$.

Assume that $\overline{\mathbf{D}}$ is invertible. This happens with probability at least $(1 - 1/(q-1))$. For CHAL queries we write $\mathbf{F}_c =: \begin{pmatrix} \overline{\mathbf{D}}\mathbf{W}_c \\ \underline{\mathbf{D}}\mathbf{W}_c + \mathbf{R}_c \end{pmatrix}$ where $\mathbf{W}_c$ is uniform random in $\mathbb{Z}_q^{k \times k}$ and $\mathbf{R}_c$ is $\mathbf{0} \in \mathbb{Z}_q^{k \times k}$ or uniform random in $\mathbb{Z}_q^{k \times k}$. In the following we will assume that $\mathbf{W}_c$ has full rank. This happens with probability at least $(1 - 1/(q-1))$.

The value $\mathbf{h}$ is uniform random in $\mathbb{Z}_q^k$, since $\mathbf{h}'$ is uniformly random and $\overline{\mathbf{F}_c}$ is an invertible $k \times k$ matrix, since $\overline{\mathbf{D}}$ and $\mathbf{W}_c$ are invertible.

If $\mathsf{m}^\star_{\hat{\jmath}+1} = 0$ the CHAL queries are distributed identically in $\mathsf{G}_{2,\hat{\jmath},1}$ and $\mathsf{G}_{2,\hat{\jmath},2}$. If $\mathsf{m}^\star_{\hat{\jmath}+1} = 1$ The reduction computes $\mathbf{h}_0$ as

$$\begin{aligned}\mathbf{h}_0 &:= \left(\sum_{j=1}^{\alpha} \mathbf{J}_{j,\mathsf{m}^\star_j}^{\top} + \mathsf{F}\left(\mathsf{m}^\star_{\lvert\hat{\jmath}}\right)\right)\mathbf{h} + \mathbf{B}_1^{\perp}\underline{\mathbf{F}_c}\mathbf{h}' \\ &= \left(\sum_{j=1}^{\alpha} \mathbf{J}_{j,\mathsf{m}^\star_j}^{\top} + \mathsf{F}\left(\mathsf{m}^\star_{\lvert\hat{\jmath}}\right)\right)\mathbf{h} + \mathbf{B}_1^{\perp}\underline{\mathbf{D}}\overline{\mathbf{D}}^{-1}\overline{\mathbf{F}_c}\mathbf{h}' + \mathbf{B}_1^{\perp}\mathbf{R}_c\mathbf{h}'\end{aligned}$$

$$= \left(\sum_{j=1}^{\alpha} \mathbf{X}_{j,\mathsf{m}_j^\star}^\top + \mathsf{F}\left(\mathsf{m}_{|\hat{\jmath}}^\star\right) \right) \mathbf{h} + \mathbf{B}_1^\perp \mathbf{R}_c \overline{\mathbf{F}_c}^{-1} \mathbf{h}$$

with

$$\mathsf{F}\left(\mathsf{m}_{|\hat{\jmath}}^\star\right) := \mathbf{B}_1^\perp \mathsf{ZF}_{\hat{\jmath}}\left(\mathsf{m}_{|\hat{\jmath}}^\star\right)^\top + \mathbf{B}_0^\perp \mathsf{OF}_{\hat{\jmath}}\left(\mathsf{m}_{|\hat{\jmath}}^\star\right)^\top.$$

If $\mathbf{R}_c = \mathbf{0}$, the reduction is simulating $\mathsf{G}_{2,\hat{\jmath},1}$. If $\mathbf{R}_c$ is uniformly random, we implicitly set $\mathsf{ZF}'_{\hat{\jmath}}(\mathsf{m}_{|\hat{\jmath}}) := \mathbf{R}_c \overline{\mathbf{F}_c}^{-1}$ and are simulating game $\mathsf{G}_{2,\hat{\jmath},2}$. □

Lemma 9 ($\mathsf{G}_{2,\hat{\jmath},2} \rightsquigarrow \mathsf{G}_{2,\hat{\jmath},3}$). *For all adversaries $\mathcal{A}$ there exists an adversary $\mathcal{B}$ with*

$$\left|\Pr\left[\mathsf{G}_{2,\hat{\jmath},2}^{\mathcal{A}} \Rightarrow 1\right] - \Pr\left[\mathsf{G}_{2,\hat{\jmath},3}^{\mathcal{A}} \Rightarrow 1\right]\right| \leq k\mathsf{Adv}_{\mathcal{U}_k,\mathsf{PGGen},1}^{\mathsf{mddh}}(\mathcal{B}) + \frac{Q_c + 2}{q-1}$$

and $T(\mathcal{B}) \approx T(\mathcal{A}) + (Q_e + Q_c) \cdot \mathsf{poly}(\lambda)$.

Proof. We define

$$\mathsf{OF}_{\hat{\jmath}+1}(\mathsf{m}_{|\hat{\jmath}+1}) := \begin{cases} \mathsf{OF}_{\hat{\jmath}}(\mathsf{m}_{|\hat{\jmath}}) + \mathsf{OF}'_{\hat{\jmath}}(\mathsf{m}_{|\hat{\jmath}}) & \text{if } \mathsf{m}_{\hat{\jmath}+1} = 0 \\ \mathsf{OF}_{\hat{\jmath}}(\mathsf{m}_{|\hat{\jmath}}) & \text{if } \mathsf{m}_{\hat{\jmath}+1} = 1 \end{cases},$$

where $\mathsf{OF}'_{\hat{\jmath}} : \{0,1\}^{\hat{\jmath}} \to \mathbb{Z}_q^{1\times k}$ is another independent random function. Since $\mathsf{OF}_{\hat{\jmath}}$ in not used in game $\mathsf{G}_{2,\hat{\jmath},3}$, $\mathsf{OF}_{\hat{\jmath}+1}$ is a random function.

The argument that the games $\mathsf{G}_{2,\hat{\jmath},2}$ and $\mathsf{G}_{2,\hat{\jmath},3}$ are computationally indistinguishable under an MDDH assumption in $\mathbb{G}_1$ is the same as in Lemma 8, just with the roles of 0 and 1 swapped. □

Lemma 10 (Optimization: $\mathsf{G}_{2,\hat{\jmath},1} \rightsquigarrow \mathsf{G}_{2,\hat{\jmath},3}$). *For all adversaries $\mathcal{A}$ there exists an adversary $\mathcal{B}$ with*

$$\left|\Pr\left[\mathsf{G}_{2,\hat{\jmath},1}^{\mathcal{A}} \Rightarrow 1\right] - \Pr\left[\mathsf{G}_{2,\hat{\jmath},3}^{\mathcal{A}} \Rightarrow 1\right]\right| \leq k\mathsf{Adv}_{\mathcal{U}_k,\mathsf{PGGen},1}^{\mathsf{mddh}}(\mathcal{B}) + \frac{Q_c + 2}{q-1}$$

and $T(\mathcal{B}) \approx T(\mathcal{A}) + (Q_e + Q_c) \cdot \mathsf{poly}(\lambda)$.

Proof. We can do the reduction of Lemmata 8 and 9 in one step using only one MDDH challenge in $\mathbb{G}_1$. This combined reduction embeds the challenge in both $\mathbf{X}_{\hat{\jmath}+1,1}$ as $\mathbf{X}_{\hat{\jmath}+1,1} := \mathbf{J}_{\hat{\jmath}+1,1} + \mathbf{B}_1^\perp \underline{\mathbf{D}}\overline{\mathbf{D}}^{-1}$ and $\mathbf{X}_{\hat{\jmath}+1,0}$ as $\mathbf{X}_{\hat{\jmath}+1,0} := \mathbf{J}_{\hat{\jmath}+1,0} + \mathbf{B}_0^\perp \underline{\mathbf{D}}\overline{\mathbf{D}}^{-1}$ and picks in each CHAL query on $\mathsf{m}^\star$ c as the index of the first CHAL query on a message with prefix $\mathsf{m}_{|\hat{\jmath}+1}^\star$. □

Lemma 11 ($\mathsf{G}_{2,\hat{\jmath},3} \rightsquigarrow \mathsf{G}_{2,\hat{\jmath}+1,0}$). *For all adversaries $\mathcal{A}$ there exists an adversary $\mathcal{B}$ with*

$$\left|\Pr\left[\mathsf{G}_{2,\hat{\jmath},3}^{\mathcal{A}} \Rightarrow 1\right] - \Pr\left[\mathsf{G}_{2,\hat{\jmath}+1,0}^{\mathcal{A}} \Rightarrow 1\right]\right| \leq 2k\mathsf{Adv}_{\mathcal{U}_k,\mathsf{PGGen},2}^{\mathsf{mddh}}(\mathcal{B}) + \frac{2}{q-1}$$

and $T(\mathcal{B}) \approx T(\mathcal{A}) + (Q_e + Q_c) \cdot \mathsf{poly}(\lambda)$.

Proof. In $\mathsf{G}_{2,\hat{\jmath},3}$ we replace the term $\mathsf{ZF}_{\hat{\jmath}+1}(\mathsf{m}_{|\hat{\jmath}+1})(\mathbf{B}_1^\perp)^\top + \mathsf{OF}_{\hat{\jmath}+1}(\mathsf{m}_{|\hat{\jmath}+1})(\mathbf{B}_0^\perp)^\top$ with $\mathsf{RF}_{\hat{\jmath}+1}(\mathsf{m}_{|\hat{\jmath}+1})$. This does not change the distribution, since $\mathbf{B}_1^\perp, \mathbf{B}_0^\perp$ is a basis of $\mathbb{Z}_q^{2k}$.

The remaining transition is the reverse of Lemma 7. □

Lemma 12 ($\mathsf{G}_{2,\alpha,0} \rightsquigarrow \mathsf{G}_3$). *For all adversaries $\mathcal{A}$ there exists an adversary $\mathcal{B}$ with*

$$\left|\Pr[\mathsf{G}_{2,\alpha,0}^{\mathcal{A}} \Rightarrow 1] - \Pr[\mathsf{G}_3^{\mathcal{A}} \Rightarrow 1]\right| \leq \frac{Q_e}{q^{2k}}$$

and $T(\mathcal{B}) \approx T(\mathcal{A}) + (Q_e + Q_c) \cdot \mathsf{poly}(\lambda)$.

Proof. Assume $\mathcal{Q}_e \cap \mathcal{Q}_c = \emptyset$; otherwise, the adversary has lost the game regardless of her output. Furthermore assume, that $\mathbf{t} \neq \mathbf{0} \in \mathbb{Z}_q^{2k}$. This happens with probability at least $(1 - 1/q^{2k})$.

In each Eval query the value $\mathsf{RF}_\alpha(\mathsf{m})\mathbf{t}$ is then distributed like a fresh random vector from $\mathbb{Z}_q^k$ the first time a tag for m is queried. We can ignore duplicated queries for m since they will be answered with the same tag. □

Lemma 13 ($\mathsf{G}_3 \rightsquigarrow \mathsf{G}_4$). *For all adversaries $\mathcal{A}$ there exists an adversary $\mathcal{B}$ with*

$$\left|\Pr[\mathsf{G}_3^{\mathcal{A}} \Rightarrow 1] - \Pr[\mathsf{G}_4^{\mathcal{A}} \Rightarrow 1]\right| \leq 2k\mathsf{Adv}^{\mathsf{mddh}}_{\mathcal{U}_k,\mathsf{PGGen},1}(\mathcal{B}) + \frac{2}{q-1}$$

and $T(\mathcal{B}) \approx T(\mathcal{A}) + (Q_e + Q_c) \cdot \mathsf{poly}(\lambda)$.

Proof. We pick a Q_c fold $\mathcal{U}_{3k,k}$-MDDH challenge $([\mathbf{D}]_1, [\mathbf{f}_1]_1, \ldots, [\mathbf{f}_{Q_c}]_1)$ and use the reduction given in Fig. 7.

<u>InitMAC:</u>
parse $\mathcal{PG} =: (\mathbb{G}_1, \mathbb{G}_2, \mathbb{G}_T, q, P_1, P_2, e)$
$\mathbf{B}_0, \mathbf{B}_1 \xleftarrow{\$} \mathcal{U}_{2k,k}$
such that $\mathbf{B}_0, \mathbf{B}_1$ is a basis of $\mathbb{Z}_q^{2k}$
for $j \in \{1, \ldots, \alpha\}$, $b \in \{0,1\}$ **do**
  $\mathbf{J}_{j,b} \xleftarrow{\$} \mathbb{Z}_q^{k \times 2k}$
  if $j \neq 1$ **then** $\mathbf{X}_{j,b} := \mathbf{J}_{j,b}$
// Implicit: For $b \in \{0,1\}$:
// $\mathbf{X}_{1,b} := \mathbf{J}_{1,b} + \left(\underline{\mathbf{D}}\overline{\mathbf{D}}^{-1}\right)^\top$
$\mathbf{x}' \xleftarrow{\$} \mathbb{Z}_q^k$
return $\mathcal{PG}$
 	
<u>FinalizeMAC($\beta \in \{0,1\}$):</u>
return $(\mathcal{C}_\mathcal{M} \cap \mathcal{Q}_\mathcal{M} = \emptyset) \wedge \beta$
	<u>Eval($\mathsf{m} \in \mathcal{S}$):</u>
	$\mathcal{Q}_\mathcal{M} := \mathcal{Q}_\mathcal{M} \cup \{\mathsf{m}\}$
	$\mathbf{t} := \mathsf{RF}(\mathsf{m}) \in \mathbb{Z}_q^{2k}$
	$\mathbf{u} := \widetilde{\mathsf{RF}}(\mathsf{m})$
	return $([\mathbf{t}]_2, [\mathbf{u}]_2)$
	
	<u>Chal($\mathsf{m}^\star \in \mathcal{S}$):</u>
	$\mathcal{C}_\mathcal{M} := \mathcal{C}_\mathcal{M} \cup \{\mathsf{m}^\star\}$
	Let this be the c-th Chal query.
	$\mathbf{h} := \overline{\mathbf{f}_c}$
	$\mathbf{h}_0 := \left(\sum_{j=1}^{\alpha} \mathbf{J}_{j,\mathsf{m}_j^\star}^\top + \mathbf{B}_1^\perp \mathsf{RF}_\alpha(\mathsf{m}^\star)^\top\right)\mathbf{h} + \underline{\mathbf{f}_c}$
	$h_1 := (\mathbf{x}')^\top \mathbf{h}$
	return $([\mathbf{h}]_1, [\mathbf{h}_0]_1, [h_1]_T)$

Fig. 7. Reduction for the transition from G_3 to G_4 to the Q_c-fold $\mathcal{U}_{3k,k}$-MDDH challenge $([\mathbf{D}]_1, [\mathbf{f}_1]_1, \ldots, [\mathbf{f}_{Q_c}]_1)$.

Assume that $\overline{\mathbf{D}}$ is invertible. This happens with probability at least $(1 - 1/(q-1))$. Write $\mathbf{f}_c =: \begin{pmatrix} \overline{\mathbf{D}}\mathbf{w}_c \\ \underline{\mathbf{D}}\mathbf{w}_c + \mathbf{r}_c \end{pmatrix}$ where $\mathbf{w}_c$ is uniform random in $\mathbb{Z}_q^k$ and $\mathbf{r}_c$ is $\mathbf{0} \in \mathbb{Z}_q^{2k}$ or uniform random in $\mathbb{Z}_q^{2k}$. Then $\mathbf{h} := \overline{\mathbf{f}_c}$ is a uniform random vector in $\mathbb{Z}_q^k$, since $\overline{\mathbf{D}}$ has full rank and $\mathbf{w}_c$ is uniformly random.

The value $\mathbf{h}_0$ is calculated as

$$\begin{aligned}\mathbf{h}_0 &:= \left(\sum_{j=1}^{\alpha} \mathbf{J}_{j,\mathsf{m}_j^\star}^\top + \mathbf{B}_1^\perp \mathsf{RF}_\alpha(\mathsf{m}^\star)^\top\right)\mathbf{h} + \underline{\mathbf{f}_c} \\ &= \left(\sum_{j=1}^{\alpha} \mathbf{J}_{j,\mathsf{m}_j^\star}^\top + \mathbf{B}_1^\perp \mathsf{RF}_\alpha(\mathsf{m}^\star)^\top\right)\mathbf{h} + \underline{\mathbf{D}}\,\overline{\mathbf{D}}^{-1}\overline{\mathbf{f}_c} + \mathbf{r}_c \\ &= \left(\sum_{j=1}^{\alpha} \mathbf{X}_{j,\mathsf{m}_j^\star}^\top + \mathbf{B}_1^\perp \mathsf{RF}_\alpha(\mathsf{m}^\star)^\top\right)\mathbf{h} + \mathbf{r}_c.\end{aligned}$$

If $\mathbf{r}_c = \mathbf{0}$, we are simulating game G_3. If $\mathbf{r}_c$ is uniform random, then $\mathbf{h}_0$ is uniform random and we are simulating game G_4. □

Lemma 14 ($\mathsf{G}_4 \rightsquigarrow \mathsf{G}_5$). *For all adversaries $\mathcal{A}$ there exists an adversary $\mathcal{B}$ with*

$$\left|\Pr[\mathsf{G}_4^{\mathcal{A}} \Rightarrow 1] - \Pr[\mathsf{G}_5^{\mathcal{A}} \Rightarrow 1]\right| \leq 2k\mathsf{Adv}^{\mathsf{mddh}}_{\mathcal{U}_k,\mathsf{PGGen},1}(\mathcal{B}) + \frac{2}{q-1}$$

and $T(\mathcal{B}) \approx T(\mathcal{A}) + (Q_e + Q_c) \cdot \mathsf{poly}(\lambda)$.

Proof. We pick a Q_c fold $\mathcal{U}_k$-MDDH challenge $\left([\mathbf{D}]_1, [\mathbf{f}_1]_1, \ldots, [\mathbf{f}_{Q_c}]_1\right)$ and use the reduction given in Fig. 8.

$\underline{\textsc{Init}_{\mathsf{MAC}}}$:
parse $\mathcal{PG} =: (\mathbb{G}_1, \mathbb{G}_2, \mathbb{G}_T, q, P_1, P_2, e)$
$\mathbf{B}_0, \mathbf{B}_1 \xleftarrow{\$} \mathcal{U}_{2k,k}$
such that $\mathbf{B}_0, \mathbf{B}_1$ is a basis of $\mathbb{Z}_q^{2k}$
for $j \in \{1, \ldots, \alpha\}$, $b \in \{0, 1\}$ **do**
$\quad \mathbf{X}_{j,b} \xleftarrow{\$} \mathbb{Z}_q^{k \times 2k}$
$\mathbf{j}' \xleftarrow{\$} \mathbb{Z}_q^k$
// Implicit: $\mathbf{x}' := \mathbf{j}' + \left(\underline{\mathbf{D}}\,\overline{\mathbf{D}}^{-1}\right)^\top$
return $\mathcal{PG}$
 	
$\underline{\textsc{Finalize}_{\mathsf{MAC}}(\beta \in \{0,1\})}$:
return $(\mathcal{C}_{\mathcal{M}} \cap \mathcal{Q}_{\mathcal{M}} = \emptyset) \wedge \beta$
	$\underline{\textsc{Eval}(\mathsf{m} \in \mathcal{S})}$:
	$\mathcal{Q}_{\mathcal{M}} := \mathcal{Q}_{\mathcal{M}} \cup \{\mathsf{m}\}$
	$\mathbf{t} := \mathsf{RF}(\mathsf{m}) \in \mathbb{Z}_q^{2k}$
	$\mathbf{u} := \widetilde{\mathsf{RF}}(\mathsf{m})$
	return $\left([\mathbf{t}]_2, [\mathbf{u}]_2\right)$
	
	$\underline{\textsc{Chal}(\mathsf{m}^\star \in \mathcal{S})}$:
	$\mathcal{C}_{\mathcal{M}} := \mathcal{C}_{\mathcal{M}} \cup \{\mathsf{m}^\star\}$
	Let this be the c-th $\textsc{Chal}$ query.
	$\mathbf{h} := \overline{\mathbf{f}_c}$
	$\mathbf{h}_0 \xleftarrow{\$} \mathbb{Z}_q^{2k}$
	$h_1 := (\mathbf{j}')^\top \mathbf{h} + \underline{\mathbf{f}_c}$
	return $\left([\mathbf{h}]_1, [\mathbf{h}_0]_1, [h_1]_T\right)$

Fig. 8. Reduction for the transition from G_4 to G_5 to the Q_c-fold $\mathcal{U}_k$-MDDH challenge $\left([\mathbf{D}]_1, [\mathbf{f}_1]_1, \ldots, [\mathbf{f}_{Q_c}]_1\right)$.

Assume that $\overline{\mathbf{D}}$ is invertible. This happens with probability at least $(1 - 1/(q-1))$. Write $\mathbf{f}_c =: \binom{\overline{\mathbf{D}}\mathbf{w}_c}{\underline{\mathbf{D}}\mathbf{w}_c + r_c}$ where $\mathbf{w}_c$ is uniform random in $\mathbb{Z}_q^k$ and r_c is 0 or uniform random in $\mathbb{Z}_q$. Then, just like in the previous Lemma, $\mathbf{h} := \overline{\mathbf{f}_c}$ is a uniform random vector in $\mathbb{Z}_q^k$, since $\overline{\mathbf{D}}$ has full rank and $\mathbf{w}_c$ is uniformly random.

The value h_1 is calculated as

$$h_1 := (\mathbf{j}')^\top \mathbf{h} + \underline{\mathbf{f}_c} = (\mathbf{j}')^\top \mathbf{h} + \underline{\mathbf{D}}\overline{\mathbf{D}}^{-1}\overline{\mathbf{f}_c} + r_c = (\mathbf{x}')^\top \mathbf{h} + r_c.$$

If $r_c = 0$, we are simulating game G_4. If r_c is uniform random, then h_1 is uniform random and we are simulating game G_5. □

Summary. To prove Theorem 1, we combine Lemmata 5–14 to change $\mathbf{h}_0$ and h_1 from real to random and then apply Lemmata 12–5 in reverse order to undo all changes to the Eval oracle to get to the $\mathsf{mPR\text{-}CMA}_{\mathsf{rand}}$ game. The Lemmata 8 and 9 resp. Lemma 10 get information theoretic arguments then. □

3.2 Tight Multi-challenge Security for the First LP MAC

Here we show how tight multi-challenge security can be obtained for the first HIBE from [28]. The MAC, given in Fig. 9, only differs in the parameter η, that is k here. Furthermore this MAC has identity space base set $\mathcal{S} = \{0,1\}^\alpha$ (for arbitrary $\alpha \in \mathbb{N}_+$) and uses $n = 3k$, $n' = k$, $\ell(p) = 1$ (thus also satisfies the delegatable, affine MAC notion) and $\ell'(l, i) = 2i\alpha$. To match the formal definition, $\mathbf{X}_{i,j,b}$ should be renamed to $\mathbf{X}_{i,2j-b}$ and $f_{i,2j-b}(\mathsf{m}) := \left(\llbracket \mathsf{m}_{|i} \rrbracket_j \stackrel{?}{=} b\right)$. In the single-challenge setting, all of these transitions are information-theoretic secure, but in the multi-challenge setting we need a MDDH-assumption in $\mathbb{G}_1$ to proof them.

Theorem 2 (Security of MAC_1). *MAC_1 is tightly $\mathsf{mHPR\text{-}CMA}$ secure under the $\mathcal{U}_k$-MDDH assumption for $\mathbb{G}_1$ and $\mathbb{G}_2$. More precisely, for all adversaries $\mathcal{A}$ there exist adversaries $\mathcal{B}_1$ and $\mathcal{B}_2$ with*

$$\begin{aligned}\mathsf{Adv}^{\mathsf{mhpr\text{-}cma}}_{\mathsf{MAC}_1,\mathsf{PGGen}}(\mathcal{A}) \le{}& \big(8k(\alpha+1)L + 8k\alpha L^2\big)\mathsf{Adv}^{\mathsf{mddh}}_{\mathcal{U}_k,\mathsf{PGGen},2}(\mathcal{B}_1)\\ &+ \big(1 + k(\alpha+4)L + k\alpha L^2\big)\mathsf{Adv}^{\mathsf{mddh}}_{\mathcal{U}_k,\mathsf{PGGen},1}(\mathcal{B}_2)\\ &+ \frac{10 + 2Q_c + (Q_c+6)\alpha(L^2+L)}{q-1} + \frac{2Q_e}{q^{2k}}\end{aligned}$$

and $T(\mathcal{B}_1) \approx T(\mathcal{B}_2) \approx T(\mathcal{A}) + (Q_e + Q_c)\cdot \mathsf{poly}(\lambda)$, where Q_e resp. Q_c denotes the number of Eval *resp.* Chal *queries of $\mathcal{A}$ and* poly *is a polynomial independent of $\mathcal{A}$.*

$\underline{\mathsf{Gen}_{\mathsf{MAC}}(\mathbb{G}_2, q, P_2):}$
$\mathbf{B} \xleftarrow{\$} \mathcal{U}_{3k,k}$
for $i \in \{1, \ldots, L\},\ j \in \{1, \ldots, i\alpha\},\ b \in \{0,1\}$ **do** $\mathbf{X}_{i,j,b} \xleftarrow{\$} \mathbb{Z}_q^{k \times 3k}$
$\mathbf{x}' \xleftarrow{\$} \mathbb{Z}_q^k$
return $\mathsf{sk}_{\mathsf{MAC}} := \left(\mathbf{B}, (\mathbf{X}_{i,j,b})_{1 \leq i \leq L, 1 \leq j \leq i\alpha, b \in \{0,1\}}, \mathbf{x}'\right)$

$\underline{\mathsf{Tag}(\mathsf{sk}_{\mathsf{MAC}}, \mathsf{m} \in \mathcal{S}^p):}$
parse $\mathsf{sk}_{\mathsf{MAC}} =: \left(\mathbf{B}, (\mathbf{X}_{i,j,b})_{1 \leq i \leq L, 1 \leq j \leq i\alpha, b \in \{0,1\}}, \mathbf{x}'\right)$
$\mathbf{s} \xleftarrow{\$} \mathbb{Z}_q^k$; $\mathbf{t} := \mathbf{Bs}$
$\mathbf{u} := \sum_{i=1}^{p} \sum_{j=1}^{i\alpha} \mathbf{X}_{i,j,[\![\mathsf{m}]\!]_j} \mathbf{t} + \mathbf{x}'$
return $\left([\mathbf{t}]_2, [\mathbf{u}]_2\right)$

$\underline{\mathsf{Ver}_{\mathsf{MAC}}(\mathsf{sk}_{\mathsf{MAC}}, \mathsf{m} \in \mathcal{S}^p, \tau):}$
parse $\mathsf{sk}_{\mathsf{MAC}} =: \left(\mathbf{B}, (\mathbf{X}_{i,j,b})_{1 \leq i \leq L, 1 \leq j \leq i\alpha, b \in \{0,1\}}, \mathbf{x}'\right)$
parse $\tau =: \left([\mathbf{t}]_2, [\mathbf{u}]_2\right)$
return $\mathbf{u} \stackrel{?}{=} \sum_{i=1}^{p} \sum_{j=1}^{i\alpha} \mathbf{X}_{i,j,[\![\mathsf{m}]\!]_j} \mathbf{t} + \mathbf{x}'$

Fig. 9. The new multi-challenge tightly secure delegatable affine MAC MAC_1.

The proof can be found in the full version. A summary of the hybrids can be found in Table 4.

3.3 Tight Multi-challenge Security for the Second LP MAC

The second MAC of [28] can be made tightly secure in a similar way to the first MAC. Details can be found in the full version.

4 Transformation to HIBE

Any mHPR-CMA affine MAC with levels can be tightly transformed to an hierarchical identity-based key encapsulation mechanism (HIBKEM) under the $\mathcal{D}_{k+\eta,k}$-MDDH assumption in $\mathbb{G}_1$ with the transformation given in Fig. 10. The transformation follows the same idea as [5]. A security proof can be found in the full version. With a QANIZK for linear subspaces we can use the idea of [22] to obtain an IND-HID-CCA-secure HIBE. Details can be found in the full version.

$\mathsf{Gen}(1^\lambda)$:

$\mathcal{PG} \xleftarrow{\$} \mathsf{PGGen}(1^\lambda)$
parse $\mathcal{PG} =: (\mathbb{G}_1, \mathbb{G}_2, \mathbb{G}_T, q, P_1, P_2, e)$
$\mathsf{sk}_{\mathsf{MAC}} \xleftarrow{\$} \mathsf{Gen}_{\mathsf{MAC}}(\mathbb{G}_2, q, P_2)$
$\mathsf{sk}_{\mathsf{MAC}} =: \left(\mathbf{B}, (\mathbf{X}_{l,i,j})_{1\le l\le \ell(p), 1\le i\le L, 1\le j\le \ell'(l,i)}, \mathbf{x}'\right)$
$\mathbf{A} \xleftarrow{\$} \mathcal{D}_{k+\eta,k}$
for $l \in \{1,\dots,\ell(L)\}$, $i\in\{1,\dots,L\}$, $j\in\{1,\dots,\ell'(l,i)\}$ **do**
  $\mathbf{Y}_{l,i,j} \xleftarrow{\$} \mathbb{Z}_q^{k\times n}$; $\mathbf{Z}_{l,i,j} := \left(\mathbf{Y}_{l,i,j}^\top \mid \mathbf{X}_{l,i,j}^\top\right)\mathbf{A}$
  $\mathbf{D}_{l,i,j} := \mathbf{X}_{l,i,j}\cdot\mathbf{B}$; $\mathbf{E}_{l,i,j} := \mathbf{Y}_{l,i,j}\cdot \mathbf{B}$
$\mathbf{y}' \xleftarrow{\$} \mathbb{Z}_q^k$; $\mathbf{z}' := \left(\mathbf{y}'^\top \mid \mathbf{x}'^\top\right)\cdot\mathbf{A}$
$\widetilde{\mathbf{Z}} := \left([\mathbf{Z}_{l,i,j}]_1\right)_{1\le l\le\ell(p),1\le i\le L,1\le j\le \ell'(l,i)}$
$\mathsf{pk} := \left(\mathcal{PG}, [\mathbf{A}]_1, \widetilde{\mathbf{Z}}, [\mathbf{z}']_1\right)$
$\widetilde{\mathsf{dk}} := \left([\mathbf{D}_{l,i,j}]_2, [\mathbf{E}_{l,i,j}]_2\right)_{1\le l\le\ell(p), 1\le i\le L, 1\le j\le \ell'(l,i)}$
$\mathsf{dk} := \left([\mathbf{B}]_2, \widetilde{\mathsf{dk}}\right)$
$\mathsf{sk} := \left(\mathsf{sk}_{\mathsf{MAC}}, (\mathbf{Y}_{l,i,j})_{1\le l\le\ell(p), 1\le i\le L, 1\le j\le \ell'(l,i)}, \mathbf{y}'\right)$
return $(\mathsf{pk}, \mathsf{dk}, \mathsf{sk})$

$\mathsf{Ext}(\mathsf{sk}, \mathsf{id} \in \mathcal{S}^p)$:

$\left(\left([\mathbf{t}_l]_2\right)_{1\le l\le\ell(p)}, [\mathbf{u}]_2\right) \xleftarrow{\$} \mathsf{Tag}(\mathsf{sk}_{\mathsf{MAC}}, \mathsf{id})$
$$\mathbf{v} := \sum_{l=1}^{\ell(p)} \left(\sum_{i=1}^{p}\sum_{j=1}^{\ell'(l,i)} f_{l,i,j}(\mathsf{id}_{|i})\mathbf{Y}_{l,i,j}\right)\mathbf{t}_l + \mathbf{y}'$$
for $l \in \{1,\dots,\ell(p)\}$, $i \in \{p+1,\dots,L\}$, $j \in \{1,\dots,\ell'(l,i)\}$ **do**
  $\mathbf{d}_{l,i,j} := \mathbf{X}_{l,i,j}\mathbf{t}_l$; $\mathbf{e}_{l,i,j} := \mathbf{Y}_{l,i,j}\mathbf{t}_l$
$\mathsf{usk}[\mathsf{id}] := \left(\left([\mathbf{t}_l]_2\right)_{1\le l\le\ell(p)}, [\mathbf{u}]_2, [\mathbf{v}]_2\right)$
$\mathsf{udk}[\mathsf{id}] := \left([\mathbf{d}_{l,i,j}]_2, [\mathbf{e}_{l,i,j}]_2\right)_{1\le l\le\ell(p), p+1\le i\le L, 1\le j\le\ell'(l,i)}$
return $(\mathsf{usk}[\mathsf{id}], \mathsf{udk}[\mathsf{id}])$

$\mathsf{Enc}(\mathsf{pk}, \mathsf{id} \in \mathcal{S}^p)$:

$\mathbf{r} \xleftarrow{\$} \mathbb{Z}_q^k$; $\mathbf{c}_0 := \mathbf{A}\mathbf{r}$
for $l \in \{1,\dots,\ell(p)\}$ **do**
$$\mathbf{c}_{1,l} := \sum_{i=1}^{p}\sum_{j=1}^{\ell'(l,i)} f_{l,i,j}(\mathsf{id}_{|i})\mathbf{Z}_{l,i,j}\mathbf{r}$$
$\mathsf{C} := \left([\mathbf{c}_0]_1, \left([\mathbf{c}_{1,l}]_1\right)_{1\le l\le\ell(p)}\right)$
$\mathsf{K} := \mathbf{z}'\cdot\mathbf{r}$
return $([\mathsf{K}]_T, \mathsf{C})$

$\mathsf{Del}(\mathsf{dk}, \mathsf{usk}[\mathsf{id}], \mathsf{udk}[\mathsf{id}], \mathsf{id} \in \mathcal{S}^p, \mathsf{id}_{p+1})$:

$\mathsf{usk}[\mathsf{id}] =: \left(\left([\mathbf{t}_l]_2\right)_{1\le l\le\ell(p)}, [\mathbf{u}]_2, [\mathbf{v}]_2\right)$
$\mathsf{udk}[\mathsf{id}] =: \left([\mathbf{d}_{l,i,j}]_2, [\mathbf{e}_{l,i,j}]_2\right)_{1\le l\le\ell(p), p+1\le i\le L, 1\le j\le\ell'(l,i)}$
for $l \in \{\ell(p)+1,\dots,\ell(p+1)\}$ **do**
  $\mathbf{t}_l := \mathbf{0}$
for $l \in \{1,\dots,\ell(p+1)\}$ **do**
  $\mathbf{s}'_l \xleftarrow{\$} \mathbb{Z}_q^{n'}$; $\mathbf{t}'_l := \mathbf{t}_l + \mathbf{B}\mathbf{s}'_l$
$\mathsf{id}' := (\mathsf{id}_1,\dots,\mathsf{id}_p,\mathsf{id}_{p+1})$
$$\mathbf{u}' := \mathbf{u} + \sum_{l=1}^{\ell(p)}\sum_{j=1}^{\ell'(l,p+1)} f_{l,p+1,j}(\mathsf{id}')\mathbf{d}_{l,p+1,j} + \sum_{l=1}^{\ell(p+1)}\left(\sum_{i=1}^{p+1}\sum_{j=1}^{\ell'(l,i)} f_{l,i,j}(\mathsf{id}'_{|i})\mathbf{D}_{l,i,j}\right)\mathbf{s}'_l$$
$$\mathbf{v}' := \mathbf{v} + \sum_{l=1}^{\ell(p)}\sum_{j=1}^{\ell'(l,p+1)} f_{l,p+1,j}(\mathsf{id}')\mathbf{e}_{l,p+1,j} + \sum_{l=1}^{\ell(p+1)}\left(\sum_{i=1}^{p+1}\sum_{j=1}^{\ell'(l,i)} f_{l,i,j}(\mathsf{id}'_{|i})\mathbf{E}_{l,i,j}\right)\mathbf{s}'_l$$
for $l \in \{1,\dots,\ell(p)\}$, $i \in \{p+2,\dots,L\}$, $j \in \{1,\dots,\ell'(l,i)\}$ **do**
  $\mathbf{d}'_{l,i,j} := \mathbf{d}_{l,i,j} + \mathbf{D}_{l,i,j}\mathbf{s}'_l$
  $\mathbf{e}'_{l,i,j} := \mathbf{e}_{l,i,j} + \mathbf{E}_{l,i,j}\mathbf{s}'_l$
for $l \in \{\ell(p)+1,\dots,\ell(p+1)\}$, $i \in \{p+2,\dots,L\}$, $j \in \{1,\dots,\ell'(l,i)\}$ **do**
  $\mathbf{d}'_{l,i,j} := \mathbf{D}_{l,i,j}\mathbf{s}'_l$; $\mathbf{e}'_{l,i,j} := \mathbf{E}_{l,i,j}\mathbf{s}'_l$
$\mathsf{usk}' := \left(\left([\mathbf{t}'_l]_2\right)_{1\le l\le\ell(p+1)}, [\mathbf{u}']_2, [\mathbf{v}']_2\right)$
$\mathsf{udk}' := \left(\left[\mathbf{d}'_{l,i,j}\right]_2, \left[\mathbf{e}'_{l,i,j}\right]_2\right)_{1\le l\le\ell(p+1), p+2\le i\le L, 1\le j\le\ell'(l,i)}$
return $(\mathsf{usk}', \mathsf{udk}')$

$\mathsf{Dec}(\mathsf{usk}[\mathsf{id}], \mathsf{id} \in \mathcal{S}^p, \mathsf{C})$:

$\mathsf{usk}[\mathsf{id}] =: \left(\left([\mathbf{t}_l]_2\right)_{1\le l\le\ell(p)}, [\mathbf{u}]_2, [\mathbf{v}]_2\right)$
parse $\mathsf{C} =: \left([\mathbf{c}_0]_1, \left([\mathbf{c}_{1,l}]_1\right)_{1\le l\le\ell(p)}\right)$
$$[\mathsf{K}]_T := e\left(\left[\mathbf{c}_0^\top\right]_1, \begin{bmatrix}\mathbf{v}\\ \mathbf{u}\end{bmatrix}_2\right) - \sum_{l=1}^{\ell(p)} e\left(\left[\mathbf{c}_{1,l}^\top\right]_1, [\mathbf{t}_l]_2\right)$$
return $[\mathsf{K}]_T$

Fig. 10. The transformation $\mathsf{HIBKEM}_{\mathsf{CPA}}$ of an affine MAC with levels to an HIBKEM.

Table 4. Summary of the hybrids for the security proof of Theorem 2. Non-duplicated EVAL queries (with $p = \hat{\imath}$) draw $\mathbf{t}$ from the set described by the second column and add the randomness $r_{\mathbf{u}}(\mathsf{m})\mathbf{t}$ to $\mathbf{u}$ or choose $\mathbf{u}$ uniform random. The CHAL queries add the term $r_{\mathbf{h}_0}(\mathsf{m}^\star)^\top \mathbf{h}$ to $\mathbf{h}_0$ (if $\mathsf{m}^\star$ has length $\geq \hat{\imath}$). The column "Transition" displays how we can switch to this hybrid from the previous one. The background colors indicate repeated transitions.

Hybrid	$\mathbf{t}$ uniform in	$r_{\mathbf{u}}(\mathsf{m})$	$r_{\mathbf{h}_0}(\mathsf{m})$	Transition
G_0	$\mathsf{Span}(\mathbf{B})$	0		Original game
G_1	$\mathsf{Span}(\mathbf{B})$	0		Identical
$\mathsf{G}_{2,\hat{\imath},0}$	$\mathsf{Span}(\mathbf{B})$	0		Identical
$\mathsf{G}_{2,\hat{\imath},1}$	$\mathbb{Z}_q^{3k}$	0		$\mathcal{U}_k$-MDDH in $\mathbb{G}_2$
$\mathsf{G}_{2,\hat{\imath},2,\hat{\jmath},0}$	$\mathbb{Z}_q^{3k}$	$\mathsf{RF}_{\hat{\imath},\hat{\jmath}}([\![\mathsf{m}]\!]_{\vert\hat{\jmath}})(\mathbf{B}^\perp)^\top$		Identical
$\mathsf{G}_{2,\hat{\imath},2,\hat{\jmath},1}$	**if** $[\![\mathsf{m}]\!]_{\hat{\jmath}+1} = 0$ **then** $\vert\ \mathsf{Span}(\mathbf{B}\vert\mathbf{B}_0)$ **else** $\lfloor \mathsf{Span}(\mathbf{B}\vert\mathbf{B}_1)$	$\mathsf{RF}_{\hat{\imath},\hat{\jmath}}([\![\mathsf{m}]\!]_{\vert\hat{\jmath}})(\mathbf{B}^\perp)^\top$		$\mathcal{U}_k$-MDDH in $\mathbb{G}_2$
$\mathsf{G}_{2,\hat{\imath},2,\hat{\jmath},2}$		$(\mathsf{ZF}_{\hat{\imath},\hat{\jmath}+1}([\![\mathsf{m}]\!]_{\vert\hat{\jmath}+1})(\mathbf{B}_0^*)^\top + \mathsf{OF}_{\hat{\imath},\hat{\jmath}}([\![\mathsf{m}]\!]_{\vert\hat{\jmath}})(\mathbf{B}_1^*)^\top)$		$\mathcal{U}_k$-MDDH in $\mathbb{G}_1$
$\mathsf{G}_{2,\hat{\imath},2,\hat{\jmath},3}$		$(\mathsf{ZF}_{\hat{\imath},\hat{\jmath}+1}([\![\mathsf{m}]\!]_{\vert\hat{\jmath}+1})(\mathbf{B}_0^*)^\top + \mathsf{OF}_{\hat{\imath},\hat{\jmath}+1}([\![\mathsf{m}]\!]_{\vert\hat{\jmath}+1})(\mathbf{B}_1^*)^\top)$		$\mathcal{U}_k$-MDDH in $\mathbb{G}_1$
$\mathsf{G}_{2,\hat{\imath},2,\hat{\jmath}+1,0}$	$\mathbb{Z}_q^{3k}$	$\mathsf{RF}_{\hat{\imath},\hat{\jmath}+1}([\![\mathsf{m}]\!]_{\vert\hat{\jmath}+1})(\mathbf{B}^\perp)^\top$		$\mathcal{U}_k$-MDDH in $\mathbb{G}_2$
$\mathsf{G}_{2,\hat{\imath},3}$	$\mathbb{Z}_q^{3k}$	uniform random	$\mathsf{RF}_{\hat{\imath}}(\mathsf{m}_{\vert\hat{\imath}})(\mathbf{B}^\perp)^\top$	Statistically close
$\mathsf{G}_{2,\hat{\imath},4}$	$\mathbb{Z}_q^{3k}$	uniform random	0	$\mathcal{U}_k$-MDDH in $\mathbb{G}_1$
$\mathsf{G}_{2,\hat{\imath},5}$	$\mathsf{Span}(\mathbf{B})$	uniform random	0	$\mathcal{U}_k$-MDDH in $\mathbb{G}_2$
G_3	$\mathsf{Span}(\mathbf{B})$	uniform random	0	$\mathcal{U}_k$-MDDH in $\mathbb{G}_1$

References

1. Abdalla, M., et al.: Searchable encryption revisited: consistency properties, relation to anonymous IBE, and extensions. In: Shoup, V. (ed.) CRYPTO 2005. LNCS, vol. 3621, pp. 205–222. Springer, Heidelberg (2005). https://doi.org/10.1007/11535218_13
2. Abe, M., Jutla, C.S., Ohkubo, M., Pan, J., Roy, A., Wang, Y.: Shorter QA-NIZK and SPS with tighter security. In: Galbraith, S.D., Moriai, S. (eds.) ASIACRYPT 2019, Part III. LNCS, vol. 11923, pp. 669–699. Springer, Cham (2019). https://doi.org/10.1007/978-3-030-34618-8_23
3. Attrapadung, N., Hanaoka, G., Yamada, S.: A framework for identity-based encryption with almost tight security. In: Iwata, T., Cheon, J.H. (eds.) ASIACRYPT 2015, Part I. LNCS, vol. 9452, pp. 521–549. Springer, Heidelberg (2015). https://doi.org/10.1007/978-3-662-48797-6_22

4. Bellare, M., Goldwasser, S.: New paradigms for digital signatures and message authentication based on non-interactive zero knowledge proofs. In: Brassard, G. (ed.) CRYPTO 1989. LNCS, vol. 435, pp. 194–211. Springer, New York (1990). https://doi.org/10.1007/0-387-34805-0_19
5. Blazy, O., Kiltz, E., Pan, J.: (Hierarchical) identity-based encryption from affine message authentication. In: Garay, J.A., Gennaro, R. (eds.) CRYPTO 2014, Part I. LNCS, vol. 8616, pp. 408–425. Springer, Heidelberg (2014). https://doi.org/10.1007/978-3-662-44371-2_23
6. Blazy, O., Kiltz, E., Pan, J.: (Hierarchical) identity-based encryption from affine message authentication. Cryptology ePrint Archive, Report 2014/581 (2014). http://eprint.iacr.org/2014/581
7. Boneh, D., Franklin, M.K.: Identity-based encryption from the weil pairing. In: Kilian, J. (ed.) CRYPTO 2001. LNCS, vol. 2139, pp. 213–229. Springer, Heidelberg (2001). https://doi.org/10.1007/3-540-44647-8_13
8. Chen, J., Wee, H.: Fully, (almost) tightly secure IBE and dual system groups. In: Canetti, R., Garay, J.A. (eds.) CRYPTO 2013, Part II. LNCS, vol. 8043, pp. 435–460. Springer, Heidelberg (2013). https://doi.org/10.1007/978-3-642-40084-1_25
9. Dodis, Y., Kiltz, E., Pietrzak, K., Wichs, D.: Message authentication, revisited. In: Pointcheval, D., Johansson, T. (eds.) EUROCRYPT 2012. LNCS, vol. 7237, pp. 355–374. Springer, Heidelberg (2012). https://doi.org/10.1007/978-3-642-29011-4_22
10. Escala, A., Herold, G., Kiltz, E., Råfols, C., Villar, J.: An algebraic framework for Diffie-Hellman assumptions. In: Canetti, R., Garay, J.A. (eds.) CRYPTO 2013, Part II. LNCS, vol. 8043, pp. 129–147. Springer, Heidelberg (2013). https://doi.org/10.1007/978-3-642-40084-1_8
11. Gay, R., Hofheinz, D., Kiltz, E., Wee, H.: Tightly CCA-secure encryption without pairings. In: Fischlin, M., Coron, J.-S. (eds.) EUROCRYPT 2016, Part I. LNCS, vol. 9665, pp. 1–27. Springer, Heidelberg (2016). https://doi.org/10.1007/978-3-662-49890-3_1
12. Gay, R., Hofheinz, D., Kohl, L.: Kurosawa-desmedt meets tight security. In: Katz, J., Shacham, H. (eds.) CRYPTO 2017, Part III. LNCS, vol. 10403, pp. 133–160. Springer, Cham (2017). https://doi.org/10.1007/978-3-319-63697-9_5
13. Gay, R., Hofheinz, D., Kohl, L., Pan, J.: More efficient (almost) tightly secure structure-preserving signatures. In: Nielsen, J.B., Rijmen, V. (eds.) EUROCRYPT 2018, Part II. LNCS, vol. 10821, pp. 230–258. Springer, Cham (2018). https://doi.org/10.1007/978-3-319-78375-8_8
14. Gentry, C., Silverberg, A.: Hierarchical ID-based cryptography. In: Zheng, Y. (ed.) ASIACRYPT 2002. LNCS, vol. 2501, pp. 548–566. Springer, Heidelberg (2002). https://doi.org/10.1007/3-540-36178-2_34
15. Gjøsteen, K., Jager, T.: Practical and tightly-secure digital signatures and authenticated key exchange. In: Shacham, H., Boldyreva, A. (eds.) CRYPTO 2018, Part II. LNCS, vol. 10992, pp. 95–125. Springer, Cham (2018). https://doi.org/10.1007/978-3-319-96881-0_4
16. Gong, J., Cao, Z., Tang, S., Chen, J.: Extended dual system group and shorter unbounded hierarchical identity based encryption. Des. Codes Crypt. **80**(3), 525–559 (2015). https://doi.org/10.1007/s10623-015-0117-z
17. Gong, J., Chen, J., Dong, X., Cao, Z., Tang, S.: Extended nested dual system groups, revisited. In: Cheng, C.-M., Chung, K.-M., Persiano, G., Yang, B.-Y. (eds.) PKC 2016, Part I. LNCS, vol. 9614, pp. 133–163. Springer, Heidelberg (2016). https://doi.org/10.1007/978-3-662-49384-7_6

18. Gong, J., Dong, X., Chen, J., Cao, Z.: Efficient IBE with tight reduction to standard assumption in the multi-challenge setting. In: Cheon, J.H., Takagi, T. (eds.) ASIACRYPT 2016, Part II. LNCS, vol. 10032, pp. 624–654. Springer, Heidelberg (2016). https://doi.org/10.1007/978-3-662-53890-6_21
19. Groth, J., Sahai, A.: Efficient non-interactive proof systems for bilinear groups. In: Smart, N. (ed.) EUROCRYPT 2008. LNCS, vol. 4965, pp. 415–432. Springer, Heidelberg (2008). https://doi.org/10.1007/978-3-540-78967-3_24
20. Hofheinz, D.: Adaptive partitioning. In: Coron, J.-S., Nielsen, J.B. (eds.) EUROCRYPT 2017, Part III. LNCS, vol. 10212, pp. 489–518. Springer, Cham (2017). https://doi.org/10.1007/978-3-319-56617-7_17
21. Hofheinz, D., Jager, T.: Tightly secure signatures and public-key encryption. In: Safavi-Naini, R., Canetti, R. (eds.) CRYPTO 2012. LNCS, vol. 7417, pp. 590–607. Springer, Heidelberg (2012). https://doi.org/10.1007/978-3-642-32009-5_35
22. Hofheinz, D., Jia, D., Pan, J.: Identity-based encryption tightly secure under chosen-ciphertext attacks. In: Peyrin, T., Galbraith, S. (eds.) ASIACRYPT 2018, Part II. LNCS, vol. 11273, pp. 190–220. Springer, Cham (2018). https://doi.org/10.1007/978-3-030-03329-3_7
23. Hofheinz, D., Koch, J., Striecks, C.: Identity-based encryption with (almost) tight security in the multi-instance, multi-ciphertext setting. In: Katz, J. (ed.) PKC 2015. LNCS, vol. 9020, pp. 799–822. Springer, Heidelberg (2015). https://doi.org/10.1007/978-3-662-46447-2_36
24. Horwitz, J., Lynn, B.: Toward hierarchical identity-based encryption. In: Knudsen, L.R. (ed.) EUROCRYPT 2002. LNCS, vol. 2332, pp. 466–481. Springer, Heidelberg (2002). https://doi.org/10.1007/3-540-46035-7_31
25. Jutla, C.S., Roy, A.: Shorter quasi-adaptive NIZK proofs for linear subspaces. In: Sako, K., Sarkar, P. (eds.) ASIACRYPT 2013, Part I. LNCS, vol. 8269, pp. 1–20. Springer, Heidelberg (2013). https://doi.org/10.1007/978-3-642-42033-7_1
26. Kiltz, E., Loss, J., Pan, J.: Tightly-secure signatures from five-move identification protocols. In: Takagi, T., Peyrin, T. (eds.) ASIACRYPT 2017, Part III. LNCS, vol. 10626, pp. 68–94. Springer, Cham (2017). https://doi.org/10.1007/978-3-319-70700-6_3
27. Kiltz, E., Wee, H.: Quasi-adaptive NIZK for linear subspaces revisited. In: Oswald, E., Fischlin, M. (eds.) EUROCRYPT 2015, Part II. LNCS, vol. 9057, pp. 101–128. Springer, Heidelberg (2015). https://doi.org/10.1007/978-3-662-46803-6_4
28. Langrehr, R., Pan, J.: Tightly secure hierarchical identity-based encryption. In: Lin, D., Sako, K. (eds.) PKC 2019, Part I. LNCS, vol. 11442, pp. 436–465. Springer, Cham (2019). https://doi.org/10.1007/978-3-030-17253-4_15
29. Langrehr, R., Pan, J.: Tightly secure hierarchical identity-based encryption. Cryptology ePrint Archive, Report 2019/058 (2019). https://eprint.iacr.org/2019/058
30. Lewko, A.: Tools for simulating features of composite order bilinear groups in the prime order setting. In: Pointcheval, D., Johansson, T. (eds.) EUROCRYPT 2012. LNCS, vol. 7237, pp. 318–335. Springer, Heidelberg (2012). https://doi.org/10.1007/978-3-642-29011-4_20
31. Lewko, A.B., Waters, B.: New techniques for dual system encryption and fully secure HIBE with short ciphertexts. In: Micciancio, D. (ed.) TCC 2010. LNCS, vol. 5978, pp. 455–479. Springer, Heidelberg (2010). https://doi.org/10.1007/978-3-642-11799-2_27
32. Lewko, A.B., Waters, B.: Why proving HIBE systems secure is difficult. In: Nguyen, P.Q., Oswald, E. (eds.) EUROCRYPT 2014. LNCS, vol. 8441, pp. 58–76. Springer, Heidelberg (2014). https://doi.org/10.1007/978-3-642-55220-5_4

33. Naor, M., Reingold, O.: On the construction of pseudo-random permutations: Luby-Rackoff revisited (extended abstract). In: 29th ACM STOC, pp. 189–199. ACM Press, May 1997
34. Waters, B.: Dual system encryption: realizing fully secure IBE and HIBE under simple assumptions. In: Halevi, S. (ed.) CRYPTO 2009. LNCS, vol. 5677, pp. 619–636. Springer, Heidelberg (2009). https://doi.org/10.1007/978-3-642-03356-8_36
35. Waters, B.: Efficient identity-based encryption without random oracles. In: Cramer, R. (ed.) EUROCRYPT 2005. LNCS, vol. 3494, pp. 114–127. Springer, Heidelberg (2005). https://doi.org/10.1007/11426639_7

Obfuscation and Applications

The Usefulness of Sparsifiable Inputs: How to Avoid Subexponential iO

Thomas Agrikola[1(✉)], Geoffroy Couteau[2], and Dennis Hofheinz[3]

[1] Karlsruhe Institute of Technology, Karlsruhe, Germany
thomas.agrikola@kit.edu
[2] IRIF, Paris-Diderot University, CNRS, Paris, France
couteau@irif.fr
[3] ETH Zurich, Zurich, Switzerland
hofheinz@inf.ethz.ch

Abstract. We consider the problem of removing subexponential reductions to indistinguishability obfuscation (iO) in the context of obfuscating probabilistic programs. Specifically, we show how to apply complexity absorption (Zhandry Crypto 2016) to the recent notion of probabilistic indistinguishability obfuscation (piO, Canetti et al. TCC 2015). As a result, we obtain a variant of piO which allows to obfuscate a large class of probabilistic programs, from polynomially secure indistinguishability obfuscation and extremely lossy functions. Particularly, our piO variant is able to obfuscate circuits with specific input domains regardless of the performed computation. We then revisit several (direct or indirect) applications of piO, and obtain

- a fully homomorphic encryption scheme (without circular security assumptions),
- a multi-key fully homomorphic encryption scheme with threshold decryption,
- an encryption scheme secure under arbitrary key-dependent messages,
- a spooky encryption scheme for all circuits,
- a function secret sharing scheme with additive reconstruction for all circuits,

all from polynomially secure iO, extremely lossy functions, and, depending on the scheme, also other (but polynomial and comparatively mild) assumptions. All of these assumptions are implied by polynomially secure iO and the (non-polynomial, but very well-investigated) exponential DDH assumption. Previously, all the above applications required to assume the *subexponential* security of iO (and more standard assumptions).

Keywords: Indistinguishability obfuscation · Extremely lossy functions · Subexponential assumptions

T. Agrikola, G. Couteau and D. Hofheinz—Supported by ERC Project PREP-CRYPTO 724307.

Work done while all authors were at Karlsruhe Institute of Technology.

A. Kiayias et al. (Eds.): PKC 2020, LNCS 12110, pp. 187–219, 2020.
https://doi.org/10.1007/978-3-030-45374-9_7

1 Introduction

Obfuscation. Code obfuscation has been formalized already in the early 2000s as a cryptographic building block, by Hada [42] and Barak et al. [5], along with a number of early positive [23,45,47,56,61] and negative [5,38,61] results. However, prior to the candidate obfuscation scheme of Garg et al. [31], only relatively few positive results on obfuscation were known.

The first candidate obfuscator from [31] changed things. Their work identified indistinguishability obfuscation (iO, cf. [5,39]) as an achievable *and* useful general notion of obfuscation: it presented a candidate indistinguishability obfuscator, along with a first highly non-trivial application. Since then, a vast number of applications have been proposed, ranging from functional [31], deniable [59], and fully homomorphic [25] encryption, over multi-party computation (e.g., [30]), to separation results (e.g., [46]). In the process, powerful techniques like "puncturing" [59] have been discovered, which have found applications even beyond obfuscation (e.g., in multi-party computation [8,36], instantiating the Fiat-Shamir paradigm [24], and verifiable random functions [9,40]). Besides, the notion of iO itself has been refined, and related to other notions of obfuscation [2,10,11,20,25,50], and various different constructions of obfuscators have been presented [3,4,13,53,54,57,63].

Subexponential Assumptions. It is currently hard to find a cryptographic primitive that can *not* be constructed from iO (in combination with another mild assumption such as the existence of one-way functions). However, some of the known iO-based constructions come only with *subexponential* reductions to iO. For instance, the only known iO-based constructions of fully homomorphic encryption [25], spooky encryption [27], and graded encoding schemes [29] suffer from reductions with a subexponential loss.

Hence, while iO has generally been recognized as an extremely powerful primitive (even to the extent being called a "central hub" for cryptography [59]), it is not at all clear if this also holds for *polynomially* secure iO. Indeed, it is conceivable that only polynomially secure iO exists, in which case much of iO's power stands in question.

More generally, subexponential reductions (in particular to iO) are undesirable. Namely, the security of existing iO constructions is still not well-understood, and in particular current state-of-the-art constructions of iO schemes (such as [4,53,54]) already require subexponential computational assumptions themselves. Hence, assuming subexponential iO is a particularly risky bet. This suspicion is confirmed in part by [58], who separate polynomial and subexponential security for virtual black-box obfuscation.

Removing subexponential assumptions in general and from iO-based constructions in particular has already explicitly been considered in [35,52] and [33,34,55] respectively. These works offer general techniques and ideas to turn subexponential reductions into polynomial ones. For instance, [34,55] offer ways to replace (subexponential) iO-based constructions with (polynomial) constructions based on functional encryption. Of course, this requires a special structure of the primitive to be implemented, and is demonstrated for several primitives, including non-interactive key exchange and short signature schemes.

Our Contribution. In this work, we are also concerned with substituting subexponential with polynomial reductions in iO-based constructions. Unlike [34,55], however, we do not follow the approach of using functional encryption directly in place of iO, but instead will employ extremely lossy functions (ELFs) [62] to "absorb" subexponential complexity.[1]

We will implement a variant of probabilistic indistinguishability obfuscation (piO, introduced in [25]) using polynomially secure iO (and ELFs). piO schemes can be used to obfuscate *probabilistic* (i.e., randomized) programs, and are currently the only way to obtain, e.g., fully homomorphic encryption (FHE) schemes without circular security assumptions [25]. However, the only previous construction of piO schemes required subexponentially secure iO [25]. Hence, our construction yields the first FHE scheme from polynomially secure iO (and ELFs). Similarly, we can turn the assumption of subexponentially secure iO into polynomially secure iO (plus ELFs) in the construction of spooky encryption from [27].

Both FHE and spooky encryption are quite powerful primitives, and we obtain several "spin-off results" by revisiting their implications. For instance, when instantiating the piO-based FHE construction of [25] with our piO scheme and a suitable public-key encryption scheme, we obtain a fully key-dependent message (KDM) secure public-key encryption scheme from (polynomially secure) iO and the exponentially secure DDH assumption (and no further assumptions). Under the same assumptions, we obtain multi-key FHE with threshold decryption and function secret sharing schemes from the spooky encryption construction from [27].

On the Plausibility of ELFs. One could argue that we trade one exponential assumption for another, and it is not clear that assuming polynomial iO and exponential DDH is any better than assuming only subexponential iO in the first place. Seconding Zhandry [62] here, we think that exponential DDH is a realistic assumption that is far more popular, better-investigated, and arguably more plausible than subexponential iO. Much of the currently deployed cryptography relies on (in fact a strong variant of) exponential DDH, because parameters are almost always chosen according to the best known attacks.

On the Number of Assumptions. Another natural observation is that iO for general circuits is already an exponential family of assumptions in itself (one for each obfuscated circuit). It might seem that this lets the challenge of relying on polynomially secure iO instead of subexponentially secure iO appear less appealing. We make two comments on that.

[1] That means that our final schemes depend on ELFs, which are currently only known to be instantiable from exponential assumptions. However, we stress that ELFs can be built from exponential variants of very standard assumptions, such as the decisional Diffie-Hellman (DDH) assumption..

- First, being an exponential family of assumptions and assuming resistance against subexponential adversaries are orthogonal issues. Many cryptographic assumptions have several dimensions of strengths, and relaxing the assumption in any of these dimensions is desirable.[2] In this work, we make progress in one important dimension. By replacing subexponential iO by polynomial iO plus exponential DDH, we effectively trade an *exponential* number of subexponential hardness assumptions in exchange for a *single* (plausible, well-studied) exponential hardness assumption (plus an exponential family of polynomial hardness assumptions).
- Second, iO being an exponential family of assumptions can be considered an artificial consequence of working on the general notion of iO for *arbitrary circuits*. When using iO in concrete constructions (e.g. in all the constructions described in this paper), one almost never needs to assume iO for all circuits. It usually suffices to assume iO for a constant number of specific circuits (namely those being obfuscated in the construction and the analysis). Hence, iO is a small number of assumptions when used for building a cryptographic primitive.

1.1 Technical Overview

The piO Construction of Canetti et al. To describe our ideas, it will be helpful to briefly review the work of Canetti et al. [25]. In a nutshell, they define the notion of piO as a way to obfuscate probabilistic programs, and show how to use piO to implement the first FHE scheme without any circular security assumption. Intuitively, where the notion of iO captures that the obfuscation $\mathsf{iO}(P)$ of a *deterministic* program P does not leak anything beyond the functionality of P, piO captures the same for *probabilistic* programs P.[3]

They also show how to implement piO with an indistinguishability obfuscator iO and a pseudorandom function (PRF) F. Namely, in order to obfuscate a probabilistic program P, Canetti et al. obfuscate the *deterministic* program P' that, on input x, runs $P(x)$ with random coins $r = F(K, x)$. Here, K is a PRF key hardcoded into P'. The security proof uses "puncturing" techniques [59] and a hybrid argument over all possible P-inputs x. More specifically, for each P-input x, separate reductions to the security of iO and F show that the execution of $P'(x)$ is secure.[4]

This proof strategy is very general and does not need to make any specific assumptions about the structure of P. (In fact, this strategy can be viewed

[2] For example, if a protocol relies on the subexponential hardness of LWE with exponential modulus-to-noise ratio, it would be desirable to achieve the same while relying only on polynomially secure LWE, even if the modulus-to-noise ratio remains exponential.

[3] This is of course an oversimplification. Also, [25] define several types of piO security that provide a tradeoff between security and achievability.

[4] Again, we are not very specific about the form of desired or assumed security. However, we believe that for this exposition, these specifics do not matter.

as a specific form of "complexity leveraging", technically similar to the conversion of selective security into adaptive security, e.g., [16].) However, the price to pay is a reduction loss which is linear in the size of the input domain (which usually is exponentially large). In particular, even after scaling security parameters suitably, Canetti et al. still require subexponentially secure iO and PRFs.

More on Previous Works to Remove Subexponentiality. There are a number of known ways to deal with subexponential reduction losses due to complexity leveraging (or related techniques). For instance, various semi-generic (pre-iO) techniques seek to achieve adaptive security (for different primitives) by establishing an algebraic or combinatorial structure on the used inputs [17,44,49,60], and can sometimes be adapted to the iO setting [48]. But like the already-mentioned, somewhat more general approaches [34,55], these works make specific assumptions about the structure of the involved computations.

A somewhat more general approach (that works for more general classes of programs) was outlined by Zhandry [62], who introduces the notion of "extremely lossy functions" (ELFs). Intuitively, an ELF is an injective function G that can be switched into an "extremely lossy mode", in which its range is polynomially small. Such an ELF can sometimes be used to "preprocess" inputs in a cryptographic scheme, with the following benefit: a security reduction can switch the ELF to extremely lossy mode, so that only a polynomial number of (preprocessed) inputs $G(x)$ need to be considered. This simplifies a potential hybrid argument over all (preprocessed) inputs $G(x)$, and can lead to a polynomial (instead of a subexponential) reduction.

However, trying to apply this strategy to the construction and reduction of Canetti et al. (as sketched above) directly fails. Namely, in their application, inputs will be inputs x to an arbitrary (probabilistic) program P; preprocessing them with an ELF will destroy their structure, and it is not clear how to run P on ELF-preprocessed inputs $G(x)$. Indeed, applying ELFs to realize piO requires fundamentally different techniques.

Main Idea: piO with Sparsifiable Inputs. Instead, we will restrict ourselves to programs P that take as input an element x from a small number of (arbitrary but efficiently samplable) distributions. In other words, all possible inputs x need to be in the range of one of a small number of efficient samplers S_i. As an example, for $i \in \{0,1\}$, sampler S_i could sample ciphertexts C that encrypt plaintext i. Moreover, we require that all inputs to a program P to be obfuscated are at some point actually sampled from some S_i according to a certain process.

Obfuscating a given probabilistic program P (that takes as inputs one or more x as above) now consists of two steps:

1. First, we *encode* all inputs x, in the sense that we compile S_i to attach a "certificate" aux to x. This certificate aux guarantees that x has really been sampled using S_i. Furthermore, the compiled sampler S_i uses preprocessed random coins of the form $G(r)$ (instead of r) for an ELF G. (When G is

in injective mode, this does not affect the distribution of sampled x.) The certificate aux additionally guarantees this choice of random coins.[5]
2. Second, we produce the actual obfuctation of the probabilistic program P as follows. We use an indistinguishability obfuscator iO to obfuscate the following (deterministic) variant P' of P: on inputs $x_1, \ldots, x_\ell$ with certificates $\mathsf{aux}_1, \ldots, \mathsf{aux}_\ell$, P' first checks the certificates aux_i and aborts if one of them is invalid. Next, P' runs $P(x_1, \ldots, x_\ell)$, with random coins $F(K, (x_i)_{i=1}^{\ell})$ for a PRF F and a hardcoded PRF key K. Finally, P' outputs P's output.

Maybe the most important property of this setup is that now the sets of inputs x_i are "sparsifiable" in the following sense. If we set G to extremely lossy mode, then only a polynomial number of different random coins r can occur. Hence, each S_i will output one of only a small number of possible samples (e.g., encryptions C generated with random coins from a small set). In that sense, the set of possible inputs x_i to P has been "sparsified", and a hybrid argument over all possible inputs as in [25] is possible with polynomial loss.

We stress that our technique of applying ELFs fundamentally differs from [62]. In [62], the constructed primitive itself ensures that G is applied on all inputs. When approaching the challenge of constructing piO, however, the input to the primitive must externally be sampled using random coins that are preprocessed with G. This process is not under the control of the primitive and therefore requires a mechanism certifying that inputs are generated according to this specific process. We implement this mechanism using the combination of compiling the sampler for the input distribution into a "certifying sampler" (step 1) and restricting correctness of the obfuscated program (step 2).

Surprisingly, our piO scheme achieves the notion of "dynamic-input piO" [25], a very strong variant of piO security. On a high level, dynamic-input piO guarantees indistinguishability between obfuscations of probabilistic programs as long as their output distributions on adversarially chosen inputs are indistinguishable. This constitutes a very strong requirement and, in fact, implies differing-inputs obfuscation [2,5], a notion for which strong impossibility results exist [7,32]. However, our obfuscator produces circuits which are only required to work on inputs certifiably generated according to a specific process. Hence, our piO scheme enjoys a restricted form of correctness. This enables us to circumvent the impossibility results [7,32].

Applications. One obvious question is of course how restrictive our assumption on input domains really is. We show that our assumptions apply to two existing piO-based constructions, with a number of interesting consequences.

First, we revisit the piO-based construction of fully homomorphic encryption from [25]. Here, piO is used to obfuscate the FHE evaluation algorithm that takes two ciphertexts (say, of two bit plaintexts b_0 and b_1) as input, and outputs a ciphertext of the NAND of the two plaintexts (i.e., $b_0 \overline{\wedge} b_1$). If we set S_b to be a sampler that samples an encryption of b, this setting perfectly fits our scheme. Hence, we obtain first a leveled homomorphic encryption (LHE) scheme,

[5] Looking ahead, this "certificate" will be implemented using a NIZK in our construction.

and from this an FHE scheme using the high-level strategy from [25]. Hence, putting this together with our piO construction, we obtain an FHE scheme from polynomially secure iO and an ELF (and no further assumptions).

We note that the above FHE scheme is also fully key-dependent message (KDM, see [14]) secure when implemented with a suitable basic public-key encryption scheme (such as the DDH-based scheme of [18]). In that case, the FHE is secure even when an encryption of its own secret key $C_{\mathsf{sk}} = \mathsf{Enc}(\mathsf{pk}, \mathsf{sk})$ is public. However, such an encryption C_{sk} can be transformed into an encryption $\mathsf{Enc}(\mathsf{pk}, f(\mathsf{sk}))$ of an arbitrary function of sk thanks to the fully homomorphic properties of the FHE scheme. This leads to a conceptually very simple fully KDM-secure encryption scheme from polynomial assumptions (and ELFs). (We stress that we do not claim novelty for this observation. The connection between FHE and KDM security has already been observed in [6] and [27] have observed that the FHE construction of Canetti et al. preserves interesting properties of the underlying encryption scheme. However, [27] do not explicitly mention KDM security, and we find these consequences interesting enough to point out.)

As our second application, we consider spooky encryption (with CRS) introduced by Dodis et al. [27]. Intuitively, a spooky encryption scheme features a particular type of homomorphism in a multi-key, multi-ciphertext setting. More precisely, given ciphertexts $\{c_i = \mathsf{Enc}(\mathsf{pk}_i, x_i)\}_i$, a spooky encryption scheme allows to produce ciphertexts $\{c'_i\}_i$ with $y_i = \mathsf{Dec}(\mathsf{sk}_i, c'_i)$ such that certain so-called "spooky" relations between between the x_i's and the y_i's hold. An important subclass of spooky relations allows to ensure that the y_i's are random subject to $\sum_i y_i = f(x_1, \dots, x_n)$, for any polynomial-time computable function f. Dodis et al. show that spooky encryption implies (among other things) function secret sharing, and they give a piO-based instantiation of spooky encryption (without the need of a CRS). At the heart of their construction is an obfuscated public "spooky evaluation" algorithm with a hardcoded decryption key. Since this algorithm also takes ciphertexts (and a public key) as input, its input domain can be sparsified much like in the FHE case.

In contrast to the FHE application, however, the spooky encryption application contains more technical subtleties. In particular, some inputs to the "spooky evaluation" algorithm may depend on other inputs, and hence sparsifying inputs needs to proceed in a certain order. The main difficulty here is to find a suitably flexible definition of sparsification; we omit the details in this overview. We note that our results of course also yield all applications of spooky encryption, only from polynomially secure iO (and ELFs). In particular, we obtain a simple protocol for function secret sharing for all functions (with additive reconstruction) from these assumptions [21].

We believe that our new notion of obfuscation will prove useful in other applications; for example, it would likely allow to improve the recent result of [26], which constructed CCA1-secure FHE from subexponentially secure iO.

Follow-Up Work. In the recent work [28], Döttling and Nishimaki define the notion universal proxy re-encryption (UPRE). UPRE schemes allow a proxy to convert any ciphertext under any public key of any existing PKE scheme into a ciphertext under any public key of any possibly different existing PKE scheme. [28] instantiate UPRE based on probabilistic IO due to [25]. UPRE for all PKE schemes (including non re-randomizable ones) requires dynamic-input pIO, which implies differing-inputs obfuscation. However, [28] observe that our notion of doubly-probabilistic IO suffices which yields an instantiation of UPRE for all PKE schemes based on polynomial IO and exponential DDH.

Organization. In Sect. 2, we introduce our notations and recall standard preliminaries. Section 3 formally introduces our new variant of piO, called dpiO. Section 4 shows how to instantiate dpiO using polynomially secure iO and ELFs. Eventually, in Sect. 5 and the full version [1] we revisit the construction of leveled homomorphic encryption from [25], using dpiO instead of piO. In the full version [1], we revisit the construction of spooky encryption from [27] using dpiO and analyze our new construction.

2 Preliminaries

Notations. Throughout this paper, λ denotes the security parameter. For a natural number $n \in \mathbb{N}$, $[n]$ denotes the set $\{1, \dots, n\}$. A probabilistic polynomial time algorithm (PPT, also denoted *efficient* algorithm) runs in time polynomial in the (implicit) security parameter λ. A positive function f is *negligible* if for any polynomial p there exists a bound $B > 0$ such that, for any integer $k \geq B$, $f(k) \leq 1/|p(k)|$. An event depending on λ occurs with *overwhelming probability* when its probability is at least $1 - \mathsf{negl}(\lambda)$ for a negligible function negl. Given a finite set S, the notation $x \stackrel{\$}{\leftarrow} S$ means a uniformly random assignment of an element of S to the variable x. The notation $\mathcal{A}^{\mathcal{O}}$ indicates that the algorithm $\mathcal{A}$ is given oracle access to $\mathcal{O}$. Let $\mathcal{C} = \{\mathcal{C}_\lambda\}_{\lambda \geq 0}$ be a family of sets of (possibly randomized) circuits, where $\mathcal{C}_\lambda$ contains circuits of size $\mathsf{poly}(\lambda)$. A circuit sampler for $\mathcal{C}$ is a distribution ensemble $D = \{D_\lambda\}_{\lambda \geq 0}$, such that D_λ ranges over triples (C_0, C_1, z) with $(C_0, C_1) \in \mathcal{C}_\lambda^2$ of identical size and taking inputs of the same length, and $z \in \{0,1\}^{\mathsf{poly}(\lambda)}$. A class of samplers $\mathbf{S}$ is a set of circuit samplers for $\mathcal{C}$.

2.1 Indistinguishability Obfuscation for General Samplers

Indistinguishability obfuscation (iO) for general samplers was introduced in [25]. This notion generalizes the classical notion of iO introduced in [5]. Informally, an iO scheme for a sampler D allows to obfuscate circuits sampled with D so that, given a sample (C_0, C_1) from D, $\mathsf{iO}(C_0) \approx \mathsf{iO}(C_1)$. The standard notion of iO is recovered by considering samplers over functionally equivalent deterministic circuits of the same size. Stronger notions of obfuscation, denoted piO, can be defined for samplers over *probabilistic* circuits, satisfying various indistinguishability notions. We recall below the general definition of [25] of piO for a class of samplers (using a different notion of correctness defined in [27]). The original correctness definition states that an efficient adversary given oracle access to either the original circuit or the obfuscation (with the restriction that no input can be queried twice), can not tell the difference.

Definition 1 (piO for a Class of Samplers [25,27]). *A uniform PPT machine* piO *is an* indistinguishability obfuscator *for a class of samplers* **S** *over a family* $\mathcal{C} = \{C_\lambda\}_{\lambda \geq 0}$ *of possibly randomized circuits if it satisfies the following conditions:*

Correctness. *For every security parameter* λ*, every circuit* $C \in C_\lambda$*, and every input* x*, the distributions of* $C(x)$ *over the random coins of* C *and of* $\mathsf{piO}(1^\lambda, C)(x)$ *over the random coins of the obfuscator are identical.*

μ**-Indistinguishability.** *For every sampler* $D = \{D_\lambda\}_{\lambda \geq 0} \in \mathbf{S}$*, and for every non-uniform PPT machine* $\mathcal{A}$*, it holds that*

$$|\Pr[(C_0, C_1, z) \xleftarrow{\$} D_\lambda : \mathcal{A}(C_0, C_1, \mathsf{piO}(1^\lambda, C_0), z) = 1]$$
$$- \Pr[(C_0, C_1, z) \xleftarrow{\$} D_\lambda : \mathcal{A}(C_0, C_1, \mathsf{piO}(1^\lambda, C_1), z) = 1]| \leq \mu(\lambda).$$

We remark that the construction of piO from [25] satisfies this notion of correctness if instantiated with a perfect puncturable PRF, see Definition 4. Note that this does not extend to multiple evaluations of the obfuscated circuit. Further, note that this notion of correctness implies that the obfuscated circuit respects the support of the original circuit.

To recover the standard notion of iO, we introduce the class $\mathbf{S}^{\mathsf{eq}}$ of samplers for functionally equivalent (possibly randomized) circuits, *i.e.*, samplers over triplets (C_0, C_1, z) such that $|C_0| = |C_1|$, and for any input x and random coin r, $C_0(x; r) = C_1(x; r)$. The standard iO notion is obtained by considering piO over the subclass $\mathbf{S}^{\mathsf{det}} \subset \mathbf{S}^{\mathsf{eq}}$ of samplers for deterministic functionally equivalent circuits. We denote by $\mathsf{Adv}_{\mathsf{iO}}(\mathcal{A})$ the advantage of a PPT adversary $\mathcal{A}$ in distinguishing between the obfuscation of functionaly equivalent deterministic circuits.

The work of [25] introduced four types of samplers over probabilistic circuits, which define four corresponding variants of piO: dynamic-input piO, worst-case piO, memoryless worst-case piO, and X-Ind piO. Informally, a dynamic-input sampler is required to output (possibly randomized) circuits C_0, C_1 such that the output of these circuits on a dynamically chosen input is computationally indistinguishable. The corresponding notion, dynamic-input piO, is the strongest notion defined in [25] and a randomized equivalent of the notion of differing-input obfuscation. Therefore, it inherits the implausibility results of differing-input obfuscation for general circuits [7,32]. On the other hand, [25] shows that the weaker notion X-Ind piO can be realized from subexponentially secure iO (and subexponentially secure one-way functions). Below, we recall the notion of dynamic-input samplers and dynamic-input piO from [25].

2.2 Dynamic-Input Samplers

Definition 2 (Dynamic-Input Indistinguishable Samplers [25]). *The class* $\mathbf{S}^{\mathsf{d\text{-}Ind}}$ *of dynamic-input samplers for a circuit family* $\mathcal{C}$ *contains all* *circuits samplers* $D = \{D_\lambda\}_{\lambda \in \mathbb{N}}$ *for* $\mathcal{C}$ *with the following properties: for every non-uniform PPT* $\mathcal{A} = (\mathcal{A}_1, \mathcal{A}_2)$*, the advantage* $\mathsf{Adv}_{\mathsf{d\text{-}Ind}}(\mathcal{A}) := \Pr[\mathsf{Exp\text{-}d\text{-}Ind}_{\mathcal{A}}(\lambda) = 1] - \frac{1}{2}$ *of* $\mathcal{A}$ *in the experiment* Exp-d-Ind *represented in Fig. 1 is negligible.*

Experiment $\mathsf{Exp\text{-}d\text{-}Ind}_{\mathcal{A}}(\lambda)$
$(C_0, C_1, z) \xleftarrow{\$} D_\lambda$
$(x, \mathsf{st}) \xleftarrow{\$} \mathcal{A}_1(C_0, C_1, z)$ // the challenge input is chosen dynamically
$y \xleftarrow{\$} C_b(x)$ for $b \xleftarrow{\$} \{0,1\}$
$b' \xleftarrow{\$} \mathcal{A}_2(\mathsf{st}, C_0, C_1, z, x, y)$
return $b = b'$

Fig. 1. Experiment Exp-d-Ind for the indistinguishability property of dynamic-input samplers.

Definition 3 (dynamic-input piO). *A uniform PPT machine is a dynamic-input* piO *scheme if it is a* piO *for the class of dynamic-input samplers* $\mathbf{S}^{\mathsf{d\text{-}Ind}}$ *over* $\mathcal{C}$ *that includes all randomized circuits.*

Note that the class $\mathbf{S}^{\mathsf{eq}}$ of samplers for functionally equivalent circuits that we defined previously, is a subclass of $\mathbf{S}^{\mathsf{d\text{-}Ind}}$: any sampler for triples (C_0, C_1, z) where C_0 and C_1 are functionally equivalent is trivially a dynamic-input sampler.

2.3 Puncturable Pseudorandom Function

A pseudorandom function (PRF) originally introduced in [37] is a tuple of PPT algorithms $\mathsf{F} = (\mathsf{F.KeyGen}, \mathsf{F.Eval})$. Let $\mathcal{K}$ denote the key space, $\mathcal{X}$ denote the domain, and $\mathcal{Y}$ denote the range. The key generation algorithm F.KeyGen on input of 1^λ, outputs a random key from $\mathcal{K}$ and the evaluation algorithm F.Eval on input of a key K and $x \in \mathcal{X}$, evaluates the function $F\colon \mathcal{K} \times \mathcal{X} \to \mathcal{Y}$. The core property of PRFs is that, on a random choice of key K, no probabilistic polynomial-time adversary should be able to distinguish $F(K, \cdot)$ from a truly random function, when given black-box access to it. Puncturable PRFs (pPRFs) have the additional property that some keys can be generated *punctured* at some point, so that they allow to evaluate the PRF at all points except for the punctured point. As observed in [19,22,51], it is possible to construct such punctured keys for the original construction from [37], which can be based on any one-way functions [43].

Definition 4 (Puncturable Pseudorandom Function [19,22,51]**).** *A* puncturable pseudorandom function (pPRF) *with punctured key space* $\mathcal{K}_p$ *is a triple of PPT algorithms* (F.KeyGen, F.Punct, F.Eval) *such that*

- $\mathsf{F.KeyGen}(1^\lambda)$ *outputs a random key* $K \in \mathcal{K}$,

- $\mathsf{F.Punct}(K, x)$, *on input* $K \in \mathcal{K}$, $x \in \mathcal{X}$, *outputs a punctured key* $K\{x\} \in \mathcal{K}_p$,
- $\mathsf{F.Eval}(K', x')$, *on input a key* K' *(punctured or not), and a point* x', *outputs an evaluation of the PRF.*

We require F *to meet the following conditions:*

Functionality Preserved Under Puncturing. *For all* $\lambda \in \mathbb{N}$, *for all* $x \in \mathcal{X}$,

$$\Pr[K \xleftarrow{\$} \mathsf{F.KeyGen}(1^\lambda), K\{x\} \xleftarrow{\$} \mathsf{F.Punct}(K, x): \\ \forall x' \in \mathcal{X} \setminus \{x\}: \mathsf{F.Eval}(K, x') = \mathsf{F.Eval}(K\{x\}, x')] = 1.$$

Pseudorandom at Punctured Points. *For all PPT adversaries* $\mathcal{A}$,

$$\mathsf{Adv}_{\mathsf{s\text{-}cPRF}}(\mathcal{A}) := \Pr[\mathsf{Exp\text{-}s\text{-}pPRF}_{\mathcal{A}}(\lambda) = 1] - \frac{1}{2}$$

is negligible, where Exp-s-cPRF *is represented Fig. 2.*

We call a pPRF F perfect, *if the distribution* $\{\mathsf{F.Eval}(K, x) \mid K \xleftarrow{\$} \mathsf{F.KeyGen}(1^\lambda)\}$ *is identical to the uniform distribution over* $\mathcal{Y}$, *for all inputs* $x \in \mathcal{X}$.[6]

Definition 4 corresponds to a selective security notion for puncturable pseudorandom functions; adaptive security can also be considered, but will not be required in our work. For ease of notation we often write $F(\cdot, \cdot)$ instead of $\mathsf{F.Eval}(\cdot, \cdot)$.

Experiment $\mathsf{Exp\text{-}s\text{-}pPRF}_{\mathcal{A}}(\lambda)$

$(x^*, \mathsf{state}) \xleftarrow{\$} \mathcal{A}(1^\lambda)$

$K \xleftarrow{\$} \mathsf{F.KeyGen}(1^\lambda)$, $K\{x^*\} \xleftarrow{\$} \mathsf{F.Punct}(K, x^*)$

$b \xleftarrow{\$} \{0,1\}$, $y_0 \leftarrow \mathsf{F.Eval}(K, x^*)$, $y_1 \xleftarrow{\$} \mathcal{Y}$

$b' \xleftarrow{\$} \mathcal{A}(\mathsf{state}, K\{x^*\}, y_b)$

return $b = b'$

Fig. 2. Selective security game for puncturable pseudorandom functions.

2.4 Extremely Lossy Function

In this section we present extremely lossy functions (ELFs) introduced in [62]. ELFs are an extremely powerful primitive for complexity absorption allowing to replace subexponential or even exponential security assumptions with polynomial ones. Informally, an ELF is a function that can be generated in two

[6] Given any pPRF F′, we can build a perfect pPRF F by sampling two keys $K_1 \xleftarrow{\$} \mathsf{F'.KeyGen}(1^\lambda)$ and $K_2 \xleftarrow{\$} \mathcal{Y}$ in the key generation algorithm and defining the evaluation algorithm to output $\mathsf{F'.Eval}(K_1, x) \oplus K_2$ on input of x, see [27].

different modes: an injective mode and an extremely lossy mode. In injective mode, the range of the ELF has exponential size whereas the range comprises only polynomially many elements in extremely lossy mode.

Definition 5 (Extremely Lossy Function [62]). *An extremely lossy function* ELF *is an algorithm* $\mathsf{ELF.Gen}$ *which, on input* (M, r)*, where* M *is an integer and* $r \in [M]$*, outputs the description of a function* $G\colon [M] \rightarrow [N]$ *such that*

- G *can be computed in time* $\mathsf{poly}(\log M)$
- *If* $r = M$*,* G *is injective with overwhelming probability (in* $\log M$*) over the randomness of* $\mathsf{ELF.Gen}(M, M)$*;*
- *For any* $r \in [M]$*,* $|G([M])| < r$ *with overwhelming probability (in* $\log M$*) over the randomness of* $\mathsf{ELF.Gen}(M, r)$*;*
- ***Indistinguishability:*** *For any large enough* M*, any polynomial* P*, and any inverse polynomial function* δ*, there exists a polynomial* Q *such that for any adversary* $\mathcal{A}$ *running in time at most* $P(\log M)$ *and any* $r \in [Q(\log M), M]$*, the advantage of* $\mathcal{A}$ *in distinguishing* $\mathsf{ELF.Gen}(M, M)$ *from* $\mathsf{ELF.Gen}(M, r)$ *is bounded by* $\delta(\log M)$.

In addition, we will consider extremely lossy functions satisfying *strong regularity*, as defined below.

Definition 6 (Strong regularity). *An* ELF *is strongly regular if for any (polynomial)* r*, the distribution* $\{x \overset{\$}{\leftarrow} [M] : G(x)\}$ *is statistically close to uniform over* $G([M])$*, with overwhelming probability over the choice of* $G \overset{\$}{\leftarrow} \mathsf{ELF.Gen}(M, r)$.

We note that, if an ELF is strongly regular, it is possible to efficiently enumerate its image: the set of values obtained by evaluating an ELF on $\lambda r \log r$ random inputs, where r is a bound on the size of its image, contains the entire image of the ELF with overwhelming probability.

Instantiating ELFs. A construction of strongly regular extremely lossy function is given in [62]. It can be based on the exponential hardness of the decision Diffie-Hellman assumption (or any of its variants, such as the decision linear assumption), which we denote eDDH. The eDDH assumption for a group generator $\mathsf{GroupGen}$ (which generates a tuple $(\mathbb{G}, p, g)$ where $\mathbb{G}$ is a group, p is its order, and g is a generator of $\mathbb{G}$) states that there exists a polynomial q such that for any time bound t and probability ε, denoting $\kappa \leftarrow \log q(t, 1/\varepsilon)$, any adversary $\mathcal{A}$ running in time at most t has advantage at most ε in distinguishing the following distributions:

$$\{(\mathbb{G}, p, g) \overset{\$}{\leftarrow} \mathsf{GroupGen}(1^\kappa), (a, b, c) \overset{\$}{\leftarrow} \mathbb{Z}_p^3 : (\mathbb{G}, g, g^a, g^b, g^c)\},$$
$$\{(\mathbb{G}, p, g) \overset{\$}{\leftarrow} \mathsf{GroupGen}(1^\kappa), (a, b) \overset{\$}{\leftarrow} \mathbb{Z}_p^2 : (\mathbb{G}, g, g^a, g^b, g^{ab})\}.$$

As noted in [62], groups based on elliptic curves are plausible candidates for groups where this assumption holds: in practical instantiations of DDH over elliptic curves, the size of the group is chosen assuming that the best attack takes time $O(\sqrt{p})$, hence disproving eDDH (which amounts to showing that there is an attack which takes time less than p^c for any constant c) would have considerable practical implications. Furthermore, relying on some form of exponential hardness assumption seems necessary, as a construction from polynomial hardness only would have surprising complexity-theoretic implications. More precisely, given access to only some super-logarithmic amount of non-determinism (i.e. $\omega(\log\log M)$ bits, where $[M]$ is the domain of the ELF), it is easy to distinguish between injective and lossy mode of the ELF. This is due to the fact that in lossy mode, the codomain of G has only polynomial size which means that the restriction of G to the set $D = [2^{\omega(\log\log M)}]$ (having super-polynomial cardinality) is guaranteed to have a collision (which is not the case in injective mode), and using only $\omega(\log\log M)$ bits of non-determinism this collision can be guessed.

2.5 Non-interactive Zero-Knowledge Proof System

A non-interactive zero-knowledge (NIZK) proof system for a language L with witness relation R enables to prove in a non-interactive manner that some statements are in L without leaking information about corresponding witnesses. NIZK proof systems were originally introduced in [15].

Definition 7 (Non-interactive zero-knowledge proof system [41]). *A non-interactive zero-knowledge (NIZK) proof system for a language* $L \in \mathsf{NP}$ *(with witness relation* R*) is a tuple of PPT algorithms* $\mathsf{NIZK} = (\mathsf{NIZK.Setup}, \mathsf{NIZK.Prove}, \mathsf{NIZK.Verify})$ *such that* $\mathsf{NIZK.Setup}$ *is a common reference string generation algorithm,* $\mathsf{NIZK.Prove}$ *is a proving algorithm* $\mathsf{NIZK.Verify}$ *is a (deterministic) verification algorithm.*

- $\mathsf{NIZK.Setup}(1^\lambda)$ *outputs a common reference string* crs.
- $\mathsf{NIZK.Prove}(\mathsf{crs}, x, w)$, *on input* crs, *a statement* x *and a witness* w, *outputs a proof* π.
- $\mathsf{NIZK.Verify}(\mathsf{crs}, x, \pi)$, *on input* crs, *a statement* x *and a proof* π, *outputs either* 1 *or* 0.

We require NIZK *to meet the following properties:*

Perfect Completeness. *For every* $(x, w) \in R$, *we have that*

$$\Pr[\mathsf{crs} \xleftarrow{\$} \mathsf{NIZK.Setup}(1^\lambda),\ \pi \xleftarrow{\$} \mathsf{NIZK.Prove}(\mathsf{crs}, x, w) : \mathsf{NIZK.Verify}(\mathsf{crs}, x, \pi) = 1] = 1.$$

Statistical Soundness. *For every* $x \notin L$ *with* $|x| = \lambda$ *and every (possibly unbounded) adversary* $\mathcal{A}$, *we have that*

$$\Pr[\mathsf{crs} \xleftarrow{\$} \mathsf{NIZK.Setup}(1^\lambda), \pi \xleftarrow{\$} \mathcal{A}(\mathsf{crs}, x) : \mathsf{NIZK.Verify}(\mathsf{crs}, x, \pi) = 1] < 2^{-\lambda}.$$

Computational Zero-Knowledge. *There exists a PPT algorithm* $\mathsf{Sim} = (\mathsf{Sim}_0, \mathsf{Sim}_1)$ *such that for every PPT adversary* $\mathcal{A}$,

$$\mathsf{Adv}_{\mathcal{ZK}}(\mathcal{A}) := |\Pr\left[\mathsf{crs} \xleftarrow{\$} \mathsf{NIZK.Setup}(1^\lambda) \colon \mathcal{A}^{\mathsf{NIZK.Prove}(\mathsf{crs},\cdot,\cdot)}(\mathsf{crs}) = 1\right] - \Pr\left[(\mathsf{crs}, \tau) \xleftarrow{\$} \mathsf{Sim}_0(1^\lambda) \colon \mathcal{A}^{\mathsf{Sim}_1'(\mathsf{crs},\tau,\cdot,\cdot)}(\mathsf{crs}) = 1\right]|$$

is negligible in λ, *where* $\mathsf{Sim}_1'(\mathsf{crs}, \tau, x, w)$ *returns* $\mathsf{Sim}_1'(\mathsf{crs}, \tau, x)$ *only if* $(x, w) \in R$.

For simplicity in the analysis we use a NIZK proof system that satisfies the following property: with overwhelming probability over the coins of $\mathsf{NIZK.Setup}(1^\lambda)$, there does not exist any pair (x, π) such that $x \notin L$ and $\mathsf{NIZK.Verify}(\mathsf{crs}, x, \pi) = 1$. We call a NIZK that satisfies this property *almost perfectly sound.* We note that there is a simple folklore method which allows to construct an almost perfectly sound NIZK proof system starting from any statistically sound NIZK proof system. Consider a $2^{-\lambda}$-statistically sound NIZK proof system, for statements $x \in \{0,1\}^n$, for some polynomial $n = n(\lambda)$. Using parallel repetitions, the soundness of the proof system can be amplified to $2^{-\lambda-n}$.[7] Then, it necessarily holds that for all possible crs except a $2^{-\lambda}$ fraction of them, there does not exist any pair (x, π) where $x \notin L$ and π is an accepting proof. To realize this, let E_x^{crs} denote the event that there exists a proof π such that $\mathsf{NIZK.Verify}(\mathsf{crs}, x, \pi) = 1$. Then, by a union bound argument, $\Pr_{\mathsf{crs}}[\exists x \in \{0,1\}^n \setminus L \colon E_x^{\mathsf{crs}}] \leq \sum_{x \in \{0,1\}^n \setminus L} \Pr_{\mathsf{crs}}[E_x^{\mathsf{crs}}] \leq 2^n \cdot 2^{-\lambda-n}$. Hence, the NIZK proof system obtained via parallel repetitions is almost perfectly sound.

In [12] Bitansky et al. showed that statistically sound NIZK proof systems can be obtained from polynomially secure indistinguishability obfuscation in conjunction with polynomially secure one-way functions.

3 Indistinguishability Obfuscation of Probabilistic Circuits over Distributions of Inputs

We first define the notion of a *sampler with input.* A sampler with input is a family of PPT algorithms which, on input x, sample from some distribution $\mathcal{D}_x$. This notion is convenient to capture the fact that, in many scenarios, the inputs to an obfuscated (probabilistic) circuit are sampled from some distribution $\mathcal{D}_x$, where x is some private input of a player.

Definition 8 (Sampler with Input). *We say that* $\mathcal{SI} = \{\mathcal{SI}_\lambda\}_{\lambda \in \mathbb{N}}$ *is a family of* samplers with input, *with input domain* $\mathcal{I} = \{\mathcal{I}_\lambda\}_{\lambda \in \mathbb{N}}$, *if for any* $\lambda \in \mathbb{N}$, $\mathcal{SI}_\lambda$ *is a set of probabilistic algorithms running in polynomial time (in* 1^λ*) with input domain* $\mathcal{I}_\lambda$ *such that for any* $S \in \mathcal{SI}_\lambda$, *and* $x \in \mathcal{I}_\lambda$, $S(x)$ *samples from* $\{0,1\}^\lambda$.

[7] That is, for any statement $x \notin L$, the probability $\Pr_{\mathsf{crs}}[\exists \pi \colon \mathsf{NIZK.Verify}(\mathsf{crs}, x, \pi) = 1] \leq 2^{-\lambda-n}$.

3.1 Doubly-Probabilistic Indistinguishability Obfuscation

Below, we define a variant of indistinguishability obfuscation, that takes into account the fact that in many applications, obfuscated (probabilistic) circuits might only have to be evaluated on inputs coming from specific distributions. This is formalized by defining an encoding procedure for a sampler with input, which additionally produces auxiliary material that an obfuscated circuit can use to verify that its inputs were produced correctly, and by restricting the correctness of the obfuscated circuit to only hold for such well-formed inputs. We also refer to this auxiliary material as "certificate".

However, this approach faces two issues. First, the inputs to an obfuscated circuit might not be sampled "all at once" from a single distribution; rather, they can come from different and independent sources. We capture this behavior by defining *ℓ-source obfuscation*, to account for the fact that different inputs might have been sampled independently. Second, when inputs are sampled by different parties, there might still be interdependencies which must be accounted for. For example, a party might sample an input (e.g. a public key of an encryption scheme), pass it to a second party, who then samples a second input from a distribution that is parametrized by the first input (e.g. a ciphertext under that public key). We handle this possibility by ordering the ℓ inputs to the obfuscated circuit, and by considering a *stateful* sampler with input S: when S is used to generate the i'th sample y_i, it receives in addition to its input a state $\mathsf{stf}(y_1, \ldots, y_{i-1})$, where stf is some fixed efficiently computable *state function* (which depends on the particular application), and the y_j are outputs sampled by the first $i-1$ sources. The state function captures the fact that a particular application might define an arbitrary communication pattern, and specifies which samples a party should have access to when generating his sample.

Additionally, we admit the possibility that a sampler produces some additional correlated output, that will not serve as input to an obfuscated circuit. Hence, there is no need to "certify" this input using the auxiliary information, and we call this output unauthenticated output. Continuing the use case from above, given a sampler producing some public key, the unauthenticated part of that sampler's output could be a corresponding secret key.

Definition 9 (Doubly-Probabilistic Indistinguishability Obfuscation (dpiO)). *Let ℓ be an integer. Let $\{\mathsf{stf}_\lambda : (\{0,1\}^\lambda \cup \{\bot\})^{\ell-1} \to \mathcal{T}_\lambda\}_{\lambda\in\mathbb{N}}$ be a family of efficiently computable functions. Let $\mathcal{SI} = \{\mathcal{SI}_\lambda\}_{\lambda\in\mathbb{N}}$ be a family of samplers with inputs, with input domain $\{\mathcal{T}_\lambda \times \mathcal{I}\}_{\lambda\in\mathbb{N}}$. Let $\mathcal{C} = \{\mathcal{C}_\lambda\}_{\lambda\in\mathbb{N}}$ be a family of (probabilistic) circuits, and let* $\mathbf{CS}$ *be a class of circuit samplers over $\mathcal{C}$. An ℓ-source* dpiO *scheme for* $(\mathsf{stf}, \mathcal{SI}, \mathcal{C}, \mathbf{CS})$ *is a triple of PPT algorithms* $(\mathsf{Setup}, \mathsf{Encode}, \mathsf{Obfuscate})$ *such that*

- $\mathsf{Setup}(1^\lambda)$*, on input the security parameter (in unary), outputs public parameters* pp*;*
- $\mathsf{Encode}(\mathsf{pp}, S)$*, on input the public parameters* pp*, and a sampler with input* $S \in \mathcal{SI}_\lambda$*, outputs an encoded sampler* S'*;*

– $\mathsf{Obfuscate}(\mathsf{pp}, S, C)$, *on input public parameters* pp, *a sampler with input* $S \in \mathcal{SI}_\lambda$, *and a circuit* $C \in \mathcal{C}_{\ell\lambda}$, *outputs a circuit* C' *of size* $\mathsf{poly}(\lambda, |C|)$. *We call* C' *an* obfuscation of C with respect to S.

We further assume that the outputs of S *on any input* (state, x) *is of the form* $(y; y')$ *(looking ahead, we will call* y *the* authenticated output, *and* y' *the* unauthenticated output*). The scheme should satisfy the three properties given below.*

Informally, the first security requirement ensures that, on any (adversarially chosen) input x, state state, and sampler with input S, the sampler S' obtained by encoding S outputs samples of the form $(y, \mathsf{aux}; y')$ where $(y; y')$ is distributed as an output of $S(\mathsf{state}, x)$, and aux does not leak any non-trivial information about the inputs. This is formalized by requiring the existence of a simulator that can simulate aux given only y.

Definition 10 (Simulatability of Encodings). *An* ℓ*-source* dpiO *scheme for* $(\mathsf{stf}, \mathcal{SI}, \mathcal{C}, \mathbf{CS})$ *satisfies* simulatability of encodings *if for any large enough* λ *and any (stateful) PPT adversary* $\mathcal{A}$, *there exists a PPT simulator* $\mathsf{Sim} = (\mathsf{Sim}_0, \mathsf{Sim}_1)$ *such that the advantage of* $\mathcal{A}$ *in distinguishing the experiments* $\mathsf{Exp}^{0\text{-enc}}$ *and* $\mathsf{Exp}^{1\text{-enc}}$ *represented on Fig. 3 is negligible. We denote by* $\mathsf{Adv}_{\mathsf{enc}}(\mathcal{A})$ *the advantage of* $\mathcal{A}$ *in this experiment.*

$\mathsf{Exp}_{\mathcal{A}}^{0\text{-enc}}(1^\lambda)$

$\mathsf{pp} \xleftarrow{\$} \mathsf{Setup}(1^\lambda)$
return $b' \leftarrow \mathcal{A}^{\mathcal{O}_0^{\mathsf{enc}}[\mathsf{pp}]}(\mathsf{pp})$

$\mathsf{Exp}_{\mathcal{A}}^{1\text{-enc}}(1^\lambda)$

$(\mathsf{pp}, \mathsf{trap}) \xleftarrow{\$} \mathsf{Sim}_0(1^\lambda)$
return $b' \leftarrow \mathcal{A}^{\mathcal{O}_1^{\mathsf{enc}}[\mathsf{pp},\mathsf{trap}]}(\mathsf{pp})$

Oracle $\mathcal{O}_0^{\mathsf{enc}}[\mathsf{pp}]$

on input (S, state, x) from $\mathcal{A}$
$S' \leftarrow \mathsf{Encode}(\mathsf{pp}, S)$
$(y, \mathsf{aux}; y') \xleftarrow{\$} S'(\mathsf{state}, x)$
return $(y, \mathsf{aux}; y')$

Oracle $\mathcal{O}_1^{\mathsf{enc}}[\mathsf{pp}, \mathsf{trap}]$

on input (S, state, x) from $\mathcal{A}$
$(y; y') \xleftarrow{\$} S(\mathsf{state}, x)$
$\mathsf{aux} \xleftarrow{\$} \mathsf{Sim}_1(\mathsf{pp}, \mathsf{trap}, S, y, \mathsf{state})$
return $(y, \mathsf{aux}; y')$

Fig. 3. Experiments $\mathsf{Exp}_{\mathcal{A}}^{0\text{-enc}}(1^\lambda)$ and $\mathsf{Exp}_{\mathcal{A}}^{1\text{-enc}}(1^\lambda)$ for the simulatability of encodings in an ℓ-source dpiO. The PPT algorithm $\mathcal{A}$ can interact polynomially many times with either $\mathcal{O}_0^{\mathsf{enc}}[\mathsf{pp}]$ or $\mathcal{O}_1^{\mathsf{enc}}[\mathsf{pp}, \mathsf{trap}]$. $\mathcal{A}$ wins the experiment when it outputs $b' = b$ in $\mathsf{Exp}_{\mathcal{A}}^{b\text{-enc}}(1^\lambda)$

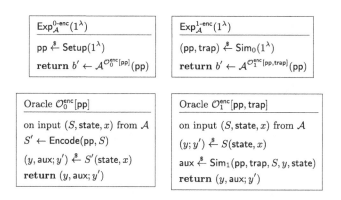

We now introduce the restricted correctness requirement. Intuitively, it states the following: in an honest scenario, the inputs $(y_1, \ldots, y_\ell)$ should be constructed using the sampler with input S. The restricted correctness property guarantees that if the inputs have indeed been constructed "according to S", then the obfuscated circuit will behave correctly, and its output distribution (taken over the coins of the obfuscator) will be (statistically) indistinguishable from the output distribution of the circuit C (taken over its internal random coins). Note that this statistical indistinguishability does not extend to multiple evaluations. Additionally, when evaluated on such inputs, the obfuscated circuit respects the support of the original circuit.

To make this definition meaningful, we need a way to let the obfuscated circuit verify that the inputs are well-formed. Note that we do not want to ensure that they were generated through S with uniformly random coins, but only that they were generated through S with *some* random coins (and some input). To make this verification possible, we let the parties generate their input using the encoded sampler S' instead. This encoded sampler should correctly sample as S, but it will in addition produce auxiliary information which can be used by the obfuscated program to verify that the inputs were honestly constructed (more formally, for a given y, that there exists an input x, coins r, and an unauthenticated part y' such that $(y; y') = S(x; r)$).

A small technicality is that we must allow the sampler with input to depend on state information, to capture the possible interdependencies between the inputs. This means that the auxiliary information will have to certify that an input was generated correctly, with respect to some state that the obfuscated circuit might not have access too (which would prevent it from verifying the certificate). However, this issue disappears by restricting the interdependencies to only involve a state computed from the previous *samples* (as opposed to more complex interdependencies which would involve, for example, the coins used to produce these samples). In this case, the obfuscated circuit can check the certificates in an incremental way: it first checks that y_1 was correctly constructed with respect to the state $\mathsf{st}_\lambda(\bot, \ldots, \bot)$, then it checks that y_2 was correctly constructed with respect to the state $\mathsf{st}_\lambda(y_1, \bot, \ldots, \bot)$, and so on.

Definition 11 (Statistical Restricted Correctness). *An ℓ-source* dpiO *scheme for* $(\mathsf{stf}, \mathcal{SI}, \mathcal{C}, \mathbf{CS})$ *satisfies* restricted correctness *if for any large enough $\lambda \in \mathbb{N}$, any $S \in \mathcal{SI}_\lambda$, $(x_1, \ldots, x_\ell) \in \mathcal{I}_\lambda^\ell$, and $C \in \mathcal{C}_{\ell\lambda}$, the advantage of any*

$\mathsf{Exp}_{\mathcal{A}}^{0\text{-rcorr}}(1^\lambda)$

- $\mathsf{pp} \xleftarrow{\$} \mathsf{Setup}(1^\lambda)$
- $S' \leftarrow \mathsf{Encode}(\mathsf{pp}, S)$
- $C' \xleftarrow{\$} \mathsf{Obfuscate}(\mathsf{pp}, S, C)$
- **for** $j \in [\ell]$ **do**
  - $\mathsf{state}_j \leftarrow \mathsf{stf}_\lambda(y_1, \ldots, y_{j-1}, \bot, \ldots)$
  - $(y_j, \mathsf{aux}_j; y_j') \leftarrow S'(\mathsf{state}_j, x_j)$
- $z \leftarrow C'(y_1, \mathsf{aux}_1, \ldots, y_\ell, \mathsf{aux}_\ell)$
- **return** $\mathcal{A}(z)$

$\mathsf{Exp}_{\mathcal{A}}^{1\text{-rcorr}}(1^\lambda)$

- **for** $j \in [\ell]$ **do**
  - $\mathsf{state}_j \leftarrow \mathsf{stf}_\lambda(y_1, \ldots, y_{j-1}, \bot, \ldots)$
  - $(y_j; y_j') \leftarrow S(\mathsf{state}_j, x_j)$
- $z \leftarrow C(y_1, \ldots, y_\ell)$
- **return** $\mathcal{A}(z)$

Fig. 4. Experiments $\mathsf{Exp}_{\mathcal{A}}^{0\text{-rcorr}}(1^\lambda)$ and $\mathsf{Exp}_{\mathcal{A}}^{1\text{-rcorr}}(1^\lambda)$ for the restricted correctness property an ℓ-source dpiO. $\mathcal{A}$ wins the experiment when it outputs $b' = b$ in $\mathsf{Exp}_{\mathcal{A}}^{b\text{-rcorr}}(1^\lambda)$ when $b \xleftarrow{\$} \{0, 1\}$.

(possibly unbounded) adversary $\mathcal{A}$ *in distinguishing the experiments* $\mathsf{Exp}^{0\text{-rcorr}}$ *and* $\mathsf{Exp}^{1\text{-rcorr}}$ *represented on Fig. 4 is negligible. We denote by* $\mathsf{Adv}_{\mathsf{rcorr}}(\mathcal{A})$ *the advantage of* $\mathcal{A}$ *in this experiment. Additionally, we require that the encoded sampler and the obfuscated circuit respect the support of the original sampler and the original circuit, respectively. That is for all* $\mathsf{pp} \leftarrow \mathsf{Setup}(1^\lambda)$ *and all* $S' \leftarrow \mathsf{Encode}(\mathsf{pp}, S)$ *and all* $C' \leftarrow \mathsf{Obfuscate}(\mathsf{pp}, S, C)$*, we have that for all inputs* (state, x)*,* $S'(\mathsf{state}, x) \in \mathsf{Supp}(S(\mathsf{state}, x))$ *and for all* $(y_1, \mathsf{aux}_1, \dots, y_\ell, \mathsf{aux}_\ell)$ *produced as in* $\mathsf{Exp}^{0\text{-rcorr}}$*,* $C'(y_1, \mathsf{aux}_1, \dots, y_\ell, \mathsf{aux}_\ell) \in \mathsf{Supp}(C(y_1, \dots, y_\ell))$.

We now introduce the indistinguishability notion. It is close in spirit to the standard indistinguishability notion for obfuscation of probabilistic circuits of [25]. However, in our scenario, the security notion must account for the fact that a set of public parameters pp is generated in a setup phase; the indistinguishability property of obfuscated circuits must therefore hold when (polynomially) many circuits are obfuscated with respect to a single string of public parameters. This suggests an oracle-based security notion.

Definition 12 (Indistinguishability with Respect to CS). *An* ℓ*-source* dpiO *scheme for* $(\mathsf{stf}, \mathcal{SI}, \mathcal{C}, \mathbf{CS})$ *satisfies* indistinguishability with respect to**CS** *if for every circuit sampler* $D = \{D_\lambda\}_{\lambda \in \mathbb{N}} \in \mathbf{CS}$*, for any large enough* λ*, the advantage of any PPT adversary* $\mathcal{A}$ *in distinguishing the experiments* $\mathsf{Exp}^{0\text{-ind}}$ *and* $\mathsf{Exp}^{1\text{-ind}}$ *represented on Fig. 5 is negligible. We denote by* $\mathsf{Adv}_{\mathsf{ind}}(\mathcal{A})$ *the advantage of* $\mathcal{A}$ *in this experiment.*

$\mathsf{Exp}_{\mathcal{A}}^{b\text{-ind}}(1^\lambda)$
$\mathsf{pp} \xleftarrow{\$} \mathsf{Setup}(1^\lambda)$
return $b' \leftarrow \mathcal{A}^{\mathcal{O}_b^{\mathsf{ind}}[\mathsf{pp}, D_\lambda](\cdot)}(\mathsf{pp})$

Oracle $\mathcal{O}_b^{\mathsf{ind}}[\mathsf{pp}, D_\lambda]$
on input S from $\mathcal{A}$
$(C_0, C_1, z) \xleftarrow{\$} D_\lambda$
$C' \xleftarrow{\$} \mathsf{Obfuscate}(\mathsf{pp}, S, C_b)$
return (C_0, C_1, z, C')

Fig. 5. Experiment $\mathsf{Exp}_{\mathcal{A}}^{b\text{-ind}}(1^\lambda)$ for the indistinguishability with respect to **CS** in an ℓ-source dpiO. The PPT algorithm $\mathcal{A}$ can interact polynomially many times with $\mathcal{O}_b^{\mathsf{ind}}[\mathsf{pp}, D_\lambda]$. The oracle $\mathcal{O}_b^{\mathsf{ind}}[\mathsf{pp}, D_\lambda]$ is stateful and has (pp, D_λ) hardcoded in its description. $\mathcal{A}$ wins the experiment when it outputs $b' = b$ in $\mathsf{Exp}_{\mathcal{A}}^{b\text{-ind}}(1^\lambda)$ when $b \xleftarrow{\$} \{0, 1\}$.

4 Construction

In this section, we will construct an ℓ-source dpiO scheme (for any constant ℓ), for samplers with input over an input domain $\mathcal{I}$ of polynomial size[8], and dynamic-input indistinguishable circuit-samplers. Our construction relies on polynomially-secure indistinguishability obfuscation, a perfect puncturable pseudorandom function, an almost perfectly sound non-interactive zero-knowledge proof system, and an extremely lossy function.

[8] We note that the output domain of such samplers can be of exponential size.

4.1 Overview

We start by providing a high-level overview of our construction. The Setup procedure generates parameters for the ELF and for the NIZK proof system. To encode a sampler with input S, we define the encoded sampler S' as follows: on input $(\mathsf{state}, x; r)$, S' computes $(y; y') \overset{\$}{\leftarrow} S(\mathsf{state}, x; G(r))$ and $\mathsf{aux} \overset{\$}{\leftarrow} \mathsf{NIZK.Prove}(y, L^{G,S}_{\mathsf{state}}, (y', x, r))$, and outputs $(y, \mathsf{aux}; y')$. Here, G is the ELF defined by the public parameters, and the language $L^{G,S}_{\mathsf{state}}$ contains all values y for which there exists (y', x, r) such that $(y; y') = S(\mathsf{state}, x, G(r))$. We call *valid input* a value $y \in L^{G,S}_{\mathsf{state}}$. Note that when G is in injective mode, $L^{G,S}_{\mathsf{state}}$ will in general be a trivial language. The simulatability of the encodings directly follows from the injectivity of G, and the zero-knowledge property of the proof system.

We construct the $\mathsf{Obfuscate}$ algorithm for a circuit C as follows (we assume a single source in this overview for simplicity). It first samples a pPRF key K for the pPRF F. Then, it returns an obfuscation of the following circuit: on input (y, aux), run $\mathsf{NIZK.Verify}$ on aux to check that y is a valid input (and output $\bot$ otherwise). Set $r \leftarrow F(K, y)$, and output $C(y; r)$. Restricted correctness follows from the correctness of the NIZK scheme. For indistinguishability between obfuscations of two dynamic-input indistinguishable circuits (C_0, C_1), we follow the standard puncturing strategy of [25]: we proceed through a sequence of hybrids, with successive modifications of the obfuscated circuit. For every possible input y, we construct a sequence of hybrids where the outputs $C_0(y; r)$ are gradually replaced by $C_1(y; r)$. Each replacement relies on the security of the iO scheme, the PRF security, and the dynamic-input indistinguishability of C_0 and C_1.

The main issue of this approach is that the number of possible inputs y (hence the number of hybrids) is exponential – indeed, this is the reason why the piO scheme of [25] requires subexponentially secure primitives (iO and PRF). To get around this issue, we first switch G to an appropriate extremely lossy mode, that the adversary cannot distinguish from the injective mode. Now, the soundness of the NIZK proof system ensures that all valid inputs y are of the form $S(\mathsf{state}, x; G(r))$ for some (x, r) (omitting y' for simplicity). For a given state, the quantity of such values is bounded by the size of the range of G (which is polynomial), times the size of the input domain $\mathcal{I}$. Therefore, in all applications where the inputs to the obfuscated circuit are sampled using private inputs from a small domain, we can base security on polynomially secure iO.

4.2 Construction

For our construction, we employ a perfectly sound NIZK proof system for the following (parametrized) language

$$L^{G,S}_{\mathsf{state}} := \{y \mid \exists (y', x, r) \colon (y; y') = S(\mathsf{state}, x; G(r))\}.$$

Let $\ell \in \mathbb{N}$ be a constant, let $\{\mathsf{stf}_\lambda \colon (\{0,1\}^\lambda \cup \{\bot\})^{\ell-1} \to \mathcal{T}_\lambda\}_\lambda$ be a family of efficiently computable state functions, and let $\mathcal{C} = \{C_\lambda\}_\lambda$ be a family of (randomized) circuits with random space $\{0,1\}^M$ (where $M = M(\lambda)$ is polynomial).

$\mathsf{Setup}(1^\lambda)$

$\mathsf{crs} \xleftarrow{\$} \mathsf{NIZK.Setup}(1^\lambda)$

$G \xleftarrow{\$} \mathsf{ELF.Gen}(M, M)$

return $\mathsf{pp} \leftarrow (\mathsf{crs}, G)$

$\mathsf{Encode}(\mathsf{pp}, S)$

define S'^{pp} as follows :

Circuit $S'^{\mathsf{pp}}(\mathsf{state}, x; r_1, r_2)$

$(y; y') \leftarrow S(\mathsf{state}, x; G(r_1))$

$\pi \xleftarrow{\$} \mathsf{NIZK.Prove}(\mathsf{crs},$

$\quad st = (G, S, \mathsf{state}, y), w = (y', x, r_1); r_2)$

return $(y, \pi; y')$

return S'^{pp}

$\mathsf{Obfuscate}(\mathsf{pp}, S, C)$

$K \xleftarrow{\$} \mathsf{F.KeyGen}(1^\lambda)$

define $\bar{C}$ as follows:

Circuit $\bar{C}[\mathsf{stf}, (\mathsf{crs}, G), S, C, K](x)$

parse $x =: ((y_1, \mathsf{aux}_1), \ldots, (y_\ell, \mathsf{aux}_\ell))$

$\mathsf{state}_j := \mathsf{stf}(y_1, \ldots, y_{j-1}, \bot, \ldots, \bot)$

if $\neg(\forall j \in [\ell]\colon \mathsf{NIZK.Verify}(\mathsf{crs}, (G, S, \mathsf{state}_j, y_j), \mathsf{aux}_j) = 1)$ **then**

$\quad$ **return** $\bot$

$r := \mathsf{F.Eval}(K, (y_1, \ldots, y_\ell))$

$y := C((y_1, \ldots, y_\ell); r)$

return y

$\Lambda \xleftarrow{\$} \mathsf{iO}(\bar{C})$

return Λ

Fig. 6. Construction of ℓ-source dpIO scheme $\mathsf{dpiO} = (\mathsf{Setup}, \mathsf{Encode}, \mathsf{Obfuscate})$.

Let $\mathcal{SI}$ be a family of samplers with input domain $\mathcal{I}$ of polynomial size. Further, let $\mathbf{S}^{\mathsf{d\text{-}Ind}}$ be the class of dynamic-input indistinguishable samplers (over $\mathcal{C}$).

Theorem 13. *If* ELF *is a strongly regular extremely lossy function,* iO *is a perfectly correct polynomially secure IO scheme,* F *is a polynomially secure perfect puncturable PRF, and* NIZK *is a perfectly sound polynomially zero-knowledge NIZK proof system for the family of languages* $\{L^{G,S}_{\mathsf{state}}\}_{\mathsf{state},G,S}$, *then* $\mathsf{dpiO} = (\mathsf{Setup}, \mathsf{Encode}, \mathsf{Obfuscate})$ *defined in Fig. 6 is an ℓ-source dpIO scheme for* $(\mathsf{stf}, \mathcal{SI}, \mathcal{C}, \mathbf{S}^{\mathsf{d\text{-}Ind}})$.

As noted in Sect. 2.5, almost perfectly correct NIZKs can be constructed from polynomially-secure indistinguishability obfuscation and extremely lossy functions. ELFs also imply the existence of one-way functions, hence of perfect puncturable PRFs [37,43]. Therefore, we get as corollary:

Corollary 14. *Assuming polynomially-secure indistinguishability obfuscation and extremely lossy functions, there exists (for any constant ℓ) an ℓ-source doubly-probabilistic indistinguishability obfuscation scheme for the class of dynamic-input circuit-samplers, and input-samplers with a polynomial size input domain.*

Proof (of Theorem 13). We prove that dpiO as defined in Fig. 6 satisfies simulatability of encodings (cf. Definition 10), statistical restricted correctness (cf. Definition 11), and indistinguishability (cf. Definition 12).

Simulatability of Encodings. We prove that there exists a PPT simulator $\mathsf{Sim} = (\mathsf{Sim}_0, \mathsf{Sim}_1)$ such that for every PPT adversary $\mathcal{A}$, the advantage $\mathsf{Adv}_{\mathsf{enc}}(\mathcal{A})$ is negligible. By the zero-knowledge property of NIZK, there exists a simulator $(\mathsf{NIZK.Sim}_0, \mathsf{NIZK.Sim}_1)$. We construct a simulator $\mathsf{Sim} = (\mathsf{Sim}_0, \mathsf{Sim}_1)$ as follows:

- Sim_0 produces the CRS using $(\mathsf{crs}, \tau) \xleftarrow{\$} \mathsf{NIZK.Sim}_0(1^\lambda)$, samples the parameters of the ELF G in injective mode, and outputs $\mathsf{pp} := (\mathsf{crs}, G)$ together with $\mathsf{trap} := \tau$.
- Sim_1 on input $(\mathsf{pp}, \mathsf{trap})$, a sampler S, a state state, and a value y sampled via $(y; y') \xleftarrow{\$} S(\mathsf{state}, x)$, Sim_1 produces a simulated proof via $\pi \xleftarrow{\$} \mathsf{NIZK.Sim}_1(\mathsf{crs}, \tau, (G, S, \mathsf{state}, y))$ and outputs $\mathsf{aux} := \pi$.

Let $\mathcal{A}$ be a PPT adversary on the simulatability property of dpiO. We prove indistinguishability between the real and the simulated distribution via a series of hybrids starting from the simulated game $\mathsf{Exp}_{\mathcal{A}}^{\text{1-enc}}(1^\lambda)$.

Game $\mathbf{G}_0$: This game is identical to $\mathsf{Exp}_{\mathcal{A}}^{\text{1-enc}}(1^\lambda)$. We remark that in this game, the tuple $(y; y')$ is produced using the adversarially chosen sampler S on input of the adversarially chosen state state and input x supplied with true randomness.

Game $\mathbf{G}_1$: This game is identical to $\mathbf{G}_0$ except for the fact that for each query (S, state, x), the sampler S is supplied with randomness $G(r)$ for uniform r (instead of true randomness). Due to the strong regularity of G and by a standard hybrid argument over all queries, the statistical distance between $\mathbf{G}_0$ and $\mathbf{G}_1$ is negligible.

Game $\mathbf{G}_2$: This game is the same as $\mathbf{G}_1$ with the difference that crs is produced honestly using $\mathsf{NIZK.Setup}(1^\lambda)$. Additionally, for each adversarial query (S, state, x), the proof π is produced honestly by $\mathsf{NIZK.Prove}(\mathsf{crs}, (G, S, \mathsf{state}, y), (y', x, r))$, where $G(r)$ are the random coins supplied to the sampler S. The view of $\mathcal{A}$ in game $\mathbf{G}_2$ is distributed exactly as in the real game $\mathsf{Exp}_{\mathcal{A}}^{\text{0-enc}}(1^\lambda)$.

We construct a PPT adversary $\mathcal{B}$ on the zero-knowledge property of NIZK. Given a CRS crs, $\mathcal{B}$ samples an ELF G in injective mode and invokes $\mathcal{A}$ on input of $\mathsf{pp} := (\mathsf{crs}, G)$. Each time $\mathcal{A}$ queries its oracle on (S, state, x), $\mathcal{B}$ draws random coins r and invokes the sampler S on input of (state, x) with random coins $G(r)$ to obtain $(y; y')$. In order to produce π, $\mathcal{B}$ calls its prove oracle on input $(G, S, \mathsf{state}, y)$ with witness (y', x, r). Therefore, if $\mathcal{B}$ is supplied with an honest CRS and honestly generated proofs, $\mathcal{B}$ perfectly simulates $\mathbf{G}_2$ for $\mathcal{A}$, else $\mathcal{B}$ perfectly simulates $\mathbf{G}_1$. Hence, $|\Pr[\mathsf{out}_2 = 1] - \Pr[\mathsf{out}_3 = 1]| \leq \mathsf{Adv}_{\mathsf{ZK}}(\mathcal{B})$. This concludes the proof.

Restricted Correctness. Let $S \in \mathbf{SI}_\lambda$ be an arbitrary sampler with input, let $y_1, \ldots, y_\ell$ be arbitrary values from the input domain $\mathcal{I}_\lambda$, and let C be a circuit from the family $\mathcal{C}_{\ell\lambda}$. To prove the correctness of dpiO, we proceed over a series of hybrids.

Game $\mathbf{G}_0$: This game is the ideal game $\mathsf{Exp}_{\mathcal{A}}^{1\text{-rcorr}}(1^\lambda)$. As the sampler S is called using true randomness whereas in $\mathsf{Exp}_{\mathcal{A}}^{0\text{-rcorr}}(1^\lambda)$ samples are generated using $G(r)$, where r is truly random, we need an intermediate hybrid.

Game $\mathbf{G}_1$: This game is identical to $\mathbf{G}_0$ with the difference that each call of the sampler S is supplied with $G(r)$ as randomness (where r is sampled uniformly for each call). Due to the strong regularity of G, and by a hybrid argument over all calls of S, the statistical distance between $\mathbf{G}_0$ and $\mathbf{G}_1$ is negligible.

Game $\mathbf{G}_2$: This game is the real game $\mathsf{Exp}_{\mathcal{A}}^{0\text{-rcorr}}(1^\lambda)$.

We now argue that the view of $\mathcal{A}$ in game $\mathbf{G}_1$ is distributed identically to its view in $\mathbf{G}_2$. $\mathbf{G}_2$ samples public parameters pp via $\mathsf{Setup}(1^\lambda)$ and S' an encoded sampler via $S' \leftarrow \mathsf{Encode}(\mathsf{pp}, S)$. Further, (y_j, aux_j) are sampled as $\mathsf{state}_j \leftarrow \mathsf{stf}(y_1, \ldots, y_{j-1}, \perp, \ldots, \perp)$ and $(y_j, \mathsf{aux}_j, y'_j) \overset{\$}{\leftarrow} S'(\mathsf{state}_j, x_j)$, for $j \in [\ell]$. Let Λ be the obfuscation $\Lambda \overset{\$}{\leftarrow} \mathsf{Obfuscate}(\mathsf{pp}, S, C)$ of the circuit C with respect to sampler S. Due to the perfect correctness of iO, Λ has the same functionality as $\bar{C}[\mathsf{stf}, (\mathsf{crs}, G), S, C, K]$, where K is a freshly generated key for the PRF F. Hence, by the perfect completeness of NIZK, on input of $((y_1, \mathsf{aux}_1), \ldots, (y_\ell, \mathsf{aux}_\ell))$, Λ evaluates the circuit C on input of $(y_1, \ldots, y_\ell)$ with random coins $F(K, (y_1, \ldots, y_\ell))$. Therefore, the view of $\mathcal{A}$ in the games $\mathbf{G}_1$ and $\mathbf{G}_2$ only differs in the fact that $\mathbf{G}_1$ supplies C with true random coins whereas $\mathbf{G}_2$ supplies C with $F(K, (y_1, \ldots, y_\ell))$ as randomness. As F is a perfect PRF, the distribution $\{F(K, (y_1, \ldots, y_\ell)) \mid K \overset{\$}{\leftarrow} \mathsf{F.KeyGen}(1^\lambda)\}$ is identical to the uniform distribution over the image of F. Therefore, the view of $\mathcal{A}$ in $\mathbf{G}_1$ and $\mathbf{G}_2$ is distributed identically.

By construction, all $S' \leftarrow \mathsf{Encode}(\mathsf{pp}, S)$ respect the support of S. Furthermore, by construction, perfect completeness of NIZK and perfect correctness of iO, for all $C' \leftarrow \mathsf{Obfuscate}(\mathsf{pp}, S, C)$ and all $(y_1, \mathsf{aux}_1, \ldots, y_\ell, \mathsf{aux}_\ell)$ produced as in $\mathsf{Exp}^{0\text{-rcorr}}$, $C'(y_1, \mathsf{aux}_1, \ldots, y_\ell, \mathsf{aux}_\ell) \in \mathsf{Supp}(C(y_1, \ldots, y_\ell))$.

Security. Let $D \in \mathbf{S}^{\mathsf{d\text{-}Ind}}$ be an arbitrary dynamic-input indistinguishable circuit sampler over $\mathcal{C}$. To prove that dpiO satisfies indistinguishability (Definition 12), we proceed over a series of hybrids. Toward contradiction, assume that there is a PPT adversary $\mathcal{A}$ distinguishing $\mathsf{Exp}_{\mathcal{A}}^{0\text{-ind}}(1^\lambda)$ from $\mathsf{Exp}_{\mathcal{A}}^{1\text{-ind}}(1^\lambda)$ with non-negligible advantage ε over the random guess after making a polynomial number Q of queries to the oracle.

Game $\mathbf{G}_0$. In this game, the challenger samples $b \overset{\$}{\leftarrow} \{0,1\}$, and sets up the experiment $\mathsf{Exp}_{\mathcal{A}}^{b\text{-ind}}(1^\lambda)$. More precisely, $\mathcal{A}$ has access to the public parameters pp and an oracle $\mathcal{O}_b^{\mathsf{ind}}[\mathsf{pp}, D_\lambda]$, that on input of a sampler with input S, draws a sample (C_0, C_1, z) from D and outputs (C_0, C_1, z) together with an obfuscation $\mathsf{Obfuscate}(\mathsf{pp}, S, C_b)$. $\mathcal{A}$ outputs a guess b' and the challenger returns 1 if $b' = b$. By assumption, $\Pr[\mathsf{out}_0 = 1] = \varepsilon$.

Game $\mathbf{G}_1$. In this game, the challenger samples G as $G \xleftarrow{\$} \mathsf{ELF.Gen}(M, t)$, where t is a polynomial such that any PPT algorithm of circuit size s has advantage at most $\varepsilon/2$ in distinguishing $\mathsf{ELF.Gen}(M, M)$ from $\mathsf{ELF.Gen}(M, t)$. The advantage of $\mathcal{A}$ in this game is therefore lower bounded by $\varepsilon/2$: $\Pr[\mathsf{out}_1 = 1] \geq \varepsilon/2$.

Game $\mathbf{G}_1'$. This game proceeds exactly as $\mathbf{G}_1$, except that after sampling $b \xleftarrow{\$} \{0,1\}$, the challenger always sets up the experiment $\mathsf{Exp}_{\mathcal{A}}^{\text{1-ind}}(1^\lambda)$. The challenger still returns 1 iff $b' = b$.

By using a standard hybrid argument over the oracle queries, we prove that $|\Pr[\mathsf{out}_1 = 1] - \Pr[\mathsf{out}_1' = 1]| \leq Q \cdot \mathsf{negl}(\lambda)$, where Q is a polynomial in λ.

Game $\mathbf{G}_{1.q}$ This game is identical to $\mathbf{G}_1$ except for the fact that the first q oracle queries are answered using an obfuscation Λ_q of C_1 instead of C_b. Hence, $\Pr[\mathsf{out}_{1.0} = 1] = \Pr[\mathsf{out}_1 = 1]$ and $\Pr[\mathsf{out}_{1.Q} = 1] = \Pr[\mathsf{out}_1' = 1]$, where Q is the number of adversarial oracle queries.

As $|\Pr[\mathsf{out}_1 = 1] - \Pr[\mathsf{out}_1' = 1]| \leq \sum_{q=1}^{Q} |\Pr[\mathsf{out}_{1.q} = 1] - \Pr[\mathsf{out}_{1.q+1} = 1]|$, it suffices to upper bound the distinguishing gap between $\mathbf{G}_{1.q}$ and $\mathbf{G}_{1.q+1}$.

We observe that due to the (almost) perfect soundness of NIZK, the obfuscated circuit in the q-th oracle answer simulates the randomized computation of the circuit $C_{q,0}$ only on well-formed inputs, i.e. on outputs of S_q using random coins from the range of G. As ELF is in extremely lossy mode, this set of well-formed inputs is *extremely sparsified.* Therefore, by the strong regularity of ELF, we can enumerate over all possible outputs at all input positions $j \in [\ell]$. Let $B_{q,j}$ be the set of all well-formed inputs for input position j:

$$B_{q,j} := \{S_q(\mathsf{stf}(y_1, \ldots, y_{j-1}), x; G(r)) \mid x \in \mathcal{I}_\lambda, r \in \{0,1\}^M, y_k \in B_k \text{ for } k \in [j-1]\}.$$

The set $B_{q,j}$ contains at most $|\mathcal{I}| \cdot t^{j-1}$ elements. Further, let $\gamma_{q,1} < \cdots < \gamma_{q,\bar{t}}$ be the ordered enumeration of all ℓ-tuples in $B_q := \prod_{j=1}^{\ell} B_{q,j}$.[9] Hence, the total number of well-formed inputs $\bar{t} = \prod_{j=1}^{\ell} |B_{q,j}| \leq (|\mathcal{I}| \cdot t^{\ell-1})^\ell \leq |\mathcal{I}|^\ell \cdot t^{(\ell^2)}$ is polynomial in λ (given that ℓ is a constant, and $|\mathcal{I}|$ and t are polynomial).

Towards proving indistinguishability between $\mathbf{G}_{1.q}$ and $\mathbf{G}_{1.q+1}$, we conduct a hybrid argument over all well-formed inputs for the obfuscation Λ_q and gradually replace the evaluation of circuit $C_{q,b}$ with $C_{q,1}$. From here on, our proof strategy is similar to the one employed in [25]. However, we only need to consider polynomially many hybrids (as we assume $|\mathcal{I}|$ to be polynomial), hence we only lose a polynomial factor to the underlying assumptions.

[9] We remark that the values of each set B_j can be computed efficiently by evaluating S on all possible inputs from $\mathcal{I} \times (\prod_{k=1}^{j-1} B_j)$ and all possible images in the range of G. Furthermore, it is possible to enumerate the image of G in polynomial time because G is strongly regular.

Game $\mathbf{G}_{1.q.i}$. In game $\mathbf{G}_{1.q.i}$ the oracle answers the q-th query using an obfuscation of the circuit

$$\bar{C}'[\mathsf{stf}, (\mathsf{crs}, G), S_q, C_{q,b}, C_{q,1}, K_q, \gamma_{q,i}]$$

that is defined in Fig. 7 using iO.

Circuit $\bar{C}'[\mathsf{stf}, (\mathsf{crs}, G), S, C_0, C_1, K, \gamma_i](x)$

parse $x =: ((y_1, \mathsf{aux}_1), \ldots, (y_\ell, \mathsf{aux}_\ell))$
$\mathsf{state}_j := \mathsf{stf}(y_1, \ldots, y_{j-1}, \bot, \ldots, \bot)$
if $\neg\,(\forall j \in [\ell]\colon \mathsf{NIZK.Verify}(\mathsf{crs}, (G, S, \mathsf{state}_j, y_j), \mathsf{aux}_j) = 1)$ **then**
  return $\bot$
$\gamma := (y_1, \ldots, y_\ell)$
if $\gamma < \gamma_i$ **then** $r := F(K, \gamma)$; **return** $C_1(\gamma; r)$
if $\gamma = \gamma_i$ **then** $r := F(K, \gamma)$; **return** $C_b(\gamma; r)$
if $\gamma > \gamma_i$ **then** $r := F(K, \gamma)$; **return** $C_b(\gamma; r)$

Fig. 7. Definition of the circuit $\bar{C}'$.

The circuits $\bar{C}[\mathsf{stf}, (\mathsf{crs}, G), S_q, C_{q,b}, K_q]$ and $\bar{C}'[\mathsf{stf}, (\mathsf{crs}, G), S_q, C_{q,0}, C_{q,1}, K_q, \gamma_{q,1}]$ are functionally equivalent (on input $x = ((y_1, \mathsf{aux}_1), \ldots, (y_\ell, \mathsf{aux}_\ell))$, both return $C_{q,b}(y_1, \ldots, y_\ell)$ with randomness $F(K_q, (y_1, \ldots, y_\ell))$). Hence, this game hop is justified by the indistinguishability property of iO, more formally there exists a PPT adversary $\mathcal{B}$ such that $|\Pr[\mathsf{out}_{1.q} = 1] - \Pr[\mathsf{out}_{1.q.1}] = 1| \leq \mathsf{Adv}_{\mathsf{iO}}(\mathcal{B})$.

We aim to reduce the game hop from $\mathbf{G}^b_{1.q.i}$ to $\mathbf{G}^b_{1.q.i+1}$ to the dynamic-input indistinguishability of the circuit sampler D_λ. For this purpose, we first need to supply $C_{q,b}$ with true randomness. Hence, we define an other series of hybrids between $\mathbf{G}_{1.q.i}$ and $\mathbf{G}_{1.q.i+1}$.

Game $\mathbf{G}_{1.q.i.1}$. This game is identical to $\mathbf{G}_{1.q.i}$ except for the fact that we use a punctured PRF key $K_q\{\gamma_{q,i}\} \xleftarrow{\$} \mathsf{F.Punct}(K_q, \gamma_{q,i})$ and obfuscate the circuit

$$\bar{C}''[\mathsf{stf}, (\mathsf{crs}, G), C_{q,0}, C_{q,1}, K_q\{\gamma_{q,i}\}, Y := C_{q,b}(\gamma_{q,i}; F(K_q, \gamma_{q,i})), \gamma_{q,i}]$$

defined in Fig. 8 using iO.

As F preserves the functionality under punctured keys, the circuits $\bar{C}'[\mathsf{stf}, (\mathsf{crs}, G), S_q, C_{q,0}, C_{q,1}, K_q, \gamma_{q,i}]$ and $\bar{C}''[\mathsf{stf}, (\mathsf{crs}, G), S_q, C_{q,0}, C_{q,1}, K_q\{\gamma_{q,i}\}, Y := C_{q,b}(\gamma_{q,i}; F(K_q, \gamma_{q,i})), \gamma_{q,i}]$ are functionally equivalent. Hence, there exists a PPT adversary $\mathcal{B}$ such that $|\Pr[\mathsf{out}_{1.q.i} = 1] - \Pr[\mathsf{out}_{1.q.i.1} = 1]| \leq \mathsf{Adv}_{\mathsf{iO}}(\mathcal{B})$.

We note that the view of $\mathcal{A}$ in game $\mathbf{G}_{1.q.i.1}$ does not depend on the PRF key K. This enables to exploit the selective security of F.

```
Circuit C̄''[stf, (crs, G), S, C_0, C_1, K{γ_i}, Y, γ_i](x)

parse x =: ((y_1, aux_1), ..., (y_ℓ, aux_ℓ))
state_j := stf(y_1, ..., y_{j-1}, ⊥, ..., ⊥)
if ¬(∀j ∈ [ℓ]: NIZK.Verify(crs, (G, S, state_j, y_j), aux_j) = 1) then
  return ⊥
γ := (y_1, ..., y_ℓ)
if γ < γ_i then r := F(K{γ_i}, γ); return C_1(γ; r)
if γ = γ_i then return Y
if γ > γ_i then r := F(K{γ_i}, γ); return C_b(γ; r)
```

Fig. 8. Definition of the circuit $\bar{C}''$.

Game $\mathbf{G}_{1.q.i.2}$. In this game we replace the randomness $F(K_q, (\gamma_{q,i}))$ by true randomness, i.e. we produce Y as follows: $Y := C_{q,b}(\gamma_{q,i}; R)$. This game hop is justified by the selective PRF property, more formally $|\Pr[\mathsf{out}_{1.q.i.1} = 1] - \Pr[\mathsf{out}_{1.q.i.2} = 1]| \leq \mathsf{Adv}_{\text{s-cPRF}}(\mathcal{B})$ for some PPT adversary $\mathcal{B}$.

Game $\mathbf{G}_{1.q.i.3}$. Game $\mathbf{G}_{1.q.i.3}$ is the same as $\mathbf{G}_{1.q.i.2}$ except for the fact that Y is produced using the circuit $C_{q,1}$, i.e. $Y := C_{q,1}(\gamma_{q,i}; R)$. This game hop is justified by the fact that the circuit sampler D_λ is a dynamic-input indistinguishable sampler.

Game $\mathbf{G}_{1.q.i.4}$. This game is the same as $\mathbf{G}_{1.q.i.3}$ with the difference that we again use pseudorandom coins to compute Y, i.e. $Y := C_{q,1}(\gamma_{q,i}; F(K_q, \gamma_{q,i}))$. For every PPT adversary $\mathcal{A}$ there exists a PPT adversary $\mathcal{B}$ such that $|\Pr[\mathsf{out}_{1.q.i.3} = 1] - \Pr[\mathsf{out}_{1.q.i.4} = 1]| \leq \mathsf{Adv}_{\text{s-cPRF}}(\mathcal{B})$.

As the pPRF F preserves functionality under punctured keys, the two circuits $\bar{C}''[\mathsf{stf}, (\mathsf{crs}, G), S_q, C_{q,0}, C_{q,1}, K_q\{\gamma_{q,i}\}, Y := C_{q,1}(\gamma_{q,i}; F(K_q, \gamma_{q,i})), \gamma_{q,i}]$ and $\bar{C}'[\mathsf{stf}, (\mathsf{crs}, G), S_q, C_{q,0}, C_{q,1}, K_q, \gamma_{q,i+1}]$ are functionally equivalent. Therefore, we have that $|\Pr[\mathsf{out}_{1.q.i.4} = 1] - \Pr[\mathsf{out}_{1.q.i+1} = 1]| \leq \mathsf{Adv}_{\mathsf{iO}}(\mathcal{B})$.

Summing up, the advantage to distinguish $\mathbf{G}_1$ and $\mathbf{G}_{1.Q}$ is bounded by $|\mathcal{I}|^\ell \cdot t^{\ell^2} \cdot \mathsf{negl}(\lambda)$. As ℓ is constant and $|\mathcal{I}|, t$ are polynomial, this quantity is negligible. As the circuit obfuscated in $\mathbf{G}_{1.Q}$ is now functionally equivalent to the circuit obfuscated in $\mathbf{G}_1^1$, the game hop to $\mathbf{G}_1'$ is justified by the indistinguishability property of iO. More formally there exists a PPT adversary $\mathcal{B}$ such that $|\Pr[\mathsf{out}_{1.Q} = 1] - \Pr[\mathsf{out}_1'] = 1| \leq \mathsf{Adv}_{\mathcal{B}}^{\mathsf{iO}}(\lambda)$. This implies that the advantage of $\mathcal{A}$ in game $\mathbf{G}_1'$ is lower bounded by $\varepsilon/2 - \mathsf{negl}(\lambda)$, which is non-negligible. However, the view of $\mathcal{A}$ in $\mathbf{G}_1'$ is perfectly independent of b, hence its advantage in this game cannot be non-zero; therefore, we reach a contradiction, which concludes the proof. □

4.3 Extension

We sketch a straightforward extension of our above construction. It follows easily by inspection that the same proof strategy would work even if the ℓ sources, which sample inputs accorded to an encoding of a sampler S with respect to public parameters pp, are not required anymore to use the *same* public parameters. The ℓ sources could even each use different public parameters $(\mathsf{pp}_1, \ldots, \mathsf{pp}_\ell)$. The modified proof for this scenario would proceed by first switching the ELFs in $(\mathsf{pp}_1, \ldots, \mathsf{pp}_\ell)$ to an extremely-lossy mode, through a sequence of ℓ hybrids. Each extremely-lossy mode is chosen so that $\mathcal{A}$ as advantage at most $\varepsilon/2\ell$ in distinguishing it from the injective mode. By a union bound, $\mathcal{A}$ has therefore advantage at most $\varepsilon/2$ in distinguishing the all-injective modes from the all-lossy modes. Then, enumerating over all possible valid inputs to an obfuscated circuit takes polynomial time as before, as each input of a source comes from a set of polynomial size. Therefore, the exact same sequence of hybrids proves security, with a polynomial loss in the underlying primitives. To adapt the security properties of our definition of dpiO to this multi-parameter setting, it suffices to let all experiments initially sample and send to the adversary ℓ public parameters $(\mathsf{pp}_1, \ldots, \mathsf{pp}_\ell)$ instead of one. In the simulatability of encodings definition (resp. in the indistinguishability definition), the adversary is allowed to specify under which public parameters it wants to receive a (real or simulated) sample $(y, \mathsf{aux}; y')$ (resp. under which public parameters it wants C_b to be obfuscated in the indistinguishability experiment).

It can prove convenient to simplify the construction in some applications to allow different sources to use different public parameters. Let us illustrate the syntax we adopt on an example: if $(\mathsf{Setup}, \mathsf{Encode}, \mathsf{Obfuscate})$ is a 5-source dpiO scheme, we denote by $\mathsf{Obfuscate}(\mathsf{pp}_1[1-3], \mathsf{pp}_2[4,5],, S, C)$ an obfuscation of a circuit C, whose first three inputs should be sampled with respect to pp_1, and whose last two inputs should be sampled with respect to pp_2. We will also sometimes slightly abuse our notation, noting that an ℓ-source dpiO scheme directly implies an i-source dpiO scheme for $i \leq \ell$, and allow an ℓ-source scheme to obfuscate a circuit C that takes $i < \ell$ inputs.

5 Leveled Homomorphic Encryption

In this section we show that our notion of dpIO from Sect. 3 can be applied to construct leveled homomorphic encryption in a similar way as in [25]. This construction leads to a transformation which operates on an encryption scheme E, satisfying IND-CPA security (and possibly other security properties, e.g., KDM security), and produces a leveled homomorphic encryption scheme that retains the security properties of E. We recall the definition of IND-CPA secure encryption schemes in the full version [1].

Let stf_λ be the trivial state function, i.e. $\mathsf{stf}\colon (y_1, y_2) \mapsto \bot$ for each $(y_1, y_2) \in (\{0,1\}^\lambda \cup \{\bot\})^2$. Let $E = (E.\mathsf{KeyGen}, E.\mathsf{Enc}, E.\mathsf{Dec})$ be an IND-CPA-secure public-key encryption scheme. Let the class $\mathcal{SI}$ contain all samplers S^{pk} that on input of a state state and an input $x \in \mathcal{I} := \{0,1\}$, produce an encryption $y := E.\mathsf{Enc}(\mathsf{pk}, x)$ and $y' := \bot$ ignoring state, where pk is a public key in the range of $E.\mathsf{KeyGen}(1^\lambda)$. Let $\mathcal{C}$ be the class of polynomially sized randomized circuits and let $\mathbf{S}^{\mathsf{d\text{-}Ind}}$ be the class of dynamic-input indistinguishable samplers over $\mathcal{C}$.

Theorem 15. *Let* (Setup, Encode, Obfuscate) *be a 2-source* dpiO *scheme for* (stf, $\mathcal{SI}, \mathcal{C}, \mathbf{S}^{\text{d-Ind}}$) *and let E be an IND-CPA secure public-key encryption scheme. Then,* LHE *as defined in Fig. 9 is an IND-CPA secure LHE scheme.*

The proof strategy is similar as in [25].Here we provide an informal sketch of the proof and refer the reader to the full version [1] for the full proof. On a high level, we want to reduce the security of LHE to the security of the underlying encryption scheme E. However, the evaluation key ek contains information (even though obfuscated) on the secret keys of each level. For the purpose of invoking the security of E on the challenge ciphertext, we need to remove this dependency on sk_0. Therefore, we gradually (starting from level L) replace the obfuscations of the circuits C with an obfuscation of *trapdoor* circuits tC that simply output samples produced by the encoded sampler S' on input of 0 (hence, not needing any information on decryption keys). These two circuits only differ in the fact that they sample from the same encoded sampler S' using (possibly) different inputs. Due to the simulatability of encodings and the IND-CPA security of E, the two circuits are dynamic-input indistinguishable. Hence, by the indistinguishability property of dpiO for $\mathbf{S}^{\text{d-Ind}}$, an honest evaluation key and an evaluation key consisting only of trapdoor circuits are indistinguishable.

$\mathsf{LHE.KeyGen}(1^\lambda, 1^L)$

for $i \in \{0, \ldots, L\}$ **do**
  $(\mathsf{pk}_i, \mathsf{sk}_i) \xleftarrow{\$} E.\mathsf{KeyGen}(1^\lambda)$
  $\mathsf{pp}_i \xleftarrow{\$} \mathsf{Setup}(1^\lambda)$
  $S'^{\mathsf{pk}_i} \leftarrow \mathsf{Encode}(\mathsf{pp}_i, S^{\mathsf{pk}_i})$
for $i \in \{1, \ldots, L\}$ **do**
  $\Lambda_i \xleftarrow{\$} \mathsf{Obfuscate}\left(\mathsf{pp}_{i-1}, S^{\mathsf{pk}_{i-1}}, C[S'^{\mathsf{pk}_i}, \mathsf{sk}_{i-1}]\right)$
$\mathsf{pk} := S'^{\mathsf{pk}_0}$, $\mathsf{sk} := \mathsf{sk}_L$, $\mathsf{ek} := (\Lambda_1, \ldots, \Lambda_L)$
return $(\mathsf{pk}, \mathsf{ek}, \mathsf{sk})$

$\mathsf{LHE.Enc}(\mathsf{pk}, m \in \{0,1\})$

parse $\mathsf{pk} =: S'^{\mathsf{pk}_0}$
$(y, \mathsf{aux}, y') \xleftarrow{\$} S'^{\mathsf{pk}_0}(\perp, m)$
return $c \leftarrow (y, \mathsf{aux})$

$\mathsf{LHE.Dec}(\mathsf{sk}, c)$

parse $\mathsf{sk} =: \mathsf{sk}_L$
parse $c =: (y, aux)$
return $E.\mathsf{Dec}(\mathsf{sk}_L, y)$

$\mathsf{LHE.Eval}(\mathsf{ek}, C, (c_1, \ldots, c_l))$

for $i \in \{1, \ldots, L\}$ **do**
  foreach gate g on level i **do**
    // let α_g, β_g denote the respective inputs
    $\gamma_g := \Lambda_i(\alpha_g, \beta_g)$

Fig. 9. Description of the LHE scheme LHE. The circuit C is defined in Fig. 10.

$C[S'^{\mathsf{pk}}, \mathsf{sk}'](x_\alpha, x_\beta)$

$\alpha \leftarrow E.\mathsf{Dec}(\mathsf{sk}', x_\alpha)$
$\beta \leftarrow E.\mathsf{Dec}(\mathsf{sk}', x_\beta)$
$(y, \mathsf{aux}, y') \xleftarrow{\$} S'^{\mathsf{pk}}(\perp, \alpha \overline{\wedge} \beta)$
return (y, aux)

$tC[S'^{\mathsf{pk}}](x_\alpha, x_\beta)$

$(y, \mathsf{aux}, y') \xleftarrow{\$} S'^{\mathsf{pk}}(\perp, 0)$
return (y, aux)

Fig. 10. Definition of the circuits C and tC.

Given these modifications, the challenge ciphertext c^* consists of an encryption of a bit b under pk_0 accompanied by some auxiliary information produced by the corresponding encoded sampler. This auxiliary information might leak information on the bit b and thereby prevents to directly employ the IND-CPA security of E. However, as dpiO satisfies simulatability of encodings, this auxiliary information can be simulated without knowledge of b and, hence, contains no information about b. Therefore, by the IND-CPA security of E, LHE is IND-CPA secure. Given our construction of dpiO from Sect. 4, we obtain the following corollary:

Corollary 16. *Assuming polynomially secure indistinguishability obfuscation and extremely lossy functions, there exists a leveled homomorphic encryption scheme.*

Note that IND-CPA secure cryptosystems, as required in our construction, can be constructed from (polynomially secure) IO and one-way function (the latter being implied by ELFs). Previously, constructions of LHE were only known from the learning with error assumption, or from *subexponentially secure* indistinguishability obfuscation (together with lossy encryption, which can be based e.g. on DDH). Using the generic transformation from leveled homomorphic encryption to fully homomorphic encryption from [25], we also get:

Corollary 17. *Assuming slightly-superpolynomially secure indistinguishability obfuscation and extremely lossy functions, there exists a fully homomorphic encryption scheme.*

Due to space limitations we state here two corollaries concerning FHE and KDM security and refer the reader to the full version [1] for a detailed discussion.

Corollary 18. *Assuming polynomially-secure indistinguishability obfuscation and extremely lossy functions, there exists a fully homomorphic encryption scheme.*

Corollary 19. *Assuming polynomially-secure indistinguishability obfuscation and eDDH, there exists a fully KDM-secure encryption scheme.*

Acknowledgments. We would like to thank the anonymous reviewers for many helpful comments.

References

1. Agrikola, T., Couteau, G., Hofheinz, D.: The usefulness of sparsifiable inputs: how to avoid subexponential io. Cryptology ePrint Archive, Report 2018/470 (2018). https://eprint.iacr.org/2018/470
2. Ananth, P., Boneh, D., Garg, S., Sahai, A., Zhandry, M.: Differing-inputs obfuscation and applications. Cryptology ePrint Archive, Report 2013/689 (2013). http://eprint.iacr.org/2013/689

3. Ananth, P., Jain, A.: Indistinguishability obfuscation from compact functional encryption. In: Gennaro, R., Robshaw, M.J.B. (eds.) CRYPTO 2015, Part I. LNCS, vol. 9215, pp. 308–326. Springer, Heidelberg (2015). https://doi.org/10.1007/978-3-662-47989-6_15
4. Ananth, P., Sahai, A.: Projective arithmetic functional encryption and indistinguishability obfuscation from degree-5 multilinear maps. In: Coron, J.-S., Nielsen, J.B. (eds.) EUROCRYPT 2017, Part I. LNCS, vol. 10210, pp. 152–181. Springer, Cham (2017). https://doi.org/10.1007/978-3-319-56620-7_6
5. Barak, B., et al.: On the (im)possibility of obfuscating programs. In: Kilian, J. (ed.) CRYPTO 2001. LNCS, vol. 2139, pp. 1–18. Springer, Heidelberg (2001). https://doi.org/10.1007/3-540-44647-8_1
6. Barak, B., Haitner, I., Hofheinz, D., Ishai, Y.: Bounded key-dependent message security. In: Gilbert, H. (ed.) EUROCRYPT 2010. LNCS, vol. 6110, pp. 423–444. Springer, Heidelberg (2010). https://doi.org/10.1007/978-3-642-13190-5_22
7. Bellare, M., Stepanovs, I., Waters, B.: New negative results on differing-inputs obfuscation. In: Fischlin, M., Coron, J.-S. (eds.) EUROCRYPT 2016, Part II. LNCS, vol. 9666, pp. 792–821. Springer, Heidelberg (2016). https://doi.org/10.1007/978-3-662-49896-5_28
8. Benhamouda, F., Lin, H.: k-round multiparty computation from k-round oblivious transfer via garbled interactive circuits. In: Nielsen, J.B., Rijmen, V. (eds.) EUROCRYPT 2018, Part II. LNCS, vol. 10821, pp. 500–532. Springer, Cham (2018). https://doi.org/10.1007/978-3-319-78375-8_17
9. Bitansky, N.: Verifiable random functions from non-interactive witness-indistinguishable proofs. In: Kalai, Y., Reyzin, L. (eds.) TCC 2017, Part II. LNCS, vol. 10678, pp. 567–594. Springer, Cham (2017). https://doi.org/10.1007/978-3-319-70503-3_19
10. Bitansky, N., Canetti, R., Kalai, Y.T., Paneth, O.: On virtual grey box obfuscation for general circuits. In: Garay, J.A., Gennaro, R. (eds.) CRYPTO 2014, Part II. LNCS, vol. 8617, pp. 108–125. Springer, Heidelberg (2014). https://doi.org/10.1007/978-3-662-44381-1_7
11. Bitansky, N., Paneth, O.: On the impossibility of approximate obfuscation and applications to resettable cryptography. In: Boneh, D., Roughgarden, T., Feigenbaum, J. (eds.) 45th ACM STOC, pp. 241–250. ACM Press, June 2013
12. Bitansky, N., Paneth, O.: ZAPs and non-interactive witness indistinguishability from indistinguishability obfuscation. In: Dodis, Y., Nielsen, J.B. (eds.) TCC 2015, Part II. LNCS, vol. 9015, pp. 401–427. Springer, Heidelberg (2015). https://doi.org/10.1007/978-3-662-46497-7_16
13. Bitansky, N., Vaikuntanathan, V.: Indistinguishability obfuscation from functional encryption. In: Guruswami, V. (ed.) 56th FOCS, pp. 171–190. IEEE Computer Society Press, October 2015
14. Black, J., Rogaway, P., Shrimpton, T.: Encryption-scheme security in the presence of key-dependent messages. In: Nyberg, K., Heys, H. (eds.) SAC 2002. LNCS, vol. 2595, pp. 62–75. Springer, Heidelberg (2003). https://doi.org/10.1007/3-540-36492-7_6
15. Blum, M., Feldman, P., Micali, S.: Non-interactive zero-knowledge and its applications (extended abstract). In: 20th ACM STOC, pp. 103–112. ACM Press, May 1988
16. Boneh, D., Boyen, X.: Efficient selective-ID secure identity-based encryption without random oracles. In: Cachin, C., Camenisch, J.L. (eds.) EUROCRYPT 2004. LNCS, vol. 3027, pp. 223–238. Springer, Heidelberg (2004). https://doi.org/10.1007/978-3-540-24676-3_14

17. Boneh, D., Boyen, X.: Secure identity based encryption without random oracles. In: Franklin, M. (ed.) CRYPTO 2004. LNCS, vol. 3152, pp. 443–459. Springer, Heidelberg (2004). https://doi.org/10.1007/978-3-540-28628-8_27
18. Boneh, D., Halevi, S., Hamburg, M., Ostrovsky, R.: Circular-secure encryption from decision Diffie-Hellman. In: Wagner, D. (ed.) CRYPTO 2008. LNCS, vol. 5157, pp. 108–125. Springer, Heidelberg (2008). https://doi.org/10.1007/978-3-540-85174-5_7
19. Boneh, D., Waters, B.: Constrained pseudorandom functions and their applications. In: Sako, K., Sarkar, P. (eds.) ASIACRYPT 2013, Part II. LNCS, vol. 8270, pp. 280–300. Springer, Heidelberg (2013). https://doi.org/10.1007/978-3-642-42045-0_15
20. Boyle, E., Chung, K.-M., Pass, R.: On extractability obfuscation. In: Lindell, Y. (ed.) TCC 2014. LNCS, vol. 8349, pp. 52–73. Springer, Heidelberg (2014). https://doi.org/10.1007/978-3-642-54242-8_3
21. Boyle, E., Gilboa, N., Ishai, Y.: Function secret sharing. In: Oswald, E., Fischlin, M. (eds.) EUROCRYPT 2015, Part II. LNCS, vol. 9057, pp. 337–367. Springer, Heidelberg (2015). https://doi.org/10.1007/978-3-662-46803-6_12
22. Boyle, E., Goldwasser, S., Ivan, I.: Functional signatures and pseudorandom functions. In: Krawczyk, H. (ed.) PKC 2014. LNCS, vol. 8383, pp. 501–519. Springer, Heidelberg (2014). https://doi.org/10.1007/978-3-642-54631-0_29
23. Canetti, R.: Towards realizing random oracles: hsh functions that hide all partial information. In: Kaliski Jr., B.S. (ed.) CRYPTO 1997. LNCS, vol. 1294, pp. 455–469. Springer, Heidelberg (1997). https://doi.org/10.1007/BFb0052255
24. Canetti, R., Chen, Y., Reyzin, L., Rothblum, R.D.: Fiat-Shamir and correlation intractability from strong KDM-secure encryption. In: Nielsen, J.B., Rijmen, V. (eds.) EUROCRYPT 2018, Part I. LNCS, vol. 10820, pp. 91–122. Springer, Cham (2018). https://doi.org/10.1007/978-3-319-78381-9_4
25. Canetti, R., Lin, H., Tessaro, S., Vaikuntanathan, V.: Obfuscation of probabilistic circuits and applications. In: Dodis, Y., Nielsen, J.B. (eds.) TCC 2015, Part II. LNCS, vol. 9015, pp. 468–497. Springer, Heidelberg (2015). https://doi.org/10.1007/978-3-662-46497-7_19
26. Canetti, R., Raghuraman, S., Richelson, S., Vaikuntanathan, V.: Chosen-ciphertext secure fully homomorphic encryption. In: Fehr, S. (ed.) PKC 2017, Part II. LNCS, vol. 10175, pp. 213–240. Springer, Heidelberg (2017). https://doi.org/10.1007/978-3-662-54388-7_8
27. Dodis, Y., Halevi, S., Rothblum, R.D., Wichs, D.: Spooky encryption and its applications. In: Robshaw, M., Katz, J. (eds.) CRYPTO 2016, Part III. LNCS, vol. 9816, pp. 93–122. Springer, Heidelberg (2016). https://doi.org/10.1007/978-3-662-53015-3_4
28. Döttling, N., Nishimaki, R.: Universal proxy re-encryption. Cryptology ePrint Archive, Report 2018/840 (2018). https://eprint.iacr.org/2018/840
29. Farshim, P., Hesse, J., Hofheinz, D., Larraia, E.: Graded encoding schemes from obfuscation. In: Abdalla, M., Dahab, R. (eds.) PKC 2018, Part II. LNCS, vol. 10770, pp. 371–400. Springer, Cham (2018). https://doi.org/10.1007/978-3-319-76581-5_13
30. Garg, S., Gentry, C., Halevi, S., Raykova, M.: Two-round secure MPC from indistinguishability obfuscation. In: Lindell, Y. (ed.) TCC 2014. LNCS, vol. 8349, pp. 74–94. Springer, Heidelberg (2014). https://doi.org/10.1007/978-3-642-54242-8_4
31. Garg, S., Gentry, C., Halevi, S., Raykova, M., Sahai, A., Waters, B.: Candidate indistinguishability obfuscation and functional encryption for all circuits. In: 54th FOCS, pp. 40–49. IEEE Computer Society Press, October 2013

32. Garg, S., Gentry, C., Halevi, S., Wichs, D.: On the implausibility of differing-inputs obfuscation and extractable witness encryption with auxiliary input. In: Garay, J.A., Gennaro, R. (eds.) CRYPTO 2014, Part I. LNCS, vol. 8616, pp. 518–535. Springer, Heidelberg (2014). https://doi.org/10.1007/978-3-662-44371-2_29
33. Garg, S., Pandey, O., Srinivasan, A.: Revisiting the cryptographic hardness of finding a nash equilibrium. In: Robshaw, M., Katz, J. (eds.) CRYPTO 2016, Part II. LNCS, vol. 9815, pp. 579–604. Springer, Heidelberg (2016). https://doi.org/10.1007/978-3-662-53008-5_20
34. Garg, S., Pandey, O., Srinivasan, A., Zhandry, M.: Breaking the sub-exponential barrier in obfustopia. In: Coron, J.-S., Nielsen, J.B. (eds.) EUROCRYPT 2017, Part III. LNCS, vol. 10212, pp. 156–181. Springer, Cham (2017). https://doi.org/10.1007/978-3-319-56617-7_6
35. Garg, S., Srinivasan, A.: Single-key to multi-key functional encryption with polynomial loss. In: Hirt, M., Smith, A. (eds.) TCC 2016, Part II. LNCS, vol. 9986, pp. 419–442. Springer, Heidelberg (2016). https://doi.org/10.1007/978-3-662-53644-5_16
36. Garg, S., Srinivasan, A.: Two-round multiparty secure computation from minimal assumptions. In: Nielsen, J.B., Rijmen, V. (eds.) EUROCRYPT 2018, Part II. LNCS, vol. 10821, pp. 468–499. Springer, Cham (2018). https://doi.org/10.1007/978-3-319-78375-8_16
37. Goldreich, O., Goldwasser, S., Micali, S.: How to construct random functions (extended abstract). In: 25th FOCS, pp. 464–479. IEEE Computer Society Press, October 1984
38. Goldwasser, S., Kalai, Y.T.: On the impossibility of obfuscation with auxiliary input. In: 46th FOCS, pp. 553–562. IEEE Computer Society Press, October 2005
39. Goldwasser, S., Rothblum, G.N.: On best-possible obfuscation. In: Vadhan, S.P. (ed.) TCC 2007. LNCS, vol. 4392, pp. 194–213. Springer, Heidelberg (2007). https://doi.org/10.1007/978-3-540-70936-7_11
40. Goyal, R., Hohenberger, S., Koppula, V., Waters, B.: A generic approach to constructing and proving verifiable random functions. In: Kalai, Y., Reyzin, L. (eds.) TCC 2017. LNCS, vol. 10678, pp. 537–566. Springer, Cham (2017). https://doi.org/10.1007/978-3-319-70503-3_18
41. Groth, J., Ostrovsky, R., Sahai, A.: Perfect non-interactive zero knowledge for NP. In: Vaudenay, S. (ed.) EUROCRYPT 2006. LNCS, vol. 4004, pp. 339–358. Springer, Heidelberg (2006). https://doi.org/10.1007/11761679_21
42. Hada, S.: Zero-knowledge and code obfuscation. In: Okamoto, T. (ed.) ASIACRYPT 2000. LNCS, vol. 1976, pp. 443–457. Springer, Heidelberg (2000). https://doi.org/10.1007/3-540-44448-3_34
43. Håstad, J., Impagliazzo, R., Levin, L.A., Luby, M.: A pseudorandom generator from any one-way function. SIAM J. Comput. **28**(4), 1364–1396 (1999)
44. Hofheinz, D., Kiltz, E.: Programmable hash functions and their applications. In: Wagner, D. (ed.) CRYPTO 2008. LNCS, vol. 5157, pp. 21–38. Springer, Heidelberg (2008). https://doi.org/10.1007/978-3-540-85174-5_2
45. Hofheinz, D., Malone-Lee, J., Stam, M.: Obfuscation for cryptographic purposes. In: Vadhan, S.P. (ed.) TCC 2007. LNCS, vol. 4392, pp. 214–232. Springer, Heidelberg (2007). https://doi.org/10.1007/978-3-540-70936-7_12
46. Hofheinz, D., Rao, V., Wichs, D.: Standard security does not imply indistinguishability under selective opening. In: Hirt, M., Smith, A. (eds.) TCC 2016, Part II. LNCS, vol. 9986, pp. 121–145. Springer, Heidelberg (2016). https://doi.org/10.1007/978-3-662-53644-5_5

47. Hohenberger, S., Rothblum, G.N., Shelat, A., Vaikuntanathan, V.: Securely obfuscating re-encryption. In: Vadhan, S.P. (ed.) TCC 2007. LNCS, vol. 4392, pp. 233–252. Springer, Heidelberg (2007). https://doi.org/10.1007/978-3-540-70936-7_13
48. Hohenberger, S., Sahai, A., Waters, B.: Replacing a random oracle: full domain hash from indistinguishability obfuscation. In: Nguyen, P.Q., Oswald, E. (eds.) EUROCRYPT 2014. LNCS, vol. 8441, pp. 201–220. Springer, Heidelberg (2014). https://doi.org/10.1007/978-3-642-55220-5_12
49. Hohenberger, S., Waters, B.: Short and stateless signatures from the RSA assumption. In: Halevi, S. (ed.) CRYPTO 2009. LNCS, vol. 5677, pp. 654–670. Springer, Heidelberg (2009). https://doi.org/10.1007/978-3-642-03356-8_38
50. Ishai, Y., Pandey, O., Sahai, A.: Public-coin differing-inputs obfuscation and its applications. In: Dodis, Y., Nielsen, J.B. (eds.) TCC 2015, Part II. LNCS, vol. 9015, pp. 668–697. Springer, Heidelberg (2015). https://doi.org/10.1007/978-3-662-46497-7_26
51. Kiayias, A., Papadopoulos, S., Triandopoulos, N., Zacharias, T.: Delegatable pseudorandom functions and applications. In: Sadeghi, A.R., Gligor, V.D., Yung, M. (eds.) ACM CCS 2013, pp. 669–684. ACM Press, November 2013
52. Li, B., Micciancio, D.: Compactness vs collusion resistance in functional encryption. In: Hirt, M., Smith, A. (eds.) TCC 2016, Part II. LNCS, vol. 9986, pp. 443–468. Springer, Heidelberg (2016). https://doi.org/10.1007/978-3-662-53644-5_17
53. Lin, H.: Indistinguishability obfuscation from SXDH on 5-linear maps and locality-5 PRGs. In: Katz, J., Shacham, H. (eds.) CRYPTO 2017, Part I. LNCS, vol. 10401, pp. 599–629. Springer, Cham (2017). https://doi.org/10.1007/978-3-319-63688-7_20
54. Lin, H., Tessaro, S.: Indistinguishability obfuscation from trilinear maps and block-wise local PRGs. In: Katz, J., Shacham, H. (eds.) CRYPTO 2017, Part I. LNCS, vol. 10401, pp. 630–660. Springer, Cham (2017). https://doi.org/10.1007/978-3-319-63688-7_21
55. Liu, Q., Zhandry, M.: Decomposable obfuscation: a framework for building applications of obfuscation from polynomial hardness. In: Kalai, Y., Reyzin, L. (eds.) TCC 2017, Part I. LNCS, vol. 10677, pp. 138–169. Springer, Cham (2017). https://doi.org/10.1007/978-3-319-70500-2_6
56. Lynn, B., Prabhakaran, M., Sahai, A.: Positive results and techniques for obfuscation. In: Cachin, C., Camenisch, J. (eds.) EUROCRYPT 2004. LNCS, vol. 3027, pp. 20–39. Springer, Heidelberg (2004). https://doi.org/10.1007/978-3-540-24676-3_2
57. Pass, R., Seth, K., Telang, S.: Indistinguishability obfuscation from semantically-secure multilinear encodings. In: Garay, J.A., Gennaro, R. (eds.) CRYPTO 2014, Part I. LNCS, vol. 8616, pp. 500–517. Springer, Heidelberg (2014). https://doi.org/10.1007/978-3-662-44371-2_28
58. Pass, R., Shelat, A.: Impossibility of VBB obfuscation with ideal constant-degree graded encodings. In: Kushilevitz, E., Malkin, T. (eds.) TCC 2016, Part I. LNCS, vol. 9562, pp. 3–17. Springer, Heidelberg (2016). https://doi.org/10.1007/978-3-662-49096-9_1
59. Sahai, A., Waters, B.: How to use indistinguishability obfuscation: deniable encryption, and more. In: Shmoys, D.B. (ed.) 46th ACM STOC, pp. 475–484. ACM Press, May/June 2014
60. Waters, B.: Efficient identity-based encryption without random Oracles. In: Cramer, R. (ed.) EUROCRYPT 2005. LNCS, vol. 3494, pp. 114–127. Springer, Heidelberg (2005). https://doi.org/10.1007/11426639_7

61. Wee, H.: On obfuscating point functions. In: Gabow, H.N., Fagin, R. (eds.) 37th ACM STOC, pp. 523–532. ACM Press, May 2005
62. Zhandry, M.: The magic of ELFs. In: Robshaw, M., Katz, J. (eds.) CRYPTO 2016, Part I. LNCS, vol. 9814, pp. 479–508. Springer, Heidelberg (2016). https://doi.org/10.1007/978-3-662-53018-4_18
63. Zimmerman, J.: How to obfuscate programs directly. In: Oswald, E., Fischlin, M. (eds.) EUROCRYPT 2015, Part II. LNCS, vol. 9057, pp. 439–467. Springer, Heidelberg (2015). https://doi.org/10.1007/978-3-662-46803-6_15

Witness Maps and Applications

Suvradip Chakraborty[1(✉)], Manoj Prabhakaran[2], and Daniel Wichs[3]

[1] Institute of Science and Technology Austria, Klosterneuburg, Austria
suvradip.chakraborty@ist.ac.at
[2] Indian Institute of Technology Bombay, Mumbai, India
mp@cse.iitb.ac.in
[3] Northeastern and NTT Research, Boston, USA
wichs@ccs.neu.edu

Abstract. We introduce the notion of *Witness Maps* as a cryptographic notion of a proof system. A *Unique Witness Map* (UWM) deterministically maps all witnesses for an **NP** statement to a single representative witness, resulting in a computationally sound, deterministic-prover, non-interactive witness independent proof system. A relaxation of UWM, called Compact Witness Map (CWM), maps all the witnesses to a small number of witnesses, resulting in a "lossy" deterministic-prover, non-interactive proof-system. We also define a *Dual Mode Witness Map* (DMWM) which adds an "extractable" mode to a CWM.

Our main construction is a DMWM for all **NP** relations, assuming sub-exponentially secure indistinguishability obfuscation ($i\mathcal{O}$), along with standard cryptographic assumptions. The DMWM construction relies on a CWM and a new primitive called *Cumulative All-Lossy-But-One Trapdoor Functions* (C-ALBO-TDF), both of which are in turn instantiated based on $i\mathcal{O}$ and other primitives. Our instantiation of a CWM is in fact a UWM; in turn, we show that a UWM implies Witness Encryption. Along the way to constructing UWM and C-ALBO-TDF, we also construct, from standard assumptions, *Puncturable Digital Signatures* and a new primitive called *Cumulative Lossy Trapdoor Functions* (C-LTDF). The former improves up on a construction of Bellare et al. (Eurocrypt 2016), who relied on sub-exponentially secure $i\mathcal{O}$ and sub-exponentially secure OWF.

As an application of our constructions, we show how to use a DMWM to construct the first *leakage and tamper-resilient signatures* with a *deterministic signer*, thereby solving a decade old open problem posed by Katz and Vaikunthanathan (Asiacrypt 2009), by Boyle, Segev and Wichs (Eurocrypt 2011), as well as by Faonio and Venturi (Asiacrypt 2016). Our construction achieves the optimal leakage rate of $1 - o(1)$.

S. Chakraborty—Work carried out while at IIT Madras.

M. Prabhakaran—Supported by the Dept. of Science and Technology, India via the Ramanujan Fellowship and an Indo-Israel Joint Research Project grant, 2018.

D. Wichs—Research supported by NSF grants CNS-1314722, CNS-1413964, CNS-1750795 and the Alfred P. Sloan Research Fellowship.

A. Kiayias et al. (Eds.): PKC 2020, LNCS 12110, pp. 220–246, 2020.
https://doi.org/10.1007/978-3-030-45374-9_8

1 Introduction

A foundational innovation of theoretical computer science has been the generalization of the notion of what a *proof* is. Interactive proofs, zero-knowledge proofs and probabilistically checkable proofs are all critical to the current theory – and practice – of computer science. In this work, we introduce and explore yet another notion of a proof, against the backdrop of recent advances in cryptography.

A conventional proof of a statement that can be verified by an efficient program is called a *witness* for the statement. Goldwasser, Micali and Rackoff, in their seminal work on interactive proofs [26], introduced the fascinating concept of zero-knowledge proof protocols which reveal no "knowledge" about the witness to a verifier, yet can soundly convince her of the existence of a witness. The notion of knowledge was formalized using *simulators*. An important direction of subsequent investigation has been to develop more rudimentary models of proofs, which when realized, offer powerful cryptographic applications. In particular, Blum, Feldman and Micali [4] introduced the notion of *non-interactive* zero-knowledge proofs (NIZK), wherein they reverted to the conventional notion of a proof being just a single message that the prover can send to the verifier, but allowed a "trusted setup" in the form of a common reference string, with respect to which the proof would be verified. Feige and Shamir [21] defined *witness indistinguishability* as a simpler notion of hiding information about the witness.

> *The central object we investigate in this paper – called a Witness Map – is an even more rudimentary notion of a proof, wherein a proof is simply an alternate representation of a witness, verified using an alternate relation.*

The prover and the verifier are required to be efficient and *deterministic*, and the proof system is required to be computationally sound. A common reference string is used to generate and verify the proofs. Instead of zero-knowledge property, we require a "lossiness" property. Specifically, in a *Compact Witness Map* (CWM), each statement has a small number of proofs that its witnesses could map to, with an important special case being that of a *Unique Witness Map* (UWM).

One may wonder if it is possible to hide the witness to any extent at all, when the prover is deterministic. But we show that if indistinguishability obfuscation ($i\mathcal{O}$) and one-way functions exist, then UWMs do exist. On the other hand, we show that the existence of UWMs imply the existence of Witness Encryption (WE). Hence UWM could be viewed as the newest member of "obfustopia," and arguably the one with the simplest definition.[1]

We extend the scope of witness maps further to define the notion of a *Dual Mode Witness Map* (DMWM). In a DMWM, a proof either allows the original

[1] We present a brief formulation (omitting some formalism) here. A UWM for an **NP** language L is specified by a distribution over polynomial time verifiable relations R^{K}, such that (1) for every $x \in L$, there is a canonical witness $w^*_{\mathsf{K},x}$ with $(x, w^*_{\mathsf{K},x}) \in R^{\mathsf{K}}$, which can be efficiently computed from any witness w for $x \in L$, and (2) it is computationally infeasible to find a pair $(x, w^*) \in R^{\mathsf{K}}$ such that $x \notin L$.

witness to be extracted (using a trapdoor) or it is lossy. Which mode a proof falls into depends on whether or not the "tag" used for constructing the proof equals a hidden tag used to derive the mapping key. In defining the lossy mode, we introduce a strong form of lossiness – called *cumulative lossiness* – which bounds the total amount of information about a witness that can be revealed by *all* the proofs using all the lossy tags. We also show how to construct a DMWM for any NP relation using a CWM and a new notion of lossy trapdoor functions (which may be of independent interest).

We show that DMWMs can be readily used to solve an open problem in the area of leakage-resilient cryptography, namely, that of constructing a leakage and tamper resilient signature scheme (where all the data and randomness used by the signer are open to leakage and tampering). A crucial aspect of our construction that helps in achieving this is that signing algorithm in our scheme is deterministic, a property it inherits from the prover in a DMWM. We also extend our results to a *continuous* leakage and tampering model.

We expand on each of these contributions in greater detail below.

1.1 Witness Maps

We introduce a new primitive called a compact/unique witness map (CWM/UWM). Informally, CWM/UWM deterministically maps all possible valid witnesses for some **NP** statement to a much smaller number of *representative witnesses*, resulting in loss of information regarding the original witness. Nevertheless, the mapping should preserve the functionality of the witnesses, namely that the representative witnesses should be efficiently verifiable and (computationally) guarantee the soundness of the statement. A particularly strong form of CWM is a Unique Witness Map (UWM), in which all the possible witnesses for a statement are mapped to a single representative witness. In other words, in a UWM the representative witness only depends on the statement being proved, but not which of the original witnesses was used to prove it.[2] While we require the CWM/UWM to be deterministic, it can depend on some public *common reference string* (CRS). A UWM is essentially equivalent to a non-interactive witness indistinguishable argument (in the CRS model) with a deterministic prover and a deterministic verifier.

Defining CWM/UWM. In more detail, a CWM consists of three algorithms $(\mathsf{setup}, \mathsf{map}, \mathsf{check})$. The setup algorithm generates a CRS K. The deterministic algorithm $\mathsf{map}(\mathsf{K}, x, w)$ takes as input a statement x and a witness w and maps it to a representative witness w^*. The algorithm $\mathsf{check}(\mathsf{K}, x, w^*)$ takes as input the statement x and the representative witness w^* and outputs 1 if it verifies and 0 otherwise. We require the standard completeness property (if w is good witness for x then $\mathsf{check}(\mathsf{K}, \mathsf{map}(\mathsf{K}, x, w)) = 1$) and computational soundness (if x is false then it's computationally hard to produce w^* such that $\mathsf{check}(\mathsf{K}, x, w^*) = 1$).

[2] Note that uniqueness is a property of the map/prover, but we do not require uniqueness for the verifier; for any given statement, there may be many representative witnesses that the verifier would accept, but the map/prover always produces a unique one.

Lastly, we require that for any true statement x the set of possible representative witnesses $\{w^* = \mathsf{map}(\mathsf{K}, x, w) \ : \ w \text{ witness for } x\}$ is small, and potentially much smaller than the set of all original witnesses w for x. In a UWM, the set of representative witnesses needs to be of size 1, meaning there is a unique representative witness for each x in the language.

Constructing UWM. We give a simple construction of a UWM from $i\mathcal{O}$ and a punctured digital signature (PDS) scheme (see below), by leveraging the framework of Sahai and Waters [41] previously used to construct NIZKs. Our construction could be seen as implementing "deterministic witness signatures," wherein the signing key is a valid witness to a statement. We remark that a notion of witness signatures exists in the literature [28], building on the notion of "Signatures of Knowledge" [12]; however, these are incomparable to our UWM construction, as they allow randomized provers, but demand extractability of the witness (and in the case of Signatures of Knowledge, simulatability as well).

Puncturable Digital Signatures (PDS). As part of our UWM construction, we rely on Puncturable Digital Signatures (PDS). This primitive allows us to create a punctured signing key that cannot be used to sign some specified message m but otherwise correctly produces signatures for all other messages $m' \neq m$. We improve upon the construction of PDS by Bellare et al. [3], who relied on *sub-exponentially secure* Indistinguishability Obfuscation and*sub-exponentially secure* one-way functions (OWF). Our construction shows that PDS is equivalent to OWF.

Implications of UWM. We show that UWMs are a powerful primitive and, in particular, imply witness encryption (WE) [23]. However, we do not know of any such implication for CWMs in general, especially if the image size of the map can be (slightly) super-polynomial.

Dual-Mode Witness Maps. We also introduce a generalization of compact/unique witness maps (CWM/UWM) that we call *dual-mode witness maps* (DMWM). In a DMWM the map and check algorithms take as input an additional tag or branch parameter b. Furthermore the setup algorithm also takes as input a special "injective branch" b^* which is used to generate the CRS along with a trapdoor td. If $b = b^*$ then the map is injective and the original witness w can be extracted from the representative witness w^* output by the map using the trapdoor td. On the other hand, the maps for all $b \neq b^*$ is *cumulatively lossy* – i.e., even taken together, they do not reveal much information about the original witness. The identity of the injective branch b^* is hidden by the CRS.

Our definition of the cumulative lossiness property for DMWM is motivated by its application to leakage and tamper resilient signatures (see below). But it is in itself a property that can be applied more broadly. In particular, we introduce the following primitives and employ them in our construction of DMWMs (in combination with CWMs).

Cumulatively Lossy Trapdoor Functions. We introduce new variants of *lossy trapdoor functions* (LTDFs) [38], which we call *cumulatively lossy trapdoor* *functions* (C-LTDFs). Recall that, in an LTDF, a function f can be sampled to either be injective (and the sampling algorithm also generates an inversion trapdoor) or lossy (the image of f is substantially smaller than the input domain) and the two modes should be indistinguishable. For C-LTDFs, we further require that arbitrarily many lossy functions taken together are jointly lossy. In other words, if we sample arbitrarily many independent lossy functions f_i then their concatenation $(f_1, \ldots, f_\ell)(x) = (f_1(x), \ldots, f_\ell(x))$ is also lossy. We can construct C-LTDFs from DDH or LWE.

We also define *cumulatively all-lossy-but-one trapdoor functions* (C-ALBO-TDFs). This is a collection of functions $f(b, \cdot)$ parametrized by a *branch index* b. We can sample f with a special injective branch b^* such that $f(b^*, \cdot)$ is injective (and we have the corresponding inversion trapdoor) but $f(b, \cdot)$ is lossy for all $b \neq b^*$. We should not be able to distinguish which branch is the injective one. Furthermore, the lossy branches $b \neq b^*$ are cumulatively lossy. Previous constructions of LTDFs with branches [38] only achieved the opposite notion of "all-but-one lossy", where there is one lossy branch and all the other branches are injective. To the best of our knowledge, constructing ALBO-LTDFs (even without the cumulative loss requirement) was previously open. We show how to boost C-LTDFs to get C-ALBO-LTDFs via $i\mathcal{O}$.

1.2 Application: Leakage and Tamper Resilient Signatures

A digital signature scheme is one of the most fundamental cryptographic primitives and is used as an important building block in many cryptographic protocols and applications. Signature schemes are used ubiquitously in practice, in a variety of settings and applications. In particular, signing keys are often embedded in smart cards and devices operated by untrusted users. Such settings admit powerful "physical attacks" exploiting numerous side-channels for leaking (e.g. power analysis, timing measurements, microwave attacks [31,32]) and tampering (see for instance [6,40]). This has led to several works over the last decade that addressed security of cryptographic primitives – and in particular of digital signature schemes – that are leakage and/or tamper resistant [9,14,19,29,33]. In this work, we address an important question that this body of work has raised again and again:

Is there a leakage and tamper resilient (LTR) signature scheme?
Is there one with a *deterministic* signing algorithm?

The significance of this question lies in the fact that it appears harder to protect against an adversary who can target the randomness used in the scheme. When the randomness is open to attacks, current state of the art can protect only against leakage attacks [9,13,17], and not against tampering attacks (as explicitly posed in [19]). Note that if the adversary can obtain signatures produced using arbitrarily tampered randomness, it can set the randomness to a constant (say, all 0s) and therefore effectively make the signing algorithm deterministic. Therefore, a natural solution is to *entirely eliminate attacks on the randomness* by constructing a LTR signature scheme with a deterministic signing algorithm. Indeed, this is the approach taken in [13], but unfortunately their solution does not offer security against tampering of the secret key.

LTR Signature Results. Our main contribution is the construction of a *leakage and tamper resilient (LTR) signature scheme* with a deterministic signing algorithm. We focus on the *bounded* leakage and tampering model of Damgård et al. [14]. In this model, the adversary can get some bounded amount of leakage on the secret key and can also tamper with the secret key some bounded number of times; these bounds can be made arbitrarily large but have to be chosen a-priori. We strengthen the model so that *only publicly known, fixed components of the scheme (namely, the code and public parameters) are fully protected.* In particular, any randomness used during computation is subject to leakage *and* tampering. The key-generation phase is also subject to leakage (but is protected from tampering). Note that tamperability of the signing randomness invalidates prior results [14,19], and motivates the need for finding a deterministic solution. A recent work of Chen et al. [13] constructs a deterministic leakage-resilient (but *not* tamper-resilient) signature scheme from $i\mathcal{O}$ and puncturable primitives. However, as we argue later, this construction does not generalize to the setting of tampering.

Our schemes achieve a leakage rate of $1 - o(1)$, where the leakage rate is defined as the ratio of the amount of leakage to the size of the secret signing key. The scheme natively only achieves selective security, where the message to be forged is chosen by the adversary at the very beginning of the attack game. Adaptive security follows via complexity leveraging. We present our construction using generic primitives discussed below. While current instantiations of these primitives rely on indistinguishability obfuscation ($i\mathcal{O}$) and either DDH or LWE, there is hope that our template can also be instantiated under weaker assumptions in the future. Our construction combines ideas from leakage-resilience [9] and tamper-resilience [19], but replaces various ingredients with our new building blocks to facilitate a deterministic solution.

We also discuss how to extend our results to the *continuous* leakage and tampering model. In this model, the key is periodically refreshed and the adversary is only bounded in the amount of leakage and tampering that can be performed in each time period, but can continuously attack the system for arbitrarily many time periods. However, in this model, we inherently cannot allow tampering of the randomness used to perform the refreshes.

Along the way toward our main result for LTR Signatures, we introduce several new cryptographic primitives and constructions, which may be of independent interest and which we now proceed to describe.

Construction Outline. We construct deterministic leakage and tamper resilient signatures directly from dual-mode witness maps (DMWM) and a leakage-resilient one-way function (which, as we shall see, can be based on general one-way functions). As mentioned above, we construct DMWMs by combining a compact witness map (CWM) for **NP**, with a C-ALBO-LTDF, constructing other primitives like PDS and C-LTDF along the way. While current instantiations of CWMs and

C-ALBO-LTDFs rely on strong assumptions (i.e., $i\mathcal{O}$ and either DDH or LWE), this does not appear inherent and there is hope that future work can find alternate instantiations based on weaker assumptions. In particular, while UWMs imply a strong primitive (namely, Witness Encryption), the same is not known for DMWM, CWM or C-ALBO-LTDF.

1.2.1 Related Work on Leakage and Tamper-Resilient Signatures

Various notions of leakage-resilient signatures (LRS) have been studied for about a decade now. Alwen, Dodis and Wichs [1] and Katz and Vaikuntanathan [29] gave initial constructions of LRS schemes in the bounded leakage model, where the leakage is allowed to happen from the entire memory of the device. The construction of [1] was in the random oracle (RO) model. [29] gave a standard model construction, which had a deterministic signing scheme as well, but which allowed only a logarithmic number of signature queries, and the total leakage allowed degraded with number of queries. Meanwhile, Faust, Kiltz, Pietrzak and Rothblum [20] gave a construction of a *stateful* LRS scheme in the "Only Computation Leaks" model of Micali and Reyzin [35]. The first full-fledged construction of fully leakage-resilient (FLR) signatures – which allowed bounded leakage from the randomness used for key-generation and signing – were proposed independently by Boyle et al. [9] and Malkin et al. [33]. Faonio et al. [17] also gave a construction of FLR signatures in the bounded retrieval model, where the secret key (and the leakage from it) may be larger than the size of a signature. In this setting, standard existential unforgeability is impossible to achieve, since the adversary can simply leak a forgery. Hence the authors only demand a graceful degradation of security to hold. Yuen et al. [42] constructed a FLR signature scheme in the selective auxiliary input leakage model, where it is assumed that the leakage is a computationally hard-to-invert function. The recent work of Chen et al. [13] gave an FLR signature scheme with a deterministic signing algorithm, and achieved selective unforgeability, relying on $i\mathcal{O}$.

Tamper resilience was addressed in [14,19]. The question of *fully* leakage and tamper resilient signatures (i.e., allowing leakage from and tampering of randomness as well as secret key) was explicitly posed as an open problem in [19]. The continual memory leakage (CML) model has been studied in [10,15,33].

Comparison with the Work of [13]**.** Recently, Chen et al. [13] constructed a deterministic leakage-resilient (but *not* tamper-resilient) signature scheme in the bounded leakage model. An important limitation of their construction is that it does not appear amenable to a *leakage-to-tamper reduction*, which relies on being able to bound the amount of information revealed by a signature using the tampered signing key, given the verification key. (Their signing key sk is a ciphertext of a symmetric-key encryption scheme and the verification key vk comprises of two obfuscated programs).

Comparison with the Work of [18]**.** Predictable argument of knowledge (PAoK) [18] are 2-round public-coin argument systems where the answer of the prover can be predicted, given the private randomness of the verifier (thus necessitating the prover to be *deterministic*). They insist on knowledge soundness from PAoK and show that a PAoK for general **NP** relations is equivalent to extractable witness encryption. In contrast, DMWM are *non-interactive.*

1.3 Technical Overview

1.3.1 Compact Witness Maps

We now sketch the main idea behind the construction of our unique witness map (UWM) scheme, which is the strongest form of compact witness maps (CWMs). Our construction essentially follows the same (abstracted out) approach of Sahai and Waters NIZKs [41]. The setup of the UWM generates a (public) CRS K. The CRS K in our construction embeds the description of an obfuscated program P, with the signing key of the Puncturable Digital Signature (PDS) scheme hard-coded in it. The obfuscated program P functions as follows: the input to the program P is a statement-witness pair, say (stmnt, w) belonging to underlying **NP** relation R_ℓ (we consider statements of size at most ℓ). The program simply checks if $R_\ell(\mathsf{stmnt}, w) = 1$, and signs the statement stmnt using the signing key sk to obtain a signature on stmnt. While generating the mapping, the mapping algorithm $\textsc{uwm}.\mathsf{map}(\mathsf{K}, \mathsf{stmnt}, w)$ runs the obfuscated program P with input (stmnt, w) to obtain a signature σ_{stmnt} on stmnt using sk. The representative witness w^* is just the signature σ_{stmnt}. The verification of the mapping is done by simply verifying the signature σ_{stmnt} (using the verification algorithm of the PDS scheme).

For proving security of the UWM scheme, we consider the notion of selective soundness[3], where the adversary announces the statement stmnt^* on which it tries to break the soundness (i.e, produce a representative witness w^*corresponding to it) of the UWM scheme, before receiving the key K. In the hybrid, we change the obfuscated program by puncturing the signing key sk at the statement stmnt^*. The consistency property of the PDS scheme ensures that the signatures output by the punctured key sk_{stmnt^*} (punctured at stmnt^*) produces the same output as the signatures generated by the original signing key sk. If the adversary could produce a witness w^* (which is nothing but a signature) corresponding to the false statement stmnt^*, this means it has managed to successfully output a forgery for the PDS scheme. Also note that, our mapping satisfies uniqueness, since (x, w) is deterministically mapped to the signature on x, independent of w.

Construction of PDS. To instantiate the UWMs described above, it remains to construct a Puncturable Digital Signature (PDS) scheme. The work of Sahai and Waters [41] implicitly constructs one using iO as a part of their construction of NIZKs, and Bellare et al. [3] makes this explicit. We show a simple construction from one-way functions. The main idea is to rely on *tree-based signatures*, where

[3] The size of the statements supported by UWM scheme is bounded (looking ahead, this will indeed be the case in our FLTR signature scheme). Hence, we can achieve adaptive soundness via a standard complexity leveraging argument, albeit incurring a sub-exponential loss in the security parameter.

every node of the tree is associated with a fresh verification/signing key of a standard (one-time) signature and a PRG seed; the seed of the parent node is used to generate the values (the verification/signing key and the seed) of each of the two children nodes. The verification key of the scheme corresponds to that of the root note and the signing key corresponds to the (signing key, seed) of the root. Each message traces out a path in the tree from a root to a leaf and the signature corresponds to a "certificate chain" consisting of signed verification keys along that path together with a signature of the message under the leaf's key. Note that the intermediate values in the tree are generated on the fly and the entire tree (which is of exponential size) is never stored all at once. Puncturing the signing key is analogous to puncturing the GGM PRF [7,8,24,30]. In particular, we remove all of the values along one path from the root to a particular leaf for the specified message on which we are puncturing, and instead give out the values of (signing key, seed) for each sibling along that path; this is sufficient to generate signatures for every other message aside from the punctured one.

UWMs Imply Witness Encryption. Lastly, we show that UWMs are a powerful cryptographic primitive and in fact imply *witness encryption* (WE) [23]. In a WE scheme, it is possible to encrypt a message m under an **NP** statement x such that, if the statement is true, then the ciphertext can be decrypted using any witness w for x. However, if x is a false statement, then the ciphertext should computationally hide the encrypted message. To construct a WE scheme from a UWM the encryption algorithm chooses a random seed z for a pseudorandom generator G and sets $y = G(z)$. It then uses a UWM to get a representative witness w^* for the statement $\hat{x}$ stating that "either x is true or y is pseudorandom", using z as the witness. It uses the Goldreich-Levin hardcore bit of w^* to blind the message m and outputs the blinded value along with y. The decryption algorithm uses the UWM to map the witness w for x into the unique witness w^* for the statement $\hat{x}$. It then computes the hardcore bit of w^* and uses it to recover the message. Intuitively, if an adversary can break WE security, then it can distinguish encryptions of 0 and 1 with non-negligible probability even if x is a false statement. This means that, using Goldreich-Levin decoding, it can compute the correct value w^* given y with non-negligible probability. Furthermore this value w^* is a valid representative witness for the statement $\hat{x}$. Since the adversary cannot break the PRG, it must also compute a valid representative witness for $\hat{x}$ if we switch y to false. But this contradicts the soundness of UWM.

1.3.2 Leakage and Tamper Resilient Signatures

We now give an overview of our leakage and tamper resilient (LTR) signature construction. The construction proceeds in 3 steps. First, we construct LTR signatures from dual-mode witness maps (DMWMs). Second, we construct DWMs from cummulatively all-lossy-but-one tradoor functions (C-ALBO-TDFs) and compact witness maps (CWMs). Thirdly, we construct C-ALBO-TDFS from DDH and LWE and iO.

LTR Signatures from DMWMs. Recall that DMWM is essentially a witness map that takes as input a branch index b. The CRS is also generated with an injective branch b^* and a trapdoor td. If the map uses the branch $b = b^*$ then it is injective and the original witness can be extracted using the trapdoor. Otherwise the map reveals very little information about the original witness. The two modes are computationally indistinguishable from each other.

Our signature scheme has the following form: The signing key is a random string x, and the verification key is $y = H(x)$, where H is a sufficiently compressing, second pre-image resistant hash function. To sign a message m, we set the branch for the DMWM to be the message m, and construct a representative witness w^* for the statement: $\exists x, y = H(x)$ using x as the original witness. Note that the signing procedure is deterministic. The verifier checks the representative witness using the DMWM scheme.

To argue selective security, we can set up the CRS of the DMWM so that the injective branch b^* is exactly the message that the adversary will forge the signature on. It remains indistinguishable to the adversary that this happened and hence the probability of forging does not change. However, now we can extract a pre-image x' such that $H(x') = y$ from the adversary's forgery. Moreover, since all the other signatures obtained by the adversary are all lossy, it would be *information-theoretically* hard to recover the original pre-image x. This holds even given some bounded additional leakage about the secret key x. It also holds even if x is tampered and then used to produce a signature since this still only provides bounded leakage on x. Therefore we recover a second pre-image $x' \neq x$ which contradicts the second pre-image resistance of H.

We also adapt our results to the continuous leakage and tampering (CLT) model. We do so by essentially taking the same construction, but using a "entropy-bounded" or "noisy" continuous-leakage-resilient (CLR) one-way relation [15] in place of the second pre-image resistant hash (which can be thought of as a leakage-resilient one-way function). We achieve security as long as the adversary cannot tamper the randomness of the refresh procedure, and this restriction is inherent.

DMWMs from CWMs via C-ALBO-TDFs. We now discuss how to construct dual-mode witness maps (DMWMs) from compact witness maps (CWMs). Recall that DMWM has branches in one of two modes: injective and lossy. On the other hand a CWM does not have any branches and is always lossy. To convert a CWM into DMWM we add a "cumulatively all-lossy-but-one trapdoor functions (C-ALBO-TDFs)". This is a family of functions $f(b, \cdot)$ parametrized by tags/branches b such that, for one special branch b^* the function $f(b^*, \cdot)$ is injective and efficiently invertible using a trapdoor, but for all other $b \neq b^*$ the functions $f(b, \cdot)$ are cumulatively lossy. The CRS of the DMWM will consist of the public key of the C-ALBO-TDF with the special injective branch b^* as well as a CRS of CWM scheme. To compute a proof for a statement y with witness w under a tag b, the prover computes $z = f(b, w)$ and then uses the CWM to prove that z was computed correctly using a valid witness w for the statement y.

Construction of C-ALBO-TDFs. Finally, we discuss how to construct *cumulative all-lossy-but-one* trapdoor functions (C-ALBO-LTDFs). We start with a simpler primitive of C-LTDFs which can be used to sample a function f_{ek} described by a public key ek. The key ek can be sampled indistinguishably in either lossy or injective mode (with a trapdoor). We require that the combination of arbitrarily many different lossy functions is cumulatively lossy.

We construct C-LTDFs by adapting a construction of LTDFs from DDH due to [38]. In that construction, the key ek is given by a matrix of group elements $g^{\boldsymbol{M}}$ where g is a generator of the group of order q and $\boldsymbol{M} \in \mathbb{Z}_q^{n \times n}$ is a matrix of exponents. For $\boldsymbol{x} \in \{0,1\}^n$ the function is defined as $f_{\mathsf{ek}}(\boldsymbol{x}) = g^{\boldsymbol{M} \cdot \boldsymbol{x}}$. If $\boldsymbol{M}$ is invertible than this function is injective and can be inverted with knowledge of $\boldsymbol{M}^{-1}$. If $\boldsymbol{M}$ is low rank (e.g., rank 1) then this function is lossy. The two modes are indistinguishable by DDH. However, if we choose many different lossy functions by choosing random rank 1 matrices each time then the scheme is not cumulatively lossy; in fact n random lossy function taken together are injective! To get a cumulative lossy scheme, we fix some public parameters $g^{\boldsymbol{A}}$ where $\boldsymbol{A} \in \mathbb{Z}_q^{n \times n}$ is a random rank 1 matrix. We then choose each fresh lossy key ek by choosing a random $\boldsymbol{R} \in \mathbb{Z}_q^{n \times n}$ and setting $\mathsf{ek} = g^{\boldsymbol{R}\boldsymbol{A}}$. Injective keys ek are still chosen as $g^{\boldsymbol{M}}$ for a random $\boldsymbol{M}$, which is invertible with overwhelming probability. It's easy to show that lossy and injective keys are indistinguishable even given the public parameters. Now if we apply many different lossy functions on the same input $\boldsymbol{x}$ we only reveal $\boldsymbol{A}\boldsymbol{x}$, which loses information about $\boldsymbol{x}$.

The above construction can also be extended to rely on the d-Linear assumption for larger d instead of DDH. We also provide an analogous construction under LWE by adapting an LTDF of [2], which relies on the "lossy mode" of LWE from [25].

We then show how to bootstrap C-LTDFs to get C-ALBO-LTDFS via iO. The idea is to obfuscate a program that, on input a branch b, applies a pseudorandom function to b to sample a fresh lossy key of a C-LTDF, except for a special branch b^* on which it outputs a (hard-coded) injective C-LTDF key. By relying on standard puncturing techniques, we show that this yields a C-ALBO-LTDF.

2 Puncturable Digital Signature Schemes

A puncturable digital signature (PDS) scheme [3] is a digital signature scheme with the additional facility to "puncture" the signing key at some arbitrary message, say, m^*. The resulting punctured signing key allows one to sign all messages except m^*. A PDS is said to be *consistent*, if a secret signing key sk and all possible punctured signing keys $\widehat{\mathsf{sk}}_{m^*}$ derived from sk, for every unpunctured message, produce the same signature, deterministically. In this paper, we shall consider only PDS schemes that are consistent, and hence shall omit that qualifier in the sequel.

The security requirement of a PDS scheme is that the (standard) existential unforgeability should hold for the punctured message m^*. Following Bellare et al. [3], we focus on *selective unforgeability*, wherein the adversary must specify the message m^* at which the signing key needs to be punctured ahead of time, i.e., before receiving the public parameters and the verification key. It then receives the punctured signing key $\widehat{\mathsf{sk}}_{m^*}$ (punctured at m^*) and the verification key of the PDS, and the goal of the adversary is produce a forgery on m^*. A formal definition is provided in the full version of our paper [11].

Below, we summarize the construction of our PDS scheme, and refer to the full version [11] for the formal details of the scheme. Our construction of the PDS relies on the *sole* assumption that one-way functions exist.

The construction follows the paradigm of extending one-time signatures into full-fledged signatures using a tree of pseudorandomly generated key pairs [27,34,37]. Each message in the message space is associated with a leaf in this tree, and the key pair at that leaf is used to exclusively sign that message. The signature on a message will also certify the leaf's verification key using a "certificate chain" that follows the path from root to leaf in the tree. Our scheme will rely on a punctured PRF to generate this tree. The signing key punctured at a message m^* will include a punctured PRF key, *punctured at all the points in the path from root to the leaf corresponding to* m^*; also it will include a small set of certificates that, for every message $m \neq m^*$, can be used to certify the verification key for the first node that is in the path from the root to the leaf corresponding to m, but not in the path from the root to the leaf corresponding to m^*. Compared to the certificate chains used in the standard signature construction, it is important in our case to *verifiably tie* the verification keys to specific nodes in the tree, because otherwise the signer with a punctured signing key can use keys for one leaf to sign the message associated with another leaf.

3 Witness Maps

In this section we formally define the new primitives called Compact Witness Maps and Dual Mode Witness Maps.

Recall that $R \subseteq \{0,1\}^* \times \{0,1\}^*$ is said to be an **NP** relation if membership in it can be computed in time polynomial in the length of the first input.

Given an **NP** relation R, we define the **NP** language $L_R := \{x \mid \exists w, (x,w) \in R\}$. When referring to $(x,w) \in R$, where R is a given **NP** relation, x is called the statement and w the witness. It will be convenient for us to consider **NP** relations parametrized with their input length: Below we let $R_\ell := R \cap \{0,1\}^\ell \times \{0,1\}^*$.

Definition 1 (Compact Witness Map (CWM)). *For $\alpha \geq 0$, an α-CWM for an* **NP** *relation R is a triple* CWM $= (\mathsf{setup}, \mathsf{map}, \mathsf{check})$ *where* setup *is a PPT algorithm and the other two are deterministic polynomial time algorithms such that:*

- $\mathsf{setup}(\kappa, \ell)$ *outputs a string* K *of length polynomial in the security parameter κ and ℓ.*
- *Completeness: For any polynomial ℓ, $\forall (x, w) \in R_{\ell(\kappa)}$, $\forall \mathsf{K} \leftarrow \mathsf{setup}(\kappa, \ell(\kappa))$,*

$$\mathsf{check}(\mathsf{K}, x, \mathsf{map}(\mathsf{K}, x, w)) = 1.$$

- *Lossiness: For any polynomial ℓ, $\forall \mathsf{K} \leftarrow \mathsf{setup}(\kappa, \ell(\kappa))$, $\forall x \in \{0,1\}^{\ell(\kappa)}$,*

$$|\{\mathsf{map}(\mathsf{K}, x, w) \mid (x, w) \in R_{\ell(\kappa)}\}| \leq 2^{\alpha}.$$

- *Soundess: For any polynomial ℓ and any PPT adversary $\mathcal{A}$, $\mathsf{Adv}_{\mathcal{A}}^{\mathrm{CWM}}(\kappa)$ defined below is negligible:*

$$\Pr_{\mathsf{K} \leftarrow \mathsf{setup}(\kappa, \ell(\kappa))}[\mathcal{A}(\mathsf{K}) \rightarrow (x^*, w^*), \mathsf{check}(\mathsf{K}, x^*, w^*) = 1, x^* \notin L_R].$$

A 0-CWM is called a Unique Witness Map *(UWM).*

The above definition has perfect security in the sense that the completeness and lossiness conditions hold for *every possible* K that CWM.setup can output with positive probability. A statistical version, where this needs to hold with all but negligible probability over the choice of K will suffice for all our applications. But for simplicity, we shall use the perfect version above. It is useful to consider a variant of the definition with a *selective soundness* guarantee, in which the adversary is required to generate x^* first (given κ, ℓ) before it gets K. For some applications (e.g., construction of a witness encryption scheme from a UWM) this level of soundness suffices. It also provides an intermediate target for constructions, as one can convert a selectively sound CWM to a standard CWM by relying on complexity leveraging (as we shall do in our construction in Sect. 3.1).

Definition 2 (Dual Mode Witness Maps (DMWM)). *An α-DMWM with tag space $\mathcal{T}$ for an* **NP** *relation R is a tuple* DMWM $= (\mathsf{setup}, \mathsf{map}, \mathsf{check}, \mathsf{extract})$ *where* setup *is a PPT algorithm and the others are deterministic polynomial time algorithms such that:*

- $\mathsf{setup}(\kappa, \ell, \mathsf{tag})$ *outputs* $(\mathsf{K}, \mathsf{td})$*, where κ is a security parameter, $\ell(\kappa)$ is a polynomial, and* $\mathsf{tag} \in \mathcal{T}$*,* K *and* td *are strings of length polynomial in κ.*

- *Completeness:* $\forall \mathsf{tag}, \mathsf{tag}' \in \mathcal{T}$ *for all polynomials* ℓ, $\forall (x, w) \in R_{\ell(\kappa)}$, $\forall \mathsf{K} \leftarrow \mathsf{setup}(\kappa, \ell(\kappa), \mathsf{tag})$,

$$\mathsf{check}(\mathsf{K}, \mathsf{tag}', x, \mathsf{map}(\mathsf{K}, \mathsf{tag}', x, w)) = 1.$$

- *Hidden Tag: For any PPT adversary* $\mathcal{A}$, $\mathsf{Adv}_{\mathcal{A}}^{\text{DMWM-hide}}(\kappa)$ *defined below is negligible:*

$$\Big| \Pr \big[\mathcal{A}(\kappa, \ell) \to (\mathsf{tag}_0, \mathsf{tag}_1, \mathsf{st}), b \leftarrow \{0,1\}, \\ (\mathsf{K}, \mathsf{td}) \leftarrow \mathsf{setup}(\kappa, \ell(\kappa), \mathsf{tag}_b), \mathcal{A}(\mathsf{K}, \mathsf{st}) \to b', b = b'\big] - \frac{1}{2}\Big|.$$

- *Extraction: For any polynomial* ℓ, *for any PPT adversary* $\mathcal{A}$, $\mathsf{Adv}_{\mathcal{A}}^{\text{DMWM}}(\kappa)$ *defined below is negligible:*

$$\mathsf{Adv}_{\mathcal{A}}^{\text{DMWM}}(\kappa) := \Pr[\mathcal{A}(\kappa, \ell) \to (\mathsf{tag}, \mathsf{st}), (\mathsf{K}, \mathsf{td}) \leftarrow \mathsf{setup}(\kappa, \ell(\kappa), \mathsf{tag}), \\ \mathcal{A}(\mathsf{K}, \mathsf{st}) \to (x^*, w^*), \mathsf{check}(\mathsf{K}, \mathsf{tag}, x^*, w^*) = 1, \\ (x^*, \mathsf{extract}(\mathsf{td}, x, w^*)) \notin R_{\ell(\kappa)}]$$

- *Cumulative Lossiness:* $\forall \mathsf{tag}, \ell$, $\forall \mathsf{K} \leftarrow \mathsf{setup}(\kappa, \ell, \mathsf{tag})$, $\forall x \in L_{R_\ell}$, *there exist (inefficient) functions* $\mathsf{compress}_{\mathsf{K},x} : \{0,1\}^* \to S_{\mathsf{K},x}$ *and* $\mathsf{expand}_{\mathsf{K},x} : S_{\mathsf{K},x} \times \{0,1\}^* \to \{0,1\}^*$ *such that* $|S_{\mathsf{K},x}| \leq 2^{\alpha(\kappa)}$, *and for all* $\mathsf{tag}' \neq \mathsf{tag}$, $\mathsf{map}(\mathsf{K}, \mathsf{tag}', x, w) = \mathsf{expand}_{\mathsf{K},x}(\mathsf{compress}_{\mathsf{K},x}(w), \mathsf{tag}')$.

3.1 Unique Witness Maps

In this section, we present a construction of 0-CWM or an UWM.

3.1.1 A UWM for Any NP Relation

Now we present the construction of our UWM system UWM for any **NP** relation R (see Fig. 1). The main building blocks of our construction are a punctured digital signature (PDS) scheme PDS and an $i\mathcal{O}$ scheme (denoted as $i\mathcal{O}$).

Theorem 1. *Let* $i\mathcal{O}$ *be a (polynomially) secure indistinguishability obfuscator for circuits and* PDS *be a (polynomially) secure consistent puncturable digital signature scheme. Then* UWM *defined in Fig. 1 is a UWM for the* **NP** *relation* R *satisfying selective soundness.*

Let PDS = $(\mathsf{keygen}, \mathsf{sign}, \mathsf{ver}, \mathsf{pkeygen}, \mathsf{psign})$ be a secure punctured digital signature scheme and $i\mathcal{O}$ be a secure indistinguishability obfuscator for circuits.

1. UWM.$\mathsf{setup}(\ell, \kappa)$: Generate $(\mathsf{sk}, \mathsf{vk}) \leftarrow$ PDS.$\mathsf{keygen}(\ell, \kappa)$. Then create an obfuscated program $P \leftarrow i\mathcal{O}(\mathsf{Endorse}_{\mathsf{sk}}^{R_\ell})$, where the program $\mathsf{Endorse}_{\mathsf{sk}}^{R_\ell}$ is as shown below. Output $\mathsf{K} = (\mathsf{vk}, P)$.
2. UWM.$\mathsf{map}(\mathsf{K}, x, w)$: Parse K as (vk, P). Output $w^* \leftarrow P(x, w)$.
3. UWM.$\mathsf{check}(\mathsf{K}, x, w^*)$: Parse K as (vk, P). Output PDS.$\mathsf{ver}(\mathsf{vk}, x, w^*)$.

Program $\mathsf{Endorse}_{\mathsf{sk}}^{R_\ell}((x, w))$

Constant: Signing key sk

Input Domain: $(x, w) \in \{0,1\}^\ell \times \{0,1\}^{\ell'}$

if $(x, w) \in R_\ell$ **then**
  output PDS.$\mathsf{sign}(\mathsf{sk}, x)$
else
  output $\perp$

Program $\mathsf{pEndorse}_{\widehat{\mathsf{sk}}_{x^*}}^{R_\ell}((x, w))$

Constant: Punctured signing key $\widehat{\mathsf{sk}}_{x^*}$

Input Domain: $(x, w) \in \{0,1\}^\ell \times \{0,1\}^{\ell'}$

if $(x, w) \in R_\ell$ and $x \neq x^*$ **then**
  output PDS.$\mathsf{psign}(\widehat{\mathsf{sk}}_{x^*}, x)$
else
  output $\perp$

Fig. 1. The UWM for an **NP** relation R. The program $\mathsf{pEndorse}_{\widehat{\mathsf{sk}}_{x^*}}^{R_\ell}$ is used only in the proof.

Proof. Firstly, we note that UWM satisfies perfect completeness (assuming $i\mathcal{O}$ and PDS are perfectly correct). Also, it satisfies uniqueness, since (x, w) is deterministically mapped to the signature on x, independent of w. Below, we shall prove that the scheme is sound as well.

Consider an adversary $\mathcal{A}$ in the definition of $\mathsf{Adv}_{\mathcal{A}}^{\text{UWM}}(\kappa)$. Note that $\mathcal{A}$ outputs a point x^* first. We consider a hybrid experiment where, after $\mathcal{A}$ outputs x^*, K is derived from a modified UWM.setup: The modified UWM.setup is only different in that instead of using $\mathsf{Endorse}_{\mathsf{sk}}^{R_\ell}$, the program $\mathsf{pEndorse}_{\widehat{\mathsf{sk}}_{x^*}}^{R_\ell}$ (also shown in Fig. 1) is used, where $\widehat{\mathsf{sk}}_{x^*} \leftarrow$ PDS.$\mathsf{pkeygen}(\mathsf{sk}, x^*)$.

We claim that the advantage $\mathcal{A}$ has in the modified experiment can only be negligibly more than that in the original experiment. For this consider, a coupled execution of the two experiments, with $\mathcal{A}$'s random tape being the same in the two executions. Then it is enough to upper bound the difference of probabilities of the condition UWM.$\mathsf{check}(\mathsf{K}, x^*, w^*) = 1 \wedge x^* \notin L_{R_\ell}$ holding in the modified experiment and in the original experiment. Fix a choice of randomness that maximizes this difference, δ. We shall describe a (non-uniform) adversary $\mathcal{A}_{i\mathcal{O}}$, which internally runs the coupled experiment with this choice of randomness for $\mathcal{A}$. Let x^* be the output of $\mathcal{A}$ with this choice. Note that for $\delta > 0$, we need $x^* \notin L_{R_\ell}$. For such x^*, observe that $\mathsf{Endorse}_{\mathsf{sk}}^{R_\ell}$ and $\mathsf{pEndorse}_{\widehat{\mathsf{sk}}_{x^*}}^{R_\ell}$ are functionally equivalent programs (for all sk). This is because, if $(x, w) \in R_\ell$, then $x \neq x^*$ and the consistency of the PDS scheme guarantees that PDS.$\mathsf{sign}(\mathsf{sk}, x) =$ PDS.$\mathsf{sign}(\widehat{\mathsf{sk}}_{x^*}, x)$.

So $\mathcal{A}_{i\mathcal{O}}$ can output the pair of programs $\mathsf{Endorse}^{R_\ell}_{\mathsf{sk}}$ and $\mathsf{pEndorse}^{R_\ell}_{\widehat{\mathsf{sk}}_{x^*}}$. It receives back an obfuscated program P and carries out the rest of the UWM security game with $\mathcal{A}$ using P. If $P \leftarrow i\mathcal{O}(\mathsf{Endorse}^{R_\ell}_{\mathsf{sk}})$, then this game is exactly the original game, and otherwise it is the modified game. Hence, $\mathcal{A}_{i\mathcal{O}}$ distinguishes between these two cases with advantage δ. Hence, by the security of $i\mathcal{O}$, δ is negligible; this in turn shows that the advantage $\mathcal{A}$ has in the modified experiment is only negligibly far from that in the original experiment.

Next, we argue that in the modified selective soundness experiment $\mathcal{A}$ has negligible advantage. Note that in the modified experiment, $\mathcal{A}$ outputs a string $x^* \in \{0,1\}^\ell$, gets back (vk, P), where $(\mathsf{vk}, \mathsf{sk}) \leftarrow$ PDS.$\mathsf{keygen}(\ell, \kappa)$, and P is generated from the punctured secret-key $\widehat{\mathsf{sk}}_{x^*}$, outputs a purported signature w^*, and wins if PDS.$\mathsf{ver}(\mathsf{vk}, x^*, w^*) = 1$. By the security of PDS, the probability of $\mathcal{A}$ winning is at most $\mathsf{Adv}^{\text{PDS}}_{\mathcal{A}}(\kappa)$, which is negligible. □

Remark 1. In the above proof, we only show selective soundness of UWM. We note that, one can transform a selectively sound UWM to an adaptively sound one using complexity leveraging, when appropriate. This can be done by choosing PDS to be $2^{-(\ell+\kappa)}$-secure punctured digital signature scheme and $i\mathcal{O}$ to be $2^{-(\ell+\kappa)}$-secure indistinguishability obfuscator for circuits respectively (i.e., the advantages $\mathsf{Adv}^{\text{PDS}}_{\mathcal{A}}(\kappa_1) \leq 2^{-(\ell+\kappa)}$ and $\mathsf{Adv}^{i\mathcal{O}}_{Samp,\mathcal{D}}(\kappa_2) \leq 2^{-(\ell+\kappa)}$, where κ_1 and κ_2 are the security parameters for PDS and $i\mathcal{O}$ respectively, and κ is the security parameter for UWM). One can set κ_1 and κ_2 to be large enough to satisfy this.

3.1.2 Implication to Witness Encryption

In this section, we show that UWM implies Witness encryption (WE). Due to space constraints, we only present a high level idea behind the construction and refer the reader to our full version [11] for the detailed description.

Intuition Behind the Construction. In a WE scheme, it is possible to encrypt a message m under an **NP** statement x such that, if the statement is true, then the ciphertext can be decrypted using any witness w for x. However, if x is a false statement, then the ciphertext should computationally hide the encrypted message. We show a construction of WE for an arbitrary **NP** language L starting from an UWM for the language $L_{OR} = L \vee L'$, where L' is another **NP** language whose YES instances are *indistinguishable* from NO instances. To WE encrypt a bit $m \in \{0,1\}$ with respect to an **NP** statement $x \in L$, we sample an YES instance from the **NP** language L'. We do so by sampling a pseudo-random string $y = G(z)$, such that z serves as a valid witness corresponding to the string y. We then consider the language $L_{OR} = L \vee L'$ which consists of instances $\hat{x}$ of the form "either $x \in L \vee y$ is pseudorandom". We use the UWM to derive a representative witness w^* for a statement corresponding to this augmented **NP** language (using witness z) and then derive the Goldreich-Levin hardcore bit of w^* to be used as a one-time pad to encrypt the bit m. The decryptor can derive the same representative witness w^* using his witness for $x \in L$ (which is also a valid witness for L_{OR}) and therefore decrypt. Intuitively, if an adversary can break WE security, then it can distinguish encryptions of 0 and 1 with non-negligible probability even if x is a false statement. This means that, using Goldreich-Levin decoding, it can compute the correct value w^* given y with non-negligible probability. Furthermore this value w^* is a valid representative witness for the statement $\hat{x}$. At this point, we switch the YES instance of L' to a NO instance (this can be done by sampling a random y, instead of a pseudorandom y), without affecting the advantage of the adversary much. Hence, it must also compute a valid representative witness for $\hat{x}$ if we switch y to false. But this contradicts the soundness of UWM. We remark that, for this reduction it suffices even if the UWM is only *selectively sound.*

3.2 New Kinds of Lossy Trapdoor Functions

3.2.1 Cumulative Lossy Trapdoor Functions

Here we introduce the notion of "cumulative" lossy trapdoor functions (C-LTDF). A (standard) lossy trapdoor function (LTDF) f can be sampled in one of two *indistinguishable* modes – *injective* or *lossy.* In the injective mode, the function f can be efficiently inverted with the knowledge of a trapdoor; whereas in the lossy mode the function statistically loses a lot of information about its input. We say that a function f with domain $\{0,1\}^n$ is (n,k)-lossy if its image size is at most 2^{n-k}. Then, mapping a random x to $f(x)$ loses at least k bits of information about x.

Now, consider the information about x revealed by $(f_1(x), \cdots, f_m(x))$, where $f_1, \cdots, f_m$ are m independently sampled functions from an (n,k)-lossy function family. According to the current definitions and constructions of LTDFs, up to $m(n-k)$ bits could be revealed about x; if $m \geq n/(n-k)$, x could be completely determined by these values.

This is where C-LTDF differs from an LTDF. In a C-LTDF, the amount of information about x that $(f_1(x), \cdots, f_m(x))$ reveals is bounded by a *cumulative loss parameter* α, *irrespective of how large* m *is.* Here the lossy functions f_i can all be sampled independently, but using the same public parameters. The formal definition follows.

Definition 3 (C-LTDF). *Let* $\kappa \in \mathbb{N}$ *be the security parameter, and* $\ell, \alpha : \mathbb{N} \to \mathbb{N}$. *A* (ℓ, α)-cumulative lossy trapdoor function family (C-LTDF) *is a tuple of (probabilistic) polynomial time algorithms* $(\mathsf{setup}, \mathsf{sample}_{\mathsf{inj}}, \mathsf{sample}_{\mathsf{loss}}, \mathsf{eval}, \mathsf{invert})$ *(the last two being deterministic), having properties as follows:*

- **Parameter Generation.** *The setup algorithm* $\mathsf{setup}(\kappa)$ *outputs a public parameter* pp.
- **Sampling: Injective mode.** *The algorithm* $\mathsf{sample}_{\mathsf{inj}}(\kappa, \mathsf{pp})$ *outputs the tuple* $(\mathsf{ek}, \mathsf{tk})$ *such that* $\mathsf{invert}(\mathsf{tk}, \mathsf{eval}(\mathsf{ek}, x)) = x$ *for all* $x \in \{0,1\}^{\ell(\kappa)}$ *(i.e.,* $\mathsf{eval}(\mathsf{ek}, \cdot)$ *computes an injective function* $f_{\mathsf{ek}}(\cdot)$ *and* $\mathsf{invert}(\mathsf{tk}, \cdot)$ *computes* $f_{\mathsf{ek}}^{-1}(\cdot)$*).*
- **Sampling: Lossy mode.** *For all* pp *in the support of* $\mathsf{setup}(\kappa)$ *there exists an (inefficient) function* $\mathsf{compress}_{\mathsf{pp}} : \{0,1\}^{\ell(\kappa)} \to R_{\mathsf{pp}}$ *with range* $|R_{\mathsf{pp}}| \leq 2^{\ell(\kappa)-\alpha(\kappa)}$, *and for all* ek *in the support of* $\mathsf{sample}_{\mathsf{loss}}(\kappa, \mathsf{pp})$ *there exists an*

(inefficient) function $\mathsf{expand}_{\mathsf{ek}}(\cdot)$ *such that the following holds: for all* $x \in \{0,1\}^{\ell(\kappa)}$ *we have* $\mathsf{eval}(\mathsf{ek}, x) = \mathsf{expand}_{\mathsf{ek}}(\mathsf{compress}_{\mathsf{pp}}(x))$.
- **Indistinguishability of modes.** *The ensembles* $\{(\mathsf{pp}, \mathsf{ek}) : \mathsf{pp} \leftarrow \mathsf{setup}(\kappa), (\mathsf{ek}, \mathsf{tk}) \leftarrow \mathsf{sample}_{\mathsf{inj}}(\kappa, \mathsf{pp})\}_{\kappa \in \mathbb{N}}$ *and* $\{(\mathsf{pp}, \mathsf{ek}) : \mathsf{pp} \leftarrow \mathsf{setup}(\kappa), \mathsf{ek} \leftarrow \mathsf{sample}_{\mathsf{loss}}(\kappa, \mathsf{pp})\}_{\kappa \in \mathbb{N}}$ *are computationally indistinguishable.*

3.2.1.1 C-LTDF from the d-Linear Assumption

Due to space constraints, we present the construction of C-LTDF from the d-linear assumption, and refer the reader to our full version [11] for the construction from LWE.

The d-linear assumption [5] is a generalization of the Decision Diffie-Hellman (DDH) assumption. For our construction, we will actually need Matrix d-Linear assumption, which is implied by the d-Linear assumption, as shown by Naor and Segev [36]. Due to space constraints, we only specify the d-Linear assumption here, and refer the reader to our full version [11] for the definition of Matrix d-Linear assumption.

Definition 4 (d-Linear assumption [5]**).** *Let* $d \geq 1$ *be an integer, and* GroupGen *be as above. We say that the* d-linear assumption *holds for* GroupGen *if the following two distributions are computationally indistinguishable:*

$$\{(g, \mathbb{G}, p, \{g_i, g_i^{r_i}\}_{i=1}^d, h, h^{\sum_{i=1}^d r_i}) : (g, \mathbb{G}, p) \leftarrow \mathsf{GroupGen}; g_i, h \xleftarrow{\$} \mathbb{G}; r_i \xleftarrow{\$} \mathbb{Z}_p\},$$
$$\{(g, \mathbb{G}, p, \{g_i, g_i^{r_i}\}_{i=1}^d, h, h^r) : (g, \mathbb{G}, p) \leftarrow \mathsf{GroupGen}; g_i, h \xleftarrow{\$} \mathbb{G}; r_i, r \xleftarrow{\$} \mathbb{Z}_p\},$$

Before specifying the assumption, we will need some additional notations as follows.

Additional Notation. Let GroupGen be a PPT algorithm that takes as input the security parameter κ and outputs the a triplet $(\mathbb{G}, p, g)$ where $\mathbb{G}$ is a group of prime order p generated by $g \in \mathbb{G}$. We denote by $\mathsf{Rk}_i(\mathbb{F}_p^{a\times b})$ the set of all $a \times b$ matrices over the field $\mathbb{F}_p$ of rank i. For a vector $\boldsymbol{x} = (x_1, \cdots x_n) \in \mathbb{F}_p^n$, we define $g^{\boldsymbol{x}}$ to be the column vector $(g^{x_1}, \cdots, g^{x_n}) \in \mathbb{G}^n$. If $M = (m_{ij})$ is a $n \times n$ matrix over $\mathbb{F}_p$, we denote by g^M the $n \times n$ matrix over $\mathbb{G}$ given by $(g^{m_{ij}})$. Given any matrix $M = (m_{ij}) \in \mathbb{F}_p^{n\times n}$ and a column vector $\boldsymbol{y} = (y_1, \cdots y_n) \in \mathbb{G}^n$, we define by $\boldsymbol{y}^M = \left(\prod_{j=1}^n y_j^{m_{1j}}, \cdots, \prod_{j=1}^n y_j^{m_{nj}}\right) \in \mathbb{G}^n$. For any matrix $R = (r_{ij}) \in \mathbb{G}^{n\times n}$ and a column vector $\boldsymbol{z} = (z_1, \cdots, z_n) \in \mathbb{F}_p^n$, we define by $R^{\boldsymbol{z}} = \left(\prod_{j=1}^n r_{1j}^{z_j}, \cdots, \prod_{j=1}^n r_{nj}^{z_j}\right) \in \mathbb{G}^n$. This naturally generalizes for two matrices as well. In other words, for two matrices $R \in \mathbb{G}^{n\times n}$ and $Z \in \mathbb{F}_p^{n\times n}$, we denote by $R^Z = (R^{\boldsymbol{z}_1}, \cdots, R^{\boldsymbol{z}_n}) \in \mathbb{G}^{n\times n}$, where each $R^{\boldsymbol{z}_i}$ $(i \in [n])$ is a column vector in $\mathbb{G}^n$ (as defined above) and for all i, $\boldsymbol{z}_i$ denotes the ith column of the matrix Z.

The Construction. Let $d \geq 1$ be a positive integer. Define the tuple C-LTDF $=$ $(\mathsf{setup}, \mathsf{sample}_{\mathsf{inj}}, \mathsf{sample}_{\mathsf{loss}}, \mathsf{eval}, \mathsf{invert})$ as follows:

1. $\mathsf{setup}(\kappa)$: On input the security parameter κ, do the following:
   - Run $\mathsf{GroupGen}(\kappa)$ to obtain the tuple $(\mathbb{G}, p, g)$.
   - Sample a random matrix $M \xleftarrow{\$} \mathsf{Rk}_d(\mathbb{Z}_p^{n\times n})$ and let $S = g^M \in \mathbb{G}^{n\times n}$.
   - Set the public parameter $\mathsf{pp} = (\mathbb{G}, p, g, S)$.
2. $\mathsf{sample}_{\mathsf{inj}}(\kappa, \mathsf{pp})$: On input pp, chooses a random matrix $M_1 \xleftarrow{\$} \mathsf{Rk}_n(\mathbb{Z}_p^{n\times n})$ and computes $S_1 = g^{M_1} \in \mathbb{G}^{n\times n}$. Set the function index as $\mathsf{ek} = S_1$ and the associated trapdoor as $\mathsf{tk} = (g, M_1)$.
3. $\mathsf{sample}_{\mathsf{loss}}(\kappa, \mathsf{pp})$: On input pp, chooses a random matrix $M_1 \xleftarrow{\$} \mathsf{Rk}_d(\mathbb{Z}_p^{n\times n})$ and computes $S_1 = S^{M_1} \in \mathbb{G}^{n\times n}$. Set the function index as $\mathsf{ek} = S_1$.
4. $\mathsf{eval}(\mathsf{ek}, \boldsymbol{x})$: On input a function index ek and an input vector $\boldsymbol{x} \in \{0,1\}^n$, compute the function $f_{\mathsf{ek}}(\boldsymbol{x}) = S_1^{\boldsymbol{x}} \in \mathbb{G}^n$.
5. $\mathsf{invert}(\mathsf{ek}, \mathsf{tk}, \boldsymbol{y})$: Given a function index $\mathsf{ek} = S_1$, the trapdoor $\mathsf{tk} = (g, M_1)$ and a vector $\boldsymbol{y} \in \mathbb{G}^n$, do the following:
   - Compute $(z_1, \cdots, z_n) = \boldsymbol{y}^{M_1^{-1}}$.
   - Let $x_i = \log_g(z_i)$ for $i = 1, \cdots, n$.
   - Output the vector $\boldsymbol{x} = (x_1, \cdots, x_n)$.

Theorem 2. *Suppose the d-Linear assumption holds for* $\mathsf{GroupGen}$. *Let* $p_{\max}(\kappa)$ *be an upper bound on the order of the group generated by* $\mathsf{GroupGen}(\kappa)$. *Then* C-LTDF *is an* $(n, (1-\epsilon)n))$*-cumulative lossy trapdoor function family, provided* $\epsilon > d \log_2 p_{\max}(\kappa)/n(\kappa)$.

Due to space constraints, we present the proof in our full version [11].

3.2.2 Cumulative All-Lossy-But-One Trapdoor Functions

For our construction of dual mode witness maps (DMWM), we will need a richer abstraction, which we call cumulative *all-lossy-but-one* trapdoor functions (C-ALBO-TDF). These functions are associated with an additional branch space $\mathcal{B} = \{\mathcal{B}_\kappa\}_{\kappa\in\mathbb{N}}$. For a C-ALBO-TDF, almost all the branches are lossy, except for one branch which is injective. This notion of C-ALBO-TDF is actually contrary to the notion of All-But-One Lossy TDF (ABO-LTDF) defined by Peikert and Waters [39]. ABO-LTDFs are also associated with many branches, all but one of which are injective. Also, note that, we do not need any additional public parameters in the definition C-ALBO-TDF, and we require that the residual leakages of different lossy functions are "correlated" via the public key (which is shared by different functions). Now, we formally define C-ALBO-TDF and state its properties as below:

Definition 5 (C-ALBO-TDF). *Let* $\kappa \in \mathbb{N}$ *be the security parameter and* $\ell, \alpha : \mathbb{N} \to \mathbb{N}$ *be functions. Also, let* $\mathcal{B} = \{\mathcal{B}_\kappa\}_{\kappa\in\mathbb{N}}$ *be a collection of sets whose elements represent the branches. An* (ℓ, α)-cumulative all-lossy-but-one lossy trapdoor function family (C-ALBO-TDF) *with branch collection* $\mathcal{B}$ *is given by a tuple of (probabilistic) polynomial time algorithms* $(\mathsf{sample}_{\mathsf{c\text{-}albo}}, \mathsf{eval}_{\mathsf{c\text{-}albo}}, \mathsf{invert}_{\mathsf{c\text{-}albo}})$ *(the last two being deterministic), as follows:*

- **Sampling a trapdoor function with given injective branch.** *For any branch* $b^* \in \mathcal{B}$*,* $\mathsf{sample}_{\text{c-albo}}(\kappa, b^*)$ *outputs the tuple* $(\mathsf{ek}, \mathsf{tk})$*, where* ek *is the function index and* tk *is its associated trapdoor.*
  - **(Injective branch).** *For the branch* b^*, $\mathsf{invert}_{\text{c-albo}}(\mathsf{tk}, b^*, \mathsf{eval}_{\text{c-albo}}(\mathsf{ek}, b^*, x)) = x$ *for all* $x \in \{0,1\}^{\ell(\kappa)}$ *(i.e.,* $\mathsf{eval}_{\text{c-albo}}(\mathsf{ek}, b^*, \cdot)$ *computes an injective function* $g_{\mathsf{ek},b^*}(\cdot)$ *over the domain* $\{0,1\}^{\ell(\kappa)}$*, and* $\mathsf{invert}_{\text{c-albo}}(\mathsf{tk}, b^*, \cdot)$ *computes* $g^{-1}_{\mathsf{ek},b^*}(\cdot)$*).*
  - **(α-Cumulative Lossy branches).** *For all* ek *there exists an (inefficient) function* $\mathsf{compress}_{\mathsf{ek}} : \{0,1\}^{\ell(\kappa)} \to R_{\mathsf{ek}}$ *with range* $|R_{\mathsf{ek}}| \leq 2^{\ell(\kappa)-\alpha(\kappa)}$*, and for all* ek, b *there exists a function* $\mathsf{expand}_{\mathsf{ek},b}(\cdot)$ *such that the following holds. For all* $b^* \in \mathcal{B}$*, all* ek *is in the support of* $\mathsf{sample}_{\text{c-albo}}(\kappa, b^*)$*, all* $b \neq b^*$ *and all* $x \in \{0,1\}^{\ell(\kappa)}$*, we have*

$$\mathsf{eval}_{\text{c-albo}}(\mathsf{ek}, b, x) = \mathsf{expand}_{\mathsf{ek},b}(\mathsf{compress}_{\mathsf{ek}}(x)).$$

- **Hidden injective branch.** $\forall b_0^*, b_1^* \in \mathcal{B}$*, the ensembles* $\{\mathsf{ek}_0 : (\mathsf{ek}_0, \mathsf{tk}_0) \leftarrow \mathsf{sample}_{\text{c-albo}}(\kappa, b_0^*)\}_{\kappa \in \mathbb{N}}$ *and* $\{\mathsf{ek}_1 : (\mathsf{ek}_1, \mathsf{tk}_1) \leftarrow \mathsf{sample}_{\text{c-albo}}(\kappa, b_1^*)\}_{\kappa \in \mathbb{N}}$ *are computationally indistinguishable.*

3.2.3 C-ALBO-TDF from $i\mathcal{O}$ and C-LTDF

In this section, we present our construction of cumulative all-lossy-but-one LTDF (C-ALBO-LTDF). We show a generic transformation from C-LTDF to C-ALBO-TDF using $i\mathcal{O}$. The main idea of our construction is as follows: We obfuscate a program that has the public parameters pp of C-LTDF hardwired in it and internally it runs either $\mathsf{sample}_{\mathsf{inj}}$ or $\mathsf{sample}_{\mathsf{loss}}$ depending on the branch b. In other words, on input a branch b, it applies a pseudorandom function to b to sample a fresh lossy branch, except for the special branch b^* on which it outputs a hard-coded injective C-LTDF key. Due to space constraints, we refer to the full version of our paper [11] for the detailed construction.

Theorem 3. *Let* C-LTDF *be a collection of* (ℓ, α)*-cumulative LTDF,* $i\mathcal{O}$ *be an indistinguishability obfuscator for circuits,* F *be a secure puncturable PRF with input space* $\mathcal{B}$*. Then the construction* C-ALBO-TDF *sketched above is a collection of* (ℓ, α)*-cumulative all-lossy-but-one trapdoor functions.*

The detailed proof of this theorem is given in full version [11].

3.3 Construction of Dual Mode Witness Maps

In this section, we present a construction of dual mode witness maps (DMWM) for any **NP** relation R_ℓ (see Fig. 2). The main building blocks of our construction are an appropriately lossy compact witness map (CWM) and a cumulatively all-lossy-but-one trapdoor function (C-ALBO-TDF).

Intuition Behind the Construction. The CRS of DMWM will consist of the function index ek of C-ALBO-TDF sampled using the special injective tag tag^*

(we require that the tag space of DMWM is same as the branch space of C-ALBO-TDF) as well as a CRS of CWM. To compute a proof for a statement x with witness w under a tag tag, the prover computes $Y = \mathsf{eval}_{\text{c-albo}}(\mathsf{ek}, \mathsf{tag}, w)$ and then uses the CWM to prove that Y was computed correctly using a valid witness w for the statement x. The completeness and soundness of DMWM follows directly from the completeness and soundness guarantees of CWM. The cumulative lossiness of DMWM follows from the cumulative lossiness of CWM and C-ALBO-TDF.

(a) Let C-ALBO-TDF = $(\mathsf{sample}_{\text{c-albo}}, \mathsf{eval}_{\text{c-albo}}, \mathsf{invert}_{\text{c-albo}})$ be collection of $(\ell, (\ell - \alpha'))$-C-ALBO-TDF, with branch space $\mathcal{B}$.

(b) Let CWM = (CWM.setup, CWM.map, CWM.check) be a α-CWM (please refer to Section 3) for the following language:

$$L := \left\{ (x, \mathsf{ek}, \mathsf{tag}, Y) \ : \exists\, w \text{ s.t. } \left(Y = \mathsf{eval}_{\text{c-albo}}(\mathsf{ek}, \mathsf{tag}, w) \ \wedge \ (x, w) \in R_\ell \right\} \right.$$

We construct DMWM = (DMWM.setup, DMWM.map, DMWM.check, DMWM.extract) with tag space $\mathcal{T} = \mathcal{B}$ for the **NP** relation R_ℓ as follows:

1. DMWM.setup$(\kappa, \ell, \mathsf{tag})$: Here $\mathsf{tag} \in \mathcal{T}$. Run CWM.setup$(\kappa, \ell)$ to output a string K' of length polynomial in the security parameter κ. Also, run $\mathsf{sample}_{\text{c-albo}}(\kappa, \mathsf{tag})$ to output the tuple $(\mathsf{ek}, \mathsf{tk})$. Set $\mathsf{K} = (\mathsf{K}', \mathsf{ek})$ and the trapdoor $\mathsf{td} = \mathsf{tk}$.
2. DMWM.map$(\mathsf{K}, \mathsf{tag}', x, w)$: Here $\mathsf{tag}' \in \mathcal{T}$. Parse K as $\mathsf{K} = (\mathsf{K}', \mathsf{ek})$, and do the following:
   - Compute $Y = \mathsf{eval}_{\text{c-albo}}(\mathsf{ek}, \mathsf{tag}', w)$, and
   - Compute $w^*_{\text{CWM}} =$ CWM.map$(\mathsf{K}', (x, \mathsf{ek}, \mathsf{tag}', Y), w)$.

   Output the representative witness $w^* = (Y, w^*_{\text{CWM}})$.
3. DMWM.check$(\mathsf{K}, \mathsf{tag}', x, w^*)$: Parse $\mathsf{K} = (\mathsf{K}', \mathsf{ek})$ and $w^* = (Y, w^*_{\text{CWM}})$. Output CWM.check$(\mathsf{K}', (x, \mathsf{ek}, \mathsf{tag}', Y), w^*_{\text{CWM}})$.
4. DMWM.extract(td, x, w^*): Parse $w^* = (Y, w^*_{\text{CWM}})$. Output $\mathsf{invert}_{\text{c-albo}}(\mathsf{td}, \mathsf{tag}, Y)$, where $(\mathsf{ek}, \mathsf{tk}) \leftarrow \mathsf{sample}_{\text{c-albo}}(\kappa, \mathsf{tag})$ was generated as part of setup using the same tag tag.

Fig. 2. Construction of DMWM for an **NP** relation R_ℓ.

Theorem 4. *Let $\alpha, \alpha' \geq 0$, and $\alpha'' = (\alpha + \alpha')$. Let* CWM *be a (selectively) sound α-CWM for the* **NP** *language L,* c-albo-tdf *let a collection of $(\ell, (\ell - \alpha'))$-cumulative all-lossy-but-one LTDF with branch space $\mathcal{B}$. Then the construction* DMWM *defined in* Fig. 2 *is α''-DMWM with tag space $\mathcal{T} = \mathcal{B}$ for the* **NP** *relation R_ℓ.*

The detailed proof of this theorem is given in full version of our paper [11].

4 Fully Leakage and Tamper-Resilient Signature Scheme

A signature scheme with setup SIG is a tuple of PPT algorithms SIG = (setup, keygen, sign, verify). The setup algorithm takes as input the security parameter κ, and outputs a set of public parameters pub, which is taken as an implicit input (along with κ) by all the other algorithms. We denote the message space (implicitly parametrized by κ) as $\mathcal{M}$. We shall require *perfect correctness*: For all pub $\leftarrow$ SIG.setup(κ), any key pair (ssk, vk) produced by SIG.keygen and all messages $m \in \mathcal{M}$, we require SIG.verify(vk, (m, SIG.sign(ssk, m))) = 1.

We define fully-leakage and tamper-resilient (FLTR) signature security, in the bounded leakage and tampering model. Before defining the model formally, we provide an informal description here. In this model, first the challenger sets up the public parameters pub, and also generates a key-pair (ssk, vk). Then, vk is given to the adversary, and as in the case of standard signature security experiment, the adversary is given access to a signing oracle and it attempts to produce a valid signature on a message which it has not queried. But in addition, the adversary has access to a leakage oracle and a tampering oracle, as described below. Leakage and tampering act on st, which consists of the signing key ssk and all the randomness used by the signing algorithm thus far. Note that here, for definitional purposes, we allow SIG.sign to be randomized, though in our construction it will be deterministic.

Leakage: The adversary can adaptively query the leakage oracle with any efficiently computable functions f and will receive f(st) in return (subject to bounds below).

Tampering: The adversary can adaptively query the tampering oracle with efficiently computable functions T, and on each such query, the tampering oracle will generate a signing key and randomness for signature: $(\widetilde{\mathsf{ssk}}, \widetilde{r}) = T(\mathsf{st})$. Subsequently, the adversary can adaptively query each signing oracle SIG.sign$(\widetilde{\mathsf{ssk}}, \cdot, \widetilde{r})$, any number of times (subject to bounds below).

Bounds on Queries: The total output length of all the leakage functions ever queried to the leakage oracle is bounded by $\lambda(\kappa)$. For tampering, there is an upper bound $t(\kappa)$ on the total number of tampering functions queried by the adversary. However, the adversary may ask an unbounded number of untampered or tampered signing queries to the signing oracle. We shall denote an FLTR signature scheme with security subject to these bounds as (λ, t)-FLTR signature scheme.

4.1 Security Model for FLTR Signatures

Definition 6 ((λ, t)-FLTR security). *We say that a signature scheme* SIG = (SIG.setup, SIG.keygen, SIG.sign, SIG.verify) *is* (λ, t)-fully-leakage and tamper-resilient (FLTR) *if for all PPT adversaries/forgers $\mathcal{F}$ there exists a negligible function* negl : $\mathbb{N} \rightarrow \{0, 1\}$ *such that* $\Pr\left[\mathsf{Success}_{\Pi,\mathcal{F}}^{(\lambda,t)\text{-}\mathsf{FLTR}}(\kappa)\right] \leq \mathsf{negl}(\kappa)$, *where* *the event* $\mathsf{Success}^{(\lambda,t)\text{-}\mathsf{FLTR}}_{\Pi,\mathcal{F}}(\kappa)$ *is defined via the following experiment between a challenger* $\mathcal{C}$ *and the forger* $\mathcal{F}$*:*

1. *Initially, the challenger* $\mathcal{C}$ *computes* $\mathsf{pub} \leftarrow \textsc{sig}.\mathsf{setup}(\kappa)$ *and* $(\mathsf{ssk}, \mathsf{vk}) \leftarrow \textsc{sig}.\mathsf{keygen}(\kappa, \mathsf{pub})$*, and sets* $\mathsf{st} = \mathsf{ssk}$.
2. *The forger on receiving* pub *and* vk*, can adaptively query the following oracles as defined below:*
   - **Signing queries:** *The signing oracle* $\textsc{sig}.\mathsf{sign}^*_{\mathsf{ssk}}(\cdot)$ *receives as input a message* $m_i \in \mathcal{M}$. *The challenger* $\mathcal{C}$ *then samples* $r_i \leftarrow \mathcal{R}$*, and computes* $\sigma_i \leftarrow \textsc{sig}.\mathsf{sign}(\mathsf{ssk}, m, r_i)$. *It appends* r_i *to* st *and outputs* σ_i.
   - **Leakage queries:** *The leakage oracle receives as input (the description of) an efficiently computable function* $f_j : \{0,1\}^* \rightarrow \{0,1\}^{\lambda_j}$*, and responds with* $f_j(\mathsf{st})$.
   - **Tampering queries:** *When the forger* $\mathcal{F}$ *(adaptively) submits the* i^{th} *tampering query* T_i*, the challenger computes* $(\widetilde{\mathsf{ssk}}_i, \widetilde{r}_i) = T_i(\mathsf{st})$. *Subsequently,* $\mathcal{F}$ *can adaptively query the tampered-signing oracle* $\textsc{sig}.\mathsf{sign}(\widetilde{\mathsf{ssk}}_i, \cdot, \widetilde{r}_i)$ *using messages in* $\mathcal{M}$. *We call these as "tampered signing queries".*
3. *Eventually,* $\mathcal{F}$ *outputs a message-signature pair* (m^*, σ^*) *as the purported forgery.*

$\mathsf{Success}^{(\lambda,t)\text{-}\mathsf{FLTR}}_{\Pi,\mathcal{F}}(\kappa)$ *denotes the event in which the following happens:*

- *The signature* σ^* *verifies with respect to the original verification key* vk*, i.e.,* $\textsc{sig}.\mathsf{verify}(\mathsf{vk}, (m^*, \sigma^*)) = 1$.
- m^* *was never queried as input to the signing or tampered signing oracle by the forger* $\mathcal{F}$.
- *The output length of all the leakage functions* $\sum_j \lambda_j$ *is at most* $\lambda(\kappa)$.
- *The number of tampering queries made by* $\mathcal{F}$ *is at most* $t(\kappa)$.

We also consider a selective variant of the above definition, where the message m^* (on which the forgery is to be produced) is declared by the adversary before receiving the public parameters pub and the verification key vk. We call this *selectively unforgeable* (λ, t)-FLTR signature scheme. We shall focus on this model in our construction (see Sect. 4.2) and note that one can convert a selectively unforgeable (λ, t)-FLTR signature scheme to an adaptively secure one by relying on complexity leveraging, when appropriate.

4.2 Construction of Our FLTR Signature Scheme

In this section, we present our construction of FLTR signature scheme. In Fig. 3, we present this construction.

1. Let SPR = (SPR.gen, SPR.eval) be a family of SPR functions from $\{0,1\}^{d(\kappa)}$ to $\{0,1\}^{m(\kappa)}$, where $m(\kappa) \ll d(\kappa)$.
2. Let DMWM = (DMWM.setup, DMWM.map, DMWM.check, DMWM.extract) be a κ-lossy dual-mode witness map (DMWM) (refer to Definition 2) with tag space $\mathcal{T} = \mathcal{M}$ for the following language:

$$L := \{(s, y) : \exists\, x \text{ s.t. } y = \text{SPR.eval}_s(x))\}$$

Define the signature scheme SIG = (SIG.setup, SIG.keygen, SIG.sign, SIG.verify) as follows:

1. SIG.setup(κ): On input κ, sample $s \leftarrow$ SPR.gen(κ). It then samples a random tag tag $\in \mathcal{T}$, computes (K, td) $\leftarrow$ DMWM.setup(κ, ℓ, tag), and discards the trapdoor tk. Set pub := (s, K).
2. SIG.keygen(κ, pub): On input the public parameters pub, it samples $x \leftarrow \{0,1\}^{d(\kappa)}$ uniformly at random, and compute $y = \text{SPR.eval}_s(x)$. Output the signing key ssk $= x$, and the verification key vk $= y$.
3. SIG.sign(ssk, m): On input a message m, do the following:
   - Set the tag tag of DMWM to be tag $= m$.
   - Re-compute the value $y = \text{SPR.eval}_s(x)$.
   - Generate a representative witness $w^* \leftarrow$ DMWM.map(K, tag, $(s, y), x$), where (s, y) is the statement and x is the corresponding witness.
   - Output the signature $\sigma = w^*$.
4. SIG.verify(vk, (m, σ)): Parse the signature σ as $\sigma = w^*$. It then sets tag $= m$ and runs DMWM.check(K, tag, $(s, y), w^*$) to check if the mapping verifies correctly. It outputs 1 if and only if the above verification evaluates to 1.

Fig. 3. Construction of FLTR Signature Scheme SIG

Theorem 5. *Let $\lambda(\kappa)$, $t(\kappa)$, $d(\kappa)$ and $m(\kappa)$ be parameters. Let* SPR *be a second pre-image resistant function mapping $d(\kappa)$ bits to $m(\kappa)$ bits, and* DMWM *be a κ-lossy* DMWM *with tag space $\mathcal{T} = \mathcal{M}$ (where $\mathcal{M}$ is the message space of* SIG*). Then the above construction* SIG *is a $(\lambda(\kappa), t(\kappa))$-*FLTR *signature scheme, as long as the parameters satisfy:*

$$0 \le \lambda(\kappa) \le d(\kappa) - \kappa(t(\kappa) + 1)) - m(\kappa) - \omega(\log \kappa).$$

Hence, the relative leakage rate is $\frac{\lambda(\kappa)}{d(\kappa)} \approx 1 - \frac{\kappa(t(\kappa)+1) - m(\kappa) - \omega(\log \kappa)}{d(\kappa)} = 1 - o(1)$, for an appropriate choice of $(\kappa(t(\kappa) + 1) - m(\kappa) - \omega(\log \kappa)) = o(d(\kappa))$. The tampering rate $\rho(\kappa)$ is $\rho(\kappa) = \frac{t(\kappa)}{d(\kappa)} = O(1/\kappa)$.

Due to space constraints, we present the proof of Theorem 5 in the full version of our paper [11].

Extension to Continuous Leakage and Tampering. Our construction can be readily extended to a model of continuous leakage and tampering, with periodic (tamper-proof) key updates. To this end, first we note that we can replace the SPR function family used in our construction with a 'entropy-bounded" or "noisy" leakage-resilient one-way relations (LR-OWR) [9,16]. Then, we show that the only modification required to upgrade our LTR signature construction to the setting of continuous leakage and tampering is to further replace the noisy LR-OWR above with its continuous leakage analogue, which we call noisy *continuous* LR-OWR (CLR-OWR), as defined by Dodis et al. [15]. Our construction bypasses the impossibility result of [22] by allowing the signing key to periodically update in between leakage and tampering queries. We refer the reader to the full version [11] for further details.

Acknowledgments. We would like to thank the anonymous reviewers of PKC 2019 for their useful comments and suggestions. We thank Omer Paneth for pointing out to us the connection between Unique Witness Maps (UWM) and Witness encryption (WE). The first author would like to acknowledge Pandu Rangan for his involvement during the initial discussion phase of the project.

References

1. Alwen, J., Dodis, Y., Wichs, D.: Leakage-resilient public-key cryptography in the bounded-retrieval model. In: Halevi, S. (ed.) CRYPTO 2009. LNCS, vol. 5677, pp. 36–54. Springer, Heidelberg (2009). https://doi.org/10.1007/978-3-642-03356-8_3
2. Alwen, J., Krenn, S., Pietrzak, K., Wichs, D.: Learning with rounding, revisited. In: Canetti, R., Garay, J.A. (eds.) CRYPTO 2013. LNCS, vol. 8042, pp. 57–74. Springer, Heidelberg (2013). https://doi.org/10.1007/978-3-642-40041-4_4
3. Bellare, M., Stepanovs, I., Waters, B.: New negative results on differing-inputs obfuscation. In: Fischlin, M., Coron, J.-S. (eds.) EUROCRYPT 2016. LNCS, vol. 9666, pp. 792–821. Springer, Heidelberg (2016). https://doi.org/10.1007/978-3-662-49896-5_28
4. Blum, M., Feldman, P., Micali, S.: Non-interactive zero-knowledge and its applications (extended abstract). In: STOC, pp. 103–112 (1988)
5. Boneh, D., Boyen, X., Shacham, H.: Short group signatures. In: Franklin, M. (ed.) CRYPTO 2004. LNCS, vol. 3152, pp. 41–55. Springer, Heidelberg (2004). https://doi.org/10.1007/978-3-540-28628-8_3
6. Boneh, D., DeMillo, R.A., Lipton, R.J.: On the importance of eliminating errors in cryptographic computations. J. Cryptol. **14**(2), 101–119 (2001)
7. Boneh, D., Waters, B.: Constrained pseudorandom functions and their applications. In: Sako, K., Sarkar, P. (eds.) ASIACRYPT 2013. LNCS, vol. 8270, pp. 280–300. Springer, Heidelberg (2013). https://doi.org/10.1007/978-3-642-42045-0_15
8. Boyle, E., Goldwasser, S., Ivan, I.: Functional signatures and pseudorandom functions. In: Krawczyk, H. (ed.) PKC 2014. LNCS, vol. 8383, pp. 501–519. Springer, Heidelberg (2014). https://doi.org/10.1007/978-3-642-54631-0_29
9. Boyle, E., Segev, G., Wichs, D.: Fully leakage-resilient signatures. In: Paterson, K.G. (ed.) EUROCRYPT 2011. LNCS, vol. 6632, pp. 89–108. Springer, Heidelberg (2011). https://doi.org/10.1007/978-3-642-20465-4_7
10. Brakerski, Z., Kalai, Y.T., Katz, J., Vaikuntanathan, V.: Overcoming the hole in the bucket: public-key cryptography resilient to continual memory leakage. In: FOCS, pp. 501–510. IEEE (2010)

11. Chakraborty, S., Prabhakaran, M., Wichs, D.: Witness maps and applications. Cryptology ePrint Archive, Report 2020/090 (2020). https://eprint.iacr.org/2020/090
12. Chase, M., Lysyanskaya, A.: On signatures of knowledge. In: Dwork, C. (ed.) CRYPTO 2006. LNCS, vol. 4117, pp. 78–96. Springer, Heidelberg (2006). https://doi.org/10.1007/11818175_5
13. Chen, Y., Wang, Y., Zhou, H.-S.: Leakage-resilient cryptography from puncturable primitives and obfuscation. In: Peyrin, T., Galbraith, S. (eds.) ASIACRYPT 2018. LNCS, vol. 11273, pp. 575–606. Springer, Cham (2018). https://doi.org/10.1007/978-3-030-03329-3_20
14. Damgård, I., Faust, S., Mukherjee, P., Venturi, D.: Bounded tamper resilience: how to go beyond the algebraic barrier. In: Sako, K., Sarkar, P. (eds.) ASIACRYPT 2013. LNCS, vol. 8270, pp. 140–160. Springer, Heidelberg (2013). https://doi.org/10.1007/978-3-642-42045-0_8
15. Dodis, Y., Haralambiev, K., López-Alt, A., Wichs, D.: Cryptography against continuous memory attacks. In: FOCS, pp. 511–520. IEEE (2010)
16. Dodis, Y., Haralambiev, K., López-Alt, A., Wichs, D.: Efficient public-key cryptography in the presence of key leakage. In: Abe, M. (ed.) ASIACRYPT 2010. LNCS, vol. 6477, pp. 613–631. Springer, Heidelberg (2010). https://doi.org/10.1007/978-3-642-17373-8_35
17. Faonio, A., Nielsen, J.B., Venturi, D.: Mind your coins: fully leakage-resilient signatures with graceful degradation. In: Halldórsson, M.M., Iwama, K., Kobayashi, N., Speckmann, B. (eds.) ICALP 2015. LNCS, vol. 9134, pp. 456–468. Springer, Heidelberg (2015). https://doi.org/10.1007/978-3-662-47672-7_37
18. Faonio, A., Nielsen, J.B., Venturi, D.: Predictable arguments of knowledge. In: Fehr, S. (ed.) PKC 2017. LNCS, vol. 10174, pp. 121–150. Springer, Heidelberg (2017). https://doi.org/10.1007/978-3-662-54365-8_6
19. Faonio, A., Venturi, D.: Efficient public-key cryptography with bounded leakage and tamper resilience. In: Cheon, J.H., Takagi, T. (eds.) ASIACRYPT 2016. LNCS, vol. 10031, pp. 877–907. Springer, Heidelberg (2016). https://doi.org/10.1007/978-3-662-53887-6_32
20. Faust, S., Kiltz, E., Pietrzak, K., Rothblum, G.N.: Leakage-resilient signatures. In: Micciancio, D. (ed.) TCC 2010. LNCS, vol. 5978, pp. 343–360. Springer, Heidelberg (2010). https://doi.org/10.1007/978-3-642-11799-2_21
21. Feige, U., Shamir, A.: Witness indistinguishable and witness hiding protocols. In: STOC, pp. 416–426 (1990)
22. Fujisaki, E., Xagawa, K.: Public-key cryptosystems resilient to continuous tampering and leakage of arbitrary functions. In: Cheon, J.H., Takagi, T. (eds.) ASIACRYPT 2016. LNCS, vol. 10031, pp. 908–938. Springer, Heidelberg (2016). https://doi.org/10.1007/978-3-662-53887-6_33
23. Garg, S., Gentry, C., Sahai, A., Waters, B.: Witness encryption and its applications. In: STOC, pp. 467–476 (2013)
24. Goldreich, O., Goldwasser, S., Micali, S.: On the cryptographic applications of random functions (extended abstract). In: Blakley, G.R., Chaum, D. (eds.) CRYPTO 1984. LNCS, vol. 196, pp. 276–288. Springer, Heidelberg (1985). https://doi.org/10.1007/3-540-39568-7_22
25. Goldwasser, S., Kalai, Y.T., Peikert, C., Vaikuntanathan, V.: Robustness of the learning with errors assumption. In: Proceedings of the Innovations in Computer Science - ICS 2010, Tsinghua University, Beijing, China, 5–7 January 2010, pp. 230–240 (2010)

26. Goldwasser, S., Micali, S., Rackoff, C.: The knowledge complexity of interactive proof-systems. In: STOC, pp. 291–304. ACM (1985)
27. Goldwasser, S., Micali, S., Rivest, R.L.: A digital signature scheme secure against adaptive chosen-message attacks. SIAM J. Comput. **17**(2), 281–308 (1988)
28. Goyal, V., Jain, A., Khurana, D.: Non-malleable multi-prover interactive proofs and witness signatures. Technical report, Cryptology ePrint Archive, Report 2015/1095 (2015)
29. Katz, J., Vaikuntanathan, V.: Signature schemes with bounded leakage resilience. In: Matsui, M. (ed.) ASIACRYPT 2009. LNCS, vol. 5912, pp. 703–720. Springer, Heidelberg (2009). https://doi.org/10.1007/978-3-642-10366-7_41
30. Kiayias, A., Papadopoulos, S., Triandopoulos, N., Zacharias, T.: Delegatable pseudorandom functions and applications. In: ACM CCS, pp. 669–684. ACM (2013)
31. Kocher, P., Jaffe, J., Jun, B.: Differential power analysis. In: Wiener, M. (ed.) CRYPTO 1999. LNCS, vol. 1666, pp. 388–397. Springer, Heidelberg (1999). https://doi.org/10.1007/3-540-48405-1_25
32. Kocher, P.C.: Timing attacks on implementations of diffie-hellman, RSA, DSS, and other systems. In: Koblitz, N. (ed.) CRYPTO 1996. LNCS, vol. 1109, pp. 104–113. Springer, Heidelberg (1996). https://doi.org/10.1007/3-540-68697-5_9
33. Malkin, T., Teranishi, I., Vahlis, Y., Yung, M.: Signatures resilient to continual leakage on memory and computation. In: Ishai, Y. (ed.) TCC 2011. LNCS, vol. 6597, pp. 89–106. Springer, Heidelberg (2011). https://doi.org/10.1007/978-3-642-19571-6_7
34. Merkle, R.C.: A digital signature based on a conventional encryption function. In: Pomerance, C. (ed.) CRYPTO 1987. LNCS, vol. 293, pp. 369–378. Springer, Heidelberg (1988). https://doi.org/10.1007/3-540-48184-2_32
35. Micali, S., Reyzin, L.: Physically observable cryptography. In: Naor, M. (ed.) TCC 2004. LNCS, vol. 2951, pp. 278–296. Springer, Heidelberg (2004). https://doi.org/10.1007/978-3-540-24638-1_16
36. Naor, M., Segev, G.: Public-key cryptosystems resilient to key leakage. In: Halevi, S. (ed.) CRYPTO 2009. LNCS, vol. 5677, pp. 18–35. Springer, Heidelberg (2009). https://doi.org/10.1007/978-3-642-03356-8_2
37. Naor, M., Yung, M.: Universal one-way hash functions and their cryptographic applications. In: STOC, pp. 33–43. ACM (1989)
38. Peikert, C., Waters, B.: Lossy trapdoor functions and their applications. In: STOC, pp. 187–196 (2008)
39. Peikert, C., Waters, B.: Lossy trapdoor functions and their applications. SIAM J. Comput. **40**(6), 1803–1844 (2011)
40. Piret, G., Quisquater, J.-J.: A differential fault attack technique against SPN structures, with application to the AES and KHAZAD. In: Walter, C.D., Koç, Ç.K., Paar, C. (eds.) CHES 2003. LNCS, vol. 2779, pp. 77–88. Springer, Heidelberg (2003). https://doi.org/10.1007/978-3-540-45238-6_7
41. Sahai, A., Waters, B.: How to use indistinguishability obfuscation: deniable encryption, and more. In: STOC, pp. 475–484. ACM (2014)
42. Yuen, T.H., Yiu, S.M., Hui, L.C.K.: Fully leakage-resilient signatures with auxiliary inputs. In: Susilo, W., Mu, Y., Seberry, J. (eds.) ACISP 2012. LNCS, vol. 7372, pp. 294–307. Springer, Heidelberg (2012). https://doi.org/10.1007/978-3-642-31448-3_22

Encryption Schemes

Memory-Tight Reductions for Practical Key Encapsulation Mechanisms

Rishiraj Bhattacharyya(✉)

NISER, HBNI, Bhubaneswar, India
rishiraj.bhattacharyya@gmail.com

Abstract. The efficiency of a black-box reduction is an important goal of modern cryptography. Traditionally, the time complexity and the success probability were considered as the main aspects of efficiency measurements. In CRYPTO 2017, Auerbach *et al.* introduced the notion of memory-tightness in cryptographic reductions and showed a memory-tight reduction of the existential unforgeability of the RSA-FDH signature scheme. Unfortunately, their techniques do not extend directly to the reductions involving intricate RO-programming. The problem seems to be inherent as all the other existing results on memory-tightness are lower bounds and impossibility results. In fact, Auerbach *et al.* conjectured that a memory-tight reduction for IND-CCA security of Hashed-ElGamal KEM is impossible.

- We refute the above conjecture. Using a simple RO simulation technique, we provide memory-tight reductions of IND-CCA security of the Cramer-Shoup and the ECIES version of Hashed-ElGamal KEM.
- We prove memory-tight reductions for different variants of Fujisaki-Okamoto Transformation. We analyze the modular transformations introduced by Hofheinz, Hövermanns and Kiltz (TCC 2017). In addition to the constructions involving implicit rejection, we present a memory-tight reduction for the IND-CCA security of the transformation $\mathsf{QFO}_{\mathsf{m}}^{\perp}$. Our techniques can withstand correctness-errors, and applicable to several lattice-based KEM candidates.

Keywords: Memory-tight reduction · Hashed-ElGamal · FO transformation

1 Introduction

Memory Efficiency of Black-Box Reductions. Black-box reduction is an imperative tool in modern cryptography. The security of any scheme S is typically argued by an algorithm $\mathtt{R}$. Given an adversary, $\mathcal{A}_S$ against S, $\mathtt{R}$ with black-box access to $\mathcal{A}$ is shown to solve some underlying hard problem $\mathcal{P}$. The efficiency of a black-box reduction is measured by the resources $\mathtt{R}$ uses, typically in terms of $\mathcal{A}$. Traditionally the reductions aimed at optimizing the time complexity and/or the success probability [4,5,11]. However, Auerbach *et al.* [3] observed that some reductions which are *tight* in success probability and

A. Kiayias et al. (Eds.): PKC 2020, LNCS 12110, pp. 249–278, 2020.
https://doi.org/10.1007/978-3-030-45374-9_9

time complexity, require a large amount of memory. If the underlying problem is memory sensitive (easier to solve with larger memory), then a memory loose reduction does not rule out the existence of an efficient adversary. They noted further that many of the standard assumptions including LPN, SVP, Discrete Logarithm Problem in prime fields, factoring are memory sensitive. Hence it is imperative to find memory-efficient reductions when the security is based on the hardness of these problems.

Unfortunately, most of the existing results on memory-tight reductions are lower bounds. In [3], authors ruled out memory-tight, restricted black-box reductions for the security of multi-signatures from unique signatures, and multicollision resistance from collision resistance. In [21], Wang *et al.* showed lower bounds for a larger class of black-box reductions including the security of public-key encryption and signature schemes in the multi-user setting. In [14], Demay *et al.* considered the indifferentiability notion in the memory restricted setting, and proved the impossibility of domain extension of hash functions (even by one bit).

On the other hand, to the best of our knowledge, the only positive result so far is the memory-efficient reduction for RSA FDH in the Random Oracle model [3]. The authors introduced new techniques for the random oracle model and showed, using pseudo-random functions and the power of rewinding the adversary once, one can prove a memory-tight reduction of the existential unforgeability of RSA-FDH from RSA assumption. Their technique seems to be generally applicable for hash and sign paradigm, where the domain of the underlying trapdoor permutation enjoys some form of homomorphism (required for applying Coron's technique [12]).

Key Encapsulation Mechanisms. A Key Encapsulation Mechanism (KEM) is a fundamental primitive to construct efficient public-key cryptosystem. Research in KEM design has been rejuvenated in the last few years due to the ongoing effort to standardize post-quantum cryptographic algorithms. While constructions of IND-CCA secure KEM in the "classical" setting have been known for years (see [15] for a comprehensive treatment), the reductions were non-tight, and required perfect correctness from the underlying public-key encryption scheme. There are numerous recent works on KEM in the quantum setting [10,16,17,19,20]. However, not much progress has been made in the classical setting until the work of Hofheinz, Hövermanns and Kiltz [16]. HHK revisited the KEM version of Fujisaki Okamoto transformations and presented a modular analysis of multiple variants. Their results, notably include, *tight* reduction (traditional sense) even when underlying public-key encryption scheme has some correctness error.

1.1 Our Contributions

In this paper, we present memory-efficient reductions of the IND-CCA security of hashed-ElGamal and other variants of Fujisaki-Okamoto transformations.

Memory-Tight Reduction for Hashed-ElGamal. Our starting point is the following conjecture of Auerbach *et al.* [3].

Conjecture 1 [3]. *Memory-tight Reduction for Hashed-ElGamal does not exist.*

In this paper, **we refute the above conjecture**. We introduce a simple "map-then-prf" technique to simulate the random oracle in a memory-efficient way. Our technique programs the Random Oracle non-adaptively, avoiding the need to tabulate the Random Oracle queries. We consider two versions of Hashed-ElGamal KEM, ECIES [1,2] and HEG [13]. We summarize these results in the following two informal theorems.

Theorem 2 (Informal). *Let* $\mathbb{G}$ *be a prime-order cyclic group. Let* $F : \{0,1\}^{\lambda+1} \times \mathbb{G} \times \mathbb{G} \to \mathcal{K}$ *be a prf. There exists a memory-tight reduction, in the random oracle model, of the* IND-CCA *security of HEG over* $\mathbb{G}$ *and* $\mathcal{K}$ *from the gap-Diffie-Hellman problem over* $\mathbb{G}$.

Theorem 3 (Informal). *Let* $\mathbb{G}, \mathbb{G}_T$ *be prime-order cyclic groups and* $\hat{e} : \mathbb{G} \times \mathbb{G} \to \mathbb{G}_T$ *be a bilinear map. Let* $F : \{0,1\}^{\lambda} \times \mathbb{G}_T \to \mathcal{K}$ *be a prf. There exists a memory-tight reduction, in the random oracle model, of the* IND-CCA *security of ECIES over* $\mathbb{G}$ *and* $\mathcal{K}$ *from the Computational-Diffie-Hellman problem over* $\mathbb{G}$.

Memory-Tight Reduction for Variants of Fujisaki-Okamoto Transformations. Fujisaki-Okamoto transformation and other related KEM constructions have gained particular importance in recent years for their applications in constructing post-quantum KEM schemes. In particular, the modular analysis in [16] has been applied widely in constructing lattice-based candidates. In this paper, we prove memory-tight reduction for three variants of Fujisaki-Okamoto transformations (described in Table 1).

We revisit the analysis in [16] and show techniques for memory-tight reductions for all the modules, even withstanding the correctness errors. We summarize the results below.

- **Transformations** $\mathrm{U}^{\not\perp}, \mathrm{U}^{\not\perp}_m, \mathrm{U}^{\perp}, \mathrm{U}^{\perp}_m$**.** In [16], the authors presented four closely related modules to construct an IND-CCA secure KEM from a public-key encryption scheme PKE. The security requirement from PKE depends on the specific variant of U. In this paper, we show new RO simulation techniques for all the four variants to convert corresponding the reductions in [16] into memory-tight ones.
- **Preprocessing Module** T**.** In [16], the transformation T was presented as the preprocessing module to convert (with a tight reduction) an IND-CPA secure public-key encryption scheme $\overline{\mathsf{PKE}}$ to a deterministic OW-PCVA secure public-key encryption scheme. We observe that the RO simulation technique of Auerbach *et al.* [3], is sufficient for a memory-tight reduction for OW-PCA security of $T[\overline{\mathsf{PKE}}]$. When applied with the new reductions for $\mathrm{U}^{\not\perp}$ and $\mathrm{U}^{\not\perp}$, this gives a memory-tight reduction for the IND-CCA security of $\mathrm{KEM}^{\not\perp}$ and $\mathrm{KEM}^{\not\perp}_m$ respectively.
- **A new intermediate module** V**.** The modules with explicit reject, (namely $U^{\perp}_m$ and $U^{\perp}$) require security relative to a ciphertext verification oracle. Unfortunately, our technique only proves OW-PCA security of T. To bridge the gap,

we present a transformation V to convert a OW-PCA deterministic public-key encryption scheme to a OW-PCVA deterministic public-key encryption scheme via a memory-efficient reduction. When applied with T and $U_m^{\perp}$, we get a memory efficient reduction (in the *classical* setting) for the scheme $\mathrm{QKEM}_m^{\perp}$ of [16] (Table 4 in [15]).

Table 1. Considered variants of Fujisaki-Okamoto transformations. $\overline{\mathsf{PKE}} = (\overline{\mathtt{Keygen}}, \overline{\mathtt{Enc}}, \overline{\mathtt{Dec}})$ is an IND-CPA secure public-key encryption scheme. In the column $\mathtt{Decap}$, s is a random string, $sk' = sk||s$.

Constructions	$\mathtt{Encap}(pk)$	$\mathtt{Decap}(sk', c)$
$\mathrm{KEM}^{\not\perp} =$ $U^{\not\perp}\left[T[\overline{\mathsf{PKE}}, \mathtt{G}], \mathtt{H}\right]$	$m \xleftarrow{\$} \mathcal{M}$ $c = \overline{\mathtt{Enc}}(pk, m, \mathtt{G}(m))$ $K = \mathtt{H}(m, c)$	$m' = \overline{\mathtt{Dec}}(sk, c)$ if $m' \neq \perp \wedge c = \overline{\mathtt{Enc}}(pk, m', \mathtt{G}(m'))$ then $K = \mathtt{H}(m', c)$ else $K = \mathtt{H}(s, c)$
$\mathrm{KEM}_m^{\not\perp} =$ $U_m^{\not\perp}\left[T[\overline{\mathsf{PKE}}, \mathtt{G}], \mathtt{H}\right]$	$m \xleftarrow{\$} \mathcal{M}$ $c = \overline{\mathtt{Enc}}(pk, m, \mathtt{G}(m))$ $K = \mathtt{H}(m)$	$m' = \overline{\mathtt{Dec}}(sk, c)$ if $m' \neq \perp \wedge c = \overline{\mathtt{Enc}}(pk, m', \mathtt{G}(m'))$ then $K = \mathtt{H}(m')$ else $K = \mathtt{H}(s, c)$
$\mathrm{QKEM}_m^{\perp} =$ $U_m^{\perp}\left[V\left[T[\overline{\mathsf{PKE}}, \mathtt{G}], \mathtt{H}'\right], \mathtt{H}\right]$	$m \xleftarrow{\$} \mathcal{M}$ $c_1 = \overline{\mathtt{Enc}}(pk, m, \mathtt{G}(m))$ $c_2 = \mathtt{H}'(m)$ $c = c_1\|\|c_2$ $K = \mathtt{H}(m)$	Parse $c = c_1\|\|c_2$, $m' = \overline{\mathtt{Dec}}(sk, c_1)$ if $m' \neq \perp \wedge c_1 = \overline{\mathtt{Enc}}(pk, m', \mathtt{G}(m')) \wedge c_2 = \mathtt{H}'(m')$ $K = \mathtt{H}(m')$ else $K = \perp$

Other Implications. Besides memory efficiency, we found two additional implications of our work. This result refutes the folklore idea that the additional hash present in the $\mathrm{QKEM}_m^{\perp}$ transformation is redundant in the classical setting [15–17]. The second implication is that V composed with T gives a OW-PCVA secure encryption scheme from an IND-CPA secure encryption scheme without the γ-spread requirement of [16].

1.2 Overview of Our Techniques

Challenges with Existing Technique. The memory-efficient technique to simulate an RO in [3] (and later suggested in [8] in the context of KEM) is to evaluate a PRF on the input. However, in the IND-CCA security reduction for key encapsulation mechanisms, the reduction often needs to adaptively program the output of the RO. Evaluating the prf directly on the query input does not provide the required programming capability.

For example, consider the basic construction of a Key Encapsulation Mechanism from a *deterministic* public-key encryption scheme $\mathsf{PKE} = (\mathtt{Gen}, \mathtt{Enc}, \mathtt{Dec})$. The public-key, secret-key of the KEM would be a key pair $(pk, sk) \leftarrow \mathtt{Gen}$. An encapsulation involves choosing a random message m, and computing

$$c = \mathtt{Enc}(pk, m), \qquad k = \mathtt{H}(m, c).$$

The output of the encapsulation is (c, k). A traditional security proof assuming $\mathtt{H}$ to be a random oracle would be to maintain a table containing the queries and corresponding responses of H queries. Whenever the adversary makes a decapsulation query on $\hat{c}$, the reduction will check the table whether it contains an entry $(\hat{m}, \hat{c}, \hat{h})$ such that $\texttt{Enc}(pk, \hat{m})$ returns $\hat{c}$. If such an entry exists, the answer tothe decapsulation query would be $\hat{h}$. Otherwise the reduction would return a randomly sampled element $\hat{h}'$, and save $(-, \hat{c}, \hat{h}')$ in the list. The first entry will be filled up when, in a future hash query, the adversary submits $(\hat{m}, \hat{c})$ where $\hat{c} = \texttt{Enc}(pk, \hat{m})$.

Now consider a memory-efficient reduction where simulation of H is performed using a prf $F(k, .)$. A hash query on $(\hat{m}, \hat{c})$ is returned with $F(k, \hat{m}, \hat{c})$. The problem arises when simulating the decapsulation query $\hat{c}$. As the entries are no longer saved in a table, the reduction cannot find the required $\hat{m}$ to complete the prf evaluation! One may attempt to solve the issue by answering the hash query with $F(k, \hat{c})$. In that case, the decapsulation queries can be answered. However, two hash queries with the same $\hat{c}$ but different $\hat{m}$ would result in a collision! Hence, this idea fails as well.

Core of our Idea: "injectively map and prf". Our method originates from the following observation. Let us call $(\hat{m}, \hat{c})$ a good pair if $\hat{c} = \texttt{Enc}(pk, \hat{m})$. In the IND-CCA security game, the answer to a decapsulation query $\hat{c}$ needs to match with the response of a hash query $(\hat{m}, \hat{c})$ only when $(\hat{m}, \hat{c})$ is a good pair. When answering hash queries on a good pair $(\hat{m}, \hat{c})$, we can "program" the output to be $F(k, m_0, \hat{c})$ (m_0 being any fixed message). For pairs which are not good, we can query an independent prf $F'(k, \hat{m}, \hat{c})$ to compute the responses. Answer to a decapsulation query on (a valid ciphertext) $\hat{c}$ will simply be $F(k, m_0, \hat{c})$. The idea can be generalized as "Apply an appropriate injective function ϕ on the input, and then apply the prf". As the composition of an injective function with a prf results into a prf, we can use the arguments of [3]. This basic technique can readily be applied to the Cramer-Shoup version of Hashed-ElGamal, as well as the modules $\mathrm{U}^{\not\perp}$, and $\mathrm{U}^{\perp}$.

Technique for $\mathbf{U}^{\not\perp}_{\mathbf{m}}, \mathbf{U}^{\perp}_{\mathbf{m}}$. In these cases, the hash function is evaluated only on m. Thus, the above idea is not applicable directly. However, as PKE is deterministic, the reduction can still construct a good pair by simply computing $\hat{c} = \texttt{Enc}(pk, \hat{m})$, and respond a hash query on $\hat{m}$ by $F(k, \hat{c})$. We no longer need to use the independent prf F', as the hash query only contains the message.

Interestingly, the technique works even if PKE has amall correctness errors. Although, $\texttt{Enc}(pk, .)$ is no longer injective, finding a collision in the output of $\texttt{Enc}(pk, .)$ implies finding a correctness error. Conditioned on no collision in the output of $\texttt{Enc}(pk, .)$, the argument of [3] goes through. However, one needs to be careful here, as pointed out in [8]. In some definition of deterministic encryption, it is easy to come up with a scheme where a ciphertext decrypts to a message which in turn encrypts to a different ciphertext. To solve the issue, we require that for every message $\hat{m}$ there exists a single ciphertext $\hat{c}$ that decrypts to $\hat{m}$. Our definition of deterministic encryption is carefully considered to maintain this property. Moreover, the schemes generated by the transformation T of [16] satisfies the definition.

Technique for ECIES. In the case of ECIES, we have a group $\mathbb{G}$ of prime order q with a generator $g \in \mathbb{G}$. A public-key is a random element X with the corresponding secret-key x such that $X = g^x$. The encapsulation involves choosing a random $y \xleftarrow{\$} \mathbb{Z}_q$ and computing

$$Y = g^y \qquad Z = Y^x \qquad k = \mathtt{H}(Z)$$

The output of the encapsulation is (Y, k). While ECIES is analogous to $U_m^{\not\perp}$, we cannot find Y from Z! Hence, we cannot "map to ciphertext space" and apply F.

Fortunately, the "map-then-prf" technique is not limited to mapping to the ciphertext space. We note, when ECIES is implemented using a pairing friendly curve, there exists a bilinear map $\hat{e} : \mathbb{G} \times \mathbb{G} \rightarrow \mathbb{G}_T$ for some $\mathbb{G}_T$. Moreover, by the bilinear property, $\hat{e}(g^x, g^y) = \hat{e}(g, g^{xy})$. We simulate the random oracle using $F(k, \hat{e}(g, .))$. The decapsulation oracle can maintain consistency by using $F(k, \hat{e}(X, .))$.

2 Notations and Preliminaries

If S is a set $|S|$ denotes the size of S. $x \xleftarrow{\$} S$ denotes the process of choosing x uniformly at random from S. $[n]$ denotes the set of first n natural numbers. Composition of two functions is denoted by $\circ$. If $\hat{F} = F \circ \phi$, then $\hat{F}(x) = F(\phi(x))$.

Algorithms and Security Games. The algorithms and complexities considered in the papers are in the RAM model. The algorithms have access to memory and constant number of registers, each having size of one word. For a deterministic (resp. probabilistic) algorithm $\mathcal{A}$, $y = \mathcal{A}(x)$ (resp $y \xleftarrow{\$} \mathcal{A}(x)$) denotes y is the (resp. uniformly sampled) output of $\mathcal{A}$ on input x. $\mathcal{A}^{\mathcal{O}}$ denotes that $\mathcal{A}$ has access to $\mathcal{O}$ as an oracle. The oracles in this paper may be *stateful*; $st_{\mathcal{O}}$ denotes the state of the RAM $\mathcal{O}$. As followed in [3], $\mathcal{A}$ with oracle access to $\mathcal{O}$ cannot access $st_{\mathcal{O}}$.

SECURITY GAMES. The results are proven in the framework of code based games of [6]. A game G consists an algorithm consists of a `main` oracle, and zero or more stateful oracles $O_1, O_2, \cdots, O_n$. If a game G is implemented using a function f, we write $G[f]$ to denote the game.

Complexity Measures. In this paper, we consider the following three complexity measures of an algorithm.

SUCCESS PROBABILITY. The success probability of an algorithm $\mathcal{A}$ in game G is defined by $\mathbf{Succ}_{\mathcal{A},G} \stackrel{def}{=} \text{Prob}[G^{\mathcal{A}} = 1]$.

TIME COMPLEXITY. The time complexity of an algorithm $\mathcal{A}$, denoted by $\text{Time}_\lambda(\mathcal{A})$, is the number of computation steps performed by $\mathcal{A}$ in the worst case over all possible input of size λ. When $\mathcal{A}$ plays a security game G, the time complexity of the game, denoted by $\text{LocalTime}_\lambda(G^{\mathcal{A}})$, is the time complexity of $\mathcal{A}$ plus the number of queries $\mathcal{A}$ makes to the oracle.[1]

[1] In [3], authors defined the local time of the game only by the number of computations of $\mathcal{A}$. In this paper we explicitly include the number of queries made to the oracle.

Memory Complexity. Following [3,21], we define the memory complexity of an algorithm $\mathcal{A}$ to be the size of the code plus the worst-case number of registers used in memory at any step in computation, over all possible input of size λ and random coins. $\text{LocalMem}_\lambda(G^{\mathcal{A}})$ denotes the memory complexity of $\mathcal{A}$ (not the oracles) in the security game G.

Reductions and Efficiency. We follow the definition of black-box reductions proposed in [18]. A cryptographic primitive $\mathcal{P}$ is a family of efficiently computable functions $f : \{0,1\}^* \to \{0,1\}^*$. Security of $\mathcal{P}$ is described using a game G. An adversary $\mathcal{A}$ is said to *$\mathcal{P}$-break f* with probability ϵ, if

$$\mathbf{Succ}_{\mathcal{A},G[f]} = \epsilon.$$

We follow the following definition of a cryptographic reduction.

Definition 1. *Let $\mathcal{P}, \mathcal{Q}$ be cryptographic primitives and G_P and G_Q be the corresponding security games respectively. A* reduction *from $\mathcal{P}$ to $\mathcal{Q}$ is a pair of algorithms* $\mathtt{C}, \mathtt{R}$ *such that*

- $\mathtt{C}^f \in \mathcal{Q}$ *for all* $f \in \mathcal{P}$
- *For all $f \in \mathcal{P}$, for all adversary $\mathcal{A}$ that $\mathcal{Q}$-breaks $\mathtt{C}^f$, the algorithm $\mathtt{R}^{\mathcal{A}}$ $\mathcal{P}$-breaks f.*

Memory-Tight Reductions. Following [3,21], we define memory-tight reductions as follows.

Definition 2. *A Cryptographic reduction* $(\mathtt{C}, \mathtt{R})$ *from $\mathcal{P}$ to $\mathcal{Q}$ is called* memory-tight, *if for all $f \in \mathcal{P}$,*

$$\mathbf{Succ}_{\mathcal{A},G_Q[\mathtt{C}^f]} \approx \mathbf{Succ}_{\mathtt{R}^{\mathcal{A}},G_P[f]}$$
$$\mathbf{LocalTime}_\lambda(\mathtt{R}^{\mathcal{A}}) \approx \mathbf{LocalTime}_\lambda(\mathcal{A})$$
$$\mathbf{LocalMem}_\lambda(\mathtt{R}^{\mathcal{A}}) \approx \mathbf{LocalMem}_\lambda(\mathcal{A})$$

Hardness Assumptions. The security proofs of Hashed-ElGamal variants are reduced from the Computational Diffie-Hellman and gap-Diffie-Hellman assumption. Consider the CDH game described in Fig. 1.

Game $\mathsf{CDH}(q, g, \mathbb{G})$	Oracle $\mathtt{DDH}(X, Y, Z)$
$x \xleftarrow{\$} \mathbb{Z}_q^*$	**if** $\exists y$ such that $Y = g^y$ and $Z = X^y$
$y \xleftarrow{\$} \mathbb{Z}_q^*$	**return** 1
$z \leftarrow \mathcal{A}(g^x, g^y)$	**else**
if $z = g^{xy}$ **return** 1	**return** 0
else **return** 0	

Fig. 1. CDH game and gap-DH game. In gap-DH game, $\mathcal{A}$ has oracle access to $\mathtt{DDH}(\cdot,\cdot,\cdot)$

Definition 3 *(gap-Diffie-Hellman Assumption). Let q be a prime. Let $\mathbb{G} = \langle g \rangle$ be a cyclic group of order q. The (t, μ, ϵ) gap-Diffie-Hellman (gap-DH) assumption states that for all adversary $\mathcal{A}$ that runs in times t and uses μ bites of memory,*

$$\mathbf{Succ}_{\mathcal{A}^{\mathrm{DDH}}, \mathrm{CDH}} \leq \epsilon$$

The Computational Diffie-Hellman assumption is defined in the same way, except the condition that $\mathcal{A}$ has no access to the DDH oracle.

Key Encapsulation Mechanism. A key encapsulation mechanism KEM consists of three algorithms; $\mathsf{Gen}, \mathsf{Encap}, \mathsf{Decap}$. The key generation algorithm Gen takes a security parameter 1^λ as input and outputs a public key pk and a secret key sk. The encapsulation algorithm Encap, on input pk, outputs a key-ciphertext pair (c, K), where $K \in \mathcal{K}$ for some non-empty set $\mathcal{K}$. c is said to be the encapsulation of K. The deterministic decapsulation algorithm Decap takes an encapsulation c as input along with sk, and outputs a key $K \in \mathcal{K}$. A PKE is called δ-correct if

$$\mathrm{Prob}[\mathsf{Decap}(sk, c) \neq K | (pk, sk) \leftarrow \mathsf{Gen}; (c, K) \leftarrow \mathsf{Encap}(pk)] \leq \delta$$

IND-CCA security of a Key Encapsulation Mechanism. We recall the IND-CCA security game for a Key Encapsulation Mechanism in Fig. 2. The IND-CCA advantage of an adversary $\mathcal{A}$ against PKE is defined as

$$\mathbf{Adv}_{\mathcal{A}, \mathsf{KEM}}^{\mathrm{IND\text{-}CCA}} \stackrel{def}{=} \left| \mathbf{Succ}_{\mathcal{A}, \mathrm{IND\text{-}CCA}} - \frac{1}{2} \right|.$$

Game IND-CCA	Oracle Decap(c)		Game COR
1: $(pk, sk) \leftarrow \mathsf{Gen}(1^\lambda)$	1: if $c = c^*$ return $\perp$		
2: $b \xleftarrow{\$} \{0, 1\}$	2: $K \leftarrow \mathsf{Decap}(sk, c)$		1: $(pk, sk) \leftarrow \mathsf{Gen}(1^\lambda)$
3: $(c^*, K_0^*) \leftarrow \mathsf{Encap}(pk)$	3: return K		2: $m \leftarrow \mathcal{A}(pk, sk)$
4: $K_1^* \xleftarrow{\$} \mathcal{K}$			3: $c \leftarrow \mathsf{Enc}(pk, m)$
5: $b' \leftarrow \mathcal{A}^{\mathsf{Decap}}(c^*, K_b^*)$			4: if $m \neq \mathsf{Dec}(sk, c)$ return 1
6: if $b = b'$ return 1			5: else return 0
7: else return 0			

Fig. 2. IND-CCA game for KEM   **Fig. 3.** Correctness game for PKE

Public-Key Encryption. A public-key encryption scheme consists of three algorithms, $\mathsf{PKE} = (\mathtt{Gen}, \mathtt{Enc}, \mathtt{Dec})$. There are three sets associated with PKE, the message space $\mathcal{M}$, the randomness space $\mathcal{R}$, and the ciphertext space $\mathcal{C}$. The key generation algorithm takes the security parameter as input and outputs a public-key, secret-key pair (pk, sk). The encryption algorithm takes the public key pk, and a message $m \in \mathcal{M}$ as input, samples a random string $r \xleftarrow{\$} \mathcal{R}$, and outputs a ciphertext.$c \leftarrow \mathtt{Enc}(pk, m, r)$. The decryption algorithm Dec, on input sk and a ciphertext c, outputs a message $m = \mathtt{Dec}(sk, c) \in \mathcal{M}$ or a special symbol $\perp \notin \mathcal{M}$. We say, c is an invalid ciphertext, if $\mathtt{Dec}(sk, c) = \perp$.

Deterministic Public Key Encryption. We call a public-key encryption scheme PKE *deterministic*, if the algorithm Enc is deterministic and for every message $m \in \mathcal{M}$, there exists a unique $c \in \mathcal{C}$ such that $\mathtt{Dec}(sk, c) = m$. We write $c \leftarrow \mathtt{Enc}(pk, m)$ for deterministic encryption.

Correctness. Following [16], we define the correctness of a public-key encryption scheme by the security game COR in Fig. 3.

Definition 4. *Let $\delta : \mathbb{N} \to [0, 1]$ be an increasing function. Consider the game* COR *in Fig. 3. A public-key encryption scheme* PKE *is called δ-correct, if for all adversary $\mathcal{A}$ with running time bounded by t,*

$$\mathbf{Succ}_{\mathcal{A},\mathsf{COR}[\mathsf{PKE}]} \leq \delta(t)$$

where the probability is taken over the randomness of Gen *and $\mathcal{A}$. Moreover, we say* PKE *is strongly $\overline{\delta}$ correct, if $\forall\ t, \delta(t) \leq \overline{\delta}$.*

Game OW-PCVA	Procedure $\mathtt{PCO}(m, c)$	Procedure $\mathtt{CVO}(c)$
1 : $(pk, sk) \leftarrow \mathtt{Gen}(1^\lambda)$	1 : **if** $m = \mathtt{Dec}(sk, c)$ **return** 1	1 : $m \leftarrow \mathtt{Dec}(sk, c)$
2 : $m \xleftarrow{\$} \mathcal{M}$	2 : **else return** 0	2 : **if** $m \in \mathcal{M}$ **return** 1
3 : $c \leftarrow \mathtt{Enc}(pk, m)$		3 : **else return** 0
4 : $m' \leftarrow \mathcal{A}^{\mathtt{PCO},\mathtt{CVO}}(pk, c)$		
5 : **if** $m' = \mathtt{Dec}(sk, c)$ **return** 1		
6 : **else return** 0		

Fig. 4. Game OW-PCVA. In the game OW-PCA (resp. OW-VA), $\mathcal{A}$ has oracle access to only PCO (resp. CVO).

Security. Following [16], we define three security games for a public-key encryption scheme, OW-PCA, OW-VA, and OW-PCVA in Fig. 4. In OW-PCA game, the adversary has oracle access to PCO. In the OW-VA game, the adversary has oracle access to CVO. In OW-PCVA game, the adversary has oracle access to both PCO and CVO. For ATK $\in$ {PCA, VA, PCVA}, we define the corresponding advantages of an adversary $\mathcal{A}$ against PKE as

$$\mathbf{Adv}^{\text{OW-ATK}}_{\mathcal{A},\mathsf{PKE}} \stackrel{def}{=} \text{Prob}[\text{OW-ATK}[\mathsf{PKE}]^{\mathcal{A}} = 1]$$

Random Oracles. An (idealized) function $\mathcal{F} : \{0,1\}^\delta \rightarrow \{0,1\}^\rho$ is said to be a *Random Oracle*, if for all $x \in \{0,1\}^\delta$, the output $\mathcal{F}(x)$ is independently and uniformly distributed over $\{0,1\}^\rho$.

Pseudo-random Functions

Definition 5. *Let $F : \{0,1\}^\lambda \times \{0,1\}^\delta \rightarrow \{0,1\}^\rho$ be a deterministic algorithm and let $\mathcal{A}$ be an algorithm. The prf advantage of $\mathcal{A}$ is defined as*

$$\mathbf{Adv}^{\mathrm{prf}}_{\mathcal{A},F} \stackrel{def}{=} |\mathbf{Succ}(\mathtt{Real}^{\mathcal{A}}) - \mathbf{Succ}(\mathtt{Random}^{\mathcal{A}})|.$$

F is said to implement a family of (t, d, ϵ)-pseudo-random functions if for all adversary $\mathcal{A}$ that runs in time t and uses memory d,

$$\mathbf{Adv}^{\mathrm{prf}}_{\mathcal{A},F} \leq \epsilon$$

Simulating Random Oracle Using PRF. If a game G is defined in the random oracle model, then one procedure of the game defines the random oracle $\mathtt{H} : \{0,1\}^\delta \rightarrow \{0,1\}^\rho$. The standard technique to implement the random oracle procedure is via lazy sampling. However, the lazy sampling technique requires $\mathcal{O}(q_h \cdot \lambda)$ additional memory where q_h is the number of $\mathtt{H}$ queries made by the adversary. In [3], the authors formalized the technique, originally suggested in [7], of simulating the Random Oracle using a prf. Let $G[\mathtt{H}]$ be a game where $\mathtt{H}$ is a random oracle used in G. Let $G[F]$ be the same game where the random oracle is implemented using a prf F. Specifically, the oracle $\mathtt{H}$ is implemented using $F(k,.)$ for a randomly sampled key k (Fig. 6).

```
Game Real
Procedure main
  k <-$ {0,1}^λ
  b <- A^{O_F}
  if b = 0
  return 1
  else
  return 0
  endif

Procedure O_F(x)
  return F(k, x)

Game Random
Procedure main
  b <- A^{O_F}
  if b = 0
  return 1
  else
  return 0
  endif

Procedure O_F(x)
  y <-$ {0,1}^ρ
  return y
```

Fig. 5. PRF security game

```
RO simulation by lazy sampling
Procedure main

Procedure H(x)
  if H(x) = ⊥
  H(x) <-$ {0,1}^ρ
  endif
  return H(x)

RO simulation using PRF
Procedure main
  k <-$ {0,1}^κ

Procedure H(x)
  return F(k, x)
```

Fig. 6. Memory efficient simulation of Random Oracle

Lemma 1 (RO simulation using prf [3]). *For all adversary $\mathcal{A}$ against G making at most q_h queries to the random oracle, there exists a $\mathcal{B}_F$ against F in the* prf *game such that*

$$\left|\mathbf{Succ}_{\mathcal{A}^{\mathtt{H}},G[\mathtt{H}]} - \mathbf{Succ}_{\mathcal{A}^{\mathtt{H}},G[F]}\right| \leq \mathbf{Adv}^{\mathrm{prf}}_{\mathcal{B}_F,F}$$

Moreover, it holds that

$$\begin{aligned}\mathbf{LocalTime}(\mathcal{B}_F) &= \mathbf{LocalTime}(\mathcal{A}) + \mathbf{LocalTime}(G) + q_h\\ \mathbf{LocalMem}(\mathcal{B}_F) &= \mathbf{LocalMem}(\mathcal{A}) + \mathbf{LocalMem}(G)\end{aligned}$$

3 Memory-Tight Reductions for Hashed-ElGamal

3.1 Cramer-Shoup Variant

Procedure $\mathtt{Gen}(1^\lambda)$	Procedure $\mathtt{Encap}(\mathrm{pk})$	Procedure $\mathtt{Decap}(\mathrm{sk}, Y)$
$(q, g, \mathbb{G}) \leftarrow \mathtt{DH}(1^\lambda)$	$(g, h) = \mathrm{pk}$	$x = sk$
$x \xleftarrow{\$} \mathbb{Z}_q^*$	$y \xleftarrow{\$} \mathbb{Z}_q^*$	$Z = Y^x$
$\mathrm{pk} = (g, g^x)$	$Y = g^y$	$K = \mathtt{H}(Y, Z)$
$\mathrm{sk} = x$	$Z = h^y$	**return** K
return $(\mathrm{pk}, \mathrm{sk})$	$K = \mathtt{H}(Y, Z)$	
	return (Y, K)	

Fig. 7. HEG: Cramer-Shoup Version of Hashed-ElGamal KEM. $\mathtt{H} : \mathbb{G} \times \mathbb{G} \rightarrow \mathcal{K}$ is a cryptographic hash function

In this section we present a memory-tight reduction of Cramer-Shoup version of hashed-ElGamal Key Encapsulation mechanism [13]. We describe the scheme in Fig. 7. $\mathbb{G}$ is a cyclic group of prime order q. Let $\mathtt{H} : \mathbb{G} \times \mathbb{G} \rightarrow \mathcal{K}$ be a hash function. Our main result in this section is the following theorem.

Theorem 4. *Let q be a prime and $\mathbb{G}$ be any gap group of order q. Let* DDH *be the Decisional Diffie Hellman oracle on $\mathbb{G}$. Let* DH *be the Diffie Hellman instance generation algorithm over $\mathbb{G}$. Let $F : \{0,1\}^\lambda \times \{0,1\} \times \mathbb{G} \times \mathbb{G} \rightarrow \mathcal{K}$ be a prf. Let Π be the HEG KEM scheme over $\mathbb{G}$ and $\mathcal{K}$, with security parameter λ.*

Let $\mathcal{A}$ be any adversary in the IND-CCA *game of Π. Suppose $\mathcal{A}$ makes q_H hash queries and q_D decapsulation queries. Then, in the random oracle model, there exists an adversary $\mathcal{B}_{DH}$ in the* gap-DH *game, and an adversary $\mathcal{B}_F$ such that*

$$\mathbf{Adv}^{\text{IND-CCA}}_{\mathcal{A},\Pi} \leq \mathbf{Adv}^{\text{gap-DH}}_{\mathcal{B}_{DH},\mathbb{G}} + \mathbf{Adv}^{\mathrm{prf}}_{\mathcal{B}_F,F}$$

Moreover, it holds that

$$\begin{aligned}
\textbf{LocalTime}(\mathcal{B}_{DH}) &\approx \textbf{LocalTime}(\mathcal{A}) + (q_H + q_D) \cdot \textbf{LocalTime}(F) + q_H \\
\textbf{LocalMem}(\mathcal{B}_{DH}) &\approx \textbf{LocalMem}(\mathcal{A}) + \textbf{LocalMem}(F) + 7\lambda + 1 \\
\textbf{LocalTime}(\mathcal{B}_F) &\approx \textbf{LocalTime}(\mathcal{A}) + \textbf{LocalTime}(\texttt{DH}) + (q_H + q_D) \\
\textbf{LocalMem}(\mathcal{B}_F) &\approx \textbf{LocalMem}(\mathcal{A}) + \textbf{LocalMem}(\texttt{DH}) + 11\lambda + 2
\end{aligned}$$

Before proving the Theorem 4, we construct a prf $\hat{F} : \{0,1\}^\lambda \times \mathbb{G} \times \mathbb{G} \to \mathcal{K}$ that we shall use in the proof.

Construction of $\hat{F}$. Let DDH be the decisional Diffie-Hellman oracle such that $\texttt{DDH}(X, Y, Z) = 1$, if (X, Y, Z) is a valid Diffie-Hellman tuple.

Construction 5. *Let $\mathbb{G}$ be a group of prime order q and let g be a generator of $\mathbb{G}$. Fix $X \in \mathbb{G}$. Let $F : \{0,1\}^\lambda \times \{0,1\} \times \mathbb{G} \times \mathbb{G} \to \mathcal{K}$. We define $\hat{F}_X : \{0,1\}^\lambda \times \mathbb{G} \times \mathbb{G} \to \mathcal{K}$ as follows*

$$\hat{F}_X(k, Y, Z) = \begin{cases} F(k, 0, Y, Z) \text{ if } \texttt{DDH}(X, Y, Z) = 0 \\ F(k, 1, Y, g) \text{ if } \texttt{DDH}(X, Y, Z) = 1 \end{cases}$$

In order to use the map then prf technique, we need the following lemma.

Lemma 2. *If F is a prf, then $\hat{F}_X$ is a prf. Moreover, for every adversary $\mathcal{B}_{\hat{F}}$ against $\hat{F}_X$, there exists a $\mathcal{B}_F$ against F such that,*

$$\begin{aligned}
\textbf{Adv}^{\text{prf}}_{\mathcal{B}_F, F} &= \textbf{Adv}^{\text{prf}}_{\mathcal{B}_{\hat{F}}, \hat{F}} \\
\textbf{LocalTime}(\mathcal{B}_F) &= \textbf{LocalTime}(\mathcal{B}_{\hat{F}}) + q \\
\textbf{LocalMem}(\mathcal{B}_F) &= \textbf{LocalMem}(\mathcal{B}_{\hat{F}}) + 2\lambda.
\end{aligned}$$

where q is the number of queries made by $\mathcal{B}_{\hat{F}}$.

Proof. Fix $X \in \mathbb{G}$. Note that for every $Y \in \mathbb{G}$, there exists a unique $Z \in G$ such that $\texttt{DDH}(X, Y, Z) = 1$. We define $\psi_X : \mathbb{G} \times \mathbb{G} \to \{0,1\} \times \mathbb{G} \times \mathbb{G}$ as

$$\psi_X(Y, Z) = \begin{cases} (0, Y, Z) \text{ if } \texttt{DDH}(X, Y, Z) = 0 \\ (1, Y, 0^\lambda) \text{ if } \texttt{DDH}(X, Y, Z) = 1 \end{cases}$$

It is easy to verify that ψ_X is an injective function. Moreover, $\hat{F}_X = F \circ \psi_X$.

Let O be the oracle of $\mathcal{B}_F$. $\mathcal{B}_F$ chooses $x \in \mathbb{Z}_q^*$, set $X = g^x$ and invokes $\mathcal{B}_{\hat{F}}$. For every query (Y, Z) of $\mathcal{B}_{\hat{F}}$, $\mathcal{B}_F$ checks whether $Y^x = Z$, computes $\psi_X(Y, Z)$ accordingly and queries O. The response of the oracle is passed to $\mathcal{B}_{\hat{F}}$. When $\mathcal{B}_{\hat{F}}$ outputs a bit b, $\mathcal{B}_F$ outputs b. This perfectly simulates the prf game of $\hat{F}_X$.

We assume the computation time of ψ_X is constant. In order to simulate the prf game of $\hat{F}_X$, $\mathcal{B}_F$ needs to compute ψ_X for q many times. Moreover, $\mathcal{B}_F$ needs store x and a temporary variable for passing the values. The lemma follows. □

The Reduction. Theorem 4 is proven via a sequence of games. Formal description of the games are given in Figs. 8 and 9.

$\mathbf{G}_0$ $\boxed{\mathbf{G}_1}$	Procedure $\mathtt{H}(Y, Z)$ in $\mathbf{G}_0$	Procedure $\mathtt{H}(Y, Z)$ in $\mathbf{G}_1$
1: $(pk, sk) \leftarrow \mathtt{Gen}(1^\lambda)$	1: **if** $\mathtt{H}(Y, Z)$ is undefined	1: **if** $Z = Y^x \wedge Y = Y^*$
2: Parse $pk = (g, X)$	2: $\mathtt{H}(Y, Z) \xleftarrow{\$} \mathcal{K}$	2: **return** K_0^*
3: Parse $sk = x$	3: **endif**	3: **else**
4: $y^* \xleftarrow{\$} \mathbb{Z}_q^*$	4: **return** $\mathtt{H}(Y, Z)$	4: **if** $\mathtt{H}(Y, Z)$ is undefined
5: $b \xleftarrow{\$} \{0, 1\}$		5: $\mathtt{H}(Y, Z) \xleftarrow{\$} \mathcal{K}$
6: $Y^* = g^{y^*}$	**Procedure $\mathtt{Decap}(Y)$ in $\mathbf{G}_0, \mathbf{G}_1$**	6: **endif**
7: $Z^* = Y^{*x}$	1: **if** $Y = Y^*$ **return** $\perp$	7: **return** $\mathtt{H}(Y, Z)$
8: $K_0^* = \mathtt{H}(Y^*, Z^*)$ $\boxed{K_0^* \xleftarrow{\$} \mathcal{K}}$	2: $Z = Y^x$	8: **endif**
9: $K_1^* \xleftarrow{\$} \mathcal{K}$	3: $K = \mathtt{H}(Y, Z)$	
10: $b^* \leftarrow \mathcal{A}^{\mathtt{Decap},\mathtt{H}}(pk, Y^*, K_b^*)$	4: **return** K	
11: **if** $b = b^*$ **return** 1		
12: **else return** 0		
13: **endif**		

Fig. 8. The games $\mathbf{G}_0$ and $\mathbf{G}_1$. In game $\mathbf{G}_1$, Line 9 in replaced by the boxed statement

Game $\mathbf{G}_0$. The game $\mathbf{G}_0$ is the original IND-CCA game.

$$\mathbf{Adv}_{\mathcal{A},\Pi}^{\text{IND-CCA}} \stackrel{def}{=} \left|\text{Prob}[\mathbf{G}_0^{\mathcal{A}} = 1] - \frac{1}{2}\right|.$$

Game $\mathbf{G}_1$: We predefine $K_0^* = \mathtt{H}(Y^*, Z^*)$ by sampling a random element from the keyspace $\mathcal{K}$. Y^* is the challenge ciphertext sent in the KEM game and $Z^* = Y^{*x}$. The hash oracle is modified to return K_0^* for the input (Y^*, Z^*). As K_0^* is still uniformly chosen at random, and the hash oracle output is consistent, there is no change in the distribution of adversary's view.

$$\text{Prob}[\mathbf{G}_0^{\mathcal{A}} = 1] = \text{Prob}[\mathbf{G}_1^{\mathcal{A}} = 1]$$

Game $\mathbf{G}_2$. In this game the oracles $\mathtt{H}$ and $\mathtt{Decap}$ are changed. We replace the random oracle by a prf $\hat{F}_X : \{0,1\}^\lambda \times \mathbb{G} \times \mathbb{G} \rightarrow \mathcal{K}$. By Lemma 1, there exists an adversary $\mathcal{B}_{\hat{F}}$ such that

$$\left|\text{Prob}[\mathbf{G}_1^{\mathcal{A}} = 1] - \text{Prob}[\mathbf{G}_2^{\mathcal{A}} = 1]\right| \leq \mathbf{Adv}_{\mathcal{B}_{\hat{F}}, \hat{F}_X}^{\text{prf}}$$

Game $\mathbf{G}_3$. We rewrite the prf evaluation of $\hat{F}_X$ using a prf F as defined in Construction 5. In the procedure $\mathtt{Decap}$ of the game $\mathbf{G}_2$, Step 2 ($Z = Y^x$) ensures that $\hat{F}_X(k, Y, Z)$ in that procedure always evaluates to $F(k, 1, Y, g)$. As the view of the adversary remains unchanged,

$$\text{Prob}[\mathbf{G}_2^{\mathcal{A}} = 1] = \text{Prob}[\mathbf{G}_3^{\mathcal{A}} = 1]$$

Game $\mathbf{G}_4$: In this game, we set a flag $\textsc{Flag}$ and abort on the event that $\mathcal{A}$ queries $\mathtt{H}$ on (Y^*, Z^*) where Y^* is the challenge in the KEM game and (X, Y^*, Z^*) is a valid diffie hellman tuple. By the fundamental lemma of game playing proofs

$$\left|\text{Prob}[\mathbf{G}_3^{\mathcal{A}} = 1] - \text{Prob}[\mathbf{G}_4^{\mathcal{A}} = 1]\right| \leq \text{Prob}[\textsc{Flag} = 1].$$

In the game $\mathbf{G}_4$, the adversary $\mathcal{A}$ is unable to compute $\mathtt{H}(Y^*, Z^*)$ using either the hash oracle or the decapsulation oracle. The decapsulation oracle outputs $\perp$ whenever the input Y is equal to Y^*. The hash oracle aborts for the input (Y^*, Z^*). This implies that the bit b is independent from the adversary's view. Hence

$$\text{Prob}[\mathbf{G}_3^{\mathcal{A}}] = \frac{1}{2}.$$

To bound $\text{Prob}[\textsc{Flag} = 1]$, we construct an algorithm $\mathcal{B}_{DH}$ against the $\mathsf{gap\text{-}DH}$ security of $\mathbb{G}$. $\mathcal{B}_{DH}$ simulates game $\mathbf{G}_4$ for $\mathcal{A}$.

$\mathsf{gap\text{-}DH}$ Adversary $\mathcal{B}_{DH}$. Formal code of $\mathcal{B}_{DH}$ is given in Fig. 10. $\mathcal{B}_{DH}$ simulates $\mathbf{G}_4$. In order to execute line 1 of the game $\mathbf{G}_4$, $\mathcal{B}_{DH}$ uses the $\mathtt{DDH}$ oracle. By the definition of $\mathsf{gap\text{-}DH}$ game, X and Y^* are uniformly and independently distributed. Hence the simulation of $\mathbf{G}_4$ is perfect. $\textsc{Flag} = 1$ implies that $\mathcal{A}$ queried $\mathtt{H}(Y, Z)$ where $Y = Y^*$ and $\mathtt{DDH}(X, Y^*, Z) = 1$. $\mathcal{B}_{DH}$ returns that Z and wins the $\mathsf{gap\text{-}DH}$ game. Hence,

$$\text{Prob}[\textsc{Flag} = 1] = \mathbf{Adv}^{\mathsf{gap\text{-}DH}}_{\mathcal{B}_{DH},G}$$

Collecting the probabilities, we get

$$\mathbf{Adv}^{\text{IND-CCA}}_{\mathcal{A},\Pi} \leq \mathbf{Adv}^{\mathsf{gap\text{-}DH}}_{\mathcal{B}_{DH},\mathbb{G}} + \mathbf{Adv}^{\text{prf}}_{\mathcal{B}_{\hat{F}},\hat{F}}$$

Efficiency of $\mathcal{B}_{DH}$. $\mathcal{B}_{DH}$ runs $\mathcal{A}$, queries $\mathtt{DDH}$ oracle for q_H many times, computes the prf F for $(q_H + q_D)$ many times. $\mathcal{O}(\text{poly}(\lambda))$ is the cost of other operations in $\mathbf{G}_4$.

$$\mathbf{LocalTime}(\mathcal{B}_{DH}) \approx \mathbf{LocalTime}(\mathcal{A}) + (q_H + q_D)\mathbf{LocalTime}(F) + q_H$$

The last q_H term in the right-hand side of the above equation is to denote the number of queries made to the $\mathtt{DDH}$ oracle.

Memory Efficiency of $\mathcal{B}_{DH}$. $\mathcal{B}_{DH}$ needs to save the code of $\mathcal{A}$, and F. In addition, counting the registers in $\mathbf{G}_4$,

$$\mathbf{LocalMem}(\mathcal{B}_{DH}) \approx \mathbf{LocalMem}(\mathcal{A}) + \mathbf{LocalMem}(F) + 7\lambda + 1$$

So far, we have proven that there exist adversaries $\mathcal{B}_{DH}$ and $\mathcal{B}_{\hat{F}}$

$$\mathbf{Adv}^{\text{IND-CCA}}_{\mathcal{A},\Pi} \leq \mathbf{Adv}^{\mathsf{gap\text{-}DH}}_{\mathcal{B}_{DH},G} + \mathbf{Adv}^{\text{prf}}_{\mathcal{B}_{\hat{F}},\hat{F}}$$

G_2	G_3	G_4
1: $(pk, sk) \leftarrow \text{Gen}(1^\lambda)$	1: $(pk, sk) \leftarrow \text{Gen}(1^\lambda)$	1: $(pk, sk) \leftarrow \text{Gen}(1^\lambda)$
2: Parse $pk = (g, X)$	2: Parse $pk = (g, X)$	2: Parse $pk = (g, X)$
3: Parse $sk = x$	3: Parse $sk = x$	3: Parse $sk = x$
4: $k \xleftarrow{\$} \{0,1\}^\lambda$	4: $k \xleftarrow{\$} \{0,1\}^\lambda$	4: $k \xleftarrow{\$} \{0,1\}^\lambda$
5: $y^* \xleftarrow{\$} \mathbb{Z}_q^*$	5: $y^* \xleftarrow{\$} \mathbb{Z}_q^*$	5: $y^* \xleftarrow{\$} \mathbb{Z}_q^*$
6: $b \xleftarrow{\$} \{0,1\}$	6: $b \xleftarrow{\$} \{0,1\}$	6: $b \xleftarrow{\$} \{0,1\}$
7: $Y^* = g^{y^*}$	7: $Y^* = g^{y^*}$	7: $Y^* = g^{y^*}$
8: $Z^* = Y^{*x}$	8: $Z^* = Y^{*x}$	8: $Z^* = Y^{*x}$
9: $K_0^* \xleftarrow{\$} \mathcal{K}$	9: $K_0^* \xleftarrow{\$} \mathcal{K}$	9: $K_0^* \xleftarrow{\$} \mathcal{K}$
10: $K_1^* \xleftarrow{\$} \mathcal{K}$	10: $K_1^* \xleftarrow{\$} \mathcal{K}$	10: $K_1^* \xleftarrow{\$} \mathcal{K}$
11: $b^* \leftarrow \mathcal{A}^{\text{Decap,H}}(pk, Y^*, K_b^*)$	11: $b^* \leftarrow \mathcal{A}^{\text{Decap,H}}(pk, Y^*, K_b^*)$	11: $b^* \leftarrow \mathcal{A}^{\text{Decap,H}}(pk, Y^*, K_b^*)$
12: **if** $b = b^*$ **return** 1	12: **if** $b = b^*$ **return** 1	12: **if** $b = b^*$ **return** 1
13: **else return** 0	13: **else return** 0	13: **else return** 0
14: **endif**	14: **endif**	14: **endif**

Procedure H(Y, Z)	Procedure H(Y, Z)	Procedure H(Y, Z)
1: **if** $Z = Y^x \wedge Y = Y^*$	1: **if** $Z = Y^x$	1: **if** $Z = Y^x$
2: **return** K_0^*	2: **if** $Y = Y^*$	2: **if** $Y = Y^*$
3: **else**	3: **return** K_0^*	3: $\text{FLAG}=1$
4: $K = \hat{F}_X(k, Y, Z)$	4: **else**	4: **Abort**
5: **return** K	5: $K = F(k, 1, Y, g)$	5: **endif**
6: **endif**	6: **endif**	6: $K = F(k, 1, Y, g)$
	7: **else**	7: **else**
	8: $K = F(k, 0, Y, Z)$	8: $K = F(k, 0, Y, Z)$
Procedure Decap(Y)	9: **endif**	9: **endif**
1: **if** $Y = Y^*$**return** $\perp$	10: **return** K	10: **return** K
2: $Z = Y^x$		
3: $K = \hat{F}_X(k, Y, Z)$		
4: **return** K	Procedure Decap(Y)	Procedure Decap(Y)
	1: **if** $Y = Y^*$**return** $\perp$	1: **if** $Y = Y^*$**return** $\perp$
	2: $Z = Y^x$	2:
	3: $K = F(k, 1, Y, g)$	3: $K = F(k, 1, Y, g)$
	4: **return** K	4: **return** K

Fig. 9. IND-CCA game of HEG: highlighted statements are the modifications from the previous game

Applying Lemma 2, we get the adversary $\mathcal{B}_F$ such that

$$\text{Adv}^{\text{prf}}_{\mathcal{B}_{\hat{F}}, \hat{F}} = \text{Adv}^{\text{prf}}_{\mathcal{B}_F, F}$$

Hence, there exist adversaries $\mathcal{B}_{DH}$ and $\mathcal{B}_F$ such that

$$\text{Adv}^{\text{IND-CCA}}_{\mathcal{A}, \Pi} \leq \text{Adv}^{\text{gap-DH}}_{\mathcal{B}_{DH}, G} + \text{Adv}^{\text{prf}}_{\mathcal{B}_F, F}$$

The following lemma finds the efficiency of $\mathcal{B}_F$

Algorithm $\mathcal{B}_{DH}(g, X, Y^*)$	Procedure $\mathtt{H}(Y, Z)$
1 : Set $pk = (g, X)$	1 : **if** $\mathtt{DDH}(X, Y, Z) = 1$
2 : $k \xleftarrow{\$} \{0, 1\}^\lambda$	2 : **if** $Y = Y^*$
3 : $K^* \xleftarrow{\$} \mathcal{K}$	3 : $\mathrm{FLAG} = 1$
4 : $b^* \leftarrow \mathcal{A}^{\mathtt{Decap},\mathtt{H}}(pk, Y^*, K^*)$	4 : Output Z
5 : *output* $\perp$.	5 : **else**
	6 : $K = F(k, 1, Y, g)$
Procedure $\mathtt{Decap}(Y)$	7 : **endif**
	8 : **else**
1 : **if** $Y = Y^*$**return** $\perp$	9 : $K = F(k, 0, Y, Z)$
2 : $K = F(k, 1, Y, g)$	10 : **endif**
3 : **return** K	11 : **return** K

Fig. 10. Diffie Hellman adversary $\mathcal{B}_{DH}$

Lemma 3

$$\mathbf{LocalTime}(\mathcal{B}_F) \approx \mathbf{LocalTime}(\mathcal{A}) + \mathbf{LocalTime}(\mathrm{DH}) + 2(q_H + q_D)$$
$$\mathbf{LocalMem}(\mathcal{B}_F) \approx \mathbf{LocalMem}(\mathcal{A}) + \mathbf{LocalMem}(\mathrm{DH}) + 11\lambda + 2$$

3.2 ECIES

Let $\mathbb{G} = \langle g \rangle$ be a cyclic group of prime order q, equipped with a pairing $\hat{e} : \mathbb{G} \times \mathbb{G} \to \mathbb{G}_T$. Let $\mathtt{H} : \mathbb{G} \to \mathcal{K}$ be a hash function. In this section, we present a memory tight reduction of the underlying Key Encapsulation Mechanism of ECIES from the Computational Diffie-Hellman assumption over $\mathbb{G}$. We describe the ECIES KEM scheme in Fig. 11. Our main result in this section is the following theorem.

Procedure $\mathtt{Gen}(1^\lambda)$	Procedure $\mathtt{Encap}(pk)$	Procedure $\mathtt{Decap}(sk, Y)$
1 : $(q, g, \mathbb{G}) \leftarrow \mathtt{DH}(1^\lambda)$	1 : $(g, X) = pk$	1 : $x = sk$
2 : $x \xleftarrow{\$} \mathbb{Z}_p^*$	2 : $y \xleftarrow{\$} \mathbb{Z}_p^*$	2 : $Z = Y^x$
3 : $pk = (g, g^x)$	3 : $Y = g^y$	3 : $K = \mathtt{H}(Z)$
4 : $sk = x$	4 : $Z = X^y$	4 : **return** K
5 : **return** (pk, sk)	5 : $K = \mathtt{H}(Z)$	
	6 : **return** (Y, K)	

Fig. 11. ECIES KEM. $\mathtt{H} : \{0, 1\}^\lambda \times \mathbb{G} \to \mathcal{K}$ is a cryptographic hash function

Theorem 6 *Let q be a prime and $\mathbb{G}$ be a group of order q equipped with a pairing $\hat{e} : \mathbb{G} \times \mathbb{G} \to \mathbb{G}_T$. Let* DH *be the Diffie Hellman instance generation algorithm over $\mathbb{G}$. Let $F : \{0,1\}^\lambda \times \mathbb{G}_T \to \mathcal{K}$ be a prf. Let $\hat{\Pi}$ be the ECIES-KEM scheme over $\mathbb{G}$ and $\mathcal{K}$, with security parameter λ.*

Let $\mathcal{A}$ be an adversary in the IND-CCA *game of $\hat{\Pi}$. Suppose $\mathcal{A}$ makes q_h hash queries and q_D decapsulation queries. Then, in the random oracle model, there exists an adversary $\mathcal{B}_{DH}$ in the* CDH *game, and an adversary $\mathcal{B}_F$ such that*

$$\mathbf{Adv}^{\text{IND-CCA}}_{\mathcal{A},\hat{\Pi}} \leq \mathbf{Adv}^{\mathsf{CDH}}_{\mathcal{B}_{DH},\mathbb{G}} + \mathbf{Adv}^{\text{prf}}_{\mathcal{B}_F,F}$$

Moreover, it holds that

$$\begin{aligned}
\mathbf{LocalTime}(\mathcal{B}_{DH}) \approx & \mathbf{LocalTime}(\mathcal{A}) + (q_H + q_D)\mathbf{LocalTime}(F) \\
& + (q_D + 3q_H)\mathbf{LocalTime}(\hat{e}) \\
\mathbf{LocalMem}(\mathcal{B}_{DH}) \approx & \mathbf{LocalMem}(\mathcal{A}) + \mathbf{LocalMem}(F) + 7\lambda + 1 \\
\mathbf{LocalTime}(\mathcal{B}_F) \approx & \mathbf{LocalTime}(\mathcal{A}) + \mathbf{LocalTime}(\mathtt{DH}) + (q_H + q_D) \\
& (q_H + q_D)\mathbf{LocalTime}(\hat{e}) \\
\mathbf{LocalMem}(\mathcal{B}_F) \approx & \mathbf{LocalMem}(\mathcal{A}) + \mathbf{LocalMem}(\mathtt{DH}) + 12\lambda + 2
\end{aligned}$$

The reduction to prove Theorem 6 is almost the same as in the previous section. The only difference is in the construction of the intermediate prf $\hat{F}$ and the reduced CDH-adversary $\mathcal{B}_{DH}$. As the details are almost same to the reduction of HEG, we only describe $\hat{F}$ and $\mathcal{B}_{DH}$ here. The reader is referred to the full version of the paper [9] for the rest of the reduction.

Construction 7 (Construction of $\hat{F}$). *Let $\mathbb{G}$ be a group of prime order q and let g be a generator of $\mathbb{G}$. Let $\hat{e} : \mathbb{G} \times \mathbb{G} \to \mathbb{G}_T$ be a bilinear map. Let $F : \{0,1\}^\lambda \times \mathbb{G}_T \to \mathcal{K}$. We define $\hat{F} : \{0,1\}^\lambda \times \mathbb{G} \to \mathcal{K}$ as follows*

$$\hat{F}(k, Z) = F(k, \hat{e}(g, Z))$$

Lemma 4. *If F is a prf, then $\hat{F}$ is a prf. Moreover, for every adversary $\mathcal{B}_{\hat{F}}$ against $\hat{F}$, there exists a $\mathcal{B}_F$ against F such that,*

$$\begin{aligned}
\mathbf{Adv}^{\text{prf}}_{\mathcal{B}_F,F} &= \mathbf{Adv}^{\text{prf}}_{\mathcal{B}_{\hat{F}},\hat{F}} \\
\mathbf{LocalTime}(\mathcal{B}_F) &= \mathbf{LocalTime}(\mathcal{B}_{\hat{F}}) + q \cdot \mathbf{LocalTime}(\hat{e}) \\
\mathbf{LocalMem}(\mathcal{B}_F) &= \mathbf{LocalMem}(\mathcal{B}_{\hat{F}}) + 2\lambda.
\end{aligned}$$

where q is the number of queries made by $\mathcal{B}_{\hat{F}}$ to its oracle.

Description of $\mathcal{B}_{DH}$: The Adversary to Game CDH. Formal code of $\mathcal{B}_{DH}$ is given in Fig. 12. $\mathcal{B}_{DH}$ gets (g, X, Y^*) as input, where X, Y^* are distributed uniformly over $\mathbb{G}$. FLAG $= 1$ implies that $\mathcal{A}$ queried $\mathtt{H}(Z)$ where (X, Y^*, Z) is

Algorithm $\mathcal{B}_{DH}((g, X, Y^*))$

- Set $pk = (g, X)$
- $k \xleftarrow{\$} \{0,1\}^\lambda$
- $K^* \xleftarrow{\$} \mathcal{K}$
- $b^* \leftarrow \mathcal{A}^{\mathtt{Decap},\mathtt{H}}(pk, Y^*, K^*)$
- *output* $\perp$.

Procedure $\mathtt{Decap}(Y)$

- **if** $Y = Y^*$ **return** $\perp$
- $K = F(k, \hat{e}(X, Y))$
- **return** K

Procedure $\mathtt{H}(Z)$

- **if** $\hat{e}(g, Z) = \hat{e}(X, Y^*)$
  - FLAG $= 1$
  - Output Z
- **else**
  - $K = F(k, \hat{e}(g, Z))$
- **return** K
- **endif**

Fig. 12. Diffie Hellman adversary $\mathcal{B}_{DH}$

a valid Diffie Hellman tuple. If FLAG is set for some query made by $\mathcal{A}$, $\mathcal{B}_{DH}$ returns that corresponding Z and wins the CDH game.

Efficiency of $\mathcal{B}_{DH}$. $\mathcal{B}_{DH}$ runs $\mathcal{A}$, computes the pairing $\hat{e}(.,.)$ oracle for $q_D + 3q_H$ many times, computes the prf F for $(q_H + q_D)$ many times. As the rest of the steps in the algorithm takes $\mathcal{O}(\text{poly}(\lambda))$ time,

$$\begin{aligned}\mathbf{LocalTime}(\mathcal{B}_{DH}) \approx& \mathbf{LocalTime}(\mathcal{A}) + (q_H + q_D)\mathbf{LocalTime}(F) \\ &+ (q_D + 3q_H)\mathbf{LocalTime}(\hat{e})\end{aligned}$$

Memory Efficiency of $\mathcal{B}_{DH}$. $\mathcal{B}_{DH}$ needs to save the code of $\mathcal{A}$, $\hat{e}$, and F. Counting the registers, we get

$$\mathbf{LocalMem}(\mathcal{B}_{DH}) = \mathbf{LocalMem}(\mathcal{A}) + \mathbf{LocalMem}(F) + 7\lambda + 1$$

4 Transformation V: OW-PCA PKE to OW-PCVA PKE

In this section, we introduce a transformation V to construct OW-PCVA secure deterministic PKE from a OW-PCA secure PKE. Our main result is a memory-tight reduction of V. The main application of V will be in Sect. 5, where we shall use V to get a memory-tight reductions of the IND-CCA security of $\text{QKEM}^\perp$ and $\text{QKEM}^\perp_m$.

4.1 The Transformation

We start with a deterministic δ-correct OW-PCA secure public key encryption scheme, $\mathsf{PKE} = (\mathtt{Gen}, \mathtt{Enc}, \mathtt{Dec})$. Let $\mathcal{M} = \{0,1\}^n$ be the message space, and $\mathcal{C}$ be

Procedure $\text{Enc}_1(pk, m)$	Procedure $\text{Dec}_1(sk, c)$
$c_1 = \text{Enc}(pk, m)$	Parse $c = (c_1, c_2)$
$c_2 = \text{H}'(m)$	$m' = \text{Dec}(sk, c_1)$
$c = c_1 \| c_2$	**if** $m' = \perp \vee \text{H}'(m') \neq c_2 \ \vee \text{Enc}(pk, m') \neq c_1$
return c	**return** $\perp$
	else return m'

Fig. 13. OW-PCVA secure encryption scheme $\mathsf{PKE}_1 = V[\mathsf{PKE}]$

the ciphertext space. Let $\text{H}' : \mathcal{M} \to \{0,1\}^\eta$ be a hash function. The transformed scheme is described as $\mathsf{PKE}_1 = (\text{Gen}, \text{Enc}_1, \text{Dec}_1)$.
Our main result of this section is the following theorem.

Theorem 8. *Let* $\mathsf{PKE} = (\text{Gen}, \text{Enc}, \text{Dec})$ *be a deterministic* δ *correct* OW-PCA *secure public key encryption scheme. Let* $\mathcal{M}$ *be the message space, and* $\mathcal{C}$ *be the ciphertext space of* PKE. *Let* PKE_1 *be the transformed public encryption scheme. Let* $F' : \{0,1\}^\lambda \times \mathcal{C} \to \{0,1\}^\eta$ *be a prf. Let* $\mathcal{A}$ *be any adversary in the* OW-PCVA *game of* PKE_1. *Suppose* $\mathcal{A}$ *makes* $q_{h'}$ *queries to* H'. *Let* q_P *denote the number of plaintext checking queries and* q_V *denote the number of validity checking queries made by* $\mathcal{A}$.

PKE_1 *is* δ*-correct. Moreover, in the random oracle model, there exists an adversary* $\mathcal{B}$ *in the* OW-PCA *game of* PKE_1, *and an adversary* $\mathcal{B}_{F'}$ *in the* prf *game of* F', *such that*

$$\mathbf{Adv}^{\text{OW-PCVA}}_{\mathcal{A},\mathsf{PKE}_1} \leq \mathbf{Adv}^{\text{OW-PCA}}_{\mathcal{B},\mathsf{PKE}} + 2 \cdot \mathbf{Adv}^{\text{prf}}_{\mathcal{B}_{F'},F'} + \frac{q_V}{2^\eta} + 2\delta(1 + q_{h'} + q_P + q_V)$$

Moreover it holds that

$$\begin{aligned}
\mathbf{LocalTime}(\mathcal{B}) \approx & \mathbf{LocalTime}(\mathcal{A}) + q_{h'}\mathbf{LocalTime}(\text{Enc}) \\
& + (1 + q_{h'} + q_V + q_P)\mathbf{LocalTime}(F') + q_P \\
\mathbf{LocalMem}(\mathcal{B}) \approx & \mathbf{LocalMem}(\mathcal{A}) + \mathbf{LocalMem}(F') \\
& + \mathbf{LocalMem}(\text{Enc}) + 8\lambda \\
\mathbf{LocalTime}(\mathcal{B}_{F'}) \approx & \mathbf{LocalTime}(\mathcal{A}) + \mathbf{LocalTime}(\text{Gen}) + (q_V + q_P)\mathbf{LocalTime}(\text{Dec}) \\
& + (1 + q_V + q_P + q_{h'})(1 + 2 \cdot \mathbf{LocalTime}(\text{Enc})) \\
\mathbf{LocalMem}(\mathcal{B}_{F'}) \approx & \mathbf{LocalMem}(\mathcal{A}) + \mathbf{LocalMem}(\text{Gen}) + +\mathbf{LocalMem}(\text{Enc}) \\
& + \mathbf{LocalMem}(\text{Dec}) + 11\lambda + 1
\end{aligned}$$

Similar to previous section, we first construct a prf $\hat{F}$.

4.2 Construction of $\hat{F}$

Construction 9. *Fix a public key* pk *of* PKE. *Let* $F' : \{0,1\}^\lambda \times \mathcal{C} \to \{0,1\}^\eta$. *We define* $\hat{F}$ *as*

$$\hat{F}(k, m) = F'(k, \text{Enc}(pk, m))$$

In order to use the map then prf technique, we need the following lemma.

Lemma 5. *Fix pk. For every* prf*-adversary $\mathcal{B}_{\hat{F}}$ against $\hat{F}$, there exists a $\mathcal{B}_{F'}$ against F' such that,*

$$\begin{aligned}\mathbf{Adv}^{\mathrm{prf}}_{\mathcal{B}_{\hat{F}},\hat{F}} &\leq \mathbf{Adv}^{\mathrm{prf}}_{\mathcal{B}_{F'},F'} + \delta(q)\\ \mathbf{LocalTime}(\mathcal{B}_{F'}) &= \mathbf{LocalTime}(\mathcal{B}_{\hat{F}}) + q \cdot \mathbf{LocalTime}(\mathtt{Enc})\\ \mathbf{LocalMem}(\mathcal{B}_{F'}) &= \mathbf{LocalMem}(\mathcal{B}_{\hat{F}}) + 3\lambda.\end{aligned}$$

where q is the number of queries made by $\mathcal{B}_{\hat{F}}$.

The main difference in Lemma 5 with the ones in the previous section is the decryption error of PKE. In other words, we can not claim that $\mathtt{Enc}(pk, .)$ is an injective function. However, if $\mathcal{B}_{\hat{F}}$ can query with messages m_1, m_2 such that $\mathtt{Enc}(pk, m_1) = \mathtt{Enc}(pk, m_2)$, implying a decryption error for either m_1 or m_2.

Proof. First, we prove that if F' is a prf, then $\hat{F}$ is a prf. Let $\mathtt{O}$ be the oracle of $\mathcal{B}_{F'}$. $\mathcal{B}_{F'}$ runs $\mathtt{Gen}$ to receive pk, sk, and invokes $\mathcal{B}_{\hat{F}}$. For every query m of $\mathcal{B}_{\hat{F}}$, $\mathcal{B}_{F'}$, computes $c = \mathtt{Enc}(pk, m)$, and checks whether $m = \mathtt{Dec}(sk, c)$. If the check fails $\mathcal{B}_{F'}$ aborts. If the check succeeds, $\mathcal{B}_{F'}$ queries $\mathtt{O}(c)$, and the response of the oracle is passed to $\mathcal{B}_{\hat{F}}$. When $\mathcal{B}_{\hat{F}}$ outputs a bit b, $\mathcal{B}_F$ outputs b.

If $\mathcal{B}_{F'}$ aborts on input m, then correctness error occurs in $\mathtt{Dec}(sk, \mathtt{Enc}(pk, m))$. By assumption, probability of this event is bounded by $\delta(q)$. Conditioned on that $\mathcal{B}_{F'}$ does not abort, the output of $\mathtt{Enc}(pk, m)$ are unique for all m queried by $\mathcal{B}_{\hat{F}}$. In that case, $\mathcal{B}_{F'}$ perfectly simulates the prf game of $\hat{F}$. When $\mathtt{O}$ is a random function, the simulation implements a random function. When $\mathtt{O}$ is implemented by F', $\mathcal{B}_{F'}$ implements $\hat{F}$. Thus we get,

$$\begin{aligned}&\mathbf{Succ}_{\mathcal{B}_{\hat{F}},\mathrm{prf}[\hat{F}]} = \mathbf{Succ}_{\mathcal{B}_{F'},\mathrm{prf}[F']} + \mathrm{Prob}[\mathcal{B}_{F'} \text{ aborts}] \leq \mathbf{Succ}_{\mathcal{B}_{F'},\mathrm{prf}[F']} + \delta(q)\\ &\implies \mathbf{Adv}^{\mathrm{prf}}_{\mathcal{B}_{\hat{F}},\hat{F}} \leq \mathbf{Adv}^{\mathrm{prf}}_{\mathcal{B}_{F'},F'} + \delta(q)\end{aligned}$$

In order to simulate the prf game of $\hat{F}$, $\mathcal{B}_F$ needs to run $\mathtt{Enc}$ for q many times. Moreover, $\mathcal{B}_F$ needs store pk, sk and a temporary variable for passing the values. The lemma follows.

4.3 Proof of Theorem 8

It is obvious that the correctness holds. We prove rest of Theorem 8 via a sequence of games. Formal description of the games are given in the Figs. 14 and 15.

Game $\mathbf{G}_0$. G_0 is the OW-PCVA security game of PKE_1.

$$\mathbf{Adv}^{\text{OW-PCVA}}_{\mathcal{A},\mathsf{PKE}_1} = \mathrm{Prob}[G_0^{\mathcal{A}} = 1]$$

$\mathbf{G_0}$, $\boxed{\mathbf{G_1}\text{-}\mathbf{G_7}}$
$(pk, sk) \xleftarrow{\$} \texttt{Gen}$
$m^* \xleftarrow{\$} \mathcal{M}$
$\boxed{k' \xleftarrow{\$} \{0,1\}^\lambda}$
$c_2 = \texttt{H}'(m^*)$
$c_1 = \texttt{Enc}(pk, m^*)$
$c^* = (c_1, c_2)$
$m \leftarrow \mathcal{A}^{\texttt{PCO},\texttt{CVO},\texttt{H}'}(pk, c^*)$
if $m^* = m$ **return** 1
else **return** 0

Game $\mathbf{G_0}$

Procedure $\texttt{PCO}(m, c)$
Parse $c = c_1 \| c_2$
$m' = \texttt{Dec}(sk, c_1)$
$c_1' = \texttt{Enc}(pk, m')$
$c_2' = \texttt{H}'(m')$
$c' = c_1' \| c_2'$
if $m' = m$ and $c' = c$
return 1
else
return 0

Procedure $\texttt{H}'(m)$
if $\texttt{H}'(m)$ is undefined
$\texttt{H}'(m) \xleftarrow{\$} \mathcal{M}$
endif
return $\texttt{H}'(m)$

Procedure $\texttt{CVO}(c)$
Parse $c = c_1 \| c_2$
$m' = \texttt{Dec}(sk, c_1)$
$c_1' = \texttt{Enc}(pk, m')$
$c_2' = \texttt{H}'(m')$
$c' = c_1' \| c_2'$
if $m' \in \mathcal{M}$ and $c' = c$
return 1
else
return 0

Fig. 14. The main function of games $\mathbf{G_0} - \mathbf{G_7}$. The boxed statement is not executed in $\mathbf{G_0}$. Right hand side figure describes the oracles in $\mathbf{G_0}$

Game $\mathbf{G_1}$. In this game, we replace $\texttt{H}'$ by prf $\hat{F}$. By Lemma 1, there exists adversary, $\mathcal{B}_{\hat{F}}$ such that

$$\left|\text{Prob}[G_1^{\mathcal{A}} = 1] - \text{Prob}[G_0^f = 1]\right| \leq \mathbf{Adv}^{\text{prf}}_{\mathcal{B}_{\hat{F}}, \hat{F}} \tag{1}$$

Game $\mathbf{G_2}$. In this game, we modify the $\texttt{PCO}(m, c = (c_1, c_2))$ oracle simulation. Instead of the decryption, $m' = \texttt{Dec}(sk, c_1)$, and equality check $m = m'$, we only check whether, $c_1 = \texttt{Enc}(pk, m)$. Notice, the condition $c_2 = \hat{F}(k', m)$ remains unchanged. Conditioned on correctness error does not happen, $c_1' = c_1 = \texttt{Enc}(pk, m)$ implies that $m' = \texttt{Dec}(sk, c_1') = m$. Hence, this change does not affect the transcript distribution until correctness error occurs in PKE.

$$\left|\text{Prob}[G_1^{\mathcal{A}} = 1] - \text{Prob}[G_2^{\mathcal{A}} = 1]\right| \leq \delta(q_P)$$

Game $\mathbf{G_3}$. In this game we replace $\hat{F}$ as defined. The change is syntactical and does not change the distribution of any output.

$$\text{Prob}[G_2^{\mathcal{A}} = 1] = \text{Prob}[G_3^{\mathcal{A}} = 1]$$

Game $\mathbf{G_4}$. In this game, we change how the oracles PCO and CVO responds. For a $\texttt{PCO}(m, c)$ query, we no longer encrypt m to compute c_2'. Instead, we run the plaintext checking oracle $\overline{\texttt{PCO}}$, provided for PKE, to check correctness of (m, c_1). If c_1 is indeed a valid ciphertext of m, then by deterministic property of PKE, $F'(k, \texttt{Enc}(pk, m))$ is equal to $F'(k, c_1)$. Hence we only check whether

Game $\mathbf{G_1}$

Procedure $\mathtt{H}'(m)$

1 : $h' = \hat{F}(k', m)$
2 : **return** h'

Procedure $\mathtt{PCO}(m, c)$

1 : Parse $c = c_1 || c_2$
2 : $m' = \mathtt{Dec}(sk, c_1)$
3 : $c_1' = \mathtt{Enc}(pk, m')$
4 : $c_2' = \hat{F}(k', m')$
5 : $c' = c_1' || c_2'$
6 : **if** $m' = m$ and $c' = c$
7 : **return** 1
8 : **else**
9 : **return** 0

Procedure $\mathtt{CVO}(c)$

1 : Parse $c = c_1 || c_2$
2 : $m' = \mathtt{Dec}(sk, c_1)$
3 : $c_1' = \mathtt{Enc}(pk, m')$
4 : $c_2' = \hat{F}(k', m')$
5 : $c' = c_1' || c_2'$
6 : **if** $m' \in \mathcal{M}$ and $c' = c$
7 : **return** 1
8 : **else**
9 : **return** 0

Game $\mathbf{G_2}$

Procedure $\mathtt{H}'(m)$

1 : $h' = \hat{F}(k', m)$
2 : **return** h'

Procedure $\mathtt{PCO}(m, c)$

1 : Parse $c = c_1 || c_2$
2 : $c_2' = \hat{F}(k', m)$
3 : **if** $c_2' = c_2 \wedge \mathtt{Enc}(pk, m) = c_1$
4 : **return** 1
5 : **else**
6 : **return** 0

Procedure $\mathtt{CVO}(c)$

1 : Parse $c = c_1 || c_2$
2 : $m' = \mathtt{Dec}(sk, c_1)$
3 : $c_1' = \mathtt{Enc}(pk, m')$
4 : $c_2' = \hat{F}(k', m')$
5 : $c' = c_1' || c_2'$
6 : **if** $m' \in \mathcal{M}$ and $c' = c$
7 : **return** 1
8 : **else**
9 : **return** 0

Game $\mathbf{G_3}$

Procedure $\mathtt{H}'(m)$

1 : $c = \mathtt{Enc}(pk, m)$
2 : $h' = F'(k', c)$
3 : **return** h'

Procedure $\mathtt{PCO}(m, c)$

1 : Parse $c = c_1 || c_2$
2 : $c_1' = \mathtt{Enc}(pk, m)$
3 : $c_2' = F'(k', c_1')$
4 : **if** $c_2' = c_2 \wedge c_1' = c_1$
5 : **return** 1
6 : **else**
7 : **return** 0

Procedure $\mathtt{CVO}(c)$

1 : Parse $c = c_1 || c_2$
2 : $m' = \mathtt{Dec}(sk, c_1)$
3 : $c_1' = \mathtt{Enc}(pk, m')$
4 : $c_2' = F'(k', c_1')$
5 : $c' = c_1' || c_2'$
6 : **if** $m' \in \mathcal{M}$ and $c' = c$
7 : **return** 1
8 : **else**
9 : **return** 0

Fig. 15. The oracles in $\mathbf{G_1}, \mathbf{G_2}, \mathbf{G_3}$

$F'(k, c_1) = c_2$. The change in $\mathtt{PCO}$ is syntactical, and does not change output distribution of the oracle.

Similarly, in $\mathtt{CVO}$, we change the computation of c_2', which is now computed as $F(k', c_1)$. If $c_1 = c_1'$, then the change is syntactical and has no effect in the check in Step 5. If $c_1 \neq c_1'$, the condition in Step 5 rejects irrespective of the value of c_2'. Hence, this change does not change the output distribution of the oracles as well.

$$\text{Prob}[G_3^{\mathcal{A}} = 1] = \text{Prob}[G_4^{\mathcal{A}} = 1]$$

Game $\mathbf{G_5}$. We change the description of the oracle $\mathtt{CVO}(c)$. We raise a flag BAD, if $c_2' = c_2$ but c_1 is not a valid ciphertext of PKE, i.e $m' \notin \mathcal{M}$ or $c_1 \neq \mathtt{Enc}(pk, m')$ where $m' = \mathtt{Dec}(c_1)$. However, we do not change the output of the oracle. $\mathtt{CVO}(c)$ still return 0 when BAD is set.

$$\text{Prob}[G_4^{\mathcal{A}} = 1] = \text{Prob}[G_5^{\mathcal{A}} = 1]$$

Game $\mathbf{G_4}$

Procedure $\mathtt{H}'(m)$

```
c = Enc(pk, m)
h' = F'(k', c)
return h'
```

Procedure $\mathtt{PCO}(m, c)$

```
Parse c = c1||c2
if PCO‾(m, c1) = 1
   c2' = F'(k', c1)
   if c2' = c2
      return 1
endif
endif
return 0
```

Procedure $\mathtt{CVO}(c)$

```
Parse c = c1||c2
m' = Dec(sk, c1)
c1' = Enc(pk, m')
c2' = F'(k', c1)
if c2' = c2 ∧ m' ∈ M ∧ c1' = c1
   return 1
else
   return 0
```

Game $\mathbf{G_5}$ $\boxed{\mathbf{G_6}}$

Procedure $\mathtt{H}'(m)$

```
c = Enc(pk, m)
h' = F'(k', c)
return h'
```

Procedure $\mathtt{PCO}(m, c)$

```
Parse c = c1||c2
if PCO‾(m, c1) = 1
   c2' = F'(k', c1)
   if c2' = c2
      return 1
endif
endif
return 0
```

Procedure $\mathtt{CVO}(c)$

```
Parse c = c1||c2
m' = Dec(sk, c1)
c1' = Enc(pk, m')
c2' = F'(k', c1)
if c2' = c2
   if m' ∉ M or c1' ≠ c1
      Bad = 1
      return 0 [return 1]
   else
      return 1
   endif
else
   return 0
```

Game $\mathbf{G_7}$

Procedure $\mathtt{H}'(m)$

```
c = Enc(pk, m)
h' = F'(k', c)
return h'
```

Procedure $\mathtt{PCO}(m, c)$

```
Parse c = c1||c2
if PCO‾(m, c1) = 1
   c2' = F'(k', c1)
   if c2' = c2
      return 1
endif
endif
return 0
```

Procedure $\mathtt{CVO}(c)$

```
Parse c = c1||c2
c2' = F'(k', c1)
if c2' = c2
   return 1
else
   return 0
```

Fig. 16. The oracles in $\mathbf{G_4}, \mathbf{G_5}, \mathbf{G_6}, \mathbf{G_7}$. $\overline{\mathtt{PCO}}$ is the plaintext checking oracle for PKE.

Game $\mathbf{G_6}$. In game $\mathbf{G_6}$, $\mathtt{CVO}(c)$ returns 1, when BAD is set. Rest of the games remain unchanged. By the fundamental lemma of game playing proofs,

$$\left|\mathrm{Prob}[G_5^{\mathcal{A}} = 1] - \mathrm{Prob}[G_6^{\mathcal{A}} = 1]\right| \leq \mathrm{Prob}[\mathrm{BAD}]$$

Note, in the game $\mathbf{G_6}$, the oracle $\mathtt{CVO}$ returns 1, if and only if $c_2 = F'(k', c_1)$.
Game $\mathbf{G_7}$. We rewrite the description of $\mathtt{CVO}(c)$. We no longer run $\mathtt{Dec}$ and $\mathtt{Enc}$. The oracle $\mathtt{CVO}(c)$ parses c as $c_1||c_2$, and returns 1 if $c_2 = F'(k', c_1)$ and returns 0 otherwise. Rest of the game remain unchanged. As the output distribution of all the procedures in $\mathbf{G_7}$ is same as that in $\mathbf{G_6}$.

$$\mathrm{Prob}[G_6^{\mathcal{A}} = 1] = \mathrm{Prob}[G_7^{\mathcal{A}} = 1]$$

Bounding Prob[$G_7^{\mathcal{A}} = 1$]. In Fig. 17, we construct an adversary $\mathcal{B}$ against OW-PCA security of PKE. $\mathcal{B}$ receives (pk, c^*), invokes $\mathcal{A}(pk, c^*)$ and perfectly simulates the game $\mathbf{G_7}$ for $\mathcal{A}$. When $\mathcal{A}$ returns a message m, $\mathcal{B}$ returns m.

$$\text{Prob}[G_7^{\mathcal{A}} = 1] = \mathbf{Adv}_{\mathcal{B}, PKE}^{\text{OW-PCA}}$$

Algorithm $\mathcal{B}^{\overline{\text{PCO}}(\cdot)}(pk, c)$	Procedure $\text{H}'(m)$
1: $\quad k' \xleftarrow{\$} \{0,1\}^\lambda$	1: $\quad c = \text{Enc}(pk, m)$
2: $\quad c_2 = F'(k', c')$	2: $\quad h' = F'(k', c)$
3: $\quad c^* = c \| c_2$	3: $\quad$ **return** h'
4: $\quad m \leftarrow \mathcal{A}^{\text{PCO}(\cdot), \text{CVO}(\cdot), \text{H}'}(pk, c^*)$	
5: $\quad$ **return** m	Procedure $\text{PCO}(m, c)$
	1: $\quad$ Parse $c = c_1 \| c_2$
Procedure $\text{CVO}(c)$	2: $\quad$ **if** $\overline{\text{PCO}}(m, c_1) = 1$
	3: $\qquad c_2' = F'(k', c_1)$
1: $\quad$ Parse $c = c_1 \| c_2$	4: $\qquad$ **if** $c_2' = c_2$
2: $\quad c_2' = F'(k', c_1)$	5: $\qquad\quad$ **return** 1
3: $\quad$ **if** $c_2' = c_2$	6: $\qquad$ **endif**
4: $\qquad$ **return** 1	7: $\quad$ **endif**
5: $\quad$ **else**	8: $\quad$ **return** 0
6: $\qquad$ **return** 0	

Fig. 17. OW-PCA adversary $\mathcal{B}$

Efficiency of $\mathcal{B}$. Algorithm $\mathcal{B}$ runs $\mathcal{A}$, queries PCO for q_P many times, runs Enc for $q_{h'}$ many times, and computes F' for $(1 + q_{h'} + q_V + q_P)$ many times. Rest of the steps take $\mathcal{O}(\text{poly}(\lambda))$ time.

$$\mathbf{LocalTime}(\mathcal{B}) = \mathbf{LocalTime}(\mathcal{A}) + q_{h'}\mathbf{LocalTime}(\text{Enc})$$
$$+ (1 + q_{h'} + q_V + q_P)\mathbf{LocalTime}(F') + \mathcal{O}(\text{poly}(\lambda)) + q_P$$

The last q_P term in the right hand side denotes the number of queries made to PCO.

Memory Efficiency of $\mathcal{B}$. $\mathcal{B}$ needs to save the code of $\mathcal{A}$, Enc, and F'. In addition, there are following λ size registers, $c^*, c_1, c_2, k', m, c, c_2', h'$.

$$\mathbf{LocalMem}(\mathcal{B}) = \mathbf{LocalMem}(\mathcal{A}) + \mathbf{LocalMem}(F')$$
$$+ \mathbf{LocalMem}(\text{Enc}) + 8\lambda$$

Bounding Prob[BAD]. To bound Prob[BAD], we construct a prf adversary $\mathcal{B}_{F'}^{(1)}$ against F'. Recall that BAD occurs when for a $\text{CVO}(c)$ query, we get

$$c_2' = c_2 \text{ and } (m' \notin \mathcal{M} \text{ or } c_1' \neq c_1)$$

where $c = c_1 \| c_2$, $m' = \text{Dec}(sk, c_1)$, $c_1' = \text{Enc}(pk, m')$, and $c_2' = F'(k', c_1)$.

Case $m' \in \mathcal{M}$ **and** $c_1' \neq c_1$. In this case correctness error occurs in PKE. Probability of this event is bounded by $\delta(q_V)$.

Case $m' \notin \mathcal{M}$. In this case, for an invalid ciphertext c_1 in PKE, $\mathcal{A}$ can produce a c_2 such that $c_2 = F'(k', c_1)$. As $\mathcal{A}$ has no direct access to $F'(k', .)$ evaluation, and c_1 is an invalid ciphertext, there is no $H'(m)$ or PCO(m, c) query in the transcript for which $F'(k', c_1)$ was evaluated. Notice that, in PCO(m, c) evaluates $F'(k', c_1)$ only when PCO$(m, c_1) = 1$, which can not occur here. So, BAD $= 1$ implies that $\mathcal{A}$ can "guess" the output of $F'(k', c_1)$ for some $c_1 \in \mathcal{C}$. For random function this can happen with probability $\frac{q_V}{2^\eta}$. If BAD happens in significantly more probability in $\mathcal{G}_5$, that can be used to break the prf security of F'.

Formal description of $\mathcal{B}_{F'}^{(1)}$ is given in Fig. 18. $\mathcal{B}_{F'}^{(1)}$ perfectly simulates game G_5 with the help of its oracle $O_{F'}$. If $\mathcal{A}$ ever submits a CVO(c) query for which BAD occurs, $\mathcal{B}_{F'}^{(1)}$ outputs 1 and halts. If no such query is made, then at the end of the simulation, $\mathcal{B}_{F'}^{(1)}$ outputs 0. If $O_{F'}$ is a random function, then for a fixed CVO(c) query, Prob$[\mathcal{B}_{F'}^{(1)} = 1]$ is at most $\frac{1}{2^\eta}$. Taking union bound over all the CVO(c) queries made by $\mathcal{A}$, when $O_{F'}$ is a random function, Prob$[\mathcal{B}_{F'}^{(1)} = 1]$ is at most $\frac{q_V}{2^\eta}$. When $O_{F'}$ is the prf F', Prob$[\mathcal{B}_{F'}^{(1)} = 1]$ is exactly Prob[BAD] in G_5.

$\mathcal{B}_{F'}^{(1)}$	Procedure H$'(m)$	Procedure CVO(c)
1: $(pk, sk) \xleftarrow{\$} \mathsf{Gen}$	1: $c = \mathsf{Enc}(pk, m)$	1: Parse $c = c_1 \| c_2$
2: $m^* \xleftarrow{\$} \mathcal{M}$	2: $h' = 0_{F'}(c)$	2: $m' = \mathsf{Dec}(sk, c_1)$
3: $c_2 = 0_{F'}(m^*)$	3: **return** h'	3: $c_1' = \mathsf{Enc}(pk, m')$
4: $c_1 = \mathsf{Enc}(pk, m^*)$		4: $c_2' = 0_{F'}(c_1)$
5: $c^* = (c_1, c_2)$	Procedure PCO(m, c)	5: **if** $c_2' = c_2$
6: BAD $= 0$	1: Parse $c = c_1 \| c_2$	6: **if** $m' \notin \mathcal{M}$ or $c_1' \neq c_1$
7: $m \leftarrow \mathcal{A}^{\mathsf{PCO,CVO,H}'}(pk, c^*)$	2: **if** $\mathsf{Enc}(pk, m) = c_1$	7: BAD $= 1$
8: **if** BAD $= 1$	3: $c_2' = 0_{F'}(c_1)$	8: **return** 0
9: **Output** 1	4: **if** $c_2' = c_2$	9: **else**
10: **else**	5: **return** 1	10: **return** 1
11: **Output** 0	6: **endif**	11: **endif**
	7: **endif**	12: **else**
	8: **return** 0	13: **return** 0

Fig. 18. The PRF adversary $\mathcal{B}_{F'}^{(1)}$

$$\mathbf{Adv}_{\mathcal{B}_{F'}^{(1)}, F'}^{\mathrm{prf}} \geq \left| \mathrm{Prob}[\mathrm{BAD}] - \frac{q_V}{2^\eta} - \delta(q_V) \right|$$

$$\implies \mathrm{Prob}[\mathrm{BAD}] \leq \mathbf{Adv}_{\mathcal{B}_{F'}^{(1)}, F'}^{\mathrm{prf}} + \frac{q_V}{2^\eta} + \delta(q_V)$$

Efficiency of $\mathcal{B}_{F'}^{(1)}$. $\mathcal{B}_{F'}^{(1)}$ runs $\mathcal{A}$ once, algorithm Gen once, algorithm Enc for $(1 + q_{h'} + q_P + q_V)$ times, and Dec for q_V times. Additionally $\mathcal{B}_{F'}^{(1)}$ queries the oracle $\mathsf{O}_{F'}$ for $(1 + q_{h'} + q_P + q_V)$ times.

$$\begin{aligned}\mathbf{LocalTime}(\mathcal{B}_{F'}^{(1)}) \approx &\mathbf{LocalTime}(\mathcal{A}) + \mathbf{LocalTime}(\mathtt{Gen}) + q_V \cdot \mathbf{LocalTime}(\mathtt{Dec}) \\ &+ (1 + q_{h'} + q_P + q_V)(1 + \mathbf{LocalTime}(\mathtt{Enc}))\end{aligned}$$

$\mathcal{B}_{F'}^{(1)}$ needs to save the code of $\mathcal{A}$, Gen, Enc, and Dec. In addition, it needs to save eight λ size and a flag of a single bit. registers.

$$\begin{aligned}\mathbf{LocalMem}(\mathcal{B}_{F'}^{(1)}) \approx &\mathbf{LocalMem}(\mathcal{A}) + \mathbf{LocalMem}(\mathtt{Gen}) + \mathbf{LocalMem}(\mathtt{Enc}) \\ &+ \mathbf{LocalMem}(\mathtt{Dec}) + 8\lambda + 1\end{aligned}$$

Finishing the Proof of Theorem 8. Collecting the probabilities of the games, we have proven so far, there exist adversaries $\mathcal{B}, \mathcal{B}_{\hat{F}}$, and $\mathcal{B}_{F'}^{(1)}$, such that

$$\mathbf{Adv}_{\mathcal{A},\mathsf{PKE}_1}^{\text{OW-PCVA}} \leq \mathbf{Adv}_{\mathcal{B},\mathsf{PKE}}^{\text{OW-PCA}} + \mathbf{Adv}_{\mathcal{B}_{\hat{F}},\hat{F}}^{\text{prf}} + \mathbf{Adv}_{\mathcal{B}_{F'}^{(1)},F'}^{\text{prf}} + \frac{q_V}{2^\eta} + \delta(q_V) + \delta(q_p)$$

Applying Lemma 5, we get a $\mathcal{B}_{F'}^{(2)}$ such that,

$$\begin{aligned}\mathbf{Adv}_{\mathcal{A},\mathsf{PKE}_1}^{\text{OW-PCVA}} \leq &\mathbf{Adv}_{\mathcal{B},\mathsf{PKE}}^{\text{OW-PCA}} + \mathbf{Adv}_{\mathcal{B}_{F'}^{(2)},F'}^{\text{prf}} + \mathbf{Adv}_{\mathcal{B}_{F'}^{(1)},F'}^{\text{prf}} + \frac{q_V}{2^\eta} \\ &+ \delta(q_V) + \delta(q_p) + \delta(1 + q_{h'} + q_P + q_V)\end{aligned}$$

Efficiency of $\mathcal{B}_{F'}^{(2)}$ is bounded using following lemma.

Lemma 6

$$\begin{aligned}\mathbf{LocalTime}(\mathcal{B}_{F'}^{(2)}) \approx &\mathbf{LocalTime}(\mathcal{A}) + \mathbf{LocalTime}(\mathtt{Gen}) + (q_V + q_P)\mathbf{LocalTime}(\mathtt{Dec}) \\ &+ (2 + 2q_V + 2q_P + q_{h'})\mathbf{LocalTime}(\mathtt{Enc}) + (1 + q_{h'} + q_P + q_V) \\ \mathbf{LocalMem}(\mathcal{B}_{F'}^{(2)}) \approx &\mathbf{LocalMem}(\mathcal{A}) + \mathbf{LocalMem}(\mathtt{Gen}) + \mathbf{LocalMem}(\mathtt{Enc}) \\ &+ \mathbf{LocalMem}(\mathtt{Dec}) + 11\lambda\end{aligned}$$

Merging $\mathcal{B}_{F'}^{(1)}$ and $\mathcal{B}_{F'}^{(2)}$ into one adversary $\mathcal{B}_{F'}$, and taking upper bound of their efficiencies, we get Theorem 8.

5 Memory-Tight Reductions for Fujisaki-Okamoto Transformation and Variants

In this section, we prove memory-tight reduction of the IND-CCA security of four different variants of the Fujisaki-Okamoto transformation, following the modular approach of [16]. Before describing the exact transformations we consider, first we recall the modules introduces in [16].

5.1 Brief Overview of Modules from [16]

We recall the modules in the top-down fashion. First we describe the transformations from a public key encryption scheme to a key encapsulation mechanisms.

Table 2. Variants of transformation U. In the column $\mathtt{Decap}$, s is a random string, $sk' = sk||s$, and $m = \mathtt{Dec}_1(sk, c)$.

Transformations & security implications	$\mathtt{Encap}(pk)$	$\mathtt{Decap}(sk', c)$
$\mathrm{U}^{\not\perp}$(OW-PCA $\Rightarrow$ IND-CCA)	$(c = \mathtt{Enc}_1(pk, m), K = \mathtt{H}(m, c))_{m \xleftarrow{\$} \mathcal{M}}$	$\mathtt{H}(m, c)$ if $m \neq \perp$ $\mathtt{H}(s, c)$ if $m = \perp$
$\mathrm{U}^{\not\perp}_{m}$(det + OW-CPA $\Rightarrow$ IND-CCA)	$(c = \mathtt{Enc}_1(pk, m), K = \mathtt{H}(m))_{m \xleftarrow{\$} \mathcal{M}}$	$\mathtt{H}(m)$ if $m \neq \perp$ $\mathtt{H}(s, c)$ if $m = \perp$
$\mathrm{U}^{\perp}$(OW-PCVA $\Rightarrow$ IND-CCA)	$(c = \mathtt{Enc}_1(pk, m), K = \mathtt{H}(m, c))_{m \xleftarrow{\$} \mathcal{M}}$	$\mathtt{H}(m, c)$ if $m \neq \perp$ $\perp$ if $m = \perp$
$\mathrm{U}^{\perp}_{m}$(det + OW-VA $\Rightarrow$ IND-CCA)	$(c = \mathtt{Enc}_1(pk, m), K = \mathtt{H}(m))_{m \xleftarrow{\$} \mathcal{M}}$	$\mathtt{H}(m)$ if $m \neq \perp$ $\perp$ if $m = \perp$

Outer Modules: $\mathrm{U}^{\not\perp}$, $\mathrm{U}^{\not\perp}_{m}$, $\mathrm{U}^{\perp}$, $\mathrm{U}^{\perp}_{m}$**.** Let $\mathsf{PKE}_1 = (\mathtt{Gen}_1, \mathtt{Enc}_1, \mathtt{Dec}_1)$ be a public key encryption scheme with the message space $\mathcal{M}$ and let $\mathtt{H} : \mathcal{M} \rightarrow \mathcal{K}$ be a hash function. Table 2 describes the variants of module U to construct a KEM using PKE_1 and $\mathtt{H}$. The transformations yield KEM of two categories. Transformations $\mathrm{U}^{\not\perp}$ and $\mathrm{U}^{\not\perp}_{m}$ are in the category of implicit rejection, as the decapsulation algorithms in these transformations do not output $\perp$, when queried with an invalid ciphertext. Transformation $\mathrm{U}^{\perp}$, $\mathrm{U}^{\perp}_{m}$ are in the category of explicit rejection, implying that the decapsulation algorithms, given any invalid ciphertext, indeed output $\perp$.

Inner Module: *T*. Let $\overline{\mathsf{PKE}} = (\mathtt{Gen}, \overline{\mathtt{Enc}}, \overline{\mathtt{Dec}})$ be an IND-CPA secure public key encryption scheme. Let $\mathcal{M} = \{0, 1\}^n$ be the message space, $\mathcal{C}$ be the ciphertext space, and $\mathcal{R}$ be the randomness space. Let $\mathtt{G} : \mathcal{M} \rightarrow \mathcal{R}$ be a hash function. The transformation T results in a deterministic public key encryption scheme $\mathsf{PKE} = T[\overline{\mathsf{PKE}}, \mathtt{G}]$. Formal description of T is given in Fig. 19.

Procedure $\mathtt{Enc}(pk, m)$	Procedure $\mathtt{Dec}(sk, c)$
$c = \overline{\mathtt{Enc}}(pk, m; \mathtt{G}(m))$	$m' = \overline{\mathtt{Dec}}(sk, c)$
return c	**if** $m' = \perp \vee \overline{\mathtt{Enc}}(pk, m'; \mathtt{G}(m')) \neq c$
	return $\perp$
	else return m'

Fig. 19. Encryption scheme $\mathsf{PKE} = T[\overline{\mathsf{PKE}}]$

5.2 Considered Variants and the Reductions

We consider three other variants of FO transformations. The variants and their modular decomposition are listed in Table 3. For each transformation we start with an IND-CPA secure public key encryption $\overline{PKE}$. We prove memory-tight reduction for each of the modules next.

Table 3. Variants of FO transformations and their modular breakup

Category	Transformation	Modular decomposition
Implicit rejection	$\mathrm{KEM}^{\not\perp}$	$\mathrm{U}^{\not\perp}[T[\overline{\mathsf{PKE}}, \mathtt{G}], \mathtt{H}]$
	$\mathrm{KEM}^{\not\perp}_m$	$\mathrm{U}^{\not\perp}_m[T[\overline{\mathsf{PKE}}, \mathtt{G}], \mathtt{H}]]$
Explicit Rejection	$\mathrm{QKEM}^{\perp}_m$	$\mathrm{U}^{\perp}_m[V[T[\overline{\mathsf{PKE}}, \mathtt{G}], \mathtt{H}'], \mathtt{H}]$

Memory-Tight Reduction for T: IND-CPA $\Rightarrow$ OW-PCA.

Theorem 10 *Let $\mathcal{A}$ be any adversary in the* OW-PCA *game of* PKE. *Suppose $\mathcal{A}$ makes q_g queries to* G. *Let q_p denote the number of plaintext checking queries made by $\mathcal{A}$. Then, in the random oracle model, there exists adversaries $\mathcal{B}$ in the* IND-CPA *game against $\overline{\mathsf{PKE}}$, and $\mathcal{B}_F$ in the* prf *game, such that*

$$\mathbf{Adv}^{\text{OW-PCA}}_{\mathcal{A},\mathsf{PKE}} \leq 3 \cdot \mathbf{Adv}^{\text{IND-CPA}}_{\mathcal{B},\overline{\mathsf{PKE}}} + \mathbf{Adv}^{\text{prf}}_{\mathcal{B}_F,F} + \frac{2q_g + 1}{|\mathcal{M}|} + \delta(q_p + q_g)$$

$$\mathbf{LocalTime}(\mathcal{B}) \approx \mathbf{LocalTime}(\mathcal{A}) + (q_g + q_p)\mathbf{LocalTime}(F)$$
$$\mathbf{LocalMem}(\mathcal{B}) \approx \mathbf{LocalMem}(\mathcal{A}) + \mathbf{LocalMem}(F)$$

The proof of the above theorem follows exactly from the proof of analogous Theorem 3.2 of [16] and using the random oracle simulation by a prf F. Moreover, from [16], we get that, if PKE is strongly $\overline{\delta}$ correct, then PKE is $\delta(q_g+q_p)$ correct where $\delta(x) = x\overline{\delta}$.

Memory-Tight Reduction for V: OW-PCA $\Rightarrow$ OW-PCVA. It follows from Theorem 8.

Memory-Tight Reduction for Variants of U. Table 2 lists four variants of U with different security implications. The memory-efficient reductions of these implications are in principle same as the proofs presented in [16]. The only difference is in the simulation of the Random Oracle H. In Table 4, we write the precise functions to be used to simulate the random oracles in the reductions. We assume the message space of the underlying encryption scheme to be $\{0,1\}^{\mu}$. $\mathtt{PCO}(m, c)$ returns 1 if c decrypts to m. $\mathtt{CVO}(c)$ returns 0 if c decrypts to $\perp$.

Table 4. Random oracle simulation for $U^{\not\perp}$, $U_m^{\not\perp}$, $U^{\perp}$, $U_m^{\perp}$. We assume $\mathcal{M} = \{0,1\}^{\mu}$ is the message space of the underlying encryption scheme

Transformation	Key Derivation	RO simulation in Hash Query	RO Simulation in Decap query
$U^{\not\perp}$	$K = \mathtt{H}(m, c)$	if $\mathtt{PCO}(m, c) = 1$ $K = F(k, 0, 0^{\mu}, c)$ else $K = F(k, 1, m, c)$	$K = F(k, 0, 0^{\mu}, c)$
$U^{\perp}$	$K = \mathtt{H}(m, c)$	if $\mathtt{PCO}(m, c) = 1$ $K = F(k, 0, 0^{\mu}, c)$ else $K = F(k, 1, m, c)$	if $\mathtt{CVO}(c) = 0$ $K = \perp$else $K = F(k, 0, 0^{\mu}, c)$
$U_m^{\not\perp}$	$K = \mathtt{H}(m)$	$K = F(k, \mathtt{Enc}_1(pk, m))$	$K = F(k, c)$
$U_m^{\perp}$	$K = \mathtt{H}(m)$	$K = F(k, \mathtt{Enc}_1(pk, m))$	if $\mathtt{CVO}(c) = 0$ $K = \perp$ else $K = F(k, c)$

Acknowledgements. We thank Eike Kiltz for encouraging us to write up and submit the work. We are thankful to the reviewers for their comments on this and the previous versions of the paper. The author is supported by *SERB ECR/2017/001974*.

References

1. Abdalla, M., Bellare, M., Rogaway, P.: DHIES: an encryption scheme based on the Diffie-Hellman problem. Contributions to IEEE P1363a, September 1998
2. Abdalla, M., Bellare, M., Rogaway, P.: The Oracle Diffie-Hellman assumptions and an analysis of DHIES. In: Naccache, D. (ed.) CT-RSA 2001. LNCS, vol. 2020, pp. 143–158. Springer, Heidelberg (2001). https://doi.org/10.1007/3-540-45353-9_12
3. Auerbach, B., Cash, D., Fersch, M., Kiltz, E.: Memory-tight reductions. In: Katz, J., Shacham, H. (eds.) CRYPTO 2017, Part I. LNCS, vol. 10401, pp. 101–132. Springer, Cham (2017). https://doi.org/10.1007/978-3-319-63688-7_4
4. Bellare, M., Boldyreva, A., Micali, S.: Public-key encryption in a multi-user setting: security proofs and improvements. In: Preneel, B. (ed.) EUROCRYPT 2000. LNCS, vol. 1807, pp. 259–274. Springer, Heidelberg (2000). https://doi.org/10.1007/3-540-45539-6_18
5. Bellare, M., Rogaway, P.: The exact security of digital signatures-how to sign with RSA and Rabin. In: Maurer, U. (ed.) EUROCRYPT 1996. LNCS, vol. 1070, pp. 399–416. Springer, Heidelberg (1996). https://doi.org/10.1007/3-540-68339-9_34
6. Bellare, M., Rogaway, P.: The security of triple encryption and a framework for code-based game-playing proofs. In: Vaudenay, S. (ed.) EUROCRYPT 2006. LNCS, vol. 4004, pp. 409–426. Springer, Heidelberg (2006). https://doi.org/10.1007/11761679_25
7. Bernstein, D.J.: Extending the Salsa20 nonce. In: Workshop Record of Symmetric Key Encryption Workshop 2011 (2011)
8. Bernstein, D.J., Persichetti, E.: Towards KEM unification. Cryptology ePrint Archive, Report 2018/526 (2018). https://eprint.iacr.org/2018/526
9. Bhattacharyya, R.: Memory-tight reductions for practical key encapsulation mechanisms. Cryptology ePrint Archive (2020). https://eprint.iacr.org/2020/075

10. Boneh, D., Dagdelen, Ö., Fischlin, M., Lehmann, A., Schaffner, C., Zhandry, M.: Random Oracles in a quantum world. In: Lee, D.H., Wang, X. (eds.) ASIACRYPT 2011. LNCS, vol. 7073, pp. 41–69. Springer, Heidelberg (2011). https://doi.org/10.1007/978-3-642-25385-0_3
11. Chatterjee, S., Menezes, A., Sarkar, P.: Another look at tightness. In: Miri, A., Vaudenay, S. (eds.) SAC 2011. LNCS, vol. 7118, pp. 293–319. Springer, Heidelberg (2012). https://doi.org/10.1007/978-3-642-28496-0_18
12. Coron, J.-S.: On the exact security of full domain hash. In: Bellare, M. (ed.) CRYPTO 2000. LNCS, vol. 1880, pp. 229–235. Springer, Heidelberg (2000). https://doi.org/10.1007/3-540-44598-6_14
13. Cramer, R., Shoup, V.: Design and analysis of practical public-key encryption schemes secure against adaptive chosen ciphertext attack. SIAM J. Comput. **33**(1), 167–226 (2003)
14. Demay, G., Gaži, P., Hirt, M., Maurer, U.: Resource-restricted indifferentiability. In: Johansson, T., Nguyen, P.Q. (eds.) EUROCRYPT 2013. LNCS, vol. 7881, pp. 664–683. Springer, Heidelberg (2013). https://doi.org/10.1007/978-3-642-38348-9_39
15. Dent, A.W.: A designer's guide to KEMs. In: Paterson, K.G. (ed.) Cryptography and Coding 2003. LNCS, vol. 2898, pp. 133–151. Springer, Heidelberg (2003). https://doi.org/10.1007/978-3-540-40974-8_12
16. Hofheinz, D., Hövelmanns, K., Kiltz, E.: A modular analysis of the Fujisaki-Okamoto transformation. In: Kalai, Y., Reyzin, L. (eds.) TCC 2017, Part I. LNCS, vol. 10677, pp. 341–371. Springer, Cham (2017). https://doi.org/10.1007/978-3-319-70500-2_12
17. Jiang, H., Zhang, Z., Chen, L., Wang, H., Ma, Z.: IND-CCA-secure key encapsulation mechanism in the quantum random oracle model, revisited. In: Shacham, H., Boldyreva, A. (eds.) CRYPTO 2018, Part III. LNCS, vol. 10993, pp. 96–125. Springer, Cham (2018). https://doi.org/10.1007/978-3-319-96878-0_4
18. Reingold, O., Trevisan, L., Vadhan, S.: Notions of reducibility between cryptographic primitives. In: Naor, M. (ed.) TCC 2004. LNCS, vol. 2951, pp. 1–20. Springer, Heidelberg (2004). https://doi.org/10.1007/978-3-540-24638-1_1
19. Saito, T., Xagawa, K., Yamakawa, T.: Tightly-secure key-encapsulation mechanism in the quantum random oracle model. In: Nielsen, J.B., Rijmen, V. (eds.) EUROCRYPT 2018, Part III. LNCS, vol. 10822, pp. 520–551. Springer, Cham (2018). https://doi.org/10.1007/978-3-319-78372-7_17
20. Targhi, E.E., Unruh, D.: Post-quantum security of the Fujisaki-Okamoto and OAEP transforms. In: Hirt, M., Smith, A. (eds.) TCC 2016, Part II. LNCS, vol. 9986, pp. 192–216. Springer, Heidelberg (2016). https://doi.org/10.1007/978-3-662-53644-5_8
21. Wang, Y., Matsuda, T., Hanaoka, G., Tanaka, K.: Memory lower bounds of reductions revisited. In: Nielsen, J.B., Rijmen, V. (eds.) EUROCRYPT 2018, Part I. LNCS, vol. 10820, pp. 61–90. Springer, Cham (2018). https://doi.org/10.1007/978-3-319-78381-9_3

Toward RSA-OAEP Without Random Oracles

Nairen Cao[1], Adam O'Neill[2], and Mohammad Zaheri[1](✉)

[1] Department of Computer Science, Georgetown University, Washington, D.C., USA
{nc645,mz394}@georgetown.edu

[2] College of Information and Computer Sciences, University of Massachusetts Amherst, Amherst, USA
adamo@cs.umass.edu

Abstract. We show new partial and full instantiation results *under chosen-ciphertext security* for the widely implemented and standardized RSA-OAEP encryption scheme of Bellare and Rogaway (EUROCRYPT 1994) and two variants. Prior work on such instantiations either showed negative results or settled for "passive" security notions like IND-CPA. More precisely, recall that RSA-OAEP adds redundancy and randomness to a message before composing two rounds of an underlying Feistel transform, whose round functions are modeled as random oracles (ROs), with RSA. Our main results are:

- Either of the two oracles (while still modeling the other as a RO) can be instantiated in RSA-OAEP under IND-CCA2 using mild standard-model assumptions on the round functions and generalizations of algebraic properties of RSA shown by Barthe, Pointcheval, and Báguelin (CCS 2012). The algebraic properties are only shown to hold at practical parameters for small encryption exponent ($e = 3$), but we argue they have value for larger e as well.
- Both oracles can be instantiated simultaneously for two variants of RSA-OAEP, called "t-clear" and "s-clear" RSA-OAEP. For this we use extractability-style assumptions in the sense of Canetti and Dakdouk (TCC 2010) on the round functions, as well as novel yet plausible "XOR-type" assumptions on RSA. While admittedly strong, such assumptions may nevertheless be necessary at this point to make positive progress.

In particular, our full instantiations evade impossibility results of Shoup (J. Cryptology 2002), Kiltz and Pietrzak (EUROCRYPT 2009), and Bitansky *et al.* (STOC 2014). Moreover, our results for s-clear RSA-OAEP yield the most efficient RSA-based encryption scheme proven IND-CCA2 in the standard model (using bold assumptions on cryptographic hashing) to date.

Electronic supplementary material The online version of this chapter (https://doi.org/10.1007/978-3-030-45374-9_10) contains supplementary material, which is available to authorized users.

A. Kiayias et al. (Eds.): PKC 2020, LNCS 12110, pp. 279–308, 2020.
https://doi.org/10.1007/978-3-030-45374-9_10

1 Introduction

In this paper, we show new partial and full instantiations *under chosen-ciphertext attack* (CCA) for the RSA-OAEP encryption scheme [10] and some variants. This helps explain why the scheme, which so far has only been shown to have such security in the random oracle (RO) model, has stood up to cryptanalysis despite the existence of "uninstantiable" RO model schemes and other negative results. It also leads to the fastest CCA-secure RSA-based public-key encryption scheme in the standard model (where one assumes standard-model properties of cryptographic hash functions) to date. We now discuss some background and motivation before an overview of our results.

1.1 Background and Motivation

In the random oracle (RO) model of Bellare and Rogaway [9], every algorithm has oracle access to the same truly random functions. This model has been enormously enabling in the design of practical protocols for various goals; examples include public-key encryption [9,10,43], digital signatures [9,11], and identity-based encryption [21]. When a RO model scheme is implemented, one "instantiates" the oracles, that is, replaces their invocations with invocations of functions with publicly-available code. Thus, there are many possible "instantiations" of a protocol, depending on the choice of the latter. To obtain a practical instantiation, it was suggested by [9] to build these functions from cryptographic hashing in an appropriate way. We call this the *canonical instantiation.* The *RO model thesis* of [9] is that if a protocol is secure in the RO model then its canonical instantiation remains secure in the standard (RO devoid) sense.

Unfortunately, the RO model thesis has been refuted in a strong sense, starting with the work of Canetti *et al.* [28]. These works show that there exist RO model schemes for which *any* instantiation, let alone the canonical one, yields a scheme that can be broken efficiently in the standard model. However, the consensus of the community is that such schemes always seem contrived or artificial in some way. Indeed, RO model schemes that have been standardized have stood up to decades of cryptanalysis. If the RO model thesis is false, what explains this? This leads to what may be called the *practical RO model thesis:* For a "practical" scheme proven secure in the RO model scheme, its canonical instantiation remains secure in the standard model. However, from a scientific standpoint this thesis is unsatisfactory because it lacks a *definition* of "practical".[1] This shortcoming is the starting point for our work.

1.2 Our Thesis

Candidate Differentiating Properties. It seems problematic to try to define practicality in the above sense. Instead, we propose some candidate properties that we conjecture to differentiate schemes to which the RO model thesis applies from those to which it does not. Here are some such properties, some of which are inspired by our work described below:

[1] Here we do not mean "practical" in the sense of efficient enough to use in practice, but rather "does not do anything contrived.".

1. There exist standard-model properties of the constituent functions that together suffice to prove security of the scheme, ideally as well as realizations of such functions under standard assumptions.
2. *Each* individual constituent function can be separately instantiated as above, while possibly modeling the others as ROs.
3. Variants of the scheme that fall under the same framework satisfy one of the above properties.
4. There exist constructions of standard-model hash functions that allow to prove security of the scheme when replacing the ROs, ideally these constructions being under standard assumptions.

THE REVISED THESIS. Our *revised RO model thesis* is that a scheme satisfying one of the above properties is such that the canonical instantiation yields a secure scheme in the standard model, where we relax the notion of instantiation to allow stronger assumptions on non-RO constituent functions. That is, "constituent functions" refers not only to those modeled as ROs but possibly other functions associated with the scheme, like RSA. Thus, one may search for novel assumptions on RSA, for example. Indeed, if one looks at the question of why some RSA-based RO scheme is secure in practice, it could very well have to do with properties of RSA (which has a lot of algebraic structure) beyond mere one-wayness. We have seen the same strategy used to explain security of schemes, without transitioning between the RO and standard models, for example with Chaum's blind signature scheme [7] and Damgård's ElGamal [33]. It was also advocated by Pandey *et al.* [54] to resolve some long-standing theoretical questions.

It is also worth mentioning that there are impossibility results in the standard model for RSA-OAEP [49] and RSA-FDH, RSA-PSS [35,36]. However, these are *black-box* impossibility results that demonstrate that a proof treating the functions as black-boxes cannot suffice. As in other areas of cryptography [2] this motivates looking at non-blackbox assumptions.

1.3 Discussion of the Properties and Our Goals

OUR FOCUS: RSA-OAEP. We focus our study on whether the RO model thesis applies to a very influential scheme, namely *RSA-OAEP* [10]. Roughly, RSA-OAEP is defined as follows. RSA-OAEP encrypts a message as $f(s\|t)$ where f is the RSA function, where for functions $\mathcal{G}$ and $\mathcal{H}$ (originally modeled as ROs) we have $s = \mathcal{G}(r) \oplus m \| 0^{\zeta}$ for randomness $r \in \{0,1\}^{\rho}$ and message $m \in \{0,1\}^{\mu}$, $t = \mathcal{H}(s) \oplus r$. (We denote $s = s_1 \| s_2$.) Thus, we would like to examine whether RSA-OAEP satisfies the properties listed above.

THE FIRST PROPERTY. Here we seek standard model properties of RSA, $\mathcal{G}$, and $\mathcal{H}$ that suffice to prove IND-CCA. For this property, we mentioned that ideally we would also have theoretical realizations of such functions under standard assumptions. We make it clear that we do not advocate *using* these theoretical realizations in practice, but they would show that the goal is not impossible to achieve. The importance of this is illustrated by the fact that the most general forms of assumptions such as correlation intractability (CI) [28] and universal computational extraction (UCE) [5,23] have been shown (likely) impossible. (But special cases of CI and UCE which suffice for the schemes considered remain plausible [5,23,25].) Unfortunately, we do not know how to achieve the first property for RSA-OAEP, even without such theoretical realizations.

THE SECOND PROPERTY. The second property asks for so-called "partial instantiations" for each one of $\mathcal{G}$ or $\mathcal{H}$, while still modeling the other as a RO. Partial instantiations are valuable because ROs are used in different ways in a scheme, and instantiating one of them isolates a property it relies on. Moreover, we ask that *every* oracle can be (separately) instantiated. This has provable implications in practice as well, as now an attacker would need to exploit weakness in the *interaction* between these functions in order to break the scheme in the standard model. In our eyes this makes a standard model attack much less plausible. We show that RSA-OAEP satisfies this property under suitable assumptions.

THE THIRD PROPERTY. The third property is more subjective than the others, as it hinges on what constitutes a scheme falling under the same framework. The aim is to capture the scheme designers' intent or their general approach. Again, the idea is not to use the modified schemes in practice necessarily (although one certainly could if the efficiency penalty is acceptable), but to validate the framework more than simply proving the original scheme is secure in the RO model. An upshot is that this approach can indeed lead to variants of the scheme that offer better security with similar efficiency. We show the third property holds for RSA-OAEP, and in fact our results for one of our variants, namely s-clear RSA-OAEP, leads to the most efficient IND-CCA secure scheme in the standard model, albeit under bold assumptions on cryptographic hashing.

THE FOURTH PROPERTY. Note that this property differs from the first in that it does not require giving higher-level properties that the hash functions should satisfy in order to make the scheme secure. Thus, it does not really give insight into what properties hash functions used in the canonical instantiation should satisfy to do this. Still, existence of such hash functions refutes uninstantiability of the scheme, showing that the job of the hash functions in making the scheme secure is at least plausible. As with the first property, we leave it as an open problem to show this for RSA-OAEP. We note that this property has been shown for other RO model schemes in, *e.g*, [46,61].

We proceed to describe our approach and results in more detail.

1.4 Using PA + IND-CPA

USING PA + IND-CPA. A common thread running through our analyses is the use of *plaintext awareness* (PA) [4,8,10]. PA captures the intuition that an adversary who produces a ciphertext must "know" the corresponding plaintext. It is not itself a notion of privacy, but, at a high level, combined with IND-CPA it implies IND-CCA. We use this approach to obtain modularity in proofs, isolate assumptions needed, and make overall analyses more tractable. Moreover, while it seems that PA necessitates using knowledge assumptions, this is somewhat inherent anyway due to black-box impossibility results discussed below.

FLAVORS AND IMPLICATIONS. PA comes in various flavors: PA-RO [4], and PA0, PA1, and PA2 [8]. PA-RO refers to a notion in the RO model, while PA0, PA1, and PA2 refer to standard model notions that differ in what extent the adversary can query its decryption or encryption oracles. (In particular, in PA2 the adversary can query for encryptions of unknown plaintexts.) Similarly, IND-CCA comes in flavors [4,56]: IND-CCA0, IND-CCA1, and IND-CCA2. We use that [4,8] show that IND-CPA + PA-RO implies IND-CCA2 in the RO model, IND-CPA + PA0 implies IND-CCA1 with one decryption query, IND-CPA + PA1 implies IND-CCA1, and IND-CPA + PA2 implies IND-CCA2.

1.5 Partial Instantiation Results

HIGH-LEVEL APPROACH. We first give partial instantiation results of RSA-OAEP under IND-CCA2. Such results have been sought after in prior work [17, 18,24] but have proven negative results or settled for weaker security notions. The heroes for us here are new generalizations of the notions of "second-input extractability" (SIE) and "common-input extractability" (CIE) proven by Barthe *et al.* [3] to hold for small-exponent RSA ($e = 3$). SIE says that an RSA image point can be inverted given a sufficiently-long (depending on e) part of the preimage, whereas CIE says that two RSA images can be inverted if the preimages share a common part. They were used by [3] where the "part" is the least-significant bits to analyze a no-redundancy, one-round version of RSA-OAEP in the RO model. The assumptions are proven via Coppersmith's algorithm to find small roots of a univariate polynomial modulo N [30].

We show that generalized versions where the "part" refers to some of the middle or most-significant bits, rather than least-significant bits, is useful for analyzing RSA-OAEP more generally. We show these versions also hold for small-exponent RSA, but based on the *bivariate* Coppersmith algorithm [15,30,31]. Moreover, despite the similarity of assumptions, our proof strategies in the partial instantiations are somewhat different than that of Barthe *et al.* [3]. Another interesting point is that while (generalized) SIE and CIE hold for $e = 3$, we argue they have practical value for larger e as well. Namely, while $e > 3$ would require an impractical "part" length using Coppersmith's technique, they could possibly hold for practical parameters via other (in particular, non-blackbox) techniques. At least, we do not see how to refute that, which could lend insight into why there is no IND-CCA2 attack on the scheme for general e.[2]

[2] Moreover, we conjecture this is different from the case of "lossiness" [48,55] as shown for RSA and used to analyze IND-CPA security of RSA-OAEP in [48]. Namely, to get sufficient lossiness it seems to inherently require large e, since the *only* way to make RSA parameters lossy is to have $e|\phi(N)$.

Results and Intuition. Namely, we show partial instantiations of both oracles $\mathcal{G}, \mathcal{H}$ under very mild assumptions on the round functions—roughly, that $\mathcal{G}$ is a pseudorandom generator and $\mathcal{H}$ is a hardcore function for RSA, respectively—in both cases assuming RSA is SIE and CIE. We first prove IND-CPA security in these cases. Interestingly, the instantiation of $\mathcal{G}$ under IND-CPA uses that RSA is SIE while the instantiation of $\mathcal{H}$ does not, the intuition being that in the latter case we assume $\mathcal{H}$ is a hardcore function so its output masks $r \in \{0,1\}^\rho$ used in the challenge ciphertext unconditionally. Now for PA-RO, in both cases we use SIE and CIE, but wrt. different bits of the input. In the case of instantiating $\mathcal{G}$, it is wrt. the redundancy bits s_2. Intuitively, for a decryption query there are two cases. Firstly, that it has a *different* r-part than the challenge and therefore this must have been queried to the RO, in which case the SIE extractor works. Secondly, that it has the *same* r-part as the challenge, but it therefore shares s_2, in which case the CIE extractor works. In the case of instantiating $\mathcal{H}$, there are again two cases for an encryption query depending on whether it shares the same s-part of the challenge or not; thus the assumption is wrt. the whole s-part.

1.6 Full Instantiation Results

High-level Approach. We next give full instantiation results for two variants of RSA-OAEP, called t-clear and s-clear RSA-OAEP. Prior results on t-clear RSA-OAEP [18] showed only partial instantiations or relatively weak security notions, and s-clear RSA-OAEP was only considered indirectly by Shoup [59] for negative results. In t-clear RSA-OAEP, a message is encrypted as $f(s_1)\|s_2\|t$ where f is the RSA function $s_1\|s_2 = \mathcal{G}(r)\oplus m\|0^\varsigma$ for randomness $r \in \{0,1\}^\rho$ and message $m \in \{0,1\}^\mu$, $t = \mathcal{H}(s_1\|s_2)\oplus r$. Here we divide s into $s_1\|s_2$, where $s_2 \in \{0,1\}^\varsigma$, so the name "$t$-clear" while consistent with prior work [18], is somewhat of a misnomer. On the other hand, in s-clear RSA OAEP a message is encrypted as $s\|f(t)$. One of the heroes for us here is a hierarchy of "extractability" notions we define and assume for the round functions, called EXT-RO, EXT0, EXT1, EXT2, roughly paralleling PA-RO, PA0, PA1, PA2 respectively, and generalizing prior work [12,26,27,34], although we mention that [34] already has our EXT1 definition. Besides this parallel, our generalizations consider adversaries that output only part of an image point or an image point along with part of a pre-image. These are bold assumptions to make on (functions constructed out of) cryptographic hash functions, but, as discussed above, we believe studying their implications is justified. In the case of s-clear, another hero is a family of new "XOR-type" assumptions we introduce, and give intuitive justifications for in light of the multiplicative structure of RSA. Again, we view part of our contribution as putting forth novel assumptions that the research community can analyze (say in the generic ring model) in the future.

We make several remarks about our results, particularly how they avoid known impossibility results, before detailing them:

- Extractability is a non-blackbox assumption (saying for every adversary there exists a non-blackbox "extractor") so we avoid the impossibility result of

Kiltz and Pietrzak [49][3]. That is, the fact we use extractable hash functions (extractability being an intuitive property used in the original RO model proof) is somewhat unavoidable.
- While extractability of $\mathcal{H}$ would *prima facie* be false, we use it only in a plausible way for a cryptographic hash function. Namely, the adversary also outputs *part of the preimage*. Extractability assumptions we use on $\mathcal{G}$, even where the adversary outputs only part of an image point, remain plausible as it is an expanding function with a sparse range (usually constructed something like $\mathcal{G}(x) = (\mathcal{H}(0\|x)\|\mathcal{H}(1\|x), \ldots)$.
- For extractability we use only bounded key-independent auxiliary input (basically, the keys for the other functions in the scheme), so we avoid the impossibility result of Bitansky *et al.* [14]. Moreover, the key-dependent auxiliary information is just one image query (at least in the proof of IND-CCA2).
- Our "XOR-type" assumptions on RSA avoid a negative result of Shoup [59], showing that there is an attack if the general trapdoor permutation is "XOR-malleable".[4]
- We typically use the various forms of extractability in combination with (at least) collision-resistance, so that the extractor returns the "right" preimage. The collision-resistant construction of [52] based on knowledge assumptions, albeit where the adversary outputs the entire image point, is on the lowest level of our hierarchy (EXT0); furthermore, it is not known to work when the adversary outputs part of the image point. Any theoretical constructions for higher levels (EXT1, EXT2) are similarly open. We hope these are targeted in future work.

Results and Intuition for t-clear. Our results for t-clear RSA-OAEP are weaker than those for s-clear RSA-OAEP. First, for t-clear we prove IND-CPA for high-entropy, public key independent messages, under mild assumptions on the round functions, namely that $\mathcal{H}$ is a hardcore function for RSA and $\mathcal{G}$ is a pseudorandom generator. Intuitively, the high-entropy requirement comes from the fact that the adversary attacking $\mathcal{H}$ needs to know r to prepare its challenge ciphertext, so the randomness of the input to $\mathcal{H}$ needs to come from m. (We could avoid it using the stronger assumption of UCE as per the result of [5], which could be viewed as a hedge.) Furthermore, m needs to be public-key independent so as to not bias the output. Then we can prove PA0 based on forms of EXT0 for $\mathcal{G}$ and $\mathcal{H}$, the intuition being that the plaintext extractor first extracts from the part $\mathcal{G}(r)$ that is left in clear by the redundancy to get r and then runs the extractor for $\mathcal{H}$ on $t \oplus r$ from which it can compute m, with the above part of the pre-image to get s. Note that when running the extractor here and below we have to be careful that the constructed extractor uses the same coins as the

[3] As acknowledged by the authors there was a bug in the proceedings version of this paper, but this has been fixed for the full version [50].

[4] In more detail, note that for s-clear the "overall" TDP (including the part output in the clear) is not partial one-way [39] so their security proof does *not* apply. In fact, Shoup [59] considers the scheme in his proof that RSA-OAEP is not IND-CCA2-secure for general one-way TDPs, exhibiting the above-mentioned attack.

starting one for consistency (otherwise we won't end up with the right extractor). We can also prove PA1, although we have to make an extractability assumption directly on the padding scheme.[5] Interestingly, even this approach does not work for PA2, which we leave completely open for t-clear (cf. Remark 14).

Results and Intuition for s-clear. We find s-clear is much more friendly to a full instantiation by making novel but plausible assumptions on RSA. One is XOR-nonmalleability (XOR-NM), saying that from $\mathcal{F}(x)$ it is hard to find some $\mathcal{F}(x')$ and z such that $z = x \oplus x'$. Another is XOR-indistinguishability (XOR-IND), saying for random x and adversarially-chosen z one cannot tell $\mathcal{F}(x)$ from $\mathcal{F}(x \oplus z)$ given "hint" $\mathcal{G}(x)$. In our results, $\mathcal{G}$ is a PRG, which we show also implies $\mathcal{G}$ is a HCF for $\mathcal{F}$. So, the notion can be viewed as an extension of the classical notion of HCF. In fact, we use XOR-IND just to show IND-CPA. The intuition is that it allows breaking the dependency of s in the input to OAEP with the input to RSA. The proofs of PA0 and PA1 are very similar, and showcase one reason s-clear is much more friendly to a full instantiation, namely it heavily depends on the extractability of $\mathcal{G}$. That is, if $\mathcal{G}$ is suitably extractable, the plaintext extractor can simply recover r and then compute the plaintext as $s \oplus \mathcal{G}(r)$. For PA2, one has to be careful as when the adversary makes an encryption query, the plaintext extractor should call the image oracle for $\mathcal{G}$, where in addition to $\mathcal{G}(x)$ for random x it receives the hint of RSA on x. We show that if RSA is XOR-IND then this implies the adversary can get the whole ciphertext as a hint to simulate the encryption oracle. Then we also have the worry about the adversary querying "mauled" ciphertexts to the extract oracle. Intuitively, if the r-part is the same then it cannot run the extractor for $\mathcal{G}$, but we show this violates XOR-NM of RSA. On the other hand, if the s-part is the same then we cannot break XOR-NM but this creates a collision for $\mathcal{G}$.

1.7 Discussion and Perspective

We summarize and compare our results to prior work in Fig. 1. Note that we get a lot of mileage from assuming the trapdoor permutation is specifically RSA, whereas prior work, which has mostly shown negative results CCA-style security notions, went for a general approach. We also highlight that while our assumptions on both RSA and the round functions for our full instantiability results are expectedly stronger than what we need for partial instantiations, they still compare favorably to prior work. In particular, while our assumption of EXT2 for $\mathcal{G}$ in our s-clear result is already "PA2-flavored," prior work [18, Definition 3.3] made CCA-style assumptions on the round functions even to obtain relatively weak notions of non-malleability. It can also be viewed as a strengthening of "adaptive" (CCA-style) security notions on one-way functions [47,54].[6] Plus, it is not clear how to get an IND-CCA2 encryption scheme from EXT2 functions in a simpler way.

[5] At a very high level, we can prove EXT0 of $\mathcal{G}, \mathcal{H}$ implies EXT0 for the padding scheme, but we do not know how to do this for EXT1 because of an "extractor blow-up" problem.

[6] These works do not precisely match our setting as [54] consider keyless functions and [47] consider functions with a trapdoor.

Scheme	Assumptions on OAEP	Assumptions on $\mathcal{F}$	Security	Size	Ref
RSA-OAEP	$\mathcal{G}$: **PRG** and $\mathcal{H}$: **RO**	**OW, SIE and CIE**	**IND-CCA2**	n	**Section 3**
RSA-OAEP	$\mathcal{G}$: **RO** and $\mathcal{H}$: **PHCF**	**OW, SIE and CIE**	**IND-CCA2**	n	**Section 3**
RSA-OAEP	$\mathcal{G}$: t-wise independent	Lossy TDP	IND-CPA	n	[48]
RSA-OAEP	$\mathcal{G}, \mathcal{H}$: UCE	OW	IND-CPA-KI	n	[5]
RSA-OAEP *t*-**clear**	$\mathcal{G}$: **PRG, EXT0 and NCR** $\mathcal{H}$: **HCF, EXT0 and CR**	**OW**	**\$IND-CCA0-KI**	$3n + 3k$	**Full version**
RSA-OAEP *t*-**clear**	OAEP : **EXT1 and NCR** $\mathcal{G}$: **PRG** and $\mathcal{H}$: **HCF**	**OW**	**\$IND-CCA1-KI**	$3n + 3k$	**Full version**
RSA-OAEP *t*-clear	$\mathcal{G}$: PRG and NCR $\mathcal{H}$: RO	OW	IND-CCA2	$n + k$	[18]
RSA-OAEP *t*-clear	$\mathcal{G}$: RO $\mathcal{H}$: NM PRG with hint	OW	IND-CCA2	$n + k$	[18]
RSA-OAEP *t*-clear	$\mathcal{G}$: PRG and NCR $\mathcal{H}$: NM PRG with hint	OW	\$NM-CPA	$n + k$	[18]
RSA-OAEP *s*-**clear**	$\mathcal{G}$: **PRG, EXT1 and NCR**	**XOR-IND0**	**IND-CCA1**	$2n + k + \mu$	**Section 6**
RSA-OAEP *s*-**clear**	$\mathcal{G}$: **PRG, EXT2 and NCR** $\mathcal{H}$: **CR**	**XOR-IND1,2 and XOR-NM0**	**IND-CCA2**	$2n + k + \mu$	**Section 6**

Fig. 1. Instantiability results for RSA-OAEP, where n is modulus length, k is security param and μ is message length. Typically $n = 2048, k = 128$ and $\mu = 128$.

1.8 Related Work

RO Model Results. Results about security of $\mathcal{F}$-OAEP for an abstract TDP $\mathcal{F}$ with applications to RSA-OAEP in the RO model were shown in [10, 39, 59]. Ultimately, these works showed RSA-OAEP is IND-CCA2 secure in the RO model assuming only one-wayness of RSA, but with a loose security reduction. Interestingly, Shoup [59] considers *s*-clear RSA-OAEP indirectly in a negative result about RSA-OAEP with a general one-way TDP. Security of *t*-clear RSA-OAEP (under the name "RSA-OAEP++") has been analyzed in the RO model by Boldyreva, Imai and Kobara [19], who show tight security in the multi-challenge setting.

Partial Instantiation Results. Canetti [24] conjectured that his notion of perfect one-wayness sufficed to instantiate *one* of the two oracles in $\mathcal{F}$-OAEP. This was disproved in general by Boldyreva and Fischlin [17], but their results do not contradict ours because they use a contrived TDP $\mathcal{F}$. Subsequently, Boldyreva and Fischlin [18] gave partial instantiations for *t*-clear $\mathcal{F}$-OAEP under stronger assumptions on the round functions.

Full Instantiation Results. Brown [22] and Paillier and Villar [53] showed negative results for proving RSA-OAEP is IND-CCA secure in restricted models, and Kiltz and Pietrzak [49] showed a general black-box impossibility result. As mentioned above, their results do not contradict ours because we use non-blackbox assumptions. Moving to weaker notions, Kiltz *et al.* [47] show IND-CPA security of RSA-OAEP using lossiness [55], while Bellare, Hoang, and Keelveedhi [5] show RSA-OAEP is IND-CPA secure for public-key independent messages assuming the round functions meet their notion of universal computational extraction. Boldyreva and Fischlin [18] show a weak form of non-malleability for t-clear $\mathcal{F}$-OAEP, again using very strong assumptions on the round functions. Lewko *et al.* [51] show IND-CPA security of the RSA PKCS v1.5 scheme, with the bounds later being corrected and improved by Smith and Zhang [60].

Candidate Instantiability Assumptions. General notions for function families geared toward instantiating ROs that have been proposed include correlation intractability [25,28], extractable hash functions [12,14,26,27], perfect one-wayness [24,29,37], seed incompressibility [42], non-malleability [1,16], and universal computational extraction (UCE) [5,6,23].

1.9 Organization

In Sect. 2, we give the preliminaries. In Sect. 3, we formalize the algebraic properties of RSA we use and our partial instantiation results for RSA-OAEP. In Sect. 4, we give a new hierarchy of extractable functions. In Sect. 5, we abstract out some properties of the OAEP padding scheme we use. Then, in Sect. 6 we give novel "XOR-type" assumptions on RSA and combine them with the above to give our full instantiation result s-clear RSA-OAEP. Due to space constraints, our results for t-clear RSA-OAEP are deferred to the supplementary materials. We also defer all detailed proofs to the supplementary materials.

2 Preliminaries and Some Generalizations

2.1 Notation and Conventions

For a probabilistic algorithm A, by $y \leftarrow_{\$} A(x)$ we mean that A is executed on input x and the output is assigned to y. We sometimes use $y \leftarrow A(x;r)$ to make A's random coins explicit. We denote by $\Pr\left[A(x) = y : x \leftarrow_{\$} X\right]$ the probability that A outputs y on input x when x is sampled according to X. We denote by $[A(x)]$ the set of possible outputs of A when run on input x. The security parameter is denoted $k \in \mathbb{N}$. Unless otherwise specified, all algorithms must run in probabilistic polynomial-time (PPT) in k, and an algorithm's running-time includes that of any overlying experiment as well as the size of its code. Integer parameters often implicitly depend on k. The length of a string s is denoted $|s|$. We denote by $s|_i^j$ the i-th least significant bits (LSB) to j-th least significant bits of s (including i-th and j-th bits), where $1 \leq i \leq j \leq |s|$. For convenience, we denote by $s|_\ell = s|_1^\ell$ the ℓ least significant bits of s and $s|^\ell = s|_{|s|-\ell}^{|s|}$ the ℓ most significant bits (MSB) of s, for $1 \leq \ell \leq |s|$. We write P_X for the distribution of random variable X and $P_X(x)$ for the probability that X puts on value x, i.e. $P_X(x) = \Pr[X = x]$. We denote by U_ℓ the uniform distribution on $\{0,1\}^\ell$. We write U_S for the uniform distribution

Game PA-RO$^{A,\mathsf{Ext}}_{\mathsf{PKE}}(k)$	**Procedure** Enc$(pk, \mathcal{M})$
$b \leftarrow_\$ \{0,1\}$; $i \leftarrow 1$; $j \leftarrow 1$	$m \leftarrow_\$ \mathcal{M}(1^k, pk)$
$(pk, sk) \leftarrow_\$ \mathsf{Kg}(1^k)$	$c \leftarrow_\$ \mathsf{Enc}^{\mathrm{RO}(\cdot,2)}(pk, m)$
$b' \leftarrow_\$ A^{\mathrm{RO}(\cdot,1),\mathrm{Enc}(pk,\cdot),\mathcal{D}(sk,\cdot)}(pk)$	$\mathbf{c}[i] \leftarrow c$; $i \leftarrow i+1$
Return $(b = b')$	Return c
Procedure RO(x, i)	**Procedure** $\mathcal{D}(sk, c)$
If $H[x] = \bot$ then $H[x] \leftarrow_\$ \{0,1\}^\ell$	If $c \in \mathbf{c}$ then return $\bot$
If $i = 1$ then	$m_0 \leftarrow \mathsf{Dec}(sk, c)$
$\mathbf{x}[j] \leftarrow x$; $\mathbf{h}[j] \leftarrow H[x]$; $j \leftarrow j+1$	$m_1 \leftarrow_\$ \mathsf{Ext}^{\mathrm{RO}(\cdot,3)}(\mathbf{x}, \mathbf{h}, \mathbf{c}, c, pk)$
Return $H[x]$	Return m_b

Fig. 2. Game to define PA-RO security.

on the set S. Vectors are denoted in boldface, for example $\mathbf{x}$. If $\mathbf{x}$ is a vector then $|\mathbf{x}|$ denotes the number of components of $\mathbf{x}$ and $\mathbf{x}[i]$ denotes its i-th component, for $1 \le i \le |\mathbf{x}|$. For convenience, we extend algorithmic notation to operate on each vector of inputs component-wise. For example, if A is an algorithm and $\mathbf{x}, \mathbf{y}$ are vectors then $\mathbf{z} \leftarrow_\$ A(\mathbf{x}, \mathbf{y})$ denotes that $\mathbf{z}[i] \leftarrow_\$ A(\mathbf{x}[i], \mathbf{y}[i])$ for all $1 \le i \le |\mathbf{x}|$. Let X be random variables taking values on a common finite domain. The min-entropy of a random variable X is $\mathrm{H}_\infty(X) = -\log(\max_x \Pr[X = x])$.

2.2 Public-Key Encryption and Its Security

Public-key Encryption. A *public-key encryption scheme* PKE with message space Msg is a tuple of algorithms (Kg, Enc, Dec). The key-generation algorithm Kg on input 1^k outputs a public key pk and matching secret key sk. The encryption algorithm Enc on inputs pk and a message $m \in \mathsf{Msg}(1^k)$ outputs a ciphertext c. The deterministic decryption algorithm Dec on inputs sk and ciphertext c outputs a message m or $\bot$. We require that for all $(pk, sk) \in [\mathsf{Kg}(1^k)]$ and all $m \in \mathsf{Msg}(1^k)$, $\mathsf{Dec}(sk, (\mathsf{Enc}(pk, m)) = m$ with probability 1.

PA-RO Security. We first define plaintext-awareness in the RO model following [4], which builds on the definition in [10] and is strictly stronger than IND-CCA2 security in general. Let PKE = (Kg, Enc, Dec) be a public key encryption scheme and let $\mathcal{M}$ be a PPT algorithm that takes as inputs 1^k and a public key pk, and outputs a message $m \in \mathsf{Msg}(1^k)$. To adversary A and extractor Ext, we associate the experiment in Fig. 2 for every $k \in \mathbb{N}$. We say that PKE is PA-RO secure if for every PPT adversary A there exists an extractor Ext such that

$$\mathbf{Adv}^{\text{pa-ro}}_{\mathsf{PKE},A,\mathsf{Ext}}(k) = 2 \cdot \Pr\left[\text{PA-RO}^{A,\mathsf{Ext}}_{\mathsf{PKE}}(k) \Rightarrow 1\right] - 1.$$

is negligible in k.

Remark 1. Our definition of plaintext awareness in the random oracle model differs from the definition given in [4] in the following way. In our definition,

Game $\text{PAI}_{\mathsf{PKE}}^{A,\mathsf{Ext}}(k)$	**Procedure** $\mathcal{D}(sk, c)$	**Procedure** $\text{Enc}(pk, \mathcal{M})$
$(pk, sk) \leftarrow_\$ \mathsf{Kg}(1^k)$	If $c \in \mathbf{c}$ then return $\perp$	$m \leftarrow_\$ \mathcal{M}(1^k, pk)$
$b \leftarrow_\$ \{0,1\}$; $i \leftarrow 1$; $\mathbf{c} \leftarrow \varepsilon$	$m_0 \leftarrow \mathsf{Dec}(sk, c)$	$c \leftarrow_\$ \mathsf{Enc}(pk, m)$
$r \leftarrow_\$ \mathsf{Coins}(k)$; $st \leftarrow (pk, r)$	$(m_1, st) \leftarrow_\$ \mathsf{Ext}(st, \mathbf{c}, c)$	$\mathbf{c}[i] \leftarrow c$; $i \leftarrow i + 1$
$b' \leftarrow A^{\mathcal{D}(sk,\cdot),\mathcal{O}}(pk; r)$	Return m_b	Return c
Return $(b = b')$		

Fig. 3. Games to define PAI security.

we are giving the extractor access to the random oracle. We observe that the analogous result of [4, Theorem 4.2] that IND-CPA and PA-RO together imply IND-CCA2 still holds for our modified definition, since in the proof the IND-CPA adversary could query its own random oracle to answer to the random oracle queries of the extractor.

We now turn to definitions of plaintext awareness in the standard model, following [8].

PA SECURITY. Let $\mathsf{PKE} = (\mathsf{Kg}, \mathsf{Enc}, \mathsf{Dec})$ be a public key encryption scheme. For PAI $\in$ {PA0, PA1, PA2}, we associate the experiment in Fig. 3 to adversary A and extractor Ext, for every $k \in \mathbb{N}$. Define the PAI advantage of A

$$\mathbf{Adv}_{\mathsf{PKE},A,\mathsf{Ext}}^{\mathsf{pai}}(k) = 2 \cdot \Pr\left[\text{PAI}_{\mathsf{PKE}}^{A,\mathsf{Ext}}(k) \Rightarrow 1\right] - 1.$$

If PAI = PA1, then $\mathcal{O} = \varepsilon$. PA0 is defined similarly to PA1, except A is only allowed to make a single decryption query. If PAI = PA2, then $\mathcal{O} = \text{Enc}$. We say that PKE is PAI secure if for every PPT adversary A with coin space Coins there exists an extractor Ext such that, $\mathbf{Adv}_{\mathsf{PKE},A,\mathsf{Ext}}^{\mathsf{pai}}(k)$ is negligible in k.

Remark 2. Our PA2 definition comes from [8]. We give PA2 adversary extra access to encryption oracle. This models the ability that IND-CCA2 adversary obtains ciphertext without knowing the randomness.

2.3 Trapdoor Permutations and Their Security

TRAPDOOR PERMUTATIONS. A trapdoor permutation family with domain TDom is a tuple of algorithms $\mathcal{F} = (\mathsf{Kg}, \mathsf{Eval}, \mathsf{Inv})$ that work as follows. Algorithm Kg on input a unary encoding of the security parameter 1^k outputs a pair (f, f^{-1}), where $f\colon \mathsf{TDom}(k) \to \mathsf{TDom}(k)$. Algorithm Eval on inputs a function f and $x \in \mathsf{TDom}(k)$ outputs $y \in \mathsf{TDom}(k)$. We often write $f(x)$ instead of $\mathsf{Eval}(f, x)$. Algorithm Inv on inputs a function f^{-1} and $y \in \mathsf{TDom}(k)$ outputs $x \in \mathsf{TDom}(k)$. We often write $f^{-1}(y)$ instead of $\mathsf{Inv}(f^{-1}, y)$. We require that for any $(f, f^{-1}) \in [\mathsf{Kg}(1^k)]$ and any $x \in \mathsf{TDom}(k)$, $f^{-1}(f(x)) = x$. We call $\mathcal{F}$ an n-bit trapdoor permutation family if $\mathsf{TDom} = \{0,1\}^n$. We will think of the RSA trapdoor permutation family [57] n-bit for simplicity, although its domain is $\mathbb{Z}_N^*$ for an n-bit integer N. Additionally, for convenience we define the following. For an ν-bit trapdoor permutation family and $\ell \in \mathbb{N}$, we define $\mathcal{F}|_\ell = (\mathsf{Kg}|_\ell, \mathsf{Eval}|_\ell, \mathsf{Inv}|_\ell)$

as the $(\nu + \ell)$-bit trapdoor permutation families such that for all $k \in \mathbb{N}$, all $(f|_\ell, f^{-1}|_\ell) \in [\mathsf{Kg}|_\ell(1^k)]$, and all $x \in \{0,1\}^{\nu+\ell}$, we have $f(x)|_\ell = f(x|^{n-\ell})\|x|_\ell$, and analogously for $\mathcal{F}|^\ell$.

2.4 Function Families and Associated Security Notions

FUNCTION FAMILIES. A function family with domain $\mathsf{F.Dom}$ and range $\mathsf{F.Rng}$ is a tuple of algorithms $\mathcal{F} = (\mathcal{K}_F, F)$ that work as follows. Algorithm $\mathcal{K}_F$ on input a unary encoding of the security parameter 1^k outputs a key K_F. Deterministic algorithm F on inputs K_F and $x \in \mathsf{F.Dom}(k)$ outputs $y \in \mathsf{F.Rng}(k)$. We alternatively write $\mathcal{F}$ as a function $\mathcal{F}\colon \mathcal{K}_F \times \mathsf{F.Dom} \to \mathsf{F.Rng}$. We call $\mathcal{F}$ an *ℓ-injective* function if for all distinct $x_1, x_2 \in \mathsf{F.Dom}(k)$ and $K_F \in [\mathcal{K}_F(1^k)]$, we have $F(K_F, x_1)|_\ell \neq F(K_F, x_2)|_\ell$.

NEAR-COLLISION RESISTANCE. Let $\mathcal{H}\colon \mathcal{K}_H \times \mathsf{HDom} \to \mathsf{HRng}$ be a function family. For $m \in \mathbb{N}$ suppose $\mathsf{HRng} = \{0,1\}^m$. For $1 \le \ell \le m$ we say $\mathcal{H}$ is *near-collision resistant* with respect to ℓ-least significant bits of the outputs (NCR$_\ell$) if for any PPT adversary A:

$$\mathbf{Adv}^{\text{n-cr}_\ell}_{\mathcal{H},A}(k) = \Pr_{K_H \leftarrow\$ \mathcal{K}_H(1^k)}\left[\begin{array}{c} (x_1, x_2) \leftarrow A(K_H) \\ x_1, x_2 \in \mathsf{HDom}(k) \end{array} \wedge \begin{array}{c} \mathcal{H}(K_H, x_1)|_\ell = \mathcal{H}(K_H, x_2)|_\ell \\ x_1 \neq x_2 \end{array}\right]$$

is negligible in k. We note that our definition differs slightly from [18] as both x_1, x_2 are adversarially chosen. In terms of feasibility, the same construction based on one-way permutations given in [18] works in our case as well. Similarly, we define NCR$^\ell$ where the adversary tries to find collision on the ℓ-most significant bits of the output.

PARTIAL HARDCORE FUNCTIONS. For convenience, we also generalize the notion of hardcore function in the following way. Let $\mathcal{F} = (\mathsf{Kg}, \mathsf{Eval}, \mathsf{Inv})$ be n-bit trapdoor permutation family. Let $\mathcal{H}\colon \mathcal{K}_H \times \{0,1\}^{n-\ell} \to \mathsf{HRng}$ be a function family, for some $\ell < n$. To attacker A, we associate the experiment in Fig. 4 for every $k \in \mathbb{N}$. We say that $\mathcal{H}$ is a *ℓ-partial hardcore function* for the trapdoor permutation family $\mathcal{F}$ if for every PPT adversary A,

$$\mathbf{Adv}^{\text{phcf}}_{\mathcal{F},\mathcal{H},A}(k) = 2 \cdot \Pr\left[\text{PHCF-DIST}^A_{\mathcal{F},\mathcal{H}}(k) \Rightarrow 1\right] - 1.$$

is negligible in k. Note if $(f(x), x|_{n-\ell})$ is a one-way function of x, then $\mathcal{H}$ is a ℓ-partial hardcore function for $\mathcal{F}$ when $\mathcal{H}$ is a computational randomness extractor [32]. This is plausible for the case that $\mathcal{F}$ is RSA when $n - \ell$ is small enough that Coppersmith's techniques do not apply. This means $n - \ell \le n(e-1)/e - \log 1/\epsilon$ such that $N^\epsilon \ge 2^k$ for security parameter k.

2.5 The OAEP Framework

OAEP PADDING SCHEME. We recall the OAEP padding scheme [10]. Let message length μ, randomness length ρ, and redundancy length ζ be integer parameters, and $\nu = \mu + \rho + \zeta$. Let $\mathcal{G}\colon \mathcal{K}_G \times \{0,1\}^\rho \to \{0,1\}^{\mu+\zeta}$ and

Game PHCF-DIST$^A_{\mathcal{F},\mathcal{H}}(k)$
$b \leftarrow_\$ \{0,1\}$; $K_H \leftarrow_\$ \mathcal{K}_H(1^k)$; $(f, f^{-1}) \leftarrow_\$ \mathsf{Kg}(1^k)$
$x \leftarrow_\$ \{0,1\}^n$; $h_0 \leftarrow H(K_H, x\|^\ell)$; $h_1 \leftarrow_\$ \mathsf{HRng}(k)$
$b' \leftarrow_\$ A(K_H, f, f(x), x\|_{n-\ell}, h_b)$
Return $(b = b')$

Fig. 4. Games to define PHCF-DIST security.

Algorithm $\mathsf{OAEP}_{(K_G,K_H)}(m\|r)$	**Algorithm** $\mathsf{OAEP}^{-1}_{(K_G,K_H)}(x)$
$s \leftarrow (m\|0^\zeta) \oplus G(K_G, r)$	$s\|t \leftarrow x$; $r \leftarrow t \oplus H(K_H, s)$
$t \leftarrow r \oplus H(K_H, s)$	$m' \leftarrow s \oplus G(K_G, r)$
$x \leftarrow s\|t$	If $m'\|_\zeta = 0^\zeta$ return $m'\|^\mu$
Return x	Else return $\perp$

Fig. 5. OAEP padding scheme $\mathsf{OAEP}[G, H]$.

$\mathcal{H}\colon \mathcal{K}_H \times \{0,1\}^{\mu+\zeta} \to \{0,1\}^\rho$ be function families. The associated *OAEP padding scheme* is a triple of algorithms $\mathsf{OAEP}[\mathcal{G}, \mathcal{H}] = (\mathcal{K}_{\mathsf{OAEP}}, \mathsf{OAEP}, \mathsf{OAEP}^{-1})$ defined as follows. On input 1^k, $\mathcal{K}_{\mathsf{OAEP}}$ returns (K_G, K_H) where $K_G \leftarrow_\$ \mathcal{K}_G(1^k)$ and $K_H \leftarrow_\$ \mathcal{K}_H(1^k)$, and $\mathsf{OAEP}, \mathsf{OAEP}^{-1}$ are as defined in Fig. 5.

OAEP Encryption Scheme and Variants. Slightly abusing notation, we denote by $\mathsf{OAEP}[\mathcal{G}, \mathcal{H}, \mathcal{F}]$ the OAEP-based encryption scheme $\mathcal{F}$-OAEP with $n = \nu$. We also consider two other OAEP-based encryption schemes, called *t-clear* and *s-clear* $\mathcal{F}$-OAEP, and denoted $\mathsf{OAEP}_{\mathsf{t\text{-}clear}}[\mathcal{G}, \mathcal{H}, \mathcal{F}|_{\zeta+\rho}]$ and $\mathsf{OAEP}_{\mathsf{s\text{-}clear}}[\mathcal{G}, \mathcal{H}, \mathcal{F}|^{\mu+\zeta}]$. Here $n = \mu$ and $n = \rho$, respectively. We often write $\mathsf{OAEP}_{\mathsf{t\text{-}clear}}$ and $\mathsf{OAEP}_{\mathsf{s\text{-}clear}}$ instead of $\mathsf{OAEP}_{\mathsf{t\text{-}clear}}[\mathcal{G}, \mathcal{H}, \mathcal{F}|_{\zeta+\rho}]$ and $\mathsf{OAEP}_{\mathsf{s\text{-}clear}}[\mathcal{G}, \mathcal{H}, \mathcal{F}|^{\mu+\zeta}]$. We typically think of $\mathcal{F}$ as RSA, and all our results apply to this case under suitable assumptions. Note that, following prior work, despite its name t-clear $\mathcal{F}$-OAEP we actually apply $\mathcal{F}$ to only the μ most significant bits of the output of the underlying padding scheme, leaving the redundancy part of s in the clear as well.

3 Partial Instantiation Results for RSA-OAEP

In this section, we give partial instantiations of either $\mathcal{G}$ or $\mathcal{H}$ for RSA-OAEP under IND-CCA2. Our results use only mild standard model properties of $\mathcal{G}$ or $\mathcal{H}$. We also use (generalizations of) algebraic properties of RSA proven by Barthe *et al.* [3] for small enough e. For example, using a 2048-bit modulus and encrypting a 128-bit AES key, our results hold for $e = 3$. They might be true for larger e; at least, they cannot be disproved. Note that our results first necessitate a separate proof of IND-CPA—the standard model IND-CPA results of Kiltz *et al.* [48] and Bellare *et al.* [5] are not suitable, the first requiring large e and the second holding only for public-key independent messages.

3.1 Algebraic Properties of RSA

We first give generalizations of algebraic properties of RSA from Barthe *et al.* [3] that we use, and their parameters. They used these assumptions to analyze security of a zero-redudancy one-round version of RSA-OAEP. We show that generalizations are useful for analyzing security of full RSA-OAEP.

SECOND-INPUT EXTRACTABILITY. Let $\mathcal{F} = (\mathsf{Kg}, \mathsf{Eval}, \mathsf{Inv})$ be a trapdoor permutation family with domain $\{0,1\}^n$. For $1 \le i \le j \le n$, we say $\mathcal{F}$ is (i,j)-*second-input-extractable* (BB (i,j)-SIE) if there exists an efficient extractor $\mathcal{E}$ such that for every $k \in \mathbb{N}$, every $f \in [\mathsf{Kg}(1^k)]$, and every $x \in \{0,1\}^n$, extractor $\mathcal{E}$ on inputs $f, f(x), x|_{i+1}^{j}$ outputs x. We often write ζ-SIE instead of $(n-\zeta, n)$-SIE.

COMMON-INPUT EXTRACTABILITY. Let $\mathcal{F} = (\mathsf{Kg}, \mathsf{Eval}, \mathsf{Inv})$ be a trapdoor permutation family with domain $\{0,1\}^n$. For $1 \le i \le j \le n$, we say $\mathcal{F}$ is (i,j)-*common-input-extractable* if there exists an efficient extractor $\mathcal{E}$ such that for every $k \in \mathbb{N}$, every $f \in [\mathsf{Kg}(1^k)]$, and every $x_1, x_2 \in \mathsf{TDom}(k)$, extractor $\mathcal{E}$ on inputs $f, f(x_1), f(x_2)$ outputs (x_1, x_2) if $x_1|_{i+1}^{j} = x_2|_{i+1}^{j}$. We often write ζ-CIE instead of $(n-\zeta, n)$-CIE.

COMPARISON TO BARTHE *et al.* Compared to [3], we generalize the notions of SIE and CIE to consider arbitrary runs of consecutive bits. That is, [3] only considers the most significant bits; *i.e.*, ζ-SIE and ζ-CIE in our notation.

PARAMETERS. Barthe *et al.* [3] show via the univariate Coppersmith algorithm [30] that RSA is ζ-SIE and ζ-CIE for sufficiently large ζ. Specifically, they show RSA is ζ_1-SIE for $\zeta_1 > n(e-1)/e$, and ζ_2-CIE for $\zeta_2 > n(e^2-1)/e^2$. We show that a generalization to runs of arbitrary consecutive bits using the *bivariate* Coppersmith algorithm [15,30,31]. Specifically, we show that RSA is (i,j)-SIE for $(j-i) > n(e-1)/e$, and (i,j)-CIE for $(j-i) > n(e^2-1)/e^2$, Due to space constraints, this is shown in the full version. Note that in our partial instantiation results for RSA-OAEP, $j-i$ refers to the length of the redundancy ζ.

3.2 Main Results

MAIN RESULTS. We now give our main results, namely partial instantiations for RSA-OAEP of either oracle $\mathcal{G}$ or $\mathcal{H}$. These results refer to IND-CCA2 security for simplicity, whereas we actually prove PA-RO + IND-CPA.

Theorem 3. Let n, μ, ζ, ρ be integer parameters. Let $\mathcal{G} : \mathcal{K}_G \times \{0,1\}^\rho \to \{0,1\}^{\mu+\zeta}$ be a pseudorandom generator and $\mathcal{H} : \{0,1\}^{\mu+\zeta} \to \{0,1\}^\rho$ be a RO. Let $\mathcal{F}$ be a family of trapdoor permutations with domain $\{0,1\}^n$, where $n = \mu + \zeta + \rho$. Suppose $\mathcal{F}$ is one-way, $(\mu+\zeta)$-second input and $(\mu+\zeta)$-common input extractable. Then $\mathsf{OAEP}[\mathcal{G}, \mathcal{H}, \mathcal{F}]$ is IND-CCA2 secure. In particular, for any adversary A, there is an adversary D and an inverter I such that

$$\mathbf{Adv}^{\text{ind-cca2}}_{\mathsf{OAEP}[\mathcal{G},\mathcal{H},\mathcal{F}],A}(k) \le 2 \cdot \mathbf{Adv}^{\text{owf}}_{\mathcal{F},I}(k) + 10 \cdot \mathbf{Adv}^{\text{prg}}_{\mathcal{G},D}(k) + \frac{2p}{2^{\mu+\zeta}} + \frac{4q}{2^{\zeta}}.$$

where q is the total number of the decryption queries and p is the total number of RO queries made by A. Furthermore, the running time of D and I are about that of A plus the time to run SIE and CIE extractors.

Theorem 4. Let n, μ, ζ, ρ be integer parameters. Let $\mathcal{H} : \mathcal{K}_H \times \{0,1\}^{\mu+\zeta} \to \{0,1\}^{\rho}$ be a hash function family and $\mathcal{G} : \{0,1\}^{\rho} \to \{0,1\}^{\mu+\zeta}$ be a RO. Let $\mathcal{F}$ be a family of trapdoor permutations with domain $\{0,1\}^n$, where $n = \mu+\zeta+\rho$. Suppose $\mathcal{F}$ is $(\rho, \rho+\zeta)$-second input and $(\rho, \rho+\zeta)$-common input extractable. Suppose further $\mathcal{H}$ is a $(\mu+\zeta)$-partial hardcore function for $\mathcal{F}$. Then $\mathsf{OAEP}[\mathcal{G}, \mathcal{H}, \mathcal{F}]$ is IND-CCA2. In particular, for any adversary $A = (A_1, A_2)$, there exists an adversary B such that

$$\mathbf{Adv}^{\text{ind-cca2}}_{\mathsf{OAEP}[\mathcal{G},\mathcal{H},\mathcal{F}],A}(k) \leq 2 \cdot \mathbf{Adv}^{\text{phcf}}_{\mathcal{F},\mathcal{H},B}(k) + \frac{2p}{2^{\rho}} + \frac{4q}{2^{\zeta}}.$$

where q the total number of the decryption queries and p is the total number of RO queries made by A. Furthermore, the running time of B is about that of A plus the time to run SIE and CIE extractors.

The proofs of both theorems follow from below.

Parameters for RSA-OAEP. We discuss when our results support RSA-OAEP encryption of an AES key of appropriate length, based on Subsect. 3.1. The main requirement is encryption exponent $e = 3$. In this case, with length 2048 bits we can use randomness and message length 128 bits, and for modulus length 4096 we can use randomness length 256. The choice that $e = 3$ is sometimes used in practice but it is an interesting open problem to extend our results to other common choices such as $e = 2^{16} + 1$. In particular, it may be possible that SIE and CIE hold in this case for the same parameters. Interestingly, we have a "flipped" situation vs. [48] who show IND-CPA security of RSA-OAEP in the standard model using *large exponent* RSA. We hope future work will help reconcile these differences.

3.3 Partial Instantiation of *G*

We first show how to instantiate $\mathcal{G}$ when modeling $\mathcal{H}$ as a RO. In particular, we show $\mathsf{OAEP}[\mathcal{G}, \mathcal{H}, \mathcal{F}]$ is IND-CPA + PA-RO when $\mathcal{G}$ is a pseudorandom generator and $\mathcal{F}$ is one-way, $(\mu+\zeta)$-SIE and $(\mu+\zeta)$-CIE.
IND-CPA Result. Under IND-CPA, we show a tight reduction when $\mathcal{G}$ is a pseudorandom generator and $\mathcal{F}$ is one-way and $(\mu+\zeta)$-SIE. Alternatively, we give result where $\mathcal{F}$ is only partial one-way, but the reduction is lossy (due to space constraints, this is shown in the full version). Note that it is shown in [38] that one-wayness of RSA implies partial one-wayness, but the reduction is even more lossy, while SIE and CIE unconditionally hold for appropriate parameters.

Theorem 5. Let n, μ, ζ, ρ be integer parameters. Let $\mathcal{G} : \mathcal{K}_G \times \{0,1\}^{\rho} \to \{0,1\}^{\mu+\zeta}$ be a pseudorandom generator and $\mathcal{H} : \{0,1\}^{\mu+\zeta} \to \{0,1\}^{\rho}$ be a RO. Let $\mathcal{F}$ be a family of trapdoor permutations with domain $\{0,1\}^n$, where

$n = \mu + \zeta + \rho$. Suppose $\mathcal{F}$ is one-way and $(\mu+\zeta)$-second input extractable. Then $\mathsf{OAEP}[\mathcal{G}, \mathcal{H}, \mathcal{F}]$ is IND-CPA. In particular, for any adversary $A = (A_1, A_2)$, there are an adversary D and an inverter I such that

$$\mathbf{Adv}^{\text{ind-cpa}}_{\mathsf{OAEP}[\mathcal{G},\mathcal{H},\mathcal{F}],A}(k) \leq 2 \cdot \mathbf{Adv}^{\text{owf}}_{\mathcal{F},I}(k) + 6 \cdot \mathbf{Adv}^{\text{prg}}_{\mathcal{G},D}(k) + \frac{2q}{2^{\mu+\zeta}}.$$

where q is the total number of RO queries made by A. Furthermore, the running time of D is about that of A and the running time of I is about that of A plus the time to run SIE extractor.

Proof Idea. Let $c = f(s\|t)$ be the challenge ciphertext. Note that, it is unlikely that A queries value s to $\mathcal{H}$ since one could use SIE extractor to invert challenge c knowing s. Thus, value t looks random to A. Moreover, we know $\mathcal{G}$ is PRG, then value s looks random. Therefore, challenge c looks random to A.

PA-RO Result. We show RSA-OAEP is PA-RO when modeling $\mathcal{H}$ as a RO if $\mathcal{G}$ is a pseudorandom generator and $\mathcal{F}$ is both second-input extractable and common-input extractable.

Theorem 6. Let n, μ, ζ, ρ be integer parameters. Let $\mathcal{G} : \mathcal{K}_G \times \{0,1\}^\rho \to \{0,1\}^{\mu+\zeta}$ be a pseudorandom generator and $\mathcal{H} : \{0,1\}^{\mu+\zeta} \to \{0,1\}^\rho$ be a RO. Let $\mathcal{F}$ be a family of trapdoor permutations with domain $\{0,1\}^n$, where $n = \mu + \zeta + \rho$. Suppose $\mathcal{F}$ is $(\mu+\zeta)$-second input and $(\mu+\zeta)$-common input extractable. Then $\mathsf{OAEP}[\mathcal{G}, \mathcal{H}, \mathcal{F}]$ is PA-RO secure. In particular, for any adversary A, there exists an adversary D and an extractor Ext such that

$$\mathbf{Adv}^{\text{pa-ro}}_{\mathsf{OAEP}[\mathcal{G},\mathcal{H},\mathcal{F}],A,\mathsf{Ext}}(k) \leq 2 \cdot \mathbf{Adv}^{\text{prg}}_{\mathcal{G},D}(k) + \frac{2q}{2^\zeta}.$$

where q is the total number of the extraction queries made by A. Furthermore, the running time of D is about that of A and the running time of Ext is about that of SIE and CIE extractors.

Proof Idea. Let $c = f(s\|t)$ be the extract query made by A. If there is a prior query s to $\mathcal{H}$, then one could use SIE or CIE extractor to extract message m. Otherwise the challenge c is invalid whp, since the ζ-lsb of $G(K_G, r)$ and s are not equal on random r whp, when $\mathcal{G}$ is PRG.

3.4 Partial Instantiation of *H*

Now, we instantiate the hash function $\mathcal{H}$ when modeling only $\mathcal{G}$ as a RO. In particular, we show $\mathsf{OAEP}[\mathcal{G}, \mathcal{H}, \mathcal{F}]$ is IND-CPA + PA-RO when $\mathcal{H}$ is a special type of hardcore function and $\mathcal{F}$ is one-way, second-input and common-input extractable. Note that Boneh [20] previously showed a simplified RSA-OAEP with one Feistel round $\mathcal{G}$ is IND-CCA2 secure and Barthe *et al.* [3] showed such a scheme does not even need redundancy, but these proof do not translate to the case of $\mathcal{H}$ as a cryptographic hash function.

IND-CPA RESULT. Under IND-CPA, we show a tight reduction when $\mathcal{H}$ is a $(\mu+\zeta)$-partial hardcore function for $\mathcal{F}$. In particular, it is plausible for $\mathcal{H}$ as a computational randomness extractor [32] and that $\mathcal{F}$ is RSA in the common setting $\rho = k$ (*e.g.*, $\rho = 128$ for modulus length $n = 2048$), since Coppersmith's technique fails.

Theorem 7. Let n, μ, ζ, ρ be integer parameters. Let $\mathcal{H} : \mathcal{K}_H \times \{0,1\}^{\mu+\zeta} \to \{0,1\}^\rho$ be a hash function family and $\mathcal{G} : \{0,1\}^\rho \to \{0,1\}^{\mu+\zeta}$ be a RO. Let $\mathcal{F}$ be a family of trapdoor permutations with domain $\{0,1\}^n$, where $n = \mu+\zeta+\rho$. Suppose $\mathcal{H}$ is a $(\mu+\zeta)$-partial hardcore function for $\mathcal{F}$. Then $\mathsf{OAEP}[\mathcal{G}, \mathcal{H}, \mathcal{F}]$ is IND-CPA. In particular, for any adversary $A = (A_1, A_2)$, there exists an adversary B such that

$$\mathbf{Adv}^{\text{ind-cpa}}_{\mathsf{OAEP}[\mathcal{G},\mathcal{H},\mathcal{F}],A}(k) \le 2 \cdot \mathbf{Adv}^{\text{phcf}}_{\mathcal{F},\mathcal{H},B}(k) + \frac{2q}{2^\rho},$$

where q is the total number of RO queries made by A. The running time of B is about that of A.

PROOF IDEA. Let $c = f(s\|t)$ be the challenge ciphertext. Note that, it is unlikely that A queries r to $\mathcal{G}$, since one can build an adversary B attacking $\mathcal{H}$. Moreover, if A does not query r to $\mathcal{G}$, value s looks random and A won't be able to obtain any information about b.

PA-RO RESULT. We show another partial instantiation result modeling only $\mathcal{G}$ as a RO. Namely, we show RSA-OAEP is PA-RO if $\mathcal{F}$ is second-input extractable, and common-input extractable. Note that this does not require any assumption on $\mathcal{H}$.

Theorem 8. Let n, μ, ζ, ρ be integer parameters. Let $\mathcal{H} : \{0,1\}^{\mu+\zeta} \to \{0,1\}^\rho$ be a hash function family and $\mathcal{G} : \mathcal{K}_G \times \{0,1\}^\rho \to \{0,1\}^{\mu+\zeta}$ be a RO. Let $\mathcal{F}$ be a family of trapdoor permutations with domain $\{0,1\}^n$, where $n = \mu+\zeta+\rho$. Suppose $\mathcal{F}$ is $(\rho, \rho+\zeta)$-second input and $(\rho, \rho+\zeta)$-common input extractable. Then $\mathsf{OAEP}[\mathcal{G}, \mathcal{H}, \mathcal{F}]$ is PA-RO secure. In particular, for any adversary A, there exists an extractor Ext such that,

$$\mathbf{Adv}^{\text{pa-ro}}_{\mathsf{OAEP}[\mathcal{G},\mathcal{H},\mathcal{F}],A,\mathsf{Ext}}(k) \le \frac{2q}{2^\zeta}.$$

where q is the total number of the extract queries made by A. The running time of Ext is about that of SIE and CIE extractors.

PROOF IDEA. Let $c = f(s\|t)$ be the extract query made by A. If there is a prior query r to $\mathcal{G}$, then one with knowledge of $\mathcal{G}(r)|_\zeta$ could use SIE or CIE extractor to extract message m. Otherwise, the challenge c is invalid whp, since the ζ-lsb of $\mathcal{G}(H(K_H, s) \oplus t)$ and s are not equal whp.

4 A Hierarchy of Extractability Notions

Intuitively, extractability of a function formalizes the idea that an adversary that produces a point in the image must "know" a corresponding preimage, as there being a non-blackbox extractor that produces one. Previous work on extractability starting with [26,27] considers a "one-shot" adversary. Inspired by the related notion of plaintext awareness for encryption schemes [4,8], we define a hierarchy of extractability notions called EXT0, EXT1, EXT2, and EXT-RO, which will in particular be useful for our full instantiation results. Even our notion of EXT0 generalizes prior work, as explained below.

EXT Functions. Let η, ζ, μ be integer parameters. Let $\mathcal{H} : \mathcal{K}_H \times \mathsf{HDom} \rightarrow \mathsf{HRng}$ be a hash function family. For EXTI $\in$ {EXT0, EXT1, EXT2}, we associate the experiment in Fig. 6 to an adversary A and extractor Ext, for every $k \in \mathbb{N}$. For any key independent auxiliary input $z \in \{0,1\}^\eta$, we define

$$\mathbf{Adv}^{(\eta,\mu)\text{-exti}_\zeta}_{\mathcal{H},\mathcal{F},A,\mathsf{Ext},z}(k) = \Pr_{\substack{K_H \leftarrow\$ \mathcal{K}_H(1^k) \\ r \leftarrow\$ \mathsf{Coins}(k)}}\left[\begin{array}{c}(\mathbf{x},\mathbf{y}) \leftarrow \mathrm{EXTI}^{A,\mathcal{E},z}_{\mathcal{H},\mathcal{F}}(K_H, r) \\ \exists i, \exists x : H(K_H, x)|_\zeta = \mathbf{y}[i] \wedge \mathbf{x}[i]|_\mu = x|_\mu \wedge H(K_H, \mathbf{x}[i])|_\zeta \neq \mathbf{y}[i]\end{array}\right]$$

We define the EXTI advantage of A to be $\mathbf{Adv}^{(\eta,\mu)\text{-exti}_\zeta}_{\mathcal{H},\mathcal{F},A,\mathsf{Ext}}(k) = \max_{z \in \{0,1\}^\eta} \mathbf{Adv}^{(\eta,\mu)\text{-exti}_\zeta}_{\mathcal{H},\mathcal{F},A,\mathsf{Ext},z}(k)$. If EXTI = EXT1, then $\mathcal{O} = \varepsilon$. Note that, in EXT1 definition, adversary A have only access to extract oracle $\mathcal{E}$. EXT0 is defined similarly to EXT1, except A is only allowed to make a single extract query. If EXTI = EXT2, then $\mathcal{O} = \mathcal{I}$, where $\mathcal{I}$ is an image oracle. We say $\mathcal{H}$ is (η,μ)-EXTI$_\zeta$ if for any PPT adversary A with coin space Coins, there exists a stateful extractor $\mathcal{E}$ such that $\mathbf{Adv}^{(\eta,\mu)\text{-exti}_\zeta}_{\mathcal{H},\mathcal{F},A,\mathsf{Ext}}(k)$ is negligible in k.

Similarly, we define the analogous notion (η,μ)-EXTI$^\zeta$ where the adversary outputs the ζ *most* significant bits of the image point. We often write η-EXTI$_\zeta$ and η-EXTI$^\zeta$ instead of $(\eta, 0)$-EXTI$_\zeta$ and $(\eta, 0)$-EXTI$^\zeta$, respectively. We also often write (η,μ)-EXTI instead of (η,μ)-EXTI$_\zeta$ when $\zeta = \log|\mathsf{HRng}|$.

Game $\mathrm{EXTI}^{A,\mathcal{E},z}_{\mathcal{H},\mathcal{F}}(K_H, r)$	**Procedure** $\mathcal{E}(x_2, y)$
$i \leftarrow 1$; $j \leftarrow 1$; $st \leftarrow \varepsilon$	If $y \in \mathbf{h}_1$ then return $\perp$
$\mathbf{x} \leftarrow \varepsilon$; $\mathbf{y} \leftarrow \varepsilon$; $\mathbf{h} \leftarrow \varepsilon$	$(st, x_1) \leftarrow \mathsf{Ext}(st, K_H, f, z, \mathbf{h}, \mathbf{w}, x_2, y; r)$
$\mathbf{h}_1 \leftarrow \varepsilon$; $\mathbf{w} \leftarrow \varepsilon$	$\mathbf{x}[i] \leftarrow x_1 \Vert x_2$; $\mathbf{y}[i] \leftarrow y$; $i \leftarrow i+1$
$(f, f^{-1}) \leftarrow\$ \mathsf{Kg}(1^k)$	Return x_1
Run $A^{\mathcal{E}(\cdot,\cdot),\mathcal{O}}(K_H, f, z; r)$	**Procedure** $\mathcal{I}(1^k)$
Return $(\mathbf{x}, \mathbf{y})$	$v \leftarrow\$ \mathsf{HDom}(k)$; $h \leftarrow H(K_H, v)$
	$\mathbf{h}[j] \leftarrow h$; $\mathbf{w}[j] \leftarrow f(v)$; $\mathbf{h}_1[j] \leftarrow h|_\zeta$; $j \leftarrow j+1$
	Return $(h, f(v))$

Fig. 6. Game to define EXTI security.

We generalized the notion of extractable functions in two ways. First, the extractor should work when the adversary outputs ζ least significant bits of an image point and μ bits of a preimage, given η bits of auxiliary information. Previous work considered $\zeta = \log|\mathsf{HRng}|$ and $\mu = 0$. Next, we give a definition of "many-times" extractability. We note that a central open problem in the theory of extractable functions to construct a "many-times" extractable function from a "one-time" extractable function, see *e.g.* [41]; the obvious approach suffers an extractor "blow-up" issue. For practical purposes, we simply formalize and assume this property for an appropriate construction from cryptographic hashing.

In the EXT2 notion, we extend the definition of EXT1 and give the adversary access to an oracle $\mathcal{I}$ that outputs the function evaluation of a random point from its domain along with an uninvertible hint about the corresponding preimage (We also consider EXT2 notion without a hint, where the uninvertable hint is an empty function). The adversary is not allowed to query any such point to the extract oracle $\mathcal{E}$. In other words, this is a form of extractability with key dependent auxiliary information that parallels PA2 for encryption schemes. Note that we avoid the impossibility result of [13] since in all of our EXT definitions, we consider only bounded independent auxiliary information.

EXT-RO FUNCTIONS. Finally, we give a notion of extractability in the RO model, inspired by PA-RO for encryption schemes. In particular, here the adversary has access to an oracle F to which it queries a sampling algorithm, the oracle returning the image of a point in the domain sampled accordingly. Moreover, instead of the adversary's random coins the extractor gets a transcript of its RO queries and responses, but *not* those made by F. Due to space constraints, we refer to the full version for the complete definition.

PLAUSIBILITY. We typically use EXT notions in tandem with other properties such as collision-resistance. In terms of feasibility, there are several constructions proposed for EXT0 with $\zeta = \log|\mathsf{HRng}|$ and $\mu = 0$ and collision-resistance in [52] based on knowledge assumptions. (In the weaker case of EXT0 with only one-wayness, which does not suffice for us, the notion is actually achievable for these parameters under standard assumptions [13].) However, for our generalizations and notions of EXT1, EXT2, we are not aware of any constructions in the standard model. Despite the fact that they are difficult to judge, it may be a reality that as a community we need to move to such assumptions in order to make progress on some difficult problems. A similar strategy was used for very different goals by Pandey *et al.* [54]. It would be interesting for future work to explore relations between our assumptions and theirs.

5 Results for Padding Schemes and OAEP

We abstract properties of the OAEP padding scheme and prove them based on corresponding notions for the round functions. Namely, we study near-collision resistance, $\mathrm{EXT0}_{\zeta+\rho}$, $\mathrm{EXT1}^{\mu+\zeta}$ and $(\zeta+\rho)$-EXT-RO. In particular, note that while the OAEP padding scheme is invertible these notions are non-trivial because we consider adversaries that only produce part of the output. Proving the other notions, $\mathrm{EXT1}_{\zeta+\rho}$, $\mathrm{EXT2}^{\mu+\zeta}$ and $\mathrm{EXT2}_{\zeta+\rho}$, in the standard model based on assumptions on the round functions remains open. However, they could be justified as assumptions by the fact that OAEP is $(\zeta+\rho)$-EXT-RO, similarly to showing a RO is UCE [5, Section 6.1]. Due to space constraints, these are shown in the full version.

6 Full Instantiation Results for s-Clear RSA-OAEP

In this section, we give full instantiation results for s-clear RSA-OAEP. Note that we are the first to consider this variant. We show that s-clear is IND-CCA2 if $\mathcal{G}$ is a pseudorandom generator, near-collision resistant, and "many-times" extractable with dependent auxiliary information, $\mathcal{H}$ is collision-resistant, and $\mathcal{F}$ meets novel "XOR-nonmalleability" and "XOR-indistinguishability" notions that seem plausible for RSA. Also note that we avoid the several impossibility results here. First, we avoid the impossibility result of [58] by using XOR-nonmalleability of $\mathcal{F}$. Second, we avoid the impossibility result of [13] since the dependent auxiliary information is bounded.

6.1 XOR Assumptions on Trapdoor Permutations and RSA

Here, we give classes of novel assumptions on RSA (and trapdoor permutations in general), which are stronger than one-wayness and needed for RSA-OAEP s-clear.

XOR-IND. Our first class of assumptions speaks to the fact that addition or XOR operations "break up" the multiplicative structure of RSA. Indeed, in a related context of arithmetic progressions on $\mathbb{Z}_N$ we have seen formal evidence of this [51,60]. It is interesting for future work to give formal evidence in our case as well. Let $\mathcal{F} = (\mathsf{Kg}, \mathsf{Eval}, \mathsf{Inv})$ be a trapdoor permutation family with domain TDom. Let $\mathcal{G} : \mathcal{K}_G \times \mathsf{TDom} \to \mathsf{GRng}$ be a function family. For $\mathrm{ATK} \in \{\mathrm{IND0}, \mathrm{IND1}, \mathrm{IND2}\}$, we associate the experiment in Fig. 7, for every $k \in \mathbb{N}$. Define the xor-atk advantage of A against $\mathcal{F}$ with the hint function family $\mathcal{G}$

$$\mathbf{Adv}^{\text{xor-atk}}_{\mathcal{F},\mathcal{G},A}(k) = 2 \cdot \Pr\left[\text{XOR-ATK}^{A}_{\mathcal{F},\mathcal{G}}(k) \Rightarrow 1\right] - 1.$$

If atk = ind0, then $\mathcal{O} = \varepsilon$. We say that $\mathcal{F}$ is XOR-IND0 with respect to hint function family $\mathcal{G}$ if for every PPT attacker A, $\mathbf{Adv}^{\text{xor-ind0}}_{\mathcal{F},\mathcal{G},A}(k)$ is negligible in k. Similarly, if atk = ind1, then $\mathcal{O} = \mathcal{C}$, where $\mathcal{C}$ is a relation checker oracle that on input y_1, y_2 and ω outputs 1, if $\omega = f^{-1}(y_1) \oplus f^{-1}(y_2)$, otherwise outputs 0. Similarly, if atk = ind2, then $\mathcal{O} = \mathcal{V}_\ell$, where $\mathcal{V}_\ell$ is an ℓ-bit image verifier oracle that on input y outputs 1, if there exists x such that $y = G(K_G, x)|_\ell$, otherwise outputs 0. Note that A is not allowed to query for the challenge to $\mathcal{V}$. We say that $\mathcal{F}$ is XOR-IND1 (resp. XOR-IND2$_\ell$) with respect to hint function family $\mathcal{G}$ if for every PPT attacker A, $\mathbf{Adv}^{\text{xor-ind1}}_{\mathcal{F},\mathcal{G},A}(k)$ (resp. $\mathbf{Adv}^{\text{xor-ind2}_\ell}_{\mathcal{F},\mathcal{G},A}(k)$) is negligible in k.

Game XOR-ATK$^A_{\mathcal{F},\mathcal{G}}(k)$
$b \leftarrow\!\!\$ \{0,1\}$; $(f, f^{-1}) \leftarrow \mathsf{Kg}(1^k)$
$K_G \leftarrow \mathcal{K}_G(1^k)$; $x \leftarrow\!\!\$ \mathsf{TDom}(k)$
$(state, z) \leftarrow\!\!\$ A_1(f, K_G, G(K_G, x))$
$y_0 \leftarrow f(x)$; $y_1 \leftarrow f(x \oplus z)$
$b' \leftarrow\!\!\$ A_2^{\mathcal{O}}(state, y_b)$
Return $(b = b')$

Fig. 7. Games to define XOR-ATK security.

Observe that the hint is *crucial*, as otherwise the assumption would trivially hold. In our results, $\mathcal{G}$ is a PRG. In this case, we show that $\mathcal{G}$ is also a HCF function for $\mathcal{F}$. In other words, the assumption in our use-case can be viewed an extension of the classical notion of HCF—$\mathcal{G}$ is "robust" not in the sense of [40], but in the sense that the view of the adversary is also indistinguishable given $\mathcal{F}$ applied to either the real input or *related one.* Note that not all hardcore functions have this property, even when $\mathcal{F}$ is partial one-way. For example, consider a hardcore function $\mathcal{G}$ that reveals first bit of its input x. Then if a partial one-way function $\mathcal{F}$ also reveals the first bit of x, XOR-indistinguishability clearly does not hold.

Theorem 9. Let $\mathcal{F}$ be a family of one-way trapdoor permutations with domain TDom. Suppose $\mathcal{G} : \mathcal{K}_G \times \mathsf{TDom} \to \mathsf{GRng}$ is a pseudorandom generator and $\mathcal{F}$ is XOR-IND0 with respect to hint function family $\mathcal{G}$. Then $\mathcal{G}$ is a hardcore function for $\mathcal{F}$ on the uniform distribution. In particular, for any adversary A, there are adversaries B, C such that

$$\mathbf{Adv}^{\mathrm{hcf}}_{\mathcal{F},\mathcal{G},U,A}(k) \leq 2 \cdot \mathbf{Adv}^{\mathrm{xor\text{-}ind0}}_{\mathcal{F},\mathcal{G},B}(k) + 2 \cdot \mathbf{Adv}^{\mathrm{prg}}_{\mathcal{G},C}(k).$$

XOR-NM0. Our second class of assumptions speak to the fact that RSA is non-malleable wrt. XOR. Intuitively, if RSA was XOR malleable, then since it is multiplicatively homomorphic it would be (something like) fully homomorphic, which is unlikely. (Although we do not claim the exact formulation of our definitions imply a formal definition of fully homomorphic.) A similar argument was made by Hofheinz for a non-malleability assumption on the Paillier trapdoor permutation (which is additively homomorphic) wrt. multiplication [Assumption 4.2][44]. Let $\mathcal{F} = (\mathsf{Kg}, \mathsf{Eval}, \mathsf{Inv})$ be a trapdoor permutation family with domain TDom. To attacker A, we associate the experiment in Fig. 8 for every $k \in \mathbb{N}$. We say that $\mathcal{F}$ is XOR-NM0 if for every PPT attacker A,

$$\mathbf{Adv}^{\mathrm{xor\text{-}nm0}}_{\mathcal{F},A}(k) = \Pr\left[\mathrm{XOR\text{-}NM0}^A_{\mathcal{F}}(k) \Rightarrow 1\right].$$

is negligible in k.
XOR-NM1. Let $\mathcal{F} = (\mathsf{Kg}, \mathsf{Eval}, \mathsf{Inv})$ be a trapdoor permutation family with domain TDom. Let $\mathcal{G} : \mathcal{K}_G \times \mathsf{TDom} \to \mathsf{GRng}$ be a hash function family.

Game XOR-NM0$^A_{\mathcal{F}}(k)$	Game XOR-NM1$^A_{\mathcal{F},\mathcal{G}}(k)$
$(f, f^{-1}) \leftarrow \mathsf{Kg}(1^k)$	$(f, f^{-1}) \leftarrow \mathsf{Kg}(1^k)$; $K_G \leftarrow \mathcal{K}_G(1^k)$
$x \leftarrow_\$ \mathsf{TDom}(k)$	$x \leftarrow_\$ \mathsf{TDom}(k)$; $z \leftarrow G(K_G, x)$
$(\omega, y') \leftarrow_\$ A(f, f(x))$	$(\alpha, st) \leftarrow_\$ A_1(f, K_G, z)$
$x' \leftarrow f^{-1}(y')$	$(\omega, y') \leftarrow_\$ A_2(st, f(x \oplus \alpha))$
If $(\omega = x \oplus x') \wedge (\omega \neq 0)$	$x' \leftarrow f^{-1}(y')$
Return 1	If $(\omega \oplus \alpha = x \oplus x') \wedge (\omega \neq 0)$ then return 1
Else return 0	Else return 0

Fig. 8. Games to define XOR-NM security.

To attacker A, we associate the experiment in Fig. 8 for every $k \in \mathbb{N}$. We say that $\mathcal{F}$ is XOR-NM1 with respect to $\mathcal{G}$ if for every PPT attacker A,

$$\mathbf{Adv}^{\text{xor-nm1}}_{\mathcal{F},\mathcal{G},A}(k) = \Pr\left[\text{XOR-NM1}^A_{\mathcal{F},\mathcal{G}}(k) \Rightarrow 1\right].$$

is negligible in k.

Relations Between Definitions. Interestingly, we show XOR-NM0 and XOR-IND1 together imply XOR-NM1.

Theorem 10. Let $\mathcal{F} = (\mathsf{Kg}, \mathsf{Eval}, \mathsf{Inv})$ be a trapdoor permutation family with domain TDom. Let $\mathcal{G} : \mathcal{K}_G \times \mathsf{TDom} \to \mathsf{GRng}$ be a function family. Suppose $\mathcal{F}$ is XOR-NM0 and XOR-IND1 with respect to $\mathcal{G}$. Then, $\mathcal{F}$ is XOR-NM1 with respect to $\mathcal{G}$. In particular, for any adversary A, there are adversaries B, C such that

$$\mathbf{Adv}^{\text{xor-nm1}}_{\mathcal{F},\mathcal{G},A}(k) \leq \mathbf{Adv}^{\text{xor-nm0}}_{\mathcal{F},\mathcal{G},B}(k) + 2 \cdot \mathbf{Adv}^{\text{xor-ind1}}_{\mathcal{F},\mathcal{G},C}(k).$$

Discussion. We caution that these are new assumptions and must be treated with care, although they have some intuitive appeal as discussed where they are introduced. It would be interesting for future work to establish theoretical constructions meeting them or show that RSA meets them under more well-studied assumptions.

6.2 Main Results

After establishing its security in the RO model, we show that s-clear RSA-OAEP is IND-CCA1 and IND-CCA2 under respective suitable assumptions. As in Sect. 3 we actually prove corresponding notions of IND-CPA + PA, yielding stronger results. The results in Section follow from those below.

IND-CCA2 Result in RO Model. First, note that the partial one-wayness result of [39] does not apply to this variant, and in fact the negative result of [59] *does* apply, demonstrating that one-wayness of the trapdoor permutation is not enough for the scheme to achieve IND-CCA2 security *even in the RO model.* We show that XOR-nonmalleability is sufficient.

Theorem 11. *Let μ, ζ, ρ be integer parameters. Let $\mathcal{F}$ be a XOR-NM0 family of one-way trapdoor permutations with domain $\{0,1\}^\rho$. Suppose $\mathcal{G} : \mathcal{K}_G \times \{0,1\}^\rho \rightarrow \{0,1\}^{\mu+\zeta}$ is a RO and $\mathcal{H} : \mathcal{K}_H \times \{0,1\}^{\mu+\zeta} \rightarrow \{0,1\}^\rho$ is collision-resistant. Then $\mathsf{OAEP}_{\text{s-clear}}[\mathcal{G}, \mathcal{H}, \mathcal{F}|^{\mu+\zeta}]$ is IND-CCA2 secure in the random oracle model. In particular, for any adversary A, there are adversaries B, C such that*

$$\mathbf{Adv}^{\text{ind-cca2}}_{\mathsf{OAEP}_{\text{s-clear}},A}(k) \leq \frac{2q}{2^\rho} + \frac{4p}{2^\zeta} + 2 \cdot \mathbf{Adv}^{\text{cr}}_{\mathcal{H},C}(k) + 4 \cdot \mathbf{Adv}^{\text{xor-nm0}}_{\mathcal{F},B}(k).$$

where p is the number of decryption-oracle queries of A and q is the total number of random-oracle queries of A and $\mathcal{M}$. Adversary B and C makes at most q random-oracle queries.

IND-CCA1 RESULT. To prove IND-CCA1, we use EXT1 and near-collision resistance of the overall OAEP padding scheme (which follows from assumptions on the round functions as per Sect. 5), as well as the assumption that $\mathcal{G}$ is a pseudorandom generator and $\mathcal{F}$ is XOR-IND (as defined in Sect. 6.1).

Theorem 12. *Let η, μ, ζ, ρ be integer parameters. Let $\mathcal{F}$ be a family of trapdoor permutations with domain $\{0,1\}^\mu$, and let $\eta = |[\mathsf{Kg}(1^k)]|$. Let $\mathcal{G} : \mathcal{K}_G \times \{0,1\}^\rho \rightarrow \{0,1\}^{\mu+\zeta}$ and $\mathcal{H} : \mathcal{K}_H \times \{0,1\}^{\mu+\zeta} \rightarrow \{0,1\}^\rho$ be function families. Suppose $\mathcal{G}$ is a pseudorandom generator, and let $\mathcal{F}$ is XOR-IND0 with respect to hint function $\mathcal{G}$ (as defined in Sect. 6.1). Also suppose $\mathsf{OAEP}[\mathcal{G}, \mathcal{H}]$ is η-EXT1$^{\mu+\zeta}$ and NCR$^{\mu+\zeta}$. Then $\mathsf{OAEP}_{\text{s-clear}}[\mathcal{G}, \mathcal{H}, \mathcal{F}|^{\mu+\zeta}]$ is IND-CCA1 secure. In particular, for any adversary A that makes q decryption queries, there exist adversaries C, D, E, and EXT1 adversary B that makes q extract queries such that for all extractors* Ext,

$$\mathbf{Adv}^{\text{ind-cca1}}_{\mathsf{OAEP}_{\text{s-clear}},A}(k) \leq 2 \cdot \mathbf{Adv}^{\eta\text{-ext1}^{\mu+\zeta}}_{\mathsf{OAEP}[\mathcal{G},\mathcal{H}],B,\mathsf{Ext}}(k) + 2 \cdot \mathbf{Adv}^{\text{n-cr}^{\mu+\zeta}}_{\mathsf{OAEP}[\mathcal{G},\mathcal{H}],C}(k) + 6 \cdot \mathbf{Adv}^{\text{xor-ind0}}_{\mathcal{F},\mathcal{G},D}(k) + 4 \cdot \mathbf{Adv}^{\text{prg}}_{\mathcal{G},E}(k).$$

IND-CCA2 RESULT. To prove IND-CCA2, we use EXT2 and near-collision resistance of $\mathcal{G}$, as well as the assumptions that $\mathcal{G}$ is a pseudorandom generator, $\mathcal{H}$ is collision-resistant and $\mathcal{F}$ is XOR-IND and XOR-NM (as defined in Sect. 6.1). Note that, EXT2 adversary only makes one image query. Thus, the dependent auxiliary information is bounded by the size of the image.

Theorem 13. *Let η, μ, ζ, ρ be integer parameters. Let $\mathcal{F}$ be a family of trapdoor permutations with domain $\{0,1\}^\mu$ and $\eta = |[\mathsf{Kg}(1^k)]| + |[\mathcal{K}_H(1^k)]|$. Let $\mathcal{G} : \mathcal{K}_G \times \{0,1\}^\rho \rightarrow \{0,1\}^{\mu+\zeta}$ and $\mathcal{H} : \mathcal{K}_H \times \{0,1\}^{\mu+\zeta} \rightarrow \{0,1\}^\rho$ be function families. Suppose $\mathcal{G}$ is PRG, NCR$_\zeta$, EXT2$_\zeta$ and η-EXT2$_\zeta$ with respect to $\mathcal{F}$, and $\mathcal{H}$ is collision-resistant. Suppose $\mathcal{F}$ is XOR-NM0, XOR-IND1 and XOR-IND2$_\zeta$ with respect to $\mathcal{G}$. Then $\mathsf{OAEP}_{\text{s-clear}}[\mathcal{G}, \mathcal{H}, \mathcal{F}|^{\mu+\zeta}]$ is IND-CCA2 secure. In particular, for any adversary A that makes q decryption queries, there exists adversaries*

$C_H, C_G, D_1, D_2, D_3, E$, and adversary B_1, B_2 that makes q extract queries such that for all extractors $\mathsf{Ext}_1, \mathsf{Ext}_2$,

$$\begin{aligned}\mathbf{Adv}^{\text{ind-cca2}}_{\mathsf{OAEP}_{s\text{-clear}},A}(k) \le 6 \cdot \mathbf{Adv}^{\eta\text{-ext2}_\zeta}_{\mathcal{G},\mathcal{F},B_1,\mathsf{Ext}_1}(k) + 18 \cdot \mathbf{Adv}^{\text{xor-ind2}_\zeta}_{\mathcal{F},\mathcal{G},D_1}(k)\\ + 10 \cdot \mathbf{Adv}^{\text{n-cr}_\zeta}_{\mathcal{G},C_G}(k) + 4 \cdot \mathbf{Adv}^{\text{cr}}_{\mathcal{H},C_H}(k) + 4 \cdot \mathbf{Adv}^{\text{xor-nm0}}_{\mathcal{F},\mathcal{G},D_3}(k)\\ + 14 \cdot \mathbf{Adv}^{\text{xor-ind1}}_{\mathcal{F},\mathcal{G},D_2}(k) + 16 \cdot \mathbf{Adv}^{\text{prg}}_{\mathcal{G},E}(k) + 24 \cdot \mathbf{Adv}^{\text{ext2}_\zeta}_{\mathcal{G},B_2,\mathsf{Ext}_2}(k)\end{aligned}$$

Efficiency. The ciphertext length is $2n+k+\mu$ where n is the length of the RSA modulus, k is the security parameter, and μ is the message length. For example, if $n = 2048$, $k = 128$, and we encrypt an AES key with $\mu = 128$ (*i.e.*, we use RSA-OAEP as a key encapsulation mechanism, which is typical in practice then the ciphertext length is 4352). It is interesting to compare this with the standard model IND-CCA2 secure key encapsulation mechanism of Kiltz *et al.* [45]. They describe their scheme based on modular squaring (factoring), but it is straightforward to derive a scheme based on RSA with large hardcore function and a cryptographic hash function being target collision-resistant, which results in the most efficient prior standard-model RSA-based encryption scheme we are aware of. It performs one "small" exponentiation wrt. e and one "full" exponentiation modulo N, so is much more computationally expensive than our scheme. Thus, one could arguably say ours is the most computationally efficient RSA-based encryption scheme under "plausible standard-model assumptions" (where one takes the liberty of making bold assumptions on cryptographic hash functions) to date. On the other hand, the scheme of [45] has ciphertext length only $2n$.

Remark 14. It is worth mentioning why we are able to get IND-CCA2 (*i.e.*, adaptive) security for s-clear RSA-OAEP but not t-clear. The point is that, in the t-clear setting, it is not even clear how to define EXT2 of OAEP in a useful way. Since OAEP is invertible, the image oracle should output only *part* of the image point. But then it is not clear how the EXT2 adversary against OAEP can simulate the encryption oracle for the PA2 adversary against t-clear RSA-OAEP. On the other hand, for EXT2 of $\mathcal{G}$, the image oracle can output the *full* image point since $\mathcal{G}$ is not invertible. This then allows proving that s-clear RSA-OAEP is PA2 directly (without using monolithic assumptions on the padding scheme not known to follow from assumptions on the round functions).

6.3 IND-CPA, PA0 and PA1 Result

We show that s-clear RSA-OAEP is IND-CPA secure under suitable assumptions. Then, we show either PA0, PA1 and PA2 security depending on the strength of assumptions on $\mathcal{G}, \mathcal{H}$ and $\mathcal{F}$. Interestingly, even our IND-CPA result uses an XOR-based assumption on the trapdoor permutation. We also give a full instantiation result for s-clear RSA-OAEP and show that it is PA0 and PA1 under suitable assumptions. We show that s-clear RSA-OAEP "inherits" the extractability of the underlying padding transform, in the form of PA1 and EXT1, as long as the latter is also near-collision resistant. Here we state the result for an abstract padding scheme rather than specifically for OAEP. Note that results for OAEP then follow from the round functions as per Sect. 5. Due to space constraints, these are shown in the full version.

6.4 PA2 Result

We give a full instantiation result for s-clear RSA-OAEP and show that it is PA2 under stronger assumptions on $\mathcal{G}, \mathcal{H}$ and $\mathcal{F}$. We note that we can reduce assumptions as per Theorem 10.

Theorem 15. Let η, μ, ζ, ρ be integer parameters. Let $\mathcal{F}$ be a family of trapdoor permutations with domain $\{0,1\}^\rho$. Let $\mathcal{G} : \mathcal{K}_G \times \{0,1\}^\rho \to \{0,1\}^{\mu+\zeta}$ and $\mathcal{H} : \mathcal{K}_H \times \{0,1\}^{\mu+\zeta} \to \{0,1\}^\rho$ be hash function families. Let $\eta = |[\mathsf{Kg}(1^k)]| + |[\mathcal{K}_H(1^k)]|$. Suppose $\mathcal{G}$ is PRG, NCR$_\zeta$, EXT2$_\zeta$ and η-EXT2$_\zeta$ with respect to $\mathcal{F}$ and $\mathcal{H}$ is collision-resistant. Suppose $\mathcal{F}$ is XOR-NM1 and XOR-IND2$_\zeta$ with respect to $\mathcal{G}$. Then $\mathsf{OAEP}_{\mathsf{s\text{-}clear}}[\mathcal{G}, \mathcal{H}, \mathcal{F}|^{\mu+\zeta}]$ is PA2 secure. In particular, for any adversary A that makes at most q decryption queries and p encryption queries, there are extractor Ext, adversaries B_F, B_G, B_H, C, D, adversary A_G, C_G that makes at most q extract queries and p image queries such that for all extractors $\mathsf{Ext}_G, \mathsf{Ext}'_G$

$$\begin{aligned}\mathbf{Adv}^{\text{pa2}}_{\mathsf{OAEP}_{\mathsf{s\text{-}clear}},A,\mathsf{Ext}}(k) \le\ & 3 \cdot \mathbf{Adv}^{\eta\text{-ext2}_\zeta}_{\mathcal{G},\mathcal{F},A_G,\mathsf{Ext}_G}(k) + 9p \cdot \mathbf{Adv}^{\text{xor-ind2}_\zeta}_{\mathcal{F},\mathcal{G},C}(k) \\ & + 6p \cdot \mathbf{Adv}^{\text{prg}}_{\mathcal{G},D}(k) + 12p \cdot \mathbf{Adv}^{\text{ext2}_\zeta}_{\mathcal{G},C_G,\mathsf{Ext}'_G}(k) \\ & + 5 \cdot \mathbf{Adv}^{\text{n-cr}_\zeta}_{\mathcal{G},B_G}(k) + 2 \cdot \mathbf{Adv}^{\text{cr}}_{\mathcal{H},B_H}(k) + 2p \cdot \mathbf{Adv}^{\text{xor-nm1}}_{\mathcal{F},\mathcal{G},B_F}(k)\end{aligned}$$

Proof Idea. Let $c = (s, y)$ be the random ciphertext that A obtains from it's encryption oracle. Let $c' = (s', y')$ be the extract query made by A. Note that if $s|_\zeta \neq s'|_\zeta$ then we use Ext_G on input $s|_\zeta$ to recover r and then m. Note that if $s|_\zeta = s'|_\zeta$ then there is 2 cases. First, if $y = y'$ then we can find collision on $\mathcal{H}$. Next, if $y \neq y'$ then we can build an XOR-NM adversary. Note that, there are two obstacles in the proof. First, EXT2 adversary need to simulate the encryption oracle for PA2 adversary using its image oracle. Moreover, PA2 adversary may query for the key-dependent messages to the encryption oracle. We were able to enable EXT2 adversary to simulate the encryption oracle assuming $\mathcal{G}$ is PRG and EXT2.

Acknowledgments. We thank the PKC reviewers for their insightful comments. Mohammad Zaheri was partially supported by NSF grant No. 1565387, No. 1149832 and No. 1718498.

References

1. Baecher, P., Fischlin, M., Schröder, D.: Expedient non-malleability notions for hash functions. In: Kiayias, A. (ed.) CT-RSA 2011. LNCS, vol. 6558, pp. 268–283. Springer, Heidelberg (2011). https://doi.org/10.1007/978-3-642-19074-2_18

2. Barak, B.: How to go beyond the black-box simulation barrier. In: 42nd FOCS, Las Vegas, NV, USA, 14–17 October 2001, pp. 106–115. IEEE Computer Society Press (2001)
3. Barthe, G., Pointcheval, D., Zanella Béguelin, S.: Verified security of redundancy-free encryption from RABIN and RSA. In: Proceedings of the 2012 ACM Conference on Computer and Communications Security, CCS 2012, pp. 724–735. ACM, New York (2012)
4. Bellare, M., Desai, A., Pointcheval, D., Rogaway, P.: Relations among notions of security for public-key encryption schemes. In: Krawczyk, H. (ed.) CRYPTO 1998. LNCS, vol. 1462, pp. 26–45. Springer, Heidelberg (1998). https://doi.org/10.1007/BFb0055718
5. Bellare, M., Hoang, V.T., Keelveedhi, S.: Instantiating random oracles via UCEs. In: Canetti, R., Garay, J.A. (eds.) CRYPTO 2013, Part II. LNCS, vol. 8043, pp. 398–415. Springer, Heidelberg (2013). https://doi.org/10.1007/978-3-642-40084-1_23
6. Bellare, M., Hoang, V.T., Keelveedhi, S.: Cryptography from compression functions: the UCE bridge to the ROM. In: Garay, J.A., Gennaro, R. (eds.) CRYPTO 2014, Part I. LNCS, vol. 8616, pp. 169–187. Springer, Heidelberg (2014). https://doi.org/10.1007/978-3-662-44371-2_10
7. Bellare, M., Namprempre, C., Pointcheval, D., Semanko, M.: The one-more-RSA-inversion problems and the security of Chaum's blind signature scheme. J. Cryptol. **16**(3), 185–215 (2003)
8. Bellare, M., Palacio, A.: Towards plaintext-aware public-key encryption without random oracles. In: Lee, P.J. (ed.) ASIACRYPT 2004. LNCS, vol. 3329, pp. 48–62. Springer, Heidelberg (2004). https://doi.org/10.1007/978-3-540-30539-2_4
9. Bellare, M., Rogaway, P.: Random oracles are practical: a paradigm for designing efficient protocols. In: Ashby, V. (ed.) ACM CCS 1993, Fairfax, Virginia, USA, 3–5 November 1993, pp. 62–73. ACM Press (1993)
10. Bellare, M., Rogaway, P.: Optimal asymmetric encryption. In: De Santis, A. (ed.) EUROCRYPT 1994. LNCS, vol. 950, pp. 92–111. Springer, Heidelberg (1995). https://doi.org/10.1007/BFb0053428
11. Bellare, M., Rogaway, P.: The exact security of digital signatures-how to sign with RSA and Rabin. In: Maurer, U. (ed.) EUROCRYPT 1996. LNCS, vol. 1070, pp. 399–416. Springer, Heidelberg (1996). https://doi.org/10.1007/3-540-68339-9_34
12. Bitansky, N., Canetti, R., Chiesa, A., Tromer, E.: From extractable collision resistance to succinct non-interactive arguments of knowledge, and back again. In: Goldwasser, S. (ed.) ITCS 2012, 8–10 January 2012, Cambridge, MA, USA, pp. 326–349. ACM (2012)
13. Bitansky, N., Canetti, R., Paneth, O., Rosen, A.: On the existence of extractable one-way functions. In: Shmoys, D.B. (ed.) 46th ACM STOC, New York, NY, USA, 31 May–3 June 2014, pp. 505–514. ACM Press (2014)
14. Bitansky, N., Canetti, R., Paneth, O., Rosen, A.: On the existence of extractable one-way functions. SIAM J. Comput. **45**(5), 1910–1952 (2016)
15. Blömer, J., May, A.: A tool kit for finding small roots of bivariate polynomials over the integers. In: Cramer, R. (ed.) EUROCRYPT 2005. LNCS, vol. 3494, pp. 251–267. Springer, Heidelberg (2005). https://doi.org/10.1007/11426639_15
16. Boldyreva, A., Cash, D., Fischlin, M., Warinschi, B.: Foundations of Non-malleable Hash and One-Way Functions. In: Matsui, M. (ed.) ASIACRYPT 2009. LNCS, vol. 5912, pp. 524–541. Springer, Heidelberg (2009). https://doi.org/10.1007/978-3-642-10366-7_31

17. Boldyreva, A., Fischlin, M.: Analysis of random oracle instantiation scenarios for OAEP and other practical schemes. In: Shoup, V. (ed.) CRYPTO 2005. LNCS, vol. 3621, pp. 412–429. Springer, Heidelberg (2005). https://doi.org/10.1007/11535218_25
18. Boldyreva, A., Fischlin, M.: On the security of OAEP. In: Lai, X., Chen, K. (eds.) ASIACRYPT 2006. LNCS, vol. 4284, pp. 210–225. Springer, Heidelberg (2006). https://doi.org/10.1007/11935230_14
19. Boldyreva, A., Imai, H., Kobara, K.: How to strengthen the security of RSA-OAEP. IEEE Trans. Inf. Theory **56**(11), 5876–5886 (2010)
20. Boneh, D.: Simplified OAEP for the RSA and Rabin functions. In: Kilian, J. (ed.) CRYPTO 2001. LNCS, vol. 2139, pp. 275–291. Springer, Heidelberg (2001). https://doi.org/10.1007/3-540-44647-8_17
21. Boneh, D., Franklin, M.K.: Identity based encryption from the Weil pairing. SIAM J. Comput. **32**(3), 586–615 (2003)
22. Brown, D.R.L.: A weak-randomizer attack on RSA-OAEP with e = 3 (2005)
23. Brzuska, C., Farshim, P., Mittelbach, A.: Indistinguishability obfuscation and UCEs: the case of computationally unpredictable sources. In: Garay, J.A., Gennaro, R. (eds.) CRYPTO 2014, Part I. LNCS, vol. 8616, pp. 188–205. Springer, Heidelberg (2014). https://doi.org/10.1007/978-3-662-44371-2_11
24. Canetti, R.: Towards realizing random oracles: hash functions that hide all partial information. In: Kaliski, B.S. (ed.) CRYPTO 1997. LNCS, vol. 1294, pp. 455–469. Springer, Heidelberg (1997). https://doi.org/10.1007/BFb0052255
25. Canetti, R., Chen, Y., Reyzin, L.: On the correlation intractability of obfuscated pseudorandom functions. In: Kushilevitz, E., Malkin, T. (eds.) TCC 2016. LNCS, vol. 9562, pp. 389–415. Springer, Heidelberg (2016). https://doi.org/10.1007/978-3-662-49096-9_17
26. Canetti, R., Dakdouk, R.R.: Extractable perfectly one-way functions. In: Aceto, L., Damgård, I., Goldberg, L.A., Halldórsson, M.M., Ingólfsdóttir, A., Walukiewicz, I. (eds.) ICALP 2008, Part II. LNCS, vol. 5126, pp. 449–460. Springer, Heidelberg (2008). https://doi.org/10.1007/978-3-540-70583-3_37
27. Canetti, R., Dakdouk, R.R.: Towards a theory of extractable functions. In: Reingold, O. (ed.) TCC 2009. LNCS, vol. 5444, pp. 595–613. Springer, Heidelberg (2009). https://doi.org/10.1007/978-3-642-00457-5_35
28. Canetti, R., Goldreich, O., Halevi, S.: The random oracle methodology, revisited. J. ACM **51**(4), 557–594 (2004)
29. Canetti, R., Micciancio, D., Reingold, O.: Perfectly one-way probabilistic hash functions (preliminary version). In: 30th ACM STOC, Dallas, TX, USA, 23–26 May 1998, pp. 131–140. ACM Press (1998)
30. Coppersmith, D.: Finding a small root of a univariate modular equation. In: Maurer, U. (ed.) EUROCRYPT 1996. LNCS, vol. 1070, pp. 155–165. Springer, Heidelberg (1996). https://doi.org/10.1007/3-540-68339-9_14
31. Coron, J.-S., Kirichenko, A., Tibouchi, M.: A note on the bivariate Coppersmith theorem. J. Cryptol. **26**(2), 246–250 (2013)
32. Dachman-Soled, D., Gennaro, R., Krawczyk, H., Malkin, T.: Computational extractors and pseudorandomness. In: Cramer, R. (ed.) TCC 2012. LNCS, vol. 7194, pp. 383–403. Springer, Heidelberg (2012). https://doi.org/10.1007/978-3-642-28914-9_22
33. Damgård, I.: Towards practical public key systems secure against chosen ciphertext attacks. In: Feigenbaum, J. (ed.) CRYPTO 1991. LNCS, vol. 576, pp. 445–456. Springer, Heidelberg (1992). https://doi.org/10.1007/3-540-46766-1_36

34. Damgård, I., Faust, S., Hazay, C.: Secure two-party computation with low communication. In: Cramer, R. (ed.) TCC 2012. LNCS, vol. 7194, pp. 54–74. Springer, Heidelberg (2012). https://doi.org/10.1007/978-3-642-28914-9_4
35. Dodis, Y., Haitner, I., Tentes, A.: On the instantiability of hash-and-sign RSA signatures. In: Cramer, R. (ed.) TCC 2012. LNCS, vol. 7194, pp. 112–132. Springer, Heidelberg (2012). https://doi.org/10.1007/978-3-642-28914-9_7
36. Dodis, Y., Oliveira, R., Pietrzak, K.: On the generic insecurity of the full domain hash. In: Shoup, V. (ed.) CRYPTO 2005. LNCS, vol. 3621, pp. 449–466. Springer, Heidelberg (2005). https://doi.org/10.1007/11535218_27
37. Fischlin, M.: Pseudorandom function tribe ensembles based on one-way permutations: improvements and applications. In: Stern, J. (ed.) EUROCRYPT 1999. LNCS, vol. 1592, pp. 432–445. Springer, Heidelberg (1999). https://doi.org/10.1007/3-540-48910-X_30
38. Fujisaki, E., Okamoto, T., Pointcheval, D., Stern, J.: RSA-OAEP is secure under the RSA assumption. In: Kilian, J. (ed.) CRYPTO 2001. LNCS, vol. 2139, pp. 260–274. Springer, Heidelberg (2001). https://doi.org/10.1007/3-540-44647-8_16
39. Fujisaki, E., Okamoto, T., Pointcheval, D., Stern, J.: RSA-OAEP is secure under the RSA assumption. J. Cryptol. **17**(2), 81–104 (2004)
40. Fuller, B., O'Neill, A., Reyzin, L.: A unified approach to deterministic encryption: new constructions and a connection to computational entropy. In: Cramer, R. (ed.) TCC 2012. LNCS, vol. 7194, pp. 582–599. Springer, Heidelberg (2012). https://doi.org/10.1007/978-3-642-28914-9_33
41. Gupta, D., Sahai, A.: On constant-round concurrent zero-knowledge from a knowledge assumption. In: Meier, W., Mukhopadhyay, D. (eds.) INDOCRYPT 2014. LNCS, vol. 8885, pp. 71–88. Springer, Cham (2014). https://doi.org/10.1007/978-3-319-13039-2_5
42. Halevi, S., Myers, S., Rackoff, C.: On seed-incompressible functions. In: Canetti, R. (ed.) TCC 2008. LNCS, vol. 4948, pp. 19–36. Springer, Heidelberg (2008). https://doi.org/10.1007/978-3-540-78524-8_2
43. Hoang, V.T., Katz, J., O'Neill, A., Zaheri, M.: Selective-opening security in the presence of randomness failures. In: Cheon, J.H., Takagi, T. (eds.) ASIACRYPT 2016. LNCS, vol. 10032, pp. 278–306. Springer, Heidelberg (2016). https://doi.org/10.1007/978-3-662-53890-6_10
44. Hofheinz, D.: All-but-many lossy trapdoor functions. In: Pointcheval, D., Johansson, T. (eds.) EUROCRYPT 2012. LNCS, vol. 7237, pp. 209–227. Springer, Heidelberg (2012). https://doi.org/10.1007/978-3-642-29011-4_14
45. Hofheinz, D., Kiltz, E., Shoup, V.: Practical chosen ciphertext secure encryption from factoring. J. Cryptol. **26**(1), 102–118 (2013)
46. Hohenberger, S., Sahai, A., Waters, B.: Replacing a random oracle: full domain hash from indistinguishability obfuscation. In: Nguyen, P.Q., Oswald, E. (eds.) EUROCRYPT 2014. LNCS, vol. 8441, pp. 201–220. Springer, Heidelberg (2014). https://doi.org/10.1007/978-3-642-55220-5_12
47. Kiltz, E., Mohassel, P., O'Neill, A.: Adaptive trapdoor functions and chosen-ciphertext security. In: Gilbert, H. (ed.) EUROCRYPT 2010. LNCS, vol. 6110, pp. 673–692. Springer, Heidelberg (2010). https://doi.org/10.1007/978-3-642-13190-5_34
48. Kiltz, E., O'Neill, A., Smith, A.: Instantiability of RSA-OAEP under chosen-plaintext attack. In: Rabin, T. (ed.) CRYPTO 2010. LNCS, vol. 6223, pp. 295–313. Springer, Heidelberg (2010). https://doi.org/10.1007/978-3-642-14623-7_16

49. Kiltz, E., Pietrzak, K.: On the security of padding-based encryption schemes – or – why we cannot prove OAEP secure in the standard model. In: Joux, A. (ed.) EUROCRYPT 2009. LNCS, vol. 5479, pp. 389–406. Springer, Heidelberg (2009). https://doi.org/10.1007/978-3-642-01001-9_23
50. Kiltz, E., Pietrzak, K.: Personal communication (2019)
51. Lewko, M., O'Neill, A., Smith, A.: Regularity of lossy RSA on subdomains and its applications. In: Johansson, T., Nguyen, P.Q. (eds.) EUROCRYPT 2013. LNCS, vol. 7881, pp. 55–75. Springer, Heidelberg (2013). https://doi.org/10.1007/978-3-642-38348-9_4
52. Bitansky, N., Canetti, R., Chiesa, A., Goldwasser, S., Lin, H., Rubinstein, A., Tromer, E.: The hunting of the SNARK. J. Cryptol. **30**, 989–1066 (2017)
53. Paillier, P., Villar, J.L.: Trading one-wayness against chosen-ciphertext security in factoring-based encryption. In: Lai, X., Chen, K. (eds.) ASIACRYPT 2006. LNCS, vol. 4284, pp. 252–266. Springer, Heidelberg (2006). https://doi.org/10.1007/11935230_17
54. Pandey, O., Pass, R., Vaikuntanathan, V.: Adaptive one-way functions and applications. In: Wagner, D. (ed.) CRYPTO 2008. LNCS, vol. 5157, pp. 57–74. Springer, Heidelberg (2008). https://doi.org/10.1007/978-3-540-85174-5_4
55. Peikert, C., Waters, B.: Lossy trapdoor functions and their applications. In: Ladner, R.E., Dwork, C. (eds.) 40th ACM STOC, Victoria, British Columbia, Canada, 17–20 May 2008, pp. 187–196. ACM Press (2008)
56. Rackoff, C., Simon, D.R.: Non-interactive zero-knowledge proof of knowledge and chosen ciphertext attack. In: Feigenbaum, J. (ed.) CRYPTO 1991. LNCS, vol. 576, pp. 433–444. Springer, Heidelberg (1992). https://doi.org/10.1007/3-540-46766-1_35
57. Rivest, R.L., Shamir, A., Adleman, L.M.: A method for obtaining digital signature and public-key cryptosystems. Commun. Assoc. Comput. Mach. **21**(2), 120–126 (1978)
58. Shoup, V.: OAEP reconsidered. In: Kilian, J. (ed.) CRYPTO 2001. LNCS, vol. 2139, pp. 239–259. Springer, Heidelberg (2001). https://doi.org/10.1007/3-540-44647-8_15
59. Shoup, V.: OAEP reconsidered. J. Cryptol. **15**(4), 223–249 (2002)
60. Smith, A., Zhang, Y.: On the regularity of lossy RSA. In: Dodis, Y., Nielsen, J.B. (eds.) TCC 2015. LNCS, vol. 9014, pp. 609–628. Springer, Heidelberg (2015). https://doi.org/10.1007/978-3-662-46494-6_25
61. Zhandry, M.: The magic of ELFs. J. Cryptol. **32**(3), 825–866 (2019)

Public-Key Puncturable Encryption: Modular and Compact Constructions

Shi-Feng Sun[1,2](✉), Amin Sakzad[1], Ron Steinfeld[1], Joseph K. Liu[1], and Dawu Gu[3](✉)

[1] Faculty of Information Technology, Monash University, Clayton, Australia
shifeng.sun@monash.edu
[2] Data61, CSIRO, Melbourne, Australia
[3] Department of Computer Science and Engineering, Shanghai Jiao Tong University, Shanghai, China
dwgu@sjtu.edu.cn

Abstract. We revisit the method of designing public-key puncturable encryption schemes and present a generic conversion by leveraging the techniques of distributed key-distribution and revocable encryption. In particular, we first introduce a refined version of identity-based revocable encryption, named *key-homomorphic identity-based revocable key encapsulation mechanism with extended correctness*. Then, we propose a generic construction of *puncturable key encapsulation mechanism* from the former by merging the idea of distributed key-distribution. Compared to the state-of-the-art, our generic construction supports unbounded number of punctures and multiple tags per message, thus achieving more *fine-grained* revocation of decryption capability. Further, it does not rely on *random oracles*, not suffer from *non-negligible* correctness error, and results in a variety of efficient schemes with distinct features. More precisely, we obtain the *first* scheme with very *compact* ciphertexts in the standard model, and the *first* scheme with support for both *unbounded* size of tags per ciphertext and *unbounded* punctures as well as *constant-time* puncture operation. Moreover, we get a comparable scheme proven secure under the standard DBDH assumption, which enjoys both faster encryption and decryption than previous works based on the same assumption, especially when the number of tags associated with the ciphertext is large.

Keywords: Functional encryption · Puncturable encryption · Forward security

1 Introduction

Public Key Encryption (PKE) is a critical cryptographic tool for protecting the confidentiality of messages transmitted over insecure communication channels, which has been widely employed in practice such as messaging services. It is commonly agreed that the standard security for PKE is indistinguishability against chosen-ciphertext attack (IND-CCA) that is guaranteed under the

A. Kiayias et al. (Eds.): PKC 2020, LNCS 12110, pp. 309–338, 2020.
https://doi.org/10.1007/978-3-030-45374-9_11

perfect secrecy of secret keys. However, as more and more cryptographic applications are performed on poorly protected mobile devices, the threat of key compromise to attackers through virus or physical access becomes more and more acute nowadays, and thus will lead to the lost of the security guarantees.

To deal with such kind of threat, numerous methods have been introduced, including key-insulated cryptography [22], threshold cryptography [21], proactive cryptography [36] and forward security [11,27]. As a promising approach, forward security has been considered in a variety of cryptographic primitives, since the initial introduction in the context of key exchange protocol [27] in 1989. However, the first forward secure PKE (FS-PKE) was proposed by Canetti et al. [11] in 2003. In general, a forward secure PKE scheme is usually equipped with an efficient update algorithm, by which the current secret key can be altered so that it cannot be used to recover *past* messages. In other words, the decryption capability for previous ciphertexts is revoked by updating the secret key.

Motivated by the problem that existing forward secure PKE schemes cannot support fine-grained revocation of decryption capability (e.g., removing decryption capability for any individual ciphertext or all ciphertexts sent during a special period), Green and Miers [26] introduced a new form of PKE—Public-key Puncturable Encryption (PPE)—for achieving forward secure asynchronous messaging. In general, this primitive supports multiple tags per message (or ciphertext), which may contain a unique message identifier (e.g., GUID) and some additional metadata (e.g., the sender identity). This feature endows the recipient with the ability of not only revoking individual ciphertext but also the entire classes of ciphertexts (e.g., all ciphertext from the same sender), so it can achieve forward security at a fine-grained level.

Briefly, PPE can be seen as a form of tag-based encryption [31] added with an efficient key-update algorithm called Puncture algorithm. In particular, this algorithm takes as input the current secret key SK and a tag t and outputs a new (punctured) secret key SK' that can decrypt all ciphertexts except for those encrypted under tag t. By this procedure, the secret key can be punctured repeatedly and sequentially on many distinct tags, thus revoking the decryption capability for the ciphertexts encrypted under (any of) these tags. Based on the Key-Policy Attribute-Based Encryption (KP-ABE) scheme [35], Green and Miers proposed the first concrete PPE scheme[1] in the random oracle model. Further to reduce the decryption cost of PPE scheme alone, they put forward a new variant of FS-PKE scheme, named Puncturable Forward Secure PKE (PFSE), by combining their PPE scheme with a variant of Canetti et al. FS-PKE scheme [11]. Subsequently, Günther et al. in [28] introduced the key encapsulation version of PFSE (PFSKEM) and proposed a generic constriction of PFSKEM from any one-time signature and hierarchical identity-based key encapsulation (HIBKEM) scheme [8] with special properties. In this work, we are more interested in PPE itself. Recently, it has been employed widely to achieve other cryptographic goals, such as constructing forward secure 0-RTT protocols [19], backward

[1] The proposed PPE scheme supports an arbitrary number of punctures, and the decryption cost is linear in the number of punctures.

private searchable encryption [10], forward secure proxy re-encryption [20], and public-key watermarking schemes [15]. This demonstrates that PPE is a useful and valuable cryptographic tool.

However, the existing PPE schemes suffer from different shortcomings. In more details, the instantiations from [12,15] are given on the basis of indistinguishability obfuscation, which are more feasibility results than practical solutions. The state-of-the-art construction is from Derler et al. [18,19], in which they introduced a relaxed variant of PPE termed Bloom Filter Encryption (BFE). Specifically, their basic construction from Identity-Based Encryption (IBE) [9] features both efficient puncture and decryption procedure, but has a large ciphertext expansion. Moreover, they presented two *generic* constructions from Ciphertext-Policy Attribute-Based Encryption (CP-ABE) [7] and Identity-Based Broadcast Encryption (IBBE) [17] under the same framework, thus achieving different tradeoffs between (public) key size and ciphertext size. For example, the design from IBBE allows us to obtain the BFE schemes with compact ciphertexts. Due to relying heavily on Bloom filter [33], however, BFE is subject to *non-negligible* correctness error. As argued in [15], this does not affect the application of BFE to designing efficient forward-secure 0-RTT protocols, but may limit its deployment in the scenarios requiring *negligible* correctness error. In addition, BFE schemes only support a *pre-determined* number of punctures, due to the inherent properties of Bloom filters, and a *unique* tag per ciphertext. This makes it less fine-grained than the PPE scheme in [26], as for example it cannot support the revocation of *all* ciphertexts from a single sender. In contrast, the scheme by Green and Miers avoids these drawbacks, but still suffers from some others, such as (1) the number of tags per ciphertext is bounded by some pre-determined parameter $d \in \mathbb{N}$ at the setup, (2) the size of both public key and ciphertext are linear in the pre-determined integer d, and (3) the security is achieved in the random oracle model.

As great effort has been made to improve the performance, security and/or functionality of attribute-based encryption (e.g., [1,2,4,14,24,34,38]) during the past decade, it is also significant to design puncturable encryption with nice features like unbounded tags (or attributes) per message. As emphasized in [34], it is highly desirable in practice to make the parameters for secret key and encryption unbounded by the public parameters fixed at setup, otherwise the public parameter size should be very huge and the scheme will be less flexible. This feature is also important for PPE applications. For example, in asynchronous messaging the decryption capability of metadata (possibly containing a huge number of attributes) encrypted with such scheme can be flexibly revoked by puncturing secret key on any type of attribute.

Based on previous discussions and the systemized work of [19], the natural questions include:

1. How to design efficient PPE schemes with as many desired features as possible (e.g., negligible correctness error, unbounded punctures and compact ciphertext)?
2. Is it possible to generically construct PPE with negligible correctness errors from other cryptographic primitives?

In this work, we make affirmative progress to above questions by leveraging the idea of distributed key-distribution and the revocation encryption technique. In particular, we propose a generic construction of puncturable key encapsulation mechanism by embedding the distributed key-distribution technique to a key encapsulation version of revocation encryption system, and thus obtain a variety of concrete PPE schemes featuring distinct characteristics. The high-level idea is described below, and the main contributions are summarized in Sect. 1.2.

1.1 Technical Overview

In a PPE scheme, the secret key is punctured gradually; the punctured secret key is updated as a new tag (to be punctured) arrives. The functionality of PPE requires that the ciphertext can be decrypted only if no tag attached to the ciphertext has been punctured. Our idea is inspired by the design of symmetric puncturable encryption [37] and the distributed symmetric key-distribution [16, 23, 32], so we concentrate on the key encapsulation version of PPE in this work. To support unbounded punctures, the intuition is to distribute an (encapsulated) symmetric key in a similar way as in [26]. Basically, the idea is to produce a share of the encryption/encapsulated key on-the-fly and to reconstruct this key from all shares for completing the decryption. Similar to [37], one share corresponds to one master secret key and each master key is used to puncture a unique tag. In this framework, the crucial point is to make sure that the share (indirectly) associated with tag t cannot be recovered once t belongs to the tag list T of the ciphertext, which implies that the encapsulated key cannot be reconstructed if some tag of the ciphertext is punctured. In other words, it is desired that the share of the encryption key with respect to t cannot be recovered if $t \in T$. We observe that it resembles revocation system [30] and can be achieved by leveraging this well-studied cryptographic tool, in which the ciphertext under revocation list T cannot be decrypted whenever user t is revoked (i.e., $t \in T$). Following this way, we realize the puncture procedure by invoking the key generation algorithm of the revocation system. In particular, each time a new tag t is to be punctured, a random value msk_t is chosen for generating a corresponding secret key sk_t and subtracted from the master secret key msk (of the revocation system). Finally, the remaining part "$msk - \sum_t sk_t$" is (implicitly) used to produce a secret key sk_0 for a distinguished tag t_0, which is excluded in all punctures and the tag list of each ciphertext. To that end, we further refine the revocation system and introduce the concept of key-homomorphic revocation system with extended correctness that is crucial for our construction (including computing sk_0) and the security proof. For more details, please refer to Sects. 2.3 and 3.

1.2 Our Contributions

In this work, we present a modular way of constructing puncturable encryption inspired by the idea of distributed key-distributions. In particular, we first introduce a variant of identity-based revocation system, named

Table 1. Comparison of public-key puncturable encryption schemes

Schemes	Public key size	Secret key size	Ciphertext overhead	Punctured key size	Unbounded	
					Punctures	Ciphertext tags
	$(\lvert\mathbb{G}\rvert, \lvert\mathbb{G}_T\rvert, H)$	$\lvert\mathbb{G}\rvert$	$(\lvert\mathbb{G}\rvert, \lambda\text{-bit})$	$\lvert\mathbb{G}\rvert$	(Y/N, #)	(Y/N, #)
[26]	$(O(n), 1, 1)$	3	$(O(\hat{n}), 0)$	$3 \cdot (i+1)$	(Y, -)	(N, n)
$[19]_{\text{IBE}}$	$(1, 0, k)$	m	$(1, k)$	$O(m)$	(N, d)	(N, 1)
$[18]_{\text{IBBE}}$	$(O(k), 1, O(k))$	m	$(2, 1)$	$O(m)$	(N, d)	(N, 1)
Sect. 4.1	$(O(n), 1, 0)$	$O(n)$	$(2, 0)$	$O(n) \cdot (i+1)$	(Y, -)	(N, n)
Sect. 4.2	$(O(n), 1, 0)$	3	$(O(n), 0)$	$3 \cdot (i+1)$	(Y, -)	(N, n)
Sect. 4.3	$(5, 1, 0)$	3	$(O(\hat{n}), 0)$	$3 \cdot (i+1)$	(Y, -)	(Y, -)
Sect. 4.4	$(O(n), 2, 0)$	$O(n)$	$(6, 0)$	$O(n) \cdot (i+1)$	(Y, -)	(N, n)

$\lvert\cdot\rvert$: the bit-length of a group element, e.g., $\lvert\mathbb{G}\rvert$; H: a hash function; λ: a security parameter; $\hat{n}$: the number of tags attached to ciphertext; n: the upper-bound of $\hat{n}$ (i.e., $|T| \leq n$); d: the upper-bound on # of allowed punctures; i = # of tags associated with the current punctured key; $m = -d \cdot \ln p/(\ln 2)^2$ is the length of Bloom filter with false positive probability p [19].

Table 2. Comparison of public-key puncturable encryption schemes

Schemes	Puncture	Encryption	Decryption*	Standard model	Negligible corr. error	Assumption
	$(H, \exp)$	$(\text{pair}, \exp_T, \exp)$	$(\text{pair}, \exp)$			
[26]	$(1, O(n))$	$(0, 1, O(\hat{n}n))$	$(3, O(\hat{n})) \cdot (i+1)$	×	√	DBDH
$[19]_{\text{IBE}}$	$(k, 0)$	$(k, k, 1)$	$(1, 0)$	×	×	BCDH
$[18]_{\text{IBBE}}$	$(k, 0)$	$(0, 1, O(k))$	$(2, 2)$	×	×	GDDHE
Sect. 4.1	$(0, O(n))$	$(0, 1, O(\hat{n}))$	$(2, O(\hat{n})) \cdot (i+1)$	√	√	q-DBDHE
Sect. 4.2	$(0, O(n))$	$(0, 1, O(n))$	$(2, O(n)) \cdot (i+1)$	√	√	DBDH
Sect. 4.3	$(0, O(1))$	$(0, 1, O(\hat{n}))$	$(3, O(\hat{n})) \cdot (i+1)$	√	√	q-MEBDH
Sect. 4.4	$(0, O(n))$	$(0, 2, O(\hat{n}))$	$(6, O(\hat{n})) \cdot (i+1)$	√	√	DLIN

$\star$: decryption is done by a secret key punctured on i tags; $\hat{n}$: the number # of tags attached to ciphertext; n: the upper-bound of $\hat{n}$ (i.e., $|T| \leq n$); $k = -\log_2 p$ is the # of H's for a Bloom filter with false positive probability p [19].

key-homomorphic identity-based revocable key encapsulation mechanism (KH-IRKEM) with extended correctness, and then propose a generic construction of *puncturable key encapsulation mechanism* (PKEM) from any such kind of KH-IRKEM scheme. Compared to the generic conversion of [19], our construction satisfies the standard correctness definition (i.e., negligible correctness error), enjoys more fine-grained revocation of decryption capability, and supports an unbounded number of punctures. Since the security and performance of our modular construction depends only on the underlying IRKEM scheme, our PKEM scheme can achieve the same level security as IRKEM without inducing additional security assumptions or computation redundancy. Based on the extensively-studied identity-based revocation systems, we also give four PKEM instantiations with distinct advantages, which are summarized as follows:

- Our first construction is the *first* PPE scheme that enjoys compact ciphertexts. Precisely, the ciphertext overhead consists of only two group elements.

Moreover, it has a faster encryption and decryption procedure (exactly decryption requires 33% less pairing computation) than the scheme by Green and Miers [26], and can be proven selectively secure in the standard model.
- Our second scheme has a comparable storage cost with [26]. Both schemes can be proven secure under the standard assumption—DBDH assumption, but our scheme enjoys more efficient encryption and decryption, especially when the number of tags encrypted is large. In more details, our encryption algorithm is independent of the number $\hat{n}$ of tags encrypted and the decryption requires 33% less pairing computation.
- Our third construction is proven secure under a stronger assumption, but features *compact* public key and *fast* puncture procedure, both of which depend not on the maximum number n of tags allowed per ciphertext. Moreover, it is the *first* scheme that has no constraint on the number of tags attached to ciphertext. It also enjoys a faster encryption algorithm compared to [26].
- As the first construction, our last scheme also features short ciphertexts, exactly consisting of six group elements. In contrast, it has a slightly slower encryption and decryption procedure, but can be proven adaptively secure based on the standard DLIN assumption, rather than a "q-type" one.

For more details on the comparison with previous works, please refer to Tables 1 and 2 as well as the analysis given in Sect. 5.

2 Background

In this section, we give the notations used in this work and recollect the syntax and security of the relevant cryptographic primitives, such as public-key puncturable encryption and identity-based revocation system.

Notations. Security parameter is denoted by λ. For a finite set S, we let $s \xleftarrow{\$} S$ be the operation of sampling s uniformly at random from S. If S is a distribution, it denotes the operation of sampling s according to S. We write $a \leftarrow \mathrm{A}(\cdot)$ to denote the process of running algorithm $\mathrm{A}(\cdot)$ and assigning the result to a. If $\mathrm{A}(\cdot)$ is randomized, we use $\mathrm{A}(x;r)$ to denote the unique output of $\mathrm{A}(\cdot)$ taking as input x and randomness r. In addition, we denote by bold uppercase $\mathbf{A}$ (resp. lowercase $\boldsymbol{x}$) a matrix (resp. vector). Unless stated otherwise, all vectors are column vectors and row vectors are written as $\boldsymbol{x}^\top$. For two vectors $\boldsymbol{x} = (x_1, x_2, \ldots, x_n) \in \mathbb{Z}_p^n$ and $\boldsymbol{y} = (y_1, y_2, \ldots, y_n) \in \mathbb{Z}_p^n$, we denote their inner product as $\langle \boldsymbol{x}, \boldsymbol{y} \rangle = \sum_{i=1}^n x_i y_i$. For a matrix $\mathbf{A} = [a_{i,j}] \in \mathbb{Z}_p^{m \times n}$ and a group element $g \in \mathbb{G}$, we write $g^{\mathbf{A}}$ to denote the matrix $[g^{a_{i,j}}] \in \mathbb{G}^{m \times n}$. Also, we use $[a, b]$ to denote the set $\{a, a+1, \ldots, b-1, b\}$ for integers $b > a \geq 0$.

2.1 Bilinear Maps

We briefly review the relevant facts about bilinear maps. Let $(\mathbb{G}_1, \mathbb{G}_2, \mathbb{G}_T)$ be multiplicative cyclic groups of prime order p, and g, h be generators of $\mathbb{G}_1$ and $\mathbb{G}_2$ respectively. An efficiently computable mapping $e : \mathbb{G}_1 \times \mathbb{G}_2 \rightarrow \mathbb{G}_T$ is a bilinear map if it satisfies the following properties:

1. Bilinearity: for all $u \in \mathbb{G}_1, v \in \mathbb{G}_2$ and $a, b \in \mathbb{Z}_p$, we have $e(u^a, v^b) = e(u, v)^{ab}$.
2. Non-degeneracy: for $g \in \mathbb{G}_1, h \in \mathbb{G}_2$, $e(g, h) \neq 1_{\mathbb{G}_T}$ whenever $g, h \neq 1_{\mathbb{G}}$.

For matrices $\mathbf{A}, \mathbf{B} \in \mathbb{Z}_p^{m \times n}$, we let $e(g^{\mathbf{A}}, h^{\mathbf{B}}) = e(g, h)^{\mathbf{A}^\top \mathbf{B}}$ hereafter.

2.2 Puncturable Key-Encapsulation Mechanism

As mentioned in [19], a full-blown public-key puncturable encryption scheme can be generically converted from any puncturable key-encapsulation mechanism (PKEM), so next we only present the syntax and security of PKEM. Following the definition given in [19], a PKEM scheme with key space $\mathcal{K}$ and tag space $\mathcal{T}$ generally consists of four polynomial time algorithms (KeyGen, Enc, Punc, Dec) with the specifications below:

- $\mathsf{KeyGen}(1^\lambda, n)$ takes as input a security parameter λ and a maximum number n of tags allowed for each ciphertext, and outputs a public and secret key pair (PK, SK). Note that $n \in \mathbb{N} \cup \{\infty\}$ and "∞" means the number of tags per ciphertext is unbounded.
- $\mathsf{Enc}(PK, T)$ takes as input a public key PK and a set of tags T such that $|T| \leq n$, and outputs an encapsulated key K and a ciphertext CT.
- $\mathsf{Punc}(SK_{i-1}, t)$ takes as input a secret key SK_{i-1} and a tag t, where $SK_0 = SK$, and outputs a new secret key SK_i that can decrypt what SK_{i-1} can except for those encrypted under tag t.
- $\mathsf{Dec}(SK_i, CT, T)$ takes as input a secret key SK_i and a ciphertext CT generated under a list of tags T, and outputs the encapsulated key K or $\perp$ (the latter indicates the decapsulation fails).

Definition 1 (Correctness). *For all $\lambda \in \mathbb{N}, n \in \mathbb{N} \cup \{\infty\}$, and $T \subseteq \mathcal{T}$ such that $|T| \leq n$, let $(PK, SK) \leftarrow \mathsf{KeyGen}(1^\lambda, n)$ and $(K, CT) \leftarrow \mathsf{Enc}(PK, T)$, then we have that $\mathsf{Dec}(SK, CT, T) = K$. Moreover, for any ℓ times of invoking $SK_i \leftarrow \mathsf{Punc}(SK_{i-1}, t')$ such that $t' \notin T$, it holds that*

$$\Pr[\mathsf{Dec}(SK_\ell, CT, T) = \perp] \leq \mathsf{negl}(\lambda),$$

where the probability is taken over the random coins of all algorithms.

Remark 1. Our syntax is slightly different from [19]. In particular, our encryption algorithm also takes as input a list of tags T instead of only PK. Thus, our puncture algorithm is operated on tag t rather than ciphertext CT. In this way, many ciphertexts under the same tag t (e.g., all ciphertexts from the same sender) can be revoked by executing the puncture algorithm once. In fact, our PKEM is more similar to the key encapsulation version of public-key puncturable encryption initialized by Green and Miers [26], which enjoys fine-grained revocation of decryption capability.

The security of PKEM is adapted from that of PPE in [26]. It is defined via an IND-PUN-ATK game, which incorporates both CPA and CCA variants. The game is played between a challenger and an adversary as follows.

Setup: On input a security parameter λ and a maximum number n of tags allowed per ciphertext, the challenger runs $(PK, SK) \leftarrow \mathsf{KeyGen}(1^\lambda, n)$. Then it returns PK and initializes two empty sets P, C and a counter $i = 0$.

Phase 1: The adversary adaptively issues the following queries

- **Puncture**(t'): On input a tag t', the challenger increments counter i, computes $SK_i \leftarrow \mathsf{Punc}(SK_{i-1}, t')$ and adds t' to P.
- **Corrupt**(): The first time the adversary issues this query, the challenger returns the most recent secret key SK_i and sets $\mathsf{C} \leftarrow \mathsf{P}$. For subsequent queries, directly returns $\perp$.
- **Decrypt**(CT, T): On input a ciphertext CT and the associated tags T, the challenger returns $K \leftarrow \mathsf{Dec}(SK_i, CT, T)$ if ATK = CCA, otherwise returns $\perp$.

Challenge: On input challenge tags $T^* \subseteq \mathcal{T}$, the challenger directly rejects if the adversary has previously issued a **Corrupt** query and $T^* \cap \mathsf{C} = \emptyset$. Otherwise, it picks $b \xleftarrow{\$} \{0, 1\}, K_1 \xleftarrow{\$} \mathcal{K}$ and computes $(K_0, CT^*) \leftarrow \mathsf{Enc}(PK, T^*)$. At last, it returns (K_b, CT^*) to the adversary.

Phase 2: This phase is the same as Phase 1 except for the following restrictions

- **Corrupt**(): Returns $\perp$ if $T^* \cap \mathsf{P} = \emptyset$.
- **Decrypt**(CT, T): Returns $\perp$ if $(CT, T) = (CT^*, T^*)$.

Guess: The adversary outputs a guess b' and wins the game if $b' = b$.

Definition 2 (Adaptive Security). *A PKEM scheme $\mathsf{PKEM} = (\mathsf{KeyGen}, \mathsf{Enc}, \mathsf{Punc}, \mathsf{Dec})$ is IND-PUN-ATK secure for ATK $\in$ {CPA, CCA} if for all probabilistic polynomial time (PPT) adversary $\mathcal{A}$, the advantage of $\mathcal{A}$ winning in the IND-PUN-ATK game is*

$$\mathsf{Adv}_{\mathcal{A},\mathsf{PKEM}}^{\text{IND-PUN-ATK}}(\lambda) = \left| \Pr[b' = b] - \frac{1}{2} \right| \leq \mathsf{negl}(\lambda),$$

where $\mathsf{negl}(\lambda)$ is a negligible function of λ.

We also define a weak security named selective security by an IND-sPUN-ATK game. It is similar to the above game except that the adversary is required to submit the challenge tag list $T^* \subseteq \mathcal{T}$ before the setup phase.

Definition 3 (Selective Security). *A PKEM scheme $\mathsf{PKEM} = (\mathsf{KeyGen}, \mathsf{Enc}, \mathsf{Punc}, \mathsf{Dec})$ is IND-sPUN-ATK secure for ATK $\in$ {CPA, CCA} if for all PPT adversary $\mathcal{A}$, the advantage of $\mathcal{A}$ winning in the IND-sPUN-ATK game is*

$$\mathsf{Adv}_{\mathcal{A},\mathsf{PKEM}}^{\text{IND-sPUN-ATK}}(\lambda) = \left| \Pr[b' = b] - \frac{1}{2} \right| \leq \mathsf{negl}(\lambda).$$

2.3 Key-Homomorphic Identity-Based Revocation Mechanism

In this part, we first recall the syntax and security of identity-based revocation scheme, and then introduce a new concept—*key-homomorphic identity-based revocable key encapsulation mechanism* (KH-IRKEM)—for our application.

In fact, we do not need a full-blown revocation encryption scheme. Instead, an identity-based revocable key encapsulation mechanism (IRKEM) is sufficient for our application, where an encapsulated key can be recovered by a receiver if and only if s/he is not revoked during the encapsulation phase.

More formally, an IRKEM scheme with master secret key space $\mathcal{MSK}$, private key space $\mathcal{SK}$, encapsulated key space $\mathcal{K}$ and identity space $\mathcal{ID}$ is comprised of a tuple of polynomial time algorithms (Params, MKGen, KeyExt, Enc, Dec):

- $\mathsf{Params}(1^\lambda, n)$ takes as input a security parameter λ and a maximum number n of revoked users, and outputs system parameters pp that is (implicitly) taken as an additional input of the rest algorithms. Note that $n \in \mathbb{N} \cup \{\infty\}$, and "$\infty$" indicates the number of revoked users is unbounded.
- $\mathsf{MKGen}(pp)$ takes as input public parameters pp and outputs a master public key mpk and a master secret key msk.
- $\mathsf{KeyExt}(msk, id)$ takes as input a master secret key msk and an identity id, outputs a private key sk_{id} for the identity id. When this algorithm is randomized, the associated random coin space is assumed to be $\mathcal{R}$.
- $\mathsf{Enc}(mpk, R)$ takes as input a master public key mpk and a list R of revoked users, where $|R| \leq n$, and outputs a symmetric key k and a ciphertext ct, such that any user with private key sk_{id} for $id \notin R$ can recover the encapsulated key k.
- $\mathsf{Dec}(sk_{id}, id, ct, R)$ takes as input a private key sk_{id} for an identity id and a ciphertext ct associated with the revocation list R, and outputs an encapsulated key k if $id \notin R$ and $\perp$ otherwise.

Definition 4 (Correctness). *For all $\lambda \in \mathbb{N}, n \in \mathbb{N} \cup \{\infty\}$, $R \subseteq \mathcal{ID}$ such that $|R| \leq n$, let $pp \leftarrow \mathsf{Params}(1^\lambda, n)$, $(mpk, msk) \leftarrow \mathsf{MKGen}(pp)$, $(k, ct) \leftarrow \mathsf{Enc}(mpk, R)$, and $sk_{id} \leftarrow \mathsf{KeyExt}(msk, id)$ for $id \notin R$, it holds that*

$$\Pr[\mathsf{Dec}(sk_{id}, id, ct, R) = k] \geq 1 - \mathsf{negl}(\lambda),$$

where the probability is taken over the randomness of the associated algorithms.

Remark 2. Similar to the definition of IBE in [5,6], we add a parameter generation algorithm to the specification of IRKEM, in order to make the public parameters explicitly distinct from the master public key. This implies that the parameters may not depend on the master secret key, although the master public key might. In this work, the parameters may include the description of groups, group generators and the like. For simplicity, we additionally assume that, as in [6], the master secret key is randomly drawn from $\mathcal{MSK}$ and the master public key is derived deterministically/probabilistically from it.

The security of IRKEM is defined by an IND-RL-ATK game, which incorporates both CPA and CCA variants. The game is played between a challenger and an adversary, which is described as follows.

Setup: On input a security parameter λ and a maximum number n of revoked users, the challenger generates $pp \leftarrow \mathsf{Params}(1^\lambda, d)$ and $(mpk, msk) \leftarrow \mathsf{MKGen}(pp)$, then returns pp, mpk and initializes an empty set $\mathcal{Q}$.

Phase 1: The adversary can adaptively issue the following queries

- **Key Extract**(id): On input an identity id, the challenger returns a corresponding private key $sk_{id} \leftarrow \mathsf{KeyExt}(msk, id)$ and adds id to $\mathcal{Q}$.
- **Decrypt**(id, ct, R): On input an identity id, a ciphertext ct and the associated revocation list R, the challenger computes sk_{id} and returns $k \leftarrow \mathsf{Dec}(sk_{id}, id, ct, R)$ if ATK = CCA, otherwise returns $\perp$.

Challenge: On input a list of revoked identities $R^* \subseteq \mathcal{ID}$, the challenger directly rejects if $\mathcal{Q} \setminus R^* \neq \emptyset$. Otherwise, it picks $b \xleftarrow{\$} \{0,1\}, k_1 \xleftarrow{\$} \mathcal{K}$ and computes $(k_0, ct^*) \leftarrow \mathsf{Enc}(mpk, R^*)$. Finally, it sends (k_b, ct^*) back to the adversary.

Phase 2: This is the same as Phase 1 except with below restrictions

- **Key Extract**(id): Returns $\perp$ if $id \notin R^*$.
- **Decrypt**(id, ct, R): Returns $\perp$ if $(ct, R) = (ct^*, R^*)$.

Guess: The adversary outputs a guess b' and wins the game if $b' = b$.

Definition 5 (Adaptive Security). *An IRKEM scheme Σ = (Params, MKGen, KeyExt, Enc, Dec) is IND-RL-ATK secure for ATK $\in$ {CPA, CCA} if for all $\lambda \in \mathbb{N}$ and PPT adversary $\mathcal{A}$, the advantage of $\mathcal{A}$ winning in the IND-RL-ATK game is*

$$\mathsf{Adv}_{\mathit{IRKEM},\mathcal{A}}^{\text{IND-RL-ATK}}(\lambda) = \left|\Pr[b' = b] - \frac{1}{2}\right| \leq \mathsf{negl}(\lambda).$$

Similar to the selective security of PKEM, we also define a selective security for IRKEM by an IND-sRL-ATK game.

Definition 6 (Selective Security). *An IRKEM scheme Σ = (Params, MKGen, KeyExt, Enc, Dec) is IND-sRL-ATK secure for ATK $\in$ {CPA, CCA} if for all $\lambda \in \mathbb{N}$ and PPT adversary $\mathcal{A}$, the advantage of $\mathcal{A}$ winning in the IND-sRL-ATK game is*

$$\mathsf{Adv}_{\mathit{IRKEM},\mathcal{A}}^{\text{IND-sRL-ATK}}(\lambda) = \left|\Pr[b' = b] - \frac{1}{2}\right| \leq \mathsf{negl}(\lambda).$$

Next we introduce the additional properties of IRKEM, desired for our applications. The first is called Extended Correctness. Informally, this property ensures that a legally encapsulated key can be computed correctly in an alternative way. It is formalized in Definition 7. To formally define this property, we will write the random coin explicitly in the encapsulation algorithm.

Definition 7 (Extended Correctness). *For all $\lambda \in \mathbb{N}, n \in \mathbb{N} \cup \{\infty\}$, $R_i \subseteq \mathcal{ID}$ such that $|R_i| \leq n$, any $pp \leftarrow \mathit{Params}(1^\lambda, n)$, $(mpk_i, msk_i) \leftarrow \mathit{MKGen}(pp)$, $(k_i, ct_i) = \mathit{Enc}(mpk_i, R_i; s_i)$, and $sk_i \leftarrow \mathit{KeyExt}(msk_i, id_i)$ for $i \in \{1,2\}$, we let $(\widehat{k}, \widehat{ct}) = \mathit{Enc}(mpk_1, R_2; s_2)$. Then an IRKEM scheme Σ is called extended correct if for $id_1 \notin R_2$ it satisfies that*

$$\Pr[\mathit{Dec}(sk_1, id_1, ct_2, R_2) = \widehat{k}] \geq 1 - \mathsf{negl}(\lambda).$$

We note that the encapsulated key $\hat{k}$ can be correctly recovered by $\hat{k} \leftarrow \mathsf{Dec}(sk_1, id_1, \widehat{ct}, R_2)$ in terms of the standard correctness (cf. Definition 4). Here, it is further required that $\hat{k}$ can be obtained by "decapsulating" other ciphertexts generated under the same revocation list and random coins. Alternatively, this property means decapsulating a ciphertext with a mismatched private key can produce a legitimate encapsulated key. Thus we are able to compute a legally encapsulated key in a different way than by running the encapsulation algorithm.

Hereafter, when the correctness is mentioned, it refers to both the regular and the extended correctness, unless stated otherwise. Now we continue to define the second property—key-homomorphism, which is critical for distributing the encapsulated key. More specifically, this property should hold with respect to both the encapsulated key and the private key, as formalized below.

Definition 8 (Key-Homomorphism). *Let Σ = (Params, MKGen, KeyExt, Enc, Dec) be an IRKEM scheme. We assume that the randomness space $\mathcal{R}$ (associated with $\mathsf{KeyExt}(\cdot)$ if it is randomized) and key spaces $\mathcal{MSK}, \mathcal{SK}$ and $\mathcal{K}$ form four groups $(\mathcal{R}, *), (\mathcal{MSK}, +), (\mathcal{SK}, \otimes)$ and $(\mathcal{K}, \odot)$. Moreover, we assume that the encapsulated key is in the form of $f(msk, s)$, where $s \in \mathcal{S}$ is the random coin consumed in the encapsulation algorithm, i.e., $(k = f(msk, s), ct) = \mathsf{Enc}(mpk, R; s)$. Then the IRKEM scheme Σ is called key-homomorphic if it satisfies the above correctness, and fulfills the following conditions for all $id \in \mathcal{ID}, msk, msk' \in \mathcal{MSK}$, $r, r' \in \mathcal{R}$ and $s \in \mathcal{S}$:*

1. $\mathsf{KeyExt}(msk, id; r) \otimes \mathsf{KeyExt}(msk', id; r') = \mathsf{KeyExt}(msk + msk', id;\ r * r')$,
2. $f(msk, s) \odot f(msk', s) = f(msk + msk', s)$.

This property plays an important role in our work, which reflects in both the construction and the security analysis. We remark that if an IRKEM Σ is correct in the sense of Definition 7 and secure (either selectively or adaptively), then $f(msk, s)$ associated with the second property of Definition 8 should depend on msk non-trivially. Otherwise, if $f(msk, s) = f'(s)$ is independent of msk and Σ is extended correct, then an adversary can break the security of Σ as follows. After receiving the master public key mpk_2 and the challenge ciphertext ct_2 and encapsulated key k_2, she generates a new (msk_1, mpk_1), chooses an $id_1 \notin R_2$ and computes $sk_1 \leftarrow \mathsf{KeyExt}(msk_1, id_1)$. Then she can recover $k_2 = \hat{k}$ by using the extended correctness property and break the security easily. Examples of such schemes can be derived from transferring the lattice-based NIPEs (the first two constructions) of [29] to IRKEMs by changing the encryption/decryption functions to encapsulation/decapsulation functions similar to Subsects. 4.1, 4.2 and 4.3. It is then easy to see that $f(msk, s)$ is independent of msk. This implies that the derived IRKEMs are not extended correct as they are proven to be secure in [29].

In the following, we first propose a generic construction of PKEM from any KH-IRKEM scheme with extended correctness, and then present several instantiations with distinct features.

3 Construction of PKEM from KH-IRKEM

In this section, we present a generic construction of PKEM from any KH-IRKEM scheme with extended correctness, as defined before. Let $\Sigma = (\mathsf{IR.Params}, \mathsf{IR.MKGen}, \mathsf{IR.KeyExt}, \mathsf{IR.Enc}, \mathsf{IR.Dec})$ be a KH-IRKEM scheme with identity space $\mathcal{ID}$, then a PKEM scheme $\Pi = (\mathsf{KeyGen}, \mathsf{Punc}, \mathsf{Enc}, \mathsf{Dec})$ with tag space $\mathcal{T} = \mathcal{ID}$ is constructed from Σ as follows.

- $\mathsf{KeyGen}(1^\lambda, n)$: On input a parameter λ and an index $n \in \mathbb{N} \cup \{\infty\}$, it first generates $pp \leftarrow \mathsf{IR.Params}(1^\lambda, n)$ and $(mpk, msk) \leftarrow \mathsf{IR.MKGen}(pp)$. Then it selects a distinguished tag $t_0 \in \mathcal{T}$, which will never be punctured and encrypted later, and produces $sk_0 \leftarrow \mathsf{IR.KeyExt}(msk, t_0)$. Finally, it outputs the public and secret key pair

$$(PK, SK) = \big((pp, mpk), (sk_0, t_0)\big).$$

- $\mathsf{Punc}(SK_{i-1}, t_i)$: On input a punctured secret key $SK_{i-1} = \big((sk_0, t_0), \ldots, (sk_{i-1}, t_{i-1})\big)$ for tags $\{t_\ell\}_{\ell=1}^{i-1}$ and a tag $t_i \in \mathcal{T} \setminus \{t_0\}$, where $SK_0 = SK$, it randomly chooses $msk_i \in \mathcal{MSK}$[2] and produces a new puncture secret key SK_i for $\{t_\ell\}_{\ell=1}^{i}$ as below:
  1. Computes $sk_0' = sk_0 \otimes \mathsf{IR.KeyExt}(-msk_i, t_0)$ and $sk_i \leftarrow \mathsf{IR.KeyExt}(msk_i, t_i)$, where sk_0 in SK_{i-1} is updated to sk_0'.
  2. Sets $SK_i = \big((sk_0', t_0), (sk_1, t_1), \ldots, (sk_{i-1}, t_{i-1}), (sk_i, t_i)\big)$, where sk_j for all $j \in [1, i-1]$ remains identical to SK_{i-1}.
- $\mathsf{Enc}(PK, T)$: On input public key $PK = (pp, mpk)$ and a list of tags T such that $|T| \leq n$ and $T \subseteq \mathcal{T} \setminus \{t_0\}$, it computes

$$(f(msk, s), ct) = \mathsf{IR.Enc}(mpk, T; s)$$

  and outputs $(K, CT) = (f(msk, s), ct)$ along with T.
- $\mathsf{Dec}(SK_i, CT, T)$: On input a punctured secret key $SK_i = \big((sk_0, t_0), \ldots, (sk_i, t_i)\big)$ and a ciphertext CT along with tags T, it returns $\perp$ if there exists $j \in [1, i]$ such that $t_j \in T$. Otherwise, it recovers the encapsulated key as:
  1. Computes $k_j = \mathsf{IR.Dec}(sk_j, t_j, CT, T)$ for all $j \in [0, i]$.
  2. Calculates $K' = \bigodot_{j=0}^{i} k_j$ and outputs K'.

The correctness follows from the (extended) correctness of the underlying KH-IRKEM scheme and its key-homomorphic properties. To be more precise, we assume that $(K, CT) = \mathsf{IR.Enc}(mpk, T; s)$ and $sk_j \leftarrow \mathsf{IR.KeyExt}(msk_j, t_j)$ such that $t_j \notin T$ for all $j \in [1, i]$. The key-homomorphic property of $\mathsf{IR.KeyExt}(\cdot, \cdot)$ indicates the current key component sk_0 (of SK_i) is in the form of $\mathsf{IR.KeyExt}(msk - \sum_{j=1}^{i} msk_j, t_0)$. Then we have that

[2] Recall that the master secret key is assumed to be randomly drawn from $\mathcal{MSK}$, as remarked in Sect. 2.3.

- $k_0 = \mathsf{IR.Dec}(sk_0, t_0, CT, T) = f(msk - \sum_{j=1}^{i} msk_j, s)$, and
- $k_j = \mathsf{IR.Dec}(sk_j, t_j, CT, T) = f(msk_j, s)$ for all $j \in [1, i]$,

where the second equalities derive from the extended correctness of KH-IRKEM scheme Σ. Finally, the key-homomorphism of $f(\cdot, \cdot)$ yields that

$$K' = f\big(msk - \sum_{j=1}^{i} msk_j, s\big) \odot \bigodot_{j=1}^{i} f(msk_j, s) = f(msk, s).$$

We remark that the ciphertext CT taken in decapsulation process is generated under mpk, while the private keys sk_j are computed from new master secret keys msk_j rather than msk. In this case, the standard correctness is insufficient, and hence the extended correctness is crucial for the correctness of our PKEM.

3.1 Security Analysis

We first show that the proposed PKEM scheme is IND-sPUN-CPA secure if the underlying IRKEM scheme is IND-sRL-CPA secure. Then we further discuss its adaptive security based on the adaptive security of the KH-IRKEM scheme.

Theorem 1. *The proposed generic construction PKEM is IND-sPUN-CPA secure, if the underlying IRKEM scheme is key-homomorphic and IND-sRL-CPA secure. More precisely, for any PPT adversary $\mathcal{A}$ against the security of our PKEM scheme, it holds that*

$$\mathrm{Adv}_{\mathsf{PKEM},\mathcal{A}}^{\text{IND-sPUN-CPA}}(\lambda) = \mathsf{Adv}_{\mathsf{IRKEM},\mathcal{B}}^{\text{IND-sRL-CPA}}(\lambda),$$

where $\mathcal{B}$ is some PPT algorithm against the security of the IRKEM scheme.

Proof. The proof is conducted through a sequence of games that starts with the real IND-sPUN-CPA game and ends with a game in which the adversary has a negligible advantage. Moreover, each two successive games are shown to be (computationally) indistinguishable. Hereafter, we let Win_i denote the event that the adversary $\mathcal{A}$ wins in game G_i. For sake of clarity, we assume that $\mathcal{A}$ makes at most q puncture queries, say $\{t_1, t_2, \ldots, t_q\}$, and at least one of them, say t_i for some $i \in [1, q]$, belongs to the set of challenge tags T^*. It is also assumed that, without loss of generality, the corrupt query is made after all q punctures. Then the current punctured secret key is sent back to $\mathcal{A}$ directly.

Game G_0: It is the real game played between a challenger and an adversary $\mathcal{A}$, as described in Sect. 2.2. In more details, $\mathcal{A}$ first submits a set of challenge tags T^* such that $|T^*| \leq n$. After that, the challenger chooses a distinguished tag $t_0 \in \mathcal{T}$ and runs $pp \leftarrow \mathsf{IR.Params}(1^\lambda, n)$, $(mpk, msk) \leftarrow \mathsf{IR.MKGen}(pp)$ and $sk_0 \leftarrow \mathsf{IR.KeyExt}(msk, t_0)$ to produce the public and secret key pair $(PK, SK) = \big((pp, mpk), (sk_0, t_0)\big)$. In addition, it initializes an empty set P for keeping track of puncture queries. Then it returns PK to the adversary $\mathcal{A}$, and answers the puncture queries and the challenge query as follows:

- **Puncture**(t_i): The challenger chooses $msk_i \xleftarrow{\$} \mathcal{MSK}$, computes $sk_i \leftarrow \mathsf{IR.KeyExt}(msk_i, t_i)$ and updates the first component sk_0 of SK_{i-1} as $sk_0 = sk_0 \otimes \mathsf{IR.KeyExt}(-msk_i, t_0)$. Then it sets $SK_i = ((sk_0, t_0), \ldots, (sk_{i-1}, t_{i-1}), (sk_i, t_i))$, where $SK_0 = SK$, and records t_i to P. Finally, it returns $SK_q = ((sk_0, t_0), (sk_1, t_1), \ldots, (sk_q, t_q))$ to $\mathcal{A}$ after all q puncture queries.
- **Challenge:** On input the challenge $T^* \subseteq \mathcal{T} \setminus \{t_0\}^3$, the challenger computes $(K_0^*, CT^*) \leftarrow \mathsf{IR.Enc}(mpk, T^*)$ and randomly chooses $K_1^* \xleftarrow{\$} \mathcal{K}$. Then it selects $b \xleftarrow{\$} \{0,1\}$ and outputs (K_b^*, CT^*).

Eventually, the adversary $\mathcal{A}$ outputs a guess b', and wins the game if $b' = b$. We get from the security definition of PKEM (cf. Definition 2) that

$$\mathsf{Adv}_{\mathsf{PKEM},\mathcal{A}}^{\text{IND-sPUN-CPA}}(\lambda) = \left|\Pr[\mathsf{Win}_0] - \frac{1}{2}\right|.$$

Game G_1**:** This game is identical to G_0, except that the master secret keys $msk_1, msk_2, \ldots, msk_q \in \mathcal{MSK}$ are sampled beforehand instead of on-the-fly and used straightforwardly to simulate the puncture queries. In particular, all queries are answered as follows:

- **Puncture**(t_i): The challenger computes $sk_i \leftarrow \mathsf{IR.KeyExt}(msk_i, t_i)$ and updates the first component of SK_{i-1} as $sk_0 = sk_0 \otimes \mathsf{IR.KeyExt}(-msk_i, t_0)$, by directly using msk_i chosen before. After that, it sets $SK_i = ((sk_0, t_0), \ldots, (sk_{i-1}, t_{i-1}), (sk_i, t_i))$ and adds t_i to P. Finally, it returns $SK_q = ((sk_0, t_0), (sk_1, t_1), \ldots, (sk_q, t_q))$ to $\mathcal{A}$ after all q puncture queries.
- **Challenge:** On input the challenge $T^* \subseteq \mathcal{T} \setminus \{t_0\}$, the challenger computes $(K_0^*, CT^*) \leftarrow \mathsf{IR.Enc}(mpk, T^*)$ and randomly picks $K_1^* \xleftarrow{\$} \mathcal{K}$. Then it outputs (K_b^*, CT^*) where b is chosen uniform randomly from $\{0,1\}$.

At last, the adversary $\mathcal{A}$ outputs her guess b'. It can be seen from the above that the way of sampling the master secret keys does not change the view of the adversary. Therefore, it holds that

$$\Pr[\mathsf{Win}_1] = \Pr[\mathsf{Win}_0].$$

Game G_2**:** It is the same as above game except that the component sk_0 of the finally corrupted secret key SK_q is generated in a different way. Briefly, sk_0 here is generated in a direct manner rather than by sequential updates (i.e., $sk_0 = sk_0 \otimes \mathsf{IR.KeyExt}(-msk_i, t_0)$). More specifically, after receiving challenge tags T^* the challenger runs $pp \leftarrow \mathsf{IR.Params}(1^\lambda, n)$ and $(mpk, msk) \leftarrow \mathsf{IR.MKGen}(pp)$, and picks in advance $msk_1, msk_2, \ldots, msk_q \in \mathcal{MSK}$ that will be used to answer the puncture queries issued by $\mathcal{A}$ later. Then it sets $msk_0 = msk - \sum_{i=1}^{q} msk_i$ and computes $sk_0 \leftarrow \mathsf{IR.KeyExt}(msk_0, t_0)$ for the distinguished tag $t_0 \in \mathcal{T}$. After that, it returns $PK = (pp, mpk)$ and simulates the puncture queries and challenge query as below:

[3] We always assume that $T^* \cap \mathsf{P} \neq \emptyset$, otherwise it will be rejected according to the security definition.

- **Puncture**(t_i): The challenger uses msk_i (chosen above) to compute $sk_i \leftarrow \mathsf{IR.KeyExt}(msk_i, t_i)$ for the i-th puncture query t_i, and records t_i to P. After receiving all q puncture queries from $\mathcal{A}$, it returns $SK_q = \big((sk_0, t_0), \ldots, (sk_q, t_q)\big)$. Recall that sk_0 is generated at the beginning.
- **Challenge:** On input the challenge T^* issued by $\mathcal{A}$, the challenger computes $(K_0^*, CT^*) \leftarrow \mathsf{IR.Enc}(mpk, T^*)$ and chooses $K_1^* \xleftarrow{\$} \mathcal{K}$. Then it chooses a random bit $b \in \{0, 1\}$ and returns (K_b^*, CT^*).

Finally, $\mathcal{A}$ outputs her guess b'. Clearly, the distribution of this game is identical to G_1, so we have

$$\Pr[\mathsf{Win}_2] = \Pr[\mathsf{Win}_1].$$

Game G_3**:** In this game, we assume that, without loss of generality, the j-th puncture query t_j is the first tag belonging to the set T^* of challenge tags. Notice that, there exists at least one puncture query contained in T^* in terms of the security definition of PKEM (cf. Definition 2), and it is easy to find the index j given T^*. Then the difference of this game from G_2 is the way of generating sk_0 and sk_j (associated with t_j).

In particular, the challenger in this game runs $pp \leftarrow \mathsf{IR.Params}(1^\lambda, n)$ and $(mpk, msk) \leftarrow \mathsf{IR.MKGen}(pp)$, chooses $msk_0, \ldots, msk_{j-1}, msk_{j+1}, \ldots, msk_q \in \mathcal{MSK}$ uniformly at random, and sets $msk_j = msk - \sum_{i=0,\neq j}^{q} msk_i$. Then it uses msk_0 to compute $sk_0 \leftarrow \mathsf{IR.KeyExt}(msk_0, t_0)$ for the distinguished tag $t_0 \in \mathcal{T}$ and uses msk_i to compute $sk_i \leftarrow \mathsf{IR.KeyExt}(msk_i, t_i)$ for the i-th puncture query t_i, where $i \in [1, q]$. As for the challenge query, it is simulated in the same way as before.

It is not difficult to see $\mathcal{A}$'s views in G_2 and G_3 are identical, as they rely essentially on the identical distributions $(msk, msk_0 = msk - \sum_{i=1}^{q} msk_i, msk_1, \ldots, msk_q)$ and $(msk, msk_0, \ldots, msk_{j-1}, msk_j = msk - \sum_{i=1,\neq j}^{q} msk_i, msk_{j+1}, \ldots, msk_q)$, respectively. Therefore, we get that

$$\Pr[\mathsf{Win}_3] = \Pr[\mathsf{Win}_2].$$

Now, what remains to do is to show the advantage of $\mathcal{A}$ winning in G_3 is negligible in λ. It is formally stated as the following lemma.

Lemma 1. *Provided that the underlying IRKEM scheme Σ is IND-sRL-CPA secure and key-homomorphic, then the advantage of $\mathcal{A}$ winning in G_3 is negligible in λ. That is,*

$$\left|\Pr[\mathsf{Win}_3] - \frac{1}{2}\right| = \mathsf{Adv}_{\mathsf{IRKEM},\mathcal{B}}^{\text{IND-sRL-CPA}}(\lambda),$$

where $\mathcal{B}$ is some PPT algorithm against the security of the IRKEM scheme.

Proof (of Lemma 1). Suppose for sake of contradiction that there is an efficient adversary $\mathcal{A}$ winning in G_3 with non-negligible advantage, then we can find an efficient algorithm $\mathcal{B}$ that succeeds to break the IND-sRL-CPA security of the underlying IRKEM scheme Σ as follows.

After receiving the set T^* of challenge tags from $\mathcal{A}$, $\mathcal{B}(1^\lambda)$ sets it as his own challenge and submits T^* to the challenger of the IRKEM scheme. Then $\mathcal{B}$ returns to $\mathcal{A}$ the response pp and mpk, such that $pp \leftarrow \mathsf{IR.Params}(1^\lambda, n)$ and $(mpk, msk) \leftarrow \mathsf{IR.MKGen}(pp)$. After that, $\mathcal{B}$ chooses uniformly at random $msk_0, \ldots, msk_{j-1}, msk_{j+1}, \ldots, msk_q$ from $\mathcal{MSK}$, and uses msk_0 to compute $sk_0 \leftarrow \mathsf{IR.KeyExt}(msk_0, t_0)$ for the distinguished tag $t_0 \in \mathcal{T}$ chosen by himself. Then $\mathcal{B}$ proceeds to simulate the puncture queries and the challenge query as follows:

- **Puncture**(t_i)**:** For the i-th puncture query t_i, $\mathcal{B}$ directly uses msk_i chosen above to generate $sk_i \leftarrow \mathsf{IR.KeyExt}(msk_i, t_i)$ if $i \neq j$. Otherwise, $\mathcal{B}$ forwards $t_j \in T^*$ to the key extraction oracle of the IRKEM scheme and gets the corresponding private key sk_j'. Then $\mathcal{B}$ computes $sk_j = sk_j' \otimes \mathsf{IR.KeyExt}(-\sum_{i=0,\neq j}^{q} msk_i, t_j)$. In addition, $\mathcal{B}$ adds t_i to P. Once finishing the simulation of all q puncture queries, $\mathcal{B}$ returns $SK_q = \big((sk_0, t_0), (sk_1, t_1), \ldots, (sk_q, t_q)\big)$ to $\mathcal{A}$.
- **Challenge:** $\mathcal{B}$ gets the response (to the challenge T^*) from the challenger of the IRKEM scheme. In particular, the response is (K_b^*, CT^*), such that $(K_0^*, CT^*) \leftarrow \mathsf{IR.Enc}(mpk, T^*)$, $K_1^* \xleftarrow{\$} \mathcal{K}$, and $b \xleftarrow{\$} \{0,1\}$. Then $\mathcal{B}$ outputs (K_b^*, CT^*) to the adversary $\mathcal{A}$.

At last, $\mathcal{B}$ outputs what $\mathcal{A}$ outputs. From the above, we can see that $\mathcal{B}$ perfectly simulates G_3, hence we have

$$\mathsf{Adv}_{\mathsf{IRKEM},\mathcal{B}}^{\text{IND-sRL-CPA}}(\lambda) = \left|\Pr[\mathcal{B}(1^\lambda, \mathsf{View}) = b] - \frac{1}{2}\right| = \left|\Pr[\mathsf{Win}_3] - \frac{1}{2}\right|,$$

where View is the view of $\mathcal{B}$ in the IRKEM game that consists of pp, mpk, sk_j' and (K_b^*, CT^*).

Putting all above equations together, we get the advantage of any PPT adversary $\mathcal{A}$ against our PKEM scheme

$$\mathsf{Adv}_{\mathsf{PKEM},\mathcal{A}}^{\text{IND-sPUN-CPA}}(\lambda) = \left|\Pr[\mathsf{Win}_3] - \frac{1}{2}\right| = \mathsf{Adv}_{\mathsf{IRKEM},\mathcal{B}}^{\text{IND-sRL-CPA}}(\lambda).$$

Theorem 2. *The proposed generic construction PKEM is IND-PUN-CPA secure, if the underlying IRKEM scheme is key-homomorphic and IND-RL-CPA secure. More precisely, for any PPT adversary $\mathcal{A}$ against the security of our PKEM scheme, it holds that*

$$\mathsf{Adv}_{\mathsf{PKEM},\mathcal{A}}^{\text{IND-PUN-CPA}}(\lambda) \leq q \cdot \mathsf{Adv}_{\mathsf{IRKEM},\mathcal{B}}^{\text{IND-RL-CPA}}(\lambda),$$

where q is the maximum number of puncture queries issued by $\mathcal{A}$ and $\mathcal{B}$ is some PPT algorithm against the security of the IRKEM scheme.

Proof (Sketch). To show the adaptive security of our PKEM scheme, we only need to guess which puncture query is belonging to the set of challenge tags T^* in the previous proof. The probability of guessing it correctly is at least $1/q$, assuming that the upper-bound on the number of puncture queries issued by $\mathcal{A}$ is q. For the detailed proof, please refer to the full version.

4 Instantiations of KH-IRKEM

In this section, we present several concrete IRKEM schemes derived from existing Identity-Based Revocation (IBR) schemes or Non-zero Inner Product Encryption (NIPE) schemes, and show that they satisfy the desired properties for our purpose. Particularly, the design of IRKEM schemes from the NIPE schemes follows the Embedding Lemma (see Proposition 1 in [3]), and thus the security of the IRKEM schemes can be reduced to the NIPE schemes. Then by applying our generic construction in Sect. 3, we obtain the first PKEM schemes that not only support unbounded number of punctures, but also features constant-size ciphertext, short public keys, or unbounded number of tags per ciphertext.

4.1 KH-IRKEM with Compact Ciphertexts

The first IRKEM scheme is derived from the NIPE scheme in [38], which is proven secure under the n-DBDHE assumption below.

q-DBDHE ASSUMPTION. Let $(\mathbb{G}, \mathbb{G}_T)$ be cyclic groups of prime order p with a symmetric bilinear pairing $e : \mathbb{G} \times \mathbb{G} \to \mathbb{G}_T$. The q-Decision Bilinear Diffie-Hellman Exponent (n-DBDHE) problem is, given

$$\left(g, g^a, g^{(a^2)}, \ldots, g^{(a^q)}, g^{(a^{q+2})}, \ldots, g^{(a^{2q})}, h, T\right)$$

where $a \xleftarrow{\$} \mathbb{Z}_p, g, h \xleftarrow{\$} \mathbb{G}$ and $T \in \mathbb{G}_T$, to decide if $T = e(g,h)^{a^{q+1}}$ or if T is randomly chosen from $\mathbb{G}_T$.

DESCRIPTION. This scheme consists of five polynomial-time algorithms (Params, MKGen, KeyExt, Enc, Dec) with the following specifications:

- $\mathsf{Params}(1^\lambda, n)$: The algorithm takes a security parameter λ and an integer $n \in \mathbb{N}$, and generates a pair of bilinear groups $(\mathbb{G}, \mathbb{G}_T)$ of prime order $p > 2^\lambda$ with bilinear map e. Then it randomly chooses $\beta, b_1, \ldots, b_n \in \mathbb{Z}_p$ and $g \in \mathbb{G}$, and computes $h = g^\beta$ and $h_i = g^{b_i}$ for all $i \in [1, n]$. Finally, it outputs the public parameters
$$pp = \left((\mathbb{G}, \mathbb{G}_T, e), g, h, \{h_i\}_{i \in [1,n]}\right).$$
- $\mathsf{MKGen}(pp)$: Given the public parameters pp, it chooses $\alpha \in \mathbb{Z}_p$ uniformly at random, and then computes and outputs the master secret key and master public key pair
$$(msk, mpk) = \left(\alpha, e(g,g)^\alpha\right).$$
- $\mathsf{KeyExt}(msk, id)$: Given a master secret key $msk = \alpha$ and an identity $id \in \mathbb{Z}_p$, this algorithm first defines a vector $\boldsymbol{x}_{id} = (x_1, \ldots, x_n) \in \mathbb{Z}_p^n$ such that $x_i = id^{i-1}$ for all $i \in [1, n]$, then it chooses $r \xleftarrow{\$} \mathbb{Z}_p$ and outputs the private key $sk_{id} = (d_1, d_2, k_1, \ldots, k_n) \in \mathbb{G}^{n+2}$ as
$$d_1 = g^\alpha h_1^r, d_2 = g^r, k_1 = h^r, k_i = \left(h_1^{-x_i} h_i\right)^r \text{ for } \forall i \in [2, n].$$

- $\mathsf{Enc}(mpk, R)$: Given a master public key mpk and a revocation list $R = \{id_1, id_2, \ldots, id_m\}$ such that $m < n$, the algorithm generates the encapsulated key $k \in \mathbb{G}_T$ and ciphertext $ct = (c_1, c_2) \in \mathbb{G}^2$ as follows:
  1. Define a vector $\boldsymbol{y}_R = (y_1, \ldots, y_n)$, where $\{y_i\}_{i\in[1,m+1]}$ are the coefficients of the polynomial $f_R(z) = \prod_{id_j \in R}(z - id_j) = \sum_{i=1}^{m+1} y_i \cdot z^{i-1}$, and all other coordinates $\{y_i\}_{i\in[m+2,n]}$ are set to 0 if $m + 1 < n$.
  2. Choose $s \xleftarrow{\$} \mathbb{Z}_p$, then compute $k = e(g, g)^{\alpha s}$, $c_1 = g^s$ and $c_2 = \left(h \prod_{i=1}^{n} h_i^{y_i}\right)^s$, and finally output (k, ct).
- $\mathsf{Dec}(sk_{id}, id, ct, R)$: Given a private key sk_{id} for an identity id and a ciphertext $ct = (c_1, c_2)$ under the revocation set R, this algorithm returns $\perp$ if $id \in R$. Otherwise, it recovers the encapsulated key k by conducting the following steps:
  1. Define the vectors $\boldsymbol{x}_{id} = (x_1, \ldots, x_n)$ and $\boldsymbol{y}_R = (y_1, \ldots, y_n)$ as before.
  2. Compute $\hat{k} = k_1 \prod_{i=2}^{n} k_i^{y_i}$ and then return

$$k' = e\left(c_1, d_1 \cdot \hat{k}^{\frac{1}{\langle \boldsymbol{x}_{id}, \boldsymbol{y}_R\rangle}}\right) \cdot e\left(c_2, d_2^{-\frac{1}{\langle \boldsymbol{x}_{id}, \boldsymbol{y}_R\rangle}}\right).$$

The regular correctness follows readily from the IBR scheme [4]. For completeness, it is analyzed in details as follows. First, we know from the definitions of $\boldsymbol{x}_{id}$ and $\boldsymbol{y}_R$ that $\langle \boldsymbol{x}_{id}, \boldsymbol{y}_R\rangle \neq 0$ *iff* $id \notin R$. Then we observe that

$$\hat{k} = h^r \prod_{i=2}^{n} \left(h_1^{-x_i y_i} \cdot h_i^{y_i}\right)^r = \left(h_1^{-\sum_{i=2}^{n} x_i y_i} \cdot \left(h \prod_{i=2}^{n} h_i^{y_i}\right)\right)^r = \left(h_1^{-\langle \boldsymbol{x}_{id}, \boldsymbol{y}_R\rangle} \cdot \left(h \prod_{i=1}^{n} h_i^{y_i}\right)\right)^r,$$

so when $id \notin R$ we have that

$$\begin{aligned} k' &= e(c_1, d_1) \cdot \left(\frac{e(c_1, \hat{k})}{e(c_2, d_2)}\right)^{\frac{1}{\langle \boldsymbol{x}_{id}, \boldsymbol{y}_R\rangle}} \\ &= e\left(g^s, g^\alpha h_1^r\right) \cdot \left(\frac{e\left(g, h_1^{-\langle \boldsymbol{x}_{id}, \boldsymbol{y}_R\rangle} \cdot h \prod_{i=1}^{n} h_i^{y_i}\right)^{rs}}{e\left(h \prod_{i=1}^{n} h_i^{y_i}, g\right)^{rs}}\right)^{\frac{1}{\langle \boldsymbol{x}_{id}, \boldsymbol{y}_R\rangle}} \\ &= e(g, g)^{\alpha s}. \end{aligned}$$

With regard to the extended correctness, it can be verified similarly. More specifically, we let $(msk', mpk') = (\alpha', e(g, g)^{\alpha'})$ be another master secret and public key pair, and $sk_{id'} = (d_1', d_2', k_1', \ldots, k_n') \leftarrow \mathsf{KeyExt}(msk', id')$ be a private key for identity id', such that

$$d_1' = g^{\alpha'} h_1^{r'},\ d_2' = g^{r'},\ k_1' = h^{r'},\ k_i' = \left(h_1^{-x_i'} h_i\right)^{r'} \text{ for } \forall i \in [2, n],$$

where $r' \xleftarrow{\$} \mathbb{Z}_p$ and $x_i' = id'^{i-1}$. Then it is easy to get via the above analysis that

$$\mathsf{Dec}(sk_{id'}, id', ct, R) = e\left(c_1, d_1' \cdot \hat{k}^{\frac{1}{\langle \boldsymbol{x}_{id'}, \boldsymbol{y}_R\rangle}}\right) \cdot e\left(c_2, d_2'^{-\frac{1}{\langle \boldsymbol{x}_{id'}, \boldsymbol{y}_R\rangle}}\right) = e(g, g)^{\alpha' s}$$

conditioned on $id' \notin R$, where $\boldsymbol{x}_{id'} = (x'_1, \ldots, x'_n)$ and $\hat{k} = k'_1 \prod_{i=2}^{n} k_i'^{y_i}$.

KEY-HOMOMORPHISM. The encapsulated key in this scheme is in the form of $f(msk, s) = e(g, g)^{msk \cdot s}$, where s is the random coin consumed in the encryption algorithm. Next, we show for any identity $id \in \mathbb{Z}_p$, master secret keys $\alpha, \alpha' \in \mathbb{Z}_p$ and randomness $r, r', s \in \mathbb{Z}_p$ that the key-homomorphic properties with respect to $\mathsf{KeyExt}(\cdot)$ and $f(\cdot)$ hold:

1. From the description above, we get that

$$\begin{aligned}
&\mathsf{KeyExt}(\alpha, id; r) \otimes \mathsf{KeyExt}(\alpha', id; r') \\
&= \left(g^{\alpha} h_1^{r}, g^{r}, h^{r}, (h_1^{-x_2} \cdot h_2)^{r}, \ldots, (h_1^{-x_n} \cdot h_n)^{r}\right) \\
&\quad \otimes \left(g^{\alpha'} h_1^{r'}, g^{r'}, h^{r'}, (h_1^{-x_2} h_2)^{r'}, \ldots, (h_1^{-x_n} h_n)^{r'}\right) \\
&= \left(g^{\alpha+\alpha'} h_1^{r+r'}, g^{r+r'}, h^{r+r'}, (h_1^{-x_2} h_2)^{r+r'}, \ldots, (h_1^{-x_n} h_n)^{r+r'}\right) \\
&= \mathsf{KeyExt}(\alpha + \alpha', id; r + r')
\end{aligned}$$

where "$\otimes$" over $\mathcal{SK} = \mathbb{G}^{n+1}$ is the coordinate-wise multiplication over $\mathbb{G}$.
2. As for $f(\cdot)$, it is clear that

$$f(\alpha, s) \odot f(\alpha', s) = e(g, g)^{\alpha s} \cdot e(g, g)^{\alpha' s} = e(g, g)^{(\alpha+\alpha')s} = f(\alpha + \alpha', s),$$

where "$\odot$" is the multiplication over $\mathbb{G}_T$.

SECURITY. The IRKEM scheme above is IND-sRL-CPA secure under the n-DBDHE assumption. This follows readily from the Embedding Lemma (see Proposition 1 in [3]) and the proof of the NIPE scheme in [38].

Now following the proposed generic construction in Sect. 3, we get the first PKEM scheme that features both unbounded punctures and constant-size ciphertexts, but subject to a bounded-number of tags per ciphertext.

4.2 KH-IRKEM with Compact Private Keys

The second IRKEM scheme is based on another NIPE scheme in [38] and proven secure under the DBDH assumption, which unlike the previous one is one of the weakest bilinear assumptions.

DBDH ASSUMPTION. Let $(\mathbb{G}, \mathbb{G}_T)$ be cyclic groups of prime order p with a symmetric bilinear pairing $e : \mathbb{G} \times \mathbb{G} \to \mathbb{G}_T$. The Decision Bilinear Diffie-Hellman (DBDH) problem is, given $\left(g, g^a, g^b, g^c, T\right)$ where $a, b, c \xleftarrow{\$} \mathbb{Z}_p, g \xleftarrow{\$} \mathbb{G}$ and $T \in \mathbb{G}_T$, to decide if $T = e(g, h)^{abc}$ or if T is a random element in $\mathbb{G}_T$.

DESCRIPTION. As before, this scheme consists of five polynomial-time algorithms $(\mathsf{Params}, \mathsf{MKGen}, \mathsf{KeyExt}, \mathsf{Enc}, \mathsf{Dec})$ as below:

- $\mathsf{Params}(1^\lambda, n)$: This algorithm takes a security parameter λ and an integer $n \in \mathbb{N}$, and generates a pair of bilinear groups $(\mathbb{G}, \mathbb{G}_T)$ of prime order $p > 2^\lambda$ with bilinear map e and generator $g \xleftarrow{\$} \mathbb{G}$. Then it randomly chooses $\beta, b_1, \ldots, b_n \in \mathbb{Z}_p$, and computes $h = g^\beta$ and $h_i = g^{b_i}$ for all $i \in [1, n]$. Finally, it outputs the public parameters

$$pp = \left((\mathbb{G}, \mathbb{G}_T, e), g, h, \{h_i\}_{i \in [1,n]}\right).$$

- $\mathsf{MKGen}(pp)$: Given the public parameters pp, it randomly chooses $\alpha \in \mathbb{Z}_p$ and outputs the master secret key and master public key pair

$$(msk, mpk) = \big(\alpha, e(g,g)^{\alpha}\big).$$

- $\mathsf{KeyExt}(msk, id)$: Given a master secret key $msk = \alpha$ and an identity $id \in \mathbb{Z}_p$, the algorithm first defines a vector $\boldsymbol{x}_{id} = (x_1, \dots, x_n) \in \mathbb{Z}_p^n$ such that $x_i = id^{i-1}$ for all $i \in [1,n]$, then it chooses $r \xleftarrow{\$} \mathbb{Z}_p$ and outputs the private key $sk_{id} = (k_0, k_1, k_2) \in \mathbb{G}^3$ as

$$k_0 = g^{\alpha} h^r,\ k_1 = \Big(\prod_{i=1}^{n} h_i^{x_i}\Big)^r,\ k_2 = g^r.$$

- $\mathsf{Enc}(mpk, R)$: Given mpk and a revocation list $R = \{id_1, id_2, \dots, id_m\}$ such that $m < n$, the algorithm generates the encapsulated key $k \in \mathbb{G}_T$ and ciphertext $ct = \big(c_0, \{c_{i,1}\}_{i\in[1,n]}\big) \in \mathbb{G}^{n+1}$ as:
  1. Define a vector $\boldsymbol{y}_R = (y_1, \dots, y_n)$, where $\{y_i\}_{i\in[1,m+1]}$ are the coefficients of the polynomial $f_R(z) = \prod_{id_j \in R}(z - id_j) = \sum_{i=1}^{m+1} y_i \cdot z^{i-1}$, and all other coordinates $\{y_i\}_{i\in[m+2,n]}$ are set to 0 if $m+1 < n$.
  2. Choose $s \xleftarrow{\$} \mathbb{Z}_p$, then compute $k = e(g,g)^{\alpha s}$, $c_0 = g^s$ and $c_{i,1} = (h^{y_i} h_i)^s$ for $\forall i \in [1,n]$, and finally output (k, ct).
- $\mathsf{Dec}(sk_{id}, id, ct, R)$: Given sk_{id} associated with id and $ct = \big(c_0, \{c_{i,1}\}_{i\in[1,n]}\big)$ associated with revocation set R, the algorithm returns $\perp$ if $id \in R$. Otherwise, it recovers the encapsulated key as follows:
  1. Define the vectors $\boldsymbol{x}_{id} = (x_1, \dots, x_n)$ and $\boldsymbol{y}_R = (y_1, \dots, y_n)$ as before.
  2. Compute $c_1 = \prod_{i=1}^{n} c_{i,1}^{x_i}$ and then return

$$k' = e\Big(c_0, k_0 \cdot k_1^{\frac{1}{\langle \boldsymbol{x}_{id}, \boldsymbol{y}_R\rangle}}\Big) \cdot e\Big(c_1, k_2^{-\frac{1}{\langle \boldsymbol{x}_{id}, \boldsymbol{y}_R\rangle}}\Big).$$

The regular correctness is verified as follows. First, we know from the definitions of $\boldsymbol{x}_{id}$ and $\boldsymbol{y}_R$ that $\langle \boldsymbol{x}_{id}, \boldsymbol{y}_R\rangle \neq 0$ *iff* $id \notin R$. Then we observe that

$$c_1 = \prod_{i=1}^{n} c_{i,1}^{x_i} = \prod_{i=1}^{n} \big(h^{x_i y_i} \cdot h_i^{x_i}\big)^s = \Big(h^{\langle \boldsymbol{x}_{id}, \boldsymbol{y}_R\rangle} \cdot \prod_{i=1}^{n} h_i^{x_i}\Big)^s,$$

so when $id \notin R$ we have that

$$\begin{aligned} k' &= e\big(c_0, k_0\big) \cdot \left(\frac{e(c_0,k_1)}{e(c_1,k_2)}\right)^{\frac{1}{\langle \boldsymbol{x}_{id}, \boldsymbol{y}_R\rangle}} \\ &= e\big(g^s, g^{\alpha} h^r\big) \cdot \left(\frac{e\Big(g, \prod_{i=1}^{n} h_i^{x_i}\Big)^{rs}}{e\Big(h^{\langle \boldsymbol{x}_{id}, \boldsymbol{y}_R\rangle} \cdot \prod_{i=1}^{n} h_i^{x_i}, g\Big)^{rs}}\right)^{\frac{1}{\langle \boldsymbol{x}_{id}, \boldsymbol{y}_R\rangle}} \\ &= e(g,g)^{\alpha s}. \end{aligned}$$

As for the extended correctness, it can be validated in a similar way, as analyzed for the first construction. Here, we omit the details.

Key-Homomorphism. In this scheme, the encapsulated key is $f(msk, s) = e(g, g)^{msk \cdot s}$ as well, where s is the encryption randomness. The group operations over e.g., $\mathcal{MSK}, \mathcal{SK}$ and $\mathcal{K}$ are defined as before. It is clear to see for all identity $id \in \mathbb{Z}_p$, any master secret keys $\alpha, \alpha' \in \mathbb{Z}_p$ and randomness $r, r', s \in \mathbb{Z}_p$, both the key-homomorphic properties with respect to $\mathsf{KeyExt}(\cdot)$ and $f(\cdot)$ hold:

1. $\mathsf{KeyExt}(\alpha, id; r) \otimes \mathsf{KeyExt}(\alpha', id; r') = \mathsf{KeyExt}(\alpha + \alpha', id;\ r + r')$
2. $f(\alpha, s) \odot f(\alpha', s) = f(\alpha + \alpha', s)$.

Security. The IRKEM scheme above is IND-sRL-CPA secure under the DBDH assumption. This can be easily shown by following the proof of [38] and the Embedding Lemma (cf. Proposition 1 in [3]).

Then by applying the conversion in Sect. 3, we obtain a PKEM scheme with "compact" secret keys. Compared to the scheme [26] under the same assumption, the communication cost is comparable, but the computation cost is better on average, especially when the number of tags encrypted is large, e.g., n. In that case, the number of exponentiation over $\mathbb{G}$ in our encryption is $\mathcal{O}(n)$ rather than $\mathcal{O}(n^2)$ as [26], and the number of pairings in decryption is d-less than [26], where d is the number of punctures corresponding to the decryption key.

4.3 KH-IRKEM Supporting Unbounded Users

Next we give the third IRKEM scheme, in which the number of users per ciphertext is unbounded compared to the previous ones. This scheme is derived from the IBR scheme in [30] and proven secure under the q-MEBDH assumption.

q-MEBDH Assumption. Let $(\mathbb{G}, \mathbb{G}_T)$ be cyclic groups of prime order p with a symmetric bilinear pairing $e : \mathbb{G} \times \mathbb{G} \to \mathbb{G}_T$. The q-decisional cDiffie-Hellman (q-MEBDH) problem is, given

$$\begin{array}{ll} & T, g, g^s, e(g,g)^\alpha \\ \forall 1 \le i, j \le q & g^{a_i},\ g^{a_i s},\ g^{a_i a_j},\ g^{\alpha/a_i^2} \\ \forall 1 \le i, j, k \le q, i \ne j & g^{a_i a_j s},\ g^{\alpha a_j/a_i^2},\ g^{\alpha a_i a_j/a_k^2},\ g^{\alpha a_i^2/a_j^2} \end{array}$$

where $\alpha, s, a_1, \ldots, a_q \xleftarrow{\$} \mathbb{Z}_p, g \xleftarrow{\$} \mathbb{G}$ and $T \in \mathbb{G}_T$, to decide if $T = e(g, g)^{\alpha s}$ or if T is a random element from $\mathbb{G}_T$.

Description. This scheme consists of five polynomial-time algorithms (Params, $\mathsf{MKGen}, \mathsf{KeyExt}, \mathsf{Enc}, \mathsf{Dec}$), which are described as follows:

- $\mathsf{Params}(1^\lambda)$: The algorithm takes a security parameter λ, and generates a tuple of bilinear groups $(\mathbb{G}, \mathbb{G}_T)$ of prime order $p > 2^\lambda$ with bilinear map e. Then it randomly chooses $b \in \mathbb{Z}_p$ and $g, h \in \mathbb{G}$, and computes $g_1 = g^b, g_2 = g^{b^2}$ and $h_1 = h^b$. At last, it outputs the public parameters

$$pp = \big((\mathbb{G}, \mathbb{G}_T, e), g, g_1, g_2, h, h_1\big).$$

- $\mathsf{MKGen}(pp)$: Given the public parameters pp, it randomly chooses $\alpha \in \mathbb{G}$ and outputs the master secret key and public key pair

$$(msk, mpk) = \big(\alpha, e(g,g)^{\alpha}\big).$$

- $\mathsf{KeyExt}(msk, id)$: Given a master secret key $msk = \alpha$ and an identity $id \in \mathbb{Z}_p$, it chooses $r \xleftarrow{\$} \mathbb{Z}_p$ and outputs the private key $sk_{id} = (k_0, k_1, k_2) \in \mathbb{G}^3$ as

$$k_0 = g^{\alpha} g_2^r, k_1 = (g_1^{id} h)^r, k_2 = g^{-r}.$$

- $\mathsf{Enc}(mpk, R)$: Given mpk and a revocation list $R = \{id_1, id_2, \ldots, id_m\}$, the algorithm selects $s, s_1, \ldots, s_m \xleftarrow{\$} \mathbb{Z}_p$ such that $s = \sum_{i=1}^{m} s_i$, and generates the encapsulated key $k \in \mathbb{G}_T$ and ciphertext $ct = \big(c_0, \{c_{i,1}, c_{i,2}\}_{i \in [1,m]}\big) \in \mathbb{G}^{2m+1}$ as follows:

$$k = e(g,g)^{\alpha s}, c_0 = g^s, c_{i,1} = g_1^{s_i}, c_{i,2} = (g_2^{id_i} h_1)^{s_i} \text{ for } \forall i \in [1, m].$$

- $\mathsf{Dec}(sk_{id}, id, ct, R)$: Given a private key sk_{id} associated with id and a ciphertext $ct = \big(c_0, \{c_{i,1}, c_{i,2}\}_{i \in [1,m]}\big)$ under the revoked set $R = \{id_1, id_2, \ldots, id_m\}$, this algorithm returns $\perp$ if $id \in R$. Otherwise, it recovers the encapsulated key by computing:

$$k' = \frac{e(c_0, k_0)}{e(\prod_{i=1}^{m} c_{i,1}^{1/(id - id_i)}, k_1) \cdot e(\prod_{i=1}^{m} c_{i,2}^{1/(id - id_i)}, k_2)}$$

The regular correctness can be verified as follows. In the case of $id \notin R$, we have that

$$\begin{aligned}
& e(\prod_{i=1}^{m} c_{i,1}^{1/(id-id_i)}, k_1) \cdot e(\prod_{i=1}^{m} c_{i,2}^{1/(id-id_i)}, k_2) \\
&= \prod_{i=1}^{m} \big(e(c_{i,1}, k_1) \cdot e(c_{i,2}, k_2)\big)^{1/(id-id_i)} \\
&= \prod_{i=1}^{m} \big(e(g^{s_i}, (g_2^{id} h_1)^r) \cdot e((g_2^{id_i} h_1)^{s_i}, g^{-r})\big)^{1/(id-id_i)} \\
&= \prod_{i=1}^{m} e(g, g_2)^{s_i r},
\end{aligned}$$

and then we get that

$$\begin{aligned}
k' &= e(g^s, g^{\alpha} g_2^r) / \prod_{i=1}^{m} e(g, g_2)^{s_i r} \\
&= e(g,g)^{\alpha s} \cdot e(g, g_2)^{sr} / e(g, g_2)^{r \cdot \sum_{i=1}^{m} s_i} \\
&= e(g,g)^{\alpha s}.
\end{aligned}$$

Regarding the extended correctness, it can be analyzed as previous constructions, so we omit the details here.

KEY-HOMOMORPHISM. In this scheme, the encapsulated key is the same as before, i.e., $f(msk, s) = e(g,g)^{msk \cdot s}$. The group operations are also defined similarly, e.g., "$\otimes$" over $\mathcal{SK} = \mathbb{G}^3$ is the coordinate-wise multiplication over $\mathbb{G}$ and $\odot$

over $\mathcal{K}$ is the multiplication over $\mathbb{G}_T$. It is easy to verify that for any identity $id \in \mathbb{Z}_p$, master secret keys $\alpha, \alpha' \in \mathbb{Z}_p$ and randomness $r, r', s \in \mathbb{Z}_p$ the following properties hold:

1. $\mathsf{KeyExt}(\alpha, id; r) \otimes \mathsf{KeyExt}(\alpha', id; r') = \mathsf{KeyExt}(\alpha + \alpha', id; r + r')$,
2. $f(\alpha, s) \odot f(\alpha', s) = f(\alpha + \alpha', s)$.

SECURITY. The IRKEM scheme presented above is IND-sRL-CPA secure under the q-MEBDH assumption. This holds straightforwardly, as this scheme is simply the key encapsulation version of the IBR scheme of [30].

By combining this scheme with our generic construction in Sect. 3, we obtain the first PKEM scheme that enjoys both compact master public key and "compact" punctured secret key. Here, the compactness of the latter means the key size depends only on the number of punctures, independent of the size of revoked set. Moreover, the number of revoked tags per ciphertext is unbounded in this scheme.

4.4 KH-IRKEM Under DLIN Assumption

Finally, we present another IRKEM scheme featuring compact ciphertexts, which is derived from the NIPE scheme of [13] (cf. Section A.2). In contrast to the construction shown in Sect. 4.1, it is proven adaptively secure under the *standard* DLIN assumption.

DLIN ASSUMPTION. Let $(\mathbb{G}_1, \mathbb{G}_2, \mathbb{G}_T)$ be cyclic groups of prime order p with a non-degenerate bilinear pairing $e : \mathbb{G}_1 \times \mathbb{G}_2 \rightarrow \mathbb{G}_T$. The Decisional Linear (DLIN) problem is to distinguish between the distributions $\left(g^{x_1}, g^{x_2}, g^{x_1 y_1}, g^{x_2 y_2}, h^{y_1+y_2}\right)$ and $\left(g^{x_1}, g^{x_2}, g^{x_1 y_1}, g^{x_2 y_2}, h^{z}\right)$, where $x_1, x_2, y_1, y_2, z \xleftarrow{\$} \mathbb{Z}_p, g \xleftarrow{\$} \mathbb{G}_1$ and $h \xleftarrow{\$} \mathbb{G}_2$.

DESCRIPTION. Similarly, this scheme is composed of five polynomial-time algorithms (Params, MKGen, KeyExt, Enc, Dec):

- $\mathsf{Params}(1^\lambda, n)$: It takes as input a security parameter λ and an integer $n \in \mathbb{N}$, and generates cyclic groups $(\mathbb{G}_1, \mathbb{G}_2, \mathbb{G}_T)$ of prime order $p > 2^\lambda$ endowed with a bilinear map e. Then it samples $g \in \mathbb{G}_1, h \in \mathbb{G}_2, a_i, b_i \in \mathbb{Z}_p$ for $i \in \{1, 2\}$, and sets
$$\mathbf{A} = \begin{pmatrix} a_1 & \\ & a_2 \\ 1 & 1 \end{pmatrix} \text{ and } \mathbf{B} = \begin{pmatrix} b_1 & \\ & b_2 \\ 1 & 1 \end{pmatrix}.$$
After that, it chooses $\mathbf{W}_1, \ldots, \mathbf{W}_n \xleftarrow{\$} \mathbb{Z}_p^{3\times 3}$ and outputs public parameters
$$pp = \left((\mathbb{G}_1, \mathbb{G}_2, \mathbb{G}_T, e), g, g^{\mathbf{A}}, \{g^{\mathbf{W}_i^\top \mathbf{A}}\}_{i\in[1,n]}, h, h^{\mathbf{B}}, \{h^{\mathbf{W}_i \mathbf{B}}\}_{i\in[1,n]}\right).$$
- $\mathsf{MKGen}(pp)$: Given the public parameters pp, it chooses $\boldsymbol{k} \xleftarrow{\$} \mathbb{Z}_p^3$, and outputs the master secret key and public key pair
$$(msk, mpk) = \left(\boldsymbol{k}, e(g, h)^{\mathbf{A}^\top \boldsymbol{k}}\right).$$

- KeyExt(msk, id): Given a master secret key $msk = \boldsymbol{k}$ and an identity $id \in \mathbb{Z}_p$, the algorithm defines a vector $\boldsymbol{x}_{id} = (x_1, \ldots, x_n) \in \mathbb{Z}_p^n$ such that $x_i = id^{i-1}$ for all $i \in [1, n]$, chooses $\boldsymbol{r} \xleftarrow{\$} \mathbb{Z}_p^2$ and outputs the private key $sk_{id} = (\boldsymbol{k}_1, \{\boldsymbol{k}_{2,i}\}_{i\in[1,n]}) \in (\mathbb{G}_2^3)^{n+1}$ as

$$\boldsymbol{k}_1 = h^{\mathbf{B}\boldsymbol{r}}, \ \boldsymbol{k}_{2,i} = h^{x_i \cdot \boldsymbol{k} + \mathbf{W}_i \mathbf{B}\boldsymbol{r}} \text{ for } \forall i \in [1, n].$$

- Enc(mpk, R): Given a master public key mpk and a revocation list $R = \{id_1, id_2, \ldots, id_m\}$ such that $m < n$, the algorithm produces the encapsulated key $k \in \mathbb{G}_T$ and ciphertext $ct = (\boldsymbol{c}_1, \boldsymbol{c}_2) \in (\mathbb{G}_1^3)^2$ as:
  1. Define a vector $\boldsymbol{y}_R = (y_1, \ldots, y_n)$, where $\{y_i\}_{i\in[1,m+1]}$ are the coefficients of the polynomial $f_R(z) = \prod_{id_j \in R}(z - id_j) = \sum_{i=1}^{m+1} y_i \cdot z^{i-1}$, and all other coordinates $\{y_i\}_{i\in[m+2,n]}$ are set to 0 if $m + 1 < n$.
  2. Select $\boldsymbol{s} \xleftarrow{\$} \mathbb{Z}_p^2$ and compute

$$k = e(g, h)^{\boldsymbol{s}^\top \mathbf{A}^\top \boldsymbol{k}}, \ \boldsymbol{c}_1 = g^{\mathbf{A}\boldsymbol{s}} \text{ and } \boldsymbol{c}_2 = g^{(\sum_{i=1}^n y_i \cdot \mathbf{W}_i^\top)\mathbf{A}\boldsymbol{s}}.$$

- Dec(sk_{id}, id, ct, R): Given a private key sk_{id} for id and a ciphertext $ct = (\boldsymbol{c}_1, \boldsymbol{c}_2)$ under revocation list R, the algorithm returns $\perp$ if $id \in R$. Otherwise, it recovers the encapsulated key k as follows:
  1. Define the vectors $\boldsymbol{x}_{id} = (x_1, \ldots, x_n)$ and $\boldsymbol{y}_R = (y_1, \ldots, y_n)$ as before.
  2. Compute $\boldsymbol{k}_2 = \prod_{i=1}^n \boldsymbol{k}_{2,i}^{y_i}$ and then output

$$k' = \left(e(\boldsymbol{c}_1, \boldsymbol{k}_2)/e(\boldsymbol{c}_2, \boldsymbol{k}_1)\right)^{\frac{1}{\langle \boldsymbol{x}_{id}, \boldsymbol{y}_R \rangle}}.$$

The regular correctness follows readily from the NIPE scheme of [13]. For completeness, we present the details below. As analyzed before, it holds that $\langle \boldsymbol{x}_{id}, \boldsymbol{y}_R \rangle \neq 0$ *iff* $id \notin R$. Further, we have that

$$\boldsymbol{k}_2 = \prod_{i=1}^n \left(h^{x_i \cdot \boldsymbol{k} + \mathbf{W}_i \mathbf{B}\boldsymbol{r}}\right)^{y_i} = h^{(\sum_{i=1}^n x_i y_i)\cdot \boldsymbol{k} + (\sum_{i=1}^n y_i \cdot \mathbf{W}_i)\mathbf{B}\boldsymbol{r}},$$

so when $id \notin R$ we get that

$$\begin{aligned} k' &= \left(\frac{e\left(g^{\mathbf{A}\boldsymbol{s}}, \ h^{(\sum_{i=1}^n x_i y_i)\cdot \boldsymbol{k} + (\sum_{i=1}^n y_i \cdot \mathbf{W}_i)\mathbf{B}\boldsymbol{r}}\right)}{e\left(g^{(\sum_{i=1}^n y_i \cdot \mathbf{W}_i^\top)\mathbf{A}\boldsymbol{s}}, \ h^{\mathbf{B}\boldsymbol{r}}\right)}\right)^{\frac{1}{\langle \boldsymbol{x}_{id}, \boldsymbol{y}_R \rangle}} \\ &= \left(\frac{e\left(g^{\mathbf{A}\boldsymbol{s}}, \ h^{(\sum_{i=1}^n x_i y_i)\cdot \boldsymbol{k}}\right) e\left(g^{\mathbf{A}\boldsymbol{s}}, \ h^{(\sum_{i=1}^n y_i \cdot \mathbf{W}_i)\mathbf{B}\boldsymbol{r}}\right)}{e\left(g^{(\sum_{i=1}^n y_i \cdot \mathbf{W}_i^\top)\mathbf{A}\boldsymbol{s}}, \ h^{\mathbf{B}\boldsymbol{r}}\right)}\right)^{\frac{1}{\langle \boldsymbol{x}_{id}, \boldsymbol{y}_R \rangle}} \\ &= e\left(g^{\mathbf{A}\boldsymbol{s}}, h^{\langle \boldsymbol{x}_{id}, \boldsymbol{y}_R \rangle \cdot \boldsymbol{k}}\right)^{\frac{1}{\langle \boldsymbol{x}_{id}, \boldsymbol{y}_R \rangle}} = e(g, h)^{\boldsymbol{s}^\top \mathbf{A}^\top \boldsymbol{k}}. \end{aligned}$$

As for the extended correctness, it can be verified as before. In particular, we let $(msk', mpk') = (\boldsymbol{k}', e(g, h)^{\mathbf{A}^\top \boldsymbol{k}'})$ be another master key pair, and $sk_{id'} = (\boldsymbol{k}_1', \{\boldsymbol{k}_{2,i}'\}_{i\in[1,n]}) \leftarrow$ KeyExt(msk', id') be a private key for id', such that

$$\boldsymbol{k}_1' = h^{\mathbf{B}\boldsymbol{r}'} \text{ and } \boldsymbol{k}_{2,i}' = h^{x_i' \cdot \boldsymbol{k}' + \mathbf{W}_i \mathbf{B}\boldsymbol{r}'} \text{ for } \forall i \in [1, n],$$

where $r' \xleftarrow{\$} \mathbb{Z}_p^2$ and $x_i' = id'^{i-1}$. Then it is not difficult to obtain that

$$\mathsf{Dec}(sk_{id'}, id', ct, R) = \left(e(\boldsymbol{c}_1, \boldsymbol{k}_2')/e(\boldsymbol{c}_2, \boldsymbol{k}_1')\right)^{\frac{1}{\langle \boldsymbol{x}_{id'}, \boldsymbol{y}_R \rangle}} = e(g,h)^{\boldsymbol{s}^\top \mathbf{A}^\top \boldsymbol{k}'}$$

conditioned on $id' \notin R$, where $\boldsymbol{x}_{id'} = (x_1', \ldots, x_n')$ and $\boldsymbol{k}_2' = \prod_{i=1}^{n} \boldsymbol{k}_{2,i}'^{\,y_i}$.

Key-Homomorphism. In this scheme, the encapsulated key is in the form of $f(msk, \boldsymbol{s}) = e(g,h)^{\boldsymbol{s}^\top \mathbf{A}^\top \boldsymbol{k}}$, where $\boldsymbol{s}$ is the random coins of the encryption algorithm. Similar to previous analysis, it is not difficult to observe that, for any $id \in \mathbb{Z}_p$, master secret keys $\boldsymbol{k}, \boldsymbol{k}' \in \mathbb{Z}_p^3$ and randomness $\boldsymbol{r}, \boldsymbol{r}', \boldsymbol{s} \in \mathbb{Z}_p^2$, the following key-homomorphic properties with respect to $\mathsf{KeyExt}(\cdot)$ and $f(\cdot)$ hold:

1. $\mathsf{KeyExt}(\boldsymbol{k}, id; \boldsymbol{r}) \otimes \mathsf{KeyExt}(\boldsymbol{k}', id; \boldsymbol{r}') = \mathsf{KeyExt}(\boldsymbol{k} + \boldsymbol{k}', id;\ \boldsymbol{r} + \boldsymbol{r}')$,
2. $f(\boldsymbol{k}, \boldsymbol{s}) \odot f(\boldsymbol{k}', \boldsymbol{s}) = f(\boldsymbol{k} + \boldsymbol{k}', \boldsymbol{s})$.

Security. This IRKEM scheme is IND-RL-CPA secure under the standard DLIN assumption. This can be argued by following the analysis of [13] and the Embedding Lemma (cf. Proposition 1 in [3]).

Then by plugging this scheme into our generic PKEM in Sect. 3, we obtain the first PKEM scheme with short ciphertext based on the standard assumption. Notice that, the other NIPE scheme (with short private key) in Section A.2 of [13] satisfies the desirable properties as well. Thus a new PKEM scheme with short secret key can be derived similarly, and we omit the details here.

5 Efficiency Comparison

In this part, we give a comprehensive comparison of our schemes with existing works [18,19,26], as shown in Tables 1 and 2 (cf. Sect. 1). In the comparison, we use terms "exp" (resp. "$\exp_T$") and "pair" to denote exponentiation in $\mathbb{G}$ (resp. $\mathbb{G}_T$) and bilinear pairing over $\mathbb{G}$, respectively. The column "unbounded punctures" (resp. ciphertext tags) in Table 1 refers to if unbounded punctures (resp. tags per ciphertext) is supported. For sake of simplicity, when comparing with the scheme of Green and Miers [26], we additionally add to their public key an element $e(g_1, g_2)$ used in their encryption, thus the pairing computation in encryption is replaced by an exponentiation in $\mathbb{G}_T$. In comparison with the basic (i.e., IBE-based) BFE scheme of [19] and the IBBE-based BFE scheme of [18], our schemes together with the scheme by Green and Miers support unbounded punctures and n tags per ciphertext for $n > 1$, rather than bounded punctures and unique tag in [18,19], but their scheme features fast puncture and decryption procedures. Moreover, our schemes do not suffer from non-negligible correctness errors and can be proven secure without random oracles. We note that, to compare with the generic IBBE-based BFE scheme in [18], we instantiate it with the efficient IBBE scheme featuring constant-size ciphertexts and private keys in [17]. In this work, our main concern is the PPE schemes with negligible correctness errors, so in the following the comparison is mainly conducted with Green and Miers's work [26].

Compared to the scheme of [26], our first scheme in Sect. 4.1 is based on a stronger assumption than [26]. It has a large size of punctured secret key (linear in the upper-bound n of tags per cipertext), but it features compact ciphertext of which the overhead consists of only 2 group elements in $\mathbb{G}$. Furthermore, it requires much fewer exponentiation evaluations for encryption, which is reduced from $O(\hat{n}n)$ to $O(\hat{n})$, and 33% less pairing computation for decryption. For the second scheme in Sect. 4.2, it also features compact[4] punctured secret key as [26]. Still, it is more efficient, especially for the case of encrypting messages under a large number of tags. Regarding the third scheme in Sect. 4.3, it enjoys the compact punctured secret key as well. In contrast, it also enjoys a short public key and allows unbounded tags per ciphertext. The disadvantage lies in that it relies on a stronger assumption q-MEBDH that appears less natural than q-DBDHE. Finally, the fourth scheme enjoys a comparable performance to the first one, but can achieve adaptive security under the standard DLIN assumption instead of a "q-type" one. More details of efficiency comparison are shown in Tables 1 and 2.

We remark that here we focus on PPE itself and conduct no comparison of the PKEM schemes with the PFSKEM scheme in [28]. PFSKEM is inspired by the PFSE scheme in [26], which essentially combines the ideas of PPE and FS-PKE [11] for further reducing the decryption cost and punctured key size of PPE that grow linearly with the number of punctures. Similarly, we can also obtain PFSE schemes with distinct features based on the proposed PKEM schemes.

In addition, we note that the decryption complexity of our PKEM schemes is linear to the occurrence number of puncture operations (see Table 2). As argued in [26], however, it can be substantially mitigated like in [25] where the decryption of ABE is securely outsourced to a third party. Moreover, as the decryption of our construction is highly parallelized, it can be further optimized.

6 Further Discussion

Following the essential idea, our generic construction of PKEM can be optimized by further refining the correctness property of KH-IRKEM. To be more precise, we can further improve the computation efficiency of both decryption and puncture procedure by removing the use of distinguished tag t_0.

In particular, the secret key SK in the optimized version is the same as the master secret key msk of the underlying IRKEM, i.e., $SK = msk$ such that $(mpk, msk) \leftarrow \mathsf{IR.MKGen}(pp)$. In the puncture procedure, the update on sk_0 (i.e., $sk_0' = sk_0 \otimes \mathsf{IR.KeyExt}(-msk_i, t_0)$) will be replaced by sequentially computing the remaining share of msk, i.e., $msk_0' = msk_0 - msk_i$, in which case the punctured secret key for tags $\{t_\ell\}_{\ell=1}^{i}$ is in the form of $SK_i = \big(msk_0', (sk_1, t_1), \ldots, (sk_i, t_i)\big)$ and msk_0 is the first component of SK_{i-1}. Note that in this case $SK_0 = msk$. For the decryption, the shared encapsulated key k_0 corresponding to tag t_0 is directly

[4] The compact here means the size of punctured secret key depends only on the number of punctures.

computed from the remaining share msk_0 of msk, instead of running the decryption algorithm of IRKEM (i.e., $k_0 \leftarrow \mathsf{IR.Dec}(sk_0, t_0, CT, T)$). To this goal, it is desired that a legally encapsulated key can be recovered correctly from msk_0 and CT along with the public parameters, as well. Therefore, the correctness property in Definition 7 needs to be further extended to include the following condition: there exists an efficiently computable key derivation function KDF, such that $\hat{k} = \mathsf{KDF}(pp, msk_1, ct_2)$. Fortunately, all our instantiations satisfy this additional property. In particular, the computation of $k_0 \leftarrow \mathsf{IR.Dec}(sk_0, t_0, CT, T)$ in the decryption will be replaced by $k_0 = \mathsf{KDF}(pp, msk_0, CT)$ and it is exactly $e(g, g^s)^{msk_0}$ in our instantiations, where g is part of pp, g^s is part of CT and s is the randomness of encryption.

As the optimized version do not change the asymptotic complexity of our PKEM schemes, we do not analyze its performance in the efficiency comparison.

7 Conclusion

We propose a generic method to construct public-key puncturable key encapsulation mechanism. Thus, we get the first modular way of designing the full-blown puncturable encryption with *negligible* correctness errors, by combining it with the standard decapsulation mechanism. To the end, we introduce a new concept of identity-based revocable encryption system, called key-homomorphic identity-based revocable key encapsulation mechanism with extended correctness. Furthermore, we present several instantiations of the new concept and obtains four concrete public-key puncturable encryption schemes with distinct features. Specifically, we get the first public-key puncturable encryption schemes with compact ciphertexts, and the first scheme allowing for both unbounded punctures and unbounded size of tag set in the ciphertext. We also get an efficient scheme based on the standard DBDH assumption that features both faster encryption and decryption when the size of tag set is large, compared to Green and Miers scheme based on the same assumption. Although we obtains some tradeoffs between distinct aspects in this work, it is still challenging to construct adaptively secure puncturable encryption scheme with e.g., both compact ciphertext and punctured keys in the standard model.

Acknowledgements. The authors would like to thank the anonymous reviewers for their comments and suggestions. Also, they are grateful to Dr. Jie Chen for the helpful discussion. This work is supported in part by the Natural Science Foundation of China (No. 61802255), the project on Security Protection Technology of Embedded Components and Control Units in Power System Terminal (2019GW–12), the Data61-Monash Collaborative Research Project, and the Australian Research Council (ARC) Discovery Project (No. DP180102199).

References

1. Attrapadung, N.: Unbounded dynamic predicate compositions in attribute-based encryption. In: Ishai, Y., Rijmen, V. (eds.) EUROCRYPT 2019, Part I. LNCS, vol. 11476, pp. 34–67. Springer, Cham (2019). https://doi.org/10.1007/978-3-030-17653-2_2
2. Attrapadung, N., Hanaoka, G., Ogawa, K., Ohtake, G., Watanabe, H., Yamada, S.: Attribute-based encryption for range attributes. In: Zikas, V., De Prisco, R. (eds.) SCN 2016. LNCS, vol. 9841, pp. 42–61. Springer, Cham (2016). https://doi.org/10.1007/978-3-319-44618-9_3
3. Attrapadung, N., Libert, B.: Functional encryption for inner product: achieving constant-size ciphertexts with adaptive security or support for negation. In: Nguyen, P.Q., Pointcheval, D. (eds.) PKC 2010. LNCS, vol. 6056, pp. 384–402. Springer, Heidelberg (2010). https://doi.org/10.1007/978-3-642-13013-7_23
4. Attrapadung, N., Libert, B., de Panafieu, E.: Expressive key-policy attribute-based encryption with constant-size ciphertexts. In: Catalano, D., Fazio, N., Gennaro, R., Nicolosi, A. (eds.) PKC 2011. LNCS, vol. 6571, pp. 90–108. Springer, Heidelberg (2011). https://doi.org/10.1007/978-3-642-19379-8_6
5. Bellare, M., Cash, D., Miller, R.: Cryptography secure against related-key attacks and tampering. In: Lee, D.H., Wang, X. (eds.) ASIACRYPT 2011. LNCS, vol. 7073, pp. 486–503. Springer, Heidelberg (2011). https://doi.org/10.1007/978-3-642-25385-0_26
6. Bellare, M., Paterson, K.G., Thomson, S.: RKA security beyond the linear barrier: IBE, encryption and signatures. In: Wang, X., Sako, K. (eds.) ASIACRYPT 2012. LNCS, vol. 7658, pp. 331–348. Springer, Heidelberg (2012). https://doi.org/10.1007/978-3-642-34961-4_21
7. Bethencourt, J., Sahai, A., Waters, B.: Ciphertext-policy attribute-based encryption. In: 2007 IEEE Symposium on Security and Privacy (S&P 2007), 20–23 May 2007, Oakland, California, USA, pp. 321–334 (2007)
8. Blazy, O., Kiltz, E., Pan, J.: (Hierarchical) identity-based encryption from affine message authentication. In: Garay, J.A., Gennaro, R. (eds.) CRYPTO 2014, Part I. LNCS, vol. 8616, pp. 408–425. Springer, Heidelberg (2014). https://doi.org/10.1007/978-3-662-44371-2_23
9. Boneh, D., Franklin, M.: Identity-based encryption from the Weil pairing. In: Kilian, J. (ed.) CRYPTO 2001. LNCS, vol. 2139, pp. 213–229. Springer, Heidelberg (2001). https://doi.org/10.1007/3-540-44647-8_13
10. Bost, R., Minaud, B., Ohrimenko, O.: Forward and backward private searchable encryption from constrained cryptographic primitives. In: Proceedings of the 2017 ACM SIGSAC Conference on Computer and Communications Security, CCS 2017, Dallas, TX, USA, 30 October–03 November 2017, pp. 1465–1482 (2017)
11. Canetti, R., Halevi, S., Katz, J.: A forward-secure public-key encryption scheme. In: Biham, E. (ed.) EUROCRYPT 2003. LNCS, vol. 2656, pp. 255–271. Springer, Heidelberg (2003). https://doi.org/10.1007/3-540-39200-9_16
12. Canetti, R., Raghuraman, S., Richelson, S., Vaikuntanathan, V.: Chosen-ciphertext secure fully homomorphic encryption. In: Fehr, S. (ed.) PKC 2017, Part II. LNCS, vol. 10175, pp. 213–240. Springer, Heidelberg (2017). https://doi.org/10.1007/978-3-662-54388-7_8
13. Chen, J., Gay, R., Wee, H.: Improved dual system ABE in prime-order groups via predicate encodings. In: Oswald, E., Fischlin, M. (eds.) EUROCRYPT 2015, Part II. LNCS, vol. 9057, pp. 595–624. Springer, Heidelberg (2015). https://doi.org/10.1007/978-3-662-46803-6_20

14. Chen, J., Gong, J., Kowalczyk, L., Wee, H.: Unbounded ABE via bilinear entropy expansion, revisited. IACR Cryptology ePrint Archive **2018**, 116 (2018)
15. Cohen, A., Holmgren, J., Nishimaki, R., Vaikuntanathan, V., Wichs, D.: Watermarking cryptographic capabilities. SIAM J. Comput. **47**(6), 2157–2202 (2018)
16. D'Arco, P., Stinson, D.R.: On unconditionally secure robust distributed key distribution centers. In: Zheng, Y. (ed.) ASIACRYPT 2002. LNCS, vol. 2501, pp. 346–363. Springer, Heidelberg (2002). https://doi.org/10.1007/3-540-36178-2_22
17. Delerablée, C.: Identity-based broadcast encryption with constant size ciphertexts and private keys. In: Kurosawa, K. (ed.) ASIACRYPT 2007. LNCS, vol. 4833, pp. 200–215. Springer, Heidelberg (2007). https://doi.org/10.1007/978-3-540-76900-2_12
18. Derler, D., Gellert, K., Jager, T., Slamanig, D., Striecks, C.: Bloom filter encryption and applications to efficient forward-secret 0-RTT key exchange. IACR Cryptology ePrint Archive **2018**, 199 (2018)
19. Derler, D., Jager, T., Slamanig, D., Striecks, C.: Bloom filter encryption and applications to efficient forward-secret 0-RTT key exchange. In: Nielsen, J.B., Rijmen, V. (eds.) EUROCRYPT 2018, Part III. LNCS, vol. 10822, pp. 425–455. Springer, Cham (2018). https://doi.org/10.1007/978-3-319-78372-7_14
20. Derler, D., Krenn, S., Lorünser, T., Ramacher, S., Slamanig, D., Striecks, C.: Revisiting proxy re-encryption: forward secrecy, improved security, and applications. In: Abdalla, M., Dahab, R. (eds.) PKC 2018, Part I. LNCS, vol. 10769, pp. 219–250. Springer, Cham (2018). https://doi.org/10.1007/978-3-319-76578-5_8
21. Desmedt, Y., Frankel, Y.: Threshold cryptosystems. In: Brassard, G. (ed.) CRYPTO 1989. LNCS, vol. 435, pp. 307–315. Springer, New York (1990). https://doi.org/10.1007/0-387-34805-0_28
22. Dodis, Y., Katz, J., Xu, S., Yung, M.: Key-insulated public key cryptosystems. In: Knudsen, L.R. (ed.) EUROCRYPT 2002. LNCS, vol. 2332, pp. 65–82. Springer, Heidelberg (2002). https://doi.org/10.1007/3-540-46035-7_5
23. Dodis, Y., Yampolskiy, A., Yung, M.: Threshold and proactive pseudo-random permutations. In: Halevi, S., Rabin, T. (eds.) TCC 2006. LNCS, vol. 3876, pp. 542–560. Springer, Heidelberg (2006). https://doi.org/10.1007/11681878_28
24. Gong, J., Waters, B., Wee, H.: ABE for DFA from k-Lin. In: Boldyreva, A., Micciancio, D. (eds.) CRYPTO 2019, Part II. LNCS, vol. 11693, pp. 732–764. Springer, Cham (2019). https://doi.org/10.1007/978-3-030-26951-7_25
25. Green, M., Hohenberger, S., Waters, B.: Outsourcing the decryption of ABE ciphertexts. In: Proceedings of the 20th USENIX Security Symposium, San Francisco, CA, USA, 8–12 August 2011 (2011)
26. Green, M.D., Miers, I.: Forward secure asynchronous messaging from puncturable encryption. In: 2015 IEEE Symposium on Security and Privacy, SP 2015, San Jose, CA, USA, 17–21 May 2015, pp. 305–320 (2015)
27. Günther, C.G.: An identity-based key-exchange protocol. In: Quisquater, J.-J., Vandewalle, J. (eds.) EUROCRYPT 1989. LNCS, vol. 434, pp. 29–37. Springer, Heidelberg (1990). https://doi.org/10.1007/3-540-46885-4_5
28. Günther, F., Hale, B., Jager, T., Lauer, S.: 0-RTT key exchange with full forward secrecy. In: Coron, J.-S., Nielsen, J.B. (eds.) EUROCRYPT 2017, Part III. LNCS, vol. 10212, pp. 519–548. Springer, Cham (2017). https://doi.org/10.1007/978-3-319-56617-7_18
29. Katsumata, S., Yamada, S.: Non-zero inner product encryption schemes from various assumptions: LWE, DDH and DCR. In: Lin, D., Sako, K. (eds.) PKC 2019. LNCS, vol. 11443, pp. 158–188. Springer, Cham (2019). https://doi.org/10.1007/978-3-030-17259-6_6

30. Lewko, A.B., Sahai, A., Waters, B.: Revocation systems with very small private keys. In: 31st IEEE Symposium on Security and Privacy, S&P 2010, Berleley/Oakland, California, USA, 16–19 May 2010, pp. 273–285 (2010)
31. MacKenzie, P., Reiter, M.K., Yang, K.: Alternatives to non-malleability: definitions, constructions, and applications. In: Naor, M. (ed.) TCC 2004. LNCS, vol. 2951, pp. 171–190. Springer, Heidelberg (2004). https://doi.org/10.1007/978-3-540-24638-1_10
32. Martin, K.M., Safavi-Naini, R., Wang, H., Wild, P.R.: Distributing the encryption and decryption of a block cipher. Des. Codes Cryptogr. **36**(3), 263–287 (2005)
33. Mitzenmacher, M.: Bloom filters. In: Encyclopedia of Database Systems, Second edn. (2018)
34. Okamoto, T., Takashima, K.: Fully secure unbounded inner-product and attribute-based encryption. In: Wang, X., Sako, K. (eds.) ASIACRYPT 2012. LNCS, vol. 7658, pp. 349–366. Springer, Heidelberg (2012). https://doi.org/10.1007/978-3-642-34961-4_22
35. Ostrovsky, R., Sahai, A., Waters, B.: Attribute-based encryption with non-monotonic access structures. In: Proceedings of the 2007 ACM Conference on Computer and Communications Security, CCS 2007, Alexandria, Virginia, USA, 28–31 October 2007, pp. 195–203 (2007)
36. Ostrovsky, R., Yung, M.: How to withstand mobile virus attacks (extended abstract). In: Proceedings of the Tenth Annual ACM Symposium on Principles of Distributed Computing, Montreal, Quebec, Canada, 19–21 August 1991, pp. 51–59 (1991)
37. Sun, S., et al.: Practical backward-secure searchable encryption from symmetric puncturable encryption. In: Proceedings of the 2018 ACM SIGSAC Conference on Computer and Communications Security, CCS 2018, Toronto, ON, Canada, 15–19 October 2018, pp. 763–780 (2018)
38. Yamada, S., Attrapadung, N., Hanaoka, G., Kunihiro, N.: A framework and compact constructions for non-monotonic attribute-based encryption. In: Krawczyk, H. (ed.) PKC 2014. LNCS, vol. 8383, pp. 275–292. Springer, Heidelberg (2014). https://doi.org/10.1007/978-3-642-54631-0_16

Secure Channels

Flexible Authenticated and Confidential Channel Establishment (fACCE): Analyzing the Noise Protocol Framework

Benjamin Dowling[1], Paul Rösler[2(✉)], and Jörg Schwenk[2]

[1] Applied Cryptography Group, Eidgenössische Technische Hochschule Zürich, Zürich, Switzerland
benjamin.dowling@inf.ethz.ch

[2] Horst-Görtz Institute for IT Security, Chair for Network and Data Security, Ruhr University Bochum, Bochum, Germany
{paul.roesler,joerg.schwenk}@rub.de

Abstract. The Noise protocol framework is a suite of channel establishment protocols, of which each individual protocol ensures various security properties of the transmitted messages, but keeps specification, implementation, and configuration relatively simple. Implementations of the Noise protocols are themselves, due to the employed primitives, very performant. Thus, despite its relative youth, Noise is already used by large-scale deployed applications such as WhatsApp and Slack. Though the Noise specification describes and claims the security properties of the protocol patterns very precisely, there has been no computational proof yet. We close this gap.

Noise uses only a limited number of cryptographic primitives which makes it an ideal candidate for reduction-based security proofs. Due to its patterns' characteristics as channel establishment protocols, and the usage of established keys within the handshake, the authenticated and confidential channel establishment (ACCE) model (Jager et al. CRYPTO 2012) seems to perfectly fit for an analysis of Noise. However, the ACCE model strictly divides protocols into two non-overlapping phases: the *pre-accept phase* (i.e., the channel establishment) and *post-accept phase* (i.e., the channel). In contrast, Noise allows the transmission of encrypted messages as soon as any key is established (for instance, before authentication between parties has taken place), and then incrementally increases the channel's security guarantees. By proposing a generalization of the original ACCE model, we capture security properties of such staged channel establishment protocols flexibly – comparably to the multi-stage key exchange model (Fischlin and Günther CCS 2014).

We give security proofs for eight of the 15 basic Noise patterns in the full version (EPRINT 2019/436) and exemplify them by the proof of the `XK` pattern in this article.

The full version of this article is available in the IACR eprint archive as article 2019/436, at https://eprint.iacr.org/2019/436.

A. Kiayias et al. (Eds.): PKC 2020, LNCS 12110, pp. 341–373, 2020.
https://doi.org/10.1007/978-3-030-45374-9_12

Keywords: Noise protocol framework · ACCE · Multi-stage · Channel establishment

1 Introduction

Noise is a protocol framework introduced by Perrin [32] for establishing confidential channels between two parties in various application scenarios that bases on a Diffie-Hellman group, a secure key derivation function (KDF), a secure hash function, and a secure authenticated encryption with associated data scheme (AEAD). Like TLS 1.2, Noise makes use of the derived keys during channel establishment, which makes an analysis with respect to *key indistinguishability* as in traditional key exchange models infeasible. Furthermore, to allow the transmission of messages as early as possible (to avoid latency costs), protocols like TLS 1.3 and Noise amalgamate handshake and channel (at cost of security guarantees for these early messages). In this work we analyze the security of patterns from the Noise framework and, since previous modeling approaches cannot be used under the aforementioned conditions, introduce the flexible ACCE model to prove fine-grained security guarantees of Noise.

The Noise Framework. The Noise protocol framework is a tool box for defining simple and lightweight protocols for homogeneous environments. In this context, homogeneous means that all parties in the environment agree upon the protocol (including mechanisms for long-term key distribution, protocol version, employed cryptographic primitives, ...). In contrast, TLS allows the establishment of a channel in highly federated environments, in which that information has not been agreed upon by the protocol participants. This induces highly complex implementations that contain version and cipher suite negotiation as well as legacy code. Noise can disregard these issues (which in TLS regularly lead to security vulnerabilities, e.g., [1,31]) but still offers multiple protocol patterns that allow a developer to choose a protocol fulfilling their application's security needs and considering the respective use case (long-term key distribution, latency, ...).

The Noise specification defines 15 core protocol patterns for different use-cases, which may consist of one, two, or three handshake messages (cf. Fig. 1) – containing ephemeral and/or long-term Diffie-Hellman shares and (if a key is already established) an AEAD ciphertext – and a channel. Each party can have a long-term DH key pair, and potentially contributes one ephemeral DH key share per protocol execution. The different patterns of Noise can hence be seen as different distributions of the corresponding two to four public DH shares to the handshake messages. The three-message patterns of Noise are novel in the sense that classical three/four-message patterns for AKE protocols typically use only one DH key exchange which is either static (TLS-DH) or ephemeral (signed DH, Station-to-Station protocol, TLS 1.3, TLS-DHE, IPsec IKE, SSH) combined with digital signatures (all of the above) or MACs (IPsec IKE Phase 2 with forward-secrecy). Noise avoids authentication with MACs or digital signatures, and provides entity authentication via long-term DH keys, key derivation, and AEAD ciphertexts.

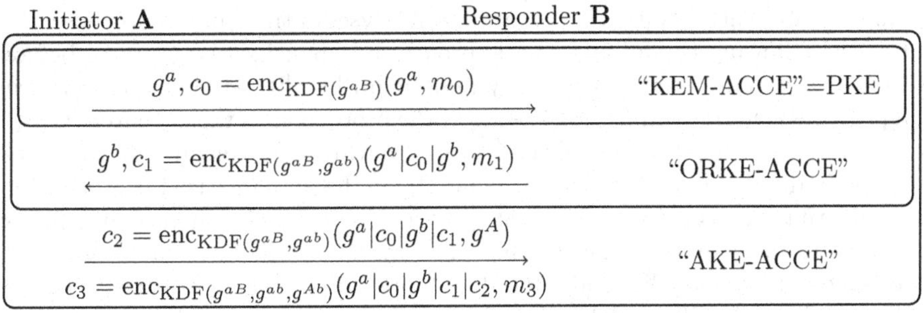

Fig. 1. The flexible structure of the Noise protocol framework, described conceptually with the `XK` pattern (three passes) that is based on the `NK` pattern (two passes), which is based on the `N` pattern (one pass). g^A and g^B denote the long-term public DH shares of parties **A** and **B**, g^a and g^b denote their ephemeral shares, and $\mathrm{enc}_k(ad, m)$ is an AEAD encryption.

As a result, Noise is for its scope even more agile than TLS, allowing tailored protocols for multiple use-cases with various security properties. Resulting from its efficiency and flexibility, Noise is used by largely deployed protocols such as WhatsApp [21,33] (for client to server communication), Wiregurard [12,13], Slack, Amazon AWS[1], and is potentially an ideal candidate for protecting the transport layer in IoT networks. Despite being distributed in applications used regularly by billions of users, there has not been a computational proof of Noise's security.[2]

Modularity in Cryptography and Real-World. Definitions and analyses in cryptography usually aim to be as modular as possible such that the results are flexibly composable. In contrast, many real-world protocols are specifically designed for one purpose such that modularity – especially regarding single components of these protocols – is not necessary and maybe even undesired (e.g., due to worse performance).

For the generic (secure) composition of a key exchange protocol with a symmetric primitive (such as a symmetric channel), the key exchange protocol needs to provide key indistinguishability for the established symmetric key (among other properties; cf., Brzuska et al. [7]). However, if this symmetric key was used by the key exchange itself, it is not indistinguishable from a random key space element anymore (as an adversary can simply check whether the challenged key was used). The same property needs to hold, and the same obstacle arises for multi-stage key exchange protocols: in order to allow for generic compositions of key exchange and symmetric protocols, the symmetric key must not be used by the key exchange protocol itself in order to maintain modular composition.

Since many real-world protocols (such as TLS 1.2, Quic, Signal, Noise, TLS 1.3 and others) disregard modularity (in the sense that key exchange and channel

[1] Both Slack and AWS use it in internal server-to-server communication.
[2] Except for the single pattern that is employed in the Wireguard protocol [13,28].

are inextricably intertwined), cryptographic analyses of these protocols chose one out of the following three bypassing approaches: 1. pausing the protocol before the key is internally used to prove key indistinguishability at that point (which still prevents generic composition results as the protocol uses the key afterwards), 2. analyzing a modified version of the protocol in which key exchange and channel are cleanly divided (which proves nothing about the actually used protocol), or 3. considering the security of the whole protocol instead of its single components by applying the ACCE model. In this work we follow the latter approach and – since no suitable ACCE model for staged protocols exist – propose a flexible and generalized ACCE model.

FLEXIBILITY AND GENERALIZATION FOR ACCE. Originally the Authenticated and Confidential Channel Establishment (ACCE) model was developed with the strict separation between key establishment and communication channel in mind. The security of ACCE, however, does not require this separation, because it only targets on the confidentiality of transmitted messages and the authentication among communicating parties.

Hence, our consideration of ACCE primitives differs from previous approaches that originated from notions of composition. We instead see fACCE as a primitive that is potentially built from authenticated key exchange (AKE) and secure channel protocols, but not necessarily *cleanly separated* into the "pre-accept" phase that establishes secrets and a "post-accept" phase that securely transmits payloadsse two phases. We directly model all communication (handshake and payload transmission) via algorithms Enc and Dec which not only capture the secure channel but also *handshake operations* for the channel establishment. As the bytes sent over the network do not need to be further specified, we simply call them *ciphertexts* even though payload is not necessarily encrypted. We similarly view a *single* dedicated session key as a legacy of instantiating ACCE protocols via the composition of AKE and channel protocols. Since there are ways to secure the transmission of payload data other than simply using a symmetric key – consider asymmetric channels that use public key cryptography – we entirely subsume session-specific information in the session state. Furthermore, we drop length-hiding property [22] since we consider it not inherent in channel protocols.

After eliminating the boundary between handshake and channel, it is important to note that a protocol that establishes a channel immediately (i.e., with the first protocol message) cannot fulfill the same security guarantees as protocols that take multiple round-trips before allowing the confidential transmission of payload. This intuition can be compared to different security levels that are achieved by key encapsulation mechanisms (KEM), one-round-key exchanges (ORKE), and authenticated key exchanges (AKE) as depicted in Fig. 1. For example, one message patterns (i.e., KEM-DEM constructions) are, among other deficiencies, subject to replay attacks if not equipped with expensive key update mechanisms such as in [19]. As a result, such attacks must be considered when designing an appropriate security model. Our model takes these different stages of security goals into account by adding flexibility to the ACCE notion.

As such we follow a similar approach as the multi-stage key exchange (MSKE) model. However, since our syntax allows for no distinction between stages (note that the MSKE model obtains new keys for each stage from the protocol), we assume the considered protocols to output a *stage number* ς with every encryption and decryption. With ς, the protocol indicates the 'security level' of the transmitted message (e.g., towards an upper layer application). In the case of an ACCE protocol in which all security properties are reached at once, this stage number is equivalent to distinguishing between the pre- and post-accept phase. In case of multi-stage protocols, a security classification can be useful information for an upper layer application that can then decide when to transmit confidential content. Since there exists no other generic indication to differentiate multiple stages based on our syntax[3], it is essentially necessary for defining security (independent of a specific protocol) that the protocol itself outputs the stage numbers. Using these output stage numbers, one can specify for each stage which properties need to be reached by the protocol in order to achieve *security*. As a result, while one security property may not be reached in an early stage (and thus the adversary could trivially attack communication in this stage), later stages may reach this security property.

Further differences from the MSKE model are that we use a generic partnering notion (instead of protocol-dependent session identifiers), define authentication flexibly (e.g., unilateral authentication does not necessarily mean server authentication), provide a metric to meaningfully compare security statements of differing yet similar protocols, and, due to the ACCE nature of our model, provide valuable security statements on channels that are built using 'internal' symmetric keys (for which composition results of the MSKE models can naturally provide no generic guarantees).[4]

CONTRIBUTIONS. Our contributions can be summarized as follows:

- We generalize and flexibilize ACCE by finding its core idea and removing remnants of historic constructions and thereby propose a model to analyze channel establishment protocols with multiple stages, fulfilling different security properties. Though this model is due to its flexibility rather complex, we consider the overall generalizations useful for future analyses.
- We prove flexible ACCE security for the majority of Noise framework's standard protocol patterns in the full version of this article [15], considering multiple fine-grained security properties of patterns. By focusing on the security of the established channels instead of the established session keys, this allows us to comprehend security claims of the Noise specification. Here we give an intuition for our overall proof approach and depict the proof of pattern `XK` in full details.

[3] One could imagine that the round-trips in the protocol may serve as stages. However, one can only define round-trips in a protocol execution if both session participants can be observed (which is not the case when considering active adversaries).

[4] The composition theorems by Fischlin and Günther [14,16,17] explicitly exclude internally used keys (such that internal keys in Quic or TLS 1.3 cannot be used for generic symmetric primitives).

1.1 Related Work

Computational security proofs for real world protocols have a long history (e.g., [11,13,14,16,27,30]). As described earlier, due to the usage of the channel key in the handshake of TLS 1.2, the ACCE model was introduced by (which was later also used in [3,6,8,9]) as a proof of key indistinguishability was impossible without considering a modified protocol variant. To further analyze the security of TLS 1.2 without client authentication, Krawczyk et al. [27] and Kohlar et al. [26] independently proposed a variant of the ACCE model.

The multi-stage key exchange (MSKE) model by Fischlin and Günther [16] extends the Bellare-Rogaway model [2] (further extended by [14,17]) similarly as we extend the original ACCE model (by allowing protocols to reach different security properties at different stages during the execution). Due to the issue of key-usage during the handshake in Noise (as in TLS 1.2 or Signal) and further model restrictions, the multi-stage key exchange cannot be applied here.

Giesen et al. [18] extended the ACCE model to consider multiple stages during a protocol execution to analyze TLS renegotiation. Besides its static security definition(s) and in addition to inheriting other unnecessary remnants of the ACCE model, all stages necessarily consist of separate handshake and channel phases (making it unapplicable for generic multi-stage protocols). Another step towards considering stages in ACCE was taken by Lychev et al. [29] and more recently by Chen et al. [10]. Their QACCE and msACCE models are, however, strongly tailored to the respectively analyzed protocols (QUIC and TLS 1.3). Blazy et al. [4] also proposed very recently a multistage ACCE model to analyze a ratcheting protocol. Similarly, their model strongly depends on the analyzed protocol, pursuing a contrary strategy to ours (i.e., a specialized instead of a generic model).

Previous to our work, Dowling and Paterson [13] examined the WireGuard key exchange protocol [12], itself based upon a single variant of Noise called pattern `IKpsk2`. They show that analyzing WireGuard in a key-indistinguishability-based security framework is impossible, as the protocol relies on an encrypted message using the established session keys to act as a key-confirmation message. They instead modify the WireGuard key exchange protocol to morally capture the key confirmation message,slightly and prove the modified construction secure. Recently Lipp et al. [28] confirmed the security of the WireGuard protocol by an automated analysis with CryptoVerif. Using this tool, they were able to produce a computational proof of security. Independently and concurrent to our work, Kobeissi et al. [24,25] published a framework for the formal verification (and automatic code generation) of Noise patterns. In particular, they formalize Noise patterns and use transition logic to create symbolic models of dynamically chosen Noise patterns to allow automatic verification using ProVerif. This is a strong indication for Noise's security but the approach and the results can barely be compared with computational, reduction-based proofs with respect to generic security models. As their verification of all base Noise patterns is conducted automatically with respect to the security statements from the Noise specification and we provide a reduction-based proof of security in a generalized, flexible computational model manually, we see these two approaches to be complementary. We note that symbolic analyses disregard the actual representation of algorithms' input and output values. Thus, in symbolic analyses, cryptographic primitives are highly idealized. Consequently, while reduction-based proofs provide relations to well studied hardness assumptions, symbolic analyses assume "unconditional" security of these primitives. Nevertheless, automatic proofs are less error-prone and better scalable which enables Kobeissi et al. [25] to apply their analysis of even more security properties (e.g., multiple variants of forward-secrecy) on far more Noise patterns than our manual approach allows.

2 Preliminaries

Here we formalize the notation and provide intuitions for security assumptions that we will utilize in our analysis of the Noise Protocol Framework. Standard assumptions and security notions such as *collision resistance* for hash functions, security of *pseudo-random functions*, and further variants of the *PRF-Oracle-Diffie-Hellman* assumption can be found in the full version [15].

2.1 Notation

The following notation will be used throughout the paper. For $q \in \mathbb{N}$ by $[q]$ we denote the set $\{1, \cdots, q\}$. For a function $F : \{0,1\}^a \to \{0,1\}^b$, a describes the input length and b describes the output length of the function. If a or b take the "value" $*$ we say that the function is defined for inputs or outputs of arbitrary length. Let S be a finite set and let $|S|$ be its size. We say a value x is chosen uniformly at random by $x \leftarrow_\$ S$. Let $\mathcal{A}$ be a probabilistic algorithm, we let $y \leftarrow_\$ \mathcal{A}(x_1, ...)$ denote running $\mathcal{A}$ on input $(x_1, ...)$ with uniformly chosen random coins, and assigning the output to y. If $\mathcal{A}$ is a deterministic algorithm, then $y \leftarrow \mathcal{A}(x_1, ...)$ denotes that y is computed by $\mathcal{A}$ using $(x_1, ...)$ as input. By $y \leftarrow_{[r]} \mathcal{A}(x_1, ...)$ we denote that a probabilistic algorithm $\mathcal{A}$ is invoked deterministically by *consuming* its random coins from r (i.e., each random coin from r is used at most once). ϵ is the empty string and $\perp$ is a special element indicating no input or no output.

2.2 The PRF-Oracle-Diffie-Hellman Assumption

Here we give the symmetric variant of the generic PRF-ODH assumption, introduced by Dowling and Paterson [13]. Our modification additionally allows to capture a "dual-PRF" like assumption necessary for the Noise Protocol Framework. The basic PRF-ODH assumption was introduced Jager et al. [22] and discussed in detail by Brendel et al. [5].

Definition 1 (Dual generic PRF-ODH Assumption). *Let G be a cyclic group of order q with generator g. Let* $\mathsf{PRF} : G \times \mathcal{M} \to \mathcal{K}$ *be a function from a* *pseudo-random function family that takes a group element $k \in G$ and a salt value $m \in \mathcal{M}$ as input, and outputs a value $y \in \mathcal{K}$. We define a second PRF family* $\mathsf{PRF}_d : \mathcal{M} \times G \to \mathcal{K}$, *by setting* $\mathsf{PRF}_d(m, e) = \mathsf{PRF}(e, m)$. *We define a security notion,* sym-lr-PRF-ODH *security, which is parameterised by:* $\mathsf{l}, \mathsf{r} \in \{\mathsf{n}, \mathsf{s}, \mathsf{m}\}$ *indicating how often the adversary is allowed to query "left" and "right" oracles (*ODHu *and* ODHv*), where* n *indicates that no query is allowed,* s *that a single query is allowed, and* m *that multiple queries are allowed to the respective oracle. Consider the following security game* $\mathcal{G}^{\mathsf{sym\text{-}lr\text{-}PRF\text{-}ODH}}_{\mathsf{PRF},G,p,\mathcal{A}}$ *between a challenger* $\mathcal{C}$ *and adversary* $\mathcal{A}$.

1. *The challenger* $\mathcal{C}$ *samples* $u, v \leftarrow_{\$} \mathbb{Z}_p$ *and provides* g, g^u, g^v *to the adversary* $\mathcal{A}$.
2. *If* $\mathsf{l} = \mathsf{m}$, $\mathcal{A}$ *can issue arbitrarily many queries to oracle* ODHu, *and if* $\mathsf{r} = \mathsf{m}$ and $\mathsf{sym} = \mathsf{Y}$ *to the oracle* ODHv. *These are implemented as follows:*
   - ODHu*: on a query of the form* (S, x), *the challenger first checks if* $S \notin G$ *and returns* $\bot$ *if this is the case. Otherwise, it computes* $y \leftarrow \mathsf{PRF}_\lambda(S^u, x)$ *and returns* y.
   - ODHv*: on a query of the form* (T, x), *the challenger first checks if* $T \notin G$ *and returns* $\bot$ *if this is the case. Otherwise, it computes* $y \leftarrow \mathsf{PRF}_\lambda(T^v, x)$ *and returns* y.
3. *Eventually,* $\mathcal{A}$ *issues a challenge query* x^*. *It is required that, for all queries* (S, x) *to* ODHu *made previously, if* $S = g^v$, *then* $x \neq x^*$. *Likewise, it is required that, for all queries* (T, x) *to* ODHv *made previously, if* $T = g^u$, *then* $x \neq x^*$. *This is to prevent trivial wins by* $\mathcal{A}$. $\mathcal{C}$ *samples a bit* $b \leftarrow_{\$} \{0, 1\}$ *uniformly at random, computes* $y_0 = \mathsf{PRF}_\lambda(g^{uv}, x^*)$, *and samples* $y_1 \leftarrow_{\$} \{0, 1\}^\lambda$ *uniformly at random. The challenger returns* y_b *to* $\mathcal{A}$.
4. *Next,* $\mathcal{A}$ *may issue (arbitrarily interleaved) queries to oracles* ODHu *and* ODHv*. These are handled as follows:*
   - ODHu*: on a query of the form* (S, x), *the challenger first checks if* $S \notin G$ *or if* $(S, x) = (g^v, x^*)$ *and returns* $\bot$ *if either holds. Otherwise, it returns* $y \leftarrow \mathsf{PRF}_\lambda(S^u, x)$.
   - ODHv*: on a query of the form* (T, x), *the challenger first checks if* $T \notin G$ *or if* $(T, x) = (g^u, x^*)$ *and returns* $\bot$ *if either holds. Otherwise, it returns* $y \leftarrow \mathsf{PRF}_\lambda(T^v, x)$.
5. *At some point,* $\mathcal{A}$ *outputs a guess bit* $b' \in \{0, 1\}$.

We say that the adversary wins $\mathcal{G}^{\mathsf{sym\text{-}lr\text{-}PRF\text{-}ODH}}_{\mathsf{PRF},G,p,\mathcal{A}}$ *if* $b' = b$ *and define the advantage function*

$$\mathsf{Adv}^{\mathsf{sym\text{-}lr\text{-}PRF\text{-}ODH}}_{\mathsf{PRF},G,p,\mathcal{A}} = |2 \cdot \Pr[b' = b] - 1|.$$

We define the advantage of $\mathcal{A}$ *in breaking the* dual *security of* PRF-ODH *as:*

$$\mathsf{Adv}^{\mathsf{d\text{-}PRF\text{-}ODH}}_{\mathsf{PRF},G,p,\mathcal{A}} = \max\left\{\mathsf{Adv}^{\mathsf{sym\text{-}lr\text{-}PRF\text{-}ODH}}_{\mathsf{PRF},G,p,\mathcal{A}}, \mathsf{Adv}^{\mathsf{sym\text{-}lr\text{-}PRF\text{-}ODH}}_{\mathsf{PRF}_d,G,p,\mathcal{A}}\right\}$$

Intuitively, the sym-lr-PRF-ODH assumption holds if the advantage $\mathsf{Adv}^{\mathsf{sym\text{-}lr\text{-}PRF\text{-}ODH}}_{\mathsf{PRF},G,p,\mathcal{A}}$ of any PPT adversary $\mathcal{A}$ is negligible. For conciseness in the advantage statements, we omit the d-PRF-ODH, and instead use sym-lr to specify which PRF-ODH assumption we use. Further used variants of the assumption are in the full version [15].

3 The Noise Protocol Framework

The Noise Protocol Framework (hereafter referred to as "Noise") is a specification that describes a framework with which two party channel establishment protocols can easily be instantiated for multiple purposes. The core of the framework is represented by the definition of 15 base protocol patterns. Each of these patterns employs only four underlying cryptographic primitives: a Diffie-Hellman group, a hash function, a key derivation function, and an AEAD cipher. Depending on how these cryptographic primitives are combined, the channel establishment protocols achieve different cryptographic properties. The main properties (in addition to confidentiality) are: 1. Authentication and integrity, 2. Key compromise impersonation (KCI) resistance, 3. Forward-secrecy, and 4. Resistance against replay attacks. Another interesting security property that is achieved by the protocols, but not explicitly claimed, is: 5. Resistance against reveals of executions' random coins.

The 15 patterns mainly differ in the setup in which they can be deployed. There are patterns that do not require the initial distribution of users' long-term public keys (and either insist on the authentication of users by transmitting these keys either in plaintext or encrypted, or alternatively disregard authentication altogether), and patterns that are based on the previous distribution of users' public keys. The out-of-band mechanism for public-key distribution is outside the scope of the specification, but one can imagine scenarios in which these keys are manually configured, can be acquired from a trusted third party, or are shipped with the respective application that uses Noise.

While historic protocols strictly separated key establishment and channel, recent specifications (such as TLS 1.3) also allow these phases to be interleaved. This allows the early transmission of payload data but results in reduced – and perhaps staged – levels of security for this data. The Noise specification provides a detailed description of security properties for the data transmission in each round-trip of the handshake and for the channel of each pattern [32].

While a key feature of Noise is the omission of a negotiation of a pattern or the negotiation of the exact employed cryptographic algorithms (in contrast to TLS, Noise is intended to be used in settings in which all participants are configured equally), recent discussions on the mailing list consider negotiation as a feature in the future[5] – which we will not regard in our analysis. Also outside the scope of our analysis, Noise allows further features such as symmetric pre-shared keys.

Implementation Assumptions. The Noise specification provides suggestions for some implementation details (but does not mandatorily require them). For our analysis, we assume that the protocol implementation follows these suggestions:

- No padding is employed (i.e., the length of the plaintext message is the same as the length of the encrypted message), and

[5] https://moderncrypto.org/mail-archive/noise/2018/001495.html.

- If an algorithm is called irregularly (an initiator receives before sending once, a party waits for ciphertext but encryption is invoked, decryption fails, ...), then the respective algorithm outputs an empty state and aborts.

Furthermore, we do not consider the associated data input on sending and receiving payload after the handshake. As our syntax intentionally makes no difference between handshake and channel, we cannot consider this additional feature of the Noise channel, as it is not provided during the handshake. Finally, we assume the protocols to output information on the current level of security (which we explain in more details below).

3.1 Noise Protocol Patterns

Here we explain the details of Noise, necessary to understand the core protocols and their properties.

A pattern is defined by the knowledge of each participant regarding the long-term public key (or static public key) of the respective partner (before the handshake and during the handshake). For unidirectional patterns, the single letter of the pattern name indicates whether the initiator's long-term public key is not defined (`N`), trans(X)mitted during the handshake (`X`), or known by the receiver in advance (`K`). It is clear that, for unidirectional patterns, the receiver's long-term public key needs to be known by the initiator in advance since otherwise no payload can be encrypted to the receiver. In the two-letter names of interactive patterns, the first letter indicates whether the initiator's long-term public key is not defined, X-mitted, or known by the responder, and the second letter indicates the same for the responder towards the initiator. So in the `XK` pattern, the initiator knows the responder's long-term public key in advance and the responder obtains the initiator's long-term public key during the handshake. At the top of Fig. 2 (in which we depict three example Noise patterns) it is denoted that the initiator knows the responder's long-term public key and the responder knows its long-term secret key for patterns `N` and `NK` a priori. For pattern `XK`, the initiator additionally knows its own key pair (of which the public key is sent to the responder during the protocol execution).

Finally, the Noise specification distinguishes whether the long-term public key is sent in plain or encrypted (for the former, the letter would be `I` instead of `X`). The specification defines all pairwise letter-combinations among the three variants `N`, `X`, `K`, the unidirectional patterns `N`, `X`, `K`, and the three variants in which the initiator sends its long-term (Identity) DH share in plaintext (i.e., `I_`).

At the left margin of Fig. 1, we depict how the Noise patterns' algorithms are invoked for party **A** (matching our generic syntax, formally defined in Sect. 5).

The handshake of a Noise pattern always starts with the initialization of the local state *st* (via Init()). This local state contains:

1. ρ: a boolean that indicates the session's role (initiator/responder),
2. `pattern`: the pattern name,
3. (X, g^X): the session owner's long-term DH exponent and DH share (optional),

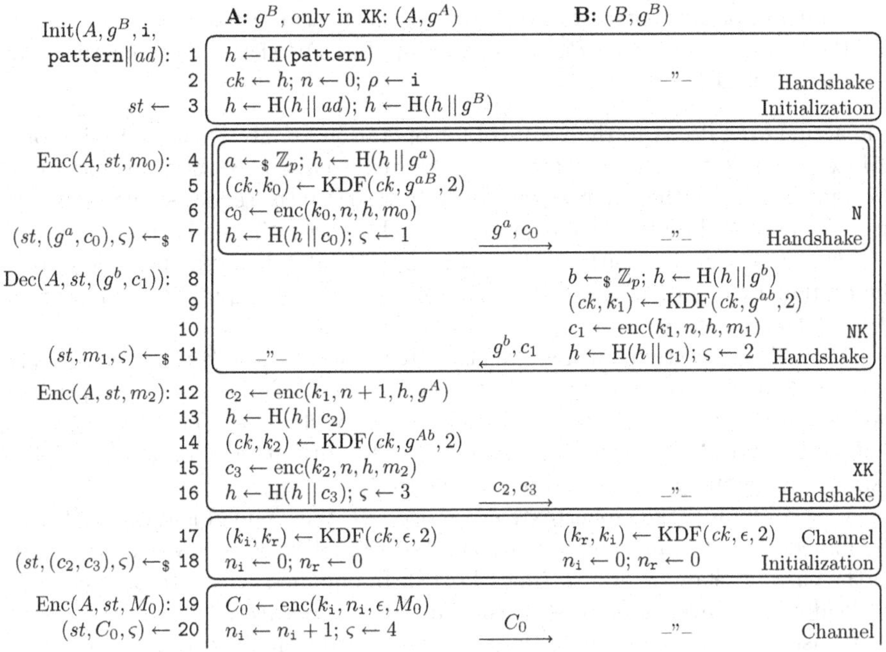

Fig. 2. Fully specified N,NK and XK patterns. m_i are payload messages sent *during* the handshake; M_i are payload messages sent *after* the handshake; ad is associated data with which the handshake is initiated; –”– denotes that the respective operations for receipt are processed (e.g., $\text{dec}(c, ..)$ for $c \leftarrow \text{enc}(..)$). Handshake initialization, channel initialization, and channel are part of all patterns. Algorithm invocations and return values in the left column depict the interaction of party **A** with the protocol (showing the protocol's syntax defined in Sect. 5). Blue marked parts are not specified by Noise but are required for our analysis (thus we assume them to be part of the protocol). (Color figure online)

4. g^Y: the intended partner's long-term public DH share (optional),
5. (x, g^x): the session's ephemeral DH exponent and DH share (optional),
6. g^y: the peer's ephemeral public DH share (optional),
7. ck: the chaining key,
8. h: the hash variable,
9. k or $k_\mathtt{i}, k_\mathtt{r}$: the encryption key(s), and
10. n or $n_\mathtt{i}, n_\mathtt{r}$: the nonce(s) for encryption.

These values are set, considering the pattern name, associated data ad, and a priori known long-term public DH shares of the partners (see Fig. 2 lines 1–4).

For each encryption (via Enc) during the handshake (i.e., before all desired security properties are reached), the following operations can be conducted:

(a) the generation of an ephemeral DH exponent and the transmission of the respective DH public share,

(b) the plain or encrypted transmission of a long-term DH share,
(c) the computation of a DH secret from a public DH share of the partner and their own DH exponent.

The actual operations in the protocol for operation (a) are 1. the sampling of a DH exponent, 2. the hashing of its public share into h, and 3. the transmission of this public share to the partner (lines 4,8). In case (b), the sender's long-term DH share is encrypted under the current key k and the resulting ciphertext is hashed into h and sent to the partner (lines 12–13).[6] If (c) a DH secret is computed, the current ck together with this DH secret are given as input to an invocation of the KDF (lines 5,9,14).

For each encryption during the handshake in which a key k was already computed, a ciphertext under this current key k is derived by encrypting a payload m or (if no payload exists yet) an empty string ϵ.[7] This ciphertext is sent to the partner and is also hashed into h. The current value of h is associated data for every encryption (lines 6–7,10–11,15–16).

After all handshake ciphertexts are processed, the channel is initialized with a symmetric key for each communication direction, derived by invoking the KDF on the current chaining key ck (lines 17–18). In one-message patterns such as `N`, payload can however only be sent from initiator to receiver.

Please note that we assume the protocol to additionally output information on the current payload transmission's level of security (represented by integer ς; lines 7,11,16,20). We proposed to add this feature to the Noise specification via the mailing list (as it could be useful to upper layer protocols). In Sect. 5, we describe why this feature is necessary for a security analysis in a generic model and in Sect. 6 we explain how this *stage counter* is naturally derived for the Noise patterns.

Flexibility in `N`, `NK`, `XK`. Figure 2 depicts the three Noise patterns `N`, `NK`, and `XK`. As it can be seen, the `XK` pattern adds one further handshake ciphertext to the `NK` pattern such that the initiator is authenticated, and the `NK` pattern adds one handshake ciphertext to the `N` pattern, such that the responder is authenticated and a bidirectional forward secure channel is established.

4 Replay Attacks, State Reveals, and Their Relation

In our model, presented in Sect. 5, we allow adversaries to reveal the secret local states of session participants. Since this slightly raises the complexity of the model – as it induces a more careful treatment of *trivial* attacks – we contextualize the meaning and explain the importance of this adversarial power (in order to justify the increased complexity), and we give an intuition for relations

[6] For patterns in which the long-term DH share is sent in plaintext, this DH share is directly hashed into h instead.

[7] Note that we use the algorithm Enc generically for sending information to the session partner. Confidentiality of payload is thereby not necessarily reached (see Sect. 5.1).

between state reveals and replay attacks on a high level (in order support comprehensibility of the model). This is aimed to give some initial motivation on how we define the model formally in the next section.

Replay Attacks in Noise. Replay attacks are an inevitable issue for early communication in many protocols – among them, many Noise patterns (e.g., patterns `N`, `NK`, and `XK`, cf., Fig. 2). When assuming long-term keys of parties to be constant (and not variable; cf., [19]), the first ciphertext in a session, sent from an initiator instance π_i^s of a party i to a responder instance $\pi_j^{t_1}$ of a party j, can be replayed to all other (responder) instances $\pi_j^{t_2}, \ldots, \pi_j^{t_n}$ of party j. As long as instances of party j are not synchronized, they will not detect this replay attack (since the ciphertext is valid for all of them). Hence, they will all accept and process this ciphertext and reply with individual (valid) ciphertexts.

We observe three conditions that allow for replay attacks and that are true for seven out of the 15 standard patterns in Noise (cf., rows in Table 1 with $\mathtt{rt} = 0$): (1) parties' long-term keys are static, (2) first ciphertexts in sessions from initiator to responder contain (confidential) payload already, and (3) there exists no (specified) synchronization mechanism among instances of a party. As a result, such ciphertexts in these patterns are inevitably potential subject to replay attacks.

Importance of State Reveal. In general – independent of replay attacks – local states of instances contain crucial session secrets. Since the primitive that we consider in this work depicts not only the initialization of a session but the session itself (in contrast to, e.g., authenticated key exchange), these considered local secrets are stored and used until a session is terminated. For settings with long session duration (e.g., IoT networks), it is reasonable to assume that adversaries gain access to some instances' local secrets during the session lifetime. As a result, a realistic model should capture this adversarial power by allowing state reveals in the security game.

If state reveals were not allowed, protocols that store valuable secrets unnecessarily in the local state (e.g., own or partners' long-term secrets) would be declared secure even though this is intuitively insecure.

State Secrets Under Replay Attacks. In the following we describe an attack against an intuitively insecure protocol that would formally be declared "secure" in a model without state reveal. Consequently, we argue that such models are unsuitable for assessing *security*.

1. An initiator instance π_i^s of party i sends the first ciphertext c_0 in a session directed to a responder instance of party j, containing an ephemeral public encryption key pk^*, and stores the respective secret key sk^* in its local state. This ciphertext is not protected against replay attacks (for the reasons given above).
2. This ciphertext c_0 is forwarded to multiple responder instances $\pi_j^{t_1}, \ldots, \pi_j^{t_n}$ of party j.

3. Each responder instance $\pi_j^{t_l}, l \in [n]$ encrypts its individual, independent, confidential reply payload under pk^* in a ciphertext $\tilde{c}^l$. We note that this payload is encrypted forward-securely as (sk^*, pk^*) are independent of i's and j's long-term keys. Each instance $\pi_j^{t_l}$ sends a replay-resistant response c_1^l back to instance π_i^s, such that c_1^l contains $\tilde{c}^l$.
4. Instance π_i^s will only receive and process one reply $c_1^{t^*}$ from an instance $\pi_j^{t^*}$ and will continue a long-lived session with it. Instance $\pi_j^{t^*}$ encrypts all further payload to π_i^s under pk^* such that sk^* remains in π_i^s's local state until the session terminates.
5. All remaining involved sessions of party j will eventually terminate due to a timeout.
6. If an attacker obtains the local state of π_i^s before its session with $\pi_j^{t^*}$ terminates, it will learn all confidential replies, encrypted in ciphertexts $\tilde{c}^1, \dots, \tilde{c}^n$ (in addition to the entire payload from $\pi_j^{t^*}$).

A model without state reveal declares all replies from instances $\pi_j^{t_1}, \dots, \pi_j^{t_n}$ "secure" even though their security crucially relies on the secrecy of π_i^s's local state. Especially since countermeasures are trivial and highly efficient[8], we consider this example protocol insecure. This intuition matches the initial idea of the (key) reveal query in the Bellare-Rogaway model [2]: "Compromise of a session key should have minimal consequences" such that it should not "leak information about other (as yet uncompromised) session keys". Since we abstractly consider all local secrets of an instance combined as a generic state *st*, this condition should hold accordingly for its reveal. For protocols with early communication (allowing for replay attacks), this condition can, however, only be met as soon as a session has exactly two participants (i.e., the session continues with exactly one responder).

Depiction in the Model. The essence of the above attack is not that messages are in danger due to replay attacks, but rather that secrets established during replay attacks may affect multiple instances. This effect must be reduced by secure protocols as far and as soon as possible. In our model, stage counters $\texttt{rp}^{\texttt{i}}, \texttt{rp}^{\texttt{r}}$ indicate how soon initiators and responders have local states that are independent of other instances' secrets (see Sect. 5.3). Thereby, we define reveals of their states harmless (for other instances) in case they are conducted after these stages are reached. Even though this independence may not be reached immediately (due to replay attacks in early communication), our model transparently indicates with these counters, how soon it is reached by protocols (see Table 1).

In our proof we explicitly emphasize the game hops in which it becomes clear that secrets are independent of others that are in revealable states of other instances.

[8] E.g., $\pi_j^{t_1}, \dots, \pi_j^{t_n}$ encrypt individual random symmetric keys $k^1, \dots, k^l$ under pk^* and encrypt their content under these symmetric keys respectively, then π_i^s can erase sk^* quickly such that its state is free of session-overlapping secrets.

5 Flexible ACCE Framework

The original ACCE model [22] and our generalization focus on the definition of *authentication* and *confidentiality* of messages, transmitted via a communication protocol (*channel establishment*). However in [22], traditional security goals like authentication and forward-secrecy are required to be reached before the actual channel is established.

Here we first provide a generic definition of the cryptographic primitive fACCE, then describe the standard execution environment in which its security is analyzed, further explain how we add flexibility to the adversary model with respect to the considered security properties, and define fACCE security.

5.1 fACCE Primitive Description

Below we define the *flexible ACCE* primitive. Intuitively, fACCE is a protocol that establishes a secure channel. Both the establishment of the channel and the transmission of payload through the channel are handled by the same algorithms. The special 'security level'-output ς of encryption and decryption signals which security properties are reached by the current algorithm invocation (e.g., to a higher level application).

Definition 2 (Flexible ACCE). *A flexible ACCE protocol* fACCE *is a tuple of algorithms* fACCE = (KGen, Init, Enc, Dec) *defined over a secret key space* $\mathcal{SK}$, *a public key space* $\mathcal{PK}$, *and a state space* $\mathcal{ST}$. *The syntax of an* fACCE *protocol is as follows:*

- KGen $\rightarrow_{\$}$ (sk, pk) *generates a long-term key pair where* $sk \in \mathcal{SK}, pk \in \mathcal{PK}$.
- $\text{Init}(sk, ppk, \rho, ad) \rightarrow_{\$} st$ *initializes a session to begin communication, where* sk *(optionally) is the caller's long-term secret key,* ppk *(optionally) is the long-term public key of the intended session partner,* $\rho \in \{\mathtt{i}, \mathtt{r}\}$ *is the session's role (i.e., initiator or responder),* ad *is data associated with this session, and* $sk \in \mathcal{SK} \cup \{\bot\}, ppk \in \mathcal{PK} \cup \{\bot\}, ad \in \{0,1\}^*, st \in \mathcal{ST}$.
- $\text{Enc}(sk, st, m) \rightarrow_{\$} (st', c, \varsigma)$ *continues the protocol execution in a session and takes message* m *to output new state* st', *ciphertext* c, *and stage* ς *that indicates the security for the transmission via* c *of the input message, where* $sk \in \mathcal{SK} \cup \{\bot\}, st, st' \in \mathcal{ST}, m, c \in \{0,1\}^*, \varsigma \in \mathbb{N}$.
- $\text{Dec}(sk, st, c) \rightarrow_{\$} (st', m, \varsigma)$ *processes the protocol execution in a session triggered by* c *and outputs new state* st', *message* m, *and stage* ς *that indicates the security for the output message during transmission via* c, *where* $sk \in \mathcal{SK} \cup \{\bot\}, st \in \mathcal{ST}, st' \in \mathcal{ST} \cup \{\bot\}, m, c \in \{0,1\}^*, \varsigma \in \mathbb{N}$. *If* $st' = \bot$ *is output, then this denotes a rejection of this ciphertext.*

We define as a convention that for output stage numbers $\varsigma = 0$, no security properties (in particular, no confidentiality) for the respectively transmitted payload has yet been reached.[9] Further we assume that the output stage numbers monotonically increase during a session (which is not a restriction).

[9] It is important to note that the first stage may not necessarily be 0, e.g. 0-RTT protocols that achieve confidentiality with the first message.

Please note that the syntax (and our security definition) leaves it to the specific protocol how far it enforces a ping-pong communication within a session. If the protocol only allows encryptions after decryptions, then we assume that the protocol enforces this by aborting on invalid algorithm invocations. If the protocol automatically responds on received ciphertexts, we assume that the environment (in our security experiment this is depicted by the adversary) handles this.

We define the correctness of an fACCE protocol below. Intuitively an fACCE protocol is correct if messages, decrypted from the established channel, were equally sent to this channel by the partner.

Definition 3 (Correctness of fACCE). *An fACCE protocol is correct if, for any two key pairs $(sk_{\mathtt{i}}, pk_{\mathtt{i}}), (sk_{\mathtt{r}}, pk_{\mathtt{r}})$ output from KGen or set to $(\bot, \bot)$ respectively, their session states $\mathrm{Init}(sk_{\mathtt{i}}, pk_{\mathtt{r}}, \mathtt{i}, ad) \rightarrow_{\$} st_{\mathtt{i}}, \mathrm{Init}(sk_{\mathtt{r}}, pk_{\mathtt{i}}, \mathtt{r}, ad) \rightarrow_{\$} st_{\mathtt{r}}$ with $ad \in \{0,1\}^*$, and message-stage-ciphertext transcripts $MSC_{\rho}, MSC_{\bar{\rho}} \leftarrow \epsilon$, it holds for all sequences of operations $((op^0, \rho^0, m^0), \ldots, (op^n, \rho^n, m^n))$ (for all $0 \le l \le n$ with $op^l \in \{e, d\}, \rho^l \in \{\mathtt{i}, \mathtt{r}\}, m^l \in \{0,1\}^*$) that are executed as follows:*

- *if $op^l = e$, invoke $\mathrm{Enc}(sk_{\rho^l}, st_{\rho^l}, m^l) \rightarrow_{\$} (st_{\rho^l}, c^l, \varsigma^l)$ and update $MSC_{\rho} \leftarrow MSC_{\rho} \| (m^l, \varsigma^l, c^l)$, or*
- *if $op^l = d$, invoke $\mathrm{Dec}(sk_{\rho^l}, st_{\rho^l}, c^l) \rightarrow_{\$} (st_{\rho^l}, m^l_*, \varsigma^l_*)$ on $(m^l_\circ, \varsigma^l_\circ, c^l) \| MSC_{\bar{\rho}} \leftarrow MSC_{\bar{\rho}}$ and update it accordingly,*

that if $m^l_* \neq \bot$, then encrypted and decrypted messages and stage outputs equal $m^l_* = m^l_\circ, \varsigma^l_* = \varsigma^l_\circ$, and that stage outputs increase monotonically ($\forall l^* < l$ with $op^l = op^{l^*} = e$ and $\rho^{l^*} = \rho^l$ it holds that $\varsigma^{l^*} \le \varsigma^l_\circ$).

5.2 Execution Environment

Here we describe the execution environment for our fACCE security experiment. In our model we allow the analysis of multiple security properties, and indeed allow these properties to be reached at different points during the protocol execution. As a consequence, one can specify for each stage which properties need to be reached by the protocol in order to achieve *security*. Since one security property may not be reached in an early stage (thus the adversary could trivially attack communication in this stage) and later stages may reach this security property, we need to separate the security experiment challenges that the adversary is to solve in each stage. We therefore define stage-specific challenge bits and freshness flags (opposed to one single challenge bit and a *static* freshness condition). The latter are dynamically checked and modified during the security game. We note that due to allowing secure and insecure stages within the same session, dependencies between messages may leak information to an attacker.

We consider a set of n_P parties each (potentially) maintaining a long-term key pair $\{(sk_1, pk_1), \ldots, (sk_{n_P}, pk_{n_P})\}$, $(sk_i, pk_i) \in \mathcal{SK} \times \mathcal{PK}$. In addition to the key pair, a variable $corr_i \in \{0,1\}$ is stored for every party $i \in [n_P]$ by the security experiment, that indicates whether sk_i was exposed to the adversary (via OCorrupt, see Sect. 5.4).

Each party can participate in up to n_S sessions. We denote both the set of variables that are specific for a session s of party i as well as the identifier of this session as π_i^s. In addition to the local variables specific to each protocol, we list the set of per-session variables that we require for our model below. In order to derive or modify a variable x of session π we write $\pi.x$ to specify this variable.

- $\rho \in \{\mathtt{i}, \mathtt{r}\}$: The role of the session in the protocol execution (i.e., initiator or responder).
- $pid \in [n_P]$: The session partner's identifier.
- ad: Data associated with this session (provided as parameter at session initialization to Init).
- $T_e[\cdot], T_d[\cdot] \in \{0,1\}^*$: Arrays of sent or received ciphertexts. After every invocation of Enc or Dec of a session π_i^s, the respective ciphertext is appended to $\pi_i^s.T_e$ or $\pi_i^s.T_d$ respectively.
- $st \in \mathcal{ST}$: All protocol-specific local variables[10].
- $rand \in \{0,1\}^*$: Any random coins used by π_i^s's protocol execution.
- $(b_1, b_2, b_3, ...)$: A vector of challenge bits the adversary is to guess (one bit for each stage).
- $(fr_1, fr_2, fr_3, ...)$: A vector of freshness flags indicating whether the security of a stage in the session is considered to have been trivially broken by adversarial behavior.

At the beginning of the game, for all sessions π_i^s the following initial values are set: $\pi_i^s.T_e$, $\pi_i^s.T_d$, $\leftarrow \epsilon$, $\pi_i^s.fr_{\varsigma^*} \leftarrow 1$ for all $\varsigma^* \in \mathbb{N}$, and $\pi_i^s.rand \leftarrow_{\$} \{0,1\}^*$, $\pi_i^s.b_{\varsigma^*} \leftarrow_{\$} \{0,1\}$ for all $\varsigma^* \in \mathbb{N}$ are sampled.

Furthermore a set of ciphertexts $Rpl \leftarrow \emptyset$ is maintained in the security game, that are declared to initiate a non-fresh (replayed) session.

Partnering. In order to define security in a flexible manner, we need to define partnering for sessions in the environment. Partnering is defined over the ciphertexts provided to/by the adversary via the oracles that let sessions encrypt and decrypt (OEnc, ODec). Intuitively, a session has an honest partner if everything that the honest partner received via ODec was sent by the session via OEnc (without modification) and vice versa, and at least one of the two parties received a ciphertext at least once[11]. This definition considers the asynchronous nature of the established channel, leading to a *matching conversation*-like partnering definition for fACCE.

Definition 4 (Honest Partner). *π_j^t is an honest partner of π_i^s if all initial variables match ($\pi_i^s.pid = j$, $\pi_j^t.pid = i$, $\pi_i^s.\rho \neq \pi_j^t.\rho$, $\pi_i^s.ad = \pi_j^t.ad$) and the received transcripts are a prefix of the partner's sent transcripts, respectively, where at least one them is not empty (i.e., for $a = |\pi_j^t.T_d|$, $b = |\pi_i^s.T_d|$ such that*

[10] See Subsect. 3.1 Noise's state definition.

[11] Note that this definition of *honest partnering* is symmetric (i.e., if a session π_i^s has an honest partner π_j^t, then this π_j^t has π_i^s as an honest partner as well).

$a > 0$ if $\pi_i^s.\rho = \mathtt{i}$ and $b > 0$ if $\pi_i^s.\rho = \mathtt{r}$ then $\forall\ 0 \leq \alpha < a : (\pi_i^s.T_e[\alpha] = \pi_j^t.T_d[\alpha])$ and $\forall\ 0 \leq \beta < b : (\pi_i^s.T_d[\beta] = \pi_j^t.T_e[\beta]))$. If π_i^s already received ciphertexts from π_j^t, then π_j^t is an honest partner of π_i^s only if there exists no other honest partner π^* of π_i^s (i.e., if $b > 0$ then there is no π^* such that π^* is an honest partner of π_i^s and $\pi^* \neq \pi_j^t$).

Please note that after encrypting without decrypting yet, the initiator may have multiple honest partners (if the resulting ciphertexts are forwarded to multiple sessions). Due to the last requirement in Definition 4, our partnering notion requires that, after decrypting once, a session must have no more than one honest partner. Thereby partnering necessarily becomes a 1-to-1 relation as soon as the initiator received once from the responder.

5.3 Flexible Security Notion

Our model enables us to analyze *levels* of authentication and confidentiality – even for different stages within one protocol execution – and thereby to distinguish precisely if and when the following goals are reached: (a) Authentication and Integrity, (b) Forward-secrecy, and (c) Resistance against replay attacks. The extended version of this work [15] additionally considers KCI resistance and resistance against randomness reveal.

Our security definition, therefore, is indexed by five integers, called counters, $(\mathtt{au}^{\mathtt{i}}, \mathtt{au}^{\mathtt{r}}, \mathtt{fs}, \mathtt{rp}^{\mathtt{i}}, \mathtt{rp}^{\mathtt{r}})$ that indicate from which stage the respective property is achieved. Since properties can be established asymmetrically (e.g., a responder authenticates itself to an unauthenticated initiator in the first stage), some counters are indexed by role $\rho \in \{\mathtt{i}, \mathtt{r}\}$ (for initiator and responder respectively). One can think of each counter as a reference 'rung' on the 'ladder' of stages from which on the specified security property is achieved by the respectively analyzed protocol. Thus, as soon as the protocol outputs a certain stage that equals a counter (the protocol says that it reached the indicated 'rung' on the 'ladder'), all messages that are transmitted thereafter (including the message just encrypted or decrypted) reach the corresponding security property.[12] Please note that some security properties, such as authentication, develop their effect in two steps (see the trivial and real attacks in the description of oracle ODec in Sect. 5.4). We describe these counters below:

1. $\mathtt{au}^{\rho}$ defines the stage required for ρ to be <u>au</u>thenticated. This means that it is hard to break the authenticity and integrity of ciphertexts *from* a party with role ρ (i.e., parties with role $\bar{\rho}$ reject ciphertexts if the origin is not an honest partner) if the stage number ς (output by Dec for the peer with $\bar{\rho}$) is greater or equal to $\mathtt{au}^{\rho}$. Note that, since our partnering notion considers FIFO channels, thereby also ciphertexts (and the order among them) are authenticated that were sent and received before $\mathtt{au}^{\rho}$ was reached.

[12] Thereby only protocols are considered that monotonically increase security properties during sessions.

2. $\mathtt{fs}$ defines the stage from which forward-secrecy (with respect to both session participants' long-term secrets) is reached. It is hard, for a stage $\varsigma \geq \mathtt{fs}$, to break the confidentiality of ciphertexts, even if both parties were corrupted.
3. $\mathtt{rp}^\rho$ defines the stage from which a fully revealed session state of ρ cannot be used to replay and reestablish the session. This means, for a session for which stage $\varsigma \geq \mathtt{rp}^\rho$ was reached, a revealed session state must not contain secrets that affect the communication's security of any non-partnered sessions (especially of other receivers). The second condition of our partnering notion (cf., Definition 4) divides partners after replay attacks occur (i.e., marks them unpartnered thereby). Hence, protocols must diverge session state(s) of previous partners in case of such replay attacks, if partnering is used to control (and forbid) session state reveals. Only replayed first ciphertext(s) from an initiator to a responder do not to divide partners according to our partnering notion. In case of such session initiating replays, other sessions' states must be diverged by the protocol as soon as their stage has $\varsigma \geq \mathtt{rp}^\rho$.

We remark that our partnering notion already defines session participants unpartnered for all but one type of replay attacks: if ciphertexts, sent by an initiator that has already received a ciphertext once, or sent by a responder, are replayed, the respective receiver is defined to have no honest partner. In a security game in which state reveals are defined to be harmless for unpartnered sessions (which is the case for our model), this induces that such replay attacks force the protocol to diverge respective receivers' session states from their previous partners' session states. As a consequence, only replays of ciphertexts, sent by an initiator to (multiple) responder(s) without any reply from the latter, must be considered harmful in our security experiment. These replay attacks cannot be prevented if the receiver's long-term secret is defined static (which we do in contrast to e.g., [19]) and the initiator has never received a ciphertext. Our definition of replay attack resistance consequently focuses on the security damage that is caused by such replay attacks: it considers how soon the secrets, established by a (replayed) ciphertext, are independent among the sender and the (other) receivers of this replayed ciphertext. Hence, a session's secrets are recovered from a replay attack if they cannot be used to obtain information on other sessions' secrets.

Besides the explained prevention of replay attacks due to our partnering notion, ciphertexts that are transmitted before a stage $\varsigma > 0$ is output are (as also explained above) authenticated as soon as authentication is reached in a later stage. Apart from this, no security guarantees are required for ciphertexts transmitted under $\varsigma = 0$.

If a property is never reached in the specified protocol, then the respective counter is set to ∞ (e.g., for protocol with unauthenticated initiators, $\mathsf{au}^\mathtt{i} = \infty$).

5.4 Adversarial Model

In order to model active attacks in our environment, the security experiment provides the OInit, OEnc, ODec oracles to an adversary $\mathcal{A}$, who can use them to control communication among sessions, together with the oracles OCorrupt, OReveal.

Since our security definition becomes simpler and more clear by considering trivial attacks during the execution of the security game (not only as a separate freshness condition evaluated after the adversary terminated), we describe the excluded trivial attacks and rewarded real attacks inline. The considered security properties are denoted as bullet point symbols below (in case they are not generically applicable).

The game maintains a win flag (to indicate whether the adversary broke authenticity or integrity of ciphertexts) and embeds challenge bits in the encryption (in order to model indistinguishability of ciphertexts). In order to win the security game, adversary $\mathcal{A}$ either has to trigger $\mathsf{win} \leftarrow 1$ or output the correct challenge bit $\pi_i^s.b_\varsigma$ of a specific session stage ς at the end of the game.

- $\mathsf{OInit}(i, s, j, \rho, ad)$ initializes a session π_i^s (if not yet initialized) of party i to be partnered with party j, invoking $\text{fACCE.Init}(sk_i, pk_j, \rho, ad) \rightarrow_{[\pi_i^s.rand]} \pi_i^s.st$ under $\pi_i^s.rand$. It also sets $\pi_i^s.\rho \leftarrow \rho$, $\pi_i^s.pid \leftarrow j$, and $\pi_i^s.ad \leftarrow ad$. This oracle provides no return value. Finally, the freshness flags are updated by invoking $\text{Fresh}_{\mathtt{fs}}()$ (see Fig. 3).
- $\mathsf{OEnc}(i, s, m_0, m_1)$ triggers the encryption of message m_b for $b = \pi_i^s.b_\varsigma$ by invoking $\text{Enc}(sk_i, \pi_i^s.st, m_b) \rightarrow_{[\pi_i^s.rand]} (st', c, \varsigma)$ for an initialized π_i^s if $|m_0| = |m_1|$ and for $\varsigma = 0$ (i.e., confidentiality is not yet achieved) it must hold that $m_0 = m_1$ as the challenge bit would otherwise be trivially leaked. It updates the session specific variables $\pi_i^s.st \leftarrow st'$, returns (c, ς) to the adversary, and appends c to $\pi_i^s.T_e$ if $c \neq \bot$.
- $\mathsf{ODec}(i, s, c)$ triggers invocation of $\text{Dec}(sk_i, \pi_i^s.st, c) \rightarrow_{[\pi_i^s.rand]} (st', m, \varsigma)$ for an initialized π_i^s and returns (m, ς) if π_i^s has no honest partner, or returns ς otherwise (since challenges from the encryption oracle would otherwise be trivially leaked). Finally c is appended to $\pi_i^s.T_d$ if decryption succeeds.

Excluding trivial attacks:

- $\mathtt{fs}$: Since decryption can change the honesty of partners, the freshness flags are updated regarding corruptions by invoking $\text{Fresh}_{\mathtt{fs}}()$ (see Fig. 3).
- $\mathtt{au}$: The consideration of trivial attacks regarding authentication are a combination of the stage at which the protocol reaches authentication and corruptions of the participants' long-term secrets. If the received ciphertext was not sent by a session of the intended partner (i.e., there exists no honest partner) and
  1. party i is corrupted (i.e., $corr_i = 1$), then all following stages are marked un-fresh ($\pi_i^s.fr_{\varsigma^*} \leftarrow 0$ for all $\varsigma \leq \varsigma^*$), since this is a KCI attack.[13]
  2. neither party i nor the session's intended partner are corrupted (i.e., $corr_i = corr_{\pi_i^s.pid} = 0$) and authentication of the partner was not reached yet (i.e., $\varsigma < \mathtt{au}^{\pi_i^s.\bar{\rho}}$), then all following stages are marked un-fresh until authentication will be reached ($\pi_i^s.fr_{\varsigma^*} \leftarrow 0$ for all $\varsigma \leq$

[13] Please note that resistance against KCI attacks is not required.

$\varsigma^* < \mathsf{au}^{\pi_i^s.\bar{\rho}}$), since this is a (temporary) trivial impersonation of the partner towards π_i^s.[14]

3. only the session's intended partner is corrupted (i.e., $corr_{\pi_i^s.pid} = 1 \neq corr_i$) and authentication of the partner was not reached yet or is reached with this received ciphertext (i.e., $\varsigma \leq \mathsf{au}^{\pi_i^s.\bar{\rho}}$), then all following stages are marked un-fresh ($\pi_i^s.fr_{\varsigma^*} \leftarrow 0$ for all $\varsigma \leq \varsigma^*$), since this is (and will continue to be) a trivial impersonation of the partner towards π_i^s.

Rewarding real attacks:

au: Similarly to detecting trivial attacks, real attacks are rewarded by considering when authentication is reached in the respective protocol execution and if the participants' long-term secrets are corrupted.
The adversary breaks authentication (and thereby $\mathsf{win} \leftarrow 1$ is set) if the received ciphertext was not sent by a session of the intended partner but was successfully decrypted (i.e., there exists no honest partner and the output state is $st' \neq \bot$), the stage is still fresh ($\pi_i^s.fr_\varsigma = 1$), and

1. this is the first authenticated ciphertext ($\varsigma = \mathsf{au}^{\pi_i^s.\bar{\rho}}$), and neither party i nor the intended partner are corrupted ($corr_i = corr_{\pi_i^s.pid} = 0$), or
2. this is a later authenticated ciphertext ($\varsigma > \mathsf{au}^{\pi_i^s.\bar{\rho}}$) and party i is not corrupted ($corr_i = 0$) as this would otherwise be a KCI attack.

- $\mathsf{OCorrupt}(i) \rightarrow sk_i$ outputs the long-term secret key sk_i of party i, sets $corr_i \leftarrow 1$, and updates the freshness flags by invoking $\mathrm{Fresh}_{\mathtt{fs}}()$.
- $\mathsf{OReveal}(i, s) \rightarrow \pi_i^s.st$ outputs the current session state $\pi_i^s.st$.

Excluding trivial attacks:

- Revealing the session-state trivially determines this session's challenge bits, since the state contains any used session keys[15]. Hence $\pi_i^s.fr_{\varsigma^*} \leftarrow 0$ is set for all stages ς^*.
- Similarly, sufficient information is leaked to determine challenge bits embedded in ciphertexts to and from *all* honest partners π_j^t (and to impersonate π_i^s towards them). As such, $\pi_j^t.fr_{\varsigma^*} \leftarrow 0$ is set for all stages ς^* of these honest partners.

rp: In case the revealed secrets enable the adversary to obtain secrets of non-partnered sessions due to a replay attack ($\varsigma < \mathtt{rp}^{\pi_i^s.\rho}$ where ς was output by π_i^s's last OEnc or ODec query) then the first ciphertext in this session is declared to induce non-fresh sessions via $Rpl \leftarrow Rpl \cup \{c\}$ where $c \leftarrow \pi_i^s.T_e[0]$

---

[14] If the partner authenticates later, then the protocol must ensure that this early trivial impersonation is detected. Consequently, this attack is not treated trivial anymore after the partner's authentication.

[15] Since we do not consider forward-secrecy within sessions, the secret session state is considered to harm security of the whole session lifetime independent of when the state is revealed.

if $\pi_i^s.\rho = \mathtt{i}$ or $c \leftarrow \pi_i^s.T_d[0]$ if $\pi_i^s.\rho = \mathtt{r}$ (such that all sessions starting with this ciphertext are also marked non-fresh)[16].

Freshness Regarding Corruptions and Replays. The definition of forward-secrecy, based on counter $\mathtt{fs}$, is straight forward: if either the own long-term secrets or the intended partner's long-term secrets were corrupted (i.e., $corr_i = 1 \vee corr_{\pi_i^s.pid} = 1$), then only stages that provide forward-secrecy are marked fresh for the respective session (i.e., $\pi_i^s.fr_{\varsigma^*} \leftarrow 0$ for all $\varsigma^* < \mathtt{fs}$). For sessions started with a ciphertext marked in set *Rpl* (i.e., initiating insecure communication due to the reveal of a replayable session), all stages are marked insecure. We formally define these properties via function $\text{Fresh}_{\mathtt{fs}}()$ (see Fig. 3).

$\text{Fresh}_{\mathtt{fs}}()$:
For all $i \in [n_P]$, for all $s \in [n_S]$:
  $\mathtt{ctr} \leftarrow \min(\varsigma^* : \pi_i^s.fr_{\varsigma^*} = 1)$
  If $corr_i = 1 \vee corr_{\pi_i^s.pid} = 1$:
    $\mathtt{ctr} \leftarrow \max(\mathtt{ctr}, \mathtt{fs})$
  If $\pi_i^s.T_e[0] \in Rpl \wedge \pi_i^s.\rho = \mathtt{i}$:
    $\mathtt{ctr} \leftarrow \infty$
  If $\pi_i^s.T_d[0] \in Rpl \wedge \pi_i^s.\rho = \mathtt{r}$:
    $\mathtt{ctr} \leftarrow \infty$
  $\pi_i^s.fr_{\varsigma^*} \leftarrow 0$ for all $\varsigma^* < \mathtt{ctr}$

Fig. 3. Function for updating freshness flags after each oracle invocation, considering long-term secrets' corruption (w.r.t. forward-secrecy) and full state reveals (w.r.t. replay attacks). The freshness flags up to (and excluding) the first secure stage are reset (e.g., for corrupted long-term keys, all stages in affected sessions are reset until forward-secrecy is reached).

5.5 Security Definition

The notion of fACCE security is captured as a game played by an adversary $\mathcal{A}$ in which the sessions are implemented as described above. At the beginning of the game, n_P long-term key pairs (pk_i, sk_i) $\forall i \in [n_P]$ are generated via fACCE. KGen and the respective public keys are provided to $\mathcal{A}$ as a parameter on the invocation (i.e., the start of the game). $\mathcal{A}$ interacts with the game via the queries described above and eventually terminates, potentially outputting a tuple (i, s, ς, b').

We can now turn to defining (in-)security of a fACCE protocol.

[16] One can easily define this trivial attack more specifically depending on whether this first ciphertext is authenticated and/or designated to a certain party. Depending on that, the secrets established by this ciphertext would only be valid among specific session (cf. [20]). For clarity and simplicity, we generically treat the ciphertext replayable solely.Please note that a state, revealed before the first ciphertext was sent/received (i.e., $c = \epsilon$), should not harm security of other sessions.

Definition 5 (Advantage in Breaking Flexible ACCE). *An adversary $\mathcal{A}$ breaks a flexible ACCE protocol* fACCE *with authentication stages* $(\mathtt{au^i}, \mathtt{au^r})$*, forward-secrecy stage* $\mathtt{fs}$*, and replayability resistance stages* $(\mathtt{rp^i}, \mathtt{rp^r})$*, when $\mathcal{A}$ terminates and outputs (i, s, ς, b'), if there either exists a session π_i^s such that $\pi_i^s.b_\varsigma = b'$, and $\pi_i^s.fr_\varsigma = 1$ (which we subsume as event* guess*), or* $\mathsf{win} = 1$*. We define the advantage of an adversary $\mathcal{A}$ breaking a flexible ACCE protocol* fACCE *as* $\mathsf{Adv}_{\mathcal{A}}^{\mathrm{fACCE}} = (2 \cdot \Pr[\mathsf{guess}] - 1) + \Pr[\mathsf{win} = 1]$.

Intuitively, a fACCE protocol is secure if it is correct and $\mathsf{Adv}_{\mathcal{A}}^{\mathrm{fACCE}}$ is negligible for all probabilistic algorithms $\mathcal{A}$ running in polynomial-time.

Necessity of Holistic Model. Our definition of flexible ACCE considers multiple security properties simultaneously (as opposed to having separate definitions for each regarded security property). In order to reduce complexity, it could seem useful to regard the security properties independently and then assemble the results. In the full version [15, Appendix B] we explain why this approach would produce more complexity, less comprehensibility, and is partially impossible.

6 Protocol Analyses

In this section, we provide an overview of our results of analyzing the Noise Protocol framework in our new fACCE model. Our main contribution is the full proofs of Noise Patterns `N`, `NN`, `NX`, `NK`, and `X`, `XN`, `XX`, `XK`. We focus on proving these two protocol "families" to demonstrate how our analysis can capture the wide variety of security properties that we show in Table 1, while also simplifying our approach by the re-use of our proof strategies. We give a detailed look of the proofs of Noise Pattern `XK` here and extend these proofs, considering further security properties in the full model, together with the proofs for the remaining mentioned patterns in the full version [15]. We present the analysis of Noise Pattern `XK` here as it comprehensibly provides an idea of the general proof structure and shows how Noise patterns can be built upon another. As the handshake of `XK` extends `NK`'s handshake, which in turn extends the handshake of `N` by a half round-trip respectively, each extension also results in further security properties (see Fig. 2 and Table 1).

Generic Proof Structure. The modular design of the Noise Protocol Framework allow us to write proofs that have a reasonably generic structure. While the proof for each specific Noise Pattern is distinct, each proof is, on a high level, split into two cases:

- The adversary has forged a ciphertext successfully , and sent it to a session that does *not* detect the forgery (or abort the protocol run). This case may be further split into multiple cases depending on which ciphertext in the Noise Pattern the adversary has managed to forge.
- The adversary has guessed the challenge bit correctly when it terminates the experiment.

We determine which $\mathsf{OCorrupt}$ queries cannot have been issued such that the attacked stage is still 'fresh' (as the adversary would otherwise be unsuccessful). Thus, each case has some queries that have not been issued to the session π_i^s and its partner session (where π_i^s either accepted the forged ciphertext, or the adversary output (i, s, ς, b')). In both cases we use a tailored $\mathsf{PRF\text{-}ODH}$ assumption, depending on which pair of queries (targeting long-term DH shares, state secrets, or, in the full model, ephemeral DH shares that depend on random coins) have *not* been issued, to replace the appropriate Diffie-Hellman public values and shared Diffie-Hellman secrets (using the ODH oracles to compute any additional secrets using the DH secret keys, if necessary). Afterwards, we iteratively replace intermediate secrets derived during the protocol execution using PRF assumptions on the underlying key derivation function. Finally, we use a single (or potentially series of) AEAD assumption(s) to replace the encryptions of ciphertexts sent to, and decryption of ciphertexts arriving at, the session π_i^s. Any adversary capable of distinguishing these changes is able to break one of the underlying assumptions used, and depending on which case we are in, either: 1. The adversary is unable to forge a ciphertext to the session π_i^s, or 2. The adversary is unable to guess the challenge bit b with non-negligible probability.

This (high-level) description effectively captures the strategy we use to prove our statements about the Noise Patterns that we analyze.

Mapping Noise's Security Statements to Our Model's Counters. Here we define the exact modeled security via the stage counters $(\mathtt{au}^{\mathtt{i}}, \mathtt{au}^{\mathtt{r}}, \mathtt{fs}, \mathtt{rp}^{\mathtt{i}}, \mathtt{rp}^{\mathtt{r}})$, $(\mathtt{kc}^{\mathtt{i}}, \mathtt{kc}^{\mathtt{r}}, \mathtt{eck}, \mathtt{rl}^{\mathtt{i}}, \mathtt{rl}^{\mathtt{r}})$[17], used in our theorems of each proof. We also explain how they relate to the round-trips in the protocol execution of the respective Noise pattern (we discuss generic mapping among stage counters and round-trips in the full version [15, Appendix C.3]). For each of the base patterns of the Noise specification, the stage at which the respective security property is reached is listed in Table 1. As stage numbers ς output by the Enc, Dec algorithms are defined as integers, we assume the Noise patterns to output a counter as stage number with every algorithm invocation, starting by 1 and always incremented by 1 until no further security properties are reached. In the case that the initiator's first ciphertext provides no confidentiality, the stage output is 0 (see column $rt = 0.5$ in Table 1) but the reply by the responder continues with $\varsigma = 2$.

The counters/round-trips for authentication and KCI resistance $(\mathtt{au}^{\rho}, \mathtt{kc}^{\rho})$ are directly lifted from the Noise specification [32]. As the definition of the remaining security properties deviate from the specification (or are not specified therein), the theorems' stage counters are defined as the first round-trips and stages that achieve the respective goals. Regarding forward-secrecy, the Noise specification differentiates among role dependent weak and strong variants of long-term secrets' corruptions. However, our consideration of forward-secrecy focuses on the relation between corruptions of long-term secrets and the reveal of sessions' random coins. Consequently, the counter $\mathtt{fs}$ is only partially derived from the Noise specification.

[17] The latter are only relevant for the proofs in the full model.

Resistance against replay attacks in the Noise specification only considers the adversary's ability to successfully let multiple sessions receive the same sent ciphertext. However, local state variables (like an ephemeral symmetric encryption key or a DH exponent), established by a ciphertext, can be exploited by an adversary to attack other sessions that sent or received the same (replayed) ciphertext. Such state variables may stay in the local state even after the replay attack "is over" (i.e., after only a unique honest partner exist). As the adversary is allowed to reveal the local state, our definition of replay attack resistance goes beyond others in the literature (e.g., [17]) and the Noise specification: it says that resistance against replay attacks is reached if the local state of a session is independent of any other session's state (except from the respective unique honest partner).

Table 1. Stages at which the respective security properties are reached. Stage x is reached (and thus returned by the protocol via output ς) at round-trip $\mathrm{RT}(x) = x/2$ (for $\mathrm{RT}(x) < rt$ no property is reached). The right half of columns depicts the counters for security properties that are only considered in the full model. $\mathtt{au}^{\rho}, \mathtt{kc}^{\rho}$ were extracted from Noise's specification [32]; $\mathtt{fs}, \mathtt{rp}^{\rho}$ are related to their definition in the specification (but adapted to our model). $\mathtt{rl}^{\rho}, \mathtt{eck}$ were defined purely with respect to the model. We give proofs for the patterns marked with a *.

	rt	$\mathtt{au}^{\mathtt{i}}$	$\mathtt{au}^{\mathtt{r}}$	fs	$\mathtt{rp}^{\mathtt{i}}$	$\mathtt{rp}^{\mathtt{r}}$	$\mathtt{kc}^{\mathtt{i}}$	$\mathtt{kc}^{\mathtt{r}}$	eck	$\mathtt{rl}^{\mathtt{i}}$	$\mathtt{rl}^{\mathtt{r}}$
N*	0	∞	∞	∞	∞	∞	∞	∞	∞	1	∞
X*	0	1	∞	∞	∞	∞	∞	∞	1	1	∞
K	0	1	∞	∞	∞	∞	∞	∞	1	1	∞
NN*	0.5	∞	∞	2	2	0	∞	∞	∞	∞	∞
NK*	0	∞	2	2	2	2	∞	2	∞	1	∞
NX*	0.5	∞	2	2	2	0	∞	2	∞	2	∞
XN*	0.5	3	∞	2	2	0	3	∞	∞	∞	3
XK*	0	3	2	2	2	2	3	2	∞	1	3
XX*	0.5	3	2	2	2	0	3	2	∞	2	3
KN	0.5	3	∞	2	2	0	3	∞	∞	∞	2
KK	0	1	2	2	2	2	3	2	1	1	2
KX	0.5	3	2	2	2	0	3	2	∞	2	2
IN	0.5	3	∞	2	2	0	3	∞	∞	∞	2
IK	0	1	2	2	2	2	3	2	1	1	2
IX	0.5	3	2	2	2	0	3	2	∞	2	2

6.1 Proof of Noise Pattern XK

Theorem 1. *Noise protocol* XK *(as in Fig. 2) is an fACCE-secure protocol with authentication levels* $\mathtt{au} = (3, 2)$*, forward-secrecy* $\mathtt{fs} = 2$*, and replay resistance* $\mathtt{rp} = (2, 2)$*. For an adversary* $\mathcal{A}$ *against the flexible ACCE security game* *(defined in Sect. 5) one can efficiently define adversaries* $\mathcal{B}_{\mathsf{coll}}$ *against the collision resistance of* H, $\mathcal{B}_{\mathsf{PRF\text{-}ODH}}$ *against the PRF-ODH assumptions* ms-PRF-ODH, sn-PRF-ODH *and* sym-ms-PRF-ODH *with respect to group* G *and* KDF, $\mathcal{B}_{\mathsf{aead}}$ *against the AEAD security of* AEAD, *and* $\mathcal{B}_{\mathsf{prf}}$ *against the PRF security of* KDF *with:*

$$\begin{aligned}\mathsf{Adv}^{\mathsf{fACCE}}_{\mathtt{XK},n_P,n_S,\mathcal{A}} \leq 3\cdot\mathsf{Adv}^{\mathsf{coll}}_{\mathrm{H},\mathcal{B}_{\mathsf{coll}}} + n_P^2 n_S\cdot\Big(\mathsf{Adv}^{\mathsf{prf}}_{\mathrm{KDF},\mathcal{B}_{\mathsf{prf}}} + \mathsf{Adv}^{\mathsf{ms\text{-}PRF\text{-}ODH}}_{\mathrm{KDF},G,p,\mathcal{B}_{\mathsf{PRF\text{-}ODH}}} \\ + \mathsf{Adv}^{\mathsf{aead}}_{\mathsf{AEAD},\mathcal{B}_{\mathsf{aead}}}\Big) + n_P^2 n_S^2\cdot\Big(\mathsf{Adv}^{\mathsf{aead}}_{\mathsf{AEAD},\mathcal{B}_{\mathsf{aead}}} + \mathsf{Adv}^{\mathsf{sym\text{-}ms\text{-}PRF\text{-}ODH}}_{\mathrm{KDF},G,p,\mathcal{B}_{\mathsf{PRF\text{-}ODH}}}\Big) \\ + n_P^2 n_S^2\cdot\Big(\max\Big\{\big(3\cdot\mathsf{Adv}^{\mathsf{prf}}_{\mathrm{KDF},\mathcal{B}_{\mathsf{prf}}} + \mathsf{Adv}^{\mathsf{ms\text{-}PRF\text{-}ODH}}_{\mathrm{KDF},G,p,\mathcal{B}_{\mathsf{PRF\text{-}ODH}}} + 4\cdot\mathsf{Adv}^{\mathsf{aead}}_{\mathsf{AEAD},\mathcal{B}_{\mathsf{aead}}}\big), \\ \big(2\cdot\mathsf{Adv}^{\mathsf{prf}}_{\mathrm{KDF},\mathcal{B}_{\mathsf{prf}}} + 3\cdot\mathsf{Adv}^{\mathsf{aead}}_{\mathsf{AEAD},\mathcal{B}_{\mathsf{aead}}} + \mathsf{Adv}^{\mathsf{sn\text{-}PRF\text{-}ODH}}_{\mathrm{KDF},G,p,\mathcal{B}_{\mathsf{PRF\text{-}ODH}}}\big)\Big\}\Big).\end{aligned}$$

Proof. We give below the proof of Noise Pattern XK. We split our analysis into three cases, depending on *how* the adversary can win the experiment. For the first two cases, the adversary causes $\mathsf{win} \leftarrow 1$ if the received ciphertext was not sent by a session of the intended partner, but was successfully decrypted in an authenticated stage by either an initiator (**Case A**) or a responder (**Case B**) session. For **Case A** $\mathcal{A}$ cannot have issued a $\mathsf{OCorrupt}(\pi_i^s.pid)$ query because breaking authentication of a corrupted peer is a trivial attack (as $\mathsf{au}^{\mathsf{r}} = 2$). Similarly, for **Case B** $\mathcal{A}$ cannot have issued a $\mathsf{OCorrupt}(\pi_i^s.pid)$ query as $\mathsf{au}^{\mathsf{i}} = 3$). Next we focus on an adversary attempting to guess the challenge bit b for any fresh session (**Case C**). **Case C** is further separated into two subcases, depending on the combination of allowable $\mathsf{OCorrupt}$ queries $\mathcal{A}$ issues, as defined in Sect. 5. We show that under such restrictions, $\mathcal{A}$ has a negligible advantage in guessing a challenge bit b for the session π_i^s. We begin with the standard fACCE experiment defined in Sect. 5, and treat **Case A**.

In **Case A Game 1**, we define an abort event that triggers if a hash collision occurs. We do so by defining an algorithm $\mathcal{B}_{\mathsf{coll}}$ that computes all hash values honestly, and aborts if there exist two evaluations $(in, \mathrm{H}(in)), (\hat{in}, \mathrm{H}(\hat{in}))$ such that $in \neq \hat{in}$, but $\mathrm{H}(in) = \mathrm{H}(\hat{in})$, outputting this pair to a hash collision challenger if found. In the next two games (**Game 2**, **Game 3**) we guess the index (i, s) of the session π_i^s, as well as the index j of the honest partner π_j^t and abort if either $\mathcal{A}$ terminates and outputs $(i^*, s^*, \varsigma, b')$ such that $(i^*, s^*) \neq (i, s)$, or if $\mathcal{A}$ initialises π_i^s such that $\pi_i^s.pid \neq j$. From now, the challenger playing the fACCE game "knows" at the beginning of the experiment the index of the session that $\mathcal{A}$ will target, and its intended partner j. In **Game 4**, we introduce an abort event $abort_{win}$ that triggers if the challenger sets $\mathsf{win} \leftarrow 1$ when the test session processes the ciphertext (g^b, c_1). The rest of the game hops in **Case A** now bound the advantage of $\mathcal{A}$ in causing $abort_{win}$ to occur.

Case A Game 5 requires careful consideration: Note that by **Game 2**, we know at the beginning of the experiment the index of session π_i^s such that (i, s, ς', b') is output by the adversary. Similarly, by **Game 3**, we know at the beginning of the experiment the index of the intended partner $\pi_i^s.pid$ of the session π_i^s. Thus, we define an algorithm $\mathcal{B}_{\mathsf{PRF\text{-}ODH}}$ that initializes a ms-PRF-ODH challenger, embeds the DH challenge keyshare g^u into the long-term public-key of party j, embeds the DH challenge keyshare g^v into the ephemeral public-key of session π_i^s, replaces the computation of $ck, k_0 \leftarrow \text{KDF}(ck, g^{aB}, 2)$ (in the session π_i^s and its partner) with uniformly random values $\widetilde{ck}, \widetilde{k_0}$, and gives $pk_j = g^u$ to the adversary with all other (honestly generated) public keys. However, $\mathcal{B}_{\mathsf{PRF\text{-}ODH}}$ must account for all sessions t such that party j must use the private key for computations. In the Noise Protocol XK, the long-term private keys are used in the following ways: In sessions where the party j acts as the initiator, they compute $ck, k_2 \leftarrow \text{KDF}(ck, g^{xu}, 2)$. Similarly, in sessions where the party acts as the responder, they compute $ck, k_0 \leftarrow \text{KDF}(ck, g^{xu}, 2)$. To simulate this computation, $\mathcal{B}_{\mathsf{PRF\text{-}ODH}}$ must instead use the ODHu oracle provided by the ms-PRF-ODH challenger, specifically querying $\mathsf{ODHu}(ck, X)$, (where X is the Diffie-Hellman public keyshare such that the private key is unknown to the challenger) which will output $\text{KDF}(ck, X^u)$. We note that $\mathbf{au}^{\mathtt{r}} = 2$, and only after processing (g^b, c_1) will π_i^s output $\varsigma = 2$, and so $\mathcal{A}$ cannot issue a $\mathsf{OCorrupt}(j)$ query before π_i^s processes ciphertext g^b, c_1. Thus we bound the probability of $\mathcal{A}$ distinguishing this change by the security of the ms-PRF-ODH assumption.

In **Case A Game 6** the challenger replaces the concretely computed values $ck, k_1 \leftarrow \text{KDF}(\widetilde{ck}, g^{ab}, 2)$ in π_i^s and its honest partner (if one exists), with uniformly random values $\widetilde{ck}, \widetilde{k_1}$. As by **Game 5**, the input $\widetilde{ck}$ is already uniformly random and independent of the protocol execution, distinguishing this game hop can be reduced to the prf security of the KDF. Note that due to this change, the state of π_i^s (containing only $\widetilde{ck}, \widetilde{k_1}$ as secrets) is independent of other sessions (making it useless to reveal their states; cf., counters $\mathtt{rp}^{\mathtt{i}} = \mathtt{rp}^{\mathtt{r}} = 2$).

Case A Game 7 proceeds identically to **Game 6**, except that the challenger flips a bit $\bar{b}$, and uses $\bar{b}$ instead of $\pi_i^s.b_1$ when responding to OEnc or ODec queries from $\mathcal{A}$ directed to sessions π_i^s or π_j^t when using the key $\widetilde{k_1}$. We do so by constructing an algorithm $\mathcal{B}_{\mathsf{aead}}$ that interacts with an aead challenger, and forwards such OEnc or ODec queries to the aead challenger. This change reduces to the aead security of the AEAD scheme, and since $\widetilde{k_1}$ is a uniformly random and independent value by **Game 6**, this replacement is sound. The additional-data field of c_1 contains $h = \text{H}(\text{H}(\text{H}(\text{H}(\text{H}(\text{H}(\mathtt{XK\_label}\|ad)\|g^B)\|g^a)\|c_0)\|g^b)$. By **Game 1** we abort the experiment if $\mathcal{A}$ causes a hash-collision to occur, and by **Game 4** we abort if no honest session owned by j has output g^b, c_1. An adversary capable of causing $\mathsf{win} \leftarrow 1$ when π_i^s processes the ciphertext g^b, c_1 can break the aead security of the underlying AEAD scheme, and thus $\mathcal{A}$ has no advantage in causing $abort_{win}$ to occur.

$$\mathsf{Adv}^{\mathsf{fACCE},\ \mathbf{Case\ A}}_{\mathtt{XK},n_P,n_S,\mathcal{A}} \leq \mathsf{Adv}^{\mathsf{coll}}_{\text{H},\mathcal{B}_{\mathsf{coll}}} + n_P^2 n_S \cdot \Big(\mathsf{Adv}^{\mathsf{ms\text{-}PRF\text{-}ODH}}_{\text{KDF},G,p,\mathcal{B}_{\mathsf{PRF\text{-}ODH}}} + \mathsf{Adv}^{\mathsf{prf}}_{\text{KDF},\mathcal{B}_{\mathsf{prf}}}$$
$$+\mathsf{Adv}^{\mathsf{aead}}_{\mathsf{AEAD},\mathcal{B}_{\mathsf{aead}}} + \mathsf{Adv}^{\mathsf{ms\text{-}PRF\text{-}ODH}}_{\text{KDF},G,p,\mathcal{B}_{\mathsf{PRF\text{-}ODH}}}\Big)$$

We can now treat **Case B**.

The first four games (**Game** $\mathbf{1, 2, 3, 4}$) proceed similarly to **Case A**. That is, we abort when a hash-collision is detected, and guess the index (i, s) of the first session π_i^s to set $\mathsf{win} \leftarrow 1$. However, in **Game 3**, we additionally guess the index (j, t) of the intended partner *session*, and abort if our guess is incorrect.

Game 4 still introduces an abort event that occurs if $\mathsf{win} \leftarrow 1$ is set in the test session, and the rest of the game hops bound the advantage of $\mathcal{A}$ in causing the abort event to occur.

Case B Game 5 again requires careful consideration: Note that by **Game 2**, we know at the beginning of the experiment the index of session π_i^s such that (i, s, ς', b') is output by the adversary and by **Game 3**, we know at the beginning of the experiment the index of the honest partner session (j, t) of the session π_i^s. We take a similar approach to **Game 5** of **Case A**. However, in this game we replace the computation of $ck, k_2 \leftarrow \text{KDF}(ck, g^{Ab}, 2)$ with uniformly random and independent values $(\widetilde{ck}, \widetilde{k_2})$ in the test session and its honest partner. Specifically, we define an algorithm $\mathcal{B}_{\mathsf{PRF\text{-}ODH}}$ that initialises a sym-ms-PRF-ODH challenger, embeds the DH challenge keyshares g^u into the long-term public-key of party i, embeds the DH challenge keyshare g^v into the ephemeral public-key of session π_j^t, replaces the computation of $ck, k_2 \leftarrow \text{KDF}(ck, g^{Ab}, 2)$ (in the session π_i^s and its partner) with uniformly random values $\widetilde{ck}, \widetilde{k_2}$, and gives $pk_i = g^u$ to the adversary with all other (honestly generated) public keys. However, $\mathcal{B}_{\mathsf{PRF\text{-}ODH}}$ must account for all sessions s such that party i must use the private key for computations. In the Noise Protocol XK, the long-term private keys are used in the following ways: In sessions where the party i acts as the initiator, they compute $ck, k_2 \leftarrow \text{KDF}(ck, g^{xu}, 2)$. Similarly, in sessions where the party acts as the responder, they compute $ck, k_0 \leftarrow \text{KDF}(ck, g^{xu}, 2)$. To simulate this computation, $\mathcal{B}_{\mathsf{PRF\text{-}ODH}}$ must instead use the ODHu oracle provided by the ms-PRF-ODH challenger, specifically querying $\mathsf{ODHu}(ck, X)$, (where X is the Diffie-Hellman public keyshare such that the private key is unknown to the challenger) which will output $\text{KDF}(ck, X^u)$. However, $\mathcal{B}_{\mathsf{PRF\text{-}ODH}}$ must account for the fact that the private key of g^v (the ephemeral public-key of π_i^s) is actually used before the computation of ck, k_2. In particular, it is used earlier in the protocol to compute $ck, k_0 := \text{KDF}(ck, g^{av})$, where g^a may have been contributed by $\mathcal{A}$. In this case, in order to compute ck, k_0, $\mathcal{B}_{\mathsf{PRF\text{-}ODH}}$ must instead use the ODHv oracle provided by the sym-ms-PRF-ODH challenger, specifically querying $\mathsf{ODHv}(ck, g^a)$, which will output $\text{KDF}(ck, g^{av})$. We note that $\mathsf{au}^{\mathsf{i}} = 3$, and only after processing (c_2, c_3) will π_i^s output $\varsigma = 3$, and so $\mathcal{A}$ cannot issue a $\mathsf{OCorrupt}(i)$ query before π_i^s processes ciphertext c_2, c_3. Thus we bound the probability of $\mathcal{A}$ distinguishing this change by the security of the sym-ms-PRF-ODH assumption. Note that other session states are (and were) independent of π_i^s's state as g^A is not stored in a state, a collision with g^b would break the above game hop, and $\widetilde{ck}, \widetilde{k_2}$ were randomly sampled (cf., counters $\mathtt{rp}^{\mathtt{i}}, \mathtt{rp}^{\mathtt{r}}$). **Case B Game 6** proceeds identically to **Game 5**, except that the challenger responds to OEnc or ODec queries directed to π_i^s or π_j^t outputting $\varsigma = 3$ from $\mathcal{A}$ (i.e. when using the key $\widetilde{k_2}$) and aborts if π_i^s decrypts c_2, c_3 successfully, but it was not output by an honest partner. This changes reduces to the AEAD security of the AEAD scheme. The additional-data field of c_3 contains $h = \text{H}(\text{H}(\text{H}(\text{H}(\text{H}(\text{H}(\text{H}(\text{H}(\mathtt{XK\_label} \| ad) \| g^B) \| g^a) \| c_0) \| g^b) \| c_1) \| c_2)$. By **Game 1** we abort the experiment if $\mathcal{A}$ causes a hash-collision to occur, and by **Game 4**

we abort if no honest session owned by j has output c_2, c_3. Now, $\mathcal{A}$ has no advantage in triggering the event $abort_{win}$ due to π_i^s processing c_2, c_3.

$$\mathsf{Adv}^{\mathsf{fACCE},\ \mathbf{Case\ B}}_{\mathrm{XK},n_P,n_S,\mathcal{A}} \leq \mathsf{Adv}^{\mathsf{coll}}_{\mathrm{H},\mathcal{B}_{\mathsf{coll}}} + n_P^2 n_S^2 \cdot \left(\mathsf{Adv}^{\mathsf{sym\text{-}ms\text{-}PRF\text{-}ODH}}_{\mathrm{KDF},G,p,\mathcal{B}_{\mathsf{PRF\text{-}ODH}}} + \mathsf{Adv}^{\mathsf{aead}}_{\mathsf{AEAD},\mathcal{B}_{\mathsf{aead}}}\right)$$

We can now treat **Case C**.

We follow now-standard procedure and define an abort event to trigger when we find a hash-collision, guess the index (i, s) of the session π_i^s, and the index (j, t) of the honest partner π_j^t. By **Case A** and **Case B**, there *must* exist such an honest partner for the beginning of stage $\varsigma = 3$. In what follows, we assume without loss of generality that π_i^s is the initiator session. The analysis where π_i^s is the responder session follows identically, except for a change in notation.

At this point, we need to split the analysis into two sub-cases:

1. **Case C.1**: $\mathcal{A}$ has not issued a $\mathsf{OCorrupt}(j)$ query during the experiment. This allows us to prove the security of all stages ciphertexts.
2. **Case C.2**: $\mathcal{A}$ has issued a $\mathsf{OCorrupt}(j)$ query *after* π_i^s decrypts g^b, c_1 successfully (outputting $\varsigma = 2$). Note that if $\mathcal{A}$ issues a $\mathsf{OCorrupt}(j)$, then $\pi_i^s.fr_1 \leftarrow 0$, and thus $\mathcal{A}$ has no advantage in outputting $(i, s, 1, b')$. This allows us to prove the security of ciphertexts belonging to stages $\varsigma \geq 2$. Note that if $\mathcal{A}$ did not ever issue a $\mathsf{OCorrupt}(j)$ query, then the security analysis reverts to **Case C.1** since $\pi_i^s.fr_1 = 1$, and we need to capture the security of the additional stages' ciphertext.

In **Case C.1 Game 4**, we replace ck, k_0 by uniformly random $\widetilde{ck}, \widetilde{k_0}$ in π_i^s and its honest partner which is reduced to the ms-PRF-ODH assumption (the challenger here acts as in **Case A, Game 5**). Here the session state is again independent of other non-partnered sessions' states. In **Game 5** and **Game 6**, we replace the values $ck, k_1 \leftarrow \mathrm{KDF}(\widetilde{ck}, g^{ab}, 2)$ with uniformly random values $\widetilde{ck}, \widetilde{k_1}$, and subsequently replace $ck, k_2 \leftarrow \mathrm{KDF}(\widetilde{ck}, g^{Ab}, 2)$ with uniformly random values $\widetilde{ck}, \widetilde{k_2}$ via the prf assumption on KDF. Similarly, in **Game 7** we replace $k_{\mathtt{i}}, k_{\mathtt{r}} \leftarrow \mathrm{KDF}(\widetilde{ck}, \epsilon, 2)$ with uniformly random values $\widetilde{k_{\mathtt{i}}}, \widetilde{k_{\mathtt{r}}}$.

In **Case C.1 Game 8** the challenger flips a bit $\bar{b}$ and uses $\bar{b}$ instead of $\pi_i^s.b_1$ when responding to $\mathsf{OEnc}(i, s, m_0, m_1)$ queries from $\mathcal{A}$ when Enc and Dec would output $\varsigma = 1$ (i.e. when using the key $\widetilde{k_0}$ replaced in **Game 4**). Specifically, the challenger constructs an algorithm $\mathcal{B}_{\mathsf{aead}}$ that interacts with an AEAD challenger in the following way: $\mathcal{B}_{\mathsf{aead}}$ acts exactly as in **Game 7** except responding to $\mathsf{OEnc}(i, s, m_0, m_1)$ or $\mathsf{ODec}(j, t, c)$ queries directed to π_i^s (or π_j^t respectively) when π_i^s or π_j^t would output $\varsigma = 1$ and instead forwards the queries to the AEAD challenger's oracles. Since $\widetilde{k_0}$ is a uniformly random and independent value (by **Game 4**), this change is sound.

Case C.1 Game 9 and **Game 10** proceed identically to **Game 8** but flip and use independent challenge bits when answering queries to OEnc if key $\widetilde{k_1}$ is used in stage $\varsigma = 2$ (**Game 9**) and when key $\widetilde{k_2}$ is used in stage $\varsigma = 3$ (**Game 10**). These changes in $\mathcal{A}$'s advantage are bound by the advantage in breaking the underlying aead assumption. Finally, in **Game 11** keys $\widetilde{k_\mathtt{i}}, \widetilde{k_\mathtt{r}}$ (replaced in **Game 7**) are used in stage $\varsigma = 4$. These changes in $\mathcal{A}$'s advantage are bound by the advantage in breaking the underlying aead assumption. In **Case C.1**, **Game 11**, the behaviour of π_i^s is independent on the test bits $\pi_i^s.b_\varsigma$ (where $\varsigma \geq 1$) and thus $\mathcal{A}$ has no advantage in guessing these challenge bits nor in causing π_i^s to set win $\leftarrow 1$.

We now treat **Case C.2**, where $\mathcal{A}$ potentially has issued a OCorrupt(j) query. Since $\mathtt{fs} = 2$, by Table 1 any adversary that issues a OCorrupt(j) sets $\pi_i^s.fr_1 \leftarrow 0$ and outputting $(i, s, 1, b')$ will lose $\mathcal{A}$ the game. Thus in **Case C.2** we do not prove the security of the first ciphertext's payload data.

Case C.2 Game 4 requires additional care: Note that by **Game 2**, we know at the beginning of the experiment the index of session π_i^s such that (i, s, ς', b') is output by the adversary and by **Game 3**, we know at the beginning of the experiment the index of the honest partner session (j, t) of the session π_i^s. We take a similar approach to **Game 5** of **Case A**. However, in this game we replace the computation of $ck, k_1 \leftarrow \text{KDF}(ck, g^{ab}, 2)$ with uniformly random and independent values $(\widetilde{ck}, \widetilde{k_1})$ in the test session and its honest partner. Specifically, we define an algorithm $\mathcal{B}_{\mathsf{PRF\text{-}ODH}}$ that initialises a sn-PRF-ODH challenger, embeds the DH challenge keyshares g^u into the ephemeral public-key of party i (g^a), embeds the DH challenge keyshare g^v into the ephemeral public-key of session π_j^t (g^b), and replaces the computation of $ck, k_1 \leftarrow \text{KDF}(ck, g^{ab}, 2)$ (in the session π_i^s and its partner) with uniformly random values $\widetilde{ck}, \widetilde{k_1}$. Note that $\mathcal{B}_{\mathsf{PRF\text{-}ODH}}$ can use its internal knowledge of the long-term private keys of party i and party j to compute $(ck, k_0) \leftarrow \text{KDF}(ck, g^{uB}, 2)$ and $(ck, k_2) \leftarrow \text{KDF}(ck, g^{Av}, 2)$. However, $\mathcal{B}_{\mathsf{PRF\text{-}ODH}}$ must account for $\mathcal{A}$ to issue OCorrupt(j) *after* π_j^t has computed the ciphertext (g^b, c_1) and instead delivering $(g^{b'}, c_1')$ to π_i^s. To simulate this computation, $\mathcal{B}_{\mathsf{PRF\text{-}ODH}}$ must instead use the ODHu oracle provided by the sn-PRF-ODH challenger, specifically querying ODHu(ck, X), (where X is the Diffie-Hellman public keyshare such that the private key is unknown to the challenger) which will output $\text{KDF}(ck, X^u)$. Thus we bound the probability of $\mathcal{A}$ distinguishing this change by the security of the sn-PRF-ODH assumption. Due to this game hop π_i^s's session state is independent of other non-partnered sessions' states.

In **Case C.2 Game 5** and **Game 6**, we replace $ck, k_2 \leftarrow \text{KDF}(\widetilde{ck}, g^{Ab}, 2)$ with uniformly random values $\widetilde{ck}, \widetilde{k_2}$, and subsequently replace $k_\mathtt{i}, k_\mathtt{r} \leftarrow \text{KDF}(\widetilde{ck}, \epsilon, 2)$ with uniformly random values $\widetilde{k_\mathtt{i}}, \widetilde{k_\mathtt{r}}$. **Case C.2**, **Game 7** proceeds similarly to **Case C.1**, **Game 9** by encrypting $m_{\bar{b}}$ for a randomly flipped bit $\bar{b}$ when Enc and Dec would output $\varsigma = 2$ (i.e. when using the key $\widetilde{k_1}$). **Case C.1**, **Game 8** proceeds similarly to **Case C.1**, **Game 10** by encrypting $m_{\bar{b}}$ for a randomly flipped bit $\bar{b}$ when Enc and Dec would output $\varsigma = 3$ (i.e. when using the key $\widetilde{k_2}$). Finally, **Game 9** proceeds identically to **Case C.1 Game 11** by encrypting $m_{\bar{b}'}$ for another randomly flipped bit $\bar{b}'$ when Enc and Dec would output $\varsigma = 4$ (i.e. when using the keys $\widetilde{k_\mathtt{i}}, \widetilde{k_\mathtt{r}}$). In **Case C.2**, **Game 9**, the behaviour of π_i^s is independent of the test bits $\pi_i^s.b_\varsigma$ (where $\varsigma \geq 2$) and thus $\mathcal{A}$ has no advantage in guessing these challenge bits nor in causing π_i^s to set $\mathsf{win} \leftarrow 1$. Thus:

$$\mathsf{Adv}^{\mathsf{fACCE,Case\ C}}_{\mathsf{XK},n_P,n_S,\mathcal{A}} \leq \mathsf{Adv}^{\mathsf{coll}}_{\mathrm{H},\mathcal{B}_{\mathsf{coll}}} + n_P^2 n_S^2 \cdot \Big(\mathsf{max}\Big\{\big(3 \cdot \mathsf{Adv}^{\mathsf{prf}}_{\mathrm{KDF},\mathcal{B}_{\mathsf{prf}}} + \mathsf{Adv}^{\mathsf{ms\text{-}PRF\text{-}ODH}}_{\mathrm{KDF},G,p,\mathcal{B}_{\mathsf{PRF\text{-}ODH}}} + 4 \cdot \mathsf{Adv}^{\mathsf{aead}}_{\mathsf{AEAD},\mathcal{B}_{\mathsf{aead}}}\big), \big(2 \cdot \mathsf{Adv}^{\mathsf{prf}}_{\mathrm{KDF},\mathcal{B}_{\mathsf{prf}}} + 3 \cdot \mathsf{Adv}^{\mathsf{aead}}_{\mathsf{AEAD},\mathcal{B}_{\mathsf{aead}}} + \mathsf{Adv}^{\mathsf{sn\text{-}PRF\text{-}ODH}}_{\mathrm{KDF},G,p,\mathcal{B}_{\mathsf{PRF\text{-}ODH}}}\big)\Big\}\Big).$$

7 Discussion

The aim of our model is explicitly not to propose the next *super-strong* notion of security (since all security properties can be analyzed optionally but not all independently), but to propose a generic model- and proof-approach.

As the main reason for basing a protocol analysis on an ACCE model is the intertwined design of the specific analyzed protocol (i.e., an atomic channel establishment), it is surprising that all previous ACCE model definitions were heavily influenced by the concept of composing a channel establishment protocol cleanly from key exchange and channel. Consequently, our results systematize and contribute to the understanding of the generic, composition-independent primitive *authenticated and confidential channel establishment.*

Acknowledgments. We thank Trevor Perrin, Sebastian Lauer, Sven Schäge, Bertram Poettering, Marc Fischlin, members of the SKECH workshop 2018, and the reviewers for insightful comments and discussions.

References

1. Aviram, N., et al.: DROWN: breaking TLS using SSLv2. In: USENIX Security (2016)
2. Bellare, M., Rogaway, P.: Entity authentication and key distribution. In: Stinson, D.R. (ed.) CRYPTO 1993. LNCS, vol. 773, pp. 232–249. Springer, Heidelberg (1994). https://doi.org/10.1007/3-540-48329-2_21
3. Bergsma, F., Dowling, B., Kohlar, F., Schwenk, J., Stebila, D.: Multi-ciphersuite security of the secure shell (SSH) protocol. In: CCS 2014 (2014)
4. Blazy, O., Bossuat, A., Bultel, X., Fouque, P.-A., Onete, C., Pagnin, E.: SAID: reshaping signal into an identity-based asynchronous messaging protocol with authenticated ratcheting. In: IEEE EuroS&P 2019 (2019)
5. Brendel, J., Fischlin, M., Günther, F., Janson, C.: PRF-ODH: relations, instantiations, and impossibility results. In: Katz, J., Shacham, H. (eds.) CRYPTO 2017. LNCS, vol. 10403, pp. 651–681. Springer, Cham (2017). https://doi.org/10.1007/978-3-319-63697-9_22
6. Brzuska, C., Jacobsen, H.: A modular security analysis of EAP and IEEE 802.11. In: Fehr, S. (ed.) PKC 2017. LNCS, vol. 10175, pp. 335–365. Springer, Heidelberg (2017). https://doi.org/10.1007/978-3-662-54388-7_12
7. Brzuska, C., Fischlin, M., Warinschi, B., Williams, S.C.: Composability of Bellare-Rogaway key exchange protocols. In: CCS 2011 (2011)

8. Brzuska, C., Smart, N.P., Warinschi, B., Watson, G.J.: An analysis of the EMV channel establishment protocol. In: CCS 2013 (2013)
9. Brzuska, C., Jacobsen, H., Stebila, D.: Safely exporting keys from secure channels. In: Fischlin, M., Coron, J.-S. (eds.) EUROCRYPT 2016. LNCS, vol. 9665, pp. 670–698. Springer, Heidelberg (2016). https://doi.org/10.1007/978-3-662-49890-3_26
10. Chen, S., Jero, S., Jagielski, M., Boldyreva, A., Nita-Rotaru, C.: Secure communication channel establishment: TLS 1.3 (over TCP fast open) vs. QUIC. Cryptology ePrint Archive, Report 2019/433 (2019). https://eprint.iacr.org/2019/433
11. Cohn-Gordon, K., Cremers, C.J.F., Dowling, B., Garratt, L., Stebila, D.: A formal security analysis of the signal messaging protocol. In: IEEE EuroS&P 2017 (2017)
12. Donenfeld, J.A.: Wireguard: next generation kernel network tunnel. In: NDSS 2017 (2017)
13. Dowling, B., Paterson, K.G.: A cryptographic analysis of the wireguard protocol. In: Preneel, B., Vercauteren, F. (eds.) ACNS 2018. LNCS, vol. 10892, pp. 3–21. Springer, Cham (2018). https://doi.org/10.1007/978-3-319-93387-0_1
14. Dowling, B., Fischlin, M., Günther, F., Stebila, D.: A cryptographic analysis of the TLS 1.3 handshake protocol candidates. In: CCS 2015 (2015)
15. Dowling, B., Rösler, P., Schwenk, J.: Flexible authenticated and confidential channel establishment (fACCE): Analyzing the noise protocol framework. Cryptology ePrint Archive, Report 2019/436 (2019). https://eprint.iacr.org/2019/436
16. Fischlin, M., Günther, F.: Multi-stage key exchange and the case of Google's QUIC protocol. In: CCS 2014 (2014)
17. Fischlin, M., Günther, F.: Replay attacks on zero round-trip time: the case of the TLS 1.3 handshake candidates. In: IEEE EuroS&P (2017)
18. Giesen, F., Kohlar, F., Stebila, D.: On the security of TLS renegotiation. In: CCS 2013 (2013)
19. Günther, F., Hale, B., Jager, T., Lauer, S.: 0-RTT key exchange with full forward secrecy. In: Coron, J.-S., Nielsen, J.B. (eds.) EUROCRYPT 2017. LNCS, vol. 10212, pp. 519–548. Springer, Cham (2017). https://doi.org/10.1007/978-3-319-56617-7_18
20. Hale, B., Jager, T., Lauer, S., Schwenk, J.: Simple security definitions for and constructions of 0-RTT key exchange. In: Gollmann, D., Miyaji, A., Kikuchi, H. (eds.) ACNS 2017. LNCS, vol. 10355, pp. 20–38. Springer, Cham (2017). https://doi.org/10.1007/978-3-319-61204-1_2
21. WhatsApp Inc., Whatsapp encryption overview (2016). https://www.whatsapp.com/security/WhatsApp-Security-Whitepaper.pdf. White paper
22. Jager, T., Kohlar, F., Schäge, S., Schwenk, J.: On the security of TLS-DHE in the standard model. In: Safavi-Naini, R., Canetti, R. (eds.) CRYPTO 2012. LNCS, vol. 7417, pp. 273–293. Springer, Heidelberg (2012). https://doi.org/10.1007/978-3-642-32009-5_17
23. Jager, T., Kohlar, F., Schäge, S., Schwenk, J.: Authenticated confidential channel establishment and the security of TLS-DHE. J. Cryptol. **30**(4), 1276–1324 (2017). https://doi.org/10.1007/s00145-016-9248-2
24. Kobeissi, N.: Noise explorer (2018). https://noiseexplorer.com/
25. Kobeissi, N., Nicolas, G., Bhargavan, K.: Noise explorer: fully automated modeling and verification for arbitrary noise protocols. In: IEEE EuroS&P 2019 (2019)
26. Kohlar, F., Schäge, S., Schwenk, J.: On the security of TLS-DH and TLS-RSA in the standard model. Cryptology ePrint Archive (2013). https://eprint.iacr.org/2013/367

27. Krawczyk, H., Paterson, K.G., Wee, H.: On the security of the TLS protocol: a systematic analysis. In: Canetti, R., Garay, J.A. (eds.) CRYPTO 2013. LNCS, vol. 8042, pp. 429–448. Springer, Heidelberg (2013). https://doi.org/10.1007/978-3-642-40041-4_24
28. Lipp, B., Blanchet, B., Bhargavan, K.: A mechanised cryptographic proof of the wireguard virtual private network protocol. In: IEEE EuroS&P 2019 (2019)
29. Lychev, R., Jero, S., Boldyreva, A., Nita-Rotaru, C.: How secure and quick is QUIC? Provable security and performance analyses. In: IEEE S&P 2015 (2015)
30. Morrissey, P., Smart, N.P., Warinschi, B.: A modular security analysis of the TLS handshake protocol. In: Pieprzyk, J. (ed.) ASIACRYPT 2008. LNCS, vol. 5350, pp. 55–73. Springer, Heidelberg (2008). https://doi.org/10.1007/978-3-540-89255-7_5
31. Möller, B., Duong, T., Kotowicz, K.: This POODLE bites: Exploiting the SSL 3.0 fallback (2014). https://www.openssl.org/~bodo/ssl-poodle.pdf
32. Perrin, T.: The noise protocol framework (2017). http://noiseprotocol.org/noise.html. Revision 33
33. Rösler, P., Mainka, C., Schwenk, J.: More is less: on the end-to-end security of group chats in signal, Whatsapp, and Threema. In: IEEE EuroS&P (2018)

Limits on the Efficiency of (Ring) LWE Based Non-interactive Key Exchange

Siyao Guo[1(✉)], Pritish Kamath[2], Alon Rosen[3], and Katerina Sotiraki[4]

[1] NYU Shanghai, Shanghai 200122, China
siyao.guo@nyu.edu
[2] TTIC, Chicago, IL 60637, USA
pritish@ttic.edu
[3] IDC Herzliya, 4610101 Herzliya, Israel
alon.rosen@idc.ac.il
[4] MIT, Cambridge, MA 02139, USA
katesot@mit.edu

Abstract. LWE based key-exchange protocols lie at the heart of post-quantum public-key cryptography. However, all existing protocols either lack the *non-interactive* nature of Diffie-Hellman key-exchange or *polynomial* LWE-modulus, resulting in unwanted efficiency overhead.

We study the possibility of designing non-interactive LWE-based protocols with *polynomial* LWE-modulus. To this end,

- We identify and formalize simple non-interactive and polynomial LWE-modulus variants of existing protocols, where Alice and Bob *simultaneously* exchange one or more (ring) LWE samples with polynomial LWE-modulus and then run individual key reconciliation functions to obtain the shared key.
- We point out central barriers and show that such non-interactive key-exchange protocols are impossible if:
  (1) the reconciliation functions first compute the inner product of the received LWE sample with their private LWE secret. This impossibility is information theoretic.
  (2) One of the reconciliation functions does not depend on the error of the transmitted LWE sample. This impossibility assumes hardness of LWE.
- We give further evidence that progress in either direction, of giving an LWE-based NIKE protocol or proving impossibility of one will lead to progress on some other well-studied questions in cryptography.

Overall, our results show possibilities and challenges in designing simple (ring) LWE-based non-interactive key exchange protocols.

S. Guo—Supported by Shanghai Eastern Young Scholar Program.
P. Kamath—Work done while at MIT, supported by NSF awards CCF-1733808, IIS-1741137 and MIT-IBM Watson AI Lab and Research Collaboration Agreement No. W1771646.
A. Rosen—Supported by ISF grant No. 1399/17 and via Project PROMETHEUS (Grant 780701).
K. Sotiraki—Research supported in part by NSF/BSF grant #1350619, an MIT-IBM grant, a DARPA Young Faculty Award, MIT Lincoln Laboratories and Analog Devices.

A. Kiayias et al. (Eds.): PKC 2020, LNCS 12110, pp. 374–395, 2020.
https://doi.org/10.1007/978-3-030-45374-9_13

1 Introduction

In 1976, Diffie and Hellman [DH76] proposed an extremely elegant key-exchange protocol, in which two parties, Alice and Bob, exchange respective group elements g^a, g^b *simultaneously*, where g is a generator of a publicly chosen group $\mathcal{G}$ and $a, b \in [|\mathcal{G}|]$ are uniformly chosen secret elements. Alice and Bob then locally perform a single group exponentiation in order to derive the shared key, g^{ab}. This simple idea lies at the foundation of public key cryptography, and has been widely used in practice throughout the years.

Two decades later, Shor [Sho94] showed that efficient quantum algorithms could, in principle, break the Diffie-Hellman key-exchange protocol, as well as other widely used assumptions (e.g. Factoring). Thus, with the development of quantum computers on the horizon, the importance of designing post-quantum secure key-exchange protocols, that can replace current standards, has been recognized. As part of this effort, the National Institute of Standards and Technology (NIST) decided to look into post-quantum cryptography standardization and is hosting a post-quantum cryptography call of proposals [NIS]. One of the major primitives that they seek is a key-encapsulation mechanism.

1.1 (Ring) LWE Based Key Exchange Protocols

A significant portion of the algorithms qualified to the second round of the NIST call for proposals [SAB+17,NAB+17,LLJ+17,PAA+17,GMZB+17] is based on the (ring) learning with errors (LWE) assumption [Reg05,LPR10]. A remarkable feature of this assumption (and consequently of the proposals) is that its *average-case* hardness is based on the *worst-case* hardness of lattice problems, which themselves are conjectured to be secure against efficient quantum algorithms.

Those proposals use two routes to achieve key-exchange, one is through public-key encryption and the other is through reconciliation. However, all of them *lack the non-interactive nature* of the key-exchange protocol of Diffie-Hellman, as explained below.

Key-Exchange Through Public-Key Encryption. In the first case, Alice samples a secret & public-key pair and sends her public-key to Bob. Then, Bob picks a desired shared key and sends it to Alice, encrypted under her public-key. Finally, Alice decrypts Bob's message to recover the shared key. While conceptually simple, this approach lacks some of the advantages of the Diffie-Hellman protocol. Firstly, Bob has complete control over the shared key. Secondly, the protocol is inherently interactive – the parties need at least two rounds of interaction.

Key-Exchange Through Reconciliation. The reconciliation approach was introduced by Ding et al. [DXL12] and Peikert [Pei14] and was implemented and improved in later works [ADPS16,BCNS14]. The most basic version of such reconciliation-based protocols has a simple description[1] (See Fig. 1): Let $\boldsymbol{A}$ be

[1] For simplicity, we only describe the LWE-based variant; the ring version is obtained by replacing $\boldsymbol{A}, \boldsymbol{x}_1, \boldsymbol{x}_2, \boldsymbol{e}_1, \boldsymbol{e}_2$ with ring elements from some chosen polynomial ring and using the corresponding polynomial multiplication.

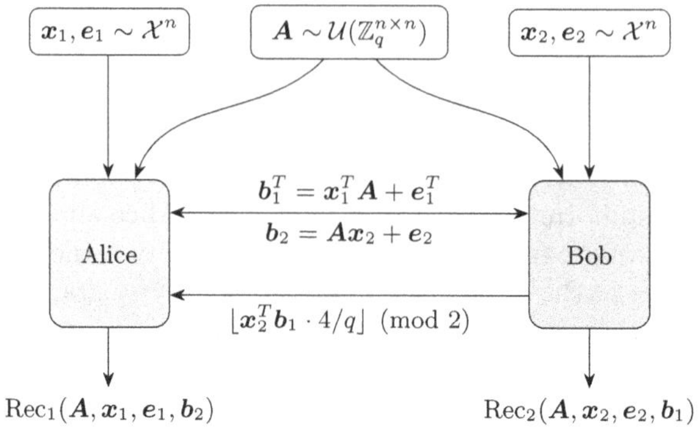

Fig. 1. Alice and Bob *simultaneously* exchange LWE samples using the same public matrix A. *After receiving* b_2, Bob sends the second most significant bit of $x_2^T b_1$ to Alice. Both players then apply their respective *key reconciliation functions* on the variables they have to produce a shared key.

a random public $n \times n$ matrix over $\mathbb{Z}_q$ where q is *polynomial* in n and let $\mathcal{X}$ be a *noise distribution*, then the parties act as follows: Alice randomly picks x_1, e_1 from $\mathcal{X}^n$ and sends $b_1 = x_1^T A + e_1$ to Bob, while Bob *simultaneously* picks random x_2, e_2 from $\mathcal{X}^n$ and sends $b_2 = Ax_2 + e_2$ to Alice. *After receiving* b_1, Bob sends to Alice the second most significant bit of $x_2^T b_1$, i.e., $\lfloor 4/q \cdot x_2^T b_1 \rfloor \pmod 2$. To agree on a common key, Alice and Bob first compute the inner product of their secret and incoming message and obtain $x_1^T Ax_2 + x_1^T e_2$ and $x_1^T Ax_2 + e_1^T x_2$ respectively. The small magnitude of Alice and Bob's secret and noise already allows them to achieve approximate agreement: the most significant bit of $x_1^T Ax_2 + x_1^T e_2$ and $x_1^T Ax_2 + e_1^T x_2$ is often the same. To achieve exact agreement, they run a simple *key reconciliation* procedure, where Bob sends the second most significant bit as an additional hint.

1.2 (Ring) LWE Based Non-interactive Key Exchange?

As discussed above, Diffie-Hellman key exchange allows parties to send their messages simultaneously or communicate in a non-interactive way (e.g. by publishing them on Alice's and Bob's public websites). In the contrast, current proposed LWE-based key exchange protocols require additional interactions. Even though the additional interaction is only a single bit (as is the case in Fig. 1), one extra round of a practical key exchange protocol may result in significant delays when used at a large scale (such as that of the internet). This motivates the main question that we study in this paper:

> *Can we have practical (ring)* LWE*-based non-interactive key exchange protocols? Or are such protocols inherently interactive?*

A Remark on LWE-Modulus. Throughout the paper, we focus on polynomial LWE-modulus. We observe that if superpolynomial LWE-modulus is to be considered, LWE-based key exchange in Fig. 1 *can be made non-interactive.* That's because the most significant bits of $\boldsymbol{x}_1^T\boldsymbol{b}_2$ and $\boldsymbol{x}_2^T\boldsymbol{b}_1$ agree with probability $1 - \Theta(nB^2/q)$, for a noise distribution $\mathcal{X}$ whose support is included in $[-B, B]$. If the modulus to noise rate is large (i.e. superpolynomial in the security parameter), then the probability of disagreement of their most significant bits is negligible, and hence the above non-interactive protocol is sufficient. However, in the case of a polynomially bounded q, the disagreement probability is non-negligible. Given the extremely demanding efficiency constraints on practical implementations[2], it would be highly desirable to have variants of such LWE-based key-exchange protocol in which the disagreement probability is negligible even in the case that q is as small as a polynomial in the security parameter. Additionally, requiring a large modulus to noise rate affects the hardness of the corresponding LWE assumption, since the worst-to-average case reductions translate this rate to the gap in the promise lattice problems [Pei09]. Namely, LWE with large modulus-to-noise rate is a stronger assumption (i.e. more susceptible to polynomial-time attacks) than LWE with a smaller modulus-to-noise rate.

1.3 Our Results

In this paper, we explore the possibility of attaining (ring) LWE-based non-interactive key exchange (NIKE) (with modulus polynomial in the security parameter).

Our Focus. We focus on the setting where Alice and Bob only send one or a few (ring) LWE samples to each other; similarly to the protocol in Fig. 1, but without the last message sent from Bob to Alice.

The main motivation for studying this setting is that perhaps it is the simplest setting which captures natural non-interactive variants of current LWE based key exchange protocols. Therefore, impossibility results will give a theoretical justification for current LWE based key exchange protocols. On the other hand, possibility results will yield Diffe-Hellman like non-interactive protocols.

Moreover, NIKE in this setting is simply characterized by two efficiently computable *key reconciliation functions* $\mathrm{Rec}_1, \mathrm{Rec}_2$, such that

- The outputs of Alice and Bob agree with each other with overwhelming probability, that is, $\mathrm{Rec}_1(\boldsymbol{A}, \boldsymbol{x}_1, \boldsymbol{e}_1, \boldsymbol{b}_2) = \mathrm{Rec}_2(\boldsymbol{A}, \boldsymbol{x}_2, \boldsymbol{e}_2, \boldsymbol{b}_1)$ holds with overwhelming probability (recall that $\boldsymbol{b}_1 := \boldsymbol{A}^T\boldsymbol{x}_1 + \boldsymbol{e}_1$ and $\boldsymbol{b}_2 := \boldsymbol{A}\boldsymbol{x}_2 + \boldsymbol{e}_2$).
- The output of the protocol is pseudo-random even when conditioned on the transcript, that is, it is hard to predict $\mathrm{Rec}_1(\boldsymbol{A}, \boldsymbol{x}_1, \boldsymbol{e}_1, \boldsymbol{b}_2)$ given $\boldsymbol{A}, \boldsymbol{b}_1, \boldsymbol{b}_2$.

Natural Choices of Reconciliation Functions. Observe that in Fig. 1, Alice and Bob achieve approximate agreement by computing $\boldsymbol{x}_1^T\boldsymbol{b}_2$ and $\boldsymbol{x}_2^T\boldsymbol{b}_1$, respectively. These values are noisy versions of $\boldsymbol{x}_1^T\boldsymbol{A}\boldsymbol{x}_2$ and their most significant bit agrees with probability $1 - \Theta(nB^2/q)$ when the support of $\mathcal{X}$ is in $[-B, B]$. Based on this observation, one may consider the following three families of reconciliation functions (in increasing order of generality).

[2] A typical size of q is $\approx 2^{13}$ and there are proposals that even use $q = 257$ [LLJ+17].

1. Rec_1 and Rec_2 are arbitrary efficient functions (not necessarily the most significant bit) on $\boldsymbol{x}_1^T \boldsymbol{b}_2$ and $\boldsymbol{x}_2^T \boldsymbol{b}_1$ respectively.
2. Rec_1 and Rec_2 are arbitrary efficient functions on $\boldsymbol{A}, \boldsymbol{x}_1, \boldsymbol{b}_2$ and $\boldsymbol{A}, \boldsymbol{x}_2, \boldsymbol{b}_1$ respectively.
3. Rec_1 and Rec_2 are arbitrary efficient functions on $\boldsymbol{A}, \boldsymbol{x}_1, \boldsymbol{e}_1, \boldsymbol{b}_2$ and $\boldsymbol{A}, \boldsymbol{x}_2, \boldsymbol{e}_2, \boldsymbol{b}_1$ respectively.

Note that the third family captures all possible reconciliation functions.

Our main results rule out the first and second families of reconciliation functions even when multiple LWE samples are exchanged, and point out central efficiency barriers for the third family.

First Result (Section 3). One natural idea to remove the interaction would be to somehow "amplify" the agreement probability by sending more LWE samples and generating more independent samples from the joint distribution $(\boldsymbol{X}, \boldsymbol{Y})$ where $\boldsymbol{X} := \boldsymbol{x}_1^T \boldsymbol{b}_2$ and $\boldsymbol{Y} := \boldsymbol{x}_2^T \boldsymbol{b}_1$, then apply Rec_1 and Rec_2 on independent samples from $\boldsymbol{X}$ and $\boldsymbol{Y}$ respectively.

In Theorem 1, we show that for any m, balanced $\text{Rec}_1, \text{Rec}_2$ (see Definition 1) and non-trivial noise distribution, $\text{Rec}_1(\boldsymbol{X}^m) = \text{Rec}_2(\boldsymbol{Y}^m)$ holds with probability at most $1 - \Omega(1/q^2)$. This implies that such reconciliation functions cannot exist (this impossibility is information theoretic and holds even for computationally inefficient reconciliation functions). Our results naturally extend to the case of ring LWE.

Second Result (Section 4). Even though the above result captures known constructions, it does not rule out a slightly more general case where the reconciliation functions depend on $\boldsymbol{A}$. Indeed, given $\boldsymbol{X}' := (\boldsymbol{A}, \boldsymbol{X})$ and $\boldsymbol{Y}' := (\boldsymbol{A}, \boldsymbol{Y})$, Alice and Bob can agree on an *insecure* random bit with probability 1 by evaluating a balanced function of $\boldsymbol{A}$ (while ignoring $\boldsymbol{X}$ and $\boldsymbol{Y}$). Of course, such protocols are not suitable for key agreement, since the common random bit is not pseudo-random conditioned on $\boldsymbol{A}$.

In Theorem 3, we show that the reconciliation functions Rec_1 and Rec_2 have to depend on the LWE noises $\boldsymbol{e}_1$ and $\boldsymbol{e}_2$ respectively. For instance, the above theorem excludes a more general case than family 2 where the reconciliation functions are of the form $\text{Rec}_1(\boldsymbol{A}, \boldsymbol{x}_1, \boldsymbol{e}_1, \boldsymbol{b}_2) = h_1(\boldsymbol{A}, \boldsymbol{x}_1, \boldsymbol{b}_2)$ and $\text{Rec}_2(\boldsymbol{A}, \boldsymbol{x}_2, \boldsymbol{e}_2, \boldsymbol{b}_1) = h_2(\boldsymbol{A}, \boldsymbol{x}_2, \boldsymbol{e}_2, \boldsymbol{b}_1)$. In particular, it rules out the case where the joint distribution is $(\boldsymbol{X}', \boldsymbol{Y}')$. However, in contrast to Theorem 1 which holds unconditionally, Theorem 3 assumes the hardness of the LWE problem. Our results extend to the case of ring LWE and to a polynomial number of samples.

Third Result (Section 5). The above two results rule out the most natural choices of key reconciliation functions based on variants of inner product, unconditionally or under the LWE assumption. In Sect. 5.1, we show that the existence of efficient Rec_1 and Rec_2, which depend on all of their inputs, cannot be ruled out (at least as long as the existence of iO is a possibility). In particular, in Theorem 4, we show that there exists an instantiation of the NIKE protocol in our framework that is based on indistinguishability obfuscation (iO) and puncturable PRFs [BZ17].

However, we identify a crucial restriction on the complexity of reconciliation functions. In Theorem 5, we show that the reconciliation functions themselves actually have to contain cryptographic hardness, in the sense that they *directly* yield weak pseudorandom functions. Therefore, the reconciliation functions have to be at least as complex as weak pseudorandom functions and hence suffer from the complexity limitations and attacks on weak pseudorandom functions. Moreover, this connection shows that any NIKE protocol based on hardness of LWE with polynomial modulus, gives rise to new constructions of weak pseudorandom functions based on the hardness of LWE with polynomial modulus. Such constructions have been an open problem almost since the introduction of the LWE assumption, and thus we view Theorem 5 as an indication that finding appropriate reconciliation functions requires new techniques.

1.4 Discussion and Open Problems

When parties exchange only LWE samples, we rule out the most natural choices of key reconciliation functions. Additionally, we point out that non-interactive key reconciliation functions, unlike interactive ones, have to be as complex as weak pseudorandom functions. Overall, our results show possibilities and challenges in designing simple (ring) LWE-based non-interactive key exchange protocols.

An interesting open direction is to understand what happens when the messages contain extra information, apart from the LWE samples. To this end, one would have to come up with a natural and simple form of messages (based on LWE) and explore the possibility of basing non-interactive key exchange on it. For instance, a natural idea is to consider LWE samples together with some *leakage* about the secrets. We remark that Theorem 5 continues to hold even if the leakage function is pseudorandom.

2 Preliminaries

We now provide some useful notation and definitions. We denote a sample drawn from $\mathcal{D}$ by $x \sim \mathcal{D}$ and a sample of the uniform distribution over S by $x \sim S$.

Definition 1. *A function $f : S \to \{0,1\}$ is called balanced respect to distribution $\mathcal{D}$ if $\mathbb{E}_{x \sim \mathcal{D}}[f(x)] = 1/2$.*

Definition 2. *A distribution $\mathcal{X}$ over $\mathbb{Z}_q$ is B-bounded if its support is included in $[-B, B]$.*

We formally define the class of all non-interactive key exchange protocols that could exist. We use $\mathsf{negl}(\lambda)$ to denote any function $g : \mathbb{R} \to \mathbb{R}$ that satisfies $g(\lambda) \leq O(n^{-c})$ for all constants $c \in \mathbb{N}$.

Definition 3. *For a security parameter $\lambda > 0$, a non-interactive key-exchange protocol consists of two* $\mathsf{poly}(\lambda)$*-time algorithms* b_1 *and* b_2 *and two* $\mathsf{poly}(\lambda)$*-time computable boolean functions* Rec_1 *and* Rec_2 *that satisfy the conditions below (where* $(\boldsymbol{r}, \boldsymbol{r}_1, \boldsymbol{r}_2)$ *is a random source where* $\boldsymbol{r}$ *is a source of shared randomness and* $\boldsymbol{r}_1$*,* $\boldsymbol{r}_2$ *are private sources of randomness of the two parties)*

1. $\Pr_{\boldsymbol{r},\boldsymbol{r}_1,\boldsymbol{r}_2}[\mathrm{Rec}_1(\boldsymbol{r}, \boldsymbol{r}_1, b_2(\boldsymbol{r}, \boldsymbol{r}_2)) = \mathrm{Rec}_2(\boldsymbol{r}, \boldsymbol{r}_2, b_1(\boldsymbol{r}, \boldsymbol{r}_1))] \geq 1 - \mathsf{negl}(\lambda)$,
2. *For any probabilistic* $\mathsf{poly}(\lambda)$*-time algorithm* $\mathcal{A}$,

$$\Pr_{\boldsymbol{r},\boldsymbol{r}_1,\boldsymbol{r}_2}[\mathcal{A}(\boldsymbol{r}, b_1(\boldsymbol{r}, \boldsymbol{r}_1), b_2(\boldsymbol{r}, \boldsymbol{r}_2)) = \mathrm{Rec}_1(\boldsymbol{r}, \boldsymbol{r}_1, b_2(\boldsymbol{r}, \boldsymbol{r}_2))] \leq \frac{1}{2} + \mathsf{negl}(\lambda).$$

Finally, we describe the Learning-with-Errors (LWE) assumption.

Definition 4. [Reg05] *The* LWE *assumption for integers* n, m, q *and noise distribution* $\mathcal{X}$ *over* $\mathbb{Z}_q$ *states that,*

$$(\boldsymbol{A}, \boldsymbol{b} := \boldsymbol{x}^T \boldsymbol{A} + \boldsymbol{e}) \approx_c (\boldsymbol{A}, \boldsymbol{u}),$$

where $\boldsymbol{A} \sim \mathbb{Z}_q^{n \times m}$, $\boldsymbol{u} \sim \mathbb{Z}_q^m$, $\boldsymbol{x} \sim \mathcal{X}^n$ *and* $\boldsymbol{e} \sim \mathcal{X}^m$.

3 (Information Theoretic) Impossibility of Amplification with Multiple Samples

Before stating the main Theorem of this section, we provide some definitions and notation.

Definition 5. *A distribution* $\mathcal{X}$ *over any group* G *(e.g.* $G = \mathbb{Z}_q$*) is* symmetric *if* $\Pr_{X \sim \mathcal{X}}[X = z] = \Pr_{X \sim \mathcal{X}}[X = -z]$ *for any* $z \in G$.

Given a distribution $\mathcal{X}$ over $\mathbb{Z}_q$, let $(\mathcal{X}^n)^*$ be the distribution of $\boldsymbol{w} = (w^{(1)}, w^{(2)}, \ldots, w^{(n)})$ drawn from $\mathcal{X}^n$ conditioned on the event that $\boldsymbol{w}$ is not a zero-divisor, that is $\gcd(w^{(1)}, w^{(2)}, \ldots, w^{(n)}, q) = 1$.

Theorem 1. *Let* $n, q \geq 1$ *be integers and* $\mathcal{X}$ *be a symmetric distribution over* $\mathbb{Z}_q$ *such that for any* $a \in \mathbb{Z}_q \setminus \{0\}$*, it holds that* $\Pr_{X \sim \mathcal{X}}[aX = 0] \leq 9/10$ *and* $\Pr_{X \sim \mathcal{X}}[aX = q/2] \leq 9/10$*. Let* $\mu_{\mathcal{X}}(X, Y)$ *be the joint distribution of*

$$X = \boldsymbol{x}_1^T \boldsymbol{A} \boldsymbol{x}_2 + \boldsymbol{x}_1^T \boldsymbol{e}_2 \text{ and } Y = \boldsymbol{x}_1^T \boldsymbol{A} \boldsymbol{x}_2 + \boldsymbol{e}_1^T \boldsymbol{x}_2,$$

where $\boldsymbol{A} \sim \mathcal{U}(\mathbb{Z}_q^{n \times n})$, $\boldsymbol{e}_1, \boldsymbol{e}_2 \sim \mathcal{X}^n$ *and* $\boldsymbol{x}_1, \boldsymbol{x}_2 \sim (\mathcal{X}^n)^*$*. Then, for any* $m \geq 1$*, and any balanced functions* $\mathrm{Rec}_1, \mathrm{Rec}_2 : \mathbb{Z}_q^m \to \{0, 1\}$ *respect to the marginal distributions of* $\mu_{\mathcal{X}}^{\otimes m}$*, it holds that*

$$\Pr_{(\boldsymbol{X},\boldsymbol{Y}) \sim \mu_{\mathcal{X}}^{\otimes m}}[\mathrm{Rec}_1(\boldsymbol{X}) = \mathrm{Rec}_2(\boldsymbol{Y})] \leq 1 - \Omega(1/q^2).$$

Our theorem also holds for the ring case with the same parameters (See Theorem 6 in Appendix A). This theorem shows that no matter how many independent samples are drawn and no matter what procedures are applied on those samples, Alice and Bob can agree with each other on a random bit with probability at most $1 - \Omega(1/q^2)$. Note that Alice and Bob have to marginally produce a uniform bit as captured in the condition that Rec_1 and Rec_2 are balanced.

Our theorem applies to the most commonly used noise distributions. For instance, the discrete Gaussian distribution $\mathcal{D}_\sigma$ with standard deviation $\sigma > 10$ satisfies the conditions of Theorem 1. First, the discrete Gaussian is a symmetric distribution. Second, if $x \sim \mathcal{D}_\sigma$, then from monotonicity of $\mathcal{D}_\sigma$, for any $a \in \mathbb{Z}_q \setminus \{0\}$, $\Pr[ax = q/2] \leq \Pr[ax = 0]$. Therefore, it is enough to show that for any $a \in \mathbb{Z}_q \setminus \{0\}$, $\Pr[ax = 0] \leq 9/10$ which is straightforward to verify[3].

Additionally, the condition of Theorem 1 that for any $a \in \mathbb{Z}_q \setminus \{0\}$, $\Pr[aX = 0] \leq 9/10$ and $\Pr[aX = q/2] \leq 9/10$ is quite mild. For instance, if $q > 2$ is prime, then this condition simplifies to the assumption that the support of $\mathcal{X}$ is not equal to $\{0\}$. Also, for general q if the support of $\mathcal{X}$ is 1/10-far from a proper subgroup or a coset of a proper subgroup of $\mathbb{Z}_q$, then this assumption is satisfied.

Notice that $\mu_{\mathcal{X}}(X, Y)$ as defined in Theorem 1 does not correspond to the joint distribution described in the introduction, since $\boldsymbol{x}_1, \boldsymbol{x}_2$ are sampled from $(\mathcal{X}^n)^*$. This is without loss of generality because if $\boldsymbol{w} \sim \mathcal{X}^n$, then the probability that $\gcd(w^{(1)}, w^{(2)}, \ldots, w^{(n)}, q) \neq 1$ is smaller than the probability that $w^{(1)}, w^{(2)}, \ldots, w^{(n)}$ all belong to a proper subgroup of $\mathbb{Z}_q$, which is less than $(9/10)^n$. So, the distribution of $(\boldsymbol{X}, \boldsymbol{Y})$ is at most $O(m/(9/10)^n)$ far from the distribution of m samples drawn as described in the introduction. Even though this is a very small change in the protocol, it will simplify our proof a lot, since in this case the value $\boldsymbol{x}_1^T \boldsymbol{A} \boldsymbol{x}_2$ is a uniform element in $\mathbb{Z}_q$[4].

Our Theorem 1 shows that in this regime, it is *information theoretically* impossible to agree on a common bit with probability $1 - o(1/q^2)$. In fact, the problem of generating common randomness by observing independent samples from two correlated distributions (or a joint distribution) is known as "Non-interactive Agreement Distillation" in the area of information theory (See Sect. 3.1) and the notion of maximal correlation exactly captures this problem (upto a polynomial factor in the error). Even though we could prove our theorem in a self-contained manner, we feel this connection provides more insight. Therefore, in the next section we present some basic facts about maximal correlation and then present a proof through this notion. In Appendix A, we also present a self-contained proof of Theorem 1 using Fourier analysis and extend this to the ring LWE case (Theorem 6).

---

[3] Note that by symmetry and monotonicity of $\mathcal{D}_\sigma$, $\Pr[ax = 0] \leq \Pr[a(|x| - 1) = 0] + \Pr[x = 0]$. Combining with the fact that $\Pr[ax = 0] + \Pr[a(|x| - 1) = 0] \leq 1$ for $a \neq 0$, and $\Pr[x = 0] \leq 1/(1 + 2e^{-1/\sigma^2})$, we conclude that $\Pr[ax = 0] \leq (1 + \Pr[x = 0])/2 \leq 9/10$ for $\sigma > 10$.

[4] If $\boldsymbol{w} = (w^{(1)}, w^{(2)}, \ldots, w^{(n)})$ such that $\gcd(w^{(1)}, w^{(2)}, \ldots, w^{(n)}, q) = 1$ and $\mathbf{u}$ is uniform in $\mathbb{Z}_q^n$, then $\boldsymbol{w}^T \mathbf{u}$ is also uniform in $\mathbb{Z}_q$.

3.1 Maximal Correlation and Non-interactive Agreement Distillation

The *Non-interactive Agreement Distillation* problem, parameterized by a joint distribution $\mu(x, y)$ is defined as follows: Two players, Alice and Bob, observe sequences $(X_1, \dots, X_m)$ and $(Y_1, \dots, Y_m)$ respectively where $\{(X_i, Y_i)\}_{i=1}^m$ are drawn i.i.d. from $\mu(x, y)$. Both players look at their share of randomness, apply a function and output a bit. Their goal is to maximize the probability that their output bits agree, while ensuring that they are marginally uniform.

Hirschfeld [Hir35] and Gebelein [Geb41] introduced the notion of *maximal correlation*, which was later studied by Rényi [Rén59]. It turns out that maximal correlation (almost tightly) captures the maximum agreement probability that the players can get.

Definition 6 (Maximal Correlation). *For a joint distribution μ over $G_A \times G_B$, its maximal correlation $\rho(\mu)$ is defined as follows,*

$$\sup_{f,g} \left\{ \mathop{\mathbb{E}}_{(x,y)\sim\mu} [f(x) \cdot g(y)] \;\middle|\; \begin{array}{l} f : G_A \to \mathbb{R}, \quad \mathbb{E}_{\mu_{G_A}}[f] = \mathbb{E}_{\mu_{G_B}}[g] = 0 \\ g : G_B \to \mathbb{R}, \, \mathrm{Var}_{\mu_{G_A}}[f] = \mathrm{Var}_{\mu_{G_B}}[g] = 1 \end{array} \right\},$$

where μ_{G_A} and μ_{G_B} are the marginal distributions of μ.

In order to analytically capture maximal correlation, let us define, for any joint distribution μ over $G_A \times G_B$, the $|G_A| \times |G_B|$ matrix M_μ given by

$$M_\mu(x, y) = \frac{\mu(x, y)}{\sqrt{\mu_A(x)\mu_B(y)}} .$$

where μ_A and μ_B are the marginal distributions of μ.

Fact 2. *The maximal correlation $\rho(\mu)$ is equal to the second largest singular value of M_μ, denoted as $\sigma_2(M_\mu)$.*[5]

In the seminal work of [Wit75], it was shown that maximal correlation actually captures (up to a square root factor), the best agreement probability that the players can get even with an infinite number of samples!

Lemma 1. *Suppose $\rho(\mu) = 1 - \varepsilon$, then for any $m \geq 1$, $f : G_A^m \to \{0, 1\}$ and $g : G_B^m \to \{0, 1\}$ with $\mathbb{E}_{\mu_X^{\otimes m}}[f] = \mathbb{E}_{\mu_Y^{\otimes m}}[g] = 1/2$, it holds that*

$$\Pr_{(\boldsymbol{X},\boldsymbol{Y})\sim\mu^{\otimes m}} [f(\boldsymbol{X}) = g(\boldsymbol{Y})] \leq 1 - \varepsilon/2. \tag{1}$$

Moreover, there exist m, f, g such that $\mathbb{E}_{\mu_X^{\otimes m}}[f] = \mathbb{E}_{\mu_Y^{\otimes m}}[g] = 1/2$ and

$$\Pr_{(\boldsymbol{X},\boldsymbol{Y})\sim\mu^{\otimes m}} [f(\boldsymbol{X}) = g(\boldsymbol{Y})] \;\geq\; 1 - \frac{\arccos(\rho(\mu))}{\pi} \;\geq\; 1 - \sqrt{2\varepsilon}. \tag{2}$$

[5] The top singular value being 1.

3.2 Bounding Maximal Correlation

Given Lemma 1, it suffices to upper bound the maximal correlation of $\mu_{\mathcal{X}}(X, Y)$. We exploit the special form of our distribution, namely that X is distributed uniformly in $\mathbb{Z}_q$ and $X - Y$ is distributed as some "noise distribution" ξ. For such distributions, the maximal correlation is much easier to analyze. In this section, we prove the following lemma.

Lemma 2. *Let $n, q \geq 1$ be integers. For a distribution $\mathcal{X}$ over $\mathbb{Z}_q$ and the joint distribution $\mu_{\mathcal{X}}$ that satisfies the conditions of Theorem 1, it holds that*

$$\rho(\mu_{\mathcal{X}}) \leq 1 - \Omega(1/q^2).$$

Theorem 1 follows immediately by combining Lemmas 1 and 2. To prove Lemma 2, we consider a more general class of joint distributions called Cayley Distributions and characterize their maximal correlation.

Definition 7 (Cayley Distributions). *A joint distribution μ over $\mathbb{Z}_q^k \times \mathbb{Z}_q^k$ is said to be a* Cayley distribution *if there exists a "noise distribution" $\xi : \mathbb{Z}_q^k \to \mathbb{R}_{\geq 0}$, such that,*

(i) $\xi(\boldsymbol{z}) = \xi(-\boldsymbol{z})$ for all $\boldsymbol{z} \in \mathbb{Z}_q^k$ and

(ii) $\mu(\boldsymbol{x}, \boldsymbol{y}) = \frac{\xi(\boldsymbol{x}-\boldsymbol{y})}{q^k}$ for all $\boldsymbol{x}, \boldsymbol{y} \in \mathbb{Z}_q^k$.[6]

A Cayley distribution can be viewed as sampling $\boldsymbol{x}$ uniformly at random in $\mathbb{Z}_q^k$, sampling $\boldsymbol{z} \sim \xi$ and setting $\boldsymbol{y} = \boldsymbol{x} + \boldsymbol{z}$. Note that a Cayley distribution μ is symmetric and has uniform marginals on $\mathbb{Z}_q^k$, so its maximal correlation is given by the second largest eigenvalue of M_μ (by Theorem 2 and the fact that for symmetric matrices, singular values are same as eigenvalues). Interestingly, the eigenvectors of M_μ can be completely characterized in a way that does not depend on the noise distribution ξ. This makes it easy to get a handle on the eigenvalues, which leads to the following lemma.

Lemma 3 (Maximal Correlation of Cayley Distributions [Lov75]**).** *For $\boldsymbol{a} \in \mathbb{Z}_q^k$, define the* character *$\chi_{\boldsymbol{a}} : \mathbb{Z}_q^k \to \mathbb{C}$ as $\chi_{\boldsymbol{a}}(\boldsymbol{x}) = e^{-2\pi i \cdot \langle \boldsymbol{a}, \boldsymbol{x} \rangle / q}$. Let μ be any Cayley distribution over $\mathbb{Z}_q^k \times \mathbb{Z}_q^k$, with associated noise function ξ. Then*

$$\rho(\mu) = \max_{\boldsymbol{a} \in Z_q^k \setminus \{\boldsymbol{0}^k\}} \mathop{\mathbb{E}}_{\boldsymbol{e} \sim \xi} [\chi_{\boldsymbol{a}}(\boldsymbol{e})].$$

We point out that Definition 7 and Lemma 3 generalize to all finite abelian groups G. However for concreteness, we only focus on our special case of $G = \mathbb{Z}_q^k$. While this lemma is standard, we include a proof for completeness.

[6] Observe that since ξ is a probability distribution over $\mathbb{Z}_q^k$, it follows that μ is also a probability distribution.

Proof. We interpret $\chi_{\boldsymbol{a}}$ as a vector in $\mathbb{C}^{q^k}$ indexed by elements in $\mathbb{Z}_q^k$. It is straightfoward to verify that $\chi_{\boldsymbol{a}} \in \mathbb{C}^{q^k}$ is an eigenvector of M_μ with corresponding eigenvalue $\mathbb{E}_{\boldsymbol{e}\sim\xi}[\chi_{\boldsymbol{a}}(\boldsymbol{e})]$. Note that since μ is a Caley distribution, $M_\mu(\boldsymbol{x},\boldsymbol{y}) = q^k \cdot \mu(\boldsymbol{x},\boldsymbol{y})$. Fix any $\boldsymbol{a} \in \mathbb{Z}_q^k$. For any $\boldsymbol{x} \in \mathbb{Z}_q^k$, it holds that

$$\begin{aligned}
(M_\mu \chi_{\boldsymbol{a}})(\boldsymbol{x}) &= \sum_{\boldsymbol{y}\in\mathbb{Z}_q^k} M_\mu(\boldsymbol{x},\boldsymbol{y}) \cdot \chi_{\boldsymbol{a}}(\boldsymbol{y}) = \sum_{\boldsymbol{y}\in\mathbb{Z}_q^k} (q^k \cdot \mu(\boldsymbol{x},\boldsymbol{y})) \cdot \chi_{\boldsymbol{a}}(\boldsymbol{y}) \\
&= \sum_{\boldsymbol{y}\in\mathbb{Z}_q^k} \xi(\boldsymbol{y}-\boldsymbol{x}) \cdot \chi_{\boldsymbol{a}}(\boldsymbol{y}) = \sum_{\boldsymbol{e}\in\mathbb{Z}_q^k} \xi(\boldsymbol{e}) \cdot \chi_{\boldsymbol{a}}(\boldsymbol{x}+\boldsymbol{e}) \\
&= \left(\sum_{\boldsymbol{e}\in\mathbb{Z}_q^k} \xi(\boldsymbol{e}) \cdot \chi_{\boldsymbol{a}}(\boldsymbol{e}) \right) \cdot \chi_{\boldsymbol{a}}(\boldsymbol{x}) \\
&= \mathop{\mathbb{E}}_{\boldsymbol{e}\sim\xi} [\chi_{\boldsymbol{a}}(\boldsymbol{e})] \cdot \chi_{\boldsymbol{a}}(\boldsymbol{x}) .
\end{aligned}$$

Note that the largest eigenvalue is $\mathbb{E}_{\boldsymbol{e}\sim\xi}[\chi_{\boldsymbol{a}}(\boldsymbol{e})] = 1$ given by $\boldsymbol{a} = \boldsymbol{0}^k$ because for any $\boldsymbol{e} \in \mathbb{Z}_q^k$, $\chi_{\boldsymbol{0}^k}(\boldsymbol{e}) = 1$ and $|\chi_{\boldsymbol{a}}(\boldsymbol{e})| \le 1$ if $\boldsymbol{a} \ne \boldsymbol{0}^k$. Hence, $\rho(\mu)$, which is the second largest eigenvalue of M_μ, is $\max_{\boldsymbol{a}\in\mathbb{Z}_q^k\setminus\{\boldsymbol{0}^k\}} \mathbb{E}_{\boldsymbol{e}\sim\xi}[\chi_{\boldsymbol{a}}(\boldsymbol{e})]$.

Proof (Proof of Lemma 2). Note that $\mu_{\mathcal{X}}$ is a Cayley distribution over $\mathbb{Z}_q \times \mathbb{Z}_q$ with associated noise distribution $\xi(z) = \Pr[\boldsymbol{x}_1^T \boldsymbol{e}_2 - \boldsymbol{e}_1^T \boldsymbol{x}_2 = z]$, where $\boldsymbol{e}_1, \boldsymbol{e}_2$ are drawn from $\mathcal{X}^n$ and $\boldsymbol{x}_1, \boldsymbol{x}_2$ are drawn from $(\mathcal{X}^n)^*$. First, $\xi(z) = \xi(-z)$ for any $z \in \mathbb{Z}_q$, since $\boldsymbol{x}_1^T \boldsymbol{e}_2$ and $\boldsymbol{e}_1^T \boldsymbol{x}_2$ are drawn from the same distribution, and so $\boldsymbol{x}_1^T \boldsymbol{e}_2 - \boldsymbol{e}_1^T \boldsymbol{x}_2$ is distributed identically to $\boldsymbol{e}_1^T \boldsymbol{x}_2 - \boldsymbol{x}_1^T \boldsymbol{e}_2$. Second, because $\boldsymbol{x}_1^T \boldsymbol{A} \boldsymbol{x}_2 + \boldsymbol{x}_1^T \boldsymbol{e}_2$ is distributed uniformly over $\mathbb{Z}_q$ and is independent from $\boldsymbol{x}_1^T \boldsymbol{e}_2 - \boldsymbol{e}_1^T \boldsymbol{x}_2$, we have that $\mu_{\mathcal{X}}(X,Y) = \Pr[\boldsymbol{x}_1^T \boldsymbol{A} \boldsymbol{x}_2 + \boldsymbol{x}_1^T \boldsymbol{e}_2 = X \textbf{ and } \boldsymbol{x}_1^T \boldsymbol{e}_2 - \boldsymbol{e}_1^T \boldsymbol{x}_2 = X - Y] = \frac{\xi(X-Y)}{q}$.

By Lemma 3, $\rho(\mu_{\mathcal{X}}) = \max_{a\in\mathbb{Z}_q\setminus\{0\}} \mathbb{E}_{e\sim\xi}[\chi_a(e)]$. Fix an arbitrary $a \in \mathbb{Z}_q\setminus\{0\}$, we need to show that $|\mathbb{E}_{e\sim\xi}[\chi_a(e)]| \le 1 - \Omega(1/q^2)$. This is implied by Claims 1 and 2 below.

Claim 1. $|\mathbb{E}_{e\sim\xi}[\chi_a(e)]| \le \max_{\boldsymbol{c}\in\mathbb{Z}_q^n\setminus\{\boldsymbol{0}^n\}} |\mathbb{E}_{\boldsymbol{e}\sim\mathcal{X}^n}[\chi_{\boldsymbol{c}}(\boldsymbol{e})]|$.

Proof. Note that

$$\begin{aligned}
|\mathop{\mathbb{E}}_{e\sim\xi}[\chi_a(e)]| &= \Big| \mathop{\mathbb{E}}_{\boldsymbol{x}_1,\boldsymbol{x}_2\sim(\mathcal{X}^n)^*} \Big[\mathop{\mathbb{E}}_{\boldsymbol{e}_1,\boldsymbol{e}_2\sim\mathcal{X}^n} [\chi_a(\boldsymbol{x}_1^T \boldsymbol{e}_2 - \boldsymbol{e}_1^T \boldsymbol{x}_2)] \Big] \Big| \\
&\le \mathop{\mathbb{E}}_{\boldsymbol{x}_1,\boldsymbol{x}_2\sim(\mathcal{X}^n)^*} \Big[\Big| \mathop{\mathbb{E}}_{\boldsymbol{e}_2\sim\mathcal{X}^n} [\chi_{a\boldsymbol{x}_1}(\boldsymbol{e}_2)] \cdot \mathop{\mathbb{E}}_{\boldsymbol{e}_1\sim\mathcal{X}^n} [\chi_{a\boldsymbol{x}_2}(-\boldsymbol{e}_1)] \Big| \Big] \\
&\le \mathop{\mathbb{E}}_{\boldsymbol{x}_1\sim(\mathcal{X}^n)^*} \Big[\Big| \mathop{\mathbb{E}}_{\boldsymbol{e}_2\sim\mathcal{X}^n} [\chi_{a\boldsymbol{x}_1}(\boldsymbol{e}_2)] \Big| \Big]
\end{aligned}$$

where the second line follows from triangle inequality and the independence of $\boldsymbol{e}_1$ and $\boldsymbol{e}_2$, the third line is because $\mathbb{E}_{\boldsymbol{e}_2\sim\mathcal{X}^n}[\chi_{a\boldsymbol{x}_1}(\boldsymbol{e}_2)]$ and $\mathbb{E}_{\boldsymbol{e}_1\sim\mathcal{X}^n}[\chi_{a\boldsymbol{x}_2}(-\boldsymbol{e}_1)]$ are reals of absolute value at most 1. Observe that for any fixed $\boldsymbol{x}_1$ from $(\mathcal{X}^n)^*$, $a\boldsymbol{x}_1 \ne \boldsymbol{0}^n$ so that $\left|\mathbb{E}_{\boldsymbol{e}_2\sim\mathcal{X}^n}[\chi_{a\boldsymbol{x}_1}(\boldsymbol{e}_2)]\right|$ is at most $\max_{\boldsymbol{c}\in\mathbb{Z}_q^n\setminus\{\boldsymbol{0}^n\}} |\mathbb{E}_{\boldsymbol{e}\sim\mathcal{X}^n}[\chi_{\boldsymbol{c}}(\boldsymbol{e})]|$ and the desired conclusion follows.

Claim 2. *For any* $\mathbf{c} \in \mathbb{Z}_q^n \setminus \{0^n\}$, $|\mathbb{E}_{e \sim \mathcal{X}^n}[\chi_{\mathbf{c}}(\mathbf{e})]| \leq 1 - \Omega(1/q^2)$.

Proof. Because each coordinate of $\mathbf{e}$ is drawn independently from $\mathcal{X}$,

$$\mathop{\mathbb{E}}_{e \sim \mathcal{X}^n}[\chi_{\mathbf{c}}(\mathbf{e})] = \prod_{i=1}^{n} \mathop{\mathbb{E}}_{z \sim \mathcal{X}}[\chi_{c_i}(z)].$$

Since $\mathcal{X}$ is symmetric, for any $i \in [n]$, $\mathbb{E}_{z \sim \mathcal{X}}[\chi_{c_i}(z)]$ is real with absolute value at most 1. Therefore, it suffices to show that $|\mathbb{E}_{z \sim \mathcal{X}}[\chi_{c_i}(z)]| \leq 1 - \Omega(1/q^2)$ for an arbitrary $i \in [n]$. Fix an $i \in [n]$ such that $c_i \neq 0$ and observe that

$$\mathop{\mathbb{E}}_{z \sim \mathcal{X}}[\chi_{c_i}(z)] \leq 1 - \Pr_{z \sim \mathcal{X}}[c_i z \neq 0] \cdot \Omega\left(\frac{1}{q^2}\right),$$

because if $c_i z \neq 0$, then the real part of $\chi_{c_i}(z)$ is at most $\cos(\frac{2\pi}{q}) \leq 1 - (1/q^2)$[7]. Similarly,

$$\mathop{\mathbb{E}}_{z \sim \mathcal{X}}[\chi_{c_i}(z)] \geq -1 + \Pr_{z \sim \mathcal{X}}[c_i z \neq q/2] \cdot \Omega\left(\frac{1}{q^2}\right)$$

holds because if $c_i z \neq q/2$, then the real part of $\chi_{c_i}(z)$ is at least $\cos(\pi + \frac{2\pi}{q}) \geq -1 + (1/q^2)$[8]. By our assumption on $\mathcal{X}$, we have that $\Pr_{z \sim \mathcal{X}}[c_i z \neq q/2] \geq 0.1$ and $\Pr_{z \sim \mathcal{X}}[c_i z \neq 0] \geq 0.1$. Hence, $|\mathbb{E}_{z \sim \mathcal{X}}[\chi_{c_i}(z)]| \leq 1 - \Omega(1/q^2)$ which concludes the proof.

For the interested reader, we provide a more self-contained proof in Appendix A which is equivalent to an unrolling of the above proof, but is much more succinct because we do not use the more general statement of Lemma 1 about maximal correlation. In Appendix A, we also give an extension of the proof to the case of Ring-LWE.

4 (Computational) Impossibility of Noise-Ignorant Key Reconciliation Functions

Let us set up some basic notation. For distributions $\mathcal{X}, \mathcal{Y}$ over G, we use $\mathrm{RD}_2(\mathcal{X}||\mathcal{Y}) = \mathbb{E}_{a \sim \mathcal{X}}[\Pr_{x \sim \mathcal{X}}[x = a] / \Pr_{y \sim \mathcal{Y}}[y = a]]$ to denote the powers of their Rényi divergence [vEH14]. We use $1 + \mathcal{X}$ to denote the distribution which samples x from $\mathcal{X}$ then outputs $1 + x$. And $\mathcal{X} + \mathcal{X}'$ is the distribution obtained as $x + x'$ for $x \sim \mathcal{X}$ and $x' \sim \mathcal{X}'$.

Theorem 3. *Let* $n \geq 1, q = \mathsf{poly}(n), m = \mathsf{poly}(n)$ *be integers and* $\mathcal{X}$ *be a noise distribution over* $\mathbb{Z}_q$ *such that* $\mathrm{RD}_2(1 + \mathcal{X}||\mathcal{X}) = 1 + \gamma$. *Let* $\mu_{\mathcal{X}}(\boldsymbol{X}, \boldsymbol{Y})$ *be the joint distribution of*

$$\boldsymbol{X} = (\boldsymbol{A}, \boldsymbol{x}_1, \boldsymbol{e}_1, \boldsymbol{b}_2) \text{ and } \boldsymbol{Y} = (\boldsymbol{A}, \boldsymbol{x}_2, \boldsymbol{b}_1),$$

[7] Because for $x \in [-\pi/2, \pi/2]$, $\cos(x) \leq 1 - x^2/(4\pi^2)$.

[8] Because for $x \in [-\pi/2, \pi/2]$, $\cos(\pi + x) \geq -1 + x^2/(4\pi^2)$.

where $\boldsymbol{A} \sim \mathcal{U}(\mathbb{Z}_q^{n\times n})$, $\boldsymbol{e}_1, \boldsymbol{e}_2 \sim \mathcal{X}^n$ *and* $\boldsymbol{x}_1, \boldsymbol{x}_2 \sim \mathcal{X}^n$, $\boldsymbol{b}_1 = \boldsymbol{x}_1^T\boldsymbol{A} + \boldsymbol{e}_1^T$ *and* $\boldsymbol{b}_2 = \boldsymbol{A}\boldsymbol{x}_2 + \boldsymbol{e}_2$.

Suppose that f *and* g *are efficiently computable boolean functions that reach key agreement with error at most* ε. *The domains of* Rec_1 *and* Rec_2 *are the support of the marginal distributions* $\mu_{\boldsymbol{X}}^{\otimes m}$ *and* $\mu_{\boldsymbol{Y}}^{\otimes m}$ *respectively. Then,* m *independent samples of* $(\boldsymbol{A}, \boldsymbol{b}_2)$ *can be efficiently distinguished from* m *independent samples* $(\boldsymbol{A}, \boldsymbol{u})$ *where* $\boldsymbol{u} \sim \mathcal{U}(\mathbb{Z}_q^n)$ *with advantage at least* $\Omega(1/q^4 m\gamma) - O(\sqrt{\varepsilon})$.

Our theorem also holds for the ring case. This theorem implies that as long as $\mathrm{RD}_2(1+\mathcal{X}||\mathcal{X})$ is polynomial in n and one party's key reconciliation function does not depend on its noise, then (ring) LWE samples (associated with error $\mathcal{X}$) are not pseudorandom. The condition of $\mathrm{RD}_2(1+\mathcal{X}||\mathcal{X})$ captures a large class of noise distributions including the discrete Gaussian distribution[9].

Let $\mathcal{X}'$ over $\mathbb{Z}_q$ be the distribution that outputs 1 with probability $\alpha = \sqrt{1/m\gamma}$ and outputs 0 otherwise. Let $\mathcal{Z} = \mathcal{U}(\mathbb{Z}_q)^{n\times n} \times \mathcal{X}^n \times \mathcal{X}^n$. Theorem 3 follows from the next two lemmas.

Lemma 4. *Let* $\{\mathbf{U}_i\}_{i=1}^m \sim \mathcal{Z}^{\otimes m}$, $\{\boldsymbol{u}_i\}_{i=1}^m, \sim \mathcal{U}(\mathbb{Z}_q^n)^{\otimes m}$, $\{\boldsymbol{u}_i'\}_{i=1}^m \sim \mathcal{U}(\mathbb{Z}_q^n)^{\otimes m}$ *and* $\{\boldsymbol{w}_i\}_{i=1}^m \sim (\mathcal{X}'^n)^{\otimes m}$. *Then,*

$$\begin{aligned}&\Pr[f(\{\mathbf{U}_i, \boldsymbol{u}_i\}_{i=1}^m) \neq f(\{\mathbf{U}_i, \boldsymbol{u}_i'\}_{i=1}^m)] \\ \leq\ &\Pr[f(\{\mathbf{U}_i, \boldsymbol{u}_i\}_{i=1}^m) \neq f(\{\mathbf{U}_i, \boldsymbol{u}_i + \boldsymbol{w}_i\}_{i=1}^m)] \cdot O\left(q^2\sqrt{m\gamma}\right).\end{aligned}$$

Lemma 5. *Let* $\boldsymbol{b}_i = \boldsymbol{A}_i\boldsymbol{x}_i + \boldsymbol{e}_i$ *and* $\boldsymbol{b}_i' = \boldsymbol{A}_i\boldsymbol{x}_i' + \boldsymbol{e}_i'$, *where* $\{\boldsymbol{A}_i\}_{i=1}^m \sim \mathcal{U}(\mathbb{Z}_q^{n\times n})^{\otimes m}$ *and* $\{\boldsymbol{x}_i\}_{i=1}^m, \{\boldsymbol{e}_i\}_{i=1}^m, \{\boldsymbol{x}_i'\}_{i=1}^m, \{\boldsymbol{e}_i'\}_{i=1}^m \sim (\mathcal{X}^n)^{\otimes m}$ *and let* $\{\boldsymbol{y}_i\}_{i=1}^m \sim (\mathcal{X}^n)^{\otimes 2}$, $\{\boldsymbol{w}_i\}_{i=1}^m \sim (\mathcal{X}'^n)^{\otimes m}$. *It holds that*

$$\Pr[f(\{\boldsymbol{A}_i, \boldsymbol{y}_i, \boldsymbol{b}_i\}_{i=1}^m) \neq f(\{\boldsymbol{A}_i, \boldsymbol{y}_i, \boldsymbol{b}_i'\}_{i=1}^m)] \geq 1/2 - 2\varepsilon, \tag{3}$$

and

$$\Pr[f(\{\boldsymbol{A}_i, \boldsymbol{y}_i, \boldsymbol{b}_i + \boldsymbol{w}_i\}_{i=1}^m) \neq f(\{\boldsymbol{A}_i, \boldsymbol{y}_i, \boldsymbol{b}_i\}_{i=1}^m)] \leq O(\sqrt{\varepsilon}). \tag{4}$$

We first prove Theorem 3 using Lemmas 4 and 5. In the rest of this section, we prove Lemmas 4 and 5. Lemma 4 is based on Fourier analysis and works for any boolean function f. Lemma 5 relies on the assumption that f, g are efficient key reconciliation functions and g does not depend on its noise.

4.1 Proof of Theorem 3

Let f and g be key reconciliation functions satisfying the conditions of Theorem 3. We wish to distinguish between m i.i.d. samples $\{(\boldsymbol{A}_i, \boldsymbol{b}_i)\}_{i=1}^m$ from m i.i.d. samples $\{(\boldsymbol{A}_i, \boldsymbol{u}_i)\}_{i=1}^m$.

[9] In particular, Bogdanov et al. [BGM+16] showed that $\mathrm{RD}_2(1 + \mathcal{D}_\sigma||\mathcal{D}_\sigma) \leq \exp(2\pi(1/\sigma)^2)$ is at most a constant for any discrete Gaussian distribution $\mathcal{D}_\sigma$ with standard deviation $\sigma \geq 1$.

First, note that if

$$|\Pr[f(\{\boldsymbol{A}_i, \boldsymbol{x}_i, \boldsymbol{e}_i, \boldsymbol{u}_i\}_{i=1}^m) = 0] - \Pr[f(\{\boldsymbol{A}_i, \boldsymbol{x}_i, \boldsymbol{e}_i, \boldsymbol{b}_i\}_{i=1}^m) = 0]| \geq \alpha/q^2,$$

where $\{\boldsymbol{x}_i\}_{i=1}^m, \{\boldsymbol{e}_i\}_{i=1}^m \sim (\mathcal{X}^n)^{\otimes m}$, there exists a polynomial time distinguisher, since $\boldsymbol{x}_i$ and $\boldsymbol{e}_i$ are efficiently sampleable.

Otherwise, from Eq. (3) of Lemma 5, we have that

$$\Pr[f(\{\boldsymbol{A}_i, \boldsymbol{x}_i, \boldsymbol{e}_i, \boldsymbol{u}_i\}_{i=1}^m) \neq f(\{\boldsymbol{A}_i, \boldsymbol{x}_i, \boldsymbol{e}_i, \boldsymbol{u}'_i\}_{i=1}^m)] \geq 2\varepsilon + 2\alpha/q^2,$$

where $\boldsymbol{u}'_i \sim \mathcal{U}(\mathbb{Z}_q^n)$. Combining this with Lemma 4, we get that

$$\Pr[f(\{\boldsymbol{A}_i, \boldsymbol{x}_i, \boldsymbol{e}_i, \boldsymbol{u}_i\}_{i=1}^m) \neq f\{\boldsymbol{A}_i, \boldsymbol{x}_i, \boldsymbol{e}_i, \boldsymbol{u}_i + \boldsymbol{w}_i\}_{i=1}^m)] \geq \Omega\left(\frac{\alpha^2}{q^4} + \frac{\alpha\varepsilon}{q^2}\right),$$

where $\boldsymbol{w}_i \sim \mathcal{X}'^n$. But, from Eq. (4) of Lemma 5, we have that

$$\Pr[f(\{\boldsymbol{A}_i, \boldsymbol{x}_i, \boldsymbol{e}_i, \boldsymbol{b}_i\}_{i=1}^m) \neq f(\{\boldsymbol{A}_i, \boldsymbol{x}_i, \boldsymbol{e}_i, \boldsymbol{b}_i + \boldsymbol{w}_i\}_{i=1}^m)] \leq O(\sqrt{\varepsilon})$$

Thus, we distinguish between m i.i.d. samples $\{(\boldsymbol{A}_i, \boldsymbol{u}_i)\}_{i=1}^m$ and $\{(\boldsymbol{A}_i, \boldsymbol{b}_i)\}_{i=1}^m$ by computing $\Pr[f(\{\boldsymbol{A}_i, \boldsymbol{x}_i, \boldsymbol{e}_i, \boldsymbol{y}_i\}_{i=1}^m) \neq f(\{\boldsymbol{A}_i, \boldsymbol{x}_i, \boldsymbol{e}_i, \boldsymbol{y}_i + \boldsymbol{w}_i\}_{i=1}^m)]$, where $\{\boldsymbol{y}_i\}_{i=1}^m$ are the challenge samples. This gives us an advantage of $\Omega(\alpha^2/q^4) - O(\sqrt{\varepsilon})$.

4.2 Proof of Lemma 4

Let $\mathsf{Re}(z)$ denote the real part of any $z \in \mathbb{C}$. We fix $\{\mathbf{U}_i\}_{i=1}^m$ and for any $\boldsymbol{u} = \{\boldsymbol{u}_i\}_{i=1}^m \in (\mathbb{Z}_q^n)^{\otimes m}$, let $F(\boldsymbol{u}) = (-1)^{f(\{(\mathbf{U}_i, \boldsymbol{u}_i)\}_{i=1}^m)}$, then

$$\Pr\left[f(\{(\mathbf{U}_i, \boldsymbol{u}_i + \boldsymbol{w}_i)\}_{i=1}^m) \neq f(\{(\mathbf{U}_i, \boldsymbol{u}_i)\}_{i=1}^m))\right] = \frac{1 - \mathbb{E}[F(\boldsymbol{u})F(\boldsymbol{u} + \boldsymbol{w})]}{2},$$

where $\boldsymbol{u} \sim \mathcal{U}(\mathbb{Z}_q^n)^{\otimes m}, \boldsymbol{w} \sim (\mathcal{X}'^n)^{\otimes m}$ and $\boldsymbol{w} = \{\boldsymbol{w}_i\}_{i=1}^m$.

For any $\boldsymbol{c} \in (\mathbb{Z}_q^n)^m$, let $\widehat{F}(\boldsymbol{c}) = \mathbb{E}_{\boldsymbol{u} \sim \mathcal{U}(\mathbb{Z}_q^n)^{\otimes m}}[F(\boldsymbol{u})\chi_{\boldsymbol{c}}(-\boldsymbol{u})]$. Note that for any $\boldsymbol{u} \in (\mathbb{Z}_q^n)^m$, $F(\boldsymbol{u}) = \sum_{\boldsymbol{c} \in (\mathbb{Z}_q^n)^m} \widehat{F}(\boldsymbol{c})\chi_{\boldsymbol{c}}(\boldsymbol{u})$. Finally, because F is real, $\mathbb{E}[F(\boldsymbol{u})F(\boldsymbol{u} + \boldsymbol{w})] = \mathbb{E}[\overline{F(\boldsymbol{u})}F(\boldsymbol{u} + \boldsymbol{w})]$.

$$
\begin{aligned}
&\mathbb{E}[\overline{F(\boldsymbol{u})}F(\boldsymbol{u} + \boldsymbol{w})] \\
&= \left|\widehat{F}(\boldsymbol{0}^{nm})\right|^2 + \sum_{\boldsymbol{c} \in (\mathbb{Z}_q^n)^m \setminus \{\boldsymbol{0}^{nm}\}} \left|\widehat{F}(\boldsymbol{c})\right|^2 \mathbb{E}[\chi_{\boldsymbol{c}}(\boldsymbol{w})] \\
&= \left|\widehat{F}(\boldsymbol{0}^{nm})\right|^2 + \sum_{\boldsymbol{c} \in (\mathbb{Z}_q^n)^m \setminus \{\boldsymbol{0}^{nm}\}} \left|\widehat{F}(\boldsymbol{c})\right|^2 \mathbb{E}[\mathsf{Re}(\chi_{\boldsymbol{c}}(\boldsymbol{w}))] \\
&\leq \left|\widehat{F}(\boldsymbol{0}^{nm})\right|^2 + \left(\max_{\boldsymbol{c} \in (\mathbb{Z}_q^n)^m \setminus \{\boldsymbol{0}^{nm}\}} \mathbb{E}[\mathsf{Re}(\chi_{\boldsymbol{c}}(\boldsymbol{w}))]\right)\left(\sum_{\boldsymbol{c} \in (\mathbb{Z}_q^n)^m \setminus \{\boldsymbol{0}^{nm}\}} \left|\widehat{F}(\boldsymbol{c})\right|^2\right) \\
&\leq \left|\widehat{F}(\boldsymbol{0}^{nm})\right|^2 + \left(\max_{\boldsymbol{c} \in (\mathbb{Z}_q^n)^m \setminus \{\boldsymbol{0}^{nm}\}} \mathbb{E}[\mathsf{Re}(\chi_{\boldsymbol{c}}(\boldsymbol{w}))]\right)\left(1 - \left|\widehat{F}(\boldsymbol{0}^{nm})\right|^2\right)
\end{aligned}
$$

where the first line is by expanding F using its Fourier representation and linearity of expectation, the second line is because $\mathbb{E}[\overline{F(\boldsymbol{u})}F(\boldsymbol{u}+\boldsymbol{w})]$ is real, and the last line uses Parseval's identity, which states that $\sum_{\boldsymbol{c}} \left|\widehat{F}(\boldsymbol{c})\right|^2 = \mathbb{E}\left[|F(\boldsymbol{u})|^2\right] = 1$.

Similarly to the analysis of Claim 2, $\max_{\boldsymbol{c}\in(\mathbb{Z}_q^n)^m\setminus\{\boldsymbol{0}^{nm}\}} \mathbb{E}[\mathsf{Re}(\chi_{\boldsymbol{c}}(\boldsymbol{w}))] \leq 1 - \Omega(\alpha/q^2)$, because for any $\boldsymbol{c} \neq \boldsymbol{0}^{nm}$, $\Pr[\boldsymbol{c}^T\boldsymbol{w} \neq 0] \geq \alpha$ and $\mathsf{Re}(\chi_{\boldsymbol{c}}(\boldsymbol{w})) \leq 1 - \Omega(1/q^2)$ whenever $\boldsymbol{c}^T\boldsymbol{w} \neq 0$. Therefore,

$$\begin{aligned}&\Pr_{\boldsymbol{u}\sim\mathcal{U}(\mathbb{Z}_q^n)^{\otimes m},\boldsymbol{w}\sim(\mathcal{X}'^n)^m}[f(\{(\mathbf{U}_i,\boldsymbol{u}_i+\boldsymbol{w}_i)\}_{i=1}^m) \neq f(\{(\mathbf{U}_i,\boldsymbol{u}_i)\}_{i=1}^m))]\\ &\geq \Omega(\alpha/q^2)\frac{1-\left|\widehat{F}(\boldsymbol{0}^{nm})\right|^2}{2}.\end{aligned}$$

Since $\Pr_{\boldsymbol{u},\boldsymbol{u}'\sim\mathcal{U}(\mathbb{Z}_q^n)^{\otimes m}}[f(\{(\mathbf{U}_i,\boldsymbol{u}_i)\}_{i=1}^m) \neq f(\{(\mathbf{U}_i,\boldsymbol{u}'_i)\}_{i=1}^m))] = \frac{1-|\widehat{F}(\boldsymbol{0}^{nm})|^2}{2}$, the lemma follows by averaging over $\{\mathbf{U}_i\}_{i=1}^m$.

4.3 Proof of Lemma 5

Let $\{\boldsymbol{y}_i\}_{i=1}^m = \{(\boldsymbol{x}''_i,\boldsymbol{e}''_i)\}_{i=1}^m$, $\boldsymbol{b}''_i = \boldsymbol{A}_i\boldsymbol{x}''_i + \boldsymbol{e}''_i$ and suppose Eq. (3) is not true, then together with the correctness condition, it holds that

$$\Pr[g(\{(\boldsymbol{A}_i,\boldsymbol{x}'_i,\boldsymbol{b}''_i)\}_{i=1}^m) = f(\{(\boldsymbol{A}_i,\boldsymbol{x}''_i,\boldsymbol{e}''_i,\boldsymbol{b}'_i)\}_{i=1}^m)] > 1/2+\varepsilon,$$

which breaks the soundness condition because an adversary can sample fresh $\{\boldsymbol{x}'_i\}_{i=1}^m \sim (\mathcal{X}^n)^{\otimes m}$ and compute $g(\{(\boldsymbol{A}_i,\boldsymbol{x}'_i,\boldsymbol{b}''_i)\}_{i=1}^m)$.
To prove Eq. (4), we first show the following two claims

Claim.

$$\begin{aligned}&\Pr[f(\{(\boldsymbol{A}_i,\boldsymbol{x}''_i,\boldsymbol{e}''_i,\boldsymbol{b}_i+\boldsymbol{w}_i)\}_{i=1}^m) \neq g(\{(\boldsymbol{A}_i,\boldsymbol{x}_i,\boldsymbol{b}''_i)\}_{i=1}^m))]\\ &\leq \sqrt{\varepsilon\cdot \mathrm{RD}_2^m(\mathcal{X}+\mathcal{X}'||\mathcal{X})}.\end{aligned}$$

Proof. We rely on two elementary properties of Rényi divergence: for any two distributions $\boldsymbol{X}$ and $\boldsymbol{Y}$ and any event E, $(\Pr[\boldsymbol{X}\in E])^2 \leq \Pr[\boldsymbol{Y}\in E]\cdot\mathrm{RD}_2(\boldsymbol{X}||\boldsymbol{Y})$, and for any m, $\mathrm{RD}_2(\boldsymbol{X}^m||\boldsymbol{Y}^m) = (\mathrm{RD}_2(\boldsymbol{X}||\boldsymbol{Y}))^m$. For any fixed choice of $\{(\boldsymbol{A}_i,\boldsymbol{x}''_i,\boldsymbol{e}''_i,\boldsymbol{x}_i)\}_{i=1}^m$, let E be the event that f disagrees with g. Then, by the properties of Rényi divergence,

$$\begin{aligned}&(\Pr[f(\{(\boldsymbol{A}_i,\boldsymbol{x}''_i,\boldsymbol{e}''_i,\boldsymbol{b}_i+\boldsymbol{w}_i)\}_{i=1}^m) \neq g(\{(\boldsymbol{A}_i,\boldsymbol{x}_i,\boldsymbol{b}''_i)\}_{i=1}^m)])^2\\ &\leq \Pr[f(\{(\boldsymbol{A}_i,\boldsymbol{x}''_i,\boldsymbol{e}''_i,\boldsymbol{b}_i)\}_{i=1}^m) \neq g(\{(\boldsymbol{A}_i,\boldsymbol{x}_i,\boldsymbol{b}''_i)\}_{i=1}^m)]\cdot\mathrm{RD}_2((\mathcal{X}+\mathcal{X}')^{\otimes m}||(\mathcal{X})^{\otimes m})\\ &= \Pr[f(\{(\boldsymbol{A}_i,\boldsymbol{x}''_i,\boldsymbol{e}''_i,\boldsymbol{b}_i)\}_{i=1}^m) \neq g(\{(\boldsymbol{A}_i,\boldsymbol{x}_i,\boldsymbol{b}''_i)\}_{i=1}^m)]\cdot(\mathrm{RD}_2(\mathcal{X}+\mathcal{X}'||\mathcal{X}))^m.\end{aligned}$$

The desired conclusion follows by averaging over $\{(\boldsymbol{A}_i,\boldsymbol{x}''_i,\boldsymbol{e}''_i,\boldsymbol{x}_i)\}_{i=1}^m$ and the fact that for any random variable z, $(\mathbb{E}[z])^2 \leq \mathbb{E}[z^2]$.

Claim. $\mathrm{RD}_2(\mathcal{X}+\mathcal{X}'||\mathcal{X}) = 1+\alpha^2\gamma$

Proof. By the definition of RD_2 and $\mathcal{X}'$,

$$\begin{aligned}
&\mathrm{RD}_2(\mathcal{X} + \mathcal{X}' \| \mathcal{X}) \\
&= \sum_{a \in G} \frac{((1-\alpha)\Pr_{X\sim\mathcal{X}}[X=a] + \alpha \Pr_{X\sim\mathcal{X}}[X+1=a])^2}{\Pr_{X\sim\mathcal{X}}[X=a]} \\
&= (1-\alpha)^2 + 2(1-\alpha)\alpha + \alpha^2 \mathrm{RD}_2(\mathcal{X}+1\|\mathcal{X}) \\
&= 1 + \alpha^2(\mathrm{RD}_2(\mathcal{X}+1\|\mathcal{X}) - 1).
\end{aligned}$$

From the correctness condition, which is

$$\Pr[f(\{(\boldsymbol{A}_i, \boldsymbol{x}_i'', \boldsymbol{e}_i'', \boldsymbol{b}_i)\}_{i=1}^m) \neq g(\{(\boldsymbol{A}_i, \boldsymbol{x}_i, \boldsymbol{b}_i'')\}_{i=1}^m)] \le \varepsilon$$

and the above two claims and union bound,

$$\begin{aligned}
&\Pr[f(\{(\boldsymbol{A}_i, \boldsymbol{x}_i'', \boldsymbol{e}_i'', \boldsymbol{b}_i + \boldsymbol{w}_i)\}_{i=1}^m) \neq f(\{(\boldsymbol{A}_i, \boldsymbol{x}_i'', \boldsymbol{e}_i'', \boldsymbol{b}_i)\}_{i=1}^m)] \\
&\le \varepsilon + \sqrt{\varepsilon(1+\alpha^2\gamma)^m}.
\end{aligned}$$

The Eq. (4) follows from our choice of $\alpha = \sqrt{1/m\gamma}$.

5 Connections to Other Cryptographic Primitives

Thus far, our results focused on specific classes of reconciliation functions showing that they are not powerful enough to give NIKE in our framework. Extending our previous results either on the positive or negative direction hits barriers. The positive direction, which is to propose a NIKE protocol that avoids our impossibility results implies cryptographic constructions still unknown from polynomial modulus LWE. In particular, a positive result would imply direct constructions of special structured weak pseudorandom functions from polynomial modulus LWE. The negative direction, which is to prove a completely general impossibility result, is ruled out if iO exists.

5.1 From iO to NIKE

Even though our results show that there are many limitations in building practical NIKE from polynomial modulus LWE, assuming indistinguishability obfuscation (iO) constructing NIKE is, at least theoretically, possible. Therefore, unless there are breakthrough advancements that rule out the possibility of construction iO, showing a general impossibility of NIKE is out of range. In this section, we sketch the iO-based construction of NIKE of Boneh and Zhandry [BZ17] and explain why it can be implemented in our framework.

Theorem 4 ([BZ17]). *Assuming a secure pseudorandom generator, a secure punctured pseudorandom function family and a secure indistinguishability obfuscator, there exists a secure* NIKE.

Additionally to the matrix $\boldsymbol{A}$, in this protocol the parties share the following *obfuscated* program:

Inputs: $\boldsymbol{b}_1, \boldsymbol{b}_2 \in \mathcal{X}, s_1, s_2 \in \mathcal{S}$
Constants: PRF
If $\boldsymbol{b}_1 = \text{PRG}(s_1)$, output $\text{PRF}(\boldsymbol{b}_1, \boldsymbol{b}_2)$.
If $\boldsymbol{b}_2 = \text{PRG}(s_2)$, output $\text{PRF}(\boldsymbol{b}_1, \boldsymbol{b}_2)$.
Otherwise, output $\perp$.

During the protocol, the parties exchange LWE samples $\boldsymbol{b}_1, \boldsymbol{b}_2$, evaluate the obfuscated program with $s_1 = (\boldsymbol{x}_1, \boldsymbol{e}_1)$ and $s_2 = (\boldsymbol{x}_2, \boldsymbol{e}_2)$ and set as their shared key the output of the obfuscated program. The LWE samples are computed from a function of the form $G_{\mathbf{M}}(\boldsymbol{x}, \boldsymbol{e}) = \mathbf{M}\boldsymbol{x} + \boldsymbol{e}$, where $\mathbf{M} \in \mathbb{Z}_q^{n \times n}$ and $\boldsymbol{x}, \boldsymbol{e}$ are sampled from a noise distribution. Directly using the LWE assumptions, which states that the output of G is indistinguishable from uniform and the fact that G is expanding, we conclude that G is a PRG. Combining this observation with the known constructions of punctured PRFs from any one-way function, we conclude that there exists a NIKE protocol assuming iO and polynomial modulus LWE.

5.2 From NIKE to Weak-PRFs

In this section, we show that reconciliation functions have to be *weak-pseudorandom functions*. A weak-pseudorandom function (weak-PRF) is an efficient function family that is indistinguishable from a random function when we have access only on random evaluations of the function. We focus on the case of boolean weak-pseudorandom functions. Formally:

Definition 8. *Let $\lambda > 0$ be a security parameter. An efficient function family ensemble $\mathcal{F} = \{\mathcal{F}_\lambda : \{0,1\}^{k(\lambda)} \to \{0,1\}\}$ is called weak-pseudorandom function family if for every probabilistic polynomial-time algorithm $\mathcal{A}$:*

$$\Pr_{f,x}[\mathcal{A}^{\mathcal{O}_f}(x) = f(x)] \leq 1/2 + \mathsf{negl}(\lambda),$$

where f is sampled uniformly at random from $\mathcal{F}_\lambda$ and $x \sim U(\{0,1\}^{k(\lambda)})$. Every query to the oracle $\mathcal{O}$ is answered with a tuple of the form $(u, f(u))$, where $u \sim \mathcal{U}(\{0,1\}^{k(\lambda)})$. We call $\left|\Pr_{f,x}[\mathcal{A}^{\mathcal{O}_f}(x) = f(x)] - 1/2\right|$ the success probability of $\mathcal{A}$.

The main theorem of this section shows that the reconciliation functions have to be sampled from a weak-PRF family.

Theorem 5. *Let $\lambda > 0$ be a security parameter and let $f(\boldsymbol{A}, \boldsymbol{x}_1, \boldsymbol{e}_1, \boldsymbol{b}_2)$ and $g(\boldsymbol{A}, \boldsymbol{x}_2, \boldsymbol{e}_2, \boldsymbol{b}_1)$ be efficient functions such that:*

- $\Pr[f(\boldsymbol{A}, \boldsymbol{x}_1, \boldsymbol{e}_1, \boldsymbol{b}_2) = g(\boldsymbol{A}, \boldsymbol{x}_2, \boldsymbol{e}_2, \boldsymbol{b}_1)] \geq 1 - \mathsf{negl}(\lambda)$
- *For every efficient probabilistic polynomial-time algorithm $\mathcal{D}$ with input $(\boldsymbol{A}, \boldsymbol{b}_1, \boldsymbol{b}_2)$:*

$$\Pr[\mathcal{D}(\boldsymbol{A}, \boldsymbol{b}_1, \boldsymbol{b}_2) = f(\boldsymbol{A}, \boldsymbol{x}_1, \boldsymbol{e}_1, \boldsymbol{b}_2)] \leq 1/2 + \mathsf{negl}(\lambda),$$

then assuming the LWE *assumption, the function families* $\mathcal{F} = \{F_{\boldsymbol{A},\boldsymbol{x}_1,\boldsymbol{e}_1} : \mathbb{Z}_q^n \to \{0,1\}\}$, *where* $F_{\boldsymbol{A},\boldsymbol{x}_1,\boldsymbol{e}_1}(\cdot) = f(\boldsymbol{A}, \boldsymbol{x}_1, \boldsymbol{e}_1, \cdot)$ *and* $\mathcal{G} = \{G_{\boldsymbol{A},\boldsymbol{x}_2,\boldsymbol{e}_2} : \mathbb{Z}_q^n \to \{0,1\}\}$, *where* $G_{\boldsymbol{A},\boldsymbol{x}_2,\boldsymbol{e}_2}(\cdot) = g(\boldsymbol{A}, \boldsymbol{x}_2, \boldsymbol{e}_2, \cdot)$ *are weak-PRF families.*

Even though we formally prove that the reconciliation functions should be pseudorandom with access to random evaluations of the functions, they have to satisfy a stronger pseudorandomness property: they should remain pseudorandom even with access to evaluations of *adversarially chosen* LWE samples. Also, our result directly generalizes to the case of *multiple* LWE samples. In fact, the above theorem can be extended to show that in a NIKE protocol where the exchanged messages are indistinguishable from uniform, reconciliation functions have to be sampled from a weak-PRF function family.

Although (weak-)PRFs are equivalent to one-way function [GGM86], the known generic constructions are highly inefficient and unstructured. Constructions of (weak-)PRFs from LWE are only known for superpolynomial modulus [BPR12,BP14] and finding a direct construction based on polynomial modulus is a very interesting open problem in the study of pseudorandom functions [BR17]. We emphasize that even though pseudorandomness is a necessary condition for a reconciliation function and identifies a barrier in building NIKE from LWE, it is definitely not sufficient. Reconciliation functions are very structured as the computation of the common key should be allowed in at least two ways, one for Alice and one for Bob.

Proof. We show that $\mathcal{F}$ is a weak-PRF family and the same analysis holds for $\mathcal{G}$. Assume that there exists a distinguisher $\mathcal{A}$ for $\mathcal{F}$ with success probability α; we use $\mathcal{A}$ to break the soundness of the NIKE protocol.

From the correctness condition of NIKE,

$$\Pr[F_{\boldsymbol{A},\boldsymbol{x}_1,\boldsymbol{e}_1}(\boldsymbol{b}_2) = g(\boldsymbol{A}, \boldsymbol{x}_2, \boldsymbol{e}_2, \boldsymbol{b}_1)] \geq 1 - \mathsf{negl}(\lambda).$$

Hence, with high probability we get evaluations of $F_{\boldsymbol{A},\boldsymbol{x}_1,\boldsymbol{e}_1}$ by sampling LWE secret and noise $\boldsymbol{x}_2, \boldsymbol{e}_2$ and computing $g(\boldsymbol{A}, \boldsymbol{x}_2, \boldsymbol{e}_2, \boldsymbol{b}_1)$. Additionally, the LWE assumption implies that these evaluations of F are computationally indistinguishable from uniform evaluations, as required by the definition of weak-PRFs. An adversary $\mathcal{D}$ that breaks the soundness condition of NIKE runs as follows:

- Run the distinguisher $\mathcal{A}$, where instead of uniform evaluations compute evaluations using LWE samples and g as above.
- Use as the challenge query $\boldsymbol{b}_2$.
- Return the output of $\mathcal{A}$.

Let us denote by $\mathcal{E}$ the event that $F_{\boldsymbol{A},\boldsymbol{x}_1,\boldsymbol{e}_1}(\boldsymbol{b}_2) = g(\boldsymbol{A}, \boldsymbol{x}_2, \boldsymbol{e}_2, \boldsymbol{b}_1)$, the success probability of $\mathcal{D}$ is equal to

$$\begin{aligned}
&\Pr[\mathcal{D}(\boldsymbol{A}, \boldsymbol{b}_1, \boldsymbol{b}_2) = F_{\boldsymbol{A},\boldsymbol{x}_1,\boldsymbol{e}_1}(\boldsymbol{b}_2)] \\
&\geq \Pr[\mathcal{D}(\boldsymbol{A}, \boldsymbol{b}_1, \boldsymbol{b}_2) = F_{\boldsymbol{A},\boldsymbol{x}_1,\boldsymbol{e}_1}(\boldsymbol{b}_2)|\mathcal{E}] \Pr[\mathcal{E}] \\
&= \Pr[\mathcal{A}(\boldsymbol{b}_2) = F_{\boldsymbol{A},\boldsymbol{x}_1,\boldsymbol{e}_1}(\boldsymbol{b}_2)] \Pr[\mathcal{E}] \\
&\geq 1/2 + \alpha - \mathsf{negl}(\lambda).
\end{aligned}$$

Hence if $\mathcal{A}$ breaks $\mathcal{F}$, then D breaks the soundness condition of NIKE.

Acknowledgements. The authors thank Martin Albrecht, Jacob Alperin-Sheriff, Leo Ducas and anonymous reviewers for useful comments and advice.

A A Self-contained Proof of Theorem 1

In Sect. 3, we use two lemmas (Lemmas 1 and 3) in order to bound the key agreement probability by $\max_{c\in\mathbb{Z}_q\setminus\{0\}} |\mathbb{E}_{e\sim\xi}[\chi_c(e)]$. In this section, we give a self-contained proof for Lemma 2 without explicitly using the notion of maximal correlation. However, this proof is essentially an unrolling of the proof using maximal correlation.

Claim 3. *For any $m \geq 1$, and balanced $f, g : \mathbb{Z}_q^m \to \{0,1\}$, it holds that*

$$\Pr[f(\boldsymbol{X}) = g(\boldsymbol{Y})] \leq \frac{1 + \max_{c\in\mathbb{Z}_q\setminus\{0\}} |\mathbb{E}_{e\sim\xi}[\chi_c(e)]|}{2}$$

where for any $z \in \mathbb{Z}_q$, $\xi(z) = \Pr[\boldsymbol{x}_1^T\boldsymbol{e}_2 - \boldsymbol{e}_1^T\boldsymbol{x}_2 = z]$.

Combining the above claim with the fact that $\max_{c\in\mathbb{Z}_q\setminus\{0\}} |\mathbb{E}_{e\sim\xi}[\chi_c(e)]| \leq 1 - \Omega(1/q^2)$ (see Claims 1 and 2), Theorem 1 follows.

Proof. Let $F(\boldsymbol{x}) = (-1)^{f(\boldsymbol{x})}$ and $G(\boldsymbol{x}) = (-1)^{g(\boldsymbol{x})}$. For any $\boldsymbol{c} \in \mathbb{Z}_q^m$, let $\hat{F}(\boldsymbol{c}) = \mathbb{E}_{\boldsymbol{x}\sim\mathcal{U}(\mathbb{Z}_q^m)}[F(\boldsymbol{x})\chi_{\boldsymbol{c}}(-\boldsymbol{x})]$ and $\hat{G}(\boldsymbol{c}) = \mathbb{E}_{\boldsymbol{x}\sim\mathcal{U}(\mathbb{Z}_q^m)}[G(\boldsymbol{x})\chi_{\boldsymbol{c}}(-\boldsymbol{x})]$. Note that for any $\boldsymbol{x} \in \mathbb{Z}_q^m$, $F(\boldsymbol{x}) = \sum_{\boldsymbol{c}\in\mathbb{Z}_q^m} \hat{F}(\boldsymbol{c})\chi_{\boldsymbol{c}}(\boldsymbol{x})$ and $G(\boldsymbol{x}) = \sum_{\boldsymbol{c}\in\mathbb{Z}_q^m} \hat{G}(\boldsymbol{c})\chi_{\boldsymbol{c}}(\boldsymbol{x})$. Observe that $\boldsymbol{X}$ is distributed uniformly and $\boldsymbol{Y} = \boldsymbol{X} + \boldsymbol{e}$.

$$\begin{aligned}
&|\mathbb{E}[\overline{F(\boldsymbol{X})}G(\boldsymbol{X}+\boldsymbol{e})]| \\
&= \left|\sum_{c\in\mathbb{Z}_q^m\setminus\{0^m\}} \hat{F}(\boldsymbol{c})\hat{G}(\boldsymbol{c})\mathbb{E}[\chi_{\boldsymbol{c}}(\boldsymbol{e})]\right| \\
&\leq \sqrt{\sum_{c\in\mathbb{Z}_q^m\setminus\{0^m\}} |\hat{F}(\boldsymbol{c})|^2 \sum_{c\neq 0^m} |\hat{G}(\boldsymbol{c})|^2}\, \max_{c\neq 0^m} |\mathbb{E}[\chi_{\boldsymbol{c}}(\boldsymbol{e})]| \\
&\leq \max_{c\in\mathbb{Z}_q^m\setminus\{0^m\}} |\mathbb{E}[\chi_{\boldsymbol{c}}(\boldsymbol{e})]| \\
&\leq \max_{c\in\mathbb{Z}_q\setminus\{0\}} |\mathbb{E}[\chi_c(\boldsymbol{e}_i)]|,
\end{aligned}$$

where $\boldsymbol{e} = (\boldsymbol{e}_1, \ldots, \boldsymbol{e}_m)$. The first equality follows by linearity of expectation and the fact that $\boldsymbol{X}$ is uniform over $\mathbb{Z}_q^m$. For the next inequality, we use triangle inequality and that $|\mathbb{E}[\chi_{\boldsymbol{c}}(\boldsymbol{e})]|$ is real, since ξ is symmetric. The next two inequalities follow by Cauchy-Schwarz and Parseval's identity, which states that $\sum_c \left|\hat{F}(c)\right|^2 = \mathbb{E}\left[|F(\boldsymbol{X})|^2\right] = 1$. The desired conclusion follows from the fact that $\Pr[f(\boldsymbol{X}) = g(\boldsymbol{Y})] = (1 + \mathbb{E}[\overline{F(\boldsymbol{X})}G(\boldsymbol{Y})])/2$.

Ring-LWE Case. We get a similar result for the Ring-LWE case. Let R_q be the ring $\mathbb{Z}_q[x]/g(x)$ where g is a polynomial of degree n over Z_q. We identify an element in R_q by its coefficient vector in $\mathbb{Z}_q^n$. We say that $\boldsymbol{w}$ is drawn from $(\mathcal{X}^n)^*$ if its coefficients are drawn from $\mathcal{X}^n$ conditioned on $\boldsymbol{w}$ being a unit of R_q.

Theorem 6. *Let $n, q \geq 1$ be integers and R_q be as above. Assume that the distribution $\mathcal{X}$ over $\mathbb{Z}_q$ is symmetric and for any $a \in \mathbb{Z}_q \setminus \{0\}$, $\Pr[az = 0] \leq 9/10$ and $\Pr[az = q/2] \leq 9/10$ and $(\mathcal{X}^n)^*$ as above.*

Let $\mu_{\mathrm{RLWE},\mathcal{X}}(\boldsymbol{X}, \boldsymbol{Y})$ be the joint distribution of

$$\boldsymbol{X} = \boldsymbol{x}_1 \cdot \boldsymbol{a} \cdot \boldsymbol{x}_2 + \boldsymbol{x}_1 \cdot \boldsymbol{e}_2 \text{ and } \boldsymbol{Y} = \boldsymbol{x}_1 \cdot \boldsymbol{a} \cdot \boldsymbol{e}_1 + \boldsymbol{x}_2 \cdot \boldsymbol{e}_1,$$

where $\cdot$ is polynomial multiplication, $\boldsymbol{a} \sim \mathcal{U}(R_q)$, $\boldsymbol{e}_1, \boldsymbol{e}_2 \sim \mathcal{X}^n$ and $\boldsymbol{x}_1, \boldsymbol{x}_2 \sim (\mathcal{X}^n)^*$. Then for any $m \geq 1$, and any balanced functions $f, g : R^m \to \{0, 1\}$ respect to the marginal distributions of $\mu_{\mathrm{RLWE},\mathcal{X}}^{\otimes m}$, it holds that

$$\Pr_{(\boldsymbol{X}^m, \boldsymbol{Y}^m) \sim \mu_{\mathrm{RLWE},\mathcal{X}}^{\otimes m}} [f(\boldsymbol{X}^m) = g(\boldsymbol{Y}^m)] \leq 1 - \Omega(1/q^2).$$

Proof. We proceed as in the LWE case by proving claims similar to Claims 1, 2 and 3. For $\boldsymbol{c} \in R_q$, we define $\chi_{\boldsymbol{c}} \colon R_q \to \mathbb{C}$ as $\chi_{\boldsymbol{c}}(\boldsymbol{x}) = e^{-2\pi i \cdot \langle \boldsymbol{c}, \boldsymbol{x} \rangle / q}$, where $\langle \boldsymbol{c}, \boldsymbol{x} \rangle$ is the inner product of the coefficient vectors of $\boldsymbol{c}, \boldsymbol{x}$ over $\mathbb{Z}_q$. Then, the following claims hold.

Claim 4. *For any $m \geq 1$ and balanced $f, g : R_q^m \to \{0, 1\}$, it holds that*

$$\Pr[f(\boldsymbol{X}^m) = g(\boldsymbol{Y}^m)] \leq \frac{1 + \max_{\boldsymbol{c} \in R_q \setminus \{\boldsymbol{0}^n\}} |\mathbb{E}_{\boldsymbol{e} \sim \xi}[\chi_{\boldsymbol{c}}(\boldsymbol{e})]|}{2}$$

where for any $\boldsymbol{z} \in R_q$, $\xi(\boldsymbol{z}) = \Pr[\boldsymbol{x}_1 \cdot \boldsymbol{e}_2 - \boldsymbol{e}_1 \cdot \boldsymbol{x}_2 = \boldsymbol{z}]$.

Claim 5. $|\mathbb{E}_{\boldsymbol{e} \sim \xi}[\chi_{\boldsymbol{a}}(\boldsymbol{e})]| \leq \max_{\boldsymbol{c} \in R_q \setminus \{\boldsymbol{0}^n\}} |\mathbb{E}_{\boldsymbol{e} \sim \mathcal{X}^n}[\chi_{\boldsymbol{c}}(\boldsymbol{e})]|$.

Claim 6. *For any $\boldsymbol{c} \in R_q \setminus \{\boldsymbol{0}^n\}$, $|\mathbb{E}_{\boldsymbol{e} \sim \mathcal{X}^n}[\chi_{\boldsymbol{c}}(\boldsymbol{e})]| \leq 1 - \Omega(1/q^2)$.*

The proofs are almost identical to the corresponding proofs of Claims 3, 2 and 1 and so we omit them.

References

[ADPS16] Alkim, E., Ducas, L., Pöppelmann, T., Schwabe, P.: Post-quantum key exchange - a new hope. In: 25th USENIX Security Symposium, USENIX Security 16, Austin, TX, USA, 10–12 August 2016, pp. 327–343 (2016)

[BCNS14] Bos, J.W., Costello, C., Naehrig, M., Stebila, D.: Post-quantum key exchange for the TLS protocol from the ring learning with errors problem. IACR Cryptology ePrint Archive 2014/599 (2014)

[BGM+16] Bogdanov, A., Guo, S., Masny, D., Richelson, S., Rosen, A.: On the hardness of learning with rounding over small modulus. In: Kushilevitz, E., Malkin, T. (eds.) TCC 2016, Part I. LNCS, vol. 9562, pp. 209–224. Springer, Heidelberg (2016). https://doi.org/10.1007/978-3-662-49096-9_9

[BP14] Banerjee, A., Peikert, C.: New and improved key-homomorphic pseudorandom functions. In: Garay, J.A., Gennaro, R. (eds.) CRYPTO 2014. LNCS, vol. 8616, pp. 353–370. Springer, Heidelberg (2014). https://doi.org/10.1007/978-3-662-44371-2_20

[BPR12] Banerjee, A., Peikert, C., Rosen, A.: Pseudorandom functions and lattices. In: Pointcheval, D., Johansson, T. (eds.) EUROCRYPT 2012. LNCS, vol. 7237, pp. 719–737. Springer, Heidelberg (2012). https://doi.org/10.1007/978-3-642-29011-4_42

[BR17] Bogdanov, A., Rosen, A.: Pseudorandom functions: three decades later. Tutorials on the Foundations of Cryptography. ISC, pp. 79–158. Springer, Cham (2017). https://doi.org/10.1007/978-3-319-57048-8_3

[BZ17] Boneh, D., Zhandry, M.: Multiparty key exchange, efficient traitor tracing, and more from indistinguishability obfuscation. Algorithmica **79**(4), 1233–1285 (2017)

[DH76] Diffie, W., Hellman, M.E.: New directions in cryptography. IEEE Trans. Inf. Theory **22**(6), 644–654 (1976)

[DXL12] Ding, J., Xie, X., Lin, X:. A simple provably secure key exchange scheme based on the learning with errors problem. Cryptology ePrint Archive, Report 2012/688 (2012). http://eprint.iacr.org/2012/688

[Geb41] Gebelein, H.: Das statistische problem der korrelation als variations-und eigenwertproblem und sein zusammenhang mit der ausgleichsrechnung. ZAMM-J. Appl. Math. Mech./Zeitschrift für Angewandte Mathematik und Mechanik **21**(6), 364–379 (1941)

[GGM86] Goldreich, O., Goldwasser, S., Micali, S.: How to construct random functions. J. ACM **33**(4), 792–807 (1986)

[GMZB+17] Garcia-Morchon, O., et al.: Round5. Technical report, National Institute of Standards and Technology (2017). https://csrc.nist.gov/projects/post-quantum-cryptography/round-2-submissions

[Hir35] Hirschfeld, H.O.: A connection between correlation and contingency. In: Mathematical Proceedings of the Cambridge Philosophical Society, vol. 31, pp. 520–524. Cambridge University Press (1935)

[LLJ+17] Lu, X., et al.: Lac. Technical report, National Institute of Standards and Technology (2017). https://csrc.nist.gov/projects/post-quantum-cryptography/round-2-submissions

[Lov75] Lovász, L.: Spectra of graphs with transitive groups. Periodica Math. Hung. **6**, 191–195 (1975)

[LPR10] Lyubashevsky, V., Peikert, C., Regev, O.: On ideal lattices and learning with errors over rings. In: Gilbert, H. (ed.) EUROCRYPT 2010. LNCS, vol. 6110, pp. 1–23. Springer, Heidelberg (2010). https://doi.org/10.1007/978-3-642-13190-5_1

[NAB+17] Naehrig, M., et al.: Frodokem. Technical report, National Institute of Standards and Technology (2017). https://csrc.nist.gov/projects/post-quantum-cryptography/round-2-submissions

[NIS] NIST. https://csrc.nist.gov/csrc/media/projects/post-quantum-cryptography/documents/call-for-proposals-final-dec-2016.pdf

[PAA+17] Poppelmann, T., et al.: Newhope. Technical report, National Institute of Standards and Technology (2017). https://csrc.nist.gov/projects/post-quantum-cryptography/round-2-submissions

[Pei09] Peikert, C.: Public-key cryptosystems from the worst-case shortest vector problem: extended abstract. In: Proceedings of the 41st Annual ACM Symposium on Theory of Computing, STOC 2009, Bethesda, MD, USA, 31 May–2 June 2009, pp. 333–342 (2009)

[Pei14] Peikert, C.: Lattice cryptography for the Internet. In: Post-Quantum Cryptography - 6th International Workshop, PQCrypto 2014, Waterloo, ON, Canada, 1–3 October 2014, Proceedings, pp. 197–219 (2014)

[Reg05] Regev, O.: On lattices, learning with errors, random linear codes, and cryptography. In: Proceedings of the 37th Annual ACM Symposium on Theory of Computing, Baltimore, MD, USA, 22–24 May 2005, pp. 84–93 (2005)

[Rén59] Rényi, A.: On measures of dependence. Acta Mathematica Hungarica **10**(3–4), 441–451 (1959)

[SAB+17] Schwabe, P., et al.: Crystals-kyber. Technical report, National Institute of Standards and Technology (2017). https://csrc.nist.gov/projects/post-quantum-cryptography/round-2-submissions

[Sho94] Shor, P.W.: Polynominal time algorithms for discrete logarithms and factoring on a quantum computer. In: Algorithmic Number Theory, First International Symposium, ANTS-I, Ithaca, NY, USA, 6–9 May 1994, Proceedings, pp. 289 (1994)

[vEH14] van Erven, T., Harremoës, P.: Rényi divergence and Kullback-Leibler divergence. IEEE Trans. Inf. Theory **60**(7), 3797–3820 (2014)

[Wit75] Witsenhausen, H.S.: On sequences of pairs of dependent random variables. SIAM J. Appl. Math. **28**(1), 100–113 (1975)

PAKEs: New Framework, New Techniques and More Efficient Lattice-Based Constructions in the Standard Model

Shaoquan Jiang[1(✉)], Guang Gong[2], Jingnan He[3,4], Khoa Nguyen[4], and Huaxiong Wang[4]

[1] Institute of Information Security, Mianyang Normal University, Mianyang, China
shaoquan.jiang@gmail.com
[2] Department of Electrical and Computer Engineering, University of Waterloo, Waterloo, ON, Canada
ggong@uwaterloo.ca
[3] State Key Laboratory of Information Security, Institute of Information Engineering of Chinese Academy of Sciences, Beijing, China
hejingnan@iie.ac.cn
[4] School of Physical and Mathematical Sciences, Nanyang Technological University, Singapore, Singapore
{khoantt,hxwang}@ntu.edu.sg

Abstract. Password-based authenticated key exchange (PAKE) allows two parties with a shared password to agree on a session key. In the last decade, the design of PAKE protocols from lattice assumptions has attracted lots of attention. However, existing solutions in the standard model do not have appealing efficiency. In this work, we first introduce a new PAKE framework. We then provide two realizations in the standard model, under the Learning With Errors (LWE) and Ring-LWE assumptions, respectively. Our protocols are much more efficient than previous proposals, thanks to three novel technical ingredients that may be of independent interests. The first ingredient consists of two approximate smooth projective hash (ASPH) functions from LWE, as well as two ASPHs from Ring-LWE. The latter are the first ring-based constructions in the literature, one of which only has a quasi-linear runtime while its function value contains $\Theta(n)$ field elements (where n is the degree of the polynomial defining the ring). The second ingredient is a new key conciliation scheme that is approximately rate-optimal and that leads to a very efficient key derivation for PAKE protocols. The third one is a new authentication code that allows to verify a MAC with a noisy key.

1 Introduction

Key exchange is a fundamental and widely used cryptographic mechanism allowing two parties to securely share a session key over a public unreliable channel. In its original form, suggested in the seminal work of Diffie and Hellman,

A. Kiayias et al. (Eds.): PKC 2020, LNCS 12110, pp. 396–427, 2020.
https://doi.org/10.1007/978-3-030-45374-9_14

key exchange does not provide authentication and security against an active adversary who has full control of the communication channel. Authenticated key exchange additionally allows each user to authenticate identities of others using either Public-key Infrastructure (PKI) such as TLS/SSL and IKE, or some pre-shared information. The pre-shared information can be either a high-entropy cryptographic key or a low-entropy password. In practice, the latter is more convenient for human users who have limited memory. The study of password authenticated key exchange (PAKE) was initiated by Bellovin and Merritt [4]. A secure PAKE protocol must resist offline dictionary attacks, in which the adversary attempts to determine the password using information from previous executions.

Related Work. Since the pioneering work of Bellovin and Merritt [4] in 1992, PAKE has been extensively studied. The first provably secure PAKE protocol was suggested in [3], but its security analysis resorts to the random oracle model (ROM). Goldreich and Lindell [13] then introduced the first construction without ROM, based on general assumptions. A reasonably efficient protocol was put forward by Katz, Ostrovsky and Yung [17], which was later abstracted by Gennaro and Lindell [11] into a framework based on smooth projective hash (SPH) functions. However, these protocols did not support mutual authentication (MA). That is, the participant cannot make sure that the party he is interacting with, is the right person. Of course, one can make it up with additional flows, but this will increase the round complexity. Jiang and Gong (JG) [16] then proposed a more efficient protocol with MA without increasing round complexity.

In this work, we are interested in PAKE protocols from lattices. The first protocol was introduced in 2009 by Katz and Vaikuntanathan (KV) [18], whose main ideas are as follows. Alice and Bob first send a CCA-secure ciphertext to each other. Then, they try to compute approximate smooth projective hashing (ASPH) values on the ciphertexts and conduct a key reconciliation to derive a session key. Their key reconciliation mechanism consists of two steps: the first step aims to extract a bit from the ASPH value which is slightly noisy, while the second step is dedicated to correct the error using error-correcting code (ECC). This mechanism is relatively inefficient as it can extract at most one bit per field element. Furthermore, the underlying CCA-secure ciphertext (hence the ASPH) is quite costly, as it includes $\omega(\log n)$ CPA-secure ciphertexts[1].

Groce and Katz (GK) [15] abstracted the JG protocol [16] into a framework for PAKE, yielding a more efficient lattice-based protocol than KV. The idea of the GK framework is as follows. Alice sends a CPA-secure encryption C of password π to Bob. Bob then computes an SPH value h on (π, C). Then, they conduct authentication via a CCA-secure encryption with randomness determined by h. This framework can be adapted into the ASPH setting using KV's ASPH with their two-step key reconciliation. A realization was given by Benhamouda *et al.* [5]. Canetti *et al.* [6] demonstrated another framework for obtaining PAKE (without ASPH), via oblivious transfer (OT). They use OT to transfer

[1] The authors actually used n CPA-secure ciphertexts.

L' bits for *each* password bit and finally achieve the authentication via the CCA-secure encryption approach [15,16].

Zhang and Yu [28] proposed a PAKE framework from a new ASPH built on a "splittable CCA-secure encryption". However, their realization is in the ROM. Another ROM-based PAKE protocol from lattices is due to Ding *et al.* [8]. In this work, we only study PAKE protocols without the ROM.

Thus, all existing PAKE frameworks have certain efficiency issues, and do not admit efficient lattice-based realizations in the standard model. Moreover, a CCA-secure encryption seems to be an essential ingredient in them. This raises two interesting questions: (1) From a theoretical point of view, is it possible to achieve a secure PAKE without relying on any CCA-secure encryption or its variant? (2) From a more practical point of view, how to design lattice-based PAKEs in the standard model with better efficiency than previous ones? Tackling these questions would likely require new technical insights.

OUR CONTRIBUTIONS AND TECHNIQUES. In this work, we answer the above two questions in the affirmative. Our contributions are threefold. First, we put forward a new framework for obtaining secure PAKE protocols that does not require any CCA-secure encryption or its variant. Second, we introduce several new technical building blocks, that enable efficient standard-model instantiations of our framework in general, and from lattices - in particular. Third, we explicitly give two realizations of our framework, based on the plain Learning With Errors (LWE) and the Ring-LWE assumptions, which enjoy security guarantees from worst-case problems in general lattices [26] and ideal lattices [19], respectively. Our PAKEs compare very favourably with previous lattice-based protocols in the standard model. We also provide implementation results of the Ring-LWE-based scheme to demonstrate its practical feasibility. To the best of our knowledge, this is the first implementation of any lattice-based PAKE in the standard model, and the performance is quite encouraging.

New PAKE Framework. Let us first discuss the high-level ideas of our new PAKE framework. It relies on an ASPH, a key reconciliation scheme and a new notion of key-fuzzy message authentication code (KF-MAC). KF-MAC allows the verification key to be slightly different from the original authentication key. We define a *generic* ASPH on top of a commitment scheme. Given secret k, input π and a value y in the commitment space (not necessarily a commitment to π), an ASPH function $\mathcal{H}$ computes the hash value $\mathcal{H}(k, \pi, y)$. If y is indeed a commitment to π with witness τ, then $\mathcal{H}(k, \pi, y)$ can also be approximated by an alternative function $\hat{\mathcal{H}}$ as $\hat{\mathcal{H}}(\tau, \alpha(k))$, where $\alpha(k)$ is called the *projection key* of k. The important property for ASPH is *smoothness*: if y is a commitment to $\pi'(\neq \pi)$, then $(\mathcal{H}(k, \pi, y), \alpha(k))$ are jointly random. We describe our PAKE framework using this generic ASPH. However, to prove the framework security, additional properties on ASPH (which will be clarified later) are required. Our PAKE framework is an integration of three basic processes below.

- Basic key exchange. Alice and Bob use ASPH $(\mathcal{H}_1, \hat{\mathcal{H}}_1, \alpha_1)$ to obtain close secrets.

1. Bob (initiator) first generates a commitment y (with witness τ_1) to password π. He then sends y to Alice.
2. Upon receiving y, Alice samples a secret k, computes and sends a projection key $\alpha_1(k)$ to Bob. She also computes a hash value $\mathcal{H}_1(k, \pi, y)$.
3. Upon receiving $\alpha_1(k)$, Bob computes $\hat{\mathcal{H}}_1(\tau_1, \alpha_1(k))$. Note that the distance between $\mathcal{H}_1(k, \pi, y)$ and $\hat{\mathcal{H}}_1(\tau_1, \alpha_1(k))$ is typically small.

- Key reconciliation. This process enables Alice (with $\mathcal{H}_1(k, \pi, y)$) and Bob (with $\hat{\mathcal{H}}_1(\tau_1, \alpha_1(k))$) to agree on a secret ξ, via a one-message key reconciliation scheme £. If no attack exists, then ξ derived by Alice and Bob will be the same. To assure this, they need to authenticate each other.
- Authentication. This process uses another ASPH $(\mathcal{H}_2, \hat{\mathcal{H}}_2, \alpha_2)$ and a projection key $V = \alpha_2(O)$ (with a hidden key O) as public parameters. Here Alice and Bob will authenticate each other and derive a session key.
  1. Alice *deterministically* computes commitment w (with witness τ_2) on password π, using randomness determined by ξ. Next, she computes KF-MAC η_0 on traffic using key $\hat{\mathcal{H}}_2(\tau_2, V)$. Finally, she sends (w, η_0) to Bob.
  2. Bob uses ξ to repeat Alice's procedure to verify (w, η_0) and compute τ_2. Then, he uses $\hat{\mathcal{H}}_2(\tau_2, V)$ to authenticate himself.

We stress that although three procedures are described separately, they can be integrated into a 3-round protocol. The pictorial outline is given in Fig. 1 and a more detailed version is in Fig. 2. For security, we require the commitment for ASPH $(\mathcal{H}_1, \hat{\mathcal{H}}_1, \alpha_1)$ to have a *trapdoor property*: with a trapdoor (but without witness τ_1), one verifies if y is a commitment of π. We call this ASPH *type-B ASPH*. We require ASPH $(\mathcal{H}_2, \hat{\mathcal{H}}_2, \alpha_2)$ to have *strong smoothness*: if w is a random (i.e., honestly generated) commitment to π, then $\hat{\mathcal{H}}_2(\tau_2, V)$ is random (given w, V, π). We call this ASPH *type-A ASPH.*

At a high level, our main strategy for proving framework security is the sequence of games: modify the protocol gradually so that the messages in the final game contain no password. Firstly, we can modify the protocol so that π in y is a dummy password. This is unnoticeable to the attacker by the commitment hiding property. Then, under this revision, y normally does not contain the correct π. If this is the case (which can be checked by the trapdoor property of type-B ASPH), then, by smoothness of $\mathcal{H}_1$, $\mathcal{H}_1(k, \pi, y)$ is random. This random distribution will propagate to ξ. Thus, on the one hand, w is a random commitment to π, and so, by the commitment hiding property, we can revise π in w to be a dummy password. On the other hand, by strong smoothness of $\hat{\mathcal{H}}_2$, KF-MAC key $\hat{\mathcal{H}}_2(\tau_2, \alpha_2(O))$ looks random to attacker, and hence, the traffic can not be tampered by KF-MAC property. In fact, an attacker can not impersonate Alice successfully either. Indeed, if he modifies Alice's message only a little, then the KF-MAC will not change and the traffic will not consistent with the KF-MAC tag. If the attacker modifies Alice's message too much (or even creates a new one), (simulated) Bob will use $\mathcal{H}_2(O, \pi, w)$ to verify the KF-MAC. By smoothness of $\mathcal{H}_2$, he will not succeed unless w contains the password π.

After modifications, protocol messages have no password. Attacker can succeed beyond trivial attacks only by constructing y or w that contains the correct π. So he can not succeed better than simply guessing the password.

New Technical Building Blocks. Together with the new framework, we also introduce three new technical ingredients that may be of independent interest.

(1) We construct a new reconciliation scheme for close secrets in $\mathbb{Z}_q^\mu$ (in Sect. 3.2). Our scheme can extract $\Theta(\log q)$ per element in $\mathbb{Z}_q$ and is proven asymptotically *rate-optimal*. It is much more efficient than all the previous two-step schemes [5,18,24], where at most one bit per element in $\mathbb{Z}_q$ can be extracted.
(2) We give an authentication code with a noisy verification key in Sect. 3.3.
(3) We provide efficient constructions of ASPHs from both plain LWE and Ring-LWE. In each setting, we construct a type-A ASPH and a type-B ASPH. The LWE-based schemes are as follows.

a. *Type-A ASPH.* For public parameters $\mathbf{B} \in \mathbb{Z}_q^{m\times(n+L)}$ and $\mathbf{g} \in \mathbb{Z}_q^m$ and an m-length error-correcting code $\mathcal{C}$ with k information symbols, the commitment to π has the form $\mathbf{w} = \mathbf{Bt} + \mathbf{g} \odot \mathcal{C}(\pi) + \mathbf{x}$, where $\odot$ is the coordinate-wise multiplication, $\mathbf{t}$ is uniformly random over $\mathbb{Z}_q^{n+L}$ and $\mathbf{x}$ is a discrete Gaussian over $\mathbb{Z}_q^m$. The commitment witness is $(\mathbf{t}, \mathbf{x})$. For secret key $\mathbf{O}$ - which is a discrete Gaussian over $\mathbb{Z}_q^{m\times L}$, the projection key is $\mathbf{O}^T\mathbf{B}$. Then, the projective hashing is computed as $\mathcal{H}(\mathbf{O}, \pi, \mathbf{w}) = \mathbf{O}^T(\mathbf{w} - \mathbf{g} \odot \mathcal{C}(\pi))$, while the alternative hashing is defined as $\hat{\mathcal{H}}((\mathbf{t}, \mathbf{x}), \mathbf{O}^T\mathbf{B}) = \mathbf{O}^T\mathbf{Bt}$. If $\mathbf{w}$ is a commitment honestly generated as above, then the two hashing values differ by $\mathbf{O}^T\mathbf{x}$ (which is short as $\mathbf{x}$ and $\mathbf{O}$ are short). For the smoothness, if w is a commitment on $\pi' \neq \pi$, then given $\mathbf{O}^T\mathbf{B}$, value $\mathbf{O}^T(\mathbf{w} - \mathbf{g} \odot \mathcal{C}(\pi))$ is statistically close to uniform over $\mathbb{Z}_q^L$ (see Theorem 2). For strong smoothness, it requires that given $\mathbf{Bt} + \mathbf{x}$ and $\mathbf{O}^T\mathbf{B}$, value $\mathbf{O}^T\mathbf{Bt}$ looks random. We prove this using hidden-bits lemma in [9].

b. *Type-B ASPH.* Type B ASPH is similar to Type A ASPH, except it needs to provide a trapdoor property for the commitment. This property is achieved via the trapdoor simulation techniques in [1,18].

The ASPHs in the ring-LWE setting essentially follow the same strategy as the LWE-based ones. However, the supporting techniques (i.e., hidden-bits lemma, trapdoor simulation and adaptive smoothness theorem) have to be rebuilt. This turns out to be highly non-trivial. Essentially, this is due to the sparseness of matrix representations for ring operations. Consequently, the random arguments for the LWE case are no longer useful. However, this rebuilding work is worth as ring-LWE ASPHs are much more efficient than LWE-based ones. A detailed informal description is presented in Sect. 5.

Efficient Lattice-Based Instantiations of PAKE in the Standard Model. When putting all building blocks together, we obtain PAKE protocols from plain LWE and Ring-LWE that are much more efficient than previous lattice-based constructions in the standard model. Table 1 provides a summary of the comparison. For simplicity, the table only counts the dominating costs.

We provide the implementation in Sect. 5.5 for our Ring-LWE-based PAKE protocol. In this proof-of-concept implementation, the Number Theory Library (NTL) [27] is employed without further optimization. To agree on a 16-byte

Table 1. Comparison among lattice-based PAKEs in the standard model. Here, $m = \Omega(n \log n)$; k is the password length; L' is the key reconciliation output length (since the output is mostly used as a key for a symmetric-key primitive, $L' \ll n$); the cost for client/server is $\sharp$ of multiplications in $\mathbb{Z}_q$; Comm is the message length in $\mathbb{Z}_q$; $\lambda > 3$.

Scheme	Client (**Mult**)	Server(**Mult**)	Comm	assum	MA	q
[5]A	$O(kL'nm)$	$O(kL'nm)$	$kL'n$	DLWE	no	$\Omega(n^3)$
[5]B	knm	$O(kL'nm)$	kn^2	DLWE	no	$\Omega(n^3)$
[6]	$O(nmk)$	$O(nmk)$	kmn	DLWE	yes	$\omega(n^2)$
[15]	$2\,nm$	$O(L'nm)$	$L'n$	DLWE	yes	$poly(n)$
[18]	$\omega(L'nm \log n)$	$\omega(L'nm \log n)$	$2L'n$	DLWE	no	$poly(n)$
Ours	nm	$O(L'nm/\log q)$	$O(\frac{L'n}{\log n} + n \log n)$	DLWE	yes	$\Omega(n^\lambda)$
Ours	$O(\frac{L'n}{\log n} + n \log^2 n)$	$O(L'n \log n)$	$O(\frac{L'n}{\log n} + n \log n)$	R-DLWE	yes	$\Omega(n^\lambda)$

session key, the bandwidth from P_i to P_j is about 40 KB and 167 KB from P_j to P_i. Generating public parameters requires about 1.31 s, while P_i's and P_j's computations cost about 0.2 s and 0.71 s, respectively. Although the efficiency is (expectedly) not competitive with the ROM protocol from [8], our implementation demonstrates that the technical ingredients introduced in this work do advance the state of the art of lattice-based PAKEs in the standard model and do bring them much closer to practice. But it still needs further improvement toward practical application. This will be our future direction.

ORGANIZATION. The rest of the paper is organized as follows. In Sect. 2, we provide necessary background on PAKEs and lattices. The technical ideas, technical building blocks and description of our new PAKE framework are presented in Sect. 3. Our LWE-based and Ring-LWE-based instantiations are provided in Sects. 4 and 5, respectively.

NOTATIONS. The transposition of matrix Γ is denoted by Γ^T; $[k]$ denotes set $\{0, \cdots, k-1\}$. Vectors are column vectors (unless stated otherwise); v_i or $\mathbf{v}[i]$ denotes the ith component of $\mathbf{v}$; $[\mathbf{v}]_1^L$ denotes the sub-vector $(v_1, \cdots, v_L)^T$ of $\mathbf{v}$. Sampling x from set S uniformly at random is denoted by $x \leftarrow S$; $A|B$ is a concatenation of A with B. $\mathbf{negl} : \mathbb{N} \to \mathbb{R}$ represents a *negligible* function: $\lim_{n\to\infty} \mathbf{negl}(n)p(n) = 0$ for any polynomial $p(n)$. The statistical distance between X_1, X_2 is $\Delta(X_1, X_2) := \frac{1}{2}\sum_x |P_{X_1}(x) - P_{X_2}(x)|$, where $P_X()$ is the probability mass function of X. We say that X_1 and X_2 are *statistically close* if $\Delta(X_1, X_2)$ is negligible. $||\mathbf{x}||$ is the Euclidean norm of $\mathbf{x}$; $||\mathbf{x}||_\infty = \max_i |x_i|$ is the ℓ_∞-norm and $\mathsf{dist}_\infty(\cdot,\cdot)$ is the distance measure under ℓ_∞-norm. $x \bmod q$ denotes the residue of $x \in \mathbb{Z}_q$ in $[0, \cdots, q)$ and $(x)_q$ denotes the residue of $x \in \mathbb{Z}_q$ in $[-q/2, q/2)$. The $\odot$ product is defined as $(a_1, \cdots, a_n) \odot (b_1, \cdots, b_n) = (a_1b_1, \cdots, a_nb_n)$. For $\mathbf{v} \in \mathbb{R}^n$, $\textsc{Diag}(\mathbf{v})$ is the diagonal matrix with v_i as the (i, i)th entry. For $m_1 \times n_1$ matrix $\mathbf{A}$ and $m_2 \times n_2$ matrix $\mathbf{B}$, the tensor product $\mathbf{A} \otimes \mathbf{B}$ is the $m_1m_2 \times n_1n_2$ matrix (C_{ij}) in the block format, where block $C_{ij} = a_{ij}\mathbf{B}$ for any $i \in [m_1], j \in [n_1]$. The (column) concatenation of vectors $\mathbf{v}_1, \ldots, \mathbf{v}_t$ is a long vector, denoted by $(\mathbf{v}_1; \mathbf{v}_2; \cdots; \mathbf{v}_t)$.

2 Preliminaries

2.1 Security Model of PAKE

In this section, we recall a formal model for a password-authenticated key exchange protocol Σ. This model is mainly adopted from Bellare *et al.* [3] with a minor revision in [15]. There are n parties $P_1, \cdots, P_n$ in the system and any two parties share a password. We will use the following notations.

- $\mathcal{D}$: This is the password dictionary. For simplicity, we assume that passwords are chosen uniformly from $\mathcal{D}$.
- $\Pi_i^{\ell_i}$: This is the ℓ_i-th instance of protocol Σ executed by party P_i. The number ℓ_i is used by P_i to distinguish these instances.
- $Flow_d$: This is the d-th message flow in the execution of protocol Σ.
- $\mathbf{sid}_i^{\ell_i}$: This is the session identifier of $\Pi_i^{\ell_i}$. It is only for the purpose of security analysis. Intuitively, two instances jointly executing Σ should share the same session identifier. The specification is available only if Σ is known.
- $\mathbf{pid}_i^{\ell_i}$: This is the party, which $\Pi_i^{\ell_i}$ is interacting with.
- $sk_i^{\ell_i}$: This is the session key derived by $\Pi_i^{\ell_i}$ after successfully executing Σ.

Partnering. Instances $\Pi_i^{\ell_i}$ and $\Pi_j^{\ell_j}$ are partnered if (1) $\mathbf{pid}_i^{\ell_i} = P_j$ and $\mathbf{pid}_j^{\ell_j} = P_i$; (2) $\mathbf{sid}_i^{\ell_i} = \mathbf{sid}_j^{\ell_j}$. The partnering is motivated to identify two instances that are jointly executing protocol Σ.

Adversarial Model. To define security, we have to specify an attacker's capabilities. Essentially, we wish to capture man-in-the-middle attacks. The protocol is secure if the adversary can not obtain anything about a session key beyond the trivial findings. Formally, the attacks are modelled through oracles that are maintained by a challenger as follows.

- **Execute**(i, ℓ_i, j, ℓ_j): When this oracle is called, it first checks whether $\Pi_i^{\ell_i}$ and $\Pi_j^{\ell_j}$ are fresh. If not, it does nothing; otherwise, a protocol execution between $\Pi_i^{\ell_i}$ and $\Pi_j^{\ell_j}$ takes place. Finally, the transcript is returned. This is an eavesdropping attack.
- **Send**(d, i, ℓ_i, M): When this oracle is called, M is sent to $\Pi_i^{\ell_i}$ as $Flow_d$. If $d = 0$ or 1, then a new instance $\Pi_i^{\ell_i}$ is created. If $d = 0$, then $M =$ "ke, $\mathsf{pid}_i^{\ell_i}$" is a key exchange request message (from an upper layer program inside P_i). In any case, $\Pi_i^{\ell_i}$ acts according to the specification of Σ.
- **Reveal**(i, ℓ_i): This oracle call assumes that $\Pi_i^{\ell_i}$ has successfully completed with a session key $sk_i^{\ell_i}$ derived. Under this, $sk_i^{\ell_i}$ is returned.
- **Test**(i, ℓ_i): This oracle is to test the secrecy of $sk_i^{\ell_i}$. The adversary is only allowed to query it once. Toward this, $\Pi_i^{\ell_i}$ must have successfully completed with $sk_i^{\ell_i}$ derived. Furthermore, $\Pi_i^{\ell_i}$ and its partnered instance (if any) should not have been issued a **Reveal** query. Then, it takes $b \leftarrow \{0, 1\}$. If $b = 1$, then $\alpha_1 = sk_i^{\ell_i}$ is provided to adversary; otherwise, a random number α_0 from the space of the session key is provided. The adversary then tries to output a guess bit b' of b. He is announced for success if $b' = b$.

Correctness. If two partnered instances both accept, they derive the same key.

Adversarial Success. Having specified the adversarial behaviour, we now define its success. This consists of authentication and secrecy.

◇ *Mutual authentication.* We first define the *semi-partnering* [15]: instances $\Pi_i^{\ell_i}$ and $\Pi_j^{\ell_j}$ are *semi-partnered* if they are partnered, or, the following conditions hold: (1) $\mathsf{sid}_i^{\ell_i}$ and $\mathsf{sid}_j^{\ell_j}$ agree except possibly for the final message flow in Σ; (2) $\mathbf{pid}_i^{\ell_i} = P_j$ and $\mathbf{pid}_j^{\ell_j} = P_i$. This relaxed partnering is defined to rule out the possible trivial attack where an attacker forwards all the messages except the final one. An attacker breaks *mutual authentication* if some $\Pi_i^{\ell_i}$ with $\mathbf{pid}_i^{\ell_i} = P_j$ has successfully completed the execution of Σ with a session key derived while there does not exist a semi-partnered instance $\Pi_j^{\ell_j}$.

◇ *Secrecy.* An adversary succeeds if $b' = b$.

We use random variable **Succ** to denote either of the above two success events. Define the advantage of adversary $\mathcal{A}$ as $\mathbf{Adv}(\mathcal{A}) := 2\Pr[\mathbf{Succ}] - 1$.

Definition 1. *A password authenticated key exchange protocol Σ is* **secure** *if it is correct and for any PPT adversary $\mathcal{A}$ that makes* **Send** *queries at most Q_s times, it holds that $\mathbf{Adv}(\mathcal{A}) \leq \frac{Q_s}{|\mathcal{D}|} + \mathbf{negl}(n)$.*

2.2 Lattices and Hard Random Lattices

We now give a brief background on lattices. Let $\mathbf{B} = \{\mathbf{b}_1, \cdots, \mathbf{b}_n\} \subset \mathbb{C}^m$ consist of n linearly independent vectors. An m-dimensional *lattice* with basis $\mathbf{B}$ is defined as $\mathcal{L}(\mathbf{B}) = \{\sum_{i=1}^n a_i \mathbf{b}_i \mid a_i \in \mathbb{Z}\}$. For lattice Λ, the Euclidean norm of its shortest non-zero vector is denoted by $\lambda_1(\Lambda)$. If we use the ℓ_∞-norm, it is denoted by $\lambda_1^\infty(\Lambda)$. The *dual lattice* of $\Lambda \subseteq \mathbb{C}^m$ is defined as $\Lambda^\vee = \{\mathbf{y} : \langle \mathbf{x}, \bar{\mathbf{y}} \rangle = \sum_i x_i y_i \in \mathbb{Z}, \forall \mathbf{x} \in \Lambda\}$, where $\bar{\mathbf{y}}$ is the complex conjugate of $\mathbf{y}$.

For $s > 0$ and $\mathbf{x} \in \mathbb{R}^m$, Gaussian function with parameter s is $\rho_s(\mathbf{x}) = \exp(-\frac{\pi||\mathbf{x}||^2}{s^2})$. The *discrete Gaussian distribution* over lattice $\Lambda \subseteq \mathbb{R}^m$ with parameter s is defined as $D_{\Lambda,s}(\mathbf{x}) = \frac{\rho_s(\mathbf{x})}{\rho_s(\Lambda)}, \forall \mathbf{x} \in \Lambda$.

For $m \geq 2$, let $H = \{\mathbf{x} \in \mathbb{C}^{\phi(m)} : x_i = \bar{x}_{m-i}, \forall i \in \mathbb{Z}_m^*\}$, where x_i in $\mathbf{x} \in H$ is indexed by $i \in \mathbb{Z}_m^*$ and $\phi(m)$ is the Euler function. We are interested in lattice $\Lambda \subseteq H$. It is an inner product space over $\mathbb{R}$, isomorphic to $\mathbb{R}^{\phi(m)}$; see [20] for details. Hence, $D_{\Lambda,s}(\mathbf{x})$ with $\Lambda \subset H$ can be defined in exactly the same way as $\Lambda \subseteq \mathbb{R}^n$. Micciancio and Regev [22] defined a quantity *smoothing parameter.*

Definition 2. *For a lattice Λ and $\epsilon > 0$, the smoothing parameter $\eta_\epsilon(\Lambda)$ is the smallest s so that $\rho_{1/s}(\Lambda^\vee \backslash \{\mathbf{0}\}) \leq \epsilon$.*

Usually, $\eta_\epsilon(\Lambda)$ is desired to be small. Then, the following result is useful.

Lemma 1. *[25] For an m-dimensional lattice Λ, $\eta_\epsilon(\Lambda) \leq \frac{\sqrt{\log(2m/(1+1/\epsilon))/\pi}}{\lambda_1^\infty(\Lambda^\vee)}$.*

The following bounds are taken from [22, Lemma 4.4] and [2, Lemma 2.4].

Lemma 2. *For $s \geq \omega(\sqrt{\log m})$ and any $\mathbf{v} \in \mathbb{R}^m$ and any $t > 0$, if $\mathbf{e} \leftarrow D_{\mathbb{Z}^m,s}$, then $P(||\mathbf{e}|| > s\sqrt{m}) \leq O(2^{-m})$ and $P(|\mathbf{v}^T\mathbf{e}| > st||\mathbf{v}||) \leq 2e^{-\pi t^2}$.*

Hard Random Lattices. For integers q, m, n and $\mathbf{A} \in \mathbb{Z}_q^{m\times n}$ of rank n, let $\Lambda^\perp(\mathbf{A}) = \{\mathbf{e} \in \mathbb{Z}^m \mid \mathbf{e}^T\mathbf{A} = \mathbf{0} \bmod q\}$ and $\Lambda(\mathbf{A}) = \{\mathbf{y} \in \mathbb{Z}^m \mid \mathbf{y} = \mathbf{A}\mathbf{s} \bmod q, \mathbf{s} \in \mathbb{Z}^n\}$. It is easy to verify that $\Lambda^\perp(\mathbf{A}) = q \cdot (\Lambda(\mathbf{A}))^\vee$ and $\Lambda(\mathbf{A}) = q \cdot (\Lambda^\perp(\mathbf{A}))^\vee$. Here is a useful lemma on $\Lambda^\perp(\mathbf{A})$.

Lemma 3. *[12] If rows of $\mathbf{A} \in \mathbb{Z}_q^{m\times n}$ generate $\mathbb{Z}_q^{1\times n}$ and $r \geq \eta_\epsilon(\Lambda^\perp(\mathbf{A}))$, then for $\mathbf{e} \leftarrow D_{\mathbb{Z}^m,r}$, $\Delta(\mathbf{e}^T\mathbf{A}, \mathbf{U}) \leq 2\epsilon$, where $\mathbf{U}$ is uniformly random in $\mathbb{Z}_q^{1\times n}$.*

3 A New PAKE Framework

3.1 Intuition

We now introduce the ideas for our PAKE framework. We need three notions: key reconciliation, key-fuzzy message authentication code (KF-MAC), and approximate smooth projective hash (ASPH). Key reconciliation is a standard notion. It allows two parties with similar secrets to agree on an identical secret. The notion of KF-MAC is new. It works like a normal MAC for the MAC generation and verification. But it also allows a receiver with a slightly noisy key to (in)validate the MAC.

We define a generic ASPH on the top of a commitment scheme. Given secret k, input π and a value y in the commitment space (but not necessarily a commitment to π), an ASPH function $\mathcal{H}$ computes the hash value $\mathcal{H}(k, \pi, y)$. If y is indeed a commitment of π with witness τ, then $\mathcal{H}(k, \pi, y)$ can also be approximated by an alternative function $\hat{\mathcal{H}}$ as $\hat{\mathcal{H}}(\tau, \alpha(k))$, where $\alpha(k)$ is called the *projection key* of k. The important property for generic ASPH is *smoothness*: if y is a commitment of $\pi'(\neq \pi)$, then $(\mathcal{H}(k, \pi, y), \alpha(k))$ are jointly random. Based on a generic ASPH, we define two types of strengthened ASPHs. Type-A ASPH is a generic ASPH with a **strong smoothness**: if w is a random commitment of π with witness τ_2, then $\hat{\mathcal{H}}_2(\tau_2, \alpha_2(O))$ appears to be random (given $(w, \alpha_2(O))$). Type-B ASPH is a generic ASPH with **trapdoor property**: with a trapdoor (but without a witness), one can check whether y is a commitment of π.

Our PAKE framework proceeds as follows. Assume that $(\mathcal{H}_1, \hat{\mathcal{H}}_1, \alpha_1)$ is a type-B ASPH and $(\mathcal{H}_2, \hat{\mathcal{H}}_2, \alpha_2)$ is a type-A ASPH.

a. *approximate key establishment.* Initiator Bob generates commitment y (and its witness τ_1) on password π. He then sends y to Alice (responder). Alice then samples a secret key k, computes and sends the projection key $\alpha_1(k)$ to Bob. At this moment, Bob and Alice can compute two close secrets: Bob computes $\hat{\mathcal{H}}_1(\tau_1, \alpha(k))$ and Alice computes $\mathcal{H}_1(k, \pi, y)$.
b. *key reconciliation.* Alice (with $\mathcal{H}_1(k, \pi, y)$) and Bob (with $\hat{\mathcal{H}}_1(\tau_1, \alpha(k))$) executes a one-message key reconciliation scheme £ to agree on a common secret ξ. This one-message σ is sent by Alice.

c. *authentication with* ξ. Alice authenticates herself. To do this, she generates a commitment w (and its witness τ_2) on π but with randomness determined by ξ. She then generates a KF-MAC on traffic using secret key $\mathcal{H}_2(\tau_2, V)$, where V is a projection key (a public parameter). She then sends w and the KF-MAC to Bob. Bob has ξ and will repeat Alice's procedure to verify the authentication. He also authenticates himself using $\mathcal{H}_2(\tau_2, V)$.
d. *key derivation.* If the authentication above succeeds, they both derive the session key sk using ξ.

Although the framework has several stages, some messages can be combined. It turns out that the overall protocol has only 3 flows (see Fig. 1), where com_i is the commitment w.r.t. $\mathcal{H}_i$.

Bob(π)	public: $V = \alpha_2(O)$	Alice(π)
$(\tau_1, y) \leftarrow \mathsf{com}_1(\pi)$	$\xrightarrow{\ y\ }$	
$\xi = \pounds_{bob}(\sigma, \hat{\mathcal{H}}_1(\tau_1, \alpha_1(k)))$ $(\tau_2, w')=\mathsf{com}_2(\pi)$ determined by ξ $w' \stackrel{?}{=} w$	$\xleftarrow{w \mid \alpha_1(k) \mid \sigma}$	Sample k $(\sigma, \xi) \leftarrow \pounds_{alice}(\mathcal{H}_1(k, \pi, y))$ $(\tau_2, w) = \mathsf{com}_2(\pi)$ determined by ξ
	KF-MACs on traffic $\Longleftrightarrow$ with key $\hat{\mathcal{H}}_2(\tau_2, \alpha_2(O))$	
output: sk determined by ξ		output: sk determined by ξ

Fig. 1. Outline of our PAKE framework

We now outline the security. The idea is to iteratively modify the protocol so that messages in the final protocol variant do not contain password π at all.

First, if $w|\alpha_1(k)|\sigma$ is attacker-generated, we modify the protocol so that Bob verifies KF-MACs using key $\mathcal{H}_2(O, \pi, w)$ (instead of $\hat{\mathcal{H}}_2(\tau_2, V)$). This is consistent as the original verification guarantees that $\hat{\mathcal{H}}_2(\tau_2, V)$ and $\mathcal{H}_2(O, \pi, w)$ are close and so the two MAC verifications give the same result. Under the change, the attacker can succeed only if w contains π; otherwise, by smoothness of $\mathcal{H}_2$, $\mathcal{H}_2(O, \pi, w)$ is random to him and so the KF-MAC will be rejected.

Then, we modify the protocol so that π in y is a dummy password. This is unnoticeable to the attacker by the commitment hiding property.

Under the above revision, y normally does not contain the correct π. If this is the case (which can be checked by the **trapdoor property** of com_1), then, by **smoothness**, $\mathcal{H}_1(k, \pi, y)$ (further ξ) is random. Thus, w is a random commitment of π. Then, by **strong smoothness**, KF-MAC key $\hat{\mathcal{H}}_2(\tau_2, \alpha_2(O))$ looks random to attacker. So we can modify π in w to a dummy password and $\hat{\mathcal{H}}_2(\tau_2, \alpha_2(O))$ to be a random key. At this moment, a skillful attacker can not modify Alice's message to fool Bob unless w contains π. Indeed, if he modifies the message too much, then (simulated) Bob will regard it as an attacker-generated message. As said above, he will fail. If he only changes a little, then (simulated) Bob will use the *same* key of Alice to verify and reject KF-MAC. Our authentication approach is different from the previous CCA-encryption approach [15,16], where the non-malleability is used to refute a modification attack.

After modifications above, protocol messages have no password and attacker can only succeed by producing y or w that contains π (beyond trivial success). Thus, he cannot succeed better than simply guessing the password.

3.2 Key Reconciliation

Key reconciliation is a mechanism that allows two parties with close secrets to share a common secret. We consider a special scenario of this problem.

Alice has a secret d uniformly random over set S and Bob has a secret d' with $\mathsf{Dist}(d, d') \leq \delta$ for a measure $\mathsf{Dist} : S \times S \rightarrow \mathbb{R}^+$ and threshold $\delta \in \mathbb{R}^+$. Then, they jointly execute a protocol Π (called *key reconciliation protocol*). In the end, they output a value $\xi \in \Xi$. *The correctness* requires that for any d, d' with $\mathsf{Dist}(d', d) \leq \delta$, Alice and Bob will agree on ξ. Protocol Π is **passively secure** with respect to (S, Ξ, δ) if the correctness holds and $H(\xi|\mathsf{trans}) = H(\xi) = \log |\Xi|$, where trans is the transcript of Π and $H()$ is the (conditional) entropy function. If Π is a one-message protocol (from Alice to Bob), it is called *one-message key reconciliation protocol.*

Trivially, $H(\xi|\mathsf{trans}) = H(\xi)$ implies that ξ and trans are independent (i.e., $P_{\xi,\mathsf{trans}} = P_\xi P_{\mathsf{trans}}$), where P_X is the distribution of X.

Lemma 4. *Let Π be a passively secure key reconciliation that has d for Alice's input, trans for the transcript and ξ for the common secret. Take $\mathsf{trans}_1 \leftarrow P_{\mathsf{trans}}$ and $\xi_1 \leftarrow P_\xi$ and $d_1 \leftarrow P_{d|(\mathsf{trans},\xi)}(\cdot|\mathsf{trans}_1, \xi_1)$. Then, $P_{d,\mathsf{trans},\xi} = P_{d_1,\mathsf{trans}_1,\xi_1}$.*

Proof. By definition of $(\mathsf{trans}_1, \xi_1)$, $P_{\mathsf{trans}_1,\xi_1} = P_{\mathsf{trans}_1} P_{\xi_1} = P_{\mathsf{trans}} P_\xi$, which equals $P_{\mathsf{trans},\xi}$, as trans and ξ are independent. Thus, for any feasible (a, b, c), $P_{d_1,\mathsf{trans}_1,\xi_1}(a, b, c) = P_{d_1|(\mathsf{trans}_1,\xi_1)}(a|b, c) \cdot P_{\mathsf{trans}_1,\xi_1}(b, c)$. This is $P_{d|(\mathsf{trans},\xi)}(a|b, c) \cdot P_{\mathsf{trans}_1,\xi_1}(b, c) = P_{d|(\mathsf{trans},\xi)}(a|b, c) \cdot P_{\mathsf{trans},\xi}(b, c) = P_{d,\mathsf{trans},\xi}(a, b, c)$. Since a, b, c are arbitrary, $P_{d,\mathsf{trans},\xi} = P_{d_1,\mathsf{trans}_1,\xi_1}$. □

A New Key Reconciliation Scheme. For close secrets over $\mathbb{Z}_q$, we show how to share a random binary sequence. We start with an example for $q = 401$. Let $d', d \in \mathbb{Z}_{401}$ with d uniformly random in $\mathbb{Z}_{401}$ and $|(d' - d)_{401}| \leq 8$. Alice has secret d and Bob has d'. They want to agree on a secret ξ. Toward this, a crucial observation is as follows. For any *integer* $f \in [0, 2^{\lfloor \log 401 \rfloor})$ with a binary representation $a_7a_6a_5 01 a_2a_1a_0$, we have $f + d' - d \mod 401 = f + (d' - d)_{401} \in [0, 256)$, which has a binary representation $a_7a_6a_5a'_4a'_3a'_2a'_1a'_0$, as $8 \leq 01a_2a_1a_0 < 16$ and $-8 \leq (d' - d)_{401} \leq 8$. Then, Alice and Bob can reconciliate as follows.

Alice samples a random $f \in [0, 256)$ of a binary form $a_7a_6a_5 01 a_2a_1a_0$. Next, she evaluates $\sigma = f + d \mod 401$ and sends it to Bob.

Upon receiving σ, Bob computes $\sigma - d' \mod 401 = f + d - d' \mod 401$. As seen above, this number has a binary form $a_7a_6a_5a'_4a'_3a'_2a'_1a'_0$. So both Alice and Bob can define the common secret as $\xi = a_7a_6a_5$.

This shared key is confidential (given σ) as d is uniformly random in $\mathbb{Z}_{401}$ and hence f in σ is masked by a one-time pad $d \in \mathbb{Z}_{401}$.

The above example can be easily generalized to general parameters. Assume that Alice has a secret $d \leftarrow \mathbb{Z}_q$ and Bob has a secret $d' \in \mathbb{Z}_q$ with $|(d'-d)_q| < \delta$ for some integer $\delta \le q/32$. They want to agree on a common secret ξ. Our scheme works as follows. Let $t = \lfloor \log q \rfloor$ and $b = \lceil \log \delta \rceil$.

Alice: 1. Alice defines $a_b = 1$ and $a_{b+1} = 0$. For $0 \le j \le t-1$ but $j \ne b, b+1$, she takes $a_j \leftarrow \{0,1\}$ and lets $f = a_{t-1} \cdots a_1 a_0$ (an integer in a binary representation). She defines $\xi = (a_{t-1}, \cdots, a_{b+2})^T$.
2. Alice sends $\sigma = (f+d) \mod q$ to Bob and sets the shared secret as ξ.

Bob: Upon σ, Bob uses d' to compute ξ as the binary form of $\lfloor \frac{(\sigma - d') \mod q}{2^{b+2}} \rfloor$. Finally, he sets the shared secret as ξ.

This protocol can be generalized. If Alice has secret $\mathbf{d} \leftarrow \mathbb{Z}_q^\mu$ and Bob has $\mathbf{d}' \in \mathbb{Z}_q^\mu$ s.t. $|(d_i - d_i')_q| \le \delta$ for $i \in [\mu]$, they can run it in parallel with input d_i, d_i' for each i to generate a vector $\boldsymbol{\xi}$. We use £ to denote this scheme, use $(\boldsymbol{\sigma}, \boldsymbol{\xi}) \leftarrow £_{alice}(\mathbf{d})$ to denote Alice's computation and $\boldsymbol{\xi} \leftarrow £_{bob}(\boldsymbol{\sigma}, \mathbf{d}')$ to denote Bob's computation, where σ_i, ξ_i are the message and common secret w.r.t. (d_i, d_i').

Lemma 5. *Alice and Bob obtain the same* $\boldsymbol{\xi}$ *with* $\boldsymbol{\xi}$ *uniformly random over* $\{0,1\}^{(t-b-2)\mu}$ *and independent of* $\boldsymbol{\sigma}$. *Also, entropy* $H(\boldsymbol{\xi}) = H(\boldsymbol{\xi}|\boldsymbol{\sigma}) \ge \mu \log \frac{q}{16\delta}$.

Proof. Let f_i be the sample of f in the ith copy of the basic protocol. Notice that $\boldsymbol{\sigma} = \mathbf{f} + \mathbf{d} \mod q$ and $\mathbf{f}$ is independent of $\mathbf{d}$. Hence, $\mathbf{d}$ is the one-time pad for $\mathbf{f}$ in $\boldsymbol{\sigma}$. Thus, $\mathbf{f}$ is independent of $\boldsymbol{\sigma}$. Also, $\boldsymbol{\xi}$ is independent of $\boldsymbol{\sigma}$ as it is determined by $\mathbf{f}$. Further, $\boldsymbol{\xi}$ is uniformly random as every bit a_{ij} of f_i for $j \ne b, b+1$ is uniformly random. Consider the correctness now. It suffices to consider the basic protocol. Since $b = \lceil \log \delta \rceil$ and f has $a_b = 1$ and $a_{b+1} = 0$, it follows that $f \pm h$ for any $0 \le h \le 2^b$ has a binary representation $a_{t-1} \cdots a_{b+2} a'_{b+1} a'_b \cdots a'_1 a'_0$. This especially implies $(f \pm h) \mod q = f \pm h$, as $0 < f \pm h < 2^t \le q$. Thus, $\lfloor \frac{f \pm h}{2^{b+2}} \rfloor = a_{t-1} \cdots a_{b+2}$. Since $|(d-d')_q| \le \delta \le 2^b$, it follows that $(\sigma - d') \mod q = f + (d-d')_q$, which has a binary representation $a_{t-1} \cdots a_{b+2} a'_{b+1} a'_b \cdots a'_1 a'_0$. Thus, $\lfloor \frac{(\sigma - d') \mod q}{2^{b+2}} \rfloor = a_{t-1} \cdots a_{b+2}$. Finally, since $2^{t-b-2} = 2^{\lfloor \log q \rfloor - \lceil \log \delta \rceil - 2} \ge \frac{q}{16\delta}$, ξ has an entropy at least $\log \frac{q}{16\delta}$ bits. □

Next lemma reflects the strength of our scheme. A proof is in the full version.

Lemma 6. *Let* $\mathbf{d}$ *be a random variable over* $\mathbb{Z}_q^\mu$, *and let* $\mathbf{e}$ *be uniformly random over* $\{-\delta, \cdots, \delta\}^\mu$. *Define* $\mathbf{d}' = \mathbf{d} + \mathbf{e} \mod q$. *Let* Π *be any protocol between Alice with input* $\mathbf{d}$ *and Bob with input* $\mathbf{d}'$, *following which they derive a shared* $\boldsymbol{\xi}$. *Assume the interaction transcript between Alice and Bob be* trans. *Then,* $H(\boldsymbol{\xi}|\mathsf{trans}) \le H(\mathbf{d}) - \mu \log(2\delta + 1)$, *where* H *is the entropy function.*

Remark. Since $\mathbf{d}$ is uniformly random over $\mathbb{Z}_q^\mu$, any key reconciliation protocol in our setting must satisfy $H(\boldsymbol{\xi}|\mathsf{trans}) \le \mu \log \frac{q}{2\delta+1}$. In comparison with this bound, our $\boldsymbol{\xi}$ loses entropy at most $\log(16\delta) - \log(2\delta+1) \le 3$ bits per coordinate.

Define *extraction bit rate* to be $\frac{H(\xi)}{\mu \log q}$. The ratio of the extraction rate between our scheme and any rate-optimal scheme is lower bounded by $\frac{\log \frac{q}{16\delta}}{\log \frac{q}{2\delta+1}} \to 1$ when $\delta = o(q)$ and hence it is asymptotically optimal. Further, our rate is asymptotically $1 - \log_q \delta$, which is a constant for δ in our concrete PAKEs.

3.3 Authentication Code for Close Secrets

Message authentication code (MAC) is a keyed function $F_K : \mathcal{M} \to \mathcal{V}$ such that without K no one can compute $F_K(M)$ for any M. For simplicity, we assume that a *normal verification* of MAC η is simply to check $\eta \stackrel{?}{=} F_K(M)$. Now we introduce a new notion of *δ-key-fuzzy* MAC, where if a verifier's secret key gets a little noisy, then he can still verify the MAC. He can accept a normal MAC while he also rejects a forged MAC. This notion is motivated by the approximate MAC [7], where the MAC is valid even if the input message gets a little noisy.

Definition 3. *A keyed deterministic function $F_K : \mathcal{M} \to \mathcal{V}$ with key space $\mathcal{K}$ is a δ-KeyFuzzy MAC (or simply, δ-KF MAC), if there exists a keyed function $\Phi_{K'} : \mathcal{V} \to \{0,1\}$ (called a fuzzy verification function) so that $\Phi_{K'}(F_K(M), M) = 1$ for any $K' \in \mathcal{K}$ with $D(K', K) \leq \delta$, where $D : \mathcal{K} \times \mathcal{K} \to \mathbb{R}$ is a distance measure.*

In this definition, we only say that a fuzzy verification function (FVF) with an approximate key can accept a MAC. For it to be useful, it needs to reject a forged MAC. This is formalized as follows in terms of one-time security.

Definition 4. *Let $F_K : \mathcal{M} \to \mathcal{V}$ be a δ-KF MAC with key space $\mathcal{K}$, distance measure D, and FVF $\Phi_{K'}$. We say that F_K is* $(1, \delta, \epsilon)$-**KF secure** *if no PPT attacker $\mathcal{A}$, after seeing any $(M, F_K(M))$, can compute MAC η of $M' \neq M$ s.t.*

$$P\big[\Phi_{K'}(\eta, M') = 1 \text{ for some } K' \in \mathcal{K} \text{ with } D(K', K) \leq \delta\big] \geq \epsilon + \mathbf{negl}(n).$$

A New $(1, \delta, \epsilon)$-KF Authentication Code. We now construct a $(1, \delta, \epsilon)$-KF authentication code. Our scheme will use an error-correcting code with a large distance. For a constant prime p, a *$[N, k, d]_p$-code* is an error-correcting code over $\mathbb{Z}_p$ with a codeword length N, minimal Hamming distance d and k information symbols. The following lemma gives a random code with a large Hamming distance (see a proof in the full paper). A random code usually is not practical as its decoding is inefficient. However, our work does not need decoding.

Lemma 7. *Let $d \leq N$. Let $\mathbf{H} \leftarrow \mathbb{Z}_p^{(N-k)\times N}$ and $\mathcal{C} \subseteq \mathbb{Z}_p^N$ be a k-dimensional subspace with $\mathbf{H}$ as its parity-check matrix (i.e., $\mathbf{Hx} = 0$ for any $\mathbf{x} \in \mathcal{C}$). Then, $\mathcal{C}$ is a $[N, k, d]_p$-code, except for a probability $N \cdot p^{d+k-N-2} \cdot 2^N$.*

Now we are ready to give our $(1, \delta, \epsilon)$-KF authentication code.

Construction. Our new fuzzy MAC scheme is as follows. Let p be a *constant* prime less than q, and $L \in \mathbb{N}$ with $p \mid L$ and $H : \{0,1\}^* \to \mathbb{Z}_p^{k_2}$ is a collision-resistant hashing. Let secret $\mathbf{d} = (d_0, \cdots, d_{L-1})^T \leftarrow \mathbb{Z}_q^L$ and message space $\mathcal{M} = \{0,1\}^*$. Assume that $\mathcal{C}_{mac} : \mathbb{Z}_p^{k_2} \to \mathbb{Z}_p^{L/p}$ is a $[L/p, k_2, \theta_{mac}L/p]_p$-code for a constant $\theta_{mac} \in (0,1)$. The authentication function $F_{\mathbf{d}}(M)$ of M is to first compute codeword $\mathbf{a} = \mathcal{C}_{mac}(H(M))$ and then define $F_{\mathbf{d}}(M) = (t_0, \cdots, t_{L/p-1})^T$, where $t_i = d_{pi+a_i}$ for $i = 0, \cdots, L/p - 1$. The normal verification of $(M, \mathbf{t})$ is to check $\mathbf{t} \stackrel{?}{=} F_{\mathbf{d}}(M)$. The fuzzy verification $\Phi_{\mathbf{d}'}(\mathbf{t}, M)$ with $||(\mathbf{d}' - \mathbf{d})_q||_\infty \le \delta$, computes $\mathbf{t}' = F_{\mathbf{d}'}(M)$ and then outputs 1 if and only if $||(\mathbf{t} - \mathbf{t}')_q||_\infty \le \delta$.

The security idea of this scheme is that the codewords for M and M' with $M \neq M'$, have a large Hamming distance (as H is collision-resistant). Hence, given the MAC of M, the MAC of M' has at least $\theta_{mac}L/p$ coordinates that are uniformly random in $\mathbb{Z}_q$. It is hard to guess them correctly with a small error.

Lemma 8. *Our scheme is a* $(1, \delta, (\frac{4\delta}{q})^{\frac{\theta_{mac}L}{p}})$*-KF MAC for* $\delta < \frac{q}{4}$, $\theta_{mac} \in (0,1)$.

Proof. Correctness holds obviously. Consider the authentication. Assume attacker $\mathcal{A}$ forges a pair $(M^*, \mathbf{t}^*)$ after seeing $(M, \mathbf{t})$ for $M^* \neq M$, where $\mathbf{t} = F_{\mathbf{d}}(M)$. As H is collision-resistant, $\mathbf{a}^* = \mathcal{C}_{mac}(H(M^*))$ and $\mathbf{a} = \mathcal{C}_{mac}(H(M))$ have a Hamming distance at least $\theta_{mac}L/p$. Let $A = \{i \mid a_i \neq a_i^*, i \in [L/p]\}$ and $\boldsymbol{\eta} = F_{\mathbf{d}}(M^*)$. Then, η_i for any $i \in A$ is independent of $(M, \mathbf{t})$. Since $\mathbf{t}^*$ is computed from $\mathcal{A}$'s view $(M, \mathbf{t})$, it follows that η_i for $i \in A$ is independent of $\mathbf{t}^*$ as well. Let $\boldsymbol{\eta}' = F_{\mathbf{d}'}(M^*)$ and so $||(\boldsymbol{\eta}' - \boldsymbol{\eta})_q||_\infty \le \delta$. Then, $P[|(t_i^* - \eta_i')_q| \le \delta : i \in A] \le P[|(t_i^* - \eta_i)_q| \le 2\delta : i \in A] \le (\frac{4\delta}{q})^{|A|}$, given $(M, \mathbf{t})$. Hence, $P[\Phi_{\mathbf{d}'}(\mathbf{t}^*, M^*) = 1 \mid (M, \mathbf{t})] \le (4\delta/q)^{\theta_{mac}L/p}$. □

3.4 Approximate Smooth Projective Hashings

We define two types of approximate smooth projective hashings (ASPH). Both of them are based on a generic ASPH below revised from [18].

Approximate Smooth Projective Hashing (Generic). We start with the definition of a general commitment.

Definition 5. *Commitment scheme* Π *is a tuple* (gen, com, ver) *with domain* $\mathbb{D}$.

- gen(1^n). *Upon* 1^n, *it generates a public-key* e.
- com$_e(m)$. *Upon public-key* e *and* $m \in \mathbb{D}$, *it executes* $(\tau, y) \leftarrow$ com$_e(m)$ *to generate commitment* y *and witness* $\tau \in \{0,1\}^*$. *Also we use* com$_e(m; \Upsilon)$ *to denote the execution with randomness* Υ.
- ver$_e(\tau, m, y)$. *To decommit* y, *sender sends* (m, τ) *to receiver who then verifies it via algorithm* ver$_e$ *and finally outputs 0 (for reject) or 1 (for accept).*

A commitment scheme $\Pi = (\mathsf{gen}, \mathsf{com}, \mathsf{ver})$ is *secure* if it satisfies the correctness, computational hiding property, and unconditional binding property.

For a commitment scheme $\Pi = (\mathsf{gen}, \mathsf{com}, \mathsf{ver})$ with domain $\mathbb{D}$, we define two NP-languages $\mathcal{L}$ and $\mathcal{L}^*$. Let $\mathcal{Y}$ be the set of all possible commitment y and $\mathcal{X} = \mathbb{D} \times \mathcal{Y}$. For $e \leftarrow \mathsf{gen}(1^n)$, define $\mathcal{L} = \{(m, y) \in \mathcal{X} \mid \exists \tau \text{ s.t. } \mathsf{ver}_e(\tau, m, y) = 1\}$; define $\mathcal{L}^*$ via an algorithm ver^*: $\mathcal{L}^* = \{(m, y) \in \mathcal{X} \mid \exists \tau \text{ s.t. } \mathsf{ver}^*_e(\tau, m, y) = 1\}$, where ver^* is chosen so that $\mathcal{L}^*$ has two properties:

1. $\mathcal{L} \subseteq \mathcal{L}^*$.
2. For any $y \in \mathcal{Y}$, there exists at most one $m \in \mathbb{D}$ so that $(m, y) \in \mathcal{L}^*$.

The approximate smooth projective hashing (generic) is described by Π, ver^* and efficient functions: $\alpha : \mathcal{K} \rightarrow \mathbb{U}, \mathcal{H} : \mathcal{K} \times \mathcal{X} \rightarrow S$ and $\hat{\mathcal{H}} : \{0,1\}^* \times \mathbb{U} \rightarrow S$, where $\mathcal{K}$ is the *key space* with distribution $D(\mathcal{K})$, $k \leftarrow D(\mathcal{K})$ is the *secret key* and $\alpha(k)$ is the *projection key*. A generic ASPH with parameter δ (or generic δ-ASPH for short) is a tuple $\mathbb{H} = (\Pi, \mathsf{ver}^*, \mathcal{H}, \hat{\mathcal{H}}, \alpha)$ with the following properties.

Correctness. For $(m, y) \in \mathcal{L}$ with witness τ and $k \leftarrow D(\mathcal{K})$ (where $D(\mathcal{K})$ is the key distribution), $P(\mathsf{Dist}[\mathcal{H}(k, m, y), \hat{\mathcal{H}}(\tau, \alpha(k))] \leq \delta) = 1 - \mathbf{negl}(n)$, where $\mathsf{Dist} : S \times S \rightarrow \mathbb{R}^+$ is a distance measure and the probability is over choices of k.

Adaptive Smoothness. Given $m \in \mathbb{D}$ and an arbitrary function $f : \mathbb{U} \rightarrow \mathcal{Y}$, let $k \leftarrow D(\mathcal{K})$ and $y = f(\alpha(k))$. If $(m, y) \in \mathcal{X} \backslash \mathcal{L}^*$, then $(\alpha(k), \mathcal{H}(k, m, y))$ is statistically close to uniform over $\mathbb{U} \times S$.

Based on generic δ-ASPH, we define two types of ASPHs, each of which has a strengthened property over a generic ASPH.

Approximate Smooth Projective Hashing (*Type A*). Type A δ-ASPH (or δ-ASPH$_A$ for short) is a generic δ-ASPH with a *strong smoothness* below.

Strong Smoothness. Given $m \in \mathbb{D}$, let $(\tau, y) \leftarrow \mathsf{com}_e(m)$, $k \leftarrow D(\mathcal{K})$ and $U \leftarrow S$. Then, $(\alpha(k), y, \hat{\mathcal{H}}(\tau, \alpha(k)))$ and $(\alpha(k), y, U)$ are indistinguishable.

The smoothness is concerned with the randomness of $\mathcal{H}(\cdot)$ while the strong smoothness is concerned with the randomness of $\hat{\mathcal{H}}(\cdot)$. In general, the former does not imply the latter. It is not hard to find ASPH with the least significant bit of $\hat{\mathcal{H}}(\cdot)$ could always be zero while $\mathcal{H}$ has the smoothness.

Approximate Smooth Projective Hashing (*Type B*). The type-B δ-ASPH is a generic δ-ASPH $(\Pi, \mathcal{H}, \hat{\mathcal{H}}, \alpha)$, except $\Pi = (\mathsf{gen}, \mathsf{com}, \mathsf{ver})$ has a trapdoor property below.

- There exists algorithm $\mathsf{sim}(1^n)$ that generates a public-key e and a trapdoor trap. Further, there exists an efficient algorithm $\mathsf{trapVer}$ so that for any (m, y), $\mathsf{trapVer}_e(\mathsf{trap}, m, y) = 1$ if and only if $(m, y) \in \mathcal{L}$. Also, there exists an efficient algorithm $\mathsf{trapVer}^*$ so that for any (m, y), $\mathsf{trapVer}^*_e(\mathsf{trap}, m, y) = 1$ if and only if $(m, y) \in \mathcal{L}^*$. In addition, $e \leftarrow \mathsf{gen}(1^n)$ and e from $\mathsf{sim}(1^n)$ are indistinguishable.

Our trapdoor differs from a trapdoor commitment, where the latter opens a commitment to any message while our trapdoor is only used to check the membership of $\mathcal{L}$ and $\mathcal{L}^*$ without a witness. Especially, it cannot recover or equivocate a commitment. For convenience, we also include sim into Π and call it a commitment with trapdoor simulation (or trapSim commitment for short).

Remark. Even if a generic ASPH is revised from [18], their ASPH (also [28]) is defined on a public-key encryption. Adaptive smoothness was introduced in [28]. But strong smoothness and trapdoor property are new here.

3.5 Our PAKE Framework

We will use the following parameters, notations and functions.

- $\mathcal{D}$ is the password dictionary; $G : \Xi \to \{0,1\}^*$ is a pseudorandom generator.
- $\mathbb{H}_1 = (\Pi_1, \mathsf{ver}_1^*, \mathcal{H}_1, \hat{\mathcal{H}}_1, \alpha_1)$ is a δ-ASPH$_B$ and $\mathbb{H}_2 = (\Pi_2, \mathsf{ver}_2^*, \mathcal{H}_2, \hat{\mathcal{H}}_2, \alpha_2)$ is a δ-ASPH$_A$, where $\Pi_1 = (\mathsf{gen}_1, \mathsf{com}_1, \mathsf{ver}_1, \mathsf{sim}_1)$ and $\Pi_2 = (\mathsf{gen}_2, \mathsf{com}_2, \mathsf{ver}_2)$. Also, $\mathbb{H}_i$ $(i = 1, 2)$ is associated with $\mathbb{D}_i, \mathcal{K}_i, S_i, \mathbb{U}_i, \mathcal{X}_i, \mathcal{L}_i$ and $\mathcal{L}_i^*$ s.t. $\mathcal{D} \subsetneq \mathbb{D}_i$.
- Let $e_i \leftarrow \mathsf{gen}_i(1^n)$ for $i = 1, 2$ and $V = \alpha_2(O)$ for $O \leftarrow D(\mathcal{K}_2)$.
- $F_K : \{0,1\}^* \to \mathcal{V}$ is $(1, \delta, \epsilon)$-KF MAC with key space S_2 and fuzzy verification function $\Phi_{K'}$.
- $\pounds$ is a one-message reconciliation scheme for Alice and Bob, w.r.t, (S_1, Ξ, δ). Alice uses her secret d to compute $(\sigma, \xi) \leftarrow \pounds_{alice}(d)$ and sends σ to Bob; Bob uses his secret d' to compute $\xi = \pounds_{bob}(\sigma, d')$; $\xi \in \Xi$ is the shared secret.

Initially, a trustee prepares parameters $\{e_i|\mathsf{ver}_i^*|\Pi_i|\mathcal{H}_i|\hat{\mathcal{H}}_i|\alpha_i\}_{i=1}^2|V|F|\pounds$. If P_i and P_j wish to establish a key, they interact as follows (see Fig. 2). For simplicity, com_{b,e_b} (resp. ver_{b,e_b}) for $b = 1, 2$ is denoted by com_b (resp. ver_b).

$P_i(\pi_{ij})$ Pub: $\{e_i|\Pi_i|\mathcal{H}_i|\hat{\mathcal{H}}_i|\alpha_i|\mathsf{ver}_i^*\}_{i=1}^2|V|F|\pounds$ $P_j(\pi_{ij})$

P_i: $(\tau_1, y) \leftarrow \mathsf{com}_1(\pi_{ij})$ $\xrightarrow{y|P_i}$

P_j: $k \leftarrow D(\mathcal{K}_1)$, $U = \alpha_1(k)$
$(\sigma, \xi) \leftarrow \pounds_{alice}(\mathcal{H}_1(k, \pi_{ij}, y))$
$\omega = w|y|U|\sigma|i|j$, $\Upsilon|sk = G(\xi)$
$(\tau_2, w) = \mathsf{com}_2(\pi_{ij}; \Upsilon)$
$\eta_0 = F_{\hat{\mathcal{H}}_2(\tau_2, V)}(\omega|0)$

$\xleftarrow{w|U|\sigma|\eta_0|P_j}$

P_i: $\xi = \pounds_{bob}(\sigma, \hat{\mathcal{H}}_1(\tau_1, U))$, $\Upsilon|sk = G(\xi)$
$\omega = w|y|U|\sigma|i|j$
$(\tau_2, w') = \mathsf{com}_2(\pi_{ij}; \Upsilon)$, $w \stackrel{?}{=} w'$
$\mathsf{ver}_2(\tau_2, \pi_{ij}, w) \stackrel{?}{=} 1$,
$\eta_0 \stackrel{?}{=} F_{\hat{\mathcal{H}}_2(\tau_2, V)}(\omega|0)$
If yes, $\eta_1 = F_{\hat{\mathcal{H}}_2(\tau_2, V)}(\omega|1)$ & output sk

$\xrightarrow{\eta_1}$ If $\eta_1 = F_{\hat{\mathcal{H}}_2(\tau_2, V)}(\omega|1)$, output sk

Fig. 2. Our PAKE framework

1. P_i samples $(\tau_1, y) \leftarrow \mathsf{com}_1(\pi_{ij})$ and sends $y|P_i$ to P_j.
2. Upon receiving $y|P_i$, P_j samples $k \leftarrow D(\mathcal{K}_1)$ and derives $U = \alpha_1(k)$ and $(\sigma, \xi) \leftarrow \pounds_{alice}(\mathcal{H}_1(k, \pi_{ij}, y))$. Then, she derives $\Upsilon|sk = G(\xi)$ and computes $(\tau_2, w) = \mathsf{com}_2(\pi_{ij}; \Upsilon)$. Next, she computes $\omega = w|y|U|\sigma|i|j$ and $\eta_0 = F_{\hat{\mathcal{H}}_2(\tau_2, V)}(\omega|0)$. Finally, she sends $w|U|\sigma|\eta_0|P_j$ to P_i.
3. Upon receiving $w|U|\sigma|\eta_0|P_j$, P_i computes $\xi = \pounds_{bob}(\sigma, \hat{\mathcal{H}}_1(\tau_1, U))$, $\Upsilon|sk = G(\xi)$, $\omega = w|y|U|\sigma|i|j$ and $(\tau_2, w') = \mathsf{com}_2(\pi_{ij}; \Upsilon)$. Then, he checks $w \stackrel{?}{=} w'$, $\eta_0 \stackrel{?}{=} F_{\hat{\mathcal{H}}_2(\tau_2, V)}(\omega|0)$, $\mathsf{ver}_2(\tau_2, \pi_{ij}, w) \stackrel{?}{=} 1$. If any of them fails, he rejects; otherwise, he sends $\eta_1 = F_{\hat{\mathcal{H}}_2(\tau_2, V)}(\omega|1)$ to P_j and sets session key sk.
4. Upon receiving η_1, P_j checks $\eta_1 \stackrel{?}{=} F_{\hat{\mathcal{H}}_2(\tau_2, V)}(\omega|1)$. If yes, she sets session key sk; otherwise, she rejects.

3.6 Correctness

Let $\mathsf{sid}_i^{\ell_i} = \mathsf{sid}_j^{\ell_j} = P_i|P_j|y|U|\sigma$. If P_i and P_j share the same sid, then y is generated by P_i while (U, σ) is generated by P_j. Hence, (σ, y, U) has the specified distribution: $(\tau_1, y) \leftarrow \mathsf{com}_1(\pi_{ij})$ and $U = \alpha_1(k)$ for $k \leftarrow D(\mathcal{K}_1)$. They will derive the same sk. Indeed, the correctness of com_1 implies $(\pi_{ij}, y) \in \mathcal{L}_1$. The correctness of ASPH$_B$ implies that $\mathsf{Dist}[\mathcal{H}_1(k, \pi_{ij}, y), \hat{\mathcal{H}}_1(\tau, \alpha_1(k))] \le \delta$. So the correctness of $\pounds$ implies P_i and P_j computes the same ξ. Since $\Upsilon|sk$ is determined by ξ and the definition of PAKE correctness assumes that both P_i and P_j accept, they both conclude with the same sk.

3.7 Security

We now state our security theorem. The main ideas have been presented at the beginning of this section and proof details will appear in the full paper.

Theorem 1. *Let $\pounds$ be a secure one-message key reconciliation w.r.t. (S_1, Ξ, δ), $G : \Xi \to \{0,1\}^*$ be a pseudorandom generator, and (F, Φ) be $(1, \delta, \epsilon)$-KF MAC with key space S_2, domain $\mathcal{M}$ and negligible ϵ. Let $\mathbb{H}_1 = (\Pi_1, \mathsf{ver}_1^*, \mathcal{H}_1, \hat{\mathcal{H}}_1, \alpha_1)$ be a δ-ASPH$_B$ on a secure trapSim-commitment $\Pi_1 = (\mathsf{gen}_1, \mathsf{com}_1, \mathsf{ver}_1, \mathsf{sim}_1)$, $\mathbb{H}_2 = (\Pi_2, \mathsf{ver}_2^*, \mathcal{H}_2, \hat{\mathcal{H}}_2, \alpha_2)$ be a δ-ASPH$_A$ on a secure commitment $\Pi_2 = (\mathsf{gen}_2, \mathsf{com}_2, \mathsf{ver}_2)$. Then, our framework is secure.*

4 LWE-Based Instantiation

4.1 The Learning with Errors Assumption

We next recall the Learning With Errors (LWE) assumption due to Regev [26]. For a vector $\mathbf{s} \in \mathbb{Z}_q^n$ and distribution χ over $\mathbb{Z}_q$, define distribution $A_{\mathbf{s},\chi}$ with m samples as follows. It chooses a matrix $\mathbf{A} \leftarrow \mathbb{Z}_q^{m \times n}$, takes $\mathbf{x} \leftarrow \chi^m$, and outputs $(\mathbf{A}, \mathbf{As} + \mathbf{x})$. The decisional LWE assumption DLWE$_{q,\chi,m,n}$ states that $(\mathbf{A}, \mathbf{As} + \mathbf{x})$ is pseudorandom when $\mathbf{s}$ is uniformly random over $\mathbb{Z}_q^n$.

For $s \in \mathbb{R}^+$, let Ψ_s be the Gaussian distribution of zero mean and standard deviation $s/\sqrt{2\pi}$. Regev [26] proved that DLWE is hard when $\chi = \Psi_s$ with $s > 2\sqrt{n}$. Usually, it is more convenient to work with $\chi = D_{\mathbb{Z}^m,s}$. Gordon et al. [14, Lemma 2] showed that the hardness of $\text{DLWE}_{q,\Psi_s,m,n}$ implies the hardness of $\text{DLWE}_{q,D_{\mathbb{Z}^m,\sqrt{2}s},m,n}$ when $s = \omega(\sqrt{\log n})$. For convenience, later we denote $\text{DLWE}_{q,D_{\mathbb{Z}^m,s},m,n}$ assumption by $\mathbf{DLWE}_{q,s,m,n}$.

4.2 Supporting Properties from LWE

Hidden-Bits Lemma from LWE. The hidden-bits lemma states that given a LWE tuple $(\mathbf{A}, \mathbf{As}+\mathbf{x})$, some linear function on $\mathbf{s}$ is confidential. This result is essentially a corollary of [9, Lemma C.6]. We now present it without a proof.

Lemma 9. *Let $L \le n$ and $\mathbf{U}^L$ be the uniformly random variable over $\mathbb{Z}_q^L$. Let $\mathbf{C} \in \mathbb{Z}_q^{L\times(n+L)}$ be an arbitrary but fixed matrix with rank L. Then, $(\mathbf{A}, \mathbf{As}+\mathbf{x}, \mathbf{Cs})$ and $(\mathbf{A}, \mathbf{As}+\mathbf{x}, \mathbf{U}^L)$ are indistinguishable under* $\text{DLWE}_{q,\beta,m,n}$ *assumption, where $\mathbf{A} \leftarrow \mathbb{Z}_q^{m\times(n+L)}, \mathbf{s} \leftarrow \mathbb{Z}_q^{n+L}$, $\mathbf{x} \leftarrow D_{\mathbb{Z}^m,\beta}$.*

Trapdoor Generation for LWE. The next lemma is adapted from [18, Lemma 3].

Lemma 10. *Let $m \ge 6n\log q$ and $n\log q = o(q^{1-\alpha})$ for constant $\alpha \in (0,1)$. Then, there is an efficient algorithm GenTrap$(1^n, 1^m, q)$ that outputs $\mathbf{A} \in \mathbb{Z}_q^{m\times n}$ and a trapdoor $\mathbf{T} \in \mathbb{Z}^{m\times m}$ such that $||\mathbf{T}|| \le O(n\log q)$ and $\mathbf{A}$ is statistically close to uniform over $\mathbb{Z}_q^{m\times n}$. Further, there exists a PPT algorithm BD$(\mathbf{T},\cdot)$ that takes $\mathbf{z} \in \mathbb{Z}_q^m$ as input and does the following: if $\mathbf{z} = \mathbf{As}+\mathbf{x}$ with $||\mathbf{x}||_\infty \le \lfloor \frac{q^{\alpha}-2}{4} \rfloor$, then output $(\mathbf{t}, \mathbf{x})$; if $\mathbf{z}$ cannot be expressed in this form, then output $\perp$.*

We require $m \ge 6n\log q$ (using [1, Theorem 3.2] with $||\mathbf{T}|| \le O(n\log q)$), while $m \ge n\log^2 q$ in [18] (using [1, Theorem 3.1]). However, their proof only requires $||\mathbf{T}|| \cdot \frac{q^{1-\alpha}-2}{4} < q/2$. We satisfy this as $||\mathbf{T}|| \le O(n\log q) = o(q^\alpha)$.

Adaptive Smoothness from LWE. The adaptive smoothness below states that for almost every $\mathbf{A} \in \mathbb{Z}_q^{m\times n'}$ and $\mathbf{h} \in \mathbb{Z}_q^m$, $\mathbf{E}^T(\mathbf{A}, \mathbf{v} - \mathbf{u}\odot\mathbf{h})$ are close to uniform for all but one codeword $\mathbf{u}$ in a m-length code $\mathcal{C}$, where $\mathbf{E}$ is discrete Gaussian and $\mathbf{v}$ is adaptively chosen (after given $\mathbf{E}^T\mathbf{A}$). The idea is to employ a similar result ([28, Lemma 19]) of [12, Lemma 8.3], under which we essentially only need to show that $\min_{\mathbf{s}\in\mathbb{Z}_q^{n+1}-\{\mathbf{0}\}} ||(\mathbf{A}, \mathbf{v}-\mathbf{u}\odot\mathbf{h})\mathbf{s}||_\infty$ is large for all but one $\mathbf{u} \in \mathcal{C}$. Let $\mathbf{s} = (s_1, \cdots, s_{n'+1})$. Notice that Lemma 11 below implies this is true when minimizing with $s_{n'+1} \ne 0$, while case $s_{n'+1} = 0$ (i.e., $\min_{\mathbf{s}'\in\mathbb{Z}_q^n-\{\mathbf{0}\}} ||\mathbf{As}'||_\infty$ is large for most of $\mathbf{A}$) is well known. The proof detail is given in the full paper.

Theorem 2. *For $\theta \in (0,1)$, let $s \ge q^{1-\frac{\theta}{3}} \cdot \omega(\sqrt{\log m})$ and $\mathcal{C}$ be a $[m,k,\theta m]_p$-code with $p < q$. Take $\mathbf{A} \leftarrow \mathbb{Z}_q^{m\times n'}, \mathbf{h} \leftarrow \mathbb{Z}_q^m$. Then, with probability $1 - 2^{-m}q^{n'-(1-\frac{\theta}{3})m} - |\mathcal{C}|^2 2^{-2m} q^{2n'+2-\theta m/3}$ (over $\mathbf{A}, \mathbf{h}$), the following is true for $\mathbf{E} \leftarrow (D_{\mathbb{Z}^m,s})^\mu$ and $\mathbf{v} = f(\mathbf{E}^T\mathbf{A})$ with an arbitrary function $f : \mathbb{Z}_q^{\mu\times n'} \to \mathbb{Z}_q^m$.*

1. $\min_{\mathbf{s}\in\mathbb{Z}_q^{n'+1}-\{\mathbf{0}\}} ||(\mathbf{A}, \mathbf{v}-\mathbf{u}\odot\mathbf{h})\mathbf{s}||_\infty \ge \lfloor \frac{q^{\theta/3}-2}{4} \rfloor$ for all but one $\mathbf{u}$ in $\mathcal{C}$;

2. $\mathbf{E}^T[\mathbf{A}, \mathbf{v} - \mathbf{u} \odot \mathbf{h}]$ *is close to uniform in* $\mathbb{Z}_q^{\mu\times(n'+1)}$ *for all but the exceptional* $\mathbf{u}$ *in item 1.*

The following lemma presents *a core technique* in this paper.

Lemma 11. *Let* $\mathbf{B} \in \mathbb{Z}_q^{m\times\nu}, \chi \in \mathbb{N}$ *and* $\mathbf{C} \in \mathbb{Z}_q^{m\times m}$ *be arbitrary but fixed matrices with* $\mathbf{C}$ *invertible. Take* $\mathbf{h} \leftarrow \mathbb{Z}_q^m$. *Let* $\mathbf{w}$ *be any random variable (maybe computed from* $\mathbf{h}, \mathbf{B}$*) over* $\mathbb{Z}_q^m$. *Assume* $\mathcal{C}$ *is a* $[m, k', \theta m]_p$*-code for a constant* $\theta \in (0, 1)$ *and* $p < q$. *Then, with probability at least* $1 - |\mathcal{C}|^2 q^{2\nu+2}(4\chi^2 q^{-\theta})^m$ *(over choices of* $\mathbf{h}$*), there is at most one* $\mathbf{u} \in \mathcal{C}$ *that* $k\mathbf{C}(\mathbf{w} - \mathbf{h} \odot \mathbf{u}) = \mathbf{B}\mathbf{s} + \mathbf{x}$ *holds for some* $(k, \mathbf{s}, \mathbf{x}) \in \mathbb{Z}_q^* \times \mathbb{Z}_q^\nu \times \mathbb{Z}_q^m$ *with* $||\mathbf{x}||_\infty < \chi$.

Proof. For any distinct $\mathbf{u}_1, \mathbf{u}_2 \in \mathcal{C}$, let $\mathbf{z}_i = \mathbf{C}(\mathbf{w} - \mathbf{h} \odot \mathbf{u}_i), i = 1, 2$. Then, $\forall \mathbf{y}_1, \mathbf{y}_2 \in \mathbb{Z}_q^m$ and $k_1, k_2 \in \mathbb{Z}_q^*$, we have

$$\begin{aligned}
&P(k_1\mathbf{z}_1 = k_1\mathbf{y}_1 \wedge k_2\mathbf{z}_2 = k_2\mathbf{y}_2) = P(\mathbf{z}_1 = \mathbf{y}_1 \wedge \mathbf{z}_2 = \mathbf{y}_2)\\
=&P(\mathbf{z}_1 = \mathbf{y}_1 \ \wedge \ (\mathbf{u}_1 - \mathbf{u}_2) \odot \mathbf{h} = \boldsymbol{\delta}), \text{ where } \boldsymbol{\delta} = \mathbf{C}^{-1}(\mathbf{y}_1 - \mathbf{y}_2)\\
\leq&P((\mathbf{u}_1 - \mathbf{u}_2) \odot \mathbf{h} = \boldsymbol{\delta})\\
\leq&P((u_{1i} - u_{2i})h_i = \delta_i, \forall i \in A) \quad (\text{where } A = \{i \mid u_{1i} \neq u_{2i}, \ i \in [m]\}) \qquad (1)\\
\leq&q^{-\theta m} \quad (\text{as } |A| \geq \theta m \text{ and } h_i \text{ is uniformly random.})
\end{aligned}$$

Let $\mathcal{Z} \subseteq \mathbb{Z}^m$ be the cube of radius $\chi - 1$ (centered at $\mathbf{0}$), and $\mathcal{S} \stackrel{def}{=} \cup_{\mathbf{s}\in\mathbb{Z}_q^\nu}(\mathbf{B}\mathbf{s} + \mathcal{Z}) \cap \mathbb{Z}^m \mod q$. Obviously, $k\mathbf{z} = \mathbf{B}\mathbf{s} + \mathbf{x}$ for $||\mathbf{x}||_\infty < \chi$ is equivalent to $k\mathbf{z} \in \mathcal{S}$. Hence, $P(k_1\mathbf{z}_1 \in \mathcal{S} \wedge k_2\mathbf{z}_2 \in \mathcal{S}) \leq |\mathcal{S}|^2 \cdot q^{-\theta m} = q^{2\nu}(4\chi^2 q^{-\theta})^m$. Since (k_1, k_2) has at most q^2 choices and $(\mathbf{u}_1, \mathbf{u}_2)$ has at most $|\mathcal{C}|^2$ choices, the bound follows. Finally, the probability bound is obtained only over choices of $\mathbf{h}$, as Eq. (1) only depends on the coins of $\mathbf{h}$ and the final result is a union bound on Eq. (1). □

Remark. The adaptiveness of $\mathbf{v}$ in Theorem 2 is important. In our PAKE, $\mathbf{E}^T\mathbf{A}$ is known to attacker. Hence, he can choose $\mathbf{v}$ based on it.

4.3 ASPHs from LWE

We will construct ASPH_A and ASPH_B with the following common parameters.

- n is the security parameter; prime modulus $q = n^\lambda$ for a constant $\lambda > \frac{3}{\theta}$ with $\theta \in (0, 1 - 1/\log p)$ and p a *constant* prime less than q; $k = o(n)$; $\delta_1 = 6n \log n$; $r_1 = 3n^{1/2}$; $r_2 = q^{1-\frac{\theta}{3}} \log n$; $\delta = q^\alpha$ (for $1 - \frac{\theta}{3} + \frac{1}{\lambda} < \alpha < 1$);

4.3.1 Construction of δ-ASPH_A

Let $L \leq n, \frac{7(n+L)}{\theta} \leq m \leq \Theta(n)$. Take $\mathbf{g} \leftarrow \mathbb{Z}_q^m$, $\mathbf{B} \leftarrow \mathbb{Z}_q^{m\times(n+L)}$. Let $\mathcal{C}$ be a $[m, k, \theta m]_p$-code, constructed from Lemma 7 with negligible failure probability $mp^{(-1+\theta+1/\log p - o(1))m}$.

The Commitment Scheme. The commitment key is $(\mathbf{B}, \mathbf{g})$. To commit $\pi \in \mathbb{Z}_p^k$, take $\mathbf{z} \leftarrow (D_{\mathbb{Z},r_1})^m$ and $\mathbf{t} \leftarrow \mathbb{Z}_q^{n+L}$. The commitment is $\mathbf{w} = \mathbf{B}\mathbf{t} + \mathbf{z} + \mathbf{g} \odot \mathcal{C}(\pi)$

with witness $\tau = (\mathbf{t}, \mathbf{z})$. The decommitment is (π, τ). Define $\mathsf{ver}(\tau, \pi, \mathbf{w}) = 1$ if and only if $\mathbf{w} = \mathbf{Bt} + \mathbf{z} + \mathbf{g} \odot \mathcal{C}(\pi)$ and $||\mathbf{z}|| \le \delta_1$. From ver, language $\mathcal{L}$ is generically defined. Define $\mathcal{L}^*$ so that $(\pi, \mathbf{w}) \in \mathcal{L}^*$ if $||(\mathbf{B}, \mathbf{w} - \mathbf{g} \odot \mathcal{C}(\pi))\mathbf{s}||_\infty < \lfloor \frac{q^{\theta/3}-2}{4} \rfloor$ for some $\mathbf{s} \in \mathbb{Z}_q^{n+L+1} - \{\mathbf{0}\}$.

Lemma 12. *Our commitment is secure under $DLWE_{q,r_1,m,n}$ assumption.*

Proof. Consider correctness first. Let $\mathbf{w} = \mathbf{Bt} + \mathbf{g} \odot \mathcal{C}(\pi) + \mathbf{z}$ be a commitment of π with $\mathbf{z} \leftarrow D_{\mathbb{Z}^m, r_1}$. Then, correctness holds if $||\mathbf{z}|| \le \delta_1$, which is true except for probability $O(2^{-m})$, by Lemma 2 (noticing $r_1\sqrt{m} = \Theta(n) = o(\delta_1)$). Hiding property directly follows from $\text{DLWE}_{q,r_1,m,n}$ assumption. The binding property follows from the properties of $\mathcal{L}^*$ (to be verified soon): $\mathcal{L} \subseteq \mathcal{L}^*$ and for any $\mathbf{w} \in \mathbb{Z}_q^m$, there is only one π so that $(\pi, \mathbf{w}) \in \mathcal{L}^*$. □

Description of δ-ASPH$_A$. We verify the required properties for $\mathcal{L}^*$.

1. $\mathcal{L} \subseteq \mathcal{L}^*$. This is obvious as $||\cdot||_\infty \le ||\cdot||$ and $\delta_1 = o(q^{\theta/3})$ using $\lambda\theta/3 > 1$.
2. *For any $\mathbf{w} \in \mathbb{Z}_q^m$, there is at most one $\pi \in \mathbb{Z}_p^k$ with $(\pi, \mathbf{w}) \in \mathcal{L}^*$.* This directly follows from Theorem 2(1) (with $n' = n + L$), where the exception probability is $O(q^{(-1/3+o(1))n})$ (negligible!).

We define $\mathcal{H}$ and $\hat{\mathcal{H}}$. For secret $\mathbf{O} \leftarrow (D_{\mathbb{Z},r_2})^{m\times L}$, let the projection key $\mathbf{V} = \mathbf{O}^T\mathbf{B}$. Let $\mathcal{H}(\mathbf{O}, \pi, \mathbf{w}) = \mathbf{O}^T(\mathbf{w} - \mathbf{g} \odot \mathcal{C}(\pi))$. If $(\pi, \mathbf{w}) \in \mathcal{L}$ with witness $\tau = (\mathbf{t}, \mathbf{z})$, let $\hat{\mathcal{H}}(\tau, \mathbf{V}) = \mathbf{Vt}$.

Correctness. Assume the closeness uses the $||\cdot||_\infty$ metric. Let $(\pi, \mathbf{w}) \in \mathcal{L}$. Then, $\mathbf{w} = \mathbf{Bt} + \mathbf{g} \odot \mathcal{C}(\pi) + \mathbf{z}$ with $||\mathbf{z}|| \le \delta_1$. For $\mathbf{O} \leftarrow (D_{\mathbb{Z},r_2})^{m\times L}$, we have $||\mathbf{Vt} - \mathbf{O}^T(\mathbf{w} - \mathbf{g} \odot \mathcal{C}(\pi))||_\infty = \max_i |\mathbf{o}_i^T\mathbf{z}| \le \delta_1 r_2 \log n = o(\delta)$ (except for a negligible probability by Lemma 2), where $\mathbf{o}_i$ is the ith column of $\mathbf{O}$.

Adaptive Smoothness. For $(\pi, \mathbf{w}) \notin \mathcal{L}^*$, $\mathcal{C}(\pi)$ is not the exceptional $\mathbf{u}$ in Theorem 2 and hence $\mathbf{O}^T(\mathbf{B}, \mathbf{w} - \mathbf{g} \odot \mathcal{C}(\pi))$ is close to uniform over $\mathbb{Z}_q^{L\times(n+L+1)}$. Further, under our setup ($n' = n + L, m \ge \frac{7(n+L)}{\theta}, k = o(n)$), the exceptional probability for Theorem 2 is $O(q^{-(1/3+o(1))n})$ (negligible).

Strong Smoothness. We need to show that $(\mathbf{O}^T\mathbf{B}, \mathbf{Bt} + \mathbf{z}, \mathbf{O}^T\mathbf{Bt})$ is indistinguishable from $(\mathbf{O}^T\mathbf{B}, \mathbf{Bt} + \mathbf{z}, \mathbf{U})$, where $(\mathbf{z}, \mathbf{t}, \mathbf{O}, \mathbf{U}) \leftarrow (D_{\mathbb{Z},r_1})^m \times \mathbb{Z}_q^{n+L} \times (D_{\mathbb{Z},r_2})^{m\times L} \times \mathbb{Z}_q^L$. This follows from Lemma 9, as $\mathbf{O}^T\mathbf{B}$ is close to uniform (well-known and also implied by Theorem 2) and hence has a rank $< L$ only negligibly.

4.3.2 Construction of δ-ASPH$_B$

δ-ASPH$_B$ is identical to δ-ASPH$_A$, except that we need a trapdoor property while strong smoothness is no longer needed. Even though, we still need to validate claims adapted from δ-ASPH$_A$ under our new parameter choices. This is shown below in the security item. The trapdoor property is from Lemma 10.

Let $\mu \in \mathbb{N}, m = 6n \log n$. Take $\mathbf{h} \leftarrow \mathbb{Z}_q^m, \mathbf{A} \leftarrow \mathbb{Z}_q^{m\times n}$. $\mathcal{C}$ is a $[m, k, \theta m]_p$-code (from Lemma 7 with a negligible failure probability $mp^{(-1+\theta+1/\log p - o(1))m}$).

trapSim-commitment Scheme. The commitment key is $(\mathbf{A}, \mathbf{h})$. The commitment to $\pi \in \mathbb{Z}_p^k$ is $\mathbf{y} = \mathbf{A}\mathbf{s} + \mathbf{x} + \mathbf{h} \odot \mathcal{C}(\pi)$ for $\mathbf{x} \leftarrow (D_{\mathbb{Z}, r_1})^m$ and $\mathbf{s} \leftarrow \mathbb{Z}_q^m$ with witness $\tau = (\mathbf{s}, \mathbf{x})$. Further, $\mathsf{ver}, \mathcal{L}$, and $\mathcal{L}^*$ are defined the same as in δ-ASPH$_A$ via equation $\mathbf{y} = \mathbf{A}\mathbf{s} + \mathbf{x} + \mathbf{h} \odot \mathcal{C}(\pi)$. The trapdoor simulation is to apply Lemma 10 to generate $\mathbf{A}$ with trapdoor $\mathbf{T} \in \mathbb{Z}^{m \times m}$, by setting $\alpha = \theta/3$ and noticing that $n \log q = o(q^{1-\theta/3})$ (as $\lambda(1 - \theta/3) \geq 2\lambda/3 \geq 2$, due to $\lambda > \frac{3}{\theta} \geq 3$).

For $(\mathbf{A}, \mathsf{T}) \leftarrow \mathsf{TrapGen}(1^n)$, membership $(\pi, \mathbf{y}) \in \mathcal{L}^*$ can be verified as follows. For each $u \in \mathbb{Z}_q^*$, try to use T to recover $(\mathbf{s}, \mathbf{x})$ so that $u(\mathbf{y} - \mathbf{h} \odot \mathcal{C}(\pi)) = \mathbf{A}\mathbf{s} + \mathbf{x}$ with $||\mathbf{x}||_\infty \leq \lfloor \frac{q^{\theta/3} - 2}{4} \rfloor$. If it succeeds for some u, then claim $(\pi, \mathbf{y}) \in \mathcal{L}^*$; otherwise, claim $(m, \mathbf{y}) \notin \mathcal{L}^*$. By Lemma 10, this decision is always correct.

Description of δ-ASPH$_B$. This is identical to δ-ASPH$_A$. For secret $\mathbf{E} \leftarrow D_{\mathbb{Z}, r_2}^{m \times \mu}$, the projection key is $\mathbf{U} = \mathbf{E}^T \mathbf{A}$. Also, let $\mathcal{H}(\mathbf{E}, \pi, \mathbf{y}) = \mathbf{E}^T(\mathbf{y} - \mathbf{h} \odot \mathcal{C}(\pi))$. If $(\pi, \mathbf{y}) \in \mathcal{L}$ with witness $\tau = (\mathbf{s}, \mathbf{x})$, let $\hat{\mathcal{H}}(\tau, \mathbf{U}) = \mathbf{U}\mathbf{s}$.

Security. Security proofs for commitment, correctness and adaptive smoothness are identical to δ-ASPH$_A$. However, we need to verify that the cited results have negligible exception probabilities under our setup. Commitment security has used Lemma 2 to correctness. In our setting, $r_1\sqrt{m} = \Theta(n\sqrt{\log n}) = o(\delta_1)$ still holds and so the result remains valid. The correctness has cited Lemma 2 which requires $\delta_1 r_1 \log n = o(\delta)$ and remains valid in our setting. Theorem 2 is cited for smoothness and property 2 of $\mathcal{L}^*$. In our setting, it only has negligible exception probability $O(q^{(-\theta/3 + o(1))m})$.

4.4 LWE-Based PAKE Instantiation

Using δ-ASPH$_B$ and δ-ASPH$_A$ just obtained, together with pseudorandom generator G, KF-MAC F (in Sect. 3.3) and reconciliation $\pounds$ (in Sect. 3.2), we can realize our PAKE framework in the LWE setting (see Fig. 3). By the security theorem of PAKE framework, we only need to make sure that each of these mechanisms is secure in our parameter choices. This is specified as follow.

- $\theta \in (0, 1 - 1/\log p)$; $q = n^\lambda$ ($\lambda > \frac{3}{\theta}$); p is *constant* prime with $p < q$; $k = o(n)$; $r_1 = 3n^{\frac{1}{2}}$, $\delta_1 = 6n \log n$, $r_2 = q^{1-\frac{\theta}{3}} \log n$, $\delta = q^\alpha$ with $1 - \frac{\theta}{3} + \frac{1}{\lambda} < \alpha < 1$.
- $G : \{0, 1\}^{L'} \rightarrow \{0, 1\}^*$ is a pseudorandom generator.
- password dictionary $\mathcal{D} \subsetneq \mathbb{Z}_p^k$.
- *Instantiate KF-MAC.* Set F_K as the $(1, \delta, (\frac{4\delta}{q})^{\theta_{mac} L/p})$-KF MAC in Sect. 3.3 with key space $\mathbb{Z}_q^L$, where $\theta_{mac} \in (0, 1 - 1/\log p)$, $L = \frac{k_2 p(1+\beta)}{1 - \theta_{mac} - 1/\log p}$ for constant $\beta > 0$ (where $k_2 = o(n)$ is the p-ary output length of H in F_K). /* In this setup, insecurity error $(\frac{4\delta}{q})^{\theta_{mac} L/p} = (4q^{\alpha-1})^{\Theta(k_2)}$ (negligible); $[L/p, k_2, \theta_{mac} L/p]_p$-code in the scheme is constructed from Lemma 7 with negligible exception probability $O(p^{-k_2 \beta} L/p)$. */
- *Instantiate* $(\mathcal{H}_1, \hat{\mathcal{H}}_1)$ *with our LWE-based* δ-ASPH$_B$: Set $m = 6n \log n$, $\mu = L' \log \frac{q}{16\delta}$ (L' is the key length of G); other parameters such as $\delta_1, \delta, r_2, r_1$ are set as above; $[m, k, \theta m]_p$-code $\mathcal{C}$ is from Lemma 7. Take $\mathbf{A} \leftarrow \mathbb{Z}_q^{m \times n}, \mathbf{h} \leftarrow \mathbb{Z}_q^m$.

/* Under our setup, $\mathcal{C}$ fails to be constructed by Lemma 7 only with negligible probability $mp^{(-1+\theta+1/\log p)m}$; our setup is consistent with parameter description in δ-ASPH$_B$ and hence the resulting scheme is secure. */

- *Instantiate* $(\mathcal{H}_2, \hat{\mathcal{H}}_2)$ *with our LWE-based* δ-ASPH$_A$: Set $m_1 = \frac{7(L+n)}{\theta}$; $\delta_1, \delta, r_2, r_1, L$ etc set as above; $[m_1, k, \theta m_1]_p$-code $\mathcal{C}_1$ is from Lemma 7. Take $\mathbf{B} \leftarrow \mathbb{Z}_q^{m_1 \times (n+L)}$ and $\mathbf{g} \leftarrow \mathbb{Z}_q^{m_1}$ as public parameters for δ-ASPH$_A$.
  /* Under our setup, $\mathcal{C}_1$ fails to be constructed by Lemma 7 only with negligible probability $m_1 p^{(-1+\theta+1/\log p)m_1}$; our setup is consistent with parameter description in δ-ASPH$_A$ and hence the resulting scheme is secure. */
- Set $\mathbf{V} = \mathbf{O}^T\mathbf{B} \in \mathbb{Z}_q^{L\times(n+L)}$ for $\mathbf{O} \leftarrow (D_{\mathbb{Z}^{m_1}, r_2})^L$ as the public projection key.
- For $\pi \in \mathbb{Z}_p^k$, define $\mathbf{g}_\pi = \mathbf{g} \odot \mathcal{C}_1(\pi)$ and $\mathbf{h}_\pi = \mathbf{h} \odot \mathcal{C}(\pi)$.
- *Instantiate* £. Set £ as the reconciliation scheme in Sect. 3.2 with μ, δ and q as above. Thus, the reconciliated key $\boldsymbol{\xi}$ has a bit-length at least $\mu \log \frac{q}{16\delta} = L'$ (fit the key length of G).

The public parameter list for our PAKE is $\mathbf{A}|\mathbf{B}|\mathbf{g}|\mathbf{h}|\mathbf{V}|F|£|\mathcal{C}|\mathcal{C}_1$. The detailed protocol is simply to plug the primitives above into our PAKE framework. This is graphically shown in Fig. 3. Since primitives are secure by our parameter clarification, our protocol is secure by Theorem 1.

$P_i(\pi_{ij})$	Pub: $\mathbf{A}\|\mathbf{B}\|\mathbf{V}\|\mathbf{g}\|\mathbf{h}\|F\|£\|\mathcal{C}\|\mathcal{C}_1$	$P_j(\pi_{ij})$
$\mathbf{x} \leftarrow D_{\mathbb{Z}^m, r_1}$, $\mathbf{s} \leftarrow \mathbb{Z}_q^n$ $\mathbf{y} = \mathbf{A}\mathbf{s} + \mathbf{x} + \mathbf{h}_{\pi_{ij}}$	$\xrightarrow{\ \mathbf{y}\|P_i\ }$	
$\boldsymbol{\xi} = £_{bob}(\boldsymbol{\sigma}, \mathbf{U}\mathbf{s})$, $\|\|\mathbf{z}\|\| \overset{?}{\leq} \delta_1$ $\omega = \mathbf{w}\|\mathbf{y}\|\mathbf{U}\|\boldsymbol{\sigma}\|i\|j\|$ $\mathbf{w} \overset{?}{=} \mathbf{B}\mathbf{t} + \mathbf{z} + \mathbf{g}_{\pi_{ij}}$, $\eta_0 \overset{?}{=} F_{\mathbf{V}\mathbf{t}}(\omega\|0)$ If yes, $\eta_1 = F_{\mathbf{V}\mathbf{t}}(\omega\|1)$ & output sk	$\xleftarrow{\ \mathbf{w}\|\mathbf{U}\|\boldsymbol{\sigma}\|\eta_0\|P_j\ }$	$\mathbf{E} \leftarrow (D_{\mathbb{Z}^m, r_2})^\mu$, $\mathbf{U} = \mathbf{E}^T\mathbf{A}$ $\mathbf{y}' = \mathbf{y} - \mathbf{h}_{\pi_{ij}}$ $(\boldsymbol{\sigma}, \boldsymbol{\xi}) \leftarrow £_{alice}(\mathbf{E}^T\mathbf{y}')$, $\omega = \mathbf{w}\|\mathbf{y}\|\mathbf{U}\|\boldsymbol{\sigma}\|i\|j\|$ $\mathbf{w} = \mathbf{B}\mathbf{t} + \mathbf{z} + \mathbf{g}_{\pi_{ij}}$, $\eta_0 = F_{\mathbf{V}\mathbf{t}}(\omega\|0)$
	$\xrightarrow{\ \eta_1\ }$	If $\eta_1 = F_{\mathbf{V}\mathbf{t}}(\omega\|1)$, output sk

Fig. 3. Our Protocol LWE-PAKE: $\mathbf{t} \leftarrow \mathbb{Z}_q^{n+L}$ and $\mathbf{z} \leftarrow D_{\mathbb{Z}^{m_1}, r_1}$ are sampled with randomness Υ where $\Upsilon|sk = G(\boldsymbol{\xi})$.

Efficiency. Note that $\mathbf{g}_{\pi_{ij}}$ and $\mathbf{h}_{\pi_{ij}}$ can be pre-computed and $D^m_{\mathbb{Z},r}$ can be sampled in $\tilde{O}(m)$ time [23]. Thus, the cost of P_i is dominated by $\mathbf{Bt}, \mathbf{Us}, \mathbf{As}$ and $\mathbf{Vt}$ which totally is about mn multiplications over $\mathbb{Z}_q$ (as $L = O(n), \mu = O(n)$ and $m_1 = o(m)$); the cost of $\mathbf{P}_j$ is dominated by $\mathbf{E}^T\mathbf{A}, \mathbf{E}^T\mathbf{y}', \mathbf{Bt}, \mathbf{Vt}$ which is $\mu mn = O(L'mn/\log q)$ multiplications. The communication cost is dominated by $(\mathbf{U}, \mathbf{w}, \mathbf{y})$ which has $O(\frac{L'n}{\log n} + n\log n)$ field elements. Finally, the authentication is provided by $(\mathbf{w}, \eta_0)$ with a cost dominated by $\mathbf{Bt}$ and $\mathbf{Vt}$, which is $(m_1 + L)(n + L) = O(n^2)$ multiplications. This is more efficient than authentication [6,15] from CCA-secure encryption, which has a cost $O(n^2 \log n)$ [21,29] in the LWE setting. Our main saving for this comes from the fact that δ-ASPH$_A$ doesn't need a trapdoor simulation so it can take $m_1 = O(n)$ while [21,29] needs this and hence the corresponding parameter is $O(n \log n)$. That is, authentication data (w, η_0) can not enable to decrypt π_{ij} and so it is different from authentication by CCA-secure encryption.

5 Instantiation from Ring-LWE

This section will present our PAKE instantiation based on Ring-LWE. This is important as it is more efficient than LWE-based one.

5.1 Basics of Rings, Ring-LWE and Operational Properties

5.1.1 Introduction to Algebraic Number Theory

We provide some facts from algebraic number theory (also see [20]). Let m be a power of 2 and $n = m/2$.

Power Basis of Cyclotomic Field. We are interested in the mth cyclotomic field $K = \mathbb{Q}(\zeta_m)$, where ζ_m is the mth primitive root of unity and has the minimal polynomial $\Phi_m(x) = x^n + 1$ with $n = m/2$. Then, K has a $\mathbb{Q}$-basis $\{1, \zeta_m, \zeta_m^2, \cdots, \zeta_m^{n-1}\}$ (called *power basis*, denoted by $\mathbf{p}$).

Canonical Embedding. $K = \mathbb{Q}(\zeta_m)$ has n embeddings $\sigma_i : K \to \mathbb{C}$, $\forall i \in \mathbb{Z}_m^*$. The *canonical embedding* $\sigma : K \to \mathbb{C}^{\phi(m)}$ is $\sigma(a) = (\sigma_i(a))_{i \in \mathbb{Z}_m^*}$ for $a \in K$. Since $\sigma_i(a) = \bar{\sigma}_{m-i}(a)$, $\sigma(a) \in H$.

Ring of Integers and Ideals. An *algebraic integer* in K is an element in it that is a root of a monic polynomial in $\mathbb{Z}[x]$. The set of all integers of K is a ring, denoted by R in this paper. For $K = \mathbb{Q}(\zeta_m)$, $R = \mathbb{Z}[\zeta_m]$. Thus, the power basis $\{1, \zeta_m, \cdots, \zeta_m^{n-1}\}$ is a $\mathbb{Z}$-basis of R.

Chinese Remainder Basis and Its Relation with Power Basis. In this paper, q is a prime with $q = 1 \mod m$ and ω_m is the mth root of 1 in $\mathbb{Z}_q^*$. let $\mathfrak{p}_i = (q, \zeta_m - \omega_m^i)$ (i.e., the ring generated by q and $\zeta_m - \omega_m^i$). By Chinese remainder theorem, for each $i \in \mathbb{Z}_m^*$, there exists $c_i \in R$ so that $c_i = 1 \mod \mathfrak{p}_i$ and $c_i = 0 \mod \mathfrak{p}_j$ for any $j \neq i$. Then, $\mathbf{c} = (c_j)_{j \in \mathbb{Z}_m^*}$ forms a basis of $R_q \stackrel{def}{=} R \bmod q$, called the *CRT basis.* Note that $c_i^2 = c_i \mod qR$, as $c_i^2 = c_i \mod \mathfrak{p}_i$ for each $i \in \mathbb{Z}_m^*$. Hence, if $a = \mathbf{c}^T\mathbf{v}, b = \mathbf{c}^T\mathbf{u} \in R_q$ for $\mathbf{v}, \mathbf{u} \in \mathbb{Z}_q^n$, then $ab = \mathbf{c}^T(\mathbf{v} \odot \mathbf{u})$. Let $\mathrm{CRT}_m = (\omega_m^{ij})_{i \in \mathbb{Z}_m^*, j \in [n]}$. Then, the power basis $\mathbf{p}$ and CRT basis $\mathbf{c}$ is connected by $\mathbf{p}^T = \mathbf{c}^T \cdot \mathrm{CRT}_m$. Thus, if $a = \mathbf{p}^T\mathbf{v}$ for some $\mathbf{v} \in \mathbb{Z}_q^n$, then $a = \mathbf{c}^T \cdot \mathrm{CRT}_m\mathbf{v}$.

Coefficient Vector Representation. For $a = \mathbf{p}^T\mathbf{v}$ with some $\mathbf{v} \in \mathbb{Z}_q^n$, we call $\mathbf{v}$ the *coefficient vector* of a under $\mathbf{p}$ and denote it by $\underline{a}$. For $\mathbf{a} \in R_q^\ell$, let $\mathbf{a} = (\mathbf{p}^T\mathbf{v}_1, \cdots, \mathbf{p}^T\mathbf{v}_\ell)^T$ for some $\mathbf{v}_i \in \mathbb{Z}_q^n$. We call $(\mathbf{v}_1; \cdots; \mathbf{v}_\ell)$ *the coefficient vector* of $\mathbf{a}$ under $\mathbf{p}$ and denote it by $\underline{\mathbf{a}}$. Similarly, we can define the *coefficient vector* of a and $\mathbf{a}$ under basis $\mathbf{c}$ and denote them by $\underset{\sim}{a}$ and $\underset{\sim}{\mathbf{a}}$ respectively. As

$\mathbf{p}^T = \mathbf{c}^T \cdot \mathrm{CRT}_m$, we know that $\underset{\sim}{a} = \mathrm{CRT}_m \cdot \underline{a}$. For $\mathbf{a} \in R_q^\ell$, we have $\underset{\sim}{\mathbf{a}} = (\mathbf{I}_\ell \otimes \mathrm{CRT}_m)\underline{\mathbf{a}}$ and $\underline{\mathbf{a}} = (\mathbf{I}_\ell \otimes \mathrm{CRT}_m^{-1})\underset{\sim}{\mathbf{a}}$.

5.1.2 Gaussian Samplings

Gaussian Distribution over $K \otimes \mathbb{R}$. Since m is a power of 2, the power basis $\mathbf{p}$ is an orthogonal basis of H (via canonical embedding σ and [20, Lemma 2.15]) and $||\zeta_m^j|| = \sqrt{n}, \forall j \in \mathbb{Z}_m^*$. Hence, Gaussian distribution over $K \otimes \mathbb{R}$ (or H via σ) with parameter ξ can be sampled as $\mathbf{z} = \sum_{i=0}^{n-1} \zeta_m^j r_j$, where $r_0, \cdots, r_{n-1}$ is i.i.d. Gaussian over $\mathbb{R}$ with parameter $\xi/\sqrt{n}$. Denote this distribution by Ψ_ξ.

Discrete Gaussian over R. Since $\mathbf{p}$ is an orthogonal basis of R (embedded into H), $\mathbf{e} = \sum_{i=0}^{n-1} \zeta_m^j e_i$ with $e_i \leftarrow D_{\mathbb{Z}, s/\sqrt{n}}$ is according to $D_{R,s}$.

5.1.3 Ring-LWE

The Learning With Errors over rings (Ring-LWE) was introduced in [19], where the worst-case hardness result was also proven. Based on basis $\mathbf{p}$, $x \in K \otimes \mathbb{R}$ can be represented as $x = \sum_i x_i \zeta_m^i$ for $x_i \in \mathbb{R}$. Also, $x \in K/qR \otimes \mathbb{R}$ can be represented as $x = \sum_i x_i \zeta_m^i$ for $x_i \in [0, q)$. Let $\mathbb{T} = K/qR \otimes \mathbb{R}$.

For $s \in R_q$ and distribution χ over $K \otimes \mathbb{R}$, a sample from distribution $A_{s,\chi}$ over $R_q \times \mathbb{T}$ consists of (a, b) with $a \leftarrow R_q, e \leftarrow \chi$ and $b = as + e \mod q$.

Decisional ring-LWE (**ring-DLWE**$_{q,\chi,m}$) states that independent samples from $A_{s,\chi}$ for $s \leftarrow R_q$ and the same number of samples uniformly over $R_q \times \mathbb{T}$ are indistinguishable. Denote this assumption with $\chi = D_{R,r}$ by **ring-DLWE**$_{q,r,m}$.

5.1.4 Matrix Representations for Operations over R_q

In this subsection, we will give some useful facts on the matrix representation over $\mathbb{Z}_q$ for elements, vector or matrix over R_q. For $b \in R_q$, define $\phi_1(b) = \mathrm{CRT}_m^{-1} \cdot \mathrm{DIAG}(\underset{\sim}{b})$, $\phi_2(b) = \mathrm{CRT}_m^T \cdot \mathrm{DIAG}(\underset{\sim}{b}) \cdot \mathrm{CRT}_m^{-T}$. Generally, for $\mathbf{D} = (d_{ij}) \in R_q^{\ell \times k}$ and $u = 1, 2$, define $\phi_u(\mathbf{D}) = (\phi_u(d_{ij}))_{1 \le i \le \ell, 1 \le j \le k}$ (a block matrix with entry (i,j) being $\phi_u(d_{ij})$). For $\mathbf{v} \in \mathbb{Z}_q^n$, define $\ddagger(\mathbf{v}) = \begin{bmatrix} v_0 & v_1 & \cdots & v_{n-1} \\ -v_{n-1} & v_0 & \cdots & v_{n-2} \\ \vdots & \vdots & \ddots & \vdots \\ -v_1 & -v_2 & \cdots & v_0 \end{bmatrix}$.

The following facts about $\phi_1, \phi_2, \ddagger$ are useful.

Lemma 13. *Let $s \in R_q, \mathbf{e}, \mathbf{b} \in R_q^\ell$ and $\mathbf{D} = (\mathbf{d}^{(1)}, \cdots, \mathbf{d}^{(k)}) \in R_q^{\ell \times k}$.*

1. $\phi_1(\mathbf{b}) = (\mathbf{I}_\ell \otimes \mathrm{CRT}_m^{-1}) \begin{bmatrix} \mathrm{DIAG}(\underset{\sim}{b_1}) \\ \vdots \\ \mathrm{DIAG}(\underset{\sim}{b_\ell}) \end{bmatrix}, \phi_2(\mathbf{b}) = (\mathbf{I}_\ell \otimes \mathrm{CRT}_m^T) \begin{bmatrix} \mathrm{DIAG}(\underset{\sim}{b_1}) \\ \vdots \\ \mathrm{DIAG}(\underset{\sim}{b_\ell}) \end{bmatrix} \mathrm{CRT}_m^{-T}$.
2. $\phi_2(\mathbf{D}) = (\mathbf{I}_\ell \otimes \mathrm{CRT}_m^T) \begin{bmatrix} \mathrm{DIAG}(\underset{\sim}{d_{11}}) & \cdots & \mathrm{DIAG}(\underset{\sim}{d_{1k}}) \\ \vdots & \ddots & \vdots \\ \mathrm{DIAG}(\underset{\sim}{d_{\ell 1}}) & \cdots & \mathrm{DIAG}(\underset{\sim}{d_{\ell k}}) \end{bmatrix} (\mathbf{I}_k \otimes \mathrm{CRT}_m^{-T})$.

3. $\underline{\mathbf{b}s} = \phi_1(\mathbf{b})\underset{\sim}{s}$.
4. $[\underline{\mathbf{e}^T\mathbf{b}}]^T = [\underline{\mathbf{e}}]^T\phi_2(\mathbf{b})$. *Further,* $((\underline{\mathbf{e}^T\mathbf{d}^{(1)}})^T, \cdots, (\underline{\mathbf{e}^T\mathbf{d}^{(k)}})^T) = [\underline{\mathbf{e}}]^T \cdot \phi_2(\mathbf{D})$.
5. $\phi_2(s) = \ddagger(\underline{s})$.

Proof. Items 1 and 2 follow by definition. For item 3, notice that for $s, b \in R_q$, $\underline{bs} = \mathrm{CRT}_m^{-1}(\underset{\sim}{b} \odot \underset{\sim}{s}) = \phi_1(b)\underset{\sim}{s}$. Generalizing to $\mathbf{b} \in R_q^\ell$ follows by definition of $\phi_1(\mathbf{b})$. For item 4, notice $(\underline{bs})^T = \underset{\sim}{s}^T\phi_1^T(b) = \underline{s}^T \cdot \mathrm{CRT}_m^T\phi_1^T(b) = \underline{s}^T\phi_2(b)$ for $s, b \in R_q$. Thus, $[\underline{\mathbf{e}^T\mathbf{b}}]^T = \sum_i[\underline{e_ib_i}]^T = \sum_i[\underline{e_i}]^T\phi_2(b_i) = [\underline{\mathbf{e}}]^T\phi_2(\mathbf{b})$. Generalizing to the second part of item 4 follows by definition of $\phi_2(\mathbf{D})$. For item 5, notice that $[\underline{bs}]^T = \underline{s}^T \cdot \ddagger(\underline{b})$ (as $x^n + 1 = 0$ in R_q). But we know that $[\underline{bs}]^T = \underline{s}^T \cdot \phi_2(b)$. Since s is arbitrary in R_q, the result follows. □

In the remaining of this section, we will present materials for ring-LWE based PAKE instantiation. Due to the space limitation, we present it in the intuitive level. The formal details appear in the full paper.

5.2 Supporting Properties from Ring-LWE

Regularity. We prove a regularity result: for discrete Gaussian $\mathbf{e}$ over R^ℓ and uniformly random $\mathbf{D}$ over $R_q^{\ell\times k}$, $\mathbf{e}^T\mathbf{D}$ is statistically close to uniform over R_q^k (for quite general k, ℓ). The strategy is as follows. By Lemma 13(4), $\mathbf{e}^T\mathbf{D}$ is represented by $[\underline{\mathbf{e}}]^T\phi_2(\mathbf{D})$. It suffices to show that $[\underline{\mathbf{e}}]^T\phi_2(\mathbf{D})$ is close to uniform in $\mathbb{Z}_q^{1\times nk}$. We use Lemma 3 (with Lemma 1) to do this. This essentially only requires to show that $\min_{\mathbf{s}\in\mathbb{Z}_q^{kn}-\{\mathbf{0}\}} ||\phi_2(\mathbf{D})\mathbf{s}||_\infty$ is large, as it implies a full column rank of $\phi_2(\mathbf{D})$ and large $\lambda_1^\infty(\Lambda(\phi_2(\mathbf{D})))$. This requirement is shown in the full paper. It should be noted that our regularity result with a special form of $\mathbf{D}$ appeared in [20] while the case of $k = 1$ is in [10].

Adaptive Smoothness-I. Given $\mathbf{a}, \mathbf{h} \leftarrow R_q^\ell$ and a $[\ell n, k, d]_p$-code $\mathcal{C}$ with large d, we show the following holds with high probability (over $\mathbf{a}, \mathbf{h}$): let $\mathbf{E}$ be discrete Gaussian over $\mathbb{Z}^{\ell n\times\mu}$ and $\mathbf{w}$ be adaptively chosen after given $\mathbf{E}^T \cdot \phi_1(\mathbf{a})$. Then,

1. $\min_{\mathbf{s}\in\mathbb{Z}_q^{n+1}-\mathbf{0}} ||\Big(\phi_1(\mathbf{a}), \underline{\mathbf{w}-\mathbf{h}_\mathbf{u}}\Big)\mathbf{s}||_\infty$ is large for all but one $\mathbf{u}$ in $\mathcal{C}$, where $\mathbf{h}_\mathbf{u} \in R_q^\ell$ is defined so that $\underset{\sim}{\mathbf{h}_\mathbf{u}} = \underset{\sim}{\mathbf{h}} \odot \mathbf{u}$;
2. $\mathbf{E}^T\Big(\phi_1(\mathbf{a}), \underline{\mathbf{w}-\mathbf{h}_\mathbf{u}}\Big)$ is close to uniform over $\mathbb{Z}_q^{\mu\times(n+1)}$ for all $\mathbf{u} \in \mathcal{C}$ but the exceptional one in item 1, where the statistical closeness is over $\mathbf{E}$.

To show item 1, it suffices to show $||\phi_1(\mathbf{a}) \cdot \mathbf{s}'||_\infty$ for any $\mathbf{s}' \in \mathbb{Z}_q^n - \{\mathbf{0}\}$ is large and the $||\cdot||_\infty$-distance from $t(\underline{\mathbf{w}-\mathbf{h}_\mathbf{u}})$ to $\mathcal{L}(\phi_1(\mathbf{a}))$, $\forall t \in \mathbb{Z}_q^*$, is large for all but one $\mathbf{u}$ in $\mathcal{C}$. The former is given by a random argument and the latter is a consequence of Lemma 11, using $\underline{\mathbf{w}-\mathbf{h}_\mathbf{u}} = (\mathbf{I}_\ell \otimes \mathrm{CRT}_m^{-1})(\underset{\sim}{\mathbf{w}} - \underset{\sim}{\mathbf{h}} \odot \mathbf{u})$. Item 2 follows from the adaptive version of Lemma 3, using item 1.

Adaptive Smoothness-II. In smoothness-I, we can extract μ random elements in $\mathbb{Z}_q$ (i.e., $\mathbf{E}^T\underline{(\mathbf{w}-\mathbf{h_u})}$) from $\mu \times n$ matrix $\mathbf{E}^T\phi_1(\mathbf{a})$. In smoothness-II, we show this extraction efficiency can be improved. Specifically, for $\mathbf{D} \leftarrow R_q^{\ell\times k}, \mathbf{h} \leftarrow R_q^\ell$ and a $[\ell n, k', d]_p$-code $\mathcal{C}$ with large d, we show the following holds with high probability (over $\mathbf{D}, \mathbf{h}$). Let $\mathbf{e}$ be discrete Gaussian in R^ℓ and $\mathbf{w}$ is adaptively chosen after given $\mathbf{e}^T\mathbf{D}$.

1. $\min_{\mathbf{s}\in\mathbb{Z}_q^{kn+L}-\mathbf{0}} ||\Big(\phi_2(\mathbf{D}), \phi_2(\mathbf{w}-\mathbf{h_u})_L\Big)\mathbf{s}||_\infty$ is large for all but one $\mathbf{u}$ in $\mathcal{C}$, where $\mathbf{h_u} \in R_q^\ell$ is defined s.t. $\underset{\sim}{\mathbf{h_u}} = \underset{\approx}{\mathbf{h}} \odot \mathbf{u}$ and $\phi_2(\mathbf{v})_L$ is the first L columns of $\phi_2(\mathbf{v})$.
2. $(\mathbf{e}^T\mathbf{D}, [\underline{\mathbf{e}^T(\mathbf{w}-\mathbf{h_u})}]_1^L)$ is close to uniform in $R_q^k \times \mathbb{Z}_q^L$ for all $\mathbf{u} \in \mathcal{C}$ but the exceptional one in item 1, where $[\mathbf{x}]_1^L$ is the first L components of vector $\mathbf{x}$ and the statistical closeness is over $\mathbf{e}$.

Here $k \in \mathbb{N}$ is arbitrary (e.g. $k = 1$ and later we will take $k = 2$). The parameter $L < n$ but we can achieve $L = \Theta(n)$. Consequently, we can now extract $\Theta(n)$ elements in $\mathbb{Z}_q$ from $\mathbf{e}^T\mathbf{D} \in R_q^k$. The proof of item 1 is given by a strengthened regularity. The idea of item 2 is to use Lemma 13(4) to study the distribution of its matrix form $[\underline{\mathbf{e}}]^T(\phi_2(\mathbf{D}), \phi_2(\mathbf{w}-\mathbf{h}_u)_L)$. This is provably close to uniform for all but one $\mathbf{u}$ by item 1 and a variant of [28, Lemma 19].

Hidden-Bits Lemma from Ring-LWE. We extend LWE-based hidden-bits lemma in Sect. 4.2 to the ring-LWE setting. It essentially says that given a redundant ring-LWE tuple, we can extract some random bits of the secret that is confidential to an attacker. Formally, for fixed $\alpha, \beta \in R_q$, let $L' = |\{i \mid (\underset{\sim}{\alpha}[i], \underset{\sim}{\beta}[i]) \neq (0,0), i \in [n]\}|$. Then, given $\mathbf{a}, \mathbf{b} \leftarrow R_q^\ell$ and $\mathbf{a}s + \mathbf{b}t + \mathbf{x}$ for $s, t \leftarrow R_q$ and $\mathbf{x}$ discrete Gaussian over R^ℓ, it holds that $[\ \underline{\alpha s + \beta t}\ ]_1^L$ is indistinguishable from uniformly random in $\mathbb{Z}_q^L$ under the ring-DLWE assumption.

Trapdoor Generation from Ring-LWE. We generalize the trapdoor generation algorithm in $\mathbb{Z}^m$ in [21] to the ring-LWE setting. The algorithm will generate a random matrix $\mathbf{D} \in R_q^{\ell\times\nu}$ together with a trapdoor $\mathbf{R}$ so that $\mathbf{R}$ can be used to decode $\mathbf{t}$ from $\mathbf{Dt} + \mathbf{x}$ when $\underline{\mathbf{x}}$ is short. Ducas and Micciancio [10] obtained the generalization for case $\nu = 1$. We obtain the result for the general ν case. Our algorithm is simply the ring version of [21]: $\mathbf{D} = (\mathbf{D}_0; \mathbf{I}_\nu \otimes \mathbf{g} - \mathbf{R}^T\mathbf{D}_0)$ for a random matrix $\mathbf{D}_0$ in $R_q^{(\ell-k\nu)\times\nu}$ and a discrete Gaussian matrix $\mathbf{R}$ in $R^{(\ell-k\nu)\times k\nu}$, where $\mathbf{g} = (1, 2, \cdots, 2^{k-1})^T$ and $k = \lceil \log q \rceil$. To show that $\mathbf{D}$ is random, it requires to show that given $\mathbf{D}_0$, $\mathbf{R}^T\mathbf{D}_0$ is statistically random. This follows by our regularity result above. The decoding property is a trivial extension of [21].

5.3 ASPHs from Ideal Lattices

In this section, we will present our construction of ASPH from ideal lattices. The idea is to extend the LWE-based schemes to the ring-LWE setting.

5.3.1 Construction of δ-ASPH$_A$

Let $L \leq n, \theta \in (0,1), k = o(n), \ell \in \mathbb{N}, p$ constant prime. Take $\mathbf{g} \leftarrow R_q^\ell$, $\mathbf{D} = (\mathbf{d}_1, \mathbf{d}_2) \leftarrow R_q^{\ell \times 2}$. Let $\mathcal{C}$ be a $[\ell n, k, \theta \ell n]_p$-code. For $\pi \in \mathbb{Z}_p^k$, define $\mathbf{g}_\pi \in R_q^\ell$ such that $\underset{\sim}{\mathbf{g}_\pi} = \underset{\sim}{\mathbf{g}} \odot \mathcal{C}(\pi)$.

The Commitment Scheme. The commitment key is $(\mathbf{D}, \mathbf{g})$. To commit to $\pi \in \mathbb{Z}_p^k$, take $\mathbf{t} \leftarrow R_q^2$ and $\mathbf{z}$ discrete Gaussian over R^ℓ. The commitment is $\mathbf{w} = \mathbf{Dt} + \mathbf{g}_\pi + \mathbf{z}$ with witness $(\mathbf{t}, \mathbf{z})$. The decommitment is $(\pi, \mathbf{t}, \mathbf{z})$. Let $\mathsf{ver}(\mathbf{t}, \mathbf{z}, \pi, \mathbf{w}) = 1$ if and only if $\mathbf{w} = \mathbf{Dt} + \mathbf{g}_\pi + \mathbf{z}$ with $||\underline{\mathbf{z}}||$ small.

Then, we define $\mathcal{L}$ and $\mathcal{L}^*$. Let $\mathcal{X} = \mathbb{Z}_p^k \times R_q^\ell$. Then, $\mathcal{L}$ is generically defined by ver. Define $\mathcal{L}^* = \{(\pi, \mathbf{w}) \in \mathcal{X} \mid ||\left(\phi_2(\mathbf{D}), \phi_2(\mathbf{w} - \mathbf{g}_\pi)_L\right)\mathbf{s}||_\infty$ is small for some $\mathbf{s} \in \mathbb{Z}_q^{2n+L} - \{\mathbf{0}\}\}$, where $\phi_2(\mathbf{v})_L$ is the first L columns of matrix $\phi_2(\mathbf{v})$.

Our commitment is secure: the hiding property directly follows from ring-DLWE assumption and binding property is implied by properties of $\mathcal{L}^*$:

(1) $\mathcal{L} \subseteq \mathcal{L}^*$. This is true as $||\left(\phi_2(\mathbf{D}), \phi_2(\mathbf{Dt} + \mathbf{z})_L\right)\mathbf{s}||_\infty$ with short $\mathbf{z}$ is small for some non-zero $\mathbf{s}$. Indeed, via Lemma 13, one can find $2n \times n$ matrix A s.t. $\phi_2(\mathbf{D})A = \phi_2(\mathbf{Dt})$. Let $\mathbf{1}_L = (1, \cdots, 1)^T$ (with L 1s), $\mathbf{1}_L^+ = (1, \cdots, 1, 0, \cdots, 0)^T$ (with L 1s and $(n-L)$ 0s). For $\mathbf{s} = (-A\mathbf{1}_L^+; \mathbf{1}_L)$, $||\left(\phi_2(\mathbf{D}), \phi_2(\mathbf{Dt} + \mathbf{z})_L\right)\mathbf{s}||_\infty = ||\phi_2(\mathbf{z})\mathbf{1}_L^+||_\infty \leq ||\underline{\mathbf{z}}||$ (small), where $\phi_2(z_i) = \ddagger(\underline{z_i})$ (Lemma 13(5)) is used.

(2) For $\mathbf{w} \in R_q^\ell$, there is at most one π so that $(\pi, \mathbf{w}) \in \mathcal{L}^*$. This follows from property 1 of adaptive smoothness-II.

Description of δ-ASPH$_A$. For secret key $\mathbf{o}$ discrete Gaussian over R^ℓ, define the projection key $\alpha(\mathbf{o}) = \mathbf{o}^T\mathbf{D}$. For $(\pi, \mathbf{w}) \in \mathcal{X}$, let $\mathcal{H}(\mathbf{o}, \pi, \mathbf{w}) = \left[\underline{\mathbf{o}^T(\mathbf{w} - \mathbf{g}_\pi)}\right]_1^L$. If $(\pi, \mathbf{w}) \in \mathcal{L}$ with witness $\tau = (\mathbf{t}, \mathbf{z})$, then let $\hat{\mathcal{H}}(\tau, \alpha(\mathbf{o})) = \left[\underline{\mathbf{o}^T\mathbf{Dt}}\right]_1^L$.

Correctness. For $(\pi, \mathbf{w}) \in \mathcal{L}$, there exists $\tau = (\mathbf{t}, \mathbf{z})$ with small $||\underline{\mathbf{z}}||$ s.t. $\mathbf{w} = \mathbf{Dt} + \mathbf{g}_\pi + \mathbf{z}$. Then, $\mathcal{H}(\mathbf{o}, \pi, \mathbf{w}) - \hat{\mathcal{H}}(\tau, \alpha(\mathbf{o})) = \left[\underline{\mathbf{o}^T\mathbf{z}}\right]_1^L = \left[\sum_{i=1}^\ell [\underline{z_i}]^T \ddagger(\underline{o_i})\right]_1^L$ (by Lemma 13(4)(5)), which is short by Lemma 2 as $\mathbf{o}$ is Gaussian and $||\underline{\mathbf{z}}||$ is small.

Adaptive Smoothness. Given π and any function $f : R_q^2 \rightarrow R_q^\ell$, let $\mathbf{o}$ discrete Gaussian over R^ℓ and $\mathbf{w} = f(\mathbf{o}^T\mathbf{D})$. If $(\pi, \mathbf{w}) \in \mathcal{X} \backslash \mathcal{L}^*$, then by definition of $\mathcal{L}^*$, $\mathbf{g}_\pi$ is not the exceptional $\mathbf{u}$ in the result of adaptive smoothness-II. Thus, $\left(\mathbf{o}^T\mathbf{D}, \left[\underline{\mathbf{o}^T(\mathbf{w} - \mathbf{g}_\mathbf{u})}\right]_1^L\right)$ is close to uniform in $R_q^2 \times \mathbb{Z}_q^L$.

Strong Smoothness. It suffices to show that $(\alpha(\mathbf{o}), \mathbf{D}, \mathbf{Dt} + \mathbf{z}, \left[\underline{\mathbf{o}^T\mathbf{Dt}}\right]_1^L)$ and $(\alpha(\mathbf{o}), \mathbf{D}, \mathbf{Dt} + \mathbf{z}, \mathbf{U})$ are indistinguishable, when $\mathbf{o}, \mathbf{z}$ discrete Gaussian over R^ℓ and $(\mathbf{t}, \mathbf{U}) \leftarrow R_q^2 \times \mathbb{Z}_q^L$. Let $(a, b) = \mathbf{o}^T\mathbf{D}$. By regularity property, with high probability, $(\underset{\sim}{a}[i], \underset{\sim}{b}[i]) \neq 0$ holds for most of i's. So strong smoothness follows from hidden-bit lemma in Sect. 5.2.

5.3.2 Construction of δ-ASPH$_B$

Let $\mu \in \mathbb{N}, \theta \in (0,1), k = o(n), \ell \in \mathbb{N}, p$ constant prime. Take $\mathbf{h}, \mathbf{a} \leftarrow R_q^\ell$. Let $\mathcal{C}$ be a $[\ell n, k, \theta \ell n]_p$-code. For $\pi \in \mathbb{Z}_p^k$, define $\mathbf{h}_\pi \in R_q^\ell$ such that $\underset{\sim}{\mathbf{h}_\pi} = \underset{\sim}{\mathbf{h}} \odot \mathcal{C}(\pi)$.

trapSim-commitment. The commitment to $\pi \in \mathbb{Z}_p^k$ using public-key $(\mathbf{a}, \mathbf{h})$ is $\mathbf{y} = \mathbf{a}s + \mathbf{h}_\pi + \mathbf{x}$ for $s \leftarrow R_q$ and $\mathbf{x}$ discrete Gaussian over R^ℓ. Details and language $\mathcal{L}$ are identical to δ-ASPH$_A$. Further, the trapdoor simulation follows.

- $\mathsf{sim}(1^n)$. Take $\mathbf{h} \leftarrow R_q^\ell$; use the trapdoor generation algorithm in Sect. 5.2 with $\nu = 1$ to generate $\mathbf{a}$ and $\mathbf{R}$ so that $\mathbf{R}$ can decode $\mathbf{a}s + \mathbf{x}$ as long as $||\mathbf{x}||$ is not large. With $\mathbf{R}$, membership $(\pi, \mathbf{y}) \in \mathcal{L}$ can be verified, by trying to decode $(s, \mathbf{x})$ so that $\mathbf{y} = \mathbf{a}s + \mathbf{x} + \mathbf{h}_\pi$.

Let $\mathcal{X} = \mathbb{Z}_p^k \times R_q^\ell$. We define $\mathcal{L}^* \subseteq \mathcal{X}$ so that $(\pi, \mathbf{y}) \in \mathcal{L}^*$ if $t(\mathbf{y} - \mathbf{h}_\pi) = \mathbf{a}s + \mathbf{x}$ for some $(t, s, \mathbf{x}) \in \mathbb{Z}_q \times R_q \times R_q^\ell$ with $\underline{\mathbf{x}}$ short and $(t, s) \neq (0, 0)$. We now verify three required properties for $\mathcal{L}^*$.

1. $\mathcal{L} \subseteq \mathcal{L}^*$. It is evident by adapting witness $(s, \mathbf{x})$ for $\mathcal{L}$ to $(1, s, \mathbf{x})$ for $\mathcal{L}^*$.
2. *Given* $\mathbf{y} \in R_q^\ell$, *there is at most one* π *with* $(\pi, \mathbf{y}) \in \mathcal{L}^*$. Notice that $t(\mathbf{y} - \mathbf{h}_\pi) = \mathbf{a}s + \mathbf{x}$ (via Lemma 13(3)) is equivalent to $t\underline{(\mathbf{y} - \mathbf{h}_\pi)} = \phi_1(\mathbf{a})\underset{\sim}{s} + \underline{\mathbf{x}}$. By adaptive smoothness-I, there is at most one π so that this holds with short $\underline{\mathbf{x}}$ and non-zero $(t, \underset{\sim}{s})$, desired.
3. For $(\mathbf{a}, \mathbf{R}) \leftarrow \mathsf{sim}(1^n)$, $(\pi, \mathbf{y}) \in \mathcal{L}^*$ can be verified using $\mathbf{R}$ as follows. For each $t \in \mathbb{Z}_q^*$, try to use $\mathbf{R}$ to recover $(s, \mathbf{x})$ so that $t(\mathbf{y} - \mathbf{h}_\pi) = \mathbf{a}s + \mathbf{x}$ for short $\mathbf{x}$. If it succeeds, then claim $(\pi, \mathbf{y}) \in \mathcal{L}^*$; otherwise, claim $(\pi, \mathbf{y}) \notin \mathcal{L}^*$. The validity of this algorithm is by the decoding capability of $\mathbf{R}$.

The commitment security is evident: the hiding property is by the ring-DLWE assumption and the binding property follows from properties 1, 2 above for $\mathcal{L}^*$.

Description of δ-ASPH$_B$. We now define $\mathcal{H}$ and $\hat{\mathcal{H}}$. Take secret $\mathbf{E}$ discrete Gaussian over $\mathbb{Z}^{n\ell \times \mu}$ and the projection key is $\mathbf{U} = \alpha(\mathbf{E}) = \mathbf{E}^T \phi_1(\mathbf{a})$. The projective hash $\mathcal{H}(\mathbf{E}, \pi, \mathbf{y}) = \mathbf{E}^T \underline{(\mathbf{y} - \mathbf{h}_\pi)}$. With witness $\tau = (s, \mathbf{x})$, define $\hat{\mathcal{H}}(\tau, \mathbf{U}) = \mathbf{U}\underset{\sim}{s}$.

<u>Correctness.</u> For $(\pi, \mathbf{y}) \in \mathcal{L}$, let $\mathbf{y} = \mathbf{a}s + \mathbf{h}_\pi + \mathbf{x}$ with short $\underline{\mathbf{x}}$. Then, by Lemma 13(3), $\mathbf{E}^T \underline{(\mathbf{y} - \mathbf{h}_\pi)} = \mathbf{E}^T \phi_1(\mathbf{a})\underset{\sim}{s} + \mathbf{E}^T \underline{\mathbf{x}} = \mathbf{U}\underset{\sim}{s} + \mathbf{E}^T \underline{\mathbf{x}}$. The correctness follows as $||\mathbf{E}^T \underline{\mathbf{x}}||_\infty$ is small by Lemma 2 (since $\mathbf{E}$ is Gaussian and $\underline{\mathbf{x}}$ is short).

<u>Smoothness.</u> For any $(\pi, \mathbf{y}) \notin \mathcal{L}^*$, $\mathbf{y}$ can not be expressed as $t(\mathbf{y} - \mathbf{h}_\pi) = \mathbf{a}s + \mathbf{x}$ with short $\underline{\mathbf{x}}$ for some $(t, s) \neq (0, 0)$. Via Lemma 13(3), $||\left(\phi_1(\mathbf{a}), \underline{\mathbf{y} - \mathbf{h}_\pi}\right)\binom{\underset{\sim}{s}}{t}||_\infty$ is large for any non-zero (t, s). By adaptive smoothness-I, $\mathbf{E}^T(\phi_1(\mathbf{a}), \underline{\mathbf{y} - \mathbf{h}_\pi})$, is close to uniform over $\mathbb{Z}_q^{\mu \times (n+1)}$.

5.4 A Ring-LWE-Based Instantiation of PAKE

We now instantiate our framework from Ring-LWE. In a nutshell, we realize the KF-MAC using the construction in Sect. 3.3 and key reconciliation scheme from Sect. 3.2, while instantiating $\mathbb{H}_1 = (\Pi_1, \mathsf{ver}_1^*, \mathcal{H}_1, \hat{\mathcal{H}}_1, \alpha_1)$ by δ-ASPH$_B$ and $\mathbb{H}_2 = (\Pi_2, \mathsf{ver}_2^*, \mathcal{H}_2, \hat{\mathcal{H}}_2, \alpha_2)$ by δ-ASPH$_A$, constructed in the last subsection. Our protocol will use the following parameters, notations and functions.

- m is a power of 2; $n = \frac{m}{2}$; $\theta \in (0,1)$; prime q; p a *constant* prime with $p < q$; $\ell_1 = \Theta(\log n)$ and $\ell_2 = \omega(1) \leq \ell_1$; $k = o(n)$; password dictionary $\mathcal{D} \subseteq \mathbb{Z}_p^k$.
- For $i = 1, 2$, let $\mathcal{C}_i$ be a $[\ell_i n, k, \theta \ell_i n]_p$-code from Lemma 7.
- $\mathbb{H}_1$ takes $\mathbf{a}, \mathbf{h} \leftarrow R_q^{\ell_1}$ as its public-key and uses code $\mathcal{C}_1$.
- $\mathbb{H}_2$ takes $\mathbf{g} \leftarrow R_q^{\ell_2}, \mathbf{D} = (d_{ij}) \leftarrow R_q^{\ell_2 \times 2}$ as its public-key and uses code $\mathcal{C}_2$. In addition, we use $\mathbf{v} = \mathbf{o}^T\mathbf{D} \in R_q^2$ with $\mathbf{o} \leftarrow (D_{R,\sqrt{n}r_2})^{\ell_2}$ as the public projection key for the PAKE framework.
- δ_1 is the bound on the noise term for the commitment in $\mathbb{H}_1$ and $\mathbb{H}_2$.
- As before, F_K is the KF-MAC in Sect. 3.3 with a fuzzy verification function $\Phi_{K'}$; G is a pseudorandom generator; £ is a reconciliation scheme for Alice and Bob, as in Sect. 3.2.

The public parameter is $\mathbf{a}|\mathbf{D}|\mathbf{v}|\mathbf{g}|\mathbf{h}|F|\pounds|\mathcal{C}_1|\mathcal{C}_2|q$. Then, the instantiated PAKE protocol between P_i and P_j is described in Fig. 4 (see Sect. 5.4 for details).

5.5 Implementation Results

Due to the space limitation, the efficiency details and comparison are given in the full paper and a summary is given in Table 1. We now provide a proof-of-concept implementation of our RLWE-PAKE scheme. The parameters are chosen as Fig. 5(a) and the output of H is 256 bits. The implementation is done on the platform of Intel Core i7-7700HQ CPU at 2.80 GHz with 7.7 GiB RAM running on the Ubuntu 16.04 LTS 64-bits operation system. Our program uses C++ language and the Number Theory Library (NTL) [27] without parallel techniques. The computational performance is presented in Fig. 5(b). In the setup phase, public parameters are generated. The columns of P_i and P_j denote the time cost

$P_i(\pi_{ij})$	Pub: $\mathbf{a}\vert\mathbf{D}\vert\mathbf{v}\vert\mathbf{g}\vert\mathbf{h}\vert F\vert\pounds\vert\mathcal{C}_1\vert\mathcal{C}_2\vert q$	$P_j(\pi_{ij})$
$\mathbf{x} \leftarrow (D_{R,\sqrt{n}r_1})^{\ell_1}, s \leftarrow R_q$ $\mathbf{y} = \mathbf{a}s + \mathbf{h}_{\pi_{ij}} + \mathbf{x}$	$\xrightarrow{\mathbf{y}\vert P_i}$	
$\boldsymbol{\xi} = \pounds_{bob}(\boldsymbol{\sigma}, \mathbf{U}\underline{s}),\ \Vert\underline{\mathbf{z}}\Vert \overset{?}{\leq} \delta_1$ $\omega = \mathbf{w}\vert\mathbf{y}\vert\mathbf{U}\vert\boldsymbol{\sigma}\vert i\vert j$ $\mathbf{w} \overset{?}{=} \mathbf{Dt} + \mathbf{g}_{\pi_{ij}} + \mathbf{z},\ \eta_0 \overset{?}{=} F_{\lfloor \mathbf{vt} \rceil_1^L}(\omega\vert 0)$ If yes, $\eta_1 = F_{\lfloor \mathbf{vt} \rceil_1^L}(\omega\vert 1)$ & output sk	$\xleftarrow{\mathbf{w}\vert\mathbf{U}\vert\boldsymbol{\sigma}\vert\eta_0\vert P_j}$	$\mathbf{E} \leftarrow (D_{\mathbb{Z},r_2})^{\ell_1 n \times \mu}$, $\mathbf{U} = \mathbf{E}^T\phi_1(\mathbf{a}),\ \mathbf{y}' = \mathbf{y} - \mathbf{h}_{\pi_{ij}}$ $(\boldsymbol{\sigma}, \boldsymbol{\xi}) \leftarrow \pounds_{alice}(\mathbf{E}^T\underline{\mathbf{y}'})$, $\mathbf{w} = \mathbf{Dt} + \mathbf{g}_{\pi_{ij}} + \mathbf{z}$ $\omega = \mathbf{w}\vert\mathbf{y}\vert\mathbf{U}\vert\boldsymbol{\sigma}\vert i\vert j,\ \eta_0 = F_{\lfloor \mathbf{vt} \rceil_1^L}(\omega\vert 0)$
	$\xrightarrow{\eta_1}$	If $\eta_1 = F_{\lfloor \mathbf{vt} \rceil_1^L}(\omega\vert 1)$, output sk

Fig. 4. Our Protocol RLWE-PAKE: $\mathbf{t} \leftarrow R_q^2$ and $\mathbf{z} \leftarrow (D_{R,\sqrt{n}r_1})^{\ell_2}$ are sampled with randomness Υ, where $\Upsilon|sk = G(\boldsymbol{\xi})$.

n	q	p	ℓ_1	ℓ_2	L	μ	k_1	k_2	r_1	r_2	L'
1024	$2^{30} + 2^{13} + 1$	13	10	10	1014	32	64	64	5.7	4571	128

(a) parameters

Setup	P_i	P_j
1.36s	0.20s	0.71s

(b) time cost

P_i (bytes)	P_j (bytes)	sk (bytes)
39990	167090	16

(c) message and sk size

Fig. 5. Performance of RLWE-PAKE

of computations by P_i and P_j respectively. The message size and session key size are listed in Fig. 5(c). It shows the message sizes by P_i and P_j respectively in order to agree on a 16 bytes session key. This is a reference implementation without optimizing. Practically, matrix multiplications can be done in parallel.

Acknowledgement. J. He was supported by scholarship from China Scholarship Council (CSC) under Grant No. 201804910203. Wang was supported by National Research Foundation, Prime Minister's Office, Singapore under its Strategic Capability Research Centres Funding Initiative and Singapore Ministry of Education under Research Grant MOE2016-T2-2-014(S). Nguyen was supported by the Gopalakrishnan-NTU Presidential Postdoctoral Fellowship 2018. Guang Gong's research is supported by NSERC SPG.

References

1. Alwen, J., Peikert, C.: Generating shorter bases for hard random lattices. In: STACS 2009. LIPIcs, vol. 3, pp. 75–86 (2009)
2. Banaszczyk, W.: Inequalites for convex bodies and polar reciprocal lattices in r^n. Discrete Comput. Geom. **13**, 217–231 (1995)
3. Bellare, M., Pointcheval, D., Rogaway, P.: Authenticated key exchange secure against dictionary attacks. In: Preneel, B. (ed.) EUROCRYPT 2000. LNCS, vol. 1807, pp. 139–155. Springer, Heidelberg (2000). https://doi.org/10.1007/3-540-45539-6_11
4. Bellovin, S.M., Merritt, M.: Encrypted key exchange: password-based protocols secure against dictionary attacks. In: IEEE S&P, pp. 72–84 (1992)
5. Benhamouda, F., Blazy, O., Ducas, L., Quach, W.: Hash proof systems over lattices revisited. In: Abdalla, M., Dahab, R. (eds.) PKC 2018. LNCS, vol. 10770, pp. 644–674. Springer, Cham (2018). https://doi.org/10.1007/978-3-319-76581-5_22
6. Canetti, R., Dachman-Soled, D., Vaikuntanathan, V., Wee, H.: Efficient Password Authenticated Key Exchange via Oblivious Transfer. In: Fischlin, M., Buchmann, J., Manulis, M. (eds.) PKC 2012. LNCS, vol. 7293, pp. 449–466. Springer, Heidelberg (2012). https://doi.org/10.1007/978-3-642-30057-8_27
7. Di Crescenzo, G., Graveman, R., Ge, R., Arce, G.: Approximate message authentication and biometric entity authentication. In: Patrick, A.S., Yung, M. (eds.) FC 2005. LNCS, vol. 3570, pp. 240–254. Springer, Heidelberg (2005). https://doi.org/10.1007/11507840_22

8. Ding, J., Alsayigh, S., Lancrenon, J., RV, S., Snook, M.: Provably secure password authenticated key exchange based on RLWE for the post-quantum world. In: Handschuh, H. (ed.) CT-RSA 2017. LNCS, vol. 10159, pp. 183–204. Springer, Cham (2017). https://doi.org/10.1007/978-3-319-52153-4_11
9. Dodis, Y., Goldwasser, S., Tauman Kalai, Y., Peikert, C., Vaikuntanathan, V.: Public-key encryption schemes with auxiliary inputs. In: Micciancio, D. (ed.) TCC 2010. LNCS, vol. 5978, pp. 361–381. Springer, Heidelberg (2010). https://doi.org/10.1007/978-3-642-11799-2_22
10. Ducas, L., Micciancio, D.: Improved short lattice signatures in the standard model. In: Garay, J.A., Gennaro, R. (eds.) CRYPTO 2014. LNCS, vol. 8616, pp. 335–352. Springer, Heidelberg (2014). https://doi.org/10.1007/978-3-662-44371-2_19
11. Gennaro, R., Lindell, Y.: A framework for password-based authenticated key exchange. In: Biham, E. (ed.) EUROCRYPT 2003. LNCS, vol. 2656, pp. 524–543. Springer, Heidelberg (2003). https://doi.org/10.1007/3-540-39200-9_33
12. Gentry, C., Peikert, C., Vaikuntanathan, V.: Trapdoors for hard lattices and new cryptographic constructions. In: STOC 2008, pp. 197–206 (2008)
13. Goldreich, O., Lindell, Y.: Session-key generation using human passwords only. In: Kilian, J. (ed.) CRYPTO 2001. LNCS, vol. 2139, pp. 408–432. Springer, Heidelberg (2001). https://doi.org/10.1007/3-540-44647-8_24
14. Gordon, S.D., Katz, J., Vaikuntanathan, V.: A group signature scheme from lattice assumptions. In: Abe, M. (ed.) ASIACRYPT 2010. LNCS, vol. 6477, pp. 395–412. Springer, Heidelberg (2010). https://doi.org/10.1007/978-3-642-17373-8_23
15. Groce, A., Katz, J.: A new framework for efficient password-based authenticated key exchange. In: CCS 2010, pp. 516–525 (2010)
16. Jiang, S., Gong, G.: Password based key exchange with mutual authentication. In: Handschuh, H., Hasan, M.A. (eds.) SAC 2004. LNCS, vol. 3357, pp. 267–279. Springer, Heidelberg (2004). https://doi.org/10.1007/978-3-540-30564-4_19
17. Katz, J., Ostrovsky, R., Yung, M.: Efficient password-authenticated key exchange using human-memorable passwords. In: Pfitzmann, B. (ed.) EUROCRYPT 2001. LNCS, vol. 2045, pp. 475–494. Springer, Heidelberg (2001). https://doi.org/10.1007/3-540-44987-6_29
18. Katz, J., Vaikuntanathan, V.: Smooth projective hashing and password-based authenticated key exchange from lattices. In: Matsui, M. (ed.) ASIACRYPT 2009. LNCS, vol. 5912, pp. 636–652. Springer, Heidelberg (2009). https://doi.org/10.1007/978-3-642-10366-7_37
19. Lyubashevsky, V., Peikert, C., Regev, O.: On ideal lattices and learning with errors over rings. J. ACM **60**(6), 43:1–43:35 (2013)
20. Lyubashevsky, V., Peikert, C., Regev, O.: A toolkit for ring-LWE cryptography. In: Johansson, T., Nguyen, P.Q. (eds.) EUROCRYPT 2013. LNCS, vol. 7881, pp. 35–54. Springer, Heidelberg (2013). https://doi.org/10.1007/978-3-642-38348-9_3
21. Micciancio, D., Peikert, C.: Trapdoors for lattices: simpler, tighter, faster, smaller. In: Pointcheval, D., Johansson, T. (eds.) EUROCRYPT 2012. LNCS, vol. 7237, pp. 700–718. Springer, Heidelberg (2012). https://doi.org/10.1007/978-3-642-29011-4_41
22. Micciancio, D., Regev, O.: Worst-case to average-case reductions based on Gaussian measures. SIAM J. Comput. **37**(1), 267–302 (2007)
23. Micciancio, D., Walter, M.: Gaussian sampling over the integers: efficient, generic, constant-time. In: Katz, J., Shacham, H. (eds.) CRYPTO 2017. LNCS, vol. 10402, pp. 455–485. Springer, Cham (2017). https://doi.org/10.1007/978-3-319-63715-0_16

24. Peikert, C.: Lattice cryptography for the internet. In: Mosca, M. (ed.) PQCrypto 2014. LNCS, vol. 8772, pp. 197–219. Springer, Cham (2014). https://doi.org/10.1007/978-3-319-11659-4_12
25. Peikert, C.: Limits on the hardness of lattice problems in ℓ_p norms. In: CCC 2007 (2007)
26. Regev, O.: On lattices, learning with errors, random linear codes, and cryptography. J. ACM **56**(6), 34:1–34:40 (2009)
27. Shoup, V.: NTL: a library for doing number theory. https://www.shoup.net/ntl/
28. Zhang, J., Yu, Y.: Two-round PAKE from approximate SPH and instantiations from lattices. In: Takagi, T., Peyrin, T. (eds.) ASIACRYPT 2017. LNCS, vol. 10626, pp. 37–67. Springer, Cham (2017). https://doi.org/10.1007/978-3-319-70700-6_2
29. Zhang, J., Yu, Y., Fan, S., Zhang, Z.: Improved lattice-based CCA2-secure PKE in the standard model. IACR Cryptology ePrint 2019:149 (2019)

Basic Primitives with Special Properties

Constraining and Watermarking PRFs from Milder Assumptions

Chris Peikert[1(✉)] and Sina Shiehian[2(✉)]

[1] Computer Science and Engineering, University of Michigan, Ann Arbor, USA
cpeikert@umich.edu

[2] Computer Science Department, University of Maryland, College Park, USA
shiayan@umich.edu

Abstract. *Constrained* pseudorandom functions (C-PRFs) let the possessor of a secret key delegate the ability to evaluate the function on certain authorized inputs, while keeping the remaining function values pseudorandom. A *constraint-hiding* constrained PRF (CHC-PRF) additionally conceals the predicate that determines which inputs are authorized. These primitives have a wealth of applications, including watermarking schemes, symmetric deniable encryption, and updatable garbled circuits.

Recent works have constructed (CH)C-PRFs from rather aggressive parameterizations of Learning With Errors (LWE) with *subexponential* modulus-noise ratios, even for relatively simple "puncturing" or NC^1 circuit constraints. This corresponds to strong lattice assumptions and inefficient constructions, and stands in contrast to LWE-based unconstrained PRFs and fully homomorphic encryption schemes, which can be based on quasi-polynomial or even (nearly) polynomial modulus-noise ratios.

In this work we considerably improve the LWE assumptions needed for building (constraint-hiding) constrained PRFs and watermarking schemes. In particular, for CHC-PRFs and related watermarking schemes we improve the modulus-noise ratio to $\lambda^{O((d+\log\lambda)\log\lambda)}$ for depth-d circuit constraints, which is merely quasi-polynomial for NC^1 circuits and closely related watermarking schemes. For (constraint-revealing) C-PRFs for NC^1 we do even better, obtaining a *nearly polynomial* $\lambda^{\omega(1)}$ ratio. These improvements are partly enabled by slightly modifying the definition of C-PRFs, in a way that is still compatible with many of their applications. Finally, as a contribution of independent interest we build CHC-PRFs for special constraint classes from *generic*, weaker assumptions: we obtain bit-fixing constraints based on the minimal assumption of one-way functions, and hyperplane-membership constraints based on key-homomorphic PRFs.

C. Peikert—This material is based upon work supported by the National Science Foundation under CAREER Award CCF-1054495 and CNS-1606362. The views expressed are those of the authors and do not necessarily reflect the official policy or position of the National Science Foundation or the Sloan Foundation.

S. Shiehian—Work was done while at the University of Michigan.

A. Kiayias et al. (Eds.): PKC 2020, LNCS 12110, pp. 431–461, 2020.
https://doi.org/10.1007/978-3-030-45374-9_15

1 Introduction

Constrained pseudorandom functions (C-PRFs), introduced concurrently and independently by [11,12,26], are PRFs in which the holder of the secret key can delegate *constrained* keys that let one evaluate the function on certain *authorized* inputs, while keeping the function values on all other inputs pseudorandom. Constrained PRFs for various constraint classes have been constructed under different assumptions, including ones where the set of authorized inputs can be specified by an arbitrary boolean circuit. (See below for details).

In the original conception and constructions of C-PRFs, a constrained key can and does reveal the constraint that determines whether an input is authorized. Boneh, Lewi, and Wu [10] introduced the notion of *constraint-hiding* constrained PRFs (CHC-PRFs), also known as private constrained PRFs, in which constrained keys conceal their underlying constraints. In particular, they considered CHC-PRFs for "punctured" constraints that authorize all but a single input. They also defined *privately programmable* PRFs (PP-PRFs), which allow the constrained key to be "programmed" to output a desired value at the punctured input, and showed that PP-PRFs can be used to build *watermarkable* PRFs [19].

1.1 Constructions and Assumptions

By now there are many constructions of constrained PRFs and their descendants, under various assumptions. The original works of [11,12,26] constructed (constraint-revealing) punctured PRFs based on the minimal assumption that one-way functions exist. Additionally, Boneh and Waters [11] constructed C-PRFs for constraints represented by arbitrary polynomial-sized circuits, under the strong assumption that cryptographic multilinear maps exist. Subsequently, Brakerski and Vaikuntanathan [17] gave a construction based on the Learning With Errors (LWE) assumption, but for which security holds only for a single constrained key. More recently, Attrapadung *et al.* [4] built C-PRFs for NC^1 constraints under number-theoretic assumptions, specifically, DDH and L-DDHI.

Moving now to constraint-hiding constrained PRFs, Boneh *et al.* [10] constructed them for arbitrary (polynomial-sized) constraining circuits, under the strong assumption that indistinguishability obfuscation (iO) exists [7,35]. LWE-based constructions soon followed, first for puncturing constraints [9], then for NC^1 circuits [18], then for all polynomial-sized circuits [15,32]. Like [17], all these LWE-based constructions are secure only for a single constrained key. However, this is an inherent limitation of CHC-PRFs for NC^1 circuits, because security for even two keys implies iO [18].

For privately programmable PRFs and watermarking schemes, the original constructions from [10,19] were based on iO. Later, Kim and Wu [27] built LWE-based watermarking schemes through a different but conceptually similar approach related to programming PRFs. Subsequently, Peikert and Shiehian [32] actually constructed LWE-based privately programmable PRFs.

1.2 LWE Error Rate

An important parameter in the LWE problem, which is related to both its concrete hardness and its connection to lattice problems, is the *error rate* α, or equivalently, the modulus-to-noise ratio $q/r = 1/\alpha$, where q is the modulus and r is the "width" of the (Gaussian) error distribution. In more detail, dimension-n LWE with error width $r \geq 2\sqrt{n}$ is at least as hard as (quantumly) approximating various worst-case lattice problems to within $\tilde{O}(n/\alpha) = \tilde{O}(q\sqrt{n})$ factors on n-dimensional lattices [31,34]. Therefore, using a smaller modulus q (equivalently, a larger error rate α) yields both a stronger security guarantee and a more efficient scheme. More concretely, according to current lattice algorithms, obtaining λ bits of security requires using a dimension $n = \lambda \cdot \tilde{\Omega}(\log(1/\alpha))$, and representing elements of $\mathbb{Z}_q$ requires $\log q = \tilde{\Omega}(\log(1/\alpha))$ bits. Therefore, LWE-based cryptographic schemes using a small error rate α (i.e., large q) suffer from large parameters and key sizes that can be cubic, or even quartic, in $\log(1/\alpha)$.

While there are LWE-based (ordinary) PRFs where the modulus is quasi-polynomial $\lambda^{\text{polylog}(\lambda)}$ [6] or even nearly polynomial $\lambda^{\omega(1)}$ [5], the current LWE-based *constrained* PRFs for punctured, NC^1, and arbitrary circuit constraints all require a *subexponential* $\exp(\text{poly}(\lambda))$ modulus (unless the domain of the PRF is restricted to quasi-polynomially long strings). It is instructive to compare this state of affairs with fully homomorphic encryption (FHE) schemes, whose underlying techniques are used in the constrained PRFs.

Without bootstrapping, state-of-the-art "leveled" FHE schemes [13,22] require a modulus that is merely *exponential in the depth* of the supported circuit class of homomorphic computations. (Bootstrapping can bring the modulus down to quasi-polynomial [13,22] or even polynomial [1,16], independent of the depth of the supported circuits.) By contrast, for constrained PRFs the modulus is *always subexponential in* λ, *regardless of the circuit depth.* In particular, NC^1 circuits induce a subexponential modulus, instead of a quasi-polynomial one as we might hope. This seems to be an artifact unrelated to the main construction and proof techniques, and raises the following natural question:

Question 1. Can we construct LWE-based (constraint-hiding) constrained PRFs with smaller-than-subexponential modulus, e.g., exponential in the depth of the circuit class?

We also point out that all of the known LWE-based watermarkable PRFs [10, 27] (excluding [33], which is not pseudorandom to the setup authority), where the latter is instantiated with LWE-based PP-PRFs [32], also need a subexponential modulus. Roughly speaking, these constructions are essentially built upon privately puncturable PRFs. This motivates the following question:

Question 2. Can we construct LWE-based watermarkable PRFs with a quasi-polynomial modulus?

1.3 Our Results

In this work, our main focus is on improving the LWE assumptions needed for constructing (single-key) constrained PRFs, including their constraint-hiding and privately programmable variants. As a contribution of independent interest, we also obtain (single-key) CHC-PRFs for bit-fixing and hyperplane-membership constraints from *generic* assumptions, namely, one-way functions and key-homomorphic PRFs, respectively.

Our main insight is that by slightly modifying the correctness requirement for constrained keys—but in a way that is still strong enough for most applications—we can construct C-PRFs using much larger LWE error rates, and hence much weaker assumptions and much smaller moduli and key sizes. In particular, we answer Question 1 in the affirmative. We also demonstrate that our new notion of correctness is sufficient for many of the applications of C-PRFs, including watermarking schemes and updatable garbled circuits; this positively answers Question 2 as well. We stress that the security level of our constructions scale proportional to the inverse of the LWE error rate; however, we note that this is a property shared by all current efficient (ordinary) lattice-based PRFs [5,6]. We now summarize our specific results.

Feasible Correctness. We first observe that satisfying a strict correctness requirement for constrained keys is the main reason previous LWE-based C-PRFs needed a subexponential modulus. In a bit more detail, the prior definitions require that, given a constrained key, it is computationally hard (or even impossible) to find an authorized input where the constrained key yields a different output than the real key. We give an alternative definition, which says that no efficient adversary, even with oracle access to the function, can *find* an input x for which *there exists* a constrained key that authorizes x yet yields a different output than the real key. (However, *after* obtaining a constrained key, an adversary may be able to find such an input.) We call this new notion *feasible correctness.*

Feasibly Correct PP-PRFs and Watermarking PRFs from LWE with Quasi-Polynomial Modulus. Our first construction under our new correctness notion is a key-injective, privately programmable PRF, based on LWE with only a quasi-polynomial modulus $q = \lambda^{O(\log^2 \lambda)}$. We plug this construction into the watermarking PRF construction of [10] and show that the resulting scheme satisfies all of the watermarking requirements presented in [27] (which are stronger than the definitions in [10]). This results in a watermarking scheme from LWE with quasi-polynomial modulus $q = \lambda^{O(\log^2 \lambda)}$, improving on the prior best of subexponential.

Feasibly Correct CHC-PRFs from LWE with Quasi-Polynomial Modulus. We next construct a feasibly correct CHC-PRF for arbitrary polynomial-sized circuit constraints, based on LWE with modulus $q = \lambda^{O((d+\log \lambda)\log \lambda)}$ where d is the depth of the supported circuit class. As an application, we instantiate the "message-embedding" construction of watermarkable PRFs from [33], which uses CHC-PRFs for log-depth constraints, with our feasibly correct CHC-PRF, thus reducing the modulus size from subexponential to quasi-polynomial $\lambda^{O(\log^2 \lambda)}$.

Feasibly Correct C-PRFs from LWE with Nearly Polynomial Modulus. Using the construction in the previous paragraph, feasibly correct CHC-PRFs for NC^1 circuits require a quasi-polynomial modulus $q = \lambda^{O(\log^2 \lambda)}$. Trivially, this construction is also a feasibly correct C-PRF for NC^1. However, we go farther by constructing such a C-PRF from LWE with only a *nearly polynomial* modulus $q = \lambda^{\omega(1)}$, by building upon the branching-program techniques of [16]. As an application, we show that we can replace regular C-PRFs with feasibly correct ones in the updatable garbled circuits construction of [2], thus reducing the modulus size from subexponential to nearly polynomial.

Bit-Fixing and Hyperplane-Membership PRFs from Generic Assumptions. As results of independent interest, we build CHC-PRFs for specific constraint classes based on *generic*, weaker assumptions than prior constructions. We consider the class of constraints that authorize inputs that lie in a specified hyperplane. For such constraints we build (feasibly correct) CHC-PRFs generically from key-homomorphic PRFs. Using the key-homomorphic PRFs of [5], we can base the security of our construction on LWE with nearly polynomial modulus $q = \lambda^{\omega(1)}$, which is significantly smaller than the quasi-polynomial $q = \lambda^{O(\log^2 \lambda)}$ that we would get by naïvely using our feasibly correct CHC-PRF for NC^1 circuits.

Lastly, for bit-fixing constraints, i.e., constraints that authorize strings matching a specified pattern in $\{0, 1, \star\}^*$ (where $\star$ denotes the wildcard symbol), we build (fully correct) CHC-PRFs based on the minimal assumption that one-way functions exist. Previously, bit-fixing PRFs were only known based on LWE with subexponential modulus [15,18,32], DDH [4], or multilinear maps [11], although the latter can securely issue more than one constrained key.

1.4 Concurrent and Independent Works

In a concurrent and independent work, Kim and Wu [28] construct watermarking PRFs from LWE with quasi-polynomial (nearly polynomial) modulus. While their security model for watermarking PRFs is an interesting strengthening of the model in [33], however, similar to [33] their PRFs do not offer full pseudorandomness in the presence of the setup authority. Furthermore, to make the LWE modulus quasi-polynomial (nearly polynomial), they have to limit the input domain of their PRFs to polylogarithmically (nearly logarithmically) long bit-strings. In comparison, both of our watermarking constructions support polynomially long bit-strings as inputs, with one satisfying the authority pseudorandom model of [27] and the other satisfying the [33] model.

In another concurrent work, Davidson, Katsumata, Nishimaki and Yamada [21] construct bit-fixing PRFs from one-way functions. Their construction is very similar to what we present in Construction 6. Later, Tsabary [36] makes an observation essentially identical to our Remark 1 and uses it to build LWE-based adaptively secure attribute based encryption for constant-width CNFs.

1.5 Techniques

Achieving Feasible Correctness. We start by reviewing why the correctness definition in current LWE-based C-PRFs leads to a subexponential modulus. In these constructions, to compute the function on an input x, first a value $\mathbf{y}_x \in \mathbb{Z}_q^m$ is computed and the final output is $\lfloor \mathbf{y}_x \rceil_p$. Using a constrained key for a depth-d constraint C that authorizes x, one can obtain $\mathbf{y}_x + \mathbf{e}_x$ where $\mathbf{e}_x$ is a B-bounded error vector for some $B = \lambda^{\tilde{O}(d)}$. For correctness we need $\lfloor \mathbf{y}_x + \mathbf{e} \rceil_p = \lfloor \mathbf{y}_x \rceil_p$, i.e., the coordinates of $\mathbf{y}_x$ should not be in the *border* interval $\frac{q}{p}(\mathbb{Z} + \frac{1}{2}) + [-B, B]$. Unfortunately, to guarantee that, given a constrained key, an adversary cannot find an input x such that $\mathbf{y}_x$ has a coordinate in the border interval, we currently do not know any solution other than making q subexponential. This is because we need to rely on the hardness of the "1-dimensional SIS problem" over $\mathbb{Z}_q$, as originally used in [17], or use a union bound over the subexponential PRF domain, as in [15].

We observe that if we can make $\mathbf{y}_x$ a pseudorandom function of x then an alternative "feasible correctness" property can be achieved. Namely, an adversary without a constrained key, but with oracle access to the PRF functionality, can only produce an x for which $\mathbf{y}_x$ has a coordinate in the border interval with probability at most $(Bp/q) \cdot \text{poly}(\lambda)$. Setting $q = Bp \cdot \lambda^{\omega(1)} = \lambda^{\tilde{O}(d)}$ yields feasible correctness.

Interestingly, we observe that the the notion of feasible correctness is compatible with many applications of C-PRFs. Most notably, the watermarking schemes based on C-PRFs maintain all of their requisite properties, because correctness only requires agreement between marked and unmarked PRFs on an overwhelming fraction of inputs. More generally (and somewhat informally), as long as a C-PRF is used in a context where it is evaluated on inputs that do not depend on the constrained key, then feasible correctness can substitute for full correctness.

Making $\mathbf{y}_x$ a pseudorandom function of x can be done by adding an independent PRF value in the computation of $\mathbf{y}_x$. In more detail, we generate a key $\kappa \leftarrow \mathsf{PRF.KG}(1^\lambda)$ for an arbitrary PRF with the same input domain as our PRF and with range $\mathbb{Z}_q^m$, and output it as part of both the master secret key and the constrained key. When evaluating the PRF on input x we compute $\mathbf{y}_x$ as before, then compute $\mathbf{y}'_x = \mathbf{y}_x + \mathsf{PRF.Eval}(\kappa, x)$ and output $\lfloor \mathbf{y}'_x \rceil_p$. Evaluation using a constrained key is similar. Using an LWE-based PRF which only requires a nearly polynomial modulus [5], we achieve feasible correctness from LWE with modulus $q = \lambda^{\tilde{O}(d)}$.

Constrained PRFs for NC^1 *Constraints.* We now describe how we construct feasibly correct (constraint-revealing) C-PRFs for NC^1 constraints from LWE with a *nearly polynomial* modulus $q = \lambda^{\omega(1)}$. Conceptually, our construction is similar to the one of [15], however we also use the technique from [16] of representing computations as branching programs. For each input x we denote by $\mathbf{M}_x$ the efficiently computable public binary matrix constructed as in [5]. These matrices have the property that for a uniformly random $\mathbf{s}$ over $\mathbb{Z}_q$, the randomized procedure which, on input x, samples a sufficiently wide Gaussian error $\mathbf{e}_x$ and outputs $\mathbf{s}\mathbf{M}_x + \mathbf{e}_x$, is pseudorandom. Our construction also crucially relies on the [16] procedure for homomorphically evaluating branching programs.

In our construction, a constrained key for a circuit C consists of the circuit C, a key κ for an auxiliary PRF, and several LWE samples $\mathbf{a}_i = \mathbf{s}(\mathbf{A}_i + C_i \cdot G) + \mathbf{e}_i$, where the C_is are the individual bits of C. Evaluating the PRF at an input x is done as follows:

- We use the "gadget homomorphisms" for branching programs with asymmetric noise growth [16] to homomorphically evaluate $U_x(\cdot)$ on the LWE samples $\mathbf{a}_i$, where $U_x(C) = C(x)$ is the branching program for a depth-universal circuit for NC^1. The result is

$$\mathbf{a}_x = \mathbf{s} \cdot \mathbf{A}_x + C(x) \cdot \mathbf{s} \cdot \mathbf{G} + \mathbf{e}_x, \tag{1}$$

  where $\mathbf{A}_x$ does not depend on C and $\mathbf{e}_x$ is polynomially bounded.
- Next, we multiply $\mathbf{a}_x$ by $\mathbf{G}^{-1}(\mathbf{A} \cdot \mathbf{M}_x)$, where $\mathbf{A}$ is a public uniformly random matrix over $\mathbb{Z}_q$, to get

$$\mathbf{b}_x = \mathbf{s} \cdot \mathbf{A}_x \cdot \mathbf{G}^{-1}(\mathbf{A} \cdot \mathbf{M}_x) + C(x) \cdot \mathbf{s} \cdot \mathbf{A} \cdot \mathbf{M}_x + \mathbf{e}', \tag{2}$$

  where $\mathbf{e}'$ is also polynomially bounded.
- Finally, we define the value of the PRF at input x to be

$$\lfloor \mathbf{s} \cdot \mathbf{A}_x \cdot \mathbf{G}^{-1}(\mathbf{A} \cdot \mathbf{M}_x) + \mathsf{PRF.Eval}(\kappa, x) \rceil_p, \tag{3}$$

  and the constrained value at x to be

$$\lfloor \mathbf{b}_x + \mathsf{PRF.Eval}(\kappa, x) \rceil_p. \tag{4}$$

Because $\mathbf{e}'$ is B-bounded for $B = \mathrm{poly}(\lambda)$, a nearly polynomial modulus $q = B \cdot \lambda^{\omega(1)} = \lambda^{\omega(1)}$ is sufficient for feasible correctness. To show that the C-PRF at unauthorized inputs x (i.e., where $C(x) = 1$) remains pseudorandom, we have to argue that the extra term $\mathbf{s} \cdot \mathbf{A} \cdot \mathbf{M}_x + \mathbf{e}'$ completely masks $\mathbf{s} \cdot \mathbf{A}_x \cdot \mathbf{G}^{-1}(\mathbf{A} \cdot \mathbf{M}_x)$. The high-level idea here is that, because $\mathbf{M}_x$ has small entries, $\mathbf{s} \cdot \mathbf{A} \cdot \mathbf{M}_x + \mathbf{e}'$ and $(\mathbf{s} \cdot \mathbf{A} + \mathbf{e}'') \cdot \mathbf{M}_x + \mathbf{e}'$ are very close to each other. Then by LWE, $(\mathbf{s} \cdot \mathbf{A} + \mathbf{e}'')$ and a uniformly chosen $\mathbf{s}'$ are indistinguishable. But as already noted, $\mathbf{s}' \cdot \mathbf{M}_x + \mathbf{e}'$ is pseudorandom, as desired.

Generic CHC-PRFs for Hyperplane Membership Constraints. We give a brief overview of our generic feasibly correct CHC-PRF construction for the class of hyperplane membership predicates. This construction can be based on any (noisy) key-homomorphic PRF. Here, for simplicity we only consider constraints of dimension 1, i.e., each constraint consists of a pair $(\alpha_0 \in \mathbb{Z}_q, \alpha_1 \in \mathbb{Z}_q)$ for some modulus q and only authorizes inputs $x \in \mathbb{Z}_q$ such that $\alpha_0 + \alpha_1 \cdot x = 0 \pmod q$. Generalizing for higher dimensions is straightforward. Let KHPRF be a key-homomorphic PRF. The master secret key consists of two keys (k_0, k_1) for KHPRF. To evaluate the PRF on an input x, we output $\mathsf{KHPRF.Eval}(k_0, x) + \mathsf{KHPRF.Eval}(x \cdot k_1, x)$. To produce a constrained key for constraint (α_0, α_1), we first sample a KHPRF key d and then output $(k_0 - \alpha_0 d, k_1 - \alpha_1 d)$ as the constrained key. It is straightforward to observe that the constrained-key (perfectly) hides (α_0, α_1). The correctness and pseudorandomness property follow from the key-homomorphism and the pseudorandomness of KHPRF. This is because

$$\begin{aligned}\mathsf{Eval}(k_0 - \alpha_1 d, x) + \mathsf{Eval}(x \cdot (k_1 - \alpha_1 d), x) = \mathsf{Eval}(k_0, x) \\ + \mathsf{Eval}(x \cdot k_1, x) - (\alpha_0 + \alpha_1 \cdot x)\mathsf{Eval}(d, x),\end{aligned} \tag{5}$$

and in particular if $\alpha_0 + \alpha_1 \cdot x \neq 0 \pmod q$ then the last term computationally hides the true value of the PRF.

2 Preliminaries

We denote row vectors by lower-case bold letters, e.g., $\mathbf{a}$. We denote matrices by upper-case bold letters, e.g., $\mathbf{A}$. The Kronecker product $\mathbf{A} \otimes \mathbf{B}$ of two matrices (or vectors) $\mathbf{A}$ and $\mathbf{B}$ is obtained by replacing each entry $a_{i,j}$ of $\mathbf{A}$ with the block $a_{i,j}\mathbf{B}$.

Depth-Universal Circuits. We use *depth-universal* circuits, i.e., universal circuits with depth $O(d)$ where d is the depth of the simulated circuit class. The construction of Cook and Hover [20] is depth-universal and has size $O(\sigma^3 \cdot d / \log d)$ for circuits of size σ and depth d.

Learning with Errors. For a positive integer dimension n and modulus q, and an error distribution χ over $\mathbb{Z}$, the LWE distribution and decision problem are defined as follows. For an $\mathbf{s} \in \mathbb{Z}^n$, the LWE distribution $A_{\mathbf{s},\chi}$ is sampled by choosing a uniformly random $\mathbf{a} \leftarrow \mathbb{Z}_q^n$ and an error term $e \leftarrow \chi$, and outputting $(\mathbf{a}, b = \langle \mathbf{s}, \mathbf{a} \rangle + e) \in \mathbb{Z}_q^{n+1}$.

Definition 1. *The decision-LWE$_{n,q,\chi}$ problem is to distinguish, with non-negligible advantage, between any desired (but polynomially bounded) number of independent samples drawn from $A_{\mathbf{s},\chi}$ for a single $\mathbf{s} \leftarrow \mathbb{Z}_q^n$, and the same number of* uniformly random *and independent samples over $\mathbb{Z}_q^{n+1}$.*

A standard instantiation of LWE is to let χ be a *discrete Gaussian* distribution (over $\mathbb{Z}$) with parameter $r = 2\sqrt{n}$. A sample drawn from this distribution has magnitude bounded by, say, $r\sqrt{n} = \Theta(n)$ except with probability at most 2^{-n}. For this parameterization, it is known that LWE is at least as hard as *quantumly* approximating certain "short vector" problems on n-dimensional lattices, in the worst case, to within $\tilde{O}(q\sqrt{n})$ factors [31,34]. Classical reductions are also known for different parameterizations [14,30].

3 Definitions

Here we recall prior definitions of constrained PRFs [32], then relax them to our new notion of *feasible* correctness.

Definition 2. *A* constrained function *for a constraint class $\mathcal{C}$ is given by a tuple of efficient algorithms* (Setup, KeyGen, Eval, Constrain, CEval) *having the following interfaces (where the domain $\mathcal{X}$, range $\mathcal{Y}$, and class $\mathcal{C}$ may depend on the security parameter):*

- Setup(1^λ), *given the security parameter λ, outputs public parameters pp.*
- KeyGen(pp), *given the public parameters pp, outputs a master secret key msk.*
- Eval(pp, msk, x), *given the master secret key and an input $x \in \mathcal{X}$, outputs some $y \in \mathcal{Y}$.*
- Constrain(pp, msk, C), *given the master secret key and a constraint $C \in \mathcal{C}$, outputs a constrained key sk_C.*
- CEval(pp, sk_C, x), *given a constrained key sk_C and an input $x \in \mathcal{X}$, outputs some $y \in \mathcal{Y}$.*

In some constructions there is no need for a Setup *algorithm, in which case the security parameter 1^λ takes the place of the public parameters pp.*

```
procedure CHCPRFReal_A(1^λ)
    C ← A(1^λ)
    pp ← Setup(1^λ)
    msk ← KeyGen(pp)
    sk_C ← Constrain(pp, msk, C)
    sk_C → A
    repeat
        x ← A
        Eval(pp, msk, x) → A
    until A halts
```

(a) The real experiment

```
procedure CHCPRFIdeal_{A,S}(1^λ)
    C ← A(1^λ)
    (pp, sk) ← S(1^λ)
    sk → A
    repeat
        x ← A
        if C(x) = true then
            CEval(pp, sk, x) → A
        else
            y ← Y; y → A
    until A halts
```

(b) The ideal experiment

Fig. 1. The real and ideal constraint-hiding constrained PRF experiments.

Definition 3. *A constrained function is a* constraint-hiding constrained PRF *(CHC-PRF) if there is a PPT simulator $\mathcal{S}$ such that, for any PPT adversary $\mathcal{A}$ (that without loss of generality never repeats an* Eval *query),*

$$\{\mathsf{CHCPRFReal}_{\mathcal{A}}(1^\lambda)\}_{\lambda \in \mathbb{N}} \stackrel{c}{\approx} \{\mathsf{CHCPRFIdeal}_{\mathcal{A},\mathcal{S}}(1^\lambda)\}_{\lambda \in \mathbb{N}}, \tag{6}$$

where CHCPRFReal *and* CHCPRFIdeal *are the respective views of $\mathcal{A}$ in the experiments defined in Fig. 1.*

We now introduce an alternative (but still sufficient for applications) notion of correctness for constrained evaluation, which we call *feasible correctness.* This requires that CEval and Eval agree on any input x that the adversary outputs after having query access to Eval, but *before* obtaining a constrained key. Correspondingly, in the simulation-based security definitions we limit the adversary to query only *unauthorized* inputs. This is because after obtaining the constrained key, it may be able to find inputs x on which CEval and Eval differ, which would allow it to distinguish the real and ideal experiments. We still call this property *simulation security*, where the restriction to unauthorized inputs is clear by the context of feasible correctness.

Definition 4. *A constrained function is* feasibly correct *if for all PPT adversaries $\mathcal{A}$ and all pp in the support of* Setup *we have*

$$\Pr\left[\begin{array}{c}\exists C \in \mathcal{C} \text{ s.t. } C(x) = true \\ \exists sk_C \in \text{support of } \mathsf{Constrain}(pp, msk, C) \text{ s.t.} \\ \mathsf{CEval}(pp, sk_C, x) \neq \mathsf{Eval}(pp, msk, x)\end{array}\right] = \operatorname{negl}(\lambda), \tag{7}$$

where $msk \leftarrow \mathsf{KeyGen}(pp)$, $x \leftarrow \mathcal{A}^{\mathsf{Eval}(pp,msk,\cdot)}(pp)$, and the probability is taken over the random coins of the KeyGen *algorithm and the random coins of the adversary $\mathcal{A}$.*

We recall the notion of key-homomorphic PRFs.

Definition 5. *A PRF* $(\mathsf{Setup}, \mathsf{Keygen}, \mathsf{Eval})$ *with domain $\mathcal{X}$, finite-group key space $\mathcal{K}$, and range $\mathbb{Z}_p^m$ for some integer modulus p and dimension m, is* noisy key homomorphic *with noise bound E if for every pp in the support of* Setup, *every two keys msk_1, msk_2 in the support of* $\mathsf{Keygen}(pp)$, *and every $x \in \mathcal{X}$, we have*

$$\mathsf{Eval}(pp, msk_1 + msk_2, x) = \mathsf{Eval}(pp, msk_1, x) + \mathsf{Eval}(pp, msk_2, x) + \mathbf{e} \tag{8}$$

for some noise vector $\mathbf{e}$ where each entry of $\mathbf{e}$ has magnitude at most E.

Theorem 1 ([5]). *Assuming the hardness of* LWE *with nearly polynomial modulus size $q = \lambda^{\omega(1)}$, there exists a noisy key-homomorphic PRF with key space $\mathbb{Z}_q^n$, range $\mathbb{Z}_p^m$ for any p for which $p/q = \operatorname{negl}(\lambda)$, and noise upper bound $E = 1$.*

4 Feasibly Correct Shift-Hiding Shiftable Functions

Recall the notion of shift-hiding shiftable functions (SHSFs) in [32] (a brief overview is available in Appendix A). Here we give a construction of what we call *feasibly correct shift-hiding shiftable functions* (FC-SHSFs) which are essentially SHSFs which satisfy *shift hiding* and *approximate shift correctness* but instead of *border avoiding* they satisfy a new notion which we call *feasible border avoiding.* Interestingly, the main building block for our FC-SHSFs is a SHSF.

4.1 Notation

Let $\mathsf{PRF} = (\mathsf{KG}, \mathsf{Eval})$ be a PRF. We can instantiate PRF based on various assumptions. In particular, the instantiation in [5] which is based on LWE with a nearly polynomial modulus, incurs no additional cost to later applications of our FC-SHSF construction. Let $U(H, x) = H(x)$ denote a depth-universal circuit for boolean circuits $H\colon \{0,1\}^\ell \to \{0,1\}^k$ of size σ and depth d, and let $U_x(\cdot) = U(\cdot, x)$. Denote the SHSFs constructed in [32] by $\mathsf{PSSHSF} = (\mathsf{Setup}, \mathsf{KeyGen}, \mathsf{Eval}, \mathsf{Shift}, \mathsf{SEval}, \mathcal{S})$ and recall that in PSSHSF the noise growth is $\lambda^{O(d \log \lambda)}$.

4.2 Construction

Here we give the tuple of algorithms $(\mathsf{Setup}, \mathsf{KeyGen}, \mathsf{Eval}, \mathsf{Shift}, \mathsf{SEval}, \mathcal{S})$ that make up our SHSF. For security parameter λ, constraint circuit size σ, and constraint circuit depth d the algorithms are parameterized by some dimension n and modulus q, and $m = n\lceil \lg q \rceil$.

Construction 1. Let $\mathcal{X} = \{0,1\}^\ell$ and $\mathcal{Y} = \mathbb{Z}_q^m$. Define:

- $\mathsf{Setup}(1^\lambda, 1^\sigma, 1^d)$: Generate PSSHSF public parameters $pp' \leftarrow \mathsf{PSSHSF}.\mathsf{Setup}(1^\lambda, 1^\sigma, 1^d)$. Output $pp := pp'$.
- $\mathsf{KeyGen}(pp)$: Generate a PRF key $\kappa \leftarrow \mathsf{PRF}.\mathsf{KG}(1^\lambda)$ and PSSHSF master secret key $msk' \leftarrow \mathsf{PSSHSF}.\mathsf{KeyGen}(1^\lambda)$. Output (κ, msk').
- $\mathsf{Eval}(pp, msk, x \in \{0,1\}^\ell)$: output

$$\mathsf{PRF}.\mathsf{Eval}(\kappa, x) + \mathsf{PSSHSF}.\mathsf{Eval}(pp', msk', x) \tag{9}$$

- $\mathsf{Shift}(pp, msk, H)$: for a shift function $H\colon \{0,1\}^\ell \to \mathbb{Z}_q^m$ whose binary decomposition $H'\colon \{0,1\}^\ell \to \{0,1\}^k$ can be implemented by a circuit of size σ, compute $sk'_H \leftarrow \mathsf{SHSF}.\mathsf{Shift}(pp', msk', H)$. Output

$$sk_H = (\kappa, sk'_H). \tag{10}$$

- $\mathsf{SEval}(pp, sk_H, x)$: On input $sk_H = (\kappa, sk'_H)$ and $x \in \{0,1\}^\ell$, output

$$\mathsf{PRF}.\mathsf{Eval}(\kappa, x) + \mathsf{PSSHSF}.\mathsf{SEval}(pp', sk'_H, x) \tag{11}$$

- $\mathcal{S}(1^\lambda, 1^\sigma, 1^d)$: Sample a PRF key $\kappa \leftarrow \mathsf{PRF}.\mathsf{KG}(1^\lambda)$, a simulated PSSHSF key $(pp', sk') \leftarrow \mathsf{PSSHSF}.\mathsf{Sim}(1^\lambda, 1^\sigma)$, and output $pp = (pp')$ and $sk = (\kappa, sk')$.

4.3 Properties

We now state the main properties of our construction that we will use in subsequent sections.

The following two lemmas follow directly from the shift-hiding and approximate shift correctness properties of PSSHSF. So, we omit the proofs of these lemmas.

procedure $\mathsf{RealKey}_{\mathcal{A}}(1^\lambda, 1^\sigma, 1^d)$
  $H \leftarrow \mathcal{A}(1^\lambda, 1^\sigma, 1^d)$
  $pp \leftarrow \mathsf{Setup}(1^\lambda, 1^\sigma, 1^d)$
  $msk \leftarrow \mathsf{KeyGen}(pp)$
  $sk \leftarrow \mathsf{Shift}(pp, msk, H)$
  $(pp, sk) \rightarrow \mathcal{A}$

(a) The real shifted key generation experiment

procedure $\mathsf{IdealKey}_{\mathcal{A}}(1^\lambda, 1^\sigma, 1^d)$
  $H \leftarrow \mathcal{A}(1^\lambda, 1^\sigma, 1^d)$
  $(pp, sk) \leftarrow \mathcal{S}(1^\lambda, 1^\sigma, 1^d)$
  $(pp, sk) \rightarrow \mathcal{A}$

(b) The random key generation experiment

Fig. 2. The real and random shifted key generation experiments.

Lemma 1 (Shift Hiding). *Assuming the hardness of $LWE_{n-1,q,\chi}$, for any PPT $\mathcal{A}$, any $\sigma = \sigma(\lambda) = \mathrm{poly}(\lambda)$ and any d,*

$$\{\mathsf{RealKey}_{\mathcal{A}}(1^\lambda, 1^\sigma, 1^d)\}_{\lambda \in \mathbb{N}} \stackrel{c}{\approx} \{\mathsf{IdealKey}_{\mathcal{A}}(1^\lambda, 1^\sigma, 1^d)\}_{\lambda \in \mathbb{N}}, \tag{12}$$

where RealKey *and* IdealKey *are the respective views of $\mathcal{A}$ in the experiments defined in Fig. 2.*

Lemma 2 (Approximate Shift Correctness). *For any shift function $H \colon \{0,1\}^\ell \rightarrow \mathbb{Z}_q^m$ whose binary decomposition $H' \colon \{0,1\}^\ell \rightarrow \{0,1\}^k$ can be represented by a boolean circuit of size σ and depth d, and any $x \in \{0,1\}^\ell$, $pp \leftarrow \mathsf{Setup}(1^\lambda, 1^\sigma, 1^d)$, $msk \leftarrow \mathsf{KeyGen}(pp)$ and $sk_H \leftarrow \mathsf{Shift}(pp, msk, H)$, we have*

$$\mathsf{SEval}(pp, sk_H, x) \approx \mathsf{Eval}(pp, msk, x) + H(x) \tag{13}$$

where the approximation hides some $\lambda^{O(d \log \lambda)}$-bounded error vector.

Lemma 3 (Feasible Border Avoiding). *If* PRF *is a pseudorandom function, then for any polynomial-time adversary $\mathcal{A}$, $i \in [m]$, $\sigma = \mathrm{poly}(\lambda)$, $d \in \mathbb{N}$, large enough $B = \lambda^{O(d \log \lambda)} \in \mathbb{N}$, primes p and q such that $q = p \cdot B \cdot \lambda^{\omega(1)}$, pp in the support of* $\mathsf{Setup}(1^\lambda, 1^\sigma, 1^d)$, *and $\beta \in \mathbb{Z}_q$, we have*

$$\Pr_{msk \leftarrow \mathsf{KeyGen}(pp)} \Big[\mathsf{Eval}(pp, msk, \mathcal{A}^{\mathsf{Eval}(pp,msk,\cdot)}(pp))_i \in \tfrac{q}{p}(\mathbb{Z} + \tfrac{1}{2}) + [\beta - B, \beta + B]\Big] \le \mathrm{negl}(\lambda). \tag{14}$$

The following is an immediate consequence of Lemma 2.

Corollary 1. *Fix the same notation as in Lemma 2. Let $\mathbf{c} \in \mathbb{Z}_q^m$ be a fixed vector. If for all $i \in [m]$ we have*

$$\mathsf{Eval}(pp, sk, x)_i \notin \tfrac{q}{p}(\mathbb{Z} + \tfrac{1}{2}) + [\mathbf{c}_i - B, \mathbf{c}_i + B], \tag{15}$$

then

$$\lfloor \mathsf{SEval}(pp, sk, x) - H(x) - \mathbf{c} \rceil_p = \lfloor \mathsf{Eval}(pp, msk, x) - \mathbf{c} \rceil_p. \tag{16}$$

5 Feasibly Correct Privately Programmable PRFs

In this section we formally define feasibly correct privately programmable PRFs (PP-PRFs) and give a construction based on our feasibly correct shiftable PRFs from Sect. 4. Our construction satisfies an additional key-injectivity property which would later be useful in watermarking constructions.

5.1 Definitions

We start by giving a variety of definitions related to "programmable functions" and privately programmable PRFs.

Definition 6. *A* programmable function *is a tuple* ($\mathsf{Setup}, \mathsf{KeyGen}, \mathsf{Eval}, \mathsf{Program}, \mathsf{PEval}$) *of efficient algorithms having the following interfaces (where the domain $\mathcal{X}$ and range $\mathcal{Y}$ may depend on the security parameter):*

- $\mathsf{Setup}(1^\lambda)$*, given the security parameter λ outputs public parameters pp.*
- $\mathsf{KeyGen}(pp)$*, given the public parameters pp, outputs a master secret key msk.*
- $\mathsf{Eval}(pp, msk, x)$*, given the master secret key and an input $x \in \mathcal{X}$, outputs some $y \in \mathcal{Y}$.*
- $\mathsf{Program}(pp, msk, (x^*, y^*))$*, given the master secret key msk and $(x^*, y^*) \in \mathcal{X} \times \mathcal{Y}$, outputs a programmed key $sk_{\mathcal{P}}$.*
- $\mathsf{PEval}(pp, sk_{\mathcal{P}}, x)$*, given a programmed key $sk_{\mathcal{P}}$ and an input $x \in \mathcal{X}$, outputs some $y \in \mathcal{Y}$.*

Definition 7. *A programmable function is* statistically programmable *if for all $\lambda \in \mathbb{N}$ and all pairs $(x^*, y^*) \in \mathcal{X} \times \mathcal{Y}$ we have*

$$\Pr_{\substack{pp \leftarrow \mathsf{Setup}(1^\lambda) \\ msk \leftarrow \mathsf{KeyGen}(pp) \\ sk_{(x^*,y^*)} \leftarrow \mathsf{Program}(pp, msk, (x^*, y^*))}} [\mathsf{PEval}(pp, sk_{(x^*,y^*)}, x^*) \neq y^*] = \mathrm{negl}(\lambda). \tag{17}$$

Definition 8. *A programmable function is* feasibly correct *if for all PPT adversaries $\mathcal{A}$ and all pp in the support of* Setup *we have*

$$\Pr\left[\begin{array}{c} \exists (x^*, y^*) \in \mathcal{X} \backslash \{x\} \times \mathcal{Y} \\ \exists sk_{(x^*,y^*)} \in \text{ support of } \mathsf{Program}(pp, msk, (x^*, y^*)) \text{ s.t.} \\ \mathsf{PEval}(pp, sk_{(x^*,y^*)}, x) \neq \mathsf{Eval}(pp, msk, x) \end{array}\right] = \mathrm{negl}(\lambda), \tag{18}$$

where $msk \leftarrow \mathsf{KeyGen}(pp)$, $x \leftarrow \mathcal{A}^{\mathsf{Eval}(pp, msk, \cdot)}(pp)$, and the probability is taken over the random coins of the KeyGen *algorithm and the random coins of the adversary $\mathcal{A}$.*

Definition 9 (Key-Injectivity). *A programmable function is key-injective if*

$$\Pr_{pp \leftarrow \mathsf{Setup}(1^\lambda)} \left[\begin{array}{c} \exists \text{ distinct } msk_1, msk_2 \in \text{ support of } \mathsf{KeyGen}, x \in \{0,1\}^\ell : \\ \mathsf{Eval}(pp, msk_1, x) = \mathsf{Eval}(pp, msk_2, x) \end{array}\right] \tag{19}$$
$$\leq \mathrm{negl}(\lambda).$$

procedure $\mathsf{RealPPRF}_{\mathcal{A}}(1^\lambda)$
$(x^*, y^*) \leftarrow \mathcal{A}(1^\lambda)$
$pp \leftarrow \mathsf{Setup}(1^\lambda)$
$msk \leftarrow \mathsf{KeyGen}(pp)$
$sk_{(x^*,y^*)} \leftarrow \mathsf{Program}(pp, msk, (x^*, y^*))$
$(pp, sk_{(x^*,y^*)}) \rightarrow \mathcal{A}$
$\mathsf{Eval}(pp, msk, x^*) \rightarrow \mathcal{A}$

(a) The real experiment

procedure $\mathsf{IdealPPRF}_{\mathcal{A},\mathcal{S}}(1^\lambda)$
$(x^*, y^*) \leftarrow \mathcal{A}(1^\lambda)$
$(pp, sk_{(x^*,y^*)}) \leftarrow \mathcal{S}(1^\lambda, (x^*, y^*))$
$(pp, sk_{(x^*,y^*)}) \rightarrow \mathcal{A}$
$y \leftarrow \mathcal{Y}$; $y \rightarrow \mathcal{A}$

(b) The ideal experiment

Fig. 3. The real and ideal experiments

Definition 10. *A programmable function is* simulation secure *if there is a PPT simulator $\mathcal{S}$ such that for any PPT adversary $\mathcal{A}$,*

$$\{\mathsf{RealPPRF}_{\mathcal{A}}(1^\lambda)\}_{\lambda\in\mathbb{N}} \overset{c}{\approx} \{\mathsf{IdealPPRF}_{\mathcal{A},\mathcal{S}}(1^\lambda)\}_{\lambda\in\mathbb{N}}, \tag{20}$$

where RealPPRF *and* IdealPPRF *are the respective views of $\mathcal{A}$ in the procedures defined in Fig. 3.*

procedure $\mathsf{RealPPRFPrivacy}_{\mathcal{A}}(1^\lambda)$
$x^* \leftarrow \mathcal{A}(1^\lambda)$
$y^* \leftarrow \mathcal{Y}$
$pp \leftarrow \mathsf{Setup}(1^\lambda)$
$msk \leftarrow \mathsf{KeyGen}(pp)$
$sk \leftarrow \mathsf{Program}(pp, msk, (x^*, y^*))$
$(pp, sk) \rightarrow \mathcal{A}$

(a) The real experiment

procedure
$\mathsf{IdealPPRFPrivacy}_{\mathcal{A},\mathcal{S}}(1^\lambda)$
$x^* \leftarrow \mathcal{A}(1^\lambda)$
$(pp, sk) \leftarrow \mathcal{S}(1^\lambda)$
$(pp, sk) \rightarrow \mathcal{A}$

(b) The ideal experiment

Fig. 4. The real and ideal privacy experiments

Definition 11. *A programmable function is* privately programmable *if there is a PPT simulator $\mathcal{S}$ such that for any PPT adversary $\mathcal{A}$,*

$$\{\mathsf{RealPPRFPrivacy}_{\mathcal{A}}(1^\lambda)\}_{\lambda\in\mathbb{N}} \overset{c}{\approx} \{\mathsf{IdealPPRFPrivacy}_{\mathcal{A}}(1^\lambda)\}_{\lambda\in\mathbb{N}}, \tag{21}$$

where RealPPRFPrivacy *and* IdealPPRFPrivacy *are the respective views of $\mathcal{A}$ in the procedures defined in Fig. 4.*

Definition 12. *A programmable function is a* feasibly correct privately programmable PRF *if it is statistically programmable, simulation secure, privately programmable, and feasibly correct.*

LWE-Based PRGs with Weak Seeds. In this construction we will need an LWE-based PRG $G \colon \mathbb{Z}_q^n \rightarrow \{0,1\}^{n_1}$ with the following property:

$$\{G(\mathbf{s}), \mathbf{s} \cdot \mathbf{A} + \mathbf{e}, \mathbf{A} : \mathbf{s}, \mathbf{e} \leftarrow \chi^n; \mathbf{A} \leftarrow \mathbb{Z}_q^{n \times m}\} \stackrel{c}{\approx} \\ \{r, \mathbf{a}, \mathbf{A} : r \leftarrow \{0,1\}^{n_1}; \mathbf{a} \leftarrow \mathbb{Z}_q^m; \mathbf{A} \leftarrow \mathbb{Z}_q^{n \times m}\}. \tag{22}$$

Such PRGs can be built when q is superpolynomial by combining the techniques in [6] and [3].

5.2 Construction of Feasibly Correct Privately Programmable PRFs

In this section we construct a feasibly correct privately programmable PRF from our shiftable function of Sect. 4. We first define the auxiliary function that the construction will use. For $(x^*, \mathbf{w}) \in \{0,1\}^\ell \times \mathbb{Z}_q^m$ define the function $H_{(x^*,\mathbf{w})} \colon \{0,1\}^\ell \to \mathbb{Z}_q^m$ as

$$H_{(x^*,\mathbf{w})}(x) = \begin{cases} \mathbf{w} & \text{if } x = x^*, \\ \mathbf{0} & \text{otherwise.} \end{cases} \tag{23}$$

Notice that $H_{(x^*,\mathbf{w})}$ has circuit size upper bounded by some $\sigma' = \mathrm{poly}(n, \log q)$ and depth at most $d' = O(\log q)$.

Construction 2. Our feasibly correct privately programmable PRF with input space $\mathcal{X} = \{0,1\}^\ell$ and output space $\mathcal{Y} = \mathbb{Z}_p^m$ where $p = \mathrm{poly}(\lambda)$, uses the FC-SHSF from Sect. 4 with parameters $n = \tilde{O}(\lambda), B = \lambda^{O(\log^2 \lambda)}$, $q = p \cdot B \cdot \lambda^{\omega(1)} = p \cdot \lambda^{O(\log^2 \lambda)}$, and is defined as follows:

- $\mathsf{Setup}(1^\lambda)$: First generate $pp' \leftarrow \mathsf{SHSF.Setup}(1^\lambda, 1^{\sigma'}, 1^{d'})$ then choose a uniformly random matrix $\mathbf{A} \in \mathbb{Z}_q^{n \times m}$, a uniformly random vector $\mathbf{r} \leftarrow \mathbb{Z}_p^m$, and output $pp := (pp', \mathbf{r}, \mathbf{A})$ we implicitly assume that pp contains the public parameters for a PRG with weak seeds which satisfies Eq. 22.
- $\mathsf{KeyGen}(pp)$: Sample $\mathbf{s} \leftarrow \chi^n$, sample $msk' \leftarrow \mathsf{SHSF.KeyGen}(pp'; G(\mathbf{s}))$. Finally, output $msk := (\mathbf{s}, msk')$.
- $\mathsf{Eval}(pp, msk = (\mathbf{s}, msk'), x \in \{0,1\}^\ell)$: Compute $\mathbf{y}_x = \mathbf{s} \cdot \mathbf{A} + \mathsf{SHSF.Eval}(pp, msk', x)$ and output $\mathbf{r} + \lfloor \mathbf{y}_x \rceil_p$.
- $\mathsf{Program}(pp, msk, (x^*, \mathbf{y}^*))$: Given $(x^*, \mathbf{y}^*) \in \{0,1\}^\ell \times \mathbb{Z}_p^m$, compute $\mathbf{w}$ as follows: choose $\mathbf{y}' \leftarrow \mathbb{Z}_q^m$ uniformly at random conditioned on $\lfloor \mathbf{y}' \rceil_p = (\mathbf{y}^* - \mathbf{r})$, let $\mathbf{a} \leftarrow \mathbf{s} \cdot \mathbf{A} + \mathbf{e}$ where $\mathbf{e} \leftarrow \chi^m$, and set

$$\mathbf{w} = \mathbf{y}' - \mathsf{SHSF.Eval}(pp, msk', x^*) - \mathbf{a} \tag{24}$$

  Compute $sk'_{(x^*,y^*)} \leftarrow \mathsf{SHSF.Shift}(pp, msk', H_{(x^*,\mathbf{w})})$. Output $sk_{(x^*,y^*)} := (\mathbf{a}, sk'_{(x^*,y^*)})$.
- $\mathsf{PEval}(pp, sk_{(x^*,y^*)} = (\mathbf{a}, sk'_{(x^*,y^*)}), x)$: output $\mathbf{r} + \lfloor \mathbf{a} + \mathsf{SHSF.SEval}(pp, sk'_{(x^*,y^*)}, x) \rceil_p$.

The proof of the following theorem is deferred to the full version of this paper.

Theorem 2. *If $\mathsf{LWE}_{n-1,q,\chi}$ is hard and* PRF *is a pseudorandom function, Construction 2 is a key-injective, feasibly correct privately programmable PRF.*

5.3 Application

In the full version of this paper we show that by instantiating the watermarking scheme of [10] with Construction 2 PP-PRFs, we get a watermarking construction from LWE with quasi-polynomial modulus $q = \lambda^{O(\log^2 \lambda)}$. This watermarking scheme satisfies all the definitions in [27] and in particular it is authority pseudorandom.

6 Feasibly Correct Constraint-Hiding Constrained PRFs

Definition 13. *A constrained function is a* feasibly correct constraint-hiding constrained PRF *if it satisfies Definition 4, and there is a PPT simulator $\mathcal{S}$ such that, for any PPT adversary $\mathcal{A}$ that never queries its* Eval *oracle on an input x for which $C(x) = true$ (and without loss of generality never repeats an* Eval *query),*

$$\{\mathsf{CHCPRFReal}_{\mathcal{A}}(1^\lambda)\}_{\lambda\in\mathbb{N}} \overset{c}{\approx} \{\mathsf{CHCPRFIdeal}_{\mathcal{A},\mathcal{S}}(1^\lambda)\}_{\lambda\in\mathbb{N}}, \tag{25}$$

where CHCPRFReal *and* CHCPRFIdeal *are the respective views of $\mathcal{A}$ in the experiments defined in Fig. 1.*

6.1 Construction

We now describe our construction of a feasibly correct CHC-PRF for domain $\mathcal{X} = \{0,1\}^\ell$ and range $\mathcal{Y} = \mathbb{Z}_p^m$, which handles constraining circuits of size σ and depth d. It uses the following components:

- A pseudorandom function $\mathsf{AuxPRF} = (\mathsf{AuxPRF.KG}, \mathsf{AuxPRF.Eval})$ having domain $\{0,1\}^\ell$ and range $\mathbb{Z}_q^m$, with key space $\{0,1\}^\kappa$.
- The feasibly correct shift hiding shiftable function $\mathsf{SHSF} = (\mathsf{Setup}, \mathsf{KeyGen}, \mathsf{Eval}, \mathsf{Shift}, \mathsf{SEval}, \mathsf{Sim})$ from Sect. 4, which has parameters q, B that appear in the analysis below.

For a boolean circuit C of size at most σ and depth upper-bound d and some $k \in \{0,1\}^\kappa$ define the function $H_{C,k} \colon \{0,1\}^\ell \to \mathbb{Z}_q^m$ as

$$\begin{aligned} H_{C,k}(x) &= C(x) \cdot \mathsf{AuxPRF.Eval}(k, x) \\ &= \begin{cases} \mathsf{AuxPRF.Eval}(k,x) & \text{if } U(C,x) = 1 \\ 0 & \text{otherwise.} \end{cases} \end{aligned} \tag{26}$$

Notice that the size of (the binary decomposition of) $H_{C,k}$ is upper bounded by

$$\sigma' = \sigma + s + \mathrm{poly}(n, \log q), \tag{27}$$

where s is the circuit size of (the binary decomposition of) $\mathsf{AuxPRF.Eval}(k,\cdot)$. And the depth of $H_{C,k}$ is upper-bounded by

$$d' = d + \delta + O(\log q), \tag{28}$$

where δ is the circuit depth of $\mathsf{AuxPRF.Eval}(k,\cdot)$. By instantiating AuxPRF with a log-depth PRF [5,6], we can set $n = \tilde{O}(\lambda)$, $B = \lambda^{O((d+\log\lambda)\log\lambda)}$, and $q = p \cdot B \cdot \lambda^{\omega(1)} = \lambda^{O((d+\log\lambda)\log\lambda)}$.

Construction 3. Our feasibly correct CHC-PRF with domain $\mathcal{X} = \{0,1\}^\ell$ and range $\mathcal{Y} = \mathbb{Z}_p^m$ is defined as follows:

- $\mathsf{Setup}(1^\lambda, 1^\sigma, 1^d)$: output $pp \leftarrow \mathsf{SHSF.Setup}(1^\lambda, 1^{\sigma'}, 1^{d'})$ where σ' and d' are defined as in Eqs. (27) and (28) respectively.
- $\mathsf{KeyGen}(pp)$: output $msk \leftarrow \mathsf{SHSF.KeyGen}(pp)$.
- $\mathsf{Eval}(pp, msk, x \in \{0,1\}^\ell)$: compute $\mathbf{y}_x = \mathsf{SHSF.Eval}(pp, msk, x)$ and output $\lfloor \mathbf{y}_x \rceil_p$.
- $\mathsf{Constrain}(pp, msk, C)$: on input a circuit C of size at most σ and depth at most d, sample a PRF key $k \leftarrow \mathsf{AuxPRF.KG}(1^\lambda)$ and output $sk_C \leftarrow \mathsf{SHSF.Shift}(pp, msk, H_{C,k})$.
- $\mathsf{CEval}(pp, sk_C, x)$: on input a constrained key sk_C and $x \in \{0,1\}^\ell$, output $\lfloor \mathsf{SHSF.SEval}(pp, sk_C, x) \rceil_p$.

6.2 Security Proof

In the full version of this paper we present the security proof of Construction 3.

Theorem 3. *Assuming that* $\mathsf{LWE}_{n-1,q,\chi}$ *is hard and* PRF *is a pseudorandom function, Construction 3 is a feasibly correct CHC-PRF.*

6.3 Applications

Watermarking in the alternative model of [33] *from LWE with quasi-polynomial modulus* Recently, [33] introduced an alternative model for watermarkable PRFs. In their model, the marking algorithm is *public* and roughly speaking, in their unremovability and correctness definition, the adversary also has access to an extraction oracle. Despite these advantages over the model considered in Sect. 5.3, their model only guarantees pseudorandomness for adversaries that don't have the master secret key, i.e., they are not *authority pseudorandom*.

In their work, they present two constructions for their models. The first construction can be instantiated based solely on LWE with polynomial modulus but it does not support embedding messages in marked keys. The second construction does support embedding messages but needs private constrained PRFs for a circuit class consisting of an arbitrary PRF. As a consequence, instantiating the second construction with state of the art lattice-based CHC-PRFs needs LWE with subexponential modulus.

We observe that the message embedding scheme constructed in [33] can be instantiated with a feasibly correct CHC-PRF instead of a regular CHC-PRF. In more detail, in the security games of this scheme, the CHC-PRF is never evaluated on points that depend on the actual description of the constrained key. Indeed, in the correctness game, the challenge CHC-PRF constrained key is not given to the adversary and instead oracle access to Eval (and CEval) is provided. In the unremovability game, the oracles provided to the adversary evaluate the CHC-PRF using the challenge constrained key on points which don't depend on the constrained key, i.e., on points that can be sampled before any constrained key is generated. In all these scenarios feasible correctness would suffice to establish the security requirements.

Now, if we use the feasibly correct CHC-PRF constructed in Sect. 6.1, the underlying LWE assumption would have modulus size $\lambda^{O(d \log \lambda)}$ where d is the depth of the constraint circuit. If we use the log-depth LWE-based PRFs with modulus size $O(\lambda^{\log \lambda})$ constructed in [5,6] as our constraint circuits then, the message embedding scheme in [33] can be instantiated based solely on LWE with a quasi-polynomial modulus $q = O(\lambda^{\log^2 \lambda})$.

Symmetric Deniable Encryption. Boneh, Lewi and Wu [10] showed that privately puncturable PRFs can be used to build a relaxed notion of symmetric deniable encryption. In more detail, their relaxed definition says that given a ciphertext encrypting an arbitrary plaintext it is possible to produce a fake secret key which decrypts the ciphertext to a random message but doesn't change the decryption of the rest of the ciphertexts. Using the current privately punctured PRFs [9,15,18,32], the deniable encryption scheme in [10] would have security based on the hardness of LWE with subexponential modulus. We observe that the construction in [10] evaluates CHC-PRFs only on random points. Consequently, in this application, we can replace CHC-PRFs with our feasibly correct CHC-PRFs. In particular, instantiating the [10] symmetric deniable encryption constriction with Construction 3 would give us a deniable symmetric encryption scheme based on LWE with quasi-polynomial modulus $q = \lambda^{O(\log^2 \lambda)}$.

7 Feasibly Correct C-PRFs for NC^1 from LWE with Nearly Polynomial Modulus

7.1 Definitions

First, we recall the definition of C-PRFs and then we define feasibly correct C-PRFs. Compared to the constraint-hiding variant discussed in Sect. 6, feasibly correct C-PRFs are weaker in the sense that they do not necessarily hide the constraint.

Definition 14. *A constrained function is a* constrained PRF *(C-PRF) if there is a PPT simulator $\mathcal{S}$ such that, for any PPT adversary $\mathcal{A}$ (that without loss of generality never repeats an* Eval *query),*

$$\{\mathsf{CPRFReal}_{\mathcal{A}}(1^\lambda)\}_{\lambda \in \mathbb{N}} \stackrel{c}{\approx} \{\mathsf{CPRFIdeal}_{\mathcal{A},\mathcal{S}}(1^\lambda)\}_{\lambda \in \mathbb{N}}, \tag{29}$$

where $\mathsf{CPRFReal}$ *and* $\mathsf{CPRFIdeal}$ *are the respective views of $\mathcal{A}$ in the experiments defined in Fig. 5.*

procedure $\mathsf{CPRFReal}_{\mathcal{A}}(1^\lambda)$
  $C \leftarrow \mathcal{A}(1^\lambda)$
  $pp \leftarrow \mathsf{Setup}(1^\lambda)$
  $msk \leftarrow \mathsf{KeyGen}(pp)$
  $sk_C \leftarrow \mathsf{Constrain}(pp, msk, C)$
  $(pp, sk_C) \rightarrow \mathcal{A}$
  repeat
    $x \leftarrow \mathcal{A}$
    $\mathsf{Eval}(pp, msk, x) \rightarrow \mathcal{A}$
  until $\mathcal{A}$ halts

(a) The real experiment

procedure $\mathsf{CPRFIdeal}_{\mathcal{A},\mathcal{S}}(1^\lambda)$
  $C \leftarrow \mathcal{A}(1^\lambda)$
  $(pp, sk_C) \leftarrow \mathcal{S}(1^\lambda, C)$
  $(pp, sk_C) \rightarrow \mathcal{A}$
  repeat
    $x \leftarrow \mathcal{A}$
    if $C(x) = \text{true}$ **then**
      $\mathsf{CEval}(pp, sk_C, x) \rightarrow \mathcal{A}$
    else
      $y \leftarrow \mathcal{Y}$; $y \rightarrow \mathcal{A}$
  until $\mathcal{A}$ halts

(b) The ideal experiment

Fig. 5. The real and ideal constrained PRF experiments.

Definition 15. *A constrained function is a* feasibly correct constrained PRF *if it satisfies Definition 4, and there is a PPT simulator $\mathcal{S}$ such that, for any PPT adversary $\mathcal{A}$ that never queries its* Eval *oracle on an input x for which $C(x) = true$ (and without loss of generality never repeats an* Eval *query),*

$$\{\mathsf{CPRFReal}_{\mathcal{A}}(1^\lambda)\}_{\lambda \in \mathbb{N}} \overset{c}{\approx} \{\mathsf{CPRFIdeal}_{\mathcal{A},\mathcal{S}}(1^\lambda)\}_{\lambda \in \mathbb{N}}, \tag{30}$$

where CPRFReal *and* CPRFIdeal *are the respective views of $\mathcal{A}$ in the experiments defined in Fig. 5.*

7.2 Notation

Let $U(H, x) = H(x)$ denote a depth-universal circuit. We define $\mathsf{BP}_{U,x}$ to be the width 5 permutation branching program that on input a boolean circuit $H\colon \{0,1\}^\ell \rightarrow \{0,1\}$ of depth d and size σ, computes $U(H, x) = H(x)$. Observe that $\mathsf{BP}_{U,x}$ has length $O(4^d)$. Let χ' be a gaussian distribution with a nearly polynomial radius $n^{\omega(1)}$.

Gadgets and Homomorphisms. Here we recall "gadgets" [29] over $\mathbb{Z}_q$ and several of their homomorphic properties, some of which were implicit in [22], and which were developed and exploited further in [8,16,23–25]. For an integer modulus q, the gadget (or powers-of-two) vector over $\mathbb{Z}_q$ is defined as

$$\mathbf{g} = (1, 2, 4, \ldots, 2^{\lceil \lg q \rceil - 1}) \in \mathbb{Z}_q^{\lceil \lg q \rceil}. \tag{31}$$

The gadget matrix is defined as $\mathbf{G}_n = \mathbf{I}_n \otimes \mathbf{g} \in \mathbb{Z}_q^{n \times m}$, where $m = n\lceil \lg q \rceil$. There is an efficiently computable function $\mathbf{G}_n^{-1}\colon \mathbb{Z}_q^{n \times m} \rightarrow \{0,1\}^{m \times m}$ with the following property:

$$\forall \mathbf{A} \in \mathbb{Z}_q^{n \times m} : \mathbf{G}_n \cdot \mathbf{G}_n^{-1}(\mathbf{A}) = \mathbf{A}. \tag{32}$$

We often drop the subscript n when it is clear from context. We use algorithm BranchEval which has the following properties.

- $\mathsf{BranchEval}(\mathsf{BP}, x, \mathbf{A})$, given a width 5 permutation branching program $\mathsf{BP}\colon \{0,1\}^\ell \to \{0,1\}$ of length L, an $x \in \{0,1\}^\ell$, and some $\mathbf{A} \in \mathbb{Z}_q^{n\times(\ell+1)m}$, outputs an integral matrix $\mathbf{R}_{\mathsf{BP},x} \in \mathbb{Z}^{(\ell+1)m\times m}$ with $\text{poly}(m)$-bounded entries for which
$$(\mathbf{A} + (1,x)\otimes \mathbf{G})\cdot \mathbf{R}_{\mathsf{BP},x} = \mathbf{A}_{\mathsf{BP}} + \mathsf{BP}(x)\cdot \mathbf{G}, \tag{33}$$
where $\mathbf{A}_{\mathsf{BP}} \in \mathbb{Z}_q^{n\times m}$ depends only on $\mathbf{A}$ and BP (and not on x).

Theorem 4 (Adapted From [5,15]**).** *Assuming the hardness of $\mathsf{LWE}_{n,q,\chi}$, there is a pair of polynomial time algorithms $\mathsf{BPPRF} = (\mathsf{Setup}, \mathsf{Eval})$ with the following interface*

- $\mathsf{Setup}(1^\lambda)$: *outputs public parameters pp.*
- $\mathsf{Eval}(pp, x)$: *on input $x \in \{0,1\}^\ell$ outputs a matrix $M_x \in \{0,1\}^{m\times m}$. This algorithm is deterministic.*

having the following property: the randomized functionality defined below,

- $\mathsf{P}(pp, \mathbf{s}, x)$: *$P$ is a randomized functionality that on input pp in the range of Setup, $\mathbf{s} \in \mathbb{Z}_q^m$ and $x \in \{0,1\}^\ell$, first samples $\mathbf{e} \leftarrow (\chi')^m$ and then outputs $\mathbf{s}\cdot\mathsf{Eval}(pp,x) + \mathbf{e} \in \mathbb{Z}_q^m$.*

is pseudorandom. In other words, for any PPT adversary $\mathcal{A}$ we have
$$\Big|\Pr_{\substack{pp\leftarrow \mathsf{Setup}(1^\lambda)\\ \mathbf{s}\leftarrow\mathbb{Z}_q^n}}[\mathcal{A}^{P(pp,\mathbf{s},\cdot)}(pp)=1] - \Pr_{pp\leftarrow\mathsf{Setup}(1^\lambda)}[\mathcal{A}^{U(\cdot)}(pp)=1]\Big| = \text{negl}(\lambda), \tag{34}$$
where $U\colon \{0,1\}^\ell \to \mathbb{Z}_q^m$ is a uniformly random function.

7.3 Construction

For security parameter λ, circuit depth d, the following construction is parametrized by some $n = \tilde{O}(\lambda)$ and $q = p\cdot B\cdot n^{\omega(1)}$ where $B = n^{\omega(1)}$ is an upper bound on the absolute value of the samples drawn from χ', and $m = n\lceil \log q\rceil = \text{poly}(n)$. Setting $p = \text{poly}(n)$ or even $p = n^{\omega(1)}$ makes $q = n^{\omega(1)} = \lambda^{\omega(1)}$. Let $\mathsf{PRF} = \{\mathsf{KG}, \mathsf{Eval}\}$ be a PRF with input domain $\mathbb{Z}_q^n$ and output range $\mathbb{Z}_q^m$.

Construction 4. Let $\mathcal{X} = \{0,1\}^\ell$ and $\mathcal{Y} = \mathbb{Z}_q^m$. Define:

- $\mathsf{Setup}(1^\lambda, 1^\sigma, 1^d)$: First sample public parameters $pp' \leftarrow \mathsf{BPPRF.Setup}(1^\lambda)$ for BPPRF. Next, sample uniformly random and independent matrices $\mathbf{A}_0 \in \mathbb{Z}_q^{n\times m}$, $\mathbf{A} \in \mathbb{Z}_q^{n\times(\sigma+1)m}$. Finally, output $pp = (pp', \mathbf{A}_0, \mathbf{A})$.
  (The n-by-m chunks of $\mathbf{A}$ will correspond to the σ bits of a circuit).
- $\mathsf{KeyGen}(pp)$: Generate a PRF key $\kappa \leftarrow \mathsf{PRF.KG}(1^\lambda)$. Sample $\mathbf{s} \leftarrow \mathbb{Z}_q^n$ and set and output the master secret key $msk = (\kappa, \mathbf{s})$.

- $\mathsf{Eval}(pp, msk, x \in \{0,1\}^\ell)$: compute

$$\mathbf{R}_0 = \mathsf{BranchEval}(\mathsf{BP}_{U,x}, 0^{\sigma+1}, \mathbf{A}) \in \mathbb{Z}^{(\sigma+1)m\times m} \tag{35}$$

  and let

$$\mathbf{A}_x = (\mathbf{A} + (1, 0^{\bar{z}}) \otimes \mathbf{G}) \cdot \mathbf{R}_0 - \mathsf{BP}_{U,x}(0^{\sigma+1}) \cdot \mathbf{G} \in \mathbb{Z}_q^{n\times m}. \tag{36}$$

  (Observe that by Equation (33), $\mathbf{A}_x = \mathbf{A}_{\mathsf{BP}}$ for the branching program $\mathsf{BP} = \mathsf{BP}_{U,x}$, and does not depend on the "dummy" ciphertext $0^{\sigma+1}$.)
  Next, let

$$\mathbf{B}_x = \mathbf{A}_x \cdot \mathbf{G}^{-1}(\mathbf{A}_0 \cdot \mathsf{BPPRF.Eval}(pp', x)). \tag{37}$$

  Finally, output

$$\lfloor \mathsf{PRF.Eval}(\kappa, x) + \mathbf{s} \cdot \mathbf{B}_x \rceil_p \tag{38}$$

- $\mathsf{Constrain}(pp, msk, C)$: for a circuit $C\colon \{0,1\}^\ell \to \{0,1\}$ of depth d and size σ, let

$$\mathbf{a} = \mathbf{s}(\mathbf{A} + (1, C) \otimes \mathbf{G}) + \mathbf{e} \tag{39}$$

  where $\mathbf{e}$ is an error vector whose entries are sampled independently from χ.
  Output

$$sk_C = (\kappa, \mathbf{a}, C). \tag{40}$$

- $\mathsf{CEval}(pp, sk_C, x)$: On input $sk_C = (\kappa, \mathbf{a}, C)$ and $x \in \{0,1\}^\ell$, compute

$$\mathbf{R}_x = \mathsf{BranchEval}(\mathsf{BP}_{U,x}, C, \mathbf{A}) \tag{41}$$

$$\mathbf{a}_x = \mathbf{a} \cdot \mathbf{R}_x. \tag{42}$$

  (By Equation (33), we have $\mathbf{a}_x \approx \mathbf{s}(\mathbf{A}_x + \mathsf{BP}_{U,x}(C) \cdot \mathbf{G})$, where we recall that $\mathsf{BP}_{U,x}(C) = C(x)$.)
  Next, compute

$$\mathbf{b}_x = \mathbf{a}_x \cdot \mathbf{G}^{-1}(\mathbf{A}_0 \cdot \mathsf{BPPRF.Eval}(pp', x)) \tag{43}$$

  Finally, output

$$\lfloor \mathsf{PRF.Eval}(\kappa, x) + \mathbf{b}_x \rceil_p. \tag{44}$$

We defer the proof of the following theorem to the full version of this paper.

Theorem 5. *If $\mathsf{LWE}_{n,q,\chi}$ is hard and* PRF *is a pseudorandom function, Construction 4 is a feasibly correct constrained PRF.*

7.4 Application

Updatable Garbled Circuits from LWE with Superpolynomial Modulus. Ananth, Cohen and Jain [2] used C-PRFs to build a cryptographic scheme that they call "updatable garbled circuits (UGC)". Specifically, they showed that a C-PRF which

- has range $\mathbb{Z}_p$ for a superpolynomially large p,
- supports point-function predicates as constraints,
- is *noisy constrained key-homomorphic*, i.e., for any two keys msk_1 and msk_2 and their respective constrained keys sk_{C_1} and sk_{C_2} and for any input x such that $C_1(x) = C_2(x) = 0$, $\mathsf{CEval}(sk_{C_1}, x_1) + \mathsf{CEval}(sk_{C_2}, x_2) = \mathsf{Eval}(msk_1 + msk_2, x) + e$ where e is bounded by some small constant,
- and has a KeyGen algorithm which simply outputs a random key from the key space,

can be used as a building block for UGCs. For their construction, they used the [17] C-PRF which satisfies all of the aforementioned properties. Since the C-PRF construction in [17] needs LWE with subexponential modulus, the security of [17] UGC construction also relies on hardness of LWE with subexponenial modulus.

We argue that in the UGC construction of [2], we can replace the [17] C-PRF with Construction 4. For this, we first notice that if we instantiate Construction 4 using [5] PRFs as the PRF (that is added before rounding) then, the resulting scheme is a noisy constrained key-homomorphic PRF. Furthermore, this instantiation has a KeyGen algorithm which samples a uniform key from its key space. Additionally, we notice that point-function predicates are in NC^1.

The last and most crucial observation is that, the UGC in [2] evaluates the C-PRF only on uniformly random inputs, both in the construction and the security definitions and games. Therefore, feasible correctness of the underlying C-PRF is enough for this UGC construction. So, we can instantiate the UGC using Construction 4. This will result in a UGC construction whose security is based on hardness of LWE with just nearly polynomial modulus $q = \lambda^{\omega(1)}$.

8 Constraint-Hiding PRFs for Hyperplane-Membership Predicates

In this section we construct constraint-hiding constrained PRFs for hyperplane-membership predicates, based solely on (approximate) key-homomorphic PRFs.

8.1 Construction

Construction 5. Let $\mathsf{KHPRF} = (\mathsf{Setup}, \mathsf{Eval})$ be a noisy key-homomorphic pseudorandom function having key space $\mathcal{K}$ (which is a finite group, with keys chosen uniformly at random), domain $\mathcal{X} = \{-D, \ldots, D\}^\ell$ for some D, range $\mathcal{Y} = \mathbb{Z}_q^m$, and homomorphism error bound E.

Our constrained PRF has domain $\mathcal{X}$ and can be constrained to membership predicates for hyperplanes

$$H_\alpha = \{x \in \mathcal{X} : \alpha_0 + \alpha_1 x_1 + \cdots + a_\ell x_\ell = 0\},$$

where $\boldsymbol{\alpha} = (\alpha_0, \alpha_1, \ldots, \alpha_\ell) \in \{-A, \ldots, A\}^{\ell+1}$. Define $B = (\ell+1)(AD+1)E$ and let $p = q/(B \cdot \lambda^{\omega(1)})$ be a divisor of q.

- $\mathsf{Setup}(1^\lambda)$: output $pp \leftarrow \mathsf{KHPRF.Setup}(1^\lambda)$.
- $\mathsf{KeyGen}(pp)$: sample KHPRF keys $k_i \leftarrow \mathcal{K}$ for $i = 0, \ldots, \ell$ and output $msk := \{k_i\}_{i=0,\ldots,\ell}$.
- $\mathsf{Eval}(pp, msk, x)$: on input $msk = \{k_i\}$ and $x \in \mathcal{X} = \{-D, \ldots, D\}^\ell$, output $\lfloor y_x \rceil_p$ where

$$y_x = \mathsf{KHPRF.Eval}(pp, k_0, x) + \sum_{i \in [\ell]} \mathsf{KHPRF.Eval}(pp, x_i k_i, x). \tag{45}$$

- $\mathsf{Constrain}(pp, msk, H_{\boldsymbol{\alpha}})$: on input $msk = \{k_i\}$ and hyperplane $H_{\boldsymbol{\alpha}}$ where $\boldsymbol{\alpha} = (\alpha_0, \alpha_1, \ldots, \alpha_\ell) \in \{-A, \ldots, A\}^{\ell+1}$, first choose a KHPRF key $d \leftarrow \mathcal{K}$ and then for each $i = 0, \ldots, \ell + 1$ define $b_i := k_i - \alpha_i d$. Output $sk_{H_\alpha} := \{b_i\}_{i=0,\ldots,\ell}$.
- $\mathsf{CEval}(pp, sk_H, x)$: on input $sk_H = \{b_i\}$ and $x \in \mathcal{X}$, output $\lfloor y_x \rceil_p$ where

$$y_x = \mathsf{KHPRF.Eval}(pp, b_0, x) + \sum_{i \in [\ell]} \mathsf{KHPRF.Eval}(pp, x_i b_i, x). \tag{46}$$

8.2 Security Proof

Theorem 6. *If* KHPRF *is a noisy key-homomorphic pseudorandom function, and the smallest prime divisor of* q *is bigger than* $(\ell+1)AD$*, then Construction 5 is a feasibly correct and simulation-secure CHC-PRF for hyperplane-membership constraints.*

Proof. This follows from Theorems 7 and 8.

Theorem 7. *If* KHPRF *is a noisy key-homomorphic pseudorandom function, then Construction 5 is feasibly correct.*

Proof. Let $msk = \{k_i\}$ be a master secret key, let $sk_{H_\alpha} = \{b_i = k_i - \alpha_i d\}$ be a constrained secret key for a hyperplane $H_{\boldsymbol{\alpha}}$, and let $x \in \mathcal{X}$ be an arbitrary input. Let y_x, y'_x be the "unrounded" values computed in Eqs. (45) and (46), respectively. If $x \in H_{\boldsymbol{\alpha}}$, i.e., $\alpha_0 + \sum_{i \in [\ell]} \alpha_i x_i = 0$, then

$$y'_x = \mathsf{KHPRF.Eval}(pp, b_0, x) + \sum_{i \in \ell} \mathsf{KHPRF.Eval}(pp, x_i b_i, x) \tag{47}$$

$$= \mathsf{KHPRF.Eval}(pp, k_0, x) + \sum_{i \in [\ell]} \mathsf{KHPRF.Eval}(pp, x_i k_i, x) \tag{48}$$

$$- (\alpha_0 + \sum_{i \in [\ell]} \alpha_i x_i) \mathsf{KHPRF.Eval}(pp, d, x) + \mathbf{e} \tag{49}$$

$$= \mathsf{KHPRF.Eval}(pp, k_0, x) + \sum_{i \in [\ell]} \mathsf{KHPRF.Eval}(pp, x_i k_i, x) + \mathbf{e} \tag{50}$$

$$= y_x + \mathbf{e}, \tag{51}$$

where the second equality is by key homomorphism, and $\mathbf{e}$ is an error vector whose entries have magnitudes at most B. Therefore, $\lfloor y'_x \rceil_p = \lfloor y_x \rceil_p$ (i.e., Eval

and CEval agree on x) unless some entry of y_x is in $\frac{q}{p}(\mathbb{Z} + \frac{1}{2}) + [-B, B]$. We next show that the probability of this event, for x output by any PPT algorithm $\mathcal{A}^{\mathsf{Eval}(pp,msk,\cdot)}$, is negligible (over the choice of msk and $\mathcal{A}$'s randomness). This follows straightforwardly from the pseudorandomness of KHPRF, and specifically the $\mathsf{KHPRF.Eval}(pp, k_0, x)$ term from Eq. (45).

Formally, we construct an adversary $\mathcal{A}'$ against the pseudorandomness of KHPRF, which has access to an oracle $\mathcal{O}$ and runs as follows:

- given public parameters pp, choose $k_1, \ldots, k_\ell \leftarrow \mathcal{K}$;
- whenever $\mathcal{A}$ makes a query $\bar{x}$, respond with $\bar{y} = \mathcal{O}(x) + \sum_{i \in [\ell]} \mathsf{KHPRF.Eval}(pp, \bar{x}_i k_i, \bar{x})$
- when $\mathcal{A}$ finally outputs an x, accept if any of the entries of $y = \mathcal{O}(x) + \sum_{i \in [\ell]} \mathsf{KHPRF.Eval}(pp, x_i k_i, x)$ belong to $\frac{q}{p}(\mathbb{Z} + \frac{1}{2}) + [-B, B]$, otherwise reject.

Clearly, if $\mathcal{O}$ is a uniformly random function, then all of the $\bar{y}$ and y are uniformly random, so by a union bound (which is needed because x might be one of the previously queried $\bar{x}$) $\mathcal{A}'$ accepts with probability at most $2Bpm \cdot \mathrm{poly}(\lambda)/q = \mathrm{negl}(\lambda)$. On the other hand, if $\mathcal{O}$ is $\mathsf{KHPRF.Eval}(\mathsf{pp}, \mathsf{k}_0, \cdot)$ (for some $k_0 \leftarrow \mathcal{K}$) then $\mathcal{A}'$ perfectly simulates the feasible correctness experiment, so the probability that $\mathcal{A}$ wins the feasible correctness game is at most the probability that $\mathcal{A}'$ accepts. By the pseudorandomness of KHPRF, the latter is negligible, as desired.

Theorem 8. *Under the hypotheses of Theorem 6, Construction 5 is simulation secure for the class of hyperplane-membership constraints.*

Proof. We need to build a simulator for adversaries that only submit unauthorized queries. The simulator $\mathcal{S}(1^\lambda, 1^\ell)$ for Construction 5, samples KHPRF keys $b_i \leftarrow \mathcal{K}$ for $i = 0, \ldots, \ell$ and outputs $\{b_i\}_{i=0,\ldots,\ell}$. Now let $\mathcal{A}$ be any polynomial-time adversary. To show that $\mathcal{S}$ satisfies Definition 3 we define a sequence of hybrid experiments and show that they are indistinguishable. Before defining the experiments in detail, we first define a particular "bad" event in all but one of them.

Definition 16. *In each of the following hybrid experiments except H_0, each query x is answered as $\lfloor y_x \rceil_p$ for some y_x that is computed in a certain way. Define* Borderline *to be the event that at least one such y_x has some coordinate in $\frac{q}{p}(\mathbb{Z} + \frac{1}{2}) + [-B, B]$.*

Hybrid H_0: This is the ideal experiment $\mathsf{Ideal}_{\mathcal{A},\mathcal{S}}$.

Hybrid H_1: This is the same as H_0, except that on every (unauthorized) query x (i.e., where $\alpha_0 + \sum_{i \in [\ell]} \alpha_i x_i \neq 0$), instead of returning a uniformly random value from $\mathbb{Z}_p^m$, we choose $y_x \leftarrow \mathbb{Z}_q^m$ and output $\lfloor y_x \rceil_p$.

Hybrid H_2: This is the same as H_1, except that we abort the experiment if Borderline happens.

Hybrid H_3: This is the same as H_2, except that we initially choose a KHPRF key $\mathbf{d} \leftarrow \mathcal{K}$ and change how (unauthorized) queries x are handled. Specifically, for any query x we answer $\lfloor y_x \rceil_p$ where

$$y_x = \mathsf{KHPRF.Eval}(pp, b_0, x) + \sum_{i\in[\ell]} \mathsf{KHPRF.Eval}(pp, x_i b_i, x) \\ + (\alpha_0 + \sum_{i\in[\ell]} \alpha_i x_i)\mathsf{KHPRF.Eval}(pp, \mathbf{d}, x). \tag{52}$$

Hybrid H_4: This is the same as H_3, except that (pp, sk) are generated as in the real experiment. Specifically, we sample $msk := \{k_i \leftarrow \mathcal{K}\}_{0\le i\le \ell}$, $\mathbf{d} \leftarrow \mathcal{K}$, and set $b_i := k_i - \alpha_i \mathbf{d}$ for $0 \le i \le \ell$.

Hybrid H_5: This is the same as H_4, except that we answer all (unauthorized) evaluation queries as in the Eval algorithm, i.e., we output $\lfloor y_x \rceil_p$ where

$$y_x = \mathsf{KHPRF.Eval}(pp, k_0, x) + \sum_{i\in[\ell]} \mathsf{KHPRF.Eval}(pp, x_i k_i, x). \tag{53}$$

Hybrid H_6: This is the same as H_5, except that we no longer abort when Borderline happens. Observe that this is exactly the real experiment $\mathsf{Real}_{\mathcal{A}}$.

We now prove that adjacent pairs of hybrid experiments are indistinguishable.

Claim. Experiments H_0 and H_1 are identical.

Proof. This follows immediately from the fact that p divides q.

Claim. Experiments H_1 and H_2 are statistically indistinguishable, in particular in H_1 the event Borderline happens with negligible probability.

Proof. This immediately follows by the fact that y_x is chosen uniformly at random from $\mathbb{Z}_q^m$ and $\frac{q}{pB} = n^{\omega(1)}$.

Claim. Assuming KHPRF is a noisy key-homomorphic PRF and the prime divisors of q are bigger than $(\ell+1)AD$, $H_2 \overset{c}{\approx} H_3$.

Proof. We need to show that in H_3, y_x is indistinguishable from uniform. Since $\mathsf{KHPRF.Eval}(pp, \mathbf{d}, x)$ is pseudorandom, all we need to prove is that $\alpha_0 + \sum_{i\in[\ell]} \alpha_i x_i$ is invertible in $\mathbb{Z}_q$. To see this recall that all queries are unauthorized and therefore $\alpha_0 + \sum_{i=1}^{\ell} \alpha_i x_i \neq 0$. On the other hand $|\alpha_0 + \sum_{i\in[\ell]} \alpha_i x_i| < (\ell+1)AD$. This proves that $\alpha_0 + \sum_{i\in[\ell]} \alpha_i x_i$ is invertible in $\mathbb{Z}_q$.

Claim. Experiments H_3 and H_4 are identical.

Proof. This follows from the fact that in both H_3 and H_4, the b_is and $\mathbf{d}$ have the same distribution, i.e., they are uniform elements in $\mathcal{K}$.

Claim. Assuming KHPRF is a noisy key-homomorphic PRF, H_4 and H_5 are identical.

Proof. We need to show that all (unauthorized) queries are answered identically in H_4 and H_5. Let y_x and y'_x be the unrounded answers to a query x in hybrids H_4 and H_5 respectively. We need to show $\lfloor y_x \rceil_p = \lfloor y'_x \rceil_p$. Since KHPRF is a noisy key-homomorphic PRF we have

$$\begin{aligned} y_x &= \mathsf{KHPRF.Eval}(pp, b_0, x) + \sum_{i \in [\ell]} \mathsf{KHPRF.Eval}(pp, x_i b_i, x) \\ &\quad + (\alpha_0 + \sum_{i \in [\ell]} \alpha_i x_i) \mathsf{KHPRF.Eval}(pp, \mathbf{d}, x) && (54) \\ &= \mathsf{KHPRF.Eval}(pp, k_0 - \alpha_0 \mathbf{d}, x) + \sum_{i \in [\ell]} \mathsf{KHPRF.Eval}(pp, x_i k_i - \alpha_i x_i \mathbf{d}, x) && (55) \\ &\quad + (\alpha_0 + \sum_{i \in [\ell]} \alpha_i x_i) \mathsf{KHPRF.Eval}(pp, \mathbf{d}, x) && (56) \\ &= \mathsf{KHPRF.Eval}(pp, k_0, x) + \sum_{i \in [\ell]} \mathsf{KHPRF.Eval}(pp, x_i k_i, x) + \mathbf{e} && (57) \\ &= y'_x + \mathbf{e}, && (58) \end{aligned}$$

where $\mathbf{e}$ is a vector with entries not bigger than $(\ell + 1)(AD + 1)E \leq B$. Since we abort when Borderline happens, the claim follows.

Claim. Assuming KHPRF is a noisy key-homomorphic PRF and the prime divisors of q are bigger than $(\ell + 1)AD$, $H_5 \overset{s}{\approx} H_6$.

Proof. By previous claims, Borderline happens with negligible probability in H_5.

This completes the proof of Theorem 8.

9 Bit Fixing PRFs from Minimal Assumptions

The class of *bit-fixing* constraints for input space $\mathcal{X} = \{0,1\}^\ell$ is the set of constraints $\mathcal{C} = \{C_v : v \in \{0,1,\star\}^\ell\}$ where $C_v(x) = \text{true}$ if and only if $x_i = v_i$ for all $i \in [\ell]$ such that $v_i \neq \star$. In other words, x must match v at every position, where $\star$ is a "wildcard" that both 0 and 1 match.

Here we construct a constraint-hiding, bit-fixing PRF (for a single constrained-key query) from the minimal assumption that PRFs exist. Let PRF = (PRF.KG, PRF.Eval) be a pseudorandom function having key space $\mathcal{K}$, domain $\mathcal{X} = \{0,1\}^\ell$, and range $\mathcal{Y}$, which we assume to be a finite (additive) group.

Construction 6. Our bit-fixing PRF with domain $\mathcal{X} = \{0,1\}^\ell$ and range $\mathcal{Y}$ is defined as follows:

- KeyGen(1^λ): sample PRF keys $msk_i^b \leftarrow \mathsf{PRF.KG}(1^\lambda)$ for $i \in [\ell]$ and $b \in \{0,1\}$, and output $msk := \{msk_i^b\}$.
- Eval$(1^\lambda, msk, x \in \{0,1\}^\ell)$: output $\sum_{i \in [\ell]} \mathsf{PRF.Eval}(msk_i^{x_i}, x)$.

- $\mathsf{Constrain}(1^\lambda, msk, v \in \{0,1,\star\})$: define and output $sk_v = \{sk_i^b\}_{i\in[\ell], b\in\{0,1\}}$, defined as follows:
  - if $v_i = b$ or $v_i = \star$ then let $sk_i^b := msk_i^b$,
  - otherwise (i.e., $v_i = 1 - b$), let $sk_i^b \leftarrow \mathsf{PRF.KG}(1^\lambda)$ be a freshly sampled key for PRF.
- $\mathsf{CEval}(1^\lambda, sk_v = \{sk_i^b\}, x)$: output $\sum_{i\in[\ell]} \mathsf{PRF.Eval}(sk_i^{x_i}, x)$.

In words, the constrained key for pattern $v \in \{0,1,\star\}^\ell$ contains exactly those msk components msk_i^b for which b "matches" v_i, with fresh PRF keys taking the place of the other msk components. In particular, it is easy to see that this ensures correct constrained evaluation on authorized inputs. Also observe that the constrained key alone hides the pattern vector *perfectly*, i.e., the distribution of sk_v is the same for all v.

9.1 Security Proof

Theorem 9. *If* PRF *is a pseudorandom function, then Construction 6 is a constraint-hiding bit-fixing PRF according to Definition 3.*

Proof. The simulator $\mathcal{S}(1^\lambda)$ for Construction 6 simply samples PRF keys $r_i^b \leftarrow \mathsf{PRF.KG}(1^\lambda)$ for $i \in [\ell], b \in \{0,1\}$ and outputs $\{r_i^b\}$. Now let $\mathcal{A}$ be any polynomial-time adversary. To show that $\mathcal{S}$ satisfies Definition 3 we define a sequence of hybrid experiments and show that they are indistinguishable.

Hybrid H_0: This is the real experiment $\mathsf{Real}_\mathcal{A}$ (see Fig. 1).
Hybrid H_1: This is the same as H_0 except that on every authorized query x (i.e., where x matches the pattern v output by $\mathcal{A}$) we answer it by $\mathsf{CEval}(pp, sk_C, x)$.
Hybrid H_2: This is the same as H_1 except that on every unauthorized query x (i.e., where x does not match the pattern v output by $\mathcal{A}$) we answer with a uniformly random element in $\mathcal{Y}$.
Hybrid H_3: This is the same as the ideal experiment $\mathsf{Ideal}_{\mathcal{A},\mathcal{S}}$.

We now show that adjacent pairs of hybrid experiments are indistinguishable. First, it follows immediately that experiments H_0 and H_1 are identical, due to the way sk_C is constructed.

Claim. If PRF is a pseudorandom function, then $H_1 \stackrel{c}{\approx} H_2$.

Proof. Let $H_{1,0} = H_1$ and define hybrid $H_{1,i}$ for $i \in [\ell]$ as follows: it is the same as H_1 except that for every query x which does not match the pattern v *in one of the first i positions*, we answer with a uniformly random element in $\mathcal{Y}$.

Clearly $H_{1,\ell} = H_2$. We show that for every $i \in [\ell]$, $H_{1,i-1} \stackrel{c}{\approx} H_{1,i}$. Notice that if $v_i = \star$ then the two experiments are identical. So assume that $v_i = b \in \{0,1\}$. Let $\mathcal{A}$ be an adversary attempting to distinguish between $H_{1,i-1}$ and $H_{1,i}$. We build an efficient adversary $\mathcal{A}'$ against the security of PRF, which has access to an oracle $\mathcal{O}$ that is either a uniformly random function $U\colon \{0,1\}^\ell \to \mathcal{Y}$ or $\mathsf{PRF.Eval}(sk, \cdot)$ for $sk \leftarrow \mathsf{PRF.KG}(1^\lambda)$. $\mathcal{A}'$ interacts with $\mathcal{A}$ in the same way as $H_{1,i-1}$, except that it does not sample msk_i^{1-b}, and on queries x for which i is the smallest index where x disagrees with the pattern v, it replies with $\sum_{j\in[\ell]\setminus\{i\}} \mathsf{PRF.Eval}(msk_j^{x_j}, x) + \mathcal{O}(x)$. Observe that if $\mathcal{O}$ is U then $\mathcal{A}$'s view is identical to $H_{1,i}$, otherwise the view is identical to $H_{1,i-1}$. Therefore, the advantage of $\mathcal{A}$ in distinguishing $H_{1,i-1}$ from $H_{1,i}$ is identical to the advantage of $\mathcal{A}'$ in attacking PRF, which by assumption is negligible, as desired.

Finally, we claim that experiments H_2 and H_3 are identical. This is because in both experiments the constrained key has the same distribution, i.e., it consists of 2ℓ independent keys for PRF.

Remark 1. We observe that any constraint-hiding bit-fixing PRF can be bootstrapped to support k-CNF formulas as constraints, where k is a constant. For input domain $\{0,1\}^\ell$, the construction is as follows:

- we generate parameters for a bit-fixing PRF with input length $(2\ell+1)^k$,
- to evaluate on an input $x \in \{0,1\}^\ell$, first, we convert x to $x' \in \{0,1\}^{(2\ell+1)^k}$ where the individual bits of x' are the result of evaluating all possible k-variable disjunctions involving the literals $F, x_1, \bar{x}_1, \cdots, x_\ell, \bar{x}_\ell$ in some specified order, then, we evaluate the bit-fixing PRF on x' and output the result,
- to generate a constrained-key for a k-CNF formula ϕ having $t \leq (2\ell+1)^k$ clauses, we generate a constrained key in the bit-fixing PRF for a pattern v where in v the positions corresponding to the clauses in ϕ are fixed to 1 and the rest of the positions are wildcard.

A Shift Hiding Shiftable Functions and Their Properties

Here we review the interface and relevant properties of *shift-hiding shiftable functions* introduced in [32]. For security parameter λ and constraint circuit size σ, shift-hiding shiftable functions are a tuple of algorithms parameterized by some $n = \mathrm{poly}(\lambda, \sigma)$ and $q = \lambda^{\mathrm{poly}(\lambda,\sigma)}$, with $m = n\lceil \lg q \rceil = \mathrm{poly}(\lambda, \sigma)$. These algorithms have the following interface.

- $\mathsf{Setup}(1^\lambda, 1^\sigma, 1^d)$: On input security parameter λ, shift circuit size σ, and shift circuit depth d, output public parameter pp.
- $\mathsf{KeyGen}(pp)$: Output the master secret key $msk = \mathbf{s}$.
- $\mathsf{Eval}(pp, msk, x)$: On input an ℓ bit string x, output $\mathbf{y} \in \mathbb{Z}_q^m$.
- $\mathsf{Shift}(pp, msk, H)$: On input a shift function $H\colon \{0,1\}^\ell \to \mathbb{Z}_q^m$, output a shifted key sk_H.
- $\mathsf{SEval}(pp, sk_H, x)$: On input a shifted key sk_H and input value $x \in \{0,1\}^\ell$, output $\mathbf{y} \in \mathbb{Z}_q^m$.
- $\mathcal{S}(1^\lambda, 1^\sigma, 1^d)$: On input security parameter λ, shift circuit size σ, and shift depth d, output simulated public parameters pp and simulated shifted key sk.

We use the following two properties of the shift-hiding shiftable functions construction of [32].

Property 1 (Shift Hiding). Assuming the hardness of $\mathrm{LWE}_{n-1,q,\chi}$ and CPA security of the GSW [22] encryption scheme, for any PPT $\mathcal{A}$, any $\sigma = \sigma(\lambda) = \mathrm{poly}(\lambda)$, and any $d = d(\lambda) = \mathrm{poly}(\lambda)$

$$\{\mathsf{RealKey}_{\mathcal{A}}(1^\lambda, 1^\sigma, 1^d)\}_{\lambda \in \mathbb{N}} \stackrel{c}{\approx} \{\mathsf{IdealKey}_{\mathcal{A}}(1^\lambda, 1^\sigma, 1^d)\}_{\lambda \in \mathbb{N}}, \tag{59}$$

where RealKey and IdealKey are the respective views of $\mathcal{A}$ in the experiments defined in Fig. 2.

Property 2 (Approximate Shift Correctness). For any shift function $H\colon \{0,1\}^\ell \to \mathbb{Z}_q^m$ whose binary decomposition $H'\colon \{0,1\}^\ell \to \{0,1\}^k$ can be represented by a boolean circuit of size σ and depth d, and any $x \in \{0,1\}^\ell$, $pp \leftarrow \mathsf{Setup}(1^\lambda, 1^\sigma, 1^d)$, $msk \leftarrow \mathsf{KeyGen}(pp)$ and $sk_H \leftarrow \mathsf{Shift}(pp, msk, H)$, we have

$$\mathsf{SEval}(pp, sk_H, x) \approx \mathsf{Eval}(pp, msk, x) + H(x) \tag{60}$$

where the approximation hides some $\lambda^{O(d \log \lambda)}$-bounded error vector.

References

1. Alperin-Sheriff, J., Peikert, C.: Faster bootstrapping with polynomial error. In: Garay, J.A., Gennaro, R. (eds.) CRYPTO 2014. LNCS, vol. 8616, pp. 297–314. Springer, Heidelberg (2014). https://doi.org/10.1007/978-3-662-44371-2_17
2. Ananth, P., Cohen, A., Jain, A.: Cryptography with updates. In: Coron, J.-S., Nielsen, J.B. (eds.) EUROCRYPT 2017. LNCS, vol. 10211, pp. 445–472. Springer, Cham (2017). https://doi.org/10.1007/978-3-319-56614-6_15
3. Applebaum, B., Cash, D., Peikert, C., Sahai, A.: Fast cryptographic primitives and circular-secure encryption based on hard learning problems. In: Halevi, S. (ed.) CRYPTO 2009. LNCS, vol. 5677, pp. 595–618. Springer, Heidelberg (2009). https://doi.org/10.1007/978-3-642-03356-8_35
4. Attrapadung, N., Matsuda, T., Nishimaki, R., Yamada, S., Yamakawa, T.: Constrained PRFs for NC^1 in traditional groups. In: Shacham, H., Boldyreva, A. (eds.) CRYPTO 2018. LNCS, vol. 10992, pp. 543–574. Springer, Cham (2018). https://doi.org/10.1007/978-3-319-96881-0_19
5. Banerjee, A., Peikert, C.: New and improved key-homomorphic pseudorandom functions. In: Garay, J.A., Gennaro, R. (eds.) CRYPTO 2014. LNCS, vol. 8616, pp. 353–370. Springer, Heidelberg (2014). https://doi.org/10.1007/978-3-662-44371-2_20
6. Banerjee, A., Peikert, C., Rosen, A.: Pseudorandom functions and lattices. In: Pointcheval, D., Johansson, T. (eds.) EUROCRYPT 2012. LNCS, vol. 7237, pp. 719–737. Springer, Heidelberg (2012). https://doi.org/10.1007/978-3-642-29011-4_42
7. Barak, B., et al.: On the (im)possibility of obfuscating programs. J. ACM **59**(2), 6:1–6:48 (2012). Preliminary version in CRYPTO 2001
8. Boneh, D., et al.: Fully key-homomorphic encryption, arithmetic circuit ABE and compact garbled circuits. In: Nguyen, P.Q., Oswald, E. (eds.) EUROCRYPT 2014. LNCS, vol. 8441, pp. 533–556. Springer, Heidelberg (2014). https://doi.org/10.1007/978-3-642-55220-5_30

9. Boneh, D., Kim, S., Montgomery, H.: Private puncturable PRFs from standard lattice assumptions. In: Coron, J.-S., Nielsen, J.B. (eds.) EUROCRYPT 2017. LNCS, vol. 10210, pp. 415–445. Springer, Cham (2017). https://doi.org/10.1007/978-3-319-56620-7_15
10. Boneh, D., Lewi, K., Wu, D.J.: Constraining pseudorandom functions privately. In: Fehr, S. (ed.) PKC 2017. LNCS, vol. 10175, pp. 494–524. Springer, Heidelberg (2017). https://doi.org/10.1007/978-3-662-54388-7_17
11. Boneh, D., Waters, B.: Constrained pseudorandom functions and their applications. In: Sako, K., Sarkar, P. (eds.) ASIACRYPT 2013. LNCS, vol. 8270, pp. 280–300. Springer, Heidelberg (2013). https://doi.org/10.1007/978-3-642-42045-0_15
12. Boyle, E., Goldwasser, S., Ivan, I.: Functional signatures and pseudorandom functions. In: Krawczyk, H. (ed.) PKC 2014. LNCS, vol. 8383, pp. 501–519. Springer, Heidelberg (2014). https://doi.org/10.1007/978-3-642-54631-0_29
13. Brakerski, Z., Gentry, C., Vaikuntanathan, V.: (Leveled) fully homomorphic encryption without bootstrapping. In: ITCS, pp. 309–325 (2012)
14. Brakerski, Z., Langlois, A., Peikert, C., Regev, O., Stehlé, D.: Classical hardness of learning with errors. In: STOC, pp. 575–584 (2013)
15. Brakerski, Z., Tsabary, R., Vaikuntanathan, V., Wee, H.: Private constrained PRFs (and more) from LWE. In: Kalai, Y., Reyzin, L. (eds.) TCC 2017. LNCS, vol. 10677, pp. 264–302. Springer, Cham (2017). https://doi.org/10.1007/978-3-319-70500-2_10
16. Brakerski, Z., Vaikuntanathan, V.: Lattice-based FHE as secure as PKE. In: ITCS, pp. 1–12 (2014)
17. Brakerski, Z., Vaikuntanathan, V.: Constrained key-homomorphic PRFs from standard lattice assumptions. In: Dodis, Y., Nielsen, J.B. (eds.) TCC 2015. LNCS, vol. 9015, pp. 1–30. Springer, Heidelberg (2015). https://doi.org/10.1007/978-3-662-46497-7_1
18. Canetti, R., Chen, Y.: Constraint-hiding constrained PRFs for NC^1 from LWE. In: Coron, J.-S., Nielsen, J.B. (eds.) EUROCRYPT 2017. LNCS, vol. 10210, pp. 446–476. Springer, Cham (2017). https://doi.org/10.1007/978-3-319-56620-7_16
19. Cohen, A., Holmgren, J., Nishimaki, R., Vaikuntanathan, V., Wichs, D.: Watermarking cryptographic capabilities. In: STOC, pp. 1115–1127 (2016)
20. Cook, S.A., Hoover, H.J.: A depth-universal circuit. SIAM J. Comput. **14**(4), 833–839 (1985)
21. Davidson, A., Katsumata, S., Nishimaki, R., Yamada, S.: Constrained PRFs for bit-fixing from OWFs with constant collusion-resistance. Cryptology ePrint Archive, Report 2018/982 (2018). https://eprint.iacr.org/2018/982
22. Gentry, C., Sahai, A., Waters, B.: Homomorphic encryption from learning with errors: conceptually-simpler, asymptotically-faster, attribute-based. In: Canetti, R., Garay, J.A. (eds.) CRYPTO 2013. LNCS, vol. 8042, pp. 75–92. Springer, Heidelberg (2013). https://doi.org/10.1007/978-3-642-40041-4_5
23. Gorbunov, S., Vaikuntanathan, V., Wee, H.: Predicate encryption for circuits from LWE. In: Gennaro, R., Robshaw, M. (eds.) CRYPTO 2015. LNCS, vol. 9216, pp. 503–523. Springer, Heidelberg (2015). https://doi.org/10.1007/978-3-662-48000-7_25
24. Gorbunov, S., Vaikuntanathan, V., Wichs, D.: Leveled fully homomorphic signatures from standard lattices. In: STOC, pp. 469–477 (2015)

25. Gorbunov, S., Vinayagamurthy, D.: Riding on asymmetry: efficient ABE for branching programs. In: Iwata, T., Cheon, J.H. (eds.) ASIACRYPT 2015. LNCS, vol. 9452, pp. 550–574. Springer, Heidelberg (2015). https://doi.org/10.1007/978-3-662-48797-6_23
26. Kiayias, A., Papadopoulos, S., Triandopoulos, N., Zacharias, T.: Delegatable pseudorandom functions and applications. In: CCS, pp. 669–684 (2013)
27. Kim, S., Wu, D.J.: Watermarking cryptographic functionalities from standard lattice assumptions. In: Katz, J., Shacham, H. (eds.) CRYPTO 2017. LNCS, vol. 10401, pp. 503–536. Springer, Cham (2017). https://doi.org/10.1007/978-3-319-63688-7_17
28. Kim, S., Wu, D.J.: Watermarking PRFs from lattices: stronger security via extractable PRFs. In: Boldyreva, A., Micciancio, D. (eds.) CRYPTO 2019. LNCS, vol. 11694, pp. 335–366. Springer, Cham (2019). https://doi.org/10.1007/978-3-030-26954-8_11
29. Micciancio, D., Peikert, C.: Trapdoors for lattices: simpler, tighter, faster, smaller. In: Pointcheval, D., Johansson, T. (eds.) EUROCRYPT 2012. LNCS, vol. 7237, pp. 700–718. Springer, Heidelberg (2012). https://doi.org/10.1007/978-3-642-29011-4_41
30. Peikert, C.: Public-key cryptosystems from the worst-case shortest vector problem. In: STOC, pp. 333–342 (2009)
31. Peikert, C., Regev, O., Stephens-Davidowitz, N.: Pseudorandomness of Ring-LWE for any ring and modulus. In: STOC, pp. 461–473 (2017)
32. Peikert, C., Shiehian, S.: Privately constraining and programming PRFs, the LWE way. In: Abdalla, M., Dahab, R. (eds.) PKC 2018. LNCS, vol. 10770, pp. 675–701. Springer, Cham (2018). https://doi.org/10.1007/978-3-319-76581-5_23
33. Quach, W., Wichs, D., Zirdelis, G.: Watermarking PRFs under standard assumptions: public marking and security with extraction queries. In: Beimel, A., Dziembowski, S. (eds.) TCC 2018. LNCS, vol. 11240, pp. 669–698. Springer, Cham (2018). https://doi.org/10.1007/978-3-030-03810-6_24
34. Regev, O.: On lattices, learning with errors, random linear codes, and cryptography. J. ACM **56**(6), 1–40 (2009). Preliminary version in STOC 2005
35. Sahai, A., Waters, B.: How to use indistinguishability obfuscation: deniable encryption, and more. In: STOC, pp. 475–484 (2014)
36. Tsabary, R.: Fully secure attribute-based encryption for t-CNF from LWE. In: Boldyreva, A., Micciancio, D. (eds.) CRYPTO 2019. LNCS, vol. 11692, pp. 62–85. Springer, Cham (2019). https://doi.org/10.1007/978-3-030-26948-7_3

Bringing Order to Chaos: The Case of Collision-Resistant Chameleon-Hashes

David Derler[1], Kai Samelin[2(✉)], and Daniel Slamanig[3]

[1] DFINITY, Zurich, Switzerland
david@dfinity.org
[2] TÜV Rheinland i-sec GmbH, Hallbergmoos, Germany
kaispapers@gmail.com
[3] AIT Austrian Institute of Technology, Vienna, Austria
daniel.slamanig@ait.ac.at

Abstract. Chameleon-hash functions, introduced by Krawczyk and Rabin at NDSS 2000, are trapdoor collision-resistant hash-functions parametrized by a public key. If the corresponding secret key is known, arbitrary collisions for the hash function can be efficiently found. Chameleon-hash functions have prominent applications in the design of cryptographic primitives, such as lifting non-adaptively secure signatures to adaptively secure ones. Recently, this primitive also received a lot of attention as a building block in more complex cryptographic applications ranging from editable blockchains to advanced signature and encryption schemes.

We observe that in latter applications various different notions of collision-resistance are used, and it is not always clear if the respective notion does really cover what seems intuitively required by the application. Therefore, we revisit existing collision-resistance notions in the literature, study their relations, and—using the example of the recent redactable blockchain proposals—discuss which practical impact different notions of collision-resistance might have. Moreover, we provide a stronger, and arguably more desirable, notion of collision-resistance than what is known from the literature. Finally, we present a surprisingly simple and efficient black-box construction of chameleon-hash functions achieving this strong notion.

1 Introduction

A chameleon-hash function (CH) is a trapdoor collision-resistant hash-function parameterized by a public key. If the corresponding secret key is known, arbitrary collisions for the hash function, i.e., distinct messages $m \neq m'$ yielding the same hash value h, can be efficiently found. Over the years, they have proven to be a very useful tool in theory, as well as practice. Exemplary, CHs are used to construct on/offline signatures [17,26,42], and to generically lift non-adaptively secure signature schemes to adaptively secure ones (cf. [42]), see e.g., Hohenberger and Waters [35]. If CHs are tightly-secure, they are used to generically

A. Kiayias et al. (Eds.): PKC 2020, LNCS 12110, pp. 462–492, 2020.
https://doi.org/10.1007/978-3-030-45374-9_16

construct tightly-secure signatures [12]. Likewise, CHs are used to generically construct strong one-time signatures as shown by Mohassel [39], inspired by a concrete construction from Pedersen commitments by Groth [30]. Zhang [46] shows how to construct IND-CCA secure public-key encryption from tag-based encryption (TBE) or identity-based encryption (IBE) and CHs. Bellare and Ristov made the interesting discovery that chameleon-hashes and Σ-protocols, i.e., three round public-coin honest-verifier zero-knowledge proofs of knowledge, are equivalent [10,11]. CHs are also used to construct sanitizable signatures [3,14,15], i.e., signatures where a designated entity can modify certain parts of a signed message without invalidating the respective signature under controlled conditions. Furthermore, CHs have been used by Steinfeld et al. [44] to extend Schnorr and RSA signatures to the universal designated-verifier setting [43]. Also, different flavors of chameleon-hashing such as (hierarchical) identity-based [5,7] or policy-based chameleon-hash functions [21,41] have been studied.

In a more applied setting, CHs have shown to be valuable to construct integrity measurement and remote attestation mechanisms (denoted chameleon attestation) [2], and are used in vehicular ad-hoc networks (VANETs) [33] or handover authentication in mobile networks [18]. More recently, CHs have been used as a means to rewrite blocks in blockchains by replacing the hash function to chain blocks and/or to hash transactions by chameleon-hashes [4,21], to which we come back in Sect. 5. This brief discussion already shows that chameleon-hashes are used in a wide spectrum of different applications requiring different strength of the respective chameleon-hash. Consequently, authors often introduce some ad-hoc notion of collision-resistance for their applications, or even ignore that applications might require a stronger notion. Subsequently, we briefly discuss the different notions which are most commonly found in the literature.

Formalizing Chameleon-Hashes. The concept of chameleon-hashing dates back to the notion of trapdoor commitments introduced by Brassard et al. [13], and was firstly coined chameleon-hashing by Krawczyk and Rabin [37] with an instantiation based on the well-known trapdoor-commitment scheme by Pedersen [40]. Later, Ateniese and de Medeiros in [6] observed that the initial collision-resistance notion (which we denote W-CollRes) is rather weak (it does not give the adversary access to any collisions), and, more importantly, it is also satisfied by chameleon-hashes suffering from a key-exposure problem. Namely, when seeing a single collision for some hash h, it allows to publicly extract the secret trapdoor. Thus, any further guarantees are lost. While this is a desirable property for the initial use in chameleon signatures [37], and is also sufficient for the lifting compiler to adaptively secure signatures [42] (as no collision is ever revealed), it is too weak for many other applications. The key-exposure freeness definition in [6] is for the specific case of public-coin chameleon-hashing (where verifying the chameleon-hash is essentially re-computing it). To address this, Ateniese et al. [4] introduced a related notion called enhanced collision-resistance (which we denote E-CollRes) for the generalized case of secret-coin chameleon-hashing (which is the setting that we also consider). The latter notion allows the adversary to see collisions, but it is not allowed to see any collision for the target hash, i.e., the hash corresponding to the collision it computes. Hence, once a single collision for a hash h is seen, an adversary can find arbitrary collisions for that particular hash h. Recently, Khalili et al. [36] have pointed out issues regarding the practicality of the concrete random-oracle model instantiation[1], proposed by Ateniese et al. in [4], and propose alternative constructions in the standard model. In another work Camenisch et al. [15] proposed an alternative collision-resistance notion which allows the adversary to see arbitrary collisions also for the target hash, but not for the target message, i.e., the message used in the collision output by the adversary has never been queried. In other words, once a collision for a message m is seen, an adversary is allowed to find arbitrary other hashes h' with the queried messages. Arguably, this notion seems more realistic as it is better compatible with practical applications (e.g., one can often make the messages unique by appending a tag/nonce), and thus we denote it as standard collision-resistance (or S-CollRes).

Motivation and Contribution. The previous discussion already illustrates that there are many different collision-resistance notions. While this does not necessarily point to an issue, we observe that it is not always clear whether the respective notion does really cover what is required by the respective application. Moreover, it is not clear if the last notion discussed above (S-CollRes) is already the most desirable notion, or, if even stronger notions are achievable, and do have practical relevance. Motivated by these observations, we provide the following contributions:

Relations among Properties. We discuss the different security notions of chameleon-hashes, and rigorously study relations among them. Most importantly, we, for the first time, clarify the picture of existing collision-resistance notions by showing implications, and separations, (cf. Fig. 1 for an overview). In the course of showing separations, we also provide a construction of a chameleon-hash satisfying the E-CollRes notion, which clearly demonstrates weaknesses of this notion.

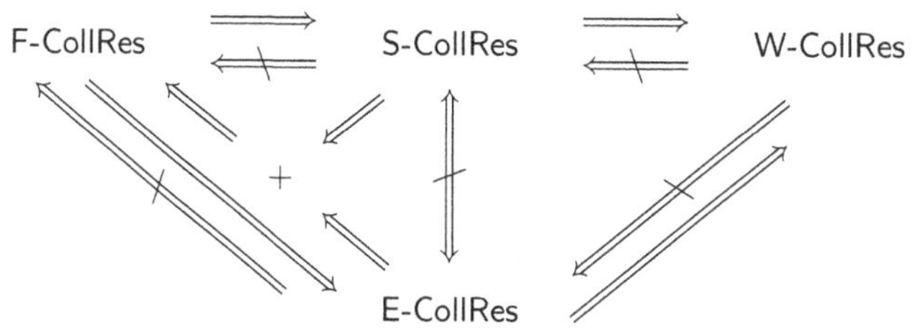

Fig. 1. Relations between CH collision-resistance properties

[1] The requirement for an invertible encoding into the group introduces an enormous efficiency penalty, and thus their instantiation is incomplete. Moreover, it is possible that their schemes do meet our stronger definition of full collision-resistance, but we neither prove nor disprove this statement here.

Stronger Notion. We find that the strongest existing collision-resistance notions, i.e., E-CollRes and S-CollRes (which are incomparable), might still be too weak for practical applications, see, e.g., Sect. 5. In particular, even if S-CollRes is satisfied, the hash values might still be malleable leaving space for potential real-world attacks. Consequently, we propose a stronger notion coined full collision-resistance (or F-CollRes for short), which enforces that the adversary cannot (except with negligible probability) output *any* new collisions and covers what one intuitively expects from collision-resistance.

Black-Box Construction. We present a simple black-box construction of a chameleon-hash function satisfying this strong F-CollRes notion. Considering the complexity of existing constructions in [4,36] which only achieve the weaker notion of E-CollRes, this is somewhat surprising. To recall, the construction from Ateniese et al. [4] starts from a public-coin chameleon-hash function that satisfies W-CollRes, uses an IND-CPA secure encryption scheme to encrypt the randomness of the chameleon-hash and then uses a true-simulation extractable (tSE) NIZK [25], which is in turn based on a NIZK and an IND-CCA secure public-key encryption scheme, to prove that the ciphertext is an encryption of the randomness. The constructions from Khalili et al. [36], which avoid the aforementioned issues with [4], are based on another new public-coin chameleon-hash function that satisfies W-CollRes and then either uses Groth-Sahai NIZK proofs [32] and the IND-CCA secure Cramer-Shoup encryption scheme [20] or a succinct non-interactive argument of knowledge (SNARK). Both constructions in [36] basically follow the generic template in [4]. In contrast, our black-box construction of a F-CollRes chameleon-hash is constructed from perfectly correct (multi-challenge) IND-CPA secure encryption, e.g., ElGamal encryption, and a simulation-sound extractable non-interactive zero-knowledge proof (SSE-NIZK), e.g., applying the compiler of Faust et al. [27] to a Fiat-Shamir transformed Σ-protocol. The basic idea is that the chameleon-hash is the encryption c of the message m and the randomness of the chameleon-hash is a NIZK proof s.t. either c correctly encrypts m under the pk of CH *or* one knows the secret key sk corresponding to pk. Interestingly, already a perfectly-binding commitment (without any hiding) is sufficient to achieve the F-CollRes notion, but instead a multi-challenge IND-CPA secure encryption scheme as a perfectly-binding commitment is used to additionally achieve the indistinguishability property of the CH, i.e., that fresh and adapted hashes are indistinguishable, a notion that is considered standard for chameleon-hashes.

Applications. We discuss how our stronger notion allows to strengthen the security of existing applications and in particular will discuss what problems may be caused by different notions of collision-resistance within recent applications to redactable blockchains [4,21]. Here, either the hash function to chain blocks in a blockchain or the hash functions to aggregate transactions within single blocks (usually by means of a Merkle-tree) are replaced by a chameleon-hash function.

2 Preliminaries

Notation. With $\lambda \in \mathbb{N}$ we denote our security parameter. All algorithms implicitly take 1^λ as an additional input. We write $a \leftarrow_r A(x)$ if the output of a probabilistic algorithm A with input x is assigned to a and use $a \leftarrow A(x)$ if A is deterministic. An algorithm is efficient, if it runs in probabilistic polynomial time (PPT) in the length of its input. All algorithms are PPT, if not explicitly mentioned otherwise. If we want to make the random coins used by an algorithm A explicit, we use the notation $a \leftarrow_r A(x;\xi)$. We write $(a;\xi) \leftarrow_r A(x)$, if we need to access the random coins ξ internally drawn by A. Most algorithms may return a special error symbol $\bot \notin \{0,1\}^*$, denoting an exception. Returning output ends execution of an algorithm or an oracle. To make the presentation in the security proofs more compact, we occasionally use $(a,\bot) \leftarrow_r A(x)$ to indicate that the second output is either ignored or not returned by A. If S is a finite set, we write $a \leftarrow_r S$ to denote that a is chosen uniformly at random from S. $\mathcal{M}$ denotes a message space of a scheme, and we generally assume that $\mathcal{M}$ is derivable from the scheme's public parameters or its public key. For a list we require that there is an injective, and efficiently reversible, encoding, that maps the list to $\{0,1\}^*$. A function $\nu : \mathbb{N} \to \mathbb{R}_{\geq 0}$ is negligible, if it vanishes faster than every inverse polynomial, i.e., $\forall k \in \mathbb{N}$, $\exists n_0 \in \mathbb{N}$ such that $\nu(n) \leq n^{-k}$, $\forall n > n_0$.

2.1 Building Blocks

We now present the building blocks we require. These include key-verifiable multi-challenge IND-CPA (mcIND-CPA) secure public-key encryption schemes Ω, digital signature schemes Σ, and non-interactive zero-knowledge proofs Π.

Public-Key Encryption Schemes. Subsequently, we define public-key encryption schemes.

Definition 1 (Public-Key Encryption Scheme). *A public-key encryption scheme Ω consists of five algorithms $\{\mathsf{PG}_\Omega, \mathsf{KG}_\Omega, \mathsf{Enc}, \mathsf{Dec}, \mathsf{KVf}_\Omega\}$, such that:*

PG_Ω. *The algorithm PG_Ω outputs the public parameters of the scheme:*

$$\mathsf{pp}_\Omega \leftarrow_r \mathsf{PG}_\Omega(1^\lambda).$$

It is assumed that pp_Ω is an implicit input to all other algorithms.

KG_Ω. *The algorithm KG_Ω outputs the key pair, on input pp_Ω:*

$$(\mathsf{sk}_\Omega, \mathsf{pk}_\Omega) \leftarrow_r \mathsf{KG}_\Omega(\mathsf{pp}_\Omega).$$

Enc. *The algorithm Enc gets as input the public key pk_Ω, and a message $m \in \mathcal{M}$ to encrypt. It outputs a ciphertext c:*

$$c \leftarrow_r \mathsf{Enc}(\mathsf{pk}_\Omega, m).$$

$\mathbf{Exp}_{\mathcal{A},\Omega}^{\mathsf{mc\text{-}IND\text{-}CPA}}(\lambda)$:
  $\mathsf{pp}_\Omega \leftarrow_r \mathsf{PG}_\Omega(1^\lambda)$
  $(\mathsf{sk}_\Omega, \mathsf{pk}_\Omega) \leftarrow_r \mathsf{KG}_\Omega(\mathsf{pp}_\Omega)$
  $b \leftarrow_r \{0,1\}$
  $a \leftarrow_r \mathcal{A}^{\mathsf{Enc}'(\mathsf{pk}_\Omega,\cdot,\cdot,b)}(\mathsf{pk}_\Omega)$
    where Enc' on input $\mathsf{pk}_\Omega, m_0, m_1, b$:
      If $m_0 \notin \mathcal{M} \vee m_1 \notin \mathcal{M} \vee |m_0| \neq |m_1|$:
        $c \leftarrow \perp$
      Else:
        $c \leftarrow_r \mathsf{Enc}(\mathsf{pk}_\Omega, m_b)$
    return c
  return 1, if $a = b$
  return 0

Fig. 2. Multi-challenge IND-CPA security

Dec. *The deterministic algorithm* Dec *outputs a message* $m \in \mathcal{M} \cup \{\perp\}$ *on input* sk_Ω*, and a ciphertext* c*:*

$$m \leftarrow \mathsf{Dec}(\mathsf{sk}_\Omega, c).$$

KVf_Ω. *The deterministic algorithm* KVf_Ω *decides whether a given public key* pk_Ω *corresponds to a given secret key* sk_Ω*:*

$$d \leftarrow \mathsf{KVf}_\Omega(\mathsf{pk}_\Omega, \mathsf{sk}_\Omega).$$

Definition 2 (Correctness). *A public key encryption scheme* Ω *is called correct, if for all security parameters* $\lambda \in \mathbb{N}$*, for all* $\mathsf{pp}_\Omega \leftarrow_r \mathsf{PG}_\Omega(1^\lambda)$*, for all* $(\mathsf{sk}_\Omega, \mathsf{pk}_\Omega) \leftarrow_r \mathsf{KG}_\Omega(\mathsf{pp}_\Omega)$*, for all* $m \in \mathcal{M}$*, for all* $c \leftarrow_r \mathsf{Enc}(\mathsf{pk}_\Omega, m)$*, we have that* $m = \mathsf{Dec}(\mathsf{sk}_\Omega, c)$ *and that for all* $\mathsf{sk}_\Omega{}'$ *we have that* $\mathsf{KVf}_\Omega(\mathsf{pk}_\Omega, \mathsf{sk}_\Omega{}') = 1 \implies m = \mathsf{Dec}(\mathsf{sk}_\Omega{}', c)$.

Definition 3 (Multi-Challenge IND-CPA Security). *A public-key encryption scheme* Ω *is multi-challenge IND-CPA secure (mcIND-CPA), if for any PPT adversary* $\mathcal{A}$ *there exists a negligible function* ν *such that:*

$$\left|\Pr\left[\mathbf{Exp}_{\mathcal{A},\Omega}^{\mathsf{mcIND\text{-}CPA}}(\lambda) = 1\right] - 1/2\right| \leq \nu(\lambda).$$

The corresponding experiment is depicted in Fig. 2.

Bellare et al. have shown, via a hybrid argument, that mcIND-CPA is equivalent to standard, i.e., "single-message", IND-CPA [8]. We opted for using mcIND-CPA, because it allows writing our proofs down more compactly, improving readability.

Digital Signature Schemes. Subsequently, we define signature schemes.

Definition 4 (Digital Signatures). *A digital signature scheme* Σ *consists of four algorithms* $\{\mathsf{PG}_\Sigma, \mathsf{KG}_\Sigma, \mathsf{Sgn}_\Sigma, \mathsf{Vrf}_\Sigma\}$ *such that:*

PG_Σ. *The algorithm* PG_Σ *outputs the public parameters*

$$\mathsf{pp}_\Sigma \leftarrow_r \mathsf{PG}_\Sigma(1^\lambda).$$

We assume that pp_Σ *contains* 1^λ *and is implicit input to all other algorithms.*

KG_Σ. *The algorithm* KG_Σ *outputs the public and private key of the signer, where* λ *is the security parameter:*

$$(\mathsf{sk}_\Sigma, \mathsf{pk}_\Sigma) \leftarrow_r \mathsf{KG}_\Sigma(\mathsf{pp}_\Sigma).$$

Sgn_Σ. *The algorithm* Sgn_Σ *gets as input the secret key* sk_Σ *and the message* $m \in \mathcal{M}$ *to sign. It outputs a signature:*

$$\sigma \leftarrow_r \mathsf{Sgn}_\Sigma(\mathsf{sk}_\Sigma, m).$$

Vrf_Σ. *The deterministic algorithm* Vrf_Σ *outputs a decision bit* $d \in \{0,1\}$*, indicating if the signature* σ *is valid, w.r.t.* pk_Σ *and* m*:*

$$d \leftarrow \mathsf{Vrf}_\Sigma(\mathsf{pk}_\Sigma, m, \sigma).$$

Definition 5 (Correctness). *A digital signature scheme* Σ *is called correct, if for all security parameters* $\lambda \in \mathbb{N}$*, for all* $\mathsf{pp}_\Sigma \leftarrow_r \mathsf{PG}_\Sigma(1^\lambda)$*, for all* $(\mathsf{sk}_\Sigma, \mathsf{pk}_\Sigma) \leftarrow_r \mathsf{KG}_\Sigma(\mathsf{pp}_\Sigma)$*, for all* $m \in \mathcal{M}$*,* $\mathsf{Vrf}_\Sigma(\mathsf{pk}_\Sigma, m, \mathsf{Sgn}_\Sigma(\mathsf{sk}_\Sigma, m)) = 1$ *is true.*

We require existential unforgeability under adaptively chosen message attacks (eUNF-CMA security). In a nutshell, unforgeability requires that an adversary $\mathcal{A}$ cannot (except with negligible probability) come up with a signature for a message m^* for which the adversary did not see any signature before, even if the adversary $\mathcal{A}$ is allowed to adaptively query for signatures on messages of its own choice.

$\mathbf{Exp}^{\mathsf{eUNF\text{-}CMA}}_{\mathcal{A},\Sigma}(\lambda)$
  $\mathsf{pp}_\Sigma \leftarrow_r \mathsf{PG}_\Sigma(1^\lambda)$
  $(\mathsf{sk}_\Sigma, \mathsf{pk}_\Sigma) \leftarrow_r \mathsf{KG}_\Sigma(\mathsf{pp}_\Sigma)$
  $\mathcal{Q} \leftarrow \emptyset$
  $(m^*, \sigma^*) \leftarrow_r \mathcal{A}^{\mathsf{Sgn}'_\Sigma(\mathsf{sk}_\Sigma, \cdot)}(\mathsf{pk}_\Sigma)$
    where Sgn'_Σ on input sk_Σ and m:
      $\sigma \leftarrow_r \mathsf{Sgn}_\Sigma(\mathsf{sk}_\Sigma, m)$
      set $\mathcal{Q} \leftarrow \mathcal{Q} \cup \{m\}$
      return σ
  return 1, if $\mathsf{Vrf}_\Sigma(\mathsf{pk}_\Sigma, m^*, \sigma^*) = 1 \ \wedge \ m^* \notin \mathcal{Q}$
  return 0

Fig. 3. Unforgeability

Definition 6 (Unforgeability). *We say a digital signature scheme* Σ *scheme is unforgeable, if for every PPT adversary* $\mathcal{A}$*, there exists a negligible function* ν *such that:*

$$\Pr\left[\mathbf{Exp}_{\mathcal{A},\Sigma}^{\mathsf{eUNF\text{-}CMA}}(\lambda) = 1\right] \leq \nu(\lambda).$$

The corresponding experiment is depicted in Fig. 3.

For Construction 1, we require that the size of signatures is independent of the size of the signed messages.

Non-interactive Proof Systems. Let L be an NP-language with associated witness relation R, i.e., such that $L = \{x \mid \exists w : R(x, w) = 1\}$. A non-interactive proof system allows to prove membership of some statement x in the language L. More formally, such a system is defined as follows.

Definition 7 (Non-interactive Proof System). *A non-interactive proof system* Π *for language* L *consists of three algorithms* $\{\mathsf{PG}_\Pi, \mathsf{Prf}_\Pi, \mathsf{Vfy}_\Pi\}$*, such that:*

PG_Π. *The algorithm* PG_Π *outputs public parameters of the scheme, where* λ *is the security parameter:*

$$\mathsf{crs}_\Pi \leftarrow_r \mathsf{PG}_\Pi(1^\lambda).$$

Prf_Π. *The algorithm* Prf_Π *outputs the proof* π*, on input of the CRS* crs_Π*, statement* x *to be proven, and the corresponding witness* w*:*

$$\pi \leftarrow_r \mathsf{Prf}_\Pi(\mathsf{crs}_\Pi, x, w).$$

Vfy_Π. *The deterministic algorithm* Vfy_Π *verifies the proof* π *by outputting a bit* $d \in \{0, 1\}$*, w.r.t. to some CRS* crs_Π *and some statement* x*:*

$$d \leftarrow \mathsf{Vfy}_\Pi(\mathsf{crs}_\Pi, x, \pi).$$

Definition 8 (Correctness). *A non-interactive proof system is called correct, if for all* $\lambda \in \mathbb{N}$*, for all* $\mathsf{crs}_\Pi \leftarrow_r \mathsf{PG}_\Pi(1^\lambda)$*, for all* $x \in L$*, for all* w *such that* $R(x, w) = 1$*, for all* $\pi \leftarrow_r \mathsf{Prf}_\Pi(\mathsf{crs}_\Pi, x, w)$*, it holds that* $\mathsf{Vfy}_\Pi(\mathsf{crs}_\Pi, x, \pi) = 1$.

In the context of (zero-knowledge) proof-systems, correctness is sometimes also referred to as completeness. In addition, we require two standard security notions for zero-knowledge proofs of knowledge: zero-knowledge and simulation-sound extractability. We define them analogously to the definitions given in [22].

Informally speaking, zero-knowledge says that the receiver of the proof π does not learn anything except the validity of the statement.

Definition 9 (Zero-Knowledge). *A non-interactive proof system* Π *for language* L *is zero-knowledge, if for any PPT adversary* $\mathcal{A}$*, there exists an PPT simulator* $\mathsf{SIM} = (\mathsf{SIM}_1, \mathsf{SIM}_2)$ *such that there exist negligible functions* ν_1 *and* ν_2 *such that*

$\mathbf{Exp}^{\mathsf{Zero\text{-}Knowledge}}_{\mathcal{A},\Pi,\mathsf{SIM}}(\lambda)$
$(\mathsf{crs}_\Pi, \tau) \leftarrow_r \mathsf{SIM}_1(1^\lambda)$
$b \leftarrow_r \{0,1\}$
$b^* \leftarrow_r \mathcal{A}^{P_b(\cdot,\cdot)}(\mathsf{crs}_\Pi)$
  where P_0 on input x, w:
    return $\pi \leftarrow_r \mathsf{Prf}_\Pi(\mathsf{crs}_\Pi, x, w)$, if $R(x,w) = 1$
    return $\perp$
  and P_1 on input x, w:
    return $\pi \leftarrow_r \mathsf{SIM}_2(\mathsf{crs}_\Pi, \tau, x)$, if $R(x,w) = 1$
    return $\perp$
return 1, if $b^* = b$
return 0

Fig. 4. Zero-Knowledge

$$\Big|\Pr\left[\mathsf{crs}_\Pi \leftarrow_r \mathsf{PG}_\Pi(1^\lambda) \;:\; \mathcal{A}(\mathsf{crs}_\Pi) = 1\right] - \Pr\left[(\mathsf{crs}_\Pi, \tau) \leftarrow_r \mathsf{SIM}_1(1^\lambda) \;:\; \mathcal{A}(\mathsf{crs}_\Pi) = 1\right]\Big| \leq \nu_1(\lambda),$$

and that

$$\left|\Pr\left[\mathbf{Exp}^{\mathsf{Zero\text{-}Knowledge}}_{\mathcal{A},\Pi,\mathsf{SIM}}(\lambda) = 1\right] - 1/2\right| \leq \nu_2(\lambda),$$

where the corresponding experiment is depicted in Fig. 4.

Simulation-sound extractability says that every adversary who is able to come up with a proof π^* for a statement must know the witness, even when seeing simulated proofs for adaptively chosen statements potentially not in L. Clearly, this implies that the proofs output by a simulation-sound extractable proof-systems are non-malleable. Note that the definition of simulation-sound extractability of [30] is stronger than ours in the sense that the adversary also gets the trapdoor ζ as input. However, in our context this weaker notion (previously also used e.g. in [1,25]) suffices.

$\mathbf{Exp}^{\mathsf{SimSoundExt}}_{\mathcal{A},\Pi,\mathcal{E}}(\lambda)$
$(\mathsf{crs}_\Pi, \tau, \zeta) \leftarrow_r \mathcal{E}_1(1^\lambda)$
$\mathcal{Q} \leftarrow \emptyset$
$(x^*, \pi^*) \leftarrow_r \mathcal{A}^{\mathsf{SIM}(\cdot)}(\mathsf{crs}_\Pi)$
  where SIM on input x:
    obtain $\pi \leftarrow_r \mathsf{SIM}_2(\mathsf{crs}_\Pi, \tau, x)$
    $\mathcal{Q} \leftarrow \mathcal{Q} \cup \{(x, \pi)\}$
    return π
$w^* \leftarrow_r \mathcal{E}_2(\mathsf{crs}_\Pi, \zeta, x^*, \pi^*)$
return 1, if $\mathsf{Vfy}_\Pi(x^*, \pi^*) = 1 \;\wedge\; R(x^*, w^*) = 0 \;\wedge\; (x^*, \pi^*) \notin \mathcal{Q}$
return 0

Fig. 5. Simulation sound extractability

Definition 10 (Simulation-Sound Extractability). *A zero-knowledge non-interactive proof system* Π *for language* L *is said to be simulation-sound extractable, if for any PPT adversary* $\mathcal{A}$*, there exists a PPT extractor* $\mathcal{E} = (\mathcal{E}_1, \mathcal{E}_2)$*, such that*

$$\Big|\Pr\left[(\mathsf{crs}_\Pi, \tau) \leftarrow_r \mathsf{SIM}_1(1^\lambda) \;:\; \mathcal{A}(\mathsf{crs}_\Pi, \tau) = 1\right] - \Pr\left[(\mathsf{crs}_\Pi, \tau, \zeta) \leftarrow_r \mathcal{E}_1(1^\lambda) \;:\; \mathcal{A}(\mathsf{crs}_\Pi, \tau) = 1\right]\Big| = 0,$$

and that there exist a negligible function ν *so that*

$$\Pr\left[\mathbf{Exp}^{\mathsf{SimSoundExt}}_{\mathcal{A},\Pi,\mathcal{E}}(\lambda)\right] = 1 \leq \nu(\lambda),$$

where the corresponding experiment is depicted in Fig. 5.

3 Chameleon-Hashes, Revisited

In this section we present the formal framework for chameleon-hashes, their security properties with a special focus on the collision-resistance notion and then show relations and separations between the security properties.

3.1 Framework

We now present the framework for chameleon-hashes. We rely on the most recent comprehensive framework by Camenisch et al. [15], which is, in turn, based upon work done by Ateniese et al. and Brzuska et al. [4,14].

Definition 11. *A chameleon-hash* CH *is a tuple of five PPT algorithms* $(\mathsf{CHPG}, \mathsf{CHKG}, \mathsf{CHash}, \mathsf{CHCheck}, \mathsf{CHAdapt})$*, such that:*

- CHPG. *The algorithm* CHPG*, on input a security parameter* λ *outputs public parameters of the scheme:*

  $$\mathsf{pp_{ch}} \leftarrow_r \mathsf{CHPG}(1^\lambda).$$

  We assume that $\mathsf{pp_{ch}}$ *is implicit input to all other algorithms.*
- CHKG. *The algorithm* CHKG*, on input the public parameters* $\mathsf{pp_{ch}}$ *outputs the private and public keys of the scheme:*

  $$(\mathsf{sk_{ch}}, \mathsf{pk_{ch}}) \leftarrow_r \mathsf{CHKG}(\mathsf{pp_{ch}}).$$
- CHash. *The algorithm* CHash *gets as input the public key* $\mathsf{pk_{ch}}$*, and a message* m *to hash. It outputs a hash* h*, and some randomness* r*:*[2]

  $$(h, r) \leftarrow_r \mathsf{CHash}(\mathsf{pk_{ch}}, m).$$

[2] We note that the randomness r is also sometimes called "check value" [4].

$\mathsf{CHCheck}$. *The deterministic algorithm* $\mathsf{CHCheck}$ *gets as input the public key* $\mathsf{pk_{ch}}$*, a message* m*, randomness* r*, and a hash* h*. It outputs a bit* $d \in \{0, 1\}$*, indicating whether the hash* h *is valid:*

$$d \leftarrow \mathsf{CHCheck}(\mathsf{pk_{ch}}, m, r, h).$$

$\mathsf{CHAdapt}$. *The algorithm* $\mathsf{CHAdapt}$ *on input of a secret key* $\mathsf{sk_{ch}}$*, the message* m*, new message* m'*, randomness* r*, and hash* h *outputs new randomness* r'*:*

$$r' \leftarrow_r \mathsf{CHAdapt}(\mathsf{sk_{ch}}, m, m', r, h).$$

Definition 12 (Correctness). *A chameleon-hash is called correct, if for all security parameters* $\lambda \in \mathbb{N}$*, for all* $\mathsf{pp_{ch}} \leftarrow_r \mathsf{CHPG}(1^\lambda)$*, for all* $(\mathsf{sk_{ch}}, \mathsf{pk_{ch}}) \leftarrow_r \mathsf{CHKG}(\mathsf{pp_{ch}})$*, for all* $m \in \mathcal{M}$*, for all* $(h, r) \leftarrow_r \mathsf{CHash}(\mathsf{pk_{ch}}, m)$*, for all* $m' \in \mathcal{M}$*, we have for all* $r' \leftarrow_r \mathsf{CHAdapt}(\mathsf{sk_{ch}}, m, m', r, h)$*, that* $1 = \mathsf{CHCheck}(\mathsf{pk_{ch}}, m, r, h) = \mathsf{CHCheck}(\mathsf{pk_{ch}}, m', r', h)$*.*

3.2 Indistinguishability

Indistinguishability requires that the randomness r does not reveal if it was obtained through CHash or $\mathsf{CHAdapt}$. Upon setup, a challenger generates a key pair $(\mathsf{sk_{ch}}, \mathsf{pk_{ch}})$ for CH (along with some public parameters), and draws a bit $b \leftarrow_r \{0, 1\}$. The challenger initializes the adversary with the $\mathsf{pk_{ch}}$ and gives the adversary access to a $\mathsf{HashOrAdapt}$ oracle, which allows the adversary to submit two messages m, m'. Depending on the bit b, the challenger then either hashes m' directly ($b = 0$), of first hashes m, and then adapts m to m' ($b = 1$). The resulting hash/randomness pair (h, r) (or (h', r'') resp.) is the oracle's output to the adversary. The adversary's objective is to guess the bit b. Note that all keys are generated honestly and the adversary gets access to a collision-finding oracle $\mathsf{CHAdapt}$ for arbitrary hashes, meaning that the adversary may also input hashes generated by the $\mathsf{HashOrAdapt}$-oracle. We stress that there may be scenarios where indistinguishability is not required or even hindering.

Definition 13 (Indistinguishability). *A chameleon-hash* CH *is indistinguishable, if for any PPT adversary* $\mathcal{A}$ *there exists a negligible function* ν *such that*

$$\left|\Pr[\mathbf{Exp}^{\mathsf{Ind}}_{\mathcal{A},\mathsf{CH}}(\lambda) = 1] - {}^1\!/_2\right| \leq \nu(\lambda),$$

where the corresponding experiment is depicted in Fig. 6.

Samelin and Slamanig recently introduced *full* indistinguishability [41], which, in turn, generalizes the notion of *strong* indistinguishability by Derler et al [21]. In their notion, the adversary is even allowed to generate the keys which are used for hashing and adapting (in the strong version, the adversary only knows all keys, but cannot generate them).

We do neither consider full nor strong indistinguishability as fundamental for chameleon-hashes, but examine these notions to achieve a more complete picture

$\mathbf{Exp}^{\mathsf{Ind}}_{\mathcal{A},\mathsf{CH}}(\lambda)$
  $\mathsf{pp_{ch}} \leftarrow_r \mathsf{CHPG}(1^\lambda)$
  $(\mathsf{sk_{ch}}, \mathsf{pk_{ch}}) \leftarrow_r \mathsf{CHKG}(\mathsf{pp_{ch}})$
  $b \leftarrow_r \{0, 1\}$
  $a \leftarrow_r \mathcal{A}^{\mathsf{HashOrAdapt}(\mathsf{sk_{ch}},\cdot,\cdot,b),\mathsf{CHAdapt}(\mathsf{sk_{ch}},\mathsf{pk_{ch}},\cdot,\cdot,\cdot)}(\mathsf{pk_{ch}})$
    where $\mathsf{HashOrAdapt}$ on input $\mathsf{sk_{ch}}, m, m', b$:
      $(h, r) \leftarrow \mathsf{CHash}(\mathsf{pk_{ch}}, m')$
      $(h', r') \leftarrow \mathsf{CHash}(\mathsf{pk_{ch}}, m)$
      $r'' \leftarrow \mathsf{CHAdapt}(\mathsf{sk_{ch}}, m, m', r', h')$
      If $r = \perp \vee r'' = \perp$, return $\perp$
      if $b = 0$:
        return (h, r)
      if $b = 1$:
        return (h', r'')
  return 1, if $a = b$
  return 0

Fig. 6. CH Indistinguishability

of the relations. The formal definitions of full and strong indistinguishability are given in the full version of this paper, where we also prove that full indistinguishability is strictly stronger than strong indistinguishability, which, in turn, is strictly stronger than indistinguishability.

3.3 Collision-Resistance

In this section we revisit existing collision-resistance notions, introduce a stronger and more desirable notion of collision-resistance dubbed *full collision-resistance* (or F-CollRes for short) and discuss how these notions differ. The main idea behind collision-resistance in general is to argue that an adversary that has no access to the secret key $\mathsf{sk_{ch}}$ cannot find any collisions, i.e,. pairs (m, r) and (m', r') and hash value h s.t. $\mathsf{CHCheck}(\mathsf{pk_{ch}}, m, r, h) = \mathsf{CHCheck}(\mathsf{pk_{ch}}, m', r', h) = 1$. In the weakest case, the adversary has no access to any other collisions, whereas in stronger notions the adversary is explicitly allowed to obtain collisions for arbitrary hashes via a $\mathsf{CHAdapt}'$ oracle (we indicate these by using boxes). We present all the different notions in Fig. 7, where we indicate the differences in the winning conditions by using boxes. In all the experiments the challenger generates a key pair $(\mathsf{sk_{ch}}, \mathsf{pk_{ch}})$ honestly (along with some public parameters) and the adversary is then initialized with $\mathsf{pk_{ch}}$. We now discuss the differences of the single collision resistance notions, where in the weakest case the adversary has no access to an $\mathsf{CHAdapt}'$ oracle (which allows the adversary to adaptively ask for collisions with messages and hashes of its own choice), but in all other cases the adversary does. To vertically align the experiments, we insert boxes for lines which are missing in one experiment but are present in the other.

$\mathbf{Exp}^{\mathsf{W\text{-}CollRes}}_{\mathcal{A},\mathsf{CH}}(\lambda)$
  $\mathsf{pp_{ch}} \leftarrow_r \mathsf{CHPG}(1^\lambda)$
  $(\mathsf{sk_{ch}}, \mathsf{pk_{ch}}) \leftarrow_r \mathsf{CHKG}(\mathsf{pp_{ch}})$
  $(m^*, r^*, m'^*, r'^*, h^*) \leftarrow_r \mathcal{A}(\mathsf{pk_{ch}})$
  return 1, if $\mathsf{CHCheck}(\mathsf{pk_{ch}}, m^*, r^*, h^*) = 1\ \wedge$
    $\mathsf{CHCheck}(\mathsf{pk_{ch}}, m'^*, r'^*, h^*) = 1\ \wedge$
    $m^* \neq m'^*$
  return 0

$\mathbf{Exp}^{\mathsf{E\text{-}CollRes}}_{\mathcal{A},\mathsf{CH}}(\lambda)$
  $\mathsf{pp_{ch}} \leftarrow_r \mathsf{CHPG}(1^\lambda)$
  $(\mathsf{sk_{ch}}, \mathsf{pk_{ch}}) \leftarrow_r \mathsf{CHKG}(\mathsf{pp_{ch}})$
  $\mathcal{Q} \leftarrow \emptyset$
  $(m^*, r^*, m'^*, r'^*, h^*) \leftarrow_r \mathcal{A}^{\mathsf{CHAdapt}'(\mathsf{sk_{ch}}, \cdot, \cdot, \cdot, \cdot)}(\mathsf{pk_{ch}})$
    where $\mathsf{CHAdapt}'$ on input $\mathsf{sk_{ch}}, m, m', r, h$:
      return $\bot$, if $\mathsf{CHCheck}(\mathsf{pk_{ch}}, m, r, h) \neq 1$
      $r' \leftarrow_r \mathsf{CHAdapt}(\mathsf{sk_{ch}}, m, m', r, h)$
      If $r' = \bot$, return $\bot$
      $\mathcal{Q} \leftarrow \mathcal{Q} \cup \{h\}$
      return r'
  return 1, if $\mathsf{CHCheck}(\mathsf{pk_{ch}}, m^*, r^*, h^*) = 1\ \wedge$
    $\mathsf{CHCheck}(\mathsf{pk_{ch}}, m'^*, r'^*, h^*) = 1\ \wedge$
    $m^* \neq m'^*\ \wedge\ h^* \notin \mathcal{Q}$
  return 0

$\mathbf{Exp}^{\mathsf{S\text{-}CollRes}}_{\mathcal{A},\mathsf{CH}}(\lambda)$
  $\mathsf{pp_{ch}} \leftarrow_r \mathsf{CHPG}(1^\lambda)$
  $(\mathsf{sk_{ch}}, \mathsf{pk_{ch}}) \leftarrow_r \mathsf{CHKG}(\mathsf{pp_{ch}})$
  $\mathcal{Q} \leftarrow \emptyset$
  $(m^*, r^*, m'^*, r'^*, h^*) \leftarrow_r \mathcal{A}^{\mathsf{CHAdapt}'(\mathsf{sk_{ch}}, \cdot, \cdot, \cdot, \cdot)}(\mathsf{pk_{ch}})$
    where $\mathsf{CHAdapt}'$ on input $\mathsf{sk_{ch}}, m, m', r, h$:
      return $\bot$, if $\mathsf{CHCheck}(\mathsf{pk_{ch}}, m, r, h) \neq 1$
      $r' \leftarrow_r \mathsf{CHAdapt}(\mathsf{sk_{ch}}, m, m', r, h)$
      If $r' = \bot$, return $\bot$
      $\mathcal{Q} \leftarrow \mathcal{Q} \cup \{m, m'\}$
      return r'
  return 1, if $\mathsf{CHCheck}(\mathsf{pk_{ch}}, m^*, r^*, h^*) = 1\ \wedge$
    $\mathsf{CHCheck}(\mathsf{pk_{ch}}, m'^*, r'^*, h^*) = 1\ \wedge$
    $m^* \neq m'^*\ \wedge\ m^* \notin \mathcal{Q}$
  return 0

$\mathbf{Exp}^{\mathsf{F\text{-}CollRes}}_{\mathcal{A},\mathsf{CH}}(\lambda)$
  $\mathsf{pp_{ch}} \leftarrow_r \mathsf{CHPG}(1^\lambda)$
  $(\mathsf{sk_{ch}}, \mathsf{pk_{ch}}) \leftarrow_r \mathsf{CHKG}(\mathsf{pp_{ch}})$
  $\mathcal{Q} \leftarrow \emptyset$
  $(m^*, r^*, m'^*, r'^*, h^*) \leftarrow_r \mathcal{A}^{\mathsf{CHAdapt}'(\mathsf{sk_{ch}}, \cdot, \cdot, \cdot, \cdot)}(\mathsf{pk_{ch}})$
    where $\mathsf{CHAdapt}'$ on input $\mathsf{sk_{ch}}, m, m', r, h$:
      return $\bot$, if $\mathsf{CHCheck}(\mathsf{pk_{ch}}, m, r, h) \neq 1$
      $r' \leftarrow_r \mathsf{CHAdapt}(\mathsf{sk_{ch}}, m, m', r, h)$
      If $r' = \bot$, return $\bot$
      $\mathcal{Q} \leftarrow \mathcal{Q} \cup \{(h, m), (h, m')\}$
      return r'
  return 1, if $\mathsf{CHCheck}(\mathsf{pk_{ch}}, m^*, r^*, h^*) = 1\ \wedge$
    $\mathsf{CHCheck}(\mathsf{pk_{ch}}, m'^*, r'^*, h^*) = 1\ \wedge$
    $m^* \neq m'^*\ \wedge\ (h^*, m^*) \notin \mathcal{Q}$
  return 0

Fig. 7. The $\mathbf{Exp}^{\mathsf{X\text{-}CollRes}}_{\mathcal{A},\mathsf{CH}}$ experiment with $\mathsf{X} \in \{\mathsf{W}, \mathsf{E}, \mathsf{S}, \mathsf{F}\}$.

Weak Collision-Resistance (W-CollRes) [37]**.** The adversary $\mathcal{A}$ wins, if it can come up with a collision for the given public key.

Enhanced Collision-Resistance (E-CollRes) [4]**.** The adversary gets access to a collision-finding oracle $\mathsf{CHAdapt}'$, which outputs a collision for adversarially chosen hashes, but also keeps track of each queried *hash* h using the list $\mathcal{Q}$. The adversary wins, if it comes up with a collision for the given public key for an adversarially chosen hash h^* never input to $\mathsf{CHAdapt}'$.

Standard Collision-Resistance (S-CollRes) [15]**.** The adversary gets access to a collision-finding oracle $\mathsf{CHAdapt}'$, which outputs a collision for the adversarially chosen hash, but also keeps track of each of the queried *messages* m and m', using the list $\mathcal{Q}$. The adversary wins, if it comes up with a collision for the given public key for an adversarially chosen h^* for which the message m^* output by the adversary was never queried to the collision-finding oracle.

Full Collision-Resistance (F-CollRes). The adversary gets access to a collision-finding oracle CHAdapt$'$, which outputs a collision for the adversarially chosen hash, but also keeps track of each of the queried *hash/message pair* (h, m) and (h, m'), using the list $\mathcal{Q}$. The adversary wins, if it comes up with a hash/message *pair* (h^*, m^*), for the given public key, never queried to or output from the collision-finding oracle.[3]

Now, we formally define security with respect to all the collision-resistance notions.

Definition 14 (X Collision-Resistance). *A chameleon-hash* CH *offers* X *collision-resistance with* X $\in$ {W, E, S, F}, *if for any PPT adversary* $\mathcal{A}$ *there exists a negligible function* ν *such that*

$$\Pr[\mathbf{Exp}_{\mathcal{A},\mathsf{CH}}^{\mathsf{X\text{-}CollRes}}(\lambda) = 1] \leq \nu(\lambda),$$

where the corresponding experiment is depicted in Fig. 7.

Discussion of the Notions. W-CollRes is the notion introduced in the first work on chameleon-hashes by Krawczyk and Rabin [37] and essentially represents the binding notion of a trapdoor-commitment scheme. Note that due to not giving access to a collision-finding oracle it gives no guarantees whatsoever if the adversary sees a single collision for any hash computed for the given public key.[4] The E-CollRes notion has been introduced by Ateniese et al. [4] and we note that there exists a definition in the setting of public-coin chameleon hashes, i.e., where the CHCheck algorithm simply re-runs the CHash, which is called key-exposure freeness [6,16]. It captures requirements similar to the ones captured by E-CollRes, but it is not directly comparable as we are considering the more general secret-coin setting. We note that the E-CollRes notion allows the adversary to come up with arbitrary collisions for hashes it has seen a collision for. The S-CollRes notion has been introduced by Camenisch et al. [15], and it captures all of the intuitive requirements of real-world applications of chameleon-hashes. Yet, it still allows the hash itself to be malleable which might still be problematic in certain applications. Finally, our new F-CollRes notion enforces that the adversary cannot (except with negligible probability) output any new collisions and seems to be the most desirable notion for collision-resistance.

3.4 Uniqueness

Camenisch et al. [15] defined a property called uniqueness. Uniqueness requires that for each hash/message pair, exactly one randomness can be found, even if the adversary $\mathcal{A}$ controls all values, but the public parameters.[5]

[3] In the case (h'^*, m'^*) is the new hash/message pair, simply switch names.

[4] A slightly stronger notion has been proposed by Zhang in [46] where the adversary sees a hash on a random message and is then given a single collision on a message of its choice. We do not cover this notion here as it seems to be tailored to the specific applications in [46] and all notions stronger than W-CollRes considered here cover more general cases.

[5] Lifting this definition to also cover those parameters is straightforward.

$\mathbf{Exp}^{\mathsf{Uniqueness}}_{\mathcal{A},\mathsf{CH}}(\lambda)$
$\mathsf{pp_{ch}} \leftarrow_r \mathsf{CHPG}(1^\lambda)$
$(\mathsf{pk}^*, m^*, r^*, r'^*, h^*) \leftarrow_r \mathcal{A}(\mathsf{pp_{ch}})$
return 1, if $\mathsf{CHCheck}(\mathsf{pk}^*, m^*, r^*, h^*) = \mathsf{CHCheck}(\mathsf{pk}^*, m^*, r'^*, h^*) = 1 \wedge r^* \neq r'^*$
return 0

Fig. 8. Uniqueness

Definition 15 (Uniqueness). *A chameleon-hash* CH *is unique, if for any PPT adversary $\mathcal{A}$ there exists a negligible function ν such that*

$$\Pr[\mathbf{Exp}^{\mathsf{Uniqueness}}_{\mathcal{A},\mathsf{CH}}(\lambda) = 1] \leq \nu(\lambda).$$

The corresponding experiment is depicted in Fig. 8.

We do not consider uniqueness as a fundamental property, as there are only very few applications requiring this notion [15,41]. However, to obtain a more complete picture with respect to the relations of the security properties, we also investigate uniqueness.

3.5 Relationships Between Properties

Below we show relations and separations between the security properties of chameleon-hashes.

Collision-Resistance Properties. We start by analyzing how the various collision-resistance notions are related.

Theorem 1. *Standard collision-resistance is strictly stronger than weak collision-resistance.*

Proof. We first prove that standard collision-resistance implies weak collision-resistance and then give a counterexample showing that the other direction of the implication does not hold.

S-CollRes $\Longrightarrow$ W-CollRes: Assume $\mathcal{A}$ to be an adversary who breaks weak collision-resistance. We now construct an adversary $\mathcal{B}$ which breaks standard collision-resistance. In particular, $\mathcal{B}$ proceeds as follows. It receives $\mathsf{pp_{ch}}$ and $\mathsf{pk_{ch}}$ from its own challenger, and uses both to initialize $\mathcal{A}$. Whenever $\mathcal{A}$ outputs a winning tuple $(m^*, r^*, m'^*, r'^*, h^*)$, $\mathcal{B}$ returns that tuple to its own challenger. As the collision-finding oracle was never queried, that tuple also makes $\mathcal{B}$ win the standard collision-resistance game with the same probability $\mathcal{A}$ wins the weak collision-resistance game.

W-CollRes $\not\Longrightarrow$ S-CollRes: The CH by Krawczyk and Rabin [37] provides a counterexample: it is weakly collision-resistant, but does not offer standard collision-resistance. Observe that it is possible to trivially extract the secret key from a collision. That collision is obtained from the collision-finding oracle in the standard collision-resistance game (cf. the full version of this paper). □

Theorem 2. *Enhanced collision-resistance is strictly stronger than weak collision-resistance.*

Proof. The proof is identical to the one of Theorem 1. □

Theorem 3. *Full collision-resistance is strictly stronger than standard collision-resistance.*

Proof. We first prove that full collision-resistance implies standard collision-resistance and then give a counterexample showing that the other direction of the implication does not hold.

F-CollRes $\implies$ S-CollRes: Assume $\mathcal{A}$ to be an adversary who breaks standard collision-resistance. Now we construct an adversary $\mathcal{B}$ which breaks full collision-resistance. In particular, $\mathcal{B}$ proceeds as follows. It receives $\mathsf{pp_{ch}}$ and $\mathsf{pk_{ch}}$ from its own challenger, and uses both to initialize $\mathcal{A}$. All queries to the collision-finding oracle are relayed to $\mathcal{B}$'s own oracle. Whenever $\mathcal{A}$ outputs a winning tuple $(m^*, r^*, m'^*, r'^*, h^*)$, $\mathcal{B}$ returns that tuple to its own challenger. As $m^* \neq m'^*$ must be true, and m^* was never queried to $\mathcal{A}$'s collision-finding oracle, this also means that (h^*, m^*) was never queried to $\mathcal{B}$'s oracle, thus meeting the winning condition.

S-CollRes $\not\Longrightarrow$ F-CollRes: The scheme by Camenisch et al. [15] provides a counterexample: it offers standard collision-resistance, but does not offer full collision-resistance. In particular, their construction is re-randomizable (cf. the full version of this paper). In more detail, to show that this construction is not fully collision-resistant, consider the following strategy: Receive $\mathsf{pk_{ch}} = (N, H)$ and $\mathsf{pp_{ch}} = e$. Compute $(h, r) \leftarrow_r \mathsf{CHash}(\mathsf{pk_{ch}}, m)$, with m random. Then, ask for an adaption (h, r, m) to (h, r', m'), for some random $m' \neq m$. Then, compute $h^* \leftarrow h2^e \mod N$, $r_1^* \leftarrow 2r \mod N$, and $r_2^* \leftarrow 2r' \mod N$. Because no collision for h^* was computed, this construction cannot be fully collision-resistant. Note, this works, as $H(m)(2r)^e \equiv h2^e \pmod N$ for any input. Also note that the attack above also breaks enhanced collision-resistance (we will later use this to derive a corollary). □

Theorem 4. *Full collision-resistance is strictly stronger than enhanced collision-resistance.*

Before we provide the proof of Theorem 4, we provide a novel construction of a chameleon-hash satisfying the E-CollRes notion that is used to separate the notions F-CollRes and E-CollRes.

Construction. Our CH presented below provides E-CollRes, but allows to efficiently find arbitrary collisions for a given hash, once a single collision was seen. However, it is not possible to find collisions for any other hash. The main idea is to encrypt a message m using a mcIND-CPA secure encryption scheme Ω and use the ciphertext as the hash. The randomness r of the chameleon-hash is the public key pk_Ω' of a freshly sampled key-pair $(\mathsf{sk}_\Omega', \mathsf{pk}_\Omega')$ of Ω, the encryption c' of a signature σ under pk_Ω' and a SSE NIZK π for the following language:

$$L := \{(\mathsf{pk}_\Omega, \mathsf{pk}_\Sigma, h, m) \mid \exists\ (\sigma, \xi)\ : \\ h = \mathsf{Enc}(\mathsf{pk}_\Omega, m;\ \xi)\ \vee\ \mathsf{Vrf}_\Sigma(\mathsf{pk}_\Sigma, h, \sigma) = 1\}. \quad (1)$$

Informally, this language requires the prover to show that it either knows the randomness ξ attesting that h is a well-formed encryption of m, *or* a valid signature σ for h. The basic idea of the construction is that when computing a hash, the witness ξ is used. The randomness includes an encryption of the signature (initially one on 0) under the public key $\mathsf{pk}_\Omega{}'$. Note that the trick is that for adaption one computes a signature σ for h, uses σ as a witness, and includes an encryption of σ under $\mathsf{pk}_\Omega{}'$ in the randomness. Clearly, now seeing a single collision allows to compute arbitrary collisions for the hash h.

This CH can be instantiated by instantiating Σ as structure-preserving signatures (SPS) in type-III bilinear groups (assuming SXDH), e.g., Groth's SPS [31]. Thus, Ω can be ElGamal [29] in one of the base-groups. The algorithm KVf_Ω is simply checking whether $g^{\mathsf{sk}_\Omega} = g^x = \mathsf{pk}_\Omega$, while for Π, a suitable instantiation is a Fiat-Shamir transformed Σ-protocol in the random-oracle model [28], which also works very well with ElGamal encryption and Groth's signature scheme.

We defer the proof of Construction 1 to the full version of this paper. We are now ready to present the proof of Theorem 4.

Proof. We first prove that full collision-resistance implies enhanced collision-resistance and then give a counterexample showing that the other direction of the implication does not hold.

$\mathsf{F\text{-}CollRes} \implies \mathsf{E\text{-}CollRes}$: Assume $\mathcal{A}$ to be an adversary who breaks the enhanced collision-resistance. We can then construct an adversary $\mathcal{B}$ which breaks the full collision-resistance. In particular, $\mathcal{B}$ proceeds as follows. It receives $\mathsf{pp}_{\mathsf{ch}}$ and $\mathsf{pk}_{\mathsf{ch}}$ from its own challenger, and uses both to initialize $\mathcal{A}$. All queries to the collision-finding oracle are relayed to $\mathcal{B}$'s own oracle. Whenever $\mathcal{A}$ outputs a winning tuple $(m^*, r^*, m'^*, r'^*, h^*)$, $\mathcal{B}$ returns that tuple to its own challenger. As $m^* \neq m'^*$ must be true, and h^* was never queried to $\mathcal{A}$'s collision-finding oracle, this also means that (h^*, m^*) was never queried to $\mathcal{B}$'s oracle, thus meeting the winning condition.

$\mathsf{E\text{-}CollRes} \not\Rightarrow \mathsf{F\text{-}CollRes}$: The scheme presented in Construction 1 gives a counterexample: it allows finding arbitrarily many collisions for a given hash h, if it sees a single one, but for no other $h' \neq h$. In more detail, to show that this construction is not fully collision-resistant, consider the following strategy. Receive $\mathsf{pk}_{\mathsf{ch}} = (\mathsf{pk}_\Omega, \mathsf{pk}_\Sigma)$ and $\mathsf{pp}_{\mathsf{ch}} = (\mathsf{pp}_\Omega, \mathsf{crs}_\Pi, \mathsf{pp}_\Sigma)$. Compute $(h, r) \leftarrow_r \mathsf{CHash}(\mathsf{pk}_{\mathsf{ch}}, m)$, with m random. Also store the secret key $\mathsf{sk}_\Omega{}'$. Then, ask for an adaption (h, r, m) to (h, r', m'), where $r' = (\pi, c'', \mathsf{pk}_\Omega{}')$, for some random m'. Then, compute $\sigma \leftarrow \mathsf{Dec}(\mathsf{sk}_\Omega{}', c'')$. Then arbitrary collisions for h are generated by executing $\mathsf{CHAdapt}$ in a similar way the owner of $\mathsf{pk}_{\mathsf{ch}}$ does for finding collisions, due to the knowledge of σ for h. Because such collisions can only be generated for already seen collisions w.r.t. h, enhanced collision-resistance holds, but full collision-resistance does not. Also note that standard collision-resistance does not hold for Construction 1 for the same reason (we will later use this to derive a corollary). □

$\underline{\mathsf{CHPG}(1^\lambda)}$: Fix a public-key encryption scheme Ω and a compatible NIZK proof system for language L in (1). Return $\mathsf{pp_{ch}} = (\mathsf{pp}_\Omega, \mathsf{pp}_\Sigma, \mathsf{crs}_\Pi)$, where

$$\mathsf{pp}_\Omega \leftarrow_r \mathsf{PG}_\Omega(1^\lambda),\ \mathsf{pp}_\Sigma \leftarrow_r \mathsf{PG}_\Sigma(1^\lambda), \text{ and } \mathsf{crs}_\Pi \leftarrow_r \mathsf{PG}_\Pi(1^\lambda).$$

$\underline{\mathsf{CHKG}(\mathsf{pp_{ch}})}$: Return $(\mathsf{sk_{ch}}, \mathsf{pk_{ch}}) = ((\mathsf{sk}_\Omega, \mathsf{sk}_\Sigma), (\mathsf{pp_{ch}}, \mathsf{pk}_\Omega, \mathsf{pk}_\Sigma, \sigma_0))$, where

$$(\mathsf{sk}_\Omega, \mathsf{pk}_\Omega) \leftarrow_r \mathsf{KG}_\Omega(\mathsf{pp}_\Omega), (\mathsf{sk}_\Sigma, \mathsf{pk}_\Sigma) \leftarrow_r \mathsf{KG}_\Sigma(\mathsf{pp}_\Sigma), \text{ and } \sigma_0 \leftarrow_r \mathsf{Sgn}_\Sigma(\mathsf{sk}_\Sigma, 0).$$

0 is considered some special invalid hash value for CH.

$\underline{\mathsf{CHash}(\mathsf{pk_{ch}}, m)}$: Parse $\mathsf{pk_{ch}}$ as $((\mathsf{pp}_\Omega, \mathsf{crs}_\Pi), \mathsf{pk}_\Omega)$, and return $(h, r) = (c, (\pi, c', \mathsf{pk}_\Omega'))$, where

$$(c; \xi) \leftarrow_r \mathsf{Enc}(\mathsf{pk}_\Omega, m), (\mathsf{sk}_\Omega', \mathsf{pk}_\Omega') \leftarrow_r \mathsf{KG}_\Omega(\mathsf{pp}_\Omega), c' \leftarrow_r \mathsf{Enc}(\mathsf{pk}_\Omega', \sigma_0), \text{ and}$$
$$\pi \leftarrow_r \mathsf{Prf}_\Pi(\mathsf{crs}_\Pi, (\mathsf{pk}_\Omega, \mathsf{pk}_\Sigma, c, m), (\bot, \xi))$$

$\underline{\mathsf{CHCheck}(\mathsf{pk_{ch}}, m, r, h)}$: Parse $\mathsf{pk_{ch}}$ as $((\mathsf{pp}_\Omega, \mathsf{crs}_\Pi), \mathsf{pk}_\Omega)$ and r as $(\pi, c', \mathsf{pk}_\Omega')$, and return 1 if the following holds, and 0 otherwise:

$$m \in \mathcal{M} \ \wedge\ \mathsf{Vfy}_\Pi(\mathsf{crs}_\Pi, (\mathsf{pk}_\Omega, \mathsf{pk}_\Sigma, h, m), \pi) = 1.$$

$\underline{\mathsf{CHAdapt}(\mathsf{sk_{ch}}, m, m', r, h)}$: Parse $\mathsf{sk_{ch}}$ as sk_Ω. Verify that $m' \in \mathcal{M}$, $\mathsf{CHCheck}(\mathsf{pk_{ch}}, m, r, h) = 1$, and return $\bot$ if not. Otherwise, return $r' = (\pi', c'', \mathsf{pk}_\Omega')$, where

$$\sigma \leftarrow_r \mathsf{Sgn}_\Sigma(\mathsf{sk}_\Sigma, h), c'' \leftarrow_r \mathsf{Enc}(\mathsf{pk}_\Omega', \sigma), \text{ and}$$
$$\pi' \leftarrow_r \mathsf{Prf}_\Pi(\mathsf{crs}_\Pi, (\mathsf{pk}_\Omega, \mathsf{pk}_\Sigma, h, m'), (\sigma, \bot)).$$

Construction 1. Enhanced Collision-Resistant Chameleon-Hash

Theorem 5. *Enhanced collision-resistance and standard collision-resistance together imply full collision-resistance.*

Proof. The theorem above is proven using a sequence of games.

Game 0: The original full collision-resistance game.

Game 1: As Game 0, we abort, if the adversary $\mathcal{A}$ outputs $(m^*, r^*, m'^*, r'^*, h^*)$ such that the winning conditions are met, but h^* was never queried to the collision-finding oracle.

Transition - Game 0 → Game 1: If this is the case, we build an adversary $\mathcal{B}$ which breaks the enhanced collision-resistance of the underlying scheme. Namely, $\mathcal{B}$ receives $\mathsf{pk_{ch}}$ and uses it to initialize $\mathcal{A}$. Every adaption query by $\mathcal{A}$ is answered by $\mathcal{B}$ using its own oracle. Once $\mathcal{A}$ outputs $(m^*, r^*, m'^*, r'^*, h^*)$, $\mathcal{B}$ returns $(m^*, r^*, m'^*, r'^*, h^*)$ to its own challenger. As h^* was never seen, $\mathcal{B}$ wins its own game. $|\Pr[S_0] - \Pr[S_1]| \leq \nu_{\mathsf{enh\text{-}collres}}(\lambda)$ follows.

Game 2: As Game 1, we abort, if the adversary $\mathcal{A}$ outputs $(m^*, r^*, m'^*, r'^*, h^*)$ such that the winning conditions are met, but m^* was never queried to the collision-finding oracle.

Transition - Game 1 → Game 2: If this is the case, we build an adversary $\mathcal{B}$ which breaks the standard collision-resistance of the underlying scheme. Namely, $\mathcal{B}$ receives $\mathsf{pk_{ch}}$ and uses it to initialize $\mathcal{A}$. Every adaption query by

$\mathcal{A}$ is answered by $\mathcal{B}$ using its own oracle. Once $\mathcal{A}$ outputs $(m^*, r^*, m'^*, r'^*, h^*)$, $\mathcal{B}$ returns $(m^*, r^*, m'^*, r'^*, h^*)$ to its own challenger. As m^* was never seen, $\mathcal{B}$ wins its own game. $|\Pr[S_1] - \Pr[S_2]| \leq \nu_{\mathsf{st\text{-}collres}}(\lambda)$ follows.

In Game 2, the adversary can no longer win the full collision-resistance game. This proves the theorem. □

The corollary below follows from the constructions used in the proofs of Theorems 3 and 4, which provide standard collision-resistance but not enhanced collision-resistance, and vice versa.

Corollary 1. *Standard collision-resistance and enhanced collision-resistance are independent.*

Additional Separations. We now prove some additional separations. We note that indistinguishability is strictly weaker than full indistinguishability (as formally shown in the full version of this paper).

Theorem 6. *Even full indistinguishability and uniqueness together do not imply weak collision-resistance.*

Proof. Assume the following contrived construction of a chameleon-hash: $\mathsf{CHPG}'(1^\lambda) := \emptyset$, $\mathsf{CHKG}'(\mathsf{pp}_{\mathsf{ch}}) := \emptyset$, $\mathsf{CHash}'(\mathsf{pk}_{\mathsf{ch}}, m) := (\emptyset, \emptyset)$, $\mathsf{CHCheck}'(\mathsf{pk}_{\mathsf{ch}}, m, r, h) :=$ **if** $h = \emptyset \wedge \mathsf{pk}_{\mathsf{ch}} = \emptyset \wedge r = \emptyset$ **then** 1 **else** 0, $\mathsf{CHAdapt}'(\mathsf{sk}_{\mathsf{ch}}, m, m', r, h) :=$ **if** $\mathsf{CHCheck}'(\mathsf{pk}_{\mathsf{ch}}, m, r, h) = 1$ **then** $\emptyset$ **else** $\perp$. Clearly, this construction is fully indistinguishable and unique. Finding collisions, however, is a trivial task. □

Theorem 7. *Even full collision-resistance and uniqueness together do not imply indistinguishability.*

Proof. Assume $\mathsf{CH} := (\mathsf{CHPG}, \mathsf{CHKG}, \mathsf{CHash}, \mathsf{CHCheck}, \mathsf{CHAdapt})$ to be a fully collision-resistant, unique, and fully indistinguishable chameleon-hash. Let $\mathsf{CH}' := (\mathsf{CHPG}', \mathsf{CHKG}', \mathsf{CHash}', \mathsf{CHCheck}', \mathsf{CHAdapt}')$ be a chameleon-hash which internally uses CH but appends m to the hash. CH' is defined as: $\mathsf{CHPG}'(1^\lambda) := \mathsf{CHPG}(1^\lambda)$, $\mathsf{CHKG}'(\mathsf{pp}_{\mathsf{ch}}) := \mathsf{CHKG}(\mathsf{pp}_{\mathsf{ch}})$, $\mathsf{CHash}'(\mathsf{pk}_{\mathsf{ch}}, m) := ((h, m), r)$ **where** $(h, r) \leftarrow_r \mathsf{CHash}(\mathsf{pk}_{\mathsf{ch}}, (m, m))$, and also $\mathsf{CHCheck}'(\mathsf{pk}_{\mathsf{ch}}, m, r, h) := \mathsf{CHCheck}(\mathsf{pk}_{\mathsf{ch}}, (m, \hat{m}), r, h')$ **where** $h' = (h, \hat{m})$, and $\mathsf{CHAdapt}'(\mathsf{sk}_{\mathsf{ch}}, m, m', r, h') := (\mathsf{CHAdapt}(\mathsf{sk}_{\mathsf{ch}}, (m, \hat{m}), (m', \hat{m}), r', h))$ **where** $h' = (h, \hat{m})$. Clearly, CH' is still fully collision-resistant and unique, but looking at the appended messages allows deciding whether an adaption has occurred. □

Theorem 8. *Even full collision-resistance and full indistinguishability together do not imply uniqueness.*

Proof. Assume $\mathsf{CH} := (\mathsf{CHPG}, \mathsf{CHKG}, \mathsf{CHash}, \mathsf{CHCheck}, \mathsf{CHAdapt})$ to be a fully collision-resistant, unique, and fully indistinguishable chameleon-hash. Let $\mathsf{CH}' := (\mathsf{CHPG}', \mathsf{CHKG}', \mathsf{CHash}', \mathsf{CHCheck}', \mathsf{CHAdapt}')$ be a chameleon-hash which internally uses CH but appends a random bit to each r.

In particular let CH' be defined as follows: $\mathsf{CHPG}'(1^\lambda) := \mathsf{CHPG}(1^\lambda)$, $\mathsf{CHKG}'(\mathsf{pp_{ch}}) := \mathsf{CHKG}(\mathsf{pp_{ch}})$, $\mathsf{CHash}'(\mathsf{pk_{ch}}, m) := (h, (r, 0))$ **where** $(h, r) \leftarrow_r \mathsf{CHash}(\mathsf{pk_{ch}}, m)$, $\mathsf{CHCheck}'(\mathsf{pk_{ch}}, m, r, h) := \mathsf{CHCheck}(\mathsf{pk_{ch}}, m, r', h)$ **where** $r = (r', \cdot)$, $\mathsf{CHAdapt}'(\mathsf{sk_{ch}}, m, m', r', h) := (\mathsf{CHAdapt}(\mathsf{sk_{ch}}, m, m', r', h), 0)$ **where** $r = (r', \cdot)$. Clearly, CH' is still fully collision-resistant and fully indistinguishable, but changing the bit in the randomness r is trivial, breaking uniqueness trivially. □

4 Fully Collision-Resistant Chameleon-Hashes

We are now ready to present our black-box construction of fully collision-resistant chameleon-hashes.

4.1 Construction

The main idea of our construction is to encrypt a message m using an mcIND-CPA secure encryption scheme and use the ciphertext as the hash, i.e., it is very close to our "contrived" construction providing enhanced collision-resistance given in Construction 1. However, it has some important, and subtle, differences.

Namely, the randomness r is a SSE NIZK attesting membership of a tuple containing the public key used for encryption, the hash, as well as the hashed message in the following NP-language:

$$L := \{(\mathsf{pk}_\Omega, h, m) \mid \exists\, (\mathsf{sk}_\Omega, \xi) \;:\; h = \mathsf{Enc}(\mathsf{pk}_\Omega, m;\, \xi) \vee \mathsf{KVf}_\Omega(\mathsf{pk}_\Omega, \mathsf{sk}_\Omega) = 1\}. \quad (2)$$

Informally, this language requires the prover to demonstrate that it either knows the randomness ξ attesting that h is a well-formed encryption of m under the CH key pk_Ω, *or* it knows a secret key sk_Ω corresponding to pk_Ω, instead of encrypting a signature and proving the verification relation. Our construction of a fully collision-resistant CH is presented as Construction 2. We note that compared to Ateniese et al. [4] we cannot use true-simulation extractable NIZKs (tSE-NIZKs) [25] and need SSE NIZKs.

4.2 Security

Subsequently, we prove the security of our CH in Construction 2.

Theorem 9. *If* Ω *is correct and* Π *is complete, then* CH *in Construction 2 is correct.*

Correctness follows from inspection and the (perfect) correctness of the used primitives.

Theorem 10. *If* Ω *is mcIND-CPA secure, and* Π *is zero-knowledge, then* CH *in Construction 2 is indistinguishable.*

In the proof, we use $\boxed{\text{frameboxes}}$ and $\rightsquigarrow$ to highlight the changes we make in the algorithms throughout a sequence of games (and we only show the changes).

$\underline{\mathsf{CHPG}(1^\lambda)}$: Fix a public-key encryption scheme Ω and a compatible NIZK proof system for language L in (2). Return $\mathsf{pp}_{\mathsf{ch}} = (\mathsf{pp}_\Omega, \mathsf{crs}_\Pi)$, where

$$\mathsf{pp}_\Omega \leftarrow_r \mathsf{PG}_\Omega(1^\lambda), \text{ and } \mathsf{crs}_\Pi \leftarrow_r \mathsf{PG}_\Pi(1^\lambda).$$

$\underline{\mathsf{CHKG}(\mathsf{pp}_{\mathsf{ch}})}$: Return $(\mathsf{sk}_{\mathsf{ch}}, \mathsf{pk}_{\mathsf{ch}}) = (\mathsf{sk}_\Omega, (\mathsf{pp}_{\mathsf{ch}}, \mathsf{pk}_\Omega))$, where

$$(\mathsf{sk}_\Omega, \mathsf{pk}_\Omega) \leftarrow_r \mathsf{KG}_\Omega(\mathsf{pp}_\Omega).$$

$\underline{\mathsf{CHash}(\mathsf{pk}_{\mathsf{ch}}, m)}$: Parse $\mathsf{pk}_{\mathsf{ch}}$ as $((\mathsf{pp}_\Omega, \mathsf{crs}_\Pi), \mathsf{pk}_\Omega)$, and return $(h, r) = (c, \pi)$, where

$$(c; \xi) \leftarrow_r \mathsf{Enc}(\mathsf{pk}_\Omega, m), \text{ and } \pi \leftarrow_r \mathsf{Prf}_\Pi(\mathsf{crs}_\Pi, (\mathsf{pk}_\Omega, h, m), (\bot, \xi)).$$

$\underline{\mathsf{CHCheck}(\mathsf{pk}_{\mathsf{ch}}, m, r, h)}$: Parse $\mathsf{pk}_{\mathsf{ch}}$ as $((\mathsf{pp}_\Omega, \mathsf{crs}_\Pi), \mathsf{pk}_\Omega)$, and r as π. Return 1, if the following holds, and 0 otherwise:

$$m \in \mathcal{M} \ \wedge \ \mathsf{Vfy}_\Pi(\mathsf{crs}_\Pi, (\mathsf{pk}_\Omega, h, m), \pi) = 1.$$

$\underline{\mathsf{CHAdapt}(\mathsf{sk}_{\mathsf{ch}}, m, m', r, h)}$: Parse $\mathsf{sk}_{\mathsf{ch}}$ as sk_Ω. Verify whether $m' \in \mathcal{M}$, and $\mathsf{CHCheck}(\mathsf{pk}_{\mathsf{ch}}, m, r, h) = 1$. Return $\bot$, if not. Otherwise, return $r' = \pi'$, where

$$\pi' \leftarrow_r \mathsf{Prf}_\Pi(\mathsf{crs}_\Pi, (\mathsf{pk}_\Omega, h, m'), (\mathsf{sk}_\Omega, \bot)).$$

Construction 2. Our Construction of a Fully Collision-Resistant CH

Proof. To prove indistinguishability, we use a sequence of games:

Game 0: The original indistinguishability game.

Game 1: As Game 0, but we modify the algorithms CHPG, CHash, and CHAdapt used inside the game:

$\underline{\mathsf{CHPG}'(1^\lambda)}$:

$$\mathsf{crs}_\Pi \leftarrow_r \mathsf{PG}_\Pi(1^\lambda) \rightsquigarrow \boxed{(\mathsf{crs}_\Pi, \tau) \leftarrow_r \mathsf{SIM}_1(1^\lambda)}.$$

$\underline{\mathsf{CHash}'(\mathsf{pk}_{\mathsf{ch}}, m)}$:

$$\pi \leftarrow_r \mathsf{Prf}_\Pi(\mathsf{crs}_\Pi, (\mathsf{pk}_\Omega, h, m), (\bot, \xi)) \rightsquigarrow \boxed{\pi \leftarrow_r \mathsf{SIM}_2(\mathsf{crs}_\Pi, \tau, (\mathsf{pk}_\Omega, h, m))}$$

$\underline{\mathsf{CHAdapt}'(\mathsf{sk}_{\mathsf{ch}}, m, m', r, h)}$:

$$\pi' \leftarrow_r \mathsf{Prf}_\Pi(\mathsf{crs}_\Pi, (\mathsf{pk}_\Omega, h, m'), (\mathsf{sk}_\Omega, \bot)) \rightsquigarrow \boxed{\pi' \leftarrow_r \mathsf{SIM}_2(\mathsf{crs}_\Pi, \tau, (\mathsf{pk}_\Omega, h, m')).}$$

Transition - Game 0 → Game 1: We bound the probability for an adversary to detect this game change by presenting a hybrid game, which, depending on a zero-knowledge challenger $\mathcal{C}^{\mathsf{zk}}$, either produces the distribution in Game 0 or Game 1, respectively. In particular, assume that we use the following changes:

$\underline{\mathsf{CHPG}''(1^\lambda)}$:

$$(\mathsf{crs}_\Pi, \tau) \leftarrow_r \mathsf{SIM}_1(1^\lambda) \rightsquigarrow \boxed{\mathsf{crs}_\Pi \leftarrow_r \mathcal{C}^{\mathsf{zk}}}.$$

$\underline{\mathsf{CHash}''(\mathsf{pk_{ch}}, m)}$:

$$\pi \leftarrow_r \mathsf{SIM}_2(\mathsf{crs}_\Pi, \tau, (\mathsf{pk}_\Omega, h, m)) \rightsquigarrow \boxed{\pi \leftarrow_r \mathcal{C}^{\mathsf{zk}}.P_b((\mathsf{pk}_\Omega, h, m), (\bot, \xi))}.$$

$\underline{\mathsf{CHAdapt}''(\mathsf{sk_{ch}}, m, m', r, h)}$:

$$\pi' \leftarrow_r \mathsf{SIM}_2(\mathsf{crs}_\Pi, \tau, (\mathsf{pk}_\Omega, h, m')) \rightsquigarrow \boxed{\pi' \leftarrow_r \mathcal{C}^{\mathsf{zk}}.P_b((\mathsf{pk}_\Omega, h, m'), (\mathsf{sk}_\Omega, \bot))}.$$

Clearly, if the challenger's internal bit is 0 we simulate the distribution in Game 0, whereas we simulate the distribution in Game 1 otherwise. We have that $|\Pr[S_0] - \Pr[S_1]| \leq \nu_{\mathsf{zk}}(\lambda)$.

Game 2: As Game 1, but we further modify the CHash algorithm as follows:

$\underline{\mathsf{CHash}'''(\mathsf{pk_{ch}}, m)}$:

$$(c; \xi) \leftarrow_r \mathsf{Enc}(\mathsf{pk}_\Omega, m) \rightsquigarrow \boxed{(c; \xi) \leftarrow_r \mathsf{Enc}(\mathsf{pk}_\Omega, 0)}.$$

Transition - Game 1 → Game 2: We bound the probability for an adversary to distinguish between two consecutive games by introducing a hybrid game which uses a multi-challenge IND-CPA challenger to interpolate between two consecutive games.

$\underline{\mathsf{CHKG}(\mathsf{pp_{ch}})''}$: Return $(\bot, \mathsf{pk_{ch}}) = (\bot, (\mathsf{pp_{ch}}, \mathsf{pk}_\Omega))$, where

$$(\mathsf{sk}_\Omega, \mathsf{pk}_\Omega) \leftarrow_r \mathsf{KG}_\Omega(\mathsf{pp}_\Omega) \rightsquigarrow \boxed{\mathsf{pk}_\Omega \leftarrow_r \mathcal{C}^{\mathsf{mc\text{-}cpa}}}.$$

$\underline{\mathsf{CHash}''''(\mathsf{pk_{ch}}, m)}$:

$$(c; \xi) \leftarrow_r \mathsf{Enc}(\mathsf{pk}_\Omega, 0) \rightsquigarrow \boxed{(c; \bot) \leftarrow_r \mathcal{C}^{\mathsf{mc\text{-}cpa}}.\mathsf{Enc}'(m, 0)}.$$

Now, depending on the challenger's bit, we either simulate Game 1 or Game 2. Thus we have that $|\Pr[S_1] - \Pr[S_{2_i}]| \leq \nu_{\mathsf{mc\text{-}cpa}}(\lambda)$

Now, the indistinguishability game is independent of the bit b, proving indistinguishability. □

Theorem 11. *If Ω is perfectly correct and mcIND-CPA secure, and Π is zero-knowledge as well as simulation-sound extractable, then* CH *in Construction 2 is fully collision-resistant.*

Proof. To prove full collision-resistance, we use a sequence of games.

Game 0: The original full collision-resistance game.

Game 1: As Game 0, but we modify the CHPG and the CHAdapt algorithm as follows:

$\underline{\mathsf{CHPG}'(1^\lambda)}$:

$$\mathsf{crs}_\Pi \leftarrow_r \mathsf{PG}_\Pi(1^\lambda) \rightsquigarrow \boxed{(\mathsf{crs}_\Pi, \tau) \leftarrow_r \mathsf{SIM}_1(1^\lambda)}.$$

$\underline{\mathsf{CHAdapt}'(\mathsf{sk}_{\mathsf{ch}}, m, m', r, h)}$:

$$\pi' \leftarrow_r \mathsf{Prf}_\Pi(\mathsf{crs}_\Pi, (\mathsf{pk}_\Omega, h, m'), (\mathsf{sk}_\Omega, \bot)) \rightsquigarrow \boxed{\pi' \leftarrow_r \mathsf{SIM}_2(\mathsf{crs}_\Pi, \tau, (\mathsf{pk}_\Omega, h, m')).}$$

Transition - Game 0 → Game 1: We bound the probability for an adversary to detect this game change by presenting a hybrid game, which, depending on a zero-knowledge challenger $\mathcal{C}^{\mathsf{zk}}$, either produces the distribution in Game 0 or Game 1, respectively.

$\underline{\mathsf{CHPG}''(1^\lambda)}$:

$$(\mathsf{crs}_\Pi, \tau) \leftarrow_r \mathsf{SIM}_1(1^\lambda) \rightsquigarrow \boxed{\mathsf{crs}_\Pi \leftarrow_r \mathcal{C}^{\mathsf{zk}}}.$$

$\underline{\mathsf{CHAdapt}''(\mathsf{sk}_{\mathsf{ch}}, m, m', r, h)}$:

$$\pi' \leftarrow_r \mathsf{SIM}_2(\mathsf{crs}_\Pi, \tau, (\mathsf{pk}_\Omega, h, m')) \rightsquigarrow \boxed{\pi' \leftarrow_r \mathcal{C}^{\mathsf{zk}}.P_b((\mathsf{pk}_\Omega, h, m'), \mathsf{sk}_\Omega)}.$$

Clearly, if the challenger's internal bit is 0 we simulate the distribution in Game 0, whereas we simulate the distribution in Game 1 otherwise. We have that $|\Pr[S_0] - \Pr[S_1]| \leq \nu_{\mathsf{zk}}(\lambda)$.

Game 2: As Game 1, but we further modify the CHPG algorithm as follows:

$\underline{\mathsf{CHPG}'''(1^\lambda)}$:

$$(\mathsf{crs}_\Pi, \tau) \leftarrow_r \mathsf{SIM}_1(1^\lambda) \rightsquigarrow \boxed{(\mathsf{crs}_\Pi, \tau, \zeta) \leftarrow_r \mathcal{E}_1(1^\lambda)}.$$

Transition - Game 1 → Game 2: Under simulation-sound extractability, Game 1 and Game 2 are indistinguishable. That is, $|\Pr[S_1] - \Pr[S_2]| = 0$.

Game 3: As Game 2, but we keep a list $\mathcal{Q}$ of all tuples (h, r, m) previously submitted to the collision-finding oracle which are accepted by the CHCheck algorithm, where h was never submitted to the collision-finding oracle before.

Transition - Game 2 → Game 3: This change is conceptual, i.e., $|\Pr[S_2] - \Pr[S_3]| = 0$.

Game 4: As Game 3, but for every valid collision $(m^*, r^*, m'^*, r'^*, h^*)$ output by the adversary we observe that either (m^*, r^*) or (m'^*, r'^*) must be a "fresh" collision, i.e., one that was never output by the collision-finding oracle. We assume, without loss of generality, that (m'^*, r'^*) is the "fresh" collision. We run $(\mathsf{sk}', \xi') \leftarrow_r \mathcal{E}_2(\mathsf{crs}_\Pi, \zeta, (\mathsf{pk}_\Omega, h^*, m'^*), r'^*)$ and abort if the extraction fails. We call this event E_1.

Transition - Game 3 → Game 4: Game 3 and Game 4 proceed identically, unless E_1 occurs. Assume, towards contradiction, that event E_1 occurs with non-negligible probability. We now construct an adversary $\mathcal{B}$ which breaks the simulation-sound extractability property of the NIZK proof system with non-negligible probability. We engage with a simulation-sound extractability challenger $\mathcal{C}^{\mathsf{sse}}$ and modify the algorithms as follows:

$\underline{\mathsf{CHPG}''''(1^\lambda):}$

$$(\mathsf{crs}_\Pi, \tau, \zeta) \leftarrow_r \mathcal{E}_1(1^\lambda) \rightsquigarrow \boxed{\mathsf{crs}_\Pi \leftarrow_r \mathcal{C}^{\mathsf{sse}}}.$$

$\underline{\mathsf{CHAdapt}'''(\mathsf{sk}_{\mathsf{ch}}, m, m', r, h):}$

$$\pi' \leftarrow_r \mathsf{SIM}_2(\mathsf{crs}_\Pi, \tau, (\mathsf{pk}_\Omega, h, m')) \rightsquigarrow \boxed{\pi' \leftarrow_r \mathcal{C}^{\mathsf{sse}}.\mathsf{SIM}(\mathsf{pk}_\Omega, h, m')}.$$

In the end we output $((\mathsf{pk}_\Omega, h^*, m'^*), r'^*)$ to the challenger. This shows that we have $|\Pr[S_3] - \Pr[S_4]| \leq \nu_{\mathsf{sse}}(\lambda)$.

Game 5: As Game 4, but we observe that if (m^*, r^*) does not correspond to a fresh collision for h^* in the above sense, then we will have an entry $(h^*, r, m) \in \mathcal{Q}$ where (m, r) is a "fresh" collision, i.e., one computed by the adversary. We run the extractor for the fresh collision, i.e., either obtain $(\mathsf{sk}'', \xi'') \leftarrow_r \mathcal{E}_2(\mathsf{crs}_\Pi, \zeta, (\mathsf{pk}_\Omega, h^*, m^*), r^*)$ or $(\mathsf{sk}'', \xi'') \leftarrow_r \mathcal{E}_2(\mathsf{crs}_\Pi, \zeta, (\mathsf{pk}_\Omega, h^*, m), r)$, respectively. In case the extraction fails, we abort. We call the abort event E_2.

Transition - Game 4 → Game 5: Analogously to the transition between Game 3 and Game 4, we argue that Game 4 and Game 5 proceed identically unless E_2 occurs which is why we do not restate the reduction to simulation-sound extractability here. We have that $|\Pr[S_4] - \Pr[S_5]| \leq \nu_{\mathsf{sse}}(\lambda)$.

Reduction to mcIND-CPA: We are now ready to construct an adversary $\mathcal{B}$ which breaks the mcIND-CPA security of the underlying Ω. Our adversary $\mathcal{B}$ proceeds as follows. It receives pp_Ω and pk_Ω from its own challenger. It embeds them straightforwardly as $\mathsf{pp}_{\mathsf{ch}}$ and $\mathsf{pk}_{\mathsf{ch}}$ to initialize $\mathcal{A}$. Now we know that we have extracted two witnesses (sk, ξ) as well as (sk'', ξ'') where one attests membership of $(\mathsf{pk}_\Omega, h^*, m'^*)$ in L and one attests membership of $(\mathsf{pk}_\Omega, h^*, m'')$ for some $m'' \neq m'^*$ in L. By the perfect correctness of the encryption scheme, we know that at most one of them can be consistent with the ciphertext contained in h^*, which implies that either sk or sk'' will be the key for the underlying encryption scheme (which of them we figure out by using KVf_Ω). With knowledge of the key, $\mathcal{B}$ trivially breaks the mcIND-CPA security of the underlying Ω by randomly sending two distinct messages to its own challenger (for encryption), simply decrypting the returned ciphertext, and answering with the correct bit. We have that $\Pr[S_5] \leq \nu_{\mathsf{mc\text{-}cpa}}(\lambda)$. This concludes the proof. □

4.3 Concrete Instantiation

A suitable instantiation for Ω is ElGamal [29]. The algorithm KVf_Ω is simply checking whether $g^{\mathsf{sk}_\Omega} = g^x = \mathsf{pk}_\Omega$. Note that for Π we only need to extract a bounded number of times (i.e., twice). To this end one may use Fiat-Shamir transformed Σ-protocols for DLOG relations in the random-oracle model [28] when additionally applying the compiler by Faust et al. [27]. In particular, Faust et al. show that such proofs are simulation-sound extractable when additionally including the statement x upon hashing in the challenge computation and if the Σ-protocol provides a property called quasi-unique responses. The latter is straightforward for the statements which need to be proven in our context. See, e.g., [23], for a detailed discussion of this transformation.

For the sake of completeness and to demonstrate how efficiently our approach can be instantiated, we provide this concrete instantiation as Construction 3. Therefore, let $(\mathbb{G}, g, q) \leftarrow_r \mathsf{GGen}(1^\lambda)$ be an instance generator which returns a prime-order, and multiplicatively written, group $\mathbb{G}$ where the DDH problem is hard, along with a generator g such that $\langle g \rangle = \mathbb{G}$. Note that an SSE NIZK for the required L in (3) can easily be obtained as an *equality* proof of two discrete logarithms together with an *or* composition of a proof of a discrete logarithm [19] of Fiat-Shamir transformed Σ-protocols discussed above.

$$L := \{(y, h, m) \mid \exists\ (x, \xi)\ :\ h = (g^\xi, m \cdot y^\xi)\ \vee\ y = g^x\}. \quad (3)$$

4.4 Comparison

Subsequently, in Table 1 we compare existing constructions of chameleon-hashes providing the W-CollRes, E-CollRes and S-CollRes notions with instantiations of our approach (in the random oracle and standard model) providing the stronger F-CollRes notion. Here E denotes an exponentiation in the respective algebraic structure, "?" denotes that it is unclear how efficient this can be realized due to requirement of an invertible onto mapping into the used group (cf. the discussion in [36]). SM and RO denote the standard and the random oracle model respectively. Furthermore, DDH, SXDH, PKoE, and OM-RSA denote the decisional

$\underline{\mathsf{CHPG}(1^\lambda)}$: Outputs the public parameters $(\mathbb{G}, g, q, H)$, where $\mathsf{pp_{ch}} = (\mathbb{G}, g, q) \leftarrow_r \mathsf{GGen}(1^\lambda)$ and a hash-function $H : \{0,1\}^* \to \mathbb{Z}_q$ (which we assume to behave like a random oracle and to be implicitly available to all algorithms below).

$\underline{\mathsf{CHKG}(\mathsf{pp_{ch}})}$: Return $(\mathsf{sk_{ch}}, \mathsf{pk_{ch}}) = (x, y)$, where $x \leftarrow_r \mathbb{Z}_q$ and $y \leftarrow g^x$.

$\underline{\mathsf{CHash}(\mathsf{pk_{ch}}, m)}$: Parse $\mathsf{pk_{ch}}$ as y, choose $(\xi, k_1, e_2, s_2) \leftarrow_r \mathbb{Z}_q^4$, set $u_{1,1} \leftarrow g^{k_1}$, $u_{1,2} \leftarrow y^{k_1}$, $u_2 \leftarrow g^{s_2} \cdot y^{-e_2}$, $e \leftarrow H((y, h, m), (u_{1,1}, u_{1,2}, u_2))$ and $e_1 \leftarrow e - e_2 \bmod q$. Then compute $s_1 \leftarrow k_1 + e_1\xi \bmod q$ and finally, return $(h, r) = (c, \pi)$, where

$$c \leftarrow (c_1, c_2) = (g^\xi, m \cdot y^\xi)\ , \text{ and } \pi \leftarrow (e_1, e_2, s_1, s_2).$$

$\underline{\mathsf{CHCheck}(\mathsf{pk_{ch}}, m, r, h)}$: Parse $\mathsf{pk_{ch}}$ as y and r as (e_1, e_2, s_1, s_2), and h as (c_1, c_2). Return 1 if the following holds, and 0 otherwise:

$$m \in \mathbb{G}\ \wedge\ e_1 + e_2 = H((y, h, m), (g^{s_1} \cdot c_1^{-e_1}, y^{s_1} \cdot (c_2/m)^{-e_1}, g^{s_2} \cdot y^{-e_2})).$$

$\underline{\mathsf{CHAdapt}(\mathsf{sk_{ch}}, m, m', r, h)}$: Parse $\mathsf{sk_{ch}}$ as x, and h as (c_1, c_2). Verify whether $m' \in \mathbb{G}$, and $\mathsf{CHCheck}(\mathsf{pk_{ch}}, m, r, h) = 1$. Return $\perp$ if not. Otherwise, choose $(k_2, e_1, s_1) \leftarrow_r \mathbb{Z}_q^3$, set $u_{1,1} \leftarrow g^{s_1} \cdot c_1^{-e_1}$, $u_{1,2} \leftarrow y^{s_1} \cdot (c_2/m')^{-e_1}$, $u_2 \leftarrow g^{k_2}$, $e \leftarrow H((y, h, m'), (u_{1,1}, u_{1,2}, u_2))$, and $e_2 \leftarrow e - e_1 \bmod q$. Finally compute $s_2 \leftarrow k_2 + e_2 x \bmod q$, and return $r' = \pi'$, where

$$\pi' \leftarrow (e_1, e_2, s_1, s_2).$$

Construction 3. Concrete instantiation of a Fully Collision-Resistant CH

Diffie-Hellman, the symmetric DDH, the power knowledge of exponent [34], and the one-more RSA inversion [9] assumptions. We also stress that for constructions relying on SXDH, for typical instantiations of type-III bilinear groups, we have that $|\mathbb{G}_2| = 2(|\mathbb{G}_1| - 1) + 1$ (where $|\cdot|$ denotes the size of the representation of a group element). Regarding our construction in the standard model, e.g., using SSE NIZKs based on Groth-Sahai NIZKs, one can use the compiler in [22] to efficiently achieve simulation-sound extractability. We, however, note that a naive instantiation of our template in the standard model would still require to include bit-wise proofs of the parts of the witness which are in $\mathbb{Z}_q$, which would, all in all, require a number of group elements in the order of $1k - 2k$ (a very rough estimate; thus we also omit the remaining costs which is indicated by "–" in Table 1). It seems that switching to a variant of ElGamal in the target group (and maybe some other tweaks) would help to work around the requirement of having bit-wise proofs. Optimizing this instantiation is not in the scope of this work and therefore we only give our rough estimates in the table. Finally, we note that we omit comparing our scheme given in Construction 1 as it is contrived and its sole purpose is to prove a separation result.

5 Application: Redactable Blockchains

While one of the major goals of blockchains is their immutability and in particular their use as an immutable append-only log, recently, starting with the work of Ateniense et al. [4], there has been an increasing interest in blockchains that allow some controlled after-the-fact modification of their content. This is motivated by illegal content that was shown to be included into the Bitcoin blockchain [38], which represents a significant challenge for law enforcement agencies [45], as well as legislations like the European General Data Protection Regulation (GDPR)

Table 1. Comparison of different chameleon-hash functions. $|\cdot|_{\text{bit}}$ refers to the bit size of the respective value which is currently believed to provide 128 bit security. We use 256bit elliptic curves for standard known order groups ($|\mathbb{G}| = 257, |\mathbb{Z}_q| = 256$), 3072bit RSA modulus for the RSA setting ($|\mathbb{Z}_N| = 3072$), and 381bit BLS12 curves for the SXDH setting ($|\mathbb{G}_1| = 382, |\mathbb{G}_2| = 763, |\mathbb{Z}_q| = 256$).

Scheme	CR	$\|h\|$	$\|h\|_{\text{bit}}$	$\|r\|$	$\|r\|_{\text{bit}}$	CHash	CHAdapt	Ass.	Model
[37]	W	$1\mathbb{G}$	256	$1\mathbb{Z}_q$	256	$2\mathrm{E}_{\mathbb{G}}$	$0\mathrm{E}_{\mathbb{G}}$	DLOG	SM
[4] (1)	E	$1\mathbb{G}$	256	$12\mathbb{G}+7\mathbb{Z}_q$	4876	$17\mathrm{E}_{\mathbb{G}}$	?	DDH	ROM
[4] (2)	E	$1\mathbb{G}_1$	382	$6\mathbb{G}_1+13\mathbb{G}_2$	12211	$51\mathrm{E}_{\mathbb{G}_1}$	?	SXDH	SM
[36] (1)	E	$1\mathbb{G}_1$	382	$9\mathbb{G}_1+4\mathbb{G}_2$	6490	$25\mathrm{E}_{\mathbb{G}_1}$	$1\mathrm{E}_{\mathbb{Z}_q}$	SXDH	SM
[36] (2)	E	$1\mathbb{G}_1$	382	$3\mathbb{G}_1$	1164	$6\mathrm{E}_{\mathbb{G}_1}$	$1\mathrm{E}_{\mathbb{Z}_q}$	PKoE	SM
[15]	S	$1\mathbb{Z}_N$	3072	$1\mathbb{Z}_N$	3072	$1\mathrm{E}_{\mathbb{Z}_N}$	$1\mathrm{E}_{\mathbb{Z}_N}$	OM-RSA	ROM
Ours	F	$2\mathbb{G}$	514	$4\mathbb{Z}_q$	1024	$6\mathrm{E}_{\mathbb{G}}$	$5\mathrm{E}_{\mathbb{G}}$	DDH	ROM
Ours	F	$2\mathbb{G}_1$	764	$\approx$1–2k $\mathbb{G}_{1/2}$	-	-	-	SXDH	SM

and the associated "right to be forgotten". Solutions to this problem may either be for the permissioned- or permissionless-blockchain setting and cryptographic in nature [4,21,41] or non-cryptographic, where in the latter case it is based on the consensus layer of the blockchain [24].

We are considering the former and focus on block-level rewriting (change entire blocks) of blockchains instead of transaction-level rewriting (change single transactions within a block) in a permissionless setting (such as Bitcoin), as this illustrates the problem with much wider implications. In the following we are using the notation used in [4], and describe a block as triple of the form $B = \langle s, x, \texttt{ctr}\rangle$, where $s \in \{0,1\}^{\lambda}$, $x \in \{0,1\}^*$ and $\texttt{ctr} \in \mathbb{N}$ and a block is valid if

$$\textbf{validblock}_q^D(B) := (H(\texttt{ctr}, G(s,x)) < D) \ \wedge \ (\texttt{ctr} < q) = 1.$$

Here, $H : \{0,1\}^* \rightarrow \{0,1\}^{2\lambda}$ and $G : \{0,1\}^* \rightarrow \{0,1\}^{2\lambda}$ are collision-resistant hash functions, and the parameters $D \in \mathbb{N}$ and $q \in \mathbb{N}$ are the difficulty level of the block and the maximum number of hash queries that a user is allowed to make in any given round of the protocol, respectively. The chaining of blocks is now done by requiring that when attaching a (valid) block $B' = \langle s', x', \texttt{ctr'}\rangle$ we have that $s' = H(\texttt{ctr}, G(s,x))$. Now to make blocks redactable, one changes the description of blocks to $B = \langle s, x, \texttt{ctr}, (h,r)\rangle$ where the new component is a chameleon-hash (h, r) and the validation predicate changes to

$$\begin{aligned}\textbf{validblock}_q^D(B) :=& (H(\texttt{ctr}, h) < D) \ \wedge \ \mathsf{CHCheck}(\mathsf{pk_{ch}}, (s,x), r, h) = 1 \ \wedge \\ & (\texttt{ctr} < q) = 1.\end{aligned}$$

Chaining is now done by requiring that when attaching a (valid) block $B' = \langle s', x', \texttt{ctr'}\rangle$ we have that $s' = H(\texttt{ctr}, h)$. Observe that now computing a collision in the chameleon-hash gives very much power as it basically allows to rewrite the entire history of the blockchain.

Ateniese et al. in [4] discuss different ways to control this power to actually compute collisions (i.e., run $\mathsf{CHAdapt}$) where 1) either $\mathsf{sk_{ch}}$ may be available to some fully trusted single party only, or 2) $\mathsf{sk_{ch}}$ is generated using a multi-party computation (MPC) protocol and $\mathsf{CHAdapt}$ is also performed in a distributed way by some set of parties. We will discuss the implications of different collision-resistance notions to this setting, which is independent of which of these two approaches is going to be used.

We recall that Ateniese et al. [4], who introduced this application, rely on E-CollRes and Derler et al. in more recent work in [21] rely on S-CollRes. Now, note that in such a permissionless setting as discussed above, where everybody is allowed to participate, it is reasonable to assume that an adversary sees the collisions computed for any blocks over some time in the system (as they will be broadcasted). Now let us discuss the single notions:

Weak Collision-Resistance (W-CollRes). A chameleon-hash providing this notion of collision-resistance provides absolutely no guarantees, as after seeing a single collision all guarantees are lost. A prime example is the Pedersen CH due to Krawczyk and Rabin [37] (cf. the full version of this paper), where a single seen collision exposes the secret key $\mathsf{sk_{ch}}$ to everybody. Clearly, this has significant consequences in the above scenario as then everybody can arbitrarily alter the blockchain.

Enhanced Collision-Resistance (E-CollRes). Recall that an adversary when attacking some hash h^* must have never input h^* to $\mathsf{CHAdapt}'$. Now, this means that if an adversary targets a specific hash and then happens to see a collision for this hash (for some reason), suddenly all guarantees are lost and arbitrary collisions could be computed. Note that our construction in Sect. 3.5 clearly demonstrates potential problems with CHs only satisfying this notion. This still represents a significant problem with this application.

Standard Collision-Resistance (S-CollRes). Recall, that an adversary is only restricted to not query message m^* (which is associated to the computed collision h^*) was never queried to the collision-finding oracle. While this still might be problematic in the redactable blockchain setting, messages can very likely be made unique by perpending a large enough random tag/nonce (note that in this could easily be done in the block format of e.g., the Bitcoin block structure). So, this notion seems suitable if the aforementioned constrained may, under certain circumstances, be guaranteed to be met, but is far away from being ideal.

Full Collision-Resistance (F-CollRes). We recall that, here, only the collision (h^*, m^*) was not generated by the collision-finding oracle, but there is no other restriction whatsoever. Consequently, this collision-resistance notion seems the "right" notion as no issues on higher levels need to be considered and very strong guarantees are already provided by the notion itself.

Acknowledgements. This work was supported by the EU's Horizon 2020 ECSEL Joint Undertaking under grant agreement n° 783119 (SECREDAS) and by the Austrian Science Fund (FWF) and netidee SCIENCE under grant agreement P31621-N38 (PROFET).

References

1. Abe, M., David, B., Kohlweiss, M., Nishimaki, R., Ohkubo, M.: Tagged one-time signatures: tight security and optimal tag size. In: Kurosawa, K., Hanaoka, G. (eds.) PKC 2013. LNCS, vol. 7778, pp. 312–331. Springer, Heidelberg (2013). https://doi.org/10.1007/978-3-642-36362-7_20
2. Alsouri, S., Dagdelen, Ö., Katzenbeisser, S.: Group-based attestation: enhancing privacy and management in remote attestation. In: Acquisti, A., Smith, S.W., Sadeghi, A.-R. (eds.) Trust 2010. LNCS, vol. 6101, pp. 63–77. Springer, Heidelberg (2010). https://doi.org/10.1007/978-3-642-13869-0_5
3. Ateniese, G., Chou, D.H., de Medeiros, B., Tsudik, G.: Sanitizable signatures. In: di Vimercati, S.C., Syverson, P., Gollmann, D. (eds.) ESORICS 2005. LNCS, vol. 3679, pp. 159–177. Springer, Heidelberg (2005). https://doi.org/10.1007/11555827_10

4. Ateniese, G., Magri, B., Venturi, D., Andrade, E.R.: Redactable blockchain - or - rewriting history in bitcoin and friends. In: EuroS&P, pp. 111–126 (2017)
5. Ateniese, G., de Medeiros, B.: Identity-based chameleon hash and applications. In: Juels, A. (ed.) FC 2004. LNCS, vol. 3110, pp. 164–180. Springer, Heidelberg (2004). https://doi.org/10.1007/978-3-540-27809-2_19
6. Ateniese, G., de Medeiros, B.: On the key exposure problem in chameleon hashes. In: Blundo, C., Cimato, S. (eds.) SCN 2004. LNCS, vol. 3352, pp. 165–179. Springer, Heidelberg (2005). https://doi.org/10.1007/978-3-540-30598-9_12
7. Bao, F., Deng, R.H., Ding, X., Lai, J., Zhao, Y.: Hierarchical identity-based chameleon hash and its applications. In: Lopez, J., Tsudik, G. (eds.) ACNS 2011. LNCS, vol. 6715, pp. 201–219. Springer, Heidelberg (2011). https://doi.org/10.1007/978-3-642-21554-4_12
8. Bellare, M., Boldyreva, A., Micali, S.: Public-key encryption in a multi-user setting: security proofs and improvements. In: Preneel, B. (ed.) EUROCRYPT 2000. LNCS, vol. 1807, pp. 259–274. Springer, Heidelberg (2000). https://doi.org/10.1007/3-540-45539-6_18
9. Bellare, M., Namprempre, C., Pointcheval, D., Semanko, M.: The one-more-RSA-inversion problems and the security of Chaum's blind signature scheme. J. Cryptol. **16**(3), 185–215 (2003). https://doi.org/10.1007/s00145-002-0120-1
10. Bellare, M., Ristov, T.: Hash functions from sigma protocols and improvements to VSH. In: Pieprzyk, J. (ed.) ASIACRYPT 2008. LNCS, vol. 5350, pp. 125–142. Springer, Heidelberg (2008). https://doi.org/10.1007/978-3-540-89255-7_9
11. Bellare, M., Ristov, T.: A characterization of chameleon hash functions and new, efficient designs. J. Cryptol. **27**(4), 799–823 (2014). https://doi.org/10.1007/s00145-013-9155-8
12. Blazy, O., Kakvi, S.A., Kiltz, E., Pan, J.: Tightly-secure signatures from chameleon hash functions. In: Katz, J. (ed.) PKC 2015. LNCS, vol. 9020, pp. 256–279. Springer, Heidelberg (2015). https://doi.org/10.1007/978-3-662-46447-2_12
13. Brassard, G., Chaum, D., Crépeau, C.: Minimum disclosure proofs of knowledge. J. Comput. Syst. Sci. **37**(2), 156–189 (1988)
14. Brzuska, C., et al.: Security of sanitizable signatures revisited. In: Jarecki, S., Tsudik, G. (eds.) PKC 2009. LNCS, vol. 5443, pp. 317–336. Springer, Heidelberg (2009). https://doi.org/10.1007/978-3-642-00468-1_18
15. Camenisch, J., Derler, D., Krenn, S., Pöhls, H.C., Samelin, K., Slamanig, D.: Chameleon-hashes with ephemeral trapdoors - and applications to invisible sanitizable signatures. In: Fehr, S. (ed.) PKC 2017. LNCS, vol. 10175, pp. 152–182. Springer, Heidelberg (2017). https://doi.org/10.1007/978-3-662-54388-7_6
16. Chen, X., Zhang, F., Kim, K.: Chameleon hashing without key exposure. In: Zhang, K., Zheng, Y. (eds.) ISC 2004. LNCS, vol. 3225, pp. 87–98. Springer, Heidelberg (2004). https://doi.org/10.1007/978-3-540-30144-8_8
17. Chen, X., Zhang, F., Susilo, W., Mu, Y.: Efficient generic on-line/off-line signatures without key exposure. In: Katz, J., Yung, M. (eds.) ACNS 2007. LNCS, vol. 4521, pp. 18–30. Springer, Heidelberg (2007). https://doi.org/10.1007/978-3-540-72738-5_2
18. Choi, J., Jung, S.: A handover authentication using credentials based on chameleon hashing. IEEE Commun. Lett. **14**(1), 54–56 (2010)
19. Cramer, R., Damgård, I., Schoenmakers, B.: Proofs of partial knowledge and simplified design of witness hiding protocols. In: Desmedt, Y.G. (ed.) CRYPTO 1994. LNCS, vol. 839, pp. 174–187. Springer, Heidelberg (1994). https://doi.org/10.1007/3-540-48658-5_19

20. Cramer, R., Shoup, V.: A practical public key cryptosystem provably secure against adaptive chosen ciphertext attack. In: Krawczyk, H. (ed.) CRYPTO 1998. LNCS, vol. 1462, pp. 13–25. Springer, Heidelberg (1998). https://doi.org/10.1007/BFb0055717
21. Derler, D., Samelin, K., Slamanig, D., Striecks, C.: Fine-grained and controlled rewriting in blockchains: chameleon-hashing gone attribute-based. In: NDSS (2019)
22. Derler, D., Slamanig, D.: Key-homomorphic signatures: definitions and applications to multiparty signatures and non-interactive zero-knowledge. Des. Codes Crypt. **87**(6), 1373–1413 (2018). https://doi.org/10.1007/s10623-018-0535-9
23. Derler, D., Slamanig, D.: Highly-efficient fully-anonymous dynamic group signatures. In: AsiaCCS, pp. 551–565 (2018)
24. Deuber, D., Magri, B., Thyagarajan, S.A.K.: Redactable blockchain in the permissionless setting. In: IEEE S&P, pp. 124–138 (2019)
25. Dodis, Y., Haralambiev, K., López-Alt, A., Wichs, D.: Efficient public-key cryptography in the presence of key leakage. In: Abe, M. (ed.) ASIACRYPT 2010. LNCS, vol. 6477, pp. 613–631. Springer, Heidelberg (2010). https://doi.org/10.1007/978-3-642-17373-8_35
26. Even, S., Goldreich, O., Micali, S.: On-line/off-line digital signatures. J. Cryptol. **9**(1), 35–67 (1996). https://link.springer.com/chapter/10.1007/0-387-34805-0_24
27. Faust, S., Kohlweiss, M., Marson, G.A., Venturi, D.: On the non-malleability of the Fiat-Shamir transform. In: Galbraith, S., Nandi, M. (eds.) INDOCRYPT 2012. LNCS, vol. 7668, pp. 60–79. Springer, Heidelberg (2012). https://doi.org/10.1007/978-3-642-34931-7_5
28. Fiat, A., Shamir, A.: How to prove yourself: practical solutions to identification and signature problems. In: Odlyzko, A.M. (ed.) CRYPTO 1986. LNCS, vol. 263, pp. 186–194. Springer, Heidelberg (1987). https://doi.org/10.1007/3-540-47721-7_12
29. ElGamal, T.: A public key cryptosystem and a signature scheme based on discrete logarithms. In: Blakley, G.R., Chaum, D. (eds.) CRYPTO 1984. LNCS, vol. 196, pp. 10–18. Springer, Heidelberg (1985). https://doi.org/10.1007/3-540-39568-7_2
30. Groth, J.: Simulation-sound NIZK proofs for a practical language and constant size group signatures. In: Lai, X., Chen, K. (eds.) ASIACRYPT 2006. LNCS, vol. 4284, pp. 444–459. Springer, Heidelberg (2006). https://doi.org/10.1007/11935230_29
31. Groth, J.: Efficient fully structure-preserving signatures for large messages. In: Iwata, T., Cheon, J.H. (eds.) ASIACRYPT 2015. LNCS, vol. 9452, pp. 239–259. Springer, Heidelberg (2015). https://doi.org/10.1007/978-3-662-48797-6_11
32. Groth, J., Sahai, A.: Efficient non-interactive proof systems for bilinear groups. In: Smart, N. (ed.) EUROCRYPT 2008. LNCS, vol. 4965, pp. 415–432. Springer, Heidelberg (2008). https://doi.org/10.1007/978-3-540-78967-3_24
33. Guo, S., Zeng, D., Xiang, Y.: Chameleon hashing for secure and privacy-preserving vehicular communications. IEEE Trans. Parallel Distrib. Syst. **25**(11), 2794–2803 (2014)
34. Hada, S., Tanaka, T.: On the existence of 3-round zero-knowledge protocols. In: Krawczyk, H. (ed.) CRYPTO 1998. LNCS, vol. 1462, pp. 408–423. Springer, Heidelberg (1998). https://doi.org/10.1007/BFb0055744
35. Hohenberger, S., Waters, B.: Short and stateless signatures from the RSA assumption. In: Halevi, S. (ed.) CRYPTO 2009. LNCS, vol. 5677, pp. 654–670. Springer, Heidelberg (2009). https://doi.org/10.1007/978-3-642-03356-8_38
36. Khalili, M., Dakhilalian, M., Susilo, W.: Efficient chameleon hash functions in the enhanced collision resistant model. Inf. Sci. **510**, 155–164 (2020)
37. Krawczyk, H., Rabin, T.: Chameleon signatures. In: NDSS, pp. 143–154 (2000)

38. Matzutt, R., et al.: A quantitative analysis of the impact of arbitrary blockchain content on bitcoin. In: Meiklejohn, S., Sako, K. (eds.) FC 2018. LNCS, vol. 10957, pp. 420–438. Springer, Heidelberg (2018). https://doi.org/10.1007/978-3-662-58387-6_23
39. Mohassel, P.: One-time signatures and chameleon hash functions. In: Biryukov, A., Gong, G., Stinson, D.R. (eds.) SAC 2010. LNCS, vol. 6544, pp. 302–319. Springer, Heidelberg (2011). https://doi.org/10.1007/978-3-642-19574-7_21
40. Pedersen, T.P.: Non-interactive and information-theoretic secure verifiable secret sharing. In: Feigenbaum, J. (ed.) CRYPTO 1991. LNCS, vol. 576, pp. 129–140. Springer, Heidelberg (1992). https://doi.org/10.1007/3-540-46766-1_9
41. Samelin, K., Slamanig, D.: Policy-based sanitizable signatures. In: Jarecki, S. (ed.) CT-RSA 2020. LNCS, vol. 12006, pp. 538–563. Springer, Cham (2020). https://doi.org/10.1007/978-3-030-40186-3_23
42. Shamir, A., Tauman, Y.: Improved online/offline signature schemes. In: Kilian, J. (ed.) CRYPTO 2001. LNCS, vol. 2139, pp. 355–367. Springer, Heidelberg (2001). https://doi.org/10.1007/3-540-44647-8_21
43. Steinfeld, R., Bull, L., Wang, H., Pieprzyk, J.: Universal designated-verifier signatures. In: Laih, C.-S. (ed.) ASIACRYPT 2003. LNCS, vol. 2894, pp. 523–542. Springer, Heidelberg (2003). https://doi.org/10.1007/978-3-540-40061-5_33
44. Steinfeld, R., Wang, H., Pieprzyk, J.: Efficient extension of standard Schnorr/RSA signatures into universal designated-verifier signatures. In: Bao, F., Deng, R., Zhou, J. (eds.) PKC 2004. LNCS, vol. 2947, pp. 86–100. Springer, Heidelberg (2004). https://doi.org/10.1007/978-3-540-24632-9_7
45. Tziakouris, G.: Cryptocurrencies - a forensic challenge or opportunity for law enforcement? An INTERPOL perspective. IEEE Secur. Privacy **16**(4), 92–94 (2018)
46. Zhang, R.: Tweaking TBE/IBE to PKE transforms with chameleon hash functions. In: Katz, J., Yung, M. (eds.) ACNS 2007. LNCS, vol. 4521, pp. 323–339. Springer, Heidelberg (2007). https://doi.org/10.1007/978-3-540-72738-5_21

Proofs and Arguments I

Concretely-Efficient Zero-Knowledge Arguments for Arithmetic Circuits and Their Application to Lattice-Based Cryptography

Carsten Baum[1] and Ariel Nof[2](✉)

[1] Aarhus University, Aarhus, Denmark
carsten.baum@outlook.com
[2] Technion, Haifa, Israel
arie.nof@cs.biu.ac.il

Abstract. In this work we present a new interactive Zero-Knowledge Argument of knowledge for general arithmetic circuits. Our protocol is based on the "MPC-in-the-head"-paradigm of Ishai et al. (STOC 2009) and follows the recent "MPC-in-the-head with Preprocessing" as proposed by Katz, Kolesnikov and Wang (ACM CCS 2018). However, in contrast to Katz et al. who used the "cut-and-choose" approach for pre-processing, we show how to incorporate the well-known "sacrificing" paradigm into "MPC-in-the-head", which reduces the proof size when working over arithmetic circuits. Our argument system uses only lightweight symmetric-key primitives and utilizes a simplified version of the so-called SPDZ-protocol.

Based on specific properties of our protocol we then show how it can be used to construct an efficient Zero-Knowledge Argument of Knowledge for instances of the Short Integer Solution (SIS) problem. We present different protocols that are tailored to specific uses of SIS, while utilizing the advantages of our scheme. In particular, we present a variant of our argument system that allows the parties to sample the circuit "on the fly", which may be of independent interest.

We furthermore implemented our Zero-Knowledge argument for SIS and show that using our protocols it is possible to run a complete interactive proof, even for general SIS instances which result in a circuit with $>10^6$ gates, in *less than 0.5 s*.

1 Introduction

Zero-Knowledge Arguments of Knowledge (ZKAoK) are interactive protocols that allow a computationally bounded prover to convince a verifier that he knows a witness for a certain statement, without revealing any further information about the witness. Since their introduction in the 80's [GMR89] these protocols have been important building blocks for applications in cryptography. While solutions for very specific languages have been plentiful, many applications

A. Kiayias et al. (Eds.): PKC 2020, LNCS 12110, pp. 495–526, 2020.
https://doi.org/10.1007/978-3-030-45374-9_17

require the use of arbitrary (algebraic) circuits in order to prove complex relationships. For example, proving that two homomorphic commitments contain the same committed message is generally an easy task, while proving knowledge of a preimage of a SHA-256 hash requires more generic solutions. Recent years saw a variety of different techniques which aim at providing such ZKAoK (see [PHGR16, GMO16, AHIV17, BBHR19, WTS+18, BCR+19] to just name a few), varying in terms of argument size, prover/verification time, interaction and assumptions. While many of these systems perform very well with large witnesses and circuit sizes, none of them are a one-size-fits-all solution.

As an example, consider the so-called Short Integer Solution (SIS) problem. Here, a verifier has a matrix $\mathbf{A}$ and a vector $\mathbf{t}$ while the prover wants to prove knowledge of a secret $\mathbf{s}$ such that $\mathbf{t} = \mathbf{A}\mathbf{s} \bmod q$ and $||\mathbf{s}||_\infty \leq \beta$. SIS and related problems are crucial building blocks for post-quantum lattice-based cryptography and constructing efficient ZKAoK with a small communication complexity and low prover's running time has long been a problem: the soundness error of current special-purpose protocols is constant, meaning that the arguments have to be repeated many times to actually be convincing to a verifier. A particular, non-standard approach has been suggested by Bendlin & Damgård [BD10], who were the first to examine arguments of knowledge for SIS using generic proof systems. They observed that for certain argument schemes, the function that is computed to validate a SIS instance has both a very low multiplication depth and low total number of multiplications, if the secret $\mathbf{s}$ is a binary vector. However, many general ZKAoK systems only provide asymptotic efficiency, meaning that they require the circuit to be big before their strengths play out [BBC+18]. Moreover, many of these approaches achieve sub-linear communication complexity at the cost of high prover's running time [AHIV17, PHGR16]. Other approaches are insecure to post-quantum attacks [WTS+18, MBKM19, BCC+16, PHGR16] or rely on knowledge assumptions that are poorly understood.

1.1 'MPC-in-the-Head' and Preprocessing

The "MPC-in-the-head" paradigm is a general technique which is used in our construction. Before outlining our contributions, we first describe this paradigm.

MPC or Secure Multiparty Computation describes a type of interactive protocol which allows to securely compute functions on secret data. No information is leaked beyond the output of the function with correctness even in the presence of dishonest participants.

MPC-in-the-head was introduced by Ishai et al. [IKOS07] as a technique to construct generic zero-knowledge proofs from MPC protocols. Here, the statement to be proven is rewritten into a circuit C, which outputs y if and only if its input w is a correct witness for the statement to be proven. The prover simulates all parties of an MPC protocol as well as their interaction *in his head.* These parties obtain a secret-sharing of the witness w as their input, run a protocol to evaluate C and send the outputs to the verifier. Moreover, the prover commits to the inputs as well as randomness and exchanged messages of each party separately, and opens a verifier-chosen subset of these commitments to the verifier. The verifier then checks if these parties were simulated correctly by the prover and that the messages and the outputs are consistent. On a very high level, this is a proof of the statement if the MPC scheme is robust against active attacks, and it is zero-knowledge due to the privacy of it.

Preprocessing is a widely used optimization of practical MPC schemes. Here, each party begins the actual protocol with shares of correlated randomness, which is itself independent of the inputs of the protocol. This correlated randomness is then used to speed up the actual computation, and due to its independence of the inputs it can be computed ahead of time. To the best of our knowledge, the first MPC-in-the-head scheme that uses preprocessing was introduced in [KKW18].

1.2 Our Contributions

In this work, we construct a new practically efficient ZKAoK for arithmetic circuits together with a multitude of techniques and apply these to construct interactive arguments for SIS. Our scheme is based on the "MPC-in-the-head" approach and uses only symmetric-key primitives. It has an argument size that only depends on non-linear gates of the circuit C and low prover running time. We implemented our construction and report on its practicality. In more details:

'MPC-in-the-Head' with Preprocessing. We first generalize the idea of [KKW18] to work over arithmetic circuits using a variant of the SPDZ MPC protocol [DPSZ12, LN17] and provide a formal proof of security to their "cut-and-choose" preprocessing heuristic. Then, we present a new construction where we replace the "cut-and-choose" mechanism with a "sacrificing"-based approach. While both approaches have similar cost per MPC instance, our "sacrificing"-based approach yields a smaller cheating probability, which means that the number of MPC instances simulated in the proof can be significantly smaller, thus *reducing* the overall communication footprint. Our scheme is highly flexible in its choice of parameters. In particular, by changing the number of parties in the underlying MPC protocol, one can alternate between achieving low communication and low running time. Our construction only requires efficient standard symmetric primitives, and thus is plausibly post-quantum secure even in the non-interactive case [DFMS19]. The two constructions can be found in Sect. 3.

Application to SIS. The MPC scheme which we use in our construction allows to perform additions and multiplications with public values "for free", meaning those do not have an impact on the size of the argument. In the SIS problem the verification of the input of the prover consists of computing a product with a public matrix $\mathbf{A}$ *and* a proof that the secret $\mathbf{s}$ contains bounded values, so the first part comes essentially for free. We initially tweak the approach of [BD10] and only allow $\mathbf{s}$ to consist of bits, which allows for a very fast argument of size using one square gate per element of $\mathbf{s}$. Then, we show how to handle more general distributions of $\mathbf{s}$ and introduce some specific optimizations to reduce communication and computation. In particular, we show how to adapt advanced techniques such as rejection sampling into the MPC-in-the-head framework, which yields a circuit with only linear gates. This is described in Sect. 5.

Experimental Results. We implemented our zero-knowledge protocol for the Binary SIS problem (i.e., where the secret $\mathbf{s}$ is a vector of bits) and ran extensive experiments with various sets of parameters – both for the SIS problem and for the simulated MPC protocol. For a 61-bit field and a matrix $\mathbf{A}$ of size 1024×4096 (which suffices for many applications such as encryption or commitments), we are able to run our argument in 1.2 s for 40-bits of statistical security when working with a single thread. When utilizing 32 threads, this reduces to only 250 ms. This shows that general lattice-based ZK arguments (which do not rely on structured lattices) are practical and can be used in real-world applications. To the best of our knowledge, we are also the first to implement ZK arguments for general SIS. The results and all the details can be found in Sect. 6.

Sampling Circuits on the Fly. A major source of optimizations to our application is the fact that our "MPC-in-the-head" protocol allows the prover and the verifier to negotiate the circuit C *during the protocol*, under certain circumstances. This fact is used by us to construct circuits "on the fly" with fewer non-linear gates, which helps to reduce the argument size. Thus, as an additional contribution of this work, we provide formal definitions for an argument system where the circuit is sampled jointly by the prover and the verifier during the execution and show how to incorporate this into our protocols. This is described in Sect. 4.

Full Version. Due to space limitations, most proofs are deferred to the full version of this work [BN19] which can be found on eprint.

2 Preliminaries

Unless stated otherwise, operations in this work are carried out over the field $\mathbb{F} = \mathbb{F}_q$ for an odd prime q. $\mathbb{F}_q$-elements are identified by the interval $[-(q-1)/2, (q-1)/2]$. $\mathbb{B}$ denotes the set $\{0, 1\}$ while $[n]$ stands for $\{1, \ldots, n\}$. We use λ as the computational and κ as the statistical security parameters, and generally assume that $q \approx poly(\lambda, \kappa)$. We use bold lower-case letters such as $\mathbf{s}$ to denote a vector and bold upper-case letters like $\mathbf{A}$ for matrices. We let $\mathbf{s}[i]$ denote the ith component of the vector $\mathbf{s}$.

2.1 Programming Model

Our notation for the circuits that we use in this paper will be similar to [BHR12]. The circuit $C = (n_{\mathtt{in}}, n_{\mathtt{out}}, n_C, L, R, F)$ is defined over $\mathbb{F}$, and each wire w will hold a value from $\mathbb{F}$ or $\perp$ initially. C has $n_{\mathtt{in}}$ input wires, $n_{\mathtt{out}}$ output wires and

$n_C \geq n_{\mathtt{in}} + n_{\mathtt{out}}$ wires in total. We define $\mathcal{I} = \{1, \ldots, n_{\mathtt{in}}\}, \mathcal{W} = \{1, \ldots, n_C\}$ and $\mathcal{O} = \{n_C - n_{\mathtt{out}} + 1, \ldots, n_C\}$. The circuit has $n_{\mathtt{gates}} = n_C - n_{\mathtt{in}}$ gates in total and we define the set $\mathcal{G} = \{n_{\mathtt{in}} + 1, \ldots, n_C\}$.

We define functions $L : \mathcal{G} \to \mathcal{W}$, $R : \mathcal{G} \to \mathcal{W} \cup \{\perp\}$ such that $L(x) < x$ as well as $L(x) < R(x) < x$ if $R(x) \neq \perp$ (i.e., the function $L(x)$ returns the index of the left input wire of the gate whereas the function $R(x)$ returns the index of the right input wire if it exists). The function $F : \mathcal{G} \times \mathbb{F} \times (\mathbb{F} \cup \{\perp\}) \to \mathbb{F}$ determines the function which is computed by each gate.

The algorithm $\mathtt{eval}(C, \mathbf{x})$ with $\mathbf{x} \in \mathbb{F}^{n_{\mathtt{in}}}$ is defined as follows:

1. For $i \in [n_{\mathtt{in}}]$ set $w_i \leftarrow \mathbf{x}[i]$.
2. For each $g \in \mathcal{G}$ set $l \leftarrow L(g), r \leftarrow R(g)$ and then $w_g \leftarrow F(g, l, r)$.
3. Output $\mathbf{y} = (w_{n_C - n_{\mathtt{out}}+1}, \ldots, w_{n_C})^\top$.

We further restrict F to compute certain functions only: (i) **Add:** On input x_1, x_2 output $x_1 + x_2$, (ii) **Mult:** On input x_1, x_2 output $x_1 \times x_2$, (iii) **CAdd:** On input x and for the hard-wired a output $x + a$, (iv) **CMult:** On input x and for the hard-wired a output $x \times a$; and (v) **Square:** On input x output x^2. We say that $C(\mathbf{x}) = \mathbf{y}$ if $\mathtt{eval}(C, \mathbf{x})$ returns the value $\mathbf{y} \in \mathbb{F}^{n_{\mathtt{out}}}$. We denote by n_{mul} and n_{sq} the number of multiplication and square gates in the circuit.

2.2 Zero-Knowledge Arguments of Knowledge

Let TM be an abbreviation for Turing Machines. An iTM is defined to be an interactive TM, i.e. a Turing Machine with a special communication tape and a PPT TM is a probabilistic polynomial-time TM. Let $L_R \subseteq \mathbb{B}^*$ be an NP language and R be its related NP-relation for circuits over $\mathbb{F}$. Thus $(x = (C, \mathbf{y}), \mathbf{w}) \in R$ iff $(C, \mathbf{y}) \in L_R$ and $\mathtt{eval}(C, \mathbf{w}) = \mathbf{y}$. We write $R_x = \{\mathbf{w} \mid (x, \mathbf{w}) \in R\}$ for the set of witnesses for a fixed x.

Honest Verifier Zero Knowledge Argument of Knowledge (HVZKAoK). Assume $(\mathcal{P}, \mathcal{V})$ is a pair of PPT iTMs and let $\xi : \mathbb{B}^* \to [0, 1]$ be a function. We say that $(\mathcal{P}, \mathcal{V})$ is a *zero-knowledge argument of knowledge* for the relation R with *knowledge error* ξ if the following properties hold:

Completeness: If $\mathcal{P}$ and $\mathcal{V}$ follow the protocol on input $x \in L_R$ and private input $\mathbf{w} \in R_x$ to $\mathcal{P}$, then $\mathcal{V}$ always outputs 1.

Knowledge Soundness: There exists a probabilistic algorithm $\mathcal{E}$ called the *knowledge extractor*, such that for every interactive prover $\hat{\mathcal{P}}$ and every $x \in L_R$, the algorithm $\mathcal{E}$ satisfies the following condition: let $\delta(x)$ the probability that $\mathcal{V}$ accepts on input x after interacting with $\hat{\mathcal{P}}$. If $\delta(x) > \xi(x)$, then upon input $x \in L_R$ and oracle access to $\hat{\mathcal{P}}$, the algorithm $\mathcal{E}$ outputs a vector $\mathbf{w} \in R_x$ in expected number of steps bounded by $O(\frac{1}{\delta(x) - \xi(x)})$.

Honest Verifier Zero-Knowledge: Let $\mathsf{view}_{\mathcal{V}}^{\mathcal{P}}(x, \mathbf{w})$ be a random variable describing the random challenge of $\mathcal{V}$ and the messages $\mathcal{V}$ receives from $\mathcal{P}$ with input $\mathbf{w}$ during the joint computation on common input x. Then, there exists a PPT simulator $\mathcal{S}$, such that for all $x \in L_R, \mathbf{w} \in R_x$: $\mathcal{S}(x) \approx_c \mathsf{view}_{\mathcal{V}}^{\mathcal{P}}(x, \mathbf{w})$.

This definition suffices, since public-coin protocols like the protocols we consider in this work, which satisfy the above properties, can be easily transformed to protocols which are zero-knowledge in general by having the verifier commit to its challenges at the beginning of the protocol. As is well known, it is possible to obtain a non-interactive zero-knowledge argument of knowledge (NIZKAoK) from any HVZKAoK via the Fiat-Shamir transformation [FS86].

2.3 Commitments and Collision-Resistant Hash Functions

We use *Commitments* and *Collision-Resistant* Hash Functions (CRHF) as buildings blocks in our constructions and thus introduce them now briefly. A commitment scheme allows one party to commit to a message m by sending a commitment value which satisfies the following two properties: (i) *Hiding:* the commitment reveals nothing about m.; and (ii) *Binding:* it is (computationally) infeasible for the committing party to open a committed message m to different message $m' \neq m$. In this work, we assume that the commitment scheme is instantiated using a cryptographic hash function such as e.g. SHA-256, which we model as a Random Oracle[1] for the purpose of giving a proof of security.

A Collision-Resistant Hash Function (CRHF) is an efficiently computable function H for which it is "hard" to find x, x' such that $H(x) = H(x')$. Usually, CRHFs are used to compress a long message into a short digest and thus for almost all messages a collision exists. CRHFs require that a collision is hard to find for any PPT algorithm.

2.4 The Short Integer Solution Problem

We will now formalize the SIS problem, which was already informally introduced in the introduction. $\mathbb{F}_q$ is the base field of the argument system. At the same time, the characteristic q will also be the modulus of the SIS instance which is defined over $\mathbb{Z}_q$. To define the Short Integer Solution problem, let $n, m \in \mathbb{N}$ be such that $n \ll m$. We naturally embed $\mathbb{Z}_q$ into $\mathbb{Z}$ by identifying each $\mod q$-number with an element from the interval $[-\frac{q-1}{2}, \frac{q-1}{2}] \subset \mathbb{Z}$. We thereby let $||\mathbf{s}||_\infty$ be the ∞-norm of the embedding of $\mathbf{s} \in \mathbb{Z}_q^m$ into the module $\mathbb{Z}^m$. Define $S_\beta^m \subset \mathbb{Z}_q^m$ as the subset of m-element vectors with ℓ_∞-norm $\leq \beta$.

Definition 1 (Short Integer Solution (SIS)). *Let m, n, q be as above and $\beta \in \mathbb{N}$. Given $\mathbf{A} \in \mathbb{Z}_q^{n \times m}$ and $\mathbf{t} \in \mathbb{Z}_q^n$, the (inhomogeneous) SIS-problem is to find $\mathbf{s} \in \mathbb{Z}_q^m$ such that $\mathbf{t} = \mathbf{A}\mathbf{s} \mod q$ and $\mathbf{s} \in S_\beta^m$.*

We collect such $(\mathbf{A}, \mathbf{s}, \mathbf{t})$ that fulfill Definition 1 in an NP-relation

$$R_{\text{SIS}}^{m,n,q,\beta} = \{(x, w) = ((\mathbf{A}, \mathbf{t}), \mathbf{s}) \mid \mathbf{s} \in S_\beta^m \wedge \mathbf{A} \in \mathbb{F}_q^{n \times m} \wedge \mathbf{t} = \mathbf{A}\mathbf{s}\}.$$

[1] This is to obtain the smallest possible argument size while avoiding attacks such as [DN19]. A generalization of our scheme without this assumption can be obtained by generating the randomness for commitments independent of the message.

In practice, one often encounters proofs that do not show exactly that $\mathbf{s} \in S_\beta^m$ even though the prover has such a value as witness. Instead, they guarantee that the bound might be a bit bigger, by a factor at most ω which usually is called *slack*. We have that $R_{\mathsf{SIS}}^{m,n,q,\beta} \subseteq R_{\mathsf{SIS}}^{m,n,q,\omega\cdot\beta}$ if $\omega \geq 1$, so any honest prover will still make the verifier accept if it proves $R_{\mathsf{SIS}}^{m,n,q,\omega\cdot\beta}$ instead. For simplicity, we also consider an instance of SIS where $\mathbf{s}$ is binary.

Definition 2 (Binary-SIS). *Let m, n, q be defined as above. Given $\mathbf{A} \in \mathbb{Z}_q^{n\times m}$ and $\mathbf{t} \in \mathbb{Z}_q^n$, the (inhomogeneous) Binary SIS-problem is to find $\mathbf{s} \in \mathbb{B}^m$ such that $\mathbf{t} = \mathbf{A}\mathbf{s} \mod q$.*

This Binary-SIS problem is not uncommon and e.g. [BD10,KTX08] used it. Its relation $R_{\mathsf{B-SIS}}^{m,n,q}$ can be defined similarly as $R_{\mathsf{SIS}}^{m,n,q,\beta}$.

3 Honest Verifier Arguments of Knowledge for Arithmetic Circuits

In this section, we introduce our honest verifier zero-knowledge argument of knowledge (HVZKAoK) protocols for satisfiability of arithmetic circuits. We begin by describing the underlying MPC protocol to securely compute an arithmetic circuit. Then, we present two HVZKAoKs based on the MPC protocol - one that relies on the "cut–and–choose" paradigm and one that uses "sacrificing". While the first is a direct extension of a recent work of [KKW18], the second one is completely new to the best of our knowledge.

3.1 The MPC Protocol

Our MPC protocol is a simplified version of the SPDZ[2] protocol [DPSZ12]. Let N denote the number of parties and let $P_1, \ldots, P_N$ denote the parties participating in the protocol.

Secret Sharing Scheme. Let $[\![x]\!]$ denote an additive sharing of x, i.e. a sharing of x consists of random $x_1, \ldots, x_N \in \mathbb{F}_q$ such that $x = \sum_{i\in[N]} x_i$, where P_i holds x_i. We define the following operations on shares:

- $\mathsf{open}([\![x]\!])$: To reveal the secret x each party broadcasts its share x_i. Upon receiving x_j from each P_j, P_i sets $x = \sum_{j\in[N]} x_j$.
- $[\![x]\!] + [\![y]\!]$: Given two shares x_i and y_i of x and y, each party P_i defines $x_i + y_i$ as its share of the result.
- $\sigma + [\![x]\!]$: Given a sharing $[\![x]\!]$ and a public constant σ, P_1 defines $x_1 + \sigma$ as its new share while other parties' shares remain the same.
- $\sigma \cdot [\![x]\!]$: Given a sharing $[\![x]\!]$ and a public constant σ, each party P_i defines $\sigma \cdot x_i$ as its share of the product.

[2] It works like SPDZ in the sense that it considers dishonest majority, uses an additive secret sharing and multiplication triples, but without the information-theoretic MAC.

Multiplications. We say that $(\llbracket a \rrbracket, \llbracket b \rrbracket, \llbracket c \rrbracket)$ is a random multiplication triple if a and b are random and $c = a \cdot b$. To multiply $\llbracket x \rrbracket$ and $\llbracket y \rrbracket$ using a preprocessed random triple $(\llbracket a \rrbracket, \llbracket b \rrbracket, \llbracket c \rrbracket)$, the parties do the following:

1. The parties compute $\llbracket \alpha \rrbracket = \llbracket x \rrbracket - \llbracket a \rrbracket$ and $\llbracket \beta \rrbracket = \llbracket y \rrbracket - \llbracket b \rrbracket$.
2. The parties run $\mathsf{open}(\llbracket \alpha \rrbracket)$ and $\mathsf{open}(\llbracket \beta \rrbracket)$ to obtain α and β.
3. Each party computes $\llbracket z \rrbracket = \llbracket c \rrbracket - \alpha \cdot \llbracket b \rrbracket - \beta \cdot \llbracket a \rrbracket + \alpha \cdot \beta$.

The above is a well-known [Bea91] technique and works because

$$\begin{aligned}\llbracket z \rrbracket &= \llbracket c \rrbracket - \alpha \cdot \llbracket b \rrbracket - \beta \cdot \llbracket a \rrbracket + \alpha \cdot \beta \\ &= \llbracket ab \rrbracket - (x-a) \cdot \llbracket b \rrbracket - (y-b) \cdot \llbracket a \rrbracket + (x-a) \cdot (y-b) \\ &= \llbracket xy \rrbracket\end{aligned}$$

Squaring. We say that $(\llbracket b \rrbracket, \llbracket d \rrbracket)$ is a random square if b is random and $d = b^2$. To compute $\llbracket x^2 \rrbracket$ given $\llbracket x \rrbracket$ using a preprocessed $(\llbracket b \rrbracket, \llbracket d \rrbracket)$, the parties do the following:

1. The parties compute $\llbracket \alpha \rrbracket = \llbracket x \rrbracket - \llbracket b \rrbracket$.
2. The parties run $\mathsf{open}(\llbracket \alpha \rrbracket)$ to obtain α.
3. Each party computes $\llbracket z \rrbracket = \alpha \cdot (\llbracket x \rrbracket + \llbracket b \rrbracket) + \llbracket d \rrbracket$.

Note that the above holds since

$$\begin{aligned}\llbracket z \rrbracket = \alpha \cdot (\llbracket x \rrbracket + \llbracket b \rrbracket) + \llbracket d \rrbracket &= (x-b) \cdot (\llbracket x \rrbracket + \llbracket b \rrbracket) + \llbracket b^2 \rrbracket \\ &= \llbracket x^2 - b^2 + b^2 \rrbracket = \llbracket x^2 \rrbracket.\end{aligned}$$

The Protocol. The above building blocks can easily be combined to securely run $\mathtt{eval}(\cdot)$ on a circuit C: after the inputs are secret-shared using $\llbracket \cdot \rrbracket$, the parties apply G as defined in Sect. 2.1 consecutively to the shares. That is, addition gates and multiplication/addition by-a-public-constant gates are computed locally, whereas multiplication and square gates are computed using the above sub-protocols.

Security. For our purpose of using a MPC protocol to establish our zero-knowledge argument, the used protocol only needs to be secure in the presence of a semi-honest adversary. Furthermore, it suffices for the protocol to be secure in the client-server broadcast model, i.e., when the parties who run the protocol (the servers) do not hold input and do not see the final output, but rather receive shares of the inputs from the clients, perform the computation by only local computation as well as sending broadcast messages to each other, and then send the output shares back to the clients.

Formally, let $\mathcal{F}_{\mathtt{tr}}$ and $\mathcal{F}_{\mathtt{sq}}$ be ideal functionalities that provide the parties with random multiplication triples and squares. We define $\mathsf{view}_{I,\pi}^{\mathcal{F}_{\mathtt{tr}},\mathcal{F}_{\mathtt{sq}}}(C)$ to be the view of a subset of parties I during the execution of a protocol π on the circuit C, in the $(\mathcal{F}_{\mathtt{tr}}, \mathcal{F}_{\mathtt{sq}})$-hybrid model and in the client-server model. The view consists of the input shares, the correlated randomness they receive from the functionalities and the messages they obtain from the other parties while evaluating C. The security of π is stated in Theorem 1, which is proven in the full version.

Theorem 1. *Let C be an arithmetic circuit over the field $\mathbb{F}$ and let π be the protocol described above. Then, for every subset of parties $I \subset \{P_1, \ldots, P_N\}$ with $|I| \leq N-1$, there exists a probabilistic polynomial-time algorithm $\mathcal{S}$ such that $\{\mathcal{S}(I, C)\} \equiv \{\mathsf{view}_{I,\pi}^{\mathcal{F}_{\mathtt{tr}}, \mathcal{F}_{\mathtt{sq}}}(C)\}$.*

3.2 HVZKAoK Protocol Using Cut and Choose

We now explain our first HVZKAoK protocol $\Pi_{\mathsf{c\&c}}$, which is based on the MPC protocol from Sect. 3.1, and which relies on the cut–and–choose technique to generate correct random multiplication triples and squares. The formal description appears in the full version.

The idea behind the protocol is that the prover $\mathcal{P}$ proves its knowledge of $\mathbf{w}$ such that $C(\mathbf{w}) = \mathbf{y}$ by simulating a secure N-party computation of the circuit over an additive sharing of $\mathbf{w}$, using the MPC protocol described above. Since $\mathcal{P}$ knows the input and thus the values on each wire of the circuit, it can simulate the execution "in the head". Since our MPC protocol uses random triples and squares supplied by the ideal functionalities $\mathcal{F}_{\mathtt{tr}}$ and $\mathcal{F}_{\mathtt{sq}}$, the prover $\mathcal{P}$ needs to play their role as well. Clearly, $\mathcal{P}$ may try to cheat in the simulated computation, aiming to cause the verifier $\mathcal{V}$ to accept false statements. This is prevented by having $\mathcal{V}$ challenging $\mathcal{P}$ in two ways. First, after $\mathcal{P}$ has committed to M sets of random triples and squares, $\mathcal{V}$ randomly selects τ of them, which are then opened to it. The remaining $M - \tau$ sets of the pre-processed data are used to support $M - \tau$ circuit computations - each with different randomness. The prover $\mathcal{P}$ performs these computations and commits to the views of the parties, to be then challenged for the second time by $\mathcal{V}$. In this second challenge, the verifier chooses a random subset of $N-1$ parties in each execution, whose views are opened and tested for consistency. If these two tests pass successfully and the output of the circuit is $\mathbf{y}$, then $\mathcal{V}$ outputs acc. Observe that $\mathcal{V}$ cannot learn any information about the witness $\mathbf{w}$ during the protocol: the opened pre-processing executions reveal only random data which is thrown away afterwards, and the $N-1$ views that are opened do not reveal anything since the MPC protocol is resilient to $N-1$ semi-honest parties. In more details, in Round 1, $\mathcal{P}$ commits to M pre-processing executions. A major source of saving here is using pseudo-randomness instead of pure randomness. Specifically, $\mathcal{P}$ chooses a seed sd_e for each execution e, from which it derives the seeds $\mathsf{sd}_{e,i}$ for each party P_i. These seeds are used to generate all the random shares held by P_i throughout the computation. Now, if execution e is selected to be tested by $\mathcal{V}$ in Round 2, then $\mathcal{P}$ can just send sd_e to $\mathcal{V}$, thereby saving communication. For the $M - \tau$ preprocessings which are used in the on-line execution in Round 3, $\mathcal{P}$ cannot send the master seed but rather will have to send $N-1$ seeds of the $N-1$ parties chosen to be opened by $\mathcal{V}$ in Round 4. Thereby the data of one of the parties is kept secret. Observe, however, that not all the data held by the parties is random. In particular, when generating a multiplication triple $[\![a_{e,k}]\!], [\![b_{e,k}]\!], [\![c_{e,k}]\!]$ (e is the execution index and k is the index of the gate for which this triple is consumed), one can use the seeds of the parties to generate the sharing of $a_{e,k}$ and $b_{e,k}$, but once these are fixed, so is $c_{e,k} = a_{e,k} \cdot b_{e,k}$. Therefore, when generating the sharing of $c_{e,k}$, it is necessary to "fix" the initial sharing derived from the random seeds. To obtain this, the prover also commits to the offset $\Delta_{e,k}$ for each execution e and multiplication gate g_k, which is added to the initial random sharing $[\![c_{e,k}]\!]$. The same applies when generating random squares. Similarly, when the sharings of the inputs are generated in Round 3, $\mathcal{P}$ can use the seeds of the parties to derive their shares, and then adjust this initial sharing by adding the offset (denoted by $\phi_{e,k}$) to obtain a correct sharing of the given input. Thus, $\mathcal{P}$ must commit to the offset on each input wire as well. To further reduce communication, we hash all the commitments together and send only the hash value to $\mathcal{V}$.

Cheating Error (Soundness). We compute the probability that $\mathcal{V}$ outputs acc when $C(\mathbf{w}) \neq \mathbf{y}$. Let c be the number of pre-processing emulations where $\mathcal{P}$ cheats (i.e., by generating incorrect squares or multiplication triples). Since τ emulations out of M are opened and tested by the verifier, we have that this step is passed without the cheating being detected with probability $\frac{\binom{M-c}{\tau}}{\binom{M}{\tau}}$. After this step, $M-\tau$ circuit computations are being simulated by the prover. In order to make the output of the protocol be $\mathbf{y}$, $\mathcal{P}$ must cheat (i.e., deviate from the specification of the MPC protocol) in $M-\tau-c$ emulations. Since $N-1$ views are being opened in each such emulation, $\mathcal{P}$ clearly will not sabotage the view of more than one party. Thus, the probability that this is not detected is $\frac{1}{N^{M-\tau-c}}$. The overall success cheating probability is therefore

$$\xi_{\mathsf{c\&c}}(M, N, \tau) = \max_{0 \leq c \leq M-\tau} \left\{ \frac{\binom{M-c}{\tau}}{\binom{M}{\tau} \cdot N^{M-\tau-c}} \right\}$$

Formal Proof. As mentioned before, the above protocol has appeared already in [KKW18] (for Boolean circuits, but extending it to Arithmetic circuits is straightforward). However, there it was described as an optimization to their baseline protocol and so was not formally proven. In the full version we therefore provide a proof that the described protocol $\Pi_{\mathsf{c\&c}}$ is an honest verifier zero-knowledge argument of knowledge.

Theorem 2. *Let H be a collision-resistant hash function and let* com *be the Random Oracle-based commitment scheme. Then, the protocol $\Pi_{\mathsf{c\&c}}$ is an HVZKAoK with knowledge error (soundness) $\xi_{\mathsf{c\&c}}(M, N, \tau)$.*

3.3 HVZKAoK Protocol Using Imperfect Preprocessing and Sacrificing

We now present our second HVZKAoK protocol Π_{sac}. In this protocol, we rely on a method where one "sacrifices" random multiplication triples and squares in order to verify the correctness of multiplication and square operations. The idea of this protocol is that $\mathcal{P}$ does not simulate the execution of a protocol to *compute* multiplication and square gates, but rather simulates an execution of a protocol to *verify* that the shares on the output wires of these gates are correctly defined. This means that now $\mathcal{P}$ will first define and commit to sharings of the values on each wire of the circuit and then will simulate an execution of a verification protocol for multiplication and square gates (recall that for other gates the computation is local and thus no verification is required). We begin by describing the verification methods used in our protocol.

Verification of a Multiplication Triple Using Another. This procedure is reminiscent to the recent work of [LN17]. Given a random triple $([\![a]\!], [\![b]\!], [\![c]\!])$, it is possible to verify the correctness of a triple $([\![x]\!], [\![y]\!], [\![z]\!])$, i.e., that $z = x \cdot y$, without revealing any information on either of the triples, in the following way:

1. The parties generate a random $\epsilon \in \mathbb{F}$.
2. The parties locally set $[\![\alpha]\!] = \epsilon[\![x]\!] + [\![a]\!]$, $[\![\beta]\!] = [\![y]\!] + [\![b]\!]$.
3. The parties run $\mathsf{open}([\![\alpha]\!])$ and $\mathsf{open}([\![\beta]\!])$ to obtain α and β.
4. The parties locally set $[\![v]\!] = \epsilon[\![z]\!] - [\![c]\!] + \alpha \cdot [\![b]\!] + \beta \cdot [\![a]\!] - \alpha \cdot \beta$.
5. The parties run $\mathsf{open}([\![v]\!])$ to obtain v and accept iff $v = 0$.

Observe that if both triples are correct multiplication triples (i.e., $z = xy$ and $c = ab$) then the parties will always accept since

$$\begin{aligned} v &= \epsilon \cdot z - c + \alpha \cdot b + \beta \cdot a - \alpha \cdot \beta \\ &= \epsilon \cdot xy - ab + (\epsilon \cdot x + a)b + (y + b)a - (\epsilon \cdot x + a)(y + b) = 0 \end{aligned}$$

In contrast, if one (or both) of the triples are incorrect, then the parties will accept with probability at most $1/|\mathbb{F}|$ as shown in Lemma 1 whose proof appears in the full version.

Lemma 1. *If $([\![a]\!], [\![b]\!], [\![c]\!])$ or $([\![x]\!], [\![y]\!], [\![z]\!])$ is an incorrect multiplication triple then the parties output* acc *in the sub-protocol above with probability* $\frac{1}{|\mathbb{F}|}$.

Verification of a Square Pair Using Another. Similarly, one can use a random square $([\![b]\!], [\![d]\!])$ to verify the correctness of a given square $([\![x]\!], [\![z]\!])$ as follows:

1. The parties generate a random $\epsilon \in \mathbb{F}$.
2. The parties locally compute $[\![\alpha]\!] = [\![x]\!] - \epsilon[\![b]\!]$.
3. The parties run $\mathsf{open}([\![\alpha]\!])$ to obtain α.
4. Each party locally computes $[\![v]\!] = [\![z]\!] - \alpha \cdot ([\![x]\!] + \epsilon[\![b]\!]) - \epsilon^2[\![d]\!]$.
5. The parties run $\mathsf{open}([\![v]\!])$ to obtain v and accept iff $v = 0$.

As before, if the squares are correct, i.e., $z = x^2$ and $d = b^2$, then the parties will accept, since

$$\begin{aligned} v &= z - \alpha \cdot (x + \epsilon \cdot b) - \epsilon^2 \cdot d \\ &= x^2 - (x - \epsilon \cdot b) \cdot (x + \epsilon \cdot b) - \epsilon^2 \cdot b^2 \\ &= x^2 - x^2 + \epsilon^2 b^2 - \epsilon^2 b^2 = 0 \end{aligned}$$

In contrast, if one of the random squares (or both) is incorrect, then the parties will accept with probability $\frac{2}{|\mathbb{F}|}$. This is shown in Lemma 2, which is proven in the full version.

Lemma 2. *If* $([\![x]\!], [\![z]\!])$ *or* $([\![b]\!], [\![d]\!])$ *is an incorrect square, then the parties output* acc *in the above protocol with probability* $\frac{2}{|\mathbb{F}|}$.

The Protocol. Our AoK protocol is formally described in Figs. 1a and 1b. In this protocol, the prover $\mathcal{P}$ first commits in Round 1 to sharings of the values on each wire of the circuit and to sharings of random multiplication triples and squares for M independent executions. As in the previous protocol, we save communication by deriving all the random shares from a single seed. Then, in Round 2, $\mathcal{V}$ challenges $\mathcal{P}$ by choosing the randomness required for the verification procedure, i.e., an ϵ value for each multiplication and square gate. Upon receiving the challenge from $\mathcal{V}$, $\mathcal{P}$ simulates M executions of the verification protocol in Round 3 and commits to the view of the parties in each execution. Then, in Round 4, $\mathcal{V}$ picks its second challenge by choosing, for each execution, $N-1$ parties whose view will be opened and tested. In Round 5, $\mathcal{P}$ sends to $\mathcal{V}$ the seeds from which the randomness of the $N-1$ parties was derived and all the messages sent to these parties from the remaining party $P_{\bar{i}_e}$. As in $\Pi_{\mathsf{C\&C}}$, for values that are fixed, i.e., inputs, multiplications and squares, $\mathcal{P}$ sends also an offset (which was committed in the first round) to "fix" the sharing to the correct value. As before, we further reduce the communication cost by hashing the commitments together and sending only the hash value. Finally, $\mathcal{V}$ accepts if and only if all commitments are correct, the view of each party was computed correctly, the verification procedures conclude with the parties holding a sharing of 0 for each multiplication/square gate and the output of the circuit is $\mathbf{y}$.

Cheating Probability (Soundness). We compute the probability that $\mathcal{V}$ outputs acc when $C(\mathbf{w}) \neq \mathbf{y}$. Observe that all the M executions are independent of each other. When considering a single instance, $\mathcal{P}$ can cheat in either computing the view of one of the parties or cheat by changing the shares on the output wire of a multiplication/square gate. In the former case, it will succeed with probability $\frac{1}{N}$ whereas in the latter case it will succeed with probability $\frac{1}{|\mathbb{F}|}$ or $\frac{2}{|\mathbb{F}|}$ (note that if there are gates of both types in the circuit, it will be more beneficial for $\mathcal{P}$ to cheat in square gates since $\frac{2}{|\mathbb{F}|} > \frac{1}{|\mathbb{F}|}$). Furthermore, the best strategy for the prover is to first cheat in multiplication/square gates and then if it didn't receive the desired challenge that will cause the verification process to end successfully, it can manipulate one of the parties' view. Thus, if there are square gates in the circuit, then the overall cheating probability is

$$\xi_{\mathsf{sac}}(M, N) = \left(\frac{2}{|\mathbb{F}|} + \left(1 - \frac{2}{|\mathbb{F}|}\right) \cdot \frac{1}{N}\right)^M = \left(\frac{2N + |\mathbb{F}| - 2}{|\mathbb{F}| \cdot N}\right)^M.$$

Similarly, if there are multiplication gates in the circuit (and no square gates), then the cheating probability is

$$\xi_{\mathsf{sac}}(M, N) = \left(\frac{1}{|\mathbb{F}|} + \left(1 - \frac{1}{|\mathbb{F}|}\right) \cdot \frac{1}{N}\right)^M = \left(\frac{N + |\mathbb{F}| - 1}{|\mathbb{F}| \cdot N}\right)^M.$$

It can be seen that the impact of $|\mathbb{F}|$ on the cheating probability in practice is not important, as the $1/N$-term will dominate the expression since $N \ll |\mathbb{F}|$.

In the full version we will give the full proof of the following.

Theorem 3. *Let H be a collision-resistant hash function and let* com *be the Random Oracle-based commitment scheme. Then the protocol Π_{sac} is a HVZKAoK with knowledge error (soundness) $\xi_{\mathsf{sac}}(M, N)$.*

3.4 Optimizations

The following optimizations can directly be made to our protocols:

1. The prover is required to send $N-1$ seeds for each execution e that was not chosen to be opened. Each of these seeds is used to generate the randomness of one party throughout the execution. As in [KKW18], we can reduce the number of seeds that are sent from $N-1$ to $\log N$ by using a binary tree.
2. We can reduce communication by verifying the correctness of the circuit's output in a batched manner, i.e., take a random linear combination of all outputs, where the randomness is chosen (as an additional challenge) by $\mathcal{V}$. Then, only the shares of this linear combination result are sent to $\mathcal{V}$.
3. Each multiplication in Π_{sac} is being verified separately. In order to save communication it is possible to batch-verify of them by opening a random linear combination of all $[\![v]\!]$-sharings.

3.5 Computation and Communication Cost

By inspecting both Π_{sac} and $\Pi_{\mathsf{c\&c}}$ one sees that for each multiplication gate $O(M \cdot N)$ multiplications in $\mathbb{F}$ must be computed. In practice, their runtime dominates those of the additions in $\mathbb{F}$ which can be optimized by carrying out multiple $\mathbb{F}$-additions over the integers before applying a modular reduction. For large enough $\mathbb{F}$ we have that $\xi_{\mathsf{sac}}(M, N) \approx (1/N)^M$, and so for statistical security parameter κ we have $M \cdot \log N = \kappa$ which means that we will approximately have to perform $O(\kappa \cdot (N/\log N) \cdot |C|)$ multiplications both at proving and verification time, but only over the field over which C is actually defined.

Next, we estimate both the practical and asymptotic communication cost of the Π_{sac} protocol[3]. Denote by $|\mathsf{hash}|, |\mathsf{sd}|$ and $|\mathsf{com}|$ the length in bits of the hash values, seeds and commitments. The communication cost of messages sent from $\mathcal{P}$ to $\mathcal{V}$ in each round is: (i) **Round 1**: $|\mathsf{hash}|$; (ii) **Round 3**: $|\mathsf{hash}|$; and

[3] The analysis for $\Pi_{\mathsf{c\&c}}$ is described in the full version.

Let H be a CRHF and com be the Random Oracle-based commitment scheme.

Inputs: Both $\mathcal{P}$ and $\mathcal{V}$ hold $\mathbf{y} \in \mathbb{F}^{n_{\text{out}}}$, a description C over $\mathbb{F}$ and parameters M, N; $\mathcal{P}$ additionally holds $\mathbf{w} \in \mathbb{F}^{n_{\text{in}}}$ such that $C(\mathbf{w}) = \mathbf{y}$.

Round 1:

1. $\mathcal{P}$ chooses a salt $\texttt{salt} \leftarrow \mathbb{B}^{\lambda}$ and does the following for each $e \in [M]$:
(a) Initialize empty strings $\mathsf{st}_e, \{\mathsf{st}_{e,i}\}_{i\in[N]}$.
(b) Choose seeds $\mathsf{sd}_e, \{\mathsf{sd}_{e,i}\}_{i\in[N]}$ and set $\mathsf{st}_{e,i} \leftarrow \mathsf{sd}_{e,i}$ for $i \in [N]$.
(c) Prepare the pre-processing data:
   - For each multiplication gate $g_k \in \mathcal{G}$:
     i. For each $i \in [N]$, use $\mathsf{sd}_{e,i}$ to generate $a_{e,k,i}, b_{e,k,i}, c_{e,k,i}$. These shares define the random sharings $[\![a_{e,k}]\!], [\![b_{e,k}]\!]$ and $[\![c_{e,k}]\!]$, where $a_{e,k} = \sum_{i=1}^{N} a_{e,k,i}$, $b_{e,k} = \sum_{i=1}^{N} b_{e,k,i}$ and $c_{e,k} = \sum_{i=1}^{N} c_{e,k,i}$.
     ii. Set $\Delta_{e,k} = a_{e,k} \cdot b_{e,k} - c_{e,k}$ and $\mathsf{st}_e \leftarrow \mathsf{st}_e \parallel \Delta_{e,k}$.
     iii. Define the random triple for g_k to be $([\![a_{e,k}]\!], [\![b_{e,k}]\!], [\![c_{e,k}]\!] + \Delta_{e,k})$.
   - For each square gate $g_k \in \mathcal{G}$:
     i. For each $i \in [N]$ use $\mathsf{sd}_{e,i}$ to generate $b_{e,k,i}$ and $d_{e,k,i}$. These shares define the random sharings $[\![b_{e,k}]\!]$ and $[\![d_{e,k}]\!]$, where $b_{e,k} = \sum_{i=1}^{N} b_{e,k,i}$ and $d_{e,k} = \sum_{i=1}^{N} d_{e,k,i}$.
     ii. Set $\Delta_{e,k} = (b_{e,k})^2 - d_{e,k}$ and $\mathsf{st}_e \leftarrow \mathsf{st}_e \parallel \Delta_{e,k}$.
     iii. Define the random square for g_k to be $([\![b_{e,k}]\!], [\![d_{e,k}]\!] + \Delta_{e,k})$.
(d) Choose a random sharing of the inputs:
   i. For each $i \in [N]$, use $\mathsf{sd}_{e,i}$ to generate $w_{e,1,i}, \ldots, w_{e,n_{\text{in}},i}$. These shares define the random sharings $[\![w_{e,1}]\!], \ldots, [\![w_{e,n_{\text{in}}}]\!]$, where $w_{e,k} = \sum_{i=1}^{N} w_{e,k,i}$.
   ii. For each input wire $k \in \mathcal{I}$ set $\phi_{e,k} = w_k - \sum_{i=1}^{N-1} w_{e,k,i}$ and $\mathsf{st}_e \leftarrow \mathsf{st}_e \parallel \phi_{e,k}$. The sharing on this wire then is $[\![w_{e,k}]\!] + \phi_{e,k}$.
(e) Simulate the computation of C gate-by-gate in topological order:
   - For each linear gate, compute the parties' output shares via the local operation described in Section 3.1.
   - For each multiplication gate $g_k \in \mathcal{G}$ with $[\![x_k]\!], [\![y_k]\!]$ as inputs:
     i. For each $i \in [N]$, use $\mathsf{sd}_{e,i}$ to generate $z_{e,k,i}$ which define the random sharing $[\![z_{e,k}]\!]$ where $z_{e,k} = \sum_{i=1}^{N} z_{e,k,i}$.
     ii. Set: $\varphi_{e,k} = x_k \cdot y_k - \sum_{i=1}^{N} z_{e,k,i}$ and $\mathsf{st}_e \leftarrow \mathsf{st}_e \parallel \varphi_{e,k}$. The sharing on the output wire is defined to be $[\![z_{e,k}]\!] + \varphi_{e,k}$.
   - For each square gate $g_k \in \mathcal{G}$ with sharing $[\![x_k]\!]$ on its input wire:
     i. For each $i \in [N]$ use $\mathsf{sd}_{e,i}$ to generate $z_{e,k,i}$. These shares define the random sharing $[\![z_{e,k}]\!]$ where $z_{e,k} = \sum_{i=1}^{N} z_{e,k,i}$.
     ii. Set: $\varphi_{e,k} = (x_k)^2 - \sum_{i=1}^{N} z_{e,k,i}$ and $\mathsf{st}_e \leftarrow \mathsf{st}_e \parallel \varphi_{e,k}$. The sharing on the output wire is defined to be $[\![z_{e,k}]\!] + \varphi_{e,k}$.
(f) Use sd_e to generate $r_e \in \mathbb{B}^{\lambda}$ and compute $\Gamma_e = \texttt{com}(\mathsf{st}_e, r_e, \texttt{salt})$.
(g) For each $i \in [N]$ use $\mathsf{sd}_{e,i}$ to generate $r_{e,i} \in \mathbb{B}^{\lambda}$ and then compute $\Gamma_{e,i} = \texttt{com}(\mathsf{st}_{e,i}, r_{e,i}, \texttt{salt})$. Then set $h_e = H(\Gamma_e \parallel \Gamma_{e,1} \parallel \cdots \parallel \Gamma_{e,N})$.
2. Compute $h_\Gamma = H(h_1 \parallel \cdots \parallel h_M)$ and send it to $\mathcal{V}$.

Fig. 1a. The "Sacrificing" based argument Π_{sac} (Part 1)

Round 2: $\mathcal{V}$ chooses sd_ι and for each $e \in [M]$ uses sd_ι to generate random coefficients $\epsilon_{e,k}$ for each multiplication/square gate g_k. $\mathcal{V}$ then sends sd_ι to $\mathcal{P}$.

Round 3: $\mathcal{P}$ performs the following steps:

1. Choose a random seed sd_E. Use sd_ι to generate random $\epsilon_{e,k}$ as $\mathcal{V}$ would do.
2. For each $e \in [M]$:
   (a) Initialize an empty string view_e.
   (b) For each multiplication gate g_k (in topological order) simulate the verification procedure described in the text using $\epsilon_{e,k}$. In addition, set: $\mathsf{view}_e \leftarrow \mathsf{view}_e \parallel \alpha_{e,k,1} \parallel \cdots \parallel \alpha_{e,k,N} \parallel \beta_{e,k,1} \parallel \cdots \parallel \beta_{e,k,N}$.
   (c) For each square gate g_k (in topological order) simulate the verification procedure described in the text using $\epsilon_{e,k}$. In addition, sets $\mathsf{view}_e \leftarrow \mathsf{view}_e \parallel \alpha_{e,k,1} \parallel \cdots \parallel \alpha_{e,k,N}$.
   (d) Let $v_{e,k,i}$ be the sharing held by party P_i at the end of the verification procedure of gate g_k. Then, for each $i \in [N]$ set: $\mathsf{view}_e \leftarrow \mathsf{view}_e \parallel v_{e,k,1} \parallel \cdots \parallel v_{e,k,N}$.
   (e) Let $o_{e,1,i}, \ldots, o_{e,n_{\text{out}},i}$ be the shares on the output wires of C held by P_i. Then, for output wire $k \in \mathcal{O}$ set: $\mathsf{view}_e \leftarrow \mathsf{view}_e \parallel o_{e,k,1} \parallel \cdots \parallel o_{e,k,N}$.
3. Generate $g_e \in \{0,1\}^\lambda$ from sd_E and set $\Pi_e = \mathtt{com}(\mathsf{view}_e, g_e, \mathtt{salt})$.
4. Compute $h_\pi = H(\Pi_1 \parallel \cdots \parallel \Pi_M)$ and send it to $\mathcal{V}$.

Round 4: For each $e \in [M]$: $\mathcal{V}$ sends a random $\bar{i}_e \in [N]$ to $\mathcal{P}$.

Round 5: For each $e \in [M]$:
Let $I_e = [N] \setminus \{\bar{i}_e\}$. Then, $\mathcal{P}$ sends the following to $\mathcal{V}$: $\mathtt{salt}$, sd_E, sd_e, $\{\mathsf{sd}_{e,i}\}_{i \in I_e}$, $\Gamma_{e,\bar{i}_e}$, $\{\phi_{e,k}\}_{k=1}^{n_{\text{in}}}$, the tuple $(\Delta_{e,k}, \varphi_{e,k}, \alpha_{e,k,\bar{i}_e}, \beta_{e,k,\bar{i}_e}, v_{e,k,\bar{i}_e})$ for each multiplication or square gate g_k, and $o_{e,1,\bar{i}_e}, \ldots, o_{e,n_{\text{out}},\bar{i}_e}$.

Output: $\mathcal{V}$ outputs acc iff all the following checks succeed:

1. For each $e \in [M]$, $\mathcal{V}$ uses $\{\mathsf{sd}_{e,i}\}_{i \in I_e}$ and the tuple received for each multiplication and square gate to compute the shares of the parties in I_e on each wire and their shares of each random triple and square. Then, it uses sd_e to compute Γ_e and uses $\{\mathsf{sd}_{e,i}\}_{i \in I_e}$ to compute $\{\Gamma_{e,i}\}_{i \in I_e}$ as an honest prover would do. Then, using $\Gamma_{e,\bar{i}_e}$ received from $\mathcal{P}$, the verifier $\mathcal{V}$ computes h_e.
   Then, $\mathcal{V}$ checks that $h_\Gamma = H(h_1 \parallel \cdots \parallel h_M)$.
2. For each $e \in [M]$, $\mathcal{V}$ computes view_e by going gate-by-gate in topological order and simulating the verification procedure using the tuple received from $\mathcal{P}$ for each multiplication and square gate, and using $\{o_{e,k,\bar{i}_e}\}_{k=1}^{n_{\text{out}}}$. Then, it computes Π_e as a honest prover would do. Finally, $\mathcal{V}$ checks that $h_\pi = H(\Pi_1 \parallel \cdots \parallel \Pi_M)$.
3. For each $e \in [M]$ and multiplication/square gate g_k, $\mathcal{V}$ checks if $\sum_{i=1}^N v_{e,k,i} = 0$.
4. For each $e \in [M]$, for each $k \in \mathcal{O}$, $\mathcal{V}$ checks that $\sum_{i=1}^N o_{e,k,i} = y_k$.

Fig. 1b. The "Sacrificing" based argument Π_{sac} (Part 2)

(iii) **Round 5**: $|\mathsf{sd}| + M \cdot (|\mathsf{sd}| + \log N \cdot |\mathsf{sd}| + |\mathtt{com}| + 4\log_2(|\mathbb{F}|) \cdot n_{mul} + 3\log_2(|\mathbb{F}|) \cdot n_{sq} + \log_2(|\mathbb{F}|) + \log_2(|\mathbb{F}|) \cdot n_{\mathtt{in}} + \log_2(|\mathbb{F}|)$.

Let $\mathsf{base}(\mathsf{hash}, \mathsf{sd}, \mathsf{com}, M, N) = 2 \cdot |\mathsf{hash}| + |\mathsf{sd}| \cdot (2 + M \log N) + |\mathsf{com}| \cdot M$ for which we only write base when the context is clear. We obtain that the overall amount of bits sent from $\mathcal{P}$'s side is $\mathsf{base} + \log_2(|\mathbb{F}|) \cdot M(4n_{mul} + 3n_{sq} + n_{\mathtt{in}} + 2)$.

Asymptotically, by setting $|\mathsf{hash}| = |\mathsf{sd}| = |\mathtt{com}| = O(\lambda)$, $\log_2(|\mathbb{F}|) = O(\log(\lambda))$ and M, N as above we get that the communication cost of $\mathcal{P}$ is $O(\log(\lambda) \cdot \kappa \cdot (|C|/\log(N)))$.

4 Sampling Circuits on the Fly

At the end of the previous section we briefly mentioned an optimization where $\mathcal{V}$ checks output correctness by looking only at a linear combination of the outputs instead of checking each output separately. In particular, this is done by having $\mathcal{V}$ choosing random coefficients which will be used to compute the linear combination *after* $\mathcal{P}$ fixes the inputs and (correlated) randomness of the simulated parties. This process can also be viewed as an interaction where the parties determine the final circuit's structure during the execution, as here the challenge chosen by $\mathcal{V}$ adds a layer on top of the initial circuit which consists of 'multiplication-by-a-constant' and addition gates. This idea, which we call "sampling the circuit on the fly" will be also used in some of the optimizations suggested for the application presented in Sect. 5. We therefore now formally establish this idea, so that security of optimizations of this kind can be derived easily without the need to re-prove security of the whole ZKAoK each time.

Although in the above example only $\mathcal{V}$ chooses the circuit that will be evaluated, we consider a broader definition where both $\mathcal{P}, \mathcal{V}$ sample the circuit together. The sampling process must begin only after $\mathcal{P}$ has committed and fixed the witness and randomness that will be used. This means that from this point on any form of cheating is possible only during the simulation of the MPC protocol to compute the sampled circuit, as the witness cannot be tailored anymore to the actually chosen circuit. We remark that although the circuit will be jointly sampled by both parties, we restrict the sampling done by $\mathcal{V}$ to be independent of the messages of $\mathcal{P}$ and to not require him to keep a secret state so that the overall protocol stays public-coin. $\mathcal{P}$, in contrast, will be allowed to make his choice depending on the witness that it committed or on other messages. At the same time, the choice of $\mathcal{P}$ should neither allow him to break the soundness nor the zero-knowledge property.

In this section, we first provide a formal definition for the notion of circuit sampling. Then, we show how to incorporate it into our argument system and finally explain (as an example) how the output linear combination optimization described above is an instantiation of the general notion and how it fits into the framework. We want to mention that, independently, Badetscher et al. [BJM19] introduced a similar concept but in an unrelated context.

4.1 Definition of Circuit Sampling

First, we define the notion of circuit sampling for an NP relation.

Definition 3. (R-circuit Sampler). *Let R be an NP relation and $S_\mathcal{P}, S_\mathcal{V}$ be two non-empty sets that can be described with a string of polynomial length (in the security parameter λ). We say that* $\mathsf{Sample} = (\mathsf{ExtWitness}, \mathsf{Response}, \mathsf{SampCircuit})$ *is an R-circuit sampler for $(x, w) \in R$ if*

$\mathsf{ExtWitness}$ *is a PPT algorithm which on input* (x, w) *outputs an extended witness* $\widehat{w}$.
$\mathsf{Response}$ *is a PPT algorithm which on input* $(x, w, \widehat{w}, \tau_{\mathcal{V}})$ *outputs* $\tau_{\mathcal{P}}$.
$\mathsf{SampCircuit}$ *is a deterministic polynomial-time algorithm which on input* $(x, \tau_{\mathcal{V}}, \tau_{\mathcal{P}})$ *outputs a circuit* C *as well as a description of a set* Y.

Furthermore, we require that membership in Y can be decided in polynomial time. We next define a security game which follows the way we embed these algorithms into our protocols. Consider the following game, which we denote by $\mathsf{Game}_{R,\mathcal{P}}((x, w), S_{\mathcal{P}}, S_{\mathcal{V}}, \lambda)$, executed with $\mathcal{P}$:

1. $\mathcal{P}$ outputs $\widehat{w}$.
2. Choose a random $\tau_{\mathcal{V}} \leftarrow S_{\mathcal{V}}$ and hand it to $\mathcal{P}$.
3. $\mathcal{P}$ outputs $\tau_{\mathcal{P}} \in S_{\mathcal{P}}$.
4. Compute $(C, Y) \leftarrow \mathsf{SampCircuit}(x, \tau_{\mathcal{P}}, \tau_{\mathcal{V}})$.
5. Output 1 iff $C(\widehat{w}) \in Y$.

To understand the game, observe that Step 1 emulates the commitment to the witness, made by $\mathcal{P}$ in the first step of our protocols, in Step 2 a challenge is chosen which is followed by the configuration chosen by $\mathcal{P}$ in Step 3. Once all the input for $\mathsf{SampCircuit}$ is gathered, (C, Y) are being determined, and $\mathcal{P}$ wins if computing the circuit C on $\widehat{w}$ yields a valid output. In the above definition there is no validation ensuring that $\tau_{\mathcal{P}}$ used in the game is valid. This can be done by $\mathsf{SampCircuit}$ outputting $Y = \emptyset$ for an *invalid* $\tau_{\mathcal{P}}$.

We have three requirements from the circuit sampler. First, an obvious requirement is that if $\mathcal{P}$ uses the correct w and chooses $\tau_{\mathcal{P}}$ honestly, then the output of the game should be 1 (except for a negligible probability).

Definition 4. (Correct R-circuit Sampler). *Let* Sample *be an* R*-circuit sampler. If when* $\mathcal{P}$ *on input* $(x, w) \in R$ *computes* $\widehat{w} \leftarrow \mathsf{ExtWitness}(x, w)$ *and* $\tau_{\mathcal{P}} \leftarrow \mathsf{Response}(x, w, \widehat{w}, \tau_{\mathcal{V}})$, *with probability negligibly close to 1 it holds that* $\mathsf{Game}_{R,\mathcal{P}}((x, w), S_{\mathcal{P}}, S_{\mathcal{V}}, \lambda) = 1$ *then we say that* Sample *is* $\mathsf{correct}$.

We furthermore require soundness. Similarly to the standard definition of it, here if $\mathcal{P}$ wins in the above game with probability $> \alpha$, then a correct witness for R can be extracted.

Definition 5. (α-sound R-circuit Sampler). *Let* Sample *be an* R*-circuit sampler. If given* $\Pr[\mathsf{Game}_{R,\mathcal{P}}((x, w), S_{\mathcal{P}}, S_{\mathcal{V}}, \lambda) = 1] > \alpha$ *(where the distribution is over* $\tau_{\mathcal{V}} \in S_{\mathcal{V}}$*), there exists a deterministic polynomial-time extractor* $\mathcal{E}(\widehat{w})$ *which outputs* $(x, w') \in R$ *then we say that* Sample *is* α*-sound.*

The definition may look similar to knowledge soundness as defined in Sect. 2.2, but there are crucial differences: $\mathcal{E}$ runs on $\widehat{w}$ in polynomial time and with probability 1. This is because extracting some w' from $\widehat{w}$ is an "easy" task (as we will see in all our circuit sampling uses) and so the only question is whether w' is valid for R or not. The definition thus says that if $\mathcal{P}$ wins with probability higher than α, then it must have used the correct witness w to compute $\widehat{w}$ which can be obtained.

Finally, we also need to ensure that the additional interaction does not leak any information about w. This is formalized in the standard way of requiring the existence of a simulator who can output an indistinguishable transcript without knowing w. Clearly, the message $\tau_{\mathcal{P}}$ should not reveal any information about $\widehat{w}$ to an outsider. However, we additionally need simulatability of $C(\widehat{w})$: the sampled circuit may enforce the relation R in different ways than a static circuit would do, which could potentially leak information.

Definition 6. (Simulatable R-circuit Sampler). *Let $(x, w) \in R$ and* Sample *be an R-circuit sampler. Then we say that* Sample *is simulatable if there exists a PPT algorithm $\mathcal{S}$ such that*

$$\{(\tau_{\mathcal{P}}, C(\widehat{w})) \leftarrow \mathcal{P}(x, w, \tau_{\mathcal{V}})\} \approx_s \{(\tau_{\mathcal{P}}, C(\widehat{w})) \leftarrow \mathcal{S}(x, \tau_{\mathcal{V}})\}$$

where $\mathcal{P}$ acts honestly as in Definition 4.

4.2 Circuit Sampling and Our ZKAoK

We now include the above approach into our second protocol Π_{sac}. The modified protocol $\Pi_{\mathsf{sac}}^{\mathrm{samp}}$ works as follows, where we highlight the additional steps:

Round 1: For each $e \in [M]$ (i.e. each MPC instance), $\mathcal{P}$ computes $\widehat{w}_e \leftarrow \mathsf{ExtWitness}(x, w)$. Then, it chooses the randomness used for the execution e (i.e., the seeds used to derive all randomness as well as the salt). Finally, $\mathcal{P}$ commits to the extended witness and the randomness and sends it to $\mathcal{V}$.

Round 2: For each $e \in [M]$, $\mathcal{V}$ samples $\tau_{\mathcal{V},e}$ as in Step 2 of the above game. It then sends $\tau_{\mathcal{V},1}, \ldots, \tau_{\mathcal{V},M}$ to $\mathcal{P}$.

Round 3: $\mathcal{P}$ locally computes $\tau_{\mathcal{P},e} \leftarrow \mathsf{Response}(x, w, \widehat{w}_e, \tau_{\mathcal{V},e})$ for each $e \in [M]$ as well as $(C_e, Y_e) \leftarrow \mathsf{SampCircuit}(x, \tau_{\mathcal{P},e}, \tau_{\mathcal{V},e})$. It uses C_e in MPC protocol instance e and sends the remaining first round messages together with $\tau_{\mathcal{P},e}$ to $\mathcal{V}$.

Round 4–Round 7: Run rounds 2–5 as in the regular protocol.

Output: Upon receiving the last message, for each $e \in [M]$ $\mathcal{V}$ recomputes $(C_e, Y_e) \leftarrow \mathsf{SampCircuit}(x, \tau_{\mathcal{P},e}, \tau_{\mathcal{V},e})$, verifies the MPC transcripts for the individual C_e and then tests that each output lies in Y_e.

The following Lemma, whose proof appears in the full version, shows that $\Pi_{\mathsf{sac}}^{\mathrm{samp}}$ is an HVZKAoK.

Lemma 3. *Let* Sample *be a correct, α-sound and simulatable R-circuit sampler for the NP-relation R. Then Π_{sac}^{samp} is a statistically complete HVZKAoK for R with knowledge error $(\alpha + (1 - \alpha) \cdot \xi_{sac}(1, N))^M$.*

To prove the lemma, the main change compared to the proof of Π_{sac} is that here the circuits are not identical throughout all instances. Fortunately, it turns out that this assumption can be relaxed without hurting the runtime of the extractor $\mathcal{E}$. Completeness and the zero-knowledge property, on the other hand, follow directly from the original proof.

Impact on the Argument Size and Runtime. As one can see from the above description, adding Circuit Sampling to the protocol Π_{sac} adds another two rounds of communication. In terms of argument size, we essentially split **Round 1** into two different parts and make two commitments instead of one which commit to preprocessed data and evaluation, but now separately. The extra cost is to send two extra commitments (thus $\mathtt{base}$ increases by $2 \cdot |\mathtt{com}|$), which is negligible in comparison to the rest of the argument.

Furthermore, it is possible to cut away the extra two rounds of communication by running the simulation C in **Round 3** only, at the expense of introducing more communication. This can be done by switching from the verification-based approach of Π_{sac} to the standard forward circuit evaluation of π where we check the triples/squares while we use them, which is possible because now evaluation is fully deterministic. This allows to perform evaluation and checking in one round in parallel. We leave a detailed analysis as future work.

4.3 Output Correctness as a Circuit Sampler

We now revisit the (briefly sketched) idea of output compression in the context of circuit sampling. Here $\mathcal{V}$ chooses random coefficients that are used to compute the linear combination of the outputs, so that only one value is eventually opened by the resulting circuit instead of $n_{\mathtt{out}}$.

We first define the three algorithms of the circuit sampler for this optimization: $\mathsf{ExtWitness}$ receives $((C, \mathbf{y}), \mathbf{w})$ as an input and returns the extended witness $\widehat{w}$, which in this case is just $\mathbf{w}$. $\mathsf{Response}$ receives as an input the tuple $((C, \mathbf{y}), \mathbf{w}, \widehat{w}, \tau_{\mathcal{V}})$, but note that in this optimization, the verifier's challenge $\tau_{\mathcal{V}}$ fully defines the circuit and thus the output of $\mathsf{Response}$ is just 1. Finally, $\mathsf{SampCircuit}$ receives $((C, \mathbf{y}), \tau_{\mathcal{V}}, \tau_{\mathcal{P}})$ as its input and returns the circuit C' and the set Y defined in the following way: The circuit C' consists of the original circuit C and the following layers which are added on top of it: (i) subtraction gates for subtracting each value on an output wire $\mathbf{y}'[k]$ by the expected public value $\mathbf{y}[k]$; (ii) 'multiplication-by-a-constant' gates for each result of the previous layer, where the constants are defined by $\tau_{\mathcal{V}}$; and (iii) addition gates for summing the results of the previous layer. The set Y consists of one value only. We summarize the construction in Fig. 2.

The three algorithms defined above satisfy the properties of the Circuit Sampler. Correctness is straightforward. Soundness of the sampler is $\frac{1}{|\mathbb{F}|}$, since if w is incorrect, then $C(w) \in Y$ with probability $\frac{1}{|\mathbb{F}|}$ because the random coefficients are uniform (see Lemma 1). Simulation follows since both $\tau_{\mathcal{P}}$ and Y are fixed.

Let $C = (n_{\mathsf{in}}, n_{\mathsf{out}}, n_C, L, R, F)$ be a circuit over $\mathbb{F}$.

ExtWitness: On input $(x = (C, \mathbf{y}), \mathbf{w})) \in R$ set $\widehat{w} := \mathbf{w}$.

SampCircuit: On input $\tau_{\mathcal{V}} = (\gamma) \in \mathbb{F}^{n_{\mathsf{out}}}$ output the circuit C' doing the following:
1. Compute $\mathbf{y}' = C(\widehat{w})$ where $\mathbf{y}' \in \mathbb{F}^{n_{\mathsf{out}}}$ and $y_1 = \sum_{i=1}^{n_{\mathsf{out}}} \gamma[i] \cdot (\mathbf{y}'[i] - \mathbf{y}[i])$.
2. Output y_1.

Furthermore output the set $Y = \{(0)\}$.

Response: Output 1.

Fig. 2. Batching the output check as a circuit sampler.

5 Proving Knowledge of SIS Instances

The protocols from Sect. 3 are *asymptotically* less communication-efficient than previous argument systems such as [AHIV17,BBC+18] as can be seen in the analysis. However, they have advantages when the circuit size is not too big or when there are many linear gates in the circuit, because the communication is dominated by the number of non-linear operations in the circuit C and has very small circuit-independent cost. In this section, we exploit this fact to implement communication-efficient arguments of knowledge for different versions of the so-called Short-Integer Solution (SIS) problem.

The section is organized as follows. We begin by presenting an interactive argument for binary secrets which does not allow any slack, which is the same as in [BD10]. The approach can be simply generalized to secrets from a larger interval, but only at the expense of vastly increasing the communication. Then, we introduce some optimizations that allow us to reduce the communication for the suggested arguments and then further squeeze down their size by introducing a slack factor. Throughout the section, for each approach that we present, we will mention what is the resulting size of the argument, based on the analysis of $\Pi_{\mathsf{sac}}^{\mathrm{samp}}$ (which is the same as that of Π_{sac}).

5.1 The Baseline Proof for SIS

We start by presenting an argument for the Binary SIS problem as introduced in Sect. 2.4. The reason behind that is because general range proofs are hard using a circuit over $\mathbb{F} = \mathbb{F}_q$ whereas they are very simple for binary values. Moreover, the protocol we design for this problem will serve as a starting point for constructions supporting secrets from larger intervals.

There are two main tasks that the protocol has to achieve, which is to show that the secret $\mathbf{s}$ is a binary vector and the correctness of the product $\mathbf{t} = \mathbf{A}\mathbf{s}$. The matrix multiplication uses a publicly known matrix, and since linear operations are free in our used MPC scheme computing $\mathbf{t}$ can be done without increasing the proof size. What remains to show is that the witness consists of bits. This test is easy to perform because $\mathbf{s}[i] \in \{0, 1\}$ is equivalent to $\mathbf{s}[i]^2 - \mathbf{s}[i] = 0$. We can therefore let the circuit C compute the square of each element of $\mathbf{s}$ and then perform a linear test. The obtained circuit is described in Fig. 3.

Witness: $\mathbf{w} = (\mathbf{s}[1], \ldots, \mathbf{s}[m]) \in \mathbb{F}^m$

Computation:

1. $\forall i \in [m]$ compute $r_i \leftarrow \mathbf{s}[i]^2$
2. $\forall j \in [n]$ compute $y_j \leftarrow \sum_{i \in [m]} a_{j,i}\mathbf{s}[i]$
3. $\forall i \in [m]$ compute $y_{i+n} \leftarrow r_i - \mathbf{s}[i]$

Output: $\hat{\mathbf{y}} \leftarrow (y_1, \ldots, y_{m+n})$

Fig. 3. A circuit representation of $R^{m,n,q}_{\mathsf{B-SIS}}$; The circuit contains m square gates, has m inputs and $m + n$ outputs.

For ease of notation we let $a_{i,j} \in \mathbb{F}$ be the element in the ith row and the jth column of $\mathbf{A}$. The circuit can be evaluated using one of the protocols from Sect. 3, with $\mathcal{V}$ testing that the circuit's output $\hat{\mathbf{y}}$ equals $(\mathbf{t}[1], \ldots, \mathbf{t}[n], 0, \cdots, 0)$. This yields a highly efficient protocol, as there are only m non-linear gates in the circuit that require communication, and all of them are square gates. Using the cost analysis from Sect. 3.5, we conclude that the total communication by $\mathcal{P}$ is $\mathtt{base} + \log q \cdot M(4m + 2)$ bits. It is immediate to extend the construction from Fig. 3 to full SIS instances (which we do in the full version) by taking the *bit-decomposition* of each input. There we show that, for secrets $\mathbf{s}$ of ∞-norm $\leq \beta$ we will have to expand the witness to contain $(\lfloor \log_2(\beta) \rfloor + 2) \cdot m$ elements and we furthermore have to evaluate as many square gates. $\mathcal{P}$ then sends $\mathtt{base} + \log q \cdot M(4m \cdot (\lfloor \log_2(\beta) \rfloor + 2) + 2)$ bits in the argument.

5.2 Amortizing Bit Tests

We now discuss an optimization which aims at reducing the argument size for the Binary SIS problem by reducing the number of non-linear gates in the circuit. Recall that in Fig. 3, we defined a circuit for this problem that has m square gates. Each of the gates was used to verify that one of m inputs is a bit. We now show how the number of square gates can be reduced to 1, at the cost of adding elements to the witness. This reduces the overall communication since adding an element to the witness increases the size of the argument per MPC instance by one field element, whereas evaluating a square gate requires sending at least two field elements (secret-shared random square, messages during evaluation of the gate etc.). The optimization uses circuit sampling where only $\mathcal{V}$ has a challenge and so only $\mathcal{V}$ is actually sampling the circuit alone.

Assume that we want to check if m input sharings $\mathbf{s}[1], \ldots, \mathbf{s}[m]$ indeed are bits, and let $|\mathbb{F}| \gg 2m$. We can implicitly define the polynomial $D(X) \in \mathbb{F}[X]$ of degree at most $m - 1$ such that $\forall i \in [m] : \; D(i) = \mathbf{s}[i]$. Furthermore, we know that there exists a polynomial $B(X) = D(X) \cdot D(X)$ of degree at most $2m - 2$ such that $\forall i \in \mathbb{F} : \; D(i)^2 = B(i)$. We thus can say that $\forall i \in [m] : \; \mathbf{s}[i] \in \mathbb{B}$ if and only if $\forall i \in [m] : \; B(i) = D(i)$.

This allows us to construct a new circuit-sampling procedure. Instead of testing all $\mathbf{s}[i]$ separately for being bits, we let the prover $\mathcal{P}$ secret-share the predetermined $B(X)$ as part of the witness. Here, by our above observation that $\forall i \in [m] : B(i) = D(i)$ it is only necessary to share the points $B(m+1), \ldots, B(2m-1)$ (in addition to sharing all $\mathbf{s}[i]$). Then, using the fact that Lagrange-interpolation requires only linear operations (so it is entirely local in the underlying MPC scheme) we let $\mathcal{V}$ send a challenge $x \in \mathbb{F}$ that is the point at which we will evaluate D, B and test that $B(x) - D(x)^2 = 0$. By the Schwartz-Zippel-Lemma, we then must have identity of $D(X)^2$ and $B(X)$ except with probability $\frac{2m-2}{|\mathbb{F}|}$. In the full version we formalize the above intuition which we show yields a circuit sampler:

Theorem 4. *The aforementioned approach yields a perfectly correct, $\frac{2m-2}{|\mathbb{F}|}$-sound and perfectly simulatable circuit sampler for the relation $R^{m,n,q}_{\mathtt{B-SIS}}$.*

Applying this optimization and using $\Pi^{\mathrm{samp}}_{\mathsf{sac}}$, we obtain that the total communication is $\mathtt{base} + \log q \cdot M(2m+4)$ bits which is approximately $\log q \cdot M(3m)$ bits smaller than the baseline approach.

5.3 Trading Argument Size for Slack

So far we have considered only arguments for SIS-instances where the gap between the norm of correct witnesses and the norm that the argument guarantees is small: if we start with $((\mathbf{A}, \mathbf{y}), \mathbf{s}) \in R^{m,n,q,\beta}_{\mathsf{SIS}}$ (i.e., $||\mathbf{s}||_\infty \leq \beta$) then the soundness guarantee is that a witness $\mathbf{s}'$ with $((\mathbf{A}, \mathbf{y}), \mathbf{s}') \in R^{m,n,q,\omega\beta}_{\mathsf{SIS}}$ could be extracted (i.e., $||\mathbf{s}||_\infty \leq \omega\beta$) where ω is a small constant. However, the argument size depends on $M \cdot m \cdot \log_2(q) \cdot \log_2(\beta)$ as we have to perform non-linear computations for the bit-decomposition of each input $\mathbf{s}[i]$. The goal of this subsection is to give an *approximate* argument of size for the $\mathbf{s}[i]$ without having to resort to bit-decomposition for each $\mathbf{s}[i]$. This would allow for a smaller number of square- or multiplication-gates as well as a more compact witness. On the other hand, the arguments will have a larger slack ω which will now also depend on the number of inputs m.

To achieve a more compact argument, we will ask the prover to show that random linear combinations of elements from $\mathbf{s}$ are small. For this we use a Lemma from [BL17] who showed that random linear combinations mod q of elements from $\mathbf{s}$ are with certain probability not much smaller than $||\mathbf{s}||_\infty$:

Lemma 4. *For all $\mathbf{s} \in \mathbb{F}_q^k$ it holds that*

$$\Pr_{\mathbf{c} \leftarrow \mathbb{B}^k}\left[|\langle \mathbf{c}, \mathbf{s}\rangle| < \frac{||\mathbf{s}||_\infty}{2}\right] \leq \frac{1}{2} \quad \& \quad \Pr_{\mathbf{C} \leftarrow \mathbb{B}^{\ell \times k}}\left[||\mathbf{C} \cdot \mathbf{s}||_\infty < \frac{||\mathbf{s}||_\infty}{2}\right] \leq 2^{-\ell}.$$

Proof. See [BL17, Lemma 2.3 & Corollary 2.4].

The above Lemma only talks about the chance of detecting a vector of high norm by seeing *one* large element in the result of the product with a random binary matrix. In the full version we extend it to the case where we always see that lots such large elements in the product $\mathbf{C} \cdot \mathbf{s}$. This is summed up as follows:

Corollary 1. *Let* $\kappa, r \in \mathbb{N}^+, \mathbf{s} \in \mathbb{F}_q^k, \beta = ||\mathbf{s}||_\infty$ *and define* $S_\kappa^\beta = \{\mathbf{h} \in \mathbb{F}_q^{r\cdot\kappa} \mid \exists T \subseteq [r\cdot\kappa] \wedge |T| > \kappa \wedge \forall i \in T: \ |\mathbf{h}[i]| \geq \frac{1}{2}\cdot\beta\}$. *If* $r \geq 5$ *then*

$$\Pr_{\mathbf{C}\leftarrow\mathbb{B}^{(r\cdot\kappa)\times k}}\left[\mathbf{C}\cdot\mathbf{s} \notin S_\kappa^\beta\right] \leq 2^{-\kappa}.$$

The above statements can directly be implemented in our argument system by the means of circuit sampling. Unfortunately, this results in a new problem, which is that we cannot output the product of $\mathbf{s}$ with a random binary matrix to $\mathcal{V}$ without necessarily leaking information about $\mathbf{s}$.

We resolve this problem using circuit sampling on the side of the prover and give two different solutions. The first idea is that $\mathcal{P}$ can compute $\mathbf{u} = \mathbf{Cs}$ and output $\mathbf{u}+$ "small" where "small" is a value of small norm. To achieve good soundness guarantees we let "small" only be polynomially bigger than $||\mathbf{u}||_\infty$ and use Rejection Sampling to hide the information from the product. Alternatively, we can allow $\mathcal{P}$ to prove knowledge of the bit decomposition of each value of $\mathbf{u} = \mathbf{Cs}$. We now describe both ideas in more detail.

1st Approach: Rejection Sampling. In this solution, we let the prover $\mathcal{P}$ add additional random elements $x_1, x_2, \ldots$ to the witness, which are supposed to be small. The verifier $\mathcal{V}$ will then, as part of his challenge in the circuit sampling, ask $\mathcal{P}$ to open a subset of $x_1, x_2, \ldots$ to show that most of the remaining ones are indeed of small size. $\mathcal{P}$ will then open sums of each $\mathbf{u}[i]$ with some x_j, subject to the constraint that this does not leak information about $\mathbf{s}$. $\mathcal{V}$ later tests that each such $\mathbf{u}[i] + x_j$ is of bounded norm.

As part of rejection sampling a prover aborts whenever the argument would leak information. But our goal is that the argument is complete with overwhelming probability. To achieve this, we use an idea which is inspired by the "imperfect proof" of [BDLN16]. There, the authors gave a protocol that showed how to prove knowledge of $\ell - \kappa$ out of ℓ SIS instances using cut-and-choose and rejection sampling. Their approach aborts only with negligible probability and turns out to be compatible with our application. The circuit sampler, on a high level, works as follows:

1. $\mathcal{P}$ will sample $x_1, \ldots, x_{16\kappa}$ uniformly at random from $[-\pi\cdot m\cdot\beta, \pi\cdot m\cdot\beta] \subset \mathbb{F}$ and commit them as part of $\widehat{w}$.
2. $\mathcal{V}$ with probability $1/2$ puts each x_i into a set E. It samples a random matrix $\mathbf{C} \in \mathbb{B}^{5\kappa\times m}$ and sends $E, \mathbf{C}$ as challenges to $\mathcal{P}$.
3. $\mathcal{P}$ now sets up a circuit C as follows:
   (a) C will output $\{x_e\}_{e\in\overline{E}}$. $\mathcal{V}$ checks that $x_e \in [-\pi\cdot m\cdot\beta, \pi\cdot m\cdot\beta]$.
   (b) Compute $\mathbf{u} = \mathbf{Cs}$ in the circuit. $\mathcal{P}$ will go through $\mathbf{u}[1], \ldots, \mathbf{u}[5\cdot\kappa]$, take the first unused $e \in E$ and test if $\mathbf{u}[i] + x_e \in [-(\pi-1)\cdot m\cdot\beta, (\pi-1)\cdot m\cdot\beta]$. If so, then it makes C output $v_i = \mathbf{u}[i] + x_e$, otherwise it removes e from E and repeats this procedure with the next-largest $e' \in E$. $\mathcal{V}$ checks that $v_i \in [-(\pi-1)\cdot m\cdot\beta, (\pi-1)\cdot m\cdot\beta]$.

We present the full sampler in the full version, together with a proof of the following Theorem.

Theorem 5. *The aforementioned approach yields a statistically correct, α-sound and perfectly simulatable circuit sampler for the relation* $R_{\text{SIS}}^{m,n,q,4\pi m\cdot\beta}$ *where* $\alpha = \max\{1/|\mathbb{F}|, 2^{-\kappa}\}$.

A drawback of this approach is the rather big slack of $4\pi \cdot m$. This slack is caused by two reasons. First, there is an inherent increase of m due to the use of Lemma 4. In addition, using Rejection Sampling means that we lose another factor $\pi = 100$. One could decrease the constant by using a discrete Gaussian distribution for the x_i as in [Lyu12], but we opted for presenting the above idea due to its simplicity. On the positive side, there are no non-linear gates in the sampled circuit and $\mathcal{P}$ will only have to add $16 \cdot \kappa$ more values to the witness, independently of β. The sampled circuit will output $\ell + 5\kappa + 1$ elements of $\mathbb{F}$, which in expectancy is around $13\kappa + 1$ (since each of the 16κ random samples is opened with probability $1/2$).

Summing up, the communication of the argument (excluding $\tau_{\mathcal{P}}$) when using $\Pi_{\mathsf{sac}}^{\mathsf{samp}}$ is $\mathsf{base} + \log_2 q \cdot M(m + 29\kappa + 1)$ bits.

2nd Approach: The Power of Random Bits. The previous solution has the disadvantage of having a comparably high slack of $4\pi m$. On the other hand, it does not use any non-linear gates. We will now show how to decrease the slack to be essentially m by reintroducing one square gate and adding computational work. To reduce the slack, we will again rely on Lemma 4. But instead of performing rejection sampling on the output, we perform a range proof for each element of the matrix product $\mathbf{u} = \mathbf{C}\mathbf{s}$. The problem that arises is that $\mathbf{C}$ is only chosen at runtime, while the committed witness must be independent of the actual values in $\mathbf{C}$. At the same time, we must construct the argument in such a way that the circuit C will not reveal any information about the product except for bounds on each value.

We resolve this problem as follows: if the witness has $||\mathbf{s}||_\infty \leq \beta$, then since $\mathbf{C} \in \mathbb{B}^{\kappa\times m}$ it must hold that $||\mathbf{C}\mathbf{s}||_\infty \leq m \cdot \beta$. Thus, letting r be the smallest integer such that $m \cdot \beta < 2^r$, it suffices for the prover to show that $\mathbf{u}[i] \in [-2^r, 2^r - 1]$ (which can be done using bit decomposition as in the generalization of Sect. 5.1). To show the inclusion $\mathcal{P}$ can add random bits $x_0^i, \ldots, x_r^i$ to the witness. Then, once the challenge is received from $\mathcal{V}$ and $\mathbf{u}$ is known to $\mathcal{P}$, it can compute the bit decomposition $\mathbf{u}[i] + 2^r = \sum_{j=0}^{r} 2^j h_j^i$ for each $i \in [\kappa]$ and tell $\mathcal{V}$ for each $j \in \{0, \ldots, r\}$ if it should use x_j^i or $1 - x_j^i$ to represent h_j^i. As all x_i^j are chosen randomly, this yields a simulatable circuit. The only issue that remains is for $\mathcal{P}$ to prove that each x_i^j is indeed a bit. For this task, we use the method presented in Sect. 5.2, which uses polynomial evaluation and requires a single non-linear gate. We describe the full circuit sampler in the full version, together with a proof of the following Theorem.

Theorem 6. *Assume that* $(q-1)/2 > 4m\beta$. *The aforementioned approach yields a perfectly correct, α-sound and perfectly simulatable circuit sampler for the relation* $R_{\text{SIS}}^{m,n,q,2m\cdot\beta+4}$ *where* $\alpha = \max\{\frac{2(r+1)\kappa-1}{|\mathbb{F}|}, 2^{-\kappa}\}$ *and r is the smallest integer such that* $m \cdot \beta \leq 2^r - 1$.

Table 1. Parameters used in the experiments for $\Pi_{\mathsf{c\&c}}$ and argument size per parameter set as a function of $\rho = m \cdot \log_2 |\mathbb{F}|$.

N	Cut-and-Choose					
	$\xi \leq 2^{-40}$			$\xi \leq 2^{-80}$		
	M	τ	Comm. of $\mathcal{P}$ (in KB)	M	τ	Comm. of $\mathcal{P}$ (in KB)
2	75	34	$31 + 0.123 \cdot \rho$	145	63	$61.1 + 0.246 \cdot \rho$
4	55	32	$22.4 + 0.069 \cdot \rho$	105	57	$44.8 + 0.144 \cdot \rho$
8	55	38	$20.7 + 0.051 \cdot \rho$	95	57	$42 + 0.114 \cdot \rho$
16	45	26	$23.4 + 0.057 \cdot \rho$	95	63	$41.5 + 0.096 \cdot \rho$
32	45	28	$23.8 + 0.051 \cdot \rho$	85	47	$50.4 + 0.114 \cdot \rho$
64	45	28	$26 + 0.051 \cdot \rho$	85	49	$53 + 0.108 \cdot \rho$

The circuit we obtain has $m + \kappa(r+1)$ inputs, one square gate and $\kappa + 2$ outputs. Then the total communication of this argument when using $\Pi_{\mathsf{sac}}^{\mathsf{samp}}$ is $\mathsf{base} + \log_2 q \cdot M(m + \kappa(r+2) + 5)$ bits.

6 Evaluation and Experimental Results

We ran extensive experiments to measure the performance of our two protocols for the Binary-SIS problem. As setup we used Amazon C5.9xlarge instances using two servers with Intel Platinum 8000 series processors (Skylake-SP) which have clock speed up to 3.4 GHZ, 36 virtual cores per server (utilized based on the experiment setup) and 72 Gb RAM. The network bandwidth between the nodes is 10 Gpbs. For our implementation we used only the baseline construction for the Binary-SIS problem presented in Sect. 5.1. Nevertheless, this includes the three general optimizations described in Sect. 3.4. Hash functions as well as commitments were implemented using SHA-256. Generation of pseudo-randomness from a seed was done using AES in counter-mode where the seed is the AES key. Thus, $|\mathsf{hash}| = |\mathsf{com}| = 256$ bits and $|\mathsf{sd}| = 128$ bits.

We used five sets of parameters for our experiments: (i) $\log_2 |\mathbb{F}| = 15$, $n = 256$ and $m = 1024$; (ii) $\log_2 |\mathbb{F}| = 15$, $n = 256$ and $m = 4096$; (iii) $\log_2 |\mathbb{F}| = 31$, $n = 512$ and $m = 2048$; (iv) $\log_2 |\mathbb{F}| = 59$, $n = 1024$ and $m = 4096$; and (v) $\log_2 |\mathbb{F}| = 61$, $n = 1024$ and $m = 4096$.

The first parameter set reflects SIS-based constructions that do not need any additional functionality. For example, they can be used to instantiate [KTX08] with a binary secret. The second parameter set is then used to study the impact of using a much larger message in the commitment scheme, which also shows how the matrix size impacts the runtimes. The third set would be a typical example for SIS-based constructions such as somewhat homomorphic commitments and allows to prove that a committed message is small. An example for an application would be the commitment scheme of [BDL+18]. The last two sets are used for applications such as somewhat homomorphic encryption schemes like [BGV14].

Table 2. Parameters used in the experiments for Π_{sac} and argument size per parameter set as a function of $\rho = m \cdot \log_2 |\mathbb{F}|$.

N	Sacrificing			
	$\xi \leq 2^{-40}$		$\xi \leq 2^{-80}$	
	M	Comm. of $\mathcal{P}$ (in KB)	M	Comm. of $\mathcal{P}$ (in KB)
2	40	$26.2 + 0.16 \cdot \rho$	80	$51.8 + 0.32 \cdot \rho$
4	20	$16 + 0.08 \cdot \rho$	40	$31.3 + 0.16 \cdot \rho$
8	14	$13.2 + 0.056 \cdot \rho$	27	$24.8 + 0.108 \cdot \rho$
16	10	$10.9 + 0.04 \cdot \rho$	20	$21.2 + 0.08 \cdot \rho$
32	8	$9.9 + 0.032 \cdot \rho$	16	$19.1 + 0.064 \cdot \rho$
64	7	$9.6 + 0.028 \cdot \rho$	14	$18.6 + 0.056 \cdot \rho$

Table 3. Best running times in MSec for different sets of SIS parameters, $\kappa = 40$.

$\log_2 \lvert\mathbb{F}\rvert$	n	m	Cut-and-Choose				Sacrificing		
			N	M	τ	Time	N	M	Time
15	256	1024	2	75	34	73.2	4	20	59.4
15	256	4096	2	75	34	295.8	4	20	252.6
31	512	2048	2	75	34	252.3	4	20	217.5
59	1024	4096	2	75	34	1010.4	2	40	1075.1
61	1024	4096	2	75	34	1204.6	2	40	1228.8

We ran experiments for 40 and 80 bits of statistical security κ. For the parameter N, i.e. the number of parties in the underlying MPC protocol, we used the values $2, 4, 8, 16, 32$ and 64. Then, given the desired level of security and N we searched for the parameters for each protocol that minimized the overall cost.

In $\Pi_{\mathsf{c\&c}}$, there are two parameters to define: M (number of pre-processing executions) and τ (number of pre-processing executions to open). To obtain these, we wrote a script that finds the minimal M and τ such that $\xi(M, N, \tau) \leq 2^{-40}$ or 2^{-80}. In Π_{sac}, we observe that for our choices of $|\mathbb{F}|$ and N, it holds that $\frac{3N+|\mathbb{F}|-3}{N \cdot |\mathbb{F}|} \approx \frac{1}{N}$ and so it suffices to choose M such that $\xi(M, N) \approx \frac{1}{N^M} \leq 2^{-40}$ or 2^{-80}.

We summarize the parameters used in our experiments in Tables 1, 2. In addition, for each set of parameters we give the size of the argument in Kbits as a formula of the SIS problem parameters $\rho = m \cdot \log_2 |\mathbb{F}|$. Observe that as the number of parties N grows, the number of MPC instances in Π_{sac} becomes much smaller than the number required in $\Pi_{\mathsf{c\&c}}$, which is translated to smaller proof size. This implies that our new 'sacrificing'-based approach *outperforms* the 'cut–and–choose'-based method for arithmetic circuits over large fields.

Running Times. In Table 3 we present the running times (in Msec.) of the two protocols for 40 bits of security respectively. The results for 80-bit of security are presented in the full version. For each set of parameters for the SIS problem we report only the best running times achieved together with the MPC protocol parameters which lead to the result. As the number of non-linear gates in this circuit is small, it is not surprising that both schemes achieve similar results. Observe that small numbers of parties in the MPC protocol lead to faster running times, in contrast to proof size which is getting smaller when the number of parties is increased.

It is worth noting that a major source of improvement we discovered was to postpone the modular reduction in the matrix multiplication to the end. That is, when the prover/verifier multiply a row in the matrix $\mathbf{A}$ with a vector of shares of $\mathbf{s}$ (which is eventually what the computed circuit does), it is highly beneficial to do the reduction modulo q only at the end of the matrix multiplication. This simple optimization alone yields an improvement of approximately 33%.

Using Multi-threads. The above results were obtained using a single thread. As computation time is the bottleneck, we examined what happens when working with multiple threads which seems to be a straightforward optimization. This experiment was run for the "toughest" instance of the SIS problem, with $\log|\mathbb{F}| = 61$, $n = 1024$ and $m = 4096$ and with the MPC protocol parameters who yielded the best running time in Table 3. The full results appear in the full version. As we discovered, using two threads already cut the running time by half and using *20 threads speeds-up the runtime by more than 80%*. As a consequence, we obtain a ZKAoK that runs in *less than 0.5 s* even for the of SIS instance with the largest parameters. This is orders of magnitude faster than any previous implementation for arithmetic circuits of the same size.

Faster Matrix Products and Structured Lattices. In this work we solely focus on unstructured matrices $\mathbf{A}$ for SIS. By micro-benchmarking the results, we observe that as the size of the matrix $\mathbf{A}$ grows, the time spent on computing the matrix multiplication becomes dominant. In particular, for the large instances, matrix multiplication takes >85% of the overall local computation time. As we use only textbook matrix multiplication, this leaves plenty of room for improvement. Furthermore, on the verifier side it is possible to batch the matrix multiplications together as only verification is needed. Another direction would be to use structured matrices i.e. structured lattices, which opens the door for FFT-like algorithms.

7 Related Work

The landscape for (lattice-based) ZK arguments has drastically changed during the past years. We will now describe how our protocol compares with other state-of-the-art arguments of knowledge in terms of communication, computation time, accuracy of the proof and the cryptographic assumptions. As most of existing work focuses only on minimizing the proof size, we can only estimate in many cases what will be the running time compared to ours. For this section, we used $N = 16$ parties in underlying MPC protocol for our scheme and set M accordingly to achieve the desired soundness. We stress that it is possible to further increase the number of parties in the underlying MPC and reduce the proof size even more, but at the cost of increasing also the running time.

Protocols for exact SIS. We subsume all protocols that prove the exact solution here. These are either based on Stern-type arguments [LNSW13], direct applications of MPC-in-the-head/IOP [AHIV17,BCR+19] or special-purpose protocols [BLS19,Beu19,YAZ+19]. Though STARKs [BBHR19] fall into the second category, we do not consider those as related work as they are rather tailored to computations with looping components. While [LNSW13] is a specific technique tailored to problems such as SIS, [AHIV17,BCR+19] require an arithmetic circuit (similar to us) for the verification of the statement. The comparison in term of proof size to these works is presented in Table 4.

Table 4. Proof sizes for Binary-SIS and 5-bit secrets, small constant slack, $\kappa = 40$.

	$\lvert\mathbb{F}\rvert \approx 2^{32}$ Binary	$\lvert\mathbb{F}\rvert \approx 2^{32}$ $\beta = 15$	$\lvert\mathbb{F}\rvert \approx 2^{61}$ Binary	$\lvert\mathbb{F}\rvert \approx 2^{61}$ $\beta = 15$
Stern [Ste96]	971 KB	7285 KB	3703 KB	27775 KB
Ligero [AHIV17]	45 KB	55 KB	55 KB	80 KB
Ours, baseline	357 KB	2138 KB	1359 KB	8148 KB
Ours, amortized	179 KB	1069 KB	680 KB	4075 KB

We did not include proof sizes for the Aurora protocol [BCR+19], as the authors there did not provide a general expression for the proof size, but rather experimental results for the binary field $\mathbb{F}_{2^{192}}$. Nevertheless, we expect them to be comparable to the sizes reported for [AHIV17]. We note that the prover running time according to their experiments is $\approx$200 s, and so is expected to be at least one order of magnitude bigger than in our protocols. The same applies to Ligero [AHIV17], which requires extensive FFT computations for large polynomials, which cause the prover's running time to be much higher than ours. We thus conclude that these approaches, which achieve sun-linear communication, outperform our approach in the non-interactive setting. However, in the interactive setting- for example, when used as a building block in a larger interactive protocol (that use e.g. lattice-based commitments) with strong runtime requirements then our computationally efficient prover is advantageous. Concurrently to this work, the works of [BLS19,Beu19,YAZ+19] have improved upon the state of the art of ZKAoK for lattice-based primitives. While it can be expected that their solutions have the same or better communication complexity than our approach for exact SIS, it is still unclear what is their computational cost, as none of these works provides an implementation. Furthermore, in comparison to their work our protocols can be used to prove arbitrary statements.

Protocols for SIS with Slack. Here, we compare with the argument system from the signature scheme of [Lyu12] (see Table 5).

We compare the proof size of [Lyu12] with our baseline protocol and with the two solutions described in Sect. 5.3. We see that in particular the 2nd protocol of Sect. 5.3 improves upon [Lyu12] for all three considered cases. This is particularly true in the cases where the gap between β and $|\mathbb{F}|$ is small, as our proof size increases as $|\mathbb{F}|$ grows whereas the size of [Lyu12] depends on the bound β but not on $|\mathbb{F}|$ when optimized correctly. At the same time, increasing β seems not to substantially change the communication complexity of either of our two proofs, whereas it has a direct impact on [Lyu12].

Table 5. Proof sizes for non-constant slack with $\log_2(|\mathbb{F}|) = 32$ and $\kappa = 40$.

Protocol	Slack	Binary SIS	SIS with $\beta = 15$
Sigma-protocol [Lyu12]	288 m	184 KB	223 KB
Ours, Approach 1 ($\kappa = 8$)	400 m	100 KB	100 KB
Ours, Approach 2 ($\kappa = 8$)	<3 m	96 KB	97 KB
Ours, Exact	1	179 KB	1069 KB

Other Approaches. Recently, del Pino et al. [dPLS19] showed how to obtain a ZK argument for our problem setting. While they have a drastically smaller proof size (in the order of 1.5 KB), their construction relies on the DLog assumption and is therefore not post-quantum secure. Moreover, their computational efficiency relies on using structured lattices, which we do not need. The same applies to Hyrax [WTS+18], Sonic [MBKM19] or Libra [XZZ+19], who rely on the DLog-assumption. Older ZK-SNARKs such as [PHGR16, BSCTV14] would offer low argument size and verification time but in addition to large keys and a high prover runtime also rely on very strong assumptions. Similarly, the work of [BCC+16] is also in the DLog setting. Its lattice-based variant [BBC+18] is so far not implemented, may have large hidden constants and itself uses ZKAoKs for SIS as building blocks.

Thanks and Acknowledgements. The authors want to thank Roey Sefi and Assi Barak for their help with the implementation as well as Carmit Hazay, Yehuda Lindell and Avishay Yanai as well as the anonymous reviewers for their helpful comments.

The work of both authors was mainly done at Bar Ilan University. Both authors acknowledge support by the BIU Center for Research in Applied Cryptography and Cyber Security in conjunction with the Israel National Cyber Bureau in the Prime Minister's Office. The work of Carsten was additionally funded by the European Research Council (ERC) under the European Unions' Horizon 2020 research and innovation programme under grant agreement No 669255 (MPCPRO).

References

[AHIV17] Ames, S., Hazay, C., Ishai, Y., Venkitasubramaniam, M.: Ligero: lightweight sublinear arguments without a trusted setup. In: Proceedings of the 2017 ACM SIGSAC Conference on Computer and Communications Security. ACM (2017)

[BBC+18] Baum, C., Bootle, J., Cerulli, A., del Pino, R., Groth, J., Lyubashevsky, V.: Sub-linear lattice-based zero-knowledge arguments for arithmetic circuits. In: Shacham, H., Boldyreva, A. (eds.) CRYPTO 2018. LNCS, vol. 10992, pp. 669–699. Springer, Cham (2018). https://doi.org/10.1007/978-3-319-96881-0_23

[BBHR19] Ben-Sasson, E., Bentov, I., Horesh, Y., Riabzev, M.: Scalable zero knowledge with no trusted setup. In: Boldyreva, A., Micciancio, D. (eds.) CRYPTO 2019. LNCS, vol. 11694, pp. 701–732. Springer, Cham (2019). https://doi.org/10.1007/978-3-030-26954-8_23

[BCC+16] Bootle, J., Cerulli, A., Chaidos, P., Groth, J., Petit, C.: Efficient zero-knowledge arguments for arithmetic circuits in the discrete log setting. In: Fischlin, M., Coron, J.-S. (eds.) EUROCRYPT 2016. LNCS, vol. 9666, pp. 327–357. Springer, Heidelberg (2016). https://doi.org/10.1007/978-3-662-49896-5_12

[BCR+19] Ben-Sasson, E., Chiesa, A., Riabzev, M., Spooner, N., Virza, M., Ward, N.P.: Aurora: transparent succinct arguments for R1CS. In: Ishai, Y., Rijmen, V. (eds.) EUROCRYPT 2019. LNCS, vol. 11476, pp. 103–128. Springer, Cham (2019). https://doi.org/10.1007/978-3-030-17653-2_4

[BD10] Bendlin, R., Damgård, I.: Threshold decryption and zero-knowledge proofs for lattice-based cryptosystems. In: Micciancio, D. (ed.) TCC 2010. LNCS, vol. 5978, pp. 201–218. Springer, Heidelberg (2010). https://doi.org/10.1007/978-3-642-11799-2_13

[BDL+18] Baum, C., Damgård, I., Lyubashevsky, V., Oechsner, S., Peikert, C.: More efficient commitments from structured lattice assumptions. In: Catalano, D., De Prisco, R. (eds.) SCN 2018. LNCS, vol. 11035, pp. 368–385. Springer, Cham (2018). https://doi.org/10.1007/978-3-319-98113-0_20

[BDLN16] Baum, C., Damgård, I., Larsen, K.G., Nielsen, M.: How to prove knowledge of small secrets. In: Robshaw, M., Katz, J. (eds.) CRYPTO 2016. LNCS, vol. 9816, pp. 478–498. Springer, Heidelberg (2016). https://doi.org/10.1007/978-3-662-53015-3_17

[Bea91] Beaver, D.: Efficient multiparty protocols using circuit randomization. In: Feigenbaum, J. (ed.) CRYPTO 1991. LNCS, vol. 576, pp. 420–432. Springer, Heidelberg (1992). https://doi.org/10.1007/3-540-46766-1_34

[Beu19] Beullens, W.: On sigma protocols with helper for MQ and PKP, fishy signature schemes and more. Cryptology ePrint Archive, Report 2019/490 (2019). https://eprint.iacr.org/2019/490

[BGV14] Brakerski, Z., Gentry, C., Vaikuntanathan, V.: (Leveled) fully homomorphic encryption without bootstrapping. ACM Trans. Comput. Theory (TOCT) **6**(3), 1–36 (2014)

[BHR12] Bellare, M., Hoang, V.T., Rogaway, P.: Foundations of garbled circuits. In: Proceedings of the 2012 ACM Conference on Computer and Communications Security. ACM (2012)

[BJM19] Badertscher, C., Jost, D., Maurer, U.: Agree-and-prove: generalized proofs of knowledge and applications. Cryptology ePrint Archive, Report 2019/662 (2019). https://eprint.iacr.org/2019/662

[BL17] Baum, C., Lyubashevsky, V.: Simple amortized proofs of shortness for linear relations over polynomial rings (2017). https://eprint.iacr.org/2017/759

[BLS19] Bootle, J., Lyubashevsky, V., Seiler, G.: Algebraic techniques for short(er) exact lattice-based zero-knowledge proofs. In: Boldyreva, A., Micciancio, D. (eds.) CRYPTO 2019. LNCS, vol. 11692, pp. 176–202. Springer, Cham (2019). https://doi.org/10.1007/978-3-030-26948-7_7

[BSCTV14] Ben-Sasson, E., Chiesa, A., Tromer, E., Virza, M.: Succinct non-interactive zero knowledge for a von Neumann architecture. In: USENIX Security Symposium (2014)

[BN19] Baum, C., Nof, A.: Concretely-efficient zero-knowledge arguments for arithmetic circuits and their application to lattice-based cryptography. Cryptology ePrint Archive, Report 2019/532 (2019). https://eprint.iacr.org/2019/532

[DFMS19] Don, J., Fehr, S., Majenz, C., Schaffner, C.: Security of the fiat-shamir transformation in the quantum random-oracle model. In: Boldyreva, A., Micciancio, D. (eds.) CRYPTO 2019. LNCS, vol. 11693, pp. 356–383. Springer, Cham (2019). https://doi.org/10.1007/978-3-030-26951-7_13

[DN19] Dinur, I., Nadler, N.: Multi-target attacks on the picnic signature scheme and related protocols. In: Ishai, Y., Rijmen, V. (eds.) EUROCRYPT 2019. LNCS, vol. 11478, pp. 699–727. Springer, Cham (2019). https://doi.org/10.1007/978-3-030-17659-4_24

[dPLS19] del Pino, R., Lyubashevsky, V., Seiler, G.: Short discrete log proofs for FHE and ring-LWE ciphertexts. In: Lin, D., Sako, K. (eds.) PKC 2019. LNCS, vol. 11442, pp. 344–373. Springer, Cham (2019). https://doi.org/10.1007/978-3-030-17253-4_12

[DPSZ12] Damgård, I., Pastro, V., Smart, N., Zakarias, S.: Multiparty computation from somewhat homomorphic encryption. In: Safavi-Naini, R., Canetti, R. (eds.) CRYPTO 2012. LNCS, vol. 7417, pp. 643–662. Springer, Heidelberg (2012). https://doi.org/10.1007/978-3-642-32009-5_38

[FS86] Fiat, A., Shamir, A.: How to prove yourself: practical solutions to identification and signature problems. In: Odlyzko, A.M. (ed.) CRYPTO 1986. LNCS, vol. 263, pp. 186–194. Springer, Heidelberg (1987). https://doi.org/10.1007/3-540-47721-7_12

[GMO16] Giacomelli, I., Madsen, J., Orlandi, C.: Faster zero-knowledge for Boolean circuits. In: USENIX Security Symposium, Zkboo (2016)

[GMR89] Goldwasser, S., Micali, S., Rackoff, C.: The knowledge complexity of interactive proof systems. SIAM J. Comput. **18**(1), 186–208 (1989)

[IKOS07] Ishai, Y., Kushilevitz, E., Ostrovsky, R., Sahai, A.: Zero-knowledge from secure multiparty computation. In: Proceedings of the Thirty-Ninth Annual ACM Symposium on Theory of Computing. ACM (2007)

[KKW18] Katz, J., Kolesnikov, V., Wang, X.: Improved non-interactive zero knowledge with applications to post-quantum signatures. In: Proceedings of the 2018 ACM SIGSAC Conference on Computer and Communications Security, CCS 2018 (2018)

[KTX08] Kawachi, A., Tanaka, K., Xagawa, K.: Concurrently secure identification schemes based on the worst-case hardness of lattice problems. In: Pieprzyk, J. (ed.) ASIACRYPT 2008. LNCS, vol. 5350, pp. 372–389. Springer, Heidelberg (2008). https://doi.org/10.1007/978-3-540-89255-7_23

[LN17] Lindell, Y., Nof, A.: A framework for constructing fast MPC over arithmetic circuits with malicious adversaries and an honest-majority. In: Proceedings of the 2017 ACM SIGSAC Conference on Computer and Communications Security, CCS 2017 (2017)

[LNSW13] Ling, S., Nguyen, K., Stehlé, D., Wang, H.: Improved zero-knowledge proofs of knowledge for the ISIS problem, and applications. In: Kurosawa, K., Hanaoka, G. (eds.) PKC 2013. LNCS, vol. 7778, pp. 107–124. Springer, Heidelberg (2013). https://doi.org/10.1007/978-3-642-36362-7_8

[Lyu12] Lyubashevsky, V.: Lattice signatures without trapdoors. In: Pointcheval, D., Johansson, T. (eds.) EUROCRYPT 2012. LNCS, vol. 7237, pp. 738–755. Springer, Heidelberg (2012). https://doi.org/10.1007/978-3-642-29011-4_43

[MBKM19] Maller, M., Bowe, S., Kohlweiss, M., Meiklejohn, S.: Sonic: zero-knowledge snarks from linear-size universal and updatable structured reference strings. In: Proceedings of the 2019 ACM SIGSAC Conference on Computer and Communications Security, pp. 2111–2128 (2019)

[PHGR16] Parno, B., Howell, J., Gentry, C., Raykova, M.: Pinocchio: nearly practical verifiable computation. Commun. ACM **59**(2) (2016)

[Ste96] Stern, J.: A new paradigm for public key identification. IEEE Trans. Inf. Theory **42**(6) (1996)

[WTS+18] Wahby, R.S., Tzialla, I., Shelat, A., Thaler, J., Walfish, M.: Doubly-efficient zkSNARKs without trusted setup. In: Proceedings of the 2018 IEEE Symposium on Security and Privacy, SP 2018 (2018)

[XZZ+19] Xie, T., Zhang, J., Zhang, Y., Papamanthou, C., Song, D.: Libra: succinct zero-knowledge proofs with optimal prover computation. In: Boldyreva, A., Micciancio, D. (eds.) CRYPTO 2019. LNCS, vol. 11694, pp. 733–764. Springer, Cham (2019). https://doi.org/10.1007/978-3-030-26954-8_24

[YAZ+19] Yang, R., Au, M.H., Zhang, Z., Xu, Q., Yu, Z., Whyte, W.: Efficient lattice-based zero-knowledge arguments with standard soundness: construction and applications. In: Boldyreva, A., Micciancio, D. (eds.) CRYPTO 2019. LNCS, vol. 11692, pp. 147–175. Springer, Cham (2019). https://doi.org/10.1007/978-3-030-26948-7_6

Updateable Inner Product Argument with Logarithmic Verifier and Applications

Vanesa Daza[1,2], Carla Ràfols[1,2], and Alexandros Zacharakis[1(✉)]

[1] Pompeu Fabra University, Barcelona, Spain
{vanesa.daza,carla.rafols,alexandros.zacharakis}@upf.edu
[2] Cybercat, Catalonia, Spain

Abstract. We propose an improvement for the inner product argument of Bootle et al. (EUROCRYPT'16). The new argument replaces the unstructured common reference string (the commitment key) by a structured one. We give two instantiations of this argument, for two different distributions of the CRS. In the designated verifier setting, this structure can be used to reduce verification from linear to logarithmic in the circuit size. The argument can be compiled to the publicly verifiable setting in asymmetric bilinear groups. The new common reference string can easily be updateable. The argument can be directly used to improve verification of Bulletproofs range proofs (IEEE SP'18). On the other hand, to use the improved argument to prove circuit satisfiability with logarithmic verification, we adapt recent techniques from Sonic (ACM CCS'19) to work with the new common reference string. The resulting argument is secure under standard assumptions (in the Random Oracle Model), in contrast with Sonic and recent works that improve its efficiency (Plonk, Marlin, AuroraLight), which, apart from the Random Oracle Model, need either the Algebraic Group Model or Knowledge Type assumptions.

Keywords: Zero Knowledge · Inner product · SNARKS · Range Proofs · Updateable

1 Introduction

Zero-Knowledge proofs have been an important primitive in the theory of cryptography since their introduction three decades ago. The classical applications of zero-knowledge proofs are numerous, including for example identification schemes, electronic voting, verifiable outsourced computation, or CCA secure public-key encryption. The common denominator of all of these is that zk-proofs are used to prove simple statements, like "this ciphertext is well-formed" or "I know a valid signature key". Although it was known that every NP statement could be proved in zero-knowledge [23], the cost of such general proofs was prohibitive and more sophisticated applications of zk-proofs were completely impractical.

A. Kiayias et al. (Eds.): PKC 2020, LNCS 12110, pp. 527–557, 2020.
https://doi.org/10.1007/978-3-030-45374-9_18

This situation has changed radically in the last few years with the introduction of pairing-based zk-SNARKs [25]. The key element of these arguments is that they are *succinct*, in fact, they are constant size, i.e. independent of the witness size and thus, very fast to verify. This is extremely powerful: in particular, a prover can show that it has executed correctly some large computation (expressed as a huge circuit) and a verifier will be convinced after doing only very few checks (e.g. computing 3 pairings in [26]). Besides their scientific interest, SNARKs have opened the door to new real-world privacy-preserving applications. Cryptocurrencies like Zcash [6] or Ethereum [36] are two of the most popular examples so far.

However, even the most efficient instantiations of pairing-based SNARKs [26,28] have a few drawbacks. On the efficiency side, the main ones are long common reference string and costly prover computation. On the security side, they are based on very strong hardness assumptions, and the setup is assumed to be trusted.

Recently, there are significant research efforts to propose alternatives which overcome some of these drawbacks following several dimensions. For instance, numerous works study how to reduce the trust in the common reference string, exploring weaker models such as subversion resistant SNARKs [1,4,17], updateable common reference strings [27] or transparent setup [5]. Although SNARKs are unbeatable in some facets, different tradeoffs are compelling depending on the application scenario.

One of the most celebrated alternatives to SNARKs are the arguments of knowledge for Arithmetic Circuit Satisfiability of Bootle et al. [10] (and Bulletproofs, the improvement thereof by Bünz et al. [12]). Their dependence on weaker assumptions (the DLOG assumption and the Random Oracle if one wants to remove interaction via Fiat-Shamir), the absence of a trusted setup and the logarithmic size of the proofs are some of its most attractive features. Unfortunately, verification time scales linearly, even when batching techniques are used. The motivation of this paper is to improve the cost of the verifier in the aforementioned works, while keeping most of its advantages.

1.1 Related Work

In [10], Bootle et al. proposed an interactive zero-knowledge argument at the heart of which lies a recursive argument for an inner product relation of committed values. The argument has very interesting properties, most notably it is transparent. The communication complexity is $\mathcal{O}_\lambda(\log |\mathcal{C}|)$[1] and the verification cost is $(\mathcal{O}_\lambda(|\mathcal{C}|))$ which is the main drawback of the scheme, since verifying is asymptotically as costly as evaluating the circuit. Prover complexity is asymptotically optimal $(\mathcal{O}_\lambda(|\mathcal{C}|))$ but it heavily uses expensive public-key operations. Bünz et al. in [12] improved the concrete efficiency of the aforementioned protocol by a constant factor.

[1] As explained in Sect. 2, $\mathcal{O}_\lambda(\cdot)$ hides linear factors that depend on the security parameter λ.

The Muggle-proofs based [37–40] proof systems build on the delegation scheme of Goldwasser, Kalai, and Rothblum [24]. These are very efficient schemes for low depth computation, whose verification and communication complexity depend on $d \log W$, where d is the circuit depth, and W its width plus some communication overhead depending on the specific instantiation. Hyrax [37] is a DLOG-based transparent instantiation with an additional cost of $\mathcal{O}_\lambda(|w|^{\frac{1}{i}})$ for some i that can be fine-tuned. Recently, Libra [38] utilized and improved techniques from [14] to achieve an asymptotically optimal prover complexity and minimize public key operations. All these schemes need either a per-circuit setup or work for log-space uniform computations. Since they are inherently interactive they rely on the Fiat-Shamir transform to yield non interactive arguments.

Probabilistically Checkable Proofs (PCP) based constructions [5,7] originate from the works of Kilian [31] and Micali [33], and are based on Interactive Oracle Proofs [8] which generalize the classical PCP proofs in the interactive setting. They are based on symmetric primitives which results in transparent, plausibly post-quantum secure constructions. The main drawback is that they are still concretely inefficient, especially as far as prover complexity is concerned. In the same family, [2,22,30] build on the MPC-in-the-head paradigm [29] and share similar properties. The most efficient one is Ligero [2] which, while having good concrete efficiency, has communication complexity $\mathcal{O}_\lambda(\sqrt{|\mathcal{C}|})$ which can be bad for moderately large computations.

The line of work of Linear PCP constructions [16,21,26,35] that originates from the seminal work of Gennaro et al. [21] and abstracted in [9], are the most efficient when considering verification time and communication. Their proof size is constant and the verification cost is $\mathcal{O}_\lambda(|x|)$ where x is the public input. Note that this is optimal since the verifier has to, at least, read the statement to be proven. The main drawback is that they need a trusted setup.

To achieve a middle ground between efficiency and trust, Groth et al. [27] defined the Updateable model. In this model, everyone can non-interactively update the setup parameters. As long as one update is honest, soundness is guaranteed. The authors also presented a scheme which is updateable, but it has a universal common reference string of size quadratic in the maximal size of all supported circuits (although from the global setup a linear, circuit-specific string can be derived). Maller et al. presented Sonic [32], which improved this to a linear CRS by exploiting the reduction of [10]. Several works [15,19,20] have tried to improve the efficiency of Sonic concretely. However, all of these, including Sonic, are secure either in the Algebraic Group Model, or under knowledge type assumptions (apart from the Random Oracle Model). Recently, [13] uses the techniques of the aforementioned results to construct a SNARK sound in groups of unknown order. When instantiated in class groups it achieves a transparent setup and asymptotically improves over STARKS [5] by a logarithmic factor.

1.2 Our Contribution

We construct a public-coin Argument of Knowledge in the Universal Updateable Model based on the work of Bootle et al. [10]. The verification complexity is

$\mathcal{O}_\lambda(|x| + \log |\mathcal{C}|)$ and communication complexity is $\mathcal{O}_\lambda(\log |\mathcal{C}|)$ where $|x|$ is the public input size. The prover is linear in $|\mathcal{C}|$ but, as in [10], it needs to perform a lot of public-key operations. The two constructions are secure, respectively, under one assumption which reduces to asymmetric DLOG and another one to asymmetric q-DLOG. They can be made non-interactive with the Fiat-Shamir heuristic. Updating and verifying updates need time $\mathcal{O}_\lambda(|\mathcal{C}|)$, and communication complexity is $\mathcal{O}_\lambda(\log |\mathcal{C}|)$ (which can be reduced to $\mathcal{O}_\lambda(\log\log |\mathcal{C}|)$) and $\mathcal{O}_\lambda(1)$, respectively.

As far as we know, all recently proposed efficient and fully-succinct updateable schemes [15,20,32] rely on the Algebraic Group Model [18] or other Knowledge Type assumptions apart from the Random Oracle Model, while in our case the Random Oracle Model and a standard assumption is enough. However, the aforementioned schemes have a better communication complexity ($\mathcal{O}_\lambda(1)$) and, while asymptotically the verifier has the same complexity ($\mathcal{O}_\lambda(\log |\mathcal{C}|)$), in their case it works mainly on the field while ours works in the group, which is less efficient. Also, while the prover complexity in [15,20,32] is quasi-linear in $|\mathcal{C}|$ and ours is linear, theirs works mainly in the field. We report some concrete numbers in Table 1 for the overhead of each scheme (we do not include concrete numbers for other schemes in communication and verification since they are constant while ours are logarithmic in $|\mathcal{C}|$).

Finally, we observe that the major overhead in the general proof system is the delegation of (public) computation regarding the circuit structure and so, for fixed languages that may be of interest, we can use the same techniques to achieve better efficiency. We demonstrate that by applying this in range proofs improving on [12]. The main overhead compared to it is that we move to bilinear groups instead of standard ones, but we exponentially reduce the verification complexity.

1.3 Our Techniques

Distribution Parameterized Vector Commitments. We revisit the use of vector commitment schemes in zero-knowledge proof systems when working in groups: instead of using the classical Pedersen commitment key which is uniformly sampled, we add some limited structure which simultaneously allows more efficient representation of the key and efficient updateability. When combined with the properties of bilinear groups, only a compressed version of it is enough to allow a verifier to perform verification tasks exponentially faster.

In particular we propose two instantiations:

- The commitment key consisting of group encodings of all monomials of a secret x, i.e., $[1], [x], [x^2], \ldots, [x^{n-1}]$.
- The commitment key consisting of group encodings of all multilinear monomials of a secret $x_1, \ldots, x_\nu$ i.e. $[1], [x_1], [x_2], [x_1 x_2], \ldots, [x_1 x_2 \cdots x_\nu]$.

The structure of both commitment keys allows to non-interactively update the parameters and thus nullifying the trapdoors x or $x_1, \ldots, x_n$. We take advantage of this structure in bilinear groups to create compressed versions of these

Table 1. Comparison of the updateable SNARKSs in terms of the most expensive operations (exponentiations and pairings). n is the number of multiplication gates, a is the number of addition gates, m is the number of wires in the circuit and M is a parameter, which determines the processed circuit's fan-in and fan-out upper bound, and can be fine-tuned to balance the computations of the prover and verifier. n' is the size of the processed circuit which in the worst case is upper bounded by $n + \frac{2m}{M-1}$. Sonic empirically assumes $n' = 3n$ for $M = 3$ in its reported numbers rather than a worst case analysis. P refers to pairing operations and E_1 to $\mathbb{G}_1$ exponentiations. We omit constant factors. Our prover is essentially only performing multi-exponentiations and we consider we need k $\mathbb{G}_1$ exponentiations to do a k-multi-exponentiation, but we note that they can be implemented with $o(k)$ exponentiations, see e.g. [10]. In the assumptions columns KT refers to Knowledge Type assumptions, AGM to the Algebraic Group Model and A-DLOG, q-A-DLOG to variants of DLOG and q-DLOG in the asymmetric group setting. All schemes are interactive and can be turned to non-interactive in the Random Oracle model.

	$\lvert\text{CRS}\rvert$	$\mathcal{P}$	$\mathcal{V}$	π	Assumptions
Sonic [32]	$36n$ $\mathbb{G}_1$	$273n$ E_1	$\mathcal{O}_\lambda(1)$	$\mathcal{O}_\lambda(1)$	AGM
Marlin [15]	$6m$ $\mathbb{G}_1$	$21m$ E_1	$\mathcal{O}_\lambda(1)$	$\mathcal{O}_\lambda(1)$	AGM or KT
Plonk [19]	$n + a$ $\mathbb{G}_1$	$9(n + a)$ E_1	$\mathcal{O}_\lambda(1)$	$\mathcal{O}_\lambda(1)$	AGM
This work	$n'\mathbb{G}_1(\mathcal{P})$ $\log n'\mathbb{G}_2(\mathcal{V})$	$(22 + 10M)n'$ E_1	$12 \log n'$ E_1 $8 \log n'$ P	$12 \log n'$ $\mathbb{G}_1$ $4 \log n'$ $\mathbb{F}$	A-DLOG or q-A-DLOG

keys of size only $\log n$. For various languages, this allows the verifier to verify statements with the help of the prover without reading the whole commitment key. This leads to exponentially faster verification of proofs with minimal overhead for the prover, at the price of moving to bilinear instead of plain DLOG groups.

Inner Program Argument with Logarithmic Verifier. Using these techniques, we modify the inner product protocol of Bootle et al. [10] for proving that for given commitments $c_1 = \mathsf{Com}(\mathbf{a})$, $c_2 = \mathsf{Com}(\mathbf{b})$ and $z \in \mathbb{F}$, it holds that $\mathbf{a}^\top \mathbf{b} = z$. More specifically, we note that the overhead of the verifier in [10] is computing a new commitment key in each of the $\log n$ rounds of the protocol, where n is the vector dimension. This key depends on the previous key and the verifiers' challenges. Instead of doing that, we only give the verifier the compressed key (which is logarithmic in n) and have the prover convince the verifier that the reduced statement is w.r.t. a new key which is the correct one.

Universally Updateable NIZK AoK. Having this powerful tool allows us to aggregate linear and quadratic constraints and thus prove general statements. We follow the techniques of [10] to reduce a statement about a circuit w.r.t. a public input to an inner product one (which need not be zero knowledge) and we can then use the improved inner product argument. More concretely, the prover convinces the verifier that $[\alpha], [\beta]$ are commitments to $\mathbf{a}, \mathbf{b}$ such that $\mathbf{a}^\top \mathbf{b} = z$.

The former vector depends on the witness and the latter on the circuit structure, is public, and both depend on a random challenge issued by the verifier.

However, computing $[\beta]$ given universal parameters that work for any circuit (of bounded size) requires $\mathcal{O}_\lambda(|\mathcal{C}|)$ time making verification linear in the computation size. To overcome this, we delegate this computation to the prover who gives a succinct proof for the correct computation of $[\beta]$. To achieve that, we assume a specific structure for the circuit (basically that the gates have bounded fan-in and fan-out) and apply techniques similar to [32] adapted to our setting. These conditions can be imposed by pre-processing the circuit appropriately without asymptotically increasing the circuit size.

We note that when we have a fixed statement, we can make things much more efficient. The blueprint of the construction remains the same and we can appropriately fine-tune the parameter generation to avoid the delegation of computation of $[\beta]$ thus achieving a concretely more efficient verifier. We show how this can be applied in Range Proofs, and reduce exponentially the verification complexity of the similar construction of [12].

2 Preliminaries

2.1 Notations

We write $x \leftarrow S$ to denote uniformly sampling from S and assigning to x. When A is an algorithm we denote with $y \leftarrow A(x)$ the assignment of the output of A with input x to y, where we uniformly sample randomness from A if it is probabilistic. We write $A(x; r)$ to explicitly refer to the randomness of A when needed. We notate with $\mathcal{O}_\lambda(\cdot)$ asymptotic complexity that hides linear factors that depend on the security parameter λ.

We denote vectors with boldface letters. If $\mathbf{v}$ is a vector, we denote with normal font its components, that is v_i is its i-th component. We denote $\mathbf{e_n} \in \mathbb{F}^n$ the n-th element of the canonical basis. The symbol $\circ$ is used for denoting pairwise product, that is $\mathbf{a} \circ \mathbf{b} = (a_1 \cdot b_1, \dots, a_n \cdot b_n)$.

Groups are written in additive notation and its elements are written implicitly: if we fix a generator $g \in \mathbb{G}$, we denote with $[r]$ the group element rg. We extend this notation to vectors of group elements by denoting $[\mathbf{r}] = ([r_1], \dots, [r_n])$. In the bilinear group setting, given some fixed generators $g_1, g_2, g_T = e(g_1, g_2)$, we use subscripts to specify the group. In this notation, $e([r]_1, [s]_2) = [rs]_T$.

Let $\mathbb{G}$ be a group of order q and $\mathbf{r} = (r_1, \dots, r_n) \in \mathbb{Z}_q^n, \mathbf{a} = (a_1, \dots, a_n) \in \mathbb{Z}_q^n$. We denote $[\mathbf{a}^\top \mathbf{r}] = \sum_{i=1}^n a_i [r_i]$, that is, $[\mathbf{a}^\top \mathbf{r}]$ is a Vector Pedersen commitment of $\mathbf{a}$ w.r.t. to commitment key $[\mathbf{r}]$. Given a vector $\mathbf{r} = (r_1, \dots, r_n)$, for even n, we denote $\mathbf{r}_{\frac{1}{2}} = (r_1, \dots, r_{n/2})$ and $\mathbf{r}_{\frac{2}{2}} = (r_{n/2+1}, \dots, r_n)$. We denote $\mathbf{x^n} = (1, x, \dots, x^{n-1})$. Finally, let $x_1, \dots, x_\nu \in \mathbb{Z}_q^n$. We denote as $\overline{\mathbf{x}}$ the vector that is constructed recursively by setting $\overline{\mathbf{x}} \leftarrow (1)$, $\{\overline{\mathbf{x}} \leftarrow (\overline{\mathbf{x}}, x_i \overline{\mathbf{x}})\}_{i \in [\nu]}$. Basically, $\mathbf{x^n}$ contains all the monomials of x up to degree $n-1$, and $\overline{\mathbf{x}}$ contains all the multilinear monomials where a "canonical" ordering has been imposed by its recursive definition.

2.2 (Zero Knowledge) Arguments

Interactive (Zero Knowledge) Arguments of Knowledge. We present the definitions and the relevant results we need for (Zero Knowledge) Arguments of Knowledge (ZKAoK). We follow the presentation of [10].

Let $\mathcal{L} \in \mathbf{NP}$ be a language and $\mathcal{R}_\mathcal{L}$ the corresponding relation for $\mathcal{L}$. A ZKAoK allows a prover to convince a verifier of knowledge of a witness w certifying membership of a public x in $\mathcal{L}$ that is $(x, w) \in \mathcal{R}_\mathcal{L}$. The zero knowledge property guarantees that the verifier learns nothing about the witness w apart from the fact that the prover knows such a witness.

Our final goal is a non-interactive argument, but we work in the interactive setting and then use standard techniques for transforming the interactive arguments to non-interactive.

Denote with $\langle \mathcal{P}(x, w), \mathcal{V}(x)\rangle$ the transcript of an execution of $\mathcal{P}$ and $\mathcal{V}$ with respective inputs x, w and x. Let $\mathsf{view}_\mathcal{V}\langle \mathcal{P}(x, w), \mathcal{V}(x)\rangle$ ($\mathsf{view}_\mathcal{P}\langle \mathcal{P}(x, w), \mathcal{V}(x)\rangle$) be the views of $\mathcal{V}$ ($\mathcal{P}$) in a protocol execution (i.e. the input, randomness and all incoming messages), and finally let $\mathsf{out}_\mathcal{V}\langle \mathcal{P}(x, w), \mathcal{V}(x)\rangle$ be the final verdict of the verifier (accept or reject).

Definition 1. *The pair $\langle \mathcal{P}, \mathcal{V}\rangle$ is a Zero Knowledge Argument of Knowledge if it is public coin, it has perfect completeness, statistical witness extended emulation and perfect honest verifier zero Knowledge as defined next.*

Definition 2. *The pair $\langle \mathcal{P}, \mathcal{V}\rangle$ has Perfect Completeness if for all $(x, w) \in \mathcal{R}_\mathcal{L}$ it holds that* $\Pr\left[\mathsf{out}_\mathcal{V}\langle \mathcal{P}(x, w), \mathcal{V}(x)\rangle = 1\right] = 1$.

Definition 3. *The pair $\langle \mathcal{P}, \mathcal{V}\rangle$ has Statistical Witness Extended Emulation if for all deterministic polynomial $\mathcal{P}^*$, there exists an expected polynomial time extractor $\mathcal{E}$, such that for all (unbounded) adversaries $\mathcal{A}$*

$$\left| \Pr\left[1 \leftarrow \mathcal{A}(tr) \;\middle|\; \begin{array}{c} (x, s) \leftarrow \mathcal{A}(1^\lambda) \wedge \\ tr \leftarrow \langle \mathcal{P}^*(x, s), \mathcal{V}(x)\rangle \end{array} \right] - \right.$$

$$\left. \Pr\left[1 \leftarrow \mathcal{A}(tr) \;\middle|\; \begin{array}{r} (x, s) \leftarrow \mathcal{A}(1^\lambda) \wedge \\ (tr, w) \leftarrow \mathcal{E}^{\langle \mathcal{P}^*(x, s), \mathcal{V}(x)\rangle}(u) \wedge \\ \textit{if } tr \textit{ is accepting then } (x, w) \in \mathcal{R}_\mathcal{L} \end{array} \right] \right| \le \mathsf{negl}(\lambda).$$

Definition 4. *An $(n_1, \ldots, n_\mu)$-tree of accepting transcripts for the pair $\langle \mathcal{P}, \mathcal{V}\rangle$ with $2\mu + 1$ rounds is a tree where:*

- *Each node of the tree in level i is labeled with the transcript of the protocol used up to $\mathcal{V}$'s i-th message.*
- *Each node in the same level i is labeled with a transcript that uses fresh (uniformly distributed and independent) randomness for the verifier's i-th challenges.*
- *Level i has n_i descendants.*
- *The leafs are labeled with transcripts that are accepted by the verifier.*

Definition 5. *The pair $\langle \mathcal{P}, \mathcal{V} \rangle$ has $(n_1, \ldots, n_\mu)$-generalized special soundness if there exists a PPT extractor $\mathcal{E}$ such that given an $(n_1, \ldots, n_\mu)$-tree of accepting transcripts for the pair $\langle \mathcal{P}, \mathcal{V} \rangle$, the extractor $\mathcal{E}$ outputs a valid witness for the statement.*

Definition 6. *An interactive proof system $\langle \mathcal{P}, \mathcal{V} \rangle$ is public coin if all messages from $\mathcal{V}$ to $\mathcal{P}$ are independent and uniformly distributed, and are uniquely defined by the randomness of the verifier alone.*

Definition 7. *A public coin interactive proof system $\langle \mathcal{P}, \mathcal{V} \rangle$ is perfect Honest Verifier Zero Knowledge (HVZK) if there exists a PPT simulator $\mathcal{S}$, such that for all PPT $\mathcal{A}$, it holds that*

$$\Pr\left[1 \leftarrow \mathcal{A}(tr) \middle| (x, w, r) \leftarrow \mathcal{A}(1^\lambda) \wedge tr \leftarrow \langle \mathcal{P}^*(x, w), \mathcal{V}(x; r) \rangle \wedge (x, w) \in \mathcal{R}_\mathcal{L}\right] =$$
$$\Pr\left[1 \leftarrow \mathcal{A}(tr) \middle| (x, w, r) \leftarrow \mathcal{A}(1^\lambda) \wedge tr \leftarrow \mathcal{S}(x, r) \wedge (x, w) \in \mathcal{R}_\mathcal{L}\right].$$

Theorem 1. *Let $\langle \mathcal{P}, \mathcal{V} \rangle$ be a $2\mu + 1$ round, public coin, interactive proof system with $(n_1, \ldots, n_\mu)$-generalized special soundness and $\prod_{i=1}^{\mu} n_i = \mathcal{O}(\lambda^c)$ for a constant c. Then $\langle \mathcal{P}, \mathcal{V} \rangle$ has witness extended emulation.*

The proof of the theorem is given in [10].

Updateable Non-interactive (Zero Knowledge) Arguments of Knowledge. Informally, a non-interactive argument system in the common reference string model is a ZK argument with two rounds where the first is a setup round to create parameters that can be reused in many proofs. The most efficient constructions for general NP statements (e.g. Groth [26]) need a very expensive and inefficient trusted setup. To deal with this, Groth et al. [27] introduced the notion of an Updateable Setup where users can non-interactively update the parameters in a way that gives us the following guarantee: if an honest update takes place, then no PPT adversary can break soundness. We follow the model of Groth et al. [27], who show that for updateability it suffices to prove that an argument is secure in the following model.

- The adversary creates setup parameters.
- An honest update on these parameters takes place.
- The adversary updates the parameters.
- Circuit specific parameters are derived publicly for a circuit $\mathcal{C}$.
- Knowledge soundness is challenged w.r.t. these parameters.

We emphasize that the circuit-specific setup is done publicly: no secret is involved in it. Anyone can take the universal parameters, and deterministically compute the circuit-specific CRS. We present the definition of Updateable Non-Interactive (Zero Knowledge) Arguments of Knowledge.

Definition 8. *An Updateable Non-Interactive (Zero Knowledge) Argument of Knowledge is a tuple of algorithms* (USetup, Update, VrfySetup, VrfyUpdate, CircuitSetup, Prove, Vrfy) *where*

- $\sigma \leftarrow \mathsf{USetup}(1^\lambda, n)$: USetup *takes as input the security parameter* λ *and an upper bound on the derived circuit size* n*, and outputs a universal CRS* σ.
- $(\sigma', \pi_{\sigma'}) \leftarrow \mathsf{Update}(\sigma)$: Update *takes as input a universal CRS* σ*, and produces a new universal CRS* σ' *along with a proof of correct update* $\pi_{\sigma'}$.
- $0/1 \leftarrow \mathsf{VrfySetup}(\sigma, 1^\lambda, n)$: VrfySetup *takes as input a universal CRS* σ*, the security parameter* λ *and* n *and outputs a bit indicating the correctness of the structure of the universal CRS.*
- $0/1 \leftarrow \mathsf{VrfyUpdate}(\sigma', \sigma, \pi_{\sigma'})$: VrfyUpdate *takes as input the new and old CRS* σ' *and* σ*, and a proof* π'_σ*, and outputs a bit indicating the correctness of the update.*
- $\sigma_\mathcal{C} \leftarrow \mathsf{CircuitSetup}(\sigma, \mathcal{C})$: *is a deterministic algorithm that takes as input the description of a circuit with size bounded by* n*, and the universal CRS and outputs circuit specific parameters* $\sigma_\mathcal{C}$.
- $\pi \leftarrow \mathsf{Prove}(\sigma_\mathcal{C}, x, w)$: *takes as input the CRS* $\sigma_\mathcal{C}$*, the public and private input* x, w*, and outputs a proof* π.
- $0/1 \leftarrow \mathsf{Vrfy}(\sigma_\mathcal{C}, x, \pi)$: *takes as input the CRS* $\sigma_\mathcal{C}$*, the public input* x *and a proof* π*, and outputs a proof indicating its validity.*

which is Perfectly Complete, Knowledge Sound and Statistically Zero Knowledge as defined next.

Definition 9. *An Updateable Non-Interactive Argument of Knowledge is Perfectly Complete if for all* λ, n

$$\Pr\left[\mathsf{VrfySetup}(\sigma, 1^\lambda, n) = 1 \,\middle|\, \sigma \leftarrow \mathsf{USetup}(1^\lambda, n)\right] = 1,$$

for all λ, n, σ

$$\Pr\left[\begin{matrix}\mathsf{VrfySetup}(\sigma', 1^\lambda, n) = 1 \wedge \\ \mathsf{VrfyUpdate}(\sigma, \sigma', \pi_{\sigma'}) = 1\end{matrix} \,\middle|\, \begin{matrix}\mathsf{VrfySetup}(\sigma, 1^\lambda, n) = 1 \wedge \\ (\sigma', \pi_{\sigma'}) \leftarrow \mathsf{Update}(\sigma)\end{matrix}\right] = 1$$

and for all $\lambda, n, \sigma, \mathcal{C}, x, w$ *where* $\mathcal{C}$ *encodes a circuit of size bounded by* n *and* $\mathcal{R}_\mathcal{C}(x, w) = 1$

$$\Pr\left[\mathsf{Vrfy}(\sigma_\mathcal{C}, x, \pi) = 1 \,\middle|\, \begin{matrix}\mathsf{VrfySetup}(\sigma, 1^\lambda, n) = 1 \wedge \\ \sigma_\mathcal{C} \leftarrow \mathsf{CircuitSetup}(\sigma, \mathcal{C}) \wedge \\ \pi \leftarrow \mathsf{Prove}(\sigma_\mathcal{C}, x, w)\end{matrix}\right] = 1.$$

Definition 10. *An Updateable Non-Interactive Argument of Knowledge is Knowledge Sound if for all stateful PPT adversaries* $\mathcal{A} = (\mathcal{A}_1, \mathcal{A}_2, \mathcal{A}_3)$*, there exists an extractor* $\mathcal{E}_\mathcal{A}$*, such that for all* λ*,* n*,* $\mathcal{C}$ *where* $\mathcal{C}$ *is a circuit of size bounded by* n

$$\Pr\left[\begin{matrix}\mathsf{VrfySetup}(\sigma_1, 1^\lambda, n) = 1 \wedge \\ \mathsf{VrfyUpdate}(\sigma_3, \sigma_2, \pi_{\sigma_3}) = 1 \wedge \\ \mathsf{Vrfy}(\sigma_\mathcal{C}, x, \pi) = 1 \wedge \\ \mathcal{C}(x, w) \neq 1\end{matrix} \,\middle|\, \begin{matrix}(\sigma_1, st_1) \leftarrow \mathcal{A}_1(1^\lambda, n) \wedge \\ (\sigma_2, \pi_{\sigma_2}) \leftarrow \mathsf{Update}(\sigma_1) \wedge \\ (\sigma_3, \pi_{\sigma_3}, st_2) \leftarrow \mathcal{A}_2(st_1, \sigma_2, \pi_{\sigma_2}) \wedge \\ \sigma_\mathcal{C} \leftarrow \mathsf{CircuitSetup}(\sigma_3, \mathcal{C}) \wedge \\ (x, \pi) \leftarrow \mathcal{A}_3(st_2, \sigma_\mathcal{C}; r) \wedge \\ w \leftarrow \mathcal{E}(\sigma_\mathcal{C}, x; r)\end{matrix}\right] \leq \mathsf{negl}(\lambda).$$

Definition 11. *An Updateable Non-Interactive Arguments of Knowledge is Statistically Zero knowledge in the Random Oracle model if there exists a pair of PPT algorithms $\mathcal{S}_1, \mathcal{S}_2$, where $\mathcal{S}_2$ is stateful, such that for all $\mathcal{A}$, and for all circuits $\mathcal{C}$ of size bounded by n, where $\mathcal{C}$ takes as input a public value x and a private value w then*

$$\Pr\left[b' = b \;\middle|\; \begin{array}{r} b \leftarrow \{0,1\} \wedge \\ \sigma \leftarrow \mathcal{A}^{H_b}(\mathsf{setup}, 1^\lambda, n) \wedge \\ \mathsf{VrfySetup}(\sigma, 1^\lambda, n) = 1 \wedge \\ \sigma_{\mathcal{C}} \leftarrow \mathsf{CircuitSetup}(\sigma, \mathcal{C}) \wedge \\ b' \leftarrow \mathcal{A}^{H_b, O_b}(\sigma_{\mathcal{C}}) \end{array} \right] \leq \frac{1}{2} + \mathsf{negl}(\lambda)$$

where H is modeled as a Random Oracle and

$$O_0(x,w) \leftarrow \begin{cases} \bot, & \textit{if } \mathcal{R}_{\mathcal{C}}(x,w) = 0 \\ \mathsf{Prove}(\sigma_{\mathcal{C}}, x, w), & \textit{otherwise} \end{cases}, \quad H_0(m) \leftarrow H(m),$$

$$O_1(x,w) \leftarrow \begin{cases} \bot, & \textit{if } \mathcal{R}_{\mathcal{C}}(x,w) = 0 \\ \mathcal{S}_1(\sigma_{\mathcal{C}}, x), & \textit{otherwise} \end{cases}, \quad H_1(m) \leftarrow \mathcal{S}_2(m).$$

Note that this definition considers adversarially created parameters, i.e. Subversion Resistant ZK [4].

From HVZK Interactive AoK to Non Interactive ZK AoK. It is well-known that we can use the Fiat-Shamir heuristic to transform any public coin Perfect HVZK interactive argument to a non-interactive full-fledged Statistical Zero Knowledge argument in the Random Oracle Model.

2.3 Updateable Commitment Schemes

We define commitment schemes which have an updateability property as well. We do this to simplify proofs in the following sections. An updateable commitment will be enough to guarantee updateability of all the protocols in this work, since all the arguments presented hold regardless of parameters *unless* there is a breach in the binding property of the commitment scheme.

Definition 12. *An Updateable Commitment Scheme is a tuple of algorithms* (Setup, VrfySetup, Update, VrfyUpdate, Com, Open) *such that*

- $\mathsf{ck} \leftarrow \mathsf{Setup}(1^\lambda, n)$ *takes as input the security parameter λ and the vector dimension n, and outputs a commitment key* ck.
- $(\mathsf{ck}', \pi_{\mathsf{ck}'}) \leftarrow \mathsf{Update}(\mathsf{ck})$: Update *takes as input a commitment key* ck *and produces a new commitment key* ck′ *and a proof of correct update $\pi_{\mathsf{ck}'}$.*
- $0/1 \leftarrow \mathsf{VrfySetup}(\mathsf{ck}, 1^\lambda, n)$: VrfySetup *takes as input a commitment key* ck, *the security parameter λ and the dimension n, and outputs a bit indicating the correctness of the structure of the key.*

- $0/1 \leftarrow \mathsf{VrfyUpdate}(\mathsf{ck}', \mathsf{ck}, \pi_{\mathsf{ck}'})$: VrfyUpdate *takes as input a new key* ck′, *an old key* ck *and a proof* $\pi_{\mathsf{ck}'}$, *and outputs a bit indicating update correctness.*
- $(c, \tau) \leftarrow \mathsf{Com}(\mathsf{ck}, \mathbf{m})$ *takes as input the commitment key and a message* $\mathbf{m} \in \mathcal{M}^n$, *and outputs a commitment* $c \in \mathcal{C}$ *and an opening trapdoor* $\tau \in \mathcal{T}$.
- $0/1 \leftarrow \mathsf{Open}(\mathsf{ck}, c, \mathbf{m}, \tau)$ *takes as input the commitment key, the message and the opening trapdoor and outputs a bit indicating the validity of the opening.*

which is Correct, Updateable Computationally Binding and Perfectly Hiding as defined next.

Definition 13. *An Updateable Commitment Scheme is correct if for all* λ, n

$$\Pr\left[\mathsf{VrfySetup}(\mathsf{ck}, 1^\lambda, n) = 1 \middle| \mathsf{ck} \leftarrow \mathsf{Setup}(1^\lambda, n)\right] = 1,$$

for all λ, n, ck

$$\Pr\left[\begin{array}{c} \mathsf{VrfySetup}(\mathsf{ck}', 1^\lambda, n) = 1 \wedge \\ \mathsf{VrfyUpdate}(\mathsf{ck}, \mathsf{ck}', \pi_{\mathsf{ck}'}) = 1 \end{array} \middle| \begin{array}{c} \mathsf{VrfySetup}(\mathsf{ck}, 1^\lambda, n) = 1 \wedge \\ (\mathsf{ck}', \pi_{\mathsf{ck}'}) \leftarrow \mathsf{Update}(\mathsf{ck}) \end{array}\right] = 1$$

and for all $\lambda, n, \mathsf{ck}, \mathbf{m}$

$$\Pr\left[\mathsf{Open}(\mathsf{ck}, c, \mathbf{m}, \tau) = 1 \middle| \begin{array}{c} \mathsf{VrfySetup}(\mathsf{ck}, 1^\lambda, n) = 1 \wedge \\ (c, \tau) \leftarrow \mathsf{Com}(\mathsf{ck}, \mathbf{m}) \end{array}\right] = 1.$$

Definition 14. *An Updateable Commitment Scheme has the Updateable Computational Binding property if for all stateful PPT* $\mathcal{A} = (\mathcal{A}_1, \mathcal{A}_2, \mathcal{A}_3)$, *and for all* λ, n

$$\Pr\left[\begin{array}{c} \mathsf{VrfySetup}(\mathsf{ck}_1, 1^\lambda, n) = 1 \wedge \\ \mathsf{VrfyUpdate}(\mathsf{ck}_3, \mathsf{ck}_2, \pi_{\mathsf{ck}_3}) = 1 \wedge \\ \mathsf{Open}(\mathsf{ck}_3, c, \mathbf{m}_1, \tau_1) = 1 \wedge \\ \mathsf{Open}(\mathsf{ck}_3, c, \mathbf{m}_2, \tau_2) = 1 \wedge \\ \mathbf{m}_1 \neq \mathbf{m}_2 \end{array} \middle| \begin{array}{r} (\mathsf{ck}_1, st_1) \leftarrow \mathcal{A}_1(1^\lambda, n) \wedge \\ (\mathsf{ck}_2, \pi_{\mathsf{ck}_2}) \leftarrow \mathsf{Update}(\mathsf{ck}_1) \wedge \\ (\mathsf{ck}_3, \pi_{\mathsf{ck}_3}, st_2) \leftarrow \mathcal{A}_2(st_1, \mathsf{ck}_2, \pi_{\mathsf{ck}_2}) \wedge \\ (c, \mathbf{m}_1, \tau_1, \mathbf{m}_2, \tau_2) \leftarrow \mathcal{A}_3(st_2) \end{array}\right] \leq \mathsf{negl}(\lambda).$$

Definition 15. *An Updateable Commitment Scheme is perfectly hiding if, for all* $\lambda, n, \mathbf{m}$, *and all* ck *s.t.* $\mathsf{VrfySetup}(\mathsf{ck}, 1^\lambda, n) = 1$, *and all* c_1

$$\Pr\left[c = c_1 \middle| (c, \tau) \leftarrow \mathsf{Com}(\mathsf{ck}, \mathbf{m})\right] = \Pr\left[c = c_1 \middle| c \leftarrow \mathcal{C}\right].$$

3 Assumptions

We present the assumptions used in this work.

Definition 16. *(DLOG Assumption) The* DLOG *Assumption holds w.r.t. a group generator* GroupGen *if for all PPT adversaries* $\mathcal{A}$

$$\Pr\left[r = r' \middle| \mathsf{pp} \leftarrow \mathsf{GroupGen}(1^\lambda) \wedge r \leftarrow \mathbb{Z}_q \wedge r' \leftarrow \mathcal{A}(\mathsf{pp}, [r])\right] \leq \mathsf{negl}(\lambda).$$

We will also consider natural extensions of the DLOG Assumption. In the n-DLOG Assumption, the adversary receives n-powers of r, $[1], [r], \ldots, [r^n]$. In the Asymmetric DLOG Assumption in asymmetric bilinear groups, the adversary receives r in both groups $[r]_1, [r]_2$. Similarly, in the asymmetric n-DLOG Assumption, the adversary receives the powers of r in both groups. In either case, its goal is to compute $r \in \mathbb{Z}_q$.

The inner product argument of Bootle et al. [10] and the argument presented in this paper are based on the generalization of the DLOG Assumption presented next but with different vector distributions. The binding property of the vector commitments used in these arguments trivially reduces to this assumption.

Definition 17. *Let $n \in \mathbb{N}$. We call $\mathcal{D}_n$ a vector distribution if it outputs in PPT time, with overwhelming probability vectors in $\mathbb{Z}_q^n$.*

In this paper, $\mathcal{D}_n$ will typically be the distribution of the key of some perfectly hiding commitment scheme. More specifically, we will consider the distributions:

$$\mathcal{U}_n : \mathbf{r} = (1, x_1, \ldots, x_{n-1}), \qquad \mathcal{PW}_n : \mathbf{r} = \left(1, x, \ldots, x^{n-1}\right),$$
$$\mathcal{ML}_{2^\nu} : \mathbf{r} = (1, x_1, x_2, x_1 \cdot x_2, \ldots, x_1 \cdots x_\nu),$$

where $x, x_i \leftarrow \mathbb{Z}_q$. The first distribution is the uniform distribution, the second is the n-Power distribution and the last one is the multilinear monomial distribution with $n = 2^\nu$. Note that in the notation we introduced before, the power and multilinear monomial distribution can also be written as $\mathcal{PW}_n : \mathbf{r} = \mathbf{x^n}, x \leftarrow \mathbb{Z}_q$ and $\mathcal{ML}_{2^\nu} : \mathbf{r} = \overline{\mathbf{x}}, \mathbf{x} \leftarrow \mathbb{Z}_q^\nu$.

Definition 18. *The $\mathcal{D}_n$-Find-Rep Assumption holds with respect to* GroupGen *for all polynomial time adversaries $\mathcal{A}$*

$$\Pr\left[[\mathbf{a}^\top \mathbf{r}] = [0] \ \wedge \ \mathbf{a} \neq \mathbf{0} \ \middle| \ \begin{array}{r} \mathsf{pp} \leftarrow \mathsf{GroupGen}(1^\lambda) \wedge \\ \mathbf{r} \leftarrow \mathcal{D}_n \wedge \\ \mathbf{a} \leftarrow \mathcal{A}(\mathsf{pp}, [\mathbf{r}]) \end{array} \right] \leq \mathsf{negl}(\lambda).$$

It is well known that the $\mathcal{U}_n$-Find-Rep (resp. $\mathcal{PW}_n$-Find-Rep) Assumption reduces to the DLOG (resp. q-DLOG) Assumption. For Multilinear Monomial distribution, we prove a similar result in Theorem 2. This assumption is inspired by the Naor-Reingold PRF [34].

In asymmetric bilinear groups, we define the Asymmetric $\mathcal{D}_n$-Find-Rep Assumption analogously except that the adversary receives $\mathbf{r}$ in both source groups $\mathbb{G}_1, \mathbb{G}_2$. We can prove similar reductions to asymmetric variants of the DLOG Assumption.

Theorem 2. *If there exists an adversary that runs in time $t(\lambda)$ and breaks the $\mathcal{ML}_{2^\nu}$-Find-Rep Assumption with probability $\epsilon(\lambda)$ with respect to a group generator* $\mathsf{BilGroupGen}(1^\lambda)$*, then there exists an adversary that breaks the Asymmetric Discrete Logarithm Assumption relative to* $\mathsf{BilGroupGen}(1^\lambda)$ *in time $\mathcal{O}_\lambda(2^\nu) + t(\lambda)$ with probability $\frac{\epsilon(\lambda)}{\nu}$.*

The proof of the theorem is presented in the full version.

4 Distribution Parameterized Vector Commitment

We can construct Updateable Commitment Schemes under the $\mathcal{D}_n$-Find-Rep assumptions we described. The Setup and Com are the same for all and they basically work as in the classical Pedersen Commitment.

We describe for the asymmetric $\mathcal{ML}_n, \mathcal{PW}_n$ distributions the algorithms related to the update (note that for $\mathcal{U}_n$, i.e. the Pedersen Vector Commitment, updateability trivially holds since the Setup is transparent). We present the $\mathcal{ML}_n$ case in detail and discuss which modifications are needed for the $\mathcal{PW}_n$ setting. For our application it is sufficient to give in $\mathbb{G}_2$ only the elements that define the commitment key, and not the whole key vector, i.e. $[\mathbf{x}]_2$ such that $\mathbf{r} = \overline{\mathbf{x}}$. Looking ahead, in the inner product argument $[\mathbf{x}]_2$ will be the compressed key the verifier has.

The update mechanism is fairly simple. To check a commitment key's structure, simply assert the various DDH relations that are implied by the $\mathcal{ML}_n$ distribution, and to update, pick a vector from $\mathcal{ML}_n$ and multiply it pairwise with the current key. NIZK PoK are used to assert that the previous randomness is taken into account in the new key and to ensure that any party updating knows its contribution to the final commitment key.

- **Setup**$(1^\lambda, n)$
  - $\mathsf{pp} \leftarrow \mathsf{GroupGen}(1^\lambda)$.
  - $\mathbf{r} \leftarrow \mathcal{ML}_n$.
  - Output $\mathsf{pp}, [\mathbf{r}]_1, [\mathbf{x}]_2 \leftarrow ([r_1]_2, [r_2]_2, \ldots, [r_{2^i}]_2, \ldots, [r_{2^\nu}]_2)$.
- **VrfySetup** $(\mathsf{pp}, [\mathbf{x}]_2, [\mathbf{r}]_1)$
  - Verify $[r_1]_1 = [1]_1$.
  - For $1 \le i \le \nu$, for $1 \le j \le 2^{i-1}$, check if $e([r_{2^{i-1}+j}]_1, [1]_2) = e([r_j]_1, [x_i]_2)$.
  - If all checks succeed output 1, otherwise output 0.
- **Update** $(\mathsf{pp}, [\mathbf{x}]_2, [\mathbf{r}]_1)$
  - $\mathbf{y} \leftarrow \mathbb{Z}_q^\nu$.
  - Compute $[\mathbf{r}']_1 \leftarrow \overline{\mathbf{y}} \circ [\mathbf{r}]_1$, $[\mathbf{x}']_2 \leftarrow \mathbf{y} \circ [\mathbf{x}]_2$.
  - For $1 \le i \le \nu$, let $\pi_i \leftarrow \mathsf{NIZKAoK}\{([x_i]_2, [x_i']_2), (y_i) : [x_i']_2 = y_i[x_i]_2\}$.
  - Output $(\mathsf{pp}, [\mathbf{x}']_2, [\mathbf{r}']_1, \pi_1, \ldots, \pi_\nu)$.
- **VrfyUpdate** $(\mathsf{pp}, [\mathbf{x}]_2, [\mathbf{x}']_2, [\mathbf{r}']_1, \pi_1, \ldots, \pi_\nu)$
  - If $\pi_1, \ldots, \pi_\nu$ are correct, output $\mathsf{VrfySetup}\,(\mathsf{pp}, [\mathbf{x}']_2, [\mathbf{r}']_1)$.
- **Com** $(\mathsf{pp}, [\mathbf{r}]_1, \mathbf{m})$
  - Pick $\rho \leftarrow \mathbb{Z}_q$.
  - Compute $c \leftarrow [(\mathbf{m}, \rho)^\top \mathbf{r}]$.
  - Output (c, τ) where $\tau \leftarrow ([\mathbf{r}]_1, \rho)$.
- **Open** $(\mathsf{pp}, [\mathbf{x}]_2, \mathbf{m}, c, \tau)$
  - Parse $\tau = ([\mathbf{r}]_1, \rho)$.
  - Output 1 iff $\mathsf{VrfySetup}\,(\mathsf{pp}, [\mathbf{x}]_2, [\mathbf{r}]_1)$ and $c = [(\mathbf{m}, \rho)^\top \mathbf{r}]$.

Theorem 3. *The $\mathcal{ML}_n$-Find-Rep Commitment scheme is Updateably Computationally Binding under the $\mathcal{ML}_n$-Find-Rep assumption, and the existence of a NIZK AoK for the relation $\mathcal{R} = \{(([x], [x']), y) \,|\, [x'] = y[x]\}$.*

The proof of the theorem is presented in the full version.

We can use a transparent scheme such as [12] to prove that an update is correctly performed, which will yield $\mathcal{O}_\lambda(\log\log n)$ proof size.

A similar construction works for the $\mathcal{PW}_n$ distribution. In this case, we simply need the element x encoded in $\mathbb{G}_2$ since this is enough to check that the key is drawn from the $\mathcal{PW}_n$ distribution. That is, for each i, it is enough to check that $e([r_i]_1, [1]_2) = e([r_{i-1}]_1, [x]_2)$. The Update and $\mathsf{VrfyUpdate}$ work in the same way but now a NIZK AoK is only needed for the element $[x]_2$.

As for concrete efficiency, the cost is dominated by the group exponentiations and the pairing operations for the verifier (the NIZK AoK statements are logarithmic in n). Setup and Update are dominated by n exponentiations in $\mathbb{G}_1$, $\mathsf{VrfySetup}$ and $\mathsf{VrfyUpdate}$ by n pairing operations, and Com and Open by one multi-exponentiation of size n in $\mathbb{G}_1$ which, if performed trivially needs n exponentiations. Proof size amounts to $\log n$ proofs of the NIZK AoK in the $\mathcal{ML}_n$ case and 1 in the $\mathcal{PW}_n$ case.

4.1 Commitments to Monomial Vectors

We will need to efficiently compute special commitments in the proof systems we present later. Specifically, given commitment schemes under $\mathcal{ML}_{2^\nu}$ and $\mathcal{PW}_{2^\nu}$ we will need to compute (non-hiding) commitments to $\mathbf{t^n}$ and $\bar{\mathbf{t}}$ where we know t and $t_1, \ldots, t_\nu$, respectively. Of course, these computations can be performed in time linear in the vector dimension, but we want to do so in sublinear (logarithmic in n) time. Since the univariate case reduces to the multilinear one by setting $t_i = t^{2^{i-1}}$, we only consider the most general case of computing $\bar{\mathbf{t}}$ when the keys are drawn from the $\mathcal{ML}_{2^\nu}$ distribution. We will need this in two different settings:

1. In the first case, let $\mathsf{ck} = (\mathsf{ck}_\mathcal{P}, \mathsf{ck}_\mathcal{V})$ be a commitment key. A prover, holding the whole commitment key $\mathsf{ck}_\mathcal{P}$, computes the commitment to $\bar{\mathbf{t}}$ w.r.t. ck, and gives it to a verifier, who holds only a compressed version of it, $\mathsf{ck}_\mathcal{V}$. It also gives a small proof that the issued commitment is a commitment to $\bar{\mathbf{t}}$ w.r.t. ck.
2. In the second case, given a commitment to $\mathbf{1^n}$ w.r.t. some commitment key $\mathsf{ck} = (\mathsf{ck}_\mathcal{P}, \mathsf{ck}_\mathcal{V})$ (which can be precomputed once), the verifier derives a commitment to $\bar{\mathbf{t}}$ w.r.t. a new commitment key $\mathsf{ck}' = (\mathsf{ck}'_\mathcal{P}, \mathsf{ck}'_\mathcal{V})$ in logarithmic time in n.

For the first case we use the following lemma:

Lemma 1. *Let* $\mathsf{ck} = (\mathsf{pp}, [\mathbf{x}]_2, [\mathbf{r}]_1)$ *be a commitment key where* $[\mathbf{r}]_1 = [\bar{\mathbf{x}}]$. *Then* $\mathsf{Com}_{\mathsf{ck}}(\bar{\mathbf{t}}) = \prod_{i=1}^{\nu}(1 + t_i x_i)[1]_1$.

Proof. We use induction on ν.

- When $\nu = 1$, we have $\bar{\mathbf{t}} = (1, t_1)$ and $\bar{\mathbf{x}} = (1, x_1)$. We get

$$\mathsf{Com}_{\mathsf{ck}}(\bar{\mathbf{t}}) = [r_1]_1 + t_1[r_2]_1 = [1]_1 + t_1 x_1[1]_1 = (1 + t_1 x_1)[1]_1.$$

– For $\nu > 1$, we have $[\mathbf{r}_\nu]_1 = (\overline{\mathbf{x}}_{\nu-1}[1]_1, x_\nu \overline{\mathbf{x}}_{\nu-1}[1]_1)$ and $\overline{\mathbf{t}} = (\overline{\mathbf{t}}_{\nu-1}, t_\nu \overline{\mathbf{t}}_{\nu-1})$ and

$$\begin{aligned}\mathsf{Com}_{\mathsf{ck}}(\overline{\mathbf{t}}) &= [\overline{\mathbf{t}}^\top \mathbf{r}_\nu]_1 = [\overline{\mathbf{t}}_{\nu-1}{}^\top \mathbf{r}_{\nu-1}]_1 + [t_\nu \overline{\mathbf{t}}_{\nu-1}{}^\top x_\nu \mathbf{r}_{\nu-1}]_1 \\ &= [\overline{\mathbf{t}}_{\nu-1}{}^\top \mathbf{r}_{\nu-1}]_1 + t_\nu x_\nu [\overline{\mathbf{t}}_{\nu-1}{}^\top \mathbf{r}_{\nu-1}]_1 \\ &= (1 + t_\nu x_\nu)[\overline{\mathbf{t}}_{\nu-1}{}^\top \mathbf{r}_{\nu-1}]_1 \\ &= (1 + t_\nu x_\nu) \prod_{i=1}^{\nu-1} (1 + t_i x_i)[1]_1,\end{aligned}$$

where the last equality follows from the induction hypothesis. ■

We take advantage of this structure by having the prover sending, for all $i \in \{1, \ldots, \nu\}$, the elements

$$[\tau_i]_1 \leftarrow \prod_{j=1}^{i} (1 + t_j x_j)[r]_1 = (1 + t_i x_i)[\tau_{i-1}]_1,$$

where $[\tau_0]_1 = [1]_1$. The verifier can then use the pairing to check

$$e(t_i[\tau_{i-1}]_1, [x_i]_2) = e([\tau_i - \tau_{i-1}]_1, [1]_2).$$

The prover needs to do $\log n$ $\mathbb{G}_1$ multi-exponentiations each of size 2^i for $i \in \{1, \ldots, \frac{n}{2}\}$, which can be implemented with n $\mathbb{G}_1$ exponentiations. The verifier needs to perform $\log n$ pairing operations and $2 \log n$ $\mathbb{G}_1$ exponentiations to verify.

For the second case, we do the following: suppose the verifier is given $\mathsf{Com}_{\mathsf{ck}_1}(\mathbf{1}) = [\mathbf{1}^\top \mathbf{r}]_1$. The verifier and the prover can compute a new verification key ck_2 as follows:

$$(\mathsf{ck}_2^{\mathcal{V}}, \mathsf{ck}_2^{\mathcal{P}}) = (([r]_1, t_1^{-1}[x_1]_2, \ldots, t_\nu^{-1}[x_\nu]_2), (\mathbf{r} \circ \overline{\mathbf{t}}^{-1})).$$

Then, we have:

$$[\mathbf{1}^\top \mathbf{r}]_1 = [(\mathbf{1} \circ \overline{\mathbf{t}})^\top (\mathbf{r} \circ \overline{\mathbf{t}}^{-1})]_1 = [\overline{\mathbf{t}}^\top (\mathbf{r} \circ \overline{\mathbf{t}}^{-1})]_1 = \mathsf{Com}_{\mathsf{ck}_2}(\overline{\mathbf{t}}).$$

The verifier needs $\log n$ $\mathbb{G}_2$ exponentiations and the prover can implicitly hold its key without computing it: when it needs to commit to $\mathbf{m}$ it can simply commit to $\mathbf{m} \circ \mathbf{t}^{-1}$ thus saving in expensive group operations.

5 Improved Inner Product Argument

In this section, we will first provide a high-level description of the inner product argument of [10], which has linear verification cost. Next, in Subsect. 5.2 we briefly discuss how to reduce the verification complexity to logarithmic in the designated verifier setting in the CRS model by changing the distribution of the commitment keys (still under the DLOG Assumption). In asymmetric bilinear groups, the construction can be "compiled" to achieve public verifiability, as discussed in Subsect. 5.3.

5.1 Inner Product Argument

We first briefly present the Inner Product Argument of [10]. The argument is a Proof of Knowledge of the openings of two (non-hiding) Vector Pedersen Commitments that satisfy an inner product relation. In [10], keys are sampled from $\mathcal{U}_n$. Formally, it is a proof of knowledge for the following language $\mathcal{L}_{\mathsf{IP}}$:

$$(\mathsf{pp}, [\mathbf{r}], [\mathbf{s}] \in \mathbb{G}^{2^\nu}, [\alpha], [\beta] \in \mathbb{G}, z \in \mathbb{Z}_q) \in \mathcal{L}_{\mathsf{IP}} \iff$$
$$\exists \mathbf{a}, \mathbf{b} \in \mathbb{Z}_q^{2^\nu} \text{ s.t. } [\alpha] = [\mathbf{a}^\top \mathbf{r}] \wedge [\beta] = [\mathbf{b}^\top \mathbf{s}] \wedge \mathbf{a}^\top \mathbf{b} = z.$$

The idea of the protocol is to reduce this statement to an equivalent one of roughly half the size.

To do that, we create new commitment keys which have size half of the original one by splitting them in half and then combining them to a new key based on a challenge issued by the verifier. That is, the new commitment key will be $[\mathbf{r}'] = c^{-1}[\mathbf{r}_{\frac{1}{2}}] + c^{-2}[\mathbf{r}_{\frac{2}{2}}]$, where c is the verifier's challenge.

In order to prevent the prover from taking advantage of the split, we first ask her to give partial commitments $[\alpha_{-1}] = [\mathbf{a}_{\frac{1}{2}}^\top \mathbf{r}_{\frac{2}{2}}]$, $[\alpha_1] = [\mathbf{a}_{\frac{2}{2}}^\top \mathbf{r}_{\frac{1}{2}}]$.

The new witness will be $\mathbf{a}' = c\mathbf{a}_{\frac{1}{2}} + c^2 \mathbf{a}_{\frac{2}{2}}$. Note that both prover and verifier can compute the commitment to this new value, for every challenge c, from the partial commitments as follows:

$$\begin{aligned}
[\alpha'] = [\mathbf{a'}^\top \mathbf{r}'] &= [(\mathbf{a}_{\frac{1}{2}} c + \mathbf{a}_{\frac{2}{2}} c^2)^\top (c^{-1}\mathbf{r}_{\frac{1}{2}} + c^{-2}\mathbf{r}_{\frac{2}{2}})] \\
&= [\mathbf{a}_{\frac{1}{2}}^\top \mathbf{r}_{\frac{1}{2}}] + [\mathbf{a}_{\frac{2}{2}}^\top \mathbf{r}_{\frac{2}{2}}] + c^{-1}[\mathbf{a}_{\frac{1}{2}}^\top \mathbf{r}_{\frac{2}{2}}] + c[\mathbf{a}_{\frac{2}{2}}^\top \mathbf{r}_{\frac{1}{2}}] \\
&= [\alpha] + c^{-1}[\alpha_{-1}] + c[\alpha_1].
\end{aligned}$$

The same procedure is done for the second commitment $[\beta] = [\mathbf{b}^\top \mathbf{s}]$ with the inverse challenge c^{-1}.

Finally, the prover sends before seeing the challenge c the values $z_{-1} = \mathbf{a}_{\frac{2}{2}}^\top \mathbf{b}_{\frac{1}{2}}$ and $z_1 = \mathbf{a}_{\frac{1}{2}}^\top \mathbf{b}_{\frac{2}{2}}$, and based on these, the new inner product is computed as $z' = z_{-1}c + z + z_1 c^{-1}$. The new statement becomes $(\mathsf{pp}, [\mathbf{r}'], [\mathbf{s}'], [\alpha'], [\beta'], z') \in \mathcal{L}_{\mathsf{IP}}$.

Straightforward calculations assert that the new witness is indeed a witness for the new statement. The prover can now simply send the new witness $\mathbf{a}', \mathbf{b}'$ with cost half of what it would take to send $\mathbf{a}, \mathbf{b}$.

To achieve logarithmic complexity, the prover and the verifier recursively proceed in reducing the statement size until it is constant. The prover finally sends the witness. Under the generalized forking lemma the protocol remains sound.

We formally present the protocol next.

IPReduce

- Common input: $\sigma = (\mathsf{pp}, [\mathbf{r}], [\mathbf{s}])$, $[\alpha]$, $[\beta]$, z.
- $\mathcal{P}$ input: $\mathbf{a}, \mathbf{b}$.
- Statement: $(\sigma, [\alpha], [\beta], z) \in \mathcal{L}_{\mathsf{IP}}$.

The prover and verifier proceed as follows:

- $\mathcal{P}$ computes

$$[\alpha_{-1}] \leftarrow [\mathbf{a}_{\frac{1}{2}}^{\top}\mathbf{r}_{\frac{2}{2}}], \qquad [\beta_{-1}] \leftarrow [\mathbf{b}_{\frac{1}{2}}^{\top}\mathbf{s}_{\frac{2}{2}}], \qquad z_{-1} \leftarrow \mathbf{a}_{\frac{2}{2}}^{\top}\mathbf{b}_{\frac{1}{2}},$$

$$[\alpha_{1}] \leftarrow [\mathbf{a}_{\frac{2}{2}}^{\top}\mathbf{r}_{\frac{1}{2}}], \qquad [\beta_{1}] \leftarrow [\mathbf{b}_{\frac{2}{2}}^{\top}\mathbf{s}_{\frac{1}{2}}], \qquad z_{1} \leftarrow \mathbf{a}_{\frac{1}{2}}^{\top}\mathbf{b}_{\frac{2}{2}}.$$

- $\mathcal{P}$ sends $[\alpha_{-1}], [\alpha_1], [\beta_{-1}], [\beta_1], z_{-1}, z_1$ and $\mathcal{V}$ replies with $c \leftarrow \mathbb{Z}_q$.
- $\mathcal{P}$ computes

$$\mathbf{a}' \leftarrow \mathbf{a}_{\frac{1}{2}}c + \mathbf{a}_{\frac{2}{2}}c^2, \qquad \mathbf{b}' \leftarrow \mathbf{b}_{\frac{1}{2}}c^{-1} + \mathbf{b}_{\frac{2}{2}}c^{-2}.$$

- $\mathcal{P}$ and $\mathcal{V}$ compute

$$[\mathbf{r}'] \leftarrow c^{-1}[\mathbf{r}_{\frac{1}{2}}] + c^{-2}[\mathbf{r}_{\frac{2}{2}}], \qquad [\mathbf{s}'] \leftarrow c[\mathbf{s}_{\frac{1}{2}}] + c^2[\mathbf{s}_{\frac{2}{2}}],$$

$$[\alpha'] \leftarrow c^{-1}[\alpha_{-1}] + [\alpha] + c^{1}[\alpha_1], \qquad [\beta'] \leftarrow c^{1}[\beta_{-1}] + [\beta] + c^{-1}[\beta_1],$$

$$z' \leftarrow z_{-1}c^{1} + z + z_1 c^{-1},$$

$$\sigma' \leftarrow (\mathsf{pp}, [\mathbf{r}'], [\mathbf{s}']).$$

- The reduced statement is $(\sigma', [\alpha'], [\beta'], z') \in \mathcal{L}_{\mathsf{IP}}$, with witness $\mathbf{a}', \mathbf{b}'$.

5.2 DV Inner Product Argument with Logarithmic Verifier

In this section we give the intuition on how to modify the above protocol with a $\mathcal{D}_n$-variant of the commitment scheme to achieve a logarithmic verifier. Full details are only given for the public verifiable scheme, which is very similar.

The linear overhead in the verifier's computation is computing the new key $\mathbf{r}'$. Having a structured commitment key allows to make this computation implicit for the verifier. If $\mathbf{r} \leftarrow \mathcal{ML}_n$, then $\mathbf{r} = (\mathbf{r}_{\frac{1}{2}}, \mathbf{r}_{\frac{2}{2}}) = (\mathbf{r}_{\frac{1}{2}}, x_\nu \mathbf{r}_{\frac{1}{2}})$. So, in the first round, the key for the next round is

$$[\mathbf{r}'] = c^{-1}[\mathbf{r}_{\frac{1}{2}}] + c^{-2}[\mathbf{r}_{\frac{2}{2}}] = (c^{-1} + x_\nu c^{-2})[\mathbf{r}_{\frac{1}{2}}].$$

The new key is now determined by $[x_1], \ldots, [x_{\nu-1}]$ and the new generator $(c^{-1} + x_\nu c^{-2})[1]$. Further, this transformation respects the structure of the key, which can again be written as $\mathbf{r}' = (\mathbf{r}'_{\frac{1}{2}}, x_{\nu-1}\mathbf{r}'_{\frac{1}{2}})$, so the same argument can be applied again.

In the designated verifier case, we let the verifier know $x_1, \ldots, x_\nu$. It does not compute or read $[\mathbf{r}']$ in each round but just checks in the last round if:

$$[r'] = \prod_{i=1}^{\nu}(c_i^{-1} + x_{\nu-i+1}c_i^{-2})[1],$$

where c_i is the challenge at round i, and $[r']$ is the key in the last round (consisting of 1 element). The same holds for the second key $[s']$. Therefore, verification requires a logarithmic number of operations.

When $\mathbf{r} \leftarrow \mathcal{PW}_n$, the verification can also be reduced to logarithmic, as the structure of the key is very similar, namely, $\mathbf{r} = (\mathbf{r}_{\frac{1}{2}}, \mathbf{r}_{\frac{2}{2}}) = (\mathbf{r}_{\frac{1}{2}}, x^{2^{\nu-1}} \mathbf{r}_{\frac{1}{2}})$. The $\mathcal{PW}_{2^\nu}$ can be seen as a special case where $x_i = x^{2^{i-1}}$.

5.3 Inner Product Argument with Logarithmic Verifier

To allow public verifiability, we work in asymmetric bilinear groups. The verifier can no longer compute

$$\prod_{i=1}^{\nu} (c_i^{-1} + x_{\nu-i+1} c_i^{-2})[1],$$

but it lets the prover compute the intermediate values in each round (which it can compute without knowledge of x_i), and the verifier uses the pairing as a DDH oracle to verify this claim.

We now present the argument formally for the $\mathcal{ML}_{2^\nu}$ distribution (for $\mathcal{PW}_n$ the argument is defined similarly and we omit the details). First, we define the language of well structured commitments. We include the generator since it will be modified in each round.

$$(\mathsf{pp}, [r]_1, [\mathbf{r}]_1, [\mathbf{x}]_2) \in \mathcal{L}_{\mathsf{Com}}^{\mathcal{ML}_{2^\nu}} \iff$$
$$[r_1]_1 = [r]_1 \wedge \forall i \in \{1, \ldots, \nu\} \, \forall j \in \{1, \ldots, 2^{i-1}\} \, [r_{2^{i-1}+j}]_1 = x_i [r_j]_1.$$

The language to be proven and the reduction step are presented next.

$$(\mathsf{pp}, [r]_1, [s]_1, [\mathbf{x}]_2, [\mathbf{y}]_2, [\alpha]_1, [\beta]_1, z) \in \mathcal{L}_{\mathsf{IP}} \iff$$
$$\exists \, [\mathbf{r}]_1, [\mathbf{s}]_1 \in \mathbb{G}^{2^\nu}, \mathbf{a}, \mathbf{b} \in \mathbb{Z}_q^{2^\nu} \text{ s.t.}$$
$$(\mathsf{pp}, [r]_1, [\mathbf{r}]_1, [\mathbf{x}]_2) \in \mathcal{L}_{\mathsf{Com}}^{\mathcal{ML}_{2^\nu}} \wedge (\mathsf{pp}, [s]_1, [\mathbf{s}]_1, [\mathbf{y}]_2) \in \mathcal{L}_{\mathsf{Com}}^{\mathcal{ML}_{2^\nu}} \wedge$$
$$[\alpha]_1 = [\mathbf{a}^\top \mathbf{r}]_1 \wedge [\beta]_1 = [\mathbf{b}^\top \mathbf{s}]_1 \wedge \mathbf{a}^\top \mathbf{b} = z.$$

PVReduce

- Common input: $\sigma = (\mathsf{pp}, [r]_1, [s]_1, [\mathbf{x}]_2, [\mathbf{y}]_2), [\alpha]_1, [\beta]_1, z$.
- $\mathcal{P}$ input: $\sigma_{\mathcal{P}} = (\mathsf{pp}, [\mathbf{r}]_1, [\mathbf{s}]_1), \mathbf{a}, \mathbf{b}$.
- Statement: $(\sigma, [\alpha]_1, [\beta]_1, z) \in \mathcal{L}_{\mathsf{IP}}$.

The prover and the verifier proceed as follows:

- $\mathcal{P}$ computes

$$[\alpha_{-1}]_1 \leftarrow [\mathbf{a}_{\frac{1}{2}}^\top \mathbf{r}_{\frac{2}{2}}]_1, \quad [\beta_{-1}]_1 \leftarrow [\mathbf{b}_{\frac{1}{2}}^\top \mathbf{s}_{\frac{2}{2}}]_1, \quad z_{-1} \leftarrow \mathbf{a}_{\frac{2}{2}}^\top \mathbf{b}_{\frac{1}{2}},$$
$$[\alpha_1]_1 \leftarrow [\mathbf{a}_{\frac{2}{2}}^\top \mathbf{r}_{\frac{1}{2}}]_1, \quad [\beta_1]_1 \leftarrow [\mathbf{b}_{\frac{2}{2}}^\top \mathbf{s}_{\frac{1}{2}}]_1, \quad z_1 \leftarrow \mathbf{a}_{\frac{1}{2}}^\top \mathbf{b}_{\frac{2}{2}}.$$

- $\mathcal{P}$ sends $[\alpha_{-1}]_1, [\alpha_1]_1, [\beta_{-1}]_1, [\beta_1]_1, z_{-1}, z_1$ and $\mathcal{V}$ replies with $c \leftarrow \mathbb{Z}_q$

- $\mathcal{P}$ computes

$$\mathbf{a}' \leftarrow \mathbf{a}_{\frac{1}{2}}c + \mathbf{a}_{\frac{2}{2}}c^2, \qquad \mathbf{b}' \leftarrow \mathbf{b}_{\frac{1}{2}}c^{-1} + \mathbf{b}_{\frac{2}{2}}c^{-2},$$
$$[\mathbf{r}']_1 \leftarrow c^{-1}[\mathbf{r}_{\frac{1}{2}}]_1 + c^{-2}[\mathbf{r}_{\frac{2}{2}}]_1, \qquad [\mathbf{s}']_1 \leftarrow c[\mathbf{s}_{\frac{1}{2}}]_1 + c^2[\mathbf{s}_{\frac{2}{2}}]_1,$$
$$[r']_1 \leftarrow [r'_1]_1, \qquad [s']_1 \leftarrow [s'_1]_1,$$
$$\sigma'_{\mathcal{P}} = (\mathsf{pp}, [\mathbf{r}']_1, [\mathbf{s}']_1).$$

- $\mathcal{P}$ sends $[r']_1, [s']_1$.
- $\mathcal{V}$ checks the following pairing equations and aborts if any fail.

$$e([r']_1 - c^{-1}[r]_1, [1]_2) = e(c^{-2}[r]_1, [x_\nu]_2),$$
$$e([s']_1 - c[s]_1, [1]_2) = e(c^2[s]_1, [y_\nu]_2).$$

- Both compute

$$[\mathbf{x}']_2 \leftarrow ([x_i]_2)_{i\in\{1,\ldots,\nu-1\}}, \qquad [\mathbf{y}']_2 \leftarrow ([y_i]_2)_{i\in\{1,\ldots,\nu-1\}},$$
$$[\alpha']_1 \leftarrow c^{-1}[\alpha_{-1}]_1 + [\alpha]_1 + c[\alpha_1]_1, \qquad [\beta']_1 \leftarrow c[\beta_{-1}]_1 + [\beta]_1 + c^{-1}[\beta_1]_1,$$
$$z' = z_{-1}c + z + z_1c^{-1},$$
$$\sigma' = (\mathsf{pp}, [r']_1, [s']_1, [\mathbf{x}']_2, [\mathbf{y}']_2).$$

- The reduced statement is $(\sigma', [\alpha']_1, [\beta']_1, z') \in \mathcal{L}_{\mathsf{IP}}$.

Theorem 4. *The protocol presented is a Public Coin, Argument of Knowledge for the relation $\mathcal{L}_{IP}$ with $\log n$ round complexity, $\mathcal{O}_\lambda(n)$ prover complexity, and $\mathcal{O}_\lambda(\log n)$ communication and verification complexity under either the $\mathcal{ML}_n$-Find-Rep or the $\mathcal{PW}_n$-Find-Rep assumptions. The argument yields a Universally Updateable Non-Interactive AoK in the Random Oracle model. In the former case the proof size of an update is $\mathcal{O}_\lambda(\log n)$ and in the latter $\mathcal{O}_\lambda(1)$.*

Proof.
Completeness: We show that each reduction round leads to a valid reduced statement. It is enough to show that the prover and verifier compute the same key. Then, we can argue as in the case with uniform keys.

First, note that $[\mathbf{r}']_1 = c^{-1}[\mathbf{r}_{\frac{1}{2}}]_1 + c^{-2}[\mathbf{r}_{\frac{2}{2}}]_1$, which means that we "combine" all pair of elements that have distance $2^{\nu-1}$. That is, for all $j \leq 2^{\nu-1}$,

$$[r'_j]_1 = c^{-1}[r_j]_1 + c^{-2}[r_{2^{\nu-1}+j}]_1.$$

Also, note that, by construction of the commitment keys for all $i \in \{1,\ldots,\nu\}$ and $j \in \{1,\ldots,2^{i-1}\}$, it holds that $[r_{2^{i-1}+j}]_1 = x_i[r_j]_1$, which means that $[r']_1 = [r'_1]_1 = c^{-1}[r_1]_1 + c^{-2}[r_{2^{\nu-1}+1}]_1 = c^{-1}[r]_1 + c^{-2}x_\nu[r]_1$ and the verifier always accepts the pairing test.

It remains to show that $(\mathsf{pp}, [r']_1, [\mathbf{r}']_1, [\mathbf{x}']_2) \in \mathcal{L}_{\mathsf{Com}}$. It is evident that $[r'_1]_1 = [r']_1$. We show that the various Diffie-Hellman Relations hold for the reduced statement.

Let $i \in \{1, \ldots, \nu - 1\}$ and $j \in \{1, \ldots, 2^{i-1}\}$. It holds that $[r'_{2^{i-1}+j}]_1 = x_i [r'_j]_1$. Indeed,

$$\begin{aligned}[r'_{2^{i-1}+j}]_1 &= c^{-1}[r_{2^{i-1}+j}]_1 + c^{-2}[r_{2^{\nu-1}+2^{i-1}+j}]_1 = c^{-1}x_i[r_j]_1 + x_\nu x_i c^{-2}[r_j]_1 \\ &= x_i(c^{-1}[r_j]_1 + x_\nu c^{-2}[r_j]_1) = x_i[r'_j]_1.\end{aligned}$$

Similar calculations show the part related to $\mathbf{s}'$. We can now argue completeness exactly as in the $\mathcal{U}_{2^\nu}$ case.

Witness extended emulation: For witness extended emulation we need to prove that, for each round, we can extract the witness, i.e. the commitment key and the commitment openings w.r.t. it. We show next how to extract the commitment keys. After having these, we can argue as in [10] except that we use the corresponding $\mathcal{D}_n$-Find-Rep Assumption.

Assume we get two accepting transcripts for different challenges c from the prover. We show that given a witness for the reduced statement, we can extract the unique valid commitment keys $[\mathbf{r}]_1, [\mathbf{s}]_1$.

Let $[\mathbf{r}'_b]_1 = c_b^{-1}[\mathbf{r}_{\frac{1}{2}}]_1 + c_b^{-2}[\mathbf{r}_{\frac{2}{2}}]_1$ be the new commitment keys for two different challenges c_0, c_1. The matrix with rows (c_b^{-1}, c_b^{-2}) for $b \in \{0, 1\}$ is invertible, so we can take appropriate linear combination and extract $[\mathbf{r}_{\frac{1}{2}}]_1$, $[\mathbf{r}_{\frac{2}{2}}]_1$. We show that this is the commitment key. First note that since the transcript is accepting, we have that for both reduced keys $[r'_{2^{i-1}+j}]_1 = x_i[r'_j]_1$ which means that $[r_{2^{i-1}+j}]_1 = x_i[r_j]_1$ and $[r_{2^{\nu-1}+2^{i-1}+j}]_1 = x_i[r_{2^{\nu-1}+j}]_1$ for all $i \le \nu - 1, j \le 2^i$. In other words $[\mathbf{r}_{\frac{1}{2}}]_1$ and $[\mathbf{r}_{\frac{2}{2}}]_1$ are valid commitment keys w.r.t. the same $[x_1]_2, \ldots, [x_{\nu-1}]_2$. By the pairing test, we have that $[r'_b]_1 = c_b^{-1}[r]_1 + c_b^{-2}x_\nu[r]_1 = c_b^{-1}[r_{\frac{1}{2},1}]_1 + c_b^{-2}[r_{\frac{2}{2},1}]_1$. This equation holds for both challenges c_b, so it should be the case that $[r_{\frac{1}{2},1}]_1 = [r]$ and $[r_{\frac{2}{2},1}]_1 = x_\nu[r]$, thus the extracted key should be the unique key determined by $[x_1]_1, \ldots, [x_\nu]_1$. We argue for $[\mathbf{s}]_1$ in the same way. After extracting the keys the extractor works exactly as in [10] to extract $\mathbf{a}, \mathbf{b}$.

Complexity: It is evident that the protocol needs ν rounds. In each round the size of the witness is decreased in half, and we perform a constant number of communication, so we have $\mathcal{O}_\lambda(\nu)$ communication complexity. The prover in round i performs $\mathcal{O}_\lambda(2^{\nu+i-1})$ computations, so the prover complexity is $\mathcal{O}_\lambda\left(\sum_{i=1}^{\nu} 2^{\nu-i+1}\right) = \mathcal{O}_\lambda(2^\nu)$, while the verifier does $\mathcal{O}_\lambda(1)$ operations and therefore its complexity is $\mathcal{O}_\lambda(\nu)$. To be more concrete, the communication complexity is $8 \log n$ elements in $\mathbb{G}_1$ and $2 \log n$ elements in $\mathbb{Z}_q$. Prover complexity is dominated by 4 times $\log n$ multi-exponentiations of sizes $\frac{n}{2^i}$ in $\mathbb{G}_1$ to compute the first 4 messages in each round and less than $4n$ $\mathbb{G}_1$ exponentiations to compute all the keys. In total, $8n$ exponentiations in $\mathbb{G}_1$ with a non optimized implementation of multi-exponentiations. ∎

6 Updateable Zero Knowledge SNARK for CSAT

We could use the improved inner product argument in a black box way to improve the verification of the zero knowledge protocol of Bootle et al. [10]. However, the source of inefficiency of verifier in [10] is twofold: the linear time needed in verifying the inner product argument, and some computation needed for the specific circuit. The latter is inherent to universal arguments since the verifier needs to, at least, read the circuit. The way to solve this is to add a circuit setup phase so the verifier will need to read the circuit only once. For a universal argument, this circuit setup should involve no secrets, that is, it should be a deterministic algorithm with input the Universal CRS and the circuit description. In this section, we give a sketch of the proof of Bootle et al. and explain where this source of inefficiency occurs in their construction. Then, we show how to overcome this using techniques similar to Sonic [32].

Roughly, the proof of [10] works as follows:

- $\mathcal{P}$ commits to its witness (a satisfying wire assignment) $\mathbf{w}$.
- $\mathcal{V}$ issues a random challenge y.
- $\mathcal{P}$ computes a polynomial $t(X) = \mathbf{q}_y(X)^\top(\mathbf{q}_y(X) \circ \mathbf{y}^\mathbf{n} + 2\mathbf{s}_y(X)) + 2K$ where $\mathbf{q}_y(X)$ is a vector of polynomials that depends on $\mathbf{w}$ and y, and $\mathbf{s}_y$ on the circuit structure and the challenge y. K is a value that depends on the public input and y. The polynomial $t(X)$ has zero constant coefficient if and only if the circuit is satisfiable w.o.p. over the choice of y. It then sends a commitment to the polynomial $t(X)$ which has constant degree (it can commit to its coefficients using standard Pedersen Commitments).
- $\mathcal{V}$ picks and sends a random challenge x to the prover. $\mathcal{V}$ then computes commitments to $\mathbf{q}_y(x)$, $\mathbf{q}_y(x) \circ \mathbf{y}^\mathbf{n}$, $\mathbf{s}_y(x)$ and K. The first two values are computed given a commitment to $\mathbf{w}$ and utilizing the homomorphic properties of the commitment scheme, and $\mathbf{s}_y$ is computed by the circuit description. K is computed efficiently by the public input.
- $\mathcal{P}$ decommits to $t_x = t(x)$. $\mathcal{V}$ checks this claim and the prover and verifier execute an inner product protocol to assert that $t(x) - 2K = \mathbf{q}_y(x)^\top(\mathbf{q}_y(x) \circ \mathbf{y}^\mathbf{n} + 2\mathbf{s}_y(x))$. This convinces the verifier that the polynomial $t(x)$ has indeed a zero constant term and that it was computed honestly, thus the verifier is convinced about the claim.

The Verifier in [10] is linear in the circuit for three reasons:

- The inner product protocol in the last step needs linear time.
- Computing a commitment to $\mathbf{q}_y(x) \circ \mathbf{y}^\mathbf{n}$ needs linear time.
- Computing a commitment to $\mathbf{s}_y(x)$ needs linear time.

The first two problems can be addressed easily: the first by using the improved inner product protocol, and the second by utilizing the structure of the $\mathcal{ML}_n$ or $\mathcal{PW}_n$ distributions to compute the commitment in logarithmic time. For the latter, the key homomorphic properties described in Subsect. 4.1 are utilized to efficiently obtain a commitment to $\mathbf{q}_y(x) \circ \mathbf{y}^\mathbf{n}$ from a commitment to $\mathbf{q}_y(x)$.

The most subtle point is computing a commitment to $\mathbf{s}_y(x)$. This depends on the circuit structure and the challenge y. We solve it by applying similar techniques as Sonic [32]. We first preprocess the circuit to impose a specific structure that allows to "commit" to it efficiently. Then we use an aggregated Grand Product protocol which we introduce in the next section to delegate the computation of $\mathbf{s}_y(x)$ to the prover. We closely follow Sonic in the handling of this issue, but we differ from it in the setting: in this work we delegate computation of a vector commitment while in Sonic the prover decommits to bivariate polynomials of specific form by utilizing a univariate polynomial commitment scheme.

We present on the full version the preprocessing for the general case which only incurs in a constant overhead and so parameters remain optimal (i.e. linear in the size of computation).

6.1 Description of the ZK Argument

We assume that the circuit is preprocessed (see the full version) and has $n-1$ multiplication gates for $n = 2^\nu$ (the last element will be used as a blinding factor). The size of the public input and output is n'. The circuit is satisfiable iff the following constraints hold

$$\mathbf{a} \circ \mathbf{b} - \mathbf{c} = \mathbf{0},$$

$$\left\{a_i + \mathbf{w_{a,i}}^\top \mathbf{c} = 0\right\}_{i \in \{n'+1,\ldots,n-1\}}, \qquad \left\{a_i + \mathbf{w_{a,i}}^\top \mathbf{c} - \chi_i = 0\right\}_{i \in \{1,\ldots,n'\}},$$

$$\left\{b_i + \mathbf{w_{b,i}}^\top \mathbf{c} = 0\right\}_{i \in \{1,\ldots,n-1\}},$$

where $\mathbf{x} = (\chi_1, \ldots, \chi_{n'})$ is the public input and $\mathbf{w_{a,i}} = \mathbf{0}$ for $i \in \{1, \ldots, n'\}$. These equations are satisfied iff the circuit is satisfiable w.r.t. the input $\mathbf{x}$.

We can aggregate these equations as follows: First, add one extra zero element $a_n = b_n = 0$ to $\mathbf{a}, \mathbf{b}, \mathbf{c}$ to make them have 2^ν elements (these will be used as a blinding factor) and two extra zero constraints $a_n + \mathbf{0}^\top \mathbf{c} - 0 = 0$, $b_n + \mathbf{0}^\top \mathbf{c} - 0 = 0$ and set

$$p_m(Y) = (\mathbf{a} \circ \mathbf{b} - \mathbf{c})^\top \mathbf{Y^n} = \mathbf{a}^\top (\mathbf{b} \circ \mathbf{Y^n}) - \mathbf{c}^\top \mathbf{Y^n},$$

$$p_a(Y) = \sum_{i=1}^{n} \left(a_i + \mathbf{w_{a,i}}^\top \mathbf{c}\right) Y^{i-1} - \sum_{i=1}^{n'} \chi_i Y^{i-1} = \mathbf{a}^\top \mathbf{Y^n} + \mathbf{c}^\top \sum_{i=1}^{n} \mathbf{w_{a,i}} Y^{i-1} - \sum_{i=1}^{n'} \chi_i Y^{i-1},$$

$$p_b(Y) = \sum_{i=1}^{n} \left(b_i + \mathbf{w_{b,i}}^\top \mathbf{c}\right) Y^{i-1} = \mathbf{b}^\top \mathbf{Y^n} + \mathbf{c}^\top \sum_{i=1}^{n} \mathbf{w_{b,i}} Y^{i-1}.$$

Now, let

$$p(Y) = p_m(Y) + Y^n p_a(Y) + Y^{2n} p_b(Y).$$

The polynomial p should be identically zero iff the circuit is satisfiable. For a fixed y, we define $\mathbf{w_a}, \mathbf{w_b}, K$ as follows:

$$\mathbf{w_a} = \sum_{i=1}^{n} \mathbf{w_{a,i}} y^{i-1}, \qquad \mathbf{w_b} = \sum_{i=1}^{n} \mathbf{w_{b,i}} y^{i-1}, \qquad K = -y^n \sum_{i=1}^{n'} \chi_i y^{i-1}. \tag{1}$$

Note that these values only depend on the circuit, the input and the challenge. We now get

$$p(y) = \mathbf{a}^\top(\mathbf{b} \circ \mathbf{y^n}) + y^n \mathbf{a}^\top \mathbf{y^n} + y^{2n}\mathbf{b}^\top \mathbf{y^n} + \mathbf{c}^\top(y^n \mathbf{w_a} + y^{2n}\mathbf{w_b} - \mathbf{y^n}) + K.$$

We can now construct polynomials

$$\mathbf{q}(X) = \mathbf{a}X + \mathbf{b}X^{-1} + \mathbf{c}X^2 + \mathbf{d}X^3,$$
$$\mathbf{s}(X) = y^n \mathbf{y^n} X^{-1} + y^{2n}\mathbf{y^n}X + (y^n \mathbf{w_a} + y^{2n}\mathbf{w_b} - \mathbf{y^n})X^{-2},$$
$$t(X) = \mathbf{q}(X)^\top(\mathbf{q}(X) \circ \mathbf{y^n} + 2\mathbf{s}(X)) + 2K.$$

Here $\mathbf{d}$ is some blinding factor chosen by the prover. The constant term of $t(X)$ equals $2p(y)$. The prover now can commit to the non-zero coefficients of t using standard Pedersen Commitment and then the verifier issues a new challenge x. The prover reveals t on this value, and the verifier needs to be convinced that the decommitted value is equivalent to computing the value on the right side. To do so, after agreeing on the (commitments of) vectors $\mathbf{q}(x), \mathbf{q}(x) \circ \mathbf{y^n} + 2\mathbf{s}(x)$, they execute an inner product protocol to assert that their inner product is $t(x) - 2K$. If that is the case, the verifier can be confident that the constant term of $t(x)$ is indeed zero, and thus the assignment satisfying. We sketch how the verifier computes the two commitments needed for the inner product protocol.

Let ck_1 be a commitment key defined in the CRS. The commitment to $\mathbf{q}(x)$ w.r.t. ck_1 can be computed by the homomorphic properties of the commitment scheme and commitments to $\mathbf{a}$, $\mathbf{b}$, $\mathbf{c}$, $\mathbf{d}$ w.r.t ck_1, which the provers issues in the first round.

Now, a commitment to $\mathbf{q}(x) \circ \mathbf{y^n} + 2\mathbf{s}(x)$ is needed to run the inner product argument. A commitment to $\mathbf{q}(x) \circ \mathbf{y^n}$, can be computed by the verifier, by deriving a new key ck_2, such that, the commitment to $\mathbf{q}(x)$ w.r.t. ck_1 is a commitment to $\mathbf{q}(x) \circ \mathbf{y^n}$ w.r.t. ck_2, as described in Subsect. 4.1. It remains to compute a commitment to $\mathbf{s}(x)$ w.r.t. ck_2.

Note that $\mathbf{s}(x)$ only depends on public values and the verifier can compute it, but would need linear time to do so. But if the verifier had commitments to $\mathbf{w_a}, \mathbf{w_b}$, it could compute the commitment to $\mathbf{s}(x)$ succinctly. To get such commitments, it delegates their computation to the prover. Assuming a preprocessed circuit, its description is given by matrices of the form $\mathbf{W_a} = \sum_{k=1}^{M} \mathbf{W_{a,k}}$ where $\mathbf{W_{a,k}}$ are matrices with, at most, one non-zero value in each column and row (respectively for $\mathbf{b}$). It follows by Eq. 1 and the structure of the preprocessed circuit matrix $\mathbf{W_a}$, that the verifier needs a commitment to

$$\mathbf{w_a} = \sum_{i=1}^{n} \mathbf{w_{a,i}} y^{i-1} = \mathbf{y^n}^\top \mathbf{W_a} = \mathbf{y^n}^\top \sum_{k=1}^{M} \mathbf{W_{a,k}} = \sum_{k=1}^{M} \sigma_k(\mathbf{y^n}) \circ \mathbf{w_{a,k}},$$

for known vectors $\mathbf{w_{a,k}}$ and permutations σ_k.

We sketch this delegation part in the next section, and provide a full description for it in the full version. A detailed description for the protocol is presented in the full version.

We state next the theorem which is the main result of our work.

Theorem 5. *There exists a Public Coin, Honest Verifier Zero Knowledge Argument of Knowledge for CSAT with* $\mathcal{O}(\log|\mathcal{C}|)$ *round complexity,* $\mathcal{O}_\lambda(|\mathcal{C}|)$ *prover complexity, and* $\mathcal{O}_\lambda(\log|\mathcal{C}|)$ *communication and verification complexity under either the* $\mathcal{ML}_{|\mathcal{C}|}$*-Find-Rep or the* $\mathcal{PW}_{|\mathcal{C}|}$*-Find-Rep assumptions. The argument yields a Universally Updateable NIZK AoK in the random oracle model. In the former case the proof size of an update is* $\mathcal{O}_\lambda(\log|\mathcal{C}|)$ *and in the latter* $\mathcal{O}_\lambda(1)$.

We note that, to achieve updateability, we rely on a NIZK AoK for proving correctness of the updates. One can be flexible in selecting such a NIZK AoK to fine tune efficiency measures. For example, one could combine the $\mathcal{ML}_{|\mathcal{C}|}$-Find-Rep scheme with [10] as the underline NIZK AoK for updateability to achieve $\mathcal{O}_\lambda(\log\log|\mathcal{C}|)$ proof size for proving correctness of an update.

7 Proof of Vector Permutation

We use techniques similar to Sonic to handle the computation regarding the structure of the circuit. We consider only the case of the left-wires for simplicity, i.e. the commitment to $\mathbf{w_a}$. The problem boils down to the following.

Let $\mathsf{ck}_1 = (\mathsf{ck}_1^{\mathcal{P}}, \mathsf{ck}_1^{\mathcal{V}}) = ([\mathbf{r}]_1, ([x_1]_2, \ldots, [x_\nu]_2))$, be a commitment key defined in the CRS, $[\omega_{a,1}]_1, \ldots, [\omega_{a,M}]_1$ be commitments to vectors $\mathbf{w_{a,1}}, \ldots, \mathbf{w_{a,M}}$ w.r.t. ck_1, $\sigma_{a,1}, \ldots, \sigma_{a,M}$ be commitments to permutations w.r.t. ck_1 (i.e. $\mathsf{Com}_{\mathsf{ck}_1}(v_{a,i})$ where $v_{a,i} = (\sigma_{a,i}(1), \ldots, \sigma_{a,i}(n))$). These commitments succinctly encode the circuit structure. Given a value y and a commitment key $\mathsf{ck}_2 = (\mathsf{ck}_2^{\mathcal{P}}, \mathsf{ck}_2^{\mathcal{V}}) = (\mathbf{r} \circ \mathbf{y}^{-\mathbf{n}}, ([x_1 y^{2^0}]_2, \ldots, [x_\nu y^{2^{\nu-1}}]_2))$, compute with the help of the prover a commitment $[\omega_a]_1$ to the vector $\mathbf{w_a} = \mathbf{w_{a,1}} \circ \sigma_{a,1}(\mathbf{y^n}) + \ldots + \mathbf{w_{a,M}} \circ \sigma_{a,M}(\mathbf{y^n})$ w.r.t. ck_2, where $\sigma_{a,i}(\mathbf{y^n}) = (y^{\sigma_{a,1}(1)-1}, \ldots, y^{\sigma_{a,M}(n)-1})$.

Note that, all the commitments that do not depend on the challenge y, can be computed once in a (deterministic) preprocessing phase, and can be reused in multiple proofs. The goal is to allow the verifier to compute the challenge dependent values in logarithmic time. These values are public and a linear time verifier could compute these on its own, though sacrifying succinctness.

The main difference with Sonic is in the setting. Sonic works with permutation polynomials, that is, polynomials of the form $p_i(X,Y) = \sum a_j X^j Y^{\sigma_i(j)}$ and the goal is to decommit to an evaluation in x, y for a polynomial $p(X,Y) = \sum_{i=1}^{M} p_i(X,Y)$, that is, the prover wants to reveal $p(x,y)$.

In both our work and Sonic, the heart of the protocol is a Permutation Argument which uses a Grand Product Argument [3,11]. We reduce the Grand Product Argument to an inner product and utilize the inner product argument of Sect. 5, while Sonic, reduces it to verifying a value of a univariate polynomial and utilizes a univariate polynomial commitment scheme.

We next sketch the delegation protocol, and in the following subsection we describe how to reduce the Grand Product to an inner product.

To proceed the prover and the verifier do the following:

- The prover helps the verifier compute a commitment to $\mathbf{y}^{-\mathbf{n}}$ w.r.t. ck_1, as explained in Subsect. 4.1.

- The prover provides values $[v_i]_1$, for $1 \leq i \leq M$, which it claims are commitments to $\sigma_{a,i}(\mathbf{y^n})$ w.r.t. ck_1.
- The prover gives $[\omega_{a,i}]_1$ and claims they are commitments to $\mathbf{w_{a,i}} \circ \sigma_{a,i}(\mathbf{y^n})$ w.r.t. ck_1.
- The prover gives $[\omega'_{a,i}]_1$ and claims they are commitments to $\mathbf{w_{a,i}} \circ \sigma_{a,i}(\mathbf{y^n}) \circ \mathbf{y^{-n}}$ w.r.t. ck_1. Equivalently, these are commitments to $\mathbf{w_{a,i}} \circ \sigma_{a,i}(\mathbf{y^n})$ w.r.t. ck_2.
- The prover and the verifier aggregate and reduce all the above claims to an inner product, which is verified by the improved inner product.
- The verifier sets $[\omega_a]_1 = [\omega'_{a,1}]_1 + \ldots + [\omega'_{a,M}]_1$ as a commitment to $\mathbf{w_a}$.

We present a sketch for reducing a Grand Product to an inner product in the next section. In the full version we present how we can aggregate all the above claims, and give a description of the protocol.

7.1 Proof of Grand Product

Let $\mathsf{ck}_1 = (\mathsf{ck}_1^{\mathcal{P}}, \mathsf{ck}_1^{\mathcal{V}}) = ([\mathbf{r}]_1, ([x_1]_2, \ldots, [x_\nu]_2))$, be a commitment key. Also, let $\mathbf{a_1} = (a_1, a_2, \ldots, a_n)$ and $\mathbf{b_1} = (b_1, b_2, \ldots, b_n)$, and $[\alpha_1]_1, [\beta_1]_1$ be commitments w.r.t. ck_1. The claim is that $\prod a_i = \prod b_i$.

Let $\mathbf{a_2} = (1, a_1, a_1a_2, \ldots, a_1 \cdots a_{n-1})$ be the vector of partial products and $\mathbf{a_3} = \mathbf{a_2} \circ \mathbf{a_1}$. We similarly define $\mathbf{b_2}, \mathbf{b_3}$. One can easily verify that $a_{3,n} = \prod_{i=1}^n a_i$ and $b_{3,n} = \prod_{i=1}^n b_i$. To convince the verifier, the prover gives commitments $[\alpha_2]_1$, $[\alpha_3]_1$, $[\beta_2]_1$, $[\beta_3]_1$ to vectors $\mathbf{a_2}$, $\mathbf{a_3}$, $\mathbf{b_2}$, $\mathbf{b_3}$ w.r.t. ck_1, convince it that they have the right form, and prove that $a_{3,n} = b_{3,n}$.

We express these requirements as a set of quadratic and linear constraints. We use different variables Y, W for the various groups of equations for presentational convenience, but we can use just one variable Y and set $W = Y^k$ for an appropriate k.

$$a_{3,n} = b_{3,n},$$

$$\begin{aligned} \mathbf{a_1} \circ \mathbf{a_2} &= \mathbf{a_3}, & \mathbf{b_1} \circ \mathbf{b_2} &= \mathbf{b_3}, \\ a_{2,1} &= 1, & b_{2,1} &= 1, \\ \{a_{2,i} &= a_{3,i-1}\}_{i=2}^n, & \{b_{2,i} &= b_{3,i-1}\}_{i=2}^n. \end{aligned}$$

We show how to reduce these equations to an inner product. We can aggregate the two Hadamard products by setting

$$p_1(Y) = \mathbf{a_1}^\top (\mathbf{a_2} \circ \mathbf{Y^n}) - \mathbf{a_3}^\top \mathbf{Y^n}, \quad p_2(Y) = \mathbf{b_1}^\top (\mathbf{b_2} \circ \mathbf{Y^n}) - \mathbf{b_3}^\top \mathbf{Y^n}.$$

We also set

$$p_3(Y) = (a_{2,1} - 1) + \sum_{i=2}^{n} (a_{2,i} - a_{3,i-1}) Y^{i-1} = \mathbf{a_2}^\top \mathbf{Y^n} - Y \mathbf{a_3}^\top (\mathbf{Y^n} - Y^{n-1} \mathbf{e_n}) - 1,$$

$$p_4(Y) = (b_{2,1} - 1) + \sum_{i=2}^{n} (b_{2,i} - b_{3,i-1}) Y^{i-1} = \mathbf{b_2}^\top \mathbf{Y^n} - Y \mathbf{b_3}^\top (\mathbf{Y^n} - Y^{n-1} \mathbf{e_n}) - 1,$$

$$p_5(Y) = a_{3,n} - b_{3,n} = \mathbf{e_n}^\top \mathbf{a_3} - \mathbf{e_n}^\top \mathbf{b_3}.$$

and $p(Y, W) = p_1(Y) + Wp_2(Y) + W^2p_3(Y) + W^3p_4(Y) + W^4p_5(Y)$. The polynomial p is identically zero if and only if the constraints are satisfied. We use the technique of Bootle et al. to embed it in the constant term of a polynomial (similarly to the previous section). The resulting polynomials are

$$\begin{aligned}
\mathbf{q}(X) &= \mathbf{a_1}X + \mathbf{a_2}X^{-1} + w\mathbf{b_1}X^2 + \mathbf{b_2}X^{-2} + \mathbf{a_3}X^3 + \mathbf{b_3}X^4, \\
\mathbf{s}(X) &= w^2\mathbf{y^n}X + w^3\mathbf{y^n}X^2 \\
&\quad + \left(-w^2y(\mathbf{y^n} - y^{n-1}\mathbf{e_n}) + w^4\mathbf{e_n} - \mathbf{y^n}\right)X^{-3} \\
&\quad + \left(-w^3y(\mathbf{y^n} - y^{n-1}\mathbf{e_n}) - w^4\mathbf{e_n} - w\mathbf{y^n}\right)X^{-4}, \\
t(X) &= \mathbf{q}(X)^\top\left(\mathbf{q}(X) \circ \mathbf{y^n} + 2\mathbf{s}(X)\right) - 2w^2 - 2w^3.
\end{aligned}$$

The verifier computes a commitment to $\mathbf{q}(x) \circ \mathbf{y^n}$ w.r.t. the new commitment key-defined by the challenge y- as in the previous section. As for the commitment of $\mathbf{s}(x)$ w.r.t. this new key, however, the verifier can compute it itself: it only needs commitments to $\mathbf{y^n}$, and to $y^{n-1}\mathbf{e_n}$ w.r.t. the new key. For the first, it is given a commitment to $[o]_1 = [\mathbf{1^n}^\top\mathbf{r}]_1$ with the initial key, ck_1, and for the second, the last group element of the initial commitment key $[r_n]_1$. The desired commitments w.r.t the new key are $[o]_1$ and $[r_n]_1$. The prover and the verifier then proceed as in the CSAT case. Both $[o]_1$ and $[r_n]_1$ can be precomputed once. The detailed protocol is given in the full version.

Extending for multiple Grand Products. It is straightforward to extend these protocol to prove simultaneously M grand products. Also we can add kM quadratic equations of the form $\mathbf{c_1} \circ \mathbf{c_2} = \mathbf{c_3}$ to include the remaining constraints needed to compute the commitments needed for the CSAT case. We include the modified system of equation in the full version.

7.2 Proof of Known Permutation

Let $[\mathbf{r}]_1$ be a commitment key of size $n = 2^\nu$, $[\alpha]_1 = [\mathbf{a}^\top\mathbf{r}]_1$, $[\beta]_1 = [\mathbf{b}^\top\mathbf{r}]_1$ and $\sigma \in S_n$ be a permutation of $\{1, \ldots, n\}$. The prover wants to convince the verifier that, for all, i $b_i = a_{\sigma(i)}$.

In the same spirit as [32], we use the proof system of [3,11]. The verifier is given as input commitments to $(1, \ldots, n)$ and $(\sigma(1), \ldots, \sigma(n))$ denoted as $[\iota]_1, [\iota^\pi]_1$ respectively, and a commitment to $\mathbf{1^n}$ denoted as $[o]$. The idea is to reduce this problem to whether two vectors have equal grand products.

The verifier issues two challenges $t, u \in \mathbb{Z}_q$ and the prover needs to convince the verifier that

$$\prod_{i=1}^{n}(b_i + t\sigma_i - u) = \prod_{i=1}^{n}(a_i + ti - u)$$

Viewing these as polynomials in u, if their respective roots $\{b_i + t\sigma_i\}_{i\in\{1,\ldots,n\}}$ and $\{a_i + ti\}_{i\in\{1,\ldots,n\}}$ are different, they will be different in a fixed u with overwhelming probability (in a sufficiently large field). Also $b_i + t\sigma_i$ will be the σ

permutation of $a_i + ti$ only if for all i $b_i = a_{\sigma(i)}$, except with negligible probability. Thus, proving the grand product of the commitments $[\beta]_1 + t[\iota^\pi]_1 - u[o]_1$ and $[\alpha]_1 + t[\iota]_1 - u[o]_1$ (which are efficiently computable for the verifier) are equal is enough.

8 Range Proofs with Logarithmic Verifier

We present a new, more efficient aggregated range proof to allow a prover to convince a verifier that it knows openings for perfectly hiding commitments which all are in a range $[0, 2^m)$. This has applications in cryptocurrencies such as Monero to privatize transactions. Our approach resembles that of Bulletproofs [12]. The difference is that, in the inner product protocol of [12], the inner product claimed is encoded in the group (i.e. $\mathbf{a}^\top \mathbf{b}[r]$) while in our setting the inner product is given as an element of $\mathbb{Z}_q$. We thus slightly modify things to work in our setting. We exploit two things to achieve logarithmic verification time: the improved inner product argument, and the ability to compute structured commitments of the form $\mathbf{t^n}$ efficiently (either with the help of the prover or by modifying the commitment key). We present the blueprint of the scheme. Details for the protocol are presented in the full version.

Let $[0, 2^m)$ be the desired range and let ν be the smallest number such that $n = 2^\nu \geq m$. We first transform the statement to a set of linear and quadratic constraints, and we then construct a suitable inner product statement that holds if and only if the statement is correct w.o.p. Let $[\gamma]_1 = v[1] + \rho_c[r_2]_1$ ($[r_2]$ is used as a blinding factor for the commitment) be a hiding commitment to v. Equivalently, we can consider this as a binding commitment to the n-dimensional vector $\mathbf{c} = (v, \rho_c, 0, \ldots, 0)$, that is, $[\gamma]_1 = [\mathbf{c}^\top \mathbf{r}]_1$ for a given commitment key $[\mathbf{r}]_1$. The prover can compute the binary representation of v padding the end with zeros. Denote the padded representation $\mathbf{a}$. It is enough for the prover to show that:

- $\mathbf{a}^\top \mathbf{2^n} = \mathbf{c}^\top \mathbf{0^n}$ (note that we define $\mathbf{0^n}$ to have 1 as its first element).
- $\mathbf{a}$ has the first $m - 1$ elements equal to either 0 or 1.
- $\mathbf{a}$ has all the other variables equal to zero.
- $\mathbf{c}$ has all but the first and second elements zero.

Now let $b_i = a_i - 1$ for $1 \leq i < m$, $b_i = 0$ for $i \geq m$. We express these constraints and aggregate them as follows:

$$\mathbf{a} \circ \mathbf{b} = \mathbf{0}, \qquad \{a_i - b_i - 1 = 0\}_{i=1}^{m-1}, \qquad \mathbf{a}^\top \mathbf{2^n} = \mathbf{c}^\top \mathbf{0^n},$$

$$\{a_i = 0\}_{i=m}^{n}, \qquad \{b_i = 0\}_{i=m}^{n}, \qquad \{c_i = 0\}_{i=3}^{n}.$$

Now let $\mathbf{Y_1} = (1, \ldots, Y^{m-2}, 0, \ldots, 0) \in \mathbb{Z}_q^n$, $\mathbf{Y_2} = (0, \ldots, 0, Y^{m-1}, \ldots, Y^{n-1}) \in \mathbb{Z}_q^n$ and $\mathbf{Y_3} = (0, 0, Y^2, \ldots, Y^{n-1}) \in \mathbb{Z}_q^n$. We define polynomials

$$p_1(Y) = \mathbf{a}^\top (\mathbf{b} \circ \mathbf{Y^n}),$$

$$p_2(Y) = \sum_{i=1}^{m-1}(a_i - b_i - 1)Y^{i-1} + \sum_{i=m}^{n} a_i Y^{i-1} = \mathbf{a}^\top \mathbf{Y^n} - \mathbf{b}^\top \mathbf{Y_1} - \mathbf{1^n}^\top \mathbf{Y_1},$$

$$p_3(Y) = \sum_{i=m}^{n} b_i Y^{i-1} = \mathbf{b}^\top \mathbf{Y_2}, \quad p_4(Y) = \sum_{i=3}^{n} c_i Y^{i-1} = \mathbf{c}^\top \mathbf{Y_3}.$$

The equations hold if and only if

$$p(Y) = p_1(Y) + Y^n p_2(Y) + Y^{2n} p_3(Y) + Y^{3n} p_4(Y) + Y^{4n}(\mathbf{a}^\top \mathbf{2^n} - \mathbf{c}^\top \mathbf{0^n}).$$

is identically zero. Similarly to the CSAT case, we define for fixed y

$$\begin{aligned}
\mathbf{q}(X) &= \mathbf{a}X + \mathbf{b}X^{-1} + \mathbf{c}X^2 + \mathbf{d}X^3,\\
\mathbf{s}(X) &= \left(y^n \mathbf{y^n} + y^{4n}\mathbf{2^n}\right) X^{-1} + \left(-y^n \mathbf{y_1} + y^{2n}\mathbf{y_2}\right) X\\
&\quad + \left(y^{3n}\mathbf{y_3} - y^{4n}\mathbf{0^n}\right) X^{-2},\\
\mathbf{t}(X) &= \mathbf{q}(x)^\top (\mathbf{q}(x) \circ \mathbf{y^n} + 2\mathbf{s}(X)) - y^n \mathbf{1^n}^\top \mathbf{y_1}.
\end{aligned}$$

Now the constant term of $t(X)$ should be zero for all Y, X if the constraints are satisfied so we proceed exactly as in the proof system of CSAT except that now it is easier to compute the vector $\mathbf{s}(x)$. In particular, the verifier can efficiently compute $\mathbf{s}(x)$, if it has commitments to $\mathbf{1^n}, (\mathbf{1^{m-1}}, \mathbf{0})$, $\mathbf{1^n} - (\mathbf{1^{m-1}}, \mathbf{0})$ and $(0, 0, 1, \ldots, 1, 1)$. By the key homomorphic properties of the commitment scheme these are commitments to $\mathbf{y^n}, \mathbf{y_1}, \mathbf{y_2}, \mathbf{y_3}$ w.r.t. the new key. The prover and verifier can efficiently compute a commitment to the vector $\mathbf{2^n}$ w.r.t to the appropriate key as described in the polynomial commitment section. Finally, note that the inner product $\mathbf{1^n}^\top \mathbf{Y_1} = 1 + y + y^2 + \ldots + y^{m-2}$ can be efficiently computed by the verifier. Indeed, assuming w.l.o.g. (otherwise apply recursively) that $m - 2 + 1 = 2^\mu$ for some μ we have that $1 + y + y^2 + \ldots + y^{2^{\mu-1}} = (1 + y^{2^0})(1 + y^{2^1}) \cdots (1 + y^{2^{\mu-1}})$, and the verifier can compute this in logarithmic time. The full protocol is presented in the full version. We note that the aggregation techniques similar to [12] can be applied in the above.

We state the main theorem for the Range Proof protocol.

Theorem 6. *There exists a Public Coin, Honest Verifier Zero Knowledge Argument of Knowledge for the language* $\mathcal{L}_{RP} = \{m, [\alpha]_1, [1]_{1,2}, [r_2]_{1,2}, \mid \exists v, \rho_c \text{ s.t. } [\alpha]_1 = v[1]_1 + \rho_c[r_2]_1 \wedge v < 2^m\}$ *with* $\log m + \mathcal{O}(1)$ *round complexity,* $\mathcal{O}_\lambda(m)$ *prover complexity, and* $\mathcal{O}_\lambda(\log m)$ *communication and verification complexity under either the* $\mathcal{ML}_m$*-Find-Rep or the* $\mathcal{PW}_m$*-Find-Rep assumptions. The argument yields a Universally Updateable NIZK AoK in the Random Oracle model. In the former case the proof size of an update is* $\mathcal{O}_\lambda(\log m)$ *and in the latter* $\mathcal{O}_\lambda(1)$.

Acknowledgements. We would like to thank the anonymous reviewers of PKC 2020 and Helger Lipmaa for useful comments on this work.

The project that gave rise to these results received the support of a fellowship from "la Caixa" Foundation (ID 100010434). The fellowship code is

LCF/BQ/DI18/11660053. This project has received funding from the European Union's Horizon 2020 research and innovation programme under the Marie Skłodowska-Curie grant agreement No. 713673. First author was supported by Project RTI2018-102112-B-I00 (AEI/FEDER,UE) and this paper is part of a project that has received funding from the European Union's Horizon 2020 research and innovation programme under grant agreement No 856879.

References

1. Abdolmaleki, B., Baghery, K., Lipmaa, H., Zajac, M.: A subversion-resistant SNARK. In: Takagi, T., Peyrin, T. (eds.) ASIACRYPT 2017. LNCS, vol. 10626, pp. 3–33. Springer, Cham (2017). https://doi.org/10.1007/978-3-319-70700-6_1
2. Ames, S., Hazay, C., Ishai, Y., Venkitasubramaniam, M.: Ligero: lightweight sublinear arguments without a trusted setup. In: Thuraisingham, B.M., Evans, D., Malkin, T., Xu, D. (eds.) ACM CCS 2017, pp. 2087–2104. ACM Press, October/November 2017. https://doi.org/10.1145/3133956.3134104
3. Bayer, S., Groth, J.: Efficient zero-knowledge argument for correctness of a shuffle. In: Pointcheval, D., Johansson, T. (eds.) EUROCRYPT 2012. LNCS, vol. 7237, pp. 263–280. Springer, Heidelberg (2012). https://doi.org/10.1007/978-3-642-29011-4_17
4. Bellare, M., Fuchsbauer, G., Scafuro, A.: NIZKs with an untrusted CRS: security in the face of parameter subversion. In: Cheon, J.H., Takagi, T. (eds.) ASIACRYPT 2016. LNCS, vol. 10032, pp. 777–804. Springer, Heidelberg (2016). https://doi.org/10.1007/978-3-662-53890-6_26
5. Ben-Sasson, E., Bentov, I., Horesh, Y., Riabzev, M.: Scalable zero knowledge with no trusted setup. In: Boldyreva, A., Micciancio, D. (eds.) CRYPTO 2019. LNCS, vol. 11694, pp. 701–732. Springer, Cham (2019). https://doi.org/10.1007/978-3-030-26954-8_23
6. Ben-Sasson, E., et al.: Zerocash: decentralized anonymous payments from bitcoin. Cryptology ePrint Archive, Report 2014/349 (2014). http://eprint.iacr.org/2014/349
7. Ben-Sasson, E., Chiesa, A., Riabzev, M., Spooner, N., Virza, M., Ward, N.P.: Aurora: transparent succinct arguments for R1CS. In: Ishai, Y., Rijmen, V. (eds.) EUROCRYPT 2019. LNCS, vol. 11476, pp. 103–128. Springer, Cham (2019). https://doi.org/10.1007/978-3-030-17653-2_4
8. Ben-Sasson, E., Chiesa, A., Spooner, N.: Interactive oracle proofs. In: Hirt, M., Smith, A. (eds.) TCC 2016. LNCS, vol. 9986, pp. 31–60. Springer, Heidelberg (2016). https://doi.org/10.1007/978-3-662-53644-5_2
9. Bitansky, N., Chiesa, A., Ishai, Y., Paneth, O., Ostrovsky, R.: Succinct non-interactive arguments via linear interactive proofs. In: Sahai, A. (ed.) TCC 2013. LNCS, vol. 7785, pp. 315–333. Springer, Heidelberg (2013). https://doi.org/10.1007/978-3-642-36594-2_18
10. Bootle, J., Cerulli, A., Chaidos, P., Groth, J., Petit, C.: Efficient zero-knowledge arguments for arithmetic circuits in the discrete log setting. In: Fischlin, M., Coron, J.-S. (eds.) EUROCRYPT 2016. LNCS, vol. 9666, pp. 327–357. Springer, Heidelberg (2016). https://doi.org/10.1007/978-3-662-49896-5_12
11. Bootle, J., Cerulli, A., Ghadafi, E., Groth, J., Hajiabadi, M., Jakobsen, S.K.: Linear-time zero-knowledge proofs for arithmetic circuit satisfiability. In: Takagi, T., Peyrin, T. (eds.) ASIACRYPT 2017. LNCS, vol. 10626, pp. 336–365. Springer, Cham (2017). https://doi.org/10.1007/978-3-319-70700-6_12

12. Bünz, B., Bootle, J., Boneh, D., Poelstra, A., Wuille, P., Maxwell, G.: Bulletproofs: short proofs for confidential transactions and more. In: 2018 IEEE Symposium on Security and Privacy, pp. 315–334. IEEE Computer Society Press, May 2018. https://doi.org/10.1109/SP.2018.00020
13. Bünz, B., Fisch, B., Szepieniec, A.: Transparent snarks from dark compilers. Cryptology ePrint Archive, Report 2019/1229 (2019). https://eprint.iacr.org/2019/1229
14. Chiesa, A., Forbes, M.A., Spooner, N.: A zero knowledge sumcheck and its applications. Cryptology ePrint Archive, Report 2017/305 (2017). http://eprint.iacr.org/2017/305
15. Chiesa, A., Hu, Y., Maller, M., Mishra, P., Vesely, N., Ward, N.: Marlin: Preprocessing zkSNARKs with universal and updatable SRS. Cryptology ePrint Archive, Report 2019/1047 (2019). https://eprint.iacr.org/2019/1047
16. Danezis, G., Fournet, C., Groth, J., Kohlweiss, M.: Square span programs with applications to succinct NIZK arguments. In: Sarkar, P., Iwata, T. (eds.) ASIACRYPT 2014. LNCS, vol. 8873, pp. 532–550. Springer, Heidelberg (2014). https://doi.org/10.1007/978-3-662-45611-8_28
17. Fuchsbauer, G.: Subversion-zero-knowledge SNARKs. In: Abdalla, M., Dahab, R. (eds.) PKC 2018. LNCS, vol. 10769, pp. 315–347. Springer, Cham (2018). https://doi.org/10.1007/978-3-319-76578-5_11
18. Fuchsbauer, G., Kiltz, E., Loss, J.: The algebraic group model and its applications. In: Shacham, H., Boldyreva, A. (eds.) CRYPTO 2018. LNCS, vol. 10992, pp. 33–62. Springer, Cham (2018). https://doi.org/10.1007/978-3-319-96881-0_2
19. Gabizon, A.: AuroraLight: improved prover efficiency and SRS size in a sonic-like system. Cryptology ePrint Archive, Report 2019/601 (2019). https://eprint.iacr.org/2019/601
20. Gabizon, A., Williamson, Z.J., Ciobotaru, O.: PLONK: permutations over Lagrange-bases for oecumencial noninteractive arguments of knowledge. Cryptology ePrint Archive, Report 2019/953 (2019). https://eprint.iacr.org/2019/953
21. Gennaro, R., Gentry, C., Parno, B., Raykova, M.: Quadratic span programs and succinct NIZKs without PCPs. In: Johansson, T., Nguyen, P.Q. (eds.) EUROCRYPT 2013. LNCS, vol. 7881, pp. 626–645. Springer, Heidelberg (2013). https://doi.org/10.1007/978-3-642-38348-9_37
22. Giacomelli, I., Madsen, J., Orlandi, C.: ZKBoo: faster zero-knowledge for boolean circuits. In: Holz, T., Savage, S. (eds.) USENIX Security 2016, pp. 1069–1083. USENIX Association, August 2016
23. Goldreich, O., Micali, S., Wigderson, A.: How to prove all NP statements in zero-knowledge and a methodology of cryptographic protocol design (extended abstract). In: Odlyzko, A.M. (ed.) CRYPTO 1986. LNCS, vol. 263, pp. 171–185. Springer, Heidelberg (1987). https://doi.org/10.1007/3-540-47721-7_11
24. Goldwasser, S., Kalai, Y.T., Rothblum, G.N.: Delegating computation: interactive proofs for muggles. In: Ladner, R.E., Dwork, C. (eds.) 40th ACM STOC, pp. 113–122. ACM Press, May 2008. https://doi.org/10.1145/1374376.1374396
25. Groth, J.: Short pairing-based non-interactive zero-knowledge arguments. In: Abe, M. (ed.) ASIACRYPT 2010. LNCS, vol. 6477, pp. 321–340. Springer, Heidelberg (2010). https://doi.org/10.1007/978-3-642-17373-8_19
26. Groth, J.: On the size of pairing-based non-interactive arguments. In: Fischlin, M., Coron, J.-S. (eds.) EUROCRYPT 2016. LNCS, vol. 9666, pp. 305–326. Springer, Heidelberg (2016). https://doi.org/10.1007/978-3-662-49896-5_11

27. Groth, J., Kohlweiss, M., Maller, M., Meiklejohn, S., Miers, I.: Updatable and universal common reference strings with applications to zk-SNARKs. In: Shacham, H., Boldyreva, A. (eds.) CRYPTO 2018. LNCS, vol. 10993, pp. 698–728. Springer, Cham (2018). https://doi.org/10.1007/978-3-319-96878-0_24
28. Groth, J., Maller, M.: Snarky signatures: minimal signatures of knowledge from simulation-extractable SNARKs. In: Katz, J., Shacham, H. (eds.) CRYPTO 2017. LNCS, vol. 10402, pp. 581–612. Springer, Cham (2017). https://doi.org/10.1007/978-3-319-63715-0_20
29. Ishai, Y., Kushilevitz, E., Ostrovsky, R., Sahai, A.: Zero-knowledge from secure multiparty computation. In: Johnson, D.S., Feige, U. (eds.) 39th ACM STOC, pp. 21–30. ACM Press, June 2007. https://doi.org/10.1145/1250790.1250794
30. Katz, J., Kolesnikov, V., Wang, X.: Improved non-interactive zero knowledge with applications to post-quantum signatures. In: Lie, D., Mannan, M., Backes, M., Wang, X. (eds.) ACM CCS 2018, pp. 525–537. ACM Press, October 2018. https://doi.org/10.1145/3243734.3243805
31. Kilian, J.: A note on efficient zero-knowledge proofs and arguments (extended abstract). In: 24th ACM STOC, pp. 723–732. ACM Press, May 1992. https://doi.org/10.1145/129712.129782
32. Maller, M., Bowe, S., Kohlweiss, M., Meiklejohn, S.: Sonic: zero-knowledge SNARKs from linear-size universal and updatable structured reference strings. In: Cavallaro, L., Kinder, J., Wang, X., Katz, J. (eds.) ACM CCS 2019, pp. 2111–2128. ACM Press, November 2019. https://doi.org/10.1145/3319535.3339817
33. Micali, S.: CS proofs (extended abstracts). In: 35th FOCS, pp. 436–453. IEEE Computer Society Press, November 1994. https://doi.org/10.1109/SFCS.1994.365746
34. Naor, M., Reingold, O.: Number-theoretic constructions of efficient pseudo-random functions. In: 38th FOCS, pp. 458–467. IEEE Computer Society Press, October 1997. https://doi.org/10.1109/SFCS.1997.646134
35. Parno, B., Howell, J., Gentry, C., Raykova, M.: Pinocchio: nearly practical verifiable computation. In: 2013 IEEE Symposium on Security and Privacy, pp. 238–252. IEEE Computer Society Press, May 2013. https://doi.org/10.1109/SP.2013.47
36. Reitwiessner, C.: zkSNARKs in a nutshell (2016). https://blog.ethereum.org/2016/12/05/zksnarks-in-a-nutshell/
37. Wahby, R.S., Tzialla, I., Shelat, A., Thaler, J., Walfish, M.: Doubly-efficient zkSNARKs without trusted setup. In: 2018 IEEE Symposium on Security and Privacy, pp. 926–943. IEEE Computer Society Press, May 2018. https://doi.org/10.1109/SP.2018.00060
38. Xie, T., Zhang, J., Zhang, Y., Papamanthou, C., Song, D.: Libra: succinct zero-knowledge proofs with optimal prover computation. In: Boldyreva, A., Micciancio, D. (eds.) CRYPTO 2019. LNCS, vol. 11694, pp. 733–764. Springer, Cham (2019). https://doi.org/10.1007/978-3-030-26954-8_24
39. Zhang, Y., Genkin, D., Katz, J., Papadopoulos, D., Papamanthou, C.: vSQL: verifying arbitrary SQL queries over dynamic outsourced databases. In: 2017 IEEE Symposium on Security and Privacy, pp. 863–880. IEEE Computer Society Press, May 2017. https://doi.org/10.1109/SP.2017.43
40. Zhang, Y., Genkin, D., Katz, J., Papadopoulos, D., Papamanthou, C.: A zero-knowledge version of vSQL. Cryptology ePrint Archive, Report 2017/1146 (2017). https://eprint.iacr.org/2017/1146

On Black-Box Extensions of Non-interactive Zero-Knowledge Arguments, and Signatures Directly from Simulation Soundness

Masayuki Abe[1], Miguel Ambrona[1(✉)], and Miyako Ohkubo[2]

[1] Secure Platform Laboratories, NTT Corporation, Tokyo, Japan
{masayuki.abe.cp,miguel.ambrona.fu}@hco.ntt.co.jp
[2] Security Fundamentals Laboratory, CSR, NICT, Tokyo, Japan
m.ohkubo@nict.go.jp

Abstract. Highly efficient non-interactive zero-knowledge arguments (NIZK) are often constructed for limited languages and it is not known how to extend them to cover wider classes of languages in general. In this work we initiate a study on black-box language extensions for conjunctive and disjunctive relations, that is, building a NIZK system for $\mathcal{L} \diamond \hat{\mathcal{L}}$ (with $\diamond \in \{\wedge, \vee\}$) based on NIZK systems for languages $\mathcal{L}$ and $\hat{\mathcal{L}}$. While the conjunctive extension of NIZKs is straightforward by simply executing the given NIZKs in parallel, it is not known how disjunctive extensions could be achieved in a black-box manner. Besides, observe that the simple conjunctive extension does not work in the case of simulation-sound NIZKs (SS-NIZKs), as pointed out by Sahai (Sahai, FOCS 1999). Our main contribution is an impossibility result that negates the existence of the above extensions and implies other non-trivial separations among NIZKs, SS-NIZKs, and labelled SS-NIZKs.

Motivated by the difficulty of such transformations, we additionally present an efficient construction of signature schemes based on unbounded simulation-sound NIZKs (USS-NIZKs) for any language without language extensions.

1 Introduction

1.1 Background

A non-interactive zero-knowledge argument system (NIZK) [8] is a beneficial building block for constructing a wide variety of cryptographic schemes and protocols. Very roughly, given an NP language $\mathcal{L}$ for certain relation R, i.e., $\mathcal{L} := \{x \mid \exists w \text{ s.t. } R(x, w) = 1\}$, a NIZK argument system for $\mathcal{L}$ allows a *prover* (who owns a pair x, w such that $R(x, w) = 1$) to convince a *verifier* of the fact that $x \in \mathcal{L}$. The communication between the two parties is unilateral and the verifier learns no new information about possible witnesses for x, except the fact that there exists one. (That is enforced by the presence of a *simulator* which,

A. Kiayias et al. (Eds.): PKC 2020, LNCS 12110, pp. 558–589, 2020.
https://doi.org/10.1007/978-3-030-45374-9_19

without any witness for x, produces an output that is indistinguishable from the proof produced by a real prover.) A NIZK system is said to be *correct* if an honest prover can always convince a verifier of a true statement. On the other hand, the system is said to be *sound* if a (possibly malicious) prover cannot convince an honest verifier of a false statement (except with negligible probability). A simulation-sound NIZK (SS-NIZK) [50] is a strengthening of NIZK whose soundness holds even in the presence of simulated proofs on arbitrary statements. SS-NIZKs receive much attention due to their usefulness in the construction of public-key encryption schemes secure against adaptive chosen message attacks [50]. Another application of SS-NIZKs is on building Threshold Password-Authenticated Key Exchange [42]. Furthermore, they have recently been used to build tightly secure CCA2 encryption in the multi-challenge and multi-user setting [37] or to design tightly secure signature schemes [29].

Thanks to a considerable and prolonged effort by the community of cryptographers, there exist NIZK systems for NP-complete languages in several settings, e.g., [8,19,25], and general constructions have been designed to strengthen them to SS-NIZK, e.g., [17,50]. Some of these settings provide very efficient NIZK systems: Schnorr proofs [43], Groth-Sahai proofs [27], Quasi-Adaptive NIZKs (QA-NIZKs) [32] that are designed for particular languages. However, when NIZK systems are used for building advanced cryptographic schemes and protocols, it is frequently assumed that a convenient language is covered by the NIZK, or that the system can be extended to support such a language. For instance, the general transformations from NIZK to unbound SS-NIZK (USS-NIZK) in [17,29] (see Definition 2.5) require the NIZK support a disjunctive statement combining two instances of certain specific languages.

Given the relevance of these works, where additional assumptions are made on the languages supported by the NIZK systems, we study *black-box language extensions* of NIZKs for conjunctive and disjunctive relations. More concretely, we consider the question of whether for some language $\hat{\mathcal{L}}$, there exists a generic compiler that on input a NIZK system for language $\mathcal{L}$, produces a NIZK system for $\mathcal{L} \diamond \hat{\mathcal{L}}$, where $\diamond \in \{\wedge, \vee\}$. Many non black-box techniques for disjunctive language extension can be found in the literature, e.g., [2,13,14,21,24,41,46], but not much is known in the case of black-box extensions, which are a relevant area of study due to their potential for building efficient and more advanced cryptographic primitives. In the settings where generic NIZKs for NP are not very efficient, using a generic transformation from a less expressive (but more efficient) NIZK may be a better approach than going through the Karp reduction.

Due to the commodity of NIZK in cryptographic design, there are strong demands to construct efficient NIZKs from various assumptions, but this is not an easy task. For instance, NIZKs for NP-complete languages based on lattice-based assumptions were known only in relaxed scenarios such as designated-verifier NIZKs [12] and preprocessing NIZKs [36], while very efficient NIZKs for limited lattice-related languages are known in the standard common reference string (CRS) model [5,45,48]. Very recently, Peikert and Shiehian finally developed a NIZK for NP based on *learning with errors* (LWE) [44]. A natural question is whether such efforts have to be done every time we want to use a new assumption. A widely useful abstraction such as black-box constructions aims to reduce the burden of cryptographic design. Its importance is remarkable in post-quantum cryptography, where several new assumptions such as isogeny-based assumptions [47,51] and multi-variable problems [56] are under investigation. Our impossibility results justify the design and study of approaches relying on particular properties of the underlying assumptions.

Note that some black-box language extensions are straightforward, e.g., a conjunctive extension can be achieved by computing both proofs and concatenating them. Others are more involved, for example, a similar approach fails in the case of disjunctive language extension, or, as pointed out by Sahai [50], the conjunctive extension does not work in the case of USS-NIZKs. Contrary to the case of conjunctive extensions, generic methods for achieving disjunction of languages in the framework of NIZKs are not known. A black-box disjunctive language extension could be a great tool for building more advanced and secure NIZK systems. Observe that NIZKs for disjunctive languages have a vast number of applications. Among them, an important example is the framework of electronic voting [14], where disjunction is used to argue that a vote is valid. In general, it is very useful in any secure function evaluation scenario where a proof of a disjunctive relation is used to guarantee that the input to each wire is either 0 or 1. Furthermore, disjunctive relations are used as a building block for achieving tight security (they often simplify the simulation in the security reduction).

1.2 Our Results

Our main contribution is a series of (im)possibility results about black-box language extensions among different types of NIZK systems. In the case of impossibility, the constructions ruled out by this work correspond to what we would normally think of as *"black-box language extensions"*.

- There exists no generic compiler that, given two NIZK systems for hard languages $\mathcal{L}$ and $\hat{\mathcal{L}}$, outputs a NIZK system for $\mathcal{L} \vee \hat{\mathcal{L}}$. This holds even if we are given stronger types of NIZKs, i.e. labelled or simulation-sound, as building blocks. This justifies existing non black-box approaches.
- It is hard to extend, in a black-box manner, a simulation-sound NIZK to cover conjunctive and disjunctive languages, or to support labels.
- Unbound simulation-soundness is hard to obtain in a black-box manner. This justifies that black-box constructions of simulation-sound NIZKs from standard NIZKs [50] are *bounded* in the number of simulations.

As it is common in all standard black-box separations, our impossibility results do not apply when extra ingredients are available. It is indeed an interesting open problem to understand what the minimal additional functionalities to achieve certain constructions are.

Additionally, we provide a construction of a secure digital signature scheme from any USS-NIZK for a hard language in NP that *does not require language extensions.* This construction is motivated by our previous impossibility results and the observation that all constructions of signatures from USS-NIZK require the underlying language be extended to support specific relations (see Table 1).

Figure 1 illustrates a more precise summary of our separations and contributions, which we further describe in the rest of this section.

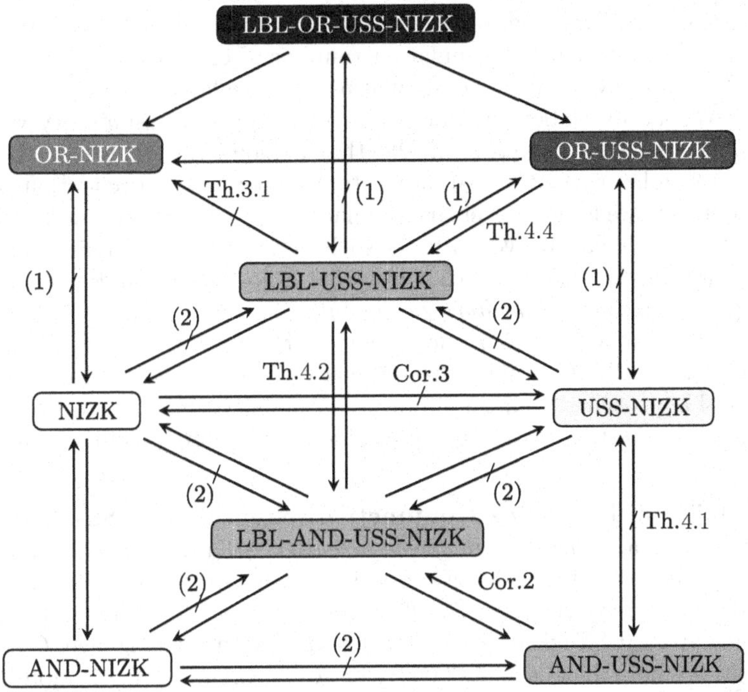

Fig. 1. Relations between variations of NIZK. Non-labelled edges correspond to straightforward black-box constructions. Separations labelled as (1) are implied by Theorem 3.1 (see Corollary 1). Those labelled as (2) are implied by Theorem 4.1 and hold in the *full-verification model* (see Definition 4.1).

Impossibility of Black-Box Disjunctive Extension of Various NIZKs. As our first contribution, we show that there is no fully black-box disjunctive language extension for NIZKs. We show this result in a stronger form by proving the absence of reductions from a labelled USS-NIZK system (see Definition 2.3) for $\mathcal{L}$ to a NIZK scheme for $\mathcal{L} \vee \hat{\mathcal{L}}$ (for any $\hat{\mathcal{L}}$). (Note that we focus on labelled USS-NIZKs for its generality.) To explain the core idea of our argument, let us define a *legitimate crs* as a crs generated with the underlying NIZK's crs generation algorithm. Roughly, our proof goes as follows: (i) we show that the prover algorithm of the disjunctive extension cannot invoke the underlying NIZK's prover on legitimate crs's (or otherwise the resulting NIZK will not be zero-knowledge); (ii) we then argue that because all calls to the underlying prover must be on non-legitimate crs's, very roughly, their trapdoor is known to the prover of the extended NIZK and thus, soundness is compromised. In Sect. 3 we formalize the previous intuition and rigorously consider other missing cases.

A bit more formally, we follow the *oracle separation paradigm*, cf., [9,23,31, 49,53] where we construct an oracle O relative to which there exists a language $\mathcal{L}$ and a secure labelled USS-NIZK system L for it, but for any language $\hat{\mathcal{L}}$, there does not exist a NIZK system M for $\mathcal{L} \vee \hat{\mathcal{L}}$ that is zero-knowledge and sound at the same time. Our contribution also includes a novel approach in the construction of an adversary against simulation soundness, exploiting the simulability of the NIZK in a reverse manner: simulating the zero-knowledge simulator with a real prover, as we elaborate below. This technique bears similarity with the *simulatable adversary paradigm* in [22] that exploits the duality of the zero-knowledge simulator and the real prover to construct a meta-reduction [10,15]. In our approach, we let the adversary simulate the oracle so that a no-instance of the language can look like a yes-instance with a certain witness. This can be done by redefining the language in such a way that a no-instance and a yes-instance are swapped (we call this *instance swapping*).

The way we simulate the oracle simplifies the analysis and results in eliminating the use of PSPACE power from the adversary, which used to be essential in standard approaches from the literature. We believe this new technique is of independent interest and could be applicable to other impossibility results.

Impossibility of Black-Box Conjunctive Extension of USS-NIZK. It is remarkable that a *conjunctive language extension* is hard to achieve in a black-box way in the case of USS-NIZKs. Specifically, in Sect. 4, we show that there is no fully black-box reduction [31,49] from a USS-NIZK system L for a hard language $\mathcal{L}$ to a USS-NIZK system M for the extended language $\mathcal{L} \wedge \hat{\mathcal{L}}$, for any arbitrary hard language $\hat{\mathcal{L}}$. (We refer to Theorem 4.1 for a more formal statement.) Here, a hard language is, in short, a language that constitutes a promise problem [18,52] consisting of a pair of disjoint, efficiently sampleable, and indistinguishable languages, $\mathcal{L}$ and $\mathcal{C}$ (see Definition 2.1). Our result also applies to the case where the extended part of the language $\hat{\mathcal{L}}$ is trivial (i.e., in BPP) as long as the inverse of its size is negligible in the security parameter.

A very high level view of our proof strategy is similar to the one for the impossibility of disjunctive extensions. However, since the simulation soundness game is interactive, when oracle queries from $\mathsf{M.PrvSim}$ run by the challenger cannot be seen by the adversary, it is more difficult to collect enough information for producing a forgery and the details of the proof differ considerably. Another important difference from the case of disjunction is that our impossibility result about the conjunctive extension is limited to what we introduce as the *full-verification model* (Definition 4.1). Namely, every proof that is created internally with the prover algorithm must then be verified by the verification algorithm.

Implications and More. Our two impossibility results, in combination with a simple analysis, allow us to discover other impossibility relations (see Fig. 1).

A remarkable one is the impossibility of fully black-box construction of USS-NIZKs from NIZKs (Corollary 3). Such an impossibility (even in the *full-verification model*) enlightens the essential difference between bounded and unbounded simulation soundness in the context of NIZKs.

Another remarkable result is fully black-box constructions of *labelled* USS-NIZKs for $\mathcal{L}$ from USS-NIZK for $\mathcal{L} \wedge \hat{\mathcal{L}}$ (Theorem 4.3) or $\mathcal{L} \vee \hat{\mathcal{L}}$ (Theorem 4.4). A heuristic way of attaching a label would be to involve it into a hash function used somewhere in the proof function. While it is possible for particular types of constructions such as those using Fiat-Shamir transformation [20], it is not necessarily trivial in other cases such as Groth-Sahai proofs [27] and Quasi-adaptive NIZKs [32] with structure-preserving property [4], even if the label is left as a non-group string. Our construction can be seen as a feasibility result: labelling is achievable in a black-box manner given USS and support for extended (conjunctive or disjunctive) languages. If either of the properties is not provided, labelling is not black-box achievable as shown in Fig. 1.

Construction of Signatures Without Language Extension. Motivated by our previous results, we show that any USS-NIZK for any hard language in NP can be used by itself *without language extensions* as a secure digital signature scheme. Our construction retains almost the same computation and space complexity and hence has a practical value. Concretely, given a USS-NIZK for any hard language $\mathcal{L}$, we construct a signature scheme that is unforgeable against adaptive chosen message attacks. We emphasize that our result does not require $\mathcal{L}$ support particular relations, which was required by related works on building signatures from USS-NIZKs, e.g., [26,34] (see Table 1). That is a sharp difference from previous works, because our impossible results suggest that such specific relations in the language cannot be achieved in a black-box way. Furthermore, the only additional building block (used to create a signature scheme for arbitrary long messages) other than USS-NIZK is an extended target-collision-resistant function that is a "secret-key-free" primitive unlike "authenticating" ones used in the literature. Note that, in theory, a signature scheme can be constructed solely from NIZK by using its common-reference generator as a one-way function. However, the resulting scheme suffers from a significant performance overhead [6] and, unlike ours, does not allow us to conclude that *upgrading a NIZK to an unbounded simulation sound NIZK requires the use of a signature-like primitive.*

Our general construction shares an idea with other works, e.g. [33]: the trapdoor for zero-knowledge simulation can be used as a signing-key and the simulated proofs should work as signatures (because the simulation function can only be invoked with the trapdoor), which are publicly verifiable with the crs bound to the trapdoor. Unforgeability is argued based on the simulation soundness property. Our result is quite general in terms of the language that the underlying USS-NIZK must support.

Table 1. Upper block: General transformations from NIZK to USS-NIZK. Lower block: Constructions of various signature schemes based on non-interactive arguments. Underlined symbols are witnesses. OSS-NIZK stands for *one-time simulation-sound NIZK*. R: relation associated to the original language. σ, $\hat{\sigma}$: common reference strings. PRF: pseudo-random function. PRG: pseudo-random generator. ENC: CPA-secure encryption. LRSIG: leakage-resilient signatures. TCR: target-collision-resistant function. SIG: signature scheme. SoK: signature of knowledge.

Ref.	Objective	Statements proved on the underlying NIZK
[50]	NIZK → OSS-NIZK	$R(x, \underline{\omega})$
[17]	NIZK → USS-NIZK	$R(x, \underline{\omega}) \vee (y{=}\mathsf{PRF}_{\underline{s}}(vk) \wedge \mathsf{Com}(\underline{s}; \underline{r}){=}\sigma) \vee (\hat{\sigma}{=}\mathsf{PRG}(\underline{s}))$
[29]	NIZK → USS-NIZK	$R(x, \underline{\omega}) \vee \underline{\sigma} = \mathsf{SIG}_{\underline{sk}}(vk)$
[7]	NIZK → SIG	$y = \mathsf{PRF}_{\underline{s}}(m) \wedge \mathsf{Com}(\underline{s}; \underline{r}) = \sigma$
[34]	USS-NIZK → LRSIG	$C = \mathsf{ENC}_{pk}(\underline{x} \| m; \underline{\omega}) \wedge y = \mathsf{TCR}_k(\underline{x})$
[26]	SE-SNARK → SoK	$R(x, \underline{\omega}) \wedge y = \mathsf{TCR}_k(m)$

1.3 Related Works

There exist several works for extending NIZKs to support disjunction of instances without reductions to NP-complete languages. In [14] Cramer et al., presented a very useful framework to extend any sigma-protocol to handle disjunctive relations among instances. The idea is to split a challenge into two so that one of them can be predicted in advance for simulating the 'no' side of the two instances. This idea applies to a wide range of NIZK constructions based on the Fiat-Shamir heuristic [20], splitting a crs into two shares allows similar ideas if some algebraic properties are available. Other works [21,41,46] follow an approach based on Groth-Sahai proofs, which can be used to prove disjunctive statements, e.g., [13,24]. Furthermore, Abdalla et al. [2] achieve disjunction through a smooth projective hash proof system [16].

Many works also try to upgrade NIZK systems to achieve simulation-soundness. Such upgrades usually require additional cryptographic primitives or the language associated to the NIZK be extended. In Table 1 we exemplify some of these transformations. The construction by Sahai in [50] is based on the generation of multiple common-reference strings of the original NIZK. It is a fully black-box construction that works for any NIZK systems and languages but results only in bounded simulation soundness that allow preliminary bounded number of queries. De Santis et al. built the first USS-NIZK in [17] by using a pseudo-random function (PRF) and a commitment scheme, in combination with a general NIZK that supports disjunction. The essential idea of this work is to prove that certain statement is true *or* the PRF was computed correctly with a secret key that was previously committed in the crs. Groth [24], followed by other works [3,13,29], combined a signature scheme and a one-time signature scheme with a NIZK system for satisfiability of relations over bilinear groups. Kiltz et al. combined randomized PRFs with a QA-NIZK based on the Matrix DH and the Kernel DH assumptions [35]. In summary, all these works for obtaining USS are non black-box, since they require specific properties.

Our last contribution is motivated by our impossibility results and the observation that the attempts from the literature to build signature schemes from USS-NIZKs require the language be extended or the use of additional primitives. For example, Bellare and Goldwasser [7] construct a signature scheme by combining a PRF and a public-key encryption scheme (as a commitment scheme) with a standard NIZK. Another attempt in [34] combines a *labelled* PKE scheme [16] with a USS-NIZK system to produce a signature scheme where messages are embedded into a label of the encryption. Libert et al. [37,38] combined a SS-QA-NIZK system with a signature scheme to achieve new functionalities. Groth and Maller [26] present a general framework for constructing signature of knowledge (SoK) schemes based on succinct simulation extractable non-interactive arguments of knowledge (SE-SNARK) requiring conjunctive extension.

2 Preliminaries

2.1 Notations

For a finite set X, we write $x \leftarrow X$ to denote that x is uniformly sampled from set X. If we need to be explicit about random coins, r, used in the sampling, we write $x \leftarrow X(r)$. For $n \in \mathbb{N}$, we denote by U_n the uniform distribution over $\{0,1\}^n$. A positive function $\epsilon : \mathbb{N} \to [0,1] \subseteq \mathbb{R}$ is called *negligible* if for every polynomial $p(x) \in \mathbb{R}[X]$ there exists a constant κ_0 s.t. $\forall \kappa \geq \kappa_0$, $\epsilon(\kappa) < 1/p(x)$.

By $y \leftarrow A(x)$ we denote a process of computation where A takes x as input and outputs y. By A^{O}, we denote oracle algorithm A that interacts with oracle O. For oracle O, we use notation $y \leftarrow \mathsf{O}(x)$ also to represent a pair of input and output, (x, y), when we need to be explicit about O. Variables with brackets $[\cdot]$ match to any value. For instance, $y \leftarrow \mathsf{O}([x])$ matches to any oracle query whose output is y and we refer to the input value by x thereafter. When the matched value will not be referred afterwards, we use $*$ and write $y \leftarrow \mathsf{O}(*)$ to mean that there exists an input to O that results in y. We also use the wildcard $[* \neq \perp] \leftarrow \mathsf{O}(x)$ to denote that O outputs something other than $\perp$ for input x.

Algorithms and oracles often implement several functions identified by an input. By $\mathsf{M}(\mathsf{func}, args)$ we mean that algorithm M works as a function specified by func taking *args* as input. Dot notation $\mathsf{M.func}$ is used as well when inputs are not important in the context.

2.2 Hard Language and Language Extension

We say that $\mathcal{L}$ is a hard language accompanied by $\mathcal{C}$ if $\mathcal{L}$ and $\mathcal{C}$ are efficiently sampleable, disjoint, and hard to distinguish. Accordingly, $(\mathcal{L}, \mathcal{C})$ constitutes a promise problem [18,52]. More formally:

Definition 2.1 (Hard Language). *Let $R_{\mathcal{L}}$ be an efficiently computable binary relation. For fixed polynomials poly_x and poly_w, let $\mathcal{L}_\kappa := \{x \in \{0,1\}^{\mathrm{poly}_x(\kappa)} \mid \exists w \in \{0,1\}^{\mathrm{poly}_w(\kappa)} : R(x,w) = 1\}$, and $\mathcal{L} := \cup_\kappa \mathcal{L}_\kappa$. Let $\mathcal{C}_\kappa \subseteq \{0,1\}^{\mathrm{poly}_x(\kappa)}$ and $\mathcal{C} := \cup_\kappa \mathcal{C}_\kappa$. Given a negligible function ϵ_{hd}, we say $\mathcal{L}$ is ϵ_{hd}-hard (with respect to $\mathcal{C}$) if for every $\kappa \in \mathbb{N}$, $\mathcal{L}_\kappa \cap \mathcal{C}_\kappa = \emptyset$ and the following properties are satisfied:*

- *For all* $\kappa \in \mathbb{N}$, *there exist efficiently sampleable distributions* $\mathcal{D}_{\mathcal{L}_\kappa}$ *and* $\mathcal{D}_{\mathcal{C}_\kappa}$ *producing elements from* $\mathcal{L}_\kappa$ *and* $\mathcal{C}_\kappa$ *respectively.*
- $\mathcal{L}$ *and* $\mathcal{C}$ *are indistinguishable, w.r.t.* $\mathcal{D}_\mathcal{L} = \{\mathcal{D}_{\mathcal{L}_\kappa}\}_{\kappa\in\mathbb{N}}$ *and* $\mathcal{D}_\mathcal{C} = \{\mathcal{D}_{\mathcal{C}_\kappa}\}_{\kappa\in\mathbb{N}}$, *i.e., for every p.p.t. algorithm* A *and for all sufficiently large* κ, *it holds*

$$|\Pr[x \leftarrow \mathcal{D}_{\mathcal{L}_\kappa} \ : \ 1 \leftarrow A(x)] - \Pr[x \leftarrow \mathcal{D}_{\mathcal{C}_\kappa} \ : \ 1 \leftarrow A(x)]| < \epsilon_{\mathsf{hd}}(\kappa).$$

When it is clear from the context, we will write $x \leftarrow \mathcal{L}_\kappa$ or $x \leftarrow \mathcal{C}_\kappa$ instead of $x \leftarrow \mathcal{D}_{\mathcal{L}_\kappa}$ or $x \leftarrow \mathcal{D}_{\mathcal{C}_\kappa}$ respectively.

Definition 2.2 (Extended Language). *Given two languages* $\mathcal{L}$ *and* $\hat{\mathcal{L}}$, *and a logical binary operator* $\diamond \in \{\wedge, \vee\}$, *an extended language (denoted by* $\mathcal{L} \diamond \hat{\mathcal{L}}$*) is defined as the union* $\cup_\kappa(\mathcal{L}_\kappa \diamond \hat{\mathcal{L}}_\kappa)$ *where* $\mathcal{L}_\kappa \diamond \hat{\mathcal{L}}_\kappa := \{(x, \hat{x}) \mid (x \in \mathcal{L}_\kappa) \diamond (\hat{x} \in \hat{\mathcal{L}}_\kappa)\}$. *The extension is said to be* non-trivial *if* $\mathcal{L}_\kappa \diamond \hat{\mathcal{L}}_\kappa \not\subseteq \mathcal{L}_{\kappa'}$ *for any* κ *and* κ'.

Note that, for any non-empty finite $\mathcal{L}_\kappa$ and $\hat{\mathcal{L}}_\kappa$, we have $\mathcal{L}_\kappa \diamond \hat{\mathcal{L}}_\kappa \not\subseteq \mathcal{L}_\kappa$. In this work, we only consider non-trivial language extensions. A language extension of a NIZK (with respect to operator $\diamond$) consists of, given languages $\mathcal{L}$ and $\hat{\mathcal{L}}$ and a NIZK scheme L for $\mathcal{L}$, build a NIZK scheme M for $\mathcal{L} \diamond \hat{\mathcal{L}}$.

2.3 Non-interactive Zero-Knowledge Argument System

In this section we present syntactical and security definitions for *labelled* NIZKs. Fixing label ℓ to a default, e.g. the empty string, results in the standard definitions for (non-labelled) NIZKs.

Definition 2.3 (Labelled Non-interactive Argument System). *A labelled non-interactive argument system for language* $\mathcal{L}$ *associated to relation* R *is a tuple of polynomial-time algorithms* $(\mathsf{Crs}, \mathsf{Prv}, \mathsf{Vrf})$ *where:*

- $\sigma \leftarrow \mathsf{Crs}(1^\kappa)$ *takes a security parameter and generates a crs,* σ.
- $\pi \leftarrow \mathsf{Prv}(\sigma, x, \ell, w)$ *takes* σ, *an instance* x, *a label* ℓ, *and a witness* w *as input and outputs a proof* π *or* $\perp$.
- $b \leftarrow \mathsf{Vrf}(\sigma, x, \ell, \pi)$ *takes* σ, *an instance* x, *a label* ℓ, *and a proof* π, *and outputs either* 1 *or* 0 *representing acceptance or rejection, respectively.*

For correctness, it is required that there exists a negligible function ϵ_{co} *in* κ *such that, for all sufficiently large* κ, *all* $(x, w) \in \{0,1\}^{\mathrm{poly}_x(\kappa)} \times \{0,1\}^{\mathrm{poly}_w(\kappa)}$ *with* $R(x, w) = 1$, *and all* $\ell \in \{0,1\}^{\mathrm{poly}_\ell(\kappa)}$, *it holds:*

$$\Pr[\sigma \leftarrow \mathsf{Crs}(1^\kappa);\ \pi \leftarrow \mathsf{Prv}(\sigma, x, \ell, w)\ :\ 1 \neq \mathsf{Vrf}(\sigma, x, \ell, \pi)] < \epsilon_{\mathsf{co}}(\kappa).$$

For soundness, it is required that there exists a negligible function ϵ *in* κ *such that, for any p.p.t. algorithm* $\mathcal{A}$ *and all sufficiently large* κ*:*

$$\Pr[\sigma \leftarrow \mathsf{Crs}(1^\kappa)\,;\ (x, \ell, \pi) \leftarrow \mathcal{A}(\sigma)\ :\ x \notin \mathcal{L}_\kappa \wedge 1 = \mathsf{Vrf}(\sigma, x, \ell, \pi)] \leq \epsilon(\kappa).$$

Definition 2.4 (Adaptive Zero-Knowledge). *A labelled non-interactive argument system* (Crs, Prv, Vrf) *is* adaptive zero-knowledge *if there exists a pair of p.p.t. algorithms* CrsSim *and* PrvSim *and a negligible function* ϵ_{azk} *in* κ *such that for every p.p.t. algorithm* $\mathcal{A}$ *and for every sufficiently large* κ,

$$\left|\Pr\left[\sigma \leftarrow \mathsf{Crs}(1^\kappa) : 1 \leftarrow \mathcal{A}^{O_1(\cdot,\cdot,\cdot)}(\sigma)\right] - \Pr\left[(\sigma,\tau) \leftarrow \mathsf{CrsSim}(1^\kappa) : 1 \leftarrow \mathcal{A}^{O_0(\cdot,\cdot,\cdot)}(\sigma)\right]\right|$$

is lower than $\epsilon_{\mathsf{azk}}(\kappa)$. *Oracles* O_1, O_0, *on input* (x,ℓ,w) *output* $\perp$ *if* $R(x,w)=0$, *and otherwise, they return* $\mathsf{Prv}(\sigma,x,\ell,w)$ *and* $\mathsf{PrvSim}(\sigma,x,\ell,\tau)$ *respectively.*

We say it is a *non-adaptive* multi-theorem zero-knowledge if the above holds when the adversary $\mathcal{A}$ is limited interact with O only before σ is generated.

Definition 2.5 (Unbounded Simulation Soundness). *A labelled non-interactive zero-knowledge argument system* $\Pi :=$ (Crs, Prv, Vrf, CrsSim, PrvSim) *for language* $\mathcal{L}$ *is unbounded simulation sound if there exists a negligible function* ϵ_{ss} *in* κ *such that, for any p.p.t. algorithm* $\mathcal{A}$,

$$\mathrm{Adv}^{\mathsf{USS}}_{\Pi,\mathcal{A}}(\kappa) := \Pr\left[\begin{array}{l}(\sigma,\tau) \leftarrow \mathsf{CrsSim}(1^\kappa) \\ (x,\ell,\pi) \leftarrow \mathcal{A}^{\mathsf{PrvSim}(\sigma,\cdot,\cdot,\tau)}(\sigma)\end{array} : \begin{array}{l}(x,\ell) \notin Q \wedge x \notin \mathcal{L}_\kappa \\ \wedge\, 1 = \mathsf{Vrf}(\sigma,x,\ell,\pi)\end{array}\right] < \epsilon_{\mathsf{ss}}(\kappa)$$

holds, where Q *is a list of queries sent to* PrvSim.

A non-interactive argument system that is zero-knowledge and unbounded simulation sound is called USS-NIZK.

We next present two lemmas related to the behavior of a zero-knowledge simulator. They state that the simulator must produce valid proofs for an overwhelming amount of yes-instances of the language (due to the *zero-knowledge property*) and valid proofs for an overwhelming amount of no-instances of the language (due to the *hardness of the language*).

Definition 2.6 (Yes-instance simulation correctness). *A non-interactive argument system* Π = (Crs, Prv, Vrf, CrsSim, PrvSim) *for language* $\mathcal{L}$ *is yes-instance simulation correct if, for any* $x \in \mathcal{L}_\kappa$ *and* $\ell \in \{0,1\}^{poly_\ell(\kappa)}$, *the probability*

$$\epsilon_{\mathsf{yes}}(\kappa) := \Pr[(\sigma,\tau) \leftarrow \mathsf{CrsSim}(1^\kappa)\ :\ 0 = \mathsf{Vrf}(\sigma,x,\mathsf{PrvSim}(\sigma,x,\ell,\tau))]$$

is negligible in κ. *The NIZK system* Π *is perfectly yes-instance simulation correct if* $\epsilon_{\mathsf{yes}}(\kappa) = 0$.

Lemma 2.1. $\epsilon_{\mathsf{yes}}(\kappa) \leq \epsilon_{\mathsf{zk}}(\kappa) + \epsilon_{\mathsf{co}}(\kappa)$.

Definition 2.7 (No-instance simulation correctness). *A non-interactive argument system* Π = (Crs, Prv, Vrf, CrsSim, PrvSim) *for* ϵ_{hd}*-hard language* $\mathcal{L}$ *accompanied by* $\mathcal{C}$ *is no-instance simulation correct if for every* $\ell \in \{0,1\}^{poly_\ell(\kappa)}$, *the probability*

$$\epsilon_{\mathsf{no}}(\kappa) := \Pr[(\sigma,\tau) \leftarrow \mathsf{CrsSim}(1^\kappa)\ ;\ x \leftarrow \mathcal{D}_{\mathcal{C}_\kappa}\ :\ 0 = \mathsf{Vrf}(\sigma,x,\mathsf{PrvSim}(\sigma,x,\ell,\tau))]$$

is negligible in κ. Π *is perfectly no-instance simulation correct if* $\epsilon_{\mathsf{no}}(\kappa) = 0$.

Observe that the yes-instance simulation correctness is universally quantified for all $x \in \mathcal{L}_\kappa$. However, the same is too restrictive in the case of no-instance simulation correctness, because, in general, a proof simulator may not produce valid proofs for a small set of no-instances without violating zero-knowledge.

Lemma 2.2. $\epsilon_{\mathsf{no}}(\kappa) \leq \epsilon_{\mathsf{zk}}(\kappa) + \epsilon_{\mathsf{co}}(\kappa) + \epsilon_{\mathsf{hd}}(\kappa)$.

We refer to the full version of this paper for a formal proof of the lemmas [1].

2.4 Fully Black-Box Constructions and Separation

We follow the framework of fully black-box constructions and separation in [31, 49]. We say that there is a fully black-box construction of primitive A based on primitive B if, given L securely implementing B as an oracle, there exists an oracle machine M such that M^{L} securely implements A.

On the other hand, to show the absence of a fully black-box construction, we use the so-called *single oracle separation technique* [31]. That is, there is no fully black-box construction of primitive A based on B if there exists an oracle O and an oracle machine L such that L^{O} securely implements B, but any oracle machine M such that M^{O} implements A, is insecure. In Sect. 3, we show an oracle O such that L^{O} is a NIZK system for $\mathcal{L}$, but any construction M^{O} of a NIZK system for language $\mathcal{L} \vee \hat{\mathcal{L}}$ is insecure (no matter what $\hat{\mathcal{L}}$ is, as long as it is hard). As we investigate constructions that do not rely on particular structures or properties, we treat $\mathcal{L}$ as a black-box as well. (Therefore, it would be more precise to denote the language as $\mathcal{L}^{\mathsf{O}}$ but we abuse notation and use $\mathcal{L}$ instead).

By $A \Rightarrow B$, we mean that there exists a fully black-box construction of B based on A. A fully black-box separation is denoted by $A \not\Rightarrow B$. If a separation holds for a restricted class of black-box constructions, we denote it by $A \not\Rightarrow_* B$. Though separations for restricted classes of black-box constructions can bring insight to a particular problem, rigorously, they are weaker than fully black-box separations, so we make it explicit.

3 Disjunctive Language Extension

We show that given a NIZK system with strong properties such as labelling and unbound simulation soundness, it is hard to disjunctively extend the language, even when compromising labelling or simulation soundness.

Theorem 3.1. *(LBL-USS-NIZK $\not\Rightarrow$ OR-NIZK) Let $\hat{\mathcal{L}}$ be a hard language. There does not exist a fully black-box construction M that converts any labelled USS-NIZK system L (for some language $\mathcal{L}$), into a NIZK scheme for $\mathcal{L} \vee \hat{\mathcal{L}}$ that is correct, adaptive zero-knowledge, and sound.*

Given the straightforward implications among NIZK, USS-NIZK, and LBL-USS-NIZK, Theorem 3.1 implies that no black-box disjunctive language extension is possible with respect to NIZK, USS-NIZK, or LBL-USS-NIZK.

Corollary 1. *It holds NIZK $\not\Rightarrow$ OR-NIZK, and USS-NIZK $\not\Rightarrow$ OR-USS-NIZK, and LBL-USS-NIZK $\not\Rightarrow$ LBL-OR-USS-NIZK.*

In the rest of this section, we prove Theorem 3.1. For that, we first describe an oracle used for constructing a hard language and a labelled USS-NIZK for it.

Definition 3.1 (Oracle O). *Oracle O_κ is equipped with two injections $H_c : \{0,1\}^\kappa \rightarrow \{0,1\}^{2\kappa}$ and $H_x : \{0,1\}^{\kappa+1} \rightarrow \{0,1\}^{2\kappa}$, and a permutation $H_p : \{0,1\}^{6\kappa} \rightarrow \{0,1\}^{6\kappa}$. Let H_c^{-1}, H_x^{-1} and H_p^{-1} be their respective inverse functions that output $\perp$ for inputs having no preimages. Oracle O_κ provides three language-related functionalities* SmplYes, SmplNo, *and* Promise, *and four NIZK-related functionalities,* Crs, Prv, PrvSim *and* Vrf *that:*

- $\mathsf{O}_\kappa(\mathsf{SmplYes}, w) \rightarrow x$: *Compute* $x \leftarrow H_x(1||w)$, *and output* x.
- $\mathsf{O}_\kappa(\mathsf{SmplNo}, w) \rightarrow x$: *Compute* $x \leftarrow H_x(0||w)$, *and output* x.
- $\mathsf{O}_\kappa(\mathsf{Promise}, x) \rightarrow 0/1$: *Output* 0 *if* $\perp \leftarrow H_x^{-1}(x)$. *Output* 1, *otherwise.*

- $\mathsf{O}_\kappa(\mathsf{Crs}, \tau) \rightarrow \sigma$: *Compute* $\sigma \leftarrow H_c(\tau)$ *and output* σ.
- $\mathsf{O}_\kappa(\mathsf{Prv}, \sigma, x, \ell, w) \rightarrow \pi/\perp$: *Output* $\pi \leftarrow H_p(\sigma||x||\ell)$. $(\star)$
- $\mathsf{O}_\kappa(\mathsf{PrvSim}, \sigma, x, \ell, \tau) \rightarrow \pi/\perp$: *Output* $\pi \leftarrow H_p(\sigma||x||\ell)$. $(\star\star)$
- $\mathsf{O}_\kappa(\mathsf{Vrf}, \sigma, x, \ell, \pi) \rightarrow 0/1$: *Output 1 if* $(\sigma||x||\ell) = H_p^{-1}(\pi)$, *else* 0.

$(\star)$ *Output* $\perp$ *instead if* $\perp \leftarrow H_c^{-1}(\sigma), x \neq H_x(1||w)$, *or* $\ell \notin \{0,1\}^{2\kappa}$.

$(\star\star)$ *Output* $\perp$ *instead if* $\sigma \neq H_c(\tau), \perp \leftarrow H_x^{-1}(x)$, *or* $\ell \notin \{0,1\}^{2\kappa}$.

We denote by O *an oracle consisting of a set of* O_κ *for all* $\kappa \in \mathbb{N}$. *Given an input,* O *defines* κ *based on the size of the second argument and checks if all other arguments follow the appropriate size. On a successful check, it forwards the input to* O_κ *and outputs the result, otherwise* O *outputs* $\perp$. *By* $\mathcal{O}$ *we denote the set of all possible oracles* O.

A query to O is *successful* if the answer is not $\perp$ (or not 0 in the case of O.Vrf). We say that a common reference string σ is *valid* (with respect to O) if there exists τ that satisfies $\sigma = H_c(\tau)$. Given σ (without τ), it is easy to assure its validity by checking that $\mathsf{O}(\mathsf{Prv}, \sigma, x, \ell, w)$ is different from $\perp$, where x can be any yes-instance and w its corresponding witness.

The oracle O can be seen as a set consisting of entries of the form (cmd, *args*, *output*) where command cmd is one of {SmplYes, SmplNo, Promise, Crs, Prv, PrvSim, Vrf}, *args* denotes inputs for each command, and *output* is the answer. Inputs and outputs may include wildcards such as $*$. Then, a set S of entries of this form is called a *partial oracle* as it can be seen as an oracle that accepts only limited inputs. A partial oracle S is called *consistent* if there exists another set S' such that $S \cup S'$ forms a complete oracle in $\mathcal{O}$. Otherwise S is called *inconsistent.* A *hybrid oracle*, denoted as $S := S_1|S_2|\cdots$, is an oracle that combines partial oracles $S_1, S_2, \ldots$ in such a way that, given a query of the form $(\mathsf{cmd}, \mathit{args})$, it first searches S_1 for matching entry $(\mathsf{cmd}, \mathit{args}, [\mathit{output}])$ and returns *output* if it exists. If no such entry is found in S_1, it searches S_2 and so forth. Note that a hybrid oracle may not be consistent.

Let L be an oracle machine that, given O as an oracle, forwards its input to O and outputs whatever O outputs. L^{O} implements a hard promise problem and a NIZK argument system for it. (Some trivial syntactical adjustments are needed to fit to the definition of NIZK in 2.3 and 2.4.) The following lemma holds for L^{O}.

Lemma 3.1. *With probability* 1 *over the choice*[1] *of* $\mathsf{O} \in \mathcal{O}$, L^{O} *implements a hard promise problem* $(\mathcal{L}, \mathcal{C})$ *for* $\mathcal{L}_\kappa := \{x \mid \exists w \in \{0,1\}^\kappa \text{ s.t. } x = H_x(1||w)\}$ *and* $\mathcal{C}_\kappa := \{x \mid \exists w \in \{0,1\}^\kappa \text{ s.t. } x = H_x(0||w)\}$. *It also implements a non-interactive zero-knowledge argument system for* $\mathcal{L}$ *that is perfectly correct, perfectly yes-instance and no-instance simulation correct. Furthermore, it is adaptive zero-knowledge and unbound simulation-sound against uniform adversaries given oracle access to* O *a polynomial number of times.*

By design of the oracle, adversaries that interact with it can only win if some *bad events* occur. It is not hard to see that these events occur with negligible probability. We refer to the full version of this paper for a formal proof [1].

We make some remarks about our design choices for O and the properties of L. It was shown in [11,55] that a simpler witness-indistinguishable oracle suffices to construct a simulation sound NIZK. It is however essential for their construction that the oracle supports an NP-complete language (or a specific disjunctive language). The NIZK implemented by the above L is deterministic but one can make it probabilistic so that (simulated) proofs have κ-bit entropy simply by attaching κ-bit randomness to the proof. The simulation soundness of L^{O} will not be directly used in our proof of impossibility. What is important here is to see that O suffices to construct a USS-NIZK for $\mathcal{L}$.

Intuition for the Impossibility. If the construction M is such that, $\mathsf{M.Crs}$ generates some σ_j by calling $\mathsf{O.Crs}$ and encoding them into $\widetilde{\sigma}$ (we name such crs's *legitimate*), we claim that the prover algorithm $\mathsf{M.Prv}$ cannot use them. Otherwise, the adaptive zero-knowledgeness will be compromised. That is, every crs that used when proving a given statement, should be generated within the prover algorithm (except for some eccentric cases that we explain later). A crucial observation is that, to prove disjunction for an instance $(x, \hat{x})$, it may be the case that $(x, \hat{x}) \in \mathcal{C}_\kappa \times \hat{\mathcal{L}}_\kappa$ and the no-instance x cannot be proven with a legitimate crs whose trapdoor is unknown to the prover. On the other hand, using a legitimate crs only for yes-instances contradicts the zero-knowledgeness

[1] Technically, for every machine $\mathcal{A}$, there exist a set of measure 0 of oracles for which $\mathcal{A}$ has a significant advantage either against the hardness of the language or the NIZK system. As it is standard after the application of the Borel-Cantelli Lemma, given that there exist countably many machines, for a measure 1 sets of oracles in $\mathcal{O}$ we can say that for all p.p.t. machines $\mathcal{A}$ our result holds.

of the underlying scheme (or the hardness of $\mathcal{L}$), because the zero-knowledge simulator does not know whether the given x is a yes or a no-instance.

Let us elaborate on this point. In the next, let $q(\kappa)$ be a (non-constant) polynomial in the security parameter that upper-bounds the number of queries to O that M^{O} performs in each invocation. Let $c > 1$ be a constant. Consider the adaptive zero-knowledge game where an adversary submits disjunctive instances $(x_j, \hat{x}_j)$ for $j = 1, \ldots, q^c$ (for certain integer c) to the challenger that produces proofs either by $\mathsf{M.Prv}$ (in the *real* world) or $\mathsf{M.PrvSim}$ (in the *simulated* world). The adversary verifies the proofs by $\mathsf{M.Vrf}$ which may make verification queries $\mathsf{O.Vrf}$ on the left-hand instance, x_j. Consider the case where instances $(x_j, \hat{x}_j)$ are taken from $\mathcal{C}_\kappa \times \hat{\mathcal{L}}_\kappa$ as pairs of $(\mathsf{no}, \mathsf{yes})$ instances, and the challenger responds with $\mathsf{M.Prv}$ in the real-world. We then define $(\mathsf{real}, \mathsf{no}, \mathsf{yes})$ as the distribution of all crs's (over the choice of instances and coins of M) that are given as input to $\mathsf{O.Vrf}$ to verify the left-hand instances x_j for $j = 1, \ldots, q^c$. We define $(\mathsf{sim}, \mathsf{no}, \mathsf{yes})$ similarly for the case the challenger respond with $\mathsf{M.PrvSim}$ in the simulated-world. Switching yes and no according to whether x_j (and $\hat{x}_j$, resp.) are chosen from $\mathcal{L}_\kappa$ or $\mathcal{C}_\kappa$ ($\hat{\mathcal{L}}_\kappa$ or $\hat{\mathcal{C}}_\kappa$, resp.), we have

$$(\mathsf{real}, \mathsf{no}, \mathsf{yes}) \overset{(\S)}{\approx} (\mathsf{sim}, \mathsf{no}, \mathsf{yes}) \overset{(\dagger)}{\approx} (\mathsf{sim}, \mathsf{yes}, \mathsf{yes}) \overset{(\ddagger)}{\approx} (\mathsf{sim}, \mathsf{yes}, \mathsf{no}) \overset{(\S)}{\approx} (\mathsf{real}, \mathsf{yes}, \mathsf{no})$$

where $\approx$ denotes indistinguishability of distributions and (§) is given by the zero-knowledge property and (†) and (‡) are given by the hardness of $\mathcal{L}$ and $\hat{\mathcal{L}}$ respectively. (Observe that $\mathsf{M.PrvSim}$ could be used to distinguish between $\mathcal{L}$ and $\mathcal{C}$ if the indistinguishability denoted by (†) did not hold). Also, observe that $(\mathsf{real}, \mathsf{no}, \mathsf{yes})$ does not contain a legitimate crs, because the real prover algorithm cannot prove on a no-instance with a legitimate crs whose trapdoor is not given. Because legitimate crs's can be identified (we refer to the *learning-phase* defined below for more details), and given the above indistinguishability relations, the same is true for $(\mathsf{real}, \mathsf{yes}, \mathsf{no})$: it does not contain legitimate crs's. Therefore, even if a witness for x_j is given, the prover must not use legitimate crs's to prove x_j.

We then argue that a NIZK system that does not use the legitimate crs for proving a given statement cannot be sound. We construct an adversary that runs the prover algorithm, $\mathsf{M.Prv}$, on $(x^*, \hat{x}^*) \in \mathcal{C}_\kappa \times \hat{\mathcal{C}}_\kappa$ and performs an *instance swapping* to fool it as if x^* was taken from $\mathcal{L}_\kappa$. This is done by giving $\mathsf{M.Prv}$ a random fake witness, w^*, for x^* and simulating O on queries involving x^*. Concretely, if $\mathsf{M.Prv}$ makes $\mathsf{O.SmplYes}$ queries on the fake witness w^* (to check its correctness), we simulate the answer by returning x^*. If $\mathsf{O.Prv}$ queries are made on x^* under a crs, σ_j, we replace the query with $\mathsf{O.PrvSim}$ using a trapdoor τ_j for σ_j. This is possible because (as we have argued above) all crs's used within $\mathsf{M.Prv}$ must have been internally generated, so their trapdoors are known. There could be a case where a legitimate crs is used to prove x^*. Recall that $(\mathsf{real}, \mathsf{yes}, \mathsf{no})$ does not include legitimate crs's, i.e., proofs with a legitimate crs will not be verified by $\mathsf{M.Vrf}$. Yet, $\mathsf{M.Prv}$ may create and verify proofs with a legitimate crs for internal use only. Therefore, the adversary must fool $\mathsf{M.Prv}$ by simulating such proofs with random strings and answering accordingly to the respective verification queries. Once $\mathsf{M.Prv}$ is done, the resulting proof $\widetilde{\pi}$ should pass the final verification since all proofs π_j embedded in $\widetilde{\pi}$ are genuine and independent of the fake witness.

Nevertheless, the above sketch ignores the possibility of a *trivial* legitimate crs whose trapdoor is also embedded to $\widetilde{\sigma}$ and available in public. Algorithm $\mathsf{M.Prv}$ may use a trivial trapdoor for no-instances and a relevant witness for yes-instances. But the witness we give to the algorithm is a fake one that does not work properly. To handle such a case, the adversary must find the trivial trapdoors in advance and use them for proofs. Although we do not know how the trivial trapdoors are encoded into $\widetilde{\sigma}$, they can be extracted by running $\mathsf{M.Prv}$ on a number of instances and observing the trapdoors used therein. Since there can be a bounded number of trivial legitimate crs's embedded in $\widetilde{\sigma}$, sufficiently repeating the proofs on random instances exhausts them with high probability.

Breaking Soundness. In the following proof, we construct adversary $\mathcal{A}$ attacking soundness of M (against a challenger $\mathcal{B}$) and use the above observation about the legitimate crs to lower bound the success probability of $\mathcal{A}$.

[Soundness Game for OR-NIZK M]
At the beginning, oracle O is chosen from $\mathcal{O}$. Then challenger $\mathcal{B}$ and adversary $\mathcal{A}$ engage in the following procedures.

Step 1: Setup Phase.

The challenger generates a common reference string by $\widetilde{\sigma} \leftarrow \mathsf{M}^{\mathsf{O}}(\mathsf{Crs}, 1^{\kappa})$. Let Q_{leg} be the list of legitimate crs's and their corresponding trapdoors (σ_j, τ_j) that have been generated in this phase, as $\sigma_j \leftarrow \mathsf{O}(\mathsf{Crs}, \tau_j)$.

Step 2: Self-learning Phase.

Given $\widetilde{\sigma}$, for every $i = 1, \ldots, q^c$, adversary $\mathcal{A}$ uniformly samples instance $(x_i, \hat{x}_i)$ and the corresponding witness $(w_i, \perp)$ from $\mathcal{L}_{\kappa} \times \hat{\mathcal{C}}_{\kappa}$ and it computes $\widetilde{\pi}_i \leftarrow \mathsf{M}^{\mathsf{O}}(\mathsf{Prv}, \widetilde{\sigma}, (x_i, \hat{x}_i), (w_i, \perp))$ and $b_i \leftarrow \mathsf{M}^{\mathsf{O}}(\mathsf{Vrf}, \widetilde{\sigma}, (x_i, \hat{x}_i), \widetilde{\pi}_i)$.
Let Q_{triv} be the list of trivial pairs of crs and trapdoor, (σ_j, τ_j), that appeared in a computation like $[* \neq \perp] \leftarrow \mathsf{O}(\mathsf{PrvSim}, \sigma_j, *, *, \tau_j)$ or $\sigma_j \leftarrow \mathsf{O}(\mathsf{Crs}, \tau_j)$ during some execution of M in this phase.

Step 3: Forgery Phase.

Sample $(x^*, \hat{x}^*) \in \mathcal{C}_{\kappa} \times \hat{\mathcal{C}}_{\kappa}$ as $w^* \leftarrow \{0,1\}^{\kappa}$, $x^* \leftarrow \mathsf{O}(\mathsf{SmplNo}, w^*)$ and $\hat{x}^* \leftarrow \hat{\mathcal{C}}_{\kappa}$
Let $\bar{x} := \mathsf{O}(\mathsf{SmplYes}, w^*)$ and apply instance swapping:
Let O' be the partial oracle given by the entries $(\mathsf{SmplYes}, w^*, x^*)$, $(\mathsf{SmplNo}, w^*, \bar{x})$, and $(\mathsf{Prv}, *, \bar{x}, *, w^*, \perp)$. Run $\mathsf{M}^{\mathsf{O}''}(\mathsf{Prv}, \widetilde{\sigma}, (x^*, \hat{x}^*), (w^*, \perp))$ where O'' is an algorithm that simulates an oracle in $\mathcal{O}$ as follows.
[Algorithm O''] Initialize Q_{intl} as an empty list.

- If a given query is defined in O', return the output accordingly.
- Given $(\mathsf{Crs}, [\tau_j])$, return $\sigma_j \leftarrow \mathsf{O}(\mathsf{Crs}, \tau_j)$ and record (σ_j, τ_j) to Q_{intl}.
- Given $(\mathsf{Prv}, [\sigma_j], x^*, [\ell_j], w^*)$ with valid σ_j:

(a) if $(\sigma_j, [\tau_j]) \in Q_{\mathsf{triv}} \cup Q_{\mathsf{intl}}$:
return $\pi_j \leftarrow \mathsf{O}(\mathsf{PrvSim}, \sigma_j, x^*, \ell_j, \tau_j)$ and add $(\mathsf{Prv}, \sigma_j, x^*, \ell_j, w^*, \pi_j)$ to O'.

(b) else:
return $\pi_j \leftarrow \{0,1\}^{6\kappa}$; add $(\mathsf{Prv}, \sigma_j, x^*, \ell_j, w^*, \pi_j)$, $(\mathsf{Vrf}, \sigma_j, x^*, \ell_j, \pi_j, 1)$ to O'.

- For every other query, forward it to O and return the output.

When M outputs a proof $\widetilde{\pi}^*$, $\mathcal{A}$ outputs $(x^*, \hat{x}^*)$ and $\widetilde{\pi}^*$ as a forgery.

Step 4: Final Verification Phase.

Challenger $\mathcal{B}$ outputs 1 (interpreted as *the adversary wins*) if $x^* \notin \mathcal{L}_\kappa$, $\hat{x}^* \notin \hat{\mathcal{L}}_\kappa$ and $1 \leftarrow \mathsf{M}^{\mathsf{O}}(\mathsf{Vrf}, \widetilde{\sigma}, (x^*, \hat{x}^*), \widetilde{\pi}^*)$; otherwise, it outputs 0 (*the adversary loses*).

Lemma 3.2. *The above adversary $\mathcal{A}$ wins the simulation soundness game of M^{O} with non-negligible probability if M is non-adaptive multi-theorem zero-knowledge and correct.*

We will use the following lemma in the proof of Lemma 3.2. It states that if an event happens for n successive independent attempts, the probability that it suddenly does not happen is upper-bounded by an inverse polynomial of n. We use this lemma to claim that, during the challenge phase, the adversary observes all trivial σ_j embedded in $\widetilde{\sigma}$ generated by the challenger.

Lemma 3.3 ([54, Fact 4.6.1])**.** *Let $X_1, \cdots X_{n+1}$ be independent Bernoulli random variables, where $Pr[X_i = 1] = p$ and $Pr[X_i = 0] = 1-p$ for $i = 1, \cdots, n+1$, and some $p \in [0,1]$. Let E be the event that the first n variables are sampled at 1, and X_{n+1} is sampled at 0. Then, $Pr[E] \leq \frac{1}{e \cdot n}$, where $e \simeq 2.71$ is the base of the natural logarithm.*

Proof (of Lemma 3.2). We analyze the probability that the forged proof passes the verification in the above game. Let $\rho_{\mathsf{zk}}(\kappa)$ and $\rho_{\mathsf{co}}(\kappa)$ denote upper-bounds for non-adaptive multi-theorem zero-knowledge and correctness for M as defined in Definitions 2.3 and 2.4, respectively. We consider these parameters as universal for all O. Let P be the probability that challenger $\mathcal{B}$ outputs 1 in the final verification phase, which is taken over the choice of O and coin flips by $\mathcal{B}$ and $\mathcal{A}$.

Our goal is to show that P is not negligible. Towards that goal, we consider a sequence of games (where each game is identical to the precedent, except for the mentioned details) that introduces arbitrarily small (though not necessarily negligible) differences in the considered probability and eventually reach the situation where $\mathcal{B}$ outputs 1 trivially. We denote the probability for the same event in Game i by P_i. In the first games (Game 0 to Game 6) we exclude events that happen only with negligible probability, simplifying the next transitions. Under the condition that these events do not happen, O'' simulates an oracle in $\mathcal{O}$ that successfully produces a correct proof on a yes instance (of the disjunctive relation). In the succeeding games (Game 7 to 9), we replace oracle O by O'', relying on the zero-knowledge property and the hardness of the languages. In the last Game 9, the adversary does nothing but creating a proof for a yes instance, which must be accepted with high probability.

Game 0: The above soundness game. So $P_0 = P$.
Game 1: For every successful query to O.PrvSim or O.Prv with respect to some σ_j, query O.Crs that generates σ_j must have been made in advance within the same execution of M or in the setup phase. Similarly, for every successful query to O.Vrf for verifying a proof, a query to O.PrvSim or O.Prv that outputs the queried proof must have been made in advance. If any of these are not the case, the game halts.
Game 2: Modify the final verification to skip the check $x^* \notin \mathcal{L}_\kappa$ and $\hat{x}^* \notin \hat{\mathcal{L}}_\kappa$.
Game 3: Halt the game if $\mathcal{A}$ observes $b_i = 0$ in the self-learning phase.
Game 4: The game halts if there has been a query on w^* or x^* or $\bar{x}$ made by M invoked in the setup and self-learning phases.
Game 5: The game halts if any of randomly assigned π_j at step (b) of O$''$ appear as a result of other O.Prv or O.PrvSim queries by the end of the forgery phase.
Game 6: The game halts if, O$''$ receives a query (PrvSim, $[\sigma_j], x^*, [\ell_j], [\tau_j]$) that there exists (Prv, $\sigma_j, x^*, \ell_j, w^*, [\pi_j]$) in O$'$, and $\pi_j \neq \pi'_j \neq \perp$ holds for $\pi'_j \leftarrow$ O(PrvSim, $\sigma_j, x^*, \ell_j, \tau_j$). The modification is to exclude a case where a trapdoor τ_j for some σ_j suddenly appears for the first time in the forgery phase while σ_j itself has appeared so far.

Claim 3.2. $|P_0 - P_6| < \varepsilon(\kappa) + q^c \rho_{\mathsf{co}}(\kappa) + 2/(eq^{c-1})$, for a negligible function $\varepsilon(\kappa)$.

Proof. We include a formal proof in the full version of this paper [1].

Game 7: Replace O in the setup and self-learning phase with algorithm O$''$ with partial oracle O$'$ defined at the end of the forgery phase after Game 4.

Since queries defined in O$'$ involve x^* or $\bar{x}$, they do not appear in the setup and forgery phase. Any queries to O$''$ not defined in O$'$ are answered by O. Thus, this modification does not introduce any relevant change and we have $P_7 = P_6$.
Game 8: In this game, we use O$''$ instead of O also in the final verification phase.

Claim 3.3. $|P_8 - P_7| < 7/eq^{c-1} + (3q^2 + 2q^{c+2})/2^{6\kappa} + 2q/2^\kappa + \hat{\epsilon}_{\mathsf{ind}}(\kappa) + 3\rho_{\mathsf{zk}}(\kappa)$.

Proof. See the end of this section.

Game 9: We then modify O$''$ so that it no longer uses O. Instead, it uses a random partial oracle R such that, O$''$ = O$'$||R is an oracle in $\mathcal{O}_\kappa$.

Since all queries to O$''$ from M.Vrf in Game 8 that answered by O are consistent with the partial oracle O$'$, the replacement by a consistent R does not change the distribution of the view of M.Vrf. Therefore, $P_9 = P_8$.

Now O$''$ is an oracle in $\mathcal{O}_\kappa$ and in Game 8, the adversary is creating a proof $\widetilde{\pi}^*$ on a (yes,no)-instance $(x^*, \hat{x}^*)$ with a correct witness with respect to O$''$. Therefore, the created proof will be accepted unless except for the correctness error. We thus have $P_9 > 1 - \rho_{\mathsf{co}}(\kappa)$.

By summing up the above differences of probabilities, we have

$$P > 1 - \left(9/(eq^{c-1}) + \hat{\epsilon}_{\mathsf{ind}}(\kappa) + 3\rho_{\mathsf{zk}}(\kappa) + (q^c + 1)\rho_{\mathsf{co}}(\kappa) + \epsilon(\kappa)\right).$$

Accordingly, if M is correct, zero-knowledge, language $\hat{\mathcal{L}}$ is hard and constant c is set so that the second term of the right-hand-side of the above inequality is small enough, $\mathcal{A}$ is successful in breaking the soundness of M with non-negligible probability in κ. □

Proof (of Claim 3.3). The view in the verification phase changes only if M.Vrf makes one of the following queries whose output differs in O and O″.

- A query $(\mathsf{PrvSim}, [\sigma_j], x^*, [\ell_j], [\tau_j])$ such that for $\pi_j \leftarrow \mathsf{O}(\mathsf{PrvSim}, \sigma_j, x^*, \ell_j, \tau_j)$, there exists $(\mathsf{Prv}, \sigma_j, x^*, \ell_j, w^*, [\pi'_j])$ in O′, with $\pi_j \neq \pi'_j$.
- A query that is not in O′ but results in a π_j that already appears in O′.
- A query included in O′.

We can bound (by a negligible function) the probability that the first two types of queries from above occur, by following similar arguments as for the transitions to Game 6 and Game 5 respectively. However, the third case requires careful analysis. In the following, we briefly present our idea for bounding the probability. First observe that O′ includes two types of queries: those involving witness w^* and those where randomly assigned proofs are verified. Informally, the first type of query will occur with low probability because, otherwise, M.Vrf would have a valid witness for a given instance, what contradicts zero-knowledge or the hardness of the language. The second type of query must also occur with low probability because, as discussed at the beginning of this section: a legitimate non-trivial σ_j cannot be used to prove a given instance, or otherwise zero-knowledgeness will be lost.

More concretely, to bound the probability of the first type of query happening, the same argument as that for Game 6 can be applied. We consider queries done by M.Vrf instead of M.Prv in the self-learning phase and the verification phase but the analysis remains the same. This gives us an upper-bound of $2q/(eq^c)$. The second type of query can be can be bounded as in the transition to Game 5, except for additional q queries made during the verification itself. We can establish a bound of $q(3q + 2q^{c+1})/2^{6\kappa}$. Finally, for the third type of query, observe that they can be splitted into: *(i)* queries including w^* and *(ii)* queries for verifying a randomly assigned proof. Queries of type *(i)*, are all of the form $(\mathsf{SmplYes}, w^*)$, (SmplNo, w^*), $(\mathsf{Prv}, *, \bar{x}, *, w^*)$, and $(\mathsf{Prv}, *, x^*, *, w^*)$. Queries of type *(ii)* are of the form $(\mathsf{Vrf}, *, x^*, *, [\pi_j])$. Let AskW (respectively VerPi) denote the event that queries of type *(i)* (respectively *(ii)*) occur.

We first bound the probability that AskW happens. Let Game 8.0 be Game 8. Let $\mathsf{AskW}_{8.i}$ denote the event that AskW happens in Game $8.i$ (defined below). It is important to observe that, at this point, the view produced by O″ with O′ is consistent, i.e., there exists a partial oracle that produces the same view, and in the forgery phase a correct proof on a (yes, no)-instance is being created with a correct witness with respect to the partial oracle.

Game 8.1: Replace M.Crs in the setup phase and M.Prv in the forgery phase respectively by M.CrsSim and M.PrvSim. Note that the trapdoor output by M.CrsSim is given to M.PrvSim.

We can show that $|\Pr[\mathsf{AskW}_{8.0}] - \Pr[\mathsf{AskW}_{8.1}]| < \rho_{\mathsf{zk}}(\kappa)$ by constructing a zero-knowledge distinguisher from adversary $\mathcal{A}$. We then claim that $\Pr[\mathsf{AskW}_{8.1}] \leq q/2^{\kappa}$. This is justified by the fact that M.PrvSim no longer takes w^* as input and hence the view of M.Vrf in the final verification is independent of w^*. Therefore, the event happens only by chance among q queries. We have that $\Pr[\mathsf{AskW}] = \Pr[\mathsf{AskW}_{8.0}] < \rho_{\mathsf{zk}}(\kappa) + q/2^{\kappa}$.

We now bound the probability of event VerPi. Suppose that we run an execution of $\mathsf{M}^{\mathsf{O}''}(\mathsf{Vrf}, \widetilde{\sigma}, \widetilde{x}, \widetilde{\pi})$ on certain input and suppose that it makes a verification query of the form $(\mathsf{Vrf}, \sigma_j, x^*, \ell_j, \pi_j)$ to O''. There are two options, either this query causes event VerPi or not, depending on whether π_j is a randomly assigned proof. However, we cannot decide which one is the case, event VerPi is not observable. This will be an obstacle if we try to construct an adversary against zero-knowledgeness as we did in previous cases. Alternatively we consider an event, VerCrs, that is observable and happens almost whenever VerPi happens. Suppose that a query $(\mathsf{Vrf}, \sigma_j, x^*, \ell_j, \pi_j)$ happens in the final verification phase. We would like to see if proof π_j was randomly assigned in step (b) of O'' or not. Observe that it is the case only if $(\sigma_j, [\tau_j]) \notin Q_{\mathsf{triv}} \cup Q_{\mathsf{intl}}$. Furthermore, if σ_j is not an internally generated crs, it must have been generated in the setup phase. Also, as σ_j appears in the final verification, it should have appeared in a verification during the self-learning phase as well. We define VerCrs as the event that in the final verification, $\mathsf{M}^{\mathsf{O}}(\mathsf{Vrf}, \widetilde{\sigma}, (x^*, \hat{x}^*), \widetilde{\pi}^*)$, a query of the following form is done: $(\mathsf{Vrf}, [\sigma_j], x^*, [\ell_j], [\pi_j])$, satisfying $\ell_j \in \{0,1\}^{2\kappa}$, $(\sigma_j, [\tau_j]) \notin Q_{\mathsf{triv}}$, and $\sigma_j \in Q_{\mathsf{nt}}$ where Q_{nt} is a list of all σ_j queried in the self-learning phase but not included in Q_{triv}. This way, event VerCrs is observable based on the view in the self-learning phase. Yet, VerCrs can differ from VerPi when a σ_j generated in the setup phase appears for the first time in the final verification. However, applying Lemma 3.3, we can upper-bound the probability for such event by q/eq^c. We thus have

$$\Pr[\mathsf{VerPi}] \leq \Pr[\mathsf{VerCrs}] + q/eq^c.$$

Now, let Game 8.0′ be Game 8 and let $\mathsf{VerCrs}_{8.i'}$ denote the event that VerCrs happens in Game $8.i'$, where:

Game 8.1′: Replace M.Crs and M.Prv with M.CrsSim and M.PrvSim, respectively. We claim that $|\Pr[\mathsf{VerCrs}_{8.0'}] - \Pr[\mathsf{VerCrs}_{8.1'}]| < \rho_{\mathsf{zk}}(\kappa) + 2q/eq^c$. To show this, we construct a zero-knowledge adversary that, given $\widetilde{\sigma}$, first executes the self-learning phase, and sends $(x^*, \hat{x}^*)$ and $(w^*, \perp)$ to the challenger. On receiving $\widetilde{\pi}^*$, the adversary runs $\mathsf{M}^{\mathsf{O}''}(\mathsf{Vrf}, \widetilde{\sigma}, (x^*, \hat{x}^*), \widetilde{\pi}^*)$ and outputs 1 if event VerCrs happens. It outputs 0, otherwise. If the challenger is working with M.Crs and M.Prv, the view in the final verification (up to the point when event VerCrs happens) distributes as in Game 8.0′. On the other hand, if the challenger is working with M.CrsSim and M.PrvSim, the view in the final verification distributes as in Game 8.1′.

In the above argument, the adversary cannot perfectly capture event VerCrs since the lists Q_{triv} and Q_{nt} that the adversary obtains from its own self-learning and uses to capture event VerCrs can be different from the ones defined for O''. This issue can be handled as follows. First, regarding σ_j in Q_{triv}, it suffices to consider those included also in Q_{leg}. This is justified by observing that the condition $(\sigma_j, [\tau_j]) \notin Q_{\mathsf{triv}} \cup Q_{\mathsf{intl}}$ is equivalent to $(\sigma_j, [\tau_j]) \notin (Q_{\mathsf{triv}} \cap Q_{\mathsf{leg}}) \cup Q_{\mathsf{intl}}$, because every $\sigma_j \in Q_{\mathsf{triv}}$ that appeared during the final verification and is not present in Q_{leg} must be in Q_{intl}. Let Q'_{triv} be the lists the adversary obtained. If $Q'_{\mathsf{triv}} \cup Q_{\mathsf{leg}}$ and $Q_{\mathsf{triv}} \cup Q_{\mathsf{leg}}$ differ, there exists $(\sigma_j, \tau_j) \in Q_{\mathsf{leg}}$ that does not appear a self-learning but does in the other self-learning. We can apply Lemma 3.3 to upper-bound the probability of having different Q_{triv} and Q'_{triv} by q/eq^c (the same argument applies to Q_{nt}). This results in adding $2q/eq^c$ to the bound, as claimed. We recall that, up to this point, $(x^*, \hat{x}^*) \in \mathcal{L}_\kappa \times \hat{\mathcal{C}}_\kappa$ with respect to oracle O'.

Game 8.2′: Sample $\hat{x}^*$ from $\hat{\mathcal{L}}_\kappa$, that is, $(x^*, \hat{x}^*)$ is chosen from (yes,yes)-instances. Any change in event VerCrs can be reduced to distinguishing $\hat{\mathcal{L}}$ and $\hat{\mathcal{C}}$. We have $|\Pr[\mathsf{VerCrs}_{8.1'}] - \Pr[\mathsf{VerCrs}_{8.2'}]| < \hat{\epsilon}_{\mathsf{ind}}(\kappa)$ where $\hat{\epsilon}_{\mathsf{ind}}(\kappa)$ is the advantage of distinguishing $\hat{\mathcal{L}}$ and $\hat{\mathcal{C}}$.

Game 8.3′: Sample x^* from $\mathcal{C}_\kappa$. That is, $(x^*, \hat{x}^*)$ is chosen from (no,yes)-instances. Due to the indistinguishability of $\mathcal{L}$ and $\mathcal{C}$, $|\Pr[\mathsf{VerCrs}_{8.2'}] - \Pr[\mathsf{VerCrs}_{8.3'}]| < q/2^\kappa$. (Note that language $\mathcal{L}$ is implemented by oracle O).

Game 8.4′: Replace $\mathsf{M.CrsSim}$ and $\mathsf{M.PrvSim}$ by $\mathsf{M.Crs}$ and $\mathsf{M.Prv}$, respectively. Note that to use $\mathsf{M.Prv}$, one needs a witness, which in this case is known. It is actually $(\perp, \hat{w})$, where $\hat{w}$ is a witness for $\hat{x}$ (received as input).
We have $|\Pr[\mathsf{VerCrs}_{8.3'}] - \Pr[\mathsf{VerCrs}_{8.4'}]| < \rho_{\mathsf{zk}}(\kappa) + 2q/eq^c$.

Since w^* is no longer given, a valid proof π_j on x^* with a legitimate non-trivial σ_j that triggers event $\mathsf{VerCrs}_{8.4'}$ can be created only by chance by guessing a relevant trapdoor or the witness, cases that have been already excluded in previous games. Therefore, we conclude that $\Pr[\mathsf{VerCrs}_{8.4'}] = 0$.
By summing up the above probabilities, we have

$$\Pr[\mathsf{VerPi}] < \Pr[\mathsf{VerCrs}] + q/eq^c < \hat{\epsilon}_{\mathsf{ind}}(\kappa) + q/2^\kappa + 2\rho_{\mathsf{zk}}(\kappa) + 5q/eq^c.$$

Finally, we have

$$\begin{aligned} |P_8 - P_7| &< 2q/eq^c + q(3q + 2q^{c+1})/2^{6\kappa} + \Pr[\mathsf{AskW}] + \Pr[\mathsf{VerPi}] \\ &< 7/eq^{c-1} + (3q^2 + 2q^{c+2})/2^{6\kappa} + 2q/2^\kappa + \hat{\epsilon}_{\mathsf{ind}}(\kappa) + 3\rho_{\mathsf{zk}}(\kappa). \end{aligned}$$ □

4 Conjunctive Language Extension

In this section, we consider non-labelled NIZKs. For that purpose, we drop the labels from the definition of O in the previous section. The internal random function H_p is adjusted to $H_p : \{0,1\}^{4\kappa} \to \{0,1\}^{4\kappa}$.

We consider a class $\mathcal{M}$ of constructions where every $\mathsf{M} \in \mathcal{M}$ satisfies the constraint that, roughly, all internally generated proofs π_j must be verified in the process of verifying the resulting proof. We call such M a construction in the *full verification model.* In the following, we use symbol $\not\Rightarrow_*$ to denote separations that hold in the full verification model.

Definition 4.1. *(Class of constructions with full verification.)* $\mathcal{M} := \{\mathsf{M}\}$ *is a class of black-box constructions of NIZK with respect to* $\mathcal{O}$ *such that, for every algorithm* $\mathsf{M} \in \mathcal{M}$, *the following condition is met: For all sufficiently large* $\kappa > 0$, *for every* $\mathsf{O} \in \mathcal{O}_\kappa$, $\widetilde{\sigma}$, $\widetilde{x}$, $\widetilde{w}$, *and query/answer pair* $[\pi_j \neq \bot] \leftarrow \mathsf{O}(\mathsf{Prv}, [\sigma_j], [x_j], [w_j])$ *observed during the execution of* $[\widetilde{\pi} \neq \bot] \leftarrow \mathsf{M}^{\mathsf{O}}(\mathsf{Prv}, \widetilde{\sigma}, \widetilde{x}, \widetilde{w})$, *there exists a query* $\mathsf{O}(\mathsf{Vrf}, \sigma_j, x_j, \pi_j)$ *during the execution of* $\mathsf{M}^{\mathsf{O}}(\mathsf{Vrf}, \widetilde{\sigma}, \widetilde{x}, \widetilde{\pi})$.

The condition captures the idea of properly using O as a proof system because whatever was proven internally by a prover is then verified by a verifier. Requiring "every" internal proof to appear also at verification is in fact needed for technical reasons. We construct an adversary that simulates proofs π_j by looking for query-answer pairs of O obtained during the challenge phase. However, such a view is only with respect to $\mathsf{M.Vrf}$ executed by the adversary itself and those with respect to $\mathsf{M.PrvSim}$ are not available, because they are executed by the challenger. So if only a subset of the internal proofs are verified in $\mathsf{M.Vrf}$, the adversary cannot simulate the distribution of the internal proofs needed to run $\mathsf{M.PrvSim}$. We do not know how to prove the separation if this condition is relaxed to, for instance, "at least one". It carries a resemblance to the constraint used in [23, footnote 9] to show a black-box separation of semantically secure encryption from chosen ciphertext secure ones. Their result applies to a class of constructions where, for every decryption query, there must exist a corresponding encryption query, or no encryption query can be made during decryption (a.k.a. the shielding model).

The following theorem can be proven by following a similar approach as the one used in the proof of Theorem 3.1. We refer to the full version of this paper [1] for a formal proof.

Theorem 4.1. *(USS-NIZK* $\not\Rightarrow_*$ *AND-USS-NIZK in the full verification model.) Given any two hard languages* $\mathcal{L}$ *and* $\hat{\mathcal{L}}$ *and any USS-NIZK system* L *for* $\mathcal{L}$, *there exists no fully black-box construction of USS-NIZK scheme* M *in class* $\mathcal{M}$ *for* $\mathcal{L} \wedge \hat{\mathcal{L}}$ *that is non-adaptive multi-theorem zero-knowledge and unbounded simulation sound.*

4.1 Constructing AND-USS-NIZK from Labelled USS-NIZK

Contrary to the impossibility in the previous section, conjunctive language extension is possible for USS-NIZKs if they support labels. Exploiting the integrity of labels, an easy solution could be the following: to prove an instance (x_1, x_2) under a label ℓ we can define a label for the USS-NIZK scheme $\ell' := x_1||x_2||\ell$

and run the prover algorithm in both pairs (x_1, ℓ') and (x_2, ℓ'). Such a simple transformation works, as long as the underlying USS-NIZK can handle the longer labels that we defined. We provide a transformation that is valid independently of the label space of the underlying NIZK as long as it supports *poly-length* labels.

For a bitstring s, let $\mathsf{f}(s)$ be a Merkle encoding of s [39] as defined by $\mathsf{f}(s) := s||\mathsf{tag}(s)$, where $\mathsf{tag}(s)$ is a bitstring representing the bit length of s minus its hamming weight. The length of $\mathsf{f}(s)$ is exactly $\mathsf{len}(s) + \lceil \log_2(\mathsf{len}(s)) \rceil$. Now, let $I(s) := \{i \,|\, \mathsf{f}(s)_i = 1\}$ where $\mathsf{f}(s)_i$ is the i-th bit of f(s). It then holds that, $I(s)$ is not empty for any s, and for different s, s', $I(s) \nsubseteq I(s')$ and vice versa.

Theorem 4.2. *(LBL-SS-NIZK ⇒ LBL-AND-SS-NIZK.) Given any two languages $\mathcal{L}$ and $\hat{\mathcal{L}}$ and two labelled USS-NIZKs for both $\mathcal{L}$ and $\hat{\mathcal{L}}$, there exists a fully black-box construction of labelled USS-NIZK for language $(\mathcal{L} \wedge \hat{\mathcal{L}})$.*

Proof. Let Π_1 and Π_2 be two labelled USS-NIZKs for $\mathcal{L}_1$ and $\mathcal{L}_2$, respectively. We construct a LBL-USS-NIZK, $\tilde{\Pi}$, for $\mathcal{L}_1 \wedge \mathcal{L}_2$ with labels of length $\mathsf{len}(\ell) := \mathrm{poly}_\ell(\kappa)$. Let u_i be the label bit-size supported by Π_i and let $u = \min(u_1, u_2)$. We require u be polynomial in κ so that polynomial number of random independent samplings from $\{0,1\}^u$ produces collisions with negligible probability. Let $v := \mathsf{len}(x_1) + \mathsf{len}(x_2) + \mathsf{len}(\ell)$ where $\mathsf{len}(x_b)$ $(b = 1, 2)$ denotes the bit length of the instances in $\mathcal{L}_b$ at security parameter κ. Let $n := v + \lceil \log_2(v) \rceil$.

- Given κ as input, $\tilde{\Pi}.\mathsf{Crs}$ runs $\sigma_{bi} \leftarrow \Pi_b.\mathsf{Crs}(1^\kappa)$ for $b \in \{1,2\}$ and $i \in [n]$ and outputs $\tilde{\sigma} := (\sigma_{11}, \sigma_{21}, \ldots, \sigma_{1n}, \sigma_{2n})$.
- Given $\tilde{\sigma}$, $\tilde{x} = (x_1, x_2)$, a label ℓ and $\tilde{w} = (w_1, w_2)$, $\tilde{\Pi}.\mathsf{Prv}$ chooses a random u-bitstring $r \leftarrow \{0,1\}^u$ and computes $\pi_{bi} \leftarrow \Pi_b.\mathsf{Prv}(\sigma_{bi}, x_b, r, w_b)$ for every $i \in I(\tilde{x}||\ell)$. It produces $\tilde{\pi}$ by concatenating all the previous proofs with r.
- Given $\tilde{\sigma}$, $\tilde{x}$, ℓ and $\tilde{\pi}$ as input, the verification algorithm $\tilde{\Pi}.\mathsf{Vrf}$ verifies the proofs included in $\tilde{\pi}$ on the corresponding σ_{bi}, $b \in \{1,2\}$, $i \in I(\tilde{x}||\ell)$. It accepts the proof if and only if all verifications succeed.

Simulators are constructed accordingly and zero knowledge holds immediately from Π_1 and Π_2. For unbound simulation soundness, suppose that, after seeing simulated proofs $\tilde{\pi}_j$ for chosen label-instance pairs $(\tilde{x}_j, \ell_j)$, an adversary outputs a proof $\tilde{\pi}^*$ (consisting of π^*_{bi} and r^*) on a fresh $(\tilde{x}^*, \ell^*)$. Let $b^* \in \{1,2\}$ be s.t. $x^*_{b^*}$ is a no-instance with respective language, which exists if the above is a valid forgery for the conjunction. Now, if there exists j s.t. $r^* = r_j$, let i^* be such that $i^* \in I(\tilde{x}^*||\ell^*)$ and $i^* \notin I(\tilde{x}_j||\ell_j)$. Otherwise, r^* is fresh, let i^* be any index from $I(\tilde{x}^*||\ell^*)$. Observe that $(\pi^*_{b^*i^*}, x^*_{b^*}, r^*)$ is a forgery against Π_{b^*} with respect to σ_{i^*}, if every r_j is unique as expected. That is because the chosen $(x^*_{b^*}, r^*)$ is a fresh instance-label pair and $x^*_{b^*}$ is a no-instance of the respective language. □

4.2 Implications and Language Preserving Reductions

We first show that a labelled USS-NIZK for $\mathcal{L}$ can be constructed from (non-labelled) USS-NIZK for $\mathcal{L} \wedge \hat{\mathcal{L}}$.

Theorem 4.3. *(AND-USS-NIZK ⇒ LBL-USS-NIZK) Given any NIZK system for $\mathcal{L} \wedge \hat{\mathcal{L}}$ that is unbounded simulation sound and adaptive zero-knowledge, there exists a fully black-box construction of LBL-USS-NIZK for $\mathcal{L}$.*

Proof. Let $\Pi := \{\mathsf{Crs}, \mathsf{Prv}, \mathsf{Vrf}, \mathsf{CrsSim}, \mathsf{PrvSim}\}$ be a USS-NIZK for $\mathcal{L} \wedge \hat{\mathcal{L}}$. It is assumed that $\hat{\mathcal{L}}$ is efficiently and uniformly sampleable (with witnesses) and includes a sufficiently large number of instances. We construct a LBL-USS-NIZK $\tilde{\Pi}$ for $\mathcal{L}$ with labels $\mathsf{len}(\ell) := \mathrm{poly}_\ell(\kappa)$ as follows. Let n be $n := \mathsf{len}(\ell) + \lceil \log_2(\mathsf{len}(\ell)) \rceil$ and function I as defined before.

- Given κ, $\tilde{\Pi}.\mathsf{Crs}$ outputs $\tilde{\sigma} := (\sigma_1, \ldots, \sigma_n)$, where $\sigma_i \leftarrow \Pi.\mathsf{Crs}(1^\kappa)$.
- Given $\tilde{\sigma}$, instance $x \in \mathcal{L}$, a label ℓ and a witness w, $\tilde{\Pi}.\mathsf{Prv}$ samples a random yes-instance $\hat{x} \leftarrow \hat{\mathcal{L}}_\kappa$ with corresponding witness $\hat{w}$. It then creates a proof $\tilde{\pi}$ by concatenating $\hat{x}$ with all proofs $\Pi.\mathsf{Prv}(\sigma_i, (x, \hat{x}), (w, \hat{w}))$ for $i \in I(\ell)$.
- The verification algorithm $\tilde{\Pi}.\mathsf{Vrf}$ verifies the proofs in $\tilde{\pi}$ with the corresponding σ_i in $i \in I(\ell)$. It accepts $\tilde{\pi}$ only if all verifications succeed.

Simulators are constructed accordingly and the zero knowledge property of $\tilde{\Pi}$ is inherited from the one by Π. For simulation soundness, consider an adversary who produces a proof $\tilde{\pi}^*$ on a fresh (x^*, ℓ^*), where x^* is a no-instance of $\mathcal{L}$. If a proof on (x^*, ℓ) was never asked by the adversary for any ℓ, $\tilde{\pi}^*$ cannot be valid due to the USS of Π. Otherwise, observe that if $\tilde{\pi}^* = (\hat{x}^*, \{\tilde{\pi}_i^*\}_{i \in I(\ell^*)})$ is valid, the USS of Π is compromised, because there must exist an index i s.t. $(x^*, \hat{x}^*)$ has not been proven with respect to σ_i, but $\tilde{\pi}_i^*$ is a valid proof for that instance. Observe that the above reasoning requires that the probability of collisions when sampling $\hat{x} \leftarrow \hat{\mathcal{L}}_\kappa$ is negligible, which is guaranteed by the assumption on $\hat{\mathcal{L}}$. □

Corollary 2. *AND-USS-NIZK ⇒ LBL-AND-USS-NIZK*

If $\hat{\mathcal{L}}$ is a *hard language* we can reduce OR-USS-NIZK to LBL-USS-NIZK.

Theorem 4.4 *(OR-USS-NIZK ⇒ LBL-USS-NIZK). Any NIZK system for $\mathcal{L} \vee \hat{\mathcal{L}}$ for a hard language $\hat{\mathcal{L}}$ that is unbound simulation sound and adaptive zero-knowledge, can be transformed into a LBL-USS-NIZK for $\mathcal{L}$ in a black-box way.*

Proof (Sketch). The transformation is analogous to the one provided in the proof of Theorem 4.3. The difference is that $\hat{x}$ is chosen to be a no-instance from $\hat{\mathcal{C}}_\kappa$ and its witness $\hat{w}$ together with $\hat{x}$ is included in the proof $\tilde{\pi}$. The verifier algorithm checks that $\hat{x} \in \hat{\mathcal{C}}_\kappa$ using $\hat{w}$. Everything else remains unchanged. □

Finally, the following result holds in the full verification model.

Corollary 3. *(NIZK $\not\Rightarrow_*$ USS-NIZK in the full verification model.) There does not exist an oracle machine M such that for every language $\mathcal{L}$ and for every NIZK Π for $\mathcal{L}$, $\mathsf{M}^{\Pi,\mathcal{L}}$ is a USS-NIZK for $\mathcal{L}$.*

Proof. Suppose that a USS-NIZK for $\mathcal{L}$ is black-box constructable from a $NIZK$ for $\mathcal{L}$ in the full verification model. Then, by applying the construction to $\mathcal{L} := (\mathcal{L}' \wedge \hat{\mathcal{L}}')$, we can construct a USS-NIZK for $(\mathcal{L}' \wedge \hat{\mathcal{L}}')$ from a $NIZK$ for $(\mathcal{L}' \wedge \hat{\mathcal{L}}')$. Since USS-NIZK implies $NIZK$, we could start from a USS-NIZK for $\mathcal{L}'$ to construct a USS-NIZK for $(\mathcal{L}' \wedge \hat{\mathcal{L}}')$, which contradicts Theorem 4.1. □

5 Signatures from USS-NIZK w/o Language Extension

We begin with a simple yet useful case where a USS-NIZK system Π for hard language $\mathcal{L}$ is *perfectly no-instance simulation correct*, i.e., $\Pi.\mathsf{PrvSim}$ works for any no-instances in $\mathcal{C}$. Let $\mathcal{H}$ be a family of functions $\mathcal{H} := \{H_\kappa : \mathcal{K}_\kappa \times \mathcal{M}_\kappa \to \mathcal{C}'_\kappa\}$ that maps messages in $\mathcal{M}_\kappa$ to a subset of no-instances $\mathcal{C}'_\kappa \subseteq \mathcal{C}_\kappa$. We construct a signature scheme $\Sigma := (\mathsf{Setup}, \mathsf{Sign}, \mathsf{Vrf})$ as follows.

$\Sigma.\mathsf{Setup}(1^\kappa)$:	$\Sigma.\mathsf{Sign}(pk, sk, m)$:	$\Sigma.\mathsf{Vrf}(pk, m, \sigma)$:
$(\sigma, \tau) \leftarrow \Pi.\mathsf{CrsSim}(1^\kappa)$	$(\sigma, K) \leftarrow pk$	$(\sigma, K) \leftarrow pk$
$K \leftarrow \mathcal{K}_\kappa$	$\tau \leftarrow sk$	$x \leftarrow H_\kappa(K, m)$
$pk := (\sigma, K)$	$x \leftarrow H_\kappa(K, m)$	$b \leftarrow \Pi.\mathsf{Vrf}(\sigma, x, \sigma)$
$sk := \tau$	$\sigma \leftarrow \Pi.\mathsf{PrvSim}(\sigma, x, \tau)$	return b
return (pk, sk)	return σ	

Since each message is mapped to a no-instance exclusively, simulation soundness is literally translated into EUF-CMA: It is hard to find new message m^* (new no-instance x^*) and valid signature σ^* (valid proof π^*) after seeing signatures σ_i (simulated proofs π_i) for arbitrary messages m_i (arbitrary no-instances x_i). Due to space constraint, we only show a formal statement below.

Theorem 5.1. *The above Σ is a EUF-CMA secure signature scheme for message space $\mathcal{M}_\kappa$ if, Π is a perfectly no-instance simulation correct USS-NIZK system for hard language $\mathcal{L}$ accompanied by $\mathcal{C}$, and $\mathcal{H}$ is a family of efficiently sampleable injections from $\mathcal{M}_\kappa$ to any $\mathcal{C}'_\kappa \subseteq \mathcal{C}_\kappa$.*

Now we proceed to more general case. We first introduce building blocks and establish some technical lemmas before presenting the construction.

Extended Target-Collision-Resistant Functions. A family of functions $\{H\}$ is target-collision-resistant if any p.p.t. adversary $\mathcal{A}$ wins in the following experiment only with negligible probability, say ϵ_{tcr}: $\mathcal{A}$ chooses an input x and it is given a random key K; $\mathcal{A}$ wins if it can produce a different input x' such that $H(K, x) = H(K, x')$. This notion was extended by Halevi and Krawczyk [28] in such a way that the adversary is allowed to select a different key for the second evaluation, i.e., the probability that the adversary comes up with a new x' and K' satisfying $H(K, x) = H(K', x')$ is upper bound by a negligible function ϵ_{etcr}. Hülsing et al. [30] considered a further extension called multi-target extended target-collision-resistant (m-eTCR) hash functions, where the above experiment is hard even if the adversary is allowed to choose several targets. More precisely:

Definition 5.1. *A family of functions $\mathcal{H} = \{H : \{0,1\}^{k(\kappa)} \times \{0,1\}^{m(\kappa)} \to \{0,1\}^{h(\kappa)}\}_{\kappa \in \mathbb{N}}$ (for certain polynomials k, m, h in κ) is said to be $\epsilon_{\mathsf{metcr}}$-multi-target extended target-collision-resistant if for every p.p.t. adversary $\mathcal{A}$ and every sufficiently large κ, it holds that*

$$\Pr\left[(\hat{x},\hat{K}) \leftarrow \mathcal{A}^{\mathsf{Key}(\cdot)}(1^\kappa) \;:\; \begin{array}{c} \exists (x_i,K_i)\in Q \text{ such that } \hat{x}\neq x_i \text{ and} \\ H(\hat{K},\hat{x}) = H(K_i,x_i) \end{array} \right] < \epsilon_{\mathsf{metcr}}(\kappa)$$

where $\mathsf{Key}(\cdot)$ *is an oracle that on input* $x_i \in \{0,1\}^{m(\kappa)}$*, samples* K_i *uniformly at random from* $\{0,1\}^{k(\kappa)}$*, stores the pair* (x_i, K_i) *in* Q *and returns* K_i*.*

Clearly, $\epsilon_{\mathsf{metcr}} \leq q \cdot \epsilon_{\mathsf{etcr}}$ holds for up to q queries. Though we use m-eTCR in our construction for simplicity of the argument, the same argument holds with standard single-target eTCR with polynomial loss in the security bound. We also note that, according to [40], eTCR can be constructed easily from TCR by appending the key to the output. That is, $H(K,m)||K$ is extended target-collision-resistant if H is target-collision-resistant.

Given a message m, we will output a no-instance by computing $x = H(K,m)$ for a randomly chosen $K \in \mathcal{K}$ and then returning $\mathcal{D}_{\mathcal{C}}(x)$. One could expect that the output of eTCR functions distributes uniformly over all possible values, but collision-resistance is not enough to guarantee such a property. (Consider an eTCR family of functions that output bitstrings where the last bit is constantly zero, i.e., non-uniform.) To overcome this limitation, we assume an additional property on the m-eTCR family: ϵ_{reg}-*regularity*. Roughly, every function in the family must be statistically close to the uniform distribution over its output.

Definition 5.2. *We say a family of functions* $\mathcal{H} = \{H : \{0,1\}^{k(\kappa)} \times \{0,1\}^{m(\kappa)} \rightarrow \{0,1\}^{h(\kappa)}\}_{\kappa\in\mathbb{N}}$ *is* ϵ_{reg}*-regular if for every sufficiently large* κ *and every* $x \in \{0,1\}^{m(\kappa)}$*, the distribution* $\mathcal{D}_x$ *defined as* $\mathcal{D}_x := (K \leftarrow \{0,1\}^{k(\kappa)}\ ;\ \mathsf{return}\ H(K,x))$ *is statistically close to the uniform distribution over* $\{0,1\}^{h(\kappa)}$*. More precisely,*

$$\Delta(\mathcal{D}_x, U_{h(\kappa)}) := \frac{1}{2} \sum_{\alpha\in\{0,1\}^{h(\kappa)}} \left| \Pr[\mathcal{D}_x = \alpha] - \underbrace{\Pr[U_{h(\kappa)} = \alpha]}_{1/2^{h(\kappa)}} \right| < \epsilon_{\mathsf{reg}}(\kappa).$$

The following lemma allows us to argue that the distribution of no-instances produced from messages is indistinguishable from yes-instances.

Lemma 5.1. *Let* $\mathcal{L}_\kappa$ *be a* ϵ_{hd}*-hard language (with respect to* $\mathcal{C}_\kappa$*) with sampling distributions* $(\mathcal{D}_{\mathcal{L}_\kappa}, \mathcal{D}_{\mathcal{C}_\kappa})$ *where* $\mathcal{D}_{\mathcal{C}_\kappa} : \{0,1\}^{h(\kappa)} \rightarrow \mathcal{C}_\kappa$ *(for certain polynomial* h *in* κ*). Let* $\mathcal{H} = \{H : \mathcal{K}_\kappa \times \mathcal{M}_\kappa \rightarrow \{0,1\}^{h(\kappa)}\}_{\kappa\in\mathbb{N}}$ *be a* $\epsilon_{\mathsf{metcr}}$*-multi-target extended target-collision-resistant function family that is* ϵ_{reg}*-regular. Consider the distribution* $\mathcal{D}_m$ *defined as* $K \leftarrow \mathcal{K}_\kappa\ ;\ \mathsf{return}\ \mathcal{D}_{\mathcal{C}_\kappa}(H(K,m))$*. For every* $m \in \mathcal{M}_\kappa$ *and every sufficiently large* κ*,* $\Delta(\mathcal{D}_m, \mathcal{D}_{\mathcal{C}_\kappa}) < \epsilon_{\mathsf{reg}}(\kappa)$*.*

Proof. Observe that for every pair of random variables X, Y and every function F whose domain is the range of X and Y, it holds[2] $\Delta(F(X), F(Y)) \leq \Delta(X, Y)$. In our case, for every $m \in \mathcal{M}_\kappa$ and every sufficiently large κ,

$$\begin{aligned}\Delta(\mathcal{D}_m, \mathcal{D}_{\mathcal{C}_\kappa}) &= \Delta(K \leftarrow \mathcal{K}_\kappa\ ;\ \mathsf{return}\ \mathcal{D}_{\mathcal{C}_\kappa}(H(K,m)),\ x \leftarrow U_{h(\kappa)}\ ;\ \mathsf{return}\ \mathcal{D}_{\mathcal{C}_\kappa}(x)) \\ &\leq \Delta(K \leftarrow \mathcal{K}_\kappa\ ;\ \mathsf{return}\ H(K,m),\ U_{h(\kappa)}) < \epsilon_{\mathsf{reg}}(\kappa).\end{aligned}$$

□

[2] We abuse notation and write $F(X)$ to denote the composition $F \circ X$, i.e., the distribution $x \leftarrow X\ ;\ \mathsf{return}\ F(x)$.

• $\Sigma.\mathsf{Setup}(1^\kappa)$:	• $\Sigma.\mathsf{Sign}(pk, sk, m)$:	• $\Sigma.\mathsf{Vrf}(pk, m, \sigma)$:
$(\sigma, \tau) \leftarrow \Pi.\mathsf{CrsSim}(1^\kappa)$	$K \leftarrow \mathcal{K}_\kappa$	parse σ as (π, K)
$pk := (\sigma, H_\kappa, \mathcal{D}_{\mathcal{C}_\kappa})$	$y := \mathcal{D}_{\mathcal{C}_\kappa}(H_\kappa(K, m))$	$y := \mathcal{D}_{\mathcal{C}_\kappa}(H_\kappa(K, m))$
$sk := \tau$	$\pi \leftarrow \Pi.\mathsf{PrvSim}(\sigma, y, \tau)$	return $\Pi.\mathsf{Vrf}(\sigma, y, \pi)$
return (pk, sk)	$\sigma := (\pi, K)$	
	return σ	

Fig. 2. Construction of signature scheme from SS-NIZK

We expect that distribution $\mathcal{D}_{\mathcal{C}_\kappa}$ is close to an injection, having small collision probability. This implies that instances in $\mathcal{C}$ have a short witness.

Definition 5.3. (Collision probability). *A function $f : \{0,1\}^{m(\kappa)} \to \{0,1\}^{n(\kappa)}$ for some polynomials m,n in κ is said have ϵ_{cp}*-collision probability *(for some function ϵ_{cp} in κ) if for every sufficiently large κ, it holds*

$$\left|\left\{x \in \{0,1\}^{m(\kappa)} : \exists y \in \{0,1\}^{m(\kappa)} \text{ such that } x \neq y \wedge f(x) = f(y)\right\}\right| < \epsilon_{\mathsf{cp}}(\kappa) \cdot 2^{m(\kappa)}.$$

Let $(\mathcal{L}_\kappa, \mathcal{C}_\kappa)$ be a ϵ_{hd}-hard promise problem over efficiently sampleable distributions $(\mathcal{D}_{\mathcal{L}_\kappa}, \mathcal{D}_{\mathcal{C}_\kappa})$ where $\mathcal{D}_{\mathcal{C}_\kappa} : \{0,1\}^{h(\kappa)} \to \mathcal{C}_\kappa$ (for certain polynomial h in κ) has ϵ_{cp}-collision probability. Let $\mathcal{H} := \{H_\kappa : \mathcal{K}_\kappa \times \mathcal{M}_\kappa \to \{0,1\}^{h(\kappa)}\}_{\kappa \in \mathbb{N}}$ be a $\epsilon_{\mathsf{metcr}}$-multi-target extended target-collision-resistant function family that is ϵ_{reg}-regular. Let $\Pi := (\mathsf{Crs}, \mathsf{Prv}, \mathsf{Vrf}, \mathsf{CrsSim}, \mathsf{PrvSim})$ be a simulation sound non-interactive zero-knowledge proof system.

Figure 2 defines the signature scheme $\Sigma := (\mathsf{Setup}, \mathsf{Sign}, \mathsf{Vrf})$. For correctness we only show the bound here.

Theorem 5.2 (Correctness). *The signature scheme Σ defined above is correct. Concretely, for every message $m \in \mathcal{M}_\kappa$ and for every sufficiently large κ,*

$$\Pr\left[\,(pk, sk) \leftarrow \Sigma.\mathsf{Setup}(1^\kappa)\,;\, \sigma \leftarrow \Sigma.\mathsf{Sign}(pk, sk, m) : 1 = \Sigma.\mathsf{Vrf}(pk, m, \sigma)\,\right] > 1 - \epsilon_{\mathsf{zk}}(\kappa) - \epsilon_{\mathsf{co}}(\kappa) - \epsilon_{\mathsf{hd}}(\kappa) - 2\epsilon_{\mathsf{reg}}(\kappa).$$

Proof. For every $m \in \mathcal{M}_\kappa$,

$$\begin{aligned}&\Pr\left[\,(pk, sk) \leftarrow \Sigma.\mathsf{Setup}(1^\kappa)\,;\, \sigma \leftarrow \Sigma.\mathsf{Sign}(pk, sk, m) : 1 = \Sigma.\mathsf{Vrf}(pk, m, \sigma)\,\right]\\ &= \Pr\left[\begin{array}{c} K \leftarrow \mathcal{K}_\kappa; (\sigma, \tau) \leftarrow \Pi.\mathsf{CrsSim}(1^\kappa) \\ y := \mathcal{D}_{\mathcal{C}_\kappa}(H_\kappa(K, m)); \pi \leftarrow \Pi.\mathsf{PrvSim}(\sigma, y, \tau)\end{array} : 1 = \Pi.\mathsf{Vrf}(\sigma, y, \pi)\right]\end{aligned}$$

which, by Lemma 5.1 (and for every sufficiently large κ) is greater or equal than

$$\Pr\left[\begin{array}{c} y \leftarrow \mathcal{D}_{\mathcal{C}_\kappa}; (\sigma, \tau) \leftarrow \Pi.\mathsf{CrsSim}(1^\kappa) \\ \pi \leftarrow \Pi.\mathsf{PrvSim}(\sigma, y, \tau)\end{array} : 1 = \Pi.\mathsf{Vrf}(\sigma, y, \pi)\right] - 2\epsilon_{\mathsf{reg}}(\kappa)$$

which, by Lemma 2.2, is greater than $1 - \epsilon_{\mathsf{zk}}(\kappa) - \epsilon_{\mathsf{co}}(\kappa) - \epsilon_{\mathsf{hd}}(\kappa) - 2\epsilon_{\mathsf{reg}}(\kappa)$. □

Theorem 5.3 (Unforgeability). *The signature scheme Σ defined above is existentially unforgeable against adaptive chosen message attacks. In particular, for every p.p.t. adversary $\mathcal{A}$ against the EUF-CMA experiment of Σ that makes at most q queries to its signing oracle, there exists a p.p.t. algorithm $\mathcal{B}$ such that*

$$\mathrm{Adv}^{\mathsf{EUF\text{-}CMA}}_{\Sigma,\mathcal{A}}(\kappa) \leq \mathrm{Adv}^{\mathsf{USS}}_{\Pi,\mathcal{B}}(\kappa) + \epsilon_{\mathsf{metcr}}(\kappa) + q\epsilon_{\mathsf{cp}}(\kappa) + 2q\epsilon_{\mathsf{reg}}(\kappa)$$

and $\mathsf{Time}(\mathcal{B}) \approx \mathsf{Time}(\mathcal{A}) + \mathsf{poly}(\kappa)$ *where* $\mathsf{poly}(\kappa)$ *is independent of* $\mathsf{Time}(\mathcal{A})$. *(Note that factor q multiplies to statistical errors only).*

Proof. For every adversary $\mathcal{A}$ against the signature scheme, we build an attacker $\mathcal{B}$ against the *simulation soundness* of the underlying Π primitive. $\mathcal{B}$ is given the security parameter κ and a common reference string σ and oracle access to $\Pi.\mathsf{PrvSim}(\sigma,\cdot,\tau)$, where τ is the trapdoor associated to σ. $\mathcal{B}$ wins the game if it can produce a valid proof on a no-instance that was not queried to its oracle. $\mathcal{B}$ sends the public key $pk = (\sigma, H_\kappa, \mathcal{D}_{\mathcal{C}_\kappa})$ to $\mathcal{A}$. $\mathcal{A}$ is allowed to ask for valid signatures of messages of its choice. On input m_i, $\mathcal{B}$ produces a valid signature by sampling $K_i \leftarrow \mathcal{K}_\kappa$, computing $y_i = \mathcal{D}_{\mathcal{C}_\kappa}(H_\kappa(K_i, m_i))$ and calling its oracle, getting $\pi_i = \Pi.\mathsf{PrvSim}(\sigma, y_i, \tau)$. Now, $\mathcal{B}$ returns $\sigma_i = (\pi_i, K_i)$ as to $\mathcal{A}$ as a signature for m_i. Eventually, $\mathcal{A}$ will come up with a pair $(\hat{m}, \hat{\sigma})$ such that $\hat{m} \neq m_i$ for every i. At this moment, $\mathcal{B}$ parses $\hat{\sigma}$ as $(\hat{\pi}, \hat{K})$ and computes $\hat{y} = \mathcal{D}_{\mathcal{C}_\kappa}(H_\kappa(\hat{K}, \hat{m}))$ and returns $(\hat{y}, \hat{\pi})$ as the solution for its challenge.

Note that $\mathcal{B}$ succeeds in simulating the EUF-CMA experiment correctly. Some signing queries can result into invalid signatures (although only with negligible probability), i.e., for some indices i, it is possible to have $\Pi.\mathsf{Vrf}(\sigma, y_i, \pi_i) = 0$. But this is not a problem, since in the real EUF-CMA experiment this event occurs with the same probability. We define the bad event, $\mathsf{Bad} \equiv$ '*There exists i such that $y_i = \hat{y}$*'. Note that, if Bad does not occur, then $\mathcal{B}$ wins if so does $\mathcal{A}$. More precisely, $\Pr[\mathcal{B} \text{ wins}] \geq \Pr[\mathcal{A} \text{ wins} \mid \neg\mathsf{Bad}] \geq \Pr[\mathcal{A} \text{ wins}] - \Pr[\mathsf{Bad}]$ or equivalently, $\Pr[\mathcal{A} \text{ wins}] \leq \Pr[\mathcal{B} \text{ wins}] + \Pr[\mathsf{Bad}]$. Note that $\Pr[\mathsf{Bad}] \leq \max_{p.p.t.\ M} \{\Pr[E_M]\}$, where for a fixed M, the probability of event E_M is defined as

$$\Pr\left[\begin{array}{l}(\sigma,\tau) \leftarrow \Pi.\mathsf{CrsSim}(1^\kappa) \\ (\hat{m},(\hat{K},\hat{\pi})) \leftarrow M^{\mathsf{Sign}(\cdot)}(\sigma, H_\kappa, \mathcal{D}_{\mathcal{C}_\kappa})\end{array} : \begin{array}{l}\exists (m_i, K_i, \pi_i) \in Q \text{ such that} \\ \mathcal{D}_{\mathcal{C}_\kappa}(H_\kappa(K_i, m_i)) = \mathcal{D}_{\mathcal{C}_\kappa}(H_\kappa(\hat{K}, \hat{m}))\end{array}\right]$$

where $\mathsf{Sign}(\cdot)$ is an oracle that, on input m_i, samples $K_i \leftarrow \mathcal{K}_\kappa$, computes $y_i = \mathcal{D}_{\mathcal{C}_\kappa}(H_\kappa(K_i, m_i))$ and $\pi_i = \Pi.\mathsf{PrvSim}(\sigma, y_i, \tau)$, adds (m_i, K_i, π_i) to Q and outputs (π_i, K_i). For every p.p.t. M, there exists a p.p.t. $\bar{M}$ such that the above probability is upper-bounded by the following ($\bar{M}$ is given the trapdoor τ):

$$\Pr\left[\begin{array}{l}(\sigma,\tau) \leftarrow \Pi.\mathsf{CrsSim}(1^\kappa) \\ (\hat{m},\hat{K}) \leftarrow \bar{M}^{\mathsf{Key}(\cdot)}(\sigma, \tau, H, \mathcal{D}_{\mathcal{C}_\kappa})\end{array} : \begin{array}{l}\exists (m_i, K_i) \in Q \text{ such that} \\ \mathcal{D}_{\mathcal{C}_\kappa}(H_\kappa(K_i, m_i)) = \mathcal{D}_{\mathcal{C}_\kappa}(H_\kappa(\hat{K}, \hat{m}))\end{array}\right]$$

where $\mathsf{Key}(\cdot)$ is an oracle that, on input m_i, samples $K_i \leftarrow \mathcal{K}_\kappa$ adds (m_i, K_i) to Q and returns K_i. Note that the sampling of the (σ, τ) using $\Pi.\mathsf{CrsSim}$ requires polynomial time, and therefore, that operation can be included inside the machine $\bar{M}$. Then, we have that $\max_{p.p.t.\ M} \{\Pr[E_M]\} \leq \max_{p.p.t.\ \bar{M}} \{\Pr[\bar{E}_{\bar{M}}]\}$ where the probability of event $\bar{E}_{\bar{M}}$ for a fixed algorithm $\bar{M}$ is defined as

$$\Pr\left[(\hat{m}, \hat{K}) \leftarrow \bar{M}^{\mathsf{Key}(\cdot)}(1^\kappa, H_\kappa, \mathcal{D}_{\mathcal{C}_\kappa}) : \begin{array}{c} \exists (m_i, K_i) \in Q \text{ such that} \\ \mathcal{D}_{\mathcal{C}_\kappa}(H_\kappa(K_i, m_i)) = \mathcal{D}_{\mathcal{C}_\kappa}(H_\kappa(\hat{K}, \hat{m})) \end{array} \right].$$

Now, let $\mathcal{X}_\kappa$ be the set of inputs to $\mathcal{D}_{\mathcal{C}_\kappa}$ that share an image, i.e.,

$$\mathcal{X}_\kappa = \{x \in \{0,1\}^{h(\kappa)} : \exists y \in \{0,1\}^{h(\kappa)} \text{ such that } x \neq y \wedge \mathcal{D}_{\mathcal{C}_\kappa}(x) = \mathcal{D}_{\mathcal{C}_\kappa}(y)\}.$$

Since $\mathcal{D}_{\mathcal{C}_\kappa}$ has ϵ_{cp}-collision probability, we have $|\mathcal{X}_\kappa| \leq \epsilon_{\mathsf{cp}} \cdot 2^{h(\kappa)}$. Now, the probability of Bad is upper-bounded by

$$\max_{p.p.t.\ \bar{M}} \left\{ \Pr\left[(\hat{m}, \hat{K}) \leftarrow \bar{M}^{\mathsf{Key}(\cdot)}(1^\kappa, H_\kappa, \mathcal{D}_{\mathcal{C}_\kappa}) : \begin{array}{c} \exists (m_i, K_i) \in Q \text{ such that} \\ H_\kappa(K_i, m_i) = H_\kappa(\hat{K}, \hat{m}) \end{array} \right] \right\} +$$
$$\max_{p.p.t.\ \bar{M}} \left\{ \Pr\left[\bot \leftarrow \bar{M}^{\mathsf{Key}(\cdot)}(1^\kappa, H_\kappa, \mathcal{D}_{\mathcal{C}_\kappa}) : \begin{array}{c} \exists (m_i, K_i) \in Q \text{ such that} \\ H_\kappa(K_i, m_i) \in \mathcal{X}_\kappa \end{array} \right] \right\}.$$

The $\epsilon_{\mathsf{metcr}}$-*multi-target extended target-collision-resistance* of function H_κ guarantees that the first summand of the above expression is upper-bounded by $\epsilon_{\mathsf{metcr}}(\kappa)$. On the other hand, if machine $\bar{M}$ performs q queries to its oracle $\mathsf{Key}(\cdot)$, the second summand is upper-bounded by $q(2\epsilon_{\mathsf{reg}}(\kappa) + \epsilon_{\mathsf{cp}}(\kappa))$, because, thanks to the ϵ_{reg}-regularity of H_κ, for every $m \in \mathcal{M}_\kappa$ (and for sufficiently large κ),

$$\Pr[K \leftarrow \mathcal{K}_\kappa : H_\kappa(K, m) \in \mathcal{X}_\kappa] < \Pr\left[x \leftarrow \{0,1\}^{h(\kappa)} : x \in \mathcal{X}_\kappa\right] + 2\epsilon_{\mathsf{reg}}(\kappa)$$

upper-bounded by $\epsilon_{\mathsf{cp}}(\kappa) + 2\epsilon_{\mathsf{reg}}(\kappa)$, so we apply the union bound over all q queries.

For every adversary $\mathcal{A}$ against the signature scheme, the described $\mathcal{B}$ is an adversary against the simulation soundness of the underlying NIZK such that

$$\mathrm{Adv}^{\mathrm{EUF\text{-}CMA}}_{\Sigma_\Pi, \mathcal{A}}(\kappa) \leq \mathrm{Adv}^{USS}_{\Pi, \mathcal{B}}(\kappa) + \epsilon_{\mathsf{metcr}}(\kappa) + q\epsilon_{\mathsf{cp}}(\kappa) + 2q\epsilon_{\mathsf{reg}}(\kappa). \qquad \square$$

Acknowledgments. We would like to thank the anonymous reviewers for their effort and valuable feedback. We also thank Carsten Baum and Kyosuke Yamashita for their helpful comments and Arnab Roy for his suggestion on labelled NIZKs.

References

1. Abe, M., Ambrona, M., Ohkubo, M.: On black-box extensions of non-interactive zero-knowledge arguments, and signatures directly from simulation soundness. Cryptology ePrint Archive, Report 2019/696 (2019)
2. Abdalla, M., Benhamouda, F., Pointcheval, D.: Disjunctions for hash proof systems: new constructions and applications. In: Oswald, E., Fischlin, M. (eds.) EUROCRYPT 2015. LNCS, vol. 9057, pp. 69–100. Springer, Heidelberg (2015). https://doi.org/10.1007/978-3-662-46803-6_3

3. Abe, M., David, B., Kohlweiss, M., Nishimaki, R., Ohkubo, M.: Tagged one-time signatures: tight security and optimal tag size. In: Kurosawa, K., Hanaoka, G. (eds.) PKC 2013. LNCS, vol. 7778, pp. 312–331. Springer, Heidelberg (2013). https://doi.org/10.1007/978-3-642-36362-7_20
4. Abe, M., Fuchsbauer, G., Groth, J., Haralambiev, K., Ohkubo, M.: Structure-preserving signatures and commitments to group elements. J. Cryptol. **29**(2), 363–421 (2016)
5. Alamati, N., Peikert, C., Stephens-Davidowitz, N.: New (and old) proof systems for lattice problems. In: Abdalla, M., Dahab, R. (eds.) PKC 2018. LNCS, vol. 10770, pp. 619–643. Springer, Cham (2018). https://doi.org/10.1007/978-3-319-76581-5_21
6. Barak, B., Mahmoody-Ghidary, M.: Lower bounds on signatures from symmetric primitives. In: FOCS 2007, pp. 680–688. IEEE Computer Society (2007)
7. Bellare, M., Goldwasser, S.: New paradigms for digital signatures and message authentication based on non-interactive zero knowledge proofs. In: Brassard, G. (ed.) CRYPTO 1989. LNCS, vol. 435, pp. 194–211. Springer, New York (1990). https://doi.org/10.1007/0-387-34805-0_19
8. Blum, M., Feldman, P., Micali, S.: Non-interactive zero-knowledge and its applications (extended abstract). In: STOC 1988, pp. 103–112. ACM (1988)
9. Boneh, D., Papakonstantinou, P., Rackoff, C., Vahlis, Y., Waters, B.: On the impossibility of basing identity based encryption on trapdoor permutations. In: FOCS, pp. 283–292. IEEE Computer Society (2008)
10. Boneh, D., Venkatesan, R.: Breaking RSA may not be equivalent to factoring. In: Nyberg, K. (ed.) EUROCRYPT 1998. LNCS, vol. 1403, pp. 59–71. Springer, Heidelberg (1998). https://doi.org/10.1007/BFb0054117
11. Brakerski, Z., Katz, J., Segev, G., Yerukhimovich, A.: Limits on the power of zero-knowledge proofs in cryptographic constructions. In: Ishai, Y. (ed.) TCC 2011. LNCS, vol. 6597, pp. 559–578. Springer, Heidelberg (2011). https://doi.org/10.1007/978-3-642-19571-6_34
12. Canetti, R., et al.: Fiat-Shamir: from practice to theory. In: STOC 2019, pp. 1082–1090 (2019)
13. Camenisch, J., Chandran, N., Shoup, V.: A public key encryption scheme secure against key dependent chosen plaintext and adaptive chosen ciphertext attacks. In: Joux, A. (ed.) EUROCRYPT 2009. LNCS, vol. 5479, pp. 351–368. Springer, Heidelberg (2009). https://doi.org/10.1007/978-3-642-01001-9_20
14. Cramer, R., Damgård, I., Schoenmakers, B.: Proofs of partial knowledge and simplified design of witness hiding protocols. In: Desmedt, Y.G. (ed.) CRYPTO 1994. LNCS, vol. 839, pp. 174–187. Springer, Heidelberg (1994). https://doi.org/10.1007/3-540-48658-5_19
15. Coron, J.-S.: Optimal security proofs for PSS and other signature schemes. In: Knudsen, L.R. (ed.) EUROCRYPT 2002. LNCS, vol. 2332, pp. 272–287. Springer, Heidelberg (2002). https://doi.org/10.1007/3-540-46035-7_18
16. Cramer, R., Shoup, V.: Universal hash proofs and a paradigm for adaptive chosen ciphertext secure public-key encryption. In: Knudsen, L.R. (ed.) EUROCRYPT 2002. LNCS, vol. 2332, pp. 45–64. Springer, Heidelberg (2002). https://doi.org/10.1007/3-540-46035-7_4
17. De Santis, A., Di Crescenzo, G., Ostrovsky, R., Persiano, G., Sahai, A.: Robust non-interactive zero knowledge. In: Kilian, J. (ed.) CRYPTO 2001. LNCS, vol. 2139, pp. 566–598. Springer, Heidelberg (2001). https://doi.org/10.1007/3-540-44647-8_33
18. Even, S., Selman, A.L., Yacobi, Y.: The complexity of promise problems with applications to public-key cryptography. Inf. Control **61**, 159–173 (1984)

19. Feige, U., Lapidot, D., Shamir, A.: Multiple non-interactive zero knowledge proofs based on a single random string (extended abstract). In: FOCS, pp. 308–317. IEEE Computer Society (1990)
20. Fiat, A., Shamir, A.: How to prove yourself: practical solutions to identification and signature problems. In: Odlyzko, A.M. (ed.) CRYPTO 1986. LNCS, vol. 263, pp. 186–194. Springer, Heidelberg (1987). https://doi.org/10.1007/3-540-47721-7_12
21. Garg, S., Gupta, D.: Efficient round optimal blind signatures. In: Nguyen, P.Q., Oswald, E. (eds.) EUROCRYPT 2014. LNCS, vol. 8441, pp. 477–495. Springer, Heidelberg (2014). https://doi.org/10.1007/978-3-642-55220-5_27
22. Gentry, C., Wichs, D.: Separating succinct non-interactive arguments from all falsifiable assumptions. In: STOC 2011, pp. 99–108. ACM (2011)
23. Gertner, Y., Malkin, T., Myers, S.: Towards a separation of semantic and CCA security for public key encryption. In: Vadhan, S.P. (ed.) TCC 2007. LNCS, vol. 4392, pp. 434–455. Springer, Heidelberg (2007). https://doi.org/10.1007/978-3-540-70936-7_24
24. Groth, J.: Simulation-sound NIZK proofs for a practical language and constant size group signatures. In: Lai, X., Chen, K. (eds.) ASIACRYPT 2006. LNCS, vol. 4284, pp. 444–459. Springer, Heidelberg (2006). https://doi.org/10.1007/11935230_29
25. Groth, J., Ostrovsky, R., Sahai, A.: Perfect non-interactive zero knowledge for NP. In: Vaudenay, S. (ed.) EUROCRYPT 2006. LNCS, vol. 4004, pp. 339–358. Springer, Heidelberg (2006). https://doi.org/10.1007/11761679_21
26. Groth, J., Maller, M.: Snarky signatures: minimal signatures of knowledge from simulation-extractable SNARKs. In: Katz, J., Shacham, H. (eds.) CRYPTO 2017. LNCS, vol. 10402, pp. 581–612. Springer, Cham (2017). https://doi.org/10.1007/978-3-319-63715-0_20
27. Groth, J., Sahai, A.: Efficient noninteractive proof systems for bilinear groups. SIAM J. Comput. **41**(5), 1193–1232 (2012)
28. Halevi, S., Krawczyk, H.: Strengthening digital signatures via randomized hashing. In: Dwork, C. (ed.) CRYPTO 2006. LNCS, vol. 4117, pp. 41–59. Springer, Heidelberg (2006). https://doi.org/10.1007/11818175_3
29. Hofheinz, D., Jager, T.: Tightly secure signatures and public-key encryption. Des. Codes Cryptograph. **80**(1), 29–61 (2016). https://doi.org/10.1007/s10623-015-0062-x
30. Hülsing, A., Rijneveld, J., Song, F.: Mitigating multi-target attacks in hash-based signatures. In: Cheng, C.-M., Chung, K.-M., Persiano, G., Yang, B.-Y. (eds.) PKC 2016. LNCS, vol. 9614, pp. 387–416. Springer, Heidelberg (2016). https://doi.org/10.1007/978-3-662-49384-7_15
31. Impagliazzo, R., Rudich, S.: Limits on the provable consequences of one-way permutations. In: STOC 1989, pp. 44–61. ACM (1989)
32. Jutla, C.S., Roy, A.: Shorter quasi-adaptive NIZK proofs for linear subspaces. In: Sako, K., Sarkar, P. (eds.) ASIACRYPT 2013. LNCS, vol. 8269, pp. 1–20. Springer, Heidelberg (2013). https://doi.org/10.1007/978-3-642-42033-7_1
33. Katz, J.: Signatures from one-way functions. Random bits; random thoughts about random things, 4 February 2010 (2010)
34. Katz, J., Vaikuntanathan, V.: Signature schemes with bounded leakage resilience. In: Matsui, M. (ed.) ASIACRYPT 2009. LNCS, vol. 5912, pp. 703–720. Springer, Heidelberg (2009). https://doi.org/10.1007/978-3-642-10366-7_41
35. Kiltz, E., Wee, H.: Quasi-adaptive NIZK for linear subspaces revisited. In: Oswald, E., Fischlin, M. (eds.) EUROCRYPT 2015. LNCS, vol. 9057, pp. 101–128. Springer, Heidelberg (2015). https://doi.org/10.1007/978-3-662-46803-6_4

36. Kim, S., Wu, D.J.: Multi-theorem preprocessing NIZKs from lattices. In: Shacham, H., Boldyreva, A. (eds.) CRYPTO 2018. LNCS, vol. 10992, pp. 733–765. Springer, Cham (2018). https://doi.org/10.1007/978-3-319-96881-0_25
37. Libert, B., Joye, M., Yung, M., Peters, T.: Concise multi-challenge CCA-secure encryption and signatures with almost tight security. In: Sarkar, P., Iwata, T. (eds.) ASIACRYPT 2014. LNCS, vol. 8874, pp. 1–21. Springer, Heidelberg (2014). https://doi.org/10.1007/978-3-662-45608-8_1
38. Libert, B., Peters, T., Yung, M.: Short group signatures via structure-preserving signatures: standard model security from simple assumptions. In: Gennaro, R., Robshaw, M. (eds.) CRYPTO 2015. LNCS, vol. 9216, pp. 296–316. Springer, Heidelberg (2015). https://doi.org/10.1007/978-3-662-48000-7_15
39. Merkle, R.C.: A certified digital signature. In: Brassard, G. (ed.) CRYPTO 1989. LNCS, vol. 435, pp. 218–238. Springer, New York (1990). https://doi.org/10.1007/0-387-34805-0_21
40. Mironov, I.: Domain extension for enhanced target collision-resistant hash functions. In: Hong, S., Iwata, T. (eds.) FSE 2010. LNCS, vol. 6147, pp. 153–167. Springer, Heidelberg (2010). https://doi.org/10.1007/978-3-642-13858-4_9
41. Malkin, T., Teranishi, I., Vahlis, Y., Yung, M.: Signatures resilient to continual leakage on memory and computation. In: Ishai, Y. (ed.) TCC 2011. LNCS, vol. 6597, pp. 89–106. Springer, Heidelberg (2011). https://doi.org/10.1007/978-3-642-19571-6_7
42. MacKenzie, P.D., Shrimpton, T., Jakobsson, M.: Threshold password-authenticated key exchange. J. Cryptol. **19**(1), 27–66 (2006)
43. Pointcheval, D., Stern, J.: Security proofs for signature schemes. In: Maurer, U. (ed.) EUROCRYPT 1996. LNCS, vol. 1070, pp. 387–398. Springer, Heidelberg (1996). https://doi.org/10.1007/3-540-68339-9_33
44. Peikert, C., Shiehian, S.: Noninteractive zero knowledge for NP from (plain) learning with errors. In: Boldyreva, A., Micciancio, D. (eds.) CRYPTO 2019. LNCS, vol. 11692, pp. 89–114. Springer, Cham (2019). https://doi.org/10.1007/978-3-030-26948-7_4
45. Peikert, C., Vaikuntanathan, V.: Noninteractive statistical zero-knowledge proofs for lattice problems. In: Wagner, D. (ed.) CRYPTO 2008. LNCS, vol. 5157, pp. 536–553. Springer, Heidelberg (2008). https://doi.org/10.1007/978-3-540-85174-5_30
46. Ràfols, C.: Stretching Groth-Sahai: NIZK proofs of partial satisfiability. In: Dodis, Y., Nielsen, J.B. (eds.) TCC 2015. LNCS, vol. 9015, pp. 247–276. Springer, Heidelberg (2015). https://doi.org/10.1007/978-3-662-46497-7_10
47. Rostovtsev, A., Stolbunov, A.: Public-key cryptosystem based on isogenies. IACR Cryptology ePrint Archive, Report 2006/145
48. Rothblum, R.D., Sealfon, A., Sotiraki, K.: Towards non-interactive zero-knowledge for NP from LWE. In: Lin, D., Sako, K. (eds.) PKC 2019. LNCS, vol. 11443, pp. 472–503. Springer, Cham (2019). https://doi.org/10.1007/978-3-030-17259-6_16
49. Reingold, O., Trevisan, L., Vadhan, S.: Notions of reducibility between cryptographic primitives. In: Naor, M. (ed.) TCC 2004. LNCS, vol. 2951, pp. 1–20. Springer, Heidelberg (2004). https://doi.org/10.1007/978-3-540-24638-1_1
50. Sahai, A.: Non-malleable non-interactive zero knowledge and adaptive chosen-ciphertext security. In: FOCS 1999, pp. 543–553. IEEE Computer Society (1999)
51. Stolbunov, A.: Constructing public-key cryptographic schemes based on class group action on a set of isogenous elliptic curves. Adv. in Math. of Comm. **4**, 215–235 (2010)

52. Sahai, A., Vadhan, S.: A complete problem for statistical zero knowledge. J. ACM **50**(2), 196–249 (2003)
53. Simon, D.R.: Finding collisions on a one-way street: can secure hash functions be based on general assumptions? In: Nyberg, K. (ed.) EUROCRYPT 1998. LNCS, vol. 1403, pp. 334–345. Springer, Heidelberg (1998). https://doi.org/10.1007/BFb0054137
54. Vahlis, E.: Cryptography: leakage resilience, black box separations, and credential-free key exchange. Ph.D. thesis, Graduate Department of Computer Science, University of Toronto (2010)
55. Yerukhimovich, A.: A study of separations in cryptography: new results and new models. Ph.D. thesis, The Faculty of the Graduate School, Department of Computer Science, University of Maryland (2011)
56. Yasuda, T., Dahan, X., Huang, Y.-J., Takagi, T., Sakurai, K.: MQ challenge: hardness evaluation of solving multivariate quadratic problems. In: NIST Workshop on Cybersecurity in a Post-Quantum World, April 2015. Cryptology ePrint Archive, Report 2015/275

On QA-NIZK in the BPK Model

Behzad Abdolmaleki[1], Helger Lipmaa[1,2(✉)], Janno Siim[1], and Michał Zając[3]

[1] University of Tartu, Tartu, Estonia
abdolmaleki.behzad.ir@gmail.com, helger.lipmaa@gmail.com,
jannosiim@gmail.com
[2] Simula UiB, Bergen, Norway
[3] Clearmatics, London, UK
m.p.zajac@gmail.com

Abstract. Recently, Bellare *et al.* defined subversion-resistance (security in the case the CRS creator may be malicious) for NIZK. In particular, a Sub-ZK NIZK is zero-knowledge, even in the case of subverted CRS. We study Sub-ZK QA-NIZKs, where the CRS can depend on the language parameter. First, we observe that subversion zero-knowledge (Sub-ZK) in the CRS model corresponds to no-auxiliary-string non-black-box NIZK in the Bare Public Key model, and hence, the use of non-black-box techniques is needed to obtain Sub-ZK. Second, we give a precise definition of Sub-ZK QA-NIZKs that are (knowledge-)sound if the language parameter but not the CRS is subverted and zero-knowledge even if both are subverted. Third, we prove that the most efficient known QA-NIZK for linear subspaces by Kiltz and Wee is Sub-ZK under a new knowledge assumption that by itself is secure in (a weaker version of) the algebraic group model. Depending on the parameter setting, it is (knowledge-)sound under different non-falsifiable assumptions, some of which do not belong to the family of knowledge assumptions.

Keywords: Bare Public Key model · No-auxiliary-string zero knowledge · Non-black-box zero knowledge · QA-NIZK · Subversion-security

1 Introduction

Zero-knowledge argument systems introduced by Goldwasser *et al.* [22] enable a prover to convince a verifier of the veracity of a statement while leaking no additional information. Blum *et al.* [6] introduced non-interactive zero-knowledge (NIZK) argument systems where the prover outputs just one message (the argument) that convinces the verifier of the truth of the statement. Unfortunately, NIZKs are impossible in the standard model [21], and thus in all such applications, one has to rely on some trust assumption like the common reference string (CRS) model stating that there exists a trusted third party who has created the CRS from a correct distribution. Other, weaker, trust models include the registered public key (RPK, [3], where the authority is trusted to check that a party knows the secret key corresponding to the public key and then store her key)

A. Kiayias et al. (Eds.): PKC 2020, LNCS 12110, pp. 590–620, 2020.
https://doi.org/10.1007/978-3-030-45374-9_20

model and the bare public key (BPK, [9], where the authority is only trusted to store the public key of each party) model. However, very few NIZKs are known in the RPK model while black-box NIZK [38] (the simulator uses adversarial algorithm only by giving inputs and receiving outputs) and even auxiliary-string non-black-box [21,42] (the simulator may use the code of the adversary, who has access to an arbitrary auxiliary string) NIZK is impossible in the BPK model.

There has been a recent surge of the research to decrease the trust in the CRS model due to the use of succinct non-interactive zero knowledge argument systems of knowledge (zk-SNARKs, [11,18,26,27,35,36,40]) in real-life applications like verifiable computation and cryptocurrencies. Recently, [2,15] constructed subversion-zero knowledge (Sub-ZK) zk-SNARKs, where the prover does not have to trust the CRS creator. According to an impossibility result of [4], this means that such SNARKs cannot have soundness when the CRS has been maliciously generated. Abdolmaleki *et al.* [2] proposed the following concrete recipe for constructing Sub-ZK zk-SNARKs: first, construct an efficient public CRS verification algorithm CV that rejects malformed CRSs. Second, when proving Sub-ZK, use a non-falsifiable knowledge assumption [10] to obtain an extractor that recovers the CRS trapdoor td from a CV-accepted CRS; td is then used by the simulator (that works when the CRS has been honestly generated) to simulate the argument. Based on this recipe, [2,15] showed that the most efficient known zk-SNARK by Groth [27] is Sub-ZK. One principal weakness of zk-SNARKs is that zk-SNARKs for languages outside of BPP have to rely on non-falsifiable assumptions, based on the impossibility result of [19]. *However, we are not aware of any prior result indicating whether non-falsifiable assumptions are needed to obtain Sub-ZK.*

Another important recent direction in the NIZK arena is that of quasi-adaptive NIZKs (QA-NIZKs, [28]). In a QA-NIZK, the CRS can depend on a language parameter ϱ, where ϱ can be thought of as a properly distributed public key of some cryptosystem. One consequence of this definition is that up to now, QA-NIZKs have been only considered in the CRS model. The dependence of CRS on correctly generated ϱ means that one can construct very efficient QA-NIZKs for non-trivial languages based on standard assumptions like KerMDH [39]. Importantly, very efficient pairing-based QA-NIZKs [1,23,28,30–32] for the linear subspace language have been constructed in the CRS model. A QA-NIZK argument system for linear subspaces allows the prover to convince the verifier that a vector of group elements[1] $[\boldsymbol{y}]_1$ belongs to the column space of a fixed public matrix $\varrho = [\boldsymbol{M}]_1 \in \mathbb{G}_1^{n \times m}$, i.e., $\boldsymbol{y} = \boldsymbol{M}\boldsymbol{x}$ for some vector $\boldsymbol{x} \in \mathbb{Z}_p^m$.

Although QA-NIZKs for other languages are known (e.g., the language of bitstrings [23] and the languages of shuffles [24], both requiring a quadratic-length CRS, and a recent QA-NIZK [12] for SSP [11], that relies on non-succinct commitment), research on QA-NIZKs has been mostly concentrated on designing efficient QA-NIZKs for linear subspaces. Such focus is motivated because of the broad applicability of QA-NIZKs for linear subspaces in the design of various cryptographic primitives (see [28,30–32] for examples and references). In addition, [14]

[1] We use pairing-based setting and the additive bracket notation of [13] (see Sect. 2).

combined SNARKs and QA-NIZKs for linear subspaces to construct an efficient pairing-based NIZK shuffle argument systems. This and other recent work [8,25, 37] that use QA-NIZKs to construct SNARKs shows that the study of different properties of QA-NIZKs can be also beneficial in the world of SNARKs.

In particular, Campanelli *et al.* [8] proposed a toolbox called LegoSNARK that allows building complex zk-SNARK arguments from other zk-SNARKs given that the building blocks of the final zk-SNARK are so-called commit-and-prove SNARKs (CP-SNARKs). A linear subspace QA-NIZK plays a crucial role in the Campanelli *et al.* framework. First, it is used in a transformation that makes commit-carrying SNARKs (CC-SNARKs), like [27], CP-SNARKs. Second, it is used as a building block in several CP-SNARKs proposed in [8]. Thus, one interested in having Sub-ZK LegoSNARK or Sub-ZK CP-SNARKs inevitably needs a Sub-ZK QA-NIZK for linear subspaces. Importantly, in [8,14], one uses a QA-NIZK to prove that an element belongs to the trivial full space; in this case, a QA-NIZK is sound by default. Instead, one has to prove that the stronger property of knowledge-soundness holds.

The main goal of the current paper is the study and construction of subversion-secure QA-NIZKs. According to the original security definitions of QA-NIZKs [28], one aims for soundness (alternatively, knowledge-soundness in applications like [8,14]) and zero-knowledge in the case when both ϱ and the CRS are honestly generated. In reality, it means that in the case of QA-NIZKs, one will have one more subversion-attack vector than in the case of SNARKs: namely, one has to consider both the case of a subverted language parameter (the Sub-PAR case) and the case of a subverted CRS. The Sub-PAR case with *honestly generated CRS* was tackled in [29] (updated full version of [28] from September 2018) where both Sub-PAR soundness and Sub-PAR zero-knowledge were shown to be achievable for a large family of subspace languages.[2] Since the simulator does not need access to a language parameter trapdoor td_ϱ, one does not have to extract td_ϱ for the simulation to be possible. Moreover, in the Sub-PAR case, the CRS is still honestly generated, which means that the simulator has access to the CRS trapdoor td.

Translated to the language of QA-NIZKs, by the impossibility result of [4], one cannot achieve both soundness and zero-knowledge in the case both ϱ and the CRS have been subverted. Therefore, in the rest of the paper, we study the slightly more relaxed case when (knowledge-)soundness holds if only ϱ has been subverted and zero-knowledge holds when both ϱ and the CRS have been subverted. It is unclear whether one can use existing techniques to construct a Sub-ZK version of the most efficient QA-NIZKs like Π_{kw} by Kiltz and Wee [31] in this case. First, ϱ has to be modeled separately from other inputs; no such parameter exists in the case of SNARKs. The existence of ϱ (and the dependence of the CRS on it) is the main reason why falsifiable QA-NIZKs are so efficient.

[2] This does not contradict the impossibility result of [4] (that achieving Sub-CRS soundness and Sub-CRS zero-knowledge at the same time is impossible for non-trivial languages) since ϱ plays a different role compared to CRS.

Second, known QA-NIZKs have a very different structure compared to SNARKs. For example, the most efficient known QA-NIZK for linear subspaces Π_{kw} by Kiltz and Wee [31] has a trapdoor matrix $\boldsymbol{K}$, but $[\boldsymbol{K}]_1$ is not explicitly given in the CRS. This means that the knowledge assumptions of [2,15] or knowledge-of-exponent assumptions [10] (that all rely on $[\alpha]_\iota$ being in the CRS for each trapdoor α) cannot be directly translated to the case of (Kiltz-Wee) QA-NIZK, and thus one seems to need quite different knowledge assumptions.

Third, another significant difference is that the soundness of efficient QA-NIZKs like [1,28,30–32] is based on standard falsifiable assumptions like KerMDH. Thus, intuitively, the use of non-falsifiable assumptions to prove Sub-ZK of a (sound) QA-NIZK seems to be less justifiable than in the case of proving Sub-ZK of zk-SNARKs since in the case of zk-SNARKs, non-falsifiable assumptions are needed to get soundness anyhow [19]. Moreover, while Bellare *et al.* had a discussion motivating the use of knowledge assumptions to obtain Sub-ZK, they did not have a formal proof of their necessity. Can one base Sub-ZK QA-NIZKs on falsifiable assumptions or prove it is impossible? (Non-subversion zero-knowledge) QA-NIZKs do not always rely on falsifiable assumptions: in the applications of QA-NIZKs in [8,14,25,37], one proves the "membership" in the full space that only makes sense under knowledge assumptions.

This brings us to the main questions of the current work:

(i) Are non-black-box techniques needed to prove Sub-ZK of NIZKs for languages outside of BPP*?*
(ii) Are (knowledge-)soundness and zero-knowledge achievable in the previously described model, i.e., only ϱ has been subverted in the case of soundness, and both ϱ and the CRS are subverted in the case of zero-knowledge? From this point on, we assume Sub-ZK QA-NIZK works in this model.
(iii) Can one obtain Sub-ZK QA-NIZKs for linear subspaces without modifying the existing constructions?

Our Contributions. We answer to the above main questions (with yes, yes, and mostly yes). It turns out that achieving Sub-ZK for state-of-the-art QA-NIZKs is considerably more complicated than for state-of-the-art SNARKs. This follows partly from the nature of QA-NIZKs (the existence of separate ϱ and pk) and from the construction of the concrete QA-NIZK. In the most relevant case ($k = 1$), it turns out that the most efficient existing QA-NIZK by Kiltz and Wee [31] is Sub-ZK (in the model described above) under a (novel) knowledge assumption given suitable algorithms that verify the correctness of both ϱ and pk. Hence, in this case, Sub-ZK comes almost for free: one only has to perform some additional computations that verify the correctness of the (language parameter and) CRS, and the proof of Sub-ZK relies on a non-falsifiable assumption.

First, we make a conceptually important observation that Sub-ZK in the CRS model, as defined in [2,4,15], is equal to *no-auxiliary-string non-black-box* zero knowledge [21] in the BPK model [9,38]. In the BPK model, the verifier (but not the prover) has a public key; and the key authority executes the functionality of an immutable bulletin board by storing the received public keys.

A zero-knowledge argument in the BPK model is either designated-verifier (the argument convinces only the designated verifier) when using the verifier's own public key or transferable (the verifier can transfer the argument to other verifiers and convince them of its validity) when using the public key pk of a third party; the latter case is essentially equivalent to the CRS model with pk being the CRS, $\mathsf{pk} = \mathsf{crs}$. The BPK model is significantly weaker than the CRS model, being arguably the weakest public key or parameter based trust model under which complicated functionalities like zero-knowledge are known to exist.

This important positive connection between no-auxiliary-string non-black-box zero knowledge and Sub-ZK was missed in the prior work on Sub-ZK; we hope it will simplify the construction and analysis of the future Sub-ZK argument systems. Because of that connection, we will usually use the abbreviation Sub-ZK to denote no-auxiliary-string non-black-box zero knowledge, but we explicitly emphasize that we are working in the BPK model.

Since three messages are needed to achieve auxiliary-string zero knowledge in the plain model for languages outside of BPP [21], it follows that in the BPK model, auxiliary-string non-black-box NIZK is possible only for languages in BPP. This provides a simple proof that one can only construct non-auxiliary-string non-black-box NIZK for languages outside of BPP and thus provides an answer to the open question (i).

In Sect. 3, we define the security of QA-NIZK arguments in the BPK model; for this, we strengthen the "strong" QA-NIZK security definitions from [29] (as updated on September 2018) that consider the case of subverted ϱ but honestly generated pk. We allow for both ϱ and pk to be subverted. We model the resulting definition of *persistent zero-knowledge* after the Sub-ZK definition of SNARKs in [2], allocating a special role for the language parameter ϱ. More precisely, we require that for any efficient malicious $\mathcal{C}$ that creates the language parameter creator and the public key, there exists an efficient extractor $\mathsf{Ext}_{\mathcal{C}}$, s.t. if $\mathcal{C}$, by using random coins r, generates a language parameter ϱ and a public key pk (since there is no auxiliary input, ϱ and pk *have* to be generated by $\mathcal{C}$) then $\mathsf{Ext}_{\mathcal{C}}$, given r, outputs the secret key sk corresponding to pk.

Since we allow both ϱ and pk to be subverted, it is possible that the subverter sets $\mathsf{sk} = \mathsf{td}_\varrho$ for td_ϱ being a trapdoor for a parameter ϱ, e.g. for Kiltz-Wee QA-NIZK, $\varrho = [\boldsymbol{M}]_1$ and $\mathsf{td}_\varrho = \boldsymbol{M}$. As we show in Sect. 4, this can result in pathological QA-NIZK argument systems that are persistent zero-knowledge but not standard zero-knowledge. (This is possible since we consider an extractor that extracts the trapdoor behind ϱ and returns this as the secret key.) Hence, we say that a QA-NIZK argument system is *no-auxiliary-string non-black-box zero-knowledge (i.e., Sub-ZK)* iff it is both standard zero-knowledge and persistent zero-knowledge.

As the next main contribution, we study a variant Π_{bpk} of the most-efficient known QA-NIZK for linear subspaces Π_{kw} by Kiltz and Wee [31] (denoted there as Π'_{as}). Π_{kw} is known to be perfectly zero-knowledge and computationally sound in the CRS model under a suitable KerMDH assumption, [31] for a matrix distribution $\mathcal{D}_k$ where k is a small security-assumption-related integer; $k = 1$ in the case of asymmetric pairings. In Π_{kw}, the CRS includes a matrix $[\bar{\boldsymbol{A}}]_2 \in \mathbb{G}_2^{k \times k}$ (assumed to be distributed according to $\mathcal{D}_k$) and the argument consists of only k group elements (thus, smaller k results in better efficiency). In the variant of Π_{kw} proposed in the current paper, pk of Π_{bpk} includes a new component $\mathsf{pk}^{\mathsf{pkv}}$ that helps to publicly check that even adversarially generated $[\bar{\boldsymbol{A}}]_2$ in pk has full rank k. In the case of many distributions $\mathcal{D}_k$ that are important in practice (we will call such distributions *efficiently verifiable*), the latter verification can be done efficiently only based on the knowledge of $[\bar{\boldsymbol{A}}]_2$ itself and thus $\mathsf{pk}^{\mathsf{pkv}}$ will be an empty string. Similarly to [2], we also define an efficient public-key verification algorithm that we denote by PKV. On top of it, we also define an efficient ϱ-verification algorithm PARV. We emphasize that we analyze Π_{kw} since it is the most efficient known QA-NIZK for linear subspaces. We leave analyzing other QA-NIZKs (that will hopefully be easier to do following our definitional framework and analysis of Π_{kw}) to the further work.

Since in the case of verifiable $\mathcal{D}_k$, we do not modify the public-key generation and the prover (thus, essentially $\Pi_{\mathsf{kw}} = \Pi_{\mathsf{bpk}}$), the (non-subversion) soundness of Π_{bpk} in the BPK model follows directly from [31]. In the non-verifiable special case $\mathcal{D}_k = \mathcal{U}_2$, we add some extra elements to pk and then prove the (non-subversion) soundness of Π_{bpk} under the SKerMDH assumption of [23]. In the subversion-case, when the language parameter could have been subverted, we prove (subverted-ϱ) soundness under KerMDH^{dl} or SKerMDH^{dl} assumption. Here, if X and Y are two assumptions, X^Y is the interactive assumption that X holds even if the adversary was given non-adaptive access to a Y oracle. See [34] for a thorough treatment of X^Y-type assumptions. Interestingly, up to now, the only non-falsifiable assumptions that have been used to construct efficient succinct NIZKs are knowledge assumptions; the use of (seemingly more standard) X^Y-type assumptions instead is one of the possibly most interesting contributions of the current paper.

As mentioned before, *knowledge-sound* QA-NIZKs are also interesting in the case when one uses them to prove the membership in the full space. We prove that Π_{bpk} is knowledge-sound by modifying a similar knowledge-soundness proof from [8] that, however, was only given in the non-subversion case, and only for $k = 1$. We use a SDL^{dl} (where SDL is the symmetric discrete logarithm assumption, [5]) assumption, like in the case of soundness proofs, to get knowledge-soundness even in the subversion case. We modify the proof of [8] so that it generalizes to arbitrary k. Moreover, knowledge-soundness will rely on both the SDL^{dl} and a hash-algebraic knowledge (HAK) assumption. In [37], Lipmaa recently defined the framework of HAK assumptions to make the algebraic group model (AGM) of Fuchsbauer *et al.* [16] more concrete and applicable. While in the AGM, it is assumed that every adversary is algebraic, a HAK assumption is defined with respect to a concrete input distribution of the adversary. I.e., a $\mathcal{D}$-HAK assumption states that if an adversary obtains an input (a vector of group elements) distributed according to a fixed distribution $\mathcal{D}$ then she knows how the group elements that she outputs depend on the input. HAK assumptions are even weaker: they allow for the case an adversary has additionally generated high min-entropy (but not necessarily uniformly random) group elements by using say elliptic-curve hashing.

Since Π_{kw} is perfectly zero-knowledge [31], we now only have to prove that it is also persistent zero-knowledge; from this, it follows that it is Sub-ZK in the BPK model. We prove that Π_{bpk} is statistically persistent zero-knowledge under either one of the two new knowledge assumptions KWKE (the *Kiltz-Wee Knowledge of Exponent* assumption) and SKWKE (the *strong* KWKE assumption)[3], assuming that its whole pk is generated by the verifier or a verifier-trusted authority—even if we are set to prove Sub-ZK that interests the prover. Intuitively, (S)KWKE guarantees that if an adversary $\mathcal{A}$ has succeeded in creating a pk accepted by PKV then one can extract corresponding $\mathsf{sk} = \boldsymbol{K}$. We prove that both assumptions hold under a *hash-algebraic knowledge* (HAK, [37]) assumption, see Theorem 1. (Here, SKWKE also relies on a computational assumption that depends on the matrix distribution $\mathcal{D}_k$ but is equal to the discrete logarithm assumption for all standard distributions $\mathcal{D}_k$.)

The proof of Theorem 1 is quite intricate. More precisely, we use a HAK assumption to extract some outputs of $\mathcal{A}$ as polynomials in indeterminates created by $\mathcal{A}$. To extract an integer sk, we use the Schwartz-Zippel lemma and let the extractor output evaluation of the polynomials at a random point. We then use the specific form of PKV to argue that such sk is correct. In the case of SKWKE, we evaluate the polynomials at two random points and use an additional reduction to a computational assumption, see Theorem 1.

Interestingly, under KWKE we only get the guarantee that the part $\mathsf{pk}^{\mathsf{zk}}$ of the pk, used either by the prover or the simulator, has been correctly computed. This, however, suffices to prove that Π_{bpk} is Sub-ZK. (Thus, Sub-ZK can be achieved even if the correctness of the whole public key cannot be verified.) Hence, in the case $\mathcal{D}_k$ is efficiently verifiable, one can get Sub-ZK essentially for free (efficiency-wise, the only added cost will be the need for a prover to verify the correctness of the public key; this can, however, be done once per public key). This is important since it means that in the case of efficiently verifiable matrix distributions, we get a stronger security property (Sub-ZK) without having to design a new, more complicated, and less efficient QA-NIZK. Arguably, in practice, one is only interested in efficiently verifiable distributions: the case $k = 1$ is the most one, and the case $k = 2$ is only needed in some applications (e.g., when one wants to rely on a weaker assumption). However, in such cases, one can usually use an efficiently verifiable distribution like $\mathcal{L}_2$ that corresponds to the 2-Lin assumption. This answers to the open questions (ii–iii).

We also show that under a stronger knowledge assumption SKWKE, one can guarantee that the whole pk has been correctly computed. However, as a drawback, the SKWKE assumption only holds if the language parameter $[\boldsymbol{M}]_1$ comes from a suitable hard distribution. The latter is, however, often the case in QA-NIZK applications, where $[\boldsymbol{M}]_1$ is a public key of a cryptographic primitive like an encryption or commitment scheme. In both cases, the soundness is guaranteed by a KerMDH assumption.

[3] It is possible to achieve the same level of security using more standard BDHKE assumption [2] by making both $[\boldsymbol{M}]_1$ and $[\boldsymbol{M}]_2$ public. Unfortunately, such a solution is less efficient; our goal was to achieve maximum efficiency.

2 Preliminaries

A random variable X has min-entropy k, $H_\infty(X) = k$, if $\max_x \Pr[X = x] = 2^{-k}$. Let PPT denote probabilistic polynomial-time. Let $\lambda \in \mathbb{N}$ be the security parameter. All adversaries will be stateful. For an algorithm $\mathcal{A}$, let $\mathrm{im}(\mathcal{A})$ be the image of $\mathcal{A}$ (the set of valid outputs of $\mathcal{A}$), let $\mathsf{RND}_\lambda(\mathcal{A})$ denote the random tape of $\mathcal{A}$ (assuming the given value of λ), and let $r \leftarrow_\$ \mathsf{RND}_\lambda(\mathcal{A})$ denote the random choice of the randomizer r from $\mathsf{RND}_\lambda(\mathcal{A})$. We denote by $\mathsf{negl}(\lambda)$ an arbitrary negligible function. We write $a \approx_\lambda b$ if $|a - b| \leq \mathsf{negl}(\lambda)$. We follow Bellare *et al.* [4] by using "cryptographic" style in security definitions where all complexity (adversaries, algorithms, assumptions) is uniform, but the adversary and the security (say, soundness) is quantified over all inputs chosen by the adversary. See [4] for a discussion.

A bilinear group generator $\mathsf{PGen}(1^\lambda)$ returns $(p, \mathbb{G}_1, \mathbb{G}_2, \mathbb{G}_T, \hat{e}, [1]_1, [1]_2)$, where $\mathbb{G}_1$, $\mathbb{G}_2$, and $\mathbb{G}_T$ are additive cyclic groups of prime order $p = 2^{\Omega(\lambda)}$, $[1]_1, [1]_2$ are generators of $\mathbb{G}_1$, $\mathbb{G}_2$, resp., and $\hat{e} : \mathbb{G}_1 \times \mathbb{G}_2 \to \mathbb{G}_T$ is a non-degenerate PPT-computable bilinear pairing. We assume the bilinear pairing to be Type-3, i.e., that there is no efficient isomorphism from $\mathbb{G}_1$ to $\mathbb{G}_2$ or from $\mathbb{G}_2$ to $\mathbb{G}_1$. We use the by now standard bracket notation, i.e., we write $[a]_\iota$ to denote ag_ι where g_ι is a fixed generator of $\mathbb{G}_\iota$. We denote $\hat{e}([a]_1, [b]_2)$ as $[a]_1[b]_2$. Thus, $[a]_1[b]_2 = [ab]_T$. We freely use the bracket notation with matrices, e.g., if $\boldsymbol{AB} = \boldsymbol{C}$ then $\boldsymbol{A}[\boldsymbol{B}]_\iota = [\boldsymbol{C}]_\iota$ and $[\boldsymbol{A}]_1[\boldsymbol{B}]_2 = [\boldsymbol{C}]_T$.

In the Bare Public Key (BPK) model [9,38], parties have access to a public file F, a polynomial-size collection of records (id, pk_{id}), where id is a string identifying a party (e.g., a verifier), and pk_{id} is her alleged public key. In a typical zero-knowledge protocol in the BPK model, a key-owning party $\mathcal{P}_{id}$ works in two stages. In stage one (the *key-generation stage*), on input a security parameter 1^λ and randomizer r, $\mathcal{P}_{id}$ outputs a public key pk_{id} and stores the corresponding secret key sk_{id}. After that, F will include (id, pk_{id}). In stage two, each party has access to F, while $\mathcal{P}_{id}$ has possible access to sk_{id} (however, the latter is not required by us). It is commonly assumed that only the verifier of a NIZK argument system in the BPK model has a public key [38]; see also Sect. 3.

In a zero-knowledge proof or argument system, a prover convinces the verifier of the veracity of a statement without leaking any side information except that the statement is true. Here, a proof (resp., an argument) system guarantees soundness against an unbounded (resp., a PPT) cheating prover. The zero-knowledge property is proven by constructing a simulator that can simulate the view of a cheating verifier without knowing the secret information (witness) of the prover. A non-interactive zero-knowledge proof or argument system [6] consists of just one message by the prover.

We will only deal with no-auxiliary-string non-black-box NIZK argument systems in the plain model, but to explain this choice, it is important to know that there are many possibility and impossibility results about zero knowledge in the BPK model. Goldreich and Oren [21] proved that three rounds are needed for auxiliary-string zero knowledge in the plain model. From this, it follows that there exists no *auxiliary-string non-black-box* NIZK argument system in the BPK model for a language $\mathscr{L}$ outside of BPP, see Lemma 1.

The *Symmetric Discrete Logarithm (SDL)* [5] *assumption* holds relative to PGen, if for any PPT $\mathcal{A}$, $\Pr\left[\mathsf{p} \leftarrow \mathsf{PGen}(1^\lambda); x \leftarrow_\$ \mathbb{Z}_p : \mathcal{A}(\mathsf{p}, [x]_1, [x]_2) = x\right] \approx_\lambda 0$.

Kernel Matrix Diffie-Hellman Assumption (KerMDH) is a well-known assumption family formally introduced in [39]. Let $\mathcal{D}_{\ell k}$ be a probability distribution over matrices in $\mathbb{Z}_p^{\ell \times k}$, where $\ell > k$. Next, we define five commonly used distributions (see [13] for references), where $a, a_i, a_{ij} \leftarrow_\$ \mathbb{Z}_p^*$: $\mathcal{U}_k$ (uniform), $\mathcal{L}_k$ (linear), $\mathcal{IL}_k$ (incremental linear), $\mathcal{C}_k$ (cascade), $\mathcal{SC}_k$ (symmetric cascade):

$$\mathcal{U}_k\colon \boldsymbol{A} = \begin{pmatrix} a_{11} & \dots & a_{1k} \\ \dots & \dots & \dots \\ a_{k1} & \dots & a_{kk} \\ a_{k+1,1} & \dots & a_{k+1,k} \end{pmatrix}, \qquad \mathcal{L}_k\colon \boldsymbol{A} = \begin{pmatrix} a_1 & 0 & \dots & 0 & 0 \\ 0 & a_2 & \dots & 0 & 0 \\ 0 & 0 & \dots & 0 & 0 \\ \dots & \dots & \dots & \dots & \dots \\ 0 & 0 & \dots & 0 & a_k \\ 1 & 1 & \dots & 1 & 1 \end{pmatrix},$$

$$\mathcal{IL}_k\colon \boldsymbol{A} = \begin{pmatrix} a & 0 & \dots & 0 & 0 \\ 0 & a+1 & \dots & 0 & 0 \\ 0 & 0 & \dots & 0 & 0 \\ \dots & \dots & \dots & \dots & \dots \\ 0 & 0 & \dots & 0 & a+k-1 \\ 1 & 1 & \dots & 1 & 1 \end{pmatrix}, \qquad \mathcal{C}_k\colon \boldsymbol{A} = \begin{pmatrix} a_1 & 0 & \dots & 0 & 0 \\ 1 & a_2 & \dots & 0 & 0 \\ 0 & 1 & \dots & 0 & 0 \\ \dots & \dots & \dots & \dots & \dots \\ 0 & 0 & \dots & 1 & a_k \\ 0 & 0 & \dots & 0 & 1 \end{pmatrix},$$

$$\mathcal{SC}_k\colon \boldsymbol{A} = \begin{pmatrix} a & 0 & \dots & 0 & 0 \\ 1 & a & \dots & 0 & 0 \\ 0 & 1 & \dots & 0 & 0 \\ \dots & \dots & \dots & \dots & \dots \\ 0 & 0 & \dots & 1 & a \\ 0 & 0 & \dots & 0 & 1 \end{pmatrix}.$$

Assume that $\mathcal{D}_{\ell k}$ outputs matrices $\boldsymbol{A}$ where the upper $k \times k$ submatrix $\bar{\boldsymbol{A}}$ is always invertible. I.e., $\mathcal{D}_{\ell k}$ is *robust*, [28]. All the above distributions can be made robust with minimal changes. Denote the lower $(\ell - k) \times k$ submatrix of $\boldsymbol{A}$ as $\underline{\boldsymbol{A}}$. Denote $\mathcal{D}_k = \mathcal{D}_{k+1,k}$.

$\mathcal{D}_{\ell k}$-KerMDH$_{\mathbb{G}_1}$ [39] holds relative to PGen, if for any PPT $\mathcal{A}$, $\Pr\left[\mathsf{p} \leftarrow \mathsf{PGen}(1^\lambda); \boldsymbol{A} \leftarrow_\$ \mathcal{D}_{\ell k}; [\boldsymbol{c}]_2 \leftarrow \mathcal{A}(\mathsf{p}, [\boldsymbol{A}]_1) : \boldsymbol{A}^\top \boldsymbol{c} = \boldsymbol{0}_k \wedge \boldsymbol{c} \neq \boldsymbol{0}_\ell\right] \approx_\lambda 0$. $\mathcal{D}_{\ell k}$-SKerMDH [23] holds relative to PGen, if for any PPT $\mathcal{A}$, $\Pr[\mathsf{p} \leftarrow \mathsf{PGen}(1^\lambda); \boldsymbol{A} \leftarrow_\$ \mathcal{D}_{\ell k}; ([\boldsymbol{c}_1]_1, [\boldsymbol{c}_2]_2) \leftarrow \mathcal{A}(\mathsf{p}, [\boldsymbol{A}]_1, [\boldsymbol{A}]_2) : \boldsymbol{A}^\top (\boldsymbol{c}_1 - \boldsymbol{c}_2) = \boldsymbol{0}_k \wedge \boldsymbol{c}_1 - \boldsymbol{c}_2 \neq \boldsymbol{0}_\ell] \approx_\lambda 0$. According to Lemma 1 of [23], if $\mathcal{D}_{\ell k}$-KerMDH holds in generic symmetric bilinear groups then $\mathcal{D}_{\ell k}$-SKerMDH holds in generic asymmetric bilinear groups. The KerMDH assumption holds also for Type-1 pairings, where $\mathbb{G}_1 = \mathbb{G}_2$, but then one needs $k \geq 2$, which affects efficiency.

Hash-Algebraic Knowledge Assumptions. The Algebraic Group Model (AGM) is a new model [16] that one can use to prove the security of a cryptographic assumption or protocol. Essentially, in AGM one assumes that each PPT algorithm (including the adversaries) is algebraic in the following sense: if the adversary $\mathcal{A}$'s input includes $[\boldsymbol{x}_\iota]_\iota$ and no other elements from the group $\mathbb{G}_\iota$ and $\mathcal{A}$ outputs group elements $[\boldsymbol{y}_\iota]_\iota$, then $\mathcal{A}$ knows matrices $\boldsymbol{N}_\iota$, such that $\boldsymbol{y}_\iota = \boldsymbol{N}_\iota \boldsymbol{x}_\iota$. Lipmaa [37] considered AGM to be as a family of algebraic knowledge assumptions. He defined the *AGM with hashing (AGMH)*, where the adversary is additionally allowed to create new group elements that have high min-entropy from the adversary's viewpoint (and in particular, without knowing their discrete logarithms). This takes into account the existence of efficient elliptic curve hashing algorithms that can be used to generate such new group elements.

Following [37], we say that a PPT algorithm $\mathcal{A}$ is *hash-algebraic (in* p*)* if there exists an efficient extractor $\mathsf{Ext}_{\mathcal{A}}$, such that for any PPT sampleable distribution $\mathcal{D}$, $\mathsf{Adv}^{\mathsf{hak}}_{\mathsf{p},\mathcal{D},\mathcal{A}}(\lambda) :=$

$$\Pr\left[\begin{array}{l} \mathsf{x} = ([\boldsymbol{x}_1]_1, [\boldsymbol{x}_2]_2) \leftarrow_{\$} \mathcal{D}; r \leftarrow_{\$} \mathsf{RND}_\lambda(\mathcal{A}); ([\boldsymbol{y}_1]_1, [\boldsymbol{y}_2]_2) \leftarrow_{\$} \mathcal{A}(\mathsf{x}; r); \\ (\boldsymbol{N}_1, \boldsymbol{N}_2, [\boldsymbol{q}_1]_1, [\boldsymbol{q}_2]_2) \leftarrow \mathsf{Ext}_{\mathcal{A}}(\mathsf{x}; r) : \\ (\boldsymbol{y}_1 \neq \boldsymbol{N}_1\binom{\boldsymbol{x}_1}{\boldsymbol{q}_1} \vee \boldsymbol{y}_2 \neq \boldsymbol{N}_2\binom{\boldsymbol{x}_2}{\boldsymbol{q}_2}) \vee (\exists \iota, s : H_\infty([q_{\iota s}]_\iota) = O(\log \lambda)) \end{array}\right].$$

A bilinear group p is *hash-algebraic* if every PPT algorithm $\mathcal{A}$ that obtains inputs from $\mathbb{G}_1/\mathbb{G}_2$ and outputs elements in $\mathbb{G}_1/\mathbb{G}_2$ is hash-algebraic. Clearly, a hash-algebraic adversary is less restricted than an algebraic adversary.

The requirement that $\mathcal{A}$ is hash-algebraic for a *concrete* $\mathcal{D}$ is a specific $(\mathsf{p}, \mathcal{D}, \mathcal{A})$-hash-algebraic knowledge (HAK) assumption stating that $\mathsf{Adv}^{\mathsf{hak}}_{\mathsf{p},\mathcal{D},\mathcal{A}}(\lambda) \approx_\lambda 0$. In AGMH, one assumes that $(\mathsf{p}, \mathcal{D}, \mathcal{A})$-HAK holds for all choices of $(\mathcal{D}, \mathcal{A})$. Alternatively, [37] calls it the p-*HAK assumption.* While proving the security of a concrete protocol in a fixed group p, it is sufficient to rely on the following assumption for a single specified distribution $\mathcal{D}$. A $(\mathsf{p}, \mathcal{D}, \mathcal{A})$-HAK assumption states that $\mathsf{Adv}^{\mathsf{hak}}_{\mathsf{p},\mathcal{D},\mathcal{A}}(\lambda) \approx_\lambda 0$. A $(\mathsf{p}, \mathcal{D})$-HAK assumption states that $\mathsf{Adv}^{\mathsf{hak}}_{\mathsf{p},\mathcal{D},\mathcal{A}}(\lambda) \approx_\lambda 0$ for all PPT $\mathcal{A}$. Analogously, the $(\mathcal{D}, \mathcal{A})$*-algebraic knowledge (AK) assumption in* p states that $\mathsf{Adv}^{\mathsf{ak}}_{\mathsf{p},\mathcal{D},\mathcal{A}}(\lambda) \approx_\lambda 0$.

Lipmaa [37] demonstrated the usefulness of the HAK assumption showing that Damgård's original Knowledge-of-Exponent (KE, [10]) assumption is secure under the DL and HAK assumptions. The opposite does not always hold: KE assumption (and its generalizations) cannot be used to extract unless each input group element $[z]_\iota$ is accompanied with a "knowledge" input $[xz]_\iota$ for random x. Thus, protocols that rely on HAK assumptions can, in principle, be more efficient than protocols that rely on KE assumptions only.

Intuitively, a security proof under the $(\mathsf{p}, \mathcal{D})$-HAK assumption constitutes essentially an AGMH security proof, but without one assuming that *all* PPT algorithms in the group p are (hash-)algebraic. Finally, according to the analysis of [37], it is sufficient to assume that $[\boldsymbol{q}_\iota]_1$ has high min-entropy while the previous approach of generic model with hashing as in [2,4,7,41] assumed that adversarially created group elements are uniformly random.

3 Defining QA-NIZK in the BPK Model

Quasi-Adaptive Non-Interactive Zero-Knowledge (QA-NIZK) argument systems [28] are quasi-adaptive in the sense that the CRS depends on a language parameter ϱ that has been sampled from a fixed distribution $\mathcal{D}_{\mathsf{p}}$. QA-NIZKs are of great interest since they are succinct and based on standard assumptions. Since QA-NIZKs have many applications, they have been a subject of intensive study, [1,23,28,30–33]. The main limitation of known QA-NIZKs is that *efficient* QA-NIZKs are only known for a restricted set of languages like the language of linear subspaces (see [12,23,24] for QA-NIZKs for other languages).

The original QA-NIZK security definitions [28] were given in the CRS model. Jutla and Roy strengthened the definitions in the full version of their paper, [29], allowing for the case when the language parameter is maliciously picked. We will lift the latter definitions to the weaker BPK model. Sometimes, the only difference compared to the definitions of [29] is in notation (a CRS will be replaced by a public key). The rest of the definitional changes are motivated by the definition of Sub-ZK zk-SNARKs in [2], e.g., a QA-NIZK in the BPK model will have a public-key verification algorithm PKV and the zero-knowledge definition mentions a subverter and an extractor. We also define a ϱ-verification algorithm PARV. Since black-box [38] and even auxiliary-input non-black-box [21] (see Lemma 1) NIZK in the BPK model is impossible we will give an explicit definition of no-auxiliary-string non-black-box NIZK.

As in [4], we will implicitly assume that the system parameters p are generated deterministically from λ; in particular, the choice of p cannot be subverted. A QA-NIZK argument system enables to prove membership in a language defined by a relation $\mathscr{R}_\varrho = \{(\mathsf{x}, \mathsf{w})\}$, which in turn is completely determined by a parameter ϱ sampled (in the honest case) from a distribution $\mathcal{D}_\mathsf{p}$. We will assume implicitly that ϱ contains p and thus not include p as an argument to algorithms that also input ϱ; recall that we assumed that p cannot be subverted. A distribution $\mathcal{D}_\mathsf{p}$ on $\mathscr{L}_\varrho$ is *witness-sampleable* [28] if there exists a PPT algorithm $\mathcal{D}'_\mathsf{p}$ that samples $(\varrho, \mathsf{td}_\varrho) \in \mathscr{R}_\mathsf{p}$ such that ϱ is distributed according to $\mathcal{D}_\mathsf{p}$.

The zero-knowledge simulator is usually required to be a single (non-black-box) PPT algorithm that works for the whole collection of relations $\mathscr{R}_\mathsf{p} = \{\mathscr{R}_\varrho\}_{\varrho \in \mathrm{im}(\mathcal{D}_\mathsf{p})}$; that is, one usually requires *uniform simulation* (see [28] for a discussion). Following [2], we accompany the universal simulator with an adversary-dependent extractor. We assume Sim also works in the case when one cannot efficiently establish whether $\varrho \in \mathrm{im}(\mathcal{D}_\mathsf{p})$. The simulator is not allowed to create new ϱ or pk but has to operate with one given to it as an input.

A tuple of PPT algorithms $\Pi = (\mathsf{PGen}, \mathsf{KGen}, \mathsf{PARV}, \mathsf{PKV}, \mathsf{P}, \mathsf{V}, \mathsf{Sim})$ is a *no-auxiliary-string non-black-box zero knowledge (Sub-ZK) QA-NIZK argument system* in the BPK model for a set of witness-relations $\mathscr{R}_\mathsf{p} = \{\mathscr{R}_\varrho\}_{\varrho \in \mathrm{Supp}(\mathcal{D}_\mathsf{p})}$, if the following Items i, ii, iv and v hold. Π is a *Sub-ZK QA-NIZK argument of knowledge*, if additionally Items iii holds. Here, PGen is the parameter generation algorithm, KGen is the public key generation algorithm, PARV is the ϱ-verification algorithm, PKV is the public-key verification algorithm, P is the prover, V is the verifier, and Sim is the simulator.

(i) **Perfect Completeness:** for any λ, $\mathsf{p} \in \mathrm{im}(\mathsf{PGen}(1^\lambda))$, PPT $\mathcal{A}$,

$$\Pr\left[\begin{array}{l} \varrho \leftarrow_\$ \mathcal{D}_\mathsf{p}; (\mathsf{pk}, \mathsf{sk}) \leftarrow \mathsf{KGen}(\varrho); (\mathsf{x}, \mathsf{w}) \leftarrow \mathcal{A}(\mathsf{pk}); \\ \pi \leftarrow \mathsf{P}(\varrho, \mathsf{pk}, \mathsf{x}, \mathsf{w}) : \mathsf{PARV}(\varrho) = 1 \wedge \mathsf{PKV}(\varrho, \mathsf{pk}) = 1 \wedge \\ ((\mathsf{x}, \mathsf{w}) \not\in \mathscr{R}_\varrho \vee \mathsf{V}(\varrho, \mathsf{pk}, \mathsf{x}, \pi) = 1) \end{array}\right] = 1 \ .$$

(ii) **Computational Quasi-Adaptive Sub-PAR Soundness:** for any $\mathsf{p} \in \mathrm{im}(\mathsf{PGen}(1^\lambda))$, and stateful PPT $\mathcal{A}$,

$$\Pr\left[\begin{array}{l}\varrho \leftarrow \mathcal{A}(\mathsf{p}); (\mathsf{pk}, \mathsf{sk}) \leftarrow \mathsf{KGen}(\varrho); (\mathsf{x}, \pi) \leftarrow \mathcal{A}(\mathsf{pk}) : \\ \mathsf{PARV}(\varrho) = 1 \wedge \mathsf{V}(\varrho, \mathsf{pk}, \mathsf{x}, \pi) = 1 \wedge \neg(\exists \mathsf{w} : \mathscr{R}_\varrho(\mathsf{x}, \mathsf{w}) = 1))\end{array}\right] \approx_\lambda 0 \ .$$

(iii) **Computational Quasi-Adaptive Sub-PAR Knowledge-Soundness:** for every PPT stateful adversary adversary $\mathcal{A}$, there exist a PPT extractor $\mathsf{Ext}_\mathcal{A}$, s.t. for all $\mathsf{p} \in \mathrm{im}(\mathsf{PGen}(1^\lambda))$,

$$\Pr\left[\begin{array}{l}r \leftarrow_\$ \mathsf{RND}_\lambda(\mathcal{A}); \varrho \leftarrow \mathcal{A}(\mathsf{p}; r); (\mathsf{pk}, \mathsf{sk}) \leftarrow \mathsf{KGen}(\varrho); \\ (\mathsf{x}, \pi) \leftarrow \mathcal{A}(\mathsf{pk}; r); \mathsf{w} \leftarrow \mathsf{Ext}_\mathcal{A}(\mathsf{p}, \mathsf{pk}; r) : \mathsf{PARV}(\varrho) = 1 \wedge \\ \mathsf{V}(\varrho, \mathsf{pk}, \mathsf{x}, \pi) = 1 \wedge \mathscr{R}_\varrho(\mathsf{x}, \mathsf{w}) = 0\end{array}\right] \approx_\lambda 0 \ .$$

A knowledge-sound argument system is called an *argument of knowledge.*

(iv) **Statistical Zero Knowledge:** for any λ, $\mathsf{p} \in \mathrm{im}(\mathsf{PGen}(1^\lambda))$, and computationally unbounded adversary $\mathcal{A}$, $|\varepsilon_0^{zk} - \varepsilon_1^{zk}| \approx_\lambda 0$, where $\varepsilon_b^{zk} :=$

$$\Pr\left[\varrho \leftarrow \mathcal{D}_\mathsf{p}; (\mathsf{pk}, \mathsf{sk}) \leftarrow \mathsf{KGen}(\varrho) : \mathcal{A}^{\mathsf{O}_b(\cdot,\cdot)}(\varrho, \mathsf{pk}) = 1 \ \right] \ .$$

The oracle $\mathsf{O}_0(\mathsf{x}, \mathsf{w})$ returns $\perp$ (reject) if $(\mathsf{x}, \mathsf{w}) \notin \mathscr{R}_\varrho$, and otherwise it returns $\mathsf{P}(\varrho, \mathsf{pk}, \mathsf{x}, \mathsf{w})$. Similarly, $\mathsf{O}_1(\mathsf{x}, \mathsf{w})$ returns $\perp$ (reject) if $(\mathsf{x}, \mathsf{w}) \notin \mathscr{R}_\varrho$, and otherwise it returns $\mathsf{Sim}(\varrho, \mathsf{pk}, \mathsf{sk}, \mathsf{x})$.

(v) **Statistical Persistent Zero Knowledge:** for any PPT subverter $\mathcal{C}$, there exists a PPT extractor $\mathsf{Ext}_\mathcal{C}$, s.t. for any λ, $\mathsf{p} \in \mathrm{im}(\mathsf{PGen}(1^\lambda))$, and computationally unbounded adversary $\mathcal{A}$, $|\varepsilon_0^{zk} - \varepsilon_1^{zk}| \approx_\lambda 0$, where

$$\varepsilon_b^{zk} := \Pr\left[\begin{array}{l}r \leftarrow_\$ \mathsf{RND}_\lambda(\mathcal{C}); (\varrho, \mathsf{pk}, \mathsf{aux}) \leftarrow \mathcal{C}(\mathsf{p}; r); \mathsf{sk} \leftarrow \mathsf{Ext}_\mathcal{C}(\mathsf{p}; r) : \\ \mathsf{PARV}(\varrho) = 1 \wedge \mathsf{PKV}(\varrho, \mathsf{pk}) = 1 \wedge \mathcal{A}^{\mathsf{O}_b(\cdot,\cdot)}(\varrho, \mathsf{pk}, \mathsf{aux}) = 1\end{array}\right] \ .$$

The oracle $\mathsf{O}_0(\mathsf{x}, \mathsf{w})$ returns $\perp$ (reject) if $(\mathsf{x}, \mathsf{w}) \notin \mathscr{R}_\varrho$, and otherwise it returns $\mathsf{P}(\varrho, \mathsf{pk}, \mathsf{x}, \mathsf{w})$. Similarly, $\mathsf{O}_1(\mathsf{x}, \mathsf{w})$ returns $\perp$ (reject) if $(\mathsf{x}, \mathsf{w}) \notin \mathscr{R}_\varrho$, and otherwise it returns $\mathsf{Sim}(\varrho, \mathsf{pk}, \mathsf{sk}, \mathsf{x})$.

Π is *statistically no-auxiliary-string*[4] *non-black-box zero knowledge (Sub-ZK)* if it is both statistically zero-knowledge and statistically persistent zero-knowledge.

Knowledge-sound QA-NIZKs are useful in situations where the witness relations $\mathscr{R}_\varrho$ are trivial in the sense that for each x, there exists a w such that $(\mathsf{x}, \mathsf{w}) \in \mathscr{R}_\varrho$. In such cases, one must argue that the prover knows this w. Knowledge-sound QA-NIZK argument systems have applications in shuffles [14] and SNARKs [8,25,37].

In their definition of strong soundness for strong QA-NIZK, Jutla and Roy [29] made the assumption that $\mathcal{C}_\varrho$ also returns td_ϱ. This assumption reminds the AGM [16], where in the security proofs, the adversary is assumed to output

[4] Auxiliary-string non-black-box ZK [21] means that definitions hold even if any $\mathsf{aux} \in \{0,1\}^{\mathsf{poly}(\lambda)}$ is given as an additional input to $\mathcal{A}$ and $\mathcal{C}_\mathsf{pk}$ (and $\mathsf{Ext}_\mathcal{C}$).

a part of her secret state but might be stronger depending on the definition of $\mathcal{D}_\mathsf{p}$. Thus, one should not make such an assumption per se but prove (say, in the AGM) that it holds. In several recent reinterpretations of AGM [37], one has reworded AGM by requiring the existence of an extractor that returns the secret state. In our Sub-PAR (knowledge-)soundness definition, we require that $\mathsf{PARV}(\varrho) = 1$ (thus, $\varrho \in \mathrm{im}(\mathcal{D}_\mathsf{p})$ and a td_ϱ exists). We do not require td_ϱ can be extracted; we only require that w can be extracted. In our security proof, the extractor of w will first extract td_ϱ by using a DL oracle; we prove knowledge-soundness under a non-falsifiable assumption (more precisely, under the $\mathrm{SDL}^{\mathrm{dl}}$ assumption that states that solving SDL is intractable even if the adversary is given non-adaptive access to a DL oracle, see Fig. 6).

More precisely, in the case of the *concrete construction* of Π_bpk, extraction of td_ϱ is needed since the Π_kw argument system [31] (and thus also the Π_bpk argument system in Sect. 5) is only sound if $\mathcal{D}_\mathsf{p}$ is witness-sampleable. In the soundness proof in [31], one obtains td_ϱ from the honest ϱ-creator. In the Sub-PAR knowledge-soundness proof in Sect. 5, we extract td_ϱ from the malicious ϱ-creator $\mathcal{A}$ and then use td_ϱ to extract w. However, we use the DL oracle to extract td_ϱ and thus will need not have to rely on witness-sampleability of $\mathcal{D}_\mathsf{p}$.

We assume that a single subverter $\mathcal{C}$ produces ϱ and pk in the case of Sub-ZK, and the extractor will get access to the code of $\mathcal{C}$ and its inputs and random coins. The extractor never works with probability 1 since $\mathcal{C}$ can randomly sample (with a non-zero but negligible probability) a well-formed pk. However, if it works, then in our constructions, the simulation will be perfect. For the sake of simplicity, we will not formalize this as perfect zero-knowledge. (One reason for this is that differently from [2], the secret key extracted by $\mathsf{Ext}_\mathcal{C}$ is not unique in our case; see discussion in Sect. 5.)

The existence of PKV is not needed in the CRS model, assuming the CRS creator is trusted by the prover, and thus PKV was not included in the prior QA-NIZK definitions. Since soundness is proved in the case pk is chosen correctly (by the verifier or a trusted third party, trusted by her), V does not need to execute PKV. However, PKV should be run by P. Similarly, the existence of PARV is not needed in the CRS model; the algorithm PARV needs to be run both by P and V. The simulator is only required to simulate correctly in the case PARV accepts ϱ and PKV accepts pk.

For Sub-ZK, we require that both standard zero-knowledge (with trusted ϱ and pk generators) and persistent zero-knowledge (with possibly subverted ϱ and pk) generators hold. The reason behind requiring both is subtle and will be explained in Sect. 4. Very briefly, since one considers a single subverter $\mathcal{C}$ that creates both ϱ and pk, persistent zero-knowledge leaves one vulnerable against the subverter who just sets $\mathsf{sk} \leftarrow \mathsf{td}_\varrho$. While this attack is not possible in the case of all QA-NIZKs, as we show in Sect. 4, one can design a QA-NIZK argument system that is persistent zero-knowledge but not standard zero-knowledge. Intuitively, requiring that the same simulator Sim also works without the knowledge of td_ϱ makes it possible to avoid such pathological cases. However, it means that persistent zero-knowledge is not a strictly stronger notion than the standard zero-knowledge, and one requires both to obtain Sub-ZK.

Comparison to Earlier Sub-ZK Definitions. Subversion-security was defined by Bellare *et al.* [4] for the CRS model; further CRS-model subversion-security definitions were given in [2,15]. As proven in [4], one cannot achieve Sub-SND (soundness even if the CRS was generated maliciously) and non-subversion zero knowledge at the same time. Thus, subsequent efforts have concentrated on achieving either Sub-SND and witness-indistinguishability [4], subversion knowledge-soundness and witness-indistinguishability [17], or Sub-ZK (zero knowledge in the case the CRS was generated maliciously) and soundness [2,4,15]. In the latter case, the CRS is trusted by the verifier V while (following the definitions of [2]) the prover checks that the CRS is well-formed by using a publicly available algorithm. Thus, Sub-ZK in the CRS model is the same as zero-knowledge in the BPK model: the CRS has to be trusted by (or, even chosen by) V and hence can be equal to the public key of an entity trusted by V (or of V herself). Since black-box NIZK [38] and even auxiliary-string non-black-box NIZK [21] in the BPK model is impossible, one has to define no-auxiliary-string non-black-box zero knowledge (Sub-ZK) as above. Bellare *et al.* [4] motivated not incorporating auxiliary strings to the definition of Sub-ZK by known impossibility results. We will formalize this (folklore, see [42] for discussion) impossibility result as the following straightforward lemma.

Lemma 1. *Auxiliary-string non-black-box NIZK in the BPK model is only possible for languages in* BPP.

Proof. The notions of (no-)auxiliary-string and (non-)-black-box zero-knowledge were defined by Goldreich and Oren [21] who proved that auxiliary-string (even non-black-box) zero-knowledge argument systems for languages outside of BPP require at least three messages in the plain model. An auxiliary-string (non-black-box) NIZK argument system in the BPK model can be interpreted as a two-message auxiliary-string (non-black-box) zero-knowledge argument system in the plain model, where the verifier creates BPK and sends it as her first message. Thus, an auxiliary-string NIZK argument system for languages outside of BPP would contradict the impossibility result of [21]. □

Auxiliary-input zero-knowledge is usually used to achieve sequential composition of interactive zero-knowledge protocols, [21]. Sub-ZK guarantees sequential security in the case of NIZK, see [2] for a proof. In particular, the main result of [2,15], reformulated in our language, is that there exist computationally knowledge-sound Sub-ZK zk-SNARKs for NP in the BPK model.

In the case of QA-NIZKs, one has to deal with two parameters, ϱ (the language parameter) and pk (the public key). As shown in [29] (updated version from September 2018), one can achieve both soundness and zero-knowledge in the case when ϱ is subverted but pk is honestly chosen. In the persistent zero-knowledge definition, we allow for subverted pk and ϱ. Due to the impossibility result of [4], we are not aiming to achieve Sub-SND. Thus, in the definition of soundness, we assume that pk is honestly generated.

$\mathsf{KGen}([\boldsymbol{M}]_1 \in \mathbb{G}_1^{n\times m})$: $\boldsymbol{A} \leftarrow_{\$} \mathcal{D}_k$; $\boldsymbol{K} \leftarrow_{\$} \mathbb{Z}_p^{n\times k}$; $\boldsymbol{C} \leftarrow \boldsymbol{K}\bar{\boldsymbol{A}} \in \mathbb{Z}_p^{n\times k}$; $[\boldsymbol{P}]_1 \leftarrow [\boldsymbol{M}]_1^\top \boldsymbol{K} \in \mathbb{Z}_p^{m\times k}$; $\mathsf{pk} \leftarrow ([\bar{\boldsymbol{A}}, \boldsymbol{C}]_2, [\boldsymbol{P}]_1)$; $\mathsf{sk} \leftarrow \boldsymbol{K}$; return $(\mathsf{pk}, \mathsf{sk})$;
$\mathsf{P}([\boldsymbol{M}]_1, \mathsf{pk}, [\boldsymbol{y}]_1, \boldsymbol{w})$: return $[\boldsymbol{\pi}]_1 \leftarrow [\boldsymbol{P}]_1^\top \boldsymbol{w} \in \mathbb{G}_1^k$;
$\mathsf{Sim}([\boldsymbol{M}]_1, \mathsf{pk}, \mathsf{sk}, [\boldsymbol{y}]_1)$: return $[\boldsymbol{\pi}]_1 \leftarrow \boldsymbol{K}^\top [\boldsymbol{y}]_1 \in \mathbb{G}_1^k$;
$\mathsf{V}([\boldsymbol{M}]_1, \mathsf{pk}, [\boldsymbol{y}]_1, [\boldsymbol{\pi}]_1)$: check that $[\boldsymbol{y}]_1^\top [\boldsymbol{C}]_2 = [\boldsymbol{\pi}]_1^\top [\bar{\boldsymbol{A}}]_2$;

Fig. 1. Kiltz-Wee QA-NIZK argument system Π_{kw} for $[\boldsymbol{y}]_1 = [\boldsymbol{M}]_1 \boldsymbol{w}$

Language of Linear Subspaces and Kiltz-Wee QA-NIZK. An important application of QA-NIZK is in the case of the following language. Assume we need to show that $[\boldsymbol{y}]_1 \in \text{colspace}([\boldsymbol{M}]_1)$, where $[\boldsymbol{M}]_1$ is sampled from a distribution $\mathcal{D}_{\mathsf{p}}$ over $\mathbb{G}_1^{n\times m}$. We assume, following [28], that (n, m) is implicitly fixed by $\mathcal{D}_{\mathsf{p}}$. That is, a QA-NIZK for linear subspaces handles languages

$$\mathscr{L}_{[\boldsymbol{M}]_1} = \left\{ [\boldsymbol{y}]_1 \in \mathbb{G}_1^n : \exists \boldsymbol{w} \in \mathbb{Z}_p^m \text{ s.t. } \boldsymbol{y} = \boldsymbol{M}\boldsymbol{w} \right\} .$$

The corresponding relation is defined as $\mathscr{R}_{[\boldsymbol{M}]_1} = \{([\boldsymbol{y}]_1, \boldsymbol{w}) \in \mathbb{G}_1^n \times \mathbb{Z}_p^m : \boldsymbol{y} = \boldsymbol{M}\boldsymbol{w}\}$. This language is useful in many applications, [8,28]. As a typical application, let $[\boldsymbol{M}]_1 = [1, \mathsf{sk}]_1^\top$ be a public key of the Elgamal cryptosystem; then ciphertext $[\boldsymbol{y}]_1 \in \mathscr{L}_{[\boldsymbol{M}]_1}$ iff it encrypts 0. Here, $[\boldsymbol{M}]_1$ comes from a KerMDH-hard witness-sampleable distribution $\mathcal{D}_{\mathsf{p}}$.

The most efficient known QA-NIZK for linear subspaces in the CRS model was proposed by Kiltz and Wee [31]. In particular, they proposed a QA-NIZK Π_{kw} that assumes that the parameter $\varrho = [\boldsymbol{M}]_1 \in \mathbb{G}_1^{n\times m}$ is sampled from a witness-sampleable distribution $\mathcal{D}_{\mathsf{p}}$. Π_{kw} results in the argument that consists of k group elements, where k is the parameter ($k = 1$ being usually sufficient in the case of asymmetric pairings) related to the underlying KerMDH distribution. More precisely, given $n > m$, the Kiltz-Wee QA-NIZK is computationally quasi-adaptively sound under the $\mathcal{D}_k$-KerMDH$_{\mathbb{G}_1}$ assumption relative to PGen, [31]. Importantly, Π_{kw} is significantly more efficient than the Groth-Sahai NIZK for the same language. For the sake of completeness, Fig. 1 describes the Kiltz-Wee QA-NIZK argument system Π_{kw} for linear subspaces in the CRS model.

Some Applications of QA-NIZK in the BPK Model. The simplest example application is that of UC-commitments from [28], where a trusted third party generates a commitment key ϱ together with a QA-NIZK public key pk, and P opens the commitments later by disclosing a QA-NIZK argument of proper commitment under the commitment key ϱ. Here, ϱ should not be generated by P (who could then equivocate) or by V (who could then extract the message). However, pk can be generated by V. This allows one, securely generated ϱ, to be used in many applications, from UC-commitments to identity-based encryption. In each such application, a trusted authority trusted by V (e.g., V herself) can create her pk that takes the particularities of that application into account.

Another, arguably much more important application, is the use of Sub-ZK QA-NIZKs in the construction of Sub-ZK SNARKs. Several recent papers

[8,14,25,37] have used QA-NIZKs for subspace language to construct SNARKs. In these cases, one proves the membership in the trivial full vector space under knowledge assumption, resulting in a statement that (say) the argument belongs to the span of certain CRS elements only like in [37] or that two commitments that possibly use different commitment keys commit to the same vectors like in [14]. To obtain Sub-ZK SNARKs (under a knowledge assumption), in such cases also the QA-NIZK has to be Sub-ZK (under a knowledge assumption).

In many other applications, it is desirable that zero-knowledge holds even if both ϱ and pk both are chosen by V (or by possibly different parties, neither of which is trusted by P). The above Sub-ZK definitions cover this more realistic scenario; in addition, they do not require V to trust ϱ. One such application is in the LegoSNARK framework by Campanelli *et al.* [8]. LegoSNARK uses QA-NIZK for linear subspace to build Commit-and-Prove (CP) SNARKs, which can be securely and efficiently combined together, creating a complex proof system able to perform well even for heterogeneous instance representation. Unfortunately, most of the modern zk-SNARKs are not CP-SNARKs. Hence [8] proposed a QA-NIZK-based transformation that builds them using any Commit-Carrying (CC) SNARK; the latter are much more common, e.g., the most efficient zk-SNARK for QAP by Groth [27] is a CC-SNARK. Despite that, Campanelli *et al.* propose a number of CP-SNARKs that are QA-NIZK-based.

4 Persistent Zero-Knowledge $\not\Rightarrow$ Zero-Knowledge

Intuitively, it seems that persistent zero-knowledge follows from the standard zero-knowledge since the set of all possible PPT subverters $\mathcal{C}$ also includes honest algorithms. However, this intuition is wrong. We will next show that one can construct pathological QA-NIZK argument systems that achieve persistent zero-knowledge, but do not satisfy the usual definition of zero-knowledge and actually leak some information about the witness.

Let us consider a slight variation of the subspace language where $\varrho = ([\boldsymbol{M}]_1, [\boldsymbol{M}]_2)$[5] and the statement is that $[\boldsymbol{y}]_1$ belongs to the subspace spanned by the matrix $[\boldsymbol{M}]_1$. Moreover, for simplicity let us take $\boldsymbol{M} \leftarrow_{\$} \mathbb{Z}_p^{2\times 1}$. Consider the QA-NIZK argument system (*a leaky QA-NIZK*) in Fig. 2. It has secret keys from the same set $\mathbb{Z}_p^{2\times 1}$, and thus, $\boldsymbol{M}$ can pass as a secret key. *Leaky QA-NIZK* does not have a public key, the argument is simply $[\pi]_1 = [w]_1$, and the verification is done by checking that $[\pi]_1^\top [\boldsymbol{M}]_2^\top = [\boldsymbol{M}w]_1^\top [1]_2 = [\boldsymbol{y}]_1^\top [1]_2$. It is not standard zero-knowledge since the simulator only knows $[\boldsymbol{M}]_1$, $[\boldsymbol{M}]_2$, and $[\boldsymbol{y}]_1 = [M_1 w, M_2 w]_1$ and outputting $[w]_1$ breaks the following symmetric computational Diffie-Hellman (CDH) assumption: given input $([1, a, b]_1, [1, a, b]_2)$ for $a \leftarrow_{\$} \mathbb{Z}_p^*$, $b \leftarrow_{\$} \mathbb{Z}_p$, it is difficult to compute $[ab]_1$. To see this, let us suppose that the symmetric CDH challenge is $[1, a, b]_1$, $[1, a, b]_2$ for $a \leftarrow_{\$} \mathbb{Z}_p^*$, $b \leftarrow_{\$} \mathbb{Z}_p$. We denote $M_1 = 1/a$, $w = b$, $M_2 = M_2' M_1 = M_2'/a$ where $M_2' \leftarrow_{\$} \mathbb{Z}_p$. We also reset

[5] Even if ϱ is maliciously created, one can efficiently check whether it has the correct form. More precisely, given $\varrho = ([\boldsymbol{M}]_1, [\boldsymbol{M}']_2)$, one can assure that $\boldsymbol{M} = \boldsymbol{M}'$ by checking $[\boldsymbol{M}]_1 [1]_2 = [1]_1 [\boldsymbol{M}']_1$ and accepting only when that is the case.

$\mathcal{D}_{\mathsf{p}}$: $\boldsymbol{M} \leftarrow_{\$} \mathbb{Z}_p^{2\times 1}$; **return** $\varrho = ([\boldsymbol{M}]_1, [\boldsymbol{M}]_2)$;
$\mathsf{KGen}(\varrho)$: **return** $(\mathsf{pk} \leftarrow \perp, \mathsf{sk} \leftarrow \mathbb{Z}_p^{2\times 1})$;
$\mathsf{Ext}_{\mathcal{C}}(\mathsf{aux}_\varrho; r)$: Extract $\mathsf{sk} = (M_1, M_2)^\top$ by using BDHKE; **return** sk;
$\mathsf{P}(\varrho, \mathsf{pk}, [\boldsymbol{y}]_1, w)$: **return** $[\pi]_1 \leftarrow [w]_1 \in \mathbb{G}_1^1$;
$\mathsf{Sim}(\varrho, \mathsf{pk}, \mathsf{sk}, [\boldsymbol{y}]_1)$: **if** $M_1^{-1}[y_1]_1 \neq M_2^{-1}[y_2]_1$ **then return** $\perp$; **else return** $[\pi]_1 \leftarrow M_1^{-1}[y_1]_1 \in \mathbb{G}_1^1$; **fi**
$\mathsf{V}(\varrho, \mathsf{pk}, [\boldsymbol{y}]_1, [\pi]_1)$: check that $[\boldsymbol{y}]_1^\top [1]_2 = [\pi]_1^\top [\boldsymbol{M}]_2^\top$;
$\mathsf{PKV}(\varrho, \mathsf{pk})$: check that $\mathsf{pk} = \perp$;

Fig. 2. A contrived leaky subspace QA-NIZK where $\varrho = ([\boldsymbol{M}]_1, [\boldsymbol{M}]_2)$

generators of $\mathbb{G}_1$ and $\mathbb{G}_2$ to be $[g]_1 = [a]_1$ and $[g]_2 = [a]_2$. Now if such simulator existed, we could run it with input $[M_1 g, M_2 g, M_1 wg, M_2 wg]_1 = [1, M_2', b, M_2' b]_1$, $[M_1 g, M_2 g]_2 = [1, M_2']_2$ and it would output $[wg]_1 = [ba]_1$; this would break the CDH assumption.

Surprisingly, simulation is possible (under a knowledge assumption) if we try to prove persistent zero-knowledge. We remind that the Bilinear Diffie-Hellman Knowledge of Exponent (BDHKE) [2] assumption says that if a PPT adversary $\mathcal{A}(\mathsf{p})$ outputs $([x]_1, [x]_2)$ on random coins r, then there exists an extractor that extracts x with an overwhelming probability given the same random coins r. Thus, assuming BDHKE and because $\mathsf{Ext}_{\mathcal{C}}$ is given access to the random coins of $\mathcal{C}$, $\mathsf{Ext}_{\mathcal{C}}$ can extract $\boldsymbol{M}$ and provide it to the simulator as sk. The simulator then computes $[w]_1 = M_1^{-1}[y_1]_1$.

We could divide $\mathcal{C}$ into $\mathcal{C}_\varrho$, which generates ϱ, and $\mathcal{C}_{\mathsf{pk}}$, which generates pk, such that the extractor only gets random coins of $\mathcal{C}_{\mathsf{pk}}$. This would make it impossible to extract $\boldsymbol{M}$. However, this will not work since we cannot exclude communication between $\mathcal{C}_\varrho$ and $\mathcal{C}_{\mathsf{pk}}$, e.g., $\mathcal{C}_\varrho$ can compute pk herself and send it to $\mathcal{C}_{\mathsf{pk}}$. $\mathcal{C}_{\mathsf{pk}}$ outputs pk without having any knowledge of sk, making extracting sk impossible.

Because of that, we adopted a different solution: namely, we require that *a Sub-ZK QA-NIZK argument system must satisfy both standard zero-knowledge and persistent zero-knowledge with respect to the same simulator.* This solution rules out the intuitively insecure arguments like the one in Fig. 2.

5 Construction of a QA-NIZK in the BPK Model

In this section, we will show that if the membership of $[\bar{\boldsymbol{A}}]_2$ in $\mathcal{D}_k$ can be efficiently verified, then a slight variant Π_{bpk} of the Kiltz-Wee QA-NIZK Π_{kw} for linear subspaces [31] is secure (including Sub-ZK) in the BPK model. More precisely, we say that the distribution $\mathcal{D}_k$ is *efficiently verifiable*, if there exists an algorithm $\mathsf{MATV}([\bar{\boldsymbol{A}}]_2)$ that outputs 1 if $\bar{\boldsymbol{A}}$ is invertible (recall that we assume that the matrix distribution is robust) and well-formed with respect to $\mathcal{D}_k$ and otherwise outputs 0. Clearly, the distributions $\mathcal{D}_1$, $\mathcal{L}_k$, $\mathcal{IL}_k$, $\mathcal{C}_k$, and $\mathcal{SC}_k$ (for any k) are verifiable, as can be seen in Fig. 3, while the verification whether $[\bar{\boldsymbol{A}}]_2$ is

$\mathsf{MATV}([\bar{\boldsymbol{A}}]_2)$ // $\mathcal{D}_k \in \{\mathcal{L}_k, \mathcal{IL}_k, \mathcal{C}_k, \mathcal{SC}_k\}$

check $[a_{11}]_2 \neq [0]_2 \wedge \ldots \wedge [a_{kk}]_2 \neq [0]_2$;
if $\mathcal{D}_k = \mathcal{L}_k$ **then** check $i \neq j \Rightarrow [a_{i,j}]_2 = [0]_2$;
elseif $\mathcal{D}_k = \mathcal{IL}_k$ **then** check $i \neq j \Rightarrow [a_{ij}]_2 = [0]_2; \forall i, [a_{i,i}]_2 = [a_{1,1}]_2 + [i-1]_2$;
elseif $\mathcal{D}_k = \mathcal{C}_k$ **then** check $i \notin \{j, j+1\} \Rightarrow [a_{ij}]_2 = [0]_2; \forall i, [a_{i+1,i}]_2 = [1]_2$;
elseif $\mathcal{D}_k = \mathcal{SC}_k$ **then** check $i \notin \{j, j+1\} \Rightarrow [a_{ij}]_2 = [0]_2$;
  $\forall i \, ([a_{i+1,i}]_2 = [1]_2 \wedge [a_{ii}]_2 = [a_{11}]_2)$; **fi**
return 1 if all checks pass and 0 otherwise;

Fig. 3. Auxiliary procedure MATV for $\mathcal{D}_k \in \{\mathcal{L}_k, \mathcal{IL}_k, \mathcal{C}_k, \mathcal{SC}_k\}$.

invertible is intractable for the distribution $\mathcal{U}_k$ if $k > 1$. Indeed, if $k = 2$ then in the latter case, one needs to test if $a_{11}a_{22} - a_{12}a_{21} = 0$, given only $[\bar{\boldsymbol{A}}]_2$; the case $k > 2$ is even more complicated. Nevertheless, we show that a slightly modified version of our construction works with the distribution $\mathcal{D}_2$.

Recall that in the BPK model, the public key pk (corresponds to the CRS in Π_{kw}) belongs either to the verifier V or to a party trusted by V. One proves computational soundness in the setting where V trusts that pk is honestly generated, i.e., that the corresponding sk is secret and pk is well-formed. Since pk is not trusted by the prover P, one proves Sub-ZK in the case of a maliciously generated pk. We assume that $[\boldsymbol{M}]_1$ is sampled by a PPT subverter, and moreover, the simulator does not know the corresponding witness $\boldsymbol{M}$ or any function of $\boldsymbol{M}$ not efficiently computable from $[\boldsymbol{M}]_1$.

To modify Π_{kw} so that it would be secure in the BPK model instead of the CRS model, the most straightforward idea is to divide pk into $\mathsf{pk}^{\mathsf{zk}} = [\boldsymbol{P}]_1$ (the part of pk that is used by P and thus intuitively needed to guarantee zero knowledge) and $\mathsf{pk}^{\mathsf{snd}} = [\bar{\boldsymbol{A}}, \boldsymbol{C}]_2$ (the part of pk is used by V and thus intuitively needed to guarantee soundness). Thus, P (resp., V) has to be assured that $\mathsf{pk}^{\mathsf{zk}}$ (resp., $\mathsf{pk}^{\mathsf{snd}}$) is generated honestly. Hence, one could use $\mathsf{pk}^{\mathsf{zk}}_{\mathsf{P}}$ from P's public key and $\mathsf{pk}^{\mathsf{snd}}_{\mathsf{V}}$ from V's public key to create an argument. However, it is not clear how to do this since both $\mathsf{pk}^{\mathsf{snd}}_{\mathsf{V}}$ and $\mathsf{pk}^{\mathsf{zk}}_{\mathsf{P}}$ depend on the same secret $\boldsymbol{K}$. Moreover, in this case, both P and V have public keys while we want to have a situation, common in the BPK model, where only V has a public key.

Instead, we assume that V's public key pk is equal to the whole CRS and then construct a public-key verification algorithm PKV. For PKV to be efficient in the case $\mathcal{D}_k$ is not efficiently verifiable, we need to add some new elements (collectively denoted as $\mathsf{pk}^{\mathsf{pkv}}$) to pk. Figure 4 describes the new QA-NIZK Π_{bpk}. The construction of PKV will be explained in Sect. 6.

We will prove that in the BPK model, Π_{bpk} is statistically persistent zero-knowledge under a novel non-falsifiable assumption, computationally quasi-adaptively Sub-PAR sound under another novel non-falsifiable assumption, and (if $\boldsymbol{M}$ has full rank) computationally quasi-adaptively Sub-PAR knowledge-sound under two non-falsifiable assumptions, one of which is novel. Some of the new non-falsifiable assumptions do not belong to the family of knowledge

$\mathsf{KGen}(\varrho := [\boldsymbol{M}]_1 \in \mathbb{G}_1^{n\times m})$: $\boldsymbol{A} \leftarrow_{\$} \mathcal{D}_k$; $\boldsymbol{K} \leftarrow_{\$} \mathbb{Z}_p^{n\times k}$; $[\boldsymbol{C}]_2 \leftarrow [\boldsymbol{K}\bar{\boldsymbol{A}}]_2 \in \mathbb{G}_2^{n\times k}$; $[\boldsymbol{P}]_1 \leftarrow [\boldsymbol{M}]_1^\top \boldsymbol{K} \in \mathbb{G}_1^{m\times k}$;
  if $\mathcal{D}_k$ is efficiently verifiable **then** $\mathsf{pk}^{\mathsf{pkv}} \leftarrow \epsilon$; **elseif** $\mathcal{D}_k = \mathcal{U}_2$ **then** $\mathsf{pk}^{\mathsf{pkv}} \leftarrow [a_{11}, a_{12}]_1$; **fi** ; $\mathsf{pk}^{\mathsf{snd}} \leftarrow [\bar{\boldsymbol{A}}, \boldsymbol{C}]_2$; $\mathsf{pk}^{\mathsf{zk}} \leftarrow [\boldsymbol{P}]_1$; $\mathsf{pk} \leftarrow (\mathsf{pk}^{\mathsf{snd}}, \mathsf{pk}^{\mathsf{zk}}, \mathsf{pk}^{\mathsf{pkv}})$; $\mathsf{sk} \leftarrow \boldsymbol{K}$;
  return $(\mathsf{pk}, \mathsf{sk})$;
$\mathsf{P}([\boldsymbol{M}]_1, \mathsf{pk}, [\boldsymbol{y}]_1, \boldsymbol{w})$: return $[\boldsymbol{\pi}]_1 \leftarrow [\boldsymbol{P}]_1^\top \boldsymbol{w} \in \mathbb{G}_1^k$;
$\mathsf{Sim}([\boldsymbol{M}]_1, \mathsf{pk}, \mathsf{sk}, [\boldsymbol{y}]_1)$: // sk is extracted by using a knowledge assumption;
  return $[\boldsymbol{\pi}]_1 \leftarrow \boldsymbol{K}^\top [\boldsymbol{y}]_1 \in \mathbb{G}_1^k$;
$\mathsf{V}([\boldsymbol{M}]_1, \mathsf{pk}, [\boldsymbol{y}]_1, [\boldsymbol{\pi}]_1)$: check that $[\boldsymbol{y}]_1^\top [\boldsymbol{C}]_2 = [\boldsymbol{\pi}]_1^\top [\bar{\boldsymbol{A}}]_2$; // $\in \mathbb{G}_T^{1\times k}$
$\mathsf{PKV}([\boldsymbol{M}]_1, \mathsf{pk})$: Return 1 only if the following checks all succeed:
  $\mathsf{pk} = (\mathsf{pk}^{\mathsf{snd}}, \mathsf{pk}^{\mathsf{zk}}, \mathsf{pk}^{\mathsf{pkv}}) \wedge \mathsf{pk}^{\mathsf{snd}} = [\bar{\boldsymbol{A}}, \boldsymbol{C}]_2 \wedge \mathsf{pk}^{\mathsf{zk}} = [\boldsymbol{P}]_1$;
  $[\boldsymbol{P}]_1 \in \mathbb{G}_1^{m\times k} \wedge [\bar{\boldsymbol{A}}]_2 \in \mathbb{G}_2^{k\times k} \wedge [\boldsymbol{C}]_2 \in \mathbb{G}_2^{n\times k}$;
  (∗) $[\boldsymbol{M}]_1^\top [\boldsymbol{C}]_2 = [\boldsymbol{P}]_1 [\bar{\boldsymbol{A}}]_2$;
  if $\mathcal{D}_k$ is efficiently verifiable **then** $\mathsf{MATV}([\bar{\boldsymbol{A}}]_2)$;
  else check $\mathsf{pk}^{\mathsf{pkv}} = [a_{11}^*, a_{12}^*]_1 \in \mathbb{G}_1^{1\times 2} \wedge [a_{11}^*]_1[1]_2 = [1]_1[a_{11}]_2 \wedge [a_{12}^*]_1[1]_2 = [1]_1[a_{12}]_2 \wedge [a_{11}^*]_1[a_{22}]_2 - [a_{12}^*]_1[a_{21}]_2 \neq [0]_T$; **fi**

Fig. 4. Sub-ZK QA-NIZK Π_{bpk} for $[\boldsymbol{y}]_1 = [\boldsymbol{M}]_1 \boldsymbol{w}$ in the BPK model, where either (1) $\mathcal{D}_k$ is efficiently verifiable or (2) $\mathcal{D}_k = \mathcal{U}_2$.

assumptions, which is an interesting result by itself. We will study new assumptions in Sect. 6, before stating and proving the security of Π_{bpk} in Sect. 7.

6 New Non-falsifiable Assumptions

We will next motivate and define the new assumptions. We will also prove the security of KWKE and SKWKE under the HAK assumptions.

KWKE and SKWKE Assumptions. In the Sub-ZK proof, we will need two different (tautological) knowledge assumptions, KWKE (Kiltz-Wee Knowledge of Exponent), and SKWKE (Strong Kiltz-Wee Knowledge of Exponent). Similarly to Sub-ZK SNARKs [2,15], the knowledge assumption is needed to equip the simulator Sim of Π_{kw} with the correct secret key $\mathsf{sk} = \boldsymbol{K}$.

The KWKE assumption guarantees that one can extract a secret key $\mathsf{sk} = \boldsymbol{K}$ from which one can compute $\mathsf{pk}^{\mathsf{zk}} = [\boldsymbol{P}]_1$ but not necessarily $\mathsf{pk}^{\mathsf{snd}}$. Since $\mathsf{pk}^{\mathsf{zk}}$ does not fix $\boldsymbol{K}$ uniquely, KWKE extracts one possible $\boldsymbol{K}$. Since for achieving Sub-ZK, it is not needed that $\mathsf{pk}^{\mathsf{snd}}$ can be computed from sk, KWKE is sufficient. To argue that KWKE is a reasonable knowledge assumption, we prove that it holds under a hash-algebraic knowledge assumption.

We also introduce a stronger knowledge assumption SKWKE that allows extracting the *unique* secret key $\boldsymbol{K}$ that was used to generate the *whole* public key pk. We prove that SKWKE holds under a HAK and a WKerMDH assumption, given that $\mathcal{D}_k$ is a WKerMDH-hard distribution. (Here, WKerMDH is a weaker variant of the well-known KerMDH distribution.) The assumption of WKerMDH-hardness often holds in practice, e.g., when ϱ corresponds to a randomly chosen public key of a cryptosystem or a commitment scheme (see Sect. 3

for an example). After that, we will prove that Π_{bpk} is Sub-ZK under either KWKE or SKWKE; in the latter case, we additionally get a guarantee that the public key is correctly formed.

We will now define the new knowledge assumptions needed in the Sub-ZK proof. In KWKE, we assume that if $\mathcal{A}$ outputs a ϱ accepted by PARV and a pk accepted by PKV, then there exists an extractor $\mathsf{Ext}_{\mathcal{A}}$ who, knowing the secret coins of $\mathcal{A}$, returns a secret key $\boldsymbol{K}$ that *could* have been used to compute $\mathsf{pk}^{\mathsf{zk}}$. SKWKE will additionally guarantee that the same $\boldsymbol{K}$ was used to compute $\mathsf{pk}^{\mathsf{snd}}$.

Definition 1. *Fix $k \geq 1$, $n > m \geq 1$, and a distribution $\mathcal{D}_k$. Let* PKV *be as in Fig. 4. Then $(\mathcal{D}_{\mathsf{p}}, k, \mathcal{D}_k)$-KWKE$_{\mathbb{G}_1}$ (resp., $\boxed{(\mathcal{D}_{\mathsf{p}}, k, \mathcal{D}_k)\text{-SKWKE}_{\mathbb{G}_1}}$) holds relative to* PGen *if for any $\mathsf{p} \in \mathrm{im}(\mathsf{PGen}(1^\lambda))$ and PPT adversary $\mathcal{A}$, there exists a PPT extractor $\mathsf{Ext}_{\mathcal{A}}$, s.t. $\mathsf{Adv}^{\boxed{\mathsf{s}}\mathsf{kwke}}_{\mathcal{D}_{\mathsf{p}},k,\mathcal{D}_k,\mathbb{G}_1,\mathsf{PGen},\mathcal{A},\mathsf{Ext}_{\mathcal{A}}}(\lambda) :=$*

$$\Pr\left[\begin{array}{l} r \leftarrow_{\$} \mathsf{RND}_\lambda(\mathcal{A}); (\varrho := [\boldsymbol{M}]_1, \mathsf{pk}) \leftarrow \mathcal{A}(\mathsf{p}; r); \boldsymbol{K} \leftarrow \mathsf{Ext}_{\mathcal{A}}(\mathsf{p}; r) : \\ \mathsf{pk} = ([\bar{\boldsymbol{A}}, \boldsymbol{C}]_2, [\boldsymbol{P}]_1, \mathsf{pk}^{\mathsf{pkv}}) \wedge \mathsf{PARV}([\boldsymbol{M}]_1) = 1 \wedge \\ \mathsf{PKV}([\boldsymbol{M}]_1, \mathsf{pk}) = 1 \wedge (\boldsymbol{P} \neq \boldsymbol{M}^\top \boldsymbol{K} \boxed{\vee \boldsymbol{C} \neq \boldsymbol{K}\bar{\boldsymbol{A}}}) \end{array}\right] \approx_\lambda 0 \ .$$

Here, the $\boxed{\textit{boxed}}$ part is only present in the definition of SKWKE.

In Theorem 1, we also need the following "weak KerMDH" assumption.

Definition 2. *$\mathcal{D}_{\ell k}$-WKerMDH$_{\mathbb{G}_1}$ holds relative to* PGen, *if for any PPT $\mathcal{A}$,* $\Pr[\mathsf{p} \leftarrow \mathsf{PGen}(1^\lambda); \boldsymbol{A} \leftarrow_{\$} \mathcal{D}_{\ell k}; \boldsymbol{c} \leftarrow \mathcal{A}(\mathsf{p}, [\boldsymbol{A}]_1) : \boldsymbol{A}^\top \boldsymbol{c} = \boldsymbol{0}_k \wedge \boldsymbol{c} \neq \boldsymbol{0}_\ell] \approx_\lambda 0$.

Clearly, $\mathcal{D}_{\ell k}$-WKerMDH$_{\mathbb{G}_1}$ is not stronger and it is ostensibly weaker than $\mathcal{D}_{\ell k}$-KerMDH$_{\mathbb{G}_1}$ since computing $\boldsymbol{c}$ may be more complicated than computing $[\boldsymbol{c}]_2$. (Although, it is easy to show that $\mathcal{D}_k$-KerMDH follows from $\mathcal{D}_k$-HAK and $\mathcal{D}_k$-WKerMDH.) The Discrete Logarithm (DL) assumption is a classical example of WKerMDH (consider matrices $\boldsymbol{A} = \left(\begin{smallmatrix} a \\ -1 \end{smallmatrix}\right)$ for $a \leftarrow_{\$} \mathbb{Z}_p$). In the case of say $\mathcal{SC}_k$, the non-trivial co-kernel element $\boldsymbol{c}$ has to satisfy $c_2 = -ac_1$ which enables to recover a; thus, $\mathcal{SC}_k$-WKerMDH is secure under the DL assumption. Similarly, in the case of $\mathcal{C}_k$, $c_2 = -a_1 c_1$.

Next, we will prove that KWKE (resp., SKWKE) holds under the $\mathcal{D}_k$-HAK (resp., $\mathcal{D}_k$-HAK and $\mathcal{D}_{\mathsf{p}}$-WKerMDH) assumption. Note that the use of WKerMDH, and thus of SKWKE, is questionable if $\mathcal{C}_\varrho$ is malicious; nevertheless, we consider this case for the sake of completeness.

Theorem 1 (Security of KWKE and SKWKE). *Assume that either $\mathcal{D}_k$ is efficiently verifiable or $\mathcal{D}_k = \mathcal{U}_2$. Assume $k/p \approx_\lambda 0$. Then*

(i) $(\mathcal{D}_{\mathsf{p}}, k, \mathcal{D}_k)$-KWKE$_{\mathbb{G}_1}$ holds under the $\mathcal{D}_k$-HAK assumption.
(ii) assuming that $\mathcal{D}_k$-HAK and $\mathcal{D}_{\mathsf{p}}$-WKerMDH$_{\mathbb{G}_1}$ hold (thus, $\varrho = [\boldsymbol{M}]_1$ comes from a WKerMDH$_{\mathbb{G}_1}$-hard distribution), $(\mathcal{D}_{\mathsf{p}}, k, \mathcal{D}_k)$-SKWKE$_{\mathbb{G}_1}$ holds.

Proof. Assume $\mathcal{A}$ is a KWKE or SKWKE adversary, s.t.: given public parameters p and randomness $r \leftarrow_{\$} \mathsf{RND}_\lambda(\mathcal{A})$, $\mathcal{A}(\mathsf{p}; r)$ outputs with probability $\varepsilon_{\mathcal{A}}$ a

$\mathsf{Ext}_{\mathcal{A}}(\mathsf{p}; r)$

$([\boldsymbol{M}]_1, \mathsf{pk}) \leftarrow \mathcal{A}(\mathsf{p}; r);$ **if** $\mathsf{PKV}([\boldsymbol{M}]_1, \mathsf{pk}) = 0$ **then return** $\perp;$ **fi** ;
$(\boldsymbol{N}_1, [\boldsymbol{q}_1]_2, \boldsymbol{N}_2, [\boldsymbol{q}_2]_2) \leftarrow \mathsf{Ext}^{hak}_{\mathcal{A}}(\mathsf{p}; r)$; Abort if this fails;
Let $\bar{\boldsymbol{A}}[i]$, $\boldsymbol{C}[i]$ be such that $\bar{\boldsymbol{A}} = \sum_{i \geq 0} \bar{\boldsymbol{A}}[i] q_{2i}$ and $\boldsymbol{C} = \sum_{i \geq 0} \boldsymbol{C}[i] q_{2i}$;
For each $i > 0$, sample random $y_i \leftarrow_{\$} \mathbb{Z}_p$;
($\sharp$)**if** $\det(\bar{\boldsymbol{A}}(\boldsymbol{y})) = 0$ **then return** $\perp;$ **fi** ; // Probability k/p
return $\boldsymbol{K} \leftarrow \boldsymbol{C}(\boldsymbol{y})\bar{\boldsymbol{A}}(\boldsymbol{y})^{-1}$;

$\mathsf{Ext}^2_{\mathcal{A}}(\mathsf{p}; r)$

$([\boldsymbol{M}]_1, \mathsf{pk}) \leftarrow \mathcal{A}(\mathsf{p}; r);$ **if** $\mathsf{PKV}([\boldsymbol{M}]_1, \mathsf{pk}) = 0$ **then return** $\perp;$ **fi** ;
$(\boldsymbol{N}_1, [\boldsymbol{q}_1]_2, \boldsymbol{N}_2, [\boldsymbol{q}_2]_2) \leftarrow \mathsf{Ext}^{hak}_{\mathcal{A}}(\mathsf{p}; r)$; Abort if this fails;
Let $\bar{\boldsymbol{A}}[i]$, $\boldsymbol{C}[i]$ be such that $\bar{\boldsymbol{A}} = \sum_{i \geq 0} \bar{\boldsymbol{A}}[i] q_{2i}$ and $\boldsymbol{C} = \sum_{i \geq 0} \boldsymbol{C}[i] q_{2i}$;
For each $i > 0$, sample $y_i \leftarrow_{\$} \mathbb{Z}_p$ and $y'_i \leftarrow_{\$} \mathbb{Z}_p$;
if $\det(\bar{\boldsymbol{A}}(\boldsymbol{y})) = 0 \vee \det(\bar{\boldsymbol{A}}(\boldsymbol{y}')) = 0$ **then return** $\perp;$ **fi** ; // Probability $\leq 2k/p$
$\boldsymbol{K} \leftarrow \boldsymbol{C}(\boldsymbol{y})\bar{\boldsymbol{A}}(\boldsymbol{y})^{-1}; \boldsymbol{K}' \leftarrow \boldsymbol{C}(\boldsymbol{y}')\bar{\boldsymbol{A}}(\boldsymbol{y}')^{-1}$;
if $\boldsymbol{K} \neq \boldsymbol{K}'$ **then return** $\boldsymbol{K} - \boldsymbol{K}'$; **else return** $\boldsymbol{K}$; **fi** ;

Fig. 5. Extractors $\mathsf{Ext}_{\mathcal{A}}(\mathsf{p}; r)$ and $\mathsf{Ext}^2_{\mathcal{A}}(\mathsf{p}; r)$ in the proof of Theorem 1

language parameter $\varrho = [\boldsymbol{M}]_1$ and public key $\mathsf{pk} = ([\bar{\boldsymbol{A}}, \boldsymbol{C}]_2, [\boldsymbol{P}]_1, \mathsf{pk}^{\mathsf{pkv}})$, such that $\mathsf{PKV}([\boldsymbol{M}]_1, \mathsf{pk}) = 1$ (in particular, $\det \bar{\boldsymbol{A}} \neq 0$ and $\boldsymbol{M}^\top \boldsymbol{C} = \boldsymbol{P}\bar{\boldsymbol{A}}$).

(i: security of KWKE**):** Assume $\mathcal{A}$ is a KWKE adversary. Let $\mathsf{Ext}^{hak}_{\mathcal{A}}$ be the extractor, existence of which is guaranteed by the $\mathcal{D}_k$-HAK assumption. Figure 5 depicts a candidate KWKE-extractor $\mathsf{Ext}_{\mathcal{A}}$, where $[q_{\iota i}]_\iota$ for $i > 0$ are group elements created by $\mathcal{A}$ (for which she does not know the discrete logarithm) in $\mathbb{G}_\iota$, and $q_{\iota 0} = 1$. Due to the $\mathcal{D}_k$-HAK assumption, $\mathsf{Ext}^{hak}_{\mathcal{A}}$ can extract $\boldsymbol{N}_\iota$ and $[\boldsymbol{q}_\iota]_\iota$, such that $\left[\begin{smallmatrix} \mathrm{vect}(\boldsymbol{M}) \\ \mathrm{vect}(\boldsymbol{P}) \end{smallmatrix}\right]_1 = \boldsymbol{N}_1 \left[\begin{smallmatrix} 1 \\ \boldsymbol{q}_1 \end{smallmatrix}\right]_1 \in \mathbb{G}_1^{mn+mk}$ and $\left[\begin{smallmatrix} \mathrm{vect}(\bar{\boldsymbol{A}}) \\ \mathrm{vect}(\boldsymbol{C}) \end{smallmatrix}\right]_2 = \boldsymbol{N}_2 \left[\begin{smallmatrix} 1 \\ \boldsymbol{q}_2 \end{smallmatrix}\right]_2 \in \mathbb{G}_2^{k^2+nk}$. Here, $\mathrm{vect}(\boldsymbol{B})$ denotes the vectorization of a matrix $\boldsymbol{B}$. Thus, e.g., $\bar{A}_{ij} = \sum_{t \geq 0} N_{k(i-1)+j,t} \boldsymbol{q}_{2t}$ and $C_{ij} = \sum_{t \geq 0} N_{k(i-1)+j+k^2,t} \boldsymbol{q}_{2t}$. Given $\boldsymbol{N}_1$ and $\boldsymbol{N}_2$, one can efficiently compute matrices $\boldsymbol{M}[j]$, $\boldsymbol{P}[j]$, $\bar{\boldsymbol{A}}[i]$ and $\boldsymbol{C}[i]$, such that the polynomials $\boldsymbol{M}(\boldsymbol{Q}_1) := \sum_{j \geq 0} \boldsymbol{M}[j] Q_{1j}$, $\boldsymbol{P}(\boldsymbol{Q}_1) := \sum_{j \geq 0} \boldsymbol{P}[j] Q_{1j}$, $\bar{\boldsymbol{A}}(\boldsymbol{Q}_2) := \sum_{i \geq 0} \bar{\boldsymbol{A}}[i] Q_{2i}$, and $\boldsymbol{C}(\boldsymbol{Q}_2) := \sum_{i \geq 0} \boldsymbol{C}[i] Q_{2i}$ satisfy $[\boldsymbol{M}]_1 = [\boldsymbol{M}(\boldsymbol{q}_1)]_1$, $[\boldsymbol{P}]_1 = [\boldsymbol{P}(\boldsymbol{q}_1)]_1$, $[\bar{\boldsymbol{A}}]_2 = [\bar{\boldsymbol{A}}(\boldsymbol{q}_2)]_2$, and $[\boldsymbol{C}]_2 = [\boldsymbol{C}(\boldsymbol{q}_2)]_2$.

We will now show that $\mathsf{Ext}_{\mathcal{A}}$ satisfies the requirements of the extractor in the definition of KWKE. Assume that $\mathcal{A}$ was successful with inputs $(\mathsf{p}; r)$. We execute $\mathsf{Ext}_{\mathcal{A}}(\mathsf{p}; r)$ and obtain either $\boldsymbol{K}$ or $\perp$. From (*) in PKV (i.e., $\boldsymbol{M}^\top \boldsymbol{C} = \boldsymbol{P}\bar{\boldsymbol{A}}$), $V(\boldsymbol{Q}_1, \boldsymbol{Q}_2) := (\sum_{j \geq 0} \boldsymbol{M}[j] Q_{1j})^\top \cdot (\sum_{i \geq 0} \boldsymbol{C}[i] Q_{2i}) - (\sum_{j \geq 0} \boldsymbol{P}[j] Q_{1j}) \cdot (\sum_{i \geq 0} \bar{\boldsymbol{A}}[i] Q_{2i})$ satisfies $V(\boldsymbol{q}_1, \boldsymbol{q}_2) = \boldsymbol{0}$. We now consider the following two cases, $V(\boldsymbol{Q}_1, \boldsymbol{Q}_2) = \boldsymbol{0}$ as a polynomial and $V(\boldsymbol{Q}_1, \boldsymbol{Q}_2) \neq \boldsymbol{0}$ but $V(\boldsymbol{q}_1, \boldsymbol{q}_2) = \boldsymbol{0}$.

Case 1: $V(\boldsymbol{Q}_1, \boldsymbol{Q}_2) = \boldsymbol{0}_{m \times k}$ *as a polynomial.* Since Q_{1j} and Q_{2i} are indeterminates for all $i, j > 0$, the coefficients V_{ij} of $Q_{1j} Q_{2i}$ of $V(\boldsymbol{Q}_1, \boldsymbol{Q}_2) =$

$\sum_{i\geq 0, j\geq 0} V_{ij} Q_{1j} Q_{2i}$ must be equal to $\mathbf{0}_{m\times k}$ for all $i, j \geq 0$. In particular,

$$\boldsymbol{P}[j] \cdot \bar{\boldsymbol{A}}[i] = \boldsymbol{M}[j]^\top \boldsymbol{C}[i] \ , \quad i \geq 0, j \geq 0 \ . \tag{1}$$

Let $\bar{\boldsymbol{A}}(\boldsymbol{Q}_2) = \sum \bar{\boldsymbol{A}}[i] Q_{2i} \in \mathbb{Z}_p^{k\times k}[\boldsymbol{Q}_2]$ be an affine multivariate matrix polynomial and let the polynomial $d(\boldsymbol{Q}_2) := \det(\bar{\boldsymbol{A}}(\boldsymbol{Q}_2)) \in \mathbb{Z}_p[\boldsymbol{Q}_2]$ be its determinant. Clearly, $\deg(d(\boldsymbol{Q}_2)) \leq k$, and $\bar{\boldsymbol{A}}(\boldsymbol{Q}_2)$ is invertible iff $d(\boldsymbol{Q}_2) \neq 0$ as a polynomial. Since $\mathsf{PKV}([\boldsymbol{M}]_1, \mathsf{pk}) = 1$, $d(\boldsymbol{Q}_2) \neq 0$ and thus $\bar{\boldsymbol{A}}(\boldsymbol{Q}_2)$ is invertible. This holds by definition for efficiently verifiable $\mathcal{D}_k$. If $\mathcal{D}_k = \mathcal{U}_2$, then $[a_{1s}]_1[1]_2 = [1]_1[a_{1s}]_2$, for $s \in \{1, 2\}$, and $[a_{11}]_1[a_{22}]_2 \neq [a_{12}]_1[a_{21}]_2$ guarantee that $d(\boldsymbol{Q}_2) \neq 0$.

By the Schwartz-Zippel lemma, $d(\boldsymbol{y}) = 0$ for uniformly sampled $y_i \leftarrow_\$ \mathbb{Z}_p$ (and thus $\mathsf{Ext}_\mathcal{A}$ aborts in step ($\sharp$)) with probability at most k/p. Thus, $\bar{\boldsymbol{A}}(\boldsymbol{y})$ is invertible with probability at least $\varepsilon_\mathcal{A} - k/p$.

Assume now that $\bar{\boldsymbol{A}}(\boldsymbol{y})$ is invertible. Define $\boldsymbol{K}(\boldsymbol{Q}_2) := \boldsymbol{C}(\boldsymbol{Q}_2)\bar{\boldsymbol{A}}^{-1}(\boldsymbol{Q}_2) = (\sum_{i\geq 0} \boldsymbol{C}[i] Q_{2i})(\sum_{i\geq 0} \bar{\boldsymbol{A}}[i] Q_{2i})^{-1} \in \mathbb{Z}_p^{n\times k}(\boldsymbol{Q}_2)$. Let $\boldsymbol{K} := \boldsymbol{K}(\boldsymbol{y})$. Since $\bar{\boldsymbol{A}}(\boldsymbol{y})$ is invertible then from Eq. (1), $\boldsymbol{P}[j] \cdot \bar{\boldsymbol{A}}(\boldsymbol{y}) = \boldsymbol{P}[j] \cdot (\sum_i \bar{\boldsymbol{A}}[i] y_i) = \boldsymbol{M}[j]^\top (\sum_i \boldsymbol{C}[i] y_i) = \boldsymbol{M}[j]^\top \boldsymbol{C}(\boldsymbol{y})$. Thus, $\boldsymbol{P}[j] = \boldsymbol{M}[j]^\top \boldsymbol{K}$, and $\boldsymbol{P}(\boldsymbol{Q}_1) = \boldsymbol{M}(\boldsymbol{Q}_1)^\top \boldsymbol{K}$. Hence, with probability $\varepsilon_{\mathsf{Ext}_\mathcal{A}} \geq \varepsilon_\mathcal{A} - k/p$, $\boldsymbol{P}(\boldsymbol{Q}_1) = \sum_{j\geq 0} \boldsymbol{P}[j] Q_{1j} = \boldsymbol{M}(\boldsymbol{Q}_1)^\top \boldsymbol{K}$. Thus, $|\varepsilon_{\mathsf{Ext}_\mathcal{A}} - \varepsilon_\mathcal{A}| \leq k/p$ and the claim follows.

Case 2: $V(\boldsymbol{X}, \boldsymbol{Q}_1, \boldsymbol{Q}_2) \neq \mathbf{0}$ but $V(\boldsymbol{x}, \boldsymbol{q}_1, \boldsymbol{q}_2) = \mathbf{0}$. Following [37], we consider separately the "non-hashing" case (the adversary creates no random elements $[q_\iota]_\iota$) and the "hashing" case (the adversary creates at least one random element that has high min-entropy).

In the non-hashing case, the verification polynomial is equal to the integer matrix $V := \boldsymbol{M}[0]^\top \boldsymbol{C}[0] - \boldsymbol{P}[0] \cdot \bar{\boldsymbol{A}}[0]$. Recall that $V(\boldsymbol{Q}_1, \boldsymbol{Q}_2) \neq \mathbf{0}$ but $V(\boldsymbol{q}_1, \boldsymbol{q}_2) = \mathbf{0}$. Since we are in the non-hashing case, there are no created group elements. Thus, the adversary cannot succeed in the non-hashing since the polynomial V is constant, and we need $V = 0$ and $V \neq 0$ at the same time.

Consider now the "hashing" case when $\mathcal{A}$ has created at least one random group element q_k (say, in $\mathbb{G}_1$). Clearly, $V(\boldsymbol{Q}_1, \boldsymbol{Q}_2)$ is a degree-1 polynomial in any indeterminate Q_k. Thus, by the Schwartz-Zippel lemma and since $H_\infty([q_{\iota s}]_\iota) = \omega(\log \lambda)$, the probability $1/2^{\sum_{\iota,s} H_\infty([q_{\iota s}]_\iota)}$ that $V(\boldsymbol{q}_1, \boldsymbol{q}_2) = 0$ is negligible. Hence, the probability that an adversary, who created at least one (high min-entropy) group element $[q_k]_1$, can make the verifier accept is negligible.

(ii: security of SKWKE**):** Let $\mathcal{A}$ be an SKWKE adversary that works in time $\tau(\lambda)$ and outputs $([\boldsymbol{M}]_1, \mathsf{pk})$ accepted by PKV with probability $\varepsilon_\mathcal{A}$. To prove that SKWKE is secure, we need to additionally show that $\boldsymbol{C} = \boldsymbol{K}\bar{\boldsymbol{A}}$. In the process, we need to assume that $\mathcal{D}_\mathsf{p}$-WKerMDH is hard against $\tau(\lambda)$-time adversaries. The general proof works exactly as in the KWKE case, except one change that we discuss below. (In particular, the Case 2 is exactly the same.) We omit other details of the proof.

More precisely, the main idea is that in the proof step (i) we already established that $\boldsymbol{C}(\boldsymbol{Q}_2) = \boldsymbol{K}(\boldsymbol{Q}_2)\bar{\boldsymbol{A}}(\boldsymbol{Q}_2)$ as polynomials. In the current step, we need to show that $\boldsymbol{C}(\boldsymbol{Q}_2) = \boldsymbol{K}\bar{\boldsymbol{A}}(\boldsymbol{Q}_2)$ holds, that is, $\boldsymbol{K}(\boldsymbol{Q}_2)$ is a constant function. To guarantee the latter, we check the value of the rational function $\boldsymbol{K}(\boldsymbol{Q}_2)$

at two positions. If the two values are different, we can break $\mathcal{D}_{\mathsf{p}}$-WKerMDH. Otherwise, w.h.p., $\boldsymbol{K}(\boldsymbol{Q}_2)$ is a constant function.

More precisely, consider the extractor $\mathsf{Ext}^2_{\mathcal{A}}$ in Fig. 5. Here, $\boldsymbol{K} = \boldsymbol{K}(\boldsymbol{y})$ and $\boldsymbol{K}' = \boldsymbol{K}(\boldsymbol{y}')$. Let $\varepsilon_{\mathcal{A}}$ be the success probability of $\mathcal{A}$. Analogously to the security proof of KWKE, with probability $\varepsilon_{\mathcal{A}} - 2k/p$, both $\bar{\boldsymbol{A}}(\boldsymbol{y})$ and $\bar{\boldsymbol{A}}(\boldsymbol{y}')$ are invertible and thus $\mathsf{Ext}^2_{\mathcal{A}}$ does not return $\perp$.

Assume now that $\mathsf{Ext}^2_{\mathcal{A}}$ does not return $\perp$. By following similar analysis as in the case (i), $\boldsymbol{P}(\boldsymbol{Q}_1) = \boldsymbol{M}(\boldsymbol{Q}_1)^\top \boldsymbol{K}$ and $\boldsymbol{P}(\boldsymbol{Q}_1) = \boldsymbol{M}(\boldsymbol{Q}_1)^\top \boldsymbol{K}'$ which means that $\boldsymbol{M}(\boldsymbol{Q}_1)^\top (\boldsymbol{K} - \boldsymbol{K}') = \boldsymbol{0}_{m \times k}$. If $\boldsymbol{K} \neq \boldsymbol{K}'$ then $\mathsf{Ext}_{\mathcal{A}}$ has computed a non-zero element $\boldsymbol{K} - \boldsymbol{K}'$ in the cokernel of $[\boldsymbol{M}]_1$ and thus broken $\mathcal{D}_{\mathsf{p}}$-WKerMDH$_{\mathbb{G}_1}$. Since breaking $\mathcal{D}_{\mathsf{p}}$-WKerMDH is hard within $\tau(\lambda)$ steps, the probability $\varepsilon_{\mathrm{WKerMDH}}$ that $\mathsf{Ext}_{\mathcal{A}}$ returns $\boldsymbol{K} - \boldsymbol{K}'$ is negligible unless $\mathcal{A}$ has computational complexity $\omega(\tau(\lambda))$. Otherwise, $\boldsymbol{K} = \boldsymbol{K}(\boldsymbol{y}) = \boldsymbol{K}(\boldsymbol{y}')$, which means $\boldsymbol{f}(\boldsymbol{y}) = \boldsymbol{f}(\boldsymbol{y}') = \boldsymbol{0}$, where $\boldsymbol{f}(\boldsymbol{Q}_2) := \boldsymbol{C}(\boldsymbol{Q}_2)\bar{\boldsymbol{A}}^{-1}(\boldsymbol{Q}_2) - \boldsymbol{K}$. Denote the (i, j)th coefficient of the matrix $\boldsymbol{f}(\boldsymbol{Q}_2)$ by $f_{ij}(\boldsymbol{Q}_2) = \sum_s C_{is}(\boldsymbol{Q}_2)\bar{A}^{-1}_{sj}(\boldsymbol{Q}_2) - K_{ij}$. Note that $f_{ij}(\boldsymbol{Q}_2) = f'_{ij}(\boldsymbol{Q}_2)/\det(\bar{\boldsymbol{A}}(\boldsymbol{Q}_2))$, where $f'_{ij}(\boldsymbol{Q}_2)$ is some polynomial of degree $\leq k$.

At this point, we know that $\det(\bar{\boldsymbol{A}}(\boldsymbol{Q}_2)) \neq 0$. Thus, $\boldsymbol{f}(\boldsymbol{Q}_2) \neq \boldsymbol{0}$ iff $\boldsymbol{C}(\boldsymbol{Q}_2) - \boldsymbol{K}\bar{\boldsymbol{A}}(\boldsymbol{Q}_2) \neq \boldsymbol{0}$. From this and the Schwartz-Zippel lemma it follows that if $f_{ij}(\boldsymbol{Q}_2) \neq 0$ then $\Pr_{\boldsymbol{y}}[f_{ij}(\boldsymbol{y}) = 0] \leq k/p$. If $\boldsymbol{f}(\boldsymbol{Q}_2) \neq \boldsymbol{0}$ then there exists at least one (i_0, j_0), s.t. $f_{i_0,j_0}(\boldsymbol{Q}_2) \neq 0$ and thus $\Pr_{\boldsymbol{y}}[f_{i_0,j_0}(\boldsymbol{y}) = 0] \leq k/p$. Thus, if $\boldsymbol{f}(\boldsymbol{Q}_2) \neq \boldsymbol{0}$ then $\Pr_{\boldsymbol{y}}[\boldsymbol{f}(\boldsymbol{y}) = \boldsymbol{0}] \leq k/p$.

Hence, with probability $\varepsilon_{\mathsf{Ext}^2_{\mathcal{A}}} \geq \varepsilon_{\mathcal{A}} - 3k/p - \varepsilon_{\mathrm{WKerMDH}}$, $\boldsymbol{C}(\boldsymbol{Q}_2) = \boldsymbol{K}\bar{\boldsymbol{A}}(\boldsymbol{Q}_2)$ and thus $\boldsymbol{P}(\boldsymbol{Q}_1) = \boldsymbol{M}(\boldsymbol{Q}_1)^\top \boldsymbol{K}$ and $\boldsymbol{C} = \boldsymbol{K}\bar{\boldsymbol{A}}$. Thus, $|\varepsilon_{\mathsf{Ext}^2_{\mathcal{A}}} - \varepsilon_{\mathcal{A}}| \leq 3k/p + \varepsilon_{\mathrm{WKerMDH}}$ and the security of SKWKE follows. □

In the case of SKWKE, we extract the *unique* $\boldsymbol{K}$ used to compute the CRS. Following a proof idea from [2], it is easy to show that under either the KWKE (and thus, also the SKWKE) assumption Π_{bpk} is Sub-ZK.

New Interactive Assumptions KerMDH^{dl} and SKerMDH^{dl}. Since in the case of efficiently verifiable $\mathcal{D}_k$, we essentially do not modify Π_{bpk} (we only define PKV), its Sub-PAR soundness *almost* follows from that of Π_{kw} [31]. The main difference is that, due to considering the subverted language parameter, we need to change how one extracts $\boldsymbol{M}$. Namely, in [31], the KerMDH adversary $\mathcal{B}$ defined in the soundness reduction obtains $([\boldsymbol{M}]_1, \boldsymbol{M})$ sampled from $\mathcal{D}'_{\mathsf{p}}$ (this relies on the witness-sampleability). In our proof of Sub-PAR soundness (Theorem 2 in Sect. 7), $\mathcal{B}$ obtains $[\boldsymbol{M}]_1 \leftarrow \mathcal{A}(\mathsf{p})$ and then uses a non-adaptive DL oracle to extract $\boldsymbol{M}$. This means that we prove Sub-PAR soundness under a new interactive non-falsifiable KerMDH^{dl} assumption; however, importantly, we do not require witness-sampleability.

Since in some applications (e.g., in the setting of symmetric pairings), one uses $\mathcal{D}_2 = \mathcal{U}_2$, we prove that if $k = 2$ and $\mathcal{D}_k = \mathcal{U}_k$, then Π_{bpk} is sound under another new interactive non-falsifiable SKerMDH^{dl} assumption. Intuitively, in this case, $\mathsf{pk}^{\mathsf{pkv}}$ contains additional elements, needed to efficiently check that $[\bar{\boldsymbol{A}}]_2$ has full rank. If $\mathcal{D}_k$ is efficiently verifiable then by definition, $\mathsf{pk}^{\mathsf{pkv}} = \varepsilon$

(empty string) is sufficient. Since for efficiency reasons, one is interested in only small values of k, we will not consider the case of non-verifiable $\mathcal{D}_k$ with $k > 2$.

In addition, we are interested in applying the QA-NIZK in the case $\boldsymbol{M}$ has rank n (i.e., the image of $\boldsymbol{M}$ is the full space). Since then soundness holds trivially, one must prove knowledge-soundness. We show that in this case, Π_{bpk} is Sub-PAR knowledge-sound under two non-falsifiable assumptions: a HAK knowledge assumption and the new interactive $\mathrm{SDL}^{\mathrm{dl}}$ assumption. The $\mathrm{KerMDH}^{\mathrm{dl}}$, $\mathrm{SKerMDH}^{\mathrm{dl}}$, and $\mathrm{SDL}^{\mathrm{dl}}$ assumptions are X^Y-type interactive assumptions as used in [20,34], where the assumption X is assumed to hold even if the adversary is given non-adaptive access (i.e., before the X challenge is chosen) to an oracle that solves the assumption Y.

The $\mathrm{SDL}^{\mathrm{dl}}$ *assumption* holds relative to PGen, if for any PPT $\mathcal{A}$,

$$\Pr\left[\mathsf{p} \leftarrow \mathsf{PGen}(1^\lambda); st \leftarrow \mathcal{A}^{\mathrm{dl}(\cdot)}(\mathsf{p}); x \leftarrow_{\$} \mathbb{Z}_p : \mathcal{A}(\mathsf{p}, st, [x]_1, [x]_2) = x\right] \approx_\lambda 0 \ .$$

Here, the oracle $\mathrm{dl}([y]_1)$ returns the discrete logarithm y of $[y]_1$.

The $\mathcal{D}_{\ell k}$-$\mathrm{KerMDH}^{\mathrm{dl}}_{\mathbb{G}_1}$ *assumption* holds relative to PGen, if for any PPT $\mathcal{A}$,

$$\Pr\left[\begin{array}{l}\mathsf{p} \leftarrow \mathsf{PGen}(1^\lambda); st \leftarrow \mathcal{A}^{\mathrm{dl}(\cdot)}(\mathsf{p}); \boldsymbol{A} \leftarrow_{\$} \mathcal{D}_{\ell k}; [\boldsymbol{c}]_2 \leftarrow \mathcal{A}(\mathsf{p}, st, [\boldsymbol{A}]_1) : \\ \boldsymbol{A}^\top \boldsymbol{c} = \boldsymbol{0}_k \wedge \boldsymbol{c} \neq \boldsymbol{0}_\ell\end{array}\right] \approx_\lambda 0 \ .$$

The $\mathcal{D}_{\ell k}$-$\mathrm{SKerMDH}^{\mathrm{dl}}$ *assumption* holds relative to PGen, if for any PPT $\mathcal{A}$,

$$\Pr\left[\begin{array}{l}\mathsf{p} \leftarrow \mathsf{PGen}(1^\lambda); st \leftarrow \mathcal{A}^{\mathrm{dl}(\cdot)}(\mathsf{p}); \boldsymbol{A} \leftarrow_{\$} \mathcal{D}_{\ell k}; \\ ([\boldsymbol{c}_1]_1, [\boldsymbol{c}_2]_2) \leftarrow \mathcal{A}(\mathsf{p}, st, [\boldsymbol{A}]_1, [\boldsymbol{A}]_2) : \boldsymbol{A}^\top(\boldsymbol{c}_1 - \boldsymbol{c}_2) = \boldsymbol{0}_k \wedge \boldsymbol{c}_1 - \boldsymbol{c}_2 \neq \boldsymbol{0}_\ell\end{array}\right] \approx_\lambda 0 \ .$$

Generic-model security proofs of $\mathrm{SDL}^{\mathrm{dl}}$ and $\mathrm{SKerMDH}^{\mathrm{dl}}$ are very similar to those of SDL and KerMDH: the field elements returned by the DL oracle are independent of the challenge and thus do not influence the rest of proof.

One could use an AK assumption instead of the $\mathrm{SDL}^{\mathrm{dl}}$ assumption. However, the AK assumption explicitly does not allow $\mathcal{A}$ to create new group elements by using elliptic-curve hashing. The $\mathrm{SDL}^{\mathrm{dl}}$ assumption allows the adversary to create such group elements, but allows access to *non-adaptive* DL oracle to extract their discrete logarithms. It is also not an expanding assumption, differently to many knowledge assumptions (e.g., the PKE assumption [26] that underlies many pairing-based SNARKs) that allow one to extract long "plaintext" from a short "ciphertext". Hence, the $\mathrm{SDL}^{\mathrm{dl}}$ assumption, while still non-falsifiable, seems to be somewhat more realistic than an AK assumption. On the other hand, we need to extract $\boldsymbol{y}$ and $\boldsymbol{\pi}$ from $\mathcal{A}$'s output after the challenge is known, adaptively. In this case, a knowledge assumption (HAK) is more realistic than an adaptive DL oracle that one could also just use to break SDL directly.

7 Security of Π_{bpk}

Theorem 2. *Let* Π_{bpk} *be the QA-NIZK argument system for linear subspaces from Fig. 4. The following statements hold in the BPK model. Assume that* $\mathcal{D}_{\mathsf{p}}$ *is such that* PARV *is efficient.*

(i) Π_{bpk} *is perfectly complete and perfectly zero-knowledge.*
(ii) *If* $(\mathcal{D}_{\mathsf{p}}, k, \mathcal{D}_k)$*-KWKE*$_{\mathbb{G}_1}$ *holds relative to* PGen *then* Π_{bpk} *is statistically persistent zero-knowledge.*
(iii) *Assume* $\mathcal{D}_k$ *is efficiently verifiable (resp.,* $\mathcal{D}_k = \mathcal{U}_2$*). If* $\mathcal{D}_k$*-KerMDH*^{dl} *(resp.,* $\mathcal{D}_k$*-SKerMDH*^{dl}*) holds relative to* PGen *then* Π_{bpk} *is computationally quasi-adaptively Sub-PAR sound.*
(iv) *Assume* $\boldsymbol{M}$ *has rank* n *(*$\boldsymbol{y} = \boldsymbol{M}\boldsymbol{w}$ *always has a solution), and that* $\mathcal{D}_k$ *is robust. If* SDL^{dl} *and* $\mathsf{KGen}([\boldsymbol{M}]_1)$*-HAK, for arbitrary efficiently computable* $[\boldsymbol{M}]_1$*, hold relative to* PGen *then* Π_{bpk} *is computationally quasi-adaptively Sub-PAR knowledge-sound.*

Proof. **(i: perfect completeness/perfect zero-knowledge):** obvious.

(ii: persistent zero-knowledge): Let $\mathcal{C}$ be a subverter that computes $([\boldsymbol{M}]_1, \mathsf{pk})$ so as to break the Sub-ZK property. That is, $\mathcal{C}(\mathsf{p}; r_{\mathcal{C}})$ outputs $([\boldsymbol{M}]_1, \mathsf{aux}_{\mathsf{pk}})$. Let $\mathcal{B}$ be the adversary from Fig. 6. Note that $\mathsf{RND}_\lambda(\mathcal{B}) = \mathsf{RND}_\lambda(\mathcal{C})$. Under the $(\mathcal{D}_{\mathsf{p}}, k, \mathcal{D}_k)$-KWKE assumption, there exists an extractor $\mathsf{Ext}^2_{\mathcal{B}}$, such that if $\mathsf{PARV}([\boldsymbol{M}]_1) = 1$ and $\mathsf{PKV}([\boldsymbol{M}]_1, \mathsf{pk}) = 1$ then $\mathsf{Ext}^2_{\mathcal{B}}(\mathsf{p}; r_{\mathcal{C}})$ outputs $\boldsymbol{K}$, such that $\boldsymbol{P} = \boldsymbol{M}^\top \boldsymbol{K}$. We construct a trivial extractor $\mathsf{Ext}_{\mathcal{C}}(\mathsf{p}; r_{\mathcal{C}})$ for $\mathcal{C}$, as depicted in Fig. 6. Clearly, $\mathsf{Ext}_{\mathcal{C}}$ returns $\mathsf{sk} = \boldsymbol{K}$, such that $\boldsymbol{P} = \boldsymbol{M}^\top \boldsymbol{K}$.

$\mathcal{B}(\mathsf{p}; r_{\mathcal{C}})$	$\mathsf{Ext}_{\mathcal{C}}(\mathsf{p}; r_{\mathcal{C}})$
$([\boldsymbol{M}]_1, \mathsf{pk}, \mathsf{aux}_{\mathcal{C}}) \leftarrow \mathcal{C}(\mathsf{p}; r_{\mathcal{C}});$ **return** $\mathsf{pk};$	**return** $\mathsf{Ext}^2_{\mathcal{B}}(\mathsf{p}; r_{\mathcal{C}});$

Fig. 6. The extractor and the constructed adversary $\mathcal{B}$ from the persistent zero-knowledge proof of Theorem 2.

Fix concrete values of λ, $\mathsf{p} \in \mathrm{im}(\mathsf{PGen}(1^\lambda))$ and $r_{\mathcal{C}} \in \mathsf{RND}_\lambda(\mathcal{C})$. Let $([\boldsymbol{M}]_1, \mathsf{pk}, \mathsf{aux}_{\mathsf{pk}}) \leftarrow \mathcal{C}(\mathsf{p}; r_{\mathcal{C}})$, and run $\mathsf{Ext}_{\mathcal{C}}(\mathsf{p}; r_{\mathcal{C}})$ to obtain $\boldsymbol{K}$. Fix $([\boldsymbol{y}]_1, \boldsymbol{w}) \in \mathscr{R}_{[\boldsymbol{M}]_1}$. It clearly suffices to show that if $\mathsf{PARV}([\boldsymbol{M}]_1) = 1$, $\mathsf{PKV}([\boldsymbol{M}]_1, \mathsf{pk}) = 1$ and $([\boldsymbol{y}]_1, \boldsymbol{w}) \in \mathscr{R}_{[\boldsymbol{M}]_1}$ then $\mathsf{O}_0([\boldsymbol{y}]_1, \boldsymbol{w}) = \mathsf{P}([\boldsymbol{M}]_1, \mathsf{pk}, [\boldsymbol{y}]_1, \boldsymbol{w}) = [\boldsymbol{P}]_1^\top \boldsymbol{w}$ and $\mathsf{O}_1([\boldsymbol{y}]_1, \boldsymbol{w}) = \mathsf{Sim}([\boldsymbol{M}]_1, \mathsf{pk}, \boldsymbol{K}, [\boldsymbol{y}]_1) = \boldsymbol{K}^\top [\boldsymbol{y}]_1$ have the same distribution. This holds since from $\mathsf{PKV}([\boldsymbol{M}]_1, \mathsf{pk}) = 1$ it follows that $\boldsymbol{P} = \boldsymbol{M}^\top \boldsymbol{K}$ and from $([\boldsymbol{y}]_1; \boldsymbol{w}) \in \mathscr{R}_{[\boldsymbol{M}]_1}$ it follows that $\boldsymbol{y} = \boldsymbol{M}\boldsymbol{w}$. Thus, $\mathsf{O}_0([\boldsymbol{y}]_1, \boldsymbol{w}) = [\boldsymbol{P}]_1^\top \boldsymbol{w} = [\boldsymbol{K}^\top \boldsymbol{M}\boldsymbol{w}]_1 = \boldsymbol{K}^\top [\boldsymbol{y}]_1 = \mathsf{O}_1([\boldsymbol{y}]_1, \boldsymbol{w})$. Hence, O_0 and O_1 have the same distribution, and thus, Π_{bpk} is persistent zero-knowledge under KWKE.

(iii: $\mathcal{D}_k$ **is efficiently verifiable, Sub-PAR soundness under** KerMDH^{dl}**):** follows directly from the soundness proof of Π_{kw} in [31]. There is only one difference: If $[\boldsymbol{M}]_1$ is not subverted (like in [31]), then one can use the witness-sampleability of $\mathcal{D}_{\mathsf{p}}$ to extract $\boldsymbol{M}$, and get a reduction to the falsifiable KerMDH assumption. In the case of Sub-PAR soundness, since the language parameter can be subverted (and thus one cannot rely on witness-sampleability), we let $\mathcal{B}$ use the DL oracle to obtain $\boldsymbol{M}$ from $[\boldsymbol{M}]_1$ and then use it in the soundness

$\mathcal{B}^{\mathsf{dl}(\cdot)}(\mathsf{p})$

$[\boldsymbol{M}]_1 \leftarrow \mathcal{A}(\mathsf{p})$; // $\boldsymbol{M} \in \mathbb{Z}_p^{n \times m}$
Use DL oracle nm times to obtain $\boldsymbol{M}$;
return $st \leftarrow \boldsymbol{M}$;

$\mathcal{B}(\mathsf{p}, st = \boldsymbol{M}, ([\boldsymbol{A}]_1, [\boldsymbol{A}]_2))$ // $([\boldsymbol{A}]_1, [\boldsymbol{A}]_2) \in \mathbb{G}_1^{(k+1)\times k} \times \mathbb{G}_2^{(k+1)\times k}$ with $\boldsymbol{A} = (a_{ij})$

Let $\boldsymbol{M}^{\perp} \in \mathbb{Z}_p^{n\times(n-m)}$ be a basis of the kernel of $\boldsymbol{M}^{\top}$;
$\boldsymbol{K}' \leftarrow_{\$} \mathbb{Z}_p^{n\times k}$; $\boldsymbol{R} \leftarrow_{\$} \mathbb{Z}_p^{(n-m-1)\times(k+1)}$;
$[\boldsymbol{A}']_2 \leftarrow \begin{pmatrix} [\boldsymbol{A}]_2 \\ \boldsymbol{R}\cdot[\boldsymbol{A}]_2 \end{pmatrix}$; // $\boldsymbol{A}' \in \mathbb{Z}_p^{(n-m+k)\times k}$
$[\boldsymbol{C}]_2 \leftarrow (\boldsymbol{K}' || \boldsymbol{M}^{\perp})[\boldsymbol{A}']_2$;
$[\boldsymbol{P}]_1 \leftarrow [\boldsymbol{M}^{\top}\boldsymbol{K}']_1$;
$\mathsf{pk}' \leftarrow ([\bar{\boldsymbol{A}}, \boldsymbol{C}]_2, [a_{11}, a_{12}, \boldsymbol{P}]_1)$;
$([\boldsymbol{y}]_1, [\boldsymbol{\pi}]_1) \leftarrow \mathcal{A}(\mathsf{pk}')$; // $[\boldsymbol{y}]_1 \in \mathbb{G}_1^n$, $[\boldsymbol{\pi}]_1 \in \mathbb{G}_1^k$
$[\boldsymbol{c}]_1^{\top} \leftarrow [(\boldsymbol{\pi}^{\top} - \boldsymbol{y}^{\top}\boldsymbol{K}') || - \boldsymbol{y}^{\top}\boldsymbol{M}^{\perp}]_1$;
Represent $[\boldsymbol{c}]_1^{\top}$ as $[\boldsymbol{c}_1^{\top} || \boldsymbol{c}_2^{\top}]_1$ with $[\boldsymbol{c}_1]_1 \in \mathbb{G}_1^{k+1}$ and $[\boldsymbol{c}_2]_1 \in \mathbb{G}_1^{n-m-1}$;
$\boldsymbol{s}_2 \leftarrow_{\$} \mathbb{Z}_p^{k+1}$; $[\boldsymbol{s}_1]_1 \leftarrow [\boldsymbol{c}_1 + \boldsymbol{R}^{\top}\boldsymbol{c}_2 + \boldsymbol{s}_2]_1$;
return $([\boldsymbol{s}_1]_1, [\boldsymbol{s}_2]_2)$;

Fig. 7. Adversary $\mathcal{B}$ in the soundness proof of Theorem 2 (reduction to $\mathrm{SKerMDH}^{\mathrm{dl}}$)

proof of [31] to get a reduction to the non-falsifiable $\mathrm{KerMDH}^{\mathrm{dl}}$ assumption. Importantly, in this case, witness-sampleability is not needed.

(iii: $\mathcal{D}_k = \mathcal{U}_2$, Sub-PAR soundness under $\mathrm{SKerMDH}^{\mathrm{dl}}$**):** In the case $\mathcal{D}_k = \mathcal{U}_2$, the proof is *similar* to the soundness proof of Π_{kw} in [31]. However, since we added $[a_{11}, a_{12}]_1$ to the public key, we reduce instead to the $\mathrm{SKerMDH}^{\mathrm{dl}}$ assumption; this complicates the proof.

Assume that $\mathcal{A}$ breaks the soundness of Π_{bpk} with probability ε. We will build an adversary $\mathcal{B}$, see Fig. 7, that breaks $\mathrm{SKerMDH}^{\mathrm{dl}}$ with probability $\geq \varepsilon - 1/p$. First, $\mathcal{B}$ uses the DL oracle to obtain $\boldsymbol{M}$ from $[\boldsymbol{M}]_1$; this is needed since $[\boldsymbol{M}]_1$ could be subverted. Here, witness-sampleability is not needed. As above, when the language parameter is generated honestly, the DL oracle is not needed, and one instead relies on the witness-sampleability of $\mathcal{D}_{\mathsf{p}}$ to obtain a reduction to the falsifiable SKerMDH assumption.

Note that in Fig. 7, $[\bar{\boldsymbol{A}}']_2 = [\bar{\boldsymbol{A}}]_2 \in \mathbb{G}_2^{k\times k}$. Define *implicitly* (since we do not know this value) $\boldsymbol{K} \leftarrow \boldsymbol{K}' + \boldsymbol{M}^{\perp}\underline{\boldsymbol{A}}'\bar{\boldsymbol{A}}^{-1} \in \mathbb{Z}_p^{n\times k}$. Thus, $[\boldsymbol{C}]_2 = (\boldsymbol{K}'||\boldsymbol{M}^{\perp})[\boldsymbol{A}']_2 = [\boldsymbol{K}'\bar{\boldsymbol{A}}' + \boldsymbol{M}^{\perp}\underline{\boldsymbol{A}}']_2 = [(\boldsymbol{K}' + \boldsymbol{M}^{\perp}\underline{\boldsymbol{A}}'\bar{\boldsymbol{A}}^{-1})\bar{\boldsymbol{A}}]_2 = [\boldsymbol{K}\bar{\boldsymbol{A}}]_2$ and $[\boldsymbol{P}]_1 = [\boldsymbol{M}^{\top}\boldsymbol{K}']_1 = [\boldsymbol{M}^{\top}(\boldsymbol{K} - \boldsymbol{M}^{\perp}\underline{\boldsymbol{A}}'\bar{\boldsymbol{A}}^{-1})]_1 = [\boldsymbol{M}^{\top}\boldsymbol{K}]_1$. Thus, pk' has the same distribution as the real public key.

With probability ε, $\mathcal{A}$ is successful, that is,

1. $\boldsymbol{y}^{\top}\boldsymbol{M}^{\perp} \neq \boldsymbol{0}_{1\times(n-m)}$ (that is, $\boldsymbol{y} \notin \mathrm{colspace}(\boldsymbol{M})$) and thus also $\boldsymbol{c} = ((\boldsymbol{\pi}^{\top} - \boldsymbol{y}^{\top}\boldsymbol{K}')|| - \boldsymbol{y}^{\top}\boldsymbol{M}^{\perp}) \neq \boldsymbol{0}_{n-m+k}$;

2. $\boldsymbol{y}^\top \boldsymbol{C} = \boldsymbol{\pi}^\top \bar{\boldsymbol{A}}$ (V accepts). Thus, $\mathbf{0}_{1\times k} = \boldsymbol{\pi}^\top \bar{\boldsymbol{A}} - \boldsymbol{y}^\top \boldsymbol{C} = \left(\boldsymbol{\pi}^\top || \mathbf{0}_{n-m}^\top\right) \boldsymbol{A}' - \boldsymbol{y}^\top \left(\boldsymbol{K}' || \boldsymbol{M}^\perp\right) \boldsymbol{A}' = \left((\boldsymbol{\pi}^\top - \boldsymbol{y}^\top \boldsymbol{K}') || - \boldsymbol{y}^\top \boldsymbol{M}^\perp\right) \boldsymbol{A}' = \boldsymbol{c}^\top \boldsymbol{A}'$.

By definition, $\boldsymbol{s}_1 - \boldsymbol{s}_2 = \boldsymbol{c}_1 + \boldsymbol{R}^\top \boldsymbol{c}_2$ and thus $(\boldsymbol{s}_1^\top - \boldsymbol{s}_2^\top)\boldsymbol{A} = (\boldsymbol{c}_1^\top + \boldsymbol{c}_2^\top \boldsymbol{R})\boldsymbol{A} = \boldsymbol{c}^\top \boldsymbol{A}' = \mathbf{0}_{1\times k}$. Since $\boldsymbol{c} \neq \mathbf{0}_{n-m+k}$ and $\boldsymbol{R}$ leaks only through $\boldsymbol{A}'$ (in the definition of $[\boldsymbol{C}]_2$) as $\boldsymbol{RA}$, $\Pr[\boldsymbol{c}_1 + \boldsymbol{R}^\top \boldsymbol{c}_2 = \mathbf{0} \mid \boldsymbol{RA}] \leq 1/p$, where the probability is over $\boldsymbol{R} \leftarrow_\$ \mathbb{Z}_p^{(n-m-1)\times(k+1)}$.

(Item iv: Sub-PAR knowledge-soundness): Our proof strategy is inspired by that of [8, App. F]. However, their proof is given for honestly generated language parameter $\varrho = [\boldsymbol{M}]_1$ and $\boldsymbol{M}$ is obtained by using witness-sampleability; we modify the proof by extracting $\boldsymbol{M}$ from ϱ by using a DL oracle. Thus, we need to use two different types of non-falsifiable assumptions: (1) the non-adaptive $\mathrm{SDL}^{\mathrm{dl}}$ assumption to extract $\boldsymbol{M}$ from $[\boldsymbol{M}]_1$, and (2) knowledge (HAK) assumptions to extract $\boldsymbol{y}$ and $\boldsymbol{\pi}$ from $[\boldsymbol{y}]_1$ and $[\boldsymbol{\pi}]_1$; we use the fact that the verification equation holds to be able to apply HAK. Moreover, we modify the proof of [8] to work for an arbitrary k.

We construct the following $\mathrm{SDL}^{\mathrm{dl}}$ adversary $\mathcal{B}$, that is given access to a non-adaptive DL oracle in the query phase and then, after that, a challenge $([x]_1, [x]_2)$, returns x. First, $\mathcal{B}$ samples r and calls $\mathcal{A}(\mathsf{p}; r)$, obtaining $[\boldsymbol{M}]_1$. $\mathcal{B}$ uses the non-adaptive DL oracle nm times, extracting the matrix $\boldsymbol{M} \in \mathbb{Z}_p^{n\times m}$.

In the challenge phase, $\mathcal{B}$ obtains $([x]_1, [x]_2)$ from the challenger. After that, $\mathcal{B}$ samples random $\boldsymbol{K}_1, \boldsymbol{K}_2 \in \mathbb{Z}_p^{n\times k}$ and sets $[\boldsymbol{K}]_\iota \leftarrow [x]_\iota \boldsymbol{K}_1 + [1]_\iota \boldsymbol{K}_2$. $\mathcal{B}$ honestly generates $\mathsf{pk} = ([\boldsymbol{P}]_1, [\bar{\boldsymbol{A}}, \boldsymbol{C}]_2)$ by setting $\boldsymbol{A} \leftarrow_\$ \mathcal{D}_k$, $[\boldsymbol{C}]_2 \leftarrow [\boldsymbol{K}]_2 \bar{\boldsymbol{A}} = \boldsymbol{K}_1 \bar{\boldsymbol{A}} [x]_2 + \boldsymbol{K}_2 \bar{\boldsymbol{A}} [1]_2 \in \mathbb{G}_2^{n\times k}$, and $[\boldsymbol{P}]_1 \leftarrow \boldsymbol{M}^\top [\boldsymbol{K}]_1 = \boldsymbol{M}^\top \boldsymbol{K}_1 [x]_1 + \boldsymbol{M}^\top \boldsymbol{K}_2 [1]_1 \in \mathbb{G}_1^{m\times k}$. Denote $\boldsymbol{P}' = \mathrm{vect}(\boldsymbol{P}) \in \mathbb{Z}_p^{mk}$. $\mathcal{B}$ sends pk to $\mathcal{A}$ who returns $[\boldsymbol{y}, \boldsymbol{\pi}]_1$.

According to the $\mathsf{KGen}([\boldsymbol{M}]_1)$-HAK assumption for arbitrary efficiently computable $[\boldsymbol{M}]_1$, given $\mathcal{A}$ who on input $(\mathsf{p}, \mathsf{pk})$, where $\mathsf{pk} \sim \mathsf{KGen}([\boldsymbol{M}]_1)$, outputs $[\boldsymbol{y}]_1 \in \mathbb{G}_1^n$ and $[\boldsymbol{\pi}]_1 \in \mathbb{G}_1^k$, we can extract $[\boldsymbol{q}]_1 \in \mathbb{G}_1^{n_q}$, $(\boldsymbol{y}_1, \boldsymbol{y}_2, \boldsymbol{y}_3)$ and $(\boldsymbol{\pi}_1, \boldsymbol{\pi}_2, \boldsymbol{\pi}_3)$, such that

$$\begin{aligned}[\boldsymbol{y}]_1 &= \boldsymbol{y}_1[1]_1 + \boldsymbol{y}_2[\boldsymbol{P}']_1 + \boldsymbol{y}_3[\boldsymbol{q}]_1 \ , \\ [\boldsymbol{\pi}]_1 &= \boldsymbol{\pi}_1[1]_1 + \boldsymbol{\pi}_2[\boldsymbol{P}']_1 + \boldsymbol{\pi}_3[\boldsymbol{q}]_1 \ ,\end{aligned} \tag{2}$$

Note that $\boldsymbol{y}_2 \in \mathbb{Z}_p^{n\times mk}$, $\boldsymbol{\pi}_2 \in \mathbb{Z}_p^{k\times mk}$, $\boldsymbol{y}_3 \in \mathbb{Z}_p^{n\times n_q}$, and $\boldsymbol{\pi}_3 \in \mathbb{Z}_p^{k\times n_q}$.

We will now write $\boldsymbol{K}' = \mathrm{vect}(\boldsymbol{K})$, $\boldsymbol{K}_1' = \mathrm{vect}(\boldsymbol{K}_1)$, $\boldsymbol{K}_2' = \mathrm{vect}(\boldsymbol{K}_2)$, $\boldsymbol{P}_1 = \boldsymbol{M}^\top \boldsymbol{K}_1$, $\boldsymbol{P}_2 = \boldsymbol{M}^\top \boldsymbol{K}_2$, $\boldsymbol{P}_1' = \mathrm{vect}(\boldsymbol{P}_1)$ and $\boldsymbol{P}_2' = \mathrm{vect}(\boldsymbol{P}_2)$. Thus, $\boldsymbol{P} = \boldsymbol{M}^\top \boldsymbol{K} = \boldsymbol{M}^\top (x\boldsymbol{K}_1 + \boldsymbol{K}_2) = x\boldsymbol{P}_1 + \boldsymbol{P}_2$ and $\boldsymbol{P}' = x\boldsymbol{P}_1' + \boldsymbol{P}_2'$. Recall $\boldsymbol{M} \in \mathbb{Z}_p^{n\times m}$, $\boldsymbol{K} \in \mathbb{Z}_p^{n\times k}$, and $\boldsymbol{P} \in \mathbb{Z}_p^{m\times k}$.

From the verification equation $[\boldsymbol{y}]_1^\top [\boldsymbol{C}]_2 = [\boldsymbol{\pi}]_1^\top [\bar{\boldsymbol{A}}]_2$. Assuming $\bar{\boldsymbol{A}}$ is invertible, $[\boldsymbol{\pi}]_1 = [\boldsymbol{K}^\top \boldsymbol{y}]_1$. From this and Eq. (2), $\boldsymbol{\pi}_1[1]_1 + \boldsymbol{\pi}_2[\boldsymbol{P}']_1 + \boldsymbol{\pi}_3[\boldsymbol{q}]_1 = [\boldsymbol{K}]_1^\top \boldsymbol{y}_1 + [\boldsymbol{K}^\top \boldsymbol{y}_2 \boldsymbol{P}']_1 + [\boldsymbol{K}^\top \boldsymbol{y}_3 \boldsymbol{q}]_1$, and thus

$$\begin{aligned}\boldsymbol{\pi}_1[1]_1 &+ \boldsymbol{\pi}_2[x\boldsymbol{P}_1' + \boldsymbol{P}_2']_1 + \boldsymbol{\pi}_3[\boldsymbol{q}]_1 \\ &= [x\boldsymbol{K}_1 + \boldsymbol{K}_2]_1^\top \boldsymbol{y}_1 + [(x\boldsymbol{K}_1 + \boldsymbol{K}_2)^\top \boldsymbol{y}_2 (x\boldsymbol{P}_1' + \boldsymbol{P}_2')]_1 + [(x\boldsymbol{K}_1 + \boldsymbol{K}_2)^\top \boldsymbol{y}_3 \boldsymbol{q}]_1 \ .\end{aligned}$$

Collecting the powers of X, we get that the verification equation states that $V(x, \boldsymbol{q}) = \boldsymbol{0}_k$, where $V(X, \boldsymbol{Q}) := \boldsymbol{a}X^2 + \boldsymbol{b}(\boldsymbol{Q})X + \boldsymbol{c}(\boldsymbol{Q})$ for

$$\begin{aligned} \boldsymbol{a} =& \boldsymbol{K}_1^\top \boldsymbol{y}_2 \boldsymbol{P}_1' , \\ \boldsymbol{b}(\boldsymbol{Q}) =& \boldsymbol{K}_1^\top (\boldsymbol{y}_1 + \boldsymbol{y}_2 \boldsymbol{P}_2') + \left(\boldsymbol{K}_2^\top \boldsymbol{y}_2 - \boldsymbol{\pi}_2 \right) \boldsymbol{P}_1' + \boldsymbol{K}_1^\top \boldsymbol{y}_3 \boldsymbol{Q} , \\ \boldsymbol{c}(\boldsymbol{Q}) =& \boldsymbol{K}_2^\top (\boldsymbol{y}_1 + \boldsymbol{y}_2 \boldsymbol{P}_2') - (\boldsymbol{\pi}_1 + \boldsymbol{\pi}_2 \boldsymbol{P}_2') + (\boldsymbol{K}_2^\top \boldsymbol{y}_3 - \boldsymbol{\pi}_3) \boldsymbol{Q} . \end{aligned}$$

Since each q_i has min-entropy $\Omega(\log \lambda)$ from the adversary's viewpoint and $V(X, \boldsymbol{Q})$ is a linear polynomial in each Q_i, from $V(x, \boldsymbol{q}) = \boldsymbol{0}_k$ it follows (by the Schwartz-Zippel lemma) with an overwhelming probability $1 - \varepsilon_q$ that $V(x, \boldsymbol{Q}) = 0$ as a polynomial and thus also $V(x, \boldsymbol{0}) = \boldsymbol{a}X^2 + \boldsymbol{b}(\boldsymbol{0})X + \boldsymbol{c}(\boldsymbol{0}) = 0$, where $\boldsymbol{b} := \boldsymbol{b}(\boldsymbol{0})$ and $\boldsymbol{b} := \boldsymbol{b}(\boldsymbol{0})$. In particular, in what follows, we can assume $\boldsymbol{y}_3 = \boldsymbol{0}$ and $\boldsymbol{\pi}_3 = \boldsymbol{0}$.

Next, let $\boldsymbol{w}$ be any solution to $\boldsymbol{y} = \boldsymbol{M}\boldsymbol{w}$; a solution exists and can be efficiently found since $\boldsymbol{M}$ has rank n. We already extracted $\boldsymbol{M}$ by using the DL oracle, while $\boldsymbol{y} = \boldsymbol{y}_1 + x\boldsymbol{d} + \boldsymbol{y}_2 \boldsymbol{P}_2'$, where $\boldsymbol{d} := \boldsymbol{y}_2 \boldsymbol{P}_1' \in \mathbb{Z}_p^n$, can be extracted if $\boldsymbol{d} = \boldsymbol{0}_n$. Thus, if $\boldsymbol{d} = \boldsymbol{0}_n$ then we can extract and return $\boldsymbol{w}$.

To show that, w.h.p., $\boldsymbol{d} = \boldsymbol{0}_n$, consider the opposite case $\boldsymbol{d} \neq \boldsymbol{0}_n$. If $\boldsymbol{a} \neq \boldsymbol{0}_k$ (this can only happen if $\boldsymbol{d} \neq \boldsymbol{0}_n$) then we have a quadratic equation $\boldsymbol{a}[x^2]_1 + \boldsymbol{b}[x]_1 + \boldsymbol{c}[1]_1 = 0$, with $\boldsymbol{a} \neq 0$, that $\mathcal{B}$ can solve for x, and thus return x.

Assume $\boldsymbol{a} = \boldsymbol{0}_k$ but $\boldsymbol{d} \neq \boldsymbol{0}_n$. This means $\boldsymbol{d} \in \mathbb{Z}_p^n$ is a non-zero element in the kernel of $\boldsymbol{K}_1^\top \in \mathbb{Z}_p^{k \times n}$. Since for $\mathcal{A}$, $\boldsymbol{K}_1$ looks uniformly random from $\mathbb{Z}_p^{k \times n}$, the question is now what is the maximum probability that for any $\boldsymbol{d} \neq \boldsymbol{0}_k$ picked by $\mathcal{A}$, $\boldsymbol{K}_1^\top \boldsymbol{d} = \boldsymbol{0}$. Obviously, unless $\boldsymbol{d} = \boldsymbol{0}_k$, this probability is equal to $\Pr[\boldsymbol{K}_1 \leftarrow_{\$} \mathbb{Z}_p^{k \times n} : \boldsymbol{K}_1^\top \boldsymbol{d} = \boldsymbol{0}_k] = p^{-k}$.

Hence, the probability of success $\varepsilon_{\mathcal{B}}$ of $\mathcal{B}$ is at least $\varepsilon_{\mathsf{w}} - \varepsilon_q - p^{-k}$, where ε_{w} is the probability of extracting w. $\square$

If the language parameter has been honestly generated, then one does not need the DL oracle to extract $\boldsymbol{M}$. Instead, as in [31], one relies on the witness-sampleability of $\mathcal{D}_{\mathsf{p}}$ to extract $\boldsymbol{M}$ and then finish the proof of Sub-PAR (knowledge-)soundness. Importantly, in the subverted case, we do not have to assume witness-sampleability.

We note SKerMDH is not secure when $k = 1$, [23].

Acknowledgments. We would like to thank Dario Fiore and anonymous reviewers for useful comments. Abdolmaleki, Lipmaa, and Siim were partially supported by the Estonian Research Council grant PRG49.

References

1. Abdalla, M., Benhamouda, F., Pointcheval, D.: Disjunctions for hash proof systems: new constructions and applications. In: Oswald, E., Fischlin, M. (eds.) EUROCRYPT 2015, Part II. LNCS, vol. 9057, pp. 69–100. Springer, Heidelberg (2015). https://doi.org/10.1007/978-3-662-46803-6_3

2. Abdolmaleki, B., Baghery, K., Lipmaa, H., Zając, M.: A subversion-resistant SNARK. In: Takagi, T., Peyrin, T. (eds.) ASIACRYPT 2017, Part III. LNCS, vol. 10626, pp. 3–33. Springer, Cham (2017). https://doi.org/10.1007/978-3-319-70700-6_1
3. Barak, B., Canetti, R., Nielsen, J.B., Pass, R.: Universally composable protocols with relaxed set-up assumptions. In: 45th FOCS, pp. 186–195 (2004)
4. Bellare, M., Fuchsbauer, G., Scafuro, A.: NIZKs with an untrusted CRS: security in the face of parameter subversion. In: Cheon, J.H., Takagi, T. (eds.) ASIACRYPT 2016, Part II. LNCS, vol. 10032, pp. 777–804. Springer, Heidelberg (2016). https://doi.org/10.1007/978-3-662-53890-6_26
5. Bichsel, P., Camenisch, J., Neven, G., Smart, N.P., Warinschi, B.: Get shorty via group signatures without encryption. In: Garay, J.A., De Prisco, R. (eds.) SCN 2010. LNCS, vol. 6280, pp. 381–398. Springer, Heidelberg (2010). https://doi.org/10.1007/978-3-642-15317-4_24
6. Blum, M., Feldman, P., Micali, S.: Non-interactive zero-knowledge and its applications (extended abstract). In: 20th ACM STOC, pp. 103–112 (2019)
7. Brown, D.R.L.: The exact security of ECDSA. Contributions to IEEE P1363a (2001). http://grouper.ieee.org/groups/1363/
8. Campanelli, M., Fiore, D., Querol, A.: LegoSNARK: modular design and composition of succinct zero-knowledge proofs. In: ACM CCS 2019, pp. 2075–2092 (2019)
9. Canetti, R., Goldreich, O., Goldwasser, S., Micali, S.: Resettable zero-knowledge (extended abstract). In: 32nd ACM STOC, pp. 235–244 (2000)
10. Damgård, I.: Towards practical public key systems secure against chosen ciphertext attacks. In: Feigenbaum, J. (ed.) CRYPTO 1991. LNCS, vol. 576, pp. 445–456. Springer, Heidelberg (1992). https://doi.org/10.1007/3-540-46766-1_36
11. Danezis, G., Fournet, C., Groth, J., Kohlweiss, M.: Square span programs with applications to succinct NIZK arguments. In: Sarkar, P., Iwata, T. (eds.) ASIACRYPT 2014, Part I. LNCS, vol. 8873, pp. 532–550. Springer, Heidelberg (2014). https://doi.org/10.1007/978-3-662-45611-8_28
12. Daza, V., González, A., Pindado, Z., Ràfols, C., Silva, J.: Shorter quadratic QA-NIZK proofs. In: Lin, D., Sako, K. (eds.) PKC 2019, Part I. LNCS, vol. 11442, pp. 314–343. Springer, Cham (2019). https://doi.org/10.1007/978-3-030-17253-4_11
13. Escala, A., Herold, G., Kiltz, E., Ràfols, C., Villar, J.: An Algebraic Framework for Diffie-Hellman Assumptions. In: Canetti, R., Garay, J.A. (eds.) CRYPTO 2013, Part II. LNCS, vol. 8043, pp. 129–147. Springer, Heidelberg (2013). https://doi.org/10.1007/978-3-642-40084-1_8
14. Fauzi, P., Lipmaa, H., Siim, J., Zając, M.: An efficient pairing-based shuffle argument. In: Takagi, T., Peyrin, T. (eds.) ASIACRYPT 2017, Part II. LNCS, vol. 10625, pp. 97–127. Springer, Cham (2017). https://doi.org/10.1007/978-3-319-70697-9_4
15. Fuchsbauer, G.: Subversion-zero-knowledge SNARKs. In: Abdalla, M., Dahab, R. (eds.) PKC 2018, Part I. LNCS, vol. 10769, pp. 315–347. Springer, Cham (2018). https://doi.org/10.1007/978-3-319-76578-5_11
16. Fuchsbauer, G., Kiltz, E., Loss, J.: The algebraic group model and its applications. In: Shacham, H., Boldyreva, A. (eds.) CRYPTO 2018, Part II. LNCS, vol. 10992, pp. 33–62. Springer, Cham (2018). https://doi.org/10.1007/978-3-319-96881-0_2
17. Fuchsbauer, G., Orrù, M.: Non-interactive zaps of knowledge. In: Preneel, B., Vercauteren, F. (eds.) ACNS 2018. LNCS, vol. 10892, pp. 44–62. Springer, Cham (2018). https://doi.org/10.1007/978-3-319-93387-0_3

18. Gennaro, R., Gentry, C., Parno, B., Raykova, M.: Quadratic span programs and succinct NIZKs without PCPs. In: Johansson, T., Nguyen, P.Q. (eds.) EUROCRYPT 2013. LNCS, vol. 7881, pp. 626–645. Springer, Heidelberg (2013). https://doi.org/10.1007/978-3-642-38348-9_37
19. Gentry, C., Wichs, D.: Separating succinct non-interactive arguments from all falsifiable assumptions. In: 43rd ACM STOC, pp. 99–108 (2011)
20. Gjøsteen, K.: A new security proof for Damgård's ElGamal. In: Pointcheval, D. (ed.) CT-RSA 2006. LNCS, vol. 3860, pp. 150–158. Springer, Heidelberg (2006). https://doi.org/10.1007/11605805_10
21. Goldreich, O., Oren, Y.: Definitions and properties of zero-knowledge proof systems. J. Cryptol. **7**(1), 1–32 (1994)
22. Goldwasser, S., Micali, S., Rackoff, C.: The knowledge complexity of interactive proof-systems (extended abstract). In: 17th ACM STOC, pp. 291–304 (1985)
23. González, A., Hevia, A., Ràfols, C.: QA-NIZK arguments in asymmetric groups: new tools and new constructions. In: Iwata, T., Cheon, J.H. (eds.) ASIACRYPT 2015, Part I. LNCS, vol. 9452, pp. 605–629. Springer, Heidelberg (2015). https://doi.org/10.1007/978-3-662-48797-6_25
24. González, A., Ráfols, C.: New techniques for non-interactive shuffle and range arguments. In: Manulis, M., Sadeghi, A.-R., Schneider, S. (eds.) ACNS 2016. LNCS, vol. 9696, pp. 427–444. Springer, Cham (2016). https://doi.org/10.1007/978-3-319-39555-5_23
25. González, A., Ràfols, C.: Sublinear pairing-based arguments with updatable CRS and weaker assumptions. Technical report 2019/326, IACR (2019) https://eprint.iacr.org/2019/326. Last Accessed 29 Mar 2019
26. Groth, J.: Short pairing-based non-interactive zero-knowledge arguments. In: Abe, M. (ed.) ASIACRYPT 2010. LNCS, vol. 6477, pp. 321–340. Springer, Heidelberg (2010). https://doi.org/10.1007/978-3-642-17373-8_19
27. Groth, J.: On the size of pairing-based non-interactive arguments. In: Fischlin, M., Coron, J.-S. (eds.) EUROCRYPT 2016, Part II. LNCS, vol. 9666, pp. 305–326. Springer, Heidelberg (2016). https://doi.org/10.1007/978-3-662-49896-5_11
28. Jutla, C.S., Roy, A.: Shorter quasi-adaptive NIZK proofs for linear subspaces. In: Sako, K., Sarkar, P. (eds.) ASIACRYPT 2013, Part I. LNCS, vol. 8269, pp. 1–20. Springer, Heidelberg (2013). https://doi.org/10.1007/978-3-642-42033-7_1
29. Jutla, C.S., Roy, A.: Shorter quasi-adaptive NIZK proofs for linear subspaces. Technical report 2013/109, International Association for Cryptologic Research (2013). http://eprint.iacr.org/2013/109. Accessed 14 Sept 2018
30. Jutla, C.S., Roy, A.: Switching lemma for bilinear tests and constant-size NIZK proofs for linear subspaces. In: Garay, J.A., Gennaro, R. (eds.) CRYPTO 2014, Part II. LNCS, vol. 8617, pp. 295–312. Springer, Heidelberg (2014). https://doi.org/10.1007/978-3-662-44381-1_17
31. Kiltz, E., Wee, H.: Quasi-adaptive NIZK for linear subspaces revisited. In: Oswald, E., Fischlin, M. (eds.) EUROCRYPT 2015, Part II. LNCS, vol. 9057, pp. 101–128. Springer, Heidelberg (2015). https://doi.org/10.1007/978-3-662-46803-6_4
32. Libert, B., Peters, T., Joye, M., Yung, M.: Non-malleability from malleability: simulation-sound quasi-adaptive NIZK proofs and CCA2-secure encryption from homomorphic signatures. In: Nguyen, P.Q., Oswald, E. (eds.) EUROCRYPT 2014. LNCS, vol. 8441, pp. 514–532. Springer, Heidelberg (2014). https://doi.org/10.1007/978-3-642-55220-5_29
33. Libert, B., Peters, T., Joye, M., Yung, M.: Compactly hiding linear spans. In: Iwata, T., Cheon, J.H. (eds.) ASIACRYPT 2015, Part I. LNCS, vol. 9452, pp. 681–707. Springer, Heidelberg (2015). https://doi.org/10.1007/978-3-662-48797-6_28

34. Lipmaa, H.: On the CCA1-security of Elgamal and Damgård's Elgamal. In: Lai, X., Yung, M., Lin, D. (eds.) Inscrypt 2010. LNCS, vol. 6584, pp. 18–35. Springer, Heidelberg (2011). https://doi.org/10.1007/978-3-642-21518-6_2
35. Lipmaa, H.: Progression-free sets and sublinear pairing-based non-interactive zero-knowledge arguments. In: Cramer, R. (ed.) TCC 2012. LNCS, vol. 7194, pp. 169–189. Springer, Heidelberg (2012). https://doi.org/10.1007/978-3-642-28914-9_10
36. Lipmaa, H.: Succinct non-interactive zero knowledge arguments from span programs and linear error-correcting codes. In: Sako, K., Sarkar, P. (eds.) ASIACRYPT 2013, Part I. LNCS, vol. 8269, pp. 41–60. Springer, Heidelberg (2013). https://doi.org/10.1007/978-3-642-42033-7_3
37. Lipmaa, H.: Simulation-extractable ZK-SNARKs revisited. Technical report 2019/612, IACR (2019). https://eprint.iacr.org/2019/612. Accessed 8 Feb 2020
38. Micali, S., Reyzin, L.: Soundness in the public-key model. In: Kilian, J. (ed.) CRYPTO 2001. LNCS, vol. 2139, pp. 542–565. Springer, Heidelberg (2001). https://doi.org/10.1007/3-540-44647-8_32
39. Morillo, P., Ràfols, C., Villar, J.L.: The kernel matrix Diffie-Hellman assumption. In: Cheon, J.H., Takagi, T. (eds.) ASIACRYPT 2016, Part I. LNCS, vol. 10031, pp. 729–758. Springer, Heidelberg (2016). https://doi.org/10.1007/978-3-662-53887-6_27
40. Parno, B., Howell, J., Gentry, C., Raykova, M.: Pinocchio: nearly practical verifiable computation. In: 2013 IEEE Symposium on Security and Privacy, pp. 238–252 (2013)
41. Stern, J., Pointcheval, D., Malone-Lee, J., Smart, N.P.: Flaws in applying proof methodologies to signature schemes. In: Yung, M. (ed.) CRYPTO 2002. LNCS, vol. 2442, pp. 93–110. Springer, Heidelberg (2002). https://doi.org/10.1007/3-540-45708-9_7
42. Wee, H.: Lower bounds for non-interactive zero-knowledge. In: Vadhan, S.P. (ed.) TCC 2007. LNCS, vol. 4392, pp. 103–117. Springer, Heidelberg (2007). https://doi.org/10.1007/978-3-540-70936-7_6

Lattice-Based Cryptography

Improved Discrete Gaussian and Subgaussian Analysis for Lattice Cryptography

Nicholas Genise[1], Daniele Micciancio[2], Chris Peikert[3], and Michael Walter[4(✉)]

[1] Rutgers University, New Brunswick, USA
[2] University of California, San Diego, San Diego, USA
[3] University of Michigan, Ann Arbor, USA
[4] IST Austria, Klosterneuburg, Austria
michael.walter@ist.ac.at

Abstract. Discrete Gaussian distributions over lattices are central to lattice-based cryptography, and to the computational and mathematical aspects of lattices more broadly. The literature contains a wealth of useful theorems about the behavior of discrete Gaussians under convolutions and related operations. Yet despite their structural similarities, most of these theorems are formally incomparable, and their proofs tend to be monolithic and written nearly "from scratch," making them unnecessarily hard to verify, understand, and extend.

In this work we present a modular framework for analyzing linear operations on discrete Gaussian distributions. The framework abstracts away the particulars of Gaussians, and usually reduces proofs to the choice of appropriate linear transformations and elementary linear algebra. To showcase the approach, we establish several general properties of discrete Gaussians, and show how to obtain all prior convolution theorems (along with some new ones) as straightforward corollaries. As another application, we describe a self-reduction for Learning With Errors (LWE) that uses a fixed number of samples to generate an unlimited number of additional ones (having somewhat larger error). The distinguishing features of our reduction are its simple analysis in our framework, and its exclusive use of discrete Gaussians without any loss in parameters relative to a prior mixed discrete-and-continuous approach.

As a contribution of independent interest, for subgaussian random matrices we prove a singular value concentration bound with explicitly

N. Genise—Supported by National Science Foundation grant SaTC-1815562. Part of this work was done at UCSD supported in part by the DARPA SafeWare program.
D. Micciancio—Supported by NSF Award 1936703.
C. Peikert—Supported in part by the Office of the Director of National Intelligence (ODNI), Intelligence Advanced Research Projects Activity (IARPA), via 2019-1902070008. The views and conclusions contained herein are those of the authors and should not be interpreted as necessarily representing the official policies, either expressed or implied, of ODNI, IARPA, or the U.S. Government.
M. Walter—Supported by the European Research Council, ERC consolidator grant (682815 - TOCNeT).

A. Kiayias et al. (Eds.): PKC 2020, LNCS 12110, pp. 623–651, 2020.
https://doi.org/10.1007/978-3-030-45374-9_21

stated constants, and we give tighter heuristics for specific distributions that are commonly used for generating lattice trapdoors. These bounds yield improvements in the concrete bit-security estimates for trapdoor lattice cryptosystems.

1 Introduction

The rapid development of lattice-based cryptography in recent years has moved the topic from a theoretical corner of cryptography to a leading candidate for post-quantum cryptography[1], while also providing advanced cryptographic functionalities like fully homomorphic encryption [Gen09]. Further appealing aspects of lattice-based cryptography are its innate parallelism and that its two foundational hardness assumptions, Short Integer Solution (SIS) and Learning With Errors (LWE), are supported by worst-case to average-case reductions (e.g., [Ajt96,Reg05]).

A very important object in lattice cryptography, and the computational and mathematical aspects of lattices more broadly, is a *discrete Gaussian* probability distribution, which (informally) is a Gaussian distribution restricted to a particular lattice (or coset thereof). For example, the strongest worst-case to average-case reductions [MR04,GPV08,Reg05] all rely centrally on discrete Gaussians and their nice properties. In addition, much of the development of lattice-based signature schemes, identity-based encryption, and other cryptosystems has centered around efficiently sampling from discrete Gaussians (see, e.g., [GPV08,Pei10,MP12,DDLL13,DLP14,MW17]), as well as the analysis of various kinds of combinations of discrete Gaussians [Pei10,BF11,MP13, AGHS13,AR16,BPMW16,GM18,CGM19,DGPY19].

By now, the literature contains a plethora of theorems about the behavior of discrete Gaussians in a variety of contexts, e.g., "convolution theorems" about sums of independent or dependent discrete Gaussians. Despite the close similarities between the proof approaches and techniques employed, these theorems are frequently incomparable and are almost always proved monolithically and nearly "from scratch." This state of affairs makes it unnecessarily difficult to understand the existing proofs, and to devise and prove new theorems when the known ones are inadequate. Because of the structural similarities among so many of the existing theorems and their proofs, a natural question is whether there is some "master theorem" for which many others are corollaries. That is what we aim to provide in this work.

1.1 Our Contributions

We present a modular framework for analyzing linear operations on discrete Gaussians over lattices, and show several applications. Our main theorem, which is the heart of the framework, is a simple, general statement about linear transformations of discrete Gaussians. We establish several natural consequences of

[1] https://csrc.nist.gov/Projects/Post-Quantum-Cryptography.

this theorem, e.g., for joint distributions of correlated discrete Gaussians. Then we show how to combine these tools in a modular way to obtain all previous discrete Gaussian convolution theorems (and some new ones) as corollaries. Notably—and in contrast to prior works—all the consequences of our main theorem follow mostly by elementary linear algebra, and do not use any additional properties (or even the definition) of the discrete Gaussian. In other words, our framework abstracts away the particulars of discrete Gaussians, and makes it easier to prove and verify many useful theorems about them.

As a novel application of our framework, we describe and tightly analyze an LWE self-reduction that, given a fixed number of LWE samples, directly generates (up to negligible statistical distance) an unlimited number of additional LWE samples with *discrete* Gaussian error (of a somewhat larger width than the original error). The ability to generate fresh, properly distributed LWE samples is often used in cryptosystems and security proofs (see [GPV08, ACPS09] for two early examples), so the tightness and simplicity of the procedure is important. The high-level idea behind prior LWE self-reductions, first outlined in [GPV08], is that a core procedure of [Reg05] can be used to generate fresh LWE samples with *continuous* Gaussian error. If desired, these samples can then be randomly rounded to have discrete Gaussian error [Pei10], but this increases the error width somewhat, and using continuous error to generate discrete samples seems unnecessarily cumbersome. We instead describe a *fully discrete* procedure, and use our framework to prove that it works for exactly the same parameters as the continuous one.

As a secondary contribution, motivated by the concrete security of "trapdoor" lattice cryptosystems, we analyze the singular values of the subgaussian matrices often used as such trapdoors [AP09, MP12]. Our analysis precisely tracks the exact constants in traditional concentration bounds for the singular values of a random matrix with independent, subgaussian rows [Ver12]. We also give a tighter heuristic bound on matrices chosen with independent subgaussian entries, supported by experimental evidence. Since the trapdoor's maximum singular value directly influences the hardness of the underlying SIS/LWE problems in trapdoor cryptosystems, our heuristic yields up to 10 more bits of security in a common parameter regime, where the trapdoor's entries are chosen independently from $\{0, \pm 1\}$ (with one-half probability on 0, and one-quarter probability on each of ± 1).[2]

1.2 Technical Overview

Linear Transformations of Discrete Gaussians. It is well known that any linear transformation of a (continuous, multivariate) Gaussian is another Gaussian.

[2] Our security analysis is a simple BKZ estimate, which is *not* a state-of-the-art concrete security analysis. However, we are only interested in the change in concrete security when changing from previous bounds to our new ones. Our point is that the underlying SIS problem is slightly harder in this trapdoor lattice regime than previously thought.

The heart of our work is a similar theorem for *discrete* Gaussians (Theorem 1). Note that we cannot hope to say anything about this in full generality, because a linear transformation of a lattice Λ may not even be a lattice. However, it is one if the kernel K of the transformation is a Λ-*subspace*, i.e., the lattice $\Lambda \cap K$ spans K (equivalently, K is spanned by vectors in Λ), so we restrict our attention to this case.

For a positive definite matrix Σ and a lattice coset $\Lambda + \mathbf{c}$, the discrete Gaussian distribution $\mathcal{D}_{\Lambda+\mathbf{c},\sqrt{\Sigma}}$ assigns to each $\mathbf{x}$ in its support $\Lambda + \mathbf{c}$ a probability proportional to $\exp(-\pi \cdot \mathbf{x}^t \Sigma^{-1} \mathbf{x})$. We show that for an arbitrary linear transformation $\mathbf{T}$, if the lattice $\Lambda \cap \ker(\mathbf{T})$ spans $\ker(\mathbf{T})$ and has smoothing parameter bounded by $\sqrt{\Sigma}$, then $\mathbf{T}$ applied to $\mathcal{D}_{\Lambda+\mathbf{c},\sqrt{\Sigma}}$ behaves essentially as one might expect from continuous Gaussians:

$$\mathbf{T}\mathcal{D}_{\Lambda+\mathbf{c},\sqrt{\Sigma}} \approx \mathcal{D}_{\mathbf{T}(\Lambda+\mathbf{c}),\mathbf{T}\sqrt{\Sigma}}.$$

The key observation for the proof is that for any point in the support of these two distributions, its probabilities under $\mathbf{T}\mathcal{D}_{\Lambda+\mathbf{c},\sqrt{\Sigma}}$ and $\mathcal{D}_{\mathbf{T}(\Lambda+\mathbf{c}),\mathbf{T}\sqrt{\Sigma}}$ differ only by a factor proportional to the Gaussian mass of some coset of $\Lambda \cap K$. But because this sublattice is "smooth" by assumption, all such cosets have essentially the same mass.

Convolutions. It is well known that the sum of two independent *continuous* Gaussians having covariances Σ_1, Σ_2 is another Gaussian of covariance Σ. We use our above-described Theorem 1 to prove similar statements for convolutions of *discrete* Gaussians. A typical such convolution is the statistical experiment where one samples

$$\mathbf{x}_1 \leftarrow \mathcal{D}_{\Lambda_1+\mathbf{c}_1,\sqrt{\Sigma_1}}, \; \mathbf{x}_2 \leftarrow \mathbf{x}_1 + \mathcal{D}_{\Lambda_2+\mathbf{c}_2-\mathbf{x}_1,\sqrt{\Sigma_2}}.$$

Based on the behavior of continuous Gaussians, one might expect the distribution of $\mathbf{x}_2$ to be close to $\mathcal{D}_{\Lambda_2+\mathbf{c}_2,\sqrt{\Sigma}}$, where $\Sigma = \Sigma_1 + \Sigma_2$. This turns out to be the case, under certain smoothness conditions on the lattices Λ_1, Λ_2 relative to the Gaussian parameters $\sqrt{\Sigma_1}, \sqrt{\Sigma_2}$. This was previously shown in [Pei10, Theorem 3.1], using a specialized analysis of the particular experiment in question.

We show how to obtain the same theorem in a higher-level and modular way, via Theorem 1. First, we show that the joint distribution of $(\mathbf{x}_1, \mathbf{x}_2)$ is close to a discrete Gaussian over $(\Lambda_1 + \mathbf{c}_1) \times (\Lambda_2 + \mathbf{c}_2)$, then we analyze the marginal distribution of $\mathbf{x}_2$ by applying the linear transformation $(\mathbf{x}_1, \mathbf{x}_2) \mapsto \mathbf{x}_2$ and analyzing the intersection of $\Lambda_1 \times \Lambda_2$ with the kernel of the transformation. Interestingly, our analysis arrives upon exactly the same hypotheses on the parameters as [Pei10, Theorem 3.1], so nothing is lost by proceeding via this generic route.

We further demonstrate the power of this approach—i.e., viewing convolutions as linear transformations of a joint distribution—by showing that it yields *all* prior discrete Gaussian convolution theorems from the literature. Indeed, we give a very general theorem on integer combinations of independent discrete Gaussians (Theorem 4), then show that several prior convolution theorems follow as immediate corollaries.

LWE Self-reduction. Recall the LWE distribution $(\mathbf{A}, \mathbf{b}^t = \mathbf{s}^t\mathbf{A} + \mathbf{e}^t \bmod q)$ where the secret $\mathbf{s} \leftarrow \mathbb{Z}_q^n$ and $\mathbf{A} \leftarrow \mathbb{Z}_q^{n\times m}$ are uniform and independent, and the entries of $\mathbf{e}$ are chosen independently from some error distribution, usually a discrete one over $\mathbb{Z}$. As described in [GPV08, ACPS09] (based on a core technique from [Reg05]), when $m \approx n \log q$ or more we can generate unlimited additional LWE samples (up to small statistical distance) with the same secret $\mathbf{s}$ and *continuous* Gaussian error, as

$$(\mathbf{a} = \mathbf{A}\mathbf{x} \in \mathbb{Z}_q^n\,,\, b = \mathbf{b}^t\mathbf{x} + \tilde{e} = \mathbf{s}^t\mathbf{a} + (\mathbf{e}^t\mathbf{x} + \tilde{e}) \bmod q)$$

for discrete Gaussian $\mathbf{x} \leftarrow \mathcal{D}_{\mathbb{Z}^m,r}$ and continuous Gaussian "smoothing error" $\tilde{e} \leftarrow \mathcal{D}_{\tilde{r}}$, for suitable parameters $r, \tilde{r}$. More specifically, the error term $\mathbf{e}^t\mathbf{x} + \tilde{e}$ is close to a continuous Gaussian $\mathcal{D}_t$, where $t^2 = (r\|\mathbf{e}\|)^2 + \tilde{r}^2$.

We emphasize that the above procedure yields samples with continuous Gaussian error. If discrete error is desired, one can then "round off" b, either naïvely (yielding somewhat unnatural "rounded Gaussian" error), or using more sophisticated randomized rounding (yielding a true discrete Gaussian [Pei10]). However, this indirect route to discrete error via a continuous intermediate step seems cumbersome and also somewhat loose, due to the extra round-off error.

An obvious alternative approach is to directly generate samples with discrete error, by choosing the "smoothing" term $\tilde{e} \leftarrow \mathcal{D}_{\mathbb{Z},\tilde{r}}$ from a discrete Gaussian. However, directly and tightly analyzing this alternative is surprisingly nontrivial, and to our knowledge it has never been proven that the resulting error is (close to) a discrete Gaussian, without incurring some loss relative to what is known for the continuous case.[3] Using the techniques developed in this paper, we give a modular proof that this alternative approach does indeed work, for the very same parameters as in the continuous case. As the reader may guess, we again express the overall error distribution as a linear transformation on some joint discrete Gaussian distribution. More specifically, the joint distribution is that of $(\mathbf{x}, \tilde{e})$ where $\mathbf{x}$ is conditioned on $\mathbf{a} = \mathbf{A}\mathbf{x}$, and the linear transformation is given by $[\mathbf{e}^t \mid 1]$ (where $\mathbf{e}^t$ is the original LWE error vector). The result then follows from our general theorem on linear transformations of discrete Gaussians (Theorem 1).

Analysis of Subgaussian Matrices. A distribution over $\mathbb{R}$ is *subgaussian* with parameter $s > 0$ if its tails are dominated by those of a Gaussian distribution of parameter s. More generally, a distribution $\mathcal{X}$ over $\mathbb{R}^n$ is subgaussian (with parameter s) if its marginals $\langle \mathcal{X}, \mathbf{u}\rangle$ are subgaussian (with the same parameter s) for every unit vector $\mathbf{u} \in \mathbb{R}^n$. We give precise concentration bounds on the singular values of random matrices whose columns, rows, or individual entries are independent subgaussians. We follow a standard proof strategy based on a union bound over an ε-net (see, e.g., [Ver12]), but we precisely track all the constant factors. For example, let $\mathbf{R} \in \mathbb{R}^{m\times n}$ be a matrix with independent subgaussian rows. First, we reduce the analysis of $\mathbf{R}$'s singular values to measuring how

[3] Of course, one can view the discrete Gaussian as a randomly rounded continuous one, but this is equivalent to the indirect, loose approach described above.

close $\mathbf{R}$ is to an isometry, specifically the norm $\|\mathbf{R}^t\mathbf{R}-\mathbf{I}_n\| = \sup_{\mathbf{u}} \|(\mathbf{R}^t\mathbf{R}-\mathbf{I}_n)\mathbf{u}\|$ where the supremum is taken over all unit vectors $\mathbf{u}$. Next, we approximate all unit vectors by an ε-net of the unit-sphere and bound the probability that $\|\mathbf{R}\mathbf{u}\|_2^2$ is too large by expressing $\|\mathbf{R}\mathbf{u}\|_2^2$ as a sum of independent terms (namely, $\|\mathbf{R}\mathbf{u}\|_2^2 = \sum_i \langle \mathbf{r}_i, \mathbf{u}\rangle^2$ where $\mathbf{r}_i$ is a row of $\mathbf{R}$). Finally, we take a union bound over the net to get a concentration bound. Lastly, we give a tighter heuristic for subgaussian matrices with independent entries from commonly used distributions in lattice-based cryptography.

1.3 Organization

The rest of the paper is organized as follows. Section 2 reviews the relevant mathematical background. Section 3 gives our general theorem on linear transformations of discrete Gaussians. Section 4 is devoted to convolutions of discrete Gaussians: we first analyze joint distributions and linear transforms of such convolutions, then show how all prior convolution theorems follow as corollaries. Section 5 gives our improved, purely discrete LWE self-reduction. Finally, Sect. 6 gives our provable and heuristic subgaussian matrix analysis; the proof of the main subgaussianity theorem appears in the full version.

2 Preliminaries

In this section we review some basic notions and mathematical notation used throughout the paper. Column vectors are denoted by lower-case bold letters ($\mathbf{a}, \mathbf{b}$, etc.) and matrices by upper-case bold letters ($\mathbf{A}, \mathbf{B}$, etc.). In addition, positive semidefinite matrices are sometimes denoted by upper-case Greek letters like Σ. The integers and reals are respectively denoted by $\mathbb{Z}$ and $\mathbb{R}$. All logarithms are base two unless specified otherwise.

Probability. We use calligraphic letters like $\mathcal{X}, \mathcal{Y}$ for probability distributions, and sometimes for random variables having such distributions. We make informal use of probability theory, without setting up formal probability spaces. We use set-like notation to describe probability distributions: for any distribution $\mathcal{X}$ over a set X, predicate P on X, and function $f\colon X \to Y$, we write $[\![f(x) \mid x \leftarrow \mathcal{X}, P(x)]\!]$ for the probability distribution over Y obtained by sampling x according to $\mathcal{X}$, conditioning on $P(x)$ being satisfied, and outputting $f(x) \in Y$. Similarly, we write $\{P(x) \mid x \leftarrow \mathcal{X}\}$ to denote the event that $P(x)$ is satisfied when x is selected according to $\mathcal{X}$, and use $\Pr\{z \leftarrow \mathcal{X}\}$ as an abbreviation for $\mathcal{X}(z) = \Pr\{x = z \mid x \leftarrow \mathcal{X}\}$. We write $f(\mathcal{X}) = [\![f(x) \mid x \leftarrow \mathcal{X}]\!]$ for the result of applying a function to a probability distribution. We let $\mathcal{U}(X)$ denote the uniform distribution over a set X of finite measure.

The *statistical distance* between any two probability distributions $\mathcal{X}, \mathcal{Y}$ over the same set is $\Delta(\mathcal{X}, \mathcal{Y}) := \sup_A |\Pr\{\mathcal{X} \in A\} - \Pr\{\mathcal{Y} \in A\}|$, where A ranges over all measurable sets. Similarly, for distributions $\mathcal{X}, \mathcal{Y}$ with the same support, their *max-log* distance [MW18] is defined as

$$\Delta_{\text{ML}}(\mathcal{X}, \mathcal{Y}) := \sup_A |\log \Pr\{\mathcal{X} \in A\} - \log \Pr\{\mathcal{Y} \in A\}|,$$

or, equivalently, $\Delta_{\text{ML}}(\mathcal{X}, \mathcal{Y}) = \sup_a |\log \Pr\{\mathcal{X} = a\} - \log \Pr\{\mathcal{Y} = a\}|$.

Distance Notation. For any two real numbers x, y, and $\varepsilon \geq 0$, we say that x *approximates* y within *relative error* ε (written $x \approx_\varepsilon y$) if $x \in [1-\varepsilon, 1+\varepsilon] \cdot y$. We also write $x \overset{\varepsilon}{\approx} y$ as an abbreviation for the symmetric relation $(x \approx_\varepsilon y) \wedge (y \approx_\varepsilon x)$, or, equivalently, $|\log x - \log y| \leq \log(1+\varepsilon) \leq \varepsilon$.

For two probability distributions $\mathcal{X}, \mathcal{Y}$ over the same set, we write $\mathcal{X} \approx_\varepsilon \mathcal{Y}$ if $\mathcal{X}(z) \approx_\varepsilon \mathcal{Y}(z)$ for every z. Similarly, we write $\mathcal{X} \overset{\varepsilon}{\approx} \mathcal{Y}$ if $\mathcal{X} \approx_\varepsilon \mathcal{Y}$ and $\mathcal{Y} \approx_\varepsilon \mathcal{X}$. The following facts are easily verified:

1. If $\mathcal{X} \approx_\varepsilon \mathcal{Y}$, then $\mathcal{Y} \approx_{\bar{\varepsilon}} \mathcal{X}$ (and therefore, $\mathcal{X} \overset{\bar{\varepsilon}}{\approx} \mathcal{Y}$) for $\bar{\varepsilon} = \varepsilon/(1-\varepsilon)$.
2. If $\mathcal{X} \approx_\varepsilon \mathcal{Y}$ and $\mathcal{Y} \approx_\delta \mathcal{Z}$ then $\mathcal{X} \approx_{\varepsilon+\delta+\varepsilon\delta} \mathcal{Z}$, and similarly for $\overset{\varepsilon}{\approx}$.
3. For any (possibly randomized) function f, $\Delta(f(\mathcal{X}), f(\mathcal{Y})) \leq \Delta(\mathcal{X}, \mathcal{Y})$, and $\mathcal{X} \approx_\varepsilon \mathcal{Y}$ implies $f(\mathcal{X}) \approx_\varepsilon f(\mathcal{Y})$.
4. If $\mathcal{X} \approx_\varepsilon \mathcal{Y}$ then $\Delta(\mathcal{X}, \mathcal{Y}) \leq \varepsilon/2$.
5. $\mathcal{X} \overset{\varepsilon}{\approx} \mathcal{Y}$ if and only if $\Delta_{\text{ML}}(\mathcal{X}, \mathcal{Y}) \leq \log(1+\varepsilon)$.

Linear Algebra. For any set of vectors $S \subseteq \mathbb{R}^n$, we write $\text{span}(S)$ for the linear span of S, i.e., the smallest linear subspace of $\mathbb{R}^n$ that contains S. For any matrix $\mathbf{T} \in \mathbb{R}^{n \times k}$, we write $\text{span}(\mathbf{T})$ for the linear span of the columns of $\mathbf{T}$, or, equivalently, the image of $\mathbf{T}$ as a linear transformation. Moreover, we often identify $\mathbf{T}$ with this linear transformation, treating them interchangeably. A matrix has *full column rank* if its columns are linearly independent.

We write $\langle \mathbf{x}, \mathbf{y} \rangle = \sum_i x_i \cdot y_i$ for the standard inner product of two vectors in $\mathbb{R}^n$. For any vector $\mathbf{x} \in \mathbb{R}^n$ and a (possibly empty) set $S \subseteq \mathbb{R}^n$, we write $\mathbf{x}_{\perp S}$ for the component of $\mathbf{x}$ orthogonal to S, i.e., the unique vector $\mathbf{x}_{\perp S} \in \mathbf{x} + \text{span}(S)$ such that $\langle \mathbf{x}_{\perp S}, \mathbf{s} \rangle = 0$ for every $\mathbf{s} \in S$.

The *singular values* of a matrix $\mathbf{A} \in \mathbb{R}^{m \times n}$ are the square roots of the first $d = \min(m, n)$ eigenvalues of its Gram matrix $\mathbf{A}^t\mathbf{A}$. We list singular values in non-increasing order, as $s_1(\mathbf{A}) \geq s_2(\mathbf{A}) \geq \cdots \geq s_d(\mathbf{A}) \geq 0$. The *spectral norm* is $\|\mathbf{A}\| := \sup_{\mathbf{x} \neq \mathbf{0}} \|\mathbf{A}\mathbf{x}\|_2 / \|\mathbf{x}\|_2$, which equals its largest singular value $s_1(\mathbf{A})$.

The (Moore-Penrose) *pseudoinverse* of a matrix $\mathbf{A} \in \mathbb{R}^{n \times k}$ of full column rank[4] is $\mathbf{A}^+ = (\mathbf{A}^t\mathbf{A})^{-1}\mathbf{A}^t$, and it is the unique matrix $\mathbf{A}^+ \in \mathbb{R}^{k \times n}$ such that $\mathbf{A}^+\mathbf{A} = \mathbf{I}$ and $\text{span}((\mathbf{A}^+)^t) = \text{span}(\mathbf{A})$. (If $\mathbf{A}$ is square, its pseudoinverse is just its inverse $\mathbf{A}^+ = \mathbf{A}^{-1}$.) For any $\mathbf{v} \in \text{span}(\mathbf{A})$ we have $\mathbf{A}\mathbf{A}^+\mathbf{v} = \mathbf{v}$, because $\mathbf{v} = \mathbf{A}\mathbf{c}$ for some vector $\mathbf{c}$.

The *tensor product* (or *Kronecker product*) of any two matrices $\mathbf{A} = (a_{i,j})$ and $\mathbf{B}$ is the matrix obtained by replacing each entry $a_{i,j}$ of $\mathbf{A}$ with the block $a_{i,j}\mathbf{B}$. It obeys the *mixed-product* property $(\mathbf{A} \otimes \mathbf{B})(\mathbf{C} \otimes \mathbf{D}) = (\mathbf{AC}) \otimes (\mathbf{BD})$ for any matrices $\mathbf{A}, \mathbf{B}, \mathbf{C}, \mathbf{D}$ with compatible dimensions.

[4] The pseudoinverse can also be defined for arbitrary matrices, but the definition is more complex, and we will not need this level of generality.

Positive (Semi)definite Matrices. A symmetric matrix $\Sigma = \Sigma^t$ is *positive semidefinite*, written $\Sigma \succeq 0$, if $\mathbf{x}^t \Sigma \mathbf{x} \geq 0$ for all vectors $\mathbf{x}$. It is *positive definite*, written $\Sigma \succ 0$, if $\mathbf{x}^t \Sigma \mathbf{x} > 0$ for all nonzero $\mathbf{x}$. Positive (semi)definiteness defines a partial ordering on symmetric matrices: we write $\Sigma \succeq \Sigma'$ (and $\Sigma' \preceq \Sigma$) if $\Sigma - \Sigma' \succeq 0$ is positive semidefinite, and similarly for $\Sigma \succ \Sigma'$.[5] For any two (not necessarily positive semidefinite) matrices $\mathbf{S}, \mathbf{T} \in \mathbb{R}^{n \times k}$, we write $\mathbf{S} \leq \mathbf{T}$ if $\mathbf{S}\mathbf{S}^t \preceq \mathbf{T}\mathbf{T}^t$.

For any matrix $\mathbf{A}$, its Gram matrix $\mathbf{A}^t\mathbf{A}$ is positive semidefinite. Conversely, a matrix Σ is positive semidefinite if and only if it can be written as $\Sigma = \mathbf{S}\mathbf{S}^t$ for some matrix $\mathbf{S}$; we write $\mathbf{S} = \sqrt{\Sigma}$, and say that $\mathbf{S}$ is a *square root* of Σ. Note that such a square root is not unique, because, e.g., $-\mathbf{S} = \sqrt{\Sigma}$ as well. We often just write $\sqrt{\Sigma}$ to refer to some arbitrary but *fixed* square root of Σ. For positive *definite* $\Sigma \succ 0$, observe that $\mathbf{S} = \sqrt{\Sigma}$ if and only if $\Sigma^{-1} = (\mathbf{S}\mathbf{S}^t)^{-1} = \mathbf{S}^{-t}\mathbf{S}^{-1}$, so $\mathbf{S}^{-t} = \sqrt{\Sigma^{-1}}$, i.e., $\sqrt{\Sigma}^{-t}$ is equivalent to $\sqrt{\Sigma^{-1}}$, and hence $\sqrt{\Sigma}^{-1}$ is equivalent to $\sqrt{\Sigma^{-1}}^t$.

Lattices. An n-dimensional *lattice* Λ is a discrete subgroup of $\mathbb{R}^n$, or, equivalently, the set $\Lambda = \mathcal{L}(\mathbf{B}) = \{\mathbf{B}\mathbf{x} \colon \mathbf{x} \in \mathbb{Z}^k\}$ of all integer linear combinations of the columns of a full-column-rank *basis* matrix $\mathbf{B} \in \mathbb{R}^{n \times k}$. The dimension k is the *rank* of Λ, and the lattice is *full rank* if $k = n$. The basis $\mathbf{B}$ is not unique; any $\mathbf{B}' = \mathbf{B}\mathbf{U}$ for $\mathbf{U} \in \mathbb{Z}^{k \times k}$ with $\det(\mathbf{U}) = \pm 1$ is also a basis of the same lattice.

A *coset* of a lattice $\Lambda \subset \mathbb{R}^n$ is a set of the form $A = \Lambda + \mathbf{a} = \{\mathbf{v} + \mathbf{a} : \mathbf{v} \in \Lambda\}$ for some $\mathbf{a} \in \mathbb{R}^n$. The *dual lattice* of Λ is the lattice $\Lambda^\vee = \{\mathbf{x} \in \operatorname{span}(\Lambda) : \langle \mathbf{x}, \Lambda \rangle \subseteq \mathbb{Z}\}$. If $\mathbf{B}$ is a basis for Λ, then $\mathbf{B}^{+t}$ is a basis for $\Lambda^\vee$. A *Λ-subspace*, also called a *lattice subspace* when Λ is clear from context, is the linear span of some set of lattice points, i.e., a subspace S for which $S = \operatorname{span}(\Lambda \cap S)$. A fundamental property of lattices (used in the proof that every lattice has a basis) is that if $\mathbf{T}$ is a linear transformation for which $\ker(\mathbf{T})$ is a Λ-subspace, then $\mathbf{T}\Lambda$ is also a lattice.[6]

The *Gram-Schmidt orthogonalization* (GSO) of a lattice basis $\mathbf{B} = \{\mathbf{b}_i\}$ is the set $\tilde{\mathbf{B}} = \{\tilde{\mathbf{b}}_i\}$ of vectors defined iteratively as $\tilde{\mathbf{b}}_i = (\mathbf{b}_i)_{\perp \{\mathbf{b}_1, \ldots, \mathbf{b}_{i-1}\}}$, i.e., the component of $\mathbf{b}_i$ orthogonal to the previous basis vectors. (Notice that the GSO is sensitive to the ordering of the basis vectors.) We define the *minimum GSO length* of a lattice as $\tilde{bl}(\Lambda) := \min_{\mathbf{B}} \max_i \|\tilde{\mathbf{b}}_i\|_2$, where the minimum is taken over all bases $\mathbf{B}$ of Λ.

For any two lattices Λ_1, Λ_2, their *tensor product* $\Lambda_1 \otimes \Lambda_2$ is the set of all sums of vectors of the form $\mathbf{v}_1 \otimes \mathbf{v}_2$ where $\mathbf{v}_1 \in \Lambda_1$ and $\mathbf{v}_2 \in \Lambda_2$. If $\mathbf{B}_1, \mathbf{B}_2$ are respectively bases of Λ_1, Λ_2, then $\mathbf{B}_1 \otimes \mathbf{B}_2$ is a basis of $\Lambda_1 \otimes \Lambda_2$.

Gaussians. Let $\mathcal{D}$ be the Gaussian probability measure on $\mathbb{R}^k$ (for any $k \geq 1$) having density function defined by $\rho(\mathbf{x}) = e^{-\pi\|\mathbf{x}\|^2}$, the Gaussian function with

[5] Notice that it is possible for $\Sigma \succeq \Sigma'$ and $\Sigma \neq \Sigma'$, and still $\Sigma \nsucc \Sigma'$.

[6] Clearly, $\mathbf{T}\Lambda$ is an additive group, and it is not too difficult to show that $\mathbf{T}\Lambda$ has a minimal nonzero element (i.e., it is discrete), so it is a lattice.

total measure $\int_{\mathbf{x}\in\mathbb{R}^k} \rho(\mathbf{x})\, d\mathbf{x} = 1$. For any (possibly non-full-rank) matrix $\mathbf{S} \in \mathbb{R}^{n\times k}$, we define the (possibly non-spherical) Gaussian distribution

$$\mathcal{D}_{\mathbf{S}} := \mathbf{S}\cdot\mathcal{D} = [\![\mathbf{S}\mathbf{x} \mid \mathbf{x} \leftarrow \mathcal{D}]\!]$$

as the image of $\mathcal{D}$ under $\mathbf{S}$; this distribution has covariance $\Sigma/(2\pi)$ where $\Sigma = \mathbf{S}\mathbf{S}^t$ is positive semidefinite. Notice that $\mathcal{D}_{\mathbf{S}}$ depends only on Σ, and not on any specific choice of the square root $\mathbf{S}$.[7] So, we often write $\mathcal{D}_{\sqrt{\Sigma}}$ instead of $\mathcal{D}_{\mathbf{S}}$. When $\Sigma = s^2\mathbf{I}$ is a scalar matrix, we often write $\mathcal{D}_s$ (observe that $\mathcal{D} = \mathcal{D}_1$).

For any Gaussian distribution $\mathcal{D}_{\mathbf{S}}$ and set $A \subseteq \operatorname{span}(\mathbf{S})$, we define $\mathcal{D}_{A,\mathbf{S}}$ as the conditional distribution (where $\mathbf{S}^{-1}(A) = \{\mathbf{x} : \mathbf{S}\mathbf{x} \in A\}$)

$$\mathcal{D}_{A,\mathbf{S}} := [\mathcal{D}_{\mathbf{S}}]_A = [\![\mathbf{y} \mid \mathbf{y} \leftarrow \mathcal{D}_{\mathbf{S}}, \mathbf{y}\in A]\!] = [\![\mathbf{S}\mathbf{x} \mid \mathbf{x} \leftarrow \mathcal{D}, \mathbf{S}\mathbf{x} \in A]\!] = \mathbf{S}\cdot[\mathcal{D}]_{\mathbf{S}^{-1}(A)}$$

whenever this distribution is well-defined.[8] Examples for which this is the case include all sets A with positive measure $\int_{\mathbf{x}\in A} d\mathbf{x} > 0$, and all sets of the form $A = L + \Lambda + \mathbf{c}$, where $L \subseteq \mathbb{R}^n$ is a linear subspace and $\Lambda + \mathbf{c} \subset \mathbb{R}^n$ is a lattice coset.

For any lattice coset $A = \Lambda + \mathbf{c}$ (and taking $\mathbf{S} = \mathbf{I}$ for simplicity), the distribution $\mathcal{D}_{\Lambda+\mathbf{c}}$ is exactly the (origin-centered) discrete Gaussian distribution given by $\Pr\{\mathbf{x} \leftarrow \mathcal{D}_A\} := \rho(\mathbf{x})/\sum_{\mathbf{y}\in A}\rho(\mathbf{y})$, as usually defined in lattice cryptography. It also follows immediately from the definition that $\mathbf{c} + \mathcal{D}_{\Lambda-\mathbf{c}}$ is the "$\mathbf{c}$-centered" discrete Gaussian $\mathcal{D}_{\Lambda,\mathbf{c}}$ that is defined and used in some works. Because of this, there is no loss of generality in dealing solely with origin-centered Gaussians, as we do in this work.

Lemma 1. *For any $A \subseteq \mathbb{R}^n$ and matrices $\mathbf{S}, \mathbf{T}$ representing linear functions where $\mathbf{T}$ is* injective *on A, we have*

$$\mathbf{T}\cdot\mathcal{D}_{A,\mathbf{S}} = \mathcal{D}_{\mathbf{T}A,\mathbf{T}\mathbf{S}}. \tag{2.1}$$

Proof. By definition of the conditioned Gaussian and the fact that $A = \mathbf{T}^{-1}(\mathbf{T}A)$, we have

$$\mathbf{T}\cdot\mathcal{D}_{A,\mathbf{S}} = \mathbf{T}\mathbf{S}\cdot[\mathcal{D}]_{\mathbf{S}^{-1}(A)} = \mathbf{T}\mathbf{S}\cdot[\mathcal{D}]_{(\mathbf{T}\mathbf{S})^{-1}(\mathbf{T}A)} = \mathcal{D}_{\mathbf{T}A,\mathbf{T}\mathbf{S}}. \qquad \square$$

We now recall the notion of the *smoothing parameter* [MR04] and its generalization to non-spherical Gaussians [Pei10].

Definition 1. *For a lattice Λ and $\varepsilon \geq 0$, we say $\eta_\varepsilon(\Lambda) \leq 1$ if $\rho(\Lambda^\vee) \leq 1 + \varepsilon$. More generally, for any matrix $\mathbf{S}$ of full column rank, we write $\eta_\varepsilon(\Lambda) \leq \mathbf{S}$ if $\Lambda \subset \operatorname{span}(\mathbf{S})$ and $\eta_\varepsilon(\mathbf{S}^+\Lambda) \leq 1$, where $\mathbf{S}^+$ is the pseudoinverse of $\mathbf{S}$. When $\mathbf{S} = s\mathbf{I}$ is a scalar matrix, we may simply write $\eta_\varepsilon(\Lambda) \leq s$.*

[7] To see this, notice that the probability under $\mathbf{S}(\mathcal{D})$ of any vector $\Sigma\mathbf{x} \in \operatorname{span}(\mathbf{S}\mathbf{S}^t) = \operatorname{span}(\mathbf{S})$ in its support is $\rho(\{\mathbf{z} : \mathbf{S}\mathbf{z} = \Sigma\mathbf{x}\}) = \rho(\mathbf{T}^t\mathbf{x} + \ker(\mathbf{S})) = \rho(\mathbf{S}^t\mathbf{x})\cdot\rho(\ker(\mathbf{T}))$ because $\mathbf{S}^t\mathbf{x}$ is orthogonal to $\ker(\mathbf{S}) = \{\mathbf{z} : \mathbf{S}\mathbf{z} = \mathbf{0}\}$. Moreover, $\rho(\ker(\mathbf{S})) = 1$ and $\rho(\mathbf{S}^t\mathbf{x}) = \rho(\|\mathbf{S}^t\mathbf{x}\|) = \rho(\sqrt{\mathbf{x}^t\Sigma\mathbf{x}})$ depends only on Σ.

[8] For any nonempty set A with zero measure, one can first define $A_\varepsilon = A + \{\mathbf{x}\colon \|\mathbf{x}\| < \varepsilon\}$, which has nonzero measure for any $\varepsilon > 0$. Then, $[\mathcal{D}_{\mathbf{S}}]_A$ is defined as the limit of $[\mathcal{D}_{\mathbf{S}}]_{A_\varepsilon}$ as $\varepsilon \to 0$, if this limit exists.

Observe that for a fixed lattice Λ, whether $\eta_\varepsilon(\Lambda) \leq \mathbf{S}$ depends only on $\Sigma = \mathbf{S}\mathbf{S}^t$, and not the specific choice of square root $\mathbf{S} = \sqrt{\Sigma}$. This is because the dual lattice $(\mathbf{S}^+\Lambda)^\vee = \mathbf{S}^t\Lambda^\vee$, so for any dual vector $\mathbf{w} = \mathbf{S}^t\mathbf{v}$ where $\mathbf{v} \in \Lambda^\vee$, $\rho(\mathbf{w}) = \exp(-\pi\|\mathbf{w}\|^2) = \exp(-\pi\mathbf{v}^t\mathbf{S}\mathbf{S}^t\mathbf{v}) = \exp(-\pi\mathbf{v}^t\Sigma\mathbf{v})$ is invariant under the choice of $\mathbf{S}$. From this analysis it is also immediate that Definition 1 is consistent with our partial ordering of matrices (i.e., $\mathbf{S} \leq \mathbf{T}$ when $\mathbf{S}\mathbf{S}^t \preceq \mathbf{T}\mathbf{T}^t$), and with the original definition [MR04] of the smoothing parameter of Λ as the smallest positive real $s > 0$ such that $\rho(s\Lambda^\vee) \leq 1 + \varepsilon$. The following lemma also follows immediately from the definition.

Lemma 2. *For any lattice Λ, $\varepsilon \geq 0$, and matrices $\mathbf{S}, \mathbf{T}$ of full column rank, we have $\eta_\varepsilon(\Lambda) \leq \mathbf{S}$ if and only if $\eta_\varepsilon(\mathbf{T}\Lambda) \leq \mathbf{T}\mathbf{S}$.*

The name "smoothing parameter" comes from the following fundamental property proved in [MR04, Reg05].

Lemma 3. *For any lattice Λ and $\varepsilon \geq 0$ where $\eta_\varepsilon(\Lambda) \leq 1$, we have $\rho(\Lambda + \mathbf{c}) \approx_\varepsilon 1/\det(\Lambda)$ for any $\mathbf{c} \in \operatorname{span}(\Lambda)$; equivalently, $(\mathcal{D} \bmod \Lambda) \approx_\varepsilon \mathcal{U} := \mathcal{U}(\operatorname{span}(\Lambda)/\Lambda)$: In particular, $\Delta(\mathcal{D} \bmod \Lambda, \mathcal{U}) \leq \varepsilon/2$ and $\Delta_{\text{ML}}(\mathcal{D} \bmod \Lambda, \mathcal{U}) \leq -\log(1 - \varepsilon)$.*

The lemma is easily generalized to arbitrary vectors $\mathbf{c}$ not necessarily in $\operatorname{span}(\Lambda)$.

Corollary 1. *For any lattice Λ and $\varepsilon \geq 0$ where $\eta_\varepsilon(\Lambda) \leq 1$, and any vector $\mathbf{c}$, we have*

$$\rho(\Lambda + \mathbf{c}) \approx_\varepsilon \frac{\rho(\mathbf{c}_{\perp\Lambda})}{\det(\Lambda)}.$$

Proof. Because $\mathbf{c}_{\perp\Lambda}$ is orthogonal to $\operatorname{span}(\Lambda)$ and $\mathbf{c}' = \mathbf{c} - (\mathbf{c}_{\perp\Lambda}) \in \operatorname{span}(\Lambda)$, we have

$$\rho(\Lambda + \mathbf{c}) = \rho(\Lambda + \mathbf{c}' + (\mathbf{c}_{\perp\Lambda})) = \rho(\mathbf{c}_{\perp\Lambda}) \cdot \rho(\Lambda + \mathbf{c}') \approx_\varepsilon \frac{\rho(\mathbf{c}_{\perp\Lambda})}{\det(\Lambda)},$$

where $\rho(\Lambda + \mathbf{c}') \approx_\varepsilon \det(\Lambda)^{-1}$ by Lemma 3. □

Finally, we recall the following bounds on the smoothing parameter.

Lemma 4 ([GPV08, Lemma 3.1]). *For any rank-n lattice Λ and $\varepsilon > 0$, we have $\eta_\varepsilon(\Lambda) \leq \tilde{bl}(\Lambda) \cdot \sqrt{\ln(2n(1 + 1/\varepsilon))/\pi}$.*

Lemma 5 ([MP13, Corollary 2.7]). *For any lattices Λ_1, Λ_2, we have*

$$\eta_{\varepsilon'}(\Lambda_1 \otimes \Lambda_2) \leq \tilde{bl}(\Lambda_1) \cdot \eta_\varepsilon(\Lambda_2),$$

where $1+\varepsilon' = (1+\varepsilon)^n$ and n is the rank of Λ_1. (Note that $\varepsilon' \approx n\varepsilon$ for sufficiently small ε.)

Quotients and Groups. Lattice cryptography typically involves integer lattices Λ that are periodic modulo some integer q, i.e., $q\mathbb{Z}^m \subseteq \Lambda \subseteq \mathbb{Z}^m$. These "$q$-ary lattices" lattices can be equivalently viewed as subgroups of $\mathbb{Z}_q^m = \mathbb{Z}^m/q\mathbb{Z}^m$. Let $\mathbf{A} \in \mathbb{Z}_q^{n\times m}$ for some $n \geq 1$ and define the lattice $\Lambda_q^\perp(\mathbf{A}) := \{\mathbf{x} \in \mathbb{Z}^m : \mathbf{A}\mathbf{x} = \mathbf{0} \bmod q\}$. We say that $\mathbf{A}$ is *primitive* if $\mathbf{A}\cdot\mathbb{Z}^m = \mathbb{Z}_q^n$.

All the results in this paper apply not only to lattices, but also to arbitrary (topologically closed) subgroups of $\mathbb{R}^n$. These are groups of the form $G = \Lambda + L$ where Λ is a lattice and L is a linear subspace. When considering such groups, one can always assume, without loss of generality, that Λ and L are mutually orthogonal because $\Lambda + L = (\Lambda_{\perp L}) + L$. Intuitively, one can think of groups $\Lambda + L$ as lattices of the form $\Lambda + \delta\Lambda_L$ where $\text{span}(\Lambda_L) = L$ and $\delta \approx 0$. Notice that $\lim_{\delta\to 0} \eta_\varepsilon(\Lambda + \delta\Lambda_L) = \eta_\varepsilon(\Lambda_{\perp L})$. For simplicity, we will focus the presentation on lattices, and leave the generalization to arbitrary groups to the reader. Results for the continuous Gaussian distribution $\mathcal{D}$ are obtained as a special case by taking the limit, for $\delta \to 0$, of $\delta\Lambda$, where Λ is an arbitrary lattice spanning the support of $\mathcal{D}$.

Subgaussian Distributions. Subgaussian distributions are those on $\mathbb{R}$ which have tails dominated by Gaussians [Ver12]. An equivalent formulation is through a distribution's moment-generating function, and the definition below is commonly used throughout lattice-based cryptography [MP12,LPR13].

Definition 2. *A real random variable X is* subgaussian *with parameter $s > 0$ if for all $t \in \mathbb{R}$,*

$$\mathbb{E}[e^{2\pi t X}] \leq e^{\pi s^2 t^2}.$$

From this we can derive a standard Gaussian concentration bound.

Lemma 6. *A subgaussian random variable X with parameter $s > 0$ satisfies, for all $t > 0$,*

$$\Pr\{|X| \geq t\} \leq 2\exp(-\pi t^2/s^2).$$

Proof. Let $\delta \in \mathbb{R}$ be arbitrary. Then,

$$\begin{aligned}\Pr\{X \geq t\} &= \Pr\{\exp(2\pi\delta X) \geq \exp(2\pi\delta t)\} \leq \exp(-2\pi\delta t)\cdot\mathbb{E}[\exp(2\pi\delta X)]\\ &\leq \exp(-2\pi\delta t + \pi\delta^2 s^2).\end{aligned}$$

This is minimized at $\delta = t/s^2$, so we have

$$\Pr\{X \geq t\} \leq \exp(-\pi t^2/s^2).$$

The symmetric case $X \leq -t$ is analogous, and the proof is completed by a union bound. □

A random *vector* $\mathbf{x}$ over $\mathbb{R}^n$ is subgaussian with parameter α if $\langle \mathbf{x}, \mathbf{u}\rangle$ is subgaussian with parameter α for all unit vectors $\mathbf{u}$. If each coordinate of a random vector is subgaussian (with a common parameter) conditioned any values of the previous coordinates, then the vector itself is subgaussian (with the same parameter). See [LPR13, Claim 2.1] for a proof.

3 Lattice Projections

We emphasize that the proof of Lemma 1 makes essential use of the injectivity of $\mathbf{T}$, and the lemma does not hold when $\mathbf{T}$ is not injective. There are two reasons for this. Consider, for simplicity, the special case where $A = \Lambda$ is a lattice and $\mathbf{S} = \mathbf{I}$. First, the set $\mathbf{T}\Lambda$ is not necessarily a lattice, and the conditional distribution $\mathcal{D}_{\mathbf{T}\Lambda,\mathbf{T}}$ may not be well defined.[9] We resolve this issue by restricting $\mathbf{T}$ to be a linear transformation whose kernel is a *lattice subspace* $P = \text{span}(P \cap \Lambda)$. Second, even when $\mathbf{T} \cdot \mathcal{D}_\Lambda$ is well defined, in general it does not equal the discrete Gaussian $\mathcal{D}_{\mathbf{T}\Lambda,\mathbf{T}}$. We address this issue by showing that these distributions are *statistically close*, assuming that the sublattice $\Lambda \cap P$ has small enough smoothing parameter.

Theorem 1. *For any $\varepsilon \in [0,1)$ defining $\bar{\varepsilon} = 2\varepsilon/(1-\varepsilon)$, matrix $\mathbf{S}$ of full column rank, lattice coset $A = \Lambda + \mathbf{a} \subset \text{span}(\mathbf{S})$, and matrix $\mathbf{T}$ such that $\ker(\mathbf{T})$ is a Λ-subspace and $\eta_\varepsilon(\Lambda \cap \ker(\mathbf{T})) \le \mathbf{S}$, we have*

$$\mathbf{T} \cdot \mathcal{D}_{A,\mathbf{S}} \overset{\bar{\varepsilon}}{\approx} \mathcal{D}_{\mathbf{T}A,\mathbf{TS}}.$$

The proof of Theorem 1 (given below) relies primarily on the following specialization to linear transformations that are *orthogonal projections* $\mathbf{x} \mapsto \mathbf{x}_{\perp P}$.

Lemma 7. *For any $\varepsilon \in [0,1)$, lattice coset $A = \Lambda + \mathbf{a}$, and lattice subspace $P = \text{span}(\Lambda \cap P)$ such that $\eta_\varepsilon(\Lambda \cap P) \le 1$, we have*

$$\Delta_{\text{ML}}((\mathcal{D}_A)_{\perp P}, \mathcal{D}_{A_{\perp P}}) \le \log \frac{1+\varepsilon}{1-\varepsilon},$$

or equivalently, $(\mathcal{D}_A)_{\perp P} \overset{\bar{\varepsilon}}{\approx} \mathcal{D}_{A_{\perp P}}$ where $\bar{\varepsilon} = 2\varepsilon/(1-\varepsilon)$.

Proof. It is immediate that both $(\mathcal{D}_A)_{\perp P}$ and $\mathcal{D}_{A_{\perp P}}$ are both well-defined distributions over $A_{\perp P}$, which is a lattice coset. For any $\mathbf{v} \in A_{\perp P}$, let $p_\mathbf{v} = \Pr\{\mathbf{v} \leftarrow (\mathcal{D}_A)_{\perp P}\}$ and $q_\mathbf{v} = \Pr\{\mathbf{v} \leftarrow \mathcal{D}_{A_{\perp P}}\}$. By definition, $q_\mathbf{v} = \rho(\mathbf{v})/\rho(A_{\perp P})$. In order to analyze $p_\mathbf{v}$, let $\Lambda_P = \Lambda \cap P$, and select any $\mathbf{w} \in A$ such that $\mathbf{w}_{\perp P} = \mathbf{v}$. Then

$$p_\mathbf{v} = \frac{\rho(\{\mathbf{x} \in A : \mathbf{x}_{\perp P} = \mathbf{v}\})}{\rho(A)} = \frac{\rho(\mathbf{w} + \Lambda_P)}{\rho(A)} \approx_\varepsilon \frac{\rho(\mathbf{w}_{\perp \Lambda_P})}{\rho(A)\det(\Lambda_P)},$$

where the last step follows by Corollary 1. By assumption, $\text{span}(\Lambda_P) = P$, so $\mathbf{w}_{\perp \Lambda_P} = \mathbf{w}_{\perp P} = \mathbf{v}$ and hence

$$p_\mathbf{v} \approx_\varepsilon \frac{\rho(\mathbf{v})}{\rho(A)\det(\Lambda_P)} = C \cdot q_\mathbf{v}$$

[9] For example, if Λ is the lattice generated by the vectors $(1,0)$ and $(\sqrt{2},1)$, and $\mathbf{T}(x,y) = x$ is the projection on the first coordinate, then $\mathbf{T}\Lambda = \mathbb{Z} + \sqrt{2}\mathbb{Z}$ is a countable but dense subset of $\mathbb{R}$. In particular, $\sum_{x \in \mathbf{T}\Lambda} \rho(x) = \infty$ and so the conditional distribution $\mathcal{D}_{\mathbf{T}\Lambda,\mathbf{T}}$ is not well defined.

for some constant $C = \rho(A_{\perp P})/(\rho(A)\det(\Lambda_P))$. Summing over all $\mathbf{v} \in A_{A_{\perp P}}$ gives $1 \approx_\varepsilon C$, or, equivalently, $C \in [1/(1+\varepsilon), 1/(1-\varepsilon)]$. It follows that

$$\frac{1-\varepsilon}{1+\varepsilon} q_\mathbf{v} \le p_\mathbf{v} \le \frac{1+\varepsilon}{1-\varepsilon} \cdot q_\mathbf{v},$$

and therefore $\Delta_{\mathrm{ML}}((\mathcal{D}_A)_{\perp P}, \mathcal{D}_{A_{\perp P}}) \le \log \frac{1+\varepsilon}{1-\varepsilon}$. □

We now prove the main theorem.

Proof (of Theorem 1). The main idea is to express Λ as $\mathbf{S}\Lambda'$ for a lattice Λ', then use the injectivity of $\mathbf{TS}$ on the subspace orthogonal to $\ker(\mathbf{TS})$, which contains $\Lambda'_{\perp \ker(\mathbf{TS})}$.

Notice that $\mathbf{a} \in A \subset \mathrm{span}(\mathbf{S})$ and $\Lambda = A - \mathbf{a} \subset \mathrm{span}(\mathbf{S})$. Therefore, we can write $A = \mathbf{S}A'$ for some lattice coset $A' = \Lambda' + \mathbf{a}'$ with $\mathbf{S}\Lambda' = \Lambda$ and $\mathbf{S}\mathbf{a}' = \mathbf{a}$. Since $\mathbf{S}$ is injective, by Lemma 1 we have

$$\mathbf{T} \cdot \mathcal{D}_{A,\mathbf{S}} = \mathbf{T} \cdot \mathcal{D}_{\mathbf{S}A',\mathbf{S}} = \mathbf{TS} \cdot \mathcal{D}_{A'}. \tag{3.1}$$

Now let $P = \ker(\mathbf{TS})$, so that $\mathbf{S}P = \mathrm{span}(\mathbf{S}) \cap \ker(\mathbf{T})$. In particular, using $\Lambda \subset \mathrm{span}(\mathbf{S})$ and the injectivity of $\mathbf{S}$, we get

$$\Lambda \cap \ker(\mathbf{T}) = \Lambda \cap \mathrm{span}(\mathbf{S}) \cap \ker(\mathbf{T}) = \Lambda \cap \mathbf{S}P = \mathbf{S}\Lambda' \cap \mathbf{S}P = \mathbf{S}(\Lambda' \cap P).$$

Using the assumption $\ker(\mathbf{T}) = \mathrm{span}(\Lambda \cap \ker(\mathbf{T}))$ we also get

$$\mathbf{S}P = \mathrm{span}(\mathbf{S}) \cap \ker(\mathbf{T}) = \mathrm{span}(\mathbf{S}) \cap \mathrm{span}(\Lambda \cap \ker(\mathbf{T})) = \mathrm{span}(\Lambda \cap \ker(\mathbf{T})).$$

It follows that $\mathbf{S}P = \mathrm{span}(\mathbf{S}(\Lambda' \cap P))$, and, since $\mathbf{S}$ is injective, $P = \mathrm{span}(\Lambda' \cap P)$. We also have

$$\eta_\varepsilon(\mathbf{S}(\Lambda' \cap P)) = \eta_\varepsilon(\Lambda \cap \ker(\mathbf{T})) \le \mathbf{S},$$

which, by definition, gives $\eta_\varepsilon(\Lambda' \cap P) \le 1$. So, the hypotheses of Lemma 7 are satisfied, and

$$\Delta_{\mathrm{ML}}((\mathcal{D}_{A'})_{\perp P}, \mathcal{D}_{A'_{\perp P}}) \le \log \frac{1+\varepsilon}{1-\varepsilon}.$$

Applying $\mathbf{TS}$ to both distributions we get that

$$\Delta_{\mathrm{ML}}(\mathbf{TS} \cdot (\mathcal{D}_{A'})_{\perp P}, \mathbf{TS} \cdot \mathcal{D}_{A'_{\perp P}}) \le \log \frac{1+\varepsilon}{1-\varepsilon}.$$

It remains to show that these are the distributions in the theorem statement. To this end, observe that $\mathbf{TSx} = \mathbf{TS}(\mathbf{x}_{\perp P})$ for any vector $\mathbf{x}$. Therefore, the first distribution equals

$$\mathbf{TS} \cdot (\mathcal{D}_{A'})_{\perp P} = \mathbf{TS} \cdot \mathcal{D}_{A'} = \mathbf{T} \cdot \mathcal{D}_{\mathbf{S}A',\mathbf{S}} = \mathbf{T} \cdot \mathcal{D}_{A,\mathbf{S}}.$$

Finally, since $\mathbf{TS}$ is injective on $A'_{\perp P}$, we can apply Lemma 1 and see that the second distribution is

$$\mathbf{TS} \cdot \mathcal{D}_{A'_{\perp P}} = \mathcal{D}_{\mathbf{TS}A',\mathbf{TS}} = \mathcal{D}_{\mathbf{T}A,\mathbf{TS}}.$$ □

Corollary 2 below, recently stated in [DGPY19], is a special case of Theorem 1. The difference is that while Corollary 2 assumes that $\mathbf{T}$ is a primitive integer matrix and $A = \Lambda = \mathbb{Z}^m$ is the integer lattice, Theorem 1 applies to arbitrary linear transformations $\mathbf{T}$ and lattice cosets $A = \Lambda + \mathbf{a} \subset \mathbb{R}^m$.

Corollary 2 ([DGPY19, Lemma 3]). *For any $\varepsilon \in (0, 1/2)$ and $\mathbf{T} \in \mathbb{Z}^{n\times m}$ such that $\mathbf{T}\mathbb{Z}^m = \mathbb{Z}^n$ and $\eta_\varepsilon(\mathbb{Z}^m \cap \ker(\mathbf{T})) \le r$, we have*

$$\Delta_{\mathrm{ML}}(\mathbf{T} \cdot \mathcal{D}_{\mathbb{Z}^m,r}\,,\, \mathcal{D}_{\mathbb{Z}^n,r\mathbf{T}}) \le 4\varepsilon.$$

4 Convolutions

This section focuses on convolutions of discrete Gaussians. The literature on lattice-based cryptography has a multitude of convolution theorems and lemmas for discrete Gaussians (e.g., [Reg05, Pei10, BF11, MP13]), most of which are formally incomparable despite the close similarity of their statements and proofs. In this section we show all of them can be obtained and generalized solely via Theorem 1 and elementary linear algebra.

First, in Sect. 4.1 we analyze the joint distribution of a convolution. Then in Sect. 4.2 we show how to obtain (and in some cases generalize) all prior discrete Gaussian convolution theorems, by viewing each convolution as a linear transformation on its joint distribution.

4.1 Joint Distributions

Here we prove several general theorems on the joint distributions of discrete Gaussian convolutions.

Theorem 2. *For any $\varepsilon \in [0, 1)$, cosets A_1, A_2 of lattices Λ_1, Λ_2 (respectively), and matrix $\mathbf{T}$ such that $\mathrm{span}(\mathbf{T}) \subseteq \mathrm{span}(\Lambda_2)$ and $\eta_\varepsilon(\Lambda_2) \le 1$, we have*

$$[\![(\mathbf{x}_1, \mathbf{x}_2) \mid \mathbf{x}_1 \leftarrow \mathcal{D}_{A_1}\,,\, \mathbf{x}_2 \leftarrow \mathcal{D}_{A_2+\mathbf{T}\mathbf{x}_1}]\!] \overset{\bar{\varepsilon}}{\approx} \mathcal{D}_A,$$

where $A = \left(\begin{smallmatrix}\mathbf{I} & \\ \mathbf{T} & \mathbf{I}\end{smallmatrix}\right) \cdot (A_1 \times A_2)$ and $\bar{\varepsilon} = 2\varepsilon/(1-\varepsilon)$.

Proof. Let $\mathbf{P}(\mathbf{x}_1, \mathbf{x}_2) = (\mathbf{x}_1, (\mathbf{x}_2)_{\perp\Lambda_2})$ be the orthogonal projection on the first n_1 coordinates and the subspace orthogonal to Λ_2, and observe that $(A_2)_{\perp\Lambda_2} = \{\mathbf{a}\}$ is a singleton set for some $\mathbf{a}$. For any fixed $\mathbf{x}_1 \in A_1$, it is straightforward to verify that

$$[\![(\mathbf{x}_1, \mathbf{x}_2) \mid \mathbf{x}_2 \leftarrow \mathcal{D}_{A_2+\mathbf{T}\mathbf{x}_1}]\!] = [\![\mathbf{x} \mid \mathbf{x} \leftarrow \mathcal{D}_A, \mathbf{P}(\mathbf{x}) = (\mathbf{x}_1, \mathbf{a})]\!].$$

Therefore, it is enough to show that $(\mathcal{D}_{A_1}, \mathbf{a}) \overset{\bar{\varepsilon}}{\approx} \mathbf{P}(\mathcal{D}_A)$. Define $\Lambda = \left(\begin{smallmatrix}\mathbf{I} & \\ \mathbf{T} & \mathbf{I}\end{smallmatrix}\right) \cdot (\Lambda_1 \times \Lambda_2)$ and $\Lambda_P = \Lambda \cap \ker(\mathbf{P}) = \{\mathbf{0}\} \oplus \Lambda_2$. Notice that $\ker(\mathbf{P}) = \{\mathbf{0}\} \oplus \mathrm{span}(\Lambda_2) = \mathrm{span}(\Lambda_P)$ (i.e., $\ker(\mathbf{P})$ is a Λ-subspace), and $\eta_\varepsilon(\Lambda_P) = \eta_\varepsilon(\Lambda_2) \le 1$. Therefore, by Theorem 1,

$$\mathbf{P}(\mathcal{D}_A) \overset{\bar{\varepsilon}}{\approx} \mathcal{D}_{\mathbf{P}(A)} = \mathcal{D}_{A_1 \times \{\mathbf{a}\}} = (\mathcal{D}_{A_1}, \mathbf{a}).$$ □

As a corollary, we get the following more symmetric statement, which says essentially that if the lattices of A_1 and A_2 are sufficiently smooth, then a pair of $\bar{\delta}$-correlated Gaussian samples over A_1 and A_2 can be produced in two different ways, depending on which component is sampled first.

Corollary 3. *For any $\varepsilon \in [0,1)$ and $\delta \in (0,1]$ with $\delta' = \sqrt{1-\delta^2}$, and any cosets A_1, A_2 of full-rank lattices $\Lambda_1, \Lambda_2 \subset \mathbb{R}^n$ (respectively) where $\eta_\varepsilon(\Lambda_1), \eta_\varepsilon(\Lambda_2) \leq \delta$, define the distributions*

$$\mathcal{X}_1 = [\![(\mathbf{x}_1, \mathbf{x}_2) \mid \mathbf{x}_1 \leftarrow \mathcal{D}_{A_1}, \ \mathbf{x}_2 \leftarrow \delta'\mathbf{x}_1 + \mathcal{D}_{A_2-\delta'\mathbf{x}_1,\delta}]\!]$$
$$\mathcal{X}_2 = [\![(\mathbf{x}_1, \mathbf{x}_2) \mid \mathbf{x}_2 \leftarrow \mathcal{D}_{A_2}, \ \mathbf{x}_1 \leftarrow \delta'\mathbf{x}_2 + \mathcal{D}_{A_1-\delta'\mathbf{x}_2,\delta}]\!].$$

Then $\mathcal{X}_1 \overset{\bar{\varepsilon}}{\approx} \mathcal{D}_{A,\sqrt{\Sigma}} \overset{\bar{\varepsilon}}{\approx} \mathcal{X}_2$, where $A = A_1 \times A_2$, $\bar{\varepsilon} = 2\varepsilon/(1-\varepsilon)$, and $\Sigma = \left(\begin{smallmatrix} \mathbf{I} & \delta'\mathbf{I} \\ \delta'\mathbf{I} & \mathbf{I} \end{smallmatrix}\right)$.

Proof. By Lemma 1, the conditional distribution of $\mathbf{x}_2$ given $\mathbf{x}_1$ in $\mathcal{X}_1$ is $\delta'\mathbf{x}_1 + \delta\mathcal{D}_{(A_2/\delta)-(\delta'/\delta)\mathbf{x}_1}$. So, $\mathcal{X}_1$ can be equivalently expressed as

$$\mathbf{S} \cdot [\![\left(\begin{smallmatrix} \mathbf{x}_1 \\ \mathbf{x}_2 \end{smallmatrix}\right) \mid \mathbf{x}_1 \leftarrow \mathcal{D}_{A_1}, \mathbf{x}_2 \leftarrow \mathcal{D}_{(A_2/\delta)-(\delta'/\delta)\mathbf{x}_1}]\!], \ \mathbf{S} = \left(\begin{smallmatrix} \mathbf{I} & \\ \delta'\mathbf{I} & \delta\mathbf{I} \end{smallmatrix}\right).$$

Since $\eta_\varepsilon(\Lambda_2/\delta) = \eta_\varepsilon(\Lambda_2)/\delta \leq 1$, we can apply Theorem 2 with $\mathbf{T} = -(\delta'/\delta)\mathbf{I}$, and get that the first distribution satisfies $\mathcal{X}_1 \overset{\bar{\varepsilon}}{\approx} \mathbf{S} \cdot \mathcal{D}_{A'}$, where $A' = \left(\begin{smallmatrix} \mathbf{I} & \\ \mathbf{T} & \mathbf{I} \end{smallmatrix}\right)(A_1 \times (A_2/\delta))$. Since $\mathbf{S}$ is injective, by Lemma 1 we have

$$\mathcal{X}_1 \overset{\bar{\varepsilon}}{\approx} \mathbf{S} \cdot \mathcal{D}_{A'} = \mathcal{D}_{\mathbf{S}A',\mathbf{S}} = \mathcal{D}_{A,\sqrt{\Sigma}}$$

where $\Sigma = \mathbf{S}\mathbf{S}^t = \left(\begin{smallmatrix} \mathbf{I} & \delta'\mathbf{I} \\ \delta'\mathbf{I} & \mathbf{I} \end{smallmatrix}\right)$. By symmetry, $\mathcal{X}_2 \overset{\bar{\varepsilon}}{\approx} \mathcal{D}_{A,\sqrt{\Sigma}}$ as well. □

Corollary 3 also generalizes straightforwardly to the non-spherical case, as follows.

Corollary 4. *For any $\varepsilon \in [0,1)$, cosets A_1, A_2 of lattices Λ_1, Λ_2 (respectively), and matrices $\mathbf{R}, \mathbf{S}_1, \mathbf{S}_2$ of full column rank where $A_1 \subset \operatorname{span}(\mathbf{S}_1)$, $\operatorname{span}(\mathbf{R}\mathbf{S}_1) \subseteq \operatorname{span}(\Lambda_2)$, and $\eta_\varepsilon(\Lambda_2) \leq \mathbf{S}_2$, we have*

$$\mathcal{X} := [\![(\mathbf{x}_1, \mathbf{x}_2) \mid \mathbf{x}_1 \leftarrow \mathcal{D}_{A_1,\mathbf{S}_1}, \ \mathbf{x}_2 \leftarrow \mathbf{R}\mathbf{x}_1 + \mathcal{D}_{A_2-\mathbf{R}\mathbf{x}_1,\mathbf{S}_2}]\!] \overset{\bar{\varepsilon}}{\approx} \mathcal{D}_{A,\mathbf{S}},$$

where $A = A_1 \times A_2$, $\bar{\varepsilon} = 2\varepsilon/(1-\varepsilon)$, and $\mathbf{S} = \left(\begin{smallmatrix} \mathbf{S}_1 & \\ \mathbf{R}\mathbf{S}_1 & \mathbf{S}_2 \end{smallmatrix}\right)$.

Proof. We proceed similarly to the proof of Corollary 3. For simplicity, substitute $\mathbf{x}_1$ with $\mathbf{S}_1\mathbf{x}_1$ where $\mathbf{x}_1 \leftarrow \mathcal{D}_{\mathbf{S}_1^+ A_1}$. Then by Lemma 1, the vector $\mathbf{x}_2$ in $\mathcal{X}$, conditioned on any value of $\mathbf{x}_1$, has distribution

$$\mathbf{R}\mathbf{S}_1\mathbf{x}_1 + \mathbf{S}_2 \cdot \mathcal{D}_{\mathbf{S}_2^+(A_2-\mathbf{R}\mathbf{S}_1\mathbf{x}_1)}.$$

So, we can express $\mathcal{X}$ equivalently as

$$\mathbf{S} \cdot [\![\left(\begin{smallmatrix} \mathbf{x}_1 \\ \mathbf{x}_2 \end{smallmatrix}\right) \mid \mathbf{x}_1 \leftarrow \mathcal{D}_{\mathbf{S}_1^+ A_1}, \ \mathbf{x}_2 \leftarrow \mathcal{D}_{\mathbf{S}_2^+(A_2-\mathbf{R}\mathbf{S}_1\mathbf{x}_1)}]\!],$$

and since $\eta_\varepsilon(\mathbf{S}_2^+ \cdot \Lambda_2) \leq 1$, we can apply Theorem 2 with lattice cosets $A_1' = \mathbf{S}_1^+ A_1, A_2' = \mathbf{S}_2^+ A_2$ and $\mathbf{T} = -\mathbf{S}_2^+ \mathbf{R} \mathbf{S}_1$. This yields $\mathcal{X} \overset{\bar{\varepsilon}}{\approx} \mathbf{S} \cdot \mathcal{D}_{A'} = \mathcal{D}_{\mathbf{S}A',\mathbf{S}}$ where

$$A' = \left(\begin{smallmatrix} \mathbf{I} & \mathbf{0} \\ \mathbf{T} & \mathbf{I} \end{smallmatrix}\right)(A_1' \times A_2')$$

and hence $\mathbf{S}A' = A$, as needed. □

The following corollary, which may be useful in cryptography, involves Gaussian distributions over lattices and uniform distributions over their (finite) quotient groups.

Corollary 5. *Let $\Lambda, \Lambda_1, \Lambda_2$ be full-rank lattices where $\Lambda \subseteq \Lambda_1 \cap \Lambda_2$ and $\eta_\varepsilon(\Lambda_1)$, $\eta_\varepsilon(\Lambda_2) \leq 1$ for some $\varepsilon > 0$, and define the distributions*

$$\mathcal{X}_1 = [\![(\mathbf{x}_1, \mathbf{x}_2) \mid \mathbf{x}_1 \leftarrow \mathcal{U}(\Lambda_1/\Lambda)\,,\ \mathbf{x}_2 \leftarrow \mathbf{x}_1 + \mathcal{D}_{\Lambda_2 - \mathbf{x}_1} \bmod \Lambda]\!],$$
$$\mathcal{X}_2 = [\![(\mathbf{x}_1, \mathbf{x}_2) \mid \mathbf{x}_2 \leftarrow \mathcal{U}(\Lambda_2/\Lambda)\,,\ \mathbf{x}_1 \leftarrow \mathbf{x}_2 + \mathcal{D}_{\Lambda_1 - \mathbf{x}_2} \bmod \Lambda]\!].$$

Then $\mathcal{X}_1 \overset{\bar{\varepsilon}}{\approx} \mathcal{X}_2$ where $\bar{\varepsilon} = 4\varepsilon/(1-\varepsilon)^2$.

Proof. We assume the strict inequality $\eta_\varepsilon(\Lambda_1) < 1$; the claim then follows in the limit. Let $\delta' \in (\eta_\varepsilon(\Lambda_1), 1)$, $\delta = \sqrt{1-\delta'^2}$, and apply Corollary 3 to $A_1 = (\delta/\delta')\Lambda_1$ and $A_2 = \delta\Lambda_2$. Notice that the hypotheses of Corollary 3 are satisfied because $\eta_\varepsilon(A_1) = \delta\eta_\varepsilon(\Lambda_1)/\delta' < \delta$ and $\eta_\varepsilon(A_2) = \delta\eta_\varepsilon(\Lambda_2) \leq \delta$. So, the distributions

$$\mathcal{X}_1' = [\![(\mathbf{x}_1, \mathbf{x}_2) \mid \mathbf{x}_1 \leftarrow \mathcal{D}_{A_1}\,,\ \mathbf{x}_2 \leftarrow \delta'\mathbf{x}_1 + \mathcal{D}_{A_2 - \delta'\mathbf{x}_1, \delta}]\!]$$
$$\mathcal{X}_2' = [\![(\mathbf{x}_1, \mathbf{x}_2) \mid \mathbf{x}_2 \leftarrow \mathcal{D}_{A_2}\,,\ \mathbf{x}_1 \leftarrow \delta'\mathbf{x}_2 + \mathcal{D}_{A_1 - \delta'\mathbf{x}_2, \delta}]\!]$$

satisfy $\mathcal{X}_1' \overset{\bar{\varepsilon}}{\approx} \mathcal{X}_2'$. Let $f \colon A_1 \times A_2 \to (\Lambda_1/\Lambda, \Lambda_2/\Lambda)$ be the function

$$f(\mathbf{x}_1, \mathbf{x}_2) = ((\delta'/\delta)\mathbf{x}_1 \bmod \Lambda, \mathbf{x}_2/\delta \bmod \Lambda).$$

It is easy to check, using Lemma 1, that

$$f(\mathcal{X}_1') = [\![(\mathbf{x}_1, \mathbf{x}_2) \mid \mathbf{x}_1 \leftarrow \mathcal{D}_{\Lambda_1, \delta'/\delta} \bmod \Lambda\,,\ \mathbf{x}_2 \leftarrow \mathbf{x}_1 + \mathcal{D}_{\Lambda_2 - \mathbf{x}_1} \bmod \Lambda]\!]$$
$$f(\mathcal{X}_2') = [\![(\mathbf{x}_1, \mathbf{x}_2) \mid \mathbf{x}_2 \leftarrow \mathcal{D}_{\Lambda_2, 1/\delta} \bmod \Lambda\,,\ \mathbf{x}_1 \leftarrow \delta'^2\mathbf{x}_2 + \mathcal{D}_{\Lambda_1 - \delta'^2\mathbf{x}_2, \delta'} \bmod \Lambda]\!]$$

and $\mathcal{X}_i = \lim_{\delta' \to 1} \mathcal{X}_i'$ for $i = 1, 2$. Since $\mathcal{X}_1' \overset{\bar{\varepsilon}}{\approx} \mathcal{X}_2'$ for all δ', we have $\mathcal{X}_1 \overset{\bar{\varepsilon}}{\approx} \mathcal{X}_2$. □

4.2 Convolutions via Linear Transformations

In this subsection we show how the preceding results can be used to easily derive all convolution theorems from previous works, for both discrete and continuous Gaussians. The main idea throughout is very simple: first express the statistical experiment as a linear transformation on some joint distribution, then apply Theorem 1. The only nontrivial step is to bound the smoothing parameter of the intersection of the relevant lattice and the kernel of the transformation, which is done using elementary linear algebra. The main results of the section are

Theorems 3 and 4; following them, we show how they imply prior convolution theorems.

The following theorem is essentially equivalent to [Pei10, Theorem 3.1], modulo the notion of distance between distributions. (The theorem statement from [Pei10] uses statistical distance, but the proof actually establishes a bound on the max-log distance, as we do here.) The main difference is in the modularity of our proof, which proceeds solely via our general tools and linear algebra.

Theorem 3. *Let $\varepsilon \in (0,1)$ define $\bar{\varepsilon} = 2\varepsilon/(1-\varepsilon)$ and $\varepsilon' = 4\varepsilon/(1-\varepsilon)^2$, let A_1, A_2 be cosets of full-rank lattices Λ_1, Λ_2 (respectively), let $\Sigma_1, \Sigma_2 \succ 0$ be positive definite matrices where $\eta_\varepsilon(\Lambda_2) \le \sqrt{\Sigma_2}$, and let*

$$\mathcal{X} = [\![(\mathbf{x}_1, \mathbf{x}_2) \mid \mathbf{x}_1 \leftarrow \mathcal{D}_{A_1, \sqrt{\Sigma_1}}, \mathbf{x}_2 \leftarrow \mathbf{x}_1 + \mathcal{D}_{A_2 - \mathbf{x}_1, \sqrt{\Sigma_2}}]\!].$$

If $\eta_\varepsilon(\Lambda_1) \le \sqrt{\Sigma_3}$ where $\Sigma_3^{-1} = \Sigma_1^{-1} + \Sigma_2^{-1} \succ 0$, then the marginal distribution $\mathcal{X}_2$ of $\mathbf{x}_2$ in $\mathcal{X}$ satisfies

$$\mathcal{X}_2 \overset{\varepsilon'}{\approx} \mathcal{D}_{A_2, \sqrt{\Sigma_1 + \Sigma_2}}.$$

In any case (regardless of $\eta_\varepsilon(\Lambda_1)$), the distribution $\mathcal{X}_1^{\mathbf{x}_2}$ of $\mathbf{x}_1$ conditioned on any $\mathbf{x}_2 \in A_2$ satisfies $\mathcal{X}_1^{\mathbf{x}_2} \overset{\bar{\varepsilon}}{\approx} \mathbf{x}_2' + \mathcal{D}_{A_1 - \mathbf{x}_2', \sqrt{\Sigma_3}}$ where $\mathbf{x}_2' = \Sigma_1(\Sigma_1 + \Sigma_2)^{-1}\mathbf{x}_2 = \Sigma_3 \Sigma_2^{-1} \mathbf{x}_2$.

Proof. Clearly, $\mathcal{X}_2 = \mathbf{P} \cdot \mathcal{X}$, where $\mathbf{P} = \begin{pmatrix} \mathbf{0} & \mathbf{I} \end{pmatrix}$. Because $\eta_\varepsilon(\Lambda_2) \le \sqrt{\Sigma_2}$, Corollary 4 implies

$$\mathcal{X} \overset{\bar{\varepsilon}}{\approx} \mathcal{D}_{A, \sqrt{\Sigma}} \quad \text{and hence} \quad \mathbf{P} \cdot \mathcal{X} \overset{\bar{\varepsilon}}{\approx} \mathbf{P} \cdot \mathcal{D}_{A, \sqrt{\Sigma}},$$

where $A = A_1 \times A_2$ and $\sqrt{\Sigma} = \begin{pmatrix} \sqrt{\Sigma_1} & \\ \sqrt{\Sigma_1} & \sqrt{\Sigma_2} \end{pmatrix}$. Then, Theorem 1 (whose hypotheses we verify below) implies that

$$\mathbf{P} \cdot \mathcal{D}_{A, \sqrt{\Sigma}} \overset{\bar{\varepsilon}}{\approx} \mathcal{D}_{\mathbf{P}A, \mathbf{P}\sqrt{\Sigma}} = \mathcal{D}_{A_2, \sqrt{\Sigma_1 + \Sigma_2}},$$

where the equality follows from the fact that $\mathcal{D}$ is insensitive to the choice of square root, and $\mathbf{R} = \mathbf{P}\sqrt{\Sigma} = \begin{pmatrix} \sqrt{\Sigma_1} & \sqrt{\Sigma_2} \end{pmatrix}$ is a square root of $\mathbf{R}\mathbf{R}^t = \Sigma_1 + \Sigma_2$. This proves the claim about $\mathcal{X}_2$.

To apply Theorem 1, for $\Lambda = \Lambda_1 \times \Lambda_2$ we require that $\ker(\mathbf{P})$ is a Λ-subspace, and that $\eta_\varepsilon(\Lambda \cap \ker(\mathbf{P})) = \eta_\varepsilon(\Lambda_1 \times \{\mathbf{0}\}) \le \sqrt{\Sigma}$. For the former, because Λ_1 is full rank we have

$$\ker(\mathbf{P}) = \operatorname{span}(\Lambda_1) \times \{\mathbf{0}\} = \operatorname{span}(\Lambda_1 \times \{\mathbf{0}\}) = \operatorname{span}(\ker(\mathbf{P}) \cap \Lambda).$$

For the latter, by definition we need to show that $\eta_\varepsilon(\Lambda') \le 1$ where $\Lambda' = \sqrt{\Sigma}^{-1} \cdot (\Lambda_1 \times \{\mathbf{0}\})$. Because

$$\sqrt{\Sigma}^{-1} = \begin{pmatrix} \sqrt{\Sigma_1}^{-1} & \\ -\sqrt{\Sigma_2}^{-1} & \sqrt{\Sigma_2}^{-1} \end{pmatrix}, \text{ we have } \Lambda' = \mathbf{S} \cdot \Lambda_1 \text{ where } \mathbf{S} = \begin{pmatrix} \sqrt{\Sigma_1}^{-1} \\ -\sqrt{\Sigma_2}^{-1} \end{pmatrix}.$$

Now $\mathbf{S}^t\mathbf{S} = \Sigma_1^{-1} + \Sigma_2^{-1} = \Sigma_3^{-1}$, so $\|\mathbf{S}\mathbf{v}\|^2 = \mathbf{v}^t\mathbf{S}^t\mathbf{S}\mathbf{v} = \|\sqrt{\Sigma_3}^{-1}\mathbf{v}\|^2$ for every $\mathbf{v}$. Therefore, $\Lambda' = \mathbf{S}\cdot\Lambda_1$ is isometric to (i.e., a rotation of) $\sqrt{\Sigma_3}^{-1}\cdot\Lambda_1$, so $\eta_\varepsilon(\Lambda') \leq 1$ is equivalent to $\eta_\varepsilon(\sqrt{\Sigma_3}^{-1}\cdot\Lambda_1) \leq 1$, which by definition is equivalent to the hypothesis $\eta_\varepsilon(\Lambda_1) \leq \sqrt{\Sigma_3}$.

To prove the claim about $\mathcal{X}_1^{\mathbf{x}_2}$ for an arbitrary $\mathbf{x}_2 \in A_2$, we work with $\mathcal{D}_{A,\sqrt{\Sigma}}$ using a different choice of the square root of $\Sigma = \left(\begin{smallmatrix}\Sigma_1 & \Sigma_1 \\ \Sigma_1 & \Sigma_1+\Sigma_2\end{smallmatrix}\right)$, namely,

$$\sqrt{\Sigma} = \begin{pmatrix}\sqrt{\Sigma_3} & \Sigma_1\sqrt{\Sigma_1+\Sigma_2}^{-t} \\ & \sqrt{\Sigma_1+\Sigma_2}\end{pmatrix} \quad \text{where} \quad \sqrt{\Sigma}^{-1} = \begin{pmatrix}\sqrt{\Sigma_3}^{-1} & \mathbf{X} \\ & \sqrt{\Sigma_1+\Sigma_2}^{-1}\end{pmatrix}$$

for $\sqrt{\Sigma_3}\mathbf{X} = -\Sigma_1(\Sigma_1+\Sigma_2)^{-1} = -\Sigma_3\Sigma_2^{-1}$; this $\sqrt{\Sigma}$ is valid because

$$\begin{aligned}\Sigma_3 + \Sigma_1(\Sigma_1+\Sigma_2)^{-1}\Sigma_1 &= (\Sigma_1^{-1}+\Sigma_2^{-1})^{-1} + \Sigma_1 - \Sigma_2(\Sigma_1+\Sigma_2)^{-1}\Sigma_1 \\ &= \Sigma_1 + (\Sigma_1^{-1}+\Sigma_2^{-1})^{-1} - (\Sigma_1^{-1}(\Sigma_1+\Sigma_2)\Sigma_2^{-1})^{-1} \\ &= \Sigma_1,\end{aligned}$$

and $\Sigma_1(\Sigma_1+\Sigma_2)^{-1} = \Sigma_3\Sigma_2^{-1}$ by a similar manipulation. Now, the distribution $\mathcal{D}_{A,\sqrt{\Sigma}}$ conditioned on any $\mathbf{x}_2 \in A_2$ is

$$\mathcal{D}_{A_1\times\{\mathbf{x}_2\},\sqrt{\Sigma}} = \sqrt{\Sigma}\cdot\mathcal{D}_{\sqrt{\Sigma}^{-1}(A_1\times\{\mathbf{x}_2\})} = \sqrt{\Sigma}\cdot(\mathcal{D}_{\sqrt{\Sigma_3}^{-1}A_1+\mathbf{X}\mathbf{x}_2}, \sqrt{\Sigma_1+\Sigma_2}^{-1}\mathbf{x}_2),$$

where the last equality follows from the fact that the second component of $\sqrt{\Sigma}^{-1}(A_1\times\{\mathbf{x}_2\})$ is fixed because $\sqrt{\Sigma}^{-1}$ is block upper-triangular. So, the conditional distribution of $\mathbf{x}_1$, which is the first component of the above distribution, is

$$\Sigma_1(\Sigma_1+\Sigma_2)^{-1}\mathbf{x}_2 + \mathcal{D}_{A_1+\sqrt{\Sigma_3}\mathbf{X}\mathbf{x}_2,\sqrt{\Sigma_3}} = \mathbf{x}_2' + \mathcal{D}_{A_1-\mathbf{x}_2',\sqrt{\Sigma_3}}.$$

Finally, because $\mathcal{X} \overset{\bar{\varepsilon}}{\approx} \mathcal{D}_{A,\sqrt{\Sigma}}$, the claim on the conditional distribution $\mathcal{X}_1^{\mathbf{x}_2}$ is established. $\square$

There are a number of convolution theorems in the literature that pertain to linear combinations of Gaussian samples. We now present a theorem that, as shown below, subsumes all of them. The proof generalizes part of the proof of [MP13, Theorem 3.3] (stated below as Corollary 6).

Theorem 4. *Let $\varepsilon \in (0,1)$, let $\mathbf{z} \in \mathbb{Z}^m \setminus \{\mathbf{0}\}$, and for $i = 1,\ldots,m$ let $A_i = \Lambda_i + \mathbf{a}_i \subset \mathbb{R}^n$ be a lattice coset and $\mathbf{S}_i \in \mathbb{R}^{n\times n}$ be such that $\Lambda_\cap = \bigcap_i \Lambda_i$ is full rank. If $\eta_\varepsilon(\ker(\mathbf{z}^t\otimes\mathbf{I}_n)\cap\Lambda) \leq \mathbf{S}$ where $\Lambda = \Lambda_1\times\cdots\times\Lambda_m$ and $\mathbf{S} = \mathrm{diag}(\mathbf{S}_1,\ldots,\mathbf{S}_m)$, then*

$$\Delta_{\mathrm{ML}}\Big(\sum_{i=1}^m z_i\mathcal{D}_{A_i,\mathbf{S}_i}, \mathcal{D}_{A',\mathbf{S}'}\Big) \leq \log\frac{1+\varepsilon}{1-\varepsilon},$$

where $A' = \sum_{i=1}^m z_iA_i$ and $\mathbf{S}' = \sqrt{\sum_{i=1}^m z_i^2\mathbf{S}_i\mathbf{S}_i^t}$.

In particular, let each $\mathbf{S}_i = s_i \mathbf{I}_n$ *for some* $s_i > 0$ *where* $\tilde{bl}(\mathrm{diag}(\mathbf{s})^{-1}(\ker(\mathbf{z}^t) \cap \mathbb{Z}^m))^{-1} \geq \eta_\varepsilon(\Lambda_\cap)$*, which is implied by* $((z_{i^*}/s_{i^*})^2 + \max_{i \neq i^*}(z_i/s_i)^2)^{-1/2} \geq \eta_\varepsilon(\Lambda_\cap)$ *where* i^* *minimizes* $|z_{i^*}/s_{i^*}| \neq 0$*. Then*

$$\Delta_{\mathrm{ML}}(\sum_{i=1}^{m} z_i \mathcal{D}_{A_i, s_i}, \mathcal{D}_{A', s'}) \leq \log \frac{1+\varepsilon'}{1-\varepsilon'},$$

where $s' = \sqrt{\sum_{i=1}^m (z_i s_i)^2}$ *and* $1 + \varepsilon' = (1+\varepsilon)^m$*.*

Proof. Let $\mathbf{Z} = \mathbf{z}^t \otimes \mathbf{I}_n$ and $A = A_1 \times \cdots \times A_m$, which is a coset of Λ, and observe that

$$\sum_{i=1}^{m} z_i \mathcal{D}_{A_i, \mathbf{S}_i} = \mathbf{Z} \cdot \mathcal{D}_{A, \mathbf{S}}.$$

Also notice that $\mathbf{Z}A = A'$, and $\mathbf{R} = \mathbf{ZS}$ is a square root of $\mathbf{RR}^t = \sum_{i=1}^m z_i^2 \mathbf{S}_i \mathbf{S}_i^t$. So, the first claim follows immediately by Theorem 1, as long as $\ker(\mathbf{Z})$ is a Λ-subspace.

To see that this is so, first observe that the lattice $Z = \ker(\mathbf{z}^t) \cap \mathbb{Z}^m$ has rank $m-1$. Then the lattice $Z \otimes \Lambda_\cap$ has rank $(m-1)n$ and is contained in $\ker(\mathbf{Z}) \cap \Lambda$, because for any $\mathbf{v} \in Z \subseteq \mathbb{Z}^m$ and $\mathbf{w} \in \Lambda_\cap$ we have $\mathbf{Z}(\mathbf{v} \otimes \mathbf{w}) = (\mathbf{z}^t \mathbf{v}) \otimes \mathbf{w} = \mathbf{0}$ and $(\mathbf{v} \otimes \mathbf{w}) \in \Lambda_\cap^m \subseteq \Lambda$. So, because $\ker(\mathbf{Z})$ has dimension $(m-1)n$ we have $\ker(\mathbf{Z}) = \mathrm{span}(Z \otimes \Lambda_\cap) = \mathrm{span}(\ker(\mathbf{Z}) \cap \Lambda)$, as desired.

For the second claim (with the first hypothesis), we need to show that $\eta_{\varepsilon'}(\ker(\mathbf{Z}) \cap \Lambda) \leq \mathbf{S} = \mathrm{diag}(\mathbf{s}) \otimes \mathbf{I}_n$. Because $Z \otimes \Lambda_\cap$ is a sublattice of $\ker(\mathbf{Z}) \cap \Lambda$ of the same rank, by Lemma 5 and hypothesis, we have

$$\begin{aligned}
\eta_{\varepsilon'}(\mathbf{S}^{-1}(\ker(\mathbf{Z}) \cap \Lambda)) &\leq \eta_{\varepsilon'}((\mathrm{diag}(\mathbf{s})^{-1} \otimes \mathbf{I}_n) \cdot (Z \otimes \Lambda_\cap)) \\
&\leq \eta_{\varepsilon'}((\mathrm{diag}(\mathbf{s})^{-1} Z) \otimes \Lambda_\cap) \\
&\leq \tilde{bl}(\mathrm{diag}(\mathbf{s})^{-1} Z) \cdot \eta_\varepsilon(\Lambda_\cap) \leq 1.
\end{aligned}$$

Finally, to see that the first hypothesis is implied by the second one, assume without loss of generality that $i^* = 1$, and observe that the vectors

$$(-\frac{z_2}{s_2}, \frac{z_1}{s_1}, 0, \ldots, 0)^t, (-\frac{z_3}{s_3}, 0, \frac{z_1}{s_1}, 0, \ldots, 0)^t, \ldots, (-\frac{z_m}{s_m}, 0, \ldots, 0, \frac{z_1}{s_1})^t$$

form a full-rank subset of $\mathrm{diag}(\mathbf{s})^{-1} Z$, and have norms at most

$$r = \sqrt{(z_{i^*}/s_{i^*})^2 + \max_{i \neq i^*}(z_i/s_i)^2}.$$

Therefore, by [MG02, Lemma 7.1] we have $\tilde{bl}(\mathrm{diag}(\mathbf{s})^{-1} Z)^{-1} \geq 1/r \geq \eta_\varepsilon(\Lambda_\cap)$, as required. $\square$

Corollary 6 (**[MP13, Theorem 3.3]**). *Let* $\mathbf{z} \in \mathbb{Z}^m \setminus \{\mathbf{0}\}$*, and for* $i = 1, \ldots, m = \mathrm{poly}(n)$ *let* $\Lambda + \mathbf{c}_i$ *be cosets of a full-rank n-dimensional lattice* Λ *and* $s_i \geq \sqrt{2}\|\mathbf{z}\|_\infty \cdot \eta_\varepsilon(\Lambda)$ *for some* $\varepsilon = \mathrm{negl}(n)$*. Then* $\sum_{i=1}^m z_i \mathcal{D}_{\Lambda + \mathbf{c}_i, s_i}$ *is within* $\mathrm{negl}(n)$ *statistical distance of* $\mathcal{D}_{Y,s}$*, where* $Y = \gcd(\mathbf{z})\Lambda + \sum_i z_i \mathbf{c}_i$ *and* $s = \sqrt{\sum_i (z_i s_i)^2}$*. In particular, if* $\gcd(\mathbf{z}) = 1$ *and* $\sum_i z_i \mathbf{c}_i \in \Lambda$*, then* $\sum z_i \mathcal{D}_{\Lambda + \mathbf{c}_i, s_i}$ *is within* $\mathrm{negl}(n)$ *statistical distance of* $\mathcal{D}_{\Lambda, s}$*.*

Proof. Apply the second part of Theorem 4 with the second hypothesis, and use the fact that $(1 + \mathrm{negl}(n))^{\mathrm{poly}(n)}$ is $1 + \mathrm{negl}(n)$. □

Theorem 4.13 from [BF11] is identical to Corollary 6, except it assumes that all the s_i equal some $s \geq \|\mathbf{z}\| \cdot \eta_\varepsilon(\Lambda)$. This also implies the second hypothesis from the second part of Theorem 4, because $\|\mathbf{z}\| \geq \sqrt{z_{i^*}^2 + \max_{i \neq i^*} z_i^2}$.

Corollary 7 ([BF11, Lemma 4.12]). *Let $\Lambda_1 + \mathbf{t}_1, \Lambda_2 + \mathbf{t}_2$ be cosets of full-rank integer lattices, and let $s_1, s_2 > 0$ be such that $(s_1^{-2} + s_2^{-2})^{-1/2} \geq \eta_\varepsilon(\Lambda_1 \cap \Lambda_2)$ for some $\varepsilon = \mathrm{negl}(n)$. Then $\mathcal{D}_{\Lambda_1+\mathbf{t}_1,s_1} + \mathcal{D}_{\Lambda_2+\mathbf{t}_2,s_2}$ is within $\mathrm{negl}(n)$ statistical distance of $\mathcal{D}_{\Lambda+\mathbf{t},s}$, where $\Lambda = \Lambda_1 + \Lambda_2$, $\mathbf{t} = \mathbf{t}_1 + \mathbf{t}_2$, and $s^2 = s_1^2 + s_2^2$.*

Proof. The intersection of full-rank integer lattices always has full rank. So, apply the second part of Theorem 4 with the second hypothesis, for $m = 2$ and $\mathbf{z} = (1, 1)^t$. □

Corollary 8 ([Reg05, Claim 3.9]). *Let $\varepsilon \in (0, 1/2)$, let $\Lambda + \mathbf{u} \subset \mathbb{R}^n$ be a coset of a full-rank lattice, and let $r, s > 0$ be such that $(r^{-2} + s^{-2})^{-1/2} \geq \eta_\varepsilon(\Lambda)$. Then $\mathcal{D}_{\Lambda+\mathbf{u},r} + \mathcal{D}_s$ is within statistical distance 4ε of $\mathcal{D}_{\sqrt{r^2+s^2}}$.*

Proof. The proof of Corollary 7 also works for any full-rank lattices $\Lambda_1 \subseteq \Lambda_2$. The corollary follows by taking $\Lambda_1 = \Lambda$ and $\Lambda_2 = \lim_{d\to\infty} d^{-1}\Lambda = \mathbb{R}^n$. □

5 LWE Self-reduction

The LWE problem [Reg05] is one of the foundations of lattice-based cryptography.

Definition 3 (LWE distribution). *Fix some parameters $n, q \in \mathbb{Z}^+$ and a distribution χ over $\mathbb{Z}$. The LWE distribution for a secret $\mathbf{s} \in \mathbb{Z}_q^n$ is*

$$\mathcal{L}_\mathbf{s} = [\![(\mathbf{a}, \mathbf{s}^t\mathbf{a} + e \bmod q) \mid \mathbf{a} \leftarrow \mathcal{U}(\mathbb{Z}_q^n), e \leftarrow \mathcal{X}]\!].$$

Given m samples $(\mathbf{a}_i, b_i = \mathbf{s}^t\mathbf{a}_i + e_i \bmod q)$ from $\mathcal{L}_\mathbf{s}$, we often group them as $(\mathbf{A}, \mathbf{b}^t = \mathbf{s}^t\mathbf{A} + \mathbf{e}^t)$, where the $\mathbf{a}_i$ are the columns of $\mathbf{A} \in \mathbb{Z}_q^{n\times m}$ and the b_i, e_i are respectively the corresponding entries of $\mathbf{b} \in \mathbb{Z}_q^m, \mathbf{e} \in \mathbb{Z}^m$.

While LWE was originally also defined for *continuous* error distributions (in particular, the Gaussian distribution $\mathcal{D}_s$), we restrict the definition to *discrete* distributions (over $\mathbb{Z}$), since discrete distributions are the focus of this work, and are much more widely used in cryptography. We refer to continuous error distributions only in informal discussion.

Definition 4 (LWE Problem). *The search problem S-LWE$_{n,q,\chi,m}$ is to recover $\mathbf{s}$ given m independent samples drawn from $\mathcal{L}_\mathbf{s}$, where $\mathbf{s} \leftarrow \mathcal{U}(\mathbb{Z}_q^n)$. The decision problem D-LWE$_{n,q,\chi,m}$ is to distinguish m independent samples drawn from $\mathcal{L}_\mathbf{s}$, where $\mathbf{s} \leftarrow \mathcal{U}(\mathbb{Z}_q^n)$, from m independent and uniformly random samples from $\mathcal{U}(\mathbb{Z}_q^{n+1})$.*

For appropriate parameters, very similar hardness results are known for search and decision $\text{LWE}_{n,q,\chi,m}$ with $\chi \in \{\mathcal{D}_s, \lfloor \mathcal{D}_s \rceil, \mathcal{D}_{\mathbb{Z},s}\}$, i.e., continuous, rounded, or discrete Gaussian error. Notably, the theoretical and empirical hardness of the problem depends mainly on $n \log q$ and the "error rate" $\alpha = s/q$, and less on m. This weak dependence on m is consistent with the fact that there is a *self-reduction* that, given just $m = O(n \log q)$ LWE samples from $\mathcal{L}_\mathbf{s}$ with (continuous, rounded, or discrete) Gaussian error of parameter s, generates *any polynomial* number of samples from a distribution statistically close to $\mathcal{L}_\mathbf{s}$ with (continuous, rounded, or discrete) Gaussian error of parameter $O(s\sqrt{m}) \cdot \eta_\varepsilon(\mathbb{Z})$, for arbitrary negligible ε. Such self-reductions were described in [GPV08, ACPS09, Pei10] (the latter for discrete Gaussian error), based on the observation that they are just special cases of Regev's core reduction [Reg05] from Bounded Distance Decoding (BDD) to LWE, and that LWE is an average-case BDD variant.

The prior LWE self-reduction for *discrete Gaussian* error, however, contains an unnatural layer of indirection: it first generates new LWE samples having *continuous* error, then randomly rounds, which by a convolution theorem yields discrete Gaussian error (up to negligible statistical distance). Below we instead give a *direct* reduction to LWE with discrete Gaussian error, which is more natural and slightly tighter, since it avoids the additional rounding that increases the error width somewhat.

Theorem 5. *Let $\mathbf{A} \in \mathbb{Z}_q^{n \times m}$ be primitive, let $\mathbf{b}^t = \mathbf{s}^t\mathbf{A} + \mathbf{e}^t \bmod q$ for some $\mathbf{e} \in \mathbb{Z}^m$, and let $r, \tilde{r} > 0$ be such that $\eta_\varepsilon(\Lambda_q^\perp(\mathbf{A})) \leq ((1/r)^2 + (\|\mathbf{e}\|/\tilde{r})^2)^{-1/2} \leq r$ for some negligible ε. Then the distribution*

$$[\![(\mathbf{a} = \mathbf{A}\mathbf{x}, b = \mathbf{b}^t\mathbf{x} + \tilde{e}) \mid \mathbf{x} \leftarrow \mathcal{D}_{\mathbb{Z}^m,r}\,,\ \tilde{e} \leftarrow \mathcal{D}_{\mathbb{Z},\tilde{r}}]\!]$$

is within negligible statistical distance of $\mathcal{L}_\mathbf{s}$ with error $\chi = \mathcal{D}_{\mathbb{Z},t}$ where $t^2 = (r\|\mathbf{e}\|)^2 + \tilde{r}^2$.

Theorem 5 is the core of the self-reduction. A full reduction between proper LWE problems follows from the fact that a uniformly random matrix $\mathbf{A} \in \mathbb{Z}_q^{n \times m}$ is primitive with overwhelming probability for sufficiently large $m \gg n$, and by choosing r and $\tilde{r}$ appropriately. More specifically, it is known [GPV08, MP12] that for appropriate parameters, the smoothing parameter of $\Lambda_q^\perp(\mathbf{A})$ is small with very high probability over the choice of $\mathbf{A}$. For example, [MP12, Lemma 2.4] implies that when $m \geq Cn \log q$ for any constant $C > 1$ and $\varepsilon \approx \varepsilon'$, we have $\eta_\varepsilon(\Lambda_q^\perp(\mathbf{A})) \leq 2\eta_{\varepsilon'}(\mathbb{Z}) \leq 2\sqrt{\ln(2(1+1/\varepsilon'))/\pi}$ except with negligible probability. So, we may choose $r = O(\sqrt{\log(1/\varepsilon')})$ for some negligible ε' and $\tilde{r} = r\|\mathbf{e}\|$ to satisfy the conditions of Theorem 5 with high probability, and the resulting error distribution has parameter $t = \sqrt{2}r\|\mathbf{e}\|$, which can be bounded with high probability for any typical LWE error distribution. Finally, there is the subtlety that in the actual LWE problem, the error distribution should be *fixed* and *known*, which is not quite the case here since $\|\mathbf{e}\|$ is secret but bounded from above. This can be handled as in [Reg05] by adding different geometrically increasing amounts of extra error. We omit the details, which are standard.

Proof (of Theorem 5). Because $\mathbf{A}$ is primitive, for any $\mathbf{a} \in \mathbb{Z}_q^n$ there exists an $\mathbf{x}^* \in \mathbb{Z}^m$ such that $\mathbf{A}\mathbf{x}^* = \mathbf{a}$, and the probability that $\mathbf{A}\mathbf{x} = \mathbf{a}$ is proportional to $\rho_r(\mathbf{x}^* + \Lambda_q^\perp(\mathbf{A}))$. Because $\eta_\varepsilon(\Lambda_q^\perp(\mathbf{A})) \leq r$, for each $\mathbf{a}$ this probability is the same (up to $\approx_\varepsilon$) by Lemma 3, and thus the distribution of $\mathbf{A}\mathbf{x}$ is within negligible statistical distance of uniform over $\mathbb{Z}_q^n$.

Next, conditioning on the event $\mathbf{A}\mathbf{x} = \mathbf{a}$, the conditional distribution of $\mathbf{x}$ is the discrete Gaussian $\mathcal{D}_{\mathbf{x}^* + \Lambda_q^\perp(\mathbf{A}), r}$. Because $b = (\mathbf{s}^t\mathbf{A} + \mathbf{e}^t)\mathbf{x} + \tilde{e} = \mathbf{s}^t\mathbf{a} + (\mathbf{e}^t\mathbf{x} + \tilde{e})$, it just remains to analyze the distribution of $\mathbf{e}^t\mathbf{x} + \tilde{e}$. By Lemma 8 below with $\Lambda = \Lambda_q^\perp(\mathbf{A})$ and $\Lambda_1 = \mathbb{Z}$, the distribution $\langle \mathbf{e}, \mathcal{D}_{\mathbf{x}^* + \Lambda_q^\perp(\mathbf{A}), r}\rangle + \mathcal{D}_{\tilde{r}}$ is within negligible statistical distance of $\mathcal{D}_{\mathbb{Z},t}$, as desired. □

We now prove (a more general version of) the core statistical lemma needed by Theorem 5, using Theorem 1. A similar lemma in which Λ_1 is taken to be $\mathbb{R} = \lim_{d\to\infty} d^{-1}\mathbb{Z}$ can be proven using Corollary 8; this yields an LWE self-reduction for continuous Gaussian error (as claimed in prior works).

Lemma 8. *Let $\mathbf{e} \in \mathbb{R}^m$, $\Lambda + \mathbf{x} \subset \mathbb{R}^m$ be a coset of a full-rank lattice, and $\Lambda_1 \subset \mathbb{R}$ be a lattice such that $\langle \mathbf{e}, \Lambda\rangle \subseteq \Lambda_1$. Also let $r, \tilde{r}, \varepsilon > 0$ be such that $\eta_\varepsilon(\Lambda) \leq s := ((1/r)^2 + (\|\mathbf{e}\|/\tilde{r})^2)^{-1/2}$. Then*

$$\Delta_{\mathrm{ML}}(\langle \mathbf{e}, \mathcal{D}_{\Lambda+\mathbf{x},r}\rangle + \mathcal{D}_{\Lambda_1,\tilde{r}}\,,\, \mathcal{D}_{\Lambda_1 + \langle \mathbf{e},\mathbf{x}\rangle, t}) \leq \log\frac{1+\varepsilon}{1-\varepsilon},$$

where $t^2 = (r\|\mathbf{e}\|)^2 + \tilde{r}^2$.

Proof. First observe that

$$\langle \mathbf{e}, \mathcal{D}_{\Lambda+\mathbf{x},r}\rangle + \mathcal{D}_{\Lambda_1,\tilde{r}} = [\mathbf{e}^t \mid 1] \cdot \mathcal{D}_{\Lambda\times\Lambda_1 + (\mathbf{x},0),\mathbf{S}}$$

where $\mathbf{S} = \begin{pmatrix} r\mathbf{I}_m & \\ & \tilde{r}\end{pmatrix}$. So, by applying Theorem 1 (whose hypotheses we verify below), we get that the above distribution is within the desired ML-distance of $\mathcal{D}_{\Lambda_1 + \langle \mathbf{e},\mathbf{x}\rangle, [r\mathbf{e}^t \mid \tilde{r}]}$, where $\mathbf{r}^t = [r\mathbf{e}^t \mid \tilde{r}]$ is a square root of $\mathbf{r}^t\mathbf{r} = (r\|\mathbf{e}\|)^2 + \tilde{r}^2 = t^2$, as desired.

To apply Theorem 1, we first need to show that

$$K = \ker([\mathbf{e}^t \mid 1]) = \{(\mathbf{v}, -\langle \mathbf{e}, \mathbf{v}\rangle) \mid \mathbf{v} \in \mathbb{R}^m\}$$

is a $(\Lambda \times \Lambda_1)$-subspace. Observe that $\Lambda' = K \cap (\Lambda \times \Lambda_1)$ is exactly the set of vectors $(\mathbf{v}, v)$ where $\mathbf{v} \in \Lambda$ and $v = -\langle \mathbf{e}, \mathbf{v}\rangle \in \Lambda_1$, i.e., the image Λ under the injective linear transformation $\mathbf{T}(\mathbf{v}) = (\mathbf{v}, -\langle \mathbf{e}, \mathbf{v}\rangle)$. So, because Λ is full rank, $\mathrm{span}(\Lambda') = K$, as needed.

Finally, we show that $s\mathbf{T} \leq \mathbf{S}$, which by hypothesis and Lemma 2 implies that $\eta_\varepsilon(\mathbf{T}\cdot\Lambda) \leq s\mathbf{T} \leq \mathbf{S}$, as desired. Equivalently, we need to show that the matrix

$$\mathbf{R} = \mathbf{S}\mathbf{S}^t - s^2\mathbf{T}\mathbf{T}^t = \begin{pmatrix} (r^2 - s^2)\mathbf{I}_m & s^2\mathbf{e} \\ s^2\mathbf{e}^t & \tilde{r}^2 - s^2e^2 \end{pmatrix}$$

is positive semidefinite, where $e = \|\mathbf{e}\|$. If $r^2 = s^2$ then $\mathbf{e} = \mathbf{0}$ and $\mathbf{R}$ is positive semidefinite by inspection, so from now on assume that $r^2 > s^2$. Sylvester's criterion says that a symmetric matrix is positive semidefinite if (and only if) all its principal minors are nonnegative.[10] First, every principal minor of $\mathbf{R}$ obtained by removing the last row and column (and possibly others) is $\det((r^2-s^2)\mathbf{I}_k) > 0$ for some k. Now consider a square submatrix of $\mathbf{R}$ wherein the last row and column have not been removed; such a matrix has the form

$$\overline{\mathbf{R}} = \begin{pmatrix} (r^2 - s^2)\mathbf{I}_k & s^2\overline{\mathbf{e}} \\ s^2\overline{\mathbf{e}}^t & \tilde{r}^2 - s^2e^2 \end{pmatrix},$$

where $\overline{\mathbf{e}}$ is some subvector of $\mathbf{e}$, hence $\|\overline{\mathbf{e}}\|^2 \le e^2$. Multiplying the last column by $r^2 - s^2 > 0$ and then subtracting from the last column the product of the first k columns with $s^2 \cdot \overline{\mathbf{e}}$, we obtain a lower-triangular matrix whose first k diagonal entries are $r^2 - s^2 > 0$, and whose last diagonal entry is

$$(\tilde{r}^2 - s^2e^2)(r^2 - s^2) - s^4\|\overline{\mathbf{e}}\|^2 \ge \tilde{r}^2r^2 - \tilde{r}^2s^2 - e^2r^2s^2 = 0,$$

where the equality follows from clearing denominators in the hypothesis $(1/s)^2 = (1/r)^2 + (e/\tilde{r})^2$. So, every principal minor of $\mathbf{R}$ is nonnegative, as desired. □

6 Subgaussian Matrices

The concrete parameters for optimized SIS- and LWE-based trapdoor cryptosystems following [MP12] depend on the largest singular value of a subgaussian random matrix with independent rows, columns, or entries, which serves as the trapdoor. The cryptosystem designer will typically need to rely on a singular value concentration bound to determine Gaussian parameters, set norm thresholds for signatures, estimate concrete security, etc. The current literature does not provide sufficiently precise concentration bounds for this purpose. For example, commonly cited bounds contains non-explicit hidden constant factors, e.g., [Ver12, Theorem 5.39] and [Ver18, Theorems 4.4.5 and 4.6.1].

In Theorem 6 (whose proof is in the full version) we present a singular value concentration bound with explicit constants, for random matrices having independent subgaussian rows. We also report on experiments to determine the singular values for commonly used distributions in lattice cryptography. Throughout this section, we use σ to denote a distribution's standard deviation and $m > n > 0$ for the dimensions of a random matrix $\mathbf{R} \in \mathbb{R}^{m\times n}$ following some particular distribution. We call a random vector $\mathbf{x} \in \mathbb{R}^n$ *σ-isotropic* if $\mathbb{E}[\mathbf{x}\mathbf{x}^t] = \sigma^2\mathbf{I}_n$.

Theorem 6. *Let $\mathbf{R} \in \mathbb{R}^{m\times n}$ be a random matrix whose rows $\mathbf{r}_i$ are independent, identically distributed, zero-mean, σ-isotropic, and subgaussian with parameter $s > 0$. Then for any $t \ge 0$, with probability at least $1 - 2e^{-t^2}$ we have*

$$\sigma(\sqrt{m} - C(s^2/\sigma^2)(\sqrt{n} + t)) \le s_n(\mathbf{R}) \le s_1(\mathbf{R}) \le \sigma(\sqrt{m} + C(s^2/\sigma^2)(\sqrt{n} + t)),$$

where $C = 8e^{1+2/e}\sqrt{\ln 9}/\sqrt{\pi} < 38$.

[10] A principal minor of a matrix is the determinant of a square submatrix obtained by removing the rows and columns having the same index set.

$\mathcal{X}$	$\bar{s}_1$	$\sigma(\sqrt{m} + C_{\mathcal{X}}(s/\sigma)^2\sqrt{n})$	observed $C_{\mathcal{X}}$	Sample Var
$\mathcal{P}$	71.26	71.43	$.99/4\pi$	.04
$\mathcal{U}\{-1,1\}$	100.74	101.01	$.99/2\pi$	.05
$\mathcal{D}_{\sqrt{2\pi}}$	100.71	101.01	$.99/2\pi$	.043
$\mathcal{D}_{\mathbb{Z},\sqrt{2\pi}}$	100.77	101.01	$.99/2\pi$	.06
$\mathcal{X}$	$\bar{s}_n$	$\sigma(\sqrt{m} - C_{\mathcal{X}}(s/\sigma)^2\sqrt{n})$	observed $C_{\mathcal{X}}$	Sample Var
$\mathcal{P}$	39.60	39.43	$.99/4\pi$	.017
$\mathcal{U}\{-1,1\}$	56.00	55.76	$.99/2\pi$	.043
$\mathcal{D}_{\sqrt{2\pi}}$	55.92	55.76	$.99/2\pi$	.036
$\mathcal{D}_{\mathbb{Z},\sqrt{2\pi}}$	56.00	55.76	$.99/2\pi$	.037

Fig. 1. Data from fifty random matrices of dimension 6144×512 for each distribution $\mathcal{X}$. The average largest and smallest singular values are respectively denoted $\bar{s}_1$ and $\bar{s}_n$, and we recorded the sample variance for each distribution's singular values. The third column is the expected singular value using each distribution's calculated $C_{\mathcal{X}}$: $1/2\pi$, $1/2\pi$, and $1/4\pi$ for discrete/continuous gaussians, $\mathcal{U}\{-1,1\}$, and $\mathcal{P}$ respectively.

Comparison. There are two commonly cited concentration bounds for the singular values of subgaussian matrices. The first is for a random matrix with independent entries.

Theorem 7 ([Ver18, Theorem 4.4.5]). *Let $\mathbf{R} \in \mathbb{R}^{m\times n}$ be a random matrix with entries drawn independently from a subgaussian distribution with parameter $s > 0$. Then, there exists some universal constant $C > 0$ such that for any $t \geq 0$, with probability at least $1 - 2e^{-t^2}$ we have*

$$s_1(\mathbf{R}) \leq C \cdot s(\sqrt{m} + \sqrt{n} + t).$$

The second theorem is for a random matrix with independent subgaussian and isotropic rows.

Theorem 8 ([Ver18, Theorem 4.6.1]). *Let $\mathbf{R} \in \mathbb{R}^{m\times n}$ be a random matrix whose rows $\mathbf{a}_i$ are independent, identically distributed, zero-mean, 1-isotropic, and subgaussian with parameter $s > 0$. Then there is a universal constant $C > 0$ such that for any $t \geq 0$, with probability at least $1 - 2e^{-t^2}$ we have*

$$\sqrt{m} - Cs^2(\sqrt{n} + t) \leq s_n(\mathbf{R}) \leq s_1(\mathbf{R}) \leq \sqrt{m} + Cs^2(\sqrt{n} + t).$$

We note that the above theorem is normalized to $\sigma = 1$. Our Theorem 6 is a more explicit version of this theorem for arbitrary σ, which scales in the appropriate way in σ, since scaling a subgaussian distribution simply scales its parameter.

6.1 Experiments

Here we present empirical data on the singular values of random matrices with independent entries drawn from commonly used distributions in lattice-based cryptography. These distributions are the continuous Gaussian, the discrete Gaussian over $\mathbb{Z}$, the uniform distribution over $\{-1, 1\}$ (denoted as $\mathcal{U}\{-1, 1\}$), and the distribution given by choosing 0 with probability 1/2 and ± 1 each with probability 1/4, which we denote $\mathcal{P}$.

First Experiment. For each distribution, we sampled fifty m-by-n (where $m = 6144$ by $n = 512$) random matrices and measured their singular values, and assumed the singular values were approximately

$$s_1 \approx \sigma\left(\sqrt{m} + C_{\mathcal{X}}(s/\sigma)^2\sqrt{n}\right)$$
$$s_n \approx \sigma\left(\sqrt{m} - C_{\mathcal{X}}(s/\sigma)^2\sqrt{n}\right)$$

where $C_{\mathcal{X}}$ is a small constant dependent on the distribution $\mathcal{X}$. The results are given in Fig. 1. We observed $C_{\mathcal{X}}(s/\sigma)^2 \approx 1$ for each distribution.

Continuous and Discrete Gaussians. The continuous Gaussian $\mathcal{D}_\sigma$ is subgaussian with parameter σ since $\mathbb{E}[e^{2\pi t\mathcal{X}}] = e^{\pi t^2\sigma^2}$ where $\mathcal{X} \sim \mathcal{D}_\sigma$. Further, the discrete Gaussian $\mathcal{D}_{\mathbb{Z},s}$ is subgaussian with parameter s, [MP12, Lemma 2.8]. Assuming that the discrete Gaussian is smooth, then one can expect the standard deviation of $\mathcal{D}_{\mathbb{Z},s}$ to be close to the standard deviation of the continuous Gaussian it approximates, $s/\sqrt{2\pi}$. This implies the ratio between the subgaussian parameter and the standard deviation of (discrete) gaussians is $\sqrt{2\pi}$. Under this assumption on the discrete Gaussian's standard deviation, we observed $C_{\text{Gaussian}} = 1/2\pi$.

Uniform over $\{-1, 1\}$. Here $\sigma = 1$ and $\mathbb{E}[e^{2\pi tX}] = \cosh 2\pi t \leq e^{2\pi^2 t^2}$, or the subgaussian parameter is at most $\sqrt{2\pi}$. We observed $C_{\mathcal{U}\{-1,1\}} = 1/2\pi$ in our experiment.

The Distribution $\mathcal{P}$. By nearly the same steps as the previous distribution, $\mathcal{P}$ is subgaussian with parameter $\sqrt{2\pi}$ and $\sigma = 1/\sqrt{2}$. Then, we observed $C_{\mathcal{P}} = 1/4\pi$.

Second Experiment. As a second experiment, we sampled $\mathcal{U}\{-1, 1\}^{32n\times n}$ and averaged its maximum singular value over 50 samples. We varied $n = 50$, 100, 200, 500, 1000 and plotted the results in Fig. 2 (red squares) graphed with the expected largest singular value (dashed blue line). We remark that we saw the same behavior for all four distributions when we varied the dimension.

6.2 Applications

Here we show how the updated singular value estimates from the previous subsection impact concrete security of lattice trapdoor schemes. As an example, we use the [MP12] trapdoor scheme with entries drawn independently from $\mathcal{P}$. That is, we consider the SIS trapdoor scheme based on $\mathbf{A} = [\bar{\mathbf{A}}|\mathbf{G} - \bar{\mathbf{A}}\mathbf{R}] \in \mathbb{Z}_q^{n\times m}$ where $\mathbf{R} \leftarrow \mathcal{P}^{(m-n\log q)\times n\log q}$ is a subgaussian matrix serving as the trapdoor[11], $\mathbf{G} = [\mathbf{I}_n|2\mathbf{I}_n|\ldots|2^{\log q-1}\mathbf{I}_n]$ is the gadget matrix, and $\bar{\mathbf{A}}$ is a truly random matrix. Further, let $s > 0$ be the width of the discrete Gaussian that we are sampling over. This $s > 0$ scales linearly with $s_1(\mathbf{R})$[12]. Since the singular values of $\mathbf{R}$ scale

[11] Trapdoor inversions are independent samples of the form $\mathbf{x} \leftarrow \mathcal{D}_{\mathbf{y}^*+\Lambda_q^\perp(\mathbf{A}),s}$.

[12] See [MP12, Section 3.4] for the further details.

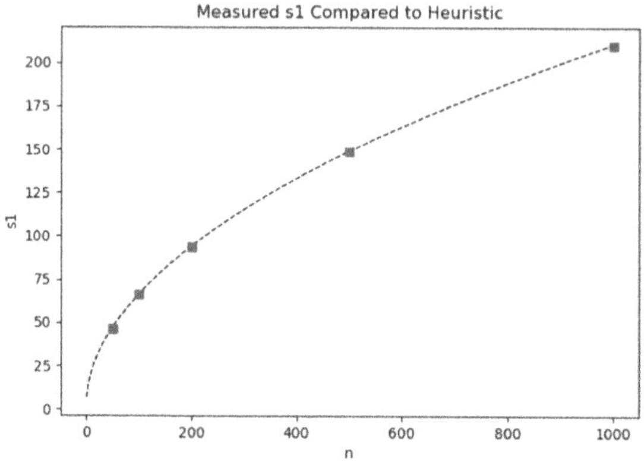

Fig. 2. Here we compare the measured largest singular value with the expectation under our heurstic, with entries from the distribution $\mathcal{X} = \{-1, 1\}$. For each $n = 50, 100, 200, 500, 1000$, the experiment sampled $N = 50$ random $32n$-by-n matrices and averaged their largest singular value. The measured sample variances were $.099, .064, .050, .048, .031$ for $n = 50, 100, 200, 500, 1000$, respectively. Also of note, the measured constant $C_{\mathcal{X}}$ approached $1/2\pi$ from below as n increased ($.92/2\pi$, $.96/2\pi$, $.97/2\pi, .99/2\pi, .99/2\pi$ for $n = 50, 100, 200, 500, 1000$). (Color figure online)

with $\sigma = 1/\sqrt{2}$, the concrete security of the underlying SIS problem increases compared to assuming the largest singular value of $\mathbf{R}$ scales with the subgaussian parameter, $s = 1$. See Fig. 3 for the difference in a commonly-used parameter regime.

In order to estimate security, we followed [APS15, ACD+18] by estimating the time-complexity of the BKZ algorithm [SE94] using sieving as its SVP oracle[13]. BKZ is expected to return a vector of length $\delta^{2n}\det(\Lambda)^{1/2n}$ for a lattice, Λ, of dimension $2n$. Also, Minkowski's theorem tells us a short enough lattice vector exists when we only use $2n$ columns of $\mathbf{A}$. In other words, breaking the trapdoor corresponds to finding a short vector in $\Lambda_q^{\perp}(\mathbf{A}_{2n}) = \{\mathbf{z} \in \mathbb{Z}^{2n} | \mathbf{A}_{2n}\mathbf{z} = \mathbf{0} \in \mathbb{Z}_q^n\}$ where $\mathbf{A}_{2n}$ is the matrix formed by the first $2n$ columns of $\mathbf{A}$.

We found the smallest block size k achieving the needed δ satisfying $s\sqrt{m} = \delta^{2n}\det(\mathbf{A}_{2n})^{\frac{1}{2n}} = \delta^{2n}\sqrt{q}$. Finally, we used the heuristic $\delta \approx (\frac{k}{2\pi e}(\pi k)^{1/k})^{\frac{1}{2(k-1)}}$ to determine the relationship between k and δ, and we set the total time complexity of BKZ with block-size k, dimension $2n$ as $8 \cdot (2n) \cdot \text{time(SVP)} = 8 \cdot (2n) \cdot 2^{.292k+16.4}$ [Che13, APS15][14].

[13] Sieving in dimension k has heuristic time-complexity $2^{.292k+16.4}$ [BDGL16].

[14] We use this simplistic method to estimate security since we are interested in the *difference* in concrete security. More sophisticated methods to estimate the concrete security of lattice-based schemes can be found in [Duc18, ADH+19].

Parameters	Original	Updated
n	512	512
q	2^{24}	2^{24}
s	2881	2037
m	24804	24804
Bit Sec.	124	136
δ	1.0046	1.0043
k	324	364

Fig. 3. The change in concrete security of the underlying SIS problem in MP12 when the trapdoor is drawn from $\mathcal{P}^{(m-n\log q)\times n\log q}$. We give the smallest BKZ block size k achieving the δ needed to find a vector of length $s\sqrt{m}$ in (a subspace of) the lattice $\Lambda_q^{\perp}(\mathbf{A})$.

References

[ACD+18] Albrecht, M.R., et al.: Estimate all the LWE, NTRU schemes! In: SCN, pp. 351–367 (2018)

[ACPS09] Applebaum, B., Cash, D., Peikert, C., Sahai, A.: Fast cryptographic primitives and circular-secure encryption based on hard learning problems. In: Halevi, S. (ed.) CRYPTO 2009. LNCS, vol. 5677, pp. 595–618. Springer, Heidelberg (2009). https://doi.org/10.1007/978-3-642-03356-8_35

[ADH+19] Albrecht, M.R., Ducas, L., Herold, G., Kirshanova, E., Postlethwaite, E.W., Stevens, M.: The general sieve kernel and new records in lattice reduction. In: Ishai, Y., Rijmen, V. (eds.) EUROCRYPT 2019, Part 2. LNCS, vol. 11477, pp. 717–746. Springer, Cham (2019). https://doi.org/10.1007/978-3-030-17656-3_25

[AGHS13] Agrawal, S., Gentry, C., Halevi, S., Sahai, A.: Discrete Gaussian leftover hash lemma over infinite domains. In: Sako, K., Sarkar, P. (eds.) ASIACRYPT 2013, Part 1. LNCS, vol. 8269, pp. 97–116. Springer, Heidelberg (2013). https://doi.org/10.1007/978-3-642-42033-7_6

[Ajt96] Ajtai, M.: Generating hard instances of lattice problems. Quaderni di Matematica **13**, 1–32 (2004). Preliminary version in STOC 1996

[AP09] Alwen, J., Peikert, C.: Generating shorter bases for hard random lattices. In: STACS, pp. 75–86 (2009)

[APS15] Albrecht, M.R., Player, R., Scott, S.: On the concrete hardness of learning with errors. J. Math. Cryptol. **9**(3), 169–203 (2015)

[AR16] Aggarwal, D., Regev, O.: A note on discrete Gaussian combinations of lattice vectors. Chicago J. Theor. Comput. Sci. (2016)

[BDGL16] Becker, A., Ducas, L., Gama, N., Laarhoven, T.: New directions in nearest neighbor searching with applications to lattice sieving. In: SODA, pp. 10–24 (2016)

[BF11] Boneh, D., Freeman, D.M.: Linearly homomorphic signatures over binary fields and new tools for lattice-based signatures. In: Catalano, D., Fazio, N., Gennaro, R., Nicolosi, A. (eds.) PKC 2011. LNCS, vol. 6571, pp. 1–16. Springer, Heidelberg (2011). https://doi.org/10.1007/978-3-642-19379-8_1

[BPMW16] Bourse, F., Del Pino, R., Minelli, M., Wee, H.: FHE circuit privacy almost for free. In: Robshaw, M., Katz, J. (eds.) CRYPTO 2016, Part 2. LNCS, vol. 9815, pp. 62–89. Springer, Heidelberg (2016). https://doi.org/10.1007/978-3-662-53008-5_3

[CGM19] Chen, Y., Genise, N., Mukherjee, P.: Approximate trapdoors for lattices and smaller hash-and-sign signatures. In: Galbraith, S.D., Moriai, S. (eds.) ASIACRYPT 2019, Part 3. LNCS, vol. 11923, pp. 3–32. Springer, Cham (2019). https://doi.org/10.1007/978-3-030-34618-8_1

[Che13] Chen, Y.: Réduction de réseau et sécurité concréte du chiffrement complétement homomorphe. Ph.D. thesis, Paris 7 (2013)

[DDLL13] Ducas, L., Durmus, A., Lepoint, T., Lyubashevsky, V.: Lattice signatures and bimodal Gaussians. In: Canetti, R., Garay, J.A. (eds.) CRYPTO 2013, Part 1. LNCS, vol. 8042, pp. 40–56. Springer, Heidelberg (2013). https://doi.org/10.1007/978-3-642-40041-4_3

[DGPY19] Ducas, L., Galbraith, S., Prest, T., Yu, Y.: Integral matrix Gram root and lattice Gaussian sampling without floats. Cryptology ePrint Archive, Report 2019/320 (2019). https://eprint.iacr.org/2019/320

[DLP14] Ducas, L., Lyubashevsky, V., Prest, T.: Efficient identity-based encryption over NTRU lattices. In: Sarkar, P., Iwata, T. (eds.) ASIACRYPT 2014, Part 2. LNCS, vol. 8874, pp. 22–41. Springer, Heidelberg (2014). https://doi.org/10.1007/978-3-662-45608-8_2

[Duc18] Ducas, L.: Shortest vector from lattice sieving: a few dimensions for free. In: Nielsen, J.B., Rijmen, V. (eds.) EUROCRYPT 2018, Part 1. LNCS, vol. 10820, pp. 125–145. Springer, Cham (2018). https://doi.org/10.1007/978-3-319-78381-9_5

[Gen09] Gentry, C.: Fully homomorphic encryption using ideal lattices. In: STOC, pp. 169–178 (2009)

[GM18] Genise, N., Micciancio, D.: Faster Gaussian sampling for trapdoor lattices with arbitrary modulus. In: Nielsen, J.B., Rijmen, V. (eds.) EUROCRYPT 2018, Part 1. LNCS, vol. 10820, pp. 174–203. Springer, Cham (2018). https://doi.org/10.1007/978-3-319-78381-9_7

[GPV08] Gentry, C., Peikert, C., Vaikuntanathan, V.: Trapdoors for hard lattices and new cryptographic constructions. In: STOC, pp. 197–206 (2008)

[LPR13] Lyubashevsky, V., Peikert, C., Regev, O.: A toolkit for ring-LWE cryptography. In: Johansson, T., Nguyen, P.Q. (eds.) EUROCRYPT 2013. LNCS, vol. 7881, pp. 35–54. Springer, Heidelberg (2013). https://doi.org/10.1007/978-3-642-38348-9_3

[MG02] Micciancio, D., Goldwasser, S.: Complexity of Lattice Problems - A Cryptographic Perspective. The Kluwer International Series in Engineering and Computer Science, vol. 671. Springer, Heidelberg (2002). https://doi.org/10.1007/978-1-4615-0897-7

[MP12] Micciancio, D., Peikert, C.: Trapdoors for lattices: simpler, tighter, faster, smaller. In: Pointcheval, D., Johansson, T. (eds.) EUROCRYPT 2012. LNCS, vol. 7237, pp. 700–718. Springer, Heidelberg (2012). https://doi.org/10.1007/978-3-642-29011-4_41

[MP13] Micciancio, D., Peikert, C.: Hardness of SIS and LWE with small parameters. In: Canetti, R., Garay, J.A. (eds.) CRYPTO 2013, Part 1. LNCS, vol. 8042, pp. 21–39. Springer, Heidelberg (2013). https://doi.org/10.1007/978-3-642-40041-4_2

[MR04] Micciancio, D., Regev, O.: Worst-case to average-case reductions based on Gaussian measures. SIAM J. Comput. **37**(1), 267–302 (2007). Preliminary version in FOCS 2004

[MW17] Micciancio, D., Walter, M.: Gaussian sampling over the integers: efficient, generic, constant-time. In: Katz, J., Shacham, H. (eds.) CRYPTO 2017, Part 2. LNCS, vol. 10402, pp. 455–485. Springer, Cham (2017). https://doi.org/10.1007/978-3-319-63715-0_16

[MW18] Micciancio, D., Walter, M.: On the bit security of cryptographic primitives. In: Nielsen, J.B., Rijmen, V. (eds.) EUROCRYPT 2018, Part 1. LNCS, vol. 10820, pp. 3–28. Springer, Cham (2018). https://doi.org/10.1007/978-3-319-78381-9_1

[Pei10] Peikert, C.: An efficient and parallel Gaussian sampler for lattices. In: Rabin, T. (ed.) CRYPTO 2010. LNCS, vol. 6223, pp. 80–97. Springer, Heidelberg (2010). https://doi.org/10.1007/978-3-642-14623-7_5

[Reg05] Regev, O.: On lattices, learning with errors, random linear codes, and cryptography. J. ACM **56**(6), 1–40 (2009). Preliminary version in STOC 2005

[SE94] Schnorr, C., Euchner, M.: Lattice basis reduction: improved practical algorithms and solving subset sum problems. Math. Program. **66**, 181–199 (1994)

[Ver12] Vershynin, R.: Introduction to the non-asymptotic analysis of random matrices. In: Compressed Sensing, pp. 210–268. Cambridge University Press (2012)

[Ver18] Vershynin, R.: High-Dimensional Probability: An Introduction with Applications in Data Science. Cambridge Series in Statistical and Probabilistic Mathematics. Cambridge University Press (2018)

Almost Tight Security in Lattices with Polynomial Moduli – PRF, IBE, All-but-many LTF, and More

Qiqi Lai[1(✉)], Feng-Hao Liu[2(✉)], and Zhedong Wang[2(✉)]

[1] School of Computer Science, Shaanxi Normal University, Xi'an, Shaanxi, China
laiqq@snnu.edu.cn

[2] Florida Atlantic University, Boca Raton, FL, USA
{fenghao.liu,wangz}@fau.edu

Abstract. Achieving tight security is a fundamental task in cryptography. While one of the most important purposes of this task is to improve the overall efficiency of a construction (by allowing smaller security parameters), many current lattice-based instantiations do not completely achieve the goal. Particularly, a super-polynomial modulus seems to be necessary in all prior work for (almost) tight schemes that allow the adversary to conduct queries, such as PRF, IBE, and Signatures. As the super-polynomial modulus would affect the noise-to-modulus ratio and thus increase the parameters, this might cancel out the advantages (in efficiency) brought from the tighter analysis. To determine the full power of tight security/analysis in lattices, it is necessary to determine whether the super-polynomial modulus restriction is inherent.

In this work, we remove the super-polynomial modulus restriction for many important primitives – PRF, IBE, All-but-many Lossy Trapdoor Functions, and Signatures. The crux relies on an improvement over the framework of Boyen and Li (Asiacrypt 16), and an almost tight reduction from LWE to LWR, which improves prior work by Alwen et al. (Crypto 13), Bogdanov et al. (TCC 16), and Bai et al. (Asiacrypt 15). By combining these two advances, we are able to derive these almost tight schemes under LWE with a polynomial modulus.

1 Introduction

Tight Security. The reduction framework is a powerful tool to analyze security of a cryptographic construction by relating its security to some suitable mathematical hard problem, such as problems of integer factoring, discrete logs, shortest vector in lattices, and many others [19,35,46]. This framework can be described roughly as follows: assume that there exists a $(t_{\mathcal{A}}, \varepsilon_{\mathcal{A}})$-adversary $\mathcal{A}$ that breaks the cryptographic construction, then we can construct a $(t_{\mathcal{B}}, \varepsilon_{\mathcal{B}})$-reduction algorithm $\mathcal{B}$ that uses $\mathcal{A}$ as a subroutine and solves the underlying hard problem.[1]

[1] We use the notation of (t, ε) to denote an algorithm that breaks a crypto system or solves a hard problem within running time t and with advantage ε.

A. Kiayias et al. (Eds.): PKC 2020, LNCS 12110, pp. 652–681, 2020.
https://doi.org/10.1007/978-3-030-45374-9_22

To evaluate how tight the security of the cryptographic scheme is with respect to the hardness of the underlying problem, we establish analysis of bounds in the form: $\varepsilon_{\mathcal{B}} \geq \varepsilon_{\mathcal{A}}/\theta$ and $t_{\mathcal{B}} \leq kt_{\mathcal{A}} + o(t_{\mathcal{A}})$, and then use $k\theta$ as a measure of tightness – the smaller this quantity is, the tighter the security can achieve. The cryptographic scheme is considered to be (1) *tight* (with respect to the underlying hard problem) if $k\theta = c$ for some constant independent of the adversary, and (2) *almost tight* (with respect to the underlying hard problem) if $k\theta = \mathsf{poly}(\lambda)$ for some small polynomial of the security parameter, independent of the adversary.

Achieving tight security is a meaningful task, particularly when one can prove the same or perhaps slightly less efficient scheme has a tight reduction than a non-tight one. From a theoretical point of view, tightness indicates that security of a crypto scheme is (extremely) closely related to the hardness of the underlying hard problem, which is the optimal case we can expect from the provable security theory. By knowing the (almost) tight relation, we would know how aggressively we can set the security parameter, which is important for practical efficiency.

This subject has drawn a large amount of attention. For symmetric key primitives, we know how to achieve almost tight pseudorandom functions (PRFs) [8,26,41] with respect to various assumptions. Later on, the community turned the focus to public-key primitives. For example, Waters [53] stated an open problem of constructing a tightly, adaptively secure IBE scheme from standard computational hardness assumptions without random oracles. In addition to IBE, progress has been made for various other schemes, including public-key encryption and signature (e.g, [5,10,24,28,32,33]).

Progress in Lattices. While research in this line is active, most results were with respect to assumptions on groups [10,24,33] or integer factorization [9,39]. For other important or post-quantum assumptions such as lattices, only a few results are known even for almost tight security. For symmetric-key primitives, there are only two almost tight PRFs from the learning with error assumption (LWE) [8,41]. For public-key primitives, Boyen and Li [16] constructed the first almost tight IBE based on LWE by using a novel application of (key) homomorphic evaluation of PRF. Later in subsequent work, Boyen and Li [17], and Libert et al. [41] generalized this technique to construct almost tight all-but-many lossy trapdoor functions (ABM-LTFs) from LWE. These results are significant, as ABM-LTFs have several important applications in constructing other primitives, such as almost tight encryption schemes that are secure against selective opening attacks and CCA2 attacks (SO-CCA2) [17], and almost tight encryption schemes with multiple challenges against CCA2 attacks [41].

Despite these excellent advances, we however notice a common drawback in all prior almost tight lattice-based results – they all require super-polynomial moduli. It is much more favorable to build schemes with a polynomial modulus, as this provides a better security guarantee, e.g., a better approximate factor of worst-case lattice problems, and thus can lead to smaller parameters resulting in better efficiency. Additionally from a theoretic point of view, it is important to determine whether a super-polynomial modulus is inherent in achieving almost tight security in lattice-based crypto. Therefore, we ask:

Can we achieve (almost) tight security in lattices with a polynomial modulus ?

1.1 Our Results

In this work, we answer this question in a positive way for the following important primitives – PRF, IBE, and ABM-LTF. In particular, we construct and prove almost tight security of all these primitives with respect to LWE with polynomial moduli. Some other almost tight constructions can also be obtained along this line as we describe several examples. (1) Similar to the work of Boyen and Li [16], our technique of IBE can be used to derive almost tight signature schemes. Moreover, our IBE can be (almost) tightly extended to CCA2-IBE. (2) We can achieve almost tight IND-SO-CCA2 secure encryption schemes from LWE with a polynomial modulus q, following the framework of [17]. (3) We can achieve almost tight encryption schemes for multiple ciphertexts against CCA2 attacks from LWE with a polynomial modulus q, following the framework of [41]. Below we summarize our main results.

1. We prove that the GGM-based PRF in [8] is almost tight with respect to LWE with a polynomial modulus. This derives the *first* almost tight lattice-based PRF with a polynomial modulus. The crux relies on a new route of reduction LWE $\rightarrow$ Q-LWR$'$ $\rightarrow$ PRF, avoiding the known non-tight approach, i.e., LWE $\rightarrow$ PRG $\rightarrow$ PRF.[2]
   Moreover, our reduction LWE $\rightarrow$ Q-LWR$'$ has advantages over existing reductions: (1) we remove the additional number-theoretic limitation on the modulus in [4]; (2) our reduction has better running time and distinguishing probability than those in the work [11,16]. See Sects. 1.2 and 3 for further discussions.
2. We then construct an almost tight adaptively secure IBE from lattices with a polynomial modulus. This improves the prior work [16] by weakening its underlying assumption, i.e., LWE for some super-polynomial modulus. To achieve this, we first improve the framework of [16], showing that an almost tight PRF (even not computable in NC1) suffices for achieving almost tight IBE with a polynomial modulus. Then the desired IBE follows by combining our almost tight PRF (not necessarily in NC1) with the improved framework.
3. We further show that our technique in Contribution 2 can be used to achieve an almost tight ABM-LTF and signatures from LWE with a polynomial modulus, improving the underlying assumption needed in the prior work [17,41].

1.2 Our Techniques

Pseudorandom Functions

In this work, we derive the first almost tight PRF with respect to LWE with a polynomial modulus. To illustrate our new ideas, we first briefly review the elegant approach by Banerjee, Peikert, and Rosen [8], who constructed the first lattice-based PRF by introducing an intermediate problem – the learning

[2] Q is the number of queries in the PRF; LWR$'$ is a variant of the LWR problem originally defined in the work [8]; Q-LWR$'$ is a multi-secret variant of LWR$'$ that includes inner products of Q secrets per sample.

with rounding (LWR) assumption, a *de-randomized* version of the LWE assumption [49]. In LWR, there is a secret vector $\boldsymbol{s} \in \mathbb{Z}_q^n$ and the target is to distinguish $(\boldsymbol{a}, \lfloor\langle\boldsymbol{a}, \boldsymbol{s}\rangle\rceil_{q\to p})$ from the uniform distribution, where $(\boldsymbol{a}, \boldsymbol{s}) \xleftarrow{\$} \mathbb{Z}_q^n \times \mathbb{Z}_q^n$, and the rounding function is taken as $\lfloor x \mod q\rceil_{q\to p} = \lfloor x(p/q)\rceil \mod p$. Since then, the work [15] and follow-up work [7] have built PRFs based on the LWE/LWR (or their variants), and different reductions from LWE to LWR have been proved for various parameters [4,6,11].

We observe that all non-GGM PRFs [7,8] cannot be proved secure under LWE with a polynomial modulus using current techniques: (1) The synthesizer in Naor-Reigold-based PRFs [45] need to use LWR with unbounded samples. However, all known reductions from LWE to LWR [4,6,8,11] with polynomial moduli require that the number of samples is bounded; (2) Other constructions such as the direct construction [8], tree-based construction [7], and the key-homomorphic PRF [7,15,41], require the modulus to be larger than the noise, which grows super-polynomially as needed in their analyses.

On the other hand, the GGM-based PRFs can be proved secure under LWE with a polynomial modulus. This is because LWR with bounded samples suffices for the GGM analysis (see [4]), and we do know reductions from LWE to LWR with a polynomial modulus [4,6,11]. However, the reduction loss in this approach depends on the number of queries Q by the PRF adversary. This work shows how to remove this dependency on Q.

Our New Idea: A New Route of Reduction

We first recall that the GGM framework [31] showed that a length-doubling PRG implies a PRF. The proof of security can be decomposed into two steps (c.f. [37]), i.e., PRG $\xrightarrow{(1)}$ Q-PRG $\xrightarrow{(2)}$ PRF, where the Q-PRG problem is to distinguish Q independent samples of PRG from Q random strings. The second step is almost tight, yet the loss in the first step depends on Q under currently known hybrid proof techniques. Therefore, any route that starts with LWE $\to$ PRG will hit this technical difficulty. To bypass this barrier, we propose a new route:

$$\boxed{\mathsf{LWE} \xrightarrow{(i)} n\text{-}\mathsf{LWE} \xrightarrow{(ii)} Q\text{-}\mathsf{LWR}' \xrightarrow{(iii)} \mathsf{PRF},}$$

where the Q-LWR′ problem asks to distinguish samples either from $(\mathbf{A}, \lfloor\boldsymbol{s}_1^t \cdot \mathbf{A}\rceil_{q\to p}, \ldots, \lfloor\boldsymbol{s}_Q^t \cdot \mathbf{A}\rceil_{q\to p})$ or from the corresponding uniform distribution, where $\boldsymbol{s}_i \leftarrow \mathbb{Z}_p^n$ for $i \in [Q]$.[3]

The reduction loss in (i) is n by a simple hybrid argument, and thus almost tight. The reduction loss in (iii) is k (the input length), which is almost tight. It is worth pointing out that the n-LWE problem is also known as the multi-secret LWE problem. As n is a system parameter that only depends on the security parameter, sometimes this version of the LWE is used as the starting point of the underlying hard problem, e.g. the work [17].

[3] The original LWR problem [8] samples the secret uniformly at random from $\mathbb{Z}_q^n$.

We next present a new analysis of n-LWE $\xrightarrow{(ii)}$ Q-LWR$'$, which can be proved *tight* (for some useful settings of parameters). To achieve this, we present a refinement of the work [4] below:

Refinement of [4]**.** We present a critical observation that the information-theoretic step of [4] can be applied to the multi-secret setting. More specifically, we take the steps as follows.

1. First, we break $\mathbf{A} \in \mathbb{Z}_q^{n\times m}$ into $(\bar{\mathbf{A}}, \boldsymbol{a}) \in \mathbb{Z}_q^{n\times(m-1)} \times \mathbb{Z}_q^n$ and switch $\bar{\mathbf{A}}$ into some lossy but indistinguishable $\tilde{\mathbf{A}}$. This incurs a security loss $\varepsilon_{n\text{-LWE}}$.
2. Then, we prove that $(\tilde{\mathbf{A}}, \lfloor \boldsymbol{s}_1{}^t \cdot \tilde{\mathbf{A}} \rceil_{q\to p}, \cdots, \lfloor \boldsymbol{s}_Q^t \cdot \tilde{\mathbf{A}} \rceil_{q\to p}, \boldsymbol{a}, \lfloor \boldsymbol{a} \cdot \boldsymbol{s}_1 \rceil_{q\to p}, \cdots,$ $\lfloor \boldsymbol{a} \cdot \boldsymbol{s}_Q \rceil_{q\to p})$ is *statistically close* to $(\tilde{\mathbf{A}}, \lfloor \boldsymbol{s}_1^t \cdot \tilde{\mathbf{A}} \rceil_{q\to p}, \cdots, \lfloor \boldsymbol{s}_Q^t \cdot \tilde{\mathbf{A}} \rceil_{q\to p}, \boldsymbol{a},$ $\lfloor \boldsymbol{u}_1 \rceil_{q\to p}, \cdots, \lfloor \boldsymbol{u}_Q \rceil_{q\to p}))$ for truly random $\{\boldsymbol{u}_i\}_{i\in[Q]}$.
3. Next, we switch $\tilde{\mathbf{A}}$ back to $\bar{\mathbf{A}}$, with another security loss $\varepsilon_{n\text{-LWE}}$.
4. Then we repeat the above steps for each column of $\mathbf{A}$.

The second step can be proved using the concept that a strong extractor extracts randomness from a block-source. It is clear that $(\boldsymbol{a}, \langle \boldsymbol{a}, \boldsymbol{s} \rangle)$ is a strong extractor. As we can show that $\boldsymbol{s}_1, \cdots, \boldsymbol{s}_Q$ form a block-source,[4] $\boldsymbol{a}$ can extract their randomness [52]. This step might incur a dependency on Q yet in the *purely information-theoretic* manner, i.e., the dependency on Q will not affect $\varepsilon_{n\text{-LWE}}$ in the multiplicative way. With appropriate parameters, we can make the statistical distance in Step 2 arbitrarily small, e.g., 2^{-n}, and the security loss in Steps 1–3 would be $2\varepsilon_{n\text{-LWE}} + 2^{-n}$. By repeating Steps 1–3 for all columns (i.e. m), we can obtain a reduction with loss $m(2\varepsilon_{n\text{-LWE}} + 2^{-n})$, which is almost tight.

Further Improvements. Next, we present two optimizations of the above approach: (1) By using a more efficient hybrid analysis, we can get rid of the dependency on m in the above argument. Particularly, if the secret $\boldsymbol{s}$ has sufficient entropy relative to m, we can extract multiple columns per hybrid, resulting in using less hybrids and thus the overall reduction can be independent of m. (2) By using a leftover hash lemma for general modulus q with a more careful analysis, we can further remove the number-theoretic restrictions in [4]. This broadens the range of parameter selections – for example, the prior analysis [4] does not cover several useful settings, e.g., $q = p^e$, where our improvement does.

Putting Things Together for PRF. Putting things together, we are able to achieve: n-LWE $\to$ PRF with reduction loss k, and similarly LWE $\to$ PRF with reduction loss kn. By applying the technique of input-domain extension by [26], we can further reduce the loss k to $\omega(\log \kappa)$ and achieve the on-the-fly security. We summarize the results as follow:

Theorem 1.1 (Informal). *With some polynomial modulus q, we have: (1) n-LWE $\to$ PRF with reduction loss $\omega(\log \kappa)$, and (2) LWE $\to$ PRF with reduction loss $n \cdot \omega(\log \kappa)$.*

[4] More precisely, we can prove that $\boldsymbol{s}_1, \cdots, \boldsymbol{s}_Q$ have high min-entropy and form a block-source, conditioned on $\lfloor \boldsymbol{s}_1^t \cdot \tilde{\mathbf{A}} \rceil_{q\to p}, \cdots, \lfloor \boldsymbol{s}_Q^t \cdot \tilde{\mathbf{A}} \rceil_{q\to p}$.

A Note on Dimension Loss. For general moduli p, q, all known reductions $\mathsf{LWE} \rightarrow (Q\text{-})\mathsf{LWR}$ ([4,6,11] and ours) incur a dimension loss, i.e., LWE with dimension ℓ implies $(Q\text{-})\mathsf{LWR}$ with dimension ranging from $O(\ell)$ to $O(\ell \log q)$. As our almost tight result $\mathsf{LWE} \rightarrow Q\text{-}\mathsf{LWR}$ can achieve dimension loss of a constant factor, in the setting of general moduli, our reduction $\mathsf{LWE} \rightarrow \mathsf{PRF}$ is better than existing non-tight analyses $\mathsf{LWE} \rightarrow \mathsf{LWR} \rightarrow \mathsf{PRF}$ [4,6,11] in terms of security loss and in some cases as well dimension loss.

For special moduli p, q such that $p|q$, the reduction $\mathsf{LWE} \rightarrow \mathsf{LWR}$ of Bai et al. [6] does not incur a dimension loss, yet their reduction running time blows up significantly (at least quadratically) as the analysis goes through a decision to search step. An alternative approach would take the LWE function $f_{\mathbf{A}}(\boldsymbol{s}, \boldsymbol{e}) = \mathbf{A} \cdot \boldsymbol{s} + \boldsymbol{e}$ as a PRG, which is indeed length expanding as we do not need $n \log q$ bits of randomness to represent $\boldsymbol{e}$. This approach would not incur a dimension loss nor impose number theoretic restrictions on the modulus q. By using these two approaches, one can get a non-tight GGM PRF with the same dimension parameter as the underlying LWE, namely ℓ.

In general, a non-tight PRF (with dimension ℓ) and a tight PRF (with dimension $O(\ell)$) are incomparable as we discuss below. On one hand, if LWE is exponentially hard, e.g., $\varepsilon_{\mathsf{LWE}}(\ell) = 2^{-\ell}$, the non-tight PRF only needs to scale up ℓ to $(\ell + \log Q)$ to accommodate the security loss of a factor Q. In this case, the non-tight PRF parameter is better than the tight one. On the other hand, if LWE is only super-polynomially hard, e.g., $\varepsilon_{\mathsf{LWE}}(\ell) = 2^{-\log^2(\ell)}$, the non-tight PRF needs to scale up ℓ to $e\ell$ where $\log e \approx \log Q / (2 \log \ell)$, in order to accommodate the security loss. As e can be an arbitrary constant depending on the adversary, the tight PRF is better in this setting.

Almost Tight IBE and ABM-LTFs from LWE with Polynomial q
Recently, Boyen and Li [16] showed how to achieve an almost tight IBE from LWE by proposing a novel technique that applies (key) homomorphic evaluation on PRF. Shortly, this technique was used to achieve $\mathsf{ABM\text{-}LTFs}$ from LWE and thus many of their applications [17,41]. However, their techniques inherently require a super-polynomial modulus in achieving almost tight security. Below, we present our new insights to remove this restriction. For simplicity of presentation, we just focus on the setting of IBE [16] and remark that the idea can be extended to the $\mathsf{ABM\text{-}LTF}$ in a similar way.

Basically, Boyen and Li [16] showed that an almost tight IBE can be constructed if (1) LWE is hard, (2) there exists an (almost) tight PRF that can be evaluated in NC1. Even though their reduction is tight from $\mathsf{LWE}+\mathsf{PRF}$, there is no known instantiation of the required PRF from LWE with a polynomial modulus. Therefore, there is no construction of pure lattice-based almost tight IBE with a polynomial modulus. How to achieve such a PRF instantiation is a natural and interesting open problem.

The GGM-PRF with our new analysis still does not solve the open problem directly, as the GGM-based construction is not known to be in NC1. Nevertheless, we bypass this issue by showing that the requirement on NC1 is not necessary. Particularly, we improve the framework of Boyen and Li [16] by showing that the following conditions are sufficient: (1) LWE is hard, (2) there exists an almost tight PRF, and (3) there exists a (leveled) fully homomorphic encryption scheme whose decryption algorithm can be computed in NC1.[5] Our desired IBE follows, as we can instantiate all the components from LWE with a polynomial modulus – the GGM-based PRF in this work for (2), and the FHE schemes [3,22] for (3). In summary, we achieve the following theorem:

Theorem 1.2 (Informal). *Assuming* LWE *is hard for some polynomial modulus q, there exists an almost tight adaptively secure* IBE *in the standard model.*

Below we highlight our new ideas. We first recall the framework of Boyen and Li [16], which can be described roughly as follows. The public key contains matrices $\mathbf{A}$ and $\mathbf{B}_1, \ldots, \mathbf{B}_k$. At various steps (in the proof), the matrices are encoded as $\mathbf{B}_i = \mathbf{A} \cdot \mathbf{R}_i + s_i \mathbf{G}$, where s_i is the i-th bit of a PRF key K and $\mathbf{R}_i$'s are random matrices with small norms. In the key derivation process, i.e., to derive $\mathsf{sk}_{\mathsf{id}}$, their scheme applies the (key) homomorphic evaluation algorithm [14] on the matrices $\{\mathbf{B}_i\}_{i \in k}$ to compute the function $\mathsf{PRF}(K, \mathsf{id})$ for some given id, resulting in $\mathbf{B}_{\mathsf{id}} = \mathbf{A} \cdot \mathbf{R}_{\mathsf{id}} + \mathsf{PRF}(K, \mathsf{id})\mathbf{G}$. Their IBE scheme [16] requires that $\|\mathbf{R}_{\mathsf{id}}\| < q$, as $\|\mathbf{R}_{\mathsf{id}}\|$ affects the quality of the SampleRight algorithm and the noise growth. As long as the PRF computation is in NC1 [16], then $\|\mathbf{R}_{\mathsf{id}}\|$ can be upper bounded by a polynomial, allowing the scheme to use a polynomial modulus q. On the other hand, if the PRF is not computable in NC1, then a super-polynomial q seems to be inherent in this approach as $\|\mathbf{R}_{\mathsf{id}}\|$ would become super-polynomial.

To bypass the technical barrier, we introduce a two-step approach that integrates homomorphic evaluation on leveled HE ciphertexts, key homomorphic evaluation on the public matrices, and Gentry's bootstrapping technique [3,29]. Given a leveled FHE (HE) that supports homomorphic computation of the PRF and has an NC1 decryption algorithm, we add an encryption of a PRF key K, i.e., $c \leftarrow \mathsf{HE.Enc}(K)$, to the public key, and encode $\mathbf{B}_i = \mathbf{A} \cdot \mathbf{R}_i + (\mathsf{sk})_i \mathbf{G}$, where $(\mathsf{sk})_i$ is the i-th bit of the decryption key of the HE scheme. Then our new key derivation process consists of the following two steps:

1. (Homomorphic Evaluation of PRF) First run $\tilde{c} = \mathsf{HE.Eval}(\mathsf{PRF}(\cdot, \mathsf{id}), c)$ to homomorphically evaluate $\mathsf{PRF}(K, \mathsf{id})$.
2. (Key Homomorphic Bootstrapping) Next run the key homomorphic evaluation of the decryption algorithm of HE on the matrices $\{\mathbf{B}_i\}_{i \in [k]}$ with the input $\tilde{c}$, i.e., evaluate $\mathsf{HE.Dec}(\mathsf{sk}, \tilde{c})$ homomorphically. Then we obtain $\mathbf{B}_{\mathsf{id}} = \mathbf{A} \cdot \mathbf{R}_{\mathsf{Dec}} + \mathsf{PRF}(K, \mathsf{id})\mathbf{G}$.

As the decryption algorithm can be computed in NC1, we know that $\|\mathbf{R}_{\mathsf{Dec}}\|$ can be bounded by a polynomial. Furthermore, we know that the required HE

[5] Actually a homomorphic encryption that supports evaluation of the PRF in (2) suffices.

can be instantiated from LWE with a polynomial modulus [3,22]. Putting all things together, we can obtain the desired IBE.

We note that our result above *does not* need the circular security assumption, as we only need a leveled HE that supports computation of the PRF, which is of a bounded depth. Moreover, in our key homomorphic bootstrapping step, the secret key of HE is information-theoretically hidden in the matrices $\mathbf{B}_i$'s. This again does not rely on the circular security assumption.

Finally, we observe that the above two-step approach can be used to improve the modulus used in prior ABM-LTF [17,41] and signatures [16]. Particularly, we achieve:

Theorem 1.3 (Informal). *Assuming* LWE *is hard for some* $q = \mathsf{poly}(\kappa)$*, there exist an almost tight* ABM-LTF *and a signature scheme with a poly modulus.*

Other Related Work. Very recently, Jager *et al.* [34] proposed a new framework to improve the size of secret key and reduction loss of the PRFs [8,40,45], yet their instantiations from lattices however, still require super-polynomial moduli.

2 Preliminaries

Notations. We let κ denote the security parameter. For an integer n, let $[n]$ denote the set $\{1, ..., n\}$. We use bold lowercase letters (e.g. $\boldsymbol{a}$) to denote vectors and bold capital letters (e.g. $\mathbf{A}$) to denote matrices. For a positive integer $q \geq 2$, let $\mathbb{Z}_q$ be the ring of integers modulo q. For a distribution or a set X, we write $x \xleftarrow{\$} X$ to denote the operation of sampling an uniformly random x according to X. For distribution X, Y, we let $\mathsf{SD}(X, Y)$ denote their statistical distance. We write $X \overset{s}{\approx} Y$ to mean that they are statistically close, and $X \overset{c}{\approx} Y$ to say that they are computationally indistinguishable. We let $\mathsf{negl}(\kappa)$ denote the set of all negligible function $\mu(\kappa) = \kappa^{-\omega(1)}$.

Definition 2.1 (Computational indistinguishability). *We say that two experiments* H_0, H_1 *are* (t, ε)*-indistinguishable with oracle access if for every distinguisher* $\mathcal{D}$ *within running time* t*, we have* $|\mathsf{Pr}[\mathcal{D}^{H_0}\mathsf{accepts}] - \mathsf{Pr}[\mathcal{D}^{H_1}\mathsf{accepts}]| < \varepsilon$*, where the probabilities are taken over the coin tosses of* H_0, H_1*.*

2.1 Learning with Error

We define the multi-secret variant of learning with error, i.e., N-LWE, and note that the standard learning with error can be denoted as 1-LWE.

Definition 2.2 (Multi-secret Learning with Errors (LWE) Assumption [49]). *Let* κ *be the security parameter,* n, m, q, N *be integers (functions of* κ*), and* $\chi = \chi(\kappa)$ *be a distribution over* $\mathbb{Z}_q$*. The* N-$\mathsf{LWE}_{n,m,q,\chi}$ *assumption with parameter* N *can be stated that for independently sampled* $\mathbf{A} \xleftarrow{\$} \mathbb{Z}_q^{n\times m}$, $\boldsymbol{u}_i \xleftarrow{\$} \mathbb{Z}_q^m$,

$\boldsymbol{s}_i \xleftarrow{\$} \mathbb{Z}_q^n$ *and* $\boldsymbol{e}_i \xleftarrow{\$} \chi^m$ *for* $i \in [N]$*, the following distributions are computationally indistinguishable:* $(\mathbf{A}, (\boldsymbol{s}_1^t \cdot \mathbf{A} + \boldsymbol{e}_1^t), \ldots, (\boldsymbol{s}_N^t \cdot \mathbf{A} + \boldsymbol{e}_N^t)) \stackrel{c}{\approx} (\mathbf{A}, \boldsymbol{u}_1^t, \ldots, \boldsymbol{u}_N^t)$*. We say* N*-*$\mathsf{LWE}_{n,m,q,\chi}$ *problem is* (t, ε)*-hard if the two distributions above are* (t, ε)*-indistinguishable.*

By a simple hybrid argument, we can derive a reduction from 1-$\mathsf{LWE}_{n,m,q}$ to N-$\mathsf{LWE}_{n,m,q}$ with a security loss with a multiplicative factor of N. The work [20, 47, 49] showed that there exist quantum/classical reductions from some worst-case lattice problems ($\mathsf{GapSVP}, \mathsf{SIVP}$) to the LWE problem.

2.2 Learning with Rounding

For any integer modulus $q > 2$, $\mathbb{Z}_q$ denotes the quotient ring of integers modulus q. We define a rounding function $\lfloor \cdot \rceil_p : \mathbb{Z}_q \rightarrow \mathbb{Z}_p$ for $q \geq p \geq 2$ as

$$\lfloor x \rceil_{q \rightarrow p} = \lfloor (p/q)\bar{x} \rceil_{q \rightarrow p},$$

where $\bar{x} \in \mathbb{Z}$ is any integer congruent to x mod q. Furthermore, $\lfloor \cdot \rceil_{q \rightarrow p}$ can be extended component-wise to vectors and matrices over $\mathbb{Z}_q$. In places where the context is clear about the modulus q, we would omit q in the notation as $\lfloor \cdot \rceil_p$ for simplicity of presentation.

Similar to the multi-secret LWE, we define a multi-secret variant for the LWR assumption, and note that the original LWR [8] can be denoted as 1-LWR.

Definition 2.3 (Multi-secret LWR). *Let* $\kappa \geq 1$ *be the security parameter,* $n, q \geq p \geq 2$*,* Q *be integers (functions of* κ*). The* Q*-*$\mathsf{LWR}_{n,m,q,p}$ *assumption states that for independently sampled* $\mathbf{A} \xleftarrow{\$} \mathbb{Z}_q^{n \times m}$*,* $\boldsymbol{u}_i \xleftarrow{\$} \mathbb{Z}_q^m$*,* $\boldsymbol{s}_i \xleftarrow{\$} \mathbb{Z}_q^n$ *with* $i \in [Q]$*, the following distributions are computationally indistinguishable:*

$$(\mathbf{A}, \lfloor \boldsymbol{s}_1^t \cdot \mathbf{A} \rceil_p, \ldots, \lfloor \boldsymbol{s}_Q^t \cdot \mathbf{A} \rceil_p) \stackrel{c}{\approx} (\mathbf{A}, \lfloor \boldsymbol{u}_1^t \rceil_p, \ldots, \lfloor \boldsymbol{u}_Q^t \rceil_p),$$

We say the Q*-*$\mathsf{LWR}_{n,m,q,p}$ *problem is* (t, ε)*-hard if the two distributions above are* (t, ε)*-indistinguishable.*

Below we define a variant of the LWR problem, namely, LWR′, which will be useful for our PRF construction.

Definition 2.4 (Multi-secret LWR′). *The* Q*-*$\mathsf{LWR}'_{n,m,q,p}$ *problem is the same as* Q*-*$\mathsf{LWR}_{n,m,q,p}$ *except that the secret vectors* $\boldsymbol{s}_1, \ldots, \boldsymbol{s}_Q$ *are sampled from* $\mathbb{Z}_p^n$*.*

2.3 Pseudorandom Function and Identity-Based Encryption

Definition 2.5 (Pseudorandom function). *Let* A *and* B *be finite sets, and let* $\mathcal{F} = \{F_i : A \rightarrow B\}$ *be a function family, endowed with efficient samplable distribution (*$\mathcal{F}, A$ *and* B *are all indexed by the security parameter* λ*). We say that* $\mathcal{F}$ *is a* (t, Q, ε)*-pseudorandom function(PRF) family if the following two experiments are* (t, ε)*-indistinguishable with oracle access up to* Q *adaptive queries: (1) Choose a function* $F \leftarrow \mathcal{F}$*, and (2) Choose a uniformly random function* $R : A \rightarrow B$*.*

Definition 2.6 (Identity-Based Encryption (IBE) [13,51]). *An identity-based encryption scheme consists of four* PPT *algorithms* (Setup, KeyGen, Enc, Dec) *defined as follows:*

- $\mathsf{Setup}(1^\kappa)$*: Given the security parameter, it outputs a master public key* mpk *and a master secret key* msk.
- $\mathsf{KeyGen}(\mathsf{msk}, \mathsf{id})$*: Given the* msk *and an identity* $\mathsf{id} \in \{0,1\}^\ell$*, it outputs the identity secret key* $\mathsf{sk}_{\mathsf{id}}$.
- $\mathsf{Enc}(\mathsf{mpk}, \mathsf{id}, m)$*: Given the* mpk*, an identity* $\mathsf{id} \in \{0,1\}^\ell$*, and a message* m*, it outputs a ciphertext* c.
- $\mathsf{Dec}(\mathsf{sk}_{\mathsf{id}}, c)$*: Given a secret key* $\mathsf{sk}_{\mathsf{id}}$ *for identity* id *and a ciphertext* c*, it outputs a plaintext* m.

The following correctness and security properties must be satisfied:

Correctness: For all security parameter κ, identity $\mathsf{id} \in \{0,1\}^\ell$ and message m, the following holds: $\Pr[\mathsf{Dec}(\mathsf{sk}_{\mathsf{id}}, \mathsf{Enc}(\mathsf{mpk}, \mathsf{id}, m)) \neq m] = \mathsf{negl}(\kappa)$, where $\mathsf{sk}_{\mathsf{id}} \leftarrow \mathsf{KeyGen}(\mathsf{msk}, \mathsf{id})$ and $(\mathsf{mpk}, \mathsf{msk}) \leftarrow \mathsf{Setup}(1^\kappa)$.

Security: We define the *adaptive* chosen-plaintext security (IND-ID-CPA) for IBE as below, where the adversary can adaptively make secret key queries.

Experiment $(\mathsf{IND\text{-}ID\text{-}CPA}^{\mathsf{IBE}}(\mathcal{A}))$

1. $(\mathsf{mpk}, \mathsf{msk}) \xleftarrow{\$} \mathsf{Setup}(1^\kappa)$.
2. $(\mathsf{id}^*, m_0, m_1) \xleftarrow{\$} \mathcal{A}_1^{\mathsf{KeyGen}(\mathsf{msk},\cdot)}(\mathsf{mpk})$ where $|m_0| = |m_1|$ and for each query id by $\mathcal{A}_1$ to $\mathsf{KeyGen}(\mathsf{msk}, \cdot)$ we have that $\mathsf{id} \neq \mathsf{id}^*$.
3. $b \xleftarrow{\$} \{0,1\}$.
4. $m^* = m_b$
5. $c^* \xleftarrow{\$} \mathsf{Enc}(\mathsf{mpk}, \mathsf{id}^*, m^*)$
6. $b' \xleftarrow{\$} \mathcal{A}_2^{\mathsf{KeyGen}(\mathsf{msk},\cdot)}(\mathsf{mpk}, c^*)$ where for each query id by $\mathcal{A}_2$ to $\mathsf{KeyGen}(\mathsf{msk}, \cdot)$ we have that $\mathsf{id} \neq \mathsf{id}^*$.
7. Output 1 if $b^* = b'$ and 0 otherwise.

Definition 2.7. *For a security parameter* κ*, let* $t = t(\kappa), q = q(\kappa)$ *and* $\varepsilon = \varepsilon(\kappa)$*. we say that an* IBE *scheme* $\mathcal{E}$ *is* (t, q, ε)-IND-ID-CPA *secure if for any* t *time adversary* $\mathcal{A}$ *makes at most* q *secret key queries and the following holds:*

$$\Pr[\mathsf{IND\text{-}ID\text{-}CPA}^{\mathsf{IBE}}(\mathcal{A}) = 1] \leq \frac{1}{2} + \varepsilon(\kappa).$$

2.4 Lattice Backgrounds

Theorem 2.8 (Trapdoor Generation [2,43]). *There is a probabilistic polynomial-time algorithm* $\mathsf{TrapGen}(1^n, q, m)$ *that for all* $m \geq m_0 = m_0(n, q) = O(n \log q)$*, outputs* $(\mathbf{A}, \mathbf{T_A})$ *s.t.* $\mathbf{A} \in \mathbb{Z}_q^{n \times m}$ *is within statistical distance* 2^{-n} *from uniform and the distribution of* $\mathbf{T_A}$ *is the Discrete Gaussian* $D_{\mathbb{Z}^m,\tau}$ *conditioned on* $\mathbf{A} \cdot \mathbf{T_A} = 0 \pmod q$ *and* $\tau = O\sqrt{n \log q \log n}$.

Theorem 2.9 ([1]). *Let $q > 2, m > n$. (i) If $s > \|\tilde{\mathbf{T}}_{\mathbf{A}}\| \cdot \omega(\sqrt{\log(m+m_1)})$. Then there exists an algorithm* SampleLeft *taking* ($\mathbf{A} \in \mathbb{Z}_q^{n\times m}, \mathbf{B} \in \mathbb{Z}^{n\times m_1}, \mathbf{T}_{\mathbf{A}}, \boldsymbol{u} \in \mathbb{Z}_q^n, s$) *as input, outputs a vector $\mathbf{d} \in \mathbb{Z}^{m+m_1}$ distributed statistically close to $D_{\Lambda_q^{\boldsymbol{u}}([\mathbf{A}|\mathbf{B}]),s}$. (ii) If $s > \|\tilde{\mathbf{T}}_{\mathbf{B}}\| \cdot \|\mathbf{R}\| \cdot \omega(\sqrt{\log m})$. Then there exists an algorithm* SampleRight *taking* ($\mathbf{A} \in \mathbb{Z}_q^{n\times k}, \mathbf{R} \in \mathbb{Z}^{k\times m}, \mathbf{B} \in \mathbb{Z}^{n\times m}, \mathbf{T}_{\mathbf{B}}, \boldsymbol{u} \in \mathbb{Z}_q^n, s$) *as input, outputs a vector $\mathbf{d} \in \mathbb{Z}^{m+k}$ distributed statistically close to $D_{\Lambda_q^{\boldsymbol{u}}([\mathbf{A}|\mathbf{AR}+\mathbf{B}]),s}$.*

Gadget Matrix. We recall the "gadget matrix" $\mathbf{G}$ defined in [43]. The "gadget matrix" $\mathbf{G} = \boldsymbol{g} \otimes \mathbf{I}_n \in \mathbb{Z}_q^{n\times n\lceil \log q\rceil}$ where $\boldsymbol{g} = (1, 2, 4, ..., 2^{\lceil \log q\rceil - 1})$.

Lemma 2.10 ([43], **Theorem 1**). *Let q be a prime, and n, m be integers with $m = n\lceil \log q\rceil$. There is a full-rank matrix $\mathbf{G} \in \mathbb{Z}_q^{n\times m}$ such that the lattice $\Lambda_q^{\perp}(\mathbf{G})$ has a publicly known trapdoor matrix $\mathbf{T}_{\mathbf{G}} \in \mathbb{Z}^{n\times m}$ with $\|\tilde{\mathbf{T}}_{\mathbf{G}}\| \le \sqrt{5}$, where $\tilde{\mathbf{T}}_{\mathbf{G}}$ is the Gram-Schmidt order orthogonalization of $\mathbf{T}_{\mathbf{G}}$.*

Lemma 2.11 ([14], **Lemma 2.1**). *There is a deterministic algorithm, denoted by $\mathbf{G}^{-1}(\cdot) : \mathbb{Z}_q^{n\times m} \to \mathbb{Z}^{m\times m}$, that takes any matrix $\mathbf{A} \in \mathbb{Z}_q^{n\times m}$ as input, and outputs the preimage $\mathbf{G}^{-1}(\mathbf{A})$ of $\mathbf{A}$ such that $\mathbf{G} \cdot \mathbf{G}^{-1}(\mathbf{A}) = \mathbf{A} \pmod q$ and $\|\mathbf{G}^{-1}(\mathbf{A})\| \le m$.*

Definition 2.12 (**δ-compatible algorithms** [54]). *We say that the deterministic algorithms* ($\mathsf{Eval}^{\mathsf{Pub}}, \mathsf{Eval}^{\mathsf{Trap}}$) *are δ-compatible for a function family $\mathcal{F} = \{f : \{0,1\}^{\ell} \to \{0,1\}\}$ if they are efficient and satisfy the following properties:*

- $\mathsf{Eval}^{\mathsf{Pub}}(f \in \mathcal{F}, \{\mathbf{A}_i \in \mathbb{Z}_q^{n\times m}\}_{i\in[\ell]}) = \mathbf{A}_f \in \mathbb{Z}^{n\times m}$.
- $\mathsf{Eval}^{\mathsf{Trap}}(f \in \mathcal{F}, \mathbf{A}, \boldsymbol{x} \in \{0,1\}^{\ell}, \{\mathbf{R}_i \in \mathbb{Z}^{m\times m}\}_{i\in[\ell]}) = \mathbf{R}_f \in \mathbb{Z}^{m\times m}$.

For any $\boldsymbol{x} = (x_1, ..., x_\ell) \in \{0,1\}^{\ell}$, we require that the following holds:

$$\mathsf{Eval}^{\mathsf{Pub}}(f, \{\mathbf{AR}_i + x_i\mathbf{G}\}_{i\in[\ell]}) = \mathbf{AR}_f + f(\boldsymbol{x})\mathbf{G} \pmod q,$$

and we have $\|\mathbf{R}_f\|_\infty \le \delta \cdot \max_{i\in[\ell]}\{\|\mathbf{R}_i\|\}$.

Lemma 2.13 (**Noise Rerandomization** [36]). *Let q, ℓ, m be positive integers and r a positive real satisfying $r > max\{\eta_\epsilon(\mathbb{Z}^m), \eta_\epsilon(\mathbb{Z}^\ell)\}$. Let $\boldsymbol{b} \in \mathbb{Z}_q^m$ be arbitrary vector and $\boldsymbol{x}$ chosen from $D_{\mathbb{Z}^m,r}$. Then for any $\mathbf{V} \in \mathbb{Z}^{m\times \ell}$ and positive real $\sigma > \mathsf{s}_1(\mathbf{V})$, there exists a PPT algorithm* $\mathsf{ReRand}(\mathbf{V}, \boldsymbol{b}+\boldsymbol{x}, r, \sigma)$ *that outputs $\boldsymbol{b}' = \boldsymbol{b}\mathbf{V} + \boldsymbol{x}' \in \mathbb{Z}_q^\ell$ where the statistical distance of the discrete Gaussian $D_{\mathbb{Z}^\ell,2r\sigma}$ and the distribution of $\boldsymbol{x}'$ is within 8ϵ.*

Fully Homomorphic Encryption. We present the syntax of (leveled fully) homomorphic encryption. A homomorphic encryption scheme HE = (HE.KeyGen, HE.Enc, HE.Dec, HE.Eval) is a quadruple of PPT algorithms as follows:

- HE.KeyGen(1^κ). Generate an encryption key ek. a public evaluation key evk, and a secret decryption key dk.
- HE.Enc(ek, μ). Generate a ciphertext ct.
- HE.Dec(dk, ct). Decrypt the ciphertext and output message μ.

- $\mathsf{HE.Eval}(\mathsf{evk}, f, \{\mathsf{ct}_i\})$. The algorithm takes evk and a function (circuit) f and a set of ciphertexts $\{\mathsf{ct}_i\}$ as input, and outputs an evaluated ciphertext ct_f.

Correctness and security follow by the standard definitions as [21,29]. If a homomorphic scheme HE supports evaluation of a class of functions $\mathcal{C}$, then it is $\mathcal{C}$-homomorphic. A fully homomorphic encryption supports evaluation of all polynomial-sized circuits. Details are deferred to full version of this paper.

Next, we present an important result, saying that for most of the LWE-based FHEs, the decryption circuits are in NC1 and can be homomorphically evaluated with a small noise growth.

Theorem 2.14 ([3,22]). *For all $n, q, m, \ell \in \mathbb{N}$, and for any sequence of matrices $(\mathbf{B}_1, ..., \mathbf{B}_\ell) \in (\mathbb{Z}_q^{n\times m})^\ell$ where $\mathbf{B}_i = \mathbf{A}\mathbf{R}_i + x_i\mathbf{G}$ for $\mathbf{A} \xleftarrow{\$} \mathbb{Z}_q^{n\times m}, \mathbf{R}_i \xleftarrow{\$} \{-1,1\}^{m\times m}, x_i \xleftarrow{\$} \{0,1\}$, the following holds. For the special decryption algorithms $f \in \{0,1\}^\ell \to \{0,1\}$ of* LWE *based FHE [3,22], $\mathsf{Eval}^{\mathsf{Pub}}(f, \mathbf{B}_1, ..., \mathbf{B}_\ell) = \mathbf{A}\mathbf{R}_f + f(\boldsymbol{x})\mathbf{G} \pmod q$, where $\boldsymbol{x} = (x_1, ..., x_\ell)$, and $\|\mathbf{R}_f\|_2 \leq O(n^{2+\varepsilon})$ for any $\varepsilon \in (0,1)$. In other word, the algorithms $(\mathsf{Eval}^{\mathsf{Pub}}, \mathsf{Eval}^{\mathsf{Trap}})$ are $O(n^{2+\varepsilon})$-compatible in this case.*

3 Almost Tight Lattice-Based PRF Under Poly Moduli

In this section, we first present an (almost) tight reduction of LWE $\to$ Q-LWR$'$ for bounded number of samples with a polynomial modulus. This new reduction serves as the core technique to prove the almost tight security of GGM PRF from LWE with polynomial modulus.

3.1 LWR with a General Modulus q

To study the LWR problem with a general modulus q, we first present a useful leftover hash lemma in a general $\mathbb{Z}_q$. In particular, we show that matrix multiplication in general $\mathbb{Z}_q$ is a good extractor, i.e. $(\mathbf{A}, \boldsymbol{s}^t\mathbf{A}) \overset{s}{\approx} (\mathbf{A}, \boldsymbol{u})$, as long as the min-entropy of $\boldsymbol{s}$ mod p' has sufficient entropy for every factor p' of q.

We note that this condition for entropy is necessary as otherwise, we can construct a simple counterexample where the output distribution of $\boldsymbol{s}^t\mathbf{A}$ is far from uniform. Consider $q = 2^{10}$, and $\boldsymbol{s}$ is sampled uniformly from $\{0,2\}^n$. It is clear that $\boldsymbol{s}$ has min-entropy n and all components of $\boldsymbol{s}$ are small, but for any vector $\boldsymbol{a} \in \mathbb{Z}_q^n$, $\langle \boldsymbol{s}, \boldsymbol{a}\rangle$ is an even number and thus the distribution of $\langle \boldsymbol{s}, \boldsymbol{a}\rangle$ over a random $\boldsymbol{a}$ is far from uniform over $\mathbb{Z}_q$.

More formally, we use the following lemma to show that this entropy condition is sufficient for extraction.

Theorem 3.1 (Randomness Extraction for General q). *Let $z, n, k, q \in \mathbb{N}$ be integers and $\varepsilon \in (0,1)$ such that*

$$k > z\log q + 3(\log(zq) + \log(1/\varepsilon)) + 2(\log q)(\log\log q) + 7.$$

Suppose $\boldsymbol{s}$ *is chosen from some distribution over* $\mathbb{Z}_q^n$ *such that* $H_\infty(\boldsymbol{s} \bmod p) \geq k$ *for any factor* p *of* q*, and* $\mathbf{A} \xleftarrow{\$} \mathbb{Z}_q^{n\times z}$*,* $\boldsymbol{u} \xleftarrow{\$} \mathbb{Z}_q^z$ *are chosen independently of* $\boldsymbol{s}$ *from the uniform distribution. Then we have:* $\Delta[(\mathbf{A}, \boldsymbol{s}^t \cdot \mathbf{A}); (\mathbf{A}, \boldsymbol{u}^t)] \leq \varepsilon$.

This theorem can be proved via Lemma 2.3 in [42]. We describe our alternative proof for completeness of presentation in the full version of this paper.

Next, we define a generalization of the weak learning with rounding (wLWR) assumption (in the form of multi-secret) in general $\mathbb{Z}_q$. Intuitively, the wLWR problem considers scenarios where the secret $\boldsymbol{s}$ comes from some high min-entropy distribution (e.g., perhaps the secret is somewhat leaked) instead of the uniform distribution.[6]

Definition 3.2 (Multi-secret wLWR). *Let* κ *be the security parameter,* $n, m, q \geq p \geq 2, \gamma, k, Q$ *be integers (functions of* κ*). The* Q*-*$\mathsf{wLWR}_{n,m,q,p}^{(\gamma,k)}$ *assumption states: let* $\{(\boldsymbol{s}_i, \mathsf{aux}_i)\}_{i\in[Q]}$ *be* Q *pairs of correlated random variables where (i) each pair is sampled independently of the others, (ii) the support of each* $\boldsymbol{s}_i \in [-\gamma, \gamma]^n$*, and (iii)* $H_\infty(\boldsymbol{s}_i \bmod p' \mid \mathsf{aux}_i) \geq k$ *for every prime factor* p' *of* q *and for* $i \in [Q]$*. Then the distributions below are computationally indistinguishable:*

$$(\{\mathsf{aux}_i\}_{i\in[Q]}, \mathbf{A}, \lfloor \boldsymbol{s}_1^t \cdot \mathbf{A} \rceil_p, \ldots, \lfloor \boldsymbol{s}_Q^t \cdot \mathbf{A} \rceil_p) \overset{c}{\approx} (\{\mathsf{aux}_i\}_{i\in[Q]}, \mathbf{A}, \lfloor \boldsymbol{u}_1 \rceil_p, \ldots, \lfloor \boldsymbol{u}_Q \rceil_p),$$

where $\mathbf{A} \xleftarrow{\$} \mathbb{Z}_q^{n\times m}, \boldsymbol{u}_1, \cdots, \boldsymbol{u}_Q \xleftarrow{\$} \mathbb{Z}_q^m$ *are chosen randomly and independently of* $\{(\boldsymbol{s}_i, \mathsf{aux}_i)\}_{i\in[Q]}$*. We say the* Q*-w*$\mathsf{LWR}_{n,m,q,p}^{(\gamma,k)}$ *problem is* (t, ε)*-hard if the two distributions above are* (t, ε)*-indistinguishable.*

We remark that contrast with the previous definition by [4] for restricted moduli, our generalized definition instead impose more condition on the secret distribution, just as required in the randomness extraction in Theorem 3.1, i.e., $\boldsymbol{s} \bmod p'$ has sufficient entropy for every factor p' of q. Intuitively, without this additional condition in general $\mathbb{Z}_q$, $\lfloor \boldsymbol{s}^t \cdot \mathbf{A} \rceil$ might be far from uniform for some $\boldsymbol{s}$ which is only guaranteed to have high min-entropy.

More formally, we establish the following main theorem to show that Q-wLWR is at least as hard as n-LWE for a wide range of parameters.

Theorem 3.3 (Hardness of Multi-secret (w)LWR). *Let* $k, \ell, n, m, p, q, \gamma, Q, \lambda$ *be positive integers,* $p_{\min}$ *be the smallest prime factor of* q*,* c *be an integer, and* χ *be a* β*-bounded distribution for some real* $\beta > 0$*, such that* $q \geq 2\beta\gamma nmp$*. Assume* n*-*$\mathsf{LWE}_{\ell,m,q,\chi}$ *problem is* (t, ε)*-hard, then we have the following:*

- *(High entropy secret).* Q-$\mathsf{wLWR}_{n,m,q,p}^{(\gamma,k)}$ *is* (t', ε')*-hard, where* $t' = t - \mathsf{poly}(\kappa), \varepsilon' = 2c\varepsilon + (Qc+1)\frac{1}{2^\lambda}$*, if* $k \geq \big(\lfloor \frac{m}{c} \rfloor + 2(\log\log q) + \ell + \lambda + 3\big)\log q + 3\log\lfloor \frac{m}{c} \rfloor + 3\lambda + 7$.

[6] In prior work [4], the wLWR problem is originally defined with respect to the secret $\boldsymbol{s}$ having sufficient min-entropy, and it is proved hard just for restricted moduli q.

– *(Uniform secret).* Q-$\mathsf{LWR}_{n,m,q,p}$ *is* (t', ε')*-hard, where* $t' = t - \mathsf{poly}(\kappa), \varepsilon' = 2c\varepsilon + (Qc+1)\frac{1}{2^\lambda}$*, if* $n \geq \frac{1}{\min\{\log(2\gamma), \log(p_{\min})\}}\Big(\Big(\lfloor \frac{m}{c} \rfloor + 2(\log\log q) + \ell + \lambda + 3\Big)\log q + 3\log\lfloor \frac{m}{c} \rfloor + 3\lambda + 7\Big)$.

The proof of this theorem relies on the use of a lossy matrix and randomness extraction alternately as we described in Sect. 1.2. Due to space limit, we defer the full proof to the supplementary material in full version of this paper.

Note that the reduction loss in Theorem 3.3 does not depend on Q in the multiplicative way, and thus can be made tight in several parameter settings. Furthermore, the hardness of ordinary wLWR, LWR and LWR′ in the general $\mathbb{Z}_q$ can be derived easily from this theorem.

As we discussed in the beginning of this section, our result in Theorem 3.3 improves the prior work [4] in the following two aspects: (1) our q does not require the additional number theoretic requirement, and (2) if the secret $\boldsymbol{s}$ has sufficient entropy, we can further improve the security loss. The work [4] can be thought as $c = m$ in our case.

Using the above theorem, we can prove the problem $\mathsf{LWR}'_{n,m,q,p}$ as a special case of the problem $\mathsf{wLWR}^{(\gamma,k)}_{n,m,q,p}$, where $\gamma = p$, and $k = n\left(\min\{\log p, \log(p_{\min})\}\right)$.

We note that by a simple calculation, $\boldsymbol{s} \xleftarrow{\$} \mathbb{Z}_p$ implies $H_\infty(\boldsymbol{s} \bmod p') \geq n\left(\min\{\log p, \log(p_{\min})\}\right)$ for any prime factor p' of q. Thus we have the following corollary.

Corollary 3.4 (Hardness of Multi-secret LWR′). *Let* $\ell, n, m, p, q, Q, \lambda$ *be positive integers,* $p_{\min}$ *be the smallest prime factor of* q*,* c *be an integer, and* χ *be a* β*-bounded distribution for some real* $\beta > 0$*, such that* $q \geq 2\beta nmp^2$*. Assume* n-$\mathsf{LWE}_{\ell,m,q,\chi}$ *problem is* (t,ε)*-hard, then* Q-$\mathsf{LWR}'_{n,m,q,p}$ *is* (t', ε')*-hard, where* $t' = t - \mathsf{poly}(\kappa), \varepsilon' = 2c\varepsilon + (Qc+1)\frac{1}{2^\lambda}$*, if* $n \geq \frac{1}{\min\{\log p, \log(p_{\min})\}}\Big(\Big(\lfloor \frac{m}{c} \rfloor + 2(\log\log q) + \ell + \lambda + 3\Big)\log q + 3\log\lfloor \frac{m}{c} \rfloor + 3\lambda + 7\Big)$.

Some Useful Setting of Parameters. Our reduction of LWE $\rightarrow$ Q-LWR′ holds for a wide range of parameters (e.g., $q = p^e$). Here we describe one example, which will be used in our almost tight PRF in Sect. 3.2.

Table 1. Simple example of parameter setting

Parameters	Description	Setting
κ	Security parameter	
n	LWR dimension	50κ
m	Number of LWR samples	$2n$
p	Modulus of LWR	κ
q	Modulus of LWE	p^6
ℓ	LWE dimension	κ
c	Reduction parameter	24
λ	Statistical loss parameter	2κ
β	LWE error bound	$\sqrt{\kappa}$

Through combining Theorem 3.3 and Corollary 3.4, together with the parameter setting in Table 1, we can directly achieve the following corollary

Corollary 3.5. *Let κ be the security parameter, $\ell, n, m, p, q, \lambda, \beta, c$ be function of κ setting above. Assume n-$\mathsf{LWE}_{\ell,m,q,\chi}$ problem is (t, ε)-hard, then Q-$\mathsf{LWR}'_{n,m,q,p}$ is (t', ε')-hard for any $Q = \mathsf{poly}(\kappa)$ and sufficient large κ, where $t' = t - \mathsf{poly}(\kappa), \varepsilon' \leq 48\varepsilon + \frac{24Q+1}{2^{2\kappa}}$.*

3.2 Lattice-Based PRF with poly Modulus

In this section, we show that the GGM-based construction [8], when instantiated under LWR' with parameters as Table 1, indeed achieves almost tight security. Thus, we achieve the first almost tight LWE-based PRF with a poly modulus.

Lattice PRF via GGM. By using the (n)-LWR' (with bounded samples) and the GGM construction, one can derive a PRF, as shown by the work [8]. For completeness, below we include the construction, parameters, and a theorem that summarizes security.

Construction. For parameters $n \in \mathbb{N}$, moduli $q \geq p \geq 2$, and input length $k \geq 1$, the family $\mathcal{F}$ consists of functions from $\{0,1\}^k$ to $\mathbb{Z}_p^n$. A function $F \in \mathcal{F}$ is indexed by some $\mathbf{A}_0, \mathbf{A}_1 \in \mathbb{Z}_q^{n \times n}$ and $\boldsymbol{s} \in \mathbb{Z}_p^n$, and is defined as

$$F(x) = F_{\boldsymbol{s},\{\mathbf{A}_i\}_{i\in\{0,1\}}}(x_1, ..., x_k); = \lfloor \cdots \lfloor \lfloor \boldsymbol{s}^t \cdot \mathbf{A}_{x_1} \rceil_p \cdot \mathbf{A}_{x_2} \rceil_p \cdots \cdot \mathbf{A}_{x_k} \rceil_p.$$

We endow $\mathcal{F}$ with the distribution where $\{\mathbf{A}_i\}_{i\in\{0,1\}}$ and $\boldsymbol{s}$ are chosen uniformly at random, and $\{\mathbf{A}_i\}_{i\in\{0,1\}}$ can be publicly known.

Parameters. Our PRF works for a wide range of parameters. For ease of our security proof, we use a concrete parameter setting following Table 1: Let κ be the security parameter, we set $n = 50\kappa, k = \kappa, p = \kappa, q = \kappa^6$.

Theorem 3.6. *Let κ be security parameter, n, k, p, q be parameters setting above, and χ be a β-bounded distribution over $\mathbb{Z}_q$ for $\beta = \sqrt{\kappa}$. Assume $\mathsf{LWE}_{\ell,2n,q,\chi}$ is (t, ε)-hard where $\ell = \kappa$. Then the family $\mathcal{F}$ constructed above is a (t', Q, ε')-PRF, where $t' = t - \mathsf{poly}(\kappa), \varepsilon' \leq 48kn\varepsilon + \frac{1}{2^\kappa}$ for sufficient large κ and any $Q = \mathsf{poly}(\kappa)$.*

Proof Sketch. As discussed in the introduction, the proof follows the steps $\mathsf{LWE} \xrightarrow{(i)} n\text{-}\mathsf{LWE} \xrightarrow{(ii)} Q\text{-}\mathsf{LWR}' \xrightarrow{(iii)} \mathsf{PRF}$. Step (i) follows from a standard hybrid argument; Step (ii) follows from Corollary 3.4 in Sect. 3.1; Step (iii) is very similar to the classic proof Q-$\mathsf{PRG} \rightarrow \mathsf{PRF}$ (see [12,31,37]). For completeness, we present the formal arguments in full version of this paper.

We can further improve the result by applying the domain extension techniques by [26], resulting in the Corollary as follows:

Corollary 3.7. *Let κ be security parameter, $n = 50\kappa, p = \kappa, q = \kappa^6, k = \kappa, \ell = \kappa, \beta = \sqrt{\kappa}$ as our setting of parameters. We have the following:*

- *Assume* n-$\mathsf{LWE}_{\ell,2n,q,\chi}$ *is* (t,ε)*-hard where* χ *is a* β*-bounded distribution over* $\mathbb{Z}_q$*. Then there exists a* (t',Q,ε')*-*PRF*, where* $t' = t - \mathsf{poly}(\kappa), \varepsilon' \le \omega(\log\kappa)\varepsilon + 2^{-\Omega(\kappa)}$ *for sufficient large* κ *and for any* $Q = \mathsf{poly}(\kappa)$*.*
- *Assume* $\mathsf{LWE}_{\ell,2n,q,\chi}$ *is* (t,ε)*-hard where* χ *is a* β*-bounded distribution over* $\mathbb{Z}_q$*. Then there exists a* (t',Q,ε')*-*PRF*, where* $t' = t - \mathsf{poly}(\kappa), \varepsilon' \le 48\kappa\omega(\log\kappa)\varepsilon + 2^{-\Omega(\kappa)}$ *for sufficient large* κ *and any* $Q = \mathsf{poly}(\kappa)$*.*

4 New Framework of Lattice-Based IBE with Tight Security Under poly Modulus

In this section, we propose a novel framework that integrates key homomorphic evaluation on the public matrices, homomorphic evaluation on leveled HE ciphertexts, bootstrapping, and our almost tight PRF in Sect. 3.2. By applying this technique, we construct an almost tight adaptively secure IBE from LWE with a polynomial modulus. Our technique can also apply to the lattice based signature scheme resulting an almost tight security under poly modulus. Due to the space, we put the construction in full version of this paper. We present our IBE construction in Sect. 4.1, and then show the tight security in Sect. 4.2, finally instantiate all the building blocks in Sect. 4.3.

4.1 IBE Construction

- $\mathsf{Setup}(1^\kappa)$ The setup algorithm takes as input a security parameter κ, It does the following:
  1. Sample a random matrix $\mathbf{A} \in \mathbb{Z}_q^{n\times m}$ along with a trapdoor basis $\mathbf{T_A} \in \mathbb{Z}^{m\times m}$ of lattice $\Lambda_q^\perp(\mathbf{A})$ by running TrapGen.
  2. Select random matrices $\mathbf{A}_0, \mathbf{A}_1 \in \mathbb{Z}_q^{n\times m}$. Run HE.KeyGen algorithm of a HE scheme $\boxed{(\mathsf{ek},\mathsf{evk},\mathsf{dk}) \leftarrow \mathsf{HE.KeyGen}}$. Set the random "PRF key" elements as $\boxed{\{\boldsymbol{d}_i\}_{i\in[k_1]}}$ where $\boxed{\boldsymbol{d}_i \xleftarrow{\$} \mathsf{HE.Enc}(\mathsf{ek},0)}$ and set "bootstrapping key" element as $\boxed{\mathsf{evk}}$. Select random "PRF input" elements
  $$\boxed{\boldsymbol{c}_0 \xleftarrow{\$} \mathsf{HE.Enc}(\mathsf{ek},0), \boldsymbol{c}_1 \xleftarrow{\$} \mathsf{HE.Enc}(\mathsf{ek},1)}$$
  uniformly at random. Select random matrices $\{\mathbf{D}_i\}_{i\in[k_2]} \in \mathbb{Z}_q^{n\times m}$. Express the decryption algorithm HE.Dec as a NAND Boolean circuit $\boxed{C_{\mathsf{Dec}}}$.
  3. Select a random vector $\boldsymbol{u} \xleftarrow{\$} \mathbb{Z}_q^n$.
  4. Select a secure pseudorandom function $\mathsf{PRF} : \{0,1\}^{k_1} \times \{0,1\}^\ell \to \{0,1\}$, express it as a NAND Boolean circuit C_{PRF} with depth $d = d(\kappa)$, and select a PRF key $K = s_1s_2...s_{k_1} \xleftarrow{\$} \{0,1\}^{k_1}$.
  5. Set $\mathsf{msk} = (\mathbf{T_A}, K)$, and output
  $$\boxed{\mathsf{mpk} = (\mathbf{A}, \{\mathbf{A}_0,\mathbf{A}_1\}, \{\boldsymbol{d}_i\}_{i\in[k_1]}, \{\mathbf{D}_i\}_{i\in[k_2]}, \{\boldsymbol{c}_0,\boldsymbol{c}_1\}, \mathsf{evk}, \boldsymbol{u}, \mathsf{PRF}, C_{\mathsf{PRF}}).}$$

- $\mathsf{KeyGen}(\mathsf{mpk}, \mathsf{msk}, \mathsf{id})$ The key generation algorithm take $\mathsf{mpk}, \mathsf{msk}$ and an identity $\mathsf{id} = x_1 x_2 ... x_\ell \in \{0,1\}^\ell$ as input, and does the following:
  1. Compute $b = \mathsf{PRF}(K, id)$.
  2. Compute $\boxed{\mathsf{ct}_{\mathsf{id}} = \mathsf{HE.Eval}(\mathsf{evk}, C_{\mathsf{PRF}}, (\{\boldsymbol{d}_i\}_{i\in[k_1]}, \{\boldsymbol{c}_{x_i}\}_{i\in[\ell]}))}$.
  3. Compute $\boxed{\mathbf{A}_{C_{\mathsf{PRF}},\mathsf{id}} = \mathsf{Eval}^{\mathsf{Pub}}(C_{\mathsf{Dec}}, (\{\mathbf{D}_i\}_{i\in[k_2]}, \{(\mathsf{ct}_{\mathsf{id}})_i \mathbf{G}\}_{i\in[k_3]}))}$, where $\boxed{(\mathsf{ct}_{\mathsf{id}})_i}$ is the i-bit of $\mathsf{ct}_{\mathsf{id}}$.
  4. Set $\mathbf{F}_{\mathsf{id},1-b} = [\mathbf{A} | \mathbf{A}_{1-b} - \mathbf{A}_{C_{\mathsf{PRF}},\mathsf{id}}] \in \mathbb{Z}_q^{n\times 2m}$.
  5. Run $\mathsf{SampleLeft}$ to sample $\boldsymbol{d}_{\mathsf{id}}$ from the discrete Gaussian distribution $D_{\Lambda_q^{\boldsymbol{u}}(\mathbf{F}_{\mathsf{id},1-b}),s}$, then $\mathbf{F}_{\mathsf{id},1-b}\boldsymbol{d}_{\mathsf{id}} = \boldsymbol{u} (\bmod q)$. Output $\mathsf{sk}_{\mathsf{id}} = (b, \boldsymbol{d}_{\mathsf{id}})$.

- $\mathsf{Enc}(\mathsf{mpk}, \mathsf{id}, \mu)$ To encrypt a message $\mu \in \{0,1\}$ with respect to an identity $\mathsf{id} = x_1 x_2 ... x_\ell \in \{0,1\}^\ell$:
  1. Compute $\boxed{\mathsf{ct}_{\mathsf{id}} = \mathsf{HE.Eval}(\mathsf{evk}, C_{\mathsf{PRF}}, (\{\boldsymbol{d}_i\}_{i\in[k_1]}, \{\boldsymbol{c}_{x_i}\}_{i\in[\ell]}))}$.
  2. Compute $\boxed{\mathbf{A}_{C_{\mathsf{PRF}},\mathsf{id}} = \mathsf{Eval}^{\mathsf{Pub}}(C_{\mathsf{Dec}}, (\{\mathbf{D}_i\}_{i\in[k_2]}, \{(\mathsf{ct}_{\mathsf{id}})_i \mathbf{G}\}))}$.
  3. Set $\mathbf{F}_{\mathsf{id},b} = [\mathbf{A} | \mathbf{A}_b - \mathbf{A}_{C_{\mathsf{PRF}},\mathsf{id}}] \in \mathbb{Z}_q^{n\times 2m}$ for $b = 0, 1$.
  4. Select two random vectors $\boldsymbol{s}_0, \boldsymbol{s}_1 \xleftarrow{\$} \mathbb{Z}_q^n$.
  5. Select two noise scalars $v_{0,0}, v_{1,0} \leftarrow D_{\mathbb{Z},\sigma_{\mathsf{LWE}}}$ and two noise vectors $\boldsymbol{v}_{0,1}, \boldsymbol{v}_{1,1} \leftarrow D_{\mathbb{Z}^{2m},\sigma}$, where σ is a gaussian parameter lager than σ_{LWE}.
  6. Compute the ciphertext $\mathsf{ct}_{\mathsf{id}} = (c_{0,0}, \boldsymbol{c}_{0,1}, c_{1,0}, \boldsymbol{c}_{1,1})$ as:

$$\begin{cases} c_{0,0} = (\boldsymbol{s}_0^t \boldsymbol{u} + v_{0,0} + \mu\lfloor q/2 \rfloor) \bmod q \\ \boldsymbol{c}_{0,1}^t = (\boldsymbol{s}_0^t \mathbf{F}_{\mathsf{id},0} + \boldsymbol{v}_{0,1}^t) \bmod q \end{cases}$$

$$\begin{cases} c_{1,0} = (\boldsymbol{s}_1^t \boldsymbol{u} + v_{1,0} + \mu\lfloor q/2 \rfloor) \bmod q \\ \boldsymbol{c}_{1,1}^t = (\boldsymbol{s}_1^t \mathbf{F}_{\mathsf{id},1} + \boldsymbol{v}_{1,1}^t) \bmod q \end{cases}$$

- $\mathsf{Dec}(\mathsf{mpk}, \mathsf{sk}_{\mathsf{id}}, \mathsf{ct}_{\mathsf{id}})$ The decryption algorithm uses the key $(b, \boldsymbol{d}_{\mathsf{id}})$ to decrypt $(c_{b,0}, \boldsymbol{c}_{b,1})$. The decryption algorithm computes $\eta = (c_{b,0} - \boldsymbol{c}_{b,1}^t \boldsymbol{d}_{\mathsf{id}}) \bmod q$. If η is closer to 0 that $\pm q/2$, then decryption algorithm outputs $\mu = 0$, otherwise, outputs $\mu = 1$.

Correctness analysis can be verified in the same way as [16]. We omit it here due to the space limit.

Parameter Setting. We now provide an instantiation that achieves both correctness a and security (Table 2).

- To ensure the condition of $\mathsf{TrapGen}$ in Theorem 2.8 and achieve the statistical distance in Lemma 4.2, we set $m = O(n \log q)$, $n \geq \kappa + \log k_2 + 5$;
- According to [3,18,21,30], there exists an HE scheme such that the decryption circuit is in NC_1, so we set $L = O(\log n)$;

Table 2. Parameter setting of IBE scheme

Parameters	Description	Setting
κ	Security parameter	
k_1	Secret key length of PRF	κ
k_2	The length of decryption key of HE	κ
k_3	Output length of HE.Eval	κ
n	Row dimension of public matrix	$\geq 2\kappa + 5$
m	Column dimension of public matrix	$O(n \log q)$
ℓ	Length of id	κ
L	Depth of HE decryption circuit	$O(\log n)$
s	Gaussian parameter of secret key	$O(n^{3+\epsilon})$
σ_{LWE}	Gaussian parameter of LWE error	$O(\sqrt{\kappa + \log \kappa})$
σ	Gaussian parameter of noise vectors in $c_{b,1}$	$2\sigma^* \cdot \sigma_{\mathsf{LWE}}$
σ^*	Parameter of ReRand algorithm	$O(n^{2+\epsilon})$
q	Modulus of LWE	$O(n^{8+\epsilon})$

- To ensure that SampleLeft in the real scheme and SampleRight in the simulation game have the statistical distance within $2^{-(\kappa+2)}/3Q_{\mathsf{id}}$ per Theorem 2.8 and Theorem 2.9, we need

$$s > \|\tilde{\mathbf{T}}_{\mathbf{A}}\| \cdot \omega(\sqrt{\log 2m}) \text{ and } s > \|\tilde{\mathbf{T}}_{\mathbf{G}}\| \cdot \|\mathbf{R}\| \cdot \omega(\sqrt{\log m}),$$

  where $\mathbf{R} = \mathbf{R}_{\mathbf{A}_{1-b}} - \mathbf{R}_{C_{\mathsf{PRF}},\mathsf{id}}$, and $n \geq \kappa + 5 + \log Q_{\mathsf{id}}$ (Q_{id} is number of key queries). According to Theorem 2.14 and the bootstrapping computation [3], the key-homomorphic evaluation algorithm of HE decryption circuit is $O(n^{2+\epsilon})$-compatible for any $\epsilon \in (0, 1)$, which means that $\|\mathbf{R}_{C_{\mathsf{PRF}},\mathsf{id}}\| \leq O(n^{2+\epsilon})$. To satisfy these conditions, we set $s = O(n^{3+\epsilon})$ and $n \geq 2\kappa + 5$ (without loss of generality, we assume $Q_{\mathsf{id}} < 2^{\kappa}$);
- To ensure Regev's quantum reduction to LWE [49], we need $\sigma_{\mathsf{LWE}} > 2\sqrt{\kappa}$;
- For ReRand algorithm to work with the statistical distance in Lemma 4.3, we need $\sigma^* > s_1([\mathbf{I}|\mathbf{R}])$, $\sigma_{\mathsf{LWE}} > max\{\eta_{\epsilon}(\mathbb{Z}^m), \eta_{\epsilon}(\mathbb{Z}^{\ell})\}$ and $\sigma = 2\sigma^* \cdot \sigma_{\mathsf{LWE}}$. According to the property of smoothing parameters (which can be found in full version of this paper) and Theorem 2.14, we set $\sigma_{\mathsf{LWE}} = O(\sqrt{\kappa + \log \kappa}), \sigma^* = O(n^{2+\epsilon})$;
- To ensure the correctness of decryption, we need $|c_{b,0} - \mathbf{c}_{b,1}^t \boldsymbol{d}_{\mathsf{id}}| < q/4$, as a result $O(s \cdot m \cdot \sigma) < q/4$. We set $q = O(n^{8+\epsilon})$ (q is not necessarily a prime).

4.2 Security

The security of the IBE scheme above can be stated by the following theorem.

Theorem 4.1. *Let the parameters be chosen as above, and χ be the distribution $\mathcal{D}_{\mathbb{Z}^m,\sigma_{\mathsf{LWE}}}$. If the $\mathsf{LWE}_{n,m,q,\chi}$ problem is $(t_{\mathsf{LWE}}, \varepsilon_{\mathsf{LWE}})$-hard, HE scheme is $(t_{\mathsf{HE}}, k_1, \varepsilon_{\mathsf{HE}})$-IND secure with decryption circuit in $\mathbf{NC}_1$ (e.g., $O(n^{2+\epsilon})$-compatible), and the PRF used in the IBE is a $(t_{\mathsf{PRF}}, Q_{\mathsf{id}}, \varepsilon_{\mathsf{PRF}})$-PRF, then the IBE scheme constructed above is $(t^*, Q_{\mathsf{id}}, \varepsilon^*)$-adaptively secure such that $\varepsilon^* \leq 2(\varepsilon_{\mathsf{LWE}} + \varepsilon_{\mathsf{PRF}}) + 3\varepsilon_{\mathsf{HE}} + 2^{-\kappa}$, and $t^* = \min\{T_{\mathsf{LWE}}, T_{\mathsf{PRF}}, T_{\mathsf{HE}}\} - \mathsf{poly}(n, m, k, Q_{\mathsf{id}}, \log q)$.*

Proof. We prove the theorem by a sequence of hybrid games. Given a PPT adversary $\mathcal{A}$, the first game is defined as the real adaptive security game. Then we will show that all the neighboring games are computationally/statistically indistinguishable. Finally we show that $\mathcal{A}$ has no advantage in the last game to complete the proof.

Before we present the hybrids, we first define the following simulation algorithms Sim.Setup, Sim.KeyGen and Sim.Enc, making essential modifications of those in the work Boyen and Li [16]. We highlight the differences in boxes.

- $\mathsf{Sim.Setup}(1^\kappa)$ The algorithm does the following:
  1. Select a matrix $\mathbf{A} \xleftarrow{\$} \mathbb{Z}_q^{n\times m}$. Run HE.KeyGen algorithm of a HE scheme $\boxed{(\mathsf{ek}, \mathsf{evk}, \mathsf{dk}) \leftarrow \mathsf{HE.KeyGen}}$. Set "bootstrapping key" element as $\boxed{\mathsf{evk}}$. Select random "PRF input" elements
  $$\boxed{\boldsymbol{c}_0 \xleftarrow{\$} \mathsf{HE.Enc}(\mathsf{ek}, 0)}, \boxed{\boldsymbol{c}_1 \xleftarrow{\$} \mathsf{HE.Enc}(\mathsf{ek}, 1)}$$
  uniformly at random. Express the decryption circuit HE.Dec as a NAND Boolean circuit $\boxed{C_{\mathsf{Dec}}}$ and express dk as $\boxed{\mathsf{dk} = (dk_1, ..., dk_{k_2})}$.
  2. Select $k_2 + 2$ low-norm matrices $\boxed{\{\mathbf{R}_{\mathbf{A}_b}\}_{b\in\{0,1\}}, \{\mathbf{R}_{\mathbf{D}_i}\}_{i\in[k_2]} \xleftarrow{\$} \{0,1\}^{m\times m}}$.
  3. Select a secure $\mathsf{PRF} : \{0,1\}^{k_1} \times \{0,1\}^\ell \to \{0,1\}$ and express it as a NAND Boolean circuit C_{PRF} with depth $d = d(\kappa)$.
  4. Select a uniformly random string $K = s_1 s_2 ... s_{k_1} \xleftarrow{\$} \{0,1\}^{k_1}$.
  5. Set $\mathbf{A}_b = \mathbf{A}\mathbf{R}_{\mathbf{A}_b} + b\mathbf{G}$ for $b = 0, 1$ and $\boxed{\mathbf{D}_i = \mathbf{A}\mathbf{R}_{\mathbf{D}_i} + dk_i\mathbf{G}}$ for $i \in [k_2]$.
  6. Set the random "PRF key" elements as $\boxed{\{\boldsymbol{d}_i\}_{i\in[k_1]}}$ where
  $\boxed{\boldsymbol{d}_i \xleftarrow{\$} \mathsf{HE.Enc}(\mathsf{ek}, s_i)}$.
  7. Set vector $\boldsymbol{u} \xleftarrow{\$} \mathbb{Z}_q^n$, and publish
  $$\boxed{\mathsf{mpk} = (\mathbf{A}, \{\mathbf{A}_0, \mathbf{A}_1\}, \{\boldsymbol{d}_i\}_{i\in[k_1]}, \{\boldsymbol{c}_0, \boldsymbol{c}_1\}, \{\mathbf{D}_i\}_{i\in[k_2]}, \mathsf{evk}, \boldsymbol{u}, \mathsf{PRF}, C_{\mathsf{PRF}})}.$$
- $\mathsf{Sim.KeyGen}(\mathsf{mpk}, \mathsf{msk}, \mathsf{id})$ Upon an input identity $\mathsf{id} = x_1 x_2 ... x_\ell \in \{0,1\}^\ell$, the algorithm uses mpk, msk to do the following:
  1. Compute $\boxed{\mathsf{ct_{id}} = \mathsf{HE.Eval}(\mathsf{evk}, C_{\mathsf{PRF}}, (\{\boldsymbol{d}_i\}_{i\in[k_1]}, \{\boldsymbol{c}_{x_i}\}_{i\in[\ell]}))}$ and
  $$\boxed{\mathbf{R}_{C_{\mathsf{PRF}},\mathsf{id}} = \mathsf{Eval}^{\mathsf{Trap}}(C_{\mathsf{Dec}}, \mathbf{A}, (\{dk_i\}_{i\in[k_2]}, \{(\mathsf{ct_{id}})_i\}_{i\in[k_3]}), (\{\mathbf{R}_{\mathbf{D}_i}\}_{i\in[k_2]}, \{[0]_i\}_{i\in[k_3]}))},$$
  where for each $i \in [k_3]$, $[0]_i$ denotes 0 matrix with dimension $m \times m$.
  2. Let $\mathsf{PRF}(K, \mathsf{id}) = b \in \{0,1\}$. Set
  $$\mathbf{F}_{\mathsf{id},1-b} = [\mathbf{A}|\mathbf{A}_{1-b} - \mathbf{A}_{C_{\mathsf{PRF}},\mathsf{id}}] = [\mathbf{A}|\mathbf{A}(\mathbf{R}_{\mathbf{A}_{1-b}} - \mathbf{R}_{C_{\mathsf{PRF}},\mathsf{id}}) + (1-2b)\mathbf{G}].$$
  3. Run SampleRight to sample $\boldsymbol{d}_{\mathsf{id}} \in D_{\Lambda_q^{\boldsymbol{u}}(\mathbf{F}_{\mathsf{id},1-b}),s}$, and output $\boxed{\mathsf{sk_{id}} = (b, \boldsymbol{d}_{\mathsf{id}})}$.

- $\mathsf{Sim.Enc}(\mathsf{mpk}, \mathsf{id}^*, \mu)$ The algorithm takes a message μ, mpk and a challenge identity id^* as input, does the following:
  1. Compute $b = \mathsf{PRF}(K, \mathsf{id}^*)$.
  2. Set $\mathbf{F}_{\mathsf{id}^*,b} = [\mathbf{A}|\mathbf{A}_b - \mathbf{A}_{C_{\mathsf{PRF}},\mathsf{id}^*}] = [\mathbf{A}|\mathbf{A}(\mathbf{R}_{\mathbf{A}_b} - \mathbf{R}_{C_{\mathsf{PRF}},\mathsf{id}^*})]$. and
  $$\mathbf{F}_{\mathsf{id}^*,1-b} = [\mathbf{A}|\mathbf{A}_{1-b} - \mathbf{A}_{C_{\mathsf{PRF}},\mathsf{id}^*}] = [\mathbf{A}|\mathbf{A}(\mathbf{R}_{\mathbf{A}_{1-b}} - \mathbf{R}_{C_{\mathsf{PRF}},\mathsf{id}^*}) + (1-2b)\mathbf{G}].$$
  3. Select random vectors $\boldsymbol{s}_b, \boldsymbol{s}_{1-b} \xleftarrow{\$} \mathbb{Z}_q^n$.
  4. Select noise scalars $v_{b,0}, v_{1-b,0} \leftarrow D_{\mathbb{Z},\sigma_{\mathsf{LWE}}}$, and noise vectors $\boxed{\boldsymbol{v}'_{b,1} \leftarrow D_{\mathbb{Z}^m,\sigma_{\mathsf{LWE}}}}$.
  5. Let $\mathbf{R} = \mathbf{R}_{\mathbf{A}_b} - \mathbf{R}_{C_{\mathsf{PRF}},\mathsf{id}^*}$, and set $\boxed{\sigma^* = \sigma/2\sigma_{\mathsf{LWE}}}$. Then invoke the ReRand algorithm to compute
  $$\boxed{\boldsymbol{v}_{b,1} = \mathsf{ReRand}([\mathbf{I}|\mathbf{R}], \boldsymbol{s}_b^t\mathbf{A} + \boldsymbol{v}'_{b,1}, \sigma_{\mathsf{LWE}}, \sigma^*) - \mathbf{F}^t_{\mathsf{id}^*,b}\boldsymbol{s}_b}.$$
  6. Select noise vectors $\boldsymbol{v}_{1-b,1} \leftarrow D_{\mathbb{Z}^{2m},\sigma}$.
  7. Set the challenge ciphertext $\mathsf{ct}_{\mathsf{id}^*} = (c_{b,0}, \boldsymbol{c}_{b,1}, c_{1-b,0}, \boldsymbol{c}_{1-b,1})$ as:
  $$\begin{cases} c_{b,0} = \left(\boldsymbol{s}_b^t\boldsymbol{u} + v_{b,0} + \mu\lfloor q/2\rfloor\right) \bmod q \\ \boldsymbol{c}_{b,1}^t = \left(\boldsymbol{s}_b^t\mathbf{F}_{\mathsf{id}^*,b} + \boldsymbol{v}_{b,1}^t\right) \bmod q \end{cases}$$
  $$\begin{cases} c_{1-b,0} = \left(\boldsymbol{s}_{1-b}^t\boldsymbol{u} + v_{1-b,0} + \mu\lfloor q/2\rfloor\right) \bmod q \\ \boldsymbol{c}_{1-b,1}^t = \left(\boldsymbol{s}_{1-b}^t\mathbf{F}_{\mathsf{id}^*,1-b} + \boldsymbol{v}_{1-b,1}^t\right) \bmod q \end{cases}$$

Now we present a sequence of games and prove that the neighboring games are indistinguishable. We follow the structure of the sequence from Boyen and Li [16], and add an additional step to incorporate the homomorphic encryption.

Game 0: This is the real adaptive security game, and all the algorithms are the same as the real game.

Game 1: This game is the same as **Game 0** except it runs $\mathsf{Sim.Setup}$ and $\mathsf{Sim.KeyGen}$ instead of Setup and KeyGen.

Game 2: This game is the same as **Game 1** except that the challenge ciphertext is generated by $\mathsf{Sim.Enc}$ rather than Enc.

Game 3: This game is the same as **Game 2** except that during the generation of challenge ciphertext, it samples $(c_{b,0}, \boldsymbol{c}_{b,1})$ uniformly random from $\mathbb{Z}_q \times \mathbb{Z}_q^{2m}$ for $b = \mathsf{PRF}(K, \mathsf{id}^*)$, and $(c_{1-b,0}, \boldsymbol{c}_{1-b,1})$ is computed by $\mathsf{Sim.Enc}$ as in **Game 2**.

Game 4: This game is the same as **Game 3** except for $b = \mathsf{PRF}(K, \mathsf{id}^*)$ it runs Enc to generate $(c_{1-b,0}, \boldsymbol{c}_{1-b,1})$ instead of using $\mathsf{Sim.Enc}$.

Game 5: This game is the same as **Game 4** except it runs Setup and KeyGen to generate mpk and $\mathsf{sk}_{\mathsf{id}^*}$.

Game 6: This game is the same as **Game 5** except that for $b = \mathsf{PRF}(K, \mathsf{id}^*)$, the challenge ciphertext part $(c_{b,0}, \boldsymbol{c}_{b,1})$ is generated by Enc rather than choosing it randomly, and $(c_{1-b,0}, \boldsymbol{c}_{1-b,1})$ is chosen randomly.

Game 7: This game is the same as **Game 6** except that it runs $\mathsf{Sim.Setup}$ and $\mathsf{Sim.KeyGen}$ to generate mpk and $\mathsf{sk}_{\mathsf{id}^*}$.

Game 8: This game is the same as **Game 7** except that for $b = \mathsf{PRF}(K, \mathsf{id}^*)$, it computes the challenge ciphertext $(c_{b,0}, \mathbf{c}_{b,1})$ by $\mathsf{Sim.Enc}$.

Game 9: This game is the same as **Game 8** except that the whole challenge ciphertext is sampled uniformly at random. As the challenge ciphertext is independent of the adversary $\mathcal{A}$, clearly in **Game 9** the adversary has no advantage.

We let W_i be the event that $\gamma' = \gamma$ at the end of the **Game** i, and set the advantage's advantage in **Game** i as $|\Pr[W_i] - 1/2|$. We prove the following lemmas, which together imply Theorem 4.1.

Lemma 4.2. *Game 0 and Game 1 are* $(T_1, \varepsilon_{\mathsf{HE}} + 2^{-(\kappa+2)})$*-indistinguishable, assuming the* HE *scheme is* $(T_{\mathsf{HE}}, \varepsilon_{\mathsf{HE}})$*-CPA secure, where* $T_1 = T_{\mathsf{HE}} - \mathsf{poly}(n, k, m, Q_{\mathsf{id}}, \log q)$.

Proof. We analyze the only four differences between **Game 0** and **Game 1:**

1. In **Game 0**, the matrix $\mathbf{A}$ is generated by $\mathsf{TrapGen}$, and the matrix $\mathbf{A}$ is chosen uniformly at random in **Game 0**. By Theorem 2.8, these two distributions of constructing matrix $\mathbf{A}$ are statistically close. More precisely, the statistical distance is within $2^{-(\kappa+2)}/3$ by our parameter setting.
2. In **Game 0**, the matrices $\{\mathbf{A}_0, \mathbf{A}_1\}$ are chosen uniformly at random from $\mathbb{Z}_q^{n\times m}$. While in **Game 1**, these matrices are computed as $\mathbf{A}_b = \mathbf{A}\mathbf{R}_{\mathbf{A}_b} + b\mathbf{G}$, for $b \in \{0,1\}$ for random low-norm matrices $\{\mathbf{R}_{\mathbf{A}_b}\}_{b\in\{0,1\}}$ from $\{0,1\}^{m\times m}$. By Theorem 3.1, the distributions of these matrices in the two games are statistically close. More precisely, the statistical distance is within $2^{-(\kappa+1)}/(3k_2+6)$ by our parameter setting.
3. In **Game 0**, the elements $\{\boldsymbol{d}_i\}_{i\in[k_1]}$ are k_1 ciphertexts $\mathsf{HE.Enc}(\mathsf{pk}, 0)$ and $\{\mathbf{D}_i\}_{i\in[k_2]}$ are chosen uniformly at random from $\mathbb{Z}_q^{n\times m}$. In **Game 1**, these elements are the ciphertexts $\mathsf{HE.Enc}(\mathsf{pk}, s_i)$ and $\{\mathbf{D}_i\}_{i\in[k_2]}$ are the matrices $\mathbf{D}_i = \mathbf{A}\mathbf{R}_{\mathbf{D}_i} + t_i\mathbf{G}$. We show the indistinguishability of the two cases by bybrid argument, we define a sequence of sub-hybirds:
   - H_0: Sample $\{\mathbf{d}_i\}_{i\in[k_1]}$ and $\{\mathbf{D}_i\}_{i\in[k_2]}$ as in **Game 0**.
   - H_1: Generate $\{\mathbf{d}_i\}_{i\in[k_1]}$ as in **Game 1**. Set $\{\mathbf{D}_i\}_{i\in[k_2]}$ as in **Game 0**.
   - H_2: Set $\{\mathbf{d}_i\}_{i\in[k_1]}$ and $\{\mathbf{D}_i\}_{i\in[k_2]}$ as in **Game 1**.

   We first show that the neighboring games H_0 and H_1 are $(T', \varepsilon_{\mathsf{HE}})$-indistinguishable by assuming that HE scheme is $(T_{\mathsf{HE}}, \varepsilon_{\mathsf{HE}})$-secure, where $T' = T_{\mathsf{HE}} - \mathsf{poly}(n, m, k, \log q)$. Then, we show that H_1 and H_2 are statistically close by Theorem 3.1.

   Without loss of generality, if there exists a distinguisher $\mathcal{D}$ can distinguish H_0 from H_1 within running time $T_{\mathcal{D}} \leq T'$ and with advantage $\varepsilon_{\mathcal{D}} \geq \varepsilon_{\mathsf{HE}}$, then we construct a reduction $\mathcal{B}$ that breaks HE as follows:
   - $\mathcal{B}$ chooses $\{\mathbf{D}_i\}_{i\in[k_2]}$ uniformly at random from $\mathbb{Z}_q^{n\times m}$.

- $\mathcal{B}$ sets $\boldsymbol{m}_0 = (s_1, ..., s_{k_1}), \boldsymbol{m}_1 = (0, ...0)$ as its challenge messages, and forwards $\boldsymbol{m}_0, \boldsymbol{m}_1$ to the challenger. $\mathcal{B}$ gets the challenge ciphertext $\mathsf{ct}^* = \{\mathsf{ct}_i\}_{i\in[k_1]}$ from the challenger, and sets $\mathsf{ct}^* = \{\boldsymbol{d}_i\}_{i\in[k_1]}$.
- $\mathcal{B}$ simulates the hybrid game (either H_0 or H_1) with $\{\boldsymbol{d}_i\}_{i\in[k_1]}, \{\mathbf{D}_i\}_{i\in[k_2]}$ and then outputs the outcome of $\mathcal{D}$.

Clearly, if the challenger encrypts $\boldsymbol{m}_0$, then $\mathcal{B}$ simulates the hybrid H_0, and otherwise, the hybrid H_1. Therefore, $\mathcal{B}$ has the same advantage as $\mathcal{D}$, i.e., $\varepsilon_{\mathcal{D}} \geq \varepsilon_{\mathsf{HE}}$, in breaking HE, and the running time of $\mathcal{B}$ is within $T_{\mathcal{D}} + \mathsf{poly}(n, m, k, \log q) \leq T_{\mathsf{HE}}$. This is a contradiction to the security of HE.

The difference between H_1 and H_2 is the generation of the matrices $\{\mathbf{D}_i\}_{i\in[k_2]}$. By Theorem 3.1, $\{\mathbf{D}_i\}_{i\in[k_2]}$ in the two cases are statistically close, and more precisely, the statistical distance of H_1 and H_2 is within $k_2 \times 2^{-(\kappa+2)}/(3k_2+6)$ by our setting of parameters.

4. In both **Game 0** and **Game 1**, the use of $\mathbf{A}_0$ or $\mathbf{A}_1$ in the key generation algorithms is decided by $b = \mathsf{PRF}(K, \mathsf{id})$. For a private key query on id in **Game 1**, let

$$\mathbf{F}_{\mathsf{id},1-b} = [\mathbf{A}|\mathbf{A}_{1-b} - \mathbf{A}_{C_{\mathsf{PRF}},\mathsf{id}}] = [\mathbf{A}|\mathbf{A}\cdot(\mathbf{R}_{\mathbf{A}_{1-b}} - \mathbf{R}_{C_{\mathsf{PRF}},\mathsf{id}}) + (1-2b)\mathbf{G}].$$

Note that the trapdoor of $\Lambda_q^{\perp}(\mathbf{G})$ is also a trapdoor of $\Lambda_q^{\perp}((1-2b)\mathbf{G})$. In **Game 0**, $\boldsymbol{d}_{\mathsf{id}}$ is generated by $\mathsf{SampleLeft}$ with the trapdoor $\mathbf{T_A}$. In **Game 1**, $\boldsymbol{d}_{\mathsf{id}}$ is generated by $\mathsf{SampleRight}$ with the trapdoor of $\Lambda_q^{\perp}((1-2b)\mathbf{G})$. By Theorem 2.9 and our setting of parameters, the statistical distance between the distributions of a single key $\boldsymbol{d}_{\mathsf{id}}$ in the two cases is bounded by $2^{-(\kappa+2)}/3Q_{\mathsf{id}}$. Therefore, from a simple union bound over Q_{id} keys, we conclude that the secret key distributions generated in these two ways are within a statistical distance up to $2^{-(\kappa+2)}/3$.

By combining the arguments above, we conclude that **Game 0** and **Game 1** are $(T_1, \varepsilon_{\mathsf{HE}} + 2^{-(\kappa+2)})$-indistinguishable, where $T_1 = T_{\mathsf{HE}} - \mathsf{poly}(n, m, k, \log q)$. □

Lemma 4.3. *Game 1 and Game 2 are* $(\infty, 2^{-(\kappa+2)}/2)$*-indistinguishable.*

Proof. The only difference between **Game 1** and **Game 2** is the way how the challenge ciphertext is generated. Particularly, in **Game 1**, the challenge ciphertext is generated by Enc, and the noise vectors are sampled from some discrete Gaussian distributions that are independent of mpk. In **Game 2** the challenge ciphertext is generated by $\mathsf{Sim.Enc}$.

By construction, Enc and $\mathsf{Sim.Enc}$ generate $(c_{b,0}, c_{1-b,0}, \boldsymbol{c}_{1-b,1})$ in the same way, so the distributions of $(c_{b,0}, c_{1-b,0}, \boldsymbol{c}_{1-b,1})$ are identical for the two cases.

By the construction of $\boldsymbol{c}_{b,1}$ in the challenge ciphertext in **Game 2**,

$$\begin{aligned} \boldsymbol{c}_{b,1}^t &= \left(\boldsymbol{s}_b^t \mathbf{F}_{\mathsf{id}^*,b} + \boldsymbol{v}_{b,1}^t\right) \bmod q \\ &= \left(\boldsymbol{s}_b^t[\mathbf{A}|\mathbf{A}(\mathbf{R}_{\mathbf{A}_b} - \mathbf{R}_{C_{\mathsf{PRF}},\mathsf{id}^*})] + \mathsf{ReRand}([\mathbf{I}|\mathbf{R}], \boldsymbol{s}_b^t\mathbf{A} + \boldsymbol{v}'_{b,1}, \sigma_{\mathsf{LWE}}, \sigma^*)\right) \bmod q \\ &= \left(\boldsymbol{s}_b^t[\mathbf{A}|\mathbf{A}\mathbf{R}] + \mathsf{ReRand}([\mathbf{I}|\mathbf{R}], \boldsymbol{s}_b^t\mathbf{A} + \boldsymbol{v}'_{b,1}, \sigma_{\mathsf{LWE}}, \sigma^*)\right) \bmod q. \end{aligned}$$

It is easy to see that the elements $s_b, \mathbf{A}, \mathbf{R}, v_{b,1}^t$ appearing in the ciphertext of **Game 2** have the same distributions as those in **Game 1**. The only difference is the generation of $v_{b,1}$. In **Game 1**, $v_{b,1}$ is sampled from $D_{\mathbb{Z}^{2m},\sigma}$. In **Game 2**, $v_{b,1}$ is the output of $\mathsf{ReRand}([\mathbf{I}|\mathbf{R}], s_b^t\mathbf{A}+v_{b,1}^{'}, \sigma_{\mathsf{LWE}}, \sigma^*)$, resulting the output gaussian parameter $r = 2\sigma_{\mathsf{LWE}} \cdot \sigma^* = \sigma$. By Lemma 2.13 and our setting of parameters, the statistical distance between the distributions of $v_{b,1}$ in the two cases is bounded by $2^{-(\kappa+2)}/2$. Therefore, the statistical distance between **Game 1** and **Game 2** is bounded by $2^{-(\kappa+2)}/2$. □

Lemma 4.4. *Game 2 and Game 3 are* $(T_3, \varepsilon_{\mathsf{LWE}})$*-indistinguishable, where* $T_3 = T_{\mathsf{LWE}} - \mathsf{poly}(n, m, k, Q_{\mathsf{id}}, \log q)$*, assuming* $\mathsf{LWE}_{n,q,\chi}$ *problem is* $(T_{\mathsf{LWE}}, \varepsilon_{\mathsf{LWE}})$*-hard.*

Proof. We show this by reduction. Assume that there exists a distinguisher $\mathcal{D}$ that distinguishes **Game 2** from **Game 3** within time $T_{\mathcal{D}} \leq T_3$ and with advantage $\varepsilon_{\mathcal{D}} \geq \varepsilon_{\mathsf{LWE}}$, then we construct a $(T_{\mathsf{LWE}}, \varepsilon_{\mathsf{LWE}})$-reduction $\mathcal{B}$ that breaks the LWE assumption. This is a contradiction to the LWE assumption.

The reduction algorithm $\mathcal{B}$ leverages $\mathcal{D}$ to break the the LWE hardness as follows: at the beginning, $\mathcal{B}$ receives the LWE challenge $(\mathbf{A}, \boldsymbol{b}) \in \mathbb{Z}_q^{n\times m} \times \mathbb{Z}_q^m$ and $(\boldsymbol{a}, b) \in \mathbb{Z}_q^n \times \mathbb{Z}_q$, which is either from $\mathcal{O}_\$$ or $\mathcal{O}_s$, where $\mathcal{O}_\$$ is the uniformly random distribution over $\mathbb{Z}_q^{n\times(m+1)} \times \mathbb{Z}_q^{m+1}$ and $\mathcal{O}_s$ is the distribution of $m+1$ LWE instances with same secret $\boldsymbol{s}$. $\mathcal{B}$ does as follows:

- Setup: Set $\mathbf{A}$ as the public matrix in mpk and $\boldsymbol{a} = \boldsymbol{u}$. Set other public parameters as **Game 2**.
- Phase 1: $\mathcal{B}$ answers the secret key queries as **Game 2**.
- Challenge: $\mathcal{B}$ computes the challenge ciphertext of id* as follows.
  1. Let $b = \mathsf{PRF}(K, \mathsf{id}^*)$. $\mathcal{B}$ sets
$$\begin{aligned}\mathbf{F}_{\mathsf{id}^*,1-b} &= [\mathbf{A}|\mathbf{A}_{1-b} - \mathbf{A}_{C_{\mathsf{PRF}},\mathsf{id}}] \\ &= [\mathbf{A}|\mathbf{A}(\mathbf{R}_{\mathbf{A}_{1-b}} - \mathbf{R}_{C_{\mathsf{PRF}},\mathsf{id}^*}) + (1-2b)\mathbf{G}].\end{aligned}$$
  2. Let $\mathbf{R} = \mathbf{R}_{\mathbf{A}_b} - \mathbf{R}_{C_{\mathsf{PRF}},\mathsf{id}^*}$. Then constructs $(c_{b,0}, \boldsymbol{c}_{b,1})$ as
$$\begin{cases} c_{b,0} = (b + \mu\lfloor q/2 \rfloor) \mod q \\ \boldsymbol{c}_{b,1}^t = (\mathsf{ReRand}([\mathbf{I}|\mathbf{R}], \boldsymbol{b}, \sigma_{\mathsf{LWE}}, \sigma^*)) \mod q \end{cases}$$
  3. $\mathcal{B}$ sets $(c_{1-b,0}, \boldsymbol{c}_{1-b,1})$ the same as **Game 2**.
- Phase 2: $\mathcal{B}$ replies the secret key queries as in **Game 2**.
- Gauss: If $\mathcal{D}$ outputs "**Game 2**", $\mathcal{B}$ decides that the challenge is from $\mathcal{O}_s$. Otherwise, $\mathcal{B}$ decides that the challenge is from $\mathcal{O}_\$$.

If $\mathcal{B}$ gets an LWE instance from the oracle $\mathcal{O}_s$, then the distributions of the elements $c_{b,0}, \boldsymbol{c}_{b,1}$ in the challenge ciphertext are the same as in **Game 2**. Therefore, $\mathcal{B}$ simulates **Game 2** for $\mathcal{D}$ in this case. On the other hand, if $\mathcal{B}$ gets an instance from the oracle $\mathcal{O}_\$$, then $c_{b,0}, \boldsymbol{c}_{b,1}$ are uniformly at random, which distribute as the case of **Game 3**. Thus $\mathcal{B}$ simulates **Game 3** in this case. As a result, the advantage of $\mathcal{B}$ is the same as that of $\mathcal{D}$, i.e., $\varepsilon_{\mathcal{D}} \geq \varepsilon_{\mathsf{LWE}}$, and the running time of $\mathcal{B}$ is at most $= T_{\mathcal{D}} + \mathsf{poly}(n, m, k, Q_{\mathsf{id}}, \log q) \leq T_{\mathsf{LWE}}$. This completes the proof. □

Lemma 4.5. *Game 3 and Game 4 are identically distributed.*

Proof. It is easy to see that the ways of generating the challenge ciphertext $c_{1-b,0}, \mathbf{c}_{1-b,1}$, from Enc and Sim.Enc, are identical. Thus, the advantages of the adversary in **Game 3** and **Game 4** are identical. □

Lemma 4.6. *Game 4 and Game 5 are* $(T_5, \varepsilon_{\mathsf{HE}} + 2^{-(\kappa+2)})$*-indistinguishable, assuming* HE *is* $(T_{\mathsf{HE}}, \varepsilon_{\mathsf{HE}})$*-CPA secure, where* $T_5 = T_{\mathsf{HE}} - \mathsf{poly}(n, m, k, Q_{\mathsf{id}}, \log q)$.

Proof. The proof is the same as Lemma 4.2. □

Lemma 4.7. *Game 5 and Game 6 are* $(T_6, 2\varepsilon_{\mathsf{PRF}})$*-indistinguishable, assuming the* PRF *is* $(T_{\mathsf{PRF}}, \varepsilon_{\mathsf{PRF}})$*-secure, where* $T_6 = T_{\mathsf{PRF}} - \mathsf{poly}(n, m, k, Q_{\mathsf{id}}, \log q)$.

Proof. Let $b = \mathsf{PRF}(K, \mathsf{id}^*)$ for the challenge identity id^*. Recall that in **Game 5**, the ciphertext component $(c_{b,0}, \mathbf{c}_{b,1})$ is uniformly random and $(c_{1-b,0}, \mathbf{c}_{1-b,1})$ is generated by Enc. In **Game 6**, the ciphertext component $(c_{b,0}, \mathbf{c}_{b,1})$ is generated by Enc and $(c_{1-b,0}, \mathbf{c}_{1-b,1})$ is uniformly random. We prove the indistinguishability between **Game 5** and **Game 6** by three steps.

First we define **Game 5'**, which is the same as **Game 5** except that it samples $b \xleftarrow{\$} \{0, 1\}$ to generate the secret keys and challenge ciphertext instead of computing it by PRF. We note that if the same identity is queried multiple times, the same b will be used. Clearly, a distinguisher between **Game 5'** and **Game 5** leads to an attacker for PRF. So **Game 5'** and **Game 5** are $(T_6', \varepsilon_{\mathsf{PRF}})$-indistinguishable.

Second, we define **Game 5''**, which is the same as **Game 5'** except that for randomly sampled b for id^*, it runs Enc to produce $(c_{b,0}, \mathbf{c}_{b,1})$ and samples $(c_{1-b,0}, \mathbf{c}_{1-b,1})$ uniformly at random. As b is uniformly at random, the advantages of the adversary in **Game 5''** and **Game 5'** are the same.

Finally, because **Game 5''** and **Game 6** are the same except that b is computed via PRF, **Game 5''** and **Game 6** are $(T_6', \varepsilon_{\mathsf{PRF}})$-indistinguishable.

The lemma follows directly by combining arguments in these three steps. □

Lemma 4.8. *Game 6 and Game 7 are* $(T_7, \varepsilon_{\mathsf{HE}} + 2^{-(\kappa+2)})$*-indistinguishable, assuming the* HE *scheme is* $(T_{\mathsf{HE}}, \varepsilon_{\mathsf{HE}})$*-CPA secure, where* $T_7 = T_{\mathsf{HE}} - \mathsf{poly}(n, m, k, Q_{\mathsf{id}}, \log q)$.

Proof. The proof is the same as the proof of Lemma 4.2. □

Lemma 4.9. *Game 7 and Game 8 are* $(\infty, 2^{-(\kappa+2)}/2)$*-indistinguishable.*

Proof. The proof is the same as the proof for Lemma 4.3. □

Lemma 4.10. *Game 8 and Game 9 are* $(T_9, \varepsilon_{\mathsf{LWE}})$*-indistinguishable, assuming* $\mathsf{LWE}_{n,q,\chi}$ *problem is* $(T_{\mathsf{LWE}}, \varepsilon_{\mathsf{LWE}})$*-hard, where* $T_9 = T_{\mathsf{LWE}} - \mathsf{poly}(n, m, k, Q_{\mathsf{id}}, \log q)$.

Proof. The proof is the same as the proof for Lemma 4.4. □

By combining all the lemmas above with the composition property of (computational) indistinguishability, we conclude that

$$|\Pr[W_0]-1/2| \le \sum_{i=0}^{8} |\Pr[W_i]-\Pr[W_{i+1}]|+|\Pr[W_9]-1/2| \le 2(\varepsilon_{\mathsf{PRF}}+\varepsilon_{\mathsf{LWE}})+3\varepsilon_{\mathsf{HE}}+2^{-\kappa},$$

and

$$\begin{aligned} t^* &= \min\{T_1, T_3, T_5, T_6, T_7, T_9\} - \mathsf{poly}(n, m, k, Q_{\mathsf{id}}, \log q) \\ &= \min\{T_{\mathsf{LWE}}, T_{\mathsf{PRF}}, T_{\mathsf{HE}}\} - \mathsf{poly}(n, m, k, Q_{\mathsf{id}}, \log q). \end{aligned}$$

□

4.3 Instantiations of LWE-based PRF and HE

We point out that all the building blocks can be instantiated under LWE with a polynomial modulus and almost tight analyses. For the PRF, we can use our construction in this work (see Corollary 3.7 in Sect. 3.2). For the homomorphic encryption, we can use the schemes [3,22] (which can be found in full version of this paper). Putting things together, we achieve the following corollary.

Corollary 4.11. *For certain* $n, m, q = \mathsf{poly}(\kappa), \chi$ *such that* $\mathsf{LWE}_{n,m,q,\chi}$ *is* $(t_{\mathsf{LWE}}, \varepsilon_{\mathsf{LWE}})$*-hard, there exists a* $(t^*, Q_{\mathsf{id}}, \varepsilon^*)$*-adaptively secure* IBE, *where* $\varepsilon^* \le \kappa\omega(\log\kappa)\,\varepsilon_{\mathsf{LWE}} + \mathsf{negl}(\kappa)$ *and* $t^* = t_{\mathsf{LWE}} - \mathsf{poly}(n, m, Q_{\mathsf{id}}, \log q)$*, for any polynomial* Q_{id}.

5 ABM-LTF with Tight Security Under poly Modulus

In this section, we present a new construction of almost tight ABM-LTF based on LWE with a polynomial modulus. This improves the work of Libert et al. [41], which requires a super-polynomial modulus. The crux of our improvement relies on our new insight as we described in Sect. 4.

Let n, m, ℓ, e, κ be integers, $q = p^e$ be a modulus such that $m \ge 2n\log q$ and $\ell < n$, where p is a large prime and $p > \kappa$. Let χ be a noise distribution, and let $\sigma_x, \sigma_e, \gamma_x, \gamma_e > 0$ be parameters. The function evaluation sampling domain is $\mathsf{D}_\kappa^E = \mathsf{D}_x^E \times \mathsf{D}_e^E$, where D_x^E (resp. D_e^E) is the set of $\boldsymbol{x}$ (resp. $\boldsymbol{e}$) in $\mathbb{Z}^n$ (resp. $\mathbb{Z}^{2m}$) with $\|\boldsymbol{x}\| \le \gamma_x\sqrt{n}\sigma_x$ (resp. $\|\boldsymbol{e}\| \le \gamma_e\sqrt{2m}\sigma_e$). Its inversion domain is $\mathsf{D}_\kappa^D = \mathsf{D}_x^D \times \mathsf{D}_e^D$, where $\mathsf{D}_{\mathsf{x}}^{\mathsf{D}}$ (resp. D_e^D) is the set of $\boldsymbol{x}$ (resp. $\boldsymbol{e}$) in $\mathbb{Z}^n$ (resp. $\mathbb{Z}^{2n}$) with $\|\boldsymbol{x}\| \le \sqrt{n}\sigma_x$ (resp. $\|\boldsymbol{e}\| \le \sqrt{2m}\sigma_e$), and its range is $\mathsf{R} = \mathbb{Z}_q^{2m}$. In this case, the function inputs are sampled from the distribution $D_{\mathsf{D}_\kappa^E} = D_{\mathbb{Z}^n,\sigma_x}^{\mathsf{D}_x^E} \times D_{\mathbb{Z}^{2m},\sigma_e}^{\mathsf{D}_e^E}$. We remark that $D_{\mathbb{Z}^n,\sigma_x}^{\mathsf{D}_x^E}$ (resp. $D_{\mathbb{Z}^{2m},\sigma_e}^{\mathsf{D}_e^E}$) is obtained by restricting the distribution $D_{\mathbb{Z}^n,\sigma_x}$ (resp. $D_{\mathbb{Z}^{2m},\sigma_e}$) to the support of D_x^E (resp. D_e^E).

Furthermore, let HE = (HE.KeyGen, HE.Enc, HE.Dec, HE.Eval) be a leveled fully homomorphic encryption scheme that can homomorphically evaluate PRF presented in Sect. 4 with polynomial modulus. Let $(\mathsf{Eval}^{\mathsf{Pub}}, \mathsf{Eval}^{\mathsf{Trap}})$ be a pair of deterministic algorithms that are δ-compatible for HE.Dec. Specifically, this δ might be $4^d m^{3/2}$ or $\tilde{O}(n^{2+\epsilon})$ according to different homomorphic evaluation algorithms according to Theorem 2.14. Furthermore, we use $k_3 \in \mathbb{N}$ to denote the output length of HE.Eval.

Construction. Below we present our construction of ABM-LTF. Our scheme modifies that of Libert et al. [41] in an essential way. To highlight our new insights, we describe our modifications in the boxes.

- **Key generation.** $\mathsf{ABM.Gen}(1^\kappa)$ does the following steps:
  1. Compute and output $\bar{\mathbf{A}} = \mathbf{C} \cdot \mathbf{B} + \mathbf{F} \in \mathbb{Z}_q^{n\times m}$ with $\mathbf{B} \xleftarrow{\$} U(\mathbb{Z}_q^{\ell\times m})$, $\mathbf{C} \xleftarrow{\$} U(\mathbb{Z}_q^{n\times \ell})$ and $\mathbf{F} \leftarrow \chi^{n\times m}$.
  2. Select a secure pseudorandom function $\mathsf{PRF} : \{0,1\}^k \times \{0,1\}^v \to \{0,1\}^\kappa$ with input length $v \in \mathbb{N}$ and key length $k \in \mathbb{N}$. Choose $K \xleftarrow{\$} \{0,1\}^k$ as an independent key for PRF. We denote by $s_i \in \{0,1\}$ the i-th bit of K.
  3. Run HE.KeyGen algorithm of a HE scheme $\boxed{(\mathsf{hek}, \mathsf{hevk}, \mathsf{hdk}) \leftarrow \mathsf{HE.KeyGen}}$. Express the decryption algorithm HE.Dec as a NAND Boolean circuit $\boxed{C_{\mathsf{Dec}}}$, and express its decryption key hdk as $\boxed{\mathsf{hdk} = (hdk_1, ..., hdk_g)}$ where $hdk_i \in \{0,1\}$ and $g \in \mathbb{N}$.
  4. Select g low-norm matrices $\{R_{\mathbf{D}i}\}_{i\in[g]} \xleftarrow{\$} \{-1,1\}^{m\times m}$.
  5. Set $\boxed{c_b \xleftarrow{\$} \mathsf{HE.Enc}(\mathsf{hek}, b)}$ for $b = 0, 1$.
  6. Set $\boxed{d_i \xleftarrow{\$} \mathsf{HE.Enc}(\mathsf{hek}, s_i)}$ for $i \in [k]$.
  7. Set $\boxed{\mathbf{D}_i = \bar{\mathbf{A}} \cdot R_{\mathbf{D}_i} + hdk_i\mathbf{G}}$ for $i \in [g]$.
  8. Output the evaluation key ek, the inversion key ik and the lossy generation key tk, which consist of

$$\mathsf{ek} = \left(\mathsf{PRF}, C_{\mathsf{PRF}}, C_{\mathsf{Dec}}, \bar{\mathbf{A}}, \{\boldsymbol{d}_i\}_{i\in[k]}, \{\mathbf{D}_i\}_{i\in[g]}, \boldsymbol{c}_0, \boldsymbol{c}_1, \mathsf{hevk}\right),$$

$$\mathsf{ik} = \left(\{\mathbf{R}_{\mathbf{D}_i}\}_{i\in[g]}, \mathsf{hdk}, K\right), \qquad \mathsf{tk} := K.$$

- **Evaluation.** $\mathsf{ABM.Eval}(\mathsf{ek}, \mathsf{t}, \mathsf{X})$ takes as inputs $\mathsf{X} := (\boldsymbol{x}, \boldsymbol{e}) \in \mathsf{D}_\kappa^E$ and the tag $\mathsf{t} = (\mathsf{t_c}, \mathsf{t_a}) \in \{0,1\}^\kappa \times \{0,1\}^v$, and proceeds as follows.
  1. For each integer $j \in [\kappa]$, let $C_{\mathsf{PRF},j} : \{0,1\}^k \times \{0,1\}^v \to \{0,1\}$ be the Boolean circuit, which evaluate the j-th bit of $\mathsf{PRF}(K, \mathsf{t_a}) \in \{0,1\}^\kappa$. Run the homomorphic evaluation algorithm of HE to obtain

$$\boxed{\mathsf{ct}_j = \mathsf{HE.Eval}(\mathsf{hevk}, C_{\mathsf{PRF},j}, (\{\boldsymbol{d}_i\}_{i\in[k]}, \{\boldsymbol{c}_{\mathsf{t_a}[i]}\}_{i\in[\ell]}))},$$

  where $\mathsf{t_a}[i]$ denotes the i-th bit of $\mathsf{t_a}$ for $i \in [\ell]$. Furthermore, run the public evaluation algorithm to obtain

$$\boxed{\mathbf{B}_{\mathsf{PRF},j} = \mathsf{Eval}^{\mathsf{Pub}}(C_{\mathsf{Dec}}, (\{\mathbf{D}_i\}_{i\in[g]}, \{(\mathsf{ct}_j)_i\mathbf{G}\}))},$$

  where $\{(\mathsf{ct}_j)_i\}_{i\in\mathbb{N}}$ denotes the bit representation of ciphertext ct_j.
  2. Define the matrix

$$\mathbf{A}_{\mathsf{t}} = \left(\bar{\mathbf{A}}, \textstyle\sum_{j\in[\kappa]} \left((-1)^{\mathsf{t_c}[j]}\mathbf{B}_{\mathsf{PRF},j} + \mathsf{t_c}[j]\mathbf{G}\right)\right) \in \mathbb{Z}_q^{n\times 2m},$$

  and compute the output $\boldsymbol{y}^t = \boldsymbol{x}^t \cdot \mathbf{A}_{\mathsf{t}} + \boldsymbol{e}^t \in \mathbb{Z}_q^{2m}$. Notice that after summation for all $j \in [\kappa]$, the coefficient of matrix $\mathbf{G}$ in the right half part of $\mathbf{A}_{\mathsf{t}}$ is just the hamming distance between $\mathsf{t_c}$ and $\mathsf{PRF}(K, \mathsf{t_a})$.

- **Inversion.** $\mathsf{ABM.Invert(ik, t, Y)}$ takes as inputs the inversion key $\mathsf{ik} = \left(\{\mathbf{R}_{\mathsf{D}_i}\}_{i\in[g]}, K\right)$, the tag $\mathsf{t} = (\mathsf{t_c}, \mathsf{t_a}) \in \{0,1\}^\kappa \times \{0,1\}^\ell$ and $\mathsf{Y} := \boldsymbol{y} \in \mathsf{R}$, and proceeds:
  1. Return $\perp$ if $\mathsf{t_c} = \mathsf{PRF}(K, \mathsf{t_a})$.
  2. Otherwise, for each $j \in [\kappa]$, run the following two algorithms:

$$\boxed{\mathsf{ct_{id}} = \mathsf{HE.Eval}(\mathsf{hevk}, C_{\mathsf{PRF},j}, (\{\boldsymbol{d}_i\}_{i\in[k]}, \{\boldsymbol{c}_{\mathsf{t_a}[i]}\}_{i\in[\ell]}))}$$

$$\boxed{\mathbf{R}_{\mathsf{PRF},j} = \mathsf{Eval}^{\mathsf{Trap}}(C_{\mathsf{Dec}}, \bar{\mathbf{A}}, (\{hdk_i\}_{i\in[g]}, \{(\mathsf{ct_{id}})_i\}_{i\in[k_3]}), \{\mathbf{R}_{\mathsf{D}_i}\}_{i\in[g]}, \{[0]_i\}_{i\in[k_3]})}$$

  and compute the matrix $\mathbf{R_t} = \sum_{j\in[\kappa]}(-1)^{\mathsf{t_c}[j]}\mathbf{R}_{\mathsf{PRF},j} \in \mathbb{Z}^{m\times m}$, where for each $i \in [k_3]$, $[0]_i$ denotes 0 matrix with dimension $m \times m$.
  3. Let h_t denote the hamming distance between $\mathsf{t_c}$ and PRF $(K, \mathsf{t_a})$. Then Compute and set $\mathbf{A_t} = \left(\bar{\mathbf{A}}, \bar{\mathbf{A}}\mathbf{R_t} + h_\mathsf{t}\mathbf{G}\right) \in \mathbb{Z}_q^{n\times 2m}$, Use the $\mathbf{G}$-trapdoor $\mathbf{R_t}$ of $\mathbf{A}$ with tag h_t to solve the unique $(\boldsymbol{x}, \boldsymbol{e}) \in \mathsf{D}_\kappa^D$ such that $\boldsymbol{y}^t = \boldsymbol{x}^t \cdot \mathbf{A} + \boldsymbol{e}^t$. This can be done by applying the LWE inversion algorithm (which can be found in full version of this paper).
- **Lossy tag generation.** $\mathsf{ABM.LTag(tk)}$ takes as input an auxiliary tag component $\mathsf{t_a} \in \{0,1\}^\ell$ and uses $\mathsf{tk} = K$ to compute and output $\mathsf{t_c} = \mathsf{PRF}(K, \mathsf{t_a}) \in \{0,1\}^\kappa$.

Below we state a theorem that summarizes what we can achieve. Due to space limit, we present the syntax of ABM-LTF and the security analysis in full version of this paper.

Theorem 5.1. *Let κ be the security parameter, $\chi = D_{\mathbb{Z},\beta/(2\sqrt{\kappa})}$ for some $\beta > 4\kappa$. Let n, m, ℓ, e be functions of κ, $q = p^e$ be a modulus such that $m \geq 2n\log q$, $n = \Omega(\ell \log q)$ and $\kappa < \ell < n$, where p is a large prime and $p > \kappa$. Let $\gamma_x \geq 3\sqrt{m/n}$, $\gamma_e \geq 3$, $\sigma_x > \Omega(n)$, $\Omega(m\sqrt{n}\kappa\delta\beta\sigma_x) \leq \sigma_e \leq q/(10\sqrt{2}\kappa\delta m)$. Then, our new construction is an l-lossy* ABM-LTF *with $l = \Omega(n \log n)$ based on* $\mathsf{LWE}_{\ell,2m,q,\chi}$.

Acknowledgements. We would like to thank Bo Yang and Mingsheng Wang for their helpful discussions. We also thank the anonymous reviewers of PKC 2020 for their insightful advices. Qiqi Lai is supported by the National Key R&D Program of China (2017YFB0802000), the National Natural Science Foundation of China (61802241, 61772326, 61802242, 61802075), the Natural Science Basic Research Plan in Shaanxi Province of China (2019JQ-360) and the National Cryptography Development Foundation during the 13th Five-year Plan Period (MMJJ20180217). Feng-Hao Liu is supported by the NSF Award CNS-1657040. Zhedong Wang is supported by the NSF Award CNS-1657040 and the National Key R&D Program of China-2017YFB0802202. Any opinions, findings, and conclusions or recommendations expressed in this material are those of the author(s) and do not necessarily reflect the views of the sponsors.

References

1. Agrawal, S., Boneh, D., Boyen, X.: Efficient lattice (H)IBE in the standard model. In: Gilbert, H. (ed.) EUROCRYPT 2010. LNCS, vol. 6110, pp. 553–572. Springer, Heidelberg (2010). https://doi.org/10.1007/978-3-642-13190-5_28
2. Ajtai, M.: Generating hard instances of lattice problems (extended abstract). In: 28th ACM STOC, pp. 99–108. ACM Press, May 1996
3. Alperin-Sheriff, J., Peikert, C.: Faster bootstrapping with polynomial error. In: Garay and Gennaro [27], pp. 297–314
4. Alwen, J., Krenn, S., Pietrzak, K., Wichs, D.: Learning with rounding, revisited - new reduction, properties and applications. In: Canetti and Garay [23], pp. 57–74
5. Attrapadung, N., Hanaoka, G., Yamada, S.: A framework for identity-based encryption with almost tight security. In: Iwata, T., Cheon, J.H. (eds.) ASIACRYPT 2015. LNCS, vol. 9452, pp. 521–549. Springer, Heidelberg (2015). https://doi.org/10.1007/978-3-662-48797-6_22
6. Bai, S., Langlois, A., Lepoint, T., Stehlé, D., Steinfeld, R.: Improved security proofs in lattice-based cryptography: using the Rényi divergence rather than the statistical distance. In: Iwata, T., Cheon, J.H. (eds.) ASIACRYPT 2015, Part I. LNCS, vol. 9452, pp. 3–24. Springer, Heidelberg (2015). https://doi.org/10.1007/978-3-662-48797-6_1
7. Banerjee, A., Peikert, C.: New and improved key-homomorphic pseudorandom functions. In: Garay and Gennaro [27], pp. 353–370
8. Banerjee, A., Peikert, C., Rosen, A.: Pseudorandom functions and lattices. In: Pointcheval and Johansson [48], pp. 719–737
9. Bellare, M., Rogaway, P.: The exact security of digital signatures-how to sign with RSA and Rabin. In: Maurer, U. (ed.) EUROCRYPT 1996. LNCS, vol. 1070, pp. 399–416. Springer, Heidelberg (1996). https://doi.org/10.1007/3-540-68339-9_34
10. Blazy, O., Kiltz, E., Pan, J.: (Hierarchical) identity-based encryption from affine message authentication. In: Garay and Gennaro [27], pp. 408–425
11. Bogdanov, A., Guo, S., Masny, D., Richelson, S., Rosen, A.: On the hardness of learning with rounding over small modulus. In: Kushilevitz, E., Malkin, T. (eds.) TCC 2016-A, Part I. LNCS, vol. 9562, pp. 209–224. Springer, Heidelberg (2016). https://doi.org/10.1007/978-3-662-49096-9_9
12. Bogdanov, A., Rosen, A.: Pseudorandom functions: three decades later. Cryptology ePrint Archive, Report 2017/652 (2017). https://eprint.iacr.org/2017/652
13. Boneh, D., Franklin, M.K.: Identity-based encryption from the weil pairing. In: Kilian, J. (ed.) CRYPTO 2001. LNCS, vol. 2139, pp. 213–229. Springer, Heidelberg (2001). https://doi.org/10.1007/3-540-44647-8_13
14. Boneh, D., et al.: Fully key-homomorphic encryption, arithmetic circuit ABE and compact garbled circuits. In: Nguyen, P.Q., Oswald, E. (eds.) EUROCRYPT 2014. LNCS, vol. 8441, pp. 533–556. Springer, Heidelberg (2014). https://doi.org/10.1007/978-3-642-55220-5_30
15. Boneh, D., Lewi, K., Montgomery, H.W., Raghunathan, A.: Key homomorphic PRFs and their applications. In: Canetti and Garay [23], pp. 410–428
16. Boyen, X., Li, Q.: Towards tightly secure lattice short signature and id-based encryption. In: Cheon and Takagi [25], pp. 404–434
17. Boyen, X., Li, Q.: All-but-many lossy trapdoor functions from lattices and applications. In: Katz and Shacham [38], pp. 298–331
18. Brakerski, Z.: Fully homomorphic encryption without modulus switching from classical GapSVP. In: Safavi-Naini and Canetti [50], pp. 868–886

19. Brakerski, Z., Goldwasser, S.: Circular and leakage resilient public-key encryption under subgroup indistinguishability - (or: quadratic residuosity strikes back). In: Rabin, T. (ed.) CRYPTO 2010. LNCS, vol. 6223, pp. 1–20. Springer, Heidelberg (2010). https://doi.org/10.1007/978-3-642-14623-7_1
20. Brakerski, Z., Langlois, A., Peikert, C., Regev, O., Stehlé, D.: Classical hardness of learning with errors. In: Boneh, D., Roughgarden, T., Feigenbaum, J. (eds.) 45th ACM STOC, pp. 575–584. ACM Press, June 2013
21. Brakerski, Z., Vaikuntanathan, V.: Efficient fully homomorphic encryption from (standard) LWE. In: Ostrovsky, R. (ed.) 52nd FOCS, pp. 97–106. IEEE Computer Society Press (2011)
22. Brakerski, Z., Vaikuntanathan, V.: Lattice-based FHE as secure as PKE. In: Naor, M. (ed.) ITCS 2014, pp. 1–12. ACM, January 2014
23. Canetti, R., Garay, J.A. (eds.): CRYPTO 2013, Part I. LNCS, vol. 8042. Springer, Heidelberg (2013). https://doi.org/10.1007/978-3-642-40041-4
24. Chen, J., Wee, H.: Fully, (almost) tightly secure IBE and dual system groups. In: Canetti, R., Garay, J.A. (eds.) CRYPTO 2013, Part II. LNCS, vol. 8043, pp. 435–460. Springer, Heidelberg (2013). https://doi.org/10.1007/978-3-642-40084-1_25
25. Cheon, J.H., Takagi, T. (eds.): ASIACRYPT 2016, Part II. LNCS, vol. 10032. Springer, Heidelberg (2016). https://doi.org/10.1007/978-3-662-53890-6
26. Döttling, N., Schröder, D.: Efficient pseudorandom functions via on-the-fly adaptation. In: Gennaro, R., Robshaw, M. (eds.) CRYPTO 2015, Part I. LNCS, vol. 9215, pp. 329–350. Springer, Heidelberg (2015). https://doi.org/10.1007/978-3-662-47989-6_16
27. Garay, J.A., Gennaro, R. (eds.): CRYPTO 2014, Part I. LNCS, vol. 8616. Springer, Heidelberg (2014). https://doi.org/10.1007/978-3-662-44371-2
28. Gay, R., Hofheinz, D., Kiltz, E., Wee, H.: Tightly CCA-Secure Encryption Without Pairings. In: Fischlin, M., Coron, J.-S. (eds.) EUROCRYPT 2016, Part I. LNCS, vol. 9665, pp. 1–27. Springer, Heidelberg (2016). https://doi.org/10.1007/978-3-662-49890-3_1
29. Gentry, C.: Fully homomorphic encryption using ideal lattices. In: Mitzenmacher [44], pp. 169–178
30. Gentry, C., Sahai, A., Waters, B.: Homomorphic encryption from learning with errors: conceptually-simpler, asymptotically-faster, attribute-based. In: Canetti and Garay [23], pp. 75–92
31. Goldreich, O., Goldwasser, S., Micali, S.: How to construct random functions (extended abstract). In: 25th FOCS, pp. 464–479. IEEE Computer Society Press, October 1984
32. Gong, J., Chen, J., Dong, X., Cao, Z., Tang, S.: Extended nested dual system groups, revisited. In: Cheng, C.-M., Chung, K.-M., Persiano, G., Yang, B.-Y. (eds.) PKC 2016, Part I. LNCS, vol. 9614, pp. 133–163. Springer, Heidelberg (2016). https://doi.org/10.1007/978-3-662-49384-7_6
33. Hofheinz, D., Jager, T.: Tightly secure signatures and public-key encryption. In: Safavi-Naini and Canetti [50], pp. 590–607
34. Jager, T., Kurek, R., Pan, J.: Simple and more efficient PRFs with tight security from LWE and matrix-DDH. Cryptology ePrint Archive, Report 2018/826, to be appear in Asiacrypt 2018. https://eprint.iacr.org/2018/826
35. Joye, M., Libert, B.: Efficient cryptosystems from 2^k-th power residue symbols. In: Johansson, T., Nguyen, P.Q. (eds.) EUROCRYPT 2013. LNCS, vol. 7881, pp. 76–92. Springer, Heidelberg (2013). https://doi.org/10.1007/978-3-642-38348-9_5

36. Katsumata, S., Yamada, S.: Partitioning via non-linear polynomial functions: more compact IBEs from ideal lattices and bilinear maps. In: Cheon and Takagi [25], pp. 682–712
37. Katz, J., Lindell, Y.: Introduction to Modern Cryptography, 2nd edn. CRC Press, Boca Raton (2014)
38. Katz, J., Shacham, H. (eds.): CRYPTO 2017, Part III. LNCS, vol. 10403. Springer, Cham (2017). https://doi.org/10.1007/978-3-319-63697-9
39. Katz, J., Wang, N.: Efficiency improvements for signature schemes with tight security reductions. In: Jajodia, S., Atluri, V., Jaeger, T. (eds.) ACM CCS 2003, pp. 155–164. ACM Press, New York (2003)
40. Lewko, A.B., Waters, B.: Efficient pseudorandom functions from the decisional linear assumption and weaker variants. In: Al-Shaer, E., Jha, S., Keromytis, A.D. (eds.) ACM CCS 2009, pp. 112–120. ACM Press, New York (2009)
41. Libert, B., Sakzad, A., Stehlé, D., Steinfeld, R.: All-but-many lossy trapdoor functions and selective opening chosen-ciphertext security from LWE. In: Katz and Shacham [38], pp. 332–364
42. Micciancio, D., Mol, P.: Pseudorandom knapsacks and the sample complexity of LWE search-to-decision reductions. In: Rogaway, P. (ed.) CRYPTO 2011. LNCS, vol. 6841, pp. 465–484. Springer, Heidelberg (2011). https://doi.org/10.1007/978-3-642-22792-9_26
43. Micciancio, D., Peikert, C.: Trapdoors for lattices: simpler, tighter, faster, smaller. In: Pointcheval and Johansson [48], pp. 700–718
44. Mitzenmacher, M. (ed.): 41st ACM STOC. ACM Press, May/June 2009
45. Naor, M., Reingold, O.: Number-theoretic constructions of efficient pseudo-random functions. In: 38th FOCS, pp. 458–467. IEEE Computer Society Press, October 1997
46. Paillier, P.: Public-key cryptosystems based on composite degree residuosity classes. In: Stern, J. (ed.) EUROCRYPT 1999. LNCS, vol. 1592, pp. 223–238. Springer, Heidelberg (1999). https://doi.org/10.1007/3-540-48910-X_16
47. Peikert, C.: Public-key cryptosystems from the worst-case shortest vector problem: extended abstract. In Mitzenmacher [44], pp. 333–342
48. Pointcheval, D., Johansson, T. (eds.): EUROCRYPT 2012. LNCS, vol. 7237. Springer, Heidelberg (2012). https://doi.org/10.1007/978-3-642-29011-4
49. Regev, O.: On lattices, learning with errors, random linear codes, and cryptography. In: Gabow, H.N., Fagin, R. (eds.) 37th ACM STOC, pp. 84–93. ACM Press, May 2005
50. Safavi-Naini, R., Canetti, R. (eds.): CRYPTO 2012. LNCS, vol. 7417. Springer, Heidelberg (2012). https://doi.org/10.1007/978-3-642-32009-5
51. Shamir, A.: Identity-based cryptosystems and signature schemes. In: Blakley, G.R., Chaum, D. (eds.) CRYPTO 1984. LNCS, vol. 196, pp. 47–53. Springer, Heidelberg (1985). https://doi.org/10.1007/3-540-39568-7_5
52. Vadhan, S.P.: Pseudorandomness. Found. Trends Theor. Comput. Sci. **7**(1–3), 1–336 (2012)
53. Waters, B.: Efficient identity-based encryption without random oracles. In: Cramer, R. (ed.) EUROCRYPT 2005. LNCS, vol. 3494, pp. 114–127. Springer, Heidelberg (2005). https://doi.org/10.1007/11426639_7
54. Yamada, S.: Asymptotically compact adaptively secure lattice IBEs and verifiable random functions via generalized partitioning techniques. In: Katz and Shacham [38], pp. 161–193

Author Index

Abdolmaleki, Behzad I-590
Abe, Masayuki I-558
Agrawal, Shweta I-34
Agrikola, Thomas I-187
Ambrona, Miguel I-558

Bai, Shi II-66
Baum, Carsten I-495
Bhattacharyya, Rishiraj I-249
Bouvier, Cyril II-483
Brakerski, Zvika II-97

Canetti, Ran II-299
Cao, Nairen I-279
Castagnos, Guilhem II-266
Catalano, Dario II-266, II-357
Chailloux, André II-453
Chakraborty, Suvradip I-220
Chan, T.-H. Hubert II-246
Costello, Craig II-505
Couteau, Geoffroy I-187

Das, Dipayan II-66
Daza, Vanesa I-527
De Feo, Luca II-187
Debris-Alazard, Thomas II-453
Derler, David I-462
Di Raimondo, Mario II-357
Dowling, Benjamin I-341
Ducas, Léo II-3

El Kaafarani, Ali II-157

Fan, Shuqin II-37
Fiore, Dario II-124, II-357

Garg, Sanjam I-123
Gay, Romain I-95, I-123
Genise, Nicholas I-623
Giacomelli, Irene II-357
Gong, Guang I-396
Gu, Dawu I-309
Guillevic, Aurore II-535
Guo, Siyao I-374

Hajiabadi, Mohammad I-123
Haque, Abida II-423
Hazay, Carmit II-328
He, Jingnan I-396
Hébant, Chloé II-597
Hiromasa, Ryo II-66
Hofheinz, Dennis I-187
Hövelmanns, Kathrin II-389

Imbert, Laurent II-483
Iovino, Vincenzo I-65

Jiang, Shaoquan I-396

Kalai, Yael II-97
Kamath, Pritish I-374
Katsumata, Shuichi II-157
Kawahara, Yuto I-3
Kiltz, Eike II-389

Laarhoven, Thijs II-3
Laguillaumie, Fabien II-266
Lai, Qiqi I-652
Langrehr, Roman I-153
Lauer, Sebastian II-567
LaVigne, Rio II-215
Libert, Benoît I-34
Lipmaa, Helger I-590
Liu, Feng-Hao I-652
Liu, Joseph K. I-309
Liu-Zhang, Chen-Da II-215
Longa, Patrick II-505

Maitra, Monosij I-34
Maurer, Ueli II-215
Meyer, Michael II-187
Micciancio, Daniele I-623
Moran, Tal II-215
Mularczyk, Marta II-215

Naehrig, Michael II-505
Nguyen, Khoa I-396
Nishimaki, Ryo I-3

Nitulescu, Anca II-124
Nof, Ariel I-495

O'Neill, Adam I-279
Ohkubo, Miyako I-558

Pan, Jiaxin I-153
Pass, Rafael II-246
Peikert, Chris I-431, I-623
Phan, Duong Hieu II-597
Pintore, Federico II-157
Pointcheval, David II-124, II-597
Prabhakaran, Manoj I-220

Ràfols, Carla I-527
Renes, Joost II-505
Rial, Alfredo I-65
Roenne, Peter B. I-65
Rosca, Miruna II-66
Rosen, Alon I-374
Rösler, Paul I-341
Ryan, Peter Y. A. I-65

Sakzad, Amin I-309, II-66
Samelin, Kai I-462
Sanders, Olivier II-628
Sarkar, Pratik II-299
Savasta, Federico II-266
Scafuro, Alessandra II-423
Schäge, Sven II-389, II-567
Schwenk, Jörg I-341, II-567
Shelat, Abhi II-328
Shi, Elaine II-246
Shiehian, Sina I-431
Siim, Janno I-590
Slamanig, Daniel I-462
Soroush, Najmeh I-65
Sotiraki, Katerina I-374
Stehlé, Damien II-66
Steinfeld, Ron I-309, II-66
Sun, Shi-Feng I-309

Titiu, Radu I-34
Tomida, Junichi I-3
Tschudi, Daniel II-215
Tucker, Ida II-266

Unruh, Dominique II-389

van Woerden, Wessel P. J. II-3
Venkitasubramaniam, Muthuramakrishnan II-328
Virdia, Fernando II-505

Walter, Michael I-623
Wang, Huaxiong I-396
Wang, Xiao II-299
Wang, Zhedong I-652
Wichs, Daniel I-220

Yang, Kang II-37
Yu, Yu II-37

Zacharakis, Alexandros I-527
Zaheri, Mohammad I-279
Zając, Michał I-590
Zhang, Jiang II-37
Zhang, Zhenfei II-66
Zhang, Zhenfeng II-37

Printed in the United States
By Bookmasters